Jean-Daniel Chiche | Rui Moreno
Christian Putensen | Andrew Rhodes
(Eds.)

Patient Safety and Quality of Care
in Intensive Care Medicine

Medizinisch Wissenschaftliche Verlagsgesellschaft

Jean-Daniel Chiche | Rui Moreno
Christian Putensen | Andrew Rhodes
(Eds.)

Patient Safety
and Quality of Care
in Intensive Care
Medicine

with contributions from:

LM Aitken | R Alvisi | R Amerling | PJD Andrews | A Artigas | D De Backer | N Badjatia | M Bauer
G Bertolini | A Biasi Cavalcanti | JF Bion | BW Böttiger | CSC Bouman | A Boumendil
FA Bozza | J Braithwaite | G Brattebø | FM Brunkhorst | DDG Bugano | M Capuzzo | M Cecconi
W Chaboyer | J Chen | E Coiera | K Colpaert | CR Cooke | JR Curtis | BH Cuthbertson
AL Cuvello Neto | KJ Deans | J Decruyenaere | J-M Dominguez-Roldan | Y Donchin | C Druml
G Dubreuil | R Endacott | A Esteban | R Ferrer | H Flaatten | J Fragata | F Frutos-Vivar
C Garcia-Alfaro | M Garrouste-Orgeas | TD Girard | ARJ Girbes | J Graf | D Grimaldi
ABJ Groeneveld | B Guidet | U Günther | N Harbord | DA Harrison | C Hartog | N Heming
F Hernandez-Hazañas | K Hillman | P Holder | MH Hooper | M Imhoff | U Janssens
JM Kahn | E Knobel | M Knobel | J Lipman | T Lisboa | Y Livne | S Lorent | M Makdisse
A Marques | GD Martich | ML Martinez | SA Mayer | DK Menon | PC Minneci | J-P Mira
X Monnet | RP Moreno | T Muders | C Natanson | A Navas | G Ntoumenopoulos
SA Nurmohamed | HM Oudemans-van Straaten | R Paterson | O Peñuelas | JG Pereira
C Pierrakos | LF Poli-de-Figueiredo | CE Pompilio | D Poole | A Pronovost | C Putensen
K Reinhart | J Rello | A Rhodes | Z Ricci | C Richard | F Rincon | JA Roberts | E Roeb
C Ronco | GD Rubenfeld | D Salgado | JIF Salluh | G Satkurunath | A Schneider
C Schwebel | E Silva | M Singer | EGM Smit | M Soares | L Soufir | A Tabah | J-L Teboul
P Teschendorf | N Theuerkauf | J-F Timsit | M Ulldemolins | A Valentin | JM Varghese
J-L Vincent | B Volpe | CS Waldmann | RR West | S West | JF Winchester | H Wrigge

 Medizinisch Wissenschaftliche Verlagsgesellschaft

Editors

Jean-Daniel Chiche, Prof.
Réanimation médicale polyvalente
Faculté de médecine Cochin Port-Royal
L'Université Paris Descartes
27, rue du Faubourg Saint-Jacques
75679 Paris Cedex 14, France

Rui P. Moreno, MD, PhD
Unidade de Cuidados Intensivos Polivalente
Hospital de Santo António dos Capuchos
Centro Hospitalar de Lisboa Central E.P.E.
Alameda de Santo António dos Capuchos
1169-050 Lisboa, Portugal

Christian Putensen, MD
Universitätsklinikum Bonn
Klinik und Poliklinik für Anästhesiologie und Operative
Intensivmedizin
Sigmund-Freud-Str. 35
53105 Bonn, Germany

Andrew Rhodes, FRCA, FRCP
Department of Intensive Care Medicine
St George's Hospital
Blackshaw Road
London SW17 0QT, UK

EUROPEAN SOCIETY
OF INTENSIVE CARE
MEDICINE

European Society of Intensive Care Medicine
40 Avenue Joseph Wybran
1070 Bruxelles, Belgium
Tel: 0032 2 559 03 50 – Fax: 0032 2 527 00 62
E-mail: public@esicm.org
www.esicm.org

MWV Medizinisch Wissenschaftliche Verlagsgesellschaft mbH & Co. KG
Zimmerstraße 11
D- 10969 Berlin
www.mwv-berlin.de

ISBN 978-3-941468-11-5

These publications are listed in: Deutsche Nationalbibliothek
Detailed bibliographical information is available via internet http://dnb.d-nb.de.

Medicine is an ever-changing science. As new research and clinical experience broaden our knowledge, changes in treatment and drug therapy are required. The editors and the publisher of this work have checked with sources believed to be reliable in their efforts to provide information that is complete and generally in accordance with the standards accepted at the time of publication. However, in view of the possibility of human error or changes in medical sciences, neither the editors nor the publisher nor any other party who has been involved in the preparation or publication of this work warrants, that the information contained herein is in every respect accurate or complete, and they disclaim all responsibility for any errors or omissions or for the results obtained from use of the information contained in this work. Readers are encouraged to confirm the information contained herein with other sources. For example and in particular, readers are advised to check the product information sheet included in the package of each drug they plan to administer to be certain that the information contained in this work is accurate and that changes have not been made in the recommended dose or in the contraindications for administration. This recommendation is of particular importance in connection with new or infrequently used drugs.

Any necessary errata are published at the publisher's website www.mwv-berlin.de.

Project management: Claudia Leonhardt, Berlin
Editorial office: Monika Laut-Zimmermann, Frauke Budig, Berlin
Copy editing: Jan K. Schwing, readytoread.de, Hamburg
Layout and typesetting: eScriptum GmbH & Co KG – Publishing Services, Berlin
Printing: druckhaus köthen GmbH, Köthen

Reply and complaints to:
MWV Medizinisch Wissenschaftliche Verlagsgesellschaft mbH & Co. KG, Zimmerstraße 11, D- 10969 Berlin, lektorat@mwv-berlin.de

Preface

This new European Society of Intensive Care Medicine (ESICM) book tackles the issues of Patient Safety and Quality of Care in Intensive Care. Although for the general public these two topics appear to be quite different they are in fact inextricably linked. In order to provide quality care there has to be an understanding of the implicit and explicit needs of our patients, taking into account their values, beliefs and ethical views. To achieve this aim, care must be provided in an effective and safe way, without errors of either commission or omission. Unfortunately safety agendas often attract negative connotations and are therefore not felt to be attractive topics for scientific societies to address and resolve. The linking of safety together with quality of care can reverse this negative spin and put a positive slant on the subject. We hope that readers of this book will come away with a refreshed view on both quality and safety agendas that will lead to an improvement in the standards of their practice.

In recent years many different institutions have driven the patient safety agenda. Politicians, insurance companies, patient organizations and commissioners of care have nurtured the idea that our hospitals should be safer than they are. Despite this, there has been a perceived lack of direction and interest from clinicians and their scientific associations. Although this is certainly not completely correct there has at the least been a lack of leadership and direction from many of the Scientific Societies. We have witnessed criticisms from many quarters about the scientific rationale and credibility behind some of the safety initiatives. These programs have all been started with the best of intentions, it is a shame that sometimes the controversy gets in the way of progress. There are many reasons underpinning this, including the way we, as clinicians, nurses and allied healthcare professionals, interact with both our patients and the healthcare systems we work in. We also live in an era that has focused too much on outcomes rather than the process of care.

The rationale for this book therefore derives from these misperceptions. We want to regain the initiative and drive forward the agenda for improving safety and increasing quality of care. This book attempts to bring together the many facets of these topics. There are chapters describing the problem from many different angles, the many related issues we face in the care of our patients, and there are then chapters that highlight some of the solutions. Through many of these chapters runs a thread that focuses on the notion that systems have to be re-designed to prevent or minimize error and that human-related factors are often the key to success. All of the chapters have been written by senior opinion-leaders from our own, as well as other societies. They are all well-known and established scientific experts in their field. This is probably the first time that such a collection of topics has been brought together in such a comprehensive fashion related specifically to the field of Intensive care Medicine. If with this exercise we can help our colleagues to prevent the loss of a single human life, then we will have achieved our aims.

As always with a collection of topics such as this, the quality of the book is a direct result of the efforts of the individual authors and of our publishing team. We, the Editors, would like to offer all of them a massive vote of gratitude. Not only have they given us a set of quality chapters, they have delivered them within a tight time schedule that means that unlike many other books this one is topical and relevant today, on the day it is published.

We hope you have as much fun reading this book as much as we have had editing it.

Rui P. Moreno (President of the ESICM)
Andrew Rhodes (President elect of the ESICM)
Jean-Daniel Chiche (Chair of the Division of Scientific Affairs)
Christian Putensen (Chair of the Editorial and Publishing Committee)

Content

Rui P. Moreno and Andrew Rhodes

Improving safety in intensive care – What does it mean?

"Primum non nocere"
Galen of Pergamum, Roman physician
and philosopher of Greek origin
(AD 129–200/217)

Introduction

A 1999 report from the Institute of Medicine (IOM) entitled "To Err is Human: Building a Safer Health System" raised the public profile of patient safety [1]. According to this report, the authors estimated that between 44,000 and 98,000 patients die every year in the United States of America as a result of clinical errors; these numbers make medical error the eighth leading cause of death in the USA, more frequent than those due to motor vehicle accidents (43,458), breast cancer (42,458) and AIDS (16,516). The costs involved in this issue are staggering, estimated to be in excess of US$ 20 billion (just for the USA).

For the purposes of the IOM Report, safety was defined as the absence of clinical error, either by commission (unintentionally doing the wrong thing) or omission (unintentionally not doing the right thing) [2] and error as the failure of a planned action to be completed as intended or the use of a wrong plan to achieve an aim; the accumulation of errors resulting in accidents [1].

Following this report, a series of authors started to use the terms safety and quality of care almost interchangeably, although the IOM defined healthcare quality as "the degree to which health services for individuals and populations increase the likelihood of desired health outcomes and are consistent with current professional knowledge" [3]. The IOM's definition is, in fact, very close to an old conceptual framework that was proposed by Avedis Donabedian, who reported that measurement of the quality of healthcare could only be made following careful observation of its structure, processes, and outcomes [4]. On top of this he also described seven pillars, or attributes, that also need to be analysed to assess the quality of care:

- Efficacy
- Effectiveness
- Efficiency
- Optimality
- Acceptability
- Legitimacy
- Equity

In other words, patient preferences are as important as social preferences and both must be taken into consideration when assessing the quality of healthcare [4].

Safety and the individual patient

As a consequence of this misperception between quality and safety of care, the awareness of the public, the media and the politicians shifted from the evaluation of the efficacy, effectiveness, efficiency, optimality, acceptability, legitimacy, and equity of medical practices (so from the quality of care) to the identification, quantification and prevention of medical error (or the adverse clinical events arising from a presumed chain of causation are attributed to the last link in that chain, usually a doctor or nurse). This misperception has subsequently been extended to the choices and decisions (or errors) that patients make themselves [5]. Most of the error-reduction efforts in healthcare have therefore focused on the doctor/patient interface, which paradoxically is a minor cause of medical accidents and incidents [6], and neglected the fact that institutional and healthcare system approaches must complement bedside strategies to reduce unsafe acts. This helps to explain why correcting the performance of individual healthcare providers rarely leads to a general improvement in patients' safety throughout a healthcare system [6–7].

Many of these issues are well known to anyone practicing in intensive care and have been repeatedly reported in the medical literature [6–9]. Furthermore it has been shown that not only are these adverse events frequent, they can result in sometimes devastating or fatal consequences [10–11]. This area has therefore become a main focus of attention in recent years with the key issues of decision-making, situation awareness, teamwork, communication, stress management and the effects of workload patterns taking their rightful place in medical journals alongside the more traditional avenues of research and development. An increased understanding of these topics is now leading to significant advances being made. Many authors have reported techniques and therapies to prevent many of the avoidable adverse consequences of critical illness. These include, but are by no means limited to, the prevention of deep vein thrombosis, stress ulceration and hyperglycaemia [12]. Indeed many have advocated that bundles of these interventions should become the standard of practice that others should compare themselves against. In parallel with this has been a greater recognition of the value of registry-type data describing practice, interventions and adverse (or beneficial) consequences. This can be typified by the increased attention paid in recent years to nosocomial infections. Whereas in the past many of these infections, sometimes even fatal, were accepted as a normal consequence of being in hospital, the publication of large-scale multinational registry data has allowed us to understand the extent of the problem and to develop patient-centred interventions [11, 13–16] for preventing it. Nowadays units can provide their own data to a relevant registry and get feedback and benchmarking data that allows the users to quantify their own quality and performance in comparison to other units of similar demographic circumstances [17].

Mr A.R., a 65-old male resident of west London, with antecedents of chronic obstructive pulmonary disease, duodenal ulceration, and a history of colonic cancer treated with surgery and chemotherapy within the last 6 months. He developed malaise and fever two days ago and presented today to the emergency department of the local hospital. On observation, he had rales in his right pulmonary field, was slightly hypotensive (mean arterial pressure 60 mmHg), tachycardic (heart rate 126 beats/minute) and febrile (39° C). He had a mild hypoxaemia (PaO_2 62 mmHg under 50 % oxygen mask), acidosis (pH 7.23), a low $PaCO_2$ (26 mmHg), leukocytosis (WBC 18.00/mm^3) and thrombocytopenia (platelets 13,000/mm^3). The attending physician referred him to the local ICU (which was full), so he was admitted to the ICU of another hospital 8 hours later.

While awaiting transfer he was given some fluid (500 ml of HES) and started on amoxycillin plus clavulanic acid 4 hours after admission.

On admission to the ICU:

Scenario a)

On admission, the patient was in severe respiratory distress; before the clinicians were able to secure his airway he had a cardiac arrest; CPR manoeuvres where immediately performed, with apparent success, a central line was inserted into the right subclavian vein (sub-clavicular approach) but unfortunately the tube was not well positioned (endobronchial in the right main bronchus). Throughout this period he had a very low oxygen saturation. The physician in charge suspected a pneumothorax – which was present – but no check of the position of tube was done for a further hour. At that time the patient was in deep coma, without measurable oxygen saturation and in shock (mean arterial pressure 35 mmHg). Despite all resuscitation manoeuvres, the patient died 11 hours later. The conclusion from the morbidity and mortality conference done one week later was that the patient died as a direct consequence of an inadequate management of the airway on admission to the ICU.

The family is not happy at all with the ICU team, and is considering whether to proceed with a lawsuit for inadequate care and gross negligence on ICU admission.

Scenario b)

On admission, the patient was in severe respiratory distress; he was immediately intubated, a central line inserted, fluid starts to achieve a CVP of 12 mmHg and then noradrenaline and dobutamine were added to correct the shock. Blood cultures were taken and antibiotic therapy changed to piperacilin/tazobactam due to the existence of immunosuppression and prior structural lung disease. According to an outcome prediction model developed to be used in patients in severe infection, sepsis and shock his probability of death before hospital discharge was 48 % [35].

During the ICU course pseudomonas aeruginosa was identified in the blood cultures and sputum from admission. The ICU course was complicated by an episode of shock due to bleeding from a duodenal ulcer two days after admission that required surgery (the patient was not on enteral nutrition at that time due to the high dose of vasopressor agents, and no prophylaxis for stress ulcer had been given). He required a tracheostomy for long-term ventilator support after a late-onset episode of ventilator-associated pneumonia (VAP) and was discharged seven weeks later to a long-term rehabilitation unit with severe residual morbidities. The family is very happy with the ICU team, who during the period have always tried to do their best.

When the morbidity and mortality conference was performed one week after discharge, several prob-

lems were identified, which may have had a significant impact on his prognosis:

- The initial treatment of the patient in the emergency department was grossly inappropriate, with a wrong estimation of the severity of the situation. This led to an incomplete and inappropriate haemodynamic resuscitation, no attempts to make an early identification of the causal agent and inadequate empirical antimicrobial therapy. Also, there was a significant delay in transferring the patient to an ICU.
- The final diagnosis: "Community-acquired pneumonia due to pseudomonas aeruginosa" was correct, but several factors lead to a bad outcome, namely:
  - The patient had inadequate antimicrobial therapy for about 8 hours after the beginning of hypotension, which per se increases his chances of death from 30 % to 80 % [36]
  - The choice of the inappropriate initial antibiotic therapy probably resulted in an excess in-hospital mortality of 39.1 %. Also, the rate of the risk of nosocomial infection was increased by 16.1 %. Overall, these factors could have resulted in an excess in-hospital mortality was 31.4 % [37]
  - Despite being a high-risk patient, no prophylactic therapy was given to prevent stress ulceration, the development of which is associated with a relative risk of death up to 4 times greater and an excess length of ICU stay of approximately 4 to 8 days [38]
  - The increase in the length of stay due to the need of prolonged mechanical ventilation was possibly associated with the development of the late VAP, which in itself added an attributable mortality of 25 % [39]

Are the two cases so different? For the individual patient described in the first case obviously yes. From the scientific point of view, according to the existing standards of practice in the emergency department and in the ICU, the potential prevalence of the mistakes described in the second case – as well as their impact on patient safety – is much more common.

When developing protocols and interventions that are designed with the aim of preventing adverse consequences for our patients, it is important to keep in mind the concept of "primum non nocere": First, do no harm [18–19]. Although this is one of the fundamental aspects of medical practice – it remains a key component of the Hippocratic Oath sworn by the majority of medical professionals – it is often forgotten. Many interventions have a good and a bad side [20–21]. Mechanical ventilation can both correct respiratory failure and also cause ventilator-induced lung injury or barotrauma. Fluid resuscitation can resuscitate shock but can also cause pulmonary oedema, the so-called circutrauma. Many new therapies or interventions get rushed into practice, with the best of intentions, only to lead to a later awareness of negative effects for some groups of patients and then a reappraisal of the situation.

The dual face of safety in intensive care: From the individual patient to populations

Although the emphasis on individualising therapy for a patient is important, it is vital that we do not forget our duty and responsibility to strive for the best possible results for the whole population of patients that we treat. In order to improve the care of a population of patients we need to identify and make use of consistent, appropriate and effective diagnostic tests and therapeutic interventions, with the aim of reducing the numbers of adverse events. This can be achieved by following strictly the indications and contraindications of the drugs that we use and avoiding where possible their off-label use [22–23].

Modern mantra dictates that we should utilise an evidenced-based doctrine to direct our clinical practice. Although this is perhaps the gold standard approach, it is not always either practical or possible. Indeed in many situations that we are faced with in daily intensive care practice the evidence available to direct our thoughts is sadly lacking in both quantity and/or quality. There are often problems translating research into clinical practice due to alterations in case mix and other methodological issues in the original studies. The end result of this is that although an intervention may be proven to be beneficial in a randomised clinical trial, the effect may not be apparent, or even be sadly lacking, when utilising the same intervention in a wider patient group in normal everyday practice. The best way to sum-

marise the available evidence, without bias, in a systematic and objective fashion remains controversial, although advances are being made [24]. Hopefully this will help close the gap between available knowledge and physicians' behaviors [22], and the understanding of the presence and size of this gap should lead to calls for both future funding and research into this area [23]. Unfortunately this whole area, due to its limitations, is prone to inappropriate influence and bias. This is especially true taking on board the recent controversies surrounding the conduct, analysis and reporting of several well-known products [25–28]. The current move to develop industry-independent corroborating trials [29–30] and also to clearly and transparently delineate the relationships between sponsor, investigator and expert opinion-maker is therefore to be encouraged and will hopefully improve this process [31].

For readers used to appraising research studies and papers it is often relatively easy to understand and quantify a likely beneficial effect on mortality from a given intervention. Indeed there are even many statistical terms that we are all familiar with that can be used to describe this effect. However, the reverse side to this is not so easy. Brennan described in his landmark New England Journal of Medicine paper the difficulties attached with quantifying mortality hazards due to inattention to safety. Without being able to grasp the size of this problem when trying to tackle the issue in our own units, other variables and indicators need to be followed. These include following the available evidence, making small-step changes in performance that can be measured, focusing our initiatives on the strengths of our staff, expecting to expend resources in an effort to improve healthcare quality, recognising the role of incident reporting on improving this quality and finally, recognising that to improve quality we need the input of many other disciplines than just our own [32].

Most of these aims can be achieved only through the development and implementation of cooperative benchmarking organisations, providing comparative feedback of the data and using meaningful endpoints [33]. We are glad that these organisations are becoming more common and foresee the need in the near future for coordination and cooperation amongst them in a common effort to increase the quality of intensive care throughout the world. If we want to perform better than at the time of the IOM report, something that so far we have obviously not achieved [34], we must view safety and effectiveness as complimentary measures, that should be taken together, not be viewed in isolation as together their effect is far more powerful than each on its own.

Finally, we should not forget that our role as physicians includes the duty of assigning available resources for healthcare in both a sensitive and equitable fashion. This is obviously specific to each of our own cultural and geopolitical settings and is therefore very different around the world. It is important to recognise that what we do today may well impact on the future and an understanding of this may help us prevent our interventions having a detrimental impact for and on the next generation of patients.

The authors

Rui P. Moreno, MD, PhD[1]
Andrew Rhodes, FRCP, FRCA[2]
 [1]Unidade de Cuidados Intensivos
 Polivalente | Hospital de Santo António
 dos Capuchos | Centro Hospitalar de Lisboa
 Central E.P.E. | Lisbon, Portugal
 [2]Consultant in Intensive Care Medicine |
 St George's Hospital | London, UK

Address for correspondence
 Rui P. Moreno
 Unidade de Cuidados Intensivos Polivalente
 Hospital de Santo António dos Capuchos
 Centro Hospitalar de Lisboa Central E.P.E.
 Alameda de Santo António dos Capuchos
 1169–050 Lisbon, Portugal
 E-mail: r.moreno@mail.telepac.pt

References

1. Kohn LT, Corrigan JM, Donaldson MS, eds. To err is human: building a safer health system. Washington DC: National Academy Press 2000.
2. Lilford R, Mohammed MA, Spiegelhalter D, Thomson R. Use and misuse of process and outcome data in managing performance of acute medical care: avoiding institutional stigma. Lancet 2004;363:1147–1154.
3. Pronovost PJ, Nolan T, Zeger S, Miller ME, Rubin H. How can clinicians measure safety and quality of acute care? Lancet 2004;363:1061–1067.
4. Donabedian A. Evaluating quality of medical care. Milbank 1996;Q 44:166–206.
5. Buetow S, Elwyn G. Patient safety and patient error. Lancet 2007;369:158–161.
6. Bion JF, Heffner JE. Challenges in the care of the acutely ill. Lancet 2004;363:970–977.
7. Angus DC, Black NA. Improving care of the critically ill: institutional and health-care system approaches. Lancet 2004;363:1314–1320.
8. Donchin Y, Gopher D, Olin M, Badihi Y, Biesky M, Sprung CL, Pizov R, Cotev S. A look into the nature and causes of human errors in the intensive care unit. Crit Care Med 1995;23: 294–300.
9. Donchin Y, Gopher D, Olin M, Badihi Y, Biesky M, Sprung CL, Pizov R, Cotev S. A look into the nature and causes of human errors in the intensive care unit. Quality and Safety in Health Care 2003;12:143–148.
10. Donchin Y, Einav Y, Morag I. The history and lessons from investigation into the nature and causes of human error in the ICU. In: Kuhlen R, Moreno R, Ranieri M, Rhodes A (eds). 25 Years of Progress and Innovation in Intensive Care Medicine. Medizinisch Wissenschaftliche Verlagsgesellschaft, Berlin 2007:369–374.
11. Valentin V, Capuzzo M, Guidet B, Moreno R, Metnitz B, Bauer P, Metnitz P, On behalf of the Research Group on Quality Improvement of the European Society of Intensive Care Medicine (ESICM) and the Sentinel Events Evaluation (SEE) study investigators. Errors in the administration of parenteral drugs – an urgent safety issue in intensive care units. Results from a multinational, prospective study. Br Med J (2009 in press).
12. Valentin A, Capuzzo M, Guidet B, Moreno RP, Dolanski L, Bauer P, Metnitz PG. Patient safety in intensive care: results from the multinational Sentinel Events Evaluation (SEE) study. Intensive Care Med 2006;32:1591–1598.
13. Brennan TA, Leape LL, Laird NM, Hebert L, Localio AR, Lawthers AG, Newhouse JP, Weiler PC, Hiatt HH. Incidence of adverse events and negligence in hospitalized patients. N Engl J Med 1991;324:370–376.
14. Vincent J-L. Give your patient a fast hug (at least) once a day. Crit Care Med 2005;33:1225–1229.
15. Berenholtz SM, Pronovost PJ, Lipsett PA, Hobson D, Earsing K, Farley JE, Milanovich S, Garrett-Mayer E, Winters BD, Rubin HR, Dorman T, Perl TM. Eliminating catheter-related bloodstream infections in the intensive care unit. Crit Care Med 2004;32:2014–2020.
16. Pronovost P, Needham D, Berenholtz S, Sinopoli D, Chu H, Cosgrove S, Sexton B, Hyzy R, Welsh R, Roth G, Bander J, Kepros J, Goeschel C. An Intervention to Decrease Catheter-Related Bloodstream Infections in the ICU. N Engl J Med 2006;355:2725–2732.

17. Gao F, Melody T, Daniels DF, Giles S, Fox S. The impact of compliance with 6-hour and 24-hour sepsis bundles on hospital mortality in patients with severe sepsis: a prospective observational study. Crit Care 2005;9:R764-R770.

18. Kaisers U, Busch T. Improving survival in acute lung injury: Is there a role for treatment bundles? Crit Care Med 2007;35:2441-2442.

19. Thomas KW. Adoption of sepsis bundles in the emergency room and intensive care unit: A model for quality improvement. Crit Care Med 2007;35:1210-1212.

20. Palomar M, Álvarez-Lerma F, Olaechea P, Morales I. Implementation of surveillance networks. In: Kuhlen R, Moreno R, Ranieri M, Rhodes A (eds). Controversies in Intensive Care Medicine. Medizinisch Wissenschaftliche Verlagsgesellschaft, Berlin 2008:353-361.

21. Singer M, Glynne P. Treating critical illness: The importance of first doing no harm. PLOS Medicine 2007;2:e167.

22. Bertolini G, Rossi C, Anghileri A, Livigni S, Addis A, Poole D. Use of Drotrecogin alfa (activated) in Italian intensive care units: the results of a nationwide survey. Intensive Care Med 2007;33:426-434.

23. Stafford RS. Regulating Off-Label Drug Use – Rethinking the Role of the FDA. N Engl J Med 2008;358:1427-1429.

24. Brunkhorst FM, Engel C, Bloos F, Meier-Hellmann A, Ragaller M, Weiler N, Moerer O, Gruendling M, Oppert M, Grond S, Olthoff D, Jaschinski U, John S, Rossaint R, Welte T, Schaefer M, Kern P, Kuhnt E, Kiehntopf M, Hartog C, Natanson C, Loeffler, Reinhart K, for the German Competence Network Sepsis (SepNet). Intensive Insulin Therapy and Pentastarch Resuscitation in Severe Sepsis. N Engl J Med 2008;358:125-139.

25. GRADE Working Group. Grading quality of evidence and strength of recommendations. Br Med J 2004;328:1-8.

26. Oeyen S. About protocols and guidelines: It's time to work in harmony! Crit Care Med 2007;35:292-293.

27. Handrigan M, Slutsky J. Funding Opportunities in Knowledge Translation: Review of the AHRQ's "Translating Research into Practice" Initiatives, Competing Funding Agencies, and Strategies for Success. Acad Emerg Med 2007;14:965-967.

28. Krumholz HM, Ross JS, Presler AH, Egilman DS. What have we learnt from Vioxx? Br Med J 2007;334:120-123.

29. Topol EJ. Failing the Public Health – Rofecoxib, Merck, and the FDA. N Engl J Med 2004;351:1707-1709.

30. Eichacker PQ, Natanson C, Danner RL. Surviving Sepsis – Practice Guidelines, Marketing Campaigns, and Eli Lilly. N Engl J Med 2006;355:1640-1642.

31. Durbin Jr CG. Is industry guiding the sepsis guidelines? A perspective. Crit Care Med 2007;35:689-691.

32. Brennan TA, Gawande A, Thomas E, Studdert D. Accidental Deaths, Saved Lives, and Improved Quality. N Engl J Med 2005;353:1405-1409.

33. Klompas M, Platt R. Ventilator-Associated Pneumonia – The Wrong Quality Measure for Benchmarking. Ann Intern Med 2007;147:803-805.

34. Altman DE, Clancy C, Blendon RJ. Improving Patient Safety – Five Years after the IOM report. N Engl J Med 2004;351:2041-2043.

35. Moreno RP, Metnitz B, Adler L, Hoechtl A, Bauer P, Metnitz PGH, SAPS 3 Investigators. Sepsis mortality prediction based on predisposition, infection and response. Intensive Care Med 2008;34:496-504.

36. Kumar A, Roberts D, Wood KE, Light B, Parrillo JE, Sharma S, Suppes R, Feinstein D, Zanotti S, Taiberg L, Gurka D, Kumar A, Cheang M. Duration of hypotension before initiation of effective antimicrobial therapy is the critical determinant of survival in human septic shock. Crit Care Med 2006;34:1589-96.

37. Garnacho-Montero J, Ortiz-Leyba C, Herrera-Melero I, Aldabó-Pallá T, Cayuela-Dominguez A, Marquez-Vacaro JA, Carbajal-Guerrero J, Garcia-Garmendia JL. Mortality and morbidity attributable to inadequate empirical antimicrobial therapy in patients admitted to the ICU with sepsis: a matched cohort study. J Antimicrob Chemother 2008;61:436-41.

38. Cook DJ, Griffith LE, Walter SD, Guyatt GH, Meade MO, Heyland DK, Kirby A, Tryba M, Canadian Critical Care Trials Group. The attributable mortality and length of intensive care unit stay of clinically important gastrointestinal bleeding in critically ill patients. Crit Care 2001;5:368-75.

39. Vallés J, Pobo A, García-Esquirol O, Mariscal D, Real J, Fernández R. Excess ICU mortality attributable to ventilator-associated pneumonia: The role of early vs late onset. Intensive Care Med 2007;33:1363-8.

A. Safety in Intensive Care Medicine

Márcio Soares, Jorge I. F. Salluh and Fernando A. Bozza

Current definitions of patient safety

Introduction

Patient safety is a major global public health concern. In developed countries, it is estimated that up to one in six patients can suffer harm while hospitalised and most of these situations are potentially preventable [1–3]. Each year in Europe, between 8 % and 12 % of patients admitted to hospitals experience care-related harm or injury [3]. In developing countries and countries in economic transition, the probability of patients being harmed in hospitals is much higher than in developed nations [4].

Patients admitted to intensive care units (ICUs) are particularly more vulnerable to suffer from adverse events as a result of severe illness itself and due to the high complexity of critical care and its multiple interventions, among other factors [5–9]. The occurrence of severe adverse events is associated with increased probability of death [8], and the vast majority of incidents occur during routine care [5]. A demand for safer care is the cornerstone of a worldwide discussion involving governmental agencies, medical societies, clinicians, patients and healthcare payers [10–13].

In this scenario, several patient safety initiatives emerged and significant continued efforts were made towards increasing patient safety. However, despite all this effort much work is still needed in the fundamentals of safety. A lack of clear and standardised definitions precludes scientifically sound measurement and evaluation of patient safety [14–15].

The need for standardised terminology and classification

Increasing concerns on patient safety have led to increased use of patient safety reporting systems. Standardised reporting systems makes possible to learn from adverse event and near miss data and to establish research priorities and compare initiatives. In the 2000 report *"To Err is Human: Building a Safer Health System"*, the Institute of Medicine (IOM) recommended that nationwide mandatory reporting systems should be established for the collection of standardised information by states on adverse events that result in death or serious harm [2]. Information and data on patient safety performance can be used to support strategies for making care safer for patients and with different purposes, from accountability to learning. A universally accepted classification of patient safety data is essential to better communicate and share knowledge on risks, hazards and patient safety events. To accomplish this goal more time and funding for the "basic science" of patient safety are clearly needed [16].

Patient safety is still an emerging field of study and there is a wide variation in definitions, terminology and classification systems used to measure and report patient safety-related issues [17–22]. The lack of an internationally agreed set of patient safety concepts limits comparative analysis of studies in this field across countries. Actually, not only a clear terminology is necessary, but also definitions of measures that identify hazards should be available to improve our ability to evaluate patient safety. In the 2003 IOM report *"Patient Safety: Achieving a New Standard of Care"*, patient safety was defined as "the prevention of harm caused by errors of commission (that result from an action that is taken) and omission (that result from an action that is not taken)" [23]. An adverse event was defined as "an event that results in unintended harm to the patient by an act of commission or omission rather than by the underlying disease or condition of the patient" [23]. "Near misses", another important concept, have been defined as "acts of commission or omission that could have harmed the patient but did not cause harm as a result of chance, prevention, or mitigation" [23]. The concept of "near misses" is extremely important as they occur much more frequently than adverse events or incidents. However, near misses have been defined in several ways and inappropriately referred to as synonymous with "potential adverse events" and "close calls", which may contribute to under-reporting.

The IOM also stated that the development of a standardised event taxonomy and common report format for submission of data related to patient safety (near misses and adverse events) is needed to allow clinicians and researchers "to aggregate the data to formulate research priorities, identify trends, and compare various approaches to patient safety" [23].

In 2004, the Dutch Institute for Healthcare Improvement (CBO) in association with several European governmental and non-governmental organisations started the Safety Improvement for Patients in Europe [SIMPATIE] project (http://www.simpatie.org) to establish a common European set of vocabulary, indicators, and reliable internal and external instruments for improving safety in healthcare. The SIMPATIE project was a

two-year project starting in February 2005 funded by European Commission on Public Health. The different tasks were set out in various work packages (WP) [24], the fourth WP (WP4) being dedicated to the development of a vocabulary and an internal indicator set for patient safety [25].

Also in 2004, the World Alliance for Patient Safety (WAPS) was created by the World Health Organization (WHO) with the aim to improve patient safety through a global initiative. WHO-WAPS (http://www.who.int/patientsafety/en) is endorsed by several governmental agencies and accrediting organisations and has established a series of priorities including the development of an internationally acceptable taxonomy for patient safety [26].

These two proposed systems to standardise key concepts, definitions and preferred terms used in patient safety issues are summarised in the following sections.

The SIMPATIE project –
A European vocabulary of patient safety

In the methodology used in WP4 to develop a European vocabulary of patient safety for the SIMPATIE project, an expert group performed a comprehensive review of existing literature [25]. A list of identified terms was discussed in telephone conferences and during a one-day meeting. A total of 24 patient safety terms were defined in a cross-cultural perspective and divided into four categories: detection of risk, analysis of risk, resulting actions and failure mode [25].

According to the SIMPATIE Project, *patient safety* is defined as "the continuous identification, analysis and management of patient-related risks and incidents in order to make patient care safer and minimise harm to patients". An *adverse event* is "an unintended and undesired occurrence in the healthcare process because of the performance or lack of it of a healthcare provider and/or the healthcare system". *Near misses* are considered "adverse events, with the capacity to cause harm but which do not have adverse consequences, because of, for instance, timely and appropriate identification and correction of potential consequences for the patient". The complete list of terms and definitions used in the "European Vocabulary on Patient Safety" is given in Table 1 [25].

Tab. 1   Definitions of the 24 terms of The SIMPATIE Project – European Vocabulary on Patient Safety.*
[reproduced from Kristensen S, Mainz J, Bartels P. Patient Safety – A Vocabulary for European Application. Aarhus, Denmark: SIMPATIE European Society for Quality in Healthcare – Office for Quality Indicators, 2007. Available at: http://www.simpatie.org]
* Terms in italics are also defined in Table 1.

Category: Detection of Risk

1. **Patient Safety**: The continuous identification, analysis and management of patient-related *risks* and *incidents* in order to make patient care safer and minimise *harm* to patients. Safety emerges from interaction of the components of the system. Improving safety depends on learning how safety emerges form such interactions.

2. **Adverse Event**: An unintended and undesired occurrence in the healthcare process because of the performance or lack of it of a healthcare provider and/or the healthcare system.

3. **Actual Event**: An *adverse event*, which causes *harm*.

4. **Near Miss** (sub-event): An *adverse event*, with the capacity to cause *harm* but which does not have *adverse consequences*, because of for instance timely and appropriate identification and correction of potential consequences for the patient.

5. **Complication**: An unintended and undesired outcome which develops as a consequence of intervention of an already present illness. It may be non preventable under the given circumstances. Please note the related definition of term number 12, "Adverse Outcome".

6. **Sentinel Event**: Sentinel reflects the seriousness of the injury and the likelihood that investigation of an event will reveal serious problems in current policies or procedures. Such occurrences signal the need for immediate investigation and response.

7. **Critical Incident**: Occurrences, which are significant or pivotal, in either a desirable or an undesirable way. Significant or pivotal means that there was significant potential for *harm* (or actual harm), but also that the event has the potential to reveal important hazards in the organisation. In other words, these incidents, whether *near misses* or *events* in which significant *harm* occurred, provide valuable opportunities to learn about individual and organisational factors that can be remedied to prevent similar incidents in the future.

8. **Complaint**: Each expression of resentment or discontent with the practice, operation or conduct of a healthcare provider made by a potential user or a user of the healthcare services or someone acting on their behalf.

9. **Reporting System**: A system which is designed to contain reports on *adverse events*. On the basis of reports analysis and communication of known causes and risk situations is possible. The system can contain reports on human and technical errors as well as organisational circumstances, which affects the occurrence of *adverse events* in the healthcare process. Reporting systems include input from all stakeholders – providers and service users.

10. **Professional Standard**: The standard of performance in particular circumstances taking into account recent insights and evidence-based norms and a standard of practice to be expected of a comparable experienced and qualified prudent practitioner in equal circumstances. Please note the related definition of term number 24, "Negligence".

Category: Analysis of Risk

11. **Harm**: Negative consequence experienced by a patient leading to: death, a permanent or temporary impairment of physical, mental or social function or a more intense or prolonged treatment.

12. **Adverse Outcome**: An unintended and undesired occurrence in the healthcare process which causes *harm* to the patient. Please note related definition of term number 5, "Complication"

13. **Risk**: The probability or chance that something undesirable will happen. A measure of the probability and severity of potential *harm*.

14. **Calculated Risk**: A deliberately and consciously taken risk in which the benefits of a treatment are deemed to offset/countervail the possible burden of serious *harm*.

15. **Barrier**: Protects people and structures from *adverse events*.

16. **Situational Awareness**: Refers to the degree to which one's perception of a situation matches reality.

Category: Resulting Actions

17. **Risk Management**: Identifying, assessing, analysing, understanding, and acting on risk issues in order to reach an optimal balance of *risk*, benefits and costs.

18. **Error Management**: An approach to manage the aftermath of an *error* with the goal of reducing future errors, avoiding negative consequences and dealing quickly with consequences once they occur.

19. **Action Plan**: Can be the result of analysis of adverse events. The Action Plan addresses system and process deficiencies; improvement strategies are developed and implemented.

20. **Culture of Safety**: An integrated pattern of individual and organisational behaviour, based upon shared beliefs and values, that continuously seeks to minimise patient harm which may result from the processes of care delivery.

21. **Human Factor**: Refers to the study of human abilities, behaviours and characteristics as they affect the design and suggested intended operation of equipment, systems, and jobs. The field concerns itself with considerations of the strengths and weaknesses of human behaviour, physical and mental abilities and how these affect the system's design.

Category: Failure Mode

22. **Error**: Preventable event leading to an adverse outcome, being either an act of commission (doing something wrong) or omission (failing to do the right thing) that leads to an undesirable outcome or has significant potential for such an outcome.

23. **Situational Factor**: The factor in a process which activates an error in the system.

24. **Negligence**: Care provided failed to meet the standard of care reasonably expected of a reasonably prudent and careful practitioner qualified to care for the patient in question. Please note the related definition of term number 10, "Professional standard"

The WHO-WAPS International Classification for Patient Safety

The International Classification for Patient Safety (ICPS) project was launched by WHO-WAPS in 2005 as an initiative to "define, harmonise and group patient safety concepts into an internationally-agreed classification in a way that is conducive to learning and improving patient safety across systems" [4,27–30]. In the first step, a panel of experts in patient safety was invited to constitute the drafting group of an initial version of ICPS. A draft based on existing classifications with initial framework, basic concepts and terms was evaluated by an international web-based two-stage Delphi modified survey to test the relevance and acceptability of the ICPS [29]. The final conceptual framework of ICPS is composed of ten major classes and concepts that group incidents into clinically meaningful categories, providing descriptive information and representing system resilience (see Fig. 1) [28].

Preferred key concepts and definitions for patient safety according to the WHO-WAPS ICPS

One of the main objectives in the development of ICPS was to provide standardised definitions and preferred terms for key concepts in patient safety [30].

According to the ICPS, a *patient* is a person who is a recipient of healthcare. *Safety* was defined as the reduction of the risk of unnecessary harm to an acceptable minimum. Therefore, *patient safety* is the reduction of the risk of unnecessary harm associated with healthcare to an acceptable minimum. Harm means an impairment of structure or function of the body and/or any deleterious effect arising therefrom, including disease, injury, suffering, disability and death, and may be physical, social or psychological. Hazard is a circumstance, agent or action with the potential to cause harm, and *circumstance* a situation or factor that may influence an event, agent or person. *Healthcare-associated harm* is harm arising from or associated with plans or actions taken during the provision of healthcare, rather than an underlying disease or injury.

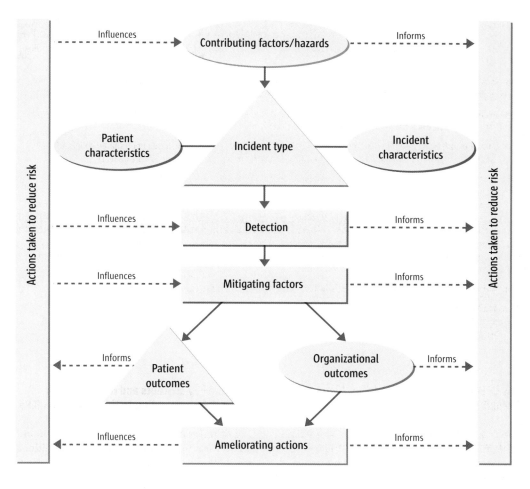

Fig. 1   Conceptual framework for the ICPS. Solid lines enclose the 10 major classes of the ICPS and represent the semantic relationships between them.
[reproduced from The World Alliance for Patient Safety Drafting Group. Towards an International Classification for Patient Safety: the conceptual framework. Int J Qual Health Care 2009; 21:2-8. The conceptual framework for International Classification for Patient Safety is the intellectual property of the World Health Organization.]

A *patient safety incident* is considered an event or circumstance which could have resulted, or did result, in unnecessary harm to a patient. The term *incident* was preferred to the term *event* since responders in the Delphi survey indicated that using *event* would be problematic because it is not generally perceived to include underlying hazards and potentially dangerous circumstances [30, 31]. *Incidents* can occur due to unintentional or deliberate acts. An *error* is a failure to carry out a planned action as intended or the application of an incorrect plan. On the other hand, a *violation* is a deliberate (even malicious) deviation from an operating procedure, standard or rule. A *patient safety incident* can be a *reportable circumstance*, a *near miss*, a *no harm incident* or a *harmful incident* (adverse event). A *reportable circumstance* is a situation in which there was significant potential for harm, but no incident occurred, and a near miss an incident which did not reach the patient. *Harmful* and *no harm incidents* are those in which an event reached a patient, resulting or not in discernable harm,

respectively. A complete list of definitions and preferred terms for 48 key concepts of the ICPS is provided in Table 2 [30].

In conclusion, the recent efforts of the WHO-WAPS ICPS and the SIMPATIE Project – European Vocabulary on Patient Safety are timely in providing a standardised terminology for patient safety. However, this should only be the starting point of a rapidly growing research field that requires strict definitions to provide reliable data and sound evidence.

Tab. 2 The International Classification for Patient Safety – List of preferred terms and definitions for key concepts. *
[reproduced from Runciman W, Hibbert P, Thomson R, Van Der Schaaf T, Sherman H, Lewalle P, on behalf of The World Alliance for Patient Safety. Towards an International Classification for Patient Safety: key concepts and terms. Int J Qual Health Care 2009;21:18–26. Oxford University Press]
* Terms in italics are also defined in Table 1.

1. **Classification**: An arrangement of *concepts* into *classes* and their subdivisions, linked so as to express the *semantic relationships* between them.

2. **Concept**: A bearer or embodiment of meaning.

3. **Class**: A group or set of like things.

4. **Semantic relationship**: The way in which things (such as *classes* or *concepts*) are associated with each other on the basis of their meaning.

5. **Patient**: A person who is a recipient of *healthcare*.

6. **Healthcare**: Services received by individuals or communities to promote, maintain, monitor or restore *health*.

7. **Health**: A state of complete physical, mental and social well-being and not merely the absence of *disease* or infirmity.

8. **Safety**: The reduction of *risk* of unnecessary *harm* to an acceptable minimum.

9. **Hazard**: A *circumstance*, *agent* or action with the potential to cause *harm*.

10. **Circumstance**: A situation or factor that may influence an *event, agent* or person(s).

11. **Event**: Something that happens to or involves a *patient*.

12. **Agent**: A substance, object or system which acts to produce change.

13. **Patient safety**: The reduction of *risk* of unnecessary *harm* associated with *healthcare* to an acceptable minimum.

14. **Healthcare-associated harm**: *Harm* arising from or associated with plans or actions taken during the provision of *healthcare*, rather than an underlying *disease* or *injury*.

15. **Patient safety incident**: An *event* or *circumstance* which could have resulted, or did result, in unnecessary *harm* to a *patient*.

16. **Error**: Failure to carry out a planned action as intended or application of an incorrect plan.

17. **Violation**: Deliberate deviation from an operating procedure, standard or rule.

18. **Risk**: The probability that an *incident* will occur.

19. **Reportable circumstance**: A situation in which there was significant potential for *harm*, but no incident occurred.

20. **Near miss**: An *incident* which did not reach the *patient*.

21. **No harm incident**: An *incident* which reached a *patient* but no discernable *harm* resulted.

22. **Harmful incident (adverse event)**: An *incident* that resulted in *harm* to a *patient*.

23. **Harm**: Impairment of structure or function of the body and/or any deleterious effect arising therefrom. *Harm* includes *disease*, *injury*, *suffering*, *disability* and death.

24. **Disease**: A physiological or psychological dysfunction.

25. **Injury**: Damage to tissues caused by an *agent* or *event*.

26. **Suffering**: The experience of anything subjectively unpleasant.

27. **Disability**: Any type of impairment of body structure or function, activity limitation and/or restriction of participation in society, associated with past or present *harm*.

28. **Contributing factor**: A *circumstance*, action or influence which is thought to have played a part in the origin or development of an *incident* or to increase the *risk* of an *incident*.

29. **Incident type**: A descriptive term for a category made up of *incidents* of a common nature, grouped because of shared, agreed features.

30. **Patient characteristics**: Selected *attributes* of a *patient*.

31. **Attributes**: Qualities, properties or features of someone or something.

32. **Incident characteristics**: Selected *attributes* of an *incident*.

33. **Adverse reaction**: Unexpected *harm* resulting from a justified action where the correct process was followed for the context in which the *event* occurred.

34. **Side effect**: A known effect, other than that primarily intended, related to the pharmacological properties of a medication.

35. **Preventable**: Accepted by the community as avoidable in the particular set of *circumstances*.

36. **Detection**: An action or *circumstance* that results in the discovery of an *incident*.

37. **Mitigating factor**: An *action* or circumstance that prevents or moderates the progression of an *incident* towards *harming a patient*.

38. **Patient outcome**: The impact upon a patient which is wholly or partially attributable to an *incident*.

39. **Degree of harm**: The severity and duration of *harm*, and any treatment implications that result from an *incident*.

40. **Organizational outcome**: The impact upon an organization which is wholly or partially attributable to an *incident*.

41. **Ameliorating action**: An action taken or *circumstances* altered to make better or compensate any *harm* after an *incident*.

42. **Actions taken to reduce risk**: Actions taken to reduce, manage or control any future *harm*, or probability of *harm*, associated with an *incident*.

43. **Resilience**: The degree to which a system continuously prevents, detects, mitigates or ameliorates *hazards* or *incidents*.

44. **Accountable**: Being held responsible

45. **Quality**: The degree to which health services for individuals and populations increase the likelihood of desired health outcomes and are consistent with current professional knowledge.

46. **System failure**: A fault, breakdown or dysfunction within an organization's operational methods, processes or infrastructure.

47. **System improvement**: The result or outcome of the culture, processes, and structures that are directed towards the prevention of system failure and the improvement of *safety* and *quality*.

48. **Root cause analysis**: A systematic iterative process whereby the factors that contribute to an *incident* are identified by reconstructing the sequence of events and repeatedly asking "Why?" until the underlying root causes have been elucidated.

Summary

A universally accepted classification of patient safety data is essential to improve communication and share knowledge on risks, hazards and patient safety events. It is also critical for gathering information and data on patient safety to support strategies aiming to improve the quality of care. Both WHO-WAPS ICPS and the SIM-PATIE Project – European Vocabulary on Patient Safety are extremely important and necessary initiatives to establish a standardisation of patient safety data. However, there are significant differences between them; only 6 preferred terms exist in both classifications and out of them, only one (risk) has a similar definition. As acknowledged by their developing organisations, they are still work in progress needing extensive clinical investigation and testing for the identification of opportunities of refinement, rather than fully developed classifications to be immediately and universally adopted.

Acknowledgements

Financial support: Institutional funds. Dr Soares and Dr Bozza are supported in part individual research grant from CNPq.

The authors

Márcio Soares, MD, PhD[1]
Jorge I. F. Salluh, MD, PhD[2]
Fernando A. Bozza, MD, PhD[3]
   [1]Intensive Care Unit | Instituto Nacional de Câncer | Rio de Janeiro, Brazil
   [2]Intensive Care Unit | Instituto Nacional de Câncer | Rio de Janeiro, Brazil
   [3]Intensive Care Unit | Instituto de Pesquisa Clinica Evandro Chagas | Fundação Oswaldo Cruz | Rio de Janeiro, Brazil

Address for correspondence
   Márcio Soares
   Instituto Nacional de Câncer
   Centro de Tratamento Intensivo – 10º Andar
   Pça. Cruz Vermelha, 23
   CEP: 20230-130
   Rio de Janeiro – RJ, Brazil
   E-mail: marciosoaresms@yahoo.com.br

References

1. Wilson RM, Runciman WB, Gibberd RW, Harrison BT, Newby L, Hamilton JD. The Quality in Australian Health Care Study. Med J Aust 1995;163:458–471.
2. Institute of Medicine. To Err is Human: Building a Safer Health System. Washington, DC: National Academy Press, 2000.
3. European Commission Website on Patient Safety. Available at: http://ec.europa.eu/health/ph_systems/patient_safety_en.htm (Accessed in February 8th, 2009).
4. World Alliance for Patient Safety forward programme 2005. Geneva: World Health Organization, 2004. Available at: http://www.who.int/patientsafety/information_centre/documents/en/index.html (Accessed in January 31st, 2009).
5. Rothschild JM, Landrigan CP, Cronin JW, Kaushal R, Lockley SW, Burdick E, et al. The Critical Care Safety Study: The incidence and nature of adverse events and serious medical errors in intensive care. Crit Care Med 2005;33:1694–1700.
6. Sinopoli DJ, Needham DM, Thompson DA, Holzmueller CG, Dorman T, Lubomski LH, et al. Intensive care unit safety incidents for medical versus surgical patients: a prospective multicenter study. J Crit Care 2007;22:177–183.
7. Harris CB, Krauss MJ, Coopersmith CM, Avidan M, Nast PA, Kollef MH, et al. Patient safety event reporting in critical care: a study of three intensive care units. Crit Care Med 2007;35:1068–1076.
8. Garrouste Orgeas M, Timsit JF, Soufir L, Tafflet M, Adrie C, Philippart F, et al. Impact of adverse events on outcomes in intensive care unit patients. Crit Care Med 2008;36:2041–2047.
9. Valentin A, Capuzzo M, Guidet B, Moreno RP, Dolanski L, Bauer P, Metnitz PG; Research Group on Quality Improvement of European Society of Intensive Care Medicine; Sentinel Events Evaluation Study Investigators. Patient safety in intensive care: results from the multinational Sentinel Events Evaluation (SEE) study. Intensive Care Med. 2006 Oct;32(10):1591–8. Epub 2006 Jul 28.
10. Pronovost PJ, Goeschel CA, Wachter RM. The wisdom and justice of not paying for "preventable complications". JAMA 2008;299:2197–2199.
11. Rosenthal MB. Nonpayment for performance? Medicare's new reimbursement rule. N Engl J Med 2007;357:1573–2575.
12. Wu AW, Sexton JB, Pronovost PJ. Partnership with patients: a prescription for ICU safety. Chest 2006;130:1291–1293.
13. McCauley K, Irwin RS. Changing the work environment in ICUs to achieve patient-focused care: the time has come. Chest 2006;130:1571–1578.
14. Pronovost PJ, Miller MR, Wachter RM. Tracking progress

in patient safety: an elusive target. JAMA 2006;296:696–699.

15. Leape LL, Berwick DM. Five years after To Err Is Human: what have we learned? JAMA 2005;293:2384–2390.

16. Moses H 3rd, Dorsey ER, Matheson DH, Thier SO. Financial anatomy of biomedical research. JAMA 2005;294:1333–1342.

17. Runciman WB. Shared meanings: preferred terms and definitions for safety and quality concepts. Med J Aust 2006;184(10 Suppl):S41-S43.

18. Chang A, Schyve PM, Croteau RJ, O'Leary DS, Loeb JM. The JCAHO patient safety event taxonomy: a standardized terminology and classification schema for near misses and adverse events. Int J Qual Health Care 2005;17:95–105.

19. National Patient Safety Agency, UK. National Reporting and Learning System. http://www.npsa.nhs.uk/patient-safety-incident-data/. (Accessed in February 8th, 2009).

20. Betz RP, Levy HB. An interdisciplinary method of classifying and monitoring medication errors. Am J Hosp Pharm 1985;42:1724–1732.

21. Woods A, Doan-Johnson S. Executive summary: toward a taxonomy of nursing practice errors. Nurs Manage 2002;33:45–48.

22. Elder NC, Dovey SM. Classification of medical errors and preventable adverse events in primary care: a synthesis of the literature. J Fam Pract 2002;51:927–932. Erratum in: J Fam Pract 2002;51:1079.

23. Institute of Medicine. Patient Safety: Achieving a New Standard of Care. Washington, DC: National Academy Press, 2003.

24. SIMPATIE Project: Results of the workpackages of the project. Available at: http://www.simpatie.org (Accessed in February 9th, 2009).

25. Kristensen S, Mainz J, Bartels P. Patient Safety – a Vocabulary for European Application. Aarhus, Denmark: SIMPATIE European Society for Quality in Healthcare – Office for Quality Indicators, 2007. Available at: http://www.simpatie.org (Accessed in February 9th, 2009).

26. The World Alliance for Patient Safety. World Health Organization. Avaliable at: http://www.who.int/patientsafety/en/ (Accessed in January 31st, 2009).

27. World Alliance for Patient Safety forward programme 2008–2009. Geneva: World Health Organization, 2008. Available at: http://www.who.int/patientsafety/information_centre/documents/en/index.html (Accessed in January 31st, 2009).

28. The World Alliance For Patient Safety Drafting Group, Sherman H, Castro G, Fletcher M; on behalf of The World Alliance for Patient Safety, et al. Towards an International Classification for Patient Safety: the conceptual framework. Int J Qual Health Care 2009;21:2–8.

29. Thomson R, Lewalle P, Sherman H, Hibbert P, Runciman W, Castro G, on behalf of The World Alliance for Patient Safety. Towards an International Classification for Patient Safety: a Delphi survey. Int J Qual Health Care 2009;21:9–17.

30. Runciman W, Hibbert P, Thomson R, Van Der Schaaf T, Sherman H, Lewalle P, on behalf of The World Alliance for Patient Safety. Towards an International Classification for Patient Safety: key concepts and terms. Int J Qual Health Care 2009;21:18–26.

31. Runciman WB, Williamson JA, Deakin A, Benveniste KA, Bannon K, Hibbert PD. An integrated framework for safety, quality and risk management: an information and incident management system based on a universal patient safety classification. Qual Saf Health Care 2006;15(Suppl 1):82–90.

Maité Garrouste-Orgeas, Alexis Tabah, Lilia Soufir, Carole Schwebel and Jean-François Timsit

How unsafe is my ICU?

Introduction

Over the past decade, healthcare quality and patient safety have emerged as major targets for improvement. Widely publicised reports from the USA, such as "Crossing the Quality Chasm" [40] and "To Err is Human" [33], showed that medical errors were common and adversely affected patient outcomes. These publications made the general public acutely aware of the inadequacies in the healthcare available to them. They also prompted healthcare providers, governments, and medical societies throughout the world to develop tools for measuring healthcare quality in all the fields of medicine. Institutions promoting error reporting were set up in Australia [49] and the US [31] in 2000, in the United Kingdom in 2003 [39], and in France in 2006 [32].

The risk of medical errors is high in emergency medicine and intensive care, where patients often have complex conditions, time is in short supply, and workloads fluctuate sharply. Thus, the risk associated with ICU admission deserves continuous attention. Safety must be defined and measurement tools devised. Indicators that reliably reflect safety and which can be monitored in daily practice must be identified. The impact of medical errors and other adverse events on patients and relatives must be investigated. Prevention strategies must be developed and evaluated. The keys to developing a culture of patient safety in the ICU must be found.

What is safety?

In "To Err is Human" [33], safety is defined as freedom from accidental injury and error as failure of a planned action to be completed as intended (i.e., error of execution) or use of a wrong plan to achieve an aim (i.e., error of planning). Two types of execution errors exist: errors of commission (unintentionally doing the wrong thing) and errors of omission (unintentionally not doing the right thing). Errors can happen at any step of patient management, including diagnosis, treatment, and prevention.

An error may or may not cause an adverse event. Adverse events are injuries resulting from a medical intervention and responsible for harm to the patient (death, life-threatening illness, disability at the time of discharge, prolongation of hospital stay, etc.) [33]. A near miss is an adverse event that either resolves spontaneously or is neutralised by voluntary action before the occurrence of consequences [1]; near misses must be detected because they are indicators of potentially unsafe steps in the patient management process. Adverse events may be due to medical errors, in which case they are preventable, or to factors that are not preventable.

In many sectors of industry, safety has been a primary concern for decades. Examples include the aviation industry and the nuclear power industry. These areas face many of the same challenges seen in the ICU: They deal with difficult tasks, require reliable evaluation tools, experience sharp variations in workload, involve complex interactions among people, operate under considerable time pressure, and can lead to life-threatening accidents. Error is a major source of these accidents: For instance, the National Aeronautics and Space Administration reported that 70 % of aviation accidents involved human errors [26].

Although some similarities exist between flying a plane and managing a patient, there are also substantial differences. Aircraft accidents are rare events that often result in multiple deaths, leading to considerable media attention and to exhaustive investigations into causal factors, whose results are used to devise corrective measures. Medical adverse events, although far more common, usually affect individual patients and are disclosed only to those directly involved. They may go unnoticed. Errors responsible for adverse events are rarely investigated and therefore rarely lead to recommendations for preventing recurrences. Many ICU patients have multiple conditions that require numerous concomitant treatments, making the consequences of errors difficult to predict. Despite these differences, some of the lessons learned in aviation are relevant to patient safety and to the prevention of medical errors [10].

Patient safety is the result of a web of factors that ensures safe practices within the framework of a safe system. The occurrence of errors can be viewed via a person approach or a systems approach. The person approach treats errors as moral issues, that is, as consequences of suboptimal work. The systems approach recognises that people are fallible and errors expected, even in the best organisations. Most errors result not from a single major failure but from a sequence of failures. These failures can be viewed as responsible for the elimination of successive protective barriers. In the Swiss cheese model, each barrier is likened to a slice of Swiss cheese, and adverse events occur only when the holes in a stack of slices line up [47]. The holes represent unsafe acts (active failures), which occur repeatedly, and the lining up of the holes represents in-built characteristics of the system (latent conditions). Most medical errors result from a combination of active failures and latent conditions. Active failures encompass slips, lapses, and mistakes. Slips and lapses are errors of execution; in slips, an action is performed improperly because a routine behaviour is misdirected, whereas in lapses a routine behaviour is forgotten. Mistakes are errors of planning: Lack of knowledge or incorrect assessments lead to the decision to perform a wrong action [47]. Active failures, especially mistakes, are favoured by understaffing and high workload [28, 29, 30], fatigue and sleep deprivation [2, 51], complexity of cases, and circumstances associated with discontinuity of care [17].

Measuring medical errors

To improve safety in ICUs, we need accurate tools for detecting defined indicators and methods for ensuring feedback to ICU staff.

A – Types of measures

One common approach to measure safety and quality of care is based on a Donabedian approach: structure (how care is organised) and process (what is done by caregivers) that influence outcome. Additionally, safety culture, i.e. collective attitude and belief of the local caregivers, has been proposed by Pronovost's team to take into account the effect on local culture on safety outcomes [6]. There are two main approaches to the evaluation and improvement of the quality of care: an improvement system in which a problem is identified, its causes investigated, and corrective measures suggested; and a monitoring system in which indicators that reflect quality of care are continuously monitored. These two approaches complement each other and are often used in combination.

B – Types of reporting of errors

Several countries, organisations, medical societies have promoted reporting systems for either
nosocomial infections or medical errors. A successful reporting system has certain characteristics: non-punitive, confidential, independent,
timely, system-oriented, responsive and incorporating expert analysis [35].

Several types of reporting exist:

- Self-reporting by the caregivers (type 1) which
  are the systems with disclosure of medical errors by medical actors. These systems are often either national. with reporting of events
  related to drugs, blood products, materials, or
  local, by prospective reporting by medical staff
  to the manager of the unit or the safety unit
  of the hospital. Currently, the type 1 system is
  associated with wide-scale under-reporting,
  partly due to the fear of blame or litigation,
  the poor safety culture of the units favoured
  by lack of feedback to the team and the workload of the staff, sometimes too busy to report.
  Nevertheless, with the knowledge of their limitations, this reporting must not be given up
  but associated with the other types of reporting. Moreover, it cannot be used to evaluate
  progress in improving patient safety. As an
  example, if the numbers of reported near
  misses decrease from 100 to 50 per 1000 patient days, it could be related to an improvement of safety but also to a modification of
  attitudes of the caregivers in signaling near
  misses or in the patients' case mix. Importantly, the magnitude and even the direction
  of the bias in reporting events could not be
  known.
- Self-reporting by the patient or the family
  (type 2) is another interesting approach. The
  underlying assumption is that patients and
  families are capable of detecting medical errors. A qualitative study identified three types
  of barriers for using patient data in quality
  improvement: organisational (lack of supporting values for patient-centred care, competing
  priorities, and lack of an effective quality improvement infrastructure), professional (clinicians and staff not being used to focusing on
  patient interaction as a quality issue, scepticism, and defensiveness), and data-related
  (lack of expertise with survey data) [11]. Nev-

ertheless, a number of French agencies have
been promoting patient reporting for several
years (http//www.has-sante.fr, http//www.
afssaps.fr). In the future, follow-up visits for
ICU patients may prove helpful for evaluating
the consequences of medical errors and the
perceptions of patients or proxies regarding
the detection of medical errors. Good communication between patients, proxies, and
healthcare providers would be expected to improve the collection of data about medical errors and their causes and consequences.

- Active reporting can be achieved using several methods. (1) Analysis of retrospective
  chart review during a mortality morbidity
  staff, or (2) the analysis of a great number of
  charts for quality control which is more difficult and time-consuming. In these two types
  of reporting, the detection of medical errors
  depends on the quality of the chart, the interpretation of the reviewers, the non-blind outcomes, and are challenging for retrieving
  long-term outcomes. Nevertheless, a root
  cause analysis can be performed, and these
  reviews promote a culture of safety within the
  ICU. Another active reporting method involves electronic alerts on electronic medical
  charts or materials, which are becoming increasingly available [43, 58, 41]. Finally, (4) local audits evaluating current practice against
  benchmarks are valuable for evaluating the
  accuracy of process indicators and constitute
  a simple improvement tool.
- It is also possible to develop a safety board in
  order to measure the safety and the consequences of the quality improvement programme within an ICU. The conception of
  the safety board must be created by a panel of
  senior and departmental leaders, physicians,
  nurses, members of the hospital performance
  improvement department, epidemiologists
  and information systems. The group should
  decide what indicators should be included in
  the safety board and what are the precise definitions of each indicator (see below).

Whatever the system used, one should know that
survey of quality of care and implementation of
quality of care programmes take time and are
costly. The process of data collection must fit into
the strategic priority of the ICU (hospital). It

Tab. 1   Examples of indicators for a safety board

Process indicators

Mechanical ventilation
- Semi-recumbent position during mechanical ventilation [55, 14]
- Overinflation of the endotracheal balloon [53]

Sedation
- Appropriate sedation [4, 14]
- Screening weaning of mechanical ventilation [55]
- Procedure of stopping sedation [55]
- Daily monitoring of sedation [55]

Medication
- Medication administered to wrong patient [53]
- Error administering anticoagulant medication [53]
- Error prescribing anticoagulant medication [53]
- Error administering vasoactive drugs [53]
- Error administering insulin [53]
- Death or serious disability associated with hypoglycaemia [35]

IV-lines
- Screening of removal of central venous catheter [14]

Management
- Appropriate use of prophylaxis against gastro-intestinal haemorrhage in patients with mechanical ventilation [55, 14]
- Appropriate use of thrombo-embolism prophylaxis [55, 14]
- Appropriate use of early enteral nutrition [14]
- Early management of severe sepsis, septic shock [14]
- Surgical intervention in traumatic brain injury with subdural and/or epidural brain trauma [14]
- Monitoring of intra-cranial pressure in severe traumatic brain injury with pathologic CT findings [14]
- Delay in surgical treatment [53]
- Change of route of quinolones IV/P [14]
- Screening of MRSA on admission [19]
- Pain management in unsedated patients [14]
- Events during ICU transport [55]

Complications
- Pneumonia associated with mechanical ventilation [14]
- Accidental extubation [12, 19, 55]
- Accidental removal of a central venous catheter [53]
- Catheter-related bloodstream infections [19, 45]
- Pneumothorax related to insertion of a central venous catheter [19, 12]
- Death or serious disability associated with intravascular air embolism [35]
- Fall [53]
- Death or serious disability associated with a haemolytic reaction due to the administration of ABO-incompatible blood or blood product [35]
- Percentage of infections with resistant organisms *(vancomycin-resistant enterococci, methicillin-resistant staphyloccus aureus)* [4]
- Pressure sores [55]

Outcome indicators

- ICU mortality rate [4]
- Hospital mortality rate [55]
- Percentage of ICU patients with ICU length of stay more than 7 days [4]
- Average ICU length of stay [4]
- Mean days on mechanical ventilation [4]
- Rate of unplanned re-admissions < 72 hours [55]
- Patient/Family satisfaction [55]

Structural indicators

Institutional variables
- Process for insuring staff competencies
- Presence of period of integration of the new health care workers
- Clear task identification
- Absenteeism, importance of the personnel turn-over

Task variables
- Availability of protocols
- Policy to prevent medication errors
- Policy to register outcome

Team variables
- Adequacy of staffing
- Nurse-to-patient ratio
- Availability of an intensive care practitioner 24 h a day
- Pharmacist presence during the ICU rounds [36]
- Communication or conflicts among teams members [23]

should obviously include the indicators asked for by the regulatory agencies. Other indicators relatively frequent in your organisation, with the highest variability, are probably the most adequate indicators because changes will be more easily visible. The results must be communicated downstream to the clinical staff and upstream to the institutional and national databases in order to enhance generalisability and to share knowledge.

C – Types of indicators

Indicators used to measure and monitor safety reflect structure, process, or outcome. Structural indicators measure aspects of technological, organisational, or human resources that are needed to supply high-quality care. Process indicators measure the way care is delivered with the resources that are available, protocols according to scientific evidence. Outcome indicators measure the consequences of healthcare in terms of mortality, quality of care, complications, or sequelae.

However, outcomes are not appropriate for comparing quality of care across units or institutions, as they depend not only on quality of care, but also on many other factors such as case mix, definitions of data quality, and random variation. At present, no reliable method exists for determining the contribution of differences in quality of care to differences in outcomes [38].

Process indicators are easiest to use and encourage changes and adherence to evidence-based standards of care. However, process indicators must be unequivocally linked to patient-centred care and outcomes. Various process indicators should be used (see Tab. 1) [9]. A multicentre study was conducted in France by the Outcomerea group to select quality-of-care indicators [52]. A large number of professionals belonging to different specialties involved in critical care used a Delphi procedure, starting with more than 500 indicators. All 14 selected indicators were process indicators (see Tab. 2).

Tab. 2 List of medical errors selected using Delphi techniques for the Iatroref study (Outcomerea group)

	Definitions
Suction circuit failure during intubation	The suction system does not work properly: The pressure decrease is not sufficient to ensure removal of pharyngeal, gastric, and/or bronchial secretions during intubation.
Laryngoscope dysfunction	The laryngoscope does not work properly: The light is not strong enough or does not turn on during laryngoscopy, assembly of the blades on the handle is difficult or impossible, there is no contact.
Medication administered to wrong patient	Medication intended for patient A is given to patient B.
Error administering anticoagulant medication	Anticoagulant therapy is not given as prescribed. The divergence may relate to the planning and/or execution of the prescription: drug given, dosage, preparation and administration modalities, dosing times, or dosing intervals.
Error prescribing anticoagulant medication	Failure to comply with recommendations (learned societies, department protocols, local drug committees) regarding the indications, dosage, administration modalities, contraindications, drug interactions, or laboratory monitoring of anticoagulant treatment.
Error administering vasoactive drugs	Vasoactive therapy is not given as prescribed. The divergence may relate to the planning and/or execution of the prescription: drug given, dosage, or preparation and administration modalities.
Error administering insulin	Insulin therapy is not given as prescribed (including as per department protocol). The divergence may relate to the planning and/or execution of the prescription: drug given, dosage, or preparation and administration modalities.
Accidental removal of a central venous catheter	Unplanned complete removal of a central venous catheter by the patient or by a healthcare worker during care or manipulation of the catheter.
Accidental extubation	Unplanned extubation
Failure to place patient in semi-recumbent position, in the absence of contraindication, during invasive mechanical ventilation with enteral nutrition	A patient receiving enteral nutrition is not kept in a 30–45 degree semi-recumbent position during invasive ventilation.
Overinflation of the endotracheal balloon	Mean pressure in the endotracheal balloon, measured using a manometer, is equal to or greater than 35 cm H_2O, relied on the charted pressures on the medical record
Pneumothorax related to insertion of a central venous catheter	Partial or complete pleural detachment by a gaseous effusion on the same side as insertion (or attempted insertion) of a catheter in the internal jugular or subclavian vein, occurring within 48 hours of insertion (or attempted insertion), diagnosed radiologically or diagnosed clinically, with a need for drainage of such urgency as to preclude previous radiography
Fall	The patient falls.

Definitions	
Delay in surgical treatment	Excessive time between the diagnosis of an acute condition requiring surgery and the surgical procedure according to good clinical practice. Surgery must be performed with no delay at all in patients who have immediately life-threatening lesions (e.g. rupture of large vessels, aortic dissection, or ectopic pregnancy). Surgery must be performed within 6 hours after the diagnosis of other lesions (e.g., compound fracture, peritonitis, or acute limb ischaemia).

Structure indicators are important for the delivery of care and finally, for outcome [57, 29, 56].

Apart from that, another important question should be answered: Have we created a safety culture in our ICU? Safety culture climate in ICUs is the sum of various factors like teamwork climate, job satisfaction, perception of management, working conditions, stress recognition. All of these items were developed through the safety attitude questionnaire, ICU version (http://www.uth.tmc.edu/schools/med/imed/patient_safety/ICU_2004.pdf). These items have been shown to be highly variable [27] between ICUs, and even in a single institution. Recent works suggest that the measure of safety climates relates to safety outcomes such as nurse turnover CRBSIs, or decubitus ulcers. Consequently they should be considered as important targets for future improvement.

How adequate are available methods for measuring safety?

The heavy workload and large number of interventions in the ICU increase opportunities for errors, and the high level of monitoring and documentation increases the likelihood of errors being recorded. Nevertheless, underreporting remains a major problem. The considerable variability of error rates across centres is probably ascribable in part to differences in reporting [5, 25]. In one study, the introduction of a new card-based reporting system increased the rate of reported events 2-fold overall and 43-fold for physician-reported events [25]! It is crucial to identify indicators that reliably reflect safety and that are sensitive to change induced by corrective measures. In other words, do those who will use the data believe that improvement in performance on the indicator will be associated with improved patient outcomes (i.e. face validity of the indicator)? If healthcare workers do not believe the indicator has face validity, they will probably not use it to improve patient safety.

In choosing the appropriate safety indicators for improvement, one should avoid 3 main classic epidemiological biases to assess performance over time: the selection, measurement and analytic biases.

- Selection bias: Select the appropriate denominator: The denominator should reflect specific case mix characteristics, as well as the intensity and timing of procedures [52, 60, 5, 20]. As an example, self-extubation rate is probably dependent on the percentage of mechanically ventilated patients. It is also dependent on the percentage of days under mechanical ventilation. If a large majority of your ICU patients are tracheostomised it is probably also dependent on the number of intubated patients.
- Measurement bias: Define the event precisely and measure it accurately: To be expressed as a rate, the numerator (event or harm) and denominator (population at risk) should be clearly defined. A surveillance system should be in place to measure both numerator and denominator. The surveillance system should include standardised data collections forms, used by trained staff. Data quality must be regularly checked (audit, control of missing data). This can be difficult given a lack of standardised definitions of events, and an unknown population at risk for a certain event.
- Analytic bias: Use appropriate statistical methods with careful adjustment on confounders: Multivariate

models and/or stratified analysis is able to take into account many confounders. Problems in selecting variables are detailed elsewhere [24, 18]. Most of time the data obtained from one patient in one particular ICU depends on the patients' characteristics but also on the ICU's characteristics. Similarly, one day of mechanical ventilation in a particular patient is much more dependent on the following day of mechanical ventilation in the same patient than on a day of mechanical ventilation in another patient. The hierarchical (day of mechanical ventilation in one patient, patient within the ICU, ICU within hospital, etc.) structure of the data also clearly needs to be taken into account.

Frequencies and impact of medical errors

Medical errors have been reported in 6.9% to 56.2% of ICU patients [21, 44, 22]. Medical errors occur in all domains of care delivery. In a 24-hour cross-sectional study performed in 205 European ICUs under the auspices of the European Society of Critical Care Medicine, 584 sentinel events affecting 391 patients of over 1,913 (38.8 per 100 patient days) were reported [60]. Medication errors contributed one third of the events (10.5 per 100 patient days) and unplanned catheter or tube removal another third (14.5 per 100 patient days). In a prospective prevalence study involving 3,611 patients, the Outcomerea group [20] found that multiple medical errors (excluding medication errors) often occurred in the same patient, the mean number per patient being 2.8 (range 1–26). Some of these errors had an independent impact on mortality that was unrelated to the severity of the acute or underlying chronic illness. The same group explored selected medical errors in 70 French ICUs. Adverse events that had clinical or therapeutic consequences occurred in 9.3% of patients and their rate was 2.12/1000 patient days. The most common medical errors were insulin administration errors. Patients who experienced more than two such events had a 3-fold increase in mortality [52].

Among all medical errors, medication errors are the most common. Their incidence varies widely, from 1.2 to 947 per 1,000 ICU patient days [42]. This wide range is mainly due to vari-ations in definitions and to inaccurate reporting. Medication administration involves giving the right drug to the patient in the right dose, at the right time and via the right route; thus, multiple opportunities for error exist. In the Sentinels Events Evaluation (SEE) study, 861 medication errors were reported in 441 of 1,328 adult ICU patients (74.5 per 100 patient days) [59]. The most common errors were administration at the wrong time (33.4 per 100 patient days) and missed medication (22.4 per 100 patient days), followed by wrong dosage (10.2 per 100 patient days), wrong drug (5.3 per 100 patient days), and wrong route (3.2 per 100 patient days). Twelve patients (0.9% of the study population) experienced permanent harm or died as a direct consequence of medication errors. Although the self-reporting method used in this study [59] carries a high risk of under-reporting, and the estimation of direct consequences of an error is a matter of considerable debate, this large European study confirmed the very high incidence of medication errors in ICUs. In an observational study [34], one preventable error occurred for every five medication doses and most errors were due to dose omission, wrong dosage, wrong drug, wrong technique, or drug-drug interactions. In the Harvard Medical Practice Study of medication errors in wards and ICUs [8], 14% of deaths were ascribed to medical errors in a population of patients accounting for 3.2% of hospitalisations. The same research group reported that 1% of medical errors were fatal and 12% life-threatening [3]. In a study of 554 human errors involving all categories of ICU treatment, about 30% of errors led to severe clinical deterioration or death [15].

Proposed list of indicators in a safety board

When choosing appropriate indicators, we balanced between the desire of a global though less precise measure of safety and a more focused but more robust one. It is usually accepted that it is preferable to reduce the quantity but not the quality of the data ... [46]. On the other hand, measures that are too narrow will not be sufficient to provide a broad view of patients safety.

In the same way, we should find a balance between a measure that is scientifically sound (that is to say precise, valid and reliable), and feasible given the existing resources. Clinicians who are concerned by the scientific validity of the outcomes measure may probably prefer process indicators, while employers and consumers may probably perceive outcome measure as important.

The safety board may probably include process and outcome indicators. The process measures need to be related to robust outcomes, the outcome measures need to be at least partly preventable.

A safety board is composed of indicators which must be chosen taking into account these prerequisites. Their measures is based on definitions. Selecting a list of indicators must be realised through a formalised consensus process involving a panel of experts. Importantly, there is no single perfect indicator or panel of indicators; each has strengths and limitations and provides different views of the quality and safety of care in the ICU. Examples of safety indicators are listed in Table 1.

- The error rate is closely associated with patient-related factors such as gender, age [34], diagnosis, disease severity, and intensity of care [34, 60, 54, 20, 59]. These factors are not amenable to preventive measures. However, they must be adjusted for when comparing ICUs or periods within the same ICU.
- Methods have been developed to adjust for case-mix differences when comparing rates of nosocomial infection [50, 62]. Similar methods are needed for medical errors, near misses, and adverse events.
- Ideally, a wide variety of safety outcomes would be tracked. Unfortunately, few safety outcomes are easy to define, easy to diagnose, common, preventable, and associated with substantial morbidity and/or mortality. As an example, the head-of-bed elevation is a well known process indicator largely accepted by many networks because it has been associated with a decrease in the risk of microbiologically confirmed ventilator-associated pneumonia in a randomised trial in a selected ICU population (7·3 per 1000 ventilator days vs. 28·4 per 1000 ventilator days, p<0.01) and appeared relatively easy to define, detect and correct. However, the difference was obvious only in the subgroup who received early enteral nutrition (significant interaction be-

tween head position and enteral feeding) [16], suggesting that the denominator of the indicator should take into account the number of patients under enteral nutrition. Moreover, the targeted backrest elevation of 45 degrees for semi-recumbent positioning is difficult to reach and a backrest elevation of 30 degrees did not prevent the development of VAP [61]. The indicator should include the way the head position is recorded. Finally, early enteral nutrition is associated with poor gastric emptying in ICU patients [48] and associated with an increase in the risk of early-onset VAP [62]. The 45-degree semi-recumbent position *in fine* is difficult to define (How to follow it? How many times a day? When? What is the optimal level of backrest elevation?), difficult to diagnose (Who measures it? No automatic detection systems), and not always associated with an increase in the risk of VAP (patient with early enteral nutrition only, if gastric emptying is not controlled).

- Several interventions (process indicators) have been shown to reduce morbidity, mortality, and cost in mechanically ventilated patients with similar advantages and pitfalls. The most accepted ones are listed in Table 1. Although the benefits in terms of mortality remain unclear, these interventions have been repeatedly demonstrated to reduce the incidence of adverse events.
- It would also be important to include structural indicators such as variables related to institution [18], to the task and to team organisation (see Tab. 1).

In conclusion, establishing a culture of safety is currently among the major challenges facing ICUs. A culture of safety is a set of beliefs, attitudes, and values shared by the entire staff. Several years after the publication of "To Err is Human", safety had improved in most healthcare institutions worldwide [36], despite persistent barriers that slowed the pace of progress [7]. At the level of institutions, disclosure of medical errors is a crucial step for improvement. One of the barriers is the difficulty of tracking progress because of unreliable or inadequate indicators.

Today, few ICU staff members fail to recognise the need for honesty with patients who are the victims of harm related to medical errors.

Patients, families, staff members, and hospital administrators should be viewed as partners in the quest for optimal patient safety.

Acknowledgements

The article was written on behalf of the OUTCOMEREA study group.

The authors

Maité Garrouste-Orgeas[1,2]
Alexis Tabah[2,3]
Lilia Soufir[4]
Carole Schwebel[3]
Jean-François Timsit, MD, PhD[2,3,5]
[1]Medical-Surgical ICU | St Joseph Hospital | Paris, France
[2]INSERM U 823 | La Tronche, France
[3]Medical polyvalent ICU | Albert Michallon university hospital | Grenoble, France
[4]Anaesthesiology department | Saint Joseph Hospital Network | Paris, France
[5]University Joseph Fourrier | Grenoble, France

Address for correspondence
Jean-François Timsit
University Joseph Fourrier, Grenoble, France
INSERM U823 "Outcome of cancers and critical illness"
Albert Bonniot Institute
38076, La Tronche CEDEX, France
E-mail: jftimsit@chu-grenoble.fr

References

1. Barach P. and Small SD. Reporting and preventing medical mishaps: lessons from non-medical near miss reporting systems. Bmj 2000;320(7237):759–63.
2. Barger LK, Ayas NT et al. Impact of extended-duration shifts on medical errors, adverse events, and attentional failures. PLoS Med 2006;3(12):e487.
3. Bates DW, Spell N et al. The costs of adverse drug events in hospitalized patients. Adverse Drug Events Prevention Study Group. Jama 1997;277(4):307–11.
4. Berenholtz SM, Dorman T et al. Qualitative review of intensive care unit quality indicators. J Crit Care 2002;17(1):1–12.
5. Berenholtz SM and Pronovost PJ. Monitoring patient safety. Crit Care Clin 2007;23(3):659–73.
6. Berenholtz SM, Pustavoitau A et al. How safe is my intensive care unit? Methods for monitoring and measurement. Curr Opin Crit Care 2007;13(6):703–8.
7. Blendon RJ, DesRoches CM et al. Views of practicing physicians and the public on medical errors. N Engl J Med 2002;347(24):1933–40.
8. Brennan TA, Leape LL et al. Incidence of adverse events and negligence in hospitalized patients. Results of the Harvard Medical Practice Study I. N Engl J Med 1991;324(6):370–6.
9. Calabrese AD, Erstad BL et al. Medication administration errors in adult patients in the ICU. Intensive Care Med 2001;27(10):1592–8.
10. Catchpole KR, Giddings AE et al. Improving patient safety by identifying latent failures in successful operations. Surgery 2007;142(1):102–10.
11. Davies E. and Cleary PD. Hearing the patient's voice? Factors affecting the use of patient survey data in quality improvement. Qual Saf Health Care 2005;14(6):428–32.
12. de Lassence A, Alberti C et al. Impact of unplanned extubation and reintubation after weaning on nosocomial pneumonia risk in the intensive care unit:a prospective multicenter study. Anesthesiology 2002;97(1):148–56.
13. de Lassence A, Timsit JF et al. Pneumothorax in the intensive care unit:incidence, risk factors, and outcome. Anesthesiology 2006;104(1):5–13.
14. Delgado MC M, Cabre Pericas L et al. Quality indicators in critically ill patients. Semicyuc, SEMICYUC 2005.
15. Donchin Y, Gopher D et al. A look into the nature and causes of human errors in the intensive care unit. Crit Care Med 1995;23(2):294–300.
16. Drakulovic MB, A. Torres, et al. Supine body position as a risk factor for nosocomial pneumonia in mechanically ventilated patients: a randomised trial. Lancet 1999;354(9193):1851–8.
17. Esmail R, Banack D et al. Is your patient ready for transport? Developing an ICU patient transport decision scorecard. Healthc 2006;Q 9 Spec No:80–6.
18. Francais A and Vesin A et al. How to conduct clinical research studies using high quality-clinical databases in the in critical care. Rev Bras Ter Intensiva 2008;20(3):296–304.
19. Garrouste Orgeas M, Soufir L et al. Can nosocomial infecions and iatrogenic events serve as quality-of-care indicators in the ICU? yearbook of intensive care and emergency medicine. JL Vincent. Berlin, Springer-Verlag: 2003;923–933.
20. Garrouste Orgeas M, Timsit JF et al. Impact of adverse events on outcomes in intensive care unit patients. Crit Care Med 2008;36(7):2041–7.
21. Giraud T, Dhainaut JF et al. Iatrogenic complications in

adult intensive care units: a prospective two-center study. Crit Care Med 1993;21(1):40–51.

22. Graf J, von den Driesch A et al. Identification and characterization of errors and incidents in a medical intensive care unit. Acta Anaesthesiol Scand 2005;49(7):930–9.

23. Guidet B, Mc-Aree C et al. [Field 3. Structural and managerial skills for improvement in safety practice. French-speaking Society of Intensive Care. French Society of Anesthesia and Resuscitation]. Ann Fr Anesth Reanim 2008;27(10):e65–70.

24. Harrell FE Jr., Lee KL et al. Multivariable prognostic models: issues in developing models, evaluating assumptions and adequacy, and measuring and reducing errors. Stat Med 1996;15(4):361–87.

25. Harris CB, Krauss MJ et al. Patient safety event reporting in critical care: a study of three intensive care units. Crit Care Med 2007;35(4):1068–76.

26. Helmreich RL. On error management: lessons from aviation. Bmj 2000;320(7237):781–5.

27. Huang DT, Clermont G et al. Perceptions of safety culture vary across the intensive care units of a single institution. Crit Care Med 2007;35(1):165–76.

28. Hugonnet S, Chevrolet JC et al. The effect of workload on infection risk in critically ill patients. Crit Care Med 2007;35(1):76–81.

29. Hugonnet S, Uckay I et al. Staffing level: a determinant of late-onset ventilator-associated pneumonia. Crit Care 2007;11(4):R80.

30. Hugonnet S, Villaveces A et al. Nurse staffing level and nosocomial infections: empirical evaluation of the case-crossover and case-time-control designs. Am J Epidemiol 2007;165(11):1321–7.

31. JCAHO. sentinel events, june 6. http/www.jcaho.org/ sentinel/senvnt_frm.html, 2000.

32. Journal officiel de la république française, m. d. l. s. e. d. l. s., arrêté du 25 avril 2006 relatif aux modalités de l'expérimentation de déclaration des évènements indésirables graves liés des soins réalisés lors d'investigations, de traitements ou d'action de prévention autres que les infections nosocomiales.

33. Kohn LT, Corrigan JM et al. To Err is Human: Building a Safer Health System. Waschington DC 2000.

34. Kopp BJ, Erstad BL et al. Medication errors and adverse drug events in an intensive care unit: direct observation approach for detection. Crit Care Med 2006;34(2):415–25.

35. Leape LL. Reporting of adverse events. N Engl J Med 2002;347(20):1633–8.

36. Leape LL and Berwick DM. Five years after To Err Is Human: what have we learned? Jama 2005;293(19):2384–90.

37. Leape LL, Cullen DJ et al. Pharmacist participation on physician rounds and adverse drug events in the intensive care unit. Jama 1999;282(3):267–70.

38. Lilford RJ, Mohammed MA et al. The measurement of active errors: methodological issues. Qual Saf Health Care 12 Suppl 2 2003:ii8–12.

39. Mayor S. English NHS to set up new reporting system for errors. Bmj 2000;320(7251):1689.

40. Medicine, I. o. Crossing the quality chasm: a new health system for the 21 st century. Washington DC National Academy Press 2001.

41. Melton GB and Hripcsak G. Automated detection of adverse events using natural language processing of discharge summaries. J Am Med Inform Assoc 2005;12(4):448–57.

42. Moyen E, Camire E et al. Clinical review: medication errors in critical care. Crit Care 2008;12(2):208.

43. Murff HJ, Patel VL et al. Detecting adverse events for patient safety research: a review of current methodologies. J Biomed Inform 2003;36(1–2):131–43.

44. Osmon S, Harris CB et al. Reporting of medical errors: an intensive care unit experience. Crit Care Med 32(3):2004;727–33.

45. Pronovost P, Needham D et al. An intervention to decrease catheter-related bloodstream infections in the ICU. N Engl J Med 2006;355(26):2725–32.

46. Pronovost PJ, Goeschel CA et al. Framework for patient safety research and improvement. Circulation 2009;119(2):330–7.

47. Reason J. Human error: models and management. Bmj 2000;320(7237):768–70.

48. Reignier J, Thenoz-Jost N et al. Early enteral nutrition in mechanically ventilated patients in the prone position. Crit Care Med 2004;32(1):94–9.

49. Runciman WB. Lessons from the Australian Patient Safety Foundation: setting up a national patient safety surveillance system – is this the right model? Qual Saf Health Care 2002;11(3):246–51.

50. Sax H and Pittet D. Interhospital differences in nosocomial infection rates: importance of case-mix adjustment. Arch Intern Med 2002;162(21):2437–42.

51. Scott LD, Rogers AE et al. Effects of critical care nurses' work hours on vigilance and patients' safety. Am J Crit Care 2006;15(1):30–7.

52. Soufir L, Alberti C et al. Incidence of iatrogenic events in intensive care units multicenter study. Intensive Care Med 2000;26:S271.

53. Soufir L, Garrouste-Orgeas M et al. Selection of indicators of iatrogenics events in intensive care units. Iatroref I. Intensive care medicine 32(Supplement 1) 2006:s11.

54. Soufir L, Garrouste-Orgeas M et al. Indicators of iatrogenic events in intensive care unit (ICU): a French multicenter study. Intensive care medicine 33(Supplement 2) 2007:S192.

55. SRLF. Recommendations of the SRLF: safety board for the intensive care units. Reanimation 12 2003:75s-86s.

56. Stone PW, Mooney-Kane C et al. Nurse working

conditions and patient safety outcomes. Med Care 2007;45(6):571–8.

57. Tarnow-Mordi WO, Hau C et al. Hospital mortality in relation to staff workload: a 4-year study in an adult intensive-care unit. Lancet 2000;356(9225):185–9.

58. Tuttle D, Holloway R et al. Electronic reporting to improve patient safety. Qual Saf Health Care 2004;13(4):281–6.

59. Valentin A, Capuzzo M et al. Errors in administration of parenteral drugs in intensive care units: multinational prospective study. Bmj 2009;338:b814.

60. Valentin A, Capuzzo M et al. Patient safety in intensive care: results from the multinational Sentinel Events Evaluation (SEE) study. Intensive Care Med 200632(10):1591–8.

61. van Nieuwenhoven CA, Vandenbroucke-Grauls C et al. Feasibility and effects of the semirecumbent position to prevent ventilator-associated pneumonia: a randomized study. Crit Care Med 2006;34(2):396–402.

62. Zahar JR, Nguile-Makao M et al. Predicting the Risk of documented Ventilator-Associated Pneumonia for Benchmarking: Construction and Validation of a Score. Crit Care Med 2009;37: in Press.

Andreas Valentin

Patient safety – What we have learned over the past years

Patient safety has generated increasing interest over the past decades in almost all areas of medicine. Looking back to 1995 and the landmark study of Donchin et al. – "A look into the nature and causes of human errors in the intensive care unit" – it has become evident that safety is a concern in the practice of intensive care medicine as well [1]. Since then, a considerable amount of research in intensive care units (ICUs) has focused on questions concerning the safety of critically ill patients. For example, searching on www.pubmed.gov with the medical subject headings "medical errors" and "intensive care units" reveals 10 references in 1998 but 50 references in 2008. Very similar to anaesthesia, one important aspect of patient safety in ICUs is the close relationship of a very complex process of care and the high potential for harm [2]. As in other high-complexity areas, such as aviation, it has turned out that the recognition of the potential for error is the first step in preventing harm and improving patient safety in ICUs. This chapter reviews recent findings related to the detection and prevention of error in the ICU as well as broader perspectives for improvements in patient safety.

Safety is not just about avoiding error

It is important to recognise that patient safety does not pertain only to the prevention of error. This definition would describe a reactive rather than a comprehensive approach. In the latter view, safety means the assurance that every patient will receive medical care that is timely, appropriate, and evidence-based. There are several examples of how patient safety is assured not only by the absence of error but by the reliable use and safe practice of processes in ICUs. Many processes in the care of critically ill patients are highly time-sensitive and thus highlight the need for proper handling at the patient site as well as in secondary areas such as the delivery of medications. For example, a multicentre study from Canada and the United States showed that only 50 % of patients with septic shock received effective antimicrobial therapy within 6 hours of documented hypotension. A negative and time-dependent effect resulting from the delayed administration of antibiotics was observed within these 6 hours and was associated with an average decrease in survival of 7.6 % for each hour of delay [3]. Another example is the prevention of catheter-related bloodstream infections in the ICU. Using a mainly educational intervention, Pronovost and colleagues demonstrated a large and sustained reduction in rates of catheter-related bloodstream infection [4]. From a broader perspective, following recommendations with respect to hand washing, full-barrier precautions during the insertion of central venous catheters, skin cleaning, avoidance of the femoral site, and removal of unnecessary catheters had a considerable impact on patient safety in the participating ICUs.

Can we measure patient safety?

For patient safety, as well as for other areas of quality assurance and improvement, an important starting point is to assess the current status of development. With respect to patient safety, this is a difficult but not unachievable task. Several methods have been described, ranging from the use of observers [1] to self-reporting systems or retrospective chart review [5]. Determining which method is more appropriate depends mainly on the underlying intention. While a method using observers will likely be restricted to scientific purposes, the use of self-reporting systems has been shown to be practicable in clinical settings [6–8]. Of note is that different methods will yield different findings [9]. Although desirable, it is not always possible to retrieve information about the number of opportunities for error and the actual incidents. This is a frequent limitation of self-reporting systems. But one considerable advantage of self-reporting systems is that contextual information is provided by the medical staff directly involved. Another important advantage is the creation of a team culture that relies on an atmosphere of assurance instead of the conventional approach of "blame and shame". It is therefore of utmost importance that medical staff be assured that they can report errors without fear of reprisal. Although team culture is an essential prerequisite for improvements in patient safety, it is obviously not an easily observable dimension. For ICUs it would be desirable to see more tools for measuring health-care climate, such as the recently published tool for measuring nursing climate [10].

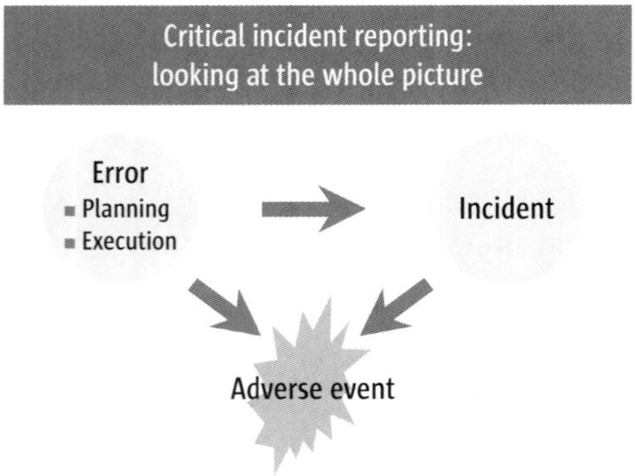

What do we need to know?

If we aim to get the most comprehensive picture of patient safety in particular settings, we not only need to look at incidents that caused harm but must also retrieve useful information on errors that did not result in subsequent harm – so-called "near misses". Fortunately, not every error leads to a critical incident or an adverse event. But in many such occurrences, a common characteristic can be found. Incidents without subsequent harm are estimated to happen 3 to 300 times more frequently than harmful events, and they provide insight into the defence barriers that prevent actual damage. Different types of events – with and without harm – can be summarised under the term "critical incident". A standardised terminology and classification schema for collecting and organising patient safety data has been developed [11]. Because improvements in patient safety will only be achieved when causes, circumstances and contributing factors of error are known and subsequently altered, it is obviously necessary to look at the whole picture of critical incidents (see Fig. 1). It is not surprising that many of the studies on patient safety in ICUs have looked at incidents irrespective of their consequences [12–16]. Such an approach aims to detect common characteristics behind the evolution of errors and to concentrate on systems which are most often the most proximal cause of error. In summary, we need to know the opportunities for error, incidence rates, causes and contributing factors as well as preventive factors of critical incidents.

| Critical incident reporting: looking at the whole picture |

Error
- Planning
- Execution

Incident

Adverse event

Fig. 1 Different types of events – with and without harm – can be summarised under the term "critical incident"

How common are critical incidents in ICUs?

It is very difficult to describe the scope of the problem in absolute numbers. As stated, different methods of error reporting or observation will produce different findings. In addition, a comparison between studies is difficult because of differences in the definition of incidents, the case mix, and the setting of ICUs. Considering the complexity of care and the high potential for harm [2], most ICUs seem to function very well. But over the last decade, several articles have revealed a serious safety problem in intensive care medicine. Donchin et al. recorded an average of 178 activities per patient per day and an estimated 1.7 errors per patient per day [1]. Another single-centre study on human errors in an ICU using predefined criteria reported 0.40 incidents per patient per day [13]. Whereas Donchin et al. used observers, the latter study was based on self-reporting of ICU staff. A multinational study on patient safety in intensive care for the European Society of Intensive Care Medicine confirmed that reports from single-centre studies reflect a widespread pattern of susceptibility to error in ICUs. In that study, 38.8 events per 100 patient days were detected in five categories – medication, lines, catheters and drains, equipment, airway, and alarms [16]. Data are shown in Table 1. A later study by the same research group focused on errors in the administration of parenteral drugs. In this multinational study, 74.5 events per 100 patient days were observed [17]. Although the willing participation of many ICUs worldwide showed that patient safety is a serious concern, there is no doubt that a detailed analysis of the causes of error and strategies to prevent it are urgently needed.

Causes of critical incidents

Any in-depth analysis of critical incidents soon reveals that two components are present when an error turns into an actual incident. Human factors and system factors combine to reduce patient safety. Human errors are estimated to be involved in approximately 70 % of medical errors. But while human factors play a major role, they are clearly less amenable to change than are system factors. The capabilities of human beings are

Tab. 1　Observed rates of events in the SEE study [with kind permission from Springer Science+Business Media: Intensive Care Med., Patient safety in intensive care: results from the multinational Sentinel Events Evaluation (SEE) study. 32(10), 2006:1591–8, Valentin A, Capuzzo M, Guidet B, Moreno RP, Dolanski L, Bauer P, et al.]

	Events per 100 patient days	Lower 95 % CI	Upper 95 % CI
Total	38.8	34.7	42.9
Lines, catheters, drains	14.5	12.0	16.9
Medication	10.5	8.6	12.4
▪ Prescription	5.7	4.4	7.1
▪ Administration	4.8	3.6	6.0
Equipment	9.2	7.4	11.1
Airway	3.3	2.4	4.3
Alarms	1.3	0.6	1.9

limited and subject to many environmental influences. Although the failure of a healthcare professional can be seen as an inevitable consequence of being human, the actual occurrence and outcome of an error are frequently due to the design of one or more systems. In a recent study from a neonatal and a paediatric ICU, it was shown that the causes of near misses were attributable to human factors alone in 5 % of cases and to work environment and system factors, either alone or in combination with one another or with human factors, in the rest [18]. It is therefore of utmost importance that system factors and work environment be designed in such a way as to prevent error or to mitigate the consequences when error does occur.

Human errors and ergonomic nightmares

With respect to human factors, the ICU has been described as a "hostile environment" [19]. Diffuse or flashy lighting, difficult access to the patient and/or equipment, a lack of space, and chaotic background noise are examples of environmental conditions with which most healthcare workers in ICUs are familiar. The negative impact of such an environment may become even greater when requirements for multitasking coupled with information overload are present. In many instances, physicians and nurses need to act like an integrated clinical database, but often without the support of a properly structured information flow and an environment designed with adherence to ergonomic principles.

System factor – Workload

In a recent multinational study on errors in the administration stage of parenteral medication, the staff of participating ICUs reported workload, stress, and fatigue as contributing factors in 33 % of medication errors [17]. The same study showed that an increased patient-to-nurse ratio and an increased occupancy rate were associated with a higher risk for medication errors. It is well known that excessive workload, extended working hours, fatigue, and sleep deprivation affect the performance of physicians and nurses [20–22]. Another example of the impact of an inappropriate workload on patient safety relates to the risk of iatrogenic infection [23]. These risks are avoidable and have a negative impact not only on patient safety but also on the safety of healthcare providers [24, 25]. Strategies to reduce such risks have been shown to be effective. In a study with interns in an ICU, an intervention to reduce the number of work hours per week and eliminate extended work shifts reduced serious errors by 26 % [26]. In a study on the effect of workload on infection risk, Hugonnet et al. found that a higher staffing level was associated with a more than 30 % reduction in infection risk in critically ill patients [23].

Demanding tasks, time pressure and emotional stress place an additional burden on medical staff in ICUs. Burnout – a psychological syndrome related to work stress – can affect the quality of patient care [27]. Although a clear association between burnout among ICU personnel and the causation of error has not been demonstrated, the reported numbers are of concern. In a national survey in French ICUs, 48 % of the physicians and 33 % of the nurses reported a high level of burnout [28, 29]. A similar survey in a Swiss ICU revealed that 49 % of the nursing team felt stressed and that 28 % of them showed a high level of burnout [30]. Knowing these facts, it is indisputably the duty of ICU managers and hos-

pital administrators to optimise schedule design and ensure appropriate levels of staffing.

Cultural factor – Safety climate

While recognising that system design is the major source of error, the question then arises: What is the culture behind these systems? A major change is necessary to overcome a culture of blame and shame and to create a new attitude toward learning. The question "Who is guilty?" should no longer be of interest; instead, the focus needs to be on the prevention and mitigation of future error. ICUs need to develop an increased alertness at all professional levels. The steps in such a development will often evolve from a culture of denial ("We don't have that kind of incident"), to a reactive culture (reaction only after things have already gone wrong), to a general attitude of risk management as an integral part of the thinking of all professionals and managers. As a prerequisite, it is necessary to abandon the unrealistic goal of perfection, to accept the limitations of human nature, and to expect errors. Error detection and recovery are integral parts of such an approach. Of note, Patel and Cohen reported recently that experts made more errors than their less experienced colleagues during a 10-hour period of ICU practice but that they recovered from those errors faster and more often [31].

The transformation of traditional patterns of behaviour, including the assignment of blame, into a new culture focused on systemic improvements in patient safety relies on an atmosphere of trust and respect that allows open communication. An encouraging result from the second multinational Sentinel Events Evaluation study (SEE 2) showed that an already existing critical incident reporting system was an independent predictor for a decreased risk of parenteral medication errors at the administration stage in ICUs [17].

In this context it is of utmost importance that responsible leaders foster teamwork, trust and individual commitment to patient care. Zohar and colleagues used a measure of healthcare climate at hospital and unit levels to investigate the influence of nurse managers and their professional peers on patient safety [10]. Evaluation of climate was based on patient orientation, professional development, and teamwork. The authors found that patient safety was maximised when both hospital and unit climates were positive. Interestingly, a compensatory effect of a positive unit climate was seen when the hospital climate was poor. This observation emphasises the need for cultural change as a key to improved patient safety. In addition, it demonstrates the relevance of efforts at the unit level.

Key elements – Routine situations and continuity of care

Contrary to popular belief, errors occur most frequently in routine situations, not in unforeseeable events. As an example, the multinational SEE 2 study revealed that 69 % of parenteral medication errors at the administration stage took place in routine situations [17]. Fortunately, every routine procedure in an ICU carries the potential to minimise the causes or at least the consequences of error. A simple organisational factor such as the routine check of perfusors and infusion pumps at nurses' shift changes was associated with a decreased risk for a medication error in SEE 2. Several studies have demonstrated that a routine procedure such as the insertion and maintenance of a central venous line is amenable to considerable improvement. Central line-associated bloodstream infection rates were reduced by educational interventions as well as the implementation of protocols and bundles relating to the insertion, access, and maintenance of central venous lines [4, 32]. Routine procedures are therefore a major starting point when looking systematically at opportunities to improve patient safety.

Another important area of concern is gaps in the continuity of care. Obviously, standard situations such as patient transport, information transfer, and shift changes are important targets for anticipatory safety strategies. For instance, intrahospital transport of patients through relatively insecure environments poses a high risk [33] and requires an adequately trained staff and appropriate precautions [34]. Another frequent routine procedure is the handover of patients between caregivers. Since this process is characterised by the communication of complex information under time pressure, a structured approach might support this task [35]. Analogous situations

in non-medical professional areas can serve as a model. Catchpole and colleagues used Formula 1 pit-stop and aviation models to develop a protocol for the handover between the operating theatre and the ICU. The authors showed that the number of technical errors, inadequate handover information, and duration of handover were reduced by using a protocol focused on leadership, task allocation, rhythm, standardised processes, checklists, awareness, anticipation, and communication [36].

It is important to note that continuity of care refers not only to the period during which a critically ill patient is admitted to the ICU. Discharge from the ICU may also entail a gap between patient needs and the provided level of care [37, 38]. The concept of critical care outreach teams [39–41] may provide an answer to these questions, but a more detailed discussion is beyond the scope of this chapter.

Summary

Patient safety is a key component of every process in intensive care medicine. Of note, patient safety consists not only in the absence of error but, even more, in the assurance that every patient will receive timely and appropriate, evidence-based medical care. Progress has been made in the awareness regarding patient safety over the past years. But as demonstrated by recent studies, there is still an urgent need for ICUs to improve the safety of such key processes as the administration of drugs and the management of central venous lines. The development of a safety culture with open communication of problems and professional exchange at all levels is the distinct responsibility of ICU leaders. Besides these cultural aspects, a clear effort is needed in many ICUs to change system factors such as workload and working environment in such a way that the system acts to prevent, rather than initiate, human error.

The author

Andreas Valentin, MD
    General and Medical ICU
    KA Rudolfstiftung
    Juchgasse 25
    1030 Vienna, Austria
    E-mail: andreas.valentin@meduniwien.ac.at

References

1. Donchin Y, Gopher D, Olin M, Badihi Y, Biesky M, Sprung CL, et al. A look into the nature and causes of human errors in the intensive care unit. Crit Care Med. 1995 Feb;23(2):294–300.
2. Webster CS. The nuclear power industry as an alternative analogy for safety in anaesthesia and a novel approach for the conceptualisation of safety goals. Anaesthesia. 2005 Nov;60(11):1115–22.
3. Kumar A, Roberts D, Wood KE, Light B, Parrillo JE, Sharma S, et al. Duration of hypotension before initiation of effective antimicrobial therapy is the critical determinant of survival in human septic shock. Crit Care Med. 2006 Jun;34(6):1589–96.
4. Pronovost P, Needham D, Berenholtz S, Sinopoli D, Chu H, Cosgrove S, et al. An intervention to decrease catheter-related bloodstream infections in the ICU. N Engl J Med. 2006 Dec 28;355(26):2725–32.
5. Beckmann U, Bohringer C, Carless R, Gillies DM, Runciman WB, Wu AW, et al. Evaluation of two methods for quality improvement in intensive care: facilitated incident monitoring and retrospective medical chart review. Crit Care Med. 2003 Apr;31(4):1006–11.
6. Frey B, Kehrer B, Losa M, Braun H, Berweger L, Micallef J, et al. Comprehensive critical incident monitoring in a neonatal-pediatric intensive care unit: experience with the system approach. Intensive Care Med. 2000 Jan;26(1):69–74.
7. Ligi I, Arnaud F, Jouve E, Tardieu S, Sambuc R, Simeoni U. Iatrogenic events in admitted neonates: a prospective cohort study. Lancet. 2008 Feb 2;371(9610):404–10.
8. Harris CB, Krauss MJ, Coopersmith CM, Avidan M, Nast PA, Kollef MH, et al. Patient safety event reporting in critical care: a study of three intensive care units. Crit Care Med. 2007 Apr;35(4):1068–76.
9. Michel P, Quenon JL, de Sarasqueta AM, Scemama O. Comparison of three methods for estimating rates of adverse events and rates of preventable adverse events in acute care hospitals. BMJ. 2004 Jan 24;328(7433):199.
10. Zohar D, Livne Y, Tenne-Gazit O, Admi H, Donchin Y. Healthcare climate: a framework for measuring and improving patient safety. Crit Care Med. 2007 May;35(5):1312–7.
11. Chang A, Schyve PM, Croteau RJ, O'Leary DS, Loeb JM. The JCAHO patient safety event taxonomy: a standardized terminology and classification schema for near misses and adverse events. Int J Qual Health Care. 2005 Apr;17(2):95–105.
12. Osmon S, Harris CB, Dunagan WC, Prentice D, Fraser VJ, Kollef MH. Reporting of medical errors: an intensive care unit experience. Crit Care Med. 2004 Mar;32(3):727–33.
13. Bracco D, Favre JB, Bissonnette B, Wasserfallen JB, Revelly JP, Ravussin P, et al. Human errors in a multidisciplinary intensive care unit: a 1-year prospective study. Intensive Care Med. 2001 Jan;27(1):137–45.
14. Herout PM, Erstad BL. Medication errors involving continuously infused medications in a surgical intensive care unit. Crit Care Med. 2004 Feb;32(2):428–32.
15. Kopp BJ, Erstad BL, Allen ME, Theodorou AA, Priestley G. Medication errors and adverse drug events in an intensive care unit: direct observation approach for detection. Crit Care Med. 2006 Feb;34(2):415–25.
16. Valentin A, Capuzzo M, Guidet B, Moreno RP, Dolanski L, Bauer P, et al. Patient safety in intensive care: results from the multinational Sentinel Events Evaluation (SEE) study. Intensive Care Med. 2006 Oct;32(10):1591–8.
17. Valentin A, Capuzzo M, Guidet B, Moreno R, Metnitz B, Bauer P, et al. Errors in administration of parenteral drugs in intensive care units: multinational prospective study. BMJ. 2009;338:b814.
18. Tourgeman-Bashkin O, Shinar D, Zmora E. Causes of near misses in critical care of neonates and children. Acta Paediatr. 2008 Mar;97(3):299–303.
19. Donchin Y, Seagull FJ. The hostile environment of the intensive care unit. Curr Opin Crit Care. 2002 Aug;8(4):316–20.
20. Barger LK, Ayas NT, Cade BE, Cronin JW, Rosner B, Speizer FE, et al. Impact of extended-duration shifts on medical errors, adverse events, and attentional failures. PLoS Med. 2006 Dec;3(12):e487.
21. Gander PH, Purnell HM, Garden A, Woodward A. Work Patterns and Fatigue-Related Risk Among Junior Doctors. Occup Environ Med. 2007 Mar 26.
22. Scott LD, Rogers AE, Hwang WT, Zhang Y. Effects of critical care nurses' work hours on vigilance and patients' safety. Am J Crit Care. 2006 Jan;15(1):30–7.
23. Hugonnet S, Chevrolet JC, Pittet D. The effect of workload on infection risk in critically ill patients. Crit Care Med. 2007 Jan;35(1):76–81.
24. Ayas NT, Barger LK, Cade BE, Hashimoto DM, Rosner B, Cronin JW, et al. Extended work duration and the risk of self-reported percutaneous injuries in interns. JAMA. 2006 Sep 6;296(9):1055–62.
25. Barger LK, Cade BE, Ayas NT, Cronin JW, Rosner B, Speizer FE, et al. Extended work shifts and the risk of motor vehicle crashes among interns. N Engl J Med. 2005 Jan 13;352(2):125–34.
26. Landrigan CP, Rothschild JM, Cronin JW, Kaushal R, Burdick E, Katz JT, et al. Effect of reducing interns' work hours on serious medical errors in intensive care units. N Engl J Med. 2004 Oct 28;351(18):1838–48.
27. Shanafelt TD, Bradley KA, Wipf JE, Back AL. Burnout and self-reported patient care in an internal medicine residency program. Ann Intern Med. 2002 Mar 5;136(5):358–67.
28. Embriaco N, Azoulay E, Barrau K, Kentish N, Pochard F, Loundou A, et al. High level of burnout in intensivists:

prevalence and associated factors. Am J Respir Crit Care Med. 2007 Apr 1;175(7):686–92.

29. Poncet MC, Toullic P, Papazian L, Kentish-Barnes N, Timsit JF, Pochard F, et al. Burnout syndrome in critical care nursing staff. Am J Respir Crit Care Med. 2007 Apr 1;175(7):698–704.

30. Verdon M, Merlani P, Perneger T, Ricou B. Burnout in a surgical ICU team. Intensive Care Med. 2008 Jan;34(1):152–6.

31. Patel VL, Cohen T. New perspectives on error in critical care. Curr Opin Crit Care. 2008 Aug;14(4):456–9.

32. Costello JM, Morrow DF, Graham DA, Potter-Bynoe G, Sandora TJ, Laussen PC. Systematic intervention to reduce central line-associated bloodstream infection rates in a pediatric cardiac intensive care unit. Pediatrics. 2008 May;121(5):915–23.

33. Gillman L, Leslie G, Williams T, Fawcett K, Bell R, McGibbon V. Adverse events experienced while transferring the critically ill patient from the emergency department to the intensive care unit. Emerg Med J. 2006 Nov;23(11):858–61.

34. Warren J, Fromm RE, Jr., Orr RA, Rotello LC, Horst HM. Guidelines for the inter- and intrahospital transport of critically ill patients. Crit Care Med. 2004 Jan;32(1):256–62.

35. Berkenstadt H, Haviv Y, Tuval A, Shemesh Y, Megrill A, Perry A, et al. Improving handoff communications in critical care: utilizing simulation-based training toward process improvement in managing patient risk. Chest. 2008 Jul;134(1):158–62.

36. Catchpole KR, de Leval MR, McEwan A, Pigott N, Elliott MJ, McQuillan A, et al. Patient handover from surgery to intensive care: using Formula 1 pit-stop and aviation models to improve safety and quality. Paediatr Anaesth. 2007 May;17(5):470–8.

37. Metnitz PG, Fieux F, Jordan B, Lang T, Moreno R, Le Gall JR. Critically ill patients readmitted to intensive care units–lessons to learn? Intensive Care Med. 2003 Feb;29(2):241–8.

38. Obel N, Schierbeck J, Pedersen L, Storgaard M, Pedersen C, Sorensen HT, et al. Mortality after discharge from the intensive care unit during the early weekend period: a population-based cohort study in Denmark. Acta Anaesthesiol Scand. 2007 Oct;51(9):1225–30.

39. Ball C, Kirkby M, Williams S. Effect of the critical care outreach team on patient survival to discharge from hospital and readmission to critical care: non-randomised population based study. BMJ. 2003 Nov 1;327(7422):1014.

40. Devita MA, Bellomo R, Hillman K, Kellum J, Rotondi A, Teres D, et al. Findings of the first consensus conference on medical emergency teams. Crit Care Med. 2006 Sep;34(9):2463–78.

41. Story DA, Shelton AC, Poustie SJ, Colin-Thome NJ, McIntyre RE, McNicol PL. Effect of an anaesthesia department led critical care outreach and acute pain service on postoperative serious adverse events. Anaesthesia. 2006 Jan;61(1):24–8.

Yael Livne and Yoel Donchin

Building a safety culture within the ICU

Increased professional demands from the ICU staff and heavy workload have lead to unnecessary medical errors which result from human behaviour. In order to influence ICU staff behaviour it is necessary to build a culture of safety in which employees perceive safety as a high priority goal across the organisational hierarchy. These perceptions are largely based on supervisory practices, and therefore supervisors have a significant role in improving safety in the ICU. We suggest employing an intervention programme that involves assessing the baseline level of safety culture with a questionnaire, followed by changing supervisory practices toward a greater emphasis on safety and a repeated measurement of the safety culture to evaluate the improvement. This approach should supplement traditional methods for reducing medical errors.

Introduction

Intensive care units (ICUs) are not young anymore. The first 3-bed ICU was established in Boston by the neurosurgeon Walter Edward Dandy in 1926. The need for such units went hand in hand with the advancement of medical technology. Respirators and monitoring equipment demand for their operation not just a reliable source of electricity and central gas supply but require the proper manpower, namely nurses and technicians with special training. This requires a thorough knowledge and understanding of the principles of respiratory physiology and haemodynamic monitoring. The nursing team in the new ICU became a partner in the treatment and were not just those fulfilling physicians' orders. Initially the ICU was a single room containing a respirator to ventilate patients who were unable to breathe and a monitor to record their heart rate. In the first years following the establishment of ICUs, the basic physiological and medical principles for treatment of critical patients were elaborated. It took a few more years to realise that a new branch of medicine was born that needed special training. Anaesthesiologists who usually perform "one-patient intensive care" during a surgical procedure were interested in the new field and with their basic training in lung physiology and their technical skills directed ICUs in many teaching hospitals around the world. Gradually it was not sufficient to have an ICU only for cardiac patients, and different medical and surgical ICUS, neurosurgical, cardiovascular, burn units and also neonatal ICUs came into being. The success was promising. Patients that were condemned to death in a hospital ward could now survive. The ability to keep a patient alive for long periods brought hope for many patients and increased the ethical demands on the team. The ICU became crowded, the workload and demands increased along with a shortage of proper manpower which increased the difficulties in coping with the multiple tasks. No wonder a new epidemic of "errors and mistakes" took the life of many patients [1]. During the rapid development of both medicine and ICUs, little attention was paid to the "human factor" of the employee at medical facilities. Reports of medical mistakes in ICUs, where patients in critical condition could not tolerate an error in their medication administration or respirator set-up, started to be published, first in the media and later in medical literature.

In order to understand the nature and causes of human error in the ICU, we asked the Center for Safety at Work and Human Factors Engineering at the Technion in Israel to study the situation at our hospital ICU. The findings showed that we do indeed err [2]. There were many factors of design and communication among the team that contributed to the errors. Despite the fact that we performed the necessary design changes, implemented new colourful drug labels and gained a better understanding of our environment, the errors still continued both for the patients and the medical teams. Therefore, we needed to look at our "system" in a different way. This new approach (which was not really new) emerged after one of our faculty (Dov Zohar) described at a conference held in our department his work done many years ago, in 1980. The work had been done in several factories in Haifa. By asking employees and their supervisors a set of questions that described the atmosphere in the factory, analysis of the questionnaires provided a picture of the safety attitude both among the employees and their supervisors. Zohar used the term "safety culture" as a measure of the social integrity of safety behaviour and what everyone understands by the word "safety" [11]. In later studies it was determined that a high level of safety culture goes hand in hand with a low rate of mishaps and errors [4, 5, 12].

In this chapter we shall introduce the concept, explain how to measure it and advise how to make the necessary change toward increasing the safety culture of your ICU. These changes can significantly reduce the error rate, not just in your ICU but in any medical facility.

What is safety culture?

It is widely accepted that the major cause of adverse events is deficiencies in system and organisation design, rather than in the behaviour of individual employees [6]. Therefore, an organisational culture perspective seems most appropriate for the study of safety in medical settings. Organisational culture refers to the norms, values, beliefs, and assumptions shared by members of an organisation. Organisational climate refers more particularly to shared perceptions on the part of employees regarding formal and informal policies, procedures and practices concerning particular aspects of the work environment, such as service, safety and quality [8]. The terms "culture" and "climate" are often used interchangeably. Based on Zohar's [11] definition of safety climate, we define *patient safety climate* as shared perceptions of the medical team members regarding the importance of patient safety in their unit. Thus, policies and procedures related to patient safety, as implemented by the unit's management, provide the source of patient safety climate perceptions.

Organisational climate can be used as a means for transforming team members' behaviour towards a greater emphasis on patient safety. In order to do so, management must realise that formal statements and declarations regarding the importance of patient safety are not enough. Employees can easily identify the real priorities in their unit based largely on their supervisor's daily behaviour. Managerial practices reflect the true priorities allocated to different, often competing, operational goals (e.g. quantity vs. quality, efficiency vs. safety). Prioritising certain role aspect informs employees of the activities likely to be rewarded and so can influence their behaviour. In other words, climate perceptions are formed on the basis of supervisory practices which indicate the true priority of patient safety [13]. Often there is inconsistency between declared and enacted priorities. For example, management announces that the primary goal is not to harm patients, but the supervisor expects his staff to avoid doing double-checks when the workload is high. In this case, employees pay more attention to implemented practices, concluding that patient safety is less important than what is formally announced and behave accordingly.

Climate can be described in terms of two parameters: level and strength. Climate level (low to high) refers to the perceived relative priority assigned to patient safety, whereas climate strength (weak to strong) refers to the consensus regarding climate perceptions within work groups. With respect to climate level, research findings show that employees' perceptions of safety climate level are directly and indirectly linked to safety outcomes, such as workforce injuries [12]. Recent evidence from healthcare supports the association between high patient safety climate among hospital nurses and reduced unsafe nursing behaviours [15]. Thus we expect the same pattern to emerge within the ICU, i.e. organisational climate level should affect patient safety outcomes.

Climate strength has implications on employee behaviour as well. Group-level consensus arises from supervisory practices that are unambiguous and stable [14]. The more coherent the pattern of managerial action, the stronger the climate will be, resulting in a strong situation that regulates employee behaviour. In a previous study, we found that climate strength moderated the relationship between patient safety climate level and nurses' safety behaviours, such that when climate was strong, climate level better predicted nurses' behaviours than when climate was weak [15]. That is, in order to influence the medical team's safety behaviour, the management's messages must be clear and consistent. For example, strictly enforcing safety procedures during morning shifts only, but not during night shifts, conveys an ambiguous message regarding the importance of patient safety, producing weak consensus with the resulting climate being weak. The probability of treatment errors is higher when patient safety climate is weak (weak consensus), as well as when it is low and strong (i.e. low priority, strong consensus). Thus, measuring climate level and strength makes it possible to identify units at high risk for errors and to take proactive steps in order to prevent them.

As organisations are inherently hierarchical in structure, there are multiple levels at which climate can be examined. Zohar [12] argued that safety climate could be construed at the group level and the organisational level. Policies and procedures established by senior management provide the primary source of organisation-level climate perceptions, whereas supervisory practices are the source of group-level climate perceptions. As supervisory roles involve some degree of discretion in policy implementation, there may be variations in climate level between sub-units of the organisation, as well as between the organisational level and unit level. In other words, the emphasis on patient safety may be greater in some units than in others. Hence, patient safety climate is expected to be somewhat different among ICUs and between the ICU and the hospital. As a result, it should be measured separately for each organisational level (i.e. ICU and hospital).

How to measure safety climate?

Patient safety climate is measured with a survey of employee perceptions regarding the priority of patient safety in their workplace. Items include a range of indicators reflecting the management's commitment to patient safety, covering declarative as well as enacted management behaviours. Item development should follow interviews with employees in order to gain an understanding of what patient safety is, how it could be achieved, what affects patient safety, what may cause an adverse event, how adverse events are dealt with, etc.

A number of instruments have been developed to measure safety climate in healthcare [3]. In order to create a scientifically accurate measure, the following issues should be considered:
1. It must focus on patient safety, not on other issues (such as employee safety).
2. Items must be related to the relevant level of analysis (organisation or unit). It is possible to generate two climate measures, one aiming at the organisation level, consisting of indicators of senior management's commitment to patient safety, and the other directed at the unit level, incorporating supervisory practices indicative of patient safety priority at the unit.
3. The survey has to be specific for each professional group (e. g. nurses, physicians, clinical

care staff, administrators etc.). The reason for this is that climate perceptions relate primarily to employees' direct supervisors and each professional group at the ICU has its own chain of command.

4. The measure should be validated by correlating it with patient safety outcomes (preferably objective measures), such as patient injuries, employee behaviours intended to maintain patient safety, or other organisational outcomes.

Appendix A presents a patient safety climate questionnaire designed for nurses, which we used in a previous study [15]. It is based on the conception that patient safety is indistinguishable from the delivery of quality care [6]. For example, in order to maintain patient safety it is not enough for a nurse to implement safety procedures, she/he must also engage in ongoing learning to update his/her professional knowledge, effectively communicate with co-workers, cooperate with team members and demonstrate a high level of caring for the patients. Therefore the questionnaire consists of questions regarding fundamental facets of the nursing role, namely professional learning, patient orientation, communication and collaboration. Following a short introduction the nurses are requested to indicate the extent to which they agree with 30 questions covering different aspects of their daily professional performance, using a five-point scale ranging from complete agreement to complete disagreement. They are requested to note only their job function in the system, as the questionnaire is anonymous.

The questionnaire consists of statements regarding nurses' perceptions of the following:

- **Patient orientation**: Behaviours directly related to patient safety (e.g. following safety procedures, avoiding dangerous shortcuts) as well as caring behaviours (e.g. providing emotional support for the patient, preserving dignity). See questions 1, 2, 5, 8, 9, 11, 13, 14, 17, 18, 19, 21, 22, 23, 24.
- **Communication and collaboration**: Effective communication with co-workers, delivering accurate and timely information among team members. See questions 7 (reversed), 10, 12, 15, 16, 20 25, 27, 28, 30.
- **Professional learning**: Continuously updating professional knowledge, familiarity with up-

to-date procedures and medications. See questions 3, 4, 6, 26, 29.

Based on the questionnaire results it is possible to look at the two "sides of the barricade". Once ICU staff members have filled in the questionnaires, the data are analysed by computing the total average of all items as well as an average score for each scale separately (e.g. patient orientation, communication and collaboration, professional learning).

The global climate score indicates the overall safety climate level. This information specifies the extent to which the ICU is at risk of human error due to unsafe staff behaviour. The lower the climate, the greater the probability of mishaps by staff members. Moreover, looking closely at the various scale scores allows identifying the specific aspects of safety climate that require improvement in order to enhance patient safety inside the ICU. It is also possible to compare the results received from different sectors within the ICU (e.g. physicians, nurses) and to plan an intervention programme accordingly. Assessing the baseline of climate perceptions can be used as a diagnostic tool, followed by interventions to improve patient safety and repeating climate measurement to evaluate the effectiveness of the intervention [13].

The results of the safety climate questionnaire can be graphically presented as shown in Figure 1. These results allow us to design an intervention that is specifically adjusted to the conditions found in the ICU. For example, if the professional learning scale shows low scores, intervention efforts should be directed at encouraging caregivers to take professional courses and to engage in ongoing learning. And if the communication and collaboration scale is significantly lower than others, resources should be allocated to enhance teamwork and effective communication among caregivers.

Since climate perceptions emerge in a process of interpreting managerial practices, intervention should involve enhancing supervisor-employee interactions concerning patient safety. This idea was employed by several researchers in designing interventions to improve safety [e.g. 13; 10]. For example, Zohar [13] introduced an intervention programme that was very effective in improving safety climate and safety performance in

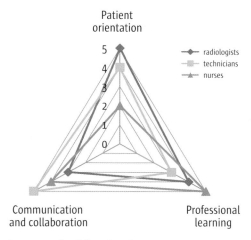

Patient
orientation

radiologists
technicians
nurses

Communication
and collaboration

Professional
learning

Fig. 1   Results of the safety climate questionnaire

The authors

Yael Livne, PhD[1]
Yoel Donchin, MD[2]
        [1]Department of Human Services
        [2]Hadassah Hebrew University |
        Medical Center | Research Center for Work |
        Safety and Human Engineering, Technion |
        Haifa, Jerusalem, Isarel

Address for correspondence
        Yoel Donchin
        Hadassah Hebrew University Medical
        Center
        PO Box 12007
        Jerusalem, Israel 91120
        E-mail: yoeld@ekmd.huji.ac.il

industrial factories. It was based on the conception that the direct supervisor has a significant role in affecting employee behaviour since he/she serves as their main source of rewards, by providing them with recognition, promotion etc. [9]. Therefore, creating a safety climate within the ICU involves changing supervisory practices toward a greater emphasis on patient safety. Following this course of action supervisors are encouraged to monitor and reward subordinates' safety behaviour on a routine basis, demonstrating a high priority for safety. The frequency of their safety-oriented interactions with employees is measured over a period of several months and presented to them as a feedback every few weeks. The continuous feedback motivates them to improve communication with employees concerning safety, which in turn leads to improved safety climate and safety behaviours.

If "to err is human", as Kohn et al. asserted a decade ago [7], then the approach to combat the error epidemic is by the adoption of methods that shall look into the human behaviour, namely methods that derive from cognitive psychology. The first step in the process is to map the strengths and weaknesses of the human component of the system, by using the safety climate questionnaire.

References

1. Brennan TA, Leape LL, Laird NM, et al. Incidence of adverse event and negligence in hospitalized patients: Results from the Harvard Medical Practice Study I. NEJM, 1991;324,370–376.
2. Donchin Y, Gopher D & Olin M. A look into the nature and causes of human error in the intensive care unit. Critical Care Medicine, 1995;5:23(2),294–300.
3. Gershon R, Stone P, Bakken S, Larson E. Measurement of organizational culture and climate in health care. J Nurs Adm 2004;34(1):33–40.
4. Griffin MA, Neal A. Perceptions of safety at work: a framework for linking safety climate to safety performance, knowledge, and motivation. J Occup Health Psychol 2000;5:347–58.
5. Hofmann DA, Stetzer A. A cross-level investigation of factors influencing unsafe behaviors and accidents. Pers Psychol, 1996;49:307–39.
6. IOM (Institute of Medicine). Crossing the quality chasm: a new health system for the 21st century. Washington DC: National Academy Press, 2001.
7. Kohn LT, Corrigan JM, Donaldson MS. To Err is Human: Building a Safer Health System. Washington DC: Institute of Medicine, National Academy Press, 1999.
8. Reichers AE, Schneider B. Climate and culture: An evolution of constructs. In B. Schneider (Ed.), Organizational climate and culture. San Francisco: Jossey-Bass, 1990.
9. Stajkovic AD, Luthans F. A meta-analysis of the effects of organizational behavior modification on task performance, 1975–95. Acad Manage J 1997;40:1122–49.
10. Thomas EJ, Sexton JB, Neilands TB, Frankel A, Helmreich

RL. The effect of executive walk rounds on nurse safety climate attitudes: a randomized trial of clinical units. BMC Health Serv Res 2005;5:28.

11. Zohar D. Safety climate in industrial organizations: theoretical and applied implications. J Appl Psychol 1980;65:96–102.

12. Zohar D. A group-level model of safety climate: Testing the effect of group climate on micro-accidents in manufacturing jobs. J Appl Psychol 2000;85:587–96.

13. Zohar D. Modifying supervisory practices to improve sub-unit safety: A leadership-based intervention model. J Appl Psychol 2002;87:156–63.

14. Zohar D. Safety climate: Conceptual and measurement issues. In J.C. Quick & L.E. Tetrick (Eds), Handbook of occupational health psychology. Washington, DC: American Psychological Association, 2003.

15. Zohar D, Livne Y, Tenne-Gazit O, Admi H, Donchin Y. Healthcare climate: a framework for measuring and improving patient safety. Crit Care Med 2007;35(5):1312–17.

Appendix A: Patient Safety Climate Survey for Nurses

PATIENT SAFETY CLIMATE SURVEY

We would like to find out how you feel about your unit's safety practices and principles, and in order to do this we ask you to complete this questionnaire.

It is important for you to be completely honest about your feelings. All responses will be treated in strict confidence and there is no requirement to put your name on the questionnaire. The responses will be processed confidentially by the review team.

It should take 10 minutes to complete this questionnaire. We would like you to indicate your company/organisation, department/ward and job function to assist us with the interpretation of the results.

Thank you for your cooperation.

Company _____

Department/ward _____

Job function _____

The following questions refer to the conditions in your ward. Please indicate your response by circling the appropriate number for each statement, in your opinion (1= Completely disagree; 5= Completely agree).

In our ward I am encouraged/required/expected to:						
1.	Know how to deal with challenging reactions from families	1	2	3	4	5
2.	Think ahead prior to every action (continuously fight the routine)	1	2	3	4	5
3.	Constantly update my professional knowledge	1	2	3	4	5
4.	Share information with team members (not to withhold information)	1	2	3	4	5
5.	Check the patient's sheet for relevant sensitivities before providing any type of medication	1	2	3	4	5
6.	Demonstrate personal resourcefulness and be able to learn on my own	1	2	3	4	5
7.	Communicate with doctors only through the nurse manager	1	2	3	4	5
8.	Comprehensively inform patients about their treatment	1	2	3	4	5
9.	Make sure every patient has comfortable surroundings (light, temperature, noise, etc.)	1	2	3	4	5
10.	Report every near-miss event (even if no harm done and not witnessed by anyone)	1	2	3	4	5
11.	Ask for explanation on every medication, so I understand its purpose and effects	1	2	3	4	5
12.	Inform a colleague when a patient complains about him/her	1	2	3	4	5
13.	Provide according to the patient's needs, even if not directly asked to	1	2	3	4	5
14.	Examine every near-miss event in order to learn from it	1	2	3	4	5
15.	Welcome criticism from doctors on professional issues	1	2	3	4	5
16.	Propose ideas to make a more comfortable environment for the patients	1	2	3	4	5
17.	Always give medications on time (even during busy hours)	1	2	3	4	5
18.	Notice any patient irregularities (even if he/she is not under my responsibility)	1	2	3	4	5
19.	Consider my colleagues' needs when coordinating vacations and absences	1	2	3	4	5

In our ward I am encouraged/required/expected to:					
20. Point out any unprofessional conduct by nurses (even if not exceptional)	1	2	3	4	5
21. Place nursing professionalism as a genuine top priority (not just as a slogan)	1	2	3	4	5
22. Invest time in clear guidance for patients (make sure they understand)	1	2	3	4	5
23. Insist that doctors rewrite unclear instructions before I carry them out	1	2	3	4	5
24. Bring to team members' attention medications which are not commonly used in the ward	1	2	3	4	5
25. Approach doctors with professional questions (not necessarily related to a specific patient)	1	2	3	4	5
26. Attend as many professional courses as possible	1	2	3	4	5
27. Frequently check my notes in the kardex	1	2	3	4	5
28. Share the workload with other team members	1	2	3	4	5
29. Attain information sources whenever a question arises, not to renounce	1	2	3	4	5
30. Significantly contribute to the development and maintenance of good working relations within the team	1	2	3	4	5

[reproduced from Zohar D, Livne Y, Tenne-Gazit O, Admi H and Donchin Y. Healthcare climate: a framework for measuring and improving patient safety. Crit Care Med 2007;35(5):1312–17]

José Fragata

Shall we publish our error rates?

Introduction

Since the publishing of the classic IOM repor, "To Err is Human", around the year 2000, medical error assumed a dominant role in both the medical and social agendas. The issue of patient safety became a major concern, on both sides of the Atlantic, and was recently considered as a civil right in a European directive in 2005. Error rates differ according to medical domains, but operating theatres and intensive medicine seem to be the areas with the higher rates and where the consequences tend to be more devastating. In intensive care medicine adverse events in patients may occur in up to 13 % to 31 % of all admissions. Errors bear profound negative consequences for patients, prolong hospital stays and aggravate costs, but even worse, undermine patient trust in healthcare staff and hospitals and ultimately lead to conflict and litigation. Since error came to be considered more of a systemic problem than the fault of careless professionals, a more sound understanding of accident trajectories has become possible, from a learning perspective, while shaming and blaming of professionals is becoming increasingly rare. This new vision opened the road to full disclosure of adverse events and medical errors in medicine, as a way to promote trust and respond to both ethical and therapeutic imperatives for patients. In this chapter I will try to support the theory behind the cul-ture of full disclosure of error rates in intensive care medicine and the practice to achieve that goal.

The dimension of error in intensive care

Before we venture into the topic of adverse events (AdEv) in the medical field it is important to define what we are talking about. According to the IOM definition [1] error is the failure of a planned action to be completed as intended (error of execution), or the use of a wrong plan to achieve an aim (error of planning) and errors may occur both by commission or omission. Some errors will produce adverse events, these being the ones that are related to treatment actions; some will have no consequences for patients, only disturb the flow and prolong the length of stay, while others will affect patient outcome to a greater or lesser extent. Some will produce permanent lesions, or even result in a patient's death. On some occasions an accident trajectory will be recovered by human and/or systemic mechanisms and no harm will be produced. These are near miss events that represent a colossal learning opportunity about error chain mechanisms. These errors have a human (two thirds of cases) or systemic origin and are preventable in around 50 % of cases, being predominantly honest, that is to say, non-negligent [2].

Errors and adverse events occur more often in intensive treatment units (ITUs) than in other wards and for several reasons – patients are severely ill and receive a great number of medical interventions, the ITU is a complex setting were different staff members interact with sophisticated equipment, often under conditions of high pressure. The error rate in ITUs is known to range between 6.9 and 31 % of all admitted cases [3–5], being mainly due to medication, ventilation, central line insertion and nosocomial infections of different etiologies [6]. Other studies reported 80 to 90 adverse events per 1,000 patient days in ITU, or 1.7 errors per patient day in intensive care, including both errors and harmful events [7]. These figures are certainly higher than the generally reported median figure of 10 % error rate for all medical fields and activities [8] relating to the complex nature of patient characteristics and tasks undertaken by professional intensive staff, despite the generally good standard of care and defence level (alarms, protocols, double checks and control measures) already in place.

But the reason why adverse events are relevant to ITU practice is not only their high prevalence, but rather their impact on different aspects of care, namely damage to patients and families, increased treatment costs, disruption of internal morale, breach of performance and quality, as well as social impact. Shall the need for monetary compensation to patients and their families arise, then anger reactions, litigation claims, reputation loss, and, above all, mistrust will undermine doctor and patient relationships that are so necessary for successful treatment. This is why error management is so important and needs to be implemented as a way to promote quality, by improving both safety and performance, while being transparent.

Safety as a dimension of performance and quality

Since Ernest Codman set the principles of quality control for hospitals back in the 1910s, and the pioneer Donabedian quality triad, Outcome,

Process and Resources, the concept of healthcare quality has developed markedly. The IOM definition lastly issued [9] has elected a broader classification, covering all aspects including, firstly, safety.

- **Safe**: avoids injuries to patients
- **Timely**: minimises waits and delays for all
- **Effective**: based on scientific evidence = results
- **Efficient**: avoids waste of equipment, supplies
- **Equitable**: not discriminatory to patients
- **Patient-centered**: responsive to patient needs and oriented to patient satisfaction

Safety emerged as the stronger component of the complex quality dimension for healthcare, and rightly so, as the everlasting Hippocratic principle of *"first, do no harm"* is still current. The exercise of a medical practice with minimal errors is not only safe in itself, but promotes efficacy (right outcome), promotes efficiency (better use of resources), is patient-centered and promotes patient satisfaction, covering in this way the full spectrum of quality. Performance is related to both complexity of the treatment tasks and the patient profiles and determines the risk of an adverse event. The risk equation stands: Risk = Complexity x Performance [10], and good performance is certainly dependent on the safety profile of the practice.

We may then conclude that safety (error avoidance) is a surrogate for good performance and, certainly, quality.

Why should error be disclosed?

There are different sets of reasons why medical errors and adverse events should be disclosed to patients, and why some barriers still persist, making widespread disclosure difficult.

After the American Medical Association's early recommendations in the fifties regarding error reporting by each hospital, the Joint Commission for the Accreditation of Hospital Organizations (JCAHO) made specific recommendations (Standard RI.1.2.2) for practitioners to disclose patient outcomes, namely unexpected adverse events, and so did the Harvard Hospital consensus statement on "When Things Go Wrong: Responding to Adverse Events" published in 2006 (IHI). Different reporting systems are presently

Tab. 1   Adverse events for compulsory reporting (Never Events)

Surgical Events	Device Events
Wrong site surgery	Contaminated device
Wrong surgery	Device malfunction
Wrong patient	Air embolism
Retained foreign bodies	
Death of a healthy patient	

in place in the US, the major difference being their voluntary or compulsory nature, varying from state to state [13]. Voluntary reporting carries the advantages of any anonymous non-accountable registry, but is mostly uncertain and unable to give a precise dimension of event rates, although being most friendly and totally dependent on individual initiative. Mandatory reports are usually oriented to events that are the most serious (not supposed to have happened) and invariably cause harm – so-called *"never events"* (see Tab. 1, as well as National Quality Forum 2005: http://www.qualityforum.org/pdf/news/txSREReportAppeals10-15-06.pdf). Another possibility, possibly the most adequate, is to keep a voluntary system and a mandatory system (only for "never events") running together, thus combining the advantages of both policies.

In regard to what constitutes error disclosure – it may just not be made at all, be made only partially, or ideally, be total, i.e. full error disclosure.

There are several reasons for full disclosure of errors and events, and they are based on ethical, therapeutic and learning grounds and supported by the imperative of professionalism.

Ethical considerations in favour of error disclosure

Beauchamp and Childress' ethical/moral principles reunite both duty-based theories and utilitarian theories and, from either perspective, error disclosure is advisable. In fact, autonomy is the first moral principle and a patient that does not know what is going on with him/her cannot make choices, namely after having been hurt, choices that might affect the future prognosis. Disclosure of errors and events serves autonomy and not doing it undermines confidence and trust

– the Hippocratic basis for classic doctor-patient relationships. Recently in the US some states have adopted the "medical apology laws" that use medical apologies to harmed patients as a misconduct waiver in court-settlement cases [14].

Other than autonomy, other ethical principles are at stake regarding error disclosure – beneficence and vulnerability – these backing the fiduciary duty of doctors towards patients *(a fiduciary is someone who has undertaken to act on behalf of another in a particular matter in circumstances which give rise to a relationship of trust and confidence)*. This fiduciary obligation of doctors means that they are in a stronger position regarding their vulnerable patients and owe them protection and altruism, and also naturally, honesty and disclosure, as part of their beneficence & non-maleficence obligations [15]. These obligations derive from the ancient Roman property law and also apply to patient care and to patients under medical responsibility.

Other than these ethical obligations towards patients there are also professional obligations, governed by professional conduct codes such as those of the American Medical Association and the JCAHO that provide guidelines for adequate medical conduct and govern professionalism [16]. These impose the duty of truth-telling to professionals in all circumstances. Therefore, disclosure of errors is not an option, it is rather a matter of good ethical positioning.

Why is disclosure a therapeutic argument?

Errors always leave scars, be they physical or psychological. An unexplained error weakens trust and leads to anger, disrupting doctor-patient relationships, and produces emotional trauma.

Apart from these trust and psychological reasons, a complication kept secret from a patient leaves him/her with no opportunity to seek help and be properly treated [16].

Learning reasons for disclosure

We have described error as an unwanted deviation from a traced plan or the choice of a wrong plan to attain an objective that was missed, but error is also a learning opportunity, as suggested by Karl Popper: "Knowledge does grow here and there by accumulation, yet far often knowledge grows by the recognition of error." This is only possible if all error episodes and even their tendencies, either provoking damage or not, are brought to attention by reporting and disclosure. This allows error trajectory study, root cause analysis and leads to the implementation of error recovery and prevention strategies. This is particularly true for near-miss situations, where an error sequence was recovered by human and or system actions, to prevent accident occurrence and harm induction. In near-miss episodes all lessons about error are present, but damage was not produced, and that makes accident dynamics much easier to study and to analyse [2].

Professionalism imposes error disclosure

What is professionalism? Professionalism was recently described as "clinical competence, communication skills, ethical understanding, upon which the aspiration of the principles of excellence, humanism, accountability and altruism is built." This represents the bridge between the technical profession and societal duty, that should be led and regulated by the profession. This most important dimension comprises knowledge and expertise, the fiduciary responsibility and altruism, and finally, professional self-regulation [17]. In the name of these professional conduct norms one must tell no lies and practise open disclosure of errors.

Now, from the patient perspective, what do patients expect after they have suffered from a medical error? Firstly, patients that suffered an injury are entitled to a prompt and competent repair of any induced lesions. Also, they expect a thorough explanation of what really happened to them and an apology or, at least, a demonstration of sorrow. These two elements – disclosure and apology – respond to different needs. Finally, they want to know what kind of measures were taken to prevent recurrences of the same type of error. Full disclosure is an ethical imperative, in line with the need to respect patients' autonomy and to maintain trustful patient-doctor relationships. Apology is a therapeutic necessity that shows our humanity and helps the patient to get over the issue and to forgive [16]. Sometimes this is not enough, as anger is just too powerful for forgiveness; nevertheless this moment of apology also helps professionals to be "cured", as second victims of an error, removing guilt and healing souls. René Leriche, a classical vascular surgeon, used to say: "Every surgeon carries with him his own cemetery – the patients he could not save – where, from time to time, he goes and prays for ..."

Yet, from the patients' perspective, different surveys support their genuine whish to know about even minor errors in the course of treatments provided to them [18, 19], and in some instances to see medical fees waived in the case of an error [20].

There seems to be no doubt that errors should be disclosed, but to what extent shall they be disclosed? Well, one should take into consideration the fact that errors are a trend and the pathway to severe accident causation, with different impact on patients; most of the time the errors we make do not produce accidents, other times we recognise the error and manage to recover it – this is a near miss –, on other occasions the consequences are only procedural, with no impact upon patients, only affecting treatment flow and costs. In a smaller number of cases damage is produced, this may be minor (incidents) or major (accidents), sometimes and in a small percentage of cases (3–5 %), these will lead to patient death. Shall we disclose every error that occurs or shall we rather be selective, making the degree of disclosure depend on the extent of the consequences? In extensive studies of the general population, over 98 % of respondents favoured that error disclosure to patients should be complete, even for minor errors [18]; however, for physicians, the disclosure rate was not more than 28 % [21], although this figure would increase in the case of patient death. In fact, and for the ITU scenar-

A

io, Vincent conducted a European survey on the rate of error disclosure by intensive care doctors, concluding that 32% would disclose fully, 63% would minimise the error and 4% would omit. Interestingly, 70% of responding doctors stated that full disclosure should always be practised [22]. Other studies in the USA and Canada, in the setting of different ethical and legal systems, revealed that doctors tended to disclose severe error with damage production, leaving out minor errors [23]. No definitive solutions are available, but ethical recommendations are in favour of disclosure of any occurring errors, regardless of the damage they might produce; however, some state that such a policy would undermine trust in the health system, and rather support that only errors impacting the patient or perceived by families should be made public [24, 25]. Using common sense and following sound ethical recommendations one should disclose more often than less and certainly, every "relevant" error factually occurring, independently of damage produced, as this policy strengthens trust and reduces potential litigation [26–28]. Above all and from a learning perspective, simple disclosure of non-damaging near misses is a tremendous opportunity for error reduction and will increase patient safety. Maybe small errors, irrelevant to patients, should be registered and studied by professionals, but need not be revealed to patients, as this is most likely unnecessary and not helpful [14].

Costs and benefits of transparency in the ITU setting

The cost/benefit trade-off of error disclosure in the ITU setting has to take into consideration the barriers and problems of disclosure, as opposed to its advantages.

Barriers to disclosure

Barriers are certainly cultural, having to do with the culture of silence in the medical community. Doctors and nurses do not harm on purpose and most errors are "honest" errors and do not result from negligent actions, so everyone finds it difficult to apologise. Saying "I feel sorry" is easy but an apology is far more difficult. Some feel

that to apologise is to recognise implicit guilt. The practitioners are not trained to hold this kind of conversation and the *shaming and blaming* culture around error makes it even more difficult [16]. Finally, the fear of medico-legal actions is always present in the doctor's mind but rarely linked to error disclosure in practice [29].

The problems surrounding error disclosure in ITUs have to do with the stressful nature of the work, involving all actors – staff, patients and families – and the fear of legal claims. However, an honest policy of disclosure seems to build trust and confidence in both the staff and the institution.

Benefits of error disclosure

The benefits are far more prevalent and involve patients, society, practitioners and institutions. Patient autonomy is reinforced, errors are detected and corrected at earlier stages and the doctor-patient relationship is improved, based on trust. Society looks upon the activity and the institution with more confidence and hospital reputation is preserved; practitioners get emotional relief by admitting error, they learn about error and more patient safety is promoted; practitioners are sued less often and when so, with less drastic consequences. Institutions see fewer legal claims and pay less for compensation while maintaining their reputation, and at the same time, patient safety is improved by this error disclosure culture [13].

There seems to be no doubt that error disclosure is desirable, therefore one would recommend publication of error rates for ITUs. This would mean that the performance portfolio for each unit would include not only the number of patients treated, the complexity or risk scoring and the survival rate associated with the practice, but also its complication rate – i.a., how many medication errors occurred, how often central lines were associated with complications, the infection rate, reintubation episodes and readmissions [30]. One may argue that this would undermine trust in service and practitioners – yet there are examples in other medical fields we can follow, such as the publication in newspapers of cardiac surgeons' mortality rates for coronary patients in the USA, which was feared to affect practices and to shift referral patterns, but did not. Rather, it promoted trust and eventually led to lowered mortality figures, just by learning and improving. This favourable result has to do with the fact that mortality figures were correctly risk-adjusted to patient profile and complexity, based on the STS (Society of Thoracic Surgeons) database. This might prove difficult for ITUs, where risk scoring has been in place for years but the population is far more diversified than in cardiac surgery. However, I am sure it would promote confidence from both practitioners and public should the process of public disclosure be properly conducted. Disclosing performance is a modern imperative, for both non-medical and medical activities, increasingly under benchmark scrutiny. Also, publishing error rates for ITUs as accountable institutions on their own will become mandatory, as error rates are performance (bad performance) surrogates; alternatively, safety rates such as survival, freedom from complications figures, zero infection goals, among others, might be presented as quality components. How to achieve this in practice is the subject of our closing chapter.

Practical issues on how to deal with error disclosure and error publication in ITUs

This is a case for increased transparency, in fact an obligation in this "flat world we live in". In fact, patient care now needs to be patient-centered and totally transparent, while patient and family empowerment in medical decision processes is requested more and more.

Error publication and disclosure are different steps of the same process of promoting more transparency within the system. Error disclosure is the *accountability* perspective, played out in a proactive and compassionate way, a way by which professionals disclose and give apologies for any errors or negative events they might be responsible for; while the publication of error rates, not errors committed by a given staff member but rather by the whole team or an institution, will represent a performance display under a *learning* perspective. Because it is proactive and not in reaction to a personal case, it is easier to handle and there is no immediate shame/blame connected to it.

This attitude is a demonstration of seriousness and concern with patient care and safety issues, while at the same time it might be a good instrument for benchmarking and reputation dissemination as well. A unit that practices individual error disclosure will have no problems in publishing its error rates, and to do so, some principles must be observed.

Orientations to correct error disclosure

Being part of a safety and reporting culture in the unit and more than an individual initiative, it must be a structured, well-defined process and similar to the "how to break bad news" approach [31]. First of all one should be sure that an error has occurred and what, if any, damage has occurred, followed by knowledge of the sequence of events – root cause analysis – to establish system responsibilities. The disclosure meeting should be prepared (define a system approach, legal and financial implications, know the full history...); then, and as soon as possible after the accident, a senior staff member should sit in a quiet room to talk with the patient or family members, a senior nurse and, eventually, other members of the team, for instance, a psychologist. A sympathetic, non-defensive, attitude should be adopted to reconstruct what has happened in simple but truthful words, promising a complete investigation and explaining how future recurrences will be prevented. Now is the time for an apology, in the form of "we feel so sorry that this has happened" in the case of a nonpreventable complication, clearly an honest error. This apology would take an even clearer form in the presence of a gross mistake, or severe damage, for instance from an institutional breach of safety, asking to "accept our apologies for this terrible accident". There is no need for self-blaming or, even worse, for blaming others, but patients or families should feel a compassionate sorrow for what happened. Silences should be well-managed and family members able to pose questions (which should be answered with full truth and simplicity) and release any emotions. This attitude might implicitly assume liability for monetary compensation, much better treated by insurance coverage, ideally within a no-fault compensation system as it exists predominantly in northern European countries. As a practical point, it will be appropriate to refrain from presenting fees before the issue is settled, as it will only aggravate feelings of anger on the part of patients and families. The conversations with families should be recorded in the clinical notes, mentioning who was present and the content of the meeting; these meetings may have to be held on different occasions, depending on the flow of the case, investigation, patient's clinical state and evolution, etc.

As a memo, the following recommendation list was proposed for the ITU scenario [30, 32].

Preparing disclosure

- *Prepare a "root cause" analysis or system approach for the accident*
- *Think about future changes to prevent recurrences*
- *Discuss with third parties the legal and financial implications of the case*
- *Prepare the "meeting" – place, moment, and people attending*

Disclosure of an error

As soon as possible after the event:

- *Choose the participants openly, asking patient and family who will be attending, make sure you are not alone, someone from the hospital should also attend*
- *Sit down, in a quiet, undisturbed place and use "body language"*
- *Be empathetic but straightforward and do not forget to apologise ("I am deeply sorry, personally and in the name of the hospital")*
- *Listen to the patient, answer questions with truth and simplicity*
- *Do not blame others or self-inflict blame on your team, just show sorrow*
- *Record the people, time and content of discussion in the notes*

Orientations to error rate publication in ITUs

ITUs should select error or accident endpoints to register prospectively and analyse over time, in order to publicise. Some are easy to measure, such as medication errors, unwanted extubation rates, nosocomial infections, device malfunctions and readmission rates. These endpoints should have a clear definition and be registered by a local risk manager. Preferably they should be presented against some form of risk complexity profile, mean length of stay, or one of the ITU scoring risk models available, for risk adjustment and to increase the meaning of data, allowing later benchmarking. Ideally, the error rate should be presented as the other side of the risk coin – the performance side – and expressed as survival rate instead of mortality, infection-free rates instead of infection, etc. This is much easier and sends out a stronger, more positive, learning message instead of the common accountability format of presenting negative results. These safety records should be presented together with other performance indicators of the unit, namely global survival, complication-free rates, length of stay, number of patients treated per bed, nursing staff ratios, etc.

Conclusion

Error publication and disclosure by ITUs is part of the process of patient safety promotion and, certainly, account for transparency in the health system, promoting trust and confidence in patient/professional relationships. Therefore, it should be generally adopted. This is a matter of professionalism and also an imperative for correct leadership, as the whole process requires a cultural change and must be led at both the individual and institutional or team level. These efforts should concentrate and focus on all parties involved – patients, as direct victims, in need of compensation and compassionate comfort, especially to mitigate the long-term consequences of errors and accidents. Professionals, the "second victims", are in search of moral support and protection from frustration, reputation and litigation losses and are ultimately the liability carriers seeking to provide fast compensation based on risk and not on fault or blame. This change would reduce the need for legal claims as the injured patient would be compensated on a pure accident or risk basis.

If all this is achieved with full transparency, namely by publication of ITU error rates, much will be gained in terms of satisfaction and, especially, additional safety for our patients, while their trust in us will only be enforced. This is the legacy Hippocrates left us, long before ITUs were even thought of, and which we are now expanding by also empowering patients' autonomy through their right to know the truth and to make informed decisions.

The author

José Fragata, MD, PhD, FECTS
   Hospital de Santa Marta | Serviço de
   Cirurgia Cardiotorácica | Lisboa, Portugal

Address for correspondence
   José Fragata
   Alameda Fernão Lopes
   Torre II – 8ª Esq
   1495–136 Miraflores, Portugal
   E-mail: jigfragata@gmail.com

References

1. Patient Safety: Achieving a new standard for care. Washington, DC: National Academy Press, 2004.
2. Fragata J, Martins L. O Erro em Medicina. Edições Almedina, Coimbra 2004.
3. Graf J, Von den Driesh A, Koch KC et al: Identification and characterization of errors and incidents in a medical intensive care unit. Acta Anaesthesiol Scand 2005;49:930–939.
4. Vriesendorp TM, DeVries JH, Vandon E et al. Evaluation of short-term consequences of hypoglycaemia in an intensive care unit. Crit Care Med 2006;34:2714–2718.
5. Giraud T, Dhainaut JF, Vaxelaire JF et al. Iatrogenic complications in adult intensive care units: a prospective two-center study. Crit Care Med 1993;21:40–51.
6. Orgeas MG, Timsit JF, Soufir L et al. Impact of adverse events on outcomes in intensive care unit patients. Crit Care Med 2008; 36:2041–2047.
7. Donchin Y, Gopher D, Olin M et al. A look into the nature and causes of human errors in the intensive care unit. Crit Care Med 1995;23:294–300.
8. To err is Human: Building a Safer Health System. Washington, DC: National Academy Press, 2000.
9. 2001. Crossing the Quality Chasm: A New Health System for the 21st Century. Washington, DC: National Academy Press.
10. Lacour-Gayet F, Clarke D, Jacobs J, Comas J et al. The Aristotle Committee The Aristotle Score: a complexity-adjusted method to evaluate surgical results. Eur J Cardiothorac Surg 2004;25:911–924.
11. Joint Commission on Accreditation of Healthcare Organizations. Patients and, when appropriate, their families are informed about the outcomes of care, including unanticipated outcomes. Standard RI 1.2.2 available at http://jcaho.org/standards_frm.html.
12. Institute for Healthcare Improvement. When things go wrong: responding to adverse events. Available at http://www.ihi.org/IHI/Topics/PatientSafety/SafetyGeneral/Literature/WhenThingsGoWrongRespondingtoAdverseEvents.htm Accesed May 18, 2006.
13. Straumanis J. Disclosure of medical error: Is it worth the risk? Pediatr Crit Care Med 2007;8 (2):S38–S43.
14. Murphy J, McEvoy MT. Revealing medical errors to your patients. Chest 2008;133(5).
15. Faunce TA, Bolsin SN. Fiduciary disclosure of medical mistakes: the duty to promptly notify patients of adverse health events. J Law Med 2005;12:478–482.
16. Leape LL. Full disclosure and apology – an idea whose time has come. The Physician Executive 2006;March-April:16–18.
17. Levitsky S. Navigating the New "Flat World" of Cardiothoracic Surgery. Ann Thorac Surg 2007;83:361–9.
18. Witman AB, Park DM, Hardin SB. How do patients want physicians to handle mistakes? A survey of internal medicine patients in an academic setting. Arch Intern Med 1996;156:2565–2569.
19. Hobgood C, Peck CR, Gilbert B et al. Medical errors – what and when: What do patients want to know? Acad Emerg Med 2002;9:1156–1161.
20. Hobgood C, Tamayo-Sarver JH, Elms A, et al. Parental preferences for error disclosure, reporting, and legal action after medical error in the care of their children. Pediatrics 2005;116:1276–1286.
21. Fischer MA, Mazor KM, Baril J et al. Learning from mistakes: factors that influence how students and residents learn from medical errors. J Gen Intern Med 2006;21:419–423.
22. Vincent JL. Information in the ICU: are we being honest with our patients? The results of a European questionnaire. Intensive Care Med 1998;24:1251–1256.
23. Gallagher TH, Waterman AD, Garbutt JM et al. US and Canadian physicians' attitudes and experiences regarding disclosing errors to patients. Arch Intern Med 2006;166:1605–1611.
24. Crane M. What to say if you made a mistake. Med Econ 2001;78:26-28, 33-36.
25. Cantor MD, Barach P, Derse A et al. Disclosing adverse events to patients. JT Comm J Qual Patient Saf 2005;31:5–12.
26. Kachalia A, Shojania KG, Hofer TP et al. Does full disclosure of medical errors affect malpractice liability? The jury is still out. JT Comm J Qual SAf 2003;29:503–511.
27. Popp PL. How will disclosure affect future litigation? ASHRM Journal 2003;23(1):5–9.
28. Mazor KM, Simon SR, Gurwitz JH. Communicating with patients about medical errors. A review of the literature. Arch Intern Med 2004;164:1690–1697.
29. Kaldjian LC, Jones EW, Rosenthal GE et al. An empiri-

cally derived taxonomy of factors affecting physicians' willingness to disclose medical errors. J Gen Intern Med 2006;21:942–948.

30. Boyle D, O'Connell D, Platt FW, et al. Disclosing errors and adverse events in the intensive care unit. Crit Care Med 2006;34:1532–1537.

31. Berlinger N, Wu AW. Subtracting insult from injury: addressing cultural expectations in the disclosure of medical error. J Med Ethics 2005;31(2):106–8.

32. Hébert PC, Levin AV, Robertson G. Bioethics for clinicians: 23. Disclosure of medical error. CMAJ 2001;164:509–513.

Ken Hillman, Jack Chen, Jeffrey Braithwaite and Enrico Coiera

Moving from safe ICUs to safe systems

The World Health Organisation (WHO) states that patient safety includes three complementary actions: preventing adverse events; mitigating their effects when they occur; and making them visible. Perhaps making them visible is the first step, as without the knowledge provided by data, problems cannot be identified, nor can the impact of preventative measures be evaluated.

Patient safety in acute hospitals was first measured in a comprehensive way in the Harvard Medical Practice Study [1, 2]. It found that 3.7% of all patients suffered harm during their hospital admission:

- 70% of events resulted in short-term disability and
- 14% of events resulted in death.

Applied across the United States, it was estimated that medical errors caused between 44,000 and 98,000 deaths annually [3]. The Quality in Australian Health Study found an adverse event rate of almost 17% of all hospital patients, with estimates between 10,000 to 14,000 potentially preventable deaths in Australia each year [4], although refinements suggested a rate of 1:10. Subsequent studies from New Zealand [5, 6] the United Kingdom [7], Denmark [8] Canada [9] and

Spain [10] estimated a similar rate of serious adverse events or potentially preventable deaths in those countries.

One of the major contributors to the high incidence of serious adverse events in acute hospitals is related to the way acute hospitals are constructed historically around individual clinicians and the individual clinician/patient relationship [11, 12]. Originally, hospitals were charitable institutions caring for the poor around the time of the crusades [13].

Soon, formal medical training in universities began in Europe. The training centred on a physician diagnosing and treating individual patients. Teamwork and systems were not emphasised. The trained physician would earn their living from treating patients who could afford their fees.

Many of them gave of their time, without payment, to also treat patients in public hospitals. The hospitals would provide continuous care with the equivalent of nursing staff, who often belonged to religious orders. Medical students and junior doctors were apprenticed to physicians in these public hospitals. In return for being trained, the apprentices would care for the patients around the clock. The specialist physicians would visit occasionally and give advice on patient management. At the heart of the system were specialist physicians. They would give freely of their time to train their apprentices as well as treating the poor. In return, the hospital provided the physician with the infrastructure to manage patients. All seemed to gain. The poor were treated without cost to them; those aspiring to be doctors were trained by the physicians. The specialists felt virtuous about their charitable work and the hospital provided a structure which was structured around the needs and convenience of the specialist physician.

Major changes in medicine and the population of patients since then challenge this historical construct. Up until the middle of the last century, there were a limited number of drugs; complex investigations were rare; surgery was confined to a limited range of operations; the specialty of anaesthetics was almost non-existent and intensive care units (ICUs) had not been established. Twenty years after the Second World War this had all changed. Antibiotics were discovered; drugs controlling cardiovascular and respiratory conditions became available; chemotherapy and radiotherapy were being used in the treatment of cancer; dialysis and other supportive interventions for chronic conditions became available; diagnostic procedures enabled us to image and understand much of the body's processes previously guessed at by external signs and symptoms; and the number of non-invasive and invasive surgical options expanded.

At about the same time, the first ICUs were established, initially to artificially ventilate patients with poliomyelitis [14]. Over the next two decades, ICUs grew out of recovery rooms and existing general wards and were eventually purpose-built. Specifically trained nursing staff began caring for patients in these units. In many countries, there are now also specifically trained critical care medical specialists, who solely practice critical care medicine [15].

The ICU was an essential incubator for the development of the specialty of critical care medicine. It enabled intensivists to develop their craft and develop the skills and knowledge unique to the specialty. However, the concept of a strictly confined space in which to treat the seriously ill is also consistent with the silos that define the historical development of acute hospitals.

There remains an emphasis on the individual skills that a doctor needs to manage an individual patient. Hospitals are still divided into specific areas – operating rooms; emergency departments; general wards; and diagnostic areas. While this lends itself, in many cases, to excellent medical practice, it also encourages territorialism and a silo mentality. Hospitals are still, in multiple ways, constructed around senior clinicians' preference.

In many countries, patients are admitted 'under' a single specialist. They 'own' their patients. This has the advantage of accountability but it also has the disadvantage that the hospital focuses on the individual doctor/patient relationship and interaction and coordination of patient care is limited. There are few patient-centred systems in hospitals.

The adverse events that result from the gap between patient needs and hospital resources are probably related more to the lack of systems designed around the patient's needs as they are related to a scarcity of staff and infrastructure. Studies have attributed 15% of adverse events to system failures [16, 17]. The significance of system failure has been emphasised in the United States Institute of Medicine's publication To Err is Human [3].

The challenge to establish more robust systems around patient care in acute hospitals will become even more urgent as we examine the changing nature of hospital patients [11, 12]. They are now older, often with multiple comorbidities, having more complex surgery and other potentially dangerous interventions.

One can gain further insight into the failure of current hospitals to warrant patient safety when serious adverse events are examined in more detail. Almost 80% of hospital cardiac arrests are preceded by slow and potentially treatable deterioration 18, 19]. Approximately half of all hospital deaths are also potentially preventable [20]. Up to 70% of all admissions to intensive care also have a clear record of slow and potentially preventable deterioration [21–23].

It has become clear that, while the specialty of intensive care manages the seriously ill within its own four walls, patients who were equally, or even more, at risk and in general wards suffer potentially preventable severe adverse events. For example, most patients who die in intensive care do so in a predictable and orchestrated way as a result of actively withholding and withdrawing treatment [24]. Unexpected cardiac arrests are almost non-existent. Patient deterioration is detected early in the ICU by skilled staff and sophisticated monitoring. Similarly, the response to acute deterioration is rapid and appropriate. The same often does not occur for patients elsewhere in the hospital. While there may be excellent individuals working in the various locations in hospitals, there is little in the way of a systematic patient-centred approach to deal with serious illness.

Another problem contributing to the high incidence of failure to recognise and intervene early in serious illness is related to poor undergraduate education around the seriously ill [25, 26]. Medical students on graduation have poor knowledge and little in the way of skills as well as minimal experience in how to manage serious illness.

Moreover, hospital physicians are increasingly specialised [15, 27] and harness sophisticated technology. Even if at one time they were trained in caring for the seriously ill, these skills have been lost over time and there are few incentives to maintain those skills.

It is against the background of an increasingly aging hospital population with multiple comorbidities, complex interventions and other treatments that the first hospital-wide systems were introduced to recognise and treat seriously ill patients early [28, 29]. The medical emergency team (MET) concept has now been adopted in many parts of the world in the form of patient-at-risk teams (PART) [23]; modified early warning scores (MEWS) [30]; outreach programmes [31]; and MET systems adopted for paediatric use [32, 33]. No one dealing with the seriously ill would question the concept that early recognition and resuscitation of patients is preferable to delaying until cardiac arrest or other serious adverse events occur. The challenge is how to identify quickly and accurately the seriously ill and probably even more importantly, how to implement successfully the system for identification and response across traditional hospital boundaries. Some studies in single hospitals have shown impressive reductions in the rate of cardiac arrest and other serious adverse events [32, 34–40]. And yet the largest randomised trial on the effect of a MET system was underpowered and did not

demonstrate a difference between the control and intervention groups [41]. There are many explanations for this, including the failure of existing criteria to accurately identify at-risk patients [42]. The methodology in some studies that failed to demonstrate a positive result may be flawed. For example, a recent study used cardiac arrests as a measure of the effectiveness of a MET system in an already highly monitored and resourced area such as the ICU [43]. Obviously, hospital-wide systems such as the MET concept were not designed to reduce serious adverse events in an area with sophisticated monitoring and staffed by experts in advanced resuscitation.

Another major factor in the success or otherwise of a rapid response concept could be the commitment and enthusiasm of the hospital in making the system work. It would not be surprising if the hospitals that showed a remarkable decrease in serious adverse events were also hospitals that were committed to converting the eminently sensible concept of providing early recognition and care for the seriously ill at an early stage into a system which worked. The studies which have shown an improvement in care were single hospitals using before/after methodology [31–36, 38, 39]. These were almost certainly hospitals committed to making the system work. Whereas the MERIT study included 23 hospitals where the results in the MET hospitals demonstrated a wide degree of success, both for markers of successful implementation as well as reductions in serious adverse events [41]. Moreover, some of the control hospitals were already behaving as MET hospitals with a large percentage of calls for non-cardiac arrest situations.

Other measures of successful implementation in the MERIT study showed variability. Approximately half of all patients with MET criteria, demonstrating serious pathophysological disturbances, had an emergency call made. Similarly, almost half of all patients with serious adverse events demonstrated antecedent vital sign abnormalities [41].

Interestingly, data from the same MERIT study demonstrated a significant correlation between the proportion of MET-like calls (defined as the early medical emergency team calls not related to a cardiac arrest and a death/total emergency team calls) (DOSE) and reduction of deaths and cardiac arrests (RESPONSE) as well as an overall decrease in mortality in hospitals with a MET system [44]. This data may go some way to shedding light on whether MET systems work. Thus, successful implementation, resulting in a higher number of MET calls, may explain some of the variability in the MERIT study.

It seems likely that in order to implement successfully a hospital-wide system we need to radically rethink the way we monitor and manage the seriously ill in hospitals [45, 46]. In order to recognise seriously ill patients earlier, we need to move away from intermittent monitoring of vital signs at irregular times as it has a high incidence of inaccurate or non-existent recordings [47]. Instead, we propose that it will be important to move toward systems of universal non-invasive monitoring of vital signs [48].

There are other components in implementing an effective MET system. Each is essential, and they complement each other. They include having an appropriate response once the at-risk patient has been identified; educating all hospital staff about the MET system so they all feel confident about activating the system; collecting data which defines and tracks the effectiveness of the MET system; and having effective ownership of the system with, among others, senior hospital executives and clinicians.

One of the first challenges of successfully implementing a MET system is to conduct a hospital-wide education programme [49]. This could take the form of strategies such as having the MET criteria and how to call for assistance printed on the back of hospital identification badges as well as similar information being widely displayed on laminated charts throughout the hospital. It should also be part of the routine orientation programme for all hospital staff.

Data collection, analysis, display and wide distribution is crucial for monitoring the extent of the problem as well as tracking the effectiveness of the intervention strategy [50]. Many data points can be collected, but it is important to track potentially preventable deaths, cardiac arrests and admissions to the ICU as these are all serious adverse events and the MET system is specifically designed to reduce them. "Potentially preventable" can be defined by one of the three serious adverse events being preceded by one or more of the MET criteria which has not resulted in a response [50].

A well-functioning MET system should reduce the number of available arrests as well as more accurately define those where a "do not resuscitate" (DNR) order should have been made. This should result in cardiac arrests being a rare event in hospitals and confined to sudden-onset arrests related to events such as ventricular fibrillation.

The other data that should be collected is the number of MET calls/1,000 admissions. This is strongly associated with reduction of potentially preventable cardiac arrests and deaths [44] and is an accurate indicator of how successful the implementation strategy has been.

Conclusion

The final essential component in successful implementation of a hospital-wide system is ownership by senior executives and clinicians in the hospital who are needed to oversee the implementation and maintenance process. In summary, safe systems require an organisation-wide approach, which means moving away from vertical silos to creating patient-focused systems, if we are to improve patient safety.

The successful introduction of a hospital-wide system such as the MET concept also assists in inspiring and facilitating other organisation-wide systems [51–56]. For example, soon after the implementation of a MET system organisations are faced with the challenge of being urgently called to patients who are plainly dying but have not been assigned a DNR order. This could facilitate a new way of identifying and managing end-of-life patients safely as well as preventing serious adverse events in patients who were not at the end of life.

Evaluating the effectiveness of system implementation presents different challenges to more conventional clinical research. Health service research is a relatively new area for critical care [57]. It provides a framework for exploring the processes and dynamics underlying complex health systems. In turn this can help provide novel frameworks for generating new knowledge about barriers and enablers to establishing and maintaining best practice within complex systems [57].

In effect, we propose that we need to have effective well-functioning MET capabilities, technical capacity to measure responses, technological systems to monitor patients via universal non-invasive monitoring of vital signs, and much more clarity of focus on patients and their care. These are necessary but not sufficient preconditions. We also need much more of an appreciation of change and how and under what circumstances it occurs [58–61], more information on how improvement takes place in complex, adaptive health systems [62], and what the underpinnings are of cultural change [63, 64] – i.e. how and under what circumstances attitudes and values on the one hand, and behaviours and practices on the other, alter or are modified in response to incentives, encouragement, rewards, and other stimuli. This type of research requires an interdisciplinary approach. The methodologies are often not simple, requiring expert statistical input and knowledge of behavioural complexity. Understanding organisational and cultural impacts requires other expertise from areas such as social psychology, sociology, medical anthropology and linguistics.

In a relatively short time, the specialty of intensive care medicine has established excellence in patient care within the four walls of the ICU to being at the vanguard of efforts to establish and evaluate organisation-wide systems to improve the care of the seriously ill. The next generation of multi-disciplinary research and practice will move us from emphasising safe ICUs to designing safe systems of care. Patients deserve nothing less.

The authors

Ken Hillman, MBBS, MD, FRCA, FJFICM, FANZCA[1,4]
Jack Chen, MBBS, PhD, MBA[1,4]
Jeffrey Braithwaite, Prof., PhD, MBA[2,4]
Enrico Coiera, Prof., MBBS, PhD[3,4]
   [1]The Simpson Centre for Health Systems Research | The University of New South Wales
   [2]Centre for Clinical Governance Research in Health | The University of New South Wales
   [3]Centre for Health Informatics | The University of New South Wales
   [4]The Institute of Health Innovation | The University of New South Wales | Sydney, Australia.

Address for correspondence
   Ken Hillman
   Critical Care Services
   Liverpool Hospital
   Locked Mailbag 7103
   Liverpool BC, NSW 1871, Australia
   E-mail: k.hillman@unsw.edu.au

References

1. Brennan TA, Leape LL, Laird NM, Herbert L, Localio AR, Lawthers AG et al. Incidence of adverse events and negligence in hospitalised patients: results of the Harvard Medical Practice Study I. N Engl J Med 1991;324:370–6

2. Leape LL, Brennan TA, Laird NM, Lawthers AG, Localio AR, Barnes BA et al. Nature of adverse events in hospitalised patients: results of the Harvard Medical Practice Study II. N Engl J Med 1991;324:377–84.

3. Kohn LT, Corrigan JM, Donaldson MS (eds). To Err is Human: Building a Safer Health System. Washington, DC: National Academy Press, 2000.

4. Wilson RM, Runciman WB, Gibberd RW, Harrison BT, Newby L, Hamilton JD. Quality in Australian Health Care Study. Med J Aust 1995;163:458–71.

5. David P, Lay-Yee R, Briant R, Ali W, Scott A, Schug S. Adverse events in New Zealand public hospitals I: occurrence and impact. N Z Med J 2002;115:U271.

6. Davis P, Lay-Yee R, Briant R, Ali W, Scott A, Schug S. Adverse events in in New Zealand public hospitals II: occurrence and impact. N Z Med J 2003;116:U624.

7. Department of Health. An organisation with a memory: report of an expert group on learning from adverse events in the NHS chaired by the Chief Medical Officer. Crownright. Department of Health, HMSO, 2000.

8. Schiøler T, Lipczak H, Pederson BL, Mogensen TS, Bech KB, Stockmarr A et al. Danish adverse events study. Incidence of adverse events in hospitals. A retrospective study of medical records. Ugeskr Laeger 2001;163:5370–8.

9. Baker GR, Norton PG, Flintolf V, Blais R, Brown A, Cox J et al. The Canadian Adverse Events Study: the incidence of adverse events among hospital patients in Canada. CMAJ 2004; 170:1678–86.

10. Aranaz-Andres JM, Aibar-Remon C, Vitaller-Murillo J, Ruiz-Lopez P, Limon-Ramirez R, Teriol-Garcia E, the ENEAS work group. Incidence of adverse events related to health care in Spain: results of the Spanish National Study of Adverse Events. J Epidemiolo Community Health 2008;62:1022–9.

11. Hillman K. The changing role of acute-care hospitals. Med J Aust 1999;170:325–8.

12. Hillman K, Chen J, Young L. The evolution of the health care system. In: DeVita M, Hillman K, Bellowo R (eds). Medical Emergency Teams: Implementation and Outcome Measurement. New York: Springer; 2006. p.104–15.

13. Abel-Smith B. The hospitals 1800–1948. London: Heinemann, 1964.

14. Lassen HCA. A preliminary report on the 1952 epidemic of poliomyelitis in Copenhagen with special reference to the treatment of acute respiratory insufficiency. Lancet 1953;1:37–41.

15. Hillman K. Critical care without walls. Curr Opin Crit Care 2002; 8:594–9.

16. Thomas EJ, Studdert DM, Runciman WB, Webb RK, Sexton EJ, Wilson RM et al. A comparison of iatrogenic injury studies in Australia and the United States I: context, methods, casemix, population, patient and hospital characteristics. Int J Qual Health Care 2000; 12:371–8.

17. World Health Organization. Progress in essential drugs and medical policy Geneva: WHO; 1998–1999. WHO/EDM/2000;2:2000.

18. Schein RM, Hazday N, Pena M, Ruben BH, Sprung CL. Clinical antecedents to in-hospital cardiopulmonary arrest. Chest 1990;98:1388–92.

19. Franklin C, Matthew J. Developing strategies to prevent inhospital cardiac arrest: analysing responses of physicians and nurses in the hours before the event. Crit Care Med 1994;22:244–7.

20. Hillman K, Bristow PJ, Chey T, Daffurn K, Jacques T, Norman SL et al. Antecedents to hospital deaths. Internal Med J 2001;31:343–8.

21. McQuillan P, Pilkington S, Allan A, Taylor B, Short A, Morgan G et al. Confidential inquiry into quality of care before admission to intensive care. BMJ 1998;316:1853–8.

22. Hillman KM, Bristow PJ, Chey T, Daffurn K, Jacques T, Norman SL et al. Duration of life-threatening antecedents prior to intensive care admission. Intensive Care Med 2002;28:1629–34.

23. Goldhill DR, Worthington L, Mulchahy A, Tarling M, Sumner A. The patient- at-risk team: identifying and managing seriously ill ward patients. Anaesthesia 1999;54:853–60.

24. Sprung CL, Eidelman LA. Worldwide similarities and differences in the forgoing of life-sustaining treatment. Intensive Care Med 1996;22:1003–5.

25. Buchman TG, Dellinger RP, Raphaely RC, Todres D. Undergraduate education in critical care medicine. Crit Care Med 1992;20:1588–603.

26. Harrison GA, Hillman KM, Fulde GWO, Jacques TC. The need for undergraduate eduction in critical care. (Results of a questionnaire to year 6 medical undergraduates, University of New South Wales and recommendations on a curriculum in critical care). Anaesth Intensive Care 1999;27:53–8.

27. Hillman K. Breaking the paradigm: the ICU without walls. In: Kuhlen R, Moreno R, Ranieri M, Rhodes A (eds). 25 Years of Progress and Innovation in Intensive Care Medicine. European Society of Intensive Care Medicine. Berlin: Medizinisch Wissenschaftliche Verlagsgesellschaft; 2007. p. 337–41.

28. Lee A, Bishop G, Hillman KM. The medical emergency team. Anaesth Intensive Care 1995;23:183–6.

29. Hourihan F, Bishop G, Hillman KM, Daffurn K. The medical emergency team: a new strategy to identify and intervene in high-risk patients. Clin Intensive Care 1995;6:269–72.

30. Stenhouse C, Coates S, Tivey M, Allsop P, Parker T. Prospective evaluation of a Modified Early Warning Score to aid earlier detection of patients developing critical illness on a general surgical ward. Brit J Anaes 2000;84:663.

31. Bright D, Walker W, Bion J. Clinical review: outreach – a strategy for improving the care of the acutely ill hospitalised patient. Crit Care 2004;8:33–40.

32. Tibballs J, Kinney S, Duk T, Oakley E, Hennessey M. Reduction of paediatric in-patient cardiac arrest and death with a medical emergency team: preliminary results. Arch Dis Child 2005;90:1148–52.

33. Brilli RJ, Gibson R, Luria JW, Wheeler TA, Shaw J, Linam M et al. Implementation of a medical emergency team in a large paediatric teaching hospital prevents respiratory and cardiopulmonary arrests outside the intensive care unit. Paediatr Crit Care Med 2007;8:236–46.

34. Buist MD, Moore GE, Bernard SA, Waxman BP, Anderson JN, Nguyen TV. Effects of a medical emergency team on reduction of incidence and mortality from unexpected cardiac arrests in hospital: preliminary study. BMJ 2002;324:387–90.

35. DeVita MA, Braithwaite RS, Mahidhara R, Stuart S, Foraida M, Simmons RL. Use of medical emergency team (MET) responses to reduce hospital cardiopulmonary arrests. Qual Saf Health Care 2004;13:251–4.

36. Bellomo R, Goldsmith D, Uchino S, Buckmaster J, Hart G, Opdam H et al. A prospective before-and-after trial of a medical emergency team. Med J Aust 2003;179:283–7.

37. Bellomo R, Goldsmith D, Uchino S, Buckmaster J, Hart G, Opdam H et al. Prospective controlled trial of effect of a medical emergency team on postoperative morbidity and mortality rates. Crit Care Med 2004;32:916–21.

38. Dacey MJ, Mirza ER, Wilcox V, Doherty M, Mello J, Boyer A et al. The effect of a rapid response team on major clinical outcome measures in a community hospital. Crit Care Med 2007;35:2076–82.

39. Kenward G, Castle N, Hodgetts T, Shaikh L. Evaluation of a medical emergency team one year after implementation. Resuscitation 2004;61:257–63.

40. Jones D, Duke G, Green J, Briedis J, Bellomo R, Casamento A et al. Medical emergency team syndromes and an approach to their management. Crit Care 2006;10:R30.

41. Hillman K, Chen J, Cretikos M, Bellomo R, Brown D, Doig G, Finfer S, Flabouris A and MERIT Study Investigators. Introduction of the medical emergency team (MET) system: a cluster randomised controlled trial. Lancet 2005;365:2091–7.

42. Duckitt RW, Buxton-Thomas R, Walker J, Cheek E, Bewick V, Venn R, Forni LG et al. Worthing physiological scoring system: derivation and validation of a physiological early-warning scoring system for medical admissions.

An observational, population based single-centre study. Br J Anaesth 2007;98:769–74.

43. Chan PS, Khalid A, Longmore LS, Berg RA, Kosiborod M, Spertus JA.. Hospital-wide code rates and mortality before and after implementation of a rapid response team. JAMA 2008;300:2506–13.

44. Chen J, Bellomo R, Flabouris A, Hillman K, Finfer S, the MERIT Study Investigators for the Simspon Centre and the ANZICS Clinical Trials Group. The relationship between early emergency team calls and serious adverse events. Crit Care Med 2009;37:148–53.

45. Thomson R. National Health Service National Patient Safety Agency. The fifth report from the Patient Safety Observatory. Safer care for the acutely ill patient: learning from serious incidents, 2007.

46. Øvretveit J, Suffoletto J-A. Improving rapid response systems: progress, issues, and future directions. J Com J Qual Patient Saf 2007;33:512–9.

47. Chen J, Hillman K, Bellomo R, Flabouris A, Finfer S, Cretikos M, the MERIT Study Investigators for the Simspon Centre and the ANZICS Clinical Trials Group. The impact of introducing a medical emergency team on the documentation of vital signs. Resuscitation 2009;80:35–43.

48. Hravnack M, Edwards L, Clontz A, Valenta C, DeVita MA, Pinsky MR. Defining the incidence of cardiorespiratory instability in patients in step-down units using an electronic integrated monitoring system. Arch Intern Med 2008;168:1300–8.

49. Hillman K, Parr M, Flabouris A, Bishop G, Stewart A. Redefining in-hospita; resuscitation: the concept of the medical emergency team. Resuscitation 2001;48:105–10.

50. Hillman K, Alexandrou E, Flabouris M, Brown D, Murphy J, Daffurn K et al. Clinical outcome indicators in acute hospital medicine. Clin Intensive Care 2000;11:89–94.

51. Kotter JP. Leading change. Boston: Harvard Business School Press, 1996.

52. van Bokhoven MA, Kok G, van der Weijden T. Designing a quality improvement intervention: a systematic approach. Qual Saf Health Care 2003;12:215–20.

53. Kotter J, Schlesinger L. Choosing strategies for change. Harv Bus Rev 2979;57–106–14.

54. Piderit SK. Rethinking resistance and recognizing ambivalence. A multidimensional view of attitudes toward an organizational change. Acad Manage J 2000;794(A):783.

55. Scott T, Mannion R, Marshall M, Davies H. Does organisational culture influence health care perform-ance? A review of the evidence. J Health Serv Res Policy 2003;8:105–17.

56. Solberg LI, Brekke ML, Fazio CJ, Fowles J, Jacobsen DN, Kittke TE et al. Lessons from experienced guideline implementers: attend to many factors and use multiple strategies. Jt Comm J Qual Improv 2000;26:171–88.

57. Hillman K, Chen J, May E. Complex intensive care unit interventions. Crit Care Med 2009;37(13):S102–6.

58. Braithwaite J. An empirical assessment of social structural and cultural change in clinical directorates. Health Care Anal 2006:14:185–93.

59. Braithwaite J. Analysing structural and cultural change in acute settings using a Giddens-Weick paradigmatic approach. Health Care Anal 2006;14:91–102.

60. Grol R. Beliefs and evidence in changing clinical practice. BMJ 1997;315:418–21.

61. Braithwaite J. Organizational change, patient-focused care: an Australian perspective. Health Serv Manage-ment Res 1995;8:172–85.

62. Braithwaite J, Runciman WR, Merry A. Towards safer, better healthcare: harnessing the natural properties of complex sociotechnical systems. Qual Saf Health Care 2008;18:37–41.

63. Callen J, Westbrook JI, Braithwaite J. Cultures in hospitals and their influence on and attitudes to, and satisfaction with, the use of clinical information systems, *Social Science & Medicine* 2007;65(3):635–9.

64. Braithwaite J, Westbrook MT, Iedema R, Mallock NA, Forsyth R, Zhang K. A tale of two hospitals: assessing cultural landscapes and compositions. Soc Sci Med 205;60:1149–62.

B. Decision making

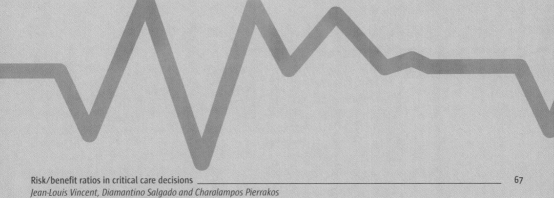

Jean-Louis Vincent, Diamantino Salgado and Charalampos Pierrakos

Risk/benefit ratios in critical care decisions

Introduction

Many aspects of everyday life carry a certain risk/benefit ratio, which we may be aware of only subconsciously, but which determines our attitude to a particular event or activity. For example, when crossing a road, we have clearly decided that the benefit of being on the other side of that road for whatever reason outweighs the risk of being run over! Obviously, the risk/benefit ratio will be very different when considering crossing a country lane with little or no traffic compared to a main road in a large, busy city. Clearly, too, assessment of the risk/benefit ratio will vary between individuals and in the same individual at different times, depending on how necessary or urgent it is to cross that road.

Risk/benefit ratios are also widely used in all fields of medicine. In the intensive care unit (ICU), many, if not all, interventions have risk/benefit ratios (acknowledged or not) which determine whether or not they should be started and/or pursued. As in the above example, risk/benefit ratios will vary depending on individual patient characteristics, and may change in the same patient during the course of the disease process. In this chapter, we will consider just a few of the most important or most frequently encountered risk/benefit decisions in the ICU.

Fluid administration

The importance of adequate fluid resuscitation is not disputed and it is well recognised that prolonged hypovolaemia can lead to multiple organ failure. However, excessive fluid administration can also have important deleterious effects. Lung oedema is often a primary concern leading to altered gas exchange and hypoxaemia. Oedema in the brain may contribute to the development of delirium, oedema in the heart may contribute to systolic and diastolic dysfunction, oedema in the abdominal wall can contribute to abdominal compartment syndrome, oedema in the gut may limit tolerance to feeding, oedema in the muscle and subcutaneous tissues may contribute to general weakness and impaired wound healing. A positive fluid balance has been associated with increased mortality in patients with pulmonary oedema [1], and in the large observational SOAP study, a positive fluid balance was an important independent indicator of worse outcome (by multivariable analysis) in critically ill patients with sepsis [2], acute respiratory failure [3] and acute renal failure [4]. In patients with acute lung injury, a conservative fluid strategy was associated with improved oxygenation and increased ventilator-free days compared to a liberal fluid strategy [5].

It is, therefore, important to consider the possible risks of fluid administration when determining whether or not to start or continue fluids. We often stop fluid challenge when we feel the potential benefit of continuing fluids is outweighed by the risk of oedema, frequently when a patient becomes hypoxaemic. Clearly the risk/benefit ratio will be influenced by individual patient factors, including the reason for fluid administration and the presence of pre-existing conditions, such as renal failure, and such decisions must be made on an individual basis.

Once a decision to administer fluids has been made, a whole new series of risk/benefit analyses comes into play regarding the risks and benefits of the individual fluids. Crystalloids (sodium chloride 0.9 % or Ringer's lactate solution) and colloids (gelatins, hydroxyethyl starch [HES], and albumin solution) are the most frequently used plasma expanding solutions in the ICU, but there is still no consensus as to which fluid type is best. In favour of crystalloids is their low cost, wide availability, and lack of anaphylactic reactions. However, due to their short life-span in the vascular compartment, and their high distribution volume in vasodilatory shock, a greater volume is needed to reach the same resuscitation goals compared to colloid solutions; consequently, there is a greater risk of aggravating pulmonary oedema and anasarca, dilutional coagulopathy, and hyperchloraemic metabolic acidosis [6]. On the other hand, colloid solutions have the same expanding performance in smaller administered volumes, and stay longer in the vascular compartment due to their ability to shift fluids from the interstitium to the vessels, which could be interesting in patients with severe oedematous states. However, there are also concerns regarding colloid use, including risks of acquired infection from human albumin (hepatitis B and C, human immunodeficiency virus, prions), and allergic reactions, coagulation abnormalities and acute kidney injury from gelatins and HES solutions [7].

No study has unequivocally shown that one solution is superior to another. In fact, recent meta-analyses showed that the different fluid types were equivalent [8, 9]. A useful recommendation would be to use crystalloids as the initial resuscitation fluid and to consider colloid solutions if there is some risk of fluid overload associated with severe hypoalbuminaemia.

Blood transfusions

The risks and benefits of blood transfusion have been widely discussed in recent years. Blood transfusions have obvious benefits in patients with life-threatening haemorrhage, but in patients with less extreme blood loss or anaemia, the risk/benefit ratio is less clear. Red blood cells are the main carrier of oxygen to the tissues and transfusions are often given in an attempt to increase tissue oxygen delivery and hence to reduce or limit tissue hypoxia. However, increased oxygen delivery does not necessarily equate to increased oxygen uptake [10]. Moreover, blood transfusions have inherent risks, including the potential transmission of diseases, such as hepatitis B and C, human immunodeficiency virus, and prions, transfusion-related immunosuppression and acute lung injury, allergic and haemolytic reactions [11]. In addition, several studies have suggested worse outcomes in patients who receive a blood transfusion during their ICU stay [12, 13], although more recent studies suggest that this may no longer be the case [14].

On the other hand, anaemia is also associated with worse outcomes in critically ill patients [15, 16]. Again, the risk/benefit ratio will depend on the individual patient and must be assessed accordingly. In the study by Hebert et al. comparing a restrictive with a liberal blood transfusion strategy, there were no differences in overall 30-day mortality rates; however, in patients aged less than 55 years and patients with APACHE II scores < 20 the restrictive strategy was associated with significantly lower 30-day mortality rates than the liberal strategy, suggesting that in such patients the risk/benefit ratio may, in general, lean towards no transfusion. Patients with septic shock and acute coronary syndromes, however, may be more likely to benefit from blood transfusion and in such patients, a higher transfusion trigger may be warranted [17].

Vasopressor agents

Fluids alone are often not sufficient to restore an adequate perfusion pressure and vasopressor support is required. However, once again, a risk/benefit assessment must be made for each patient to assess the optimal choice of agent and when and for how long they should be administered. While vasopressor agents are clearly beneficial in raising arterial pressure, they may alter the distribution of blood flow and also increase cellular oxygen requirements, thus potentially precipitating or worsening regional hypoxia. Different vasopressors have different effects on haemodynamic parameters and on regional perfusion. Dopamine and norepinephrine are the vasopressors most frequently used in patients with septic shock. While the beneficial effects of both on arterial pressure are evident, each has its own potentially negative effects. For example, dopamine may increase heart rate, can produce tachyarrhythmias, and may suppress pituitary function. Recent observational studies have given conflicting results suggested that dopamine may be associated with worse [18] or better [19] outcomes in patients with sepsis. Norepinephrine may be more effective than dopamine in restoring haemodynamic stability [20], but is more likely to cause excessive vasoconstriction and decreased organ perfusion. Current data are unable to determine which vasopressor is superior and choice will be based on personal experience, severity of shock, and baseline cardiovascular status.

Vasopressin is another vasopressor that has recently been investigated in critically ill patients. In healthy individuals, vasopressin has few vasopressor effects, but it is very important in controlling vascular tone in shock states. Administration of vasopressin in catecholamine-resistant septic shock may restore physiologic hormone levels, increase vascular tone, and reduce vasopressor requirements [21]. Despite the beneficial results on shock reversal and reduction of vasopressors, vasopressin may be associated with serious adverse events, especially when used in high doses (> 0.04 U/min), which could be exacerbated in hypovolaemic subjects. The most common undesirable effects associated with vasopressin administration are arterial pulmonary hypertension, and decreases in heart rate, cardiac output and oxygen delivery, hepato-splanchnic ischaemia, thrombocytopenia, and skin necrosis [22]. Low doses of vasopressin (0.01–0.04 U/min) may be associated with fewer side effects. The recent VASST study showed that a combination of low-dose vasopressin and norepinephrine had the same safety profile as norepinephrine alone in the treatment of patients with septic shock, and was associated with reduced mortality in a subgroup of patients with less severe septic shock who required less than 15 µg/min of norepinephrine [23].

Tight blood sugar control

In an important study, Van den Berghe et al. [24] reported that tight control of blood glucose concentrations (using insulin to maintain blood glucose between 80–110 mg/dl) in surgical intensive care patients was associated with improved survival. The same group later extended these findings to medical ICU patients [25], and this strategy was widely incorporated into clinical practice. However, these studies were conducted in a single ICU, and randomised multicentre studies have failed to duplicate these initial results [7, 26]. Moreover, in these subsequent studies, tight glucose control has been widely associated with a higher incidence of potentially harmful hypoglycaemia [7, 26, 27]. Recent studies suggest that variability in blood glucose concentrations may be more important than the actual blood glucose concentration [28]. Until the results of further studies are available, it would, thus, appear sensible to find a balance between the potentially beneficial effects of tight glucose control and the risks of hypoglycaemia by targeting a glucose concentration of less than 150 mg/dl [29, 30].

Endotracheal intubation versus non-invasive ventilation

Non-invasive ventilation (NIV) has been widely promoted as offering a means of reducing the risks associated with endotracheal intubation, such as ventilator-associated pneumonia and ventilator-induced lung injury. However, while NIV has been widely used and is recommended as first-line management in patients with hypercapnic respiratory failure [31], predominantly associated with acute exacerbations of chronic obstructive pulmonary disease, use of NIV in hypoxaemic respiratory failure is controversial and stud-

Tab. 1 Some of the indications and contraindications when considering patients for NIV

Indications	Need for ventilatory support
	■ Dyspnoea (moderate or severe)
	■ Tachypnoea, use of accessory muscles, etc.
	Altered gas exchange
	■ $PaCO_2 > 50$ mmHg AND pH <7.32 OR
	■ $PaO_2/FiO_2 < 200$ mmHg (CPAP?)
	No contraindication
Contraindications	Respiratory arrest – apnoea
	Lack of collaboration – agitation
	Inability to protect the airway
	Copious secretions, inefficient cough
	Unstable haemodynamic status, myocardial ischaemia, arrhythmias
	Local problem – severe facial trauma, epistaxis, etc.

ies have yielded conflicting results [32, 33]. One of the reasons for these apparent differences may be the heterogeneous nature of acute respiratory failure, which can be the end-point of multiple pathological processes [34], and while NIV may be beneficial in some of these conditions, such as cardiogenic pulmonary oedema [35], it may be less effective in others, e.g. acute respiratory distress syndrome [32]. Timing may also be an important issue in assessing whether NIV is appropriate as patients need to be sick enough to benefit but not so sick that they need immediate intubation [36]. The risks of NIV include respiratory and even cardiac arrest, and indications and contra-indications need to be carefully weighed in any patient being considered for NIV (see Tab. 1).

High positive end-expiratory pressure (PEEP) levels in acute lung injury (ALI)

PEEP is a mainstay therapy for patients with ALI and acute respiratory distress syndrome (ARDS). PEEP can be used to open and keep atelectatic lung areas opened [37]. However the "ideal" PEEP level is a great subject of debate. Firstly, mechanical ventilation has been associated with worsening of lung injury (ventilator-induced lung injury) and inflammation, which is directly linked to the degree of pressure and tidal volume secondary to cyclical alveolar opening and closing [38]. Secondly, high intrathoracic pressures have been as-

sociated with haemodynamic decompensation causing acute *cor pulmonale* [39]. Strategies to reduce tidal volumes and limit airway pressures have consistently reduced mortality in patients with ARDS, and are recommended standards of care [40–42].

Two recent randomised controlled trials, the LOV and EXPRESS studies, tested the effect of ventilating patients with ARDS with high PEEP levels [43, 44]; both failed to show a mortality reduction. Nonetheless, the EXPRESS study reported that patients in the high PEEP group had more ventilator-free and organ-failure-free days. In a recent systematic review, we observed reduced mortality rates in ARDS patients ventilated with high PEEP levels [45].

It is, therefore, reasonable to consider high PEEP, since low tidal volume (< 6 ml/ideal body weight) and limited plateau pressure (< 35 cm-H_2O) are maintained in patients with severe ARDS [46]. We also need to look at cardiac function and limit pressures as much as possible in patients with right ventricular dysfunction.

Duration of antibiotic therapy

Antibiotics are an essential aspect of therapy in any bacterial infection and in sepsis. A decision needs to be made, however, regarding the optimal duration of therapy. Clearly, antibiotics must be given long enough to ensure eradication of the infecting agent without risk of resurgence, but longer courses can be associated with increased risks of adverse effects, increased costs, and potentially increased risk of emergence of antimicrobial-resistant organisms. Several studies have suggested that reducing the duration of antibiotic administration can be associated with a reduced development of antimicrobial resistance [47, 48]. Recently, it has been suggested that biomarkers of infection, such as procalcitonin, may be helpful in guiding duration of therapy. Christ-Crain et al. reported reduced antibiotic use in patients with lower respiratory tract infections [49] and community-acquired pneumonia [50] in whom decisions to start and continue antibiotic use were made according to procalcitonin levels. In a study in septic patients, Nobre et al. randomly assigned patients to a group managed according to serial procalcitonin levels and a group managed according to current standard practice. Patients in the procalcitonin group had a 3.5-day shorter median duration of antibiotic therapy and a 2-day shorter duration of ICU stay than the control group. The mortality rates and rates of recurrence of the primary infection were similar in the two groups [51].

Selective decontamination of oropharyngeal and digestive tract

Pneumonia is the principal type of nosocomial infection in the critically ill patient, and aspiration of oropharyngeal contents is an important factor in the development of ventilator-associated pneumonia (VAP), a condition which is associated with an increased risk of death [52].

Strategies designed to reduce the oropharyngeal microbial burden could be interesting for preventing VAP. Reduced respiratory infections have been reported after the use of prophylactic antibiotic regimens, such as selective decontamination of the digestive tract (SDD) and selective oropharyngeal decontamination (SOD) [53, 54]. However, most studies were underpowered to detect any benefits on survival. In addition, there is considerable concern that this technique may be associated with the emergence and selection of multiresistant bacteria [55]. This effect could be particularly harmful in the ICU where the risk of development of multiresistant organisms is

increasingly high [56]. Recently, a multicentre randomised Dutch study tested SOD and SDD in a mixed ICU population [57]. The authors documented a modest absolute mortality reduction at 28 days after several statistical adjustments that reduced the final impact of the study.

Thus, any decision to implement SOD or SDD regimens must be counterbalanced with the risk of selection of multiresistant organisms and cost. Use of such measures may be more interesting in units with a high prevalence of VAP and where multiresistant organisms are not considered a major problem [58].

Activated protein C

In a multicentre, randomised controlled trial, administration of activated protein C in patients with severe sepsis was associated with improved survival [59]. However, being a natural anticoagulant, it is perhaps not surprising that treatment with activated protein C is associated with an increased risk of bleeding. In the original PROWESS study, the data suggested that one additional serious bleeding event would occur for every 66 patients treated [59]. In an analysis of 2,786 adult patients treated with activated protein C, Bernard et al. reported that 2.8% of patients had a serious bleeding event during the infusion period and 5.3% during the 28-day study period [60]; 43% of the bleeding events during drug infusion were procedure-related. In the open-label ENHANCE study [61], serious bleeding rates were increased compared with patients in PROWESS, and based on these data, Farmer calculated that one serious adverse bleeding event would occur for every 16 patients treated [62]. However, the risks of bleeding are particularly high in certain groups of patients predisposed to bleeding and during procedures. In assessing whether or not to give activated protein C, the absolute and relative contraindications (see Tab. 2) must therefore be carefully noted.

Sedative agents

Sedative agents have been widely used in the ICU to supposedly improve patient comfort. However, deep sedation is not without its risks, including

Tab. 2   Absolute and relative contraindications related to bleeding risk when considering therapy with activated protein C

Absolute contraindications	▪ Active internal bleeding
	▪ Recent (within 3 months) haemorrhagic stroke
	▪ Recent (within 2 months) intracranial or intraspinal surgery, or severe head trauma
	▪ Trauma with an increased risk of life-threatening bleeding
	▪ Presence of an epidural catheter
	▪ Intracranial neoplasm or mass lesion or evidence of cerebral herniation
Relative contraindications	▪ Concurrent therapeutic dosing of heparin to treat an active thrombotic or embolic event
	▪ Platelet count < 30,000 x 10^6/l, even if it is increased after transfusions
	▪ Prothrombin time-INR > 3.0
	▪ Recent (within 6 weeks) gastrointestinal bleeding
	▪ Recent administration (within 3 days) of thrombolytic therapy
	▪ Recent administration (within 7 days) of oral anticoagulants or glycoprotein IIb/IIIa inhibitors
	▪ Recent administration (within 7 days) of aspirin >650 mg per day or other platelet inhibitors
	▪ Recent (within 3 months) ischaemic stroke
	▪ Intracranial arteriovenous malformation or aneurysm
	▪ Known bleeding diathesis
	▪ Chronic severe hepatic disease
	▪ Any other condition in which bleeding constitutes a significant hazard or would be particularly difficult to manage because of its location

the psychological effects of a loss of contact of the patients with their environment, higher incidence of delirium, respiratory and myocardial depression, altered gut function, and reduced mobility associated with an increased risk of ICU-acquired weakness, thrombophlebitis, and decubitus ulcers. In addition, many sedative agents have immunosuppressant effects leading to an increased risk of infection. Kress and co-workers showed that daily interruption of sedative infusions in mechanically ventilated patients reduced the duration of mechanical ventilation and shortened ICU length of stay [63]. Small amounts of sedation may be necessary in some patients at some time during their ICU stay, but by ensuring adequate pain relief and improving communication with patients, we can increasingly aim for minimal sedation.

Steroids in septic shock

The use of steroids in patients with sepsis has swung like a pendulum from widespread use to no use and back again [64]. Forty years ago, high-dose steroids were used in septic patients because it was believed that their anti-inflammatory properties could be useful. However, two large double-blind randomised controlled trials later failed to confirm these findings [65, 66], and steroids fell out of favour until a study by Annane et al. [67] suggested that moderate doses of steroids could improve outcomes in patients with severe sepsis and relative adrenal insufficiency. However, the recent multicentre, randomised Corticus study [68], failed to demonstrate any improvement in survival or reversal of shock, although it included patients with less severe illness than the early study by Annane et al. [67]. Importantly too, patients treated with steroids had higher rates of superinfection and hyperglycaemia than placebo-treated patients. Steroid use has also been associated with an increased risk of neuromuscular weakness in ICU patients [69]. Clearly, no drug is without risks, and although steroids may have a place in a select group of patients with severe septic shock [64], the risks of secondary infection, hyperglycaemia, and ICU-acquired weakness need to be carefully weighed against any possible benefit.

Enteral versus parenteral nutrition

Adequate nutritional support is considered an essential part of patient care. Despite efforts to ensure adequate caloric intake, patients frequently continue to lose muscle body mass as a consequence of catabolism induced by the disease process, and malnutrition is highly prevalent in hospitalised patients and associated with increased morbidity and mortality [70]. Early enteral nutrition is considered the first choice in critically ill patients to counteract this deficit. However, several clinical situations can make it difficult to deliver the total calorie requirements using eneteral nutrition, such as haemodynamic instability, ileus, transfers, enteral feeding tube displacement, etc. Total or partial parenteral support is considered as an alternative in patients where enteral feeding is not sufficient, either because of intolerance or contraindication. Parenteral nutrition may also be used in combination with enteral feeding to deliver optimal nutritional support. Parenteral nutrition may be associated with higher risks due to the insertion and presence of the feeding catheter per se, but there are also specific problems related to the parenteral solution, including electrolyte disorders, hyperglycaemia, altered liver function tests, and risks of worsening pulmonary gas exchange [71]. However, meta-analyses have not demonstrated higher risks with parenteral nutrition in critically ill patients [72, 73]. In fact, clinical practice guidelines indicate that patients who fail to reach target nutritional requirements should receive additional parenteral nutrition [74].

While the association of enteral and parenteral nutrition seems to be an acceptable alternative in those patients unable to reach optimal caloric support by the enteral route alone, care should be taken to avoid overfeeding and excessive hyperglycaemia, which can equally be associated with complications [75].

ICU admission

Even ICU admission can have its risks! This is perhaps especially true for patients with haematological cancers, who have worse outcomes than other ICU patients [76]. ICU patients benefit from a better surveillance with higher nurse-to-patient ratios, but the ICU is associated with a greater risk of nosocomial infection, particularly dangerous for immunosuppressed haematology patients. The risk of developing infections with multiresistant bacteria such as methicillin-resistant *Staphylococcus aureus* (MRSA) or extended spectrum beta-lactamase (ESBL)-producing bacteria is also greater [56, 77]. Other ICU-associated risks include stress-induced gastrointestinal bleeding, complications related to insertion of intravenous catheters, sleep disorders and ICU psychosis. Medical error rates, e.g. related to incorrect medication, may also be higher in ICUs than in other hospital units, largely because of the greater need for high-risk interventions and medications [78, 79].

Summary and conclusion

The above list is just a small example of some of the key topics in intensive care in which a risk/benefit analysis must be made. There are many, many more. Indeed, perhaps the only intervention without risks is a friendly smile and a few comforting words! The recent emphasis on good, evidence-based medicine has encouraged us all to look a little more closely at what we are doing, to be able to justify our use of interventions both globally and in individual patients. Increased awareness of the risks and benefits of various interventions has led to a reduction in iatrogenicity; for example, blood transfusions are used less liberally, invasive haemodynamic monitoring with pulmonary artery catheters is now replaced wherever possible by non-invasive techniques, sedation is more often minimal than excessive, etc. Evidence for and against many of the interventions used in the ICU is still lacking [80], and more good quality randomised trials are needed to provide data to support or oppose much of what we do. In the meantime, a careful assessment of the risks and benefits of each procedure and intervention in each patient will help maximise outcomes and limit adverse effects.

Acknowledgements

Dr. Salgado is supported by grants from the post-graduate scholarship program of the Coordenação Aperfeiçoamento de Pessoal de Nivél Superior (CAPES) – Brazilian Ministry of Education, and from the Federal University of Rio de Janeiro.

The authors

Jean-Louis Vincent, Prof.
Diamantino Salgado, MD
Charalampos Pierrakos, MD
  Department of Intensive Care | Erasme Hospital |
  Université libre de Bruxelles, Belgium

Address for correspondence
  Jean-Louis Vincent
  Department of Intensive Care
  Erasme University Hospital
  Université Libre de Bruxelles
  Route de Lennik 808
  1070 Bruxelles, Belgium
  E-mail: jlvincen@ulb.ac.be

References

1. Schuller D, Mitchell JP, Calandrino FS, Schuster DP. Fluid balance during pulmonary edema: Is fluid gain a marker or a cause of poor outcome? Chest 1991; 100:1068–1075.
2. Vincent JL, Sakr Y, Sprung CL, Ranieri VM, Reinhart K, Gerlach H et al. Sepsis in European intensive care units: results of the SOAP study. Crit Care Med 2006; 34(2):344–353.
3. Sakr Y, Vincent JL, Reinhart K, Groeneveld J, Michalopoulos A, Sprung CL et al. High tidal volume and positive fluid balance are associated with worse outcome in acute lung injury. Chest 2005; 128(5):3098–3108.
4. Payen D, de Pont AC, Sakr Y, Spies C, Reinhart K, Vincent JL. A positive fluid balance is associated with a worse outcome in patients with acute renal failure. Crit Care 2008; 12(3):R74.
5. Wiedemann HP, Wheeler AP, Bernard GR, Thompson BT, Hayden D, DeBoisblanc B et al. Comparison of two fluid-management strategies in acute lung injury. N Engl J Med 2006; 354(24):2564–2575.
6. Aber TS, Hosac AM, Veach MP, Pierre YW. Fluid therapy in the critically ill. Journal of Pharmacy Practice 2002; 15:114–123.
7. Brunkhorst FM, Engel C, Bloos F, Meier-Hellmann A, Ragaller M, Weiler N et al. Intensive insulin therapy and pentastarch resuscitation in severe sepsis. N Engl J Med 2008; 358(2):125–139.
8. Bunn F, Trivedi D, Ashraf S. Colloid solutions for fluid resuscitation. Cochrane Database Syst Rev 2008;(1):CD001319.
9. Perel P, Roberts I. Colloids versus crystalloids for fluid resuscitation in critically ill patients. Cochrane Database Syst Rev 2007;(4):CD000567.
10. Hebert PC, Van der Linden P, Biro G, Hu LQ. Physiologic aspects of anemia. Crit Care Clin 2004; 20(2):187–212.
11. Kleinman S, Chan P, Robillard P. Risks associated with transfusion of cellular blood components in Canada. Transfus Med Rev 2003; 17(2):120–162.
12. Vincent JL, Baron JF, Reinhart K, Gattinoni L, Thijs L, Webb A et al. Anemia and blood transfusion in critically ill patients. J A M A 2002; 288(12):1499–1507.
13. Corwin HL, Gettinger A, Pearl RG, Fink MP, Levy MM, Abraham E et al. The CRIT Study: Anemia and blood transfusion in the critically ill–current clinical practice in the United States. Crit Care Med 2004; 32(1):39–52.
14. Vincent JL, Sakr Y, Sprung CL, Harboe S, Damas P. Are blood transfusions associated with greater mortality rates? Anesthesiology 2008; 108:31–39.
15. Carson JL, Duff A, Poses RM, Berlin JA, Spence RK, Trout R et al. Effect of anaemia and cardiovascular disease on surgical mortality and morbidity. Lancet 1996; 348(9034):1055–1060.
16. Carson JL, Noveck H, Berlin JA, Gould SA. Mortality and morbidity in patients with very low postoperative Hb levels who decline blood transfusion. Transfusion 2002; 42(7):812–818.
17. Hebert PC, Tinmouth A, Corwin HL. Controversies in RBC transfusion in the critically ill. Chest 2007; 131(5):1583–1590.
18. Sakr Y, Reinhart K, Vincent JL, Sprung CL, Moreno R, Ranieri VM et al. Does dopamine administration in shock influence outcome? Results of the Sepsis Occurrence in Acutely Ill Patients (SOAP) Study. Crit Care Med 2006; 34(3):589–597.
19. Povoa PR, Carneiro AH, Ribeiro OS, Pereira AC. Influence of vasopressor agent in septic shock mortality. Results from the Portuguese Community-Acquired Sepsis Study (SACiUCI study). Crit Care Med 2009;37(2):410–416.
20. Martin C, Papazian L, Perrin G, Saux P, Gouin F. Norepinephrine or dopamine for the treatment of hyperdynamic septic shock? Chest 1993; 103:1826–1831.
21. Landry DW, Oliver JA. The pathogenesis of vasodilatory shock. N Engl J Med 2001; 345(8):588–595.
22. Lange M, Ertmer C, Westphal M. Vasopressin vs. terlipressin in the treatment of cardiovascular failure in sepsis. Intensive Care Med 2008; 34(5):821–832.
23. Russell JA, Walley KR, Singer J, Gordon AC, Hebert PC, Cooper DJ et al. Vasopressin versus norepinephrine infusion in patients with septic shock. N Engl J Med 2008; 358(9):877–887.
24. Van den Berghe G, Wouters P, Weekers F, Verwaest C, Bruyninckx F, Schetz M et al. Intensive insulin therapy in the critically ill patient. N Engl J Med 2001; 345:1359–1367.
25. Van den Berghe G, Wilmer A, Hermans G, Meersseman W, Wouters PJ, Milants I et al. Intensive insulin therapy in the medical ICU. N Engl J Med 2006; 354(5):449–461.

26. NICE-SUGAR Study Investigators, Finfer S, Chittock DR, SU SY, Blair D, Foster D et al. Intensive versus conventional glucose control in critically ill patients. N Engl J Med 2009;360(13):1283–1297.

27. Wiener RS, Wiener DC, Larson RJ. Benefits and risks of tight glucose control in critically ill adults: a meta-analysis. JAMA 2008; 300(8):933–944.

28. Ali NA, O'Brien JM, Jr., Dungan K, Phillips G, Marsh CB, Lemeshow S et al. Glucose variability and mortality in patients with sepsis. Crit Care Med 2008; 36(8):2316–2321.

29. Dellinger RP, Levy MM, Carlet JM, Bion J, Parker MM, Jaeschke R et al. Surviving Sepsis Campaign: International guidelines for management of severe sepsis and septic shock: 2008. Intensive Care Med 2008; 34(1):17–60.

30. Krinsley JS, Preiser JC. Moving beyond tight glucose control to safe effective glucose control. Crit Care 2008; 12(3):149.

31. British Thoracic Society. Non-invasive ventilation in acute respiratory failure. Thorax 2002; 57(3):192–211.

32. Ferrer M, Esquinas A, Leon M, Gonzalez G, Alarcon A, Torres A. Noninvasive ventilation in severe hypoxemic respiratory failure: a randomized clinical trial. Am J Respir Crit Care Med 2003; 168(12):1438–1444.

33. Martin TJ, Hovis JD, Costantino JP, Bierman MI, Donahoe MP, Rogers RM et al. A randomized, prospective evaluation of noninvasive ventilation for acute respiratory failure. Am J Respir Crit Care Med 2000; 161(3 Pt 1):807–813.

34. Antonelli M, Pennisi MA, Montini L. Clinical review: Noninvasive ventilation in the clinical setting–experience from the past 10 years. Crit Care 2005; 9(1):98–103.

35. Vital FM, Saconato H, Ladeira MT, Sen A, Hawkes CA, Soares B et al. Non-invasive positive pressure ventilation (CPAP or bilevel NPPV) for cardiogenic pulmonary edema. Cochrane Database Syst Rev 2008;(3):CD005351.

36. Truwit JD, Bernard GR. Noninvasive ventilation–don't push too hard. N Engl J Med 2004; 350(24):2512–2515.

37. Haitsma JJ, Lachmann B. Lung protective ventilation in ARDS: the open lung maneuver. Minerva Anestesiol 2006; 72(3):117–132.

38. Ranieri VM, Suter PM, Tortorella C, De Tullio R, Dayer JM, Brienza A et al. Effect of mechanical ventilation on inflammatory mediators in patients with acute respiratory distress syndrome: a randomized controlled trial. J A M A 1999; 282(1):54–61.

39. Vieillard-Baron A. Is right ventricular function the one that matters in ARDS patients? Definitely yes. Intensive Care Med 2009; 35(1):4–6.

40. Dellinger RP, Levy MM, Carlet JM, Bion J, Parker MM, Jaeschke R et al. Surviving Sepsis Campaign: International guidelines for management of severe sepsis and septic shock: 2008. Crit Care Med 2008; 36:296–327.

41. The ARDS Network. Ventilation with lower tidal volumes as compared with traditional tidal volumes for acute lung injury and the acute respiratory distress syndrome. N Engl J Med 2000; 342(18):1301–1308.

42. Gattinoni L, Pesenti A. The concept of "baby lung". Intensive Care Med 2005; 31(6):776–784.

43. Meade MO, Cook DJ, Guyatt GH, Slutsky AS, Arabi YM, Cooper DJ et al. Ventilation strategy using low tidal volumes, recruitment maneuvers, and high positive end-expiratory pressure for acute lung injury and acute respiratory distress syndrome: a randomized controlled trial. JAMA 2008; 299(6):637–645.

44. Mercat A, Richard JC, Vielle B, Jaber S, Osman D, Diehl JL et al. Positive end-expiratory pressure setting in adults with acute lung injury and acute respiratory distress syndrome: a randomized controlled trial. JAMA 2008; 299(6):646–655.

45. Phoenix S, Paravastu S, Columb M, Vincent JL, Nirmalan M. Does a higher positive end-expiratory pressure decrease mortality in acute respiratory distress syndrome? A systematic review and meta-analysis. Anesthesiology. 2009;110(5):1098–105.

46. Gattinoni L, Caironi P. Refining ventilatory treatment for acute lung injury and acute respiratory distress syndrome. JAMA 2008; 299(6):691–693.

47. Chastre J, Wolff M, Fagon JY, Chevret S, Thomas F, Wermert D et al. Comparison of 8 vs 15 days of antibiotic therapy for ventilator-associated pneumonia in adults: a randomized trial. JAMA 2003; 290(19):2588–2598.

48. Marra AR, de Almeida SM, Correa L, Silva M, Jr., Martino MD, Silva CV et al. The effect of limiting antimicrobial therapy duration on antimicrobial resistance in the critical care setting. Am J Infect Control 2009;37(3):204–209.

49. Christ-Crain M, Jaccard-Stolz D, Bingisser R, Gencay MM, Huber PR, Tamm M et al. Effect of procalcitonin-guided treatment on antibiotic use and outcome in lower respiratory tract infections: cluster-randomised, single-blinded intervention trial. Lancet 2004; 363(9409):600–607.

50. Christ-Crain M, Stolz D, Bingisser R, Muller C, Miedinger D, Huber PR et al. Procalcitonin-guidance of antibiotic therapy in community-acquired pneumonia: A randomized trial. Am J Respir Crit Care Med 2006; 174:84–93.

51. Nobre V, Harbarth S, Graf JD, Rohner P, Pugin J. Use of procalcitonin to shorten antibiotic treatment duration in septic patients: a randomized trial. Am J Respir Crit Care Med 2008; 177(5):498–505.

52. Rello J, Ollendorf DA, Oster G, Vera-Llonch M, Bellm L, Redman R et al. Epidemiology and outcomes of ventilator-associated pneumonia in a large US database. Chest 2002; 122(6):2115–2121.

53. Bergmans DC, Bonten MJ, Gaillard CA, Paling JC, van der Geest S, van Tiel FH et al. Prevention of ventilator-associated pneumonia by oral decontamination: a prospective, randomized, double-blind, placebo-controlled study. Am J Respir Crit Care Med 2001; 164(3):382–388.

54. de Jonge E, Schultz MJ, Spanjaard L, Bossuyt PMM, Vroom MB, Dankert J et al. Effects of selective decon-

tamination of the digestive tract on mortality and the acquisition of resistant bacteria in intensive care patients. Lancet 2003; 362:1011–1016.

55. Lingnau W, Berger J, Javorsky F, Fille M, Allerberger F, Benzer H. Changing bacterial ecology during a five-year period of selective intestinal decontamination. J Hosp Infect 1998; 39(3):195–206.

56. Zhanel GG, DeCorby M, Laing N, Weshnoweski B, Vashisht R, Tailor F et al. Antimicrobial-resistant pathogens in intensive care units in Canada: results of the Canadian National Intensive Care Unit (CAN-ICU) study, 2005–2006. Antimicrob Agents Chemother 2008; 52(4):1430–1437.

57. de Smet AM, Kluytmans JA, Cooper BS, Mascini EM, Benus RF, van der Werf TS et al. Decontamination of the digestive tract and oropharynx in ICU patients. N Engl J Med 2009; 360(1):20–31.

58. Vincent JL. Selective digestive decontamination: for everyone, everywhere? Lancet 2003; 362(9389):1006–1007.

59. Bernard GR, Vincent JL, Laterre PF, LaRosa SP, Dhainaut JF, Lopez-Rodriguez A et al. Efficacy and safety of recombinant human activated protein C for severe sepsis. N Engl J Med 2001; 344:699–709.

60. Bernard GR, Macias WL, Joyce DE, Williams MD, Bailey J, Vincent JL. Safety assessment of drotrecogin alfa (activated) in the treatment of adult patients with severe sepsis. Crit Care 2003; 7:155–163.

61. Vincent JL, Bernard GR, Beale R, Doig C, Putensen C, Dhainaut JF et al. Drotrecogin alfa (activated) treatment in severe sepsis from the global open-label trial EN-HANCE. Crit Care Med 2005; 33:2266–2277.

62. Farmer JC. Drotrecogin alfa (activated) treatment in severe sepsis: a "journal club" review of the global EN-HANCE trial. Crit Care Med 2005; 33(10):2428–2431.

63. Kress JP, Pohlman AS, O'Connor MF, Hall JB. Daily interruption of sedative infusions in critically ill patients undergoing mechanical ventilation. N Engl J Med 2000; 342(20):1471–1477.

64. Vincent JL. Steroids in Sepsis: Another swing of the pendulum in our clinical trials. Crit Care 2008; 12:141.

65. Bone RC, Fisher CJJ, Clemmer TP, Slotman GJ, Metz CA, Balk RA. A controlled clinical trial of high-dose methylprednisolone in the treatment of severe sepsis and septic shock. N Engl J Med 1987; 317:653–658.

66. The Veterans Administration Systemic Sepsis Cooperative Study Group. Effect of high-dose glucocorticoid therapy on mortality in patients with clinical signs of systemic sepsis. N Engl J Med 1987; 317:659–665.

67. Annane D, Sebille V, Charpentier C, Bollaert PE, Francois B, Korach JM et al. Effect of treatment with low doses of hydrocortisone and fludrocortisone on mortality in patients with septic shock. J A M A 2002; 288:862–871.

68. Sprung CL, Annane D, Keh D, Moreno R, Singer M, Freivogel K et al. Hydrocortisone therapy for patients with septic shock. N Engl J Med 2008; 358(2):111–124.

69. Steinberg KP, Hudson LD, Goodman RB, Hough CL, Lanken PN, Hyzy R et al. Efficacy and safety of corticosteroids for persistent acute respiratory distress syndrome. N Engl J Med 2006; 354(16):1671–1684.

70. Pichard C, Kyle UG, Morabia A, Perrier A, Vermeulen B, Unger P. Nutritional assessment: lean body mass depletion at hospital admission is associated with an increased length of stay. Am J Clin Nutr 2004; 79(4):613–618.

71. Marik PE, Pinsky M. Death by parenteral nutrition. Intensive Care Med 2003; 29(6):867–869.

72. Simpson F, Doig GS. Parenteral vs. enteral nutrition in the critically ill patient: a meta-analysis of trials using the intention to treat principle. Intensive Care Med 2005; 31(1):12–23.

73. Braunschweig CL, Levy P, Sheean PM, Wang X. Enteral compared with parenteral nutrition: a meta-analysis. Am J Clin Nutr 2001; 74(4):534–542.

74. Kreymann KG, Berger MM, Deutz NE, Hiesmayr M, Jolliet P, Kazandjiev G et al. ESPEN Guidelines on Enteral Nutrition: Intensive care. Clin Nutr 2006; 25(2):210–223.

75. Heidegger CP, Darmon P, Pichard C. Enteral vs. parenteral nutrition for the critically ill patient: a combined support should be preferred. Curr Opin Crit Care 2008; 14(4):408–414.

76. Taccone FS, Artigas AA, Sprung CL, Moreno R, Sakr Y, Vincent JL. Characteristics and outcomes of cancer patients in European ICUs. Crit Care 2009; 13(1):R15.

77. Streit JM, Jones RN, Sader HS, Fritsche TR. Assessment of pathogen occurrences and resistance profiles among infected patients in the intensive care unit: report from the SENTRY Antimicrobial Surveillance Program (North America, 2001). Int J Antimicrob Agents 2004; 24(2):111–118.

78. Cullen DJ, Sweitzer BJ, Bates DW, Burdick E, Edmondson A, Leape LL. Preventable adverse drug events in hospitalized patients: a comparative study of intensive care and general care units. Crit Care Med 1997; 25(8):1289–1297.

79. Rothschild JM, Landrigan CP, Cronin JW, Kaushal R, Lockley SW, Burdick E et al. The Critical Care Safety Study: The incidence and nature of adverse events and serious medical errors in intensive care. Crit Care Med 2005; 33(8):1694–1700.

80. Vincent JL. Is the current management of severe sepsis and septic shock really evidence based? PLoS Med 2006; 3(9):e346.

Ariane Boumendil and Bertrand Guidet

Safe triage decision

Introduction

The aim of the intensive care unit (ICU) is to support patients with potential or definite organ failure. Intensive care is expensive, accounting for a large part of hospital expenditures. According to the introduction section of the 1999 guidelines for ICU admission published by the American College of Critical Care Medicine (ACCCM), "because of utilization of expensive resources, ICU should in general be reserved for those patients with reversible conditions who have a reasonable prospect of substantial recovery." If there is no prospect of recovery then such care is inappropriate, as it will prolong life in an undignified manner. A common concern of every developed country is the fact that healthcare needs tend to be endless, whereas funds allocated to the healthcare system are not; in this context efficient use of ICUs has become a priority.

Decisions regarding whom to admit and whom to exclude from ICUs is a process known as "triage". Triage is influenced by a myriad of factors, which can be classified into three groups depending on whether they relate to the ICU admission request (pre-triage phase), the evaluation by the intensivist (triage, strictly speaking), or the availability of ICU beds (post-triage phase) [1]. Therefore, triage does not only concern intensivists, but any physician that might request an ICU admission.

Emergency physicians often have to decide whether to address a patient to the ICU. Studies of ICU admission rarely take into account the pre-triage phase [2].

As with any other medical treatment, the decision to admit a patient to an ICU should be based on the concept of potential benefit. To be fair, the decision should be the same whether the admission is requested in one centre or another. The decision should thus be based on objective criteria and on a comprehensive assessment of the patient using standardized tools.

In practice, however, we wonder how physicians evaluate patients, how they identify patients "who benefit the most", how they define and predict benefit, if patients are part of the decisions. In the first part of this chapter we will review existing recommendations; in the second part, we will summarise the criteria actually used by physicians to decide whether or not to admit a patient to the ICU based on a review of published studies; finally, we will discuss the outcome of admitted versus refused patients.

A search on pubmed using the keywords "critical care" or "intensive care" combined with "admission" or "triage" brought up 10,717 articles (770 reviews). Most of the papers focus on a specific disease or treatment. Combining the previous search with the keyword "criteria", the number of articles is reduced to 1,823, including 142 reviews.

Suggested criteria

Existing guidelines and recommendations for ICU admission

There are few published recommendations regarding admission of patients to the ICU. Intensivists have little to guide them in the rationing of critical care services [3]. The most popular guidelines are those published and periodically updated by the ACCCM [4, 5].

Critical care societies' recommendations

The guidelines for ICU admission, discharge, and triage issued by the Society of Critical Care Medicine in 1999 [5] lists 48 specific diagnoses and 26 objective criteria (see Tab. 1) that should lead to ICU admission, and detail a prioritisation model which defines patients that will benefit most from the ICU. The authors state that patients "too sick" and "too well" to benefit from critical care services must be identified and thus recommend that physicians should be familiar with tools for assessing severity of illness and prognosis of critically ill patients. It is also specified in the manuscript that institutions should adapt these guidelines to their specific local requirements.

Other publications: An example [6]

This publication is an adaptation of English guidelines completed by several recommendations on different types of organ support. The introduction of the paper summarises the most important factors to be considered for assessing suitability for admission to the ICU, namely:

- Diagnosis
- Severity of illness
- Age
- Coexisting disease
- Physiological reserve
- Prognosis
- Availability of suitable treatment
- Response to treatment to date
- Recent cardiopulmonary arrest
- Anticipated quality of life
- Patient's wishes

Tab. 1 Diagnosis and objective parameters models [reproduced from Task Force of the American College of Critical Care Medicine, Society of Critical Care Medicine. Guidelines for intensive care unit admission, discharge, and triage. Critical Care Medicine, 1999. 27(3):633–8]

Diagnosis Model

A Cardiac System
1 Acute myocardial infarction with complications
2 Cardiogenic shock
3 Complex arrhythmias requiring close monitoring and intervention
4 Acute congestive heart failure with respiratory failure and/or requiring haemodynamic support
5 Hypertensive emergencies
6 Unstable angina, particularly with dysrhythmias, haemodynamic instability, or persistent chest pain
7 S/P cardiac arrest
8 Cardiac tamponade or constriction with haemodynamic instability
9 Dissecting aortic aneurysms
10 Complete heart block

B Pulmonary System
1 Acute respiratory failure requiring ventilatory support
2 Pulmonary emboli with haemodynamic instability
3 Patients in an intermediate care unit who are demonstrating respiratory deterioration
4 Need for nursing/respiratory care not available in lesser care areas such as floor or intermediate care unit
5 Massive haemoptysis
6 Respiratory failure with imminent intubation

C Neurologic Disorders
1 Acute stroke with altered mental status
2 Coma: metabolic, toxic, or anoxic
3 Intracranial haemorrhage with potential for herniation
4 Acute subarachnoid haemorrhage
5 Meningitis with altered mental status or respiratory compromise

6   Central nervous system or neuromuscular disorders with deteriorating neurologic or pulmonary function

7   Status epilepticus

8   Brain-dead or potentially brain-dead patients who are being aggressively managed while determining organ donation status

9   Vasospasm

10   Severely head-injured patients

D   Drug Ingestion and Drug Overdose

1   Haemodynamically unstable drug ingestion

2   Drug ingestion with significantly altered mental status with inadequate airway protection

3   Seizures following drug ingestion

E   Gastrointestinal Disorders

1   Life-threatening gastrointestinal bleeding including hypotension, angina, continued bleeding, or with comorbid conditions

2   Fulminant hepatic failure

3   Severe pancreatitis

4   Esophageal perforation with or without mediastinitis

F   Endocrine

1   Diabetic ketoacidosis complicated by haemodynamic instability, altered mental status, respiratory insufficiency, or severe acidosis

2   Thyroid storm or myxoedema coma with haemodynamic instability

3   Hyperosmolar state with coma and/or haemodynamic instability

4   Other endocrine problems such as adrenal crises with haemodynamic instability

5   Severe hypercalcaemia with altered mental status, requiring haemodynamic monitoring

6   Hypo- or hypernatraemia with seizures, altered mental status

7   Hypo- or hypermagnesaemia with haemodynamic compromise or dysrhythmias

8   Hypo- or hyperkalaemia with dysrhythmias or muscular weakness

9   Hypophosphataemia with muscular weakness

G   Surgical

1   Post-operative patients requiring haemodynamic monitoring/ventilatory support or extensive nursing care

H   Miscellaneous

1   Septic shock with haemodynamic instability

2   Haemodynamic monitoring

3   Clinical conditions requiring ICU-level nursing care

4   Environmental injuries (lightning, near-drowning, hypo-/hyperthermia)

5   New/experimental therapies with potential for complications

Objective Parameters Model

Vital Signs

*   Pulse < 40 or > 150 beats/minute

*   Systolic arterial pressure < 80 mm Hg or 20 mm Hg below the patient's usual pressure

*   Mean arterial pressure < 60 mm Hg

*   Diastolic arterial pressure > 120 mm Hg

*   Respiratory rate > 35 breaths/minute

Laboratory Values (newly discovered)

*   Serum sodium < 110 mEq/L or > 170 mEq/L

*   Serum potassium < 2.0 mEq/L or > 7.0 mEq/L

* PaO_2 < 50 mm Hg

*   pH < 7.10 or > 7.7

*   Serum glucose > 800 mg/dl

*   Serum calcium > 15 mg/dl

*   Toxic level of drug or other chemical substance in a haemodynamically or neurologically compromised patient

Radiography/Ultrasonography/Tomography (newly discovered)

*   Cerebral vascular haemorrhage, contusion or subarachnoid haemorrhage with altered mental status or focal neurological signs

*   Ruptured viscera, bladder, liver, esophageal varices or uterus with haemodynamic instability

*   Dissecting aortic aneurysm

* Myocardial infarction with complex arrhythmias, haemodynamic instability or congestive heart failure

* Sustained ventricular tachycardia or ventricular fibrillation

* Complete heart block with haemodynamic instability

Physical Findings (acute onset)

* Unequal pupils in an unconscious patient

* Burns covering > 10 % BSA

* Anuria

* Airway obstruction

* Coma

* Continuous seizures

* Cyanosis

* Cardiac tamponade

Although the authors mention that age itself should not be a barrier to admission, they advise physicians to keep in mind that "increasing age is associated with diminishing physiological reserve and an increasing chance of serious coexisting illness."

The few published guidelines or recommendations regarding admission of patients to intensive care leave decisions to individual physicians; criteria used may thus vary a lot. Some physicians may think their duty is to preserve life regardless of consciousness or cost, some may think that there is medical futility in some patients and these biases surely slip into decisions.

Criteria used

Criteria identified through questionnaires

Physicians should select patients who are likely to benefit from ICU care; accordingly, the most frequently mentioned criterion for rationing healthcare is a small expected benefit [7].

Age certainly is a factor considered by physicians in the admission of acutely ill medical patients to critical care units, but not the most determinant. In response to a hypothetical case scenario, Nuckton et al. [8] asked physicians to admit one of two patients – aged 56 and 82 – to a last available critical care unit bed. When age was the only difference between the two patients, over 80 % of respondents chose the younger patient for admission and 6.2 % abstained. Following the provision of more detailed medical and social information, however, only 53.5 % chose the younger patient and 5.3 % continued to abstain. In a ranking of several admission factors, age was found to be of less importance than severity of presenting illness, previous medical history and "do not resuscitate" status, but of more importance than patient motivation, ability to contribute to society, family support and ability to pay for care.

In response to a questionnaire [9], over 300 Swiss physicians ranked factors used to assess patients for admission to the ICU in the following decreasing order of importance:

■ Prognosis of underlying disease
■ Prognosis of acute illness
■ Patient's wishes
■ Bed used to the prejudice of another patient
■ Number of available beds
■ Current nursing workload
■ Policy of intensive care unit
■ Legal liability
■ Patient's functional status
■ Family's wishes
■ Patient's age
■ Cost relative to expected outcome
■ Patient's compliance with medical recommendations
■ Drug misuse
■ Other, less determinant factors (chronic alcoholism, psychiatric disease, emotional state, religious beliefs, socio-economic characteristics)

In this study eight clinical vignettes involving hypothetical patients were submitted to physicians. One scenario (myocardial infarction) was designed to elicit an acceptance rate close to 100 %; only 94 % of the physicians chose to admit the patient. In another scenario (respiratory failure in the presence of relapse with acute leukaemia) refusal was expected from most doctors, yet 82 % of respondents admitted the patient.

Criteria used by intensivists to decide whether to admit or refuse patients to ICU

Studies of triage [10–16] have focused on the general population of patients referred for ICU admission and on evaluations made by intensivists only. Seven studies (6 in Europe, 1 in Asia) [10–14, 17, 18] compared admitted to refused patients [10, 11]. Case mix and data collected vary from one study to another; for instance, pre-admission status [11, 13, 18] and severity of illness of the patients were not recorded in all studies. The refusal rate shows a high variability across hospitals as it ranges from 23% to 72%. Factors associated with ICU refusal included older age [10, 12, 14, 17]; underlying diseases [10, 11, 17, 18]; dependency [11, 13]; nonsurgical status [16, 17]; reason for ICU admission request [14, 16]; and organisational factors such as a full unit [11–13], the location of the patient [13], the experience of the intensivist [13], and the time of the request [11].

Patients or family wishes are no prognostic factors of ICU admission although they are mentioned as important factors to consider in published recommendations [6].

Specificity of old patients

Patients over 80 years of age have various and often complicated health states. They can have a great number of diagnosable disorders. A disorder in one organ system can weaken another system and lead to disability, dependence, or death. Effects of the disorders are magnified by social disadvantage and geriatric symptoms. Common geriatric symptoms such as falls, mobility problems, weight or appetite loss and frailty require particular attention. For instance, a measure of frailty based on clinical judgment has been reported to predict loss of self-sufficiency and death. To be fair, decisions of ICU admission of old patients should be based on comprehensive evaluation of all dimensions of the health state of those patients, enabling the evaluation of the benefit of an ICU hospitalisation. Decisions of ICU admission of old patients should also definitely take into account patients wishes.

To our knowledge, only two French studies addressed ICU triage in patients older than 80 years, one being a single centre-study [19] and the other a multicentre study [20]. In the first study (n = 180) the refusal rate was 72% and factors independently associated with ICU refusal were age above 85, non-surgical status, and a full unit. Greater self-sufficiency was associated with ICU admission [19]. Using data from the second study, it has been shown that Emergency and ICU physicians were extremely reluctant to consider ICU admission of patients aged 80 and over, despite the presence of potential ICU admission criteria adapted from guidelines published by the American Society of Critical Care Medicine [20].

What happens to refused patients?

Compared to that of admitted patients, hospital mortality is higher among patients considered too sick to benefit and lower among patients considered too well to benefit. Interestingly enough, mortality differences between ICU admitted and non admitted patients are reduced in the long term. It means that the beneficial effect of ICU treatment partly vanishes after hospital discharge and that questions the "liberal ICU admission policy" (see Tab. 2) [21].

Sprung et al. [12] showed that secondary ICU admission is of poor prognosis. Simchen et al. [22] estimated that 5.5% of hospitalised patients had potential ICU admission condition, among those patients only 27% were hospitalised in a critical care unit, 24% in a high dependency care unit and about 50% in other medical wards. The authors also showed that 3-day mortality was higher for patients admitted in medical wards. Vanhecke et al. [23] prospectively studied outcome of over 300 patients considered for, but not admitted to the ICU. During the study period, 1,655 patients were evaluated for ICU admission of which 21% were not admitted. The 6-month mortality of patients not admitted was 36%, which was similar to the mortality rate of admitted patients. Factors independently associated with 6-month death in patients not admitted were enrolment in hospice at the time of evaluation, choice to decline ICU and severity of illness (assessed by APACHE II).

Tab. 2   Mortality according to ICU admission decision

	n (%)	Hospital mortality	Observed/ expected mortality	Long-term mortality (endpoint)
Metcalfe (UK) [15]				
Admitted	480 (74 %)	35 %		37 % (3 months)
Refused	165 (26 %)	38 %		46 % (3 months)
Sprung (Israel) [12]				
Admitted	290 (76 %)	14 %		
Refused	92 (24 %)	46 %		
Joynt (Hong Kong) [14]				
Admitted	388		0.93	
Refused	236 (38 %)			
■ Too sick to benefit			1.28	
■ Too well to benefit			0.39	
Garrouste (France) [13]				
Admitted	437	29 %		
Refused	137 (24 %)	38 %		
■ Too sick to benefit	51	81 %		
■ Too well to benefit	76	9 %		
■ No bed available	9	28 %		
■ Family refused the option of ICU	1	0 %		
Garrouste (France) [19]				
Admitted	48	62 %		71 % (one year)
Refused	132 (73 %)			
■ Too sick to benefit	79	71 %		87 % (one year)
■ Too well to benefit	51	18 %		47 % (one year)
■ Family refused the option of ICU	2			

Conclusion

Reports from prospective studies show that the most determinant factors of ICU admission are concordant with those published in medical recommendations. Some of recommended factors, however, are not listed among those used by clinicians to decide whether to admit or refuse ICU admission; patients' wishes, for instance, are rarely accounted for. Moreover, recommendations as well as prospective studies focus on the general population although specific populations, such as old patients, require particular attention. Decisions regarding ICU admission are highly variable from one centre to another and certainly more variable in old patients than in younger ones. Larger scale prospective studies are needed to establish specific recommendations. The prospective multicentre study Intensive Care Elderly-CUB-Réa (ICECub) was designed to determine criteria used for admission of patients over 80 to the ICU from the emergency department (ED) and to evaluate patients' outcome according to physicians' decisions. 2,646 patients over 80 requiring intensive care staying in 15 EDs in the Paris area between November 2004 and January 2006 were included in the study. Patients were mostly women (62.6 %). Median age was 86 years; 25 % of patients were aged under 83 and 10 % over 95 years. The majority of patients lived in their own homes. 58.8 % of patients were independent in all six major activities of daily living and 14.4 % were dependent in all activities. Four out of 5 patients had a chronic illness, 1 out of 5 had dementia. The median number of medications was 5. Notably, information was rarely missing. Severity could be estimated in 94 % of patients. Only 13 % of patients were admitted to the ICU. The major determinants used by physicians for ICU admission will be compared to those declared by the same physicians in response to a questionnaire sent before the beginning of the prospective study.

The authors

Ariane Boumendil, PhD[1,2]
Bertrand Guidet, MD[1,2,3]

[1]Inserm, Unité de Recherche en Épidémiologie Systèmes d'Information et Modélisation (U707) | Paris, France
[2]Université Pierre et Marie Curie | Faculté de Médecine Pierre et Marie Curie | Unité de Recherche en Épidémiologie Systèmes d'Information et Modélisation | Paris, France
[3]Assistance Publique – Hôpitaux de Paris | Hôpital Saint-Antoine | Medical ICU | Paris, France

Address for correspondence
Bertrand Guidet
Medical ICU
Hôpital Saint Antoine
184 rue du Faubourg Saint Antoine
75012 Paris, France
E-mail: bertrand.guidet@sat.aphp.fr

References

1. Levin PD and Sprung CL The process of intensive care triage. Intensive Care Med, 2001. 27(9):1441–5.
2. Boumendil A et al. Should elderly patients be admitted to the intensive care unit? Intensive Care Med, 2007. 33(7): p. 1252–1262.
3. Truog RD et al. Rationing in the intensive care unit. Crit Care Med, 2006. 34(4):958–63; quiz 971.
4. Consensus statement on the triage of critically ill patients. Society of Critical Care Medicine Ethics Committee. Journal of the American Medical Association, 1994. 271(15):1200–3.
5. Guidelines for intensive care unit admission, discharge, and triage. Task Force of the American College of Critical Care Medicine, Society of Critical Care Medicine. Critical Care Medicine, 1999. 27(3):633–8.
6. Smith G and Nielsen M. ABC of intensive care. Criteria for admission. BMJ, 1999. 318(7197):1544–7.
7. Hurst SA et al. Prevalence and Determinants of Physician Bedside Rationing: Data from Europe. J Gen Intern Med, 2006.
8. Nuckton TJ and List ND. Age as a factor in critical care unit admissions. Arch Intern Med, 1995. 155(10):1087–92.
9. Escher M, Perneger TV and Chevrolet JC. National questionnaire survey on what influences doctors' decisions about admission to intensive care. Bmj, 2004. 329(7463):425.
10. Azoulay E et al. Compliance with triage to intensive care recommendations. Critical Care Medicine, 2001. 29(11):2132–6.
11. Garrouste-Orgeas M et al. Predictors of intensive care unit refusal in French intensive care units: a multiple-center study. Crit Care Med, 2005. 33(4):750–5.
12. Sprung CL et al. Evaluation of triage decisions for intensive care admission. Critical Care Medicine, 1999. 27(6):1073–9.
13. Garrouste-Orgeas M et al. Triaging patients to the ICU: a pilot study of factors influencing admission decisions and patient outcomes. Intensive Care Medicine, 2003. 29(5):774–81.
14. Joynt GM et al. Prospective evaluation of patients refused admission to an intensive care unit: triage, futility and outcome. Intensive Care Medicine, 2001. 27(9):1459–65.
15. Metcalfe MA, Slogget A and McPherson K. Mortality among appropriately referred patients refused admission to intensive-care units. Lancet, 1997. 350(9070):7–11.
16. Sprung CL and Eidelman LA. Triage decisions for intensive care in terminally ill patients. Intensive Care Med, 1997. 23(10):1011–4.
17. Frisho-Lima P. et al. Rationing critical care – what happens to patients who are not admitted? Theor Surg, 1994. 9(4):208–11.
18. Thiery G et al. Outcome of cancer patients considered for intensive care unit admission: a hospital-wide prospective study. J Clin Oncol, 2005. 23(19):4406–13.
19. Garrouste-Orgeas M et al. Decision-making process, outcome, and 1-year quality of life of octogenarians referred for intensive care unit admission. Intensive Care Med, 2006. 32(7):1045–51.
20. Garrouste-Orgeas M, Boumendil A, Pateron D, Aegerter P, Somme D, Tabassome S, Guidet G. Selection of ICU

admission criteria for patients aged 80 years and over and compliance of emergency and ICU physicians with the selected criteria: An observational multicenter prospective study. Crit Care Med 2009 (in press).

21. Keenan SP et al. Intensive care unit admission has minimal impact on long-term mortality. Crit Care Med, 2002. 30(3):501–7.

22. Simchen E et al. Survival of critically ill patients hospitalized in and out of intensive care units under paucity of intensive care unit beds. Crit Care Med, 2004. 32(8): p. 1654–61.

23. Vanhecke TE et al. Outcomes of patients considered for, but not admitted to, the intensive care unit. Crit Care Med, 2008. 36(3):812–7.

C. Culture and behaviour

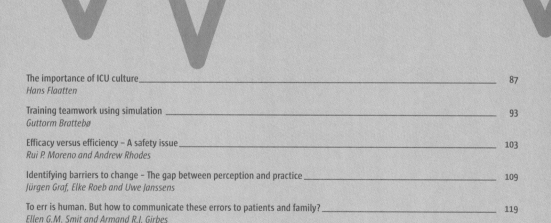

Hans Flaatten

The importance of ICU culture

More often one needs to ask, "What goes on here?" rather than, "What is wrong; and how can it be made better?"
                        Avedis Donabedian 1966 [1]

The so-called "culture" of the ICU may in several ways influence both the quality of care and patient safety. The meaning of the word "ICU culture" is probably obscure for many ICU physicians, but is nevertheless deeply embedded in us all. After all, consultants and trainees alike, we all share the common workplace: our ICU.

The culture of a workplace is often defined as the complex pattern of beliefs, values, attitudes, norms and unspoken assumptions of all the people that behave and work together. The local working culture is powerful, and will often remain even if teams change and individual personnel come and go. The working culture of an organisation has also been described as *"analogous to the personality in the individual"* [2] or *"the ways things are done here"* [3].

There is a lot we do not know regarding the local ICU culture. Firstly, culture is probably different from unit to unit, even within a country. Variations between countries are probably also significant. Secondly, to link elements in the ICU culture to any outcome measure is difficult.

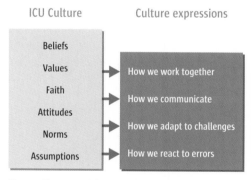

Fig. 1   Elements of the ICU culture, and the way this may be expressed

The culture itself may be hard to define and measure. However, the culture may lead to different expressions, and this relationship is illustrated in Figure 1. These expressions are more visible, can be measured in different ways, and have recently been the subject of a number of investigations. The way the ICU expresses itself has been used to identify a safety culture. This means that a culture oriented towards patient safety can be identified in different ways.

Recently, large healthcare organisations like the Department of Health (UK) and Institute of Medicine (USA)

have drawn attention to deficiencies in the way healthcare is given and urged for more focus on patient safety. This year the WHO too has made patient safety a major focus area also within the field of surgery [4].

Different organisational cultures

There have been several attempts to further describe and categorise working culture in general. In the paper "A typology of organisational cultures" Westrum categorizes the local culture by how the organisation deals with process information [2]. The underlying idea here is that the leaders, by the way they handle information, shape a unit's culture. Three types of culture are described: the "pathological" or power-oriented culture, the "bureaucratic" or rule-oriented culture and the "generative" or performance-oriented culture (see Tab. 1). Although such a classification may seem a bit caricatured, most will find patterns here to recognise from working environments at home. From a safety standpoint it is, however, not necessarily true that generative organisation culture is always the best. This is, among several factors, also dependent on what kind of goals the organisation wants to achieve (and safety may not be a goal). In general, however, a performance-oriented organisation is usually more creative, open and "solution-oriented", making the process safer.

Can we measure safety culture?

Safety climate, measures of elements that compose a "safety culture", has been evaluated in many ways. Along with other "high-risk" industry like the oil business, nuclear energy and aviation, healthcare is today usually included in this context. There is not a universal definition of what describes a safety culture. In the UK the Department of Health [5] has described this as a culture where:

- The staff have a constant and active awareness of the potential for things to go wrong
- The culture is open and fair
- The culture encourages people to speak up about mistakes
- The staff is able to learn about what is going wrong and then put things right

A number of general surveys to explore an organisation's safety climate have been developed, and some of these are transformed to cover healthcare as well. In a review from 2005, nine different surveys were found [6]. They differ regarding the target they addressed (individuals or groups), if psychometrics were performed and how they were used (inter- or intra-institution, inter-industry comparisons, etc.). Only a few had been used to evaluate associations between patient safety climate and various process measures claimed to be associated with patient outcome. Just one survey had been used to explore possible relations between safety climate score and patient outcome [7].

Several questionnaires are available on the web, and one of the most frequently cited is the Safety Attitudes Questionnaire [8]. This questionnaire has separate versions including one specifically addressing ICU personnel.

Tab. 1   The three types of organisational culture according to Westrum [2]

Pathological	Bureucratic	Generative
Power-oriented	Rule-oriented	Performance-oriented
Cooperation: low	Cooperation: moderate	Cooperation: high
Messengers shot	Messengers ignored	Messengers trained
Responsibilities shirked	Responsibilities narrowed	Risks are shared
Bridging discouraged	Bridging tolerated	Bridging encouraged
Failure → scapegoating	Failure → justice	Failure → inquiry
Novelty crushed	Novelty → problems	Novelty implemented

Studies on ICU culture

In Europe, probably the first large study conducted regarding ICU culture and its possible effects on quality and outcome was the EURICUS I study [9]. In that study, 89 ICUs in 12 European countries prospectively collected data during a 4-month period. One of the main objectives was to define performance indicators for evaluating the effectiveness of organisation and management of an ICU. One of the dimensions studied was a sub-investigation on the ICU culture. Mortality ratio corrected for severity of illness was used as a measure of outcome (SMR). They could demonstrate a higher SMR with process-orientated compared to result-orientated ICUs both for patients with low risk of death as well as in those with high risk of death. Overall, European ICUs were found on average to be more result-oriented and the staff members of the ICUs were found to have a relatively low need for security.

Often surveys on safety cultures have been performed at the hospital level, assuming a uniform culture throughout the organisation. This may not be true, and recently results from four ICUs in a single institution have revealed significant variations [10]. That study also showed that nursing directors tended to overestimate their own personnel's safety score.

Some elements in the ICU culture may be more important for patient safety. This relates in particular to teamwork, how different personnel groups communicate, use of checklists in daily patient care and how the ICUs handle adverse events.

Teamwork

Attitudes among pilots and health workers regarding safety have been studied, also in comparison with surgeons, anaesthesiologists and intensive care physicians [11]. In that study, pilot attitudes differed from physicians regarding teamwork and hierarchy. While only 55 % of the surgeons advocated a flat hierarchy, 94 % of the pilots and ICU personnel advocated this.

Some of the results from the EURICUS I study may indicate an effect from differences in how personnel groups within the ICU cooperate and work together. However, in general, there is little hard evidence linking teamwork to patient outcome. Results from education research with medical students in a simulator setting have provided results that link rating of team skills and clinical team performance [12]. An observational study on teamwork performance during resuscitation of the newborn has revealed an association of team behaviour and adherence to national guidelines [13].

In the field of surgery a recent study from San Diego investigated the effect of teamwork on several 30-day outcome variables. Standard methods to assess intraoperative team behaviour were used, and the association with patient outcome analysed. The study found increased odds of complications and death related to less sharing of information during the intraoperative phases, and to reduced briefing and information sharing during the handoff phases [14]. In intensive care teams, performance-related outcome differences have yet to be demonstrated using a proper study design. However, the message from other areas in medicine may indicate that the ICU may also gain from improved quality of teamwork.

Communications

In some studies the act of communication has been studied separately from teamwork performance. A study from a surgical department in Kentucky found that organisational factors like teamwork, safety climate and work conditions measured with various survey instruments had no influence on risk-adjusted surgical outcome. Communication and collaboration between attending and resident doctors, however, influenced patient morbidity [15]. Such findings emphasise the specific importance of the physician's role in decision-making in providing high-quality care.

Checklist

Extensive uses of checklists have been documented in other high-risk sectors for decades. The use of checklists probably started in aviation more than 60 years ago in order to assure a standardised control by the pilots in the cockpit before departure. Gradually checklists have been used also in various aspects of medical care as cognitive aids to help health personnel to perform or prepare for various tasks.

Checklists may serve different purposes, from simple medical equipment checklists ("laundry lists") to complex checklists in flowchart models in order to accomplish specific tasks. An example here is a clinical algorithm to make a diagnosis [16]. Checklists are assumed to increase the quality of patient care. Most checklists, however, usually demonstrate increased quality of the processes. Improved clinical outcome as a result of using checklists has been more difficult to demonstrate.

In a large prospective study involving 108 ICUs, Pronovost et al. found a profound effect of simple interventions for preventing catheter-related infections. Using a mixture of different techniques, also involving a sort of checklist (hand washing, full barrier precautions during insertion, disinfection of the skin with clorhexidine and avoiding the femoral site if possible), they could demonstrate a large reduction in catheter-related infections, results that were sustained after four years [17].

Error reporting

Reporting and reacting to adverse events ("error") has been viewed as an important part of an ICU oriented towards a safety culture. The increased complexity of intensive care has increased the possibilities for errors to occur. To report adverse events may contribute in many ways towards a safety culture. The three most important aspects are:

- Provide an overview of the number and type of adverse events in the ICU.
- Use reported events to prevent similar events in the future (analyse events and take action).
- To establish and promote event reporting, create a more open attitude towards adverse

events, shifting the focus from individual to system performance.

We all know from personal experiences that error is a frequent occurrence in the ICU [18] and that the number of reported events usually underestimates the true number [19]. Most adverse events may have little or no influence on the clinical course of our patients, and some events may be detected at an early stage and hence counteractive measures may be taken. Still a number of adverse events continue and result in significantly increased patient morbidity and mortality. The number of adverse events contributing to patient mortality is obscure in most ICUs. The contribution may be present in different ways from being a direct cause of death to contributing in various degrees to patient death.

How often do adverse events occur in the ICU? The large ESICM-initiated prevalence study on adverse events in the ICU was launched to provide an answer to this question. In 205 ICUs 1,905 patients were included. 38.8 (95% confidence interval 34.7–42.9) events per 100 patients were observed during 24 hours [20].

An incidence reporting system has been standard procedure in our department since 1997 [18]. In contrast to a point-prevalence study, this allows us to provide real incidence numbers over time. The ICU, the post-cardiac surgery ICU and the ordinary recovery unit participate in this registry. Results from 1997 to 2006 (10 years) for 3,100 reported events are shown in Table 2. Interestingly, incidence/patient varies between the units, but when corrected for length of stay much of the differences disappear.

Can the use of reporting system decrease the occurrence of adverse events? No firm evidence exists in the literature, but it is tempting to hypothesise that an increased awareness of adverse events, and a systematic approach to decrease their occurrence, will prevent adverse events from happening. By analysing the accumulated

Tab. 2 Adverse events incidence, Haukeland University Hospital 1997–2006

	General ICU	Cardiac ICU	Postoperative unit
Events per 100 patients	40 (39.2–42.2)	9 (9.6–9.3)	0.96 (0.90–1.03)
Events per 100 days	8.2 (7.8–8.6)	8.6 (8–9.3)	3.3 (3.1–3.5)

events reported in our own department, however, no such effect could be observed. The linearity over time of reported events in all three reporting units makes us conclude that reporting and working with events in itself has not diminished our event rate. Does this indicate an unsafe ICU? No-one can answer this question. In the same period we have had a constant decrease in SMR, indicating improved outcome. This one ICU experience clearly demonstrates the difficulty in linking a safety issue (event reporting) to a hard outcome like survival.

Conclusion

The evidence suggests a profound influence of the ICU culture on patient safety. This may take different forms, from the way we communicate, to the organisation of work in the ICU. The potential to improve safety through changes in culture is probably present in most ICUs, but is often difficult to measure. Using safety climate surveys and possibly external input in the form of audits or other performance measures with a focus on safety, may concentrate of areas of improvements.

The author

Hans Flaatten, MD, PhD
Department of Anaesthesia and Intensive Care
Haukeland University Hospital
5021 Bergen, Norway
E-mail: hans.flaatten@helse-bergen.no

References

1. Donabedian A. Evaluating the quality of medical care. 1966. Milbank Q. 2005;83:691–729.
2. Westrum R. A typology of organisational cultures. Qual Saf Health Care. 2004;13 Suppl 2:ii22–7.
3. Davies HT, Nutley SM, Mannion R. Organisational culture and quality of health care. Qual Health Care. 2000;9:111–119.
4. WHO. Safe Surgery Saves Lives. 2009 http://www.who.int/patientsafety/safesurgery/en/
5. Department of Health (UK). An organisation with a memory. 2000. www.dh.gov/uk/en/
6. Colla JB, Bracken AC, Kinney LM, Weeks WB. Measuring patient safety climate: a review of surveys. Qual Saf Health Care. 2005;14:364–366.
7. Sexton JB, Helmreich RL, Neilands TB et al. The Safety Attitudes Questionnaire: psychometric properties, benchmarking data, and emerging research. BMC Health Serv Res. 2006;6:44.
8. The University of Texas Centre of Excellence for Patients Safety. Surveys and tools. 2009 http://www.uth.tmc.edu/schools/med/imed/patient_safety/survey&tools.htm
9. Miranda DR, DW R, WB S, V F. Organisation and Management of Intensive Care. Berlin: Springer; 1997:286.
10. Huang DT, Clermont G, Sexton JB et al. Perceptions of safety culture vary across the intensive care units of a single institution. Crit Care Med. 2007;35:165–176.
11. Sexton JB, Thomas EJ, Helmreich RL. Error, stress, and teamwork in medicine and aviation: cross sectional surveys. BMJ. 2000;320:745–749.
12. Wright MC, Phillips-Bute BG, Petrusa ER, Griffin KL, Hobbs GW, Taekman JM. Assessing teamwork in medical education and practice: Relating behavioural teamwork ratings and clinical performance. Med Teach. 2008;1–9.
13. Thomas EJ, Sexton JB, Lasky RE, Helmreich RL, Crandell DS, Tyson J. Teamwork and quality during neonatal care in the delivery room. J Perinatol. 2006;26:163–169.
14. Mazzocco K, Petitti DB, Fong KT et al. Surgical team behaviours and patient outcomes. Am J Surg. 2008
15. Davenport DL, Henderson WG, Mosca CL, Khuri SF, Mentzer RMJ. Risk-adjusted morbidity in teaching hospitals correlates with reported levels of communication and collaboration on surgical teams but not with scale measures of teamwork climate, safety climate, or working conditions. J Am Coll Surg. 2007;205:778–784.
16. Hales BM, Pronovost PJ. The checklist – a tool for error management and performance improvement. J Crit Care. 2006;21:231–235.
17. Pronovost P. Interventions to decrease catheter-related bloodstream infections in the ICU: the Keystone Intensive Care Unit Project. Am J Infect Control. 2008;36:S171.e1–5.
18. Flaatten H, Hevroy O. Errors in the intensive care unit (ICU). Experiences with an anonymous registration. Acta Anaesthesiol Scand. 1999;43:614–617.
19. Donchin Y, Gopher D, Olin M et al. A look into the nature and causes of human errors in the intensive care unit. Crit Care Med. 1995;23:294–300.
20. Valentin A, Capuzzo M, Guidet B et al. Patient safety in intensive care: results from the multinational Sentinel Events Evaluation (SEE) study. Intensive Care Med. 2006;32:1591–1598.

Guttorm Brattebø

Training teamwork using simulation

The well-being of patients in the intensive care unit (ICU) depends heavily on the healthcare workers that are involved in their treatment, in addition to the sophisticated equipment and effective medicines that are in use. Despite both professional education and written procedures, adverse events are fairly common in such dynamic and complex environments. The investigation of adverse events in aviation has clearly shown that it is human factors and suboptimal team cooperation that often lead to disasters. Therefore the aviation industry developed the concept of crew resource management (CRM) to address the problems of leadership, communication, and cooperation. The same causes of errors and lack of quality have been identified in medicine, and CRM training and the use of simulations have been applied to the operation room environment, as in full-scale anaesthesia simulators, in the delivery room, and the trauma bay. Hence, the use of simulation to improve teamwork seems to be a sound strategy for improving care. On the other hand, simulation is just an educational method, with many strengths and certain limitations. Simulation training is especially useful for training the non-clinical skills mentioned, and actually requires no fancy or expensive technical equipment. This paper discusses the background for targeting improved teamwork as a strategy to reduce adverse events in emergency situations, such as in the ICU. Based on the au-thor's experience in trauma simulation, some practical advice is given on how to start simple simulation training programmes.

Modern medicine is very complex and intensive care with its sophisticated technical equipment and advanced treatment options is among the more challenging clinical environments in a hospital. While this gives hope for effectively treating very severe conditions, it also increases the possibilities for unwanted harm to patients. Such events have been labelled adverse events (AE), and may occur in as much as 5–10 % of all hospital admissions [1–3]. Based on thorough investigations of adverse events there are reasons to believe that a significant proportion of them could have been prevented theoretically, since the root causes often are inter-personal issues, especially communication [4–7]. While only a small proportion of adverse events result in death, they cause significant morbidity, suffering and costs. Some of the common examples of management care problems are given in Table 1.

This situation can and must be changed, but unfortunately healthcare lags behind other high-risk industries in its attention to ensuring basic safety for our patients. Therefore, dramatic, sys-

Tab. 1   Some examples of care management problems
[reproduced from How to investigate and analyse
clinical incidents: Clinical Risk Unit and Association
of Litigation and Risk Management protocol,
Vincent C, Taylor-Adams S, Chapman EJ, Hewett
D, Prior S, Strange P, et al. 320:777–81, 2000, with
permission from BMJ Publishing Group Ltd.]

- Failure to monitor, observe, or act
- Delay in diagnosis
- Incorrect risk assessment
  (for example, of suicide or self-harm)
- Inadequate handover
- Failure to note faulty equipment
- Failure to carry out preoperative checks
- Not following an agreed protocol
  (without clinical justification)
- Not seeking help when necessary
- Failure to adequately supervise a junior staff
  member
- Incorrect protocol applied
- Treatment given to incorrect body site
- Wrong treatment given

tem-wide changes are required to improve safety for people receiving healthcare. In some parts of the world patient injuries are followed by a search for the individual healthcare worker that was thought to have "caused" the injury. This is not in accordance with our current understanding of how injury to patients nearly always is the result of bad system designs [1, 6, 9, 10]. Focus must shift from blaming the individual person treating the patient to trying to prevent harm by improved system design. Special attention should be spent on communication and using proven medication safety practices, e.g. in intensive care [1, 11, 12].

Mandatory reporting systems for severe injuries and death, and voluntary and protected reporting for minor injuries and incidents will help us to learn from adverse events [6, 13]. Senior staff must display an open mind toward patient safety and, e.g. by self-reporting their own errors and adverse events, present an example that juniors can follow. Raised and clear standards and expectations for safety will also help us create a safety culture, with safety as a declared, serious aim.

There is scientific support for the relation between teamwork and patient safety in highly dy-

namic domains such as intensive care units (ICU), surgical theatres, and trauma rooms [14–16].

In recent years the importance of well-functioning teams has been identified as a crucial factor in both the causation and prevention of adverse events [14, 16]. Investigations have also shown that human factors like suboptimal team cooperation, lack of leadership and clear communication lead to disasters [7, 17, 18]. Team training and simulator use is often mentioned as one important way of reducing the risk of patient harm [1, 19, 20]. It is human nature to err, but equally important as our tendency to, for example, forget important details, is our ability to spot abnormalities and to create instant solutions and better alternatives to meet the challenges ahead e.g. "bridging the gaps". Pattern recognition and mental simulation has been pointed out as the basis for expert behaviour [21–23]. The ability for this can be trained in a simulator environment. The opportunity to "learn by doing" rarely presents itself in modern medicine when one considers the handling of seldom-occurring crises, and it would also hardly be acceptable from a patient safety perspective [19]. For example, can trauma teams be expected to function efficiently and smoothly when treating challenging major trauma cases even though the teams have often not received previous training [24]. Team members are usually sufficiently trained professionals individually, but with limited experience in teamwork [25].

In obstetrics, another dynamic domain of medicine, the British confidential enquiries into maternal and child health in December 2007 concluded that "... the assessors were struck by the number of health care professionals who appeared to fail to be able to identify and manage common medical conditions or potential emergencies outside their immediate area of expertise. Resuscitation skills were also considered poor in an unacceptably high number of cases." Further: "In many cases the care provided was hampered by a lack of cross disciplinary or cross agency working and problems with communication. These included: Poor or non-existent team working, inappropriate delegation to junior staff, inappropriate or too short consultations by phone, the lack of sharing of relevant information between health professionals, including between General Practitioners (GPs) and the maternity team, poor interpersonal skills." [26].

In trauma, studies indicate that as many as one-fourth of trauma deaths are preventable, and that most treatment errors and protocol deviations occur in the admission phase. Improving the systems for treating severely injured patients can significantly reduce the proportion of preventable deaths [27]. Regarding teamwork, the most difficult tasks to improve seem to be leadership, communication and cooperation [7, 18, 25, 28].

Based on an extensive literature review Manser identified some safety-relevant aspects of teamwork that are listed in Table 2 [14]. The nature of many medical emergency teams and the conditions they are supposed to function under pose specific challenges to optimal team function because conditions change (dynamism), teams may be assembled *ad hoc*, work together only for a brief period, consist of many professions, and therefore must integrate various professional cultures [14, 30]. The obvious answer to these issues is to give such teams the opportunity to train together as a team. In the military there is a slogan: "Train as you fight!" This is most suitable for emergency teams as well.

Communication seems to be one of the key elements in teamwork, and several ideas have been put forward trying to describe a format for optimal communication in clinical settings. The so-called SBAR (situation, background, assessment & recommendations) is one simple but effective way of structuring communication [31]. Various models of the relationship between specific communication practices and patient safety have been proposed [32, 33]. The practices brought forward are also in good agreement with the ANTS models [23, 28].

In their review of contributory factors underlying critical incidents, Reader and colleagues found an overlap between the non-technical skills requirements for the ICU and anaesthesia, with both domains having a need for good teamwork, situation awareness, task management and decision-making skills [22]. Further they recommend that non-technical skill training programmes should be integrated with the technical aspects of a domain when professionals have an adequate level of technical competence. Then the cognitive load of having to learn both technical and non-technical skills simultaneous-

Tab. 2 Aspects of teamwork relevant to patient safety [modified from 14, 21, 23, 29]

Aspects	Characteristics
Quality of collaboration	Mutual respect and trust
Shared mental models	Shared perception of a situation, and understanding of team structure, tasks, and team roles
Coordination	Adaptive coordination (e.g. shift between explicit and implicit coordination; increased information exchange and planning in critical situations)
Communication	Openness of communication and exchange of information
	Quality of communication (e.g. shared frames of reference)
	Specific communication practices (e.g. team briefing, closed-loop, SBAR)
Leadership	Leadership style (value contributions from staff, encourage participation in decision-making)
	Adaptive leadership behaviour (e.g. increased explicit behaviour in critical situations)
Situational awareness	Actively seeking information, recognising and understanding data and information (e.g. pattern recognition)
	Anticipation
Decision making	Identifying options
	Balancing risks and mental simulation
	Re-evaluation and change of solution/decision

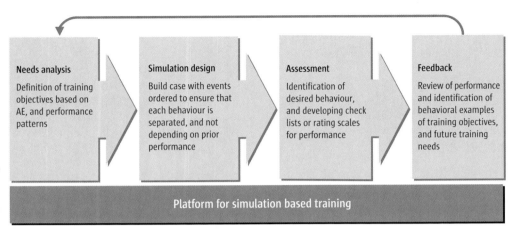

Fig. 1　Description of taxonomy in simulation training, with the different design steps from needs analysis to feedback and identification of future traning needs [modified from Fernandez R, Kozlowski SWJ, Shapiro MJ, Salas E. Toward a definition of teamwork in emergency medicine. Acad Emerg Med 2008;15:1104–12.]

ly will be reduced. Reader and colleagues' review argues that the framework of non-technical skill categories identified in the ANTS taxonomy also is pertinent to the ICU environment [22].

It is thus reasonable to agree that there is good scientific evidence for using simulation to improve teamwork. The next issue is then to decide how to develop a simulation programme to achieve better team performance. Fernandez and colleagues have described a very useful model for defining teamwork in emergency medicine, including some key recommendations to guide the implementation of their proposed taxonomy into routine simulation-based training [34]. Salas and colleagues also provide evidence-based principles for the planning, implementation and evaluation of team training programmes based on extensive reviews of the literature [20]. Some of the questions to be answered before a simulator training programme is constructed are listed in Figure 1.

The most basic aspect is the assessment of the educational needs: What problem, threat or procedure is to be addressed in the training? Simulation is a method that can be used in many different ways, and hence it is important to decide on the educational goals that are to be achieved. Then one has to build the simulation case or scenario to be simulated. It is strongly recommended to construct clinical problems that the participants can identify from their own experience, so

that they "believe" in the case. This must include certain events that can trigger the wanted behaviour. These triggers should be independent of each other. Then there is the need for a checklist or scale for evaluating the performance of the teams. This is very important for the feedback. The list must describe which behaviour one wishes to observe. One must also decide on whether the patient should be "allowed to die" during the simulation. Perhaps there are more effective ways of making the team realise that they have not performed to standards, than letting them "fail" by losing the patient.

The most important part of the simulation is the debriefing and the feedback session immediately after the simulation. In the BEST programme we usually place the participants in a horseshoe formation, so that everybody can see each other's faces when discussing. Be sure to have enough time for debriefing and keep all participants together. The main purpose is to give the participants a possibility for reflection and discussion on their performance. This is also the reason for running two simulations consecutively, so that the teams will have the opportunity to demonstrate improvement based on the feedback and discussions. Regarding clinical feedback, Jack Ende's excellent discussion of this many years ago is still valid [29]. Especially the need for using non-evaluating language, dealing

Tab. 3 Guidelines for feedback in medical education
[Ende J. Feedback in clinical medical education.
JAMA 250:777–81, © (1983) American Medical
Association. All rights reserved.]

Feedback should

- be undertaken with the teacher and trainee working as allies, with common goals
- be well-timed and expected
- be based on first-hand data
- be regulated in quantity and limited to behaviours that are remediable
- be phrased in descriptive non-evaluative language
- deal with specific performances, not generalisations
- offer subjective data, labelled as such
- deal with decisions and actions, rather than assumed intentions or interpretations

with specific and observed behaviour, and aiming at decisions and actions and not assumed intentions, is important. Ende's main guidelines for clinical feedback are listed in Table 3.

When building a simulation-based training programme one must also determine on which technological level the simulator or simulation should be placed: high-fidelity versus low-fidelity simulation. There are a number of quite fancy and highly sophisticated simulators on the marked, with a vast possibility for complicated responses to various inputs like medications. These simulators rely on computer programmes, where different algorithms are constructed based on different physiological models. The strengths of these sophisticated simulators are that they are more real and can be subjected to more procedures. On the other hand, they are very expensive, must be programmed and sometimes there is need for a second person just to take care of the technical issues [35]. It is our experience that it is possible to run effective team training using simple and regular resuscitation mannequins available in most departments. Experienced teams will not need a very expensive mannequin to train inter-personal skills. Furthermore, regardless of the possibility of future close-to-reality simulators, simulation training is and will always be an artificial situation, not real life. This is also the experience from a US-based programme that has been running local team training in obstetrics at rural hospitals in Oregon [36].

Pitfalls

It is tempting just focusing on the medical procedures and specific clinical problems. Then the physicians in the team certainly could go on arguing, citing publications and sources for (contradictory) information for hours. However, from my point of view, the medical content is not the most important issue in a simulation exercise. The crucial point is to be able to pose certain challenges that will demand demonstration of skills in communication, cooperation and leadership. Therefore, the focus must be on these team behaviours explicitly. On the other hand, a case that can be identified as relevant, and a team composition that reflects what is normally the situation when such a team works together, will help the team acting more as if the simulation was a real situation. Often some team members are reluctant to become engaged because they find the training situation artificial, but if other team members (especially physicians) act appropriately, this usually makes the team exercise develop and resemble a real case.

An example of the briefing and case presentation for a BEST trauma team simulation is given in Box 1. In this set-up we use a low-fidelity "dead" mannequin or a live model, where clinical information and parameters are given verbally by the facilitator on demand [29 and www.bestnet. no]. One obvious advantage to this solution is the facilitator's ability to adjust the patient's response and progression of the case to the specific team's decisions and actual performance. The structure for team debriefing and reflection used in the BEST programme after the simulation is described in Box 2.

Box 1:
Information for trauma team before the simulation

You are a member of the trauma team, about to take part in a simulated multi-trauma admission. The patient is a simple resuscitation mannequin, but a facilitator will give all relevant information when prompted during the session. Clinical data will be given after the relevant procedure has been performed. You will have to simulate any invasive procedures and clinical examinations, and say aloud what you are doing, e.g. "I am auscultating the chest, what do I hear?" Everything that you might do in this situation should be carried out as normal, e.g. connecting monitoring devices and performing relevant X-rays. Intravenous drugs or fluids should be prepared as normal but not delivered into the venous cannulas. Please note that the main purpose of the simulation is to train team communication, cooperation and leadership during the initial resuscitation and stabilisation of the patient. After the training there will be a discussion and feedback session, before a second simulator run. The simulations will be videotaped, intended for possible help in the debriefing.

Clinical scenario

The patient is a 24-year-old male who approx. 30 minutes ago drove his car into a concrete wall at high speed. He was not wearing a seat belt, and the car had no airbag. He has open airways, is breathing spontaneously at a rate of 24 a minute, reacting to painful stimuli by eye opening, swearing, and localising pain. He is bleeding from his nose and mouth, and from an open leg fracture. Please go ahead and perform an initial assessment and resuscitation.

Box 2:
The structure for team debriefing and reflection used in the BEST programme (www.bestnet.no)

1. **Participants' own opinions on the simulation in general**

Have a short session in which all participants have the possibility for "tension release".

Let them comment briefly on questions like "How did the simulation affect you?" and ask the participants to focus especially on the positive aspects of the simulation. The team leader is the last person to comment on the performance, so that the team is not "silenced" by the leader before they are able to make their remarks.

2. **Short feedback from instructor focusing on the successful aspects**

Explain to the participants that feedback related to the professional content will be given in connection with the review of the videotape.

3. **The professional content in the simulation**

Order of actions, decisions to be made, efforts to initiate, equipment needed. Give all the participants a chance to suggest improvements. The instructor then sums up by writing all the suggestions on a whiteboard. This is an important part of the feedback session as the participants by proposing improvements themselves will be responsible for running the emergency room. This is usually a good time for the instructor to give a short feedback on the professional content.

4. **Show some of the video**

Everyone wants to see themselves on the video, and at the same time they are a bit frightened by the proposition. It might be a good idea to show the first six to seven minutes of the video only commenting in general terms. Further on, the feedback session should focus on the objectives stated for the simulation. In our course the main objectives are improved cooperation, communication, and leadership behaviour. It might be a good idea to start every round with a brief definition of successful objectives. Normally every team will have a short theoretical introduction to communication and communication problems before the simulation.

5. **Summary & closing remarks**

It seems urgent that every participant leave the room with a feeling that they all had a chance to comment on the simulation. Remember that it is the team that should be the main focus, not individuals. Closing the session should therefore include questions like "Are there any other experiences, aspects, etc. that you think haven't been touched upon and that you want to comment on?" It might also be a good idea to ask if the theoretical introduction was consistent with the experiences the participants had during the simulations.

Use of video

Recording a video of the simulation can be useful for highlighting certain aspects of the team's performance. However, there is no need for sophisticated audio-visual equipment. A simple video camera will do, preferably fitted with a wide-angle lens, since many treatment rooms are rather small. A wireless microphone is also nice to have, since it will enhance the sound quality of the communication if it is placed above the "patient". We also recommend placing the camera high in the room, with the "patient" centred, maintaining a steady view throughout the session. Trying to follow e.g. the team leader or specific procedures will often result in a busy "music video" like recording that will be difficult to follow during the viewing. Likewise, it is highly recommended to test the equipment for sound, light, recording quality, battery capacity, and replay on the actual projector or TV set to be used prior to the training session.

The BEST trauma team training course

The one-day multi-professional course with simulated trauma patients is organised locally at each hospital, and the training takes place in each hospital's own trauma room. The one-day course consists of three hours of lectures and case discussions, followed by four hours of practical training. All personnel involved in trauma treatment participate in the lectures, which are followed by the simulation where two of the hospital's own trauma teams participate in two simulation sessions each. The course focuses on the need for optimal team function and a strict and hierarchical progression in patient assessment and treatment. The theory is based on current best practice principles, but the course elaborates significantly more on communication, cooperation and leadership. Case stories and instructors are from identifiable hospital levels. Discussions and didactical exchange of ideas and experience is encouraged throughout the course. Training is done in the trauma room using a standard resuscitation mannequin as the simulated patient. After a brief review of the emergency call to the medical dispatch centre the team is given a few minutes to plan and prepare for admitting the simulated patient.

The teams use their own familiar team set-up and procedures, and all necessary disposable equipment. Each team member plays his/her own professional role. A short report from the ambulance crew is also given to the participants before the simulated patient arrives, to encourage preparations. The preparation and treatment of the simulated victim is videotaped. During the simulation the instructor will give the physiological data after each monitoring or diagnostic procedure is properly performed.

After approx. 20–30 minutes, or when the patient and team are ready to leave the emergency room for e. g. the OP theatre or XR lab, the instructor stops the simulation. After the simulation the complete team is debriefed in a separate room (without observers), reviewing the video using a structured format focusing on what went well and what can be improved. This session normally takes 30–40 minutes. A second simulation is then carried out with the same team, but with a new case. Debriefing is done again, and finally the team is encouraged to summarise areas of potential improvement discovered during the simulation and discussions. If possible, the staff not participating in the simulation discuss case stories in a theoretical format during the simulations. The simulation case histories are based on real cases, with appropriate XR films and lab results. After the course all educational material (on CD-ROM) is left at the hospital and the hospital is encouraged and allowed to copy and edit this material, in order to arrange local training.

Conclusion

For the last 12 years the BEST Foundation has used interdisciplinary team training based on AE reports, and firmly believes that such training increases the teams' ability to prevent adverse events [37–39]. Building team resilience to error is perhaps the most effective strategy in our strive for safer healthcare, and simulator team training should be further explored and refined to meet the demands for cost-effectiveness.

The author

Guttorm Brattebø, MD
    Department of Anaesthesia & Intensive Care
    Haukeland University Hospital
    5021 Bergen, Norway
    E-mail: guttorm.bratteboe@helse-bergen.no

References

1. Kohn LT, Corrigan JM, Donaldson MS. To err is human: building a safer health system. Washington, DC: National Academy Press, 1999.
2. Baker GR, Norton PG, Flintoft V, Blais R, Brown A, Cox J, et al. The Canadian adverse events study: the incidence of adverse events among hospital patients in Canada. CMAJ 2004;170:1678–86.
3. Schioler T, Lipczak H, Pedersen BL, Mogensen TS, Bech KB, Stockmarr A, et al. Danish adverse event study. (Incidence of adverse events in hospitals. A retrospective study of medical records). Ugeskr Laeger 2001;163:5370–8.
4. The joint commission. Root causes of sentinel events. http:// www.jointcommission.org/NR/rdonlyres/FA465646–5F5F-4543-AC8FE8AF6571E372/0/root_cause_se.jpg.
5. Stein-Parbury J, Liaschenko J. Understanding collaboration between nurses and physicians as knowledge at work. Am J Crit Care 2007;16:470–7.
6. Pronovost PJ, Thompson DA, Holzmueller CG, Lubomski LH, Dorman T, Dickman F, et al. Toward learning from patient safety reporting systems. J Crit Care 2006;21:305–15.
7. Williams R, Silverman R, Schwind C, Fortune JB, Sutyak J, Horvath KD, et al. Surgeon information transfer and communication: factors affecting quality and efficiency of inpatient care. Ann Surg 2007;245:159–71.
8. Vincent C, Taylor-Adams S, Chapman EJ, Hewett D, Prior S, Strange P, et al. How to investigate and analyse clinical incidents: Clinical Risk Unit and Association of Litigation and Risk Management protocol. BMJ 2000;320:320:777–81.
9. van Beuzekom M, Akerboom SP, Boer F. Assessing system failures in operating rooms and intensive care units. Qual Saf Health Care 2007;16;45–50.
10. Catchpole KR, Giddings AE, Wilkinson M, Hirst G, Dale T, de Leval MR. Improving patient safety by identifying latent failures in successful operations. Surgery 2007;142:102–10.
11. Pronovost P, Weast B, Schwarz M, Wyskiel RM, Prow D, Milanovich SN, et al. Medication reconciliation: a practical tool to reduce the risk of medication errors. J Crit Care 2003;18:201–5.
12. Kozer E, Seto W, Verjee Z, Parshuram C, Khattak S, Koren G, et al. Prospective observational study on the incidence of medication errors during simulated resuscitation in a paediatric emergency department. BMJ 2004;329;1321–5.
13. Berwick DM. Errors today and errors tomorrow. N Engl J Med 2003;348:2570–2.
14. Manser T. Teamwork and patient safety in dynamic domains of healthcare: a review of the literature. Acta Anaesthesiol Scand 2009;53:143–51.
15. Reader TW, Flin R, Cuthbertson BH. Communication skills and error in the intensive care unit. Curr Opin Crit Care 2007;13:732–6.
16. Jain M, Miller L, Belt D, King D, Berwick DM. Decline in ICU adverse events, nosocomial infections and cost through a quality improvement initiative focusing on teamwork and culture change. Qual Saf Healthcare 2006;15:235–9.
17. Christian CK, Gustafson ML, Roth EM, Sheridan TB, Gandhi TK, Dwyer K, et al. A prospective study of patient safety in the operating room. Surgery 2006;139:159–73.
18. Greenberg C, Regenbogen S, Studdert D, Lipsitz SR, Rogers SO, Zinner MJ, et al. Patterns of communication breakdown resulting in injury to surgical patients. J Am Coll Surg 2007;204:533–40.
19. Perkins GD. Simulation in resuscitation training. Resuscitation 2007;73:202–11.
20. Salas E, DiazGranados D, Weaver SJ, King H. Does team training work? Principles for health care. Acad Emerg Med 2008;15:1002–9.
21. Klein G. The sources of power: how people make decisions. Massachusetts: MIT Press, 1998.
22. Reader T, Flin R, Lauche K, Cuthbertson BH. Nontechnical skills in the intensive care unit. Br J Anaesth 2006;96:551–9.
23. Flin R, Maran N. Identifying and training non-technical skills for teams in acute medicine Qual Saf Health Care 2004;13(Suppl 1):i80-i84.
24. Wisborg T, Rønning TH, Beck VB, Brattebø G. Preparing teams for low-frequency emergecies in Norwegian hospitals. Acta Anaesthesiol Scand 2003: 47:1248–50.
25. Sexton JB, Thomas EJ, Helmreich RL. Error, stress, and teamwork in medicine and aviation: cross sectional surveys. BMJ 2000;320:745–9.
26. Lewis G (ed). Executive summary and key recommendations. The confidential enquiry into maternal and child health (CEMACH). The seventh report on confidential enquiries into maternity deaths in the UK: 2003–2005. CEMACH: London, 2007. www.cemach.org.uk.
27. Esposito TJ, Sanddal TL, Reynolds SA, Sanddal ND. Effect of a voluntary trauma system on preventable death and inappropriate care in a rural state. J Trauma 2003;54:663–70
28. Fletcher GCL, McGeorge P, Flin RH, Glavin RJ, Maran NJ. The role of non-technical skills in anaesthesia: a review of current literature. Br J Anaesth 2002;88:418–29.
29. Ende J. Feedback in clinical medical education. JAMA 1983;250:777–81.
30. Malhotra S, Jordan D, Shortliffe E, Patel VL. Workflow modelling in critical care: piecing together your own puzzle. J Biomed Inform 2007;40:81–92.
31. Leonard M, Graham S, Bonacum D. The human factor: the critical importance of effective teamwork and communication in providing safe care. Qual Saf Health Care 2004;13(suppl 1):i85-i90.

C

32. Lingard L, Whyte S, Espin S, Baker GR, Orser B, Doran D. Towards safer interprofessional communication: constructing a model of "utility" from preoperative team briefings. J Interprof Care 2006;20:471–83.

33. Pronovost PJ, Berenholtz SM, Dorman T, et al. Improving communications in the ICU using daily goals. J Crit Care 2003;18:71–5.

34. Fernandez R, Kozlowski SWJ, Shapiro MJ, Salas E. Toward a definition of teamwork in emergency medicine. Acad Emerg Med 2008;15:1104–12.

35. Kyle RR, Murray WB (eds). Clinical simulation: operations, engineering and management. Burlington, MA: Academic Press, 2008.

36. Guise JM, Segel S. Teamwork in obstetric critical care. Best Pract Res Clin Obstet Gynaecol 2008;22:937–51.

37. Wisborg T, Brattebø G. Keeping the spirit high: why trauma team training is (sometimes) implemented. Acta Anaesthesiol Scand 2008;52:437–41.

38. Wisborg T, Brattebø G, Brinchmann-Hansen Å, Uggen PE, Hansen KS. Effects of nationwide training of multi-professional trauma teams in Norwegian hospitals. J Trauma 2008;64:1613–8.

39. Kyrkjebø JM, Brattebø G, Smith-Strøm H. Improving patient safety by using interprofessional simulation training in health professional education. J Interprof Care 2006;20:1–10.

Rui P. Moreno and Andrew Rhodes

Efficacy versus efficiency – A safety issue

"Good doctors use both individual clinical expertise and the best available external evidence and neither alone is enough. Without clinical expertise, practice risks becoming tyrannised by external evidence, for even excellent external evidence may be inapplicable to or inappropriate for an individual patient."
David Sackett

Introduction

The increased public awareness that patient safety may be an important and relevant issue, that followed the publication in 1999 of the report from the Institute of Medicine (IOM) entitled "To Err is Human: Building a Safer Health System" [1], created a series of opportunities for all the participants in healthcare to look for opportunities to provide better care. This problem is of special concern to intensive care specialists due to the unique frailties of the critically ill population. Intensivists deal with fragile populations, an increasing number of old and chronically disabled patients, who are often suffering from acute life-threatening diseases, where minutes can make the difference between life and death. Despite the growing and aging population that intensive care is faced with there are insufficient num-

bers of trained nurses and doctors willing to work in this specialty which adds to the demands of everyday practice and makes the stresses of caring more acute. This is confounded by the workload patterns that many clinicians have to utilise in order to cope with the growing workload [2]. All of these issues ensure that improving awareness of patient safety is vitally important to our practice.

Intensive care has evolved as a discrete specialty over the last fifty or so years. Pioneering work by Vladimir Negovsky to set up the first scientific institution dedicated to reanimatology [3] and then amongst others Bjørn Ibsen and Hans Christian Larssen in 1952 at Blegdams Fever Hospital in Copenhagen, developed the practice of a physiologically based organ support specialty, which soon came to the forefront of hospital practice and is now present in some form in virtually every hospital in the world. This reliance on physiological data to drive therapeutic protocols has meant that innovative treatments have thrived, however, has also brought a new set of issues; namely how to assess evidence-based approaches, grade the recommendations and ensure bedside practice changes so that benefits seen in clinical research trials can be translated into improved outcomes for the patients.

A consequence of these changes is the increased pressure on scientists to generate the best possible scientific evidence using state-of-the-art procedures and methods and translating this knowledge to the bedside by educating clinicians and adapting the evidence to a more widespread use (implying the application of data to different populations). Finally these results have to be evaluated in how they have impacted and changed normal clinical practice. It is interesting to reflect on how this takes us back to the seven pillars of quality as defined by Avedis Donabedian [4]:

- Efficacy
- Effectiveness
- Efficiency
- Optimality
- Acceptability
- Legitimacy
- Equity

This definition was later followed by a call for action by the IOM in the publication "Crossing the Quality Chasm". This document described the need for nationwide changes in information technology (IT) infrastructure as a means of decreasing medical errors, improving the quality of care, and promoting the evolution of US hospitals into 21st-century healthcare institutions [5]. In this report, the IOM proposed 6 domains of quality:

1. Safety (avoiding injuries to patients from the care that is intended to help them)
2. Effectiveness (providing services based on scientific knowledge to all who could benefit, and refraining from providing services to those not likely to benefit)
3. Patient-centred (providing care that is respectful of and responsive to individual patient preferences, needs, and values, and ensuring that patient values guide all clinical decisions)
4. Timeliness (reducing waits and sometimes harmful delays for both those who receive and those who give care
5. Efficiency (avoiding waste, including waste of equipment, supplies, ideas, and energy)
6. Equitably (providing care that does not vary in quality because of personal characteristics such as gender, ethnicity, geographic location, and socioeconomic status) [6]

The objective of this chapter is to deal with the first two of these pillars, efficacy and effectiveness, and discuss how the link between them is one of the key issues in assuring the quality of medical practices and interventions.

Establishing efficiency in medicine

For many years, the standard of practice for generating evidence in modern medicine has been the randomised controlled trial (RCT), where patients (or groups of patients) are randomised into two (or more) interventions, usually without the researcher and the patient knowing in which groups he or she was included (double blindness). Data cleaning and analysis are done blindly, without breaking the identification of the groups. All these efforts are made to minimise bias and to use chance alone to distribute – among the various groups of patients – unknown variables that could eventually be able to act – as confounders or effect modifiers – in the relationship between the intervention and the outcome of interest [7]. Also, it has been demonstrated that other types of design, such as meta-analysis, can not predict with accuracy the result of a subsequent RCT [8].

Unfortunately, there are many problems in the design of RCTs, especially in the patients who are critically ill, as described very elegantly some years ago by Paul Hébert [9]. These problems include:

- difficulties in the definition of diseases and syndromes,
- a heterogeneous population of patients undergoing a variety of therapeutic interventions, and
- outcomes that may not be able to discriminate between beneficial and risky therapies.

These difficulties are made worse by the heterogeneity of study sites and by the fact that in order to increase the probability of a (economically desirable) positive outcome, companies usually adopt very stringent eligibility criteria (both for inclusion and for exclusion) and opt for outcomes that are not always the most clinically important. Also, the biological efficacy of the intervention is not systematically measured, which could partly explain some of the negative results from RCTs in sepsis [10]. Additional problems can arise from the feasibility of the RCT, namely in cost-effectiveness and in ethical terms. For all of these reasons, although RCTs are often seen as the highest level of evidence available in medicine, it is essential to always consider the quality of the study, the consistency of the results across studies, and the directness of the evidence, as well as the appropriateness of the study design. All four components (study design, study quality, consistency between studies and directness of the effect) should always considered and weighted before a conclusion is made [11].

With all of these issues in mind, it is perhaps not surprising that the regulatory agencies (EMEA, FDA, etc.) who have to appraise evidence in order to licence (allow) drugs to be marketed have developed mechanisms to try to circumvent these problems. These mechanisms include the requirement for more than one RCT to authorise the introduction of a new drug into severely ill patients and experience has shown that this is probably a very sensitive and wise decision [12]. Clearly, more investigation is needed to learn how to understand early on the potential for harm during a RCT, as pointed out by several researchers, either by having more active institutional review boards [13], different study designs [14] or by using more complex statistical techniques [15, 16]. Additional problems occur even after the conclusion of the RCT, due to bias in publication and in the dissemination process, where it has been clearly demonstrated that negative studies will have a significantly lower probability of being published in a high-impact journal or within a reasonable period of time [17, 18], have a higher chance of incomplete reporting of outcomes associated with statistical non-significance of the results [19] and their later use in being part of a summary publication, either as a systematic review, a meta-analysis or a guideline [20–22].

Moving to the real world:
From efficacy towards efficiency

At the end of the process, a definitive assessment of the risk/benefit balance of any new intervention needs to be performed, and a recommendation made, before more widespread use can happen. Often this process results in a request for further research to be performed before a definitive recommendation can be made. We must remember that this balance is strongly influenced by the expected benefits (not equal for all diseases, depending on their severity and on the existence of alternatives) and the expected risks (that can vary from mild discomfort to death). It should be remembered that when this balance is not properly weighed and appreciated significant problems arise, as in the infamous case of thalidomide. The degree of safety required, therefore, is heavily dependent on the patient characteristics that relate to the intervention being studied. For instance, some patients need more protection than others, and these include the elderly, the frail, the immuno-suppressed and the critically ill.

The art, or science, of developing evidence-based clinical practice recommendations is therefore very difficult and fraught with controversy. Recommendations must be specific to a certain patient group and to a certain practice setting. Unfortunately this is in counter-distinction to the needs and requirements of industry whose priorities are often to sell the drug or technology widely and not necessarily specifically to the patient group originally studied. These controversies are frequently debated in our medical journals, often pertaining to issues related to our practice in intensive care medicine. There are now a series of mechanisms available that are designed to help in objectively appraising the available evidence. In theory these should allow for a clear, open and transparent process. These include the GRADE working group [11] or the Cochrane Database of systematic reviews.

Even with these processes in place, the translation of research through recommendations to change bedside clinical practice is not good. To move from what is known about the benefits, the risks and the limitations of a certain intervention when applied in a very strict, usually not generalisable cohort of patients to the real world, where patient selection is different, severity of illness very heterogeneous, comorbidities the rule and not the exception, co-interventions and co-treatments usually the case, is difficult. All these issues interact with the effect (or the side effects) of the intervention in the real world, as can be seen with interventions such as statins [23, 24].

It can therefore be seen that although the RCT remains our gold standard mechanism for obtaining data, it has many limitations. In order for data to be translated from research studies to clinical practice we have to be sure that the patient we are treating is similar to the original cohort studied. Analysis of screening logs and

Gant charts from many trials shows how difficult this is. Many studies screen many times more patients than they actually enrol. This changes the population characteristics significantly; the population studied in many RCTs tends to be young, male, white, suffering from a single condition and using a single treatment while most patients in our ICUs usually have multiple illnesses, take multiple medications and are either too young or too old to have been included in clinical trials. Consequently, efficacy is not the same as effectiveness [25]. A treatment is effective if it works in real life in non-ideal circumstances. In real life, medications will be used in doses and frequencies never studied and in patient groups never assessed in the trials, often in combination with other medications that have not been tested for interactions, and off-label uses. For these reasons, and by an innate bias between the appraisal of evidence and their own past experiences and beliefs [26], most orthodox medicine is not evidence-based [27] and anecdotes are often used as evidence [28].

Finally, the process does not end when the new intervention is in the market. The effect of off-label use, different levels of co-existent diseases, the appearance of very rare (but sometimes fatal) secondary effects all can change the balance against the intervention and the indications or contraindications of the intervention. At the extreme, this process may lead to the need to withdrawal of the intervention from the market after a certain time period. Frequently we find that our systems are not well designed to cope adequately with this problem, as a long list of drugs can demonstrate [15]. Effectiveness, as defined by Donabedian as *"the extent to which a drug achieves its intended effect in the usual clinical setting"* need to be evaluated, therefore, through observational studies of real practice. This requires registries and longer-term data acquisition systems that follow through the research trials into clinical practice.

On behalf of our patients we should always remember the lessons from the past; thalidomide and congenital abnormalities, rofecoxib and heart attacks and stroke, rosiglitazone and heart attacks, trovafloxacin and liver failure amongst many others. This also applies to recent interventions closer to home, for example (very) tight glycaemic control, use of starches. It is necessary to always keep in mind the quote usually attributed to Hippocrates, that the first duty of a physicians is "First, do no harm".

The authors

Rui P. Moreno, MD, PhD[1]
Andrew Rhodes, FRCP, FRCA[2]
[1]Unidade de Cuidados Intensivos Polivalente | Hospital de Santo António dos Capuchos | Centro Hospitalar de Lisboa Central E.P.E. | Lisbon, Portugal
[2]Department of Intensive Care Medicine | St George's Healthcare NHS Trust | London, UK

Address for correspondence
Rui P. Moreno
Unidade de Cuidados Intensivos Polivalente
Hospital de Santo António dos Capuchos
Centro Hospitalar de Lisboa Central E.P.E.
Alameda de Santo António dos Capuchos
1169–050 Lisbon, Portugal
E-mail: r.moreno@mail.telepac.pt

References

1. Kohn LT, Corrigan JM, Donaldson MS, eds. To err is human: building a safer health system. Washington DC: National Academy Press 2000.
2. Angus DC, Kelley MA, Schmitz RJ, White A, Popovich J, for the Committee in Manpower for Pulmonary and Critical Care Societies (COMPACCS). Caring for the critically ill patient. Current and projected workforce requirements for care of the critically ill and patients with pulmonary disease: can we meet the requirements of an aging population? 284 2000;21.
3. Negovsky VA. Essays on Reanimatology. Moscow: MIR Publishers, 1986.
4. Donabedian A. The seven pillars of quality. Arch Pathol Lab Med 1990;114:1115–8.
5. Weir CR, Hicken BL, Rappaport HS, Nebeker JR. Crossing the Quality Chasm: The Role of Information Technology Departments. Am J Med Qual 2006;21:382–93.
6. Committee on Quality of Healthcare in America IoM. Crossing the quality chasm: a new health system for the 21st century. Washington: National Academy Press, 2001.
7. Greenland S, Morgenstern H. Ecological bias, confounding, and effect modification. Int J Epidemiol 1989;18:269–74.
8. LeLorier J, Gregoire G, Benhaddad A, Lapierre J, Derderian F. Discrepancies between meta-analysis and

subsequent large randomized, controlled trials. N Engl J Med 1997;337:536–42.

9. Hébert PC, Cook DJ, Wells G, Marshall J. The Design of Randomized Clinical Trials in Critically Ill Patients. Chest 2002;121:1290–300.

10. Ziegler EJ, Fisher CJ, Sprung CL, et al. Treatment of gram-negative bacteremia and septic shock with ha-1a human monoclonal antibody against endotoxin. A randomized, double-blind, placebo-controlled trial. N Engl J Med 1991;324:429–36.

11. GRADE Working Group. Grading quality of evidence and strength of recommendations. Br Med J 2004;328:1–8.

12. Carlet J. Prescribing indications based on successful clinical trials in sepsis: a difficult exercise. Crit Care Med 2006;34:525–9.

13. Matot I, Pizov R, Sprung CL. Evaluation of Institutional Review Board review and informed consent in publications of human research in critical care medicine. Crit Care Med 1998;26:1596–602.

14. Minneci PC, Eichacker PQ, Danner RL, Banks SM, Natanson C, Deans KJ. The importance of usual care control groups for safety monitoring and validity during critical care research. Intensive Care Med 2008;34:942–7.

15. Liu JP. Rethinking statistical approaches to evaluating drug safety. Yonsei Med J 2007;48:895–900.

16. Fleming TR. Identifying and Addressing Safety Signals in Clinical Trials. N Engl J Med 2008;359:1400–2.

17. Stern JM, Simes RJ. Publication bias: evidence of delayed publication in a cohort study of clinical research projects. Br Med J 1997;315:640–5.

18. Easterbrook PJ, Berlin JA, Gopalan R, Matthews DR. Publication bias in clinical research. Lancet 1991;337:867–72.

19. Chan A-W, Altman DG. Identifying outcome reporting bias in randomised trials on PubMed: review of publications and survey of authors. Br Med J 2005;330:753.

20. Grégoire G, Derderian F, Le Lorier J. Selecting the language of the publications included in a meta-analysis: is there a tower of babel bias? J Clin Epidemiol 1995;48:159–63.

21. Singer M. The Surviving Sepsis guidelines: evidence-based...or evidence-biased? Critical Care and Resuscitation 2006;8:244–5.

22. Detsky AS. Sources of bias for authors of clinical practice guidelines. Can Med Assoc J 2006;175:1033,5.

23. Tinetti ME. Over-the-Counter Sales of Statins and Other Drugs for Asymptomatic Conditions. N Engl J Med 2008;358:2728–32.

24. Armitage J. The safety of statins in clinical practice. Lancet 2007;DOI:10.1016/S0140.

25. Haynes B. Can it work? Does it work? Is it worth it? Br Med J 1999;319:652–3.

26. Grol R. Beliefs and evidence in changing clinical practice. Br Med J 1997;315:418–21.

27. Garrow JS. How much of orthodox medicine is evidence based? Br Med J 2007;335.

28. Aronson JK. Anecdotes as evidence. We need guidelines for reporting anecdotes of suspected adverse drug reactions. Br Med J 2003;326.

Jürgen Graf, Elke Roeb and Uwe Janssens

Identifying barriers to change –
The gap between perception and practice

Introduction

The modern intensive care unit (ICU) constitutes what psychologists have termed a *"cognitively complex environment"* [1, 2], i.e. an environment where the number of pieces of information required by an operator to make a correct decision often exceeds the five or seven that can be held in conscious working memory simultaneously [3]. Although complex systems are known to be failure-prone, the susceptibility of failure is not universally acknowledged by medical staff. In a recent survey in teaching hospitals in the United States, 30 % of the physicians and nurses working in the ICU denied committing errors, and many healthcare providers report that error is not handled appropriately in their hospital [4].

Evolutions and frameworks in medicine were not only adopted early by intensivists but extensively promoted to facilitate patient care and accelerate professional development. Growth of *evidence-based medicine* and related *critical appraisal*, as well as the role of *health services research* with its applied reasoning strategies and technologies that were quickly incorporated into intensive care medicine may serve as prominent examples [5, 6].

The application of evidence-based medicine and recent research findings into daily practice is of major concern in intensive care medicine today [7, 8]. Consequent-

ly, several of the landmark studies in the field of intensive care medicine have been incorporated in recommendations and practice guidelines [9, 10]. However, there appears to be a considerable gap between guidelines, recommendations and expert consent with regard to best current practice and daily therapy in our intensive care units [11–14]. Once again, what is already known is not always what is actually done.

A variety of barriers resident on various levels of the healthcare system including (but not limited to) economic, organisational, administrative, professional and personal aspects may hinder successful implementation of change. There is already widespread recognition that – although often evidence-based – guidelines and recommendations do not find their way into clinical practice [15]. This neglect to adopt best practice is not unique to the field of intensive care medicine [16]. Deliberating about this failure to adhere to best clinical practice led to the cognition that detailed comprehension of the various obstacles is essential to improve clinical performance [17]. Indeed, perception may play a key role for both the recognition of suboptimal or substandard care and the identification of barriers to change.

This chapter will thus provide the reader with a brief theoretical introduction what perception (really) is and how people's (and healthcare professionals') senses may function, i.e. how humans perceive themselves and their reality. Although this reasoning is usually found in the area of cognitive or behavioural sciences we believe that understanding of some basic elements related to human decision-making, adoption or rejection of rules and guidelines, and human interaction with authorities is essential prior to the elaboration on mechanisms to implement changes of clinical practice. Subsequently we will present a short example of change interlaced with aspects that stem from the presented theoretical framework.

The goal of this chapter is twofold
- to provide a deeper understanding of the human mind, decision-making and its weaknesses;
- to present a theoretical framework for change that is – after customisation – applicable to a variety of settings, enabling tailored and goal-oriented interventions at various levels.

Where we are (and who, if at all) – The theory of perception, reality and practice

"What perception is, everyone will know better by reflecting on what he does himself, when he sees, hears, feels, etc., or thinks, than by any discourse of mine. Whoever reflects what passes in his own mind cannot miss it: And if he does not reflect, all the words in the world, cannot make him have any notion of it."

John Locke, *An Essay Concerning Human Understanding, Book II, Chapter ix, § 2*

Perception is referred to as a cognitive process which is used to transfer information from the environment into the brain and mind, where it is further handled and related to other information. Perception can be characterised as either internal perception (*proprioception*) which gives us information from inside our body (how we feel, e.g. warm, cold, hungry, thirsty, pain), and external or sensory perception (*exteroception*), which is using our senses of sight, hearing, touch, smell, and taste, to discover our environment. Some philosophers and psychologists propose that this processing gives rise to particular mental states (*cognitivism*) whilst others propose a direct path back into the external world in the form of action (*radical behaviourism*). Often in psychology the sensory perception is referred to as cognitive psychology.

Historically, the most important philosophical problems posed by perception concerned the epistemology of perception, which is basically the question of how we can gain knowledge via perception or cognition. However, comprehensive contemplation of perception requires the acceptance one of a variety of metaphysical (ontological) perspectives. These include, but are not limited to, forms of so-called *indirect realism, direct realism* and *anti-realistic* theories (e.g. Idealism and Skepticism). Enactivism, a third theory of perception, attempts to find a middle path between realist and anti-realist theories. In *Enactivism* organism and environment are structurally coupled and codetermined. This leads to a dynamic interplay between an organism's sensorimotor capabilities and its environment resulting in *reality*. Thus, perception is no longer a passive process determined entirely by the features of an independently existing world [18].

The *"common sense"* philosophy established in the 18th century recognised that there is a strong belief in the existence of a "real world" beyond our minds and imaginations and that we can truly know things about the world around us – "our" *reality*. Interestingly, *"reality"* in a philosophical sense viewed from a more ontological point encompasses two conceptually interrelated aspects once again: the nature of reality itself, and the coexisting interdependence between mind and reality [19].

Practice – i.e. a customary action, manner or habit – represents just another perception of reality obliged by subjective assessment. Thus everyone basically creates or perceives his or her (or its) own reality in daily living (or practice).

Cognitive psychology – Probability of bias and misperception

Cognitive psychology concentrates on mental processes including how people think, perceive, remember and learn. As a domain of the larger field of cognitive science, cognitive psychology is related to other disciplines including neuroscience, philosophy, and linguistics. In contrast to the more theoretical, philosophical framework outlined above the main interest of cognitive psychology is how people acquire, process and store information. Cognitive psychology finds ample opportunities for target-oriented research such as ways to improve memory, how to increase decision-making accuracy, and how to structure educational curricula to enhance learning. Cognitive psychology is concerned with internal mental states, in contrast to behaviourism which is mainly interested in observable behaviours. Compared with psychoanalysis cognitive psychology is based on truly scientific methods to study mental processes instead of the application of rather subjective assessment instruments.

Research in cognitive psychology has demonstrated a variety of cognitive biases such as statistical reasoning, social attribution and memory. Tversky and Kahneman were among the first to claim that a better understanding of three heuristics (representativeness, availability of instances or scenarios, and adjustment from an anchor) and of the biases to which they lead could improve judgments and decisions in situations of uncertainty [20]. Nevertheless, this point of view has been repeatedly challenged. Humans develop cognitive biases for a variety of reasons: They may help the brain to process information quickly, for example, even when that processing is sometimes erroneous [21]. Many social psychologists have dedicated a great deal of time to understanding cognitive bias, since it is an important part of the human mind and ultimately, of human behaviour [22].

Cognitive biases are common to all humans, and many of them follow predictable and obvious patterns. Nevertheless, good data exist to suggest that under some circumstances everybody develops a tendency to react unforeseeably, often in a way that seems surprising when viewed from a more detached perspective [23–25]. Cognitive biases may be characterised according to their principle structure, possible inferences or resultant. Many different forms of cognitive bias have been ascribed by social scientists, with the following characterising more or less frequently encountered groups:

- *Bandwagon effect* – the tendency to do or believe things because many other people do or believe the same. Often related to group thinking.
- *Omission bias* – tendency to prefer a more harmful act of omission to a potentially less harmful act of commission.

- *Loss aversion* – the tendency for people to strongly prefer avoiding losses over acquiring gains.
- *Selective perception* – the tendency for expectations to affect perception.
- *Anchoring* – the tendency to rely too heavily, or "anchor" on one trait or piece of information when making decisions.
- *Projection* – the tendency to assume that other people think like we do.
- *Confirmation bias* – the tendency to ignore information which does not fit with the own beliefs while agreeable information is weighted more heavily.
- *Fundamental attribution error* – in which people ascribe behaviours to people's personalities, rather than social and environmental factors.

Understanding and recognising cognitive bias in ourselves and in others is a very useful skill. If one accounts for bias when evaluating a situation or someone's retelling of an event, one can make more accurate decisions which are based on fact, rather than on (mis-)perception generated solely by the mind. Cognitive bias may prove a powerful force in decision-making, especially in groups, and it may also skew the perspective of people and their environment. Thus, cognitive biases and intentional or non-intentional (mis-)perception of one's cognition may be of particular interest, acknowledging the gap between perception and practice.

Thus we may conclude and acuminate our short philosophical detour: Not everything that is visible will be perceived in practice and not all practice that is perceived will be truly visible.

Change management

Different interventions have been developed to enhance the implementation of research findings or innovations into daily clinical practice [17, 26]. All interventions can be dissected into various components describing and targeting aspects of relevance for change. A rather instructive and comprehensive process is presented by Bokhoven and colleagues [27] which is outlined in Figure 1. All who want to implement change should emphasise the importance of the problem analysis preceding the design of an intervention. Targeting the implementation of improved nutri-

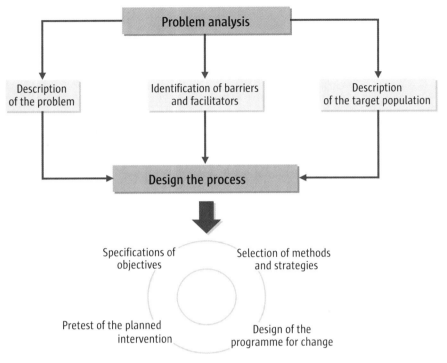

Fig. 1   Outline of the implementation of change, with emphasis on a stepwise approach which is of utmost importance to truly customise and tailor the interventions to the specific needs of the targeted healthcare professionals and their environment.

tional support in the critically ill Simpson and Doig identified the assessment of available resources, the recognition of the importance of different types of barriers for different sites, the potential for combinations of interventions to have a synergistic effect on practice change, and the potential for combinations of interventions to actually reduce workload, to be of interest [28].

In Figure 2 basic needs for and stages of change on the individual level are outlined, based on findings that individual behaviour change usually takes place in specific orders [27]. Similar approaches have been formulated for changes on the organisational level (see Fig. 3). Some groups and organisations specifically address the effectiveness and efficiency of change management in a variety of settings, concluding in their findings that the effectiveness of most interventions is heterogeneous and limited [29, 30]. Among the different approaches, combined and multifaceted efforts seem the most promising [15]. Those in-

terventions tailored to overcome specific barriers are more likely to result in sustained change and thus improvement of practice [27, 31].

Identifying barriers to change – Structured barrier analysis

A variety of potential barriers to change and performance improvement have already been identified. The Cochrane Effective Practice and Organisation of Care Group (EPOC) has classified barriers into the following categories [32]:

1. Information management clinical uncertainty
2. Sense of competence
3. Perceptions of liability
4. Patient expectations
5. Standards of practice
6. Financial discentives
7. Administrative constraints
8. Others

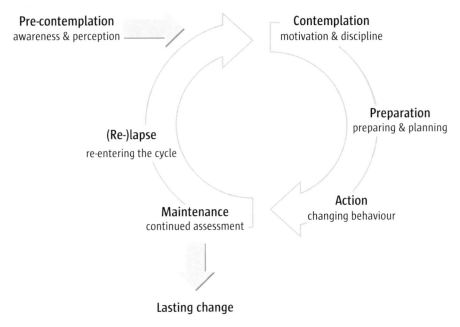

Pre-contemplation
awareness & perception

Contemplation
motivation & discipline

Preparation
preparing & planning

(Re-)lapse
re-entering the cycle

Action
changing behaviour

Maintenance
continued assessment

Lasting change

Fig. 2   Pre-contemplation – individuals may not acknowledge that a problem exists at all. At this stage a convincing (and comprehensible) reason for change needs to be firmly established. Awareness and perception are indispensable to move any further from this point. Contemplation is characterised by an ambivalent yet indecisive mind. Motivation and discipline are necessary for the affected healthcare professionals to accept, adopt and understand the proposed changes. The establishment of a sound framework may lead to the stage of preparation, i.e. formulating concrete plans for change. In the stage of action changing individuals' behaviour begins. The target population decides whether to maintain the new behaviour or to relapse into former habits. It is then essential to facilitate the stage of maintenance to achieve lasting change. Continued maintenance provides psychological rewards (positive feedback) for the accomplished task. If somebody is able to maintain this state, change is likely to be lasting. Lapse and relapse are viewed as intrinsic to any change and do not infer failure. It does not mean that lapse or relapse is desirable or even invariably expected. It simply means that behaviour change is difficult, and it is unreasonable to expect anyone to be able to modify a habit perfectly unwanted thoughts or slips.

Organisational and external barriers include the lack of resources, staff, interest or leadership, aspects associated with the regulatory environment or reimbursement mechanisms [33, 34]. On the individual level, physicians often lack awareness and familiarity with definitions and guidelines [35], fear the loss of therapeutic autonomy or simply disagree with the content of guidelines or recommendation and thus disregard their acquisition [36]. To complicate matters further, physicians usually miss the skills and expertise for the structured implementation of changes, and personal concerns may lead to a biased cognition [37]. Unfortunately current evidence based on the analysis of 15 randomised controlled clinical trials is insufficient to ascribe whether barriers were valid, which were the most important barriers, whether all barriers were identified and if they had been addressed successfully by the intervention applied [32]. Moreover, priorities which barriers are most important in impeding change in a specific environment are missing. Thus, currently no universally applicable outline for barrier analysis can be proposed. However, a selection of aspects and elements that should have been acknowledged in a structured barrier analysis is compiled in Table 1. Given the paucity of information with regard to successful barrier analysis and identification strategies, any initiative has to start with a rigorous problem analysis utilising e.g. focus group inter-

Noticing the problem

Searching for possible responses

Evaluating alternatives

Deciding to adopt action based on selected responses

Initiating action – requires policy change and resources

Implementation – changing work behaviour and relationships

Institutionalising the change – becoming routine part of the organisation

Fig. 3   Change at the organisational level according to Goodman et al. [45]. Basic elements are found in both individual and organisational changes. This diagram serves to emphasise the need for a structured approach with appreciation of the different stages of change because depending on the stage the key actors at which the intervention is targeted can vary considerably [27].

views, brainstorming, literature review, and audit, to name only a few. This may be adjusted adopting existing improvement interventions [27, 31] but should not be limited to the already known. This is where we leave known territory and have to trust our individual perception again, asking ourselves "what is known on the topic", "what is done in clinical practice", and "why (and where) a gap exists". Basically, this is the meaning of "tailored" or "individualized" intervention: It is the reflection of needs and possibilities eventually followed by goal-oriented interventions.

Berenholtz and coworkers provide a nice and instructive example for such a process [38]: A checklist to eliminate catheter-related bloodstream infections was implemented but lacked

effectiveness. In the next step – a structured barrier analysis – the compliance of the healthcare professionals (i.e. the intensivists undertaking the intervention) was found to be poor. Thus an individualised intervention was carried out: The patients' nurses were empowered to cancel all interventions not in accordance with the checklist. The analysis that followed revealed 100 % compliance with the checklist and a subsequent clinically relevant decrease in catheter-related bloodstream infections [38].

Conclusion – Bridging the gap between perception and practice

Although a variety of techniques aimed towards behaviour change have been applied in the healthcare setting, none has been found to be ubiquitously applicable [39]. This may in part be explained by the diversity of healthcare settings with their specific needs (and barriers). Currently, most of the applied interventions are intuitively designed, lack firm scientific basis, formal validation and show heterogeneous results. Nevertheless, more and more organisations worldwide propose the adoption of quality improvement collaborations in different healthcare settings. Although the evidence underlying these strategies is positive it is still limited and the effects cannot be predicted with certainty.

Prior to the design of an intervention aimed towards implementation of change an explicit problem analysis is inevitable. Strategies to identify and finally overcome barriers for change should include – but are not limited to – brainstorming, focus group interviews, external audit, and structured assessment processes and tools.

Successful examples of how to overcome barriers, thereby introducing sustained changes with improved patient outcomes, do indeed exist in various settings [40–42] and should serve to motivate each of us to put efforts into improvement and change of both our healthcare system and our individual behaviour.

Driving improvements in intensive care medicine is the repeated adjustment of all aspects surrounding patient care and patient management involving all relevant people in order to meet predefined goals. Due to the dynamic nature of the diagnostic and therapeutic armamentarium and the constantly increasing knowledge in medical sciences the development of guidelines, update of recommendations and need for changes in daily practice will be a continuous challenge in the foreseeable future.

Tab. 1 Barriers potentially affecting change in practice

Level	Attributes
Individual level	■ Missing perception ■ Insufficient awareness ■ Missing knowledge ■ Wrong attitude ■ Lack of motivation for change ■ Poor communication ■ Poor education ■ Tradition and faith ■ Poor patient acceptance
Organisational level	■ Missing resources ■ No access to peer support ■ Missing reward ■ Not enough time ■ Poor staff loyalty ■ Missing skills ■ Lack of alternatives
Societal (national) level	■ Missing regulations ■ Other focus, priority ■ No (financial) incentives ■ Not enough support ■ Not enough pressure towards quality

Epilogue – Would this pass the real-life check in the majority of ICUs?

Implementing change to improve patients' outcomes indeed is an honourable task no intensivist would deny and we all welcome the many approaches that have been outlined to improve patient care. Nevertheless, there may be oblique reasons for the observed insufficiencies in many of the ICUs, hospitals and healthcare systems all over the world.

In most countries no incentives exist for good or even better healthcare, within or outside the ICU. A reimbursement system that is solely driven by diagnosis-related groups (DRG) may provoke the wrong incentives with regard to the outcome of the individual patient. For example, except for length of stay, DRGs are virtually independent from patient outcomes in the German reimbursement system.

Considering change most intensivists are currently stuck between a rock and a hard place: Although good evidence exists that e.g. a nurse should not be responsible for more than two patients during nightshifts [43], this is rarely the reality. Without doubt intensivists will continue to undertake all efforts in order to maximise the benefit for their patients while minimising harm,

albeit working in a yet imperfect system. A principal problem that has been neglected throughout this chapter – and in many of the cited studies – is the lack of resources, especially the lack of qualified healthcare professionals to really improve and implement change. Most of the initiatives that we referred to were most likely not resource-neutral (although that has rarely been reported)! Nevertheless, our ICUs are not without financial restrictions, and most of us face the dramatic rationing in healthcare during everyday practice. The same societal and governmental initiatives that often promote improvement in patient safety and patient outcomes restrict the reimbursement of the healthcare system. Resource allocation – it's a jungle out there [44]!

The authors

Jürgen Graf, PD, MD[1]
Elke Roeb, Prof. MD[2]
Uwe Janssens, Prof. MD, FESC[3]
[1]Department of Anaesthesiology and Intensive Care | Philipps University Marburg | Marburg, Germany

[2]Department of Internal Medicine II |
Section of Gastroenterology and Intensive
Care Medicine | Justus Liebig University
Gießen | Gießen, Germany
[3]Medical Clinic | St. Antonius Hospital
Eschweiler | Eschweiler, Germany

Address for correspondence
Jürgen Graf
Department of Anaesthesiology and
Intensive Care
Philipps University Marburg
Baldingerstraße 1
35043 Marburg, Germany
E-mail: jgraf@gmx.de

References

1. Hicks FD, Merritt SL, Elstein AS. Critical thinking and clinical decision making in critical care nursing: a pilot study. Heart Lung 2003 May;32(3):169-80.

2. Hillman K, Chen J, May E. Complex intensive care unit interventions. Crit Care Med 2009 Jan;37(1 Suppl):S102-S106.

3. Miller GA. The magical number seven plus or minus two: some limits on our capacity for processing information. Psychol Rev 1956 Mar;63(2):81-97.

4. Sexton JB, Thomas EJ, Helmreich RL. Error, stress and teamwork in medicine and aviation: cross-sectional surveys. BMJ 2000;320:745-9.

5. Pronovost PJ, Jenckes MW, Dorman T, Garrett E, Breslow MJ, Rosenfeld BA, et al. Organizational characteristics of intensive care units related to outcomes of abdominal aortic surgery. JAMA 1999 Apr 14;281(14):1310-7.

6. Berenholtz S, Pronovost PJ. Barriers to translating evidence into practice. Curr Opin Crit Care 2003 Aug;9(4):321-5.

7. Curtis JR, Cook DJ, Wall RJ, Angus DC, Bion J, Kacmarek RM, et al. Intensive care unit quality improvement: a ‚how-to‘ guide for the interdisciplinary team. Crit Care Med 2006;34:211-8.

8. Frutiger A. Driving improvements: Quality management in the ICU. In: Sibbald WJ, Bion JF, editors. Evaluating critical care. Using health services research to improve quality.New York, Berlin, Heidelberg: Springer; 2001. p. 321-35.

9. Dellinger RP, Carlet JM, Masur H, Gerlach H, Calandra T, Cohen J, et al. Surviving Sepsis Campaign guidelines for management of severe sepsis and septic shock. Crit Care Med 2004;32:858-73.

10. Winters B, Dorman T. Patient-safety and quality initiatives in the intensive-care unit. Curr Opin Anaesthesiol 2006 Apr;19(2):140-5.

11. Gao F, Melody T, Daniels DF, Giles S, Fox S. The impact of compliance with 6-hour and 24-hour sepsis bundles on hospital mortality in patients with severe sepsis: a prospective observational study. Crit Care 2005;9:R764-R770.

12. Pittet D, Simon A, Hugonnet S, Pessoa-Silva CL, Sauvan V, Perneger TV. Hand hygiene among physicians: performance, beliefs, and perceptions. Ann Intern Med 2004 Jul 6;141(1):1-8.

13. Brunkhorst FM, Engel C, Ragaller M, Welte T, Rossaint R, Gerlach H, et al. Practice and perception–a nationwide survey of therapy habits in sepsis. Crit Care Med 2008 Oct;36(10):2719-25.

14. Reeve BK, Cook DJ. Semirecumbency among mechanically ventilated patients: A multicenter observational study. Clin Intensive Care 1999;10:241-4.

15. Grol R, Wensing M. What drives change? Barriers to and incentives for achieving evidence-based practice. Med J Aust 2004 Mar 15;180(6 Suppl):S57-S60.

16. Schuster M, McGlynn E, Brook R. How good is the quality of health care in the United States. Milbank Q 1998;76:517-63.

17. Grol R, Grimshaw J. From best evidence to best practice: effective implementation of change in patients' care. Lancet 2003;362:1225-30.

18. Varela F, Thompson E, Rosch E. The embodied mind – Cognitive Science and human experience. Massachusetts Institute of Technology; 1991.

19. Schumacher R. Perception and Reality. Paderborn: Mentis; 2004.

20. Tversky A, Kahneman D. Judgment under Uncertainty: Heuristics and Biases. Science 1974 Sep 27;185(4157):1124-31.

21. Kahneman D, Tversky A. On the reality of cognitive illusions. Psychol Rev 1996 Jul;103(3):582-91.

22. Elstein AS. Heuristics and biases: selected errors in clinical reasoning. Acad Med 1999 Jul;74(7):791-4.

23. Glockner A, Betsch T. Multiple-reason decision making based on automatic processing. J Exp Psychol Learn Mem Cogn 2008 Sep;34(5):1055-75.

24. Moskowitz AJ, Kuipers BJ, Kassirer JP. Dealing with uncertainty, risks, and tradeoffs in clinical decisions. A cognitive science approach. Ann Intern Med 1988 Mar;108(3):435-49.

25. Aberegg SK, Haponik EF, Terry PB. Omission bias and decision making in pulmonary and critical care medicine. Chest 2005;128:1497-505.

26. Grol R. Successes and failures in the implementation of evidence-based guidelines for clinical practice. Med Care 2001;39(Suppl 2):46-54.

27. van Bokhoven MA, Kok G, van der WT. Designing a quality improvement intervention: a systematic approach. Qual Saf Health Care 2003 Jun;12(3):215-20.

28. Simpson F, Doig GS. The relative effectiveness of practice change interventions in overcoming common barriers

to change: a survey of 14 hospitals with experience implementing evidence-based guidelines. J Eval Clin Pract 2007 Oct;13(5):709–15.

29. Grimshaw JM, Thomas RE, MacLennan G, Fraser C, Ramsay CR, Vale L, et al. Effectiveness and efficiency of guideline dissemination and implementation strategies. Health Technol Assess 2004 Feb;8(6):iii-72.

30. Shojania KG, Grimshaw JM. Evidence-based quality improvement: the state of the science. Health Aff (Millwood) 2005 Jan;24(1):138–50.

31. Bosch M, van der WT, Wensing M, Grol R. Tailoring quality improvement interventions to identified barriers: a multiple case analysis. J Eval Clin Pract 2007 Apr;13(2):161–8.

32. Shaw B, Cheater F, Baker R, Gillies C, Hearnshaw H, Flottorp S, et al. Tailored interventions to overcome identified barriers to change: effects on professional practice and health care outcomes. Cochrane Database Syst Rev 2005;(3):CD005470.

33. Dijkstra R, Wensing M, Thomas R, Akkermans R, Braspenning J, Grimshaw J, et al. The relationship between organisational characteristics and the effects of clinical guidelines on medical performance in hospitals, a eta-analysis. BMC Health Serv Res 2006;6:53.

34. Gosden T, Forland F, Kristiansen IS, Sutton M, Leese B, Giuffrida A, et al. Capitation, salary, fee-for-service and mixed systems of payment: effects on the behaviour of primary care physicians. Cochrane Database Syst Rev 2000;(3):CD002215.

35. Poeze M, Ramsay G, Gerlach H, Rubulotta F, Levy M. An international sepsis survey: a study of doctors' knowledge and perception about sepsis. Crit Care 2004;8:R409-R413.

36. Cabana MD, Rand CS, Powe NR, Wu AW, Wilson MH, Abboud PA, et al. Why don't physicians follow clinical practice guidelines? A framework for improvement. JAMA 1999 Oct 20;282(15):1458–65.

37. Cabana MD, Rand CS, Powe NR, Wu AW, Wilson MH, Abboud PA, et al. Why don't physicians follow clinical practice guidelines? A framework for improvement. JAMA 1999 Oct 20;282(15):1458–65.

38. Berenholtz SM, Pronovost PJ, Lipsett PA, Hobson D, Earsing K, Farley JE, et al. Eliminating catheter-related bloodstream infections in the intensive care unit. Crit Care Med 2004 Oct;32(10):2014–20.

39. Smith WR. Evidence for the effectiveness of techniques To change physician behavior. Chest 2000 Aug;118(2 Suppl):8S-17S.

40. Pronovost P, Needham DM, Berenholtz S, Sinopoli D, Chu H, Cosgrove S, et al. An intervention to decrease catheter-related bloodstream infections in the ICU. N Engl J Med 2006;355:2725–32.

41. DuBose JJ, Inaba K, Shiflett A, Trankiem C, Teixeira PG, Salim A, et al. Measurable outcomes of quality improvement in the trauma intensive care unit: the impact of a daily quality rounding checklist. J Trauma 2008 Jan;64(1):22–7.

42. Jain M, Miller L, Belt D, King D, Berwick DM. Decline in ICU adverse events, nosocomial infections and cost through a quality improvement initiative focusing on teamwork and culture change. Qual Saf Health Care 2006 Aug;15(4):235–9.

43. Amaravadi RK, Dimick JB, Pronovost PJ, Lipsett PA. ICU nurse-to-patient ratio is associated with complications and resource use after esophagectomy. Intensive Care Med 2000 Dec;26(12):1857–62.

44. Hawkes N. Resource allocation–it's a jungle out there. BMJ 2009;338:b77.

45. Goodman RM, Steckler A, Kegler MC. Mobilizing organizations for health enhancement: theories of organizational change. In: Glanz K, Lewis FM, Rimer BK, editors. Health behaviour and health education: theory, research and practice. 2nd ed. San Francisco: Jossey-Bass; 1997. p. 287–312.

Ellen G.M. Smit and Armand R.J. Girbes

To err is human. But how to communicate these errors to patients and family?

Introduction

Doctors, like pilots in aviation, operate in a complex environment, especially in an emergency department, operating theatre and the intensive care unit (ICU). Critical care presents substantial patient safety challenges. It is fast-paced, complex and commonly requires urgent high-risk decision-making often with incomplete data by physicians with varying levels of critical care training. These factors may lead to a higher medical error rate than elsewhere in the hospital. Moreover, critically ill patients are more vulnerable to iatrogenic injury due to their severity of illness, high-risk interventions and different interacting medication in a state of multiple organ failure. The Institute of Medicine (IOM) reported in 1999's "To Err is Human" that medical errors cause an estimated 44,000–98,000 deaths each year in the US [1], based on retrospective chart studies in three states with extrapolation to a national level. Although important, scientifically sound comments on this report can be made questioning its accurateness, the objective of the IOM report remains to stimulate a national effort to improve patient safety [2–6]. The IOM report outlined four key areas of action:

1. heightened awareness and establishment of a national focus regarding patient safety;
2. mandatory and immediate reporting of errors to enhance the current voluntary reporting system,

facilitate learning and expedite the implementation of corrective actions;
3. setting safety standards via oversight organisations, group purchasers and health professional groups;
4. creation of safety systems within healthcare organisations to enhance the implementation of safe practices at the level of health care delivery.

All over the world this report was used to stimulate a change in policy and study the feasibility of implementing the report's recommendations. But it may also help to establish a necessary change in views of practising physicians and the public on medical errors. According to a report from December 2002, neither physicians nor the public named medical errors as one of the largest problems in healthcare today. Surprisingly, 29 % of physicians reported having seen an error in the previous year and 60 % of them believed it likely to reoccur the following year [7]. However, quality programmes and patient safety are now an increasingly important issue in medicine. Safety programmes in health care organisations are developed and use of quality indicators is common. The ultimate goal of error reporting is prevention and the creation of a learning organisation, and expressly not the disqualification or punishment of individuals. A system and environment within the ICU that enhance recognition and reporting of errors are prerequisites for admitting and communicating errors to the patient and/or family. Clear definitions of errors, adverse events, management of errors, and incidence and nature of human errors are necessary. An error is defined as a planned act not completed as intended, or the use of a wrong plan of action to achieve a specific aim. An adverse event is defined as an injury to a patient resulting from medical care rather than the patient's underlying disease. An error may or may not result in an adverse event. In the literature near miss and complication is also used, with the further qualification of inevitable, preventable and blameworthy [6,8].

Management of errors

James Reason decribed the different ways of how human errors can be viewed [9]. Two approaches to the problem of human fallibility exist: the person and the system approaches. The person approach remains the dominant tradition in medicine, although it has serious shortcomings. It focuses on the errors of individuals, blaming them for forgetfulness, inattention or weakness; it uncouples a person's acts from any institutional responsibility. The system approach concentrates on the conditions under which individuals work and tries to build defences to avert errors or mitigate their effects. Errors are seen as consequences rather than causes, having their origins in "upstream" systemic factors. The important issue is, however, not who blundered, but how and why the defences failed. Only then can measures be taken to prevent a similar event. Defences, barriers and safe guards occupy a key position in the system approach. High technology and reliable organisations have many defensive layers: Some are engineered, others rely on people and others depend on procedures and administrative controls. Their function is to protect potential victims from local hazards. In the ideal world each slice is intact, in reality it is comparable to the slices of a Swiss cheese. It has many holes, and these holes can shift their location. The presence of a hole does not automatically cause a bad outcome, but when creating a line-up of holes an accident happens. A comparison between aviation and medicine in management of errors is often made. Pilots and doctors both operate in a complex environment where errors can lead to disasters for individuals. As a result,

aviation has developed standardised methods of investigating, documenting and disseminating errors and their lessons, and uses Standard Operating Procedures (SOP) before a flight [10]. The milieu in the hospital is more complex and less predictable than in the cockpit, with differing specialties interacting to treat a patient whose condition and response may partially have unknown characteristics. Only a few studies reported on the incidence, nature and cause of human medical errors and adverse events in the intensive care unit [11, 12]. The limited number of reports in this area may be related, at least in part, to the fear of legal liability. Observations during routine daily activities and error reporting by physicians and nurses immediately after an error discovery were used. In a one-year observational study in 391 patients Rothschild et al. found 120 adverse events in 79 patients (20.2 %), as well as 223 serious errors. Among the adverse events, 13 % were life-threatening or fatal. Among the serious errors, 11 % were potentially life-threatening [13]. Medications were involved in a large proportion of incidents. Failure to carry out intended treatment correctly was another leading category. Many of the errors could be attributed to problems of communication. Other contributing factors include frequent interruptions of work and organisational factors: for example, lack of clarity on the responsibility for a second check of medication. Barriers in reporting include administrative paperwork and lack of encouragement by the management.

Disclosure of adverse events to the patients and their families

Despite the fact that in recent years, an increase in attention to frankness regarding errors in medical care can be observed, healthcare workers do not demonstrate sufficient frankness in all cases. Although in a recent report, most faculty and resident physicians were inclined to report harm-causing hypothetical errors, only a minority has actually reported an error [14]. This gap between attitude and practice regarding error reporting was also previously observed by Kaldjian in a cross-sectional survey of faculty physicians, residents and medical students, although physicians with a higher level of traing were more will-

To err is human. But how to communicate these errors to patients and family?

C

ing to disclose errors [15]. However, patients and family highly appreciate honesty and openness [16, 17]. Facilitating factors like accountability, honesty, trust, reduction of malpractice risk, restitution, truth-telling, fiduciary relationship and avoidance of cover-ups were recognised [18]. A context for error disclosure, like reporting errors to institutions to improve patient safety, discussion of errors among physicians to enhance learning and informing patients as a normal part of patient care, may further enhance frank communication about errors. However, professional repercussions, legal liability, blame, lack of confidentiality, a negative patient or family reaction, humiliation, perfectionism, guilt, lack of anonymity and absence of a supportive forum for diclosure are factors that impede disclosure of errors [18, 19]. Stokes et al. showed some of the barriers to disclosure in the emergency department of the Johns Hopkins Hospital [20]. In general terms, it was found difficult to admit that one has made a mistake of any kind, particularly in medicine where the physician is required to act in the best interest of the patient and may not harm the patient. By admitting a mistake one might lose reputation and the respect of colleagues. Vincent published in 1998 the results of a European questionnaire about information-giving in the ICU [21]. Of the 1,272 questionnaires 504 were completed and analysed in 16 western European countries. Of the respondents, 25 % reported giving complete information to patients, although 35 % felt they should. There was a significant geographical and religious difference in attitudes between doctors. Physicians from the Netherlands were more likely to give complete information compared to physicians from Greece, Spain and Italy. Male doctors were more likely to give the exact story than female doctors, and Protestants were more likely than their Catholic or agnostic counterparts to do so. Big differences exist in how physicians discuss errors with patients. In the report by Galagher et al. 56 % of all respondents indicated that they avoid the word "error" in the communication with the patient [22]. In this study it also appeared that physicians had less difficulty to regret (61 %) than to make an apology (33 %). A study among pediatricians about medical error disclosure showed a marked variation in how they would disclose. There was considerable uncertainty

about when and how to disclose an error. "Often" was chosen for a less than complete disclosure. This was partly influenced by the nature of the error and how apparent the error was to the patients and their parents. When offering an apology, the amount of information given and details about prevention in future was variable, which conflicts with the professional standards [23].

The fear of lawsuits has been growing more prominent over the last years and the idea of "anything you say can be used against you" is prevalent. But the opposite may be true [16]. Poor handling after an incident may be decisive for legal action being taken. It is of significance to acknowledge the importance of a (sincere) apology from the physician to the patient and/or relatives, to normalise the relationship ("Sorry Works! Coalition"; www.sorryworks.net). Apart from the issue of blame, an expression of sorrow and compassion is also of importance in any case where incidents or complications occur.

Professional standards, however, are clear and dictate full disclosure of adverse events. The American College of Physicians ethics manual reads, "… physicians should disclose to patients information about procedural or judgment errors made in the course of care if such information is material to the patient's well-being [24]. Errors do not necessarily constitute improper, negligent, or unethical behavior, but failure to disclose them may." The Joint Commission on the Accreditation of Healthcare Organizations states that: "Patients and when appropriate, their families, are informed about the outcomes of care, including unanticipated outcomes" [25]. The different medical organisations have developed their own codes for dealing with medical errors, which concentrate on prompt, honest and clear communication. Failing to communicate effectively with patients following errors could reduce patient trust in physicians' integrity and may increase the likelihood of a lawsuit.

An open disclosure policy promotes patient safety due to initiation of incident investigation, changing of procedures and prevention of future occurrence. The patient develops a greater trust in the medical profession as a whole. The number of studies examining the patient and family point of view in error disclosure is low, but it is essential to know their experiences to guide communication. Overall, open disclosure is seen as positive and crucial to resolving an adverse event. It increases patient satisfaction, trust and results in a more positive emotional response, and physicians are less likely to change. It reduces the likelihood of legal advice being sought, although this was influenced by the severity of the clinical outcome of the adverse event [26]. Patients want to be told about medical errors, even if there is nothing that can be done about it anymore. They want a detailed explanation, responsibility to be acknowledged, a sincere apology and assurances that steps will be taken to prevent recurrences [27]. Iedema et al. found more or less the same in Australia [28]. Almost all participants appreciated the opportunity to meet with the staff and hear their explanation. A number of suggestions was proposed in the management of error disclosure to patients and their families. An adverse event must be promptly disclosed. The meeting must have a level of formality as an indicator of respect. The communication must be constant and supportive and an apology and tangible support, including counseling and additional clinical treatment, should be given. Interviewees saw the opportunity to meet with staff closely involved in the incident as important and denial of this opportunity was regarded as negative. They also indicated that mentioning improvements to the clinical practice to rule out recurrence of the adverse event must be included in the meeting.

Guideline for disclosing errors and adverse events

It is difficult to formulate a guideline for communicating all the different errors. The optimal communication in a specific situation is dependent of many factors like cultural behavior, religion and geographical differences. Disclosure of adverse events and/or errors should be considered a complex social event and it can be seen as bringing bad news. Therefore, a similar approach can be used. What is crucial is that healthcare workers acknowledge the importance of frankness, honesty and openess, and know how to cope with that. This includes coping with human emotions like loss of face, lack of courage, and sense of guilt. Training skills may be of help [29]. In clinical reality, errors and adverse events are mostly not a matter of black and white, and

gradations into multiple smaller parts of the error or adverse event exist. The information provided is always about what happened, how it could happen and what the follow-up is. Prepare very well for the meeting with the patient and/or family and do not rush. Be aware of how to attune to the needs and intellectual and emotional level of the patient and/or family and adapt your vocabulary accordingly. During the first phase it is important to apologise for the event, say only what you know and promise a thorough investigation. Empathy and compassion are appropriate attitudes at this moment. Keep the family informed about the progress of information. Initial practical problems should be fixed. During the second phase, the investigation, the involvement of external experts and moving quickly is of importance. When the investigations indeed demonstrate errors (or negligence), this should be discussed with the family. It must then be made clear that the organisation takes responsibility, and an apology is an important measure to normalise the relationship with the patient and/or relatives. The right attitude is necessary: Disclosure is about patient care and families. It is not about medical and insurance professionals or lawsuits. The meeting with the patient and/or family should be in a neutral place. Take care that you have time and provide food, drinks, mints, tissues in a clean room with comfortable chairs and a good temperature. Be at the level of the patient and/or family during the discussion and turn off your telephone. Take a chair in a good position so you can have good eye contact with every member of the group. Bring at least one member of the nursing staff. Talk slowly and don't dominate the conversation. Silences are okay, and give time to absorb and digest the information you provide. Make eye contact with every member of the group at time points of the meeting and give appropriate emotional support. Say sorry if it is appropriate to say so and admit fault if you did make a mistake. Reflection of demonstrated emotions by the family is generally of use: e.g. "I can see you are angry." It is also important to explain how future patients are going to take advantage of what you have learned from the error.

Baile et al. gave a six-step protocol, called SPIKES, for delivering bad news in oncology, which can be helpful as a guide in disclosing ad-

To err is human. But how to communicate these errors to patients and family?

C

verse events [30]. Step 1 stands for S = "Setting up the interview." The physician must be well-prepared, have knowledge of facts and earlier conversations and be aware of possible emotions of the patient/family. Also, the physician must be aware of his/her own feelings of frustration, fear and feelings of incompetence (justified or not). The meeting place must be quiet, without the chance of disturbance by others and provide the possibility to sit down together. Try to get eye contact and inform the patient/family in the course of the conversation. There must be a certain level of formality as an indicator of respect. During Step 2, P = "Before you tell ask principle". Ask for the experiences of the patient/family so that you can correspond to the already known details and communication. At Step 3, I = "Get an invitation" the patient and/or family want to know the current situation and they will explicitly ask for information. There is a difference in the amount of details people want to know and it is important to meet that request. This can change in time and it is important to give a next opportunity. Step 4, K = "Knowledge to give information". Give the details of the adverse event in the perspective of the patient/family know how and possible amount of coping. Step 5 is E = Give rise to emotions. Time for reflection of emotion and empathy gives space for future planning of treatment. Acknowledge responsibility for the adverse event and offer an apology. Also give tangible support. Finally, Step 6, S is about "Strategy and summary". Plan the next step in conversation and future treatment. Give feedback about planned action to rule out re-occurrence of the adverse event, and on the improvement of certain procedures.

Conclusion

In medicine, to err is human. The Institute of Medicine report has stimulated an international effort to improve patient safety. Nevertheless, errors and adverse events happen and will continue to happen. It is important to create a constructive error handling culture with propositions for improvement and a learning organisation. Constructive error handling behaviors are associated with lower levels of adverse outcomes. It is only in such an environment that the fulfilment of the professional standard that propagates full disclosure of adverse events can be successful. The communication with patient and family requires the physician to be able to cope appropriately with such situations. Key words are: openness, honesty, and clear and timely communication with compassion. Disclosure is about patient care, the humanity of medical actions, and families. It is not about medical and insurance professionals or lawsuits.

The authors

Ellen G.M. Smit, MD
Armand R.J. Girbes, MD, PhD, Professor in Intensive Care Medicine
    Department of Intensive Care | University Hospital VU Medical Center | Amsterdam, The Netherlands

Address for correspondence
    Armand R.J. Girbes
    Department of Intensive Care
    University Hospital VU Medical Center
    P.O. Box 7057
    1007 MB Amsterdam, The Netherlands
    E-mail: arj.girbes@vumc.nl and
            a.girbes@planet.nl

References

1. Kohn LT, Corrigan JM, Donaldson MS eds. Committee on Quality of Health Care in America, Institute of Medicine. To err is human:building a safer health care system. Washington DC: National Academy Press; 1999
2. Brennan TA. The Institute of Medicine Report on medical errors- Could it do harm? NEJM 2000; 342:1123–1125
3. Richardson WC, Berwick DM, Cris Bisgard J. The Institute of Medicine Report on medical errors, coorespondence. NEJM 2000; 343:663–665
4. Leape LL. Institute of Medicine medical error figures are not exaggerated. JAMA 2000; 284 (1):95–97
5. Andrus CH, Villasenor EG, Kettele JB, Roth R, Sweeney AM, Matolo NM. "To err is human": uniformly reporting medical errors and near misses, a naïve, costly, and misdirected goal. J Am Coll Surg; 2003; 196: 911–918
6. Public Policy Committee. American College of Clinical Pharmacology response to the Institute of Medicine Report "To err is human: building a safer health system". J Clin Pharm 2000; 40: 1075–1078
7. Blendon RJ, DesRoches CM, Brodie M et al. Views of

practicing physicians and the public on medical erros. NEJM 2002; 347:1933–1940.

8. Boyle D, O'Connell D, Platt FW, Albert RK. Disclosing errors and adverse events in the intensive care unit. CCM 2006;34: 1532–1537

9. Reason J. Human Errors:models and managent. WJM 2000; 172: 393–396

10. Helmreich RL. On error management: lessons from aviation. BMJ 2000; 320: 781–785

11. Donchin Y, Gopher D, Olin M, Badihi Y, Biesky M, Sprung CL et al. A look into the nature and causes of human errors in the intensive care unit. Qual. Saf. H ealth Care 2003; 12: 143–147

12. Alvarez G, Coiera E. Interdisciplinary communication: an uncharted source of medical error? J of Crit Care 2006; 21: 236–242

13. Rothschild JM, Landrigan CP, Cronin JW, Kaushal R, Lockley SW, Burdick E et al. The critical care safety study: the incidence and nature of adverse events and serious medical errors in intensive care. CCM 2005; 33: 1694–1700

14. Kaldjian LC, Jones EW, Wu BJ et al. reporting medical errors to improve patient safety. A survey of physicians inteaching hospitals. Arch Intern Med 2008; 168:40–46

15. Kaldjian LC, Jones EW, Wu BJ et al. Disclosing medical errors to patients: attitudes and practices of physicians and trainees. JGIM 2007; 22:988–996

16. Vincent C, Young M, Phillips A. Why do people sue doctors? A study of patients and relatives taking legal action. Lancet 1994; 343: 1609–1613

17. Gallagher TH, Waterman AD, Ebers AG et al. Patients' and physicians attitudes regarding disclosure of medical errors. JAMA 2003; 289:1001–1007

18. Kadjian LC, Jones EW, Rosenthal GE et al. An emperically derived taxonomy of factors affecting physicians' willingness to disclose medical errors. J Gen Intern Med 2006; 21:942–948

19. Sanghera IS, Franklin BD, Dhillon S. The attitudes and beliefs of healthcare professionals on the causes and reporting of medication errors in a UK intensive care unit. Anaesthesia 2007;62: 53–61

20. Stokes SL, Wu AW, Pronovost PJ. Ethical and practical aspects of disclosing adverse events in the emergency department Emerg Med Clin of N Am 2006; 24: 703–714

21. Vincent JL. Information in the ICU: are we being honest with our patients? The results of a European questionnaire. Int Care Med 1998; 24: 1251–1256

22. Gallagher TH, Garbutt JM, Waterman AD et al. Choosing your words carefully: how physicians would disclose harmful medical errors to patients. Arch Intern Med 2006; 166:1585–1593

23. Loren DJ, Klein EJ, Garbutt J, Krauss MJ, Fraser V, Dunagan C et al. Medical error disclosure among pediatricians, choosing carefully what we might say to parents. Arch Pediatr Adolesc Med 2008; 162: 922–927

24. American College of Physicians. Ethics manual. Ann Intern Med 1998; 128: 576–594

25. Joint Commission on the accreditation of Health care organizations. Standard 2001

26. Mazor KM, Simon SR, Yood RA, Martinson BC, Gunther MJ, Reed GW et al. Health plan members' views about disclosure of medical errors. Ann of Int Med 2004; 140:409–418

27. Manser T, Staender S. Aftermath of an adverse event: supporting health care professionals to meet patient expectations through open disclosure. Acta Anaesth Scand 2005;49: 728–734

28. Iedema R, Sorensen R, Manias E, et al. Patients' and family members' experiences of open disclosure following advese events. Int J Qual Health Care 2008; 20:421–432

29. Reader TW, Flin R, Cuthbertson BH. Communication skills and error in the intensive care unit. Curr Op in Crit Care 2007; 13: 732–736

30. Baile WF, Buckman R, Lenzi R. SPIKES – A six step protocol for delivering bad news: application to the patient with cancer. Oncologist 2000; 5: 302–311

D. Structure and processes

Antoine Pronovost and Gordon D. Rubenfeld

Quality in critical care

Quality is an elusive term to define, and yet most clinicians think they can recognise it. Whether we define quality as suitability for purpose, absence of defects, or conformity to specifications, we all strive in our daily encounters to deliver quality care. A number of approaches used to define, measure, and improve quality will be discussed herein.

Models of quality

The Donabedian model has been used to describe quality in three domains: structure, process and outcome [1]. To use a service-related analogy, a well-known restaurant rating guide measures quality along 3 domains: décor, service, and food, which, to some degree, parallel the Donabedian model. As in healthcare, the measured domains of restaurant quality do not always move together. It is easy to imagine a restaurant with outstanding food and very poor service. Whether or not such a restaurant is deemed "high quality" or not depends, to some degree, on what the consumer is looking for. The same is true in the domains of quality measurement in healthcare.

The National Quality Measures Clearinghouse [2] has further refined the definition of the relevant five domains (see Tab. 1). While the first three NQMC categories are similar to the

Tab. 1 The National Quality Measures Clearinghouse five domains of quality

Structure of care	A feature of a healthcare organisation or clinician relevant to its capacity to provide health care
Process of care	Healthcare service provided to, on behalf of, or by a patient appropriately based on scientific evidence of efficacy or effectiveness
Outcome of care	Health state of a patient resulting from healthcare
Experience of care	Patient's or enrollee's report concerning observations of and participation in healthcare
Access to care	Patient's or enrollee's attainment of timely and appropriate healthcare

Donabedian model, it is interesting to note the appearance of two distinct domains. First, the experience of care is specifically distinguished from outcomes of care as its own domain, highlighting the importance of patient perceptions.

Likewise, access to care reflects the importance of timing in the provision of healthcare, and highlights the operational importance of meeting peak demands for key healthcare services. Thus quality does not apply exclusively to those patients already within the system, but also those seeking to access it.

Structure measures of quality in critical care

Material resources can help define the structure of an intensive care unit (ICU). These might include specific equipment that is not generally available in most other parts of the hospital, such as ventilators and invasive monitoring devices. However, given the implicit difficulty in defining an ICU, it is no surprise that a vast spectrum of structural definitions exists: In some cases, long-term weaning institutions and step-up units are included in the definition. Attempts to define the structure of the ICU through surveys of practice have resulted in heterogeneous results [3, 4, 5]. Some consensus exists on the guidelines and recommendations around ICU structure, but in the absence of compelling evidence, these are based mostly on expert opinion [6, 7]. Clinicians generally agree that the physical structure impacts the process of care, but the magnitude and nature of this impact is difficult to define, and is seldom measured. However, one retrospective study on the impact of decanting the ICU to a temporary location during renovation indicated worsening outcomes during decanting [8]. Furthermore, quality indicators worsened as decanting continued, suggesting that they were not simply the result of a physical move to a new location, but reflected the staff's decreasing ability to compensate for suboptimal workspace over time.

Human resources should also be aligned with goals of critical care, and their organisation falls under the umbrella of structure. Based on current evidence, a closed, intensivist-led model is generally acknowledged to provide improved outcomes [9, 10, 11], at reduced costs [12]. While most of the literature supports the benefits of in-tensivist staffing, a recent study concluded that this model increased mortality [65]. However, this study was limited by a number of factors [13], most important of which was that the model studied "care by an intensivist", not care in an "intensivist-led ICU". Given the preponderance of evidence in favour of intensivist-led ICUs, it is unlikely that a single study will dramatically alter the general consensus on the benefits of this model. However, the excellent performance of some units that are not intensivist-led suggests that these units have identified alternative strategies to deliver high-quality care that should be explored [13].

Process measures of quality in critical care

Process measures are particularly useful when specific interventions are known to improve patient care in a robust and quantifiable manner. Unfortunately, even for conditions such as sepsis and ARDS for which there are established guidelines, the number of supported interventions is very limited and still debatable in some cases [14]. Recent conflicting results from confirmatory trials will make it even more difficult for intensivists to adopt specific process measures as markers of quality of care [15].

There is still, however, strong reason to support monitoring processes of care. The first is the well-recognised Hawthorne effect, which suggests that performance improves under monitoring. Named after a process improvement intervention at a Western Electric Company plant in Hawthorne, Illinois, this phenomenon generally credits change during observation to the observation itself rather than any specific intervention [16]. A number of studies indicate that performance of medical professionals improves under conditions of change and observation [17, 18], even if the cause of these effects is not always understood, nor the magnitude predicted.

The second reason to consider process measures is that they can help focus improvement on *continuity* of care, and highlight the importance of each link in the chain of care by providing clinicians with actionable behaviours. In one example, a communication tool was used to structure the format of daily rounds in order to specifically address issues relevant to patient care plans [19].

This resulted in a significant improvement in awareness of daily goals by nurses and residents (from 10 to 90%), and a decrease in patients' average length of stay from 2.2 to 1.1 days. While the study was not powered to capture mortality improvement, the decreased length of stay suggests that better communication did have an impact on patient care. Such an approach has promoted use of a checklist in the ICU, and the idea is garnering momentum throughout medicine [20]. None of the other domains of quality provide frontline clinicians with specific activities to perform in the same way as process measures of care.

Outcome measures of quality in critical care

Patient-centred outcomes may be the ultimate quality measure in medicine. Mortality and health-related quality of life are fundamentally the markers of quality that patients and payers will value. Almost by definition, high-quality medical care is care that will result in improved patient outcomes. Mortality, or the probability of death measured at a fixed point, is the most common outcome variable in critical care. Usually, this is measured at ICU discharge, hospital discharge, or at a fixed number of days after ICU admission. Endpoints close to ICU admission (7-day mortality, for example) are most likely to detect the effect of critical care but are not clinically significant [21]. Measuring mortality 5 years after critical illness would arguably be more clinically relevant, but might miss important effects of critical care that would be washed out by 5 years. Recent evidence has focused on the effects of critical illness on long-term survival and quality of life, however, there is scanty evidence linking specific therapies in the ICU with these outcomes [22].

There are several limitations to using outcomes to measure the performance of intensive care. The use of risk-adjusted mortality remains a key component in attempts to define, report, and improve quality of care [23, 24]. Risk adjustment is designed to address the problem of confounding, that is, centres with sicker patients will have worse outcomes and appear to deliver worse care. By adjusting for severity of illness in a multivariate model, the baseline risk of death is mathematically equalised between institutions. The

remaining differences in outcome are attributed to differences in structure and process of care. This is often expressed as a standardised mortality ratio (SMR) – the ratio of observed deaths to the number of deaths predicted by the risk adjustment model.

Unfortunately, there is now an extensive body of literature that demonstrates that risk-adjusted outcome is neither a reliable nor a valid technique for identifying high or poor quality hospitals because of residual confounding, bias due to referral, upcoding of severity, and chance [25, 26, 27, 28, 29]. These limitations are poorly recognised, as evidenced by a recent, widely publicised attempt to identify the "100 Top Hospitals" and their ICUs using risk-adjusted outcomes based on administrative (non-physiologic) data from the Medicare Provider Analysis and Review database [30] and from the Joint Commission on Accreditation of Healthcare Organisations' (JCAHO) recent decision to add risk-adjusted length of stay and mortality to the ICU core measures of quality of care.

Another limitation to outcome measures is that they are usually limited to mortality and, perhaps, length of stay. There are, of course, many other outcomes that matter to patients, their families, and clinicians. Although instruments exist to assess a variety of other outcomes, they are not measured routinely, are not captured by standard electronic databases, and are more difficult to assess than simple measures like mortality and length of stay. These include medical error rates, nosocomial infections, patient and family satisfaction, provider burnout, quality of dying and death, and long-term health-related quality of life [31, 32, 22].

Although there are clear benefits to feeding back process and outcome data to individually motivated institutions, the promise of using this information as a tool to improve healthcare quality by informing marketplace decisions has not been fully realised [33]. Between 1991 and 1997, all 30 non-federal hospitals in greater metropolitan Cleveland participated in the Cleveland Health Quality Choice (CHQC) programme. Every 6 months, models were used to analyse whether participating hospitals' observed in-hospital mortality rates were greater or less than expected and these results were distributed in a public report. While there was a trend over a 7-year period for hospitals with poor risk-adjusted outcomes to lose market share, this effect was not statistically or clinically significant [34]. Therefore, the benefit of feeding back outcome data to hospitals does not seem to be mediated by changes in market share. In addition to pointing out the lack of evidence supporting the claim that public distribution of quality data improves care, a recent review raised the possibility of unintended negative consequences from reporting quality measures [35]. These included shifting of high-risk patients to adjacent healthcare systems that are not being assessed and denial of care to patients perceived at high risk for bad outcomes. An important question remains unresolved: If risk-adjusted quality measures are useful to catalyse local quality improvement measures, is their effectiveness in this role linked to making the quality data public?

Quality from a business perspective

A number of concepts can readily be adopted from well-established business literature surrounding quality. Arguably the most important is defining quality as the suitability for purpose as defined by the customer. There are some limitations to applying strict business notions of quality to healthcare. For example, the payer is rarely the consumer of healthcare and this complicates targeting of the correct customer. In addition, quality factors that customers may be most willing to pay for may be the least medically beneficial to them as demonstrated by the success of direct-to-consumer pharmaceutical marketing.

Quality improvement

While quality improvement has advanced over the last 4 decades, a number of methodologies are new to the healthcare setting. A number of these hold particular potential because they better embrace the multi-disciplinary practice that is at the core of quality in critical care. Thus, the focus has shifted from a single intervention to the entire process of care. Two tools readily deployed in the business setting will be discussed here: theory of constraints (TOC) and Lean Operations.

Theory of constraints

Dr. Eliyahu Goldratt originally developed the theory of constraints (TOC), and while it is consistent with other operation management frameworks such as just-in-time delivery and the critical path method [36], its distinguishing features are flexibility and its intuitive character (once central concepts are understood). The first step in applying TOC is to identify "the goal", which is usually to maximise the profitability of a private firm. Healthcare, by contrast, must generally look to softer measures of success, but most stakeholders can agree that the goal is to maximise healthcare delivery for a given set of resources. TOC prescribes five steps to frame the process [37]:

1. Identify the constraint: The constraint is also commonly referred to as the bottleneck because it is the resource that determines the rate-limiting step for the entire process chain.
2. Decide how to exploit the constraint: Maximise bottleneck productivity, and minimise bottleneck waste.
3. Subordinate all other processes to the constraint: Adapt other processes to ensure that the bottleneck is never idle, because an hour lost at the bottleneck is an hour lost *for the entire system*.
4. Elevate the constraint: Increase the capacity of the bottleneck. Costs generally limit this option because the bottleneck should be the most expensive resource.
5. If, as a result of these steps, the constraint has moved, return to Step 1.

TOC is a useful tool because it focuses users on global measures which are appropriate for a system that depends on the efficient integration of an entire chain of activities: Managers are encouraged to ignore local optima which generally drive decisions in "silo" environments.

Additionally, TOC helps to identify the negative effects of batching. Batching occurs when downstream processes sit idle until a "batch" is ready. For example, in a pastry shop where a cake decorator is the bottleneck, he might wait for a batch of 12 cakes, only to be overwhelmed by the workload when it is finally ready. One option would be to create a buffer to keep the decorator busy at all times, but this would increase inventory and negatively impact cake freshness. Another, preferable option would be to reduce the number of items in a batch, ideally to a single cake. There are many examples of batching within hospitals, including:

- porters waiting for multiple items before they transport them,
- pharmacists preparing similar medications together, or
- physicians writing multiple orders at once.

All of these can have unintended, negative consequences, which can be identified and corrected with TOC.

Furthermore, TOC sensitises practitioners to the importance of variability in conjunction with dependent events. Variability refers to distribution around a mean (standard deviation is a familiar measure of this dispersion). In a system with dependent events (where one step cannot be competed before its predecessor), excess variability will eventually result in an idle bottleneck. Reducing variability is critical to efficiency. For example, most ICUs do not target 100 % occupancy because this would eliminate their ability to accommodate peak demand. The degree to which a unit can operate close to maximal capacity is directly proportional to the degree to which it can *limit* variability. Units that manage variability by smoothing elective surgery admissions on a daily or hourly basis can operate much closer to full capacity [38, 39], and likely experience reduced nursing stress and increased patient safety [40].

Lean operations

Lean principles have been applied to many different industries, and are highly appropriate to healthcare. Lean, despite its name, is not geared at reducing workforce numbers [41] because it requires frontline worker buy-in to succeed: These employees best comprehend the limitations of the workspace, and have the best improvement ideas. If workers are disengaged or threatened, the project will fail.

Additionally, Lean takes the patient perspective, in order to consider the series of interactions involved in patient care. Value-stream mapping refers to the use of simple symbols to represent sequential steps in a process, and it is very effective in identifying and reducing points of complexity (or handover) in patient care. Mayo's Luther-Midelfort hospital reports that 56 % of its medication errors occur at such "interfaces of care" [40].

Furthermore, Lean utilises the concept of value-added activity. Activities such as transport, waiting, rework, and inspection are generally classified as non-value added (NVA). Processes can be improved by reducing or eliminating these activities. When determining value-added vs. NVA work, the Lean approach proposes that we take the perspective of the customer (the patient in the case of healthcare), to ask whether that individual would be willing to pay out of pocket for an activity. For example, a patient would probably be willing to pay for physical examination and diagnostic tests to allow caregivers to deliver appropriate care. However, patients would probably not want to pay for redundant testing or correction of medical errors. Such a perspective helps focus on which activities promote quality of care.

Standardisation

Lean principles indicate that unnecessary variation in practice causes uncertainty, and increases error. The goal of standardisation is to find the current single best "way to safely complete an activity with the proper outcome and the highest quality" [41]. While clinicians routinely argue that they require some breadth of clinical scope in order to properly address the individual nature of their patient, it is clear that practice types often vary unnecessarily [42]. However, there is evidence of costly and non-beneficial variation in critical care practice between individual physicians [43]. Wennberg identified three different types of unwarranted variation in the medical setting: variations in effective care and patient safety, variations in preference sensitive care, and variations in supply sensitive care [44]. Variations in effective care and patient safety refer to those that occur in the face of established support for one therapy with very little downside to its application. In such cases, failure to treat according to "standard" represents an under-use. Variation in preference-sensitive care refers to areas where *patient* preference should drive the decision; unfortunately geographic patterns suggest that it is the clinicians who drive discrepancies [44]. Finally, variations in supply-sensitive care are revealed by different rates of consumption of healthcare by people who have the same chronic condition, but live in different geographic areas. This is perplexing not only because it is inconsistent with medical evidence and theory, but also because it appears in conflict with equity.

While it might not always be possible to standardise the outcome, the growing support for checklists [19, 20] indicates that it is worth considering standardising the process by which major components of their care are delivered. Evidence indicates that checklists are effective as a behaviour change tool in specific circumstances, but only if they are completed before the patient care process occurs. One can consider the example of a young driver learning to change lanes. Her checklist might include:

1. check mirrors,
2. signal,
3. check blind spots, and
4. steer smoothly to the new lane.

As the driver becomes more accustomed to this activity, the checklist would likely become obsolete. However, it would be inappropriate for the young driver to change lanes and subsequently pull over to physically check off the boxes on the list. Firstly, this step would occur too late to be of any benefit, and secondly, it would be too onerous to warrant adoption. Thus, to prevent being

victims of their own success, checklists in medicine must be integrated into the processes at the right time and place to benefit outcome, and integrated into medical records in the right way to avoid wasted effort.

Quality improvement implementation strategies

Quality improvement implementation in healthcare exists under a variety of synonyms including process improvement, knowledge translation, guideline implementation, and implementation science. Ultimately, the goal of all of these interventions is to improve the quality of care and to reduce the gap between knowledge and practice. There is an extensive literature on the effectiveness of various strategies to accomplish these goals (see Tab. 2). Least effective is probably the most widely used, namely, traditional medical education through lectures and written materials. Audit and feedback via benchmarking has been used in a number of industries to identify best practices and facilitate their dissemination. Applying established benchmarks to ICU processes is particularly attractive because processes are notoriously difficult to identify and promote in the ICU. Zimmerman applied benchmarking to identify high-performing ICUs by utilisation of resources, and matching to patient needs [45]. This allows for the identification of policies and practices such as step-down units that better fa-

Tab. 2   Quality improvement implementation strategies

	Description
Bundles	Packaging established and related interventions together in order to facilitate retention and implementation
Protocols	Structured orders that allow non-physician clinicians to titrate therapies according to specified criteria
Checklists	Reminder list to be reviewed prior to a procedure or on daily rounds
Audit and feedback	Periodic assessment and distribution of quality measures to clinical team
Automatic functions	Computerised decision-making or error checking
Social marketing	Using advertising tools (posters, emails) to disseminate information and provide encouragement to change behaviour
Thought leaders and academic detailing	Engaging high-impact, well-respected individuals to influence their peers

cilitate the matching of patient needs to deployed resources. However, broader attempts to benchmark clinically relevant interventions such as ventilator-associated pneumonia bundles have been met with limited success because of difficulties standardising and quantifying the benefit of interventions [46]. It is crucial that the recipients of feedback data buy in to the relevance and accuracy of the data. The pharmaceutical industry is tremendously effective at changing clinical behaviour through various marketing techniques. These techniques have been adapted for less mercenary purposes through social marketing and academic detailing to influence clinical behaviour.

The evidence base supporting the efficacy or cost-effectiveness of quality improvement in healthcare is not overwhelming. The most thorough review of implementation strategies [47] concluded that "[t]here is an imperfect evidence base to support decisions about which guideline dissemination and implementation strategies are likely to be efficient under different circumstances. Decision-makers need to use considerable judgement about how best to use the limited resources they have for clinical governance and related activities to maximise population benefits." There is even less evidence to guide quality improvement strategies in the evidence-challenged, multi-disciplinary, and heterogeneous clinical population of critical care.

Study designs to evaluate quality improvement

Quasi-experimental designs are often used in quality improvement because of their greater flexibility than a traditional randomised controlled trial (see Tab. 3). More importantly, their advantages and disadvantages should be described to support their appropriate use. Quasi-experimental designs have been applied to many fields in social sciences including education, criminology, and psychology [48]. However, these techniques are being applied with increasing frequency to critical care as a focus emerges for QI and operational effectiveness.

Quasi-experimental designs include:

- observational studies where no intervention takes place,
- time series which help to identify trends in a population,
- uncontrolled before-and-after trials which compare results before and after a QI intervention, as well as
- controlled before-and-after studies which provide a comparison arm (though not as rigorous a control as provided by an RCT).

Recent examples of quasi-experimental designs in critical care include a number of high-profile studies [20, 49, 50, 51, 52].

Quasi-experimental designs are best suited to a number of different settings. The first is where randomisation at the patient level is impossible

Tab. 3   Study design alternatives for evaluating implementation strategies

Study design	Method
Observational	Qualitative and quantitative description of care
Time series	Continuous evaluation over time to detect trends – the intervention may be continuous or intermittent
Uncontrolled before-after	Simple comparison between patients cared for during specified periods before and after an intervention
Controlled before-after	Attempt to control for secular changes in patient population by identifying similar patients who are not exposed to the implementation strategy
Cross-sectional	Comparing care at a number of different sites using different implementation strategies
Patient randomised trials	Randomising individual patients to different implementation strategies
Cluster randomised trials	Entire ICUs, clinics, physician practices, or hospitals are randomised to different implementation strategies

because the intervention is targeted instead at a system. The second is where patient-level randomisation is challenging because the patient-level intervention is more easily implemented and evaluated in a group. Additionally, quasi-experimental designs have other advantages over an RCT including simpler administration and decreased costs. Finally, they prevent contamination of the control arm, and improve buy-in where ethical concerns exist around patient level randomisation.

Quasi-experimental designs are now more frequently utilised in the critical care literature. In fact, all of the data we have on the structure of critical care including intensivist staffing, volume targets for mechanically ventilated patients, and nursing ratios come from quasi-experimental and observational data [10]. In one particular example, the MERIT study adopted cluster randomisation because it would have been impossible not to contaminate the control arm of a trial evaluating outreach teams [53]. Understandably, when implementation of complex guidelines requires training of the entire ICU staff, it is preferable to adopt a cluster-randomised structure in order to avoid contamination of the control arm [54].

In general, quasi-experimental designs will require some form of multivariate analysis, and must account for clustering. Careful attention must be paid to how cases will be clustered (by hospital, by unit, by physician, by nurse) or statistical analysis will be weakened (likely resulting in an erroneously low p value). Sample size and power are related to both the number of clusters and the number of patients. One paper elegantly demonstrated that the number of patients recruited must increase significantly as the cluster size increases [55]. Thus the design effect (ratio of the total number of subjects required using cluster randomisation to that required with simple randomisation) increases with cluster size. In fact, as cluster size increases, most of the patient variation occurs between clusters, while patients within a cluster display increased intracluster correlation. This helps explain why cluster RCTs will always require a greater number of patients for a given outcome.

A number of limitations are particularly important for quasi-experimental designs. The first is the impact of secular (non-periodic) trends in the study population, and in such cases time is of-

ten the greatest confounder. The second is the potential for regression to the mean. Regression to the mean is often exemplified by the "sports cover jinx" whereby athletes portrayed on the cover of a publication are "bound" to see their performance suffer in the following year. The statistical explanation for this observation is that the athletes likely had an exceptional year in order to warrant attention, and that the performance in the following year will be much closer to their average, thus representing a relative decline. Likewise, outliers are likely to move towards their mean performance: Low performers will improve and high performers will decline. Additionally, quasi-experimental designs hold the potential for observation bias, as they are generally unblinded. This results in the potential for differential data collection, between pre- and post-intervention observations.

Finally and perhaps most importantly, there is the potential for residual confounding. If unidentified variables are closely correlated with the outcome of interest, the intervention might erroneously be thought to have changed the outcome. Thus, in quasi-experimental designs, it is crucial to look carefully at what other factors may have influenced the outcome. In one study analysing the impact of booster seat promotion in a number of communities, analysis considered the overall effectiveness of the intervention using a generalised linear mixed model, adjusting for child level variables (age, sex), car level variables (driver sex, driver seat belt use), and incorporating the effects of clustering at the levels of car, site, and community [56].

Quasi-experimental designs present some difficulties with respect to generalisability. First, single-centre before-after studies are particularly difficult to generalise, owing to the vast amount of inter-centre variability. Second, studies that simply observe standard care lack an explicit intervention, and further raise the difficulty of applying findings to another centre. Furthermore, there is the potential for undescribed co-interventions, which may be responsible for the result, and therefore represent a powerful example of residual confounding. These factors in combination make it very difficult to draw a causal link between the intervention and the outcome, because quasi-experimental designs lack the mechanistic link to identify *what* worked. For example, one observational study of ventilatory outcomes in an

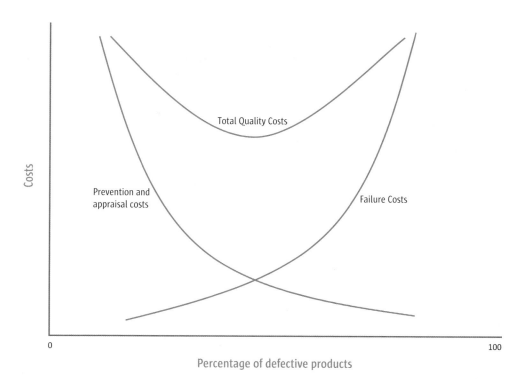

Fig. 1   The traditional perspective on product quality suggests that total costs are minimised at the point where quality improvement costs are offset by a greater reduction in failure costs [modified from Hilton, Managerial Accounting, 6th edition, McGraw-Hill, 2005].

ICU claimed $3 million savings by implementing an outcomes manager nurse, but it was not clear which of the multiple interventions, including increased tracheotomy rate, was the cause of this improvement [57].

Quasi-experimental designs are thus best applied to hypothesis generation, proof of effectiveness, and implementation of research, *but not to proof of efficacy* except in cases where randomisation is impossible. For example, while a time series quality improvement study to evaluate the effectiveness of an intervention to increase use of activated protein C for appropriate patients with septic shock is reasonable, this study design is inappropriate for initial testing of drug efficacy.

Cost of quality

Investing in quality improvement involves an initial higher cost, but some proportion of this in-

vestment is returned through a combination of reduced error, improved efficiency, or higher customer willingness-to-pay. Significant disagreement exists over the curve of investment in quality: Some evidence supports diminishing returns on investments, while other proponents of quality support ever-improving outcome measures. The traditional perspective on quality improvement suggests that investment in quality will decrease total costs at least initially, as costs of failure are reduced [58] (see Fig. 1). More recently, experts have argued that improvement in quality will *always* reduce costs because they will reduce both "costs of quality" such as inspection (which would not be necessary if quality was always within specification), and "costs of poor quality" such as re-work [59] (see Fig. 2). However, within healthcare, it has been difficult to identify one single appropriate methodology to calculate QI costs, thus rendering any cost-effectiveness analysis difficult [60].

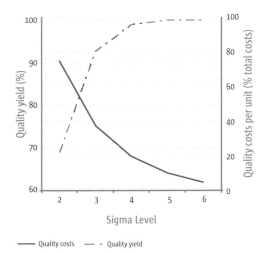

Sigma Level

—— Quality costs   — - Quality yield

Fig. 2   Lean methodology suggests that as quality im-
proves, avoidable costs are reduced dramatically
even when quality is already high [data from
Caldwell C, Brexler J, Gillem T. Lean-Six Sigma for
Healthcare: A Senior Leader Guide to Improving
Cost and Throuput. Wilwaukee (WI): ASQ Quality
Press; 2005].

Quality improvement and ethics

Because quality improvement is often pursued
through methodology that is distinctly different
from traditional research, it is on occasion unclear to what degree ethics boards should be involved, or whether informed consent is necessary
for subject participation.

Some have indicated that the *intent* to publish
might help distinguish QI from research, and
thus QI should be exempt from consent when it
is not intended for publication. While this might
provide a convenient heuristic, such reasoning is
not robust enough to meet the needs of the situation [61]. Firstly, intent can change: data that
was analysed with no intention of publication
can be submitted because of interesting findings,
thereby making any determination of original
intent very difficult. Secondly, many QI initiatives are worthy of publication from the outset,
which would essentially classify any such study
as research.

There are compelling reasons to allow QI to
occur in some cases without ethics board involvement; for example, the use of an anonymous da-

tabase to collect clinical outcomes or implementation of reminders to increase handwashing. By
contrast, plans to use a new patient monitoring
device, such as jugular venous bulb oxygen monitoring, would indeed constitute research, even
if presented as "simply an elevation of the new
standard of care", and would definitely warrant
consent. Between these examples lie a number
of more ambiguous scenarios which should be
reviewed by an ethics board.

In determining what QI does constitute research, the Johns Hopkins study of catheter-related bloodstream infections provides an excellent example of this blurry distinction [62]. In this
case, the local institutional review board (IRB)
classified the study as exempt from review and
waived the need for informed consent. However,
after publication of the results, a complaint was
filed with the Office for Human Research Protec-
tions, which subsequently found that the study
was *not* exempt because it required an intervention (although very low-risk, and consistent with
the standard of care), and was not limited to "only
the analysis of de-identified data already collected for medical care". In retrospect, it was recommended that a more appropriate solution would
have been for the study to be reviewed and expedit-
ed by the IRB chair alone because its intervention
exposed participants to only minimal risk [60].

One of the dangers of making the burden of
QI research too onerous is that either research
will decrease [63], or QI will be permitted only
if the results are not measured – an absurd and
unscientific proposition. "Unintentionally, these
requirements may lead those planning or conducting such initiatives to avoid the designation
of 'research' by producing knowledge that is of
limited applicability." [61]

QI, by its nature and methodology, seeks to
alter the system. It is positioned at the interface
between the clinician, making local patient decisions, and the manager, making global decisions for the hospital. This provides an inherent tension between the need for fidelity to the
patient, and stewardship for the hospital [64]. Clinicians engaged in these activities should have
a thorough understanding of the relevant definitions of minimal risk, protected health information, and the criteria for waived consent. When
engaged in quality improvement exercises, ethics
review is always a conservative option.

Conclusion

Defining and measuring quality is challenging but highly valuable in the ICU setting. While quality care will continue to rely on traditional RCTs to provide evidence of benefit at the individual patient level, it is likely that other modalities will play a greater role in quality improvement over the next decade as we attempt to improve the system. These include established operational methodologies such as Theory of Constraints and Lean Operations. They also include the careful selection and application of quasi-experimental designs to appropriate questions. Ethical concerns apply to QI just as in any research, and the nature of QI presents specific challenges. Some criteria can be applied to determine whether IRB approval is necessary, or whether waived consent might be appropriate, but there is still a great degree of debate over these topics as relates to QI in critical care.

The authors

Antoine Pronovost, MD, MBA, FRCPC[1]
Gordon D. Rubenfeld, MD, MSc[2]
[1]Anaesthesia and Critical Care | St Michael's Hospital | Department of Anaesthesia | University of Toronto | Toronto, Canada
[2]Program in Trauma, Emergency, and Critical Care | Sunnybrook Health Sciences Centre | Interdepartmental Division of Critical Care | Department of Medicine | University of Toronto | Toronto, Canada

Address for correspondence
Antoine Pronovost
Department of Anaesthesia
St Michael's Hospital
30 Bond Street
Toronto, Ontario, Canada
M5B IW8
E-mail: pronovosta@smh.toronto.on.ca

References

1. Donabedian A. The quality of care. How can it be assessed? JAMA 1988;260(12):1743–1748.
2. http://www.qualitymeasures.ahrq.gov/resources/glossary.aspx
3. Groeger JS, Strosberg MA, Halpern NA, Raphaely RC, Kaye WE, Guntupalli KK et a. Descriptive analysis of critical care units in the United States. Crit Care Med 1992;20(6):846–63.
4. Future Workforce Needs in Pulmonary and Critical Care Medicine. Cambridge: Abt Associates; 1998.
5. Vincent JL, Suter P, Bihari D, Bruining H. Organization of intensive care units in Europe: lessons from the EPIC study. Intensive Care Med 1997;23(11):1181–4.
6. Haupt MT, Bekes CE, Brilli RJ, Carl LC, Gray AW, Jastremski MS. Critical care services and personnel: recommendations based on a system of categorization into two levels of care. Crit Care Med 1999;27(2):422–6.
7. Standards of evidence for the safety and effectiveness of critical care monitoring devices and related interventions. Coalition for Critical Care Excellence: Consensus Conference on Physiologic Monitoring Devices. Crit Care Med 1995;23(10):1756–63.
8. Flaatten H. Effects of a major structural change to the intensive care unit on the quality and outcome after intensive care. Quality and Safety in Health Care 2005;14:270–2.
9. Chang SY. Multz AS. Hall JB. Critical care organization. Crit Care Clin 2005 Jan;21(1):43–53.
10. Pronovost PJ, Angus DC, Dorman T, Robinson KA, Dremsizov TT, Young TL. Physician staffing patterns and clinical outcomes in critically ill patients: a systematic review. JAMA 2002;288:2151–62.
11. Young MP, Birkmeyer JD. Potential reduction in mortality rates using an intensivist model to manage intensive care units. Eff Clin Pract 2000;3:284–9.
12. Pronovost PJ, Needham DM, Waters H, Birkmeyer CM, Calinawan JR, Birkmeyer JD. Intensive care unit physician staffing: Financial modeling of the Leapfrog standard. Crit Care Med 2006;34(3 Suppl):S18–24.
13. Rubenfeld GD, Angus DC. Are Intensivists Safe? Ann Intern Med 2008;148:877–9.
14. Eichacker PQ, Gerstenberger EP, Banks SM, Cui X, Natanson C. Meta-analysis of acute lung injury and acute respiratory distress syndrome trials testing low tidal volumes. Am J Respir Crit Care Med 2002 Dec 1;166(11):1510–4.
15. The NICE-SUGAR Study Investigators. Intensive versus Conventional Glucose Control in Critically Ill Patients. NEJM 2009 March 26;360(13):1283–97.
16. Gale, EAM. The Hawthorne studies – a fable for our time? Q J Med 2004;97:439–449.
17. Martin AR, Wolf MA, Thibodeau LA, Dzau V Braunwald E. A trial of two strategies to modify the test-ordering behaviour of medical residents. NEJM 1980;303:1330–6.
18. Multiple Risk Factor Trial Research Group. Multiple Risk Factor Intervention Trial. Risk factor changes and mortality results. JAMA 1982;248:1465–77.
19. Pronovost P, Berenholtz S, Dorman T, Lipsett PA, Simmonds T, Haraden C. Improving Communication in the ICU Using Daily Goals. J Crit Care 2003 Jun;18 (2):71–5.

20. Haynes AB, Weiser TG, Berry WR, Lipsitz SR, Breizat AHS, Dellinger EP, et al. A Surgical Safety Checklist to Reduce Morbidity and Mortality in a Global Population. N Engl J Med 2009 Jan 29;360:491–9.

21. Rubenfeld GD, Angus DC, Pinsky MR, Curtis JR, Connors AF, Jr., Bernard GR. Outcomes research in critical care: Results of the american thoracic society critical care assembly workshop on outcomes research. The members of the outcomes research workshop. Am J Respir Crit Care Med 1999;160:358–367.

22. Angus DC, Carlet J, editors. Surviving intensive care. Berlin: Springer-Verlag; 2002.

23. Hadorn D, Keeler E, Rogers W, Brook R. Assessing the performance of mortality prediction models. Santa Monica, CA: Rand; 1993.

24. Iezzoni LI. Risk adjustment for measuring health care outcomes. Ann Arbor, Mich.: Health Administration Press; 1994.

25. Chassin MR, Hannan EL, DeBuono BA. Benefits and hazards of reporting medical outcomes publicly. NEJM 1996;334:394–8.

26. Escarce JJ, Kelley MA. Admission source to the medical intensive care unit predicts hospital death independent of apache ii score. JAMA 1990;264:2389–94.

27. Park RE, Brook RH, Kosecoff J, Keesey J, Rubenstein L, Keeler E, Kahn KL, Rogers WH, Chassin MR. Explaining variations in hospital death rates. Randomness, severity of illness, quality of care. JAMA 1990;264:484–490.

28. Hofer TP, Hayward RA. Identifying poor-quality hospitals. Can hospital mortality rates detect quality problems for medical diagnoses? Med Care 1996;34:737–753.

29. Thomas JW, Hofer TP. Research evidence on the validity of risk-adjusted mortality rate as a measure of hospital quality of care. Med Care Res Rev 1998;55:371–404.

30. 100 top hospitals(tm): ICU benchmarks for success – 2000. 2003 [cited 2003 Oct 3 2003]. Available from: http://www.100tophospitals.com/studies/icu00/methodology.asp.

31. Heyland DK, Rocker GM, Dodek PM, Kutsogiannis DJ, Konopad E, Cook DJ, Peters S et al.. Family satisfaction with care in the intensive care unit: Results of a multiple center study. Crit Care Med 2002;30:1413–8.

32. Curtis JR, Patrick DL, Engelberg RA, Norris K, Asp C, Byock I. A measure of the quality of dying and death. Initial validation using after-death interviews with family members. J Pain Symptom Manage 2002;24:17–31.

33. Hannan EL, Kilburn H, Jr., Racz M, Shields E, Chassin MR. Improving the outcomes of coronary artery bypass surgery in New York State. JAMA 1994;271:761–6.

34. Baker DW, Einstadter D, Thomas C, Husak S, Gordon NH, Cebul RD. The effect of publicly reporting hospital performance on market share and risk-adjusted mortality at high-mortality hospitals. Med Care 2003;41:729–740.

35. Werner RM, Asch DA. The unintended consequences of publicly reporting quality information. JAMA 2005;293:1239–44.

36. Levy FK, Thompson GL, Wiest JD. The ABCs of the Critical Path Method. Harvard Business Review. 1963.

37. Goldratt E. The Goal. 2nd ed. Great Barrington (MA): North River Press; 1992.

38. McManus ML, Long MC, Cooper A, Litvak E. Theory Accurately Models the Need for Critical Care Resources. Anesthesiology 2004;100:1271–6.

39. McManus ML, Long MC, Cooper A, Mandell J, Berwick DM, Pagano M, Litvak E. Variability in surgical caseload and access to intensive care services. Anesthesiology 2003 Jun;98(6):1491–6.

40. Litvak E, Buerhaus PI, Davidoff F, Long MC, McManus ML, Berwick DM. Managing unnecessary variability in patient demand to reduce nursing stress and improve patient safety. Joint Commission Journal on Quality & Patient Safety. 2005 Jun;31(6):330–8.

41. Graban M. Lean Hospitals. New York: CRC Press; 2009.

42. Morris AH. Iatrogenic Illness: A Call for Decision Support Tools to Reduce Unnecessary Variation Quality and Safety in Health Care 2004;13:80–81.

43. Garland A, Shaman Z, Baron J, Connors AF. Physician-attributable Differences in Intensive Care Unit Costs. Am J Respir Crit Care Med 2006 Sep14;174:1206–10.

44. Wennberg JE. Unwarranted variations in healthcare delivery: implications for academic medical centres. BMJ 2002 October;325(26):961–964.

45. Zimmerman JE, Alzola C, Von Rueden KT. The Use of Benchmarking to Identify Top Performing Critical Care Units: A Preliminary Assessment of Their Policies and Practices. J Crit Care 2003 Jun;18(2): 76–86.

46. Zilberberg MD, Shorr AF, Kollef MH. Implementing quality improvements in the intensive care unit: Ventilator bundle as an example. Crit Care Med 2009;37:305–309.

47. Grimshaw JM, Thomas RE, MacLennan G, Fraser C, Ramsay CR, Vale L et al. Effectiveness and efficiency of guideline dissemination and implementation strategies. Health Technol Assess 2004;8(6):1–72.

48. Campbell DT, Stanley JC. Experimental and Quasi-experimental Designs for Research. New York: Rand McNally and Co; 1963.

49. Pronovost P, Needham D, Berenholtz S, Sinopoli D, Chu H, Cosgrove S et al. An intervention to decrease catheter-related bloodstream infections in the ICU. NEJM 2006 Dec 28;355(26):2725–32.

50. de Smet AM, Kluytmans JA, Cooper BS, Mascini EM, Benus RF, van der Werf TS et al. Decontamination of the digestive tract and oropharynx in ICU patients. NEJM 2009 Jan 1;360(1):20–31.

51. Ferrer R, Artigas A, Levy MM, Blanco J, González-Díaz G, Garnacho-Montero J et al. Improvement in process of care and outcome after a multicenter severe sepsis educational program in Spain. JAMA 2008 May 21;299(19):2294–303.

52. Chan PS, Khalid A, Longmore LS, Berg RA, Kosiborod M, Spertus JA. Hospital-wide code rates and mortality before and after implementation of a rapid response team. JAMA 2008 Dec 3;300(21):2506–13.

53. MERIT study investigators. Introduction of the medical emergency team (MET) system: a cluster-randomised controlled trial. Lancet 2005 June 16;365(9477):2091–7.

54. Martin CM, Doig GS, Heyland DK, Morrison T, Sibbald WJ. Multicentre, cluster-randomized clinical trial of algorithms for critical-care enteral and parenteral therapy (ACCEPT). CMAJ 2004 Jan 20;170(2):197–204.

55. Kerry SM, Bland JM. Sample Size in Cluster Randomization. BMJ 1998;316;549.

56. Ebel BE, Koepsell TD, Bennett EE, Rivara FP. Use of child booster seats in motor vehicles following a community campaign: a controlled trial. JAMA. 2003;289(7):879–884.

57. SM Burns, S Earven, C Fisher, R Lewis, P Merrell. Implementation of an institutional program to improve clinical and financial outcomes of mechanically ventilated patients. CCM 2003 December;31(12):2752–63.

58. Hilton, Managerial Accounting, 6th edition, McGraw-Hill, 2005.

59. Caldwell C, Brexler J, Gillem T. Lean-Six Sigma for Healthcare: A Senior Leader Guide to Improving Cost and Throuput. Wilwaukee (WI): ASQ Quality Press; 2005.

60. Brown SES, Chin MH, Huang ES. Estimating costs of quality improvement for outpatient healthcare organisations: a practical methodology. Qual Saf Health Care 2007;16;248–251.

61. Casarett D, Karlawish JHT, Sugarman J. Determining When Quality Improvement Initiatives Should Be Considered Research: Proposed Criteria and Potential Implications. JAMA 2000;283(17):75–2280.

62. Miller FG, Emmanuel EJ. Quality-Improvement Research and Informed Consent. NEJM 2008;358(8) 765–7.

63. Kass N, Pronovost PF, Sugarman J, Goeschel CA, Lubomski LH, Faden R. Controversy and Quality Improvement: Lingering Questions About Ethics, Oversight, and Patient Safety Research. Jt Comm J Qual Patient Saf 2008 Jun;34(6):349–53.

64. Rie MA, Kofke WA. Nontherapeutic quality improvement: The conflict of organizational ethics and societal rule of law. Crit Care Med 2007; 35(Suppl):S66–84.

65. Levy MM, Rapoport J, Lemeshow S, Chalfin DB, Phillips G, Danis M. Association between Critical Care Physician Management and Patient Mortality in the Intensive Care Unit. Ann Intern Med 2008;148:801–809.

Daniele Poole and Guido Bertolini

Outcome-based benchmarking in the ICU Part I: Statistical tools for the creation and validation of severity scores

Introduction

Benchmark is a term derived from industry that indicates a standard, often established from outside the productive process as the level of excellence to compare with, on which the performance of a company can be measured. Hence, the key aim of benchmarking is to learn and improve through comparison, and possibly competition, with others. In medicine, benchmarking has assumed the meaning of a tool for the continuous improvement of the quality. Several indicators have been proposed as standards for benchmarking, either in terms of process of care or outcome [1, 2]. In the field of critical care medicine severity-of-illness scoring systems, first developed in the late seventies to early eighties, have become rapidly popular and have spread worldwide, becoming the main tool for outcome-based benchmarking of intensive care units (ICUs).

As already stated in 1981 by the APACHE researchers, prognostic models are not designed to assist physicians in making decisions on individual patients, but rather to classify groups of patients on the basis of their severity.[3] Thus, the comparison of observed and score-predicted hospital mortality should, in theory, provide a measure of ICU performance and hence a means for benchmarking.

In the early eighties the APACHE [3] and the SAPS [4] were created by panels of experts who selected and weighed the items which constitute the scores, relying on their personal experience and knowledge. Thereafter, variables selection and weight for prognostic scores, such as the MPM [5–7] and the following versions of the SAPS [8–10] and the APACHE [11–14], were based on multiple logistic regression analysis. Whether these scores were created by experts or developed from cohorts of critically ill patients (ranging from few hundreds scoring systems to several tens of thousands), they all shared the same ambitious objective: to correctly predict hospital mortality, even independently from the setting the score was developed in. In other words, they were meant to become a standard for ICU benchmarking.

Thus, to analyse and discuss the possibilities and the limits of applying the outcome-based benchmarking idea to the intensive care world, it is essential to fully understand the methodological problems related to the development, validation, and exploitation of severity-of-illness scoring systems.

This article has been divided into two parts: The first one regards the description of the statistical methods for the creation and validation of a severity score, perhaps a difficult task for clinicians. In the second part, we discuss the results of validation studies of the most widely used severity scores, trying to analyse their intrinsic limits and to better spot their field of application.

The multivariate logistic regression model

Bivariate analysis evaluates the correlation existing between two variables (sometimes it is improperly called univariate analysis), but it is scarcely useful to make predictions when many factors influence the outcome, particularly when some of them are related to each other. In this case multivariable analysis is the statistical tool of choice, as has been nicely explained in an article by M.H. Katz [15]. To give an example the author reports the results of research that investigated the relation between periodontal disease and coronary heart disease [16]. Bivariate analysis showed that patients affected by periodontitis had a significantly increased risk of coronary heart disease, which suggested that risk factors for coronary heart disease were associated with periodontal disease. Actually, when important predictors of coronary disease (such as demographics, socioeconomic status, and clinical risk factors) were accounted for by means of multivariate analysis, periodontal disease turned out not to be significantly related to the outcome. Thus, multivariate analysis estimates the influence on outcome of the potential predictors, one related to the other.

An important feature of multivariate analysis is that when two or more predictors are related to each other, the model is able to assess the true weight of each variable. For example, suppose we want to investigate the influence of diabetes and hypertension on the occurrence of myocardial infarction. A question may well be raised: Is diabetes *per se* able to increase the probability of myocardial infarction, or is this association indirectly explained by the presence of more patients with hypertension among diabetics than in non-diabetics? Multivariate analysis accounts for the predictive weight of the portion of hypertension yielded by diabetes, allowing the estimation of the net weight of the latter.

Conveniently, we have at our disposal statistical models to perform multivariate analysis whatever the dependent variable. Specifically, the logistic regression model is used when dealing with a dichotomous (or binary) outcome (e.g.

disease yes or no, dead or alive, etc.) and consequently it has been widely adopted to build severity scores. Suppose we are dealing with a binary outcome (dependent variable, Y), that yields either a positive (1) or a negative (0) result, and a single predictor (independent variable, X) with values that range from 1 to 10 (see Tab. 1). For each value of the predictor we will have some patients who experience outcome 1 (e.g. hospital mortality) and others outcome 0 (alive at hospital discharge), we can thus calculate the observed frequencies of outcome 1 for each value of the predictor (fifth column of Table 1).

We can then describe the relation between the independent and dependent variables with the *logistic function*:

$$(1)\ P_{Y|X} = \exp^{(\beta_0 + \beta_1 X_1)} / (1 + \exp^{(\beta_0 + \beta_1 X_1)})$$

Where $P_{Y|X}$ is the probability of Y given the corresponding value of X (sixth column in Table 1), β_0 and β_1 are the intercept and the slope of the *logistic regression equation* we use to correlate Y and X. In our example, running the logistic regression on our data the best estimation of the coefficients is $\beta_0 = -2.990$ and $\beta_1 = 0.653$. We can then estimate the probabilities of Y for each value of X with these coefficients. In Figure 1 the observed frequencies of Y (in black) and those calculated through the logistic function (in grey), are plotted against X. It is clear how the grey line "fits" the frequencies of the observed values.

When multiple independent variables are considered the equation becomes:

$$(2)\ P_{Y|X1,X2,...Xn} = \exp^{(\beta_0 + \beta_1 X_1 + \beta_2 X_2 + ... + \beta_n X_n)} /$$
$$(1 + \exp^{(\beta_0 + \beta_1 X_1 + \beta_2 X_2 + ... + \beta_n X_n)})$$

where $(\beta_0 + \beta_1 X_1 + \beta_2 X_2 + ... + \beta_n X_n)$ is called the logit.

Multivariate regression models are a powerful tool to determine an outcome; the more causal factors are known and included in the model, the more accurate predictions can be made [17]. Unfortunately, it is virtually impossible to include all predictive factors in a prognostic model and several problems limit the generalisability of predictions to populations different from the one the prognostic model has been developed in.

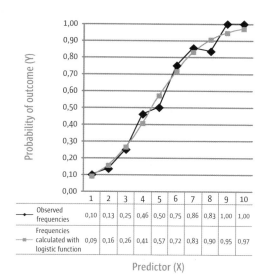

	1	2	3	4	5	6	7	8	9	10
Observed frequencies	0,10	0,13	0,25	0,46	0,50	0,75	0,86	0,83	1,00	1,00
Frequencies calculated with logistic function	0,09	0,16	0,26	0,41	0,57	0,72	0,83	0,90	0,95	0,97

Predictor (X)

Fig. 1   Probability of outcome plotted against increasing
values of the score. Observed frequencies in black,
frequencies calculated through the logit function
in gray

How to build a prognostic model

The selection of the score generation sample

The first step in the creation of a prognostic model is to select a sample of ICU patients that will
be used for the generation of the score, that we
may call the development sample. As a consequence, the level of care provided in this cohort
should represent the standard by which other
ICUs will measure their own performance. In a
consensus conference on mortality prediction
models, held in Santa Monica, California in 1993,
it was recommended that sampling should have
been "performed in a reasonably representative
manner, preferably randomly" [18]. However, it
is quite difficult to satisfy this condition and this
is the first shortcoming of commonly used severity scores. Actually, the ICUs participating in a
project for the creation of a new severity score are
usually selected among those that are willing,
able, and invited to participate in the study; thus,
there is a clear selection bias that does not allow
the argument that the level of care provided by
the participating ICUs is the standard nor that
these ICUs are representative of "all" other ICUs.

An attempt to limit this kind of bias was made
in the study carried out in the United States between 1998 and 1999 that led to the creation of
the APACHE III score, randomising 26 US hospitals among those eligible to take part in the
study and forming the final cohort of 40 volunteer tertiary care institutions [12]. Even under
such circumstances, the random sample of ICUs
was indeed representative of self-selected units.
The selection bias underlying the common methodology for the choice of the development sample
raises the first question on the generalisability of
the available prognostic models.

The selection of prognostic variables

The selection of prognostic variables to test in the
multivariate model is a key process in the development of a severity score. An easy strategy to
spot only important prognostic variables, thus
reducing the number of candidates, is to use sequential variable selection techniques which analyse the entire set of variables keeping in the
model only those that are statistically linked to
the outcome. Nevertheless, if the variable selection strategy is based solely on these automatic
procedures, the results will be most likely unreliable, due to several drawbacks of these automa-
tisms. Thus, other statistical and clinical criteria
should be adopted [17, 19, 20]. In many cases,
before automatic techniques are applied, data are
screened by means of bivariate analysis, assessing the association of each variable with hospital
mortality. However, this methodology should be
used with caution when predictors are not truly
independent from each other, and confounding
is believed to be present [21]. Thus, results of statistical analyses used for variable selection should
always be strictly evaluated by researchers and
clinical plausibility verified [22].

The creation of the score

Once important prognostic variables have been
selected they are included in the multivariate logistic regression model, and coefficients are calculated for each variable. Coefficients are then
transformed into scores for each variable, following different methodologies, but generally round-

ing decimals to the closest integer. In most cases, another regression analysis is then run, including the total score (the sum of the value of each item) as the only independent variable and hospital mortality as the dependent variable. This will yield specific coefficients for the score. As an example, the logit (i.e. the natural logarithm of $P/(1-P)$) for the SAPS II was equal to: $\beta_0+\beta_1$ (SAPS II) plus a second explanatory variable that accounted for the skewness of the distribution of the SAPS II in the development sample [8]. To apply the score to a different sample its value is calculated for each single patient and the corresponding logit is computed, and converted into probability of hospital mortality. Finally, the single-patient probabilities are summed up, providing the expected number of deaths for the entire sample, according to Equation 1.

Pitfalls in the development of prognostic models

Although the various steps for the creation of a prognostic model may appear linear, the development of good score is quite a difficult task. It should be clear that the aim of the prognostic model is to predict accurately in settings different from the one it was developed in. If a model, no matter how statistically sophisticated, does not fulfil this purpose, then it is useless. To say it with the words of Altman and Royston, "usefulness is determined by how well a model works in practice, not by how many zeroes there are in the associated P-values" [17]. When creating a prognostic model, researchers are dealing with a sample drawn from a population that is the real ground for the application of the model. When too many variables are included in the model, the risk of including variables which are statistically linked with the outcome only by chance, or which are important prognostic factors only in that specific sample (also called idiosyncrasies), increases [20, 23]. Obviously, the more statistically significant variables are included in the model, the better the model will fit the data. However, the very high price that could be paid for this choice is the skewing of the predictive ability once the score is applied in a different setting. Statisticians call this shortcoming overfitting, and some have labelled it as "the curse of prognostic models" [24], since it is a frequent and serious problem. To re-

duce the risk of overfitting, it is advisable to keep the number of variables included in the model low. A rule of thumb suggests that when dealing with a binary outcome there should be at least 10 to 20 events (i.e. hospital deaths) for each independent variable tested [17, 20]. Actually, a complex model, with a high number of prognostic factors compared to the number of events, runs a considerable risk of overfitting, thus parsimony is a desired property of any score [17, 22, 23]. The inclusion of a high number of variables has another unfavourable effect: It increases the chance that the independent variables are not uncorrelated but depend on each other (e.g. blood pressure and cardiac output); statisticians call this condition multicollinearity. In this case, although the coefficients are still reliably measured, their confidence intervals become inflated and this may limit their utility in estimating the weight of single independent variables [25, 26].

On the other hand, a model that lacks important prognostic variables is labelled underfitted. In this case the ability of the model to correctly predict the outcome is poor and predictions of the values of the dependent variable are distorted [25].

When dealing with important prognostic variables we should remember that we are trying to extract from a sample prognostic information which should allow us to make predictions in the target population. This raises the issue of the representativeness of the sample, which we have briefly discussed earlier in this paper. Prognostic scores usually do not include information regarding social, economic, and healthcare features, which can be very different in different countries and geographic areas. These factors, most likely, influence hospital mortality (the dependent variable in severity scores) irrespective of ICU performance. When context-sensitive variables in the development sample and the target population are homogeneous, and all important clinical variables are included, the prognostic model will make reliable predictions. But when the model is applied to a very different population, important context-sensitive variables may vary significantly, and alter the predictive accuracy of the score.

The validation of a prognostic model

Measures of predictive accuracy of a prognostic model: Calibration and discrimination

In this context, calibration is defined as the ability of the model to correctly estimate the probability of the event (i.e. hospital mortality). It is typically measured with goodness-of-fit statistics that summarise the discrepancy between observed values and those expected under the model.

The classical approach is based on the goodness-of-fit test proposed by Hosmer and Lemeshow. Observations (that is, patients) are grouped in strata, say, deciles, with equal risk of hospital mortality (e.g. 0–9%, 10–19%, etc.) or equal number of patients [19, 25, 27, 28]. Then the observed and expected mortality are formally compared across the deciles. When the test is statistically significant (i.e., low p value), it means that the numbers of expected and observed deaths are significantly different and hence the calibration is considered poor. A shortcoming of this approach is that when the sample size is too small or too large the test can be, respectively, underpowered, with the chance to give falsely reassuring high p value, or overpowered, thus detecting clinically irrelevant, but statistically significant differences [29]. For this reason, it is advisable to plot expected against observed mortality and to not just look at statistical results, and to report tables with the number of expected and observed deaths stratified by deciles (contingency tables) [18].

Other valuable statistical tools are available for goodness-of-fit assessment, such as the Cox calibration regression [19, 30–32]. The relation between the observed and expected probabilities of outcome is assessed using a further logistic regression in which the dependent variable is the outcome of interest (i.e. hospital mortality) while the independent variable is the natural logarithm of the odds of the probability given by the prognostic model under scrutiny:

$$(3)\ P_Y = \exp^{\beta 0+\beta 1 * \ln\,(\text{pred}/(1-\text{pred}))} /$$

$$(1 - \exp^{\beta 0+\beta 1 * \ln\,(\text{pred}\,/(1-\text{pred}))})$$

Where $\beta 0$ and $\beta 1$ are the Cox regression coefficients, and "pred" is the expected probability provided by the prognostic model. With a few algebra

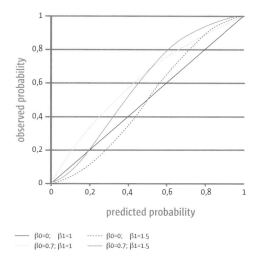

Fig. 2   Four examples of corresponding curves of Cox regression coefficients are reported

steps it is easy to demonstrate that when the intercept $\beta_0 = 0$ and the slope $\beta_1 = 1$, then the equation (2) simplifies to $P_Y = $ pred, that is to say that a perfect calibration is achieved. In Figure 2 we report some possible combinations of the Cox coefficients. If $\beta_0 = 0$ and β_1 varies (e.g. $\beta_1 = 1.5$), the extreme values will yield opposite trends (over- and under-predictions) quantitatively identical, thus the overall prediction will not be affected, but the calibration of extremes values would be poor. In other words, when β_0 equals 0 the overall percentages of observed and predicted events are identical. On the other hand, when β_0 is negative the model globally over-predicts, when it is positive the model globally under-predicts. The β_1 coefficient measures how far the average slope is from the diagonal.

Unlike the Hosmer-Lemeshow statistics, the Cox coefficients provide a quantitative measure of calibration, and thus are more informative about the true calibration of the model and should be preferred [33].

Discrimination is the ability of a score to correctly differentiate patients who died from patients who survived. This means that when the prognostic model discriminates fairly, an ICU patient randomly selected among those who died in the hospital will have more chances of carrying a higher score than a patient randomly selected

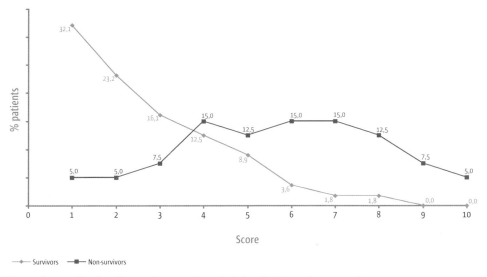

Fig. 3   Frequencies of survivors and non-survivors plotted against increasing score values

among survivors [34]. Discrimination of severity scores is usually assessed through the area under the receiver operating characteristics (ROC) curve [35, 36], although it is not the only statistical test available for this purpose.

In Figure 3 we plotted the frequencies of the survivors and non-survivors from Table 1 against increasing values of the prognostic score.

Let us set some arbitrary score thresholds. Those patients with scores higher than the

Tab. 1   Frequencies of outcome related to increasing values of the predictor. In the last column the probabilities of outcome are calculated with the logistic function.

Value of the predictor (independent variable)	Subjects	Outcome (dependent variable)		Proportion of outcome		Proportion calculated (fit) outcome = 1
		1	0	1	0	
1	20	2	18	0.10	0.90	0.09
2	15	2	13	0.13	0.87	0.16
3	12	3	9	0.25	0.75	0.26
4	13	6	7	0.46	0.54	0.41
5	10	5	5	0.50	0.50	0.57
6	8	6	2	0.75	0.25	0.72
7	7	6	1	0.86	0.14	0.83
8	6	5	1	0.83	0.17	0.90
9	3	3	0	1.00	0.00	0.95
10	2	2	0	1.00	0.00	0.97
Total	96	40	56			

threshold (right of the cut-off point) will have a prediction of death, while those with scores lower than the threshold (left of the cut-off point) will be prognosticated as survivors. If we assume as the discriminative threshold a score value greater than 1, then 95% of non-survivors and 68% of survivors will have a prediction of death (right of the threshold line); this equals 95% sensitivity and 32% specificity. Choosing a threshold of > 8 instead, the sensitivity and the specificity will be 13% and 100%, respectively. The threshold of > 3 seems to give a better combination, with 82% and 71%, respectively.

However, we are interested in the discriminative ability of the score across the total range of observed values. We reach this result plotting the sensitivity against specificity. If we consider only the 3 thresholds we have selected for the example, we will have 3 points in the graph which indicate the relation between the sensitivity and specificity for specific threshold values of the classification model or classifier (the prognostic model in our case). If all the values of the classifier and thus many points are reported, we can build the ROC curve [36].

In Figure 4 we have built a ROC curve with the data from Table 1. The bisector defines a classifier that has the same chance of discriminating

positive and negative outcomes as the flip of a coin. The more the curve rises from the diagonal to the northwest of the graph, the more it improves its discriminative ability.

The area under the curve (AUC) is a measure of discrimination. When the curve follows the vertical axis to the end, and then the horizontal superior axis, discrimination is perfect and the AUC is 1. In this case the classifier defines two populations that do not overlap. As mentioned above, the diagonal line does not provide any discriminative information, and since it divides the total area into halves, its value is 0.5. In this instance the two populations overlap perfectly.

There are other statistical tools to assess discrimination such as the concordance index and the Somer's D rank correlation index, as valuable as ROC analysis, but their use is less common [23, 37, 38].

Acknowledgements

On behalf of the GiViTI group; Gruppo Italiano per la Valutazione degli Interventi in Terapia Intensiva (Italian Group for the Evaluation of Interventions in Intensive Care Medicine). The study was entirely funded by GiViTI – Istituto di Ricerche Farmacologiche Mario Negri. GiViTI is the recipient of unrestricted grants from: Draeger Italia, Bellco, BRAHMS, and Astellas, which did not have any role in this study.

The authors

Daniele Poole, MD[1]
Guido Bertolini, MD[2]
[1]Servizio Anestesia e Rianimazione |
Ospedale Civile San Martino | Belluno, Italy
[2]Istituto di Ricerche Farmacologiche
"Mario Negri" | Centro di Ricerche Cliniche
per le Malattie Rare Aldo e Cele Daccò |
Ranica, Bergamo, Italy

Address for correspondence
Daniele Poole
S. Martino Hospital
Viale Europa, 3
32100 Belluno, Italy
E-mail: danest@libero.it

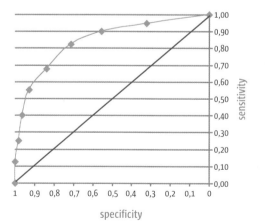

score	> 0	> 1	> 2	> 3	> 4	> 5	> 6	> 7	> 8	> 10
sens	1	0,95	0,9	0,825	0,675	0,55	0,4	0,25	0,125	0
spec	0	0,321	0,554	0,714	0,839	0,929	0,964	0,982	1	1

Fig. 4   ROC curve, sensitivity (sens) and specificity (spec) values for the data in Table 1

References

1. Harting BP, Talbot TR, Dellit TH, Hebden J, Cuny J, Greene WH, Segreti J. University HealthSystem Consortium quality performance benchmarking study of the insertion and care of central venous catheters. Infect Control Hosp Epidemiol 2008;29:440–442.

2. Wiles NJ, Scott DG, Barrett EM, Merry P, Arie E, Gaffney K, Silman AJ, Symmons DP. Benchmarking: the five year outcome of rheumatoid arthritis assessed using a pain score, the Health Assessment Questionnaire, and the Short Form-36 (SF-36) in a community and a clinic based sample. Ann Rheum Dis 2001;60:956–961.

3. Knaus WA, Zimmerman JE, Wagner DP, Draper EA, Lawrence DE. APACHE-acute physiology and chronic health evaluation: a physiologically based classification system. Crit Care Med 1981;9:591–597.

4. Le Gall JR, Loirat P, Alperovitch A, Glaser P, Granthil C, Mathieu D, Mercier P, Thomas R, Villers D. A simplified acute physiology score for ICU patients. Crit Care Med 1984;12:975–977.

5. Lemeshow S, Teres D, Pastides H, Avrunin JS, Steingrub JS. A method for predicting survival and mortality of ICU patients using objectively derived weights. Crit Care Med 1985;13: 519–525.

6. Lemeshow S, Teres D, Klar J, Avrunin JS, Gehlbach SH, Rapoport J. Mortality Probability Models (MPM II) based on an international cohort of intensive care unit patients. Jama 1993;270:2478–2486.

7. Higgins TL, Teres D, Copes WS, Nathanson BH, Stark M, Kramer AA. Assessing contemporary intensive care unit outcome: an updated Mortality Probability Admission Model (MPM0-III). Crit Care Med 2007;35:827–835.

8. Le Gall JR, Lemeshow S, Saulnier F. A new Simplified Acute Physiology Score (SAPS II) based on a European/ North American multicenter study. Jama 1993;270:2957–2963.

9. Moreno RP, Metnitz PG, Almeida E, Jordan B, Bauer P, Campos RA, Iapichino G, Edbrooke D, Capuzzo M, Le Gall JR. SAPS 3–From evaluation of the patient to evaluation of the intensive care unit. Part 2: Develop-ment of a prognostic model for hospital mortality at ICU admission. Intensive Care Med 2005;31:1345–1355.

10. Metnitz PG, Moreno RP, Almeida E, Jordan B, Bauer P, Campos RA, Iapichino G, Edbrooke D, Capuzzo M, Le Gall JR. SAPS 3 – From evaluation of the patient to evaluation of the intensive care unit. Part 1: Objectives, methods and cohort description. Intensive Care Med 2005;31:1336–1344.

11. Knaus WA, Draper EA, Wagner DP, Zimmerman JE. APACHE II: a severity of disease classification system. Crit Care Med 1985;13:818–829.

12. Knaus WA, Wagner DP, Draper EA, Zimmerman JE, Bergner M, Bastos PG, Sirio CA, Murphy DJ, Lotring T, Damiano A, et al. The APACHE III prognostic system. Risk prediction of hospital mortality for critically ill hospitalized adults. Chest 1991;100:1619–1636.

13. Zimmerman JE, Kramer AA, McNair DS, Malila FM, Shaffer VL. Intensive care unit length of stay: Benchmarking based on Acute Physiology and Chronic Health Evaluation (APACHE) IV. Crit Care Med 2006;34:2517–2529.

14. Zimmerman JE, Kramer AA, McNair DS, Malila FM. Acute Physiology and Chronic Health Evaluation (APACHE) IV: hospital mortality assessment for today's critically ill patients. Crit Care Med 2006;34:1297–1310.

15. Katz MH. Multivariable analysis: a primer for readers of medical research. Ann Intern Med 2003;138:644–650.

16. Hujoel PP, Drangsholt M, Spiekerman C, DeRouen TA. Periodontal disease and coronary heart disease risk. Jama 2000;284:1406–1410.

17. Altman DG, Royston P. What do we mean by validating a prognostic model? Stat Med 2000;19:453-473.

18. Hadorn D, Keeler EB, Rogers WH, Brook HB. (1993) Assessing the Performance of Mortality Prediction Models. Final Report for HCFA Severity Project. In: Editor (eds) Book Assessing the Performance of Mortality Prediction Models. Final Report for HCFA Severity Project. City, pp. Accessed on June 2008 at: http://www. rand.org/pubs/monograph_reports/MR2181/.

19. Miller ME, Hui SL, Tierney WM. Validation techniques for logistic regression models. Stat Med 1991;10:1213-1226.

20. Babyak MA. What you see may not be what you get: a brief, nontechnical introduction to overfitting in regression-type models. Psychosom Med 2004;66:411–421.

21. Sun GW, Shook TL, Kay GL. Inappropriate use of bivariable analysis to screen risk factors for use in multivariable analysis. J Clin Epidemiol 1996;49:907–916.

22. Sauerbrei W. The use of resampling methods to simplify regression models in medical statistics. Appl Statist 1999;48, Part 3:313–329.

23. Harrell FE, Jr., Lee KL, Mark DB. Multivariable prognostic models: issues in developing models, evaluating assumptions and adequacy, and measuring and reducing errors. Stat Med 1996;15:361–387.

24. Steyeberg E, Harrel FE. Interactive textbooks on clinical symptom research. Chapter 8: statistical models for prognostication. In: Editor (eds) Book Interactive textbooks on clinical symptom research. Chapter 8: statistical models for prognostication. City, pp. http://symptomresearch.nih.gov/chapter_8/sec6/cess6pg2.htm (Accessed February 2009).

25. Glantz SA, Slinker BK. Primer of Applied Regression and Analysis of Variance. McGraw-Hill, 2001.

26. Concato J, Feinstein AR, Holford TR. The risk of determining risk with multivariable models. Ann Intern Med 1993;118:201–210.

27. Lemeshow S, Hosmer DW, Jr. A review of goodness of fit statistics for use in the development of logistic regression models. Am J Epidemiol 1982;115:92–106.

28. Hosmer DW, Lemeshow S. Applied logistic regression. John Wiley & Sons, Inc., 2000.

29. Kramer AA, Zimmerman JE. Assessing the calibration of mortality benchmarks in critical care: The Hosmer-Lemeshow test revisited. Crit Care Med 2007;35:2052–2056.

30. Cox D. Two further applications of a model for a method of binary regression. Biometrika 1958;45:562–565.

31. Seillier-Moiseiwitsch F. Predictive diagnostics for logistic models. Stat Med 1996;15:2149–2160.

32. Peek N, Arts DG, Bosman RJ, van der Voort PH, de Keizer NF. External validation of prognostic models for critically ill patients required substantial sample sizes. J Clin Epidemiol 2007;60:491–501.

33. Harrison DA, Brady AR, Parry GJ, Carpenter JR, Rowan K. Recalibration of risk prediction models in a large multicenter cohort of admissions to adult, general critical care units in the United Kingdom. Crit Care Med 2006;34:1378–1388.

34. Zweig MH, Campbell G. Receiver-operating characteristic (ROC) plots: a fundamental evaluation tool in clinical medicine. Clin Chem 1993;39:561–577.

35. Hanley JA, McNeil BJ. The meaning and use of the area under a receiver operating characteristic (ROC) curve. Radiology 1982;143:29–36.

36. Fawcett T. (2005) An introduction to ROC analysis. In: Editor (eds) Book An introduction to ROC analysis. City, pp. Accessed February 2009 at: http://tsam-fich.wdfiles.com/local–files/apuntes/ROCintro.pdf

37. Harrell FE, Jr., Lee KL, Califf RM, Pryor DB, Rosati RA. Regression modelling strategies for improved prognostic prediction. Stat Med 1984;3:143–152.

38. Harrell FE, Jr., Califf RM, Pryor DB, Lee KL, Rosati RA. Evaluating the yield of medical tests. Jama 1982;247:2543–2546.

Daniele Poole and Guido Bertolini

Outcome-based benchmarking in the ICU Part II: Use and limitations of severity scores in critical care

In the previous section we have introduced the statistical principles on which the creation and validation of severity scores are based. In the following, we will deal with the application of prognostic models in critical care, highlighting the lack of standards for the parameters that should guide researchers in their validation studies and the inadequacy of some statistical tools currently used.

Internal validation

The internal validation of a prognostic model verifies the statistical correctness of the model and performs an evaluation of its predictive ability. Usually, the original dataset is split into a development sample, for the generation of the model, and a validation sample, in which the model predictions will be tested (data splitting) [1, 2]. We can then calculate the probability of death of each patient ($P_{Y|X}$ see Part I, Equation 1) with the coefficients generated by the regression model. The predicted hospital mortality generated by the model in the validation sample is then compared with the observed hospital mortality in the same sample. This can be done graphically, plotting observed against predicted death frequencies, and statistically, by calculating the observed over expected ratio (i.e. the standardised mortality ratio, or SMR) and its confidence intervals, or using calibration tests such as the Cox regression or the Hosmer-Lemeshow statistic and assessing discrimination with the ROC curve analysis or other techniques.

A different approach used to generate development and validation samples is cross-validation, which is basically a repeated data-splitting [1, 2]. For example, a subset, say one-tenth of the sample, is used as the validation dataset, while the remaining data is used to develop the model. This procedure can be repeated many times, changing development and validation samples at every run, both generating final model coefficients and providing internal validation. This technique uses the entire dataset to build the model, without renouncing part of the sample for data-splitting.

When these techniques are performed at random, as has been done for the majority of severity scores [3–7], although being an empiric control for errors in logistic regression [8], they provide little information on the predictive ability of the score, since the development and validation samples will have virtually the same features [1].

Other, better methodologies such as bootstrapping and leave-one-out cross-validation are available for validation, but rarely used by researchers who developed scores for the ICU patients [1, 2].

If a prognostic model includes the most important predictors, is not seriously overfitted and has been correctly built, it should adequately predict in a setting with a different case mix (e.g. different severity, different ages, different comorbidity patterns, etc.). Unfortunately, we are not able to foretell if the model accounts for all important variables and if the degree of overfitting is critical. Thus, good calibration and discrimination assessed with internal validation do not guarantee the transportability of the model into different contexts, which is the ultimate objective of a severity score. Actually, it is well known that before using a model for any purpose, its predictive ability should have been tested (assessing calibration and discrimination) in a sample different from the one it was developed in, a process called external validation [9].

External validation

Lack of criteria for the assessment of adequate external validation

It is commonly stated that to be useful a score should provide accurate predictions in the settings in which it is applied, a condition verified by means of external validation. But what does accurate mean? To assess accuracy we rely on the discrimination and the calibration abilities. Severity scores discriminate fairly in most validation studies, but physicians' predictive ability seems to discriminate adequately as well [10]. Thus, discrimination does not appear to be an obstacle for severity score external validation. Unlike discrimination, calibration measured by means of the most commonly used statistical tool, the Hosmer-Lemsehow statistic, has turned out to be poor in most validation studies. Unfortunately, this test does not provide a quantitative estimation of calibration, but just a p value that is obviously sensitive to sample size: The larger the sample the more likely a difference will turn out to be statistically significant, even if not clinically relevant, and calibration will resultingly be poor. This was

quite evident in a recalibration study of four severity scores in a population of 141,106 patients of the United Kingdom [11]. After recalibration, just looking at the calibration plots the prognostic models appeared to perform very well. Nevertheless, the chi-square value of the Hosmer-Lemeshow statistics was high (statistically significant difference between the observed and the predicted outcome). In the study, supported by a panel of expert statisticians, the Cox calibration values (see Part I) of the recalibrated scores were also reported: The mean intercept (α or β_0) was equal to o for all the recalibrated scores, while the mean slope (β_1) ranged between 0.99 and 1.00, values that instead quantified a negligible deviation from ideal calibration.

Thus, in the literature concerning external validation mostly insufficient objective measures of calibration have been applied, leaving, for the most part, a better (though subjective) assessment of calibration to the evaluation of contingency tables, which report the number of observed and predicted deaths across risk deciles, and calibration plots of observed against predicted probabilities of death. We can conclude that a threshold for accuracy has never been clearly established, and consequently the concept of clinical usefulness of severity scores that should underlie external validation studies is not well defined. In some instances it is absolutely clear from calibration plots and contingency tables reporting expected and observed hospital deaths that calibration is poor. In other cases, however, it is difficult to draw definitive conclusions. As an example, we can look at the APACHE III validation study by Zimmerman et al., carried out on 37,668 patients admitted to 285 ICUs in the United States between 1993 and 1996 [12]. The p of the Hosmer-Lemeshow statistic was < 0.0001, indicating a poor calibration. The calibration plot showed mortality overprediction in the highest risk percentiles and underprediction in the lowest risk percentiles, which ranged from +4.2 % (23 patients) to −4.3 % (49 patients), respectively. This oscillating pattern determined a global equivalence between observed and predicted deaths with an SMR of 1.01. Compared to other external validation studies [11, 13], this seems to be a better result although it appears that some problem underlying the model exists. The question is if this prognostic model should have been considered adequately validated and in which settings it could be reliably applied.

The choice of the best external validation sample

To further investigate this matter, let us go back to the UK recalibration study [11]. The APACHE III tested in the sample showed a clear underprediction, with Cox coefficients $\beta_0 = 0.44$ and $\beta_1 = 0.83$ (Cox calibration plot in Figure 1). We can hypothesise to explain this different behaviour of APACHE III in the US and UK samples. The crucial point is that the score was developed in the United States, on a sample of ICUs at least in part chosen by randomisation, from a reasonable number of patients (about 17,000) [5]. The predictive ability turns out to be better when the score is tested in a sample from the same country, which has a higher chance of being homogeneous in terms of unmeasured context-sensitive variables and suffers less from the influence of overfitting although it still may play a role. Conversely, scores that have been developed in international cohorts, such as the SAPS II, SAPS 3, and the MPM II [3, 4, 7, 14], could have less chances of predicting accurately when tested in the individual countries that participated in the development study.

This brings us back to the issue of the selection of the development sample which we dealt with at the beginning of Part I. Those statisticians who are concerned with the clinical applicability of prognostic models warn that the target population for a severity score should be predefined to permit the selection of a representative sample for the development of the score: In other words, we should know in advance to which patients we want to apply the score [15].

The results of the attempt to validate a severity score in a setting very different from the development sample are illustrated in the following example. In a validation study of APACHE III performed in a sample of 1,734 patients from 10 Brazilian ICUs the overall SMR was 1.67, and the calibration plot showed a large underprediction (i.e. excess in observed mortality) across all deciles of risk [16]. In this case we do not know to what extent the high SMR value is the result of the influence of unmeasured important context predictors or of a difference in quality of care

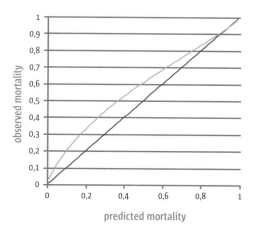

Fig. 1   Calibration curve of APACHE III according to the Cox regression (β_0=0.44, β_1=0.83) in a large sample of ICU patients from the UK [data from Harrison DA, Brady AR, Parry GJ, Carpenter JR, Rowan K. Recalibration of risk prediction models in a large multicenter cohort of admissions to adult, general critical care units in the United Kingdom. Crit Care Med 2006;34:1378–1388]

provided in the two countries. When the development and the validation settings are homogenous, instead, poor calibration can reasonably be ascribed mainly to the variables included in the model, which are more closely linked to hospital performance.

Another good example of the effects of heterogeneity between the score's original dataset and the target population arises from the application of the APACHE II in 1,962 patients admitted to a single university hospital ICU in India [17]. Observed deaths were far more than predicted, with the greatest differences arising from the lowest three deciles of risk. It is remarkable that the first five admission diagnoses in that sample were: severe falciparum malaria, poisoning, diabetic ketoacidosis, tetanus, and obstetric disorders. Interestingly, the APACHE III researchers in a 1998 publication wisely stated: "The system also has inadequate data to adjust and predict mortality for diseases that rarely occur in the U.S., such as malaria, tetanus, snakebite, or acute renal failure due to toxemia of pregnancy" [12]. The issue of the transportability of a prognostic model across international borders has already been raised in the past [18, 19], but clear indications on the matter have not been provided yet.

In light of these considerations, the creation of a global score appears to be a very difficult mission to accomplish. Nevertheless, in 2005 a new international severity score, SAPS 3, that included in the development cohort patients from seven different geographic areas (Australasia, Central/South America, Western Europe, Eastern Europe, Northern Europe, Southern Europe and Mediterranean countries, North America), was published [4, 14].

The results of the analysis of the predictive ability of the SAPS 3 across the geographic subgroups of the development cohort were very informative. The SMR values ranged from 0.84 to 1.30 and four out of seven SMRs significantly diverged from the ideal value 1 line (see Fig. 2). A score generated from such a heterogeneous sample is most likely underfitted because the model does not account for difficult-to-measure context-sensitive variables which influence the weight of score predictors and are not equally distributed in different subsets of the development sample. Thus, the resulting coefficients in the model could have been distorted and the predictions biased. Moreover, it is likely that the model has been overfitted to adequately describe the high degree of heterogeneity of the sample. In other

words, variables that are linked to the outcome in some geographic areas could be only background noise in others, thus altering the predictions in these settings. In this case, which sample would be the best for an external validation study?

Customisation strategies for severity scores

Even if we do not consider the inappropriate tool of the Hosmer-Lemeshow statistic to assess calibration, and only rely on calibration plots and contingency tables, still numerous national multicentre external validation studies demonstrated unsatisfactory performance of the severity scores under scrutiny [11, 13, 20–27]. If we assess calibration visually or by looking at contingency tables, the best, albeit improvable, result was probably achieved by the APACHE III score when it was tested in the United States (i.e. the country it was developed in) [12, 28]. Studies investigating the generalisability of the SAPS II, MPM II, and APACHE II and III when they were tested outside the United States instead provided deluding results. In several of these studies, the model equations were modified to adapt the fit to the external validation sample, through a mathematical procedure called customisation or recalibration [11, 23, 29–32]. We recognise two different

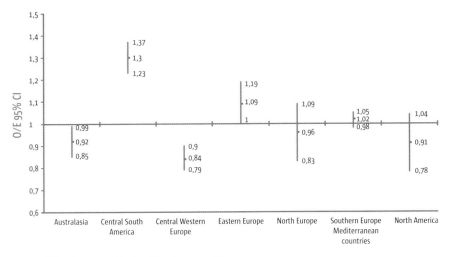

Fig. 2   SMR values for SAPS 3 in different geographic areas
[modified from Moreno et al.: SAPS 3 – From evaluation of the patient to evaluation of the intensive care unit. Part 2: Development of a prognostic model for hospital mortality at ICU admission. Intensive Care Med 2005;31:1345–1355]

levels of customisation. In first-level customisation a logistic regression is run using the variables of the prognostic model as predictors [29, 33, 34]. In this case cut-off points for continuous variables are not modified; however, we think that a customisation which includes the revision of these cut-off points should also be considered as a further level of customisation. First-level customisation leads to the generation of new variable coefficients specifically for the external validation sample. In other words, using this approach the score is almost entirely rebuilt, leaving to the original score the fundamental responsibility of selecting the variables included in the model. In our opinion, from a merely statistical perspective this methodology is questionable, although it might be the only solution when dealing with small-size databases.

With second-level customisation we recalibrate the score as a whole, which implies that the relative weight of the variables in computing the score remains unchanged, and the researcher just tries to correct the weight of the whole score in predicting mortality.

From a statistical perspective, this could be considered quite reasonable only if the score demonstrated a fairly constant over- or under-prediction of the event across risk deciles. If we apply the Cox regression analysis in this condition, we will find that the β_0 coefficient is substantially different from 0, while the β_1 value is not so far from 1 (see Fig. 3). The assumption in this case is that the relative weight of variables in the model is constant [29]. The recalibration of a severity score does not allow reliable predictions if the original model has been seriously overfitted. Thus, we believe that the recalibrated model should receive an external validation before its use is recommended.

Arguments used to explain poor performance of a model

The case mix differences

When a severity score calibration turns out to be unsatisfactory in a validation study, the authors frequently explain this by means of difference in case mix between the score generation sample and their study sample. Different case mix means

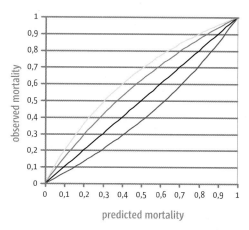

Fig. 3 β_1 always = 1; β_0 = 0.8, 0.5, 0, –0.5 top to bottom

a different composition in terms of specific subsets, e.g. surgical vs. medical, frequency of trauma, etc., many of which are accounted for by the score. Actually, simulation studies have demonstrated how the variation of the case mix resulted in the skewing of predictions [35, 36]. Theoretically, since the score adjusts for the variables in the model, their different pattern in the development and validation sample should not affect the correctness of the predictions. Thus, it is likely that when in comparison with the development sample a specific case-mix is connected to a different frequency of important unmeasured variables, the consequence could be a deterioration of prognostic power.

A different case mix of the validation sample could also corrupt the predictive ability of the severity score when the model has been overfitted to the development data. In this instance, variables correlated with the outcome by chance alone or specific to the generation sample are included in the model. When tested in the validation sample the coefficients of these variables will have an influence on the total score of each patient, although being prognostically meaningless.

So both under- and overfitting can explain poor calibration in external validation studies when a different case mix exists compared to the development sample. However, it should always be remembered that the objective of a prognostic model is to give reliable predictions in the samples to which it is applied, and if it does not reach this objective, it is of little or no use at all [1].

The different prevalence of outcome

Calibration can be defined as the correspondence of predicted probabilities with observed outcomes [37]. Consistently with this definition, when the case mix is kept constant and hospital mortality rate varied, the statistical tool used to assess calibration is able to detect the deviations from the predictions, and thus different ICU performances [33]. Some authors interpret this behaviour as a justification for poor calibration in external validation studies on samples with different outcome frequencies compared to the score development sample [20, 38]. They might have been misled by a simulation study that demonstrated how generating different mortality rates by varying the case mix caused a deterioration of the APACHE II predictive ability, although the quality of care was kept constant [36, 39]. This study only demonstrated how the APACHE II was not able to account for the variability ascribable to different case mixes. Thus, we should not use the argument of different hospital mortality prevalence to justify an unsuccessful external validation study.

The aging of the score

As time passes by, the evolution of medical technology, organisation of healthcare systems, patients' demography, etc., change. Thus it is reasonable to argue that a severity score developed many years earlier may need an update. It should also be acknowledged that the period from data collection for a new severity score to the first external validation study usually spans several years. We will consider two examples concerning this issue. The SAPS 3 score was developed in a sample of patients admitted to ICU in 2002, it was published in 2005 [4, 14], but to date no adequately sized external validation study has been published yet. The APACHE III was developed on patients admitted to ICU from 1988 through 1989, published in 1991 [5]; the first adequate validation study was published in 1998 and performed on a sample of patients admitted to ICU

between 1993 and 1996 [12]. Thus, how long will a severity score provide accurate predictions before it is time to bring it up to date? Another question is whether new is always better than old. Actually, when both APACHE II (published in 1985) [40] and APACHE III were tested in a large sample of ICU patients from the UK, the latter turned out to calibrate clearly worse than the former (Cox coefficients β_0 and β_1 equaled 0.44 and 0.83 for APACHE III, 0.28 and 0.93 for APACHE II) [11]. In a recent paper the SAPS II, published in 1993, performed as well as the latest versions of the APACHE and MPM [41]. It is also puzzling that sometimes old scores that are expected to overpredict mortality in contemporary settings (an "old" score should in theory overpredict mortality as the consequence of the improvement with time of healthcare assistance) turn out to underpredict [11, 14]. These results bear witness to the complexity of the mechanisms that underlie the predictive ability of models used for prognostication in critical care. If the aging of prognostic models was only a matter of different weight of the single items (this implies that the most important prognostic factors have been included in the score), instead of creating a new score it might be enough to recalibrate the coefficients of previous equations, possibly adding new variables. This kind of methodology was substantially followed in building the latest version of the MPM score [42] while in other cases the introduction of new variables into the model was preferred [6].

Conclusion

Results of external validation studies frequently provide contrasting results. The good or bad performance detected is sometimes the consequence of the influence of sample size on the Hosmer-Lemeshow statistics, while other times it depends on the degree of homogeneity between the development and the validation dataset. Interestingly, different authors have opposite opinions on the calibration of a score in the same dataset, indicating a high degree of subjectivity in the evaluation of the score's predictivity [12, 19, 43, 44]. However, it would be desirable that no uncertainty existed on whether the difference between the observed and predicted mortality rates in a specific ICU was the result of the provided quality of care or of a poorly performing severity score.

Unfortunately, this condition is infrequently satisfied and rarely a convincing external validation is demonstrated. The best results have been probably reached with the APACHE III score that was wisely developed in a US sample, at least in part randomly selected, representative of the target population. Actually, in published studies concerning several tens of thousands of patients, despite the high values of the Hosmer-Lemeshow chi-square values, subjective evaluation of calibration plots shows acceptable results although perfect calibration is not reached [12, 28]. However, since recent unpublished data suggested a deterioration of its predictive ability, a new version of the score, based on the framework of the APACHE III, was created [6]. Recently, a retrospective external validation study on a large US sample was published. Once again, calibration plots illustrated an acceptable, though improvable, performance [41].

Many unsatisfactory results in the field of severity scores, as well as uncertainty concerning the development and validation process, call for more specific recommendations since the latest generic guidelines on these issues were given in 1993 [9]. There are several crucial points that need to be clarified, ranging from the predefinition of the target population to allow a correct selection of the development sample, to the choice of the external validation sample; from the definition of the size of the external validation sample (both in terms of participating ICUs and patients) to the selection of the statistical tools and the definition of standardised parameters to assess the performance of the model; from the time that should elapse before the accuracy of predictions in a specific setting is checked to the methodologies for the recalibration of a score. Further, it would be useful that indications concerning reporting, for researchers who want to publish their results, were also provided.

Finally, it should be remarked that a great contribution to the improvement of benchmarking has been provided by permanent, high-quality databases [45]. In fact, compared with the rapid evolution of medicine, the time required for the creation of a severity score is so long as to frustrate its usefulness [46, 47]. Permanent databases, instead, provide a constantly updated dataset, and yearly predictions based on these data do not suffer from the aging that commonly affects severity scores. Moreover, when the predictions concern ICUs that were part of a homogeneous development sample (e.g. a homogeneous national dataset), unmeasured context variables can be considered less influential and the model suffers little from overfitting. Another advantage of permanent national databases is that the personnel of the joining ICUs are familiar with data collection and thus the quality of data should be higher.

One last consideration: We share the opinion that prognostic models should not be used for reimbursement policies or to decide on the distribution of resources to single units, because this would induce a high risk of biased data collection [48]. This brings us back to what we believe should be the main objective of a prognostic model: to be a tool for ICUs to evaluate the provided quality of care, spot critical points, apply corrective interventions, and assess their results – a process called benchmarking.

Acknowledgements

On behalf of the GiViTI group; Gruppo Italiano per la Valutazione degli Interventi in Terapia Intensiva (Italian Group for the Evaluation of Interventions in Intensive Care Medicine). The study was entirely funded by GiViTI – Istituto di Ricerche Farmacologiche Mario Negri. GiViTI is the recipient of unrestricted grants from: Draeger Italia, Bellco, BRAHMS, and Astellas, which did not have any role in this study.

The authors

Daniele Poole, MD[1]
Guido Bertolini, MD[2]
[1]Servizio Anestesia e Rianimazione |
Ospedale Civile San Martino | Belluno, Italy
[2]Istituto di Ricerche Farmacologiche
"Mario Negri" | Centro di Ricerche Cliniche
per le Malattie Rare Aldo e Cele Daccò |
Ranica, Bergamo, Italy

Address for correspondence
Daniele Poole
S. Martino Hospital
Viale Europa, 3
32100 Belluno, Italy
E-mail: danest@libero.it

References

1. Altman DG, Royston P. What do we mean by validating a prognostic model? Stat Med 2000;19:453–473.
2. Harrell FE, Jr., Lee KL, Mark DB. Multivariable prognostic models: issues in developing models, evaluating as-

sumptions and adequacy, and measuring and reducing errors. Stat Med 1996;15:361–387.

3. Le Gall JR, Lemeshow S, Saulnier F. A new Simplified Acute Physiology Score (SAPS II) based on a European/North American multicenter study. Jama 1993;270:2957–2963.

4. Moreno RP, Metnitz PG, Almeida E, Jordan B, Bauer P, Campos RA, Iapichino G, Edbrooke D, Capuzzo M, Le Gall JR. SAPS 3 – From evaluation of the patient to evaluation of the intensive care unit. Part 2: Development of a prognostic model for hospital mortality at ICU admission. Intensive Care Med 2005;31:1345–1355.

5. Knaus WA, Wagner DP, Draper EA, Zimmerman JE, Bergner M, Bastos PG, Sirio CA, Murphy DJ, Lotring T, Damiano A, et al. The APACHE III prognostic system. Risk prediction of hospital mortality for critically ill hospitalized adults. Chest 1991;100:1619–1636.

6. Zimmerman JE, Kramer AA, McNair DS, Malila FM. Acute Physiology and Chronic Health Evaluation (APACHE) IV: hospital mortality assessment for today's critically ill patients. Crit Care Med 2006;34:1297–1310.

7. Lemeshow S, Teres D, Klar J, Avrunin JS, Gehlbach SH, Rapoport J. Mortality Probability Models (MPM II) based on an international cohort of intensive care unit patients. Jama 1993;270:2478–2486.

8. Glantz SA, Slinker BK. Primer of Applied Regression and Analysis of Variance. McGraw-Hill, 2001.

9. Hadorn D, Keeler EB, Rogers WH, Brook HB. (1993) Assessing the Performance of Mortality Prediction Models. Final Report for HCFA Severity Project. In: Editor (eds) Book Assessing the Performance of Mortality Prediction Models. Final Report for HCFA Severity Project. City, pp. Accessed on June 2008 at: http://www.rand.org/pubs/monograph_reports/MR2181/

10. Sinuff T, Adhikari NK, Cook DJ, Schunemann HJ, Griffith LE, Rocker G, Walter SD. Mortality predictions in the intensive care unit: comparing physicians with scoring systems. Crit Care Med 2006;34:878–885.

11. Harrison DA, Brady AR, Parry GJ, Carpenter JR, Rowan K. Recalibration of risk prediction models in a large multicenter cohort of admissions to adult, general critical care units in the United Kingdom. Crit Care Med 2006;34:1378–1388.

12. Zimmerman JE, Wagner DP, Draper EA, Wright L, Alzola C, Knaus WA. Evaluation of acute physiology and chronic health evaluation III predictions of hospital mortality in an independent database. Crit Care Med 1998;26:1317–1326.

13. Livingston BM, MacKirdy FN, Howie JC, Jones R, Norrie JD. Assessment of the performance of five intensive care scoring models within a large Scottish database. Crit Care Med 2000;28:1820–1827.

14. Metnitz PG, Moreno RP, Almeida E, Jordan B, Bauer P, Campos RA, Iapichino G, Edbrooke D, Capuzzo M, Le Gall JR. SAPS 3 – From evaluation of the patient to evaluation of the intensive care unit. Part 1: Objectives, methods and cohort description. Intensive Care Med 2005;31:1336–1344.

15. Wyatt JC, Altman DG. Prognostic models: clinically useful or quickly forgotten? Bmj 1995;311:1539–1541.

16. Bastos PG, Sun X, Wagner DP, Knaus WA, Zimmerman JE. Application of the APACHE III prognostic system in Brazilian intensive care units: a prospective multicenter study. Intensive Care Med 1996;22:564–570.

17. Nimgaonkar A, Karnad DR, Sudarshan S, Ohno-Machado L, Kohane I. Prediction of mortality in an Indian intensive care unit. Comparison between APACHE II and artificial neural networks. Intensive Care Med 2004;30:248–253.

18. Teres D. The value and limits of severity adjusted mortality for ICU patients. J Crit Care 2004;19:257–263.

19. Teres D, Lemeshow S. As American as apple pie and APACHE. Acute Physiology and Chronic Health Evaluation. Crit Care Med 1998;26:1297–1298.

20. Beck DH, Smith GB, Pappachan JV, Millar B. External validation of the SAPS II, APACHE II and APACHE III prognostic models in South England: a multicentre study. Intensive Care Med 2003;29:249–256.

21. Cook DA. Performance of APACHE III models in an Australian ICU. Chest 2000;118:1732–1738.

22. Moreno R, Miranda DR, Fidler V, Van Schilfgaarde R. Evaluation of two outcome prediction models on an independent database. Crit Care Med 1998;26:50–61.

23. Apolone G, Bertolini G, D'Amico R, Iapichino G, Cattaneo A, De Salvo G, Melotti RM. The performance of SAPS II in a cohort of patients admitted to 99 Italian ICUs: results from GiViTI. Gruppo Italiano per la Valutazione degli interventi in Terapia Intensiva. Intensive Care Med 1996;22:1368–1378.

24. Metnitz PG, Valentin A, Vesely H, Alberti C, Lang T, Lenz K, Steltzer H, Hiesmayr M. Prognostic performance and customization of the SAPS II: results of a multicenter Austrian study. Simplified Acute Physiology Score. Intensive Care Med 1999;25:192–197.

25. Metnitz PG, Lang T, Vesely H, Valentin A, Le Gall JR. Ratios of observed to expected mortality are affected by differences in case mix and quality of care. Intensive Care Med 2000;26:1466–1472.

26. Moreno R, Morais P. Outcome prediction in intensive care: results of a prospective, multicentre, Portuguese study. Intensive Care Med 1997;23:177–186.

27. Pappachan JV, Millar B, Bennett ED, Smith GB. Comparison of outcome from intensive care admission after adjustment for case mix by the APACHE III prognostic system. Chest 1999;115:802–810.

28. Sirio CA, Shepardson LB, Rotondi AJ, Cooper GS, Angus DC, Harper DL, Rosenthal GE. Community-wide assessment of intensive care outcomes using a physiologically based prognostic measure: implications for critical care delivery from Cleveland Health Quality Choice. Chest 1999;115:793–801.

29. Steyerberg EW, Borsboom GJ, van Houwelingen HC, Eijkemans MJ, Habbema JD. Validation and updating of predictive logistic regression models: a study on sample size and shrinkage. Stat Med 2004;23:2567–2586.

30. Moreno R, Apolone G. Impact of different customization strategies in the performance of a general severity score. Crit Care Med 1997;25:2001–2008.

31. Le Gall JR, Neumann A, Hemery F, Bleriot JP, Fulgencio JP, Garrigues B, Gouzes C, Lepage E, Moine P, Villers D. Mortality prediction using SAPS II: an update for French intensive care units. Crit Care 2005;9:R645–652.

32. Rivera-Fernandez R, Vazquez-Mata G, Bravo M, Aguayo-Hoyos E, Zimmerman J, Wagner D, Knaus W. The Apache III prognostic system: customized mortality predictions for Spanish ICU patients. Intensive Care Med 1998;24:574–581.

33. Zhu BP, Lemeshow S, Hosmer DW, Klar J, Avrunin J, Teres D. Factors affecting the performance of the models in the Mortality Probability Model II system and strategies of customization: a simulation study. Crit Care Med 1996;24:57–63.

34. Peek N, Arts DG, Bosman RJ, van der Voort PH, de Keizer NF. External validation of prognostic models for critically ill patients required substantial sample sizes. J Clin Epidemiol 2007;60:491–501.

35. Murphy-Filkins R, Teres D, Lemeshow S, Hosmer DW. Effect of changing patient mix on the performance of an intensive care unit severity-of-illness model: how to distinguish a general from a specialty intensive care unit. Crit Care Med 1996;24:1968–1973.

36. Glance LG, Osler TM, Papadakos P. Effect of mortality rate on the performance of the Acute Physiology and Chronic Health Evaluation II: a simulation study. Crit Care Med 2000;28:3424–3428.

37. Miller ME, Hui SL, Tierney WM. Validation techniques for logistic regression models. Stat Med 1991;10:1213–1226.

38. Capuzzo M, Moreno RP, Le Gall JR. Outcome prediction in critical care: the Simplified Acute Physiology Score models. Curr Opin Crit Care 2008;14:485–490.

39. Glance RG, Osler TM, Papadakos P. Cannot draw generic conclusions from a single study. Authors reply to Wagner D.P. Crit Care Med 2001;29:1095–1096.

40. Knaus WA, Draper EA, Wagner DP, Zimmerman JE. APACHE II: a severity of disease classification system. Crit Care Med 1985;13:818–829.

41. Kuzniewicz MW, Vasilevskis EE, Lane R, Dean ML, Trivedi NG, Rennie DJ, Clay T, Kotler PL, Dudley RA. Variation in ICU risk-adjusted mortality: impact of methods of assessment and potential confounders. Chest 2008;133:1319–1327.

42. Higgins TL, Teres D, Copes WS, Nathanson BH, Stark M, Kramer AA. Assessing contemporary intensive care unit outcome: an updated Mortality Probability Admission Model (MPM0-III). Crit Care Med 2007;35:827–835.

43. Rowan KM, Kerr JH, Major E, McPherson K, Short A, Vessey MP. Intensive Care Society's APACHE II study in Britain and Ireland–II: Outcome comparisons of intensive care units after adjustment for case mix by the American APACHE II method. Bmj 1993;307:977–981.

44. Wagner DP. Cannot draw generic conclusions from a single study. Crit Care Med 2001;29:1095–1096.

45. Bertolini G. From national to global outcome research in the intensive care unit: a challenge to win. Crit Care Med 2008;36:336–337.

46. Black N. Developing high quality clinical databases. Bmj 1997;315:381–382.

47. Black N. High-quality clinical databases: breaking down barriers. Lancet 1999;353:1205–1206.

48. Selker HP. Systems for comparing actual and predicted mortality rates: characteristics to promote cooperation in improving hospital care. Ann Intern Med 1993;118:820–822.

Jeremy M. Kahn

Volume and outcome in intensive care

Introduction

The classic model of healthcare quality posits three interrelated domains: structure, process and outcome [1]. Outcome describes the degree to which care results in the intended effect. The typical healthcare outcomes of interest include survival, health-related quality of life, patient and family satisfaction, quality of death and dying, and costs. Process describes the degree to which care is grounded in the best available evidence, such as whether or not patients receive therapies proven to improve outcomes. Structure, perhaps the least well understood of the three domains, describes the degree to which healthcare is organised to best support the other two domains. In recent years a great deal of research has been dedicated to better understanding the role of structure in quality, especially in the intensive care unit (ICU) [2]. Examples of healthcare structures associated with improved ICU outcomes and processes of care include intensivist physician staffing [3], multi-disciplinary care teams [4], low nurse-to-patient ratios [5] and trained clinical pharmacists [6].

A recent addition to the list of healthcare structures thought to be associated with quality is patient volume [7]. We can broadly define volume as the number of clinical encounters for a specific medical condition seen by a healthcare provider in a given unit of time. The no-

tion that volume might be associated with quality is an outgrowth of the industrial management and operations research fields, in which task performance clearly improves with time and repetition [8]. It stands to reason that healthcare, which is both extremely complex and highly technical, might contain volume-quality relationships as well. Indeed, the majority of volume-outcome studies in healthcare show that caseload, both at the hospital and physician level, is strongly associated with quality in predictable ways [9]. Volume-outcome relationships are particularly well-defined in the surgical literature, where higher caseload is associated with improved survival in coronary artery bypass grafting (CABG), cancer surgery, and aortic abdominal aneurism repair, among others [10, 11]. Several relatively new publications demonstrate that strong volume-outcome relationships exist in the ICU as well [12–24]. These studies have important implications for both clinical care and health policy. Understanding volume-outcome relationships can provide insight into quality improvement, performance measurement, and the organisation of critical care services.

Volume-outcome: Evidence

The healthcare literature contains many examples of volume-outcome relationships. A 2002 systematic review found 135 volume-outcome studies in 27 different clinical conditions [9]. Seventy-one percent of studies found a significant inverse relationship between hospital volume and mortality; that is, higher volume was associated with lower mortality. Sixty-nine percent of studies found a significant inverse relationship between physician volume and outcome. The strongest associations were found for acquired-immunodeficiency syndrome (AIDS) and high-risk surgical cases, including surgical treatment of pancreatic cancer, esophageal cancer, and abdominal aortic aneurisms. Volume-outcome relationships for coronary artery bypass grafting, percutaneous coronary interventions, and carotid endarterectomy were consistently present but less strong. Subsequent to that systematic review, several high-profile studies were published demonstrating strong volume-outcome relationships in trauma and pulmonary embolism, among others [25, 26].

A common thread throughout these studies is that the disease states and syndromes are high-risk. Morbidity and mortality in AIDS, cardiothoracic surgery, and cancer surgery are extremely high, and most if not all of these patients are at one time admitted to an ICU. Consequently, these data provide indirect evidence that volume is associated with outcome in intensive care. Although for surgical procedures it is often assumed that the observed volume-outcome effect is due to surgical skill, in fact it could be the quality of intensive care following the surgery.

Complementing the indirect evidence in high-risk medical and surgical patients are several recent studies that directly examine volume-outcome relationships in ICU populations (see Tab. 1). These studies are unique in that patient inclusion was conditional on admission to an ICU. Each study examined a different patient population, used a different measure of volume and performed the analysis in slightly different ways, making a formal meta-analysis impossible. Still, it is possible to come to some broad conclusions. Ten of the 13 studies found a significant inverse relationship between volume and outcome, strongly supporting the existence of volume-out-

come relationships in the ICU. Of the three negative studies, two (Jones et al. and Moran et al.) included all intensive care unit patients, rather than select patients at the highest risk of death [12, 20]. Consistent with the surgical literature, it is likely that the volume-outcome relationship is strongest in patients with a high mortality risk. Indeed, the only positive study in all ICU patients [16] found a significant relationship only in high-risk patients, defined by a simplified acute physiology score $\geq$ 30), not in the general ICU population [16]. Many of the studies showing an extremely strong volume-outcome relationship were in patients at the highest risk of death, including patients with acute respiratory failure requiring mechanical ventilation [15], cardiac arrest [24], and haematological malignancy [22].

Effect sizes varied between studies, but generally relative risks comparing high-volume hospitals to low-volume hospitals ranged from 0.60 to 0.80, indicating that critical care in a high-volume hospital is associated with a 20% to 40% reduction in the risk of death. Given the large numbers of critically ill patients receiving care in low-volume hospitals throughout the world, the number of preventable deaths attributable to care in a low-volume hospital is large. One study estimated that as many as 20,000 deaths in the United States are attributable to receiving critical care in a small-volume hospital [15]. Thus far only one study in critical care examined physician volume, showing a decrease in mortality among ICU patients with pneumonia admitted to large-volume physicians [21]. The limited evidence about physician volume in critical care stands in contrast to the large body of literature suggesting the importance of surgeon volume in addition to hospital volume for high-risk surgeries [27].

All but one study (Needham et al.) used clinical data to risk-adjust patient outcomes [17]. Case mix varies widely between hospitals of different sizes, and accurate risk adjustment is essential in obtaining unbiased estimates of the volume-outcome effect [28]. It is possible that the study by Needham et al. was negative because the authors could not adequately control for differences in severity of illness between high- and low-volume hospitals. This phenomenon was demonstrated in a recent ICU volume-outcome study which compared volume-outcome analyses us-

Tab. 1   Volume-outcome studies in intensive care.

Reference	Population	Volume level	Hospitals (n)	Patients (n)	Clinical risk adjustment?	Effect?*
Jones, 1995 [12]	All intensive care	ICU	26	8,796	Yes	No
Pronovost, 1999 [13]	Aortic aneurism repair	Hospital	39	2,987	Yes	Yes
Durairaj, 2005 [14]	Select diagnoses	Hospital	29	43,635	Yes	Yes†
Kahn, 2006 [15]	Invasive mechanical ventilation	Hospital	37	20,241	Yes	Yes
Glance, 2006 [16]	All intensive care	ICU	76	70,757	Yes	Yes‡
Needham, 2006 [17]	Invasive mechanical ventilation	Hospital	95	20,219	No	No
Peelen, 2008 [18]	Severe sepsis	ICU	29	4,605	Yes	Yes
Nguyen, 2007 [19]	Invasive mechanical ventilation	ICU	33	41,747	Yes	Yes
Moran, 2008 [20]	All intensive care	Hospital	NR	223,129	Yes	No
Lin, 2008 [21]	Pneumonia	Physician	NR	87,479	Yes	Yes
Lecuyer [22]	Haematological malignancy	ICU	28	1,752	Yes	Yes
Kahn, 2009 [23]	Invasive mechanical ventilation	Hospital	169	30,677	Yes	Yes
Carr, 2009 [24]	Post-cardiac arrest	Hospital	39	4,674	Yes	Yes

ICU = intensive care unit; NR = not reported
* Clinically and statistically significant inverse association between volume and mortality.
† Significant for patients with gastrointestinal diagnoses (n = 12,881) but not patients with neurologic or respiratory diagnoses.
‡ Significant for high-risk patients (defined as SAPS II score ≥ 30) but not all ICU patients.

ing administrative risk adjustment (i.e. age, gender, and co-morbidities obtained through billing data), clinical risk adjustment (i.e. a severity score derived from physiologic and laboratory values) and instrumental variables, a statistical technique that can account for unmeasured confounding [23]. A significant volume-outcome relationship was observed using instrumental variables and clinical risk adjustment but not administrative risk adjustment, highlighting the need for valid risk adjustment in this area.

How are volume and outcome related?

Taken together, these studies strongly support the existence of a volume-outcome relationship in critical care.

However, questions remain about the etiology of the observed association. Several potential mechanisms underlie the volume-outcome relationship in critical care (and healthcare in general): clinical experience, selective referral, and unmeasured system-level factors [29]. A conceptual model for these mechanisms is shown in Figure 1. In the model, the association between volume and outcome runs in two directions: Higher patient volume might cause outcomes to improve, or improved outcomes might result in higher patient volumes. It is important to differentiate these potential etiologies underlying the volume-outcome relations, as each has different implications for clinical care and health policy in critical care.

Under the first scenario, the clinical experience gained with increased volume translates into better outcomes. This is the classic "practice-makes-perfect" model for volume-outcome – as clinicians do more of something, they naturally get better at it. Several aspects of critical care are likely to improve with experience. Much of intensive care hinges on accurate diagnosis of clinical syndromes such as sepsis and acute lung injury (ALI) [30]. As physicians gain experience in the ICU they might get better at recognising these syndromes, and thus are more likely to use

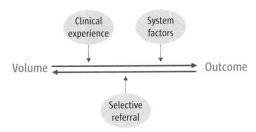

Fig. 1 Conceptual model of volume-outcome relationships in healthcare. The observed volume-outcome
effect could be due to clinical experience, selective referral or system factors.

evidence-based therapies such as activated protein C for severe sepsis [31] and lung-protective
ventilation for ALI [26]. Many elements of critical
care are technically complex, such as ventilator
management and haemodynamic monitoring.
Accurate interpretation of complex physiologic
data might improve over time, allowing for directed therapeutic interventions [32]. Finally, clinical experience might increase efficiency in the
ICU. Given a set amount of time with each patient, efficient clinicians might be able to spend
more time focusing on less immediately press-
ing aspects of care, such as appropriate preventive measures that are strongly associated with
outcome [33].

In the second scenario, increased volume
leads to better outcomes through the mechanism
of selective referral. Under selective referral, patients are differentially referred to high-quality
physicians and hospitals, resulting in increased
volume. An example of selective referral would
be if cardiologists preferentially sent patients requiring CABG surgery to surgeons known to be
of high quality, independent of their actual experience. In the ICU, selective referral might occur
if community hospitals preferentially transferred
their patients to regional referral centres with excellent outcomes. Although selective referral is
a potentially important mechanism for volume-
outcome relationships, it is unlikely that it will
explain a great deal of what we observe in critical
care. For selective referral to occur it is first necessary for providers to identify high-quality providers. Accurately identifying high-quality ICUs
is extremely challenging even with sophisticated computer models [34], let alone simple ob-

servation. Additionally, experiments with public
reporting of hospital quality information show
that patients generally do not gravitate toward
high-quality providers as we might expect [35].
In the Cleveland Health Quality Choice project, a
multi-hospital benchmarking and public reporting initiative in the United States, neither high-
quality nor low-quality providers saw a meaningful change in their market share after the public reporting of risk-adjusted outcome data [36].
The assumptions of selective referral, that we
can identify high-quality hospitals and that patients will go to those hospitals, are unlikely to
hold true.

A third possible mechanism complicating interpretation of volume-outcome relationships is
the existence of unmeasured system-level factors.
Under this scenario, volume does not cause improved outcome, but rather volume is a marker for other unmeasured structures that are related to outcome. Care structures and processes
thought to be associated with outcome in the ICU
include protocols for weaning and sedation [37–
39], multidisciplinary teams [4], and low nurse-
to-patient ratios [5]. Rather that improving quality
through clinical experience, high-volume ICUs
might simply be better at implementing these
care processes compared to low-volume ICUs.
Under this scenario, a volume-outcome study
that completely accounted for all important system-level factors would be negative, in that it
would show so significant effect after controlling
for structural elements associated with outcome.
No study to date controls for all potential system-
level factors, so unmeasured system factors remain a potentially important mechanism of the
volume-outcome effect independent of clinical
experience [40].

Implications of volume-outcome relationships

Volume-outcome relationships have important
implications for clinical care and health policy.
Although there is significant overlap, the response to volume-outcome relationships in large
part depends on the predominant mechanism
underlying the volume-outcome effect (see
Fig. 2). Depending on the predominant mechanism, clinicians and policy-makers can use volume-outcome relationships to inform quality im-

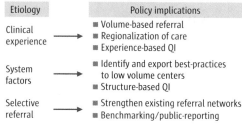

Etiology	Policy implications
Clinical experience	■ Volume-based referral ■ Regionalization of care ■ Experience-based QI
System factors	■ Identify and export best-practices to low volume centers ■ Structure-based QI
Selective referral	■ Strengthen existing referral networks ■ Benchmarking/public-reporting

Fig. 2 Policy implications of volume-outcome relation-ships based on potential etiology. QI = quality improvement

provement activities, regional healthcare delivery systems, and benchmarking activities.

Quality improvement

Volume-outcome relationships give important insight about priorities for ICU quality improve-ment activities. If the association between vol-ume and outcome is due to system-level factors, efforts could be focused toward identifying those factors and exporting them to low-volume sites. For example, protocolised care for sedation and ventilator management are strongly associated with outcome and might be easily adopted at low-volume centres [41]. Less evidence exists that a multi-disciplinary model of care involving phar-macists, nutritionists, physical therapists and respiratory therapists improves outcomes. But as more evidence emerges, multidisciplinary care might be a key structure for implementation at low-volume hospitals.

Quality improvement can benefit from vol-ume-outcome relationships even if the mecha-nism is clinical experience rather than system-level factors, especially if the volume is associ-ated with outcome at the level of the individu-al physician. Volume is easily measurable, and ICUs could identify their low-volume providers with little time or investment. Quality improve-ment activities could then be geared directly to-ward those individuals. Under a more aggressive strategy, ICUs could restrict clinical privileges to only those providers meeting certain volume benchmarks (i.e. a certain number of patients in the ICU per year).

Regionalisation of care

If volume-outcome relationships are primarily due to clinical experience, then regionalisation of care might improve outcome for patients with critical illnesses. Regionalisation would involve identifying high-performing hospitals and then routinely transferring critically ill patients to those hospitals [42]. Centralising care would lead to greater clinical experience at high-volume sites, theoretically improving outcomes both for patients already admitted to high-volume hospi-tals and patients transferred into high-volume hospitals from low-volume centres. Regionalisa-tion of care is associated with improved survival in trauma care and neonatology, syndromes that are not only similar to adult critical care and but also have established volume-outcome relation-ships [43, 44]. Regionalisation could also improve efficiency in critical care by taking advantage of economies of scale [45]. Economies of scale exist when per-patient costs become lower with each additional patient. As large ICUs expand to meet the demands of regionalisation, critical care might become less costly overall.

At this time there is little direct evidence that regionalisation will save lives in critical care. Simulation data suggest that regionalisation in the United States is feasible and potentially ben-eficial [46]. Yet the United States lacks a central regulatory authority to institute and enforce re-gionalisation. Some countries like the United Kingdom and Canada formally stratify hospi-tals based on the level of critical care they pro-vide, but do not systematically transfer patients from low-level to high-level hospitals [47, 48]. Regionalisation also might result in unintend-ed adverse consequences that might offset the potential benefit. Regionalising care could over-whelm the resources at large-volume hospitals or reduce the critical care capability at low-vol-ume hospitals, increasing mortality for patients left behind [49]. Regionalisation would also mean large-scale inter-hospital transfer of criti-cally ill patients. Although most studies show that inter-hospital transfer is safe, adverse events during transport could worsen outcomes [50, 51]. Additionally, little is known about the psy-chosocial strain on families that might accom-pany routine inter-hospital transfer of critically ill patients [52].

More evidence is needed before critical care is regionalised in a manner similar to neonatal and trauma care. However, the consistent association between volume and outcome in critical care provides compelling evidence that reorganising the system of critical care by moving patients to high-quality centres might improve survival. Volume-outcome relationships provide important conceptual support for regionalisation and highlight the need for future study.

Benchmarking and public reporting

Benchmarking and public reporting are quality improvement strategies related to quality measurement. Simple benchmarking involves comparing quality measures between providers, while public reporting involves publicising that quality data to payers and patients as well as providers. Together, benchmarking and public reporting might improve quality by stimulating quality improvement at low-performing sites or by increasing market share at high-performing sites [53]. Volume-outcome relationships can help inform this process. If volume is tightly linked to risk-adjusted quality, then providers could be benchmarked on their volume in addition to their outcome. Volume data rather than outcome data could be publicly reported, obviating the need for complex risk adjustment tools. This process has been endorsed by some quality groups in the United States, and volume-based benchmarking is ongoing in the US for some surgical procedures [54].

Benchmarking and public reporting are particularly useful if selective referral is the primary mechanism underlying the volume-outcome relationship. Selective referral implies that patients and providers are already able to recognise high-quality providers and gravitate towards them. Simply standardising and strengthening that process could be an easy means toward improving outcomes. Already between 10 and 20 % of admissions to an ICU involve a transfer between facilities [55]. It may be possible to improve outcomes by reinforcing the existing ad hoc system of inter-hospital transfers even without introducing a formal system of regionalised care [56, 57].

Although benchmarking and public reporting are potentially effective means to improve quality in healthcare, there are several caveats

that must be addressed before they can be routinely applied. First, more evidence is needed that benchmarking actually produces measurable gains in quality. What data exist are mixed, with some public reporting initiatives resulting in higher quality care and others not [36, 58, 59]. Second, public reporting of quality information might have important adverse consequences [60]. Providers might avoid taking on high-risk cases, potentially worsening quality for complex patients or widening healthcare disparities [61]. Finally volume-based benchmarking measures ignore the fact that even some low-volume providers can provide high-quality care. Benchmarking using solely volume as the quality indicator might actually guide patients away from high-performing providers and toward low-performing providers [62]. As the science of quality measurement evolves, benchmarking and public reporting might play a greater future role. Until that time, the role of volume-outcome relationships in the benchmarking process should be considered theoretical at best.

Limitations of volume as a quality measure

There are several important limitations to consider when interpreting volume-outcome studies and using these studies to affect health policy. First, volume does not automatically equal quality. Volume is simply a marker for quality. High-volume ICUs do not necessarily provide the best care, nor are improvements in quality guaranteed as ICUs increase their annual caseload [63]. This phenomenon is well-demonstrated in studies of surgery and neonatal outcomes showing that regionalisation based one volume standards would not be as effective as regionalisation based on outcome standards [62, 64]. Rather than providing definitive evidence of high quality, volume-outcome relationships are best understood as tools to guide local and regional quality improvement activities [40].

Secondly, volume is not a static measure. Provider volumes change from year to year or even month to month. Accounting for dynamic changes in volume over time using longitudinal data analysis can markedly affect the results of volume studies [65]. To this point we have mainly considered average volume, which ignores changes over time. Alternative measures such as cumulative volume (the total number of clinical encounters up to the encounter of interest) may be just as important and more relevant from a patient perspective. Similarly, average volume is highly dependent on the time horizon. A large time horizon (e.g. years) will give equal credit to high-volume periods in the distant past, while a short time horizon (e.g. months) will give more credit to high-volume periods that are recent. The right measure of volume, and the right time horizon, are dependent on the clinical question of interest [66]. If we want to benchmark a surgical procedure with a steep learning curve and little loss of skills over time, then cumulative volume may be most important. But if we want to benchmark critical care, in which the learning curve is likely to be slower and skills are rapidly lost over time, then average volume with a short time horizon may be of interest. In cases when volumes change rapidly over time, a single static measure of volume per provider may be inappropriate. Whenever evaluating volume-outcome studies it is essential to understand exactly what measure of volume is under consideration and make sure it closely aligns with the clinical question.

Future directions

Although much is known about the volume-outcome relationship in critical care, more research is needed to better understand how this relationship can guide health policy and clinical practice. First, additional volume-outcome studies are needed in diverse health systems and different patient populations. The bulk of published ICU volume-outcome studies were performed in the United States and addressed broad populations of critically ill patients. Future studies could focus on specific diseases as well as examining more diverse health systems, particularly health systems in developing nations. Secondly, more detailed studies are needed to uncover the mechanism of the volume-outcome effect. Existing studies generally control for variation in patient-level factors but fail to entirely capture ICU-specific factors such as protocol use and multidisciplinary care. Future studies that comprehensively examine the effect of ICU factors on the volume-outcome relationship will help differentiate

the mechanisms behind the observed relationship. Thirdly, more work is needed examining changes in volume over time. Rather than consider an average volume over the study period, investigators can examine how changes in volume impact quality. Such research will help policy-makers anticipate the effects of regionalising critical care, which is certain to require large-scale changes in hospital volume. Finally, research is needed into the interaction between physician volume and ICU volume in critical care. At least one study in the cancer literature suggests that both physician and hospital volume are independently important, but data from critical care are lacking [27].

Conclusions

Interest in quality measurement and quality improvement among clinicians, heathcare administrators and policy-makers is certain to increase over the coming years. The gaps between evidence and practice are large, patients are not receiving therapies proven to save lives, and the healthcare system frequently fails to deliver care in an effective and efficient manner. As we work to improve health care quality, volume-outcome analyses can help inform decisions with regard to quality improvement and the organisation of critical care services. A greater understanding of the role of volume in quality will provide important insight into the relationship between structure, process and outcome in the ICU.

The author

Jeremy M. Kahn MD, MS[1,2]
  [1]Division of Pulmonary | Allergy and Critical Care | Center for Clinical Epidemiology and Biostatistics | University of Pennsylvania School of Medicine | Philadelphia, Pennsylvania, USA
  [2]Leonard Davis Institute of Health Economics | University of Pennsylvania | Philadelphia, Pennsylvania, USA

Address for correspondence
Jeremy M. Kahn
Assistant Professor of Medicine and Critical Care
Center for Clinical Epidemiology and Biostatistics
723 Blockley Hall
423 Guardian Drive
Philadelphia PA 19104, US
E-mail: jmkahn@mail.med.upenn.edu

References

1. Donabedian A. The quality of medical care. Science 1978;200:856–864.
2. Carmel S, Rowan K. Variation in intensive care unit outcomes: a search for the evidence on organziational factors. Curr Opin Crit Care 2001;7:284–296.
3. Pronovost PJ, Angus DC, Dorman T, Robinson KA, Dremsizov TT, Young TL. Physician staffing patterns and clinical outcomes in critically ill patients: a systematic review. JAMA 2002;288:2151–2162.
4. Young MP, Gooder VJ, Oltermann MH, Bohman CB, French TK, James BC. The impact of a multidisciplinary approach on caring for ventilator-dependent patients. Int J Qual Health Care 1998;10:15–26.
5. Tarnow-Mordi WO, Hau C, Warden A, Shearer AJ. Hospital mortality in relation to staff workload: a 4-year study in an adult intensive-care unit. Lancet 2000;356:185–189.
6. MacLaren R, Bond CA, Martin SJ, Fike D. Clinical and economic outcomes of involving pharmacists in the direct care of critically ill patients with infections. Crit Care Med 2008;36:3184–3189.
7. Kahn JM. Volume, outcome, and the organization of intensive care. Crit Care 2007;11:129.
8. Liker J. The Toyota Way. New York: McGraw-Hill; 2004.
9. Halm EA, Lee C, Chassin MR. Is volume related to outcome in health care? A systematic review and methodologic critique of the literature. Ann Intern Med 2002;137:511–520.
10. Begg CB, Cramer LD, Hoskins WJ, Brennan MF. Impact of hospital volume on operative mortality for major cancer surgery. JAMA 1998;280:1747–1751.
11. Birkmeyer JD, Siewers AE, Finlayson EV, Stukel TA, Lucas FL, Batista I, et al. Hospital volume and surgical mortality in the United States. N Engl J Med 2002;346:1128–1137.
12. Jones J, Rowan K. Is there a relationship between the volume of work carried out in intensive care and its outcome? Int J Technol Assess Health Care 1995;11:762–769.
13. Pronovost PJ, Jenckes MW, Dorman T, Garrett E, Breslow MJ, Rosenfeld BA, et al. Organizational characteristics of intensive care units related to outcomes of abdominal aortic surgery. JAMA 1999;281:1310–1317.
14. Durairaj L, Torner JC, Chrischilles EA, Vaughan Sarrazin MS, Yankey J, Rosenthal GE. Hospital Volume-Outcome Relationships Among Medical Admissions to ICUs. Chest 2005;128:1682–1689.
15. Kahn JM, Goss CH, Heagerty PJ, Kramer AA, O'Brien CR, Rubenfeld GD. Hospital volume and the outcomes of mechanical ventilation. N Engl J Med 2006;355:41–50.
16. Glance LG, Li Y, Osler TM, Dick A, Mukamel DB. Impact of patient volume on the mortality rate of adult intensive care unit patients. Crit Care Med 2006;34:1925–1934.
17. Needham DM, Bronskill SE, Rothwell DM, Sibbald WJ, Pronovost PJ, Laupacis A, et al. Hospital volume and mortality for mechanical ventilation of medical and surgical patients: A population-based analysis using administrative data. Crit Care Med 2006;34:2349–2354.
18. Peelen L, De Keizer NF, Peek N, Scheffer GJ, Van der Voort PH, De Jonge E. The influence of volume and ICU organization on hospital mortality in patients admitted with severe sepsis: a retrospective multicenter cohort study. Crit Care 2007;11:R40.
19. Nguyen YL, Chiche JD, Aegerter P, Kahn JM, Martel P, Guidet B, et al. Impact of hospital volume on the outcome of mechanical ventilation in French ICUs. Intensive Care Med 2007;33:S102.
20. Moran JL, Bristow P, Solomon PJ, George C, Hart GK. Mortality and length-of-stay outcomes, 1993–2003, in the binational Australian and New Zealand intensive care adult patient database. Crit Care Med 2008;36:46–61.
21. Lin HC, Xirasagar S, Chen CH, Hwang YT. Physician's case volume of intensive care unit pneumonia admissions and in-hospital mortality. Am J Respir Crit Care Med 2008;177:989–994.
22. Lecuyer L, Chevret S, Guidet B, Aegerter P, Martel P, Schlemmer B, et al. Case volume and mortality in haematological patients with acute respiratory failure. Eur Respir J 2008;32:748–754.
23. Kahn JM, Ten Have TR, Iwashyna TJ. The relationship between hospital volume and mortality in mechanical ventilation: an instrumental variable analysis. Health Serv Res 2009 (in press).
24. Carr BG, Kahn JM, Merchant RM, Kramer AA, Neumar RW. Inter-hospital variability in post-cardiac arrest mortality. Resuscitation 2009;80:30–34.
25. Nathens AB, Jurkovich GJ, Maier RV, Grossman DC, MacKenzie EJ, Moore M, et al. Relationship between trauma center volume and outcomes. JAMA 2001;285:1164–1171.
26. Aujesky D, Mor MK, Geng M, Fine MJ, Renaud B, Ibrahim SA. Hospital volume and patient outcomes in pulmonary embolism. CMAJ 2008;178:27–33.
27. Birkmeyer JD, Stukel TA, Siewers AE, Goodney PP, Wennberg DE, Lucas FL. Surgeon volume and operative mortality in the United States. N Engl J Med 2003;349:2117–2127.
28. Tsai AC, Votruba M, Bridges JF, Cebul RD. Overcoming

bias in estimating the volume-outcome relationship. Health Serv Res 2006;41:252–264.

29. Luft HS, Hunt SS, Maerki SC. The volume-outcome relationship: practice-makes-perfect or selective-referral patterns? Health Serv Res 1987;22:157–182.

30. Rubenfeld GD, Christie JD. The epidemiologist in the intensive care unit. Intensive Care Med 2004;30:4–6.

31. Bernard GR, Vincent JL, Laterre PF, LaRosa SP, Dhainaut JF, Lopez-Rodriguez A, et al. Efficacy and safety of recombinant human activated protein C for severe sepsis. N Engl J Med 2001;344:699–709.

32. Vincent JL, Pinsky MR, Sprung CL, Levy M, Marini JJ, Payen D, et al. The pulmonary artery catheter: in medio virtus. Crit Care Med 2008;36:3093–3096.

33. Eggimann P, Harbarth S, Constantin MN, Touveneau S, Chevrolet JC, Pittet D. Impact of a prevention strategy targeted at vascular-access care on incidence of infections acquired in intensive care. Lancet 2000;355:1864–1868.

34. Glance LG, Osler TM, Dick A. Rating the quality of intensive care units: is it a function of the intensive care unit scoring system? Crit Care Med 2002;30:1976–1982.

35. Marshall MN, Shekelle PG, Leatherman S, Brook RH. The public release of performance data: what do we expect to gain? A review of the evidence. JAMA 2000;283:1866–1874.

36. Baker DW, Einstadter D, Thomas C, Husak S, Gordon NH, Cebul RD. The effect of publicly reporting hospital performance on market share and risk-adjusted mortality at high-mortality hospitals. Med Care 2003;41:729–740.

37. Ely EW, Baker AM, Dunagan DP, Burke HL, Smith AC, Kelly PT, et al. Effect on the duration of mechanical ventilation of identifying patients capable of breathing spontaneously. N Engl J Med 1996;335:1864–1869.

38. Lellouche F, Mancebo J, Jolliet P, Roeseler J, Schortgen F, Dojat M, et al. A multicenter randomized trial of computer-driven protocolized weaning from mechanical ventilation. Am J Respir Crit Care Med 2006;174:894–900.

39. Brook AD, Ahrens TS, Schaiff R, Prentice D, Sherman G, Shannon W, et al. Effect of a nursing-implemented sedation protocol on the duration of mechanical ventilation. Crit Care Med 1999;27:2609–2615.

40. Epstein AM. Volume and outcome–it is time to move ahead. N Engl J Med 2002;346:1161–1164.

41. Randolph AG, Pronovost P. Reorganizing the delivery of intensive care could improve efficiency and save lives. J Eval Clin Pract 2002;8:1–8.

42. Barnato AE, Kahn JM, Rubenfeld GD, McCauley K, Fontaine D, Frassica JJ, et al. Prioritizing the organization and management of intensive care services in the United States: the PrOMIS Conference. Crit Care Med 2007;35:1003–1011.

43. MacKenzie EJ, Rivara FP, Jurkovich GJ, Nathens AB, Frey KP, Egleston BL, et al. A national evaluation of the effect of trauma-center care on mortality. N Engl J Med 2006;354:366–378.

44. Cifuentes J, Bronstein J, Phibbs CS, Phibbs RH, Schmitt SK, Carlo WA. Mortality in low birth weight infants according to level of neonatal care at hospital of birth. Pediatrics 2002;109:745–751.

45. Jacobs P, Rapoport J, Edbrooke D. Economies of scale in British intensive care units and combined intensive care/high dependency units. Intensive Care Med 2004;30:660–664.

46. Kahn JM, Linde-Zwirble WT, Wunsch H, Barnato AE, Iwashyna TJ, Roberts MS, et al. Potential value of regionalized intensive care for mechanically ventilated medical patients. Am J Respir Crit Care Med 2008;177:285–291.

47. Critical Care Stakeholder Forum. Quality critical care: beyond "Comprehensive critical care". London: United Kingdom National Health Service; 2005.

48. Ontario Critical Care LHIN Leadership Table. Inventory of critical care services. Toronto: Ontario Ministry of Health and Long Term Care; 2006.

49. Iwashyna TJ, Kramer AA, Kahn JM. Intensive care unit occupancy and patient outcomes. Critical Care Medicine 2009 (in press).

50. Fan E, MacDonald RD, Adhikari NK, Scales DC, Wax RS, Stewart TE, et al. Outcomes of interfacility critical care adult patient transport: a systematic review. Crit Care 2006;10:R6.

51. Seymour CW, Kahn JM, Schwab CW, Fuchs BD. Adverse events during rotary-wing transport of mechanically ventilated patients: a retrospective cohort study. Crit Care 2008;12:R71.

52. Azoulay E, Pochard F, Kentish-Barnes N, Chevret S, Aboab J, Adrie C, et al. Risk of post-traumatic stress symptoms in family members of intensive care unit patients. Am J Respir Crit Care Med 2005;171:987–994.

53. Epstein AM. Public release of performance data: a progress report from the front. JAMA 2000;283:1884–1886.

54. Birkmeyer JD, Finlayson EV, Birkmeyer CM. Volume standards for high-risk surgical procedures: potential benefits of the Leapfrog initiative. Surgery 2001;130:415–422.

55. Zimmerman JE, Kramer AA, McNair DS, Malila FM. Acute Physiology and Chronic Health Evaluation (APACHE) IV: hospital mortality assessment for today's critically ill patients. Crit Care Med 2006;34:1297–1310.

56. Iwashyna TJ, Christie JD, Kahn JM, Asch DA. Uncharted paths: hospital networks in critical care. Chest 2009 (in press).

57. Iwashyna TJ, Christie JD, Moody JS, Kahn JM, Asch DA. The structure of critical care transfer networks. Med Care 2009 (in press).

58. Lindenauer PK, Remus D, Roman S, Rothberg MB, Benjamin EM, Ma A, et al. Public reporting and pay for performance in hospital quality improvement. N Engl J Med 2007;356:486–496.

59. Hibbard JH, Stockard J, Tusler M. Hospital performance reports: impact on quality, market share, and reputation. Health Aff (Millwood) 2005;24:1150–1160.

60. Werner RM, Asch DA. The unintended consequences of publicly reporting quality information. JAMA 2005;293:1239–1244.

61. Werner RM, Asch DA, Polsky D. Racial profiling: the unintended consequences of coronary artery bypass graft report cards. Circulation 2005;111:1257–1263.

62. Glance LG, Osler TM, Mukamel DB, Dick AW. Estimating the potential impact of regionalizing health care delivery based on volume standards versus risk-adjusted mortality rate. Int J Qual Health Care 2007.

63. Sowden AJ, Sheldon TA. Does volume really affect outcome? Lessons from the evidence. J Health Serv Res Policy 1998;3:187–190.

64. Rogowski JA, Horbar JD, Staiger DO, Kenny M, Carpenter J, Geppert J. Indirect vs direct hospital quality indicators for very low-birth-weight infants. JAMA 2004;291:202–209.

65. French B, Heagerty PJ. Marginal mark regression analysis of recurrent marked point process data. Biometrics 2008.

66. Kulkarni GS, Laupacis A, Urbach DR, Fleshner NE, Austin PC. Varied definitions of hospital volume did not alter the conclusions of volume-outcome analyses. J Clin Epidemiol 2008.

Ruth Endacott

Documenting care in the ICU – An expert witness view

Introduction

A health record is defined as "any electronic or paper information recorded about a person for the purpose of managing their health care" [1] and includes handwritten and electronic records, correspondence between clinicians, laboratory results, radiographs, printouts from monitoring equipment, consent forms and e-mails/text messages [2]. Health records provide evidence of health professionals' involvement with patients [3] and demonstrate the delivery of safe and effective care based on current evidence, best practice and, where applicable, validated research [4, 5]. However, documentation of care seems to raise the spectre of error; five of the Nine Patient Safety Solutions proposed by the World Health Organisation [6] are at least partly aimed at improving accuracy in patient documentation, whilst, in a single site study, Donchin and colleagues [7] found the majority of errors in the ICU relate to communication. Of note, it is acknowledged that patient records have the potential to identify the largest number of clinical incidents, as distinct from any formal reporting system, and provide the richest source of data on such incidents [8]. The expert witness (EW) will review all aspects of medical documentation when called upon, by the court, to come to a judgment about the standard of care provided to the patient. In this context,

the medical record has been described as providing "a window on the clinical judgment being exercised at the time" [2]. This chapter does not attempt to discuss specific aspects of legal process as these are mostly country-specific and addressed elsewhere, for example, see Szalados 2007 [9].

Background

Use of records

Health records are used primarily to communicate details of the patient's previous and current management to enable continuity of care and hence should provide a contemporaneous record. Documentation of aspects of management also increasingly provides primary or secondary measure in research, for example, to examine end-of-life care in the ICU [10, 11] or adequacy of vital signs monitoring [12, 13, 14]. Medical records may also be accessed to assess quality of care [15, 16] or to validate billing requests [17]. Increasingly, patients are exercising their right to access their records [2]; in the UK patients also have the right to have factual inaccuracies rectified or deleted [1], although patients do not have the right to ask for professional opinion to be changed. Any such changes to the medical record should be signed and dated.

Recent developments in record-keeping

Recent years have seen two areas of developments in documentation of care: firstly, a shift to partial or total electronic format for care documentation [18–21] and secondly, increased adoption of protocols to underpin care [22]. Both of these have medico-legal implications, as discussed later in the chapter.

The extent of electronic transfer of patient data in the ICU ranges from simple bedside or remote monitoring of patients to full paperless clinical information systems (CIS) providing complete patient documentation at the bedside. Reported benefits of computerised information systems include: increased accuracy [18], reduced staff time spent recording common ICU data, positive perceptions of staff [19], improvements in the patient problem list through automated scanning of narrative records [20] and improved communication of ICU core measures to clinicians managing the patient [21] although the impact of this on patient outcomes is yet to be established [21]. However, the preference of physicians to use verbal communication remains problematic [23]; of note, replacing telephone reporting of lab results with electronic results reporting in an ED resulted in up to 45% of 'urgent' results not being accessed [24].

The impact of computerised physician order entry (CPOE) on accuracy of prescribing is, as yet, inconsistent [25, 26, 27], although there do seem to be benefits for ICU length of stay [28] and efficiency of workflow [29]. However, computer entry can mean that the task is undertaken away from the bedside [30], depending on the system specification. Undertaking tasks outside of the context in which they originated is identified as one factor that increases the potential for error [31].

The automated transmission of patient data via PDA is promoted as one way of improving communication of patient deterioration and documentation [32], although Carroll et al. [33] found only a modest improvement in documentation with the use of PDAs. Alongside increased use of electronic forms of documentation, protocol use has increased [22] although the extent of adherence is variable [22, 34].

Common areas of error in patient documentation

Common errors in patient documentation include [2]:
- Failing to record negative events, discussions regarding risks and benefits of treatment options, drug allergies or adverse reactions, investigation results
- Altering records after the event
- Illegible entries
- Insertion of derogatory comments
- Not reading the notes when seeing a patient

Errors in ICU patient documentation fall into two categories: acts of omission [35] and acts of commission. Omissions identified include: vital signs assessed but not documented [36], medications omitted for non-therapeutic reasons [37] and absence of end-of-life decision-making documented in patient records [38].

Reported errors of commission are dominated by prescribing [39] or labelling [40] medication errors. Prescribing errors have also been found in ICU transfer reports, with one study reporting errors in 26% of all prescriptions on ICU transfer reports [41]. This same study reported some form of documentation error in 62% of all transfer reports [41]. Ambiguities in the terminology used by clinicians have been highlighted in research studies [42, 43] and medico-legal cases [44].

Medico-legal perspectives

The medical record has been described as "the physician's best defense or the plaintiff's 'Exhibit A'" [17], with the oft-cited mantra that care "if it wasn't documented, it was not done." Review of records by the EW will inform judgments regarding the appropriateness, necessity, adequacy and effectiveness of assessment, interventions and communication. A useful guiding principle is the question regarding "information management" used in root cause analysis: "To what degree is all necessary information available when needed? accurate? complete? unambiguous?" [45]. The SOAP acronym [2] may also be used to evaluate the quality and completeness of the medical record. The record should include:

Subjective information – what the patient says
Objective information – what the clinician detects: examination and investigation results
Assessment – conclusions drawn by the clinician, usually including differential diagnosis
Problem list and Plan – management and follow-up

An expert witness will generally examine the records for assessment, interventions and communication. Detailed questions asked by the EW are provided in the following box.

Sample questions used by the EW to examine patient documentation

Assessment
Have the clinicians done everything they should – is there evidence to support the adequacy of the clinical assessment?
Where aspects of assessment are delegated to more junior (medical or nursing) staff, is any guidance provided in the form of acceptable parameters?
If a professional judgment is made regarding assessment, for example, change (particularly: decrease) in frequency of observation or decision not to rouse the patient overnight for observation, is it clear who made the decision?

Interventions
Are interventions guided by the assessment? Is there a clear process from assessment via (tentative) diagnosis to intervention?
Where there is a choice of interventions is a rationale provided for decisions?
If interventions deviate from previous plans, is there a clear rationale? If the patient or family request such a deviation, is this noted, with time and date of the conversation?
Is there a plan (timeframe and parameters) for evaluation of interventions?
Is there evidence of informed consent for treatment where this is required?

Communication
Is all communication between clinicians and family documented?
Are the patient and family wishes, where known, clearly stated with date and time?

Are any differences in opinion between clinicians documented?
Are any threats to patient safety clearly documented?

Where the critical care clinicians are receiving patient assessment data from patients outside of the critical care unit, the same standards will apply. Submission of patient data to ICU clinicians confers shared responsibility for monitoring of the patients, given that "these data are immediately available to any member of the hospital healthcare team with access to the hospital intranet" [32]. Moreover, the ability to transmit patient data, radiographs and test results has become the expected standard [46].

A number of questions would be asked by an expert witness during review of electronic records for medico-legal purposes. Depending on the incident under investigation the EW may examine: availability of adequate terminals for viewing records; the quality of data; adequacies of the system; processes for dealing with 'information overload'; expectation of processes to monitor trends; access to evidence for decision-making; accountability/reporting processes and the accuracy, timeliness and completeness of patient data.

Key to assessing the accuracy of records is a review of processes to avoid and/or detect the "silent errors" [30] that can occur in data entry/retrieval and data communication/coordination. Questions to be probed include the following: how are steps taken to ensure that drugs that look similar and appear side by side on a computer screen are selected correctly? How do clinicians still get to see the 'whole picture' of the patient as depicted manually on a large 24-hour ICU chart, when having to switch between a number of windows in the electronic record [30]? What checks and balances are embedded in the electronic system, for example, pharmacist checking of prescriptions [25–27]?

If protocols are used to underpin clinical decisions, the EW would make a judgment regarding whether the protocols were: available, workable, intelligible, correct and in routine use at the time of the incident. However, where there is evidence of wide variation in content of protocols [e.g. 34, 35] this should be reflected in the expert witness judgment.

Records will also be examined by the EW for any evidence of alteration; this immediately undermines the trustworthiness of the patient record and discredits the signatory. As it is impossible to determine whether such changes were made before or after the fact, it is common for hospital policy to explicitly ban use of correction fluid in patient records. One of the advantages of more complex clinical information systems is the ability to 'lock' the record after the patient episode [47], preventing subsequent amendment.

When reviewing patient records, it is common for other areas of potential unsafe practice (for example, inadequate staffing or skill mix) to be uncovered. Of note, the review of 3,600 reports submitted to the Australian Incident Monitoring System identified that 81 % of adverse events resulted from inappropriate staff numbers or skill mix [48]. Review of staffing rotas and patient case mix may be investigated by the EW to provide an opinion on the climate of support; this is particularly pertinent if the incident under investigation involved junior medical or nursing staff.

Patient safety initiatives emphasise the need to distinguish between system or organisational failure and human error. Similarly, in the medico-legal context the EW will distinguish between practices that are customary in the organisation/unit (custom and practice) and practices that occurred during the incident giving rise to the malpractice claim/criminal case. This allows the EW to judge whether the scenario leading to the investigation was 'an accident waiting to happen'.

Areas investigated related to 'custom and practice' and the specific incident

Custom and practice
Context in which patients are managed:
Staff support
Staff training
Staffing levels
Systems for accessing patient information
Systems and processes routinely used to identify and mitigate risks to patient or staff safety
Adherence to accepted standards for documentation of care
Adherence to standards for use of electronic records

Specific incident
The actions of individuals related to the specific incident:
Was the standard of care appropriate, for that patient, in those circumstances?

Were available protocols used?
Were standards for supporting junior staff upheld?
Was assessment documented appropriately?

Judgment against a standard

An expert witness provides evidence to the court regarding accepted standards of practice. The 'expected standard' against which patient management is judged may be national or international and single or multi-professional. Where practice deviates from the standard (protocol, clinical guideline) specific reasons for amending or omitting interventions should be documented [49]. Standards specifically relating to documentation of patient care include: use of the problem list [2, 50], guidance for confidentiality with electronic records [51]. However, these standards would only be relevant if they were publicly available and commonly in use at the time of the incident.

The 'standard' against which the EW comes to a judgement is what would be reasonably expected, not necessarily what the individual EW would have done. This is sometimes referred to as the 'substitution test' – would another individual from the same professional group, possessing comparable qualifications and experience, behave in the same way in similar circumstances?

Conclusion

In summary, the quality of patient documentation in intensive care is of paramount importance in enabling continuity of the right care at the right time for the patient. Accountability for documentation of care rests not only with the individual clinician but also with those responsible for designating documentation structures and processes. Review of patient records for medico-legal purposes will often reveal unexpected problems; the areas explored in this chapter are worth reviewing in each intensive care unit as part of a regular audit cycle.

The author

Ruth Endacott
Professor of Critical Care Nursing
La Trobe University and University of Plymouth, Melbourne
Drake Circus
Plymouth PL4 8AA, UK
E-mail: ruth.endacott@plymouth.ac.uk

References

1. The Data Protection Act 1998 www.hmso.gov.uk
2. Medical Protection Society. MPS Guide to Good Records. 2008; Medical Protection Society, London
3. Griffith R. Putting the record straight: the importance of documentation. British Journal of Community Nursing. 2004; 9(3): 122–125
4. Nursing and Midwifery Council Advice Sheet on Record Keeping. 2007 NMC; London
5. General Medical Council. Good Medical Practice. 2006; GMC
6. World Health Organisation. Nine Solutions for Patient Safety. 2007; WHO
7. Donchin Y, Gopher D, Olin M, Badihi Y, Biesky M, Sprung CL, Pizov R, Cotev S. A look into the nature and causes of human errors in the intensive care unit. Crit Care Med 1995; 23(2): 294–300
8. Hogan H, Olsen S, Scobie S, Chapman E, Sachs R, McKee M et al. What can we learn about patient safety from information sources within an acute hospital: a step on the ladder of integrated risk management? Qual Saf Health Care 2008; 17: 209–215
9. Szalados, JE. Legal issues in the practice of critical care medicine: A practical approach. Critical Care Medicine 2007; 35(2): S44-S58
10. Glavan BJ, Engelberg RA, Downey L, Curtis JR. Using the medical record to evaluate the quality of end-of-life-care in the intensive care unit. Crit Care Med 2008; 36:1138-46
11. Cohen S, Sprung CL, Sjokvist P, Lippert A, Ricou B, Baras M, Hovilehto S, Maia P, Phelan D, Reinhart K, Werdan K, Bulow HH Communication of end of life decisions in European intensive care units—the Ethicus Study. Intensive Care Med 2005; 31:1215–1221
12. McQuillan P, Pilkington S, Allan A, et al. Confidential inquiry into quality of care before admission to intensive care. BMJ 1998; 316(7158):1853–1858
13. Goldhill DR, Worthington L, Mulcahy A, Tarling M, Sumner A The patient at risk team: identifying and managing seriously ill ward patients. Anaesthesia 1999; 54: 853–60

14. Odell M. Rechner IJ. Kapila A. Even T. Oliver D. Davies CWH. Milsom L. Forster A. Rudman K. The effect of a critical care outreach service and an early warning scoring system on respiratory rate recording on the general wards. Resuscitation 2007; 74(3): 470–475
15. Nelson JE, Mulkerin CM, Adams LL, Pronovost PJ Improving comfort and communication in the ICU: a practical new tool for palliative care performance, measurement and feedback. Quality and Safety in Health Care 2006; 15: 264–271
16. Najjr-Pellet J, Janquet O, Jambou P, Fabry J. Quality assessment in intensive care units: proposal for a scoring system in ternms of structure and process. Intensive Care Med 2008; 34: 278–285
17. Quinn C. The Medical Record as a Forensic Resource. Jones & Bartlett Pubs, 2005
18. Zanier ER, Ortolano F, Ghisoni L, Colombo A, Losappio S, Stocchetti N. Intracranial pressure monitoring in intensive care: clinical advantages of a computerized system over manual recording. Crit Care 2007; Jan 18; 11(1): R7
19. Donati A, Gabbanelli V, Pantanetti S, Carletti P, Principi T, Marini B, Nataloni S, Sambo G, Pelaia P. The impact of a clinical information system in an intensive care unit. J Clin Monit Comput 2008; 22:31–36
20. Meystre S, Haug P. Improving the sensitivity of the problem list in an intensive care unit by using Natural Language Processing. AMIA Annu Symp Proc. 2006; 2006: 554–558
21. Wahl W, Talsma A, Dawson C, Dickinson S, Pennington K, Wilson D, Arbabi S, Taheri P. Use of computerized ICU documentation to capture ICU core measures Surgery 2006; 140(4): 684–690
22. Quenot J-P, Mentec H, Feihl F, Annane D, Melot C and the TECLA Study Group. Bedside adherence to clinical practice guidelines in the intensive care unit: the TECLA study. Intensive Care Med 2008; 34: 1393–1400
23. Brown PJ, Borowitz SM, Novicoff W. Information exchange in the NICU: what sources of patient data do physicians prefer to use? International Journal of Medical Informatics 2004; 73(4): 349–355
24. Kilpatrick ES, Holding S. Use of computer terminals on wards to access emergency test results: a retrospective audit. BMJ 2001;322:1101–3
25. Shulman R, Singer M, Goldstone J et al. Medication errors: a prospective cohort study of hand-written and computerised physician order entry in the intensive care unit. Crit Care 2005; 9: R516–21
26. Nebeker JR, Hoffman JM, Weir CR, Bennett CL, Hurdle JF. High rates of adverse drug events in a highly computerized hospital. Arch Intern Med. 2005; 165(10): 1111–6
27. Han YY, Carcillo JA, Venkataraman ST, Clark RS, Watson RS, Nguyen TC, Bayir H, Orr RA. Unexpected increased mortality after implementation of a commercially sold

computerized physician order system. Pediatrics 2005; 116(6): 1506–12

28. Sintchenko V, Iredell JR, Gilbert GL, Coiera E. Handheld computer-based decision support reduces patient length of stay and antibiotic prescribing in critical care. J Am Med Inform Assoc. 2005; 12(4): 398–402

29. Ali NA, Mekhijan HS, Kuehn PL, Bentley TD, Kumar R, Ferketich AK, Hoffman SP. Specificity of computerized physician order entry has a significant effect on the efficiency of work-flow for critically ill patients. Crit Care Med 2005; 33(1): 110–4

30. Ash JS, Berg M, Coiera E. Some Unintended Consequences of Information Technology in Health Care: The Nature of Patient Care Information System-related Errors. J Am Med Inform Assoc. 2004;11:104–112

31. Reason J Beyond the organisational accident: the need for "error wisdom" on the frontline. Qual Saf Health Care 2004; 13(Suppl II):ii28–ii3332.   Smith GB, Prytherch DR, Schmidt P, Featherstone PI, Knight D, Clements G, Mohammed MA. Hospital-wide physiological surveillance–A new approach to the early identification and management of the sick patient. Resuscitation 2006; 71(1): 19–28

33. Carroll AE, Tarczy-Hornoch P, Reilly E, Christakis DA. The effect of Point-of-Care Personal Digital Assistant use on resident documentation discrepancies. Pediatrics 2004; 113(3) 450–454

34. Zhukovsky DS, Hwang JP, Palmer JL, Willey J, Flamm AL, Smith ML. Wide variation in content of inpatient do-not-resuscitate order forms used at National Cancer Institute-designated cancer centers in the United States. Support Care Cancer 2009; 17: 109–115

35. Hayward RA, Asch SM, Hogan MM et al Sins of omission: getting too little medical care may be the greatest threat to patient safety. Journal of General Internal Medicine 2005; 20: 686–91

36. Endacott R, Kidd T, Chaboyer W, Edington J. Recognition and communication of patient deterioration in a regional hospital: a multi-methods study. Australian Critical Care 2007; 20(3): 100–105

37. Kester L, Stoller JK. (2003) Prevalence and Causes of Medication Errors: A Review. Clinical Pulmonary Medicine, 10(6): 322–326

38. Sprung CL, Woodcock T, Sjokvist P, Ricou B, Bulow H-H, Lippert D et al. Reason, considerations, difficulties and documentation off end-of-life decisions in European intensive care units: the ETHICUS study. Intens Care Med 2008; 34: 271–277

39. Ridley SA, Booth SA, Thompson CM. Prescription errors in UK critical care units. Anaesthesia 2004; 59: 1193–2000

40. Wheeler DW, Degnan BA, Schmi JS, Burnstein RM, Menon DK, Gupta AK. Variability in the concentrations of intravenous drug infusions prepared in a critical care unit. Intensive Care Med 2008; 34: 1441–1447

41. Perren A, Conte P, De Bitonti N, Limono C, Merlani P. from the ICU to the ward: cross-checking of the physician's transfer report by intensive care nurses. Intensive Care Medicine 2008; 34: 2054–61

42. Zeleznik J, Agard-Henriques B, Schnebel B, Smith DL (2003) Terminology used by different health care providers to document skin ulcers; the blind men and the elephant. Journal of Wound, Ostomy and Continence Nursing 30(6): 324–333

43. Morandi A, Pandharipande P, Trabucchi M, Rozzini R, Mistraletti G, Trompeo AC et al. Understanding international differences in terminology for delirium and other types of acute brain dysfunction in critically ill patients. Intensive Care Medicine 2008; 34:1907–1915

44. Lyons M (2008) Do classical origins of medical terms endanger patients? The Lancet. 371: 1321–1322

45. Root Cause Analysis. Joint Commission on the Accreditation of Healthcare Organizations (JCAHO) http://www.jointcommission.org/SentinelEvents/ Forms/ accessed 11 February 2009

46. Reng M. The role of information technology in the ICU. In: Kuhlen R, Moreno R, Ranieri M, Rhodes A (eds) 25 Years of Progress and Innovation in Intensive Care Medicine 2007; 375–382]

47. Fraenkel D Clinical Information systems. In: Bersten AD, Soni N, Oh TE. Oh's Intensive Care Manual (5th ed.) 2003; Butterworth Heineman, Edinburgh

48. Beckmann U, Baldwin I, Hart GK, Runciman WB. The Australian Incident Monitoring Study in Intensive Care: AIMS-ICU. An analysis of the first year of reporting. Anaesth Intensive Care1996 24:320–9

49. Weintraub MI. Thrombolysis (Tissue Plasminogen Activator) in Stroke: A Medicolegal Quagmire Stroke. 2006; 37:1917–1922

50. Pronovost P, Berenholtz S, Dorman T, Lipsett PA, Simmonds T, Haraden C. Improving Communication in the ICU using daily goals. Journal of Critical Care 2003;18(2)71–75

51. NHS. Code of Practice for Confidentiality: specific guidance for record-keeping. Accessible at: http://www.connectingforhealth.nhs.uk

Maurizia Capuzzo, Andreas Valentin and Raffaele Alvisi

Open versus closed units

Introduction

According to PubMed, the definition of Intensive Care Unit (ICU), introduced in 1966, is a hospital unit providing continuous surveillance and care to acutely ill patients. In 1992, intensive care given in the ICU was defined as advanced and highly specialised care provided to medical or surgical patients whose conditions are life-threatening and require comprehensive care and constant monitoring. The physicians who have training in intensive care medicine are referred to as intensivists.

The principles of intensive care medicine are the same principles as those of general medicine and general surgery. The intensivists do not perform unique procedures, they are not specialists of a specific organ or apparatus like neurologists or nephrologists, but they are specialists of acuity, severity of the illness and risk of the patient [1, 2]. They have to deal with critically ill patients who have one or more organ dysfunction or failure and need early diagnoses as well as early and adequate treatments. Moreover, these patients must be viewed in an overall perspective, taking into account the interrelated functions of the various organ systems. In such a context, any sophisticated technology may help the intensivist but cannot replace his/her competence, skill, and experience.

The ICU requires an organisation suitable to the tasks given. Generally, medium-sized hospitals need at least one multidisciplinary, i.e. mixed, medical-surgical, centralised ICU, while large hospitals in metropolitan cities as well as university hospitals may have ICUs for different specialties and subspecialties (like coronary, neurological, trauma, paediatric care). In a survey organised by the Working Group on Outcome of the Health Services Research and Outcome Section of the European Society of Intensive Care Medicine (ESICM) in 2008, and administered via the internet, the percentages of mixed ICUs admitting both medical and surgical patients were 100 % in Central & South America and in Australasia, 85.7 % in Southern Europe & Mediterranean Countries and in Northern Europe, 75 % in Central & Western Europe, 71 % in Eastern Europe, but only 40 % in North America.

The organisation of the ICU differs significantly between countries, and sometimes within the same country. This phenomenon may be due at least in part to the different kinds of legal certification, or to the lack of a legal certification, of intensive care for intensivists in the various countries. The European Directive on the Recognition of Professional Qualifications [3] did not explicitly identify intensive care medicine as a medical specialty, and, only in 2008, the European Union of Medical Specialties endorsed the proposal of the ESICM that

Tab. 1 Physician activities performed in the ICU according to the definition of open and closed units

Activity	Performed or prescribed by	
	in closed ICU	in open ICU
Preadmission evaluation	intensivist	primary physician
Decision to admit the patient to ICU	intensivist	primary physician
Writing orders	intensivist	primary physician ± consultants
Daily rounds	intensivist ± nurses	primary physician ± nurses
Prescription of medications	intensivist	primary physician
Prescription of laboratory analysis	intensivist	primary physician
Management of mechanical ventilation	intensivist/nurse	primary physician/nurse
Decision to perform surgery	intensivist with surgeon	primary physician ± surgeon
Night and weekend coverage	team of intensivists	non-intensivist
Decision to discharge the patient from ICU	intensivist	primary physician
Administrative functions attributed to ICU	intensivist	primary physician's service

intensive care medicine should be recognised in the European Directive on the Recognition of Professional Qualifications as a 'Particular Medical Competence'. This term does not mandate a particular structure for intensive care medicine training or practice, and is compatible with all forms currently available in Europe. In fact, only in a few countries, such as Spain, Switzerland, Australia and New Zealand, intensive care medicine is a primary medical specialty, like pneumology and surgery, accessed directly after undergraduate medical training [4]. In other countries, intensive care medicine may be classified as a subspecialty from a single discipline – anaesthesia being the most frequent – as in Denmark, Italy, Norway and Sweden, or from multiple disciplines, like in Germany and the USA [5]. The concept of intensive care medicine as a supraspecialty, which implies multidisciplinary access from a range of base specialties, is adopted in Belgium, Ireland, Netherlands, Portugal and UK. Moreover, to make the puzzle even more fuzzy, there are countries where the different models coexist, as in Austria and France [5].

The wide differences between countries in training and certification of intensive care may have influenced the organisation of ICUs, the management being provided by intensivists in the countries where intensive care medicine is a well defined and certified medical specialty, or otherwise, by the primary physician attending to the patient.

Definition of open and closed models

The organisation models of ICU are commonly described as "open" or "closed" [6]. Table 1 summarises the activities performed by either the intensivist or the primary physician according to the two models of ICU organisation.

In an "open" ICU, the primary physician chooses whether to admit the patient, prescribes treatments and maintains the responsibility for any patient management decisions. The primary physician may require the consultation of an intensivist, if available, as well as of other specialists. One of the pros of this model is that the continuity of care is maintained, because the primary physician who knows the medical history of the patient is facilitated in taking decisions. It has been claimed that the open model respects the relationship between the patient and the physician/surgeon, but its consequence is rather that there are periods of time when the patients may simply not be cared for, as is the case when the primary physician is engaged in different activities in the hospital or is away from the hospital (for instance at night). The ICU patients who are unstable require the continuous presence of a competent physician, 24 hours a day and 7 days a week [7]. In fact, the sudden development of a life-threatening condition (pneumothorax can be taken as an example) necessitates immediate decisions. The open model is adopted in many US hospitals, where the private health insurance system favours the direct relationship between the patient and the physician/surgeon.

In most of the European countries or in Australia and New Zealand, the ICUs are "closed" or "intensivist-led" units where the intensivist takes on the senior role while the patient's primary physician acts as a consultant for the period of the patient's stay in the ICU. Moreover, the closed model requires a team of full-time intensivists to guarantee presence at night and during weekends, and a full-time medical director. It has been claimed that this model should provide optimal resident training, facilitate adoption of protocols and guidelines, and allow rapid adjustments of treatment and early interventions to treat complications. On the other hand, the continuous presence of an intensivist is essential to guarantee the multidisciplinary approach needed by the patients with interrelated complex multiple organ dysfunction or failure. The consultation of other specialists may be necessary, so the intensivists must be able to communicate and cooperate with colleagues of the same as well as other disciplines. Finally, in the closed model, the intensivist performs preadmission evaluation and is responsible for admission or refusal of the patients (so called "triage"), as well as for any treatment given to the ICU patients.

The history of intensive care units

The reason for the existence of different models of ICU organisation seems to be related to the history of intensive care in different cultures. Generally speaking, according to the books and media available to the public, we can find two different descriptions of the emergence of intensive care units.

In Great Britain and North America

Florence Nightingale (1820–1910), who was a nurse during the Crimean War in 1854, first identified the necessity to separate the seriously wounded soldiers from those less seriously wounded. She reduced mortality from 40% to 2% on the battlefield, creating the concept of intensive care. By definition, the unit was open, because the aim was to facilitate nursing management.

In 1923, W.E. Dandy helped to establish the first American ICU for postoperative neurosurgical patients, but the modern surgical ICU suitable for treating patients needing prolonged care was developed in the 1960s [8]. Surgical ICUs spread as a logical adjunct to ambitious surgical procedures, and medical ICUs developed subsequently.

A survey performed in the USA in 1991 showed that critical care medicine certification of the medical director and attending staff of the ICU increased as hospital size increased, although 22% of ICUs participating in the survey used a closed model and only 44% of all units stated that their directors were certified [9].

The percentage of hospital beds devoted to ICU averaged 8% in the USA in 1991 [9]. In 2000, in comparison with 1985, the number of ICU hospital beds in acute care hospitals with at least one ICU was increased by 26.2%, while the number of hospital beds was decreased by 26.4% [10]. The finding that generally 13% of acute care hospital beds are ICU beds suggests that at least some low-severity patients needing a lower level of medical care are admitted to those US ICUs.

In continental Europe

The polio epidemic which occurred in Denmark in 1952 represented a tremendous challenge for the health system: On one day, up to 70 young patients presented respiratory failure due to muscular paralysis [11]. The only treatment available at the time was a tank or cuirass ventilator, but the number of those devices was not great enough to treat all patients. Epidemiologist Dr H.C.A. Lassen consulted anaesthetist Dr B. Ibsen for the care of their patients [12]. As a consequence, they organised a management of the respiratory failure based on tracheostomy and manual positive pressure ventilation with a rubber bag [11]. The manpower for manual artificial ventilation was guaranteed by 200 medical students for several weeks. As a result, mortality dropped and, at the same time, the development of the mechanical ventilator was strongly stimulated [13]. Of course, it was comfortable to collect the patients needing ventilation in a centralised place. Thus, the introduction of artificial ventilation during the polio epidemic is generally considered as the European birth of intensive care, and the unit where physicians and nurses observed and treated those patients 24 hours a day, created by Ibsen [14], is regarded as the first European ICU.

Generally, ICUs are closed in Europe as well as in Australia and New Zealand. In the European Prevalence of Infection in Intensive Care (EPIC) study performed in 1992, Italy and Spain had the highest number of ICUs with a full-time doctor, while the Netherlands and Finland had the lowest number. In 67.2% of the ICUs there was an ICU director, Greece and Spain having the highest number and the United Kingdom and Ireland the lowest [15].

A recommendation of a task force of the ESICM claimed in 1997 that the director of the ICU should be an intensivist and that a qualified intensivist should be present 24 hours a day [16].

Effects of open or closed units on outcomes

In the current period of evidence-based medicine, we would expect the scientific literature to have answered the obvious question on which model, open or closed, is associated with better outcomes, and should therefore be preferred. Unfortunately, the issue appears really complex with respect to an appropriate methodological design of a study aimed at answering that question.

Methodological issues

The outcome of highest relevance should at least be hospital, not ICU, mortality, as reported in one old study [17]. In fact, the ICU is just one of the units of the entire health institution which is the hospital, and the aim of the hospital is to discharge people recovered, admitted or not to the ICU during the course of their illness. Moreover, not all patients discharged alive from the ICU leave the hospital alive: In-hospital post-ICU mortality is a well-known phenomenon [18–19].

Hospital discharge as the end point allows circumvention of the effect of ICU discharge policy, which can be strongly influenced by the discharge facilities present in the institution. Hospital mortality could also be influenced by the availability of skilled nursing rehabilitation facilities and nursing homes [20]; nevertheless, mortality at a fixed time, which should be preferred, is unpractical to collect.

Another interesting outcome could be length of stay. In fact, if open and closed ICUs are equally effective on hospital mortality, one of the two models could be associated with shorter length of stay. The information would be relevant, especially if the shortening concerns the length of the ICU stay because the ICU is the most expensive unit in the hospital. Considering the costs of each non-ICU day as reference, the cost of the first day in the ICU has been found to be associated with a 4-fold increase and that of each of the subsequent days in the ICU with a 2.5-fold increase [21].

One of the difficulties in evaluating an association between open or closed models and the outcomes arises from the high number of studies devoted to the analysis of only one of the ICU's organisational aspects. There are studies analysing: clinical rounds by an ICU physician [22–23], presence of a full-time intensivist [24–25], 24-h intensivist cover [26–27], managerial activity of the ICU medical director [28], or intensivist-to-ICU-bed ratio [29]. Moreover, in real life, things may be more complicated: For instance, in the case of a lack of reciprocal trust between intensivists and primary physicians, the primary physician may postpone intensivist consultation until it is impossible to avoid it, which is late in the course of the patient's illness. On the other hand, in settings with good cooperation between intensivists and primary physicians, the intensivist may take care of, and responsibility for, the patient even if the consultation is not mandatory. As a result, that open unit may be similar to a closed one.

Other possible limitations of studies devoted to the topic can be summarised as follows. First, to use historical controls or before-after study design, even when adjusting for common patient confounding variables like age, diagnosis and severity of illness, may not cover residual confounders, as well as the so-called temporal

Tab. 2 Studies comparing open and closed ICU models. Type of patients mixed: medical and surgical

Author	Type of patients	N. of patients in unit		Hospital mortality	Adjusted significance
		open	closed		
Li et al. [35]	Mixed	463	491	32 % vs 30 %	p 0.01
Reynolds et al. [36]	Septic shock	100	112	74 % vs 57 %	p < 0.05
Carson et al. [37]	Medical	124	121	23 % vs 31 %	NS
Manthous et al. [38]	Medical	459	471	34 % vs 25 %	p 0.002
Multz et al. [39]*	Medical	95	185	38 % vs 28 %	p < 0.04
Ghorra et al. [40]	Surgical	125	149	20 % vs 9 %	NS
Hanson et al. [41]* °	Surgical	100	100	6 % vs 4 %	NS
Baldock et al. [42]	Medical	295	330	28 % vs 20 %	p 0.005

* simultaneous cohort; ° study patients randomly selected from an ICU database

trend, which may be affected by the spreading of increased knowledge also through education [30]. On the other hand, the studies comparing simultaneous cohorts may be influenced by the case mix which is always difficult to adjust to, while randomisation is not practicable. Secondly, studies presented only as abstracts and never published in any peer-reviewed journals may suggest poor quality of data collection or design, and should be considered of lower value. Thirdly, studies performed on paediatric ICUs [31–33] may be of value, but should be confirmed in adult ICUs, because adults and children are different populations.

Findings reported in the scientific literature

A systematic review, performed on the period 1965–2001, selected 26 relevant observational studies examining ICU attending physician staffing strategies and the outcomes of hospital and ICU mortality and length of stay [34]. The ICUs were grouped according to physician staffing into the following two groups: high-intensity (mandatory intensivist consultation or care directed by the intensivist) and low-intensity (no intensivist or elective intensivist consultation). High-intensity staffing was associated with lower risk of hospital mortality (OR 0.71, with a 95 % confidence interval CI 0.62–0.82). Moreover, high-intensity staffing reduced both ICU and hospital length of

stay adjusted for case mix in two of 18 and 13 studies, respectively.

The hospital mortality recorded in the studies performed in single institutions [35–42] is reported in Table 2. Most of them investigated the effects of the change from the open to the closed model and five of them reported a significant reduction in hospital mortality when the adjustment for confounding variables was done. Moreover, some of them found a reduction of ICU length of stay [38–39, 41] or resource use [40–41], but others did not [37]. Unfortunately, some of them may be underpowered and lead to inadequate conclusions [43].

Considering only the articles on adult patients admitted to more than one ICU, the number of studies devoted to the comparison between open and closed ICU models is not high. In 1998, Multz et al. [39] in an elegant study used a prospective cohort analysis on data collected in two ICUs (one open and one closed) of two institutions, and a retrospective analysis comparing outcomes before and after the unit closure in one of the two institutions. They demonstrated that, with a lack of any significant difference in hospital mortality, the ICU length of stay was statistically and clinically shorter in the closed ICU. The difference in the number of admissions was related to the number of beds allocated to medical patients in the ICUs (10 in the open vs. 15 in the closed ICU). Interestingly, the retrospective comparison of the closed ICU with the time when it was open confirmed significantly shorter ICU length of stay and duration of mechanical ventilation with the closed model.

The largest study investigating the effect of ICU organisation on patient outcome included all Maryland hospitals that performed abdominal aortic surgery from 1994 to 1996, and considered the patients aged 30 years or older who underwent that type of surgery in the period [22]. Information about the organisation of the ICUs was collected using a questionnaire administered to the ICU directors and the analysis was performed on 39 hospitals and 2,606 patients. The multivariate analysis showed that not having daily rounds by an ICU physician vs. having daily rounds by an ICU physician was independently associated with a 3-fold increase in hospital mortality (OR 3.0, 95% CI 1.9–4.9). Moreover, not having daily rounds by an ICU physician was also associated with a mean increase of 83% (95% CI 48%-126%) in ICU length of stay. The sample size of the study and the mortality of the surgery considered allowed enough statistical power, and the daily round of ICU physician seems to be a reliable marker for intensivist team care, even if the authors did not clearly define the ICUs as open or closed [22]. Interestingly, a recent paper performed on the Hospital Outcome Cohort of the SAPS 3 Database [44], used to develop the SAPS 3 Admission Score [45], added a new piece to the jigsaw puzzle of ICU activities. Rothen et al. [46] found that the presence of interprofessional clinical rounds (i.e. participation of both physicians and nurses) in a given unit was associated with a 2.7 times (95% CI 1.2–6.2) higher chance that this unit belonged to the group of "most efficient" ICUs rather than to the group of "least efficient" ICUs. The study of Pronovost et al. [22] may be criticised for the following limitations: ICU admission presumed according to the country habits but not clearly demonstrated, lack of any severity scoring system to adjust for patient severity of illness, analysis performed on a hospital basis but lack of information about the care received before and after ICU, and, particularly, the low number of patients collected in the hospitals without daily rounds by an ICU physician. Nevertheless, the large administrative database, the well-defined procedure considered and the adjustment for surgery (elective, urgent or emergency) suggests a true effect of the presence of an ICU physician.

The effect of daily rounds by an ICU physician on another type of surgery has been investigated in 31 hospitals [23] in the same area, during an overlapping period, and using the same survey instrument as in the study of Pronovost et al. [22]. Again, having daily rounds by an ICU physician after oesophageal resection was associated with a decreased length of stay and decreased hospital costs, even if hospital mortality was not affected. The small sample size did not provide enough statistical power to detect the effect of organisation on hospital mortality [23].

In a study evaluating patients admitted to the ICU with intracerebral haemorrhage, Diringer et al. [25] compared the hospital mortality of those admitted to two neurologic ICUs having full-time intensivists with that of those admitted to 40 general ICUs (23% having full-time intensivists). Their multivariate logistic regression analysis showed that having a full-time intensivist was an independent predictor of lower hospital mortality (OR 0.388; 95% CI 0.22–0.67). Unfortunately, only two neurologic ICUs were considered, and the participation in the study of general ICUs was on a voluntary basis, within a national program to assess ICU performance. On the other hand, the protective effect of active involvement of full-time ICU physicians (direct care of ICU patients or mandatory consultation on all ICU admissions) on ICU length of stay was also recorded in a subsequent study performed on project IMPACT data [25].

In a recent comparison between 30 open and 38 closed (intensivist-led) ICUs involving 6,789 trauma patients [47], the adjusted relative risk of death in closed compared with open ICUs was 0.78 (95% CI 0.58–1.04). Nevertheless, it was significantly lower for patients aged ≥ 55 y admitted to closed ICUs (OR 0.55; 95% CI 0.39–0.77), as well as for those admitted to ICUs whose director was board-certified in surgery and critical care (OR 0.67; 95% CI 0.50–0.90). Unfortunately, the sample size (1561 in open and 5228 in closed ICUs) may have been responsible for a type II error. Moreover, it is surprising to note that, despite the definition of the intensivist-led model, the ICU team had the sole authority to write orders in only 8% of the closed ICUs.

Finally, an analysis on the patients with acute lung injury admitted to 24 ICUs in the USA (391 to 11 open and 684 to 13 closed units) demonstrated that, after adjusting for potential confounders, the patients receiving care in closed ICUs had significantly lower hospital mortality (OR 0.68; 95% CI 0.53–0.89; p 0.004) than those treated in open ICUs [48]. Surprisingly, protocols for patients requiring mechanical ventilation were available in 58% of closed and in 80% of open ICUs (p 0.28], but high tidal volume ventilation (> 12 ml/kg of predicted body weight) on the third day was applied significantly less frequently in closed than in open ICUs (10% vs. 31%, respectively; p < 0.001) and the reverse was true for protective lung ventilation (< 6.5 ml/kg of predicted body weight), applied in 5% vs. 11% of patients, respectively (p < 0.004).

Completely different findings were reported in a recent article assessing the association between critical care physician management and hospital mortality in the IMPACT database [49]. The organisation of the ICU was defined according to the answer given by trained data entry personnel to the following question: Was the patient managed by a critical care physician/team? The 123 ICUs surveyed were divided into three groups according to the percentage of patients managed by ICU physicians for the entire ICU stay (≥ 95%; between 95% and 5%; ≤ 5%), while the patients managed by ICU physicians for only a part of the ICU stay were excluded. The ICUs where ≥ 95% of patients were managed by ICU physicians were larger and in larger hospitals than the others. The standardised mortality ratio was higher for the patients admitted to ICUs where ≥ 95% of patients were managed by ICU physicians in comparison with the patients admitted to ICUs where ≤ 5% of patients were managed by ICU physicians (OR 1.09; 95% CI 1.05–1.13 and 0.91; 0.88–0.94, respectively). A random-effects logistic regression model including 59,106 patients managed by ICU physicians for the entire ICU stay and 59,106 patients not managed by ICU physicians, with the addition of an expanded SAPS II and the inclusion of a propensity score, produced a significant OR of 1.4. Unfortunately, 55% of the former and 62% of the latter patients were admitted to ICUs where the percentage of patients managed by ICU physicians for the entire ICU stay was between 5% and 95%. The authors concluded that they were not able to demonstrate any survival benefit associated with the management by ICU physicians, even if they

acknowledged their inability to identify patients managed by full-time non-resident intensivists [49]. Many comments raising concerns about the study were published: They suggested the presence of unmeasured confounders like urban vs. rural, academic vs. community institutions, or patient socioeconomic status [50], lack of adjustment for strong predictors of death as clinical estimation of prognosis [51], or residual confounding concerning both physician certification and presence of the intensivist [52] and ICU volume [53]. In fact, for an European physician it is difficult to understand how an ICU can provide critical care management only to a percentage of the patients admitted, because the ICU team has to manage 100% of the patients. Moreover, the definition of a critical care physician included physicians recognised by the institution as critical care physicians, those having passed the critical care medicine board examination and those qualified to take the examination. And to be qualified to take an examination does not mean to have passed it.

Factors influencing ICU organisation

The decision to adopt an open or closed model, which in the past was mainly based on the historical background of different countries, may at present be viewed mainly as political. From a clinical point of view, two arguments strongly favour the closed model:

- The complexity of medicine, and especially of intensive care medicine, has so dramatically increased over the last decades that it is difficult to hypothesise that a primary physician/ surgeon may be as competent as a full-time intensivist [7];
- The continuous presence of the intensivist in the ICU should allow the frequent reappraisal of the patients' clinical condition, and more rapid weaning from mechanical ventilation and vasoactive support, reducing both ICU length of stay and costs.

Despite these positive impacts, there are some political and economic factors which may influence the decision to adopt a closed model.

When the patient is managed by the intensivist, the primary physician may lose the strongest stimulus for learning, which is to be responsible for the care of sick patients [54]. As a consequence of the lack of the need to maintain intensive care medicine competence, the primary physician's knowledge will become obsolete. Moreover, the intensivist may tend to exclude the primary physician from decision-making, whilst the primary physician has the obligation toward the patient and the family to take care of the patient over the entire course of hospital stay, and must be able to guarantee continuity of care. Finally, the primary physicians will not get paid for intensive care unless they provide it [54]. Of course, this issue may not be a consideration in countries with a national health service funded by taxpayers, but it may be highly relevant where there is only private insurance.

The intensivist in a closed ICU has the responsibility of evaluating each patient before admission, as well as deciding on admission to and discharge from the ICU. Carlson et al. [37] found that the severity of illness of patients admitted to ICUs with the same medical specialisation was significantly higher when the ICU was closed than when it was open. Given the general admission policy of the intensivist (to admit the most seriously ill patients among those with a chance for recovery), it can happen that there is no bed available for a patient scheduled for surgery, or that the low-risk surgical patient admitted for monitoring is discharged at night to admit a new patient. Both the surgeon and the hospital administration will be dissatisfied with such management associated with postponed surgery. Moreover, as far as the economic aspect is concerned, the closed model implies additional costs for full-time physician teams, especially when covering on site 24 hours, 7 days a week. Even if a reduced length of ICU stay [22, 39] and a reduced number of consults [40] has been reported for closed ICUs, the effect on costs is not clear [55]. In addition, variable costs may be strongly influenced by the individual intensivists working in the ICU [56].

Although it has been calculated that the implementation of intensivist-model ICUs would save approximately 58,850 lives each year in the USA [57], a relevant argument against the full adoption of a closed model is that there are not enough intensivists to provide full-time staffing for all units throughout the USA, and demand will grow as the population ages and the use of ICUs increases [58]. An attempt to solve the prob-

lem may be offered by telemedicine [59–60]. Nevertheless, some stakeholders have already suggested the adoption of a closed model. The Leapfrog Group, a coalition of more than 170 public and private US organisations that provide health care to more than 36 million people, has made ICU physician staffing an important quality indicator for its beneficiaries. A recent article reported that only 4 % of US ICUs provide intensivist management that meets the full Leapfrog standards [61].

Finally, other caveats remain when the full-time on-site intensivist team model with night and weekend coverage is adopted in a given country. In fact, considering that the total volume of ICU activity correlates with risk-adjusted mortality, and that the higher the high-risk volume of activity, the lower the adjusted mortality of patient population [62], the problem of a low volume of activity will remain both for the ICUs (i.e. rural or small hospital ICUs) and for individual intensivists working in those ICUs. Moreover, the risk of fatigue, exhaustion and burnout attributed to prolonged periods of stressful work cannot be overlooked, and neither should the fact that such hard work may make intensive care medicine a less desirable specialty for young physicians.

Towards the future

The present organisation of ICUs in Europe is mainly based on the concept of an ICU team under the supervision of a physician with specific competence, that is the intensivist, who is responsible for patient care while the patient is in the ICU. The debate is moving toward other aspects, such as the presence of a team of full-time intensivists on-site 24 hours, 7 days a week [26–27, 63], or the out-of-hours on-site coverage by in-training physicians [64]. In fact, there are studies demonstrating an increased mortality of patients admitted to ICUs during weekends and week nights [65–66], especially in teaching hospitals [67]. This finding was not confirmed in ICUs with on-site coverage provided 24 hours, 7 days a week, by on-site board-certified intensivists [68], and in France [69], where ICU admission from the community by the French Emergency Medical Service may guarantee first aid by an experienced physician even if physicians-in-training may cover some ICUs. As a consequence, it seems that a lower level of ICU staffing may be responsible for the higher mortality of patients admitted to the

ICU out-of-hours, but the greater severity of illness as well as the lower level of staffing in other ancillary services may also play a role [64].

The language is subject to changes over time. Therefore, it should be noted that a new meaning of the open and closed unit models has recently appeared in the scientific literature, especially in Italy [70]. The new meaning of a "closed" ICU refers to highly restrictive visiting policies, limiting the admission and attendance of family members, while the new meaning of an "open" ICU refers to a unit oriented toward the implementation of non-restrictive visiting policies and committed to removing barriers like those of time and relationships [71]. In the future, the concept of open and closed visiting policies will possibly become more widespread, due to the increasing attention devoted to patients and families [72] in view of patient-centred care.

A final remark concerns the evolving role of the intensivist, apart from the issue of open or closed ICUs. The complexity of intensive, and generally, of medical treatments is pushing towards a change of the role of the intensivist, who is becoming the leader who directs and orchestrates the multidisciplinary approach to the patient. In other words, he/she is responsible for the care of the ICU patient, without being alone in taking decisions, but supported by the active role played by other specialists. Therefore, the ability of the intensivist to discuss and cooperate with colleagues of different disciplines will become more and more relevant in the future.

The authors

Maurizia Capuzzo, MD[1]
Andreas Valentin, MD[2]
Raffaele Alvisi, MD[1]
[1]Department of Anaesthesiology and Intensive Care Medicine | University Hospital of Ferrara | Ferrara, Italy
[2]General and Medical Intensive Care Unit | II Medical Department | KA Rudolfstiftung | Vienna, Austria

Address for correspondence

Maurizia Capuzzo
Department of Anaesthesiology and Intensive Care Medicine
University Hospital of Ferrara
Corso Giovecca 203
44100 Ferrara, Italy
E-mail: cpm@unife.it

References

1. Fisher MM. Critical care, specialty without frontiers. Crit Care Clin 1997;13:235–43
2. Rubenfeld GD, Angus DC. Are intensivists safe? Ann Intern Med 2008;148:877–9
3. Directive 2005/36/EC of the European Parliament and of the Council of 7 September on the recognition of professional qualifications. Official journal of the European Union 30.9.2005 L 255/22-L 255/141
4. Domínguez-Roldán J-M. Specialty of intensive care: Primary specialty vs supraspecialty. In: Kuhlen R, Moreno R, Ranieri M, Rhodes A (Eds.). Controversies in Intensive Care Medicine. MVV Medizinisch Wissenschaftliche Verlagsgesellschaft. Berlin, 2008. pp 421–429
5. Barrett H, Bion JF. An international survey of training in adult intensive care medicine. Intensive Care Med 2005;31:553–61
6. Takkala J. Organisation of intensive care. In: Kuhlen R, Moreno R, Ranieri M, Rhodes A (Eds.). 25 Years of Progress and Innovation in Intensive Care Medicine. MVV Medizinisch Wissenschaftliche Verlagsgesellschaft. Berlin, 2007. pp 343–50
7. Vincent JL. Need for intensivists in intensive care units. Lancet 2000;356:695–6
8. Mizock BA, Weil MH. Introduction: History and destiny of critical care medicine. In: Carlson RW, Geheb MA (Eds). Principles & practice of medical intensive care. WB Saunders Company, Philadelphia, 1993. pp1–7
9. Groeger JS, Strosberg MA, Halpern NA, Raphaely RC, Kaye WE, Guntupalli KK, et al. Descriptive analysis of critical care units in the United States. Crit Care Med 1992;20:846–63
10. Halpern NA, Pastores SM, Greenstein RJ. Critical care medicine in the United States 1985–2000: An analysis of bed numbers, use, and costs. Crit Care Med 2004;32:1254–9
11. Lassen HCA. A preliminary report on the 1952 epidemic of poliomyelitis in Copenhagen with special references to the treatment of acute respiratory insufficiency. Lancet;1953:i:37–41
12. Suter PM. History of intensive care medicine in Europe: A few landmarks. In: Kuhlen R, Moreno R, Ranieri M, Rhodes A (Eds.). 25 Years of Progress and Innovation in Intensive Care Medicine. MVV Medizinisch Wissenschaftliche Verlagsgesellschaft. Berlin, 2007. pp 329–32
13. Engström CG. Treatment of severe cases of respiratory paralysis by the Engstrom universal respirator. Br Med J 1954;2:666–9
14. Ibsen B. Treatment of respiratory complications in poliomyelitis; the anaesthetist's viewpoint. Dan Med Bull 1954;1:9–12
15. Vincent JL, Suter P, Binari D, Bruining H. Organization of intensive care units in Europe: lessons from the EPIC study. Intensive Care Med 1997;23:1181–4

16. Ferdinande P. Recommendations on minimal requirements for intensive care departments. Intensive Care Med 1997;23:226–32

17. Brown JJ, Sullivan G. Effect on ICU mortality of a full-time critical care specialist. Chest 1989;96:127–9

18. Iapichino G, Morabito A, Mistraletti G, Ferla L, Radrizzani D, Miranda DR. Determinants of post-intensive care mortality in high-level treated critically ill patients. Intensive Care Med 2003; 29:1751–1756

19. Azoulay E, Adrie C, De Lassence A, Pochard F, Moreau D, Thiery G, et al. Determinants of postintensive care unit mortality: A prospective multicenter study. Crit Care Med 2003;31:428–32

20. Sirio CA, Shepardson LB, Rotondi AJ, Cooper GS, Angus DC, Harper DL, Rosenthal GE. Community-wide assessment of intensive care outcomes using a physiologically based prognostic measure. Implications for critical care delivery from Cleveland Health Quality Choice. Chest. 1999;115:793–801

21. Rapoport J, Teres D, Zhao Y, Lemeshow S. Length of stay data as a guide to hospital economic performance for ICU patients. Med Care 2003;41:386–97

22. Pronovost PJ, Jenckes MW, Dorman T, Garrett E, Breslow MJ, Rosenfeld BA et al. Organizational characteristics of intensive care units related to outcomes of abdominal aortic surgery. JAMA 1999;281:1310–7

23. Dimick JB, Pronovost PJ, Heitmiller RF, Lipsett PA. Intensive care unit physician staffing is associated with decreased length of stay, hospital cost, and complications after esophageal resection. Crit Care Med 2001;29:753–8

24. Diringer MN, Edwards DF. Admission to a neurologic/neurosurgical intensive care unit is associated with reduced mortality rate after intracerebral hemorrhage. Crit Care Med 2001;29:635–40

25. Higgins TL, McGee WT, Steingrub JS, Rapoport J, Lemeshow S, Teres D. Early indicators of prolonged intensive care unit stay: Impact of illness severity, physician staffing, and pre-intensive care unit length of stay. Crit Care Med 2003;31:45–51

26. Blunt MC, Burchett KR. Out-of-hours consultant cover and case-mix-adjusted mortality in intensive care. Lancet 2000;356:735–6

27. Gajic O, Afessa B, Hanson AC, Krpata T, Yilmaz M, Mohamed SF et al. Effects of 24-hour mandatory versus on demand critical care specialist on quality of care and family and provider satisfaction in the intensive care unit of a teaching hospital. Crit Care Med 2008;36:36–44

28. Mallick R, Strosberg M, Lambrinos J, Groeger JS. The intensive care unit medical director as manager. Impact on performance. Med Care 995;33:611–24

29. Dara SI, Afessa B. Intensivist-to-Bed Ratio. Association with outcomes in the medical ICU. Chest 2005;128:567–72

30. Ferrer R, Artigas A, Levy MM, Blanco J, González-Díaz G, Garnacho-Montero J, et al. Improvement in process of care and outcome after a multicenter severe sepsis educational program in Spain. JAMA 2008;299:2294–303

31. Pollack MM, Katz RW, Ruttimann UE, Getson PR. Improving the outcome and efficiency of intensive care: the impact of an intensivist. Crit Care Med 1988;16:11–7

32. Pollack MM, Cuerdon TT, Patel KM, Ruttimann UE, Getson PR, Levetown M. Impact of quality-of-care factors on pediatric intensive care unit mortality. JAMA 1994;272:941–6

33. Goh AYT, Lum LCS, Abdel-Latif MEA. Impact of 24 hour critical care physician staffing on case-mix adjusted mortality in paediatric intensive care. Lancet 2001;357:445–6

34. Pronovost PJ, Nagus DC, Dorman T, Robinson KA, Dremsizov TT, Young TL. Physician staffing patterns and clinical outcomes in critically ill patients. A systematic review. JAMA 2002;288:2151–62

35. Li TC, Phillips MC, Shaw L, Cook EF, Natanson C, Goldman L. On-site physician staffing in a community hospital intensive care unit. JAMA 1984;252:2023–7

36. Reynolds HN, Haupt MT, Thill-Baharozian MC, Carlson RW. Impact of critical care physician staffing on patients with septic shock in a university hospital medical intensive care unit. JAMA 1988;260:3446–50.

37. Carson SS, Stocking C, Podsadecki T, Christenson J, Pohlman A, McRae S et al. Effects of organizational change in the medical intensive care unit of a teaching hospital. JAMA 1996;276:322–8

38. Manthous CA, Amoateng-Adjepong Y, al- Kharrat T, Jacob B, Alnuaimat HM, Chatila W et al. Effects of a medical intensivist on patient care in a community teaching hospital. Mayo Clin Proc 1997;72:391–9

39. Multz AS, Chalfin DB, Samson IM, Dantzker DR, Fein AM; Steinberg HN, et al. A "closed" Medical Intensive Care Unit (MICU) improves resource utilization when compared with an "open" MICU. Am J Respir Crit Care Med 1998;157:1468–73

40. Ghorra S, Reinert SE, Cioffi W, Buczko G, Simms HH. Analysis of the effect of conversion from open to closed surgical intensive care unit. Ann Surg 1999;229:163–71

41. Hanson, CW III, Deutschman CS, Anderson, HL III, Reilly PM, Behringer EC, Schwab CW, et al. Effects of an organized critical care service on outcomes and resource utilization: A cohort study. Crit Care Med 1999;27:270–4

42. Baldock G, Foley P, Brett S. The impact of organisational change on outcome in an intensive care unit in the United Kingdom. Intensive Care Med 2001;27:865–72

43. Halpern SD, Karlawish JH, Berlin JA. The continuing unethical conduct of underpowered clinical trials. JAMA 2002;288:358–62

44. Metnitz PGH, Moreno RP, Almeida E, Jordan B, Bauer P, Abizanda Campos R, et al. SAPS 3 – From Evaluation of the Patient to Evaluation of the ICU. Part 1. Objectives,

methods and cohort description. Intensive Care Med 2005;31:1336–44

45. Moreno RP, Metnitz PGH, Almeida E, Jordan B, Bauer P, Abizanda Campos R, et al. SAPS 3 – From Evaluation of the Patient to Evaluation of the ICU. Part 2. Development of a prognostic model for hospital mortality at ICU admission. Intensive Care Med 2005;31:1345–55

46. Rothen HU, Stricker K, Einfalt J, Bauer P, Metnitz PGH, Moreno RP et al. Variability in outcome and resource use in intensive care units. Intensive Care Med 2007;33:1329–36

47. Nathens AB, Rivara FP, MacKenzie EJ, Maier RV, Wang J, Egleston B, et al. The impact of an intensivist-model ICU on trauma-related mortality. Ann Surg 2006;244: 545–54

48. Treggiari MM, Martin DP, Yanez DN, Cladwell E, Hudson LD, Rubenfeld GD. Effect of intensive care unit organizational model and structure on outcomes in patients with acute lung injury. Am J Respir Crit Care Med 2007;685–90

49. Levy MM, Rapoport J, Lemeshow S, Chalfin DB, Phillips G, Danis M. Association between Critical care Physician Management and Patient Mortality in the Intensive Care Unit. Ann Intern Med 2008;148:801–9

50. Higgins TL, Nathanson B, Teres D. What conclusions should be drawn between critical care physician management and patient mortality in the intensive care unit? Ann Intern Med 2008;149:767

51. Arends JJ, Vandenbroucke JP. What conclusions should be drawn between critical care physician management and patient mortality in the intensive care unit? Ann Intern Med 2008;149:768–9

52. Manthous C, Amoateng-Adjepong Y. What conclusions should be drawn between critical care physician management and patient mortality in the intensive care unit? Ann Intern Med 2008;149:770

53. Marik P, Myburgh J. What conclusions should be drawn between critical care physician management and patient mortality in the intensive care unit? Ann Intern Med 2008;149:770–1

54. Trunkey DD. An unacceptable concept. Ann Surg 1999;229:172–3

55. Pronovost PJ, Needham DM, Waters H, Birkmeyer CM, Calinawan JR, Birkmeyer JD, et al. Intensive care unit physician staffing: financial modeling of the Leapfrog standard. Crit Care Med. 2006 Mar;34(3 Suppl):S18–24.

56. Garland A, Shaman Z, Baron J, Connors AF. Physician-attributable differences in intensive care unit costs. Am J Respir Crit Care Med 2006;174:1206–10

57. Young MP, Birkmeyer JD. Potential reduction in mortality rates using an intensivist model to manage intensive care units. Eff Clin Pract 2000;3:284–9

58. Angus DC, Kelley MA, Schmitz RJ, White A, Popovic J Jr.

Current and projected workforce requirements for care of the critically ill and patients with pulmonary disease: can we meet the requirements of an ageing population? JAMA 2000;284:2762–70

59. Rosenfeld BA, Dorman T, Breslow MJ, Pronovost P, Jenckes M, Zhang N, et al Intensive care unit telemedicine: alternate paradigm for providing continuous intensivist care. Crit Care Med 2000;28:3925–31

60. Breslow MJ, Rosenfeld BA, Doerfler M, Burke G, Yates G, Stone DJ, et al. Effect of a multiple-site intensive care unit telemedicine program on clinical and economic outcomes: an alternative paradigm for intensivist staffing. Crit Care Med. 2004;32:31–8

61. Angus DC, Shorr AF, White A, Dremsizov TT, Schmitz RJ, Kelley MA. Critical care delivery in the United States: distribution of services and compliance with Leapfrog recommendations. Crit Care Med 2006;34:1016–24

62. Iapichino G, Gattinoni L, Radrizzani D, Simini B, Bertolini G, Ferla L et al. Volume of activity and occupancy rate in intensive care units: Association with mortality. Intensive Care Med 2004;30:290–7

63. Buchardi H, Moerer O. Twenty-four hour presence of physicians in the ICU. Crit Care 2001;5:131–7

64. Arabi Y. Pro/Con debate: Should 24/7 in-house intensivist coverage be implemented? Crit Care 2008;12:216

65. Bell CM, Redelmeier DA. Mortality among patients admitted to hospitals on weekends as compared with weekdays. N Engl J Med 2001, 345:663–8

66. Uusaro A, Kari A, Ruokonen E. The effects of ICU admissions and discharge times on mortality in Finland. Intensive Care Med 2003;29:2144–8

67. Cram P, Hillis SL, Barnett M, Rosenthal GE. Effects of weekend admission and hospital teaching status on in-hospital mortality. Am J Med 2004;117:151–7

68. Arabi Y, Alshimemeri A, Taher S. Weekend and weeknight admissions have the same outcome of weekday admissions to an intensive care unit with onsite intensivist coverage. Crit Care Med 2006;34:605–11

69. Luyt CE, Combes A, Aegerter P, Guidet B, Trouillet JL, Gibert C, Chastre J. Mortality among patients admitted to intensive care units during weekday day shifts compared with « off » hours. Crit Care Med 2007;35:3–11

70. Giannini A. Open intensive care units: the case in favour. Minerva Anestesiol. 2007;73:299–305

71. Ramsey P, Cathelyn J, Gugliotta B, Glenn LL. Restricted versus open ICUs. Nurs Manage 2000;31:42–4

72. Kleinpell RM. Visiting hours in the intensive care unit: more evidence that open visitation is beneficial. Crit Care Med 2008;36:334–5

Brian H. Cuthbertson and Paul Holder

Quality and safety in critical care: Rapid response, medical emergency or outreach teams?

Introduction

All those who work in the acute hospital setting are aware that critical events occur all too commonly. The rate of these adverse events has been previously quoted to be approximately 4% [1] and rates of almost five times this number have been reported in the subgroup of high-risk patients [2]. It is also well recognised that many serious adverse events such as death, cardiac arrest and unplanned admission to intensive care units (ICU) are preceded by a period of physiological instability that can be detected by simple observations which can be undertaken by members of the healthcare team with relatively little training. It is an unfortunate fact that in too many of these situations the warnings go unrecognised, either because appropriate monitoring processes are not undertaken or because the information has not been recognised and acted on appropriately, and that a slow and progressive physiological deterioration continues unchecked until a serious adverse outcome ensues [3]. Whilst lack of recognition of the deteriorating patient on the general ward is probably the greatest problem, a lack of appropriate knowledge and skills (in such matters as oxygen therapy, fluid resuscitation, appropriate monitoring) and lack of involvement at an appropriate juncture of more senior staff, are also key deficiencies [4]. If patients who are deteriorating and are at risk can be identified earlier and their underlying pathology addressed, then it may be possible to avoid an adverse outcome such as death, cardiac arrest and unplanned admission to ICU. Whilst these outcomes are clearly the most significant, there are other less tangible adverse outcomes to consider. The human cost also extends to staff that may experience shame, guilt or depression after making an error, with litigation and complaints adding to the burden. Those whose confidence has been affected will work less effectively and efficiently and indeed may leave the profession representing a huge waste of time and resources, not to mention the human costs. Adverse events carry a high financial penalty, in the UK the consequent prolonged hospital stays cost £ 2,000 million a year and litigation costs are in the region of £ 400 million annually [5], with the inclusion of lost income, disability and medical expenses taking the estimated cost in the USA to between $ 17,000 and $ 29,000 million annually [6]. It is clear that potentially avoidable adverse events must be eliminated, or at least minimised, from modern medical care. It is the role of all involved in healthcare to engage in the process of quality improvement to identify and address areas within their area of practice that can help to achieve this goal. The question of how we detect patients at risk of deterioration and work to reverse the processes responsible will be discussed here.

One possible method of improving identification and management of these patients is to utilise the available expertise of those who regularly care for the critically ill patients in higher dependency areas of the hospital such as intensive care, thus providing the highest possible level of care irrespective of the patients' locations. The idea of critical care outreach has been suggested in many forms. The Medical Emergency Team (MET) concept was developed in Liverpool, New South Wales in 1989 and has been widely utilised in Australian hospitals since the 1990s [7]. This concept involves the approach of senior medical and nursing staff from critical care areas being called by any member of staff when a predefined set of physiological parameters cut points are breached or when there is specific concern about a deteriorating patient, so-called track and trigger systems (TTs). Subsequently the concept of a specialist response team being summoned to the deteriorating patient as a result of these scores triggering, has been implemented and studied in many different forms and in many different settings around the world. More recently, many powerful political bodies in different countries have called for the universal introduction of rapid response teams as part of patient safety initiatives examples of this are the Institute for Healthcare Improvement's Six Million Lives campaign in the USA and the Scottish Patient Safety Programme.

The evidence

Preistly et al. performed a randomised step-wedge trial of critical care outreach in a general hospital. A nurse consultant led their team with a team of experienced nurses providing 24-hour cover. Ward staff used a locally devised patient-at-risk scoring system to trigger referral. This study found a significant reduction in hospital mortality in wards where the service operated compared to those where it did not. Analysis of whether outreach increased the length of hospital stay was equivocal, and data on cardiac arrest rates, do-not-resuscitate orders and ICU admissions are not included [8].

Ball published the results of a non-randomised population based study, in which they compare historical controls with patients cared for by a nurse-only outreach team, which was available for 12 hours per day. The operational policy of this team appears to be limited to those patients who have been previously discharged from the ICU rather than including new patients. They report that after the introduction of the outreach team there was a significant increase in survival to hospital discharge and a significant decrease in ICU readmission. However, this decrease in readmission rate only returned the unit to the national average [9].

Garcea et al. published a retrospective observational study, comparing before and after introduction of outreach covering surgical wards. The team comprised 2 senior nurses and a nurse consultant; the service had an ICU consultant as the lead clinician though their level of involvement is not defined. The team's remit involved the follow-up of ICU/HDU discharges and education of ward staff with respect to the recognition of the sick patient; however, this was later expanded to include the direct referral of patients highlighted by an early warning scoring system. They tentatively conclude that outreach teams may have a favourable impact on mortality rate amongst readmissions to critical care, but suggest that more data is needed from multicentre trials [10].

Bellomo et al. performed a prospective, controlled before-and-after trial to examine the effect of the introduction of an intensive care unit-based medical emergency team in a large teaching hospital. The team evaluated and treated any patient who was deemed to be at risk of developing an adverse outcome by nursing, paramedical or medical staff. The authors concluded that the introduction of the MET was associated with a significant reduction in the number of adverse events, postoperative mortality rate and mean duration of hospital stay. They suggest that the MET was associated with major cost savings and increased efficiency of hospital care. The authors note that the decrease in adverse events was only partly accounted for by the interventions of the MET and that the increased awareness of the significance and consequences of physiological instability brought about by the introduction of the MET lead to an improvement in care [11].

Buist et al. report a non-randomised, population-based study before and after the introduction of a MET into a teaching hospital. The results demonstrate a significant decrease in the incidence of, and mortality from, unexpected cardiac arrests. The study also shows an increase in unplanned admissions to the intensive care unit after the introduction of the MET, although the statistical significance of this is not stated. One problem raised by the authors was that the control and study periods were separated by some three years [12].

Bristow et al. published a prospective cohort comparison of three hospitals. The hospitals were similarly sized public hospitals. At hospital 1, the cardiac arrest team was replaced by a MET, at hospitals 2 and 3, the arrest team operated as previously. Statistical adjustment was made for the differences in case mix between hospitals. The results show that the MET hospital had fewer unanticipated ICU/HDU admissions; however, there was no difference in either the in-hospital arrest rate or total death rate [13].

Leary and Ridley examined the effects of an outreach service on re-admissions to ICU, by comparing the numbers and reasons for re-admission before and after the introduction of outreach in their hospital. They concluded that their study could detect no change in numbers or reasons for readmissions, and state that other parameters should be used to examine the effectiveness of the outreach service, despite reduction in ICU readmissions being one of the highlighted aims of outreach [14].

The MERIT study arguably represents the best available evidence in the sphere of outreach. In this study large Australian hospitals with an ICU and emergency department that did not use the MET system were identified and offered the opportunity to participate in the study. The 23 hospitals that agreed to participate were randomised to receive standardised MET implementation (twelve hospitals) or to be controls (eleven) and thus operate entirely as previously with no indication that a study was being undertaken. Over a period of four months an educational strategy was undertaken to prepare the study hospitals for the introduction of the MET, this included education of staff about calling criteria, identification of the patient at risk and the importance of rapidly calling the MET should any of the calling criteria be met (no education on the management of the acutely unwell patient was given). After MET implementation was complete an impressive system of reminders was continued to ensure that calling criteria were not forgotten or overlooked. The study protocol required that the MET should be at least the equivalent of the pre-existing cardiac arrest team and should

consist of at least one doctor and a nurse from the emergency department or ICU. The study results showed that the introduction of a MET system did not significantly reduce the incidence of any of the study outcomes (cardiac arrest, unexpected death or unplanned ICU admission). The authors point out three main flaws in their studies ability to disprove the null hypothesis. Firstly, they suggest that the six-month study period was inadequate. Secondly, that in the control hospitals the cardiac arrest teams is often called to critically ill patients who have not suffered a cardiac arrest and thus are acting as informal METs. The final point is that the study demonstrated that even in MET hospitals that were cogniscent of their participation in a trial that monitoring, documentation and responses to changes in vital signs were not adequate, this despite the educational programme undertaken, and suggest that a rigorous continuing educational programme is required [15]. The other likely, but less emphasised reason for failure to demonstrate an improvement in outcome was that the MET intervention did not work.

In April 2003, the NHS Research and Development Service Delivery and Organisation programme called for an evaluation of critical care outreach services (CCOS) and track and trigger systems as applied throughout England. The evaluation comprised five substudies:

- a review of evaluative studies,
- a national survey covering the introduction, implementation and current models across England,
- an interrupted time series to explore their impact,
- a matched cohort analysis to evaluate their impact, and
- a qualitative evaluation [16].

The report found that there was a wide variety of systems in use; however, the use of TTs was not universal across the surveyed hospitals nor within an individual hospital. Furthermore the authors concluded that there was little evidence for the validity, reliability and utility of any currently used TTs. Comparably with the state of TTs this report identified that there was a wide variation in the structure and function of CCOS applied across the country possibly as an attempt to address local issues and concerns. The study demonstrated that in hospitals with a CCOS there was a significant decrease in CPR rates during the 24 hours prior to admission. This finding could represent a positive effect of CCOS preventing physiological deterioration; however, the very plausible alternatives of more widespread use of "do not attempt resuscitation" orders and recognition of futility of ICU admission after arrest are also discussed and likely. Another statistically significant result was the reduction in the number of out-of-hours admissions to the ICU, which could reflect a positive effect of CCOS. The final positive outcome measure that achieved statistical significance was the decrease in acute severity of illness scores of patients admitted from the wards when CCOS were in use; again, other alternative explanations than earlier appropriate admission are possible, particularly the sickest patients being removed after futile admission to ICU is avoided, or pre-transfer stabilisation of patients by the CCOS. Whilst the alternative explanations of these positive findings exist they could well be perceived to be positive effects of CCOS in their own right, especially the avoidance of distressing and expensive intervention in the cases of patients who will clearly derive no benefit. The negative findings of this study are possibly more telling, there was no evidence for an association between the use of CCOS and mortality or readmission rates for patients discharged alive from the ICU. As part of the conclusion of this report the authors point out that the CCOS depend on an appropriate activation by an effective mechanism and call for research to focus on improved TTS.

Whilst we can not say that the currently available evidence demonstrates a beneficial effect of outreach or other response teams, we can say that the current systems of patient care are failing some of the sickest patients to their extreme detriment. There is no doubt that there are a large number of preventable adverse events that are preceded by a detectable period of physiological instability. It has been shown that the recognition and documentation of these precedents is inadequate. Furthermore, the traditional response to this situation, when detected, is inadequate in many cases. There are many documented explanations for these failings including disempowered nursing staff who record continuing deterioration without directly intervening; junior medical staff who have little formal training in the in-

creasingly complex areas of resuscitation of the critically ill; and senior medical staff who, even if they were experts in resuscitation, do not have sufficient opportunity to maintain their knowledge and skills in that area, and furthermore cannot be available at the patients' bedside throughout their hospital stay.

Implementing a rapid response to the unwell patient

Track and trigger systems (TTS)

We must ensure firstly that the deteriorating patient is recognised as early as possible; current recommendations in many countries are that TTS should be used in all clinical areas to identify the failing patient despite the lack of supportive evidence. The main function of TTS is to al-

Airway
If threatened

Breathing
All respiratory arrests
Respiratory rate < 5 breaths per minute
Respiratory rate > 36 breaths per minute

Circulation
All cardiac arrests
Pulse rate < 40 beats per minute
Pulse rate < 140 beats per minute
Systolic blood pressure < 90 mmHg

Neurology
Sudden fall in level of consciousness
(fall in GCS of > 2 points)
Repeated or extended seizures

Other
Any patient you are worried about that does not fit the above criteria

Fig. 1 MET calling criteria [reprinted from The Lancet, 365, MERIT study investigators. Introduction of the medical emergency team (MET) system: a cluster-randomised controlled trial, 2091–97, 2005, with permission from Elsevier]

Quality and safety in critical care: Rapid response, medical emergency or outreach teams?

D

low recognition of any patient who has developed or who has the potential to develop critical illness, this recognition then allows appropriate and timely intervention. Simply implementing the use of these systems has been shown to increase the frequency of physiological monitoring on general wards [17], which could alone be considered to increase the likelihood of healthcare workers identifying and acting upon abnormality.

TTS are of four broad subtypes:

1. **Single parameter systems** – These utilise periodic observation of specified vital signs which are recorded and compared with a given set of predefined thresholds, when any of the thresholds are reached a response algorithm is activated. Examples of this type (such as the MET calling criteria see Fig. 1) are simple to use and therefore have better reproducibility; however, they do not allow the patient's progress to be followed (which technically speaking makes them solely a trigger system) and do not allow for a graded response. These

systems are thought to have low sensitivity, low positive predictive value, but high specificity.

2. **Multiple parameter systems** – As above, but in this case the activation of the response algorithm requires more than one criterion to be met or may produce a differing response depending on how many thresholds have been breached. These systems (such as PART see Fig. 2) allow for continued monitoring of a patient's clinical progress and a graded response strategy for varying levels of physiological derangement. They may lack reproducibility due to human calculation failures; however, this can be avoided with the introduction of electronic calculation systems using PDAs. These systems have been shown to have high sensitivity but low specificity at the lower end of their scoring range. Sensitivity is reduced and specificity increases as the number of abnormal variables increases.

3. **Aggregate scoring systems** – A score is assigned to the obtained physiological values depend-

---

A: The senior ward nurse should contact the responsible doctor and inform them of a patient with: **any 3 or more** of the following:

Respiratory Rate ≥ 25 breaths/min (or < 10)
Arterial systolic pressure < 90 mmHg
Heart Rate ≥ 110 beats/min (or < 55)
not **fully** alert and orientated
oxygen saturation < 90%
urine output < 100 ml over last 4h
or
a patient not **fully** alert and orientated **and**
respiratory rate ≥ 35 breaths/min
or
heart rate ≥ 140 beats/min

Unless immediate management improves the patient, the doctor should consider calling the team. Exceptionally (in emergency when responsible doctor not immediately available) the senior ward nurse may contact the team directly.

B: A doctor of registrar grade or above may call the team for any seriously ill patient causing acute concern. This will normally be done after discussion with the patient's consultant. The consultant responsible for the patient must be informed as soon as practical that the team has been called.

Fig. 2   The PART protocol [reproduced from The patient-at-risk team: identifying and managing seriously ill ward patients. Goldhill DR, Worthington L, Mulcahy A et al. Anaesthesia 1999;54: 853–60, with permission of Blackwell Publishing Ltd.]

ing on the degree of derangement when compared with predetermined normal values. The score then indicates whether or not the response algorithm is activated and may also produce a graded response. These systems (such as SEWS see Fig. 3 and 4) allows monitoring of clinical progress. Again, these systems are prone to human error. They can produce a range of sensitivities and specificities depending on the scoring system utilised, but it is possible to achieve both high sensitivity and specificity with the correct cut point.

4. **Combination systems** – These use single or multiple parameter systems in combination with aggregate scoring.

Available TTS have been validated in various clinical settings to demonstrate their ability to identify the at-risk patient. Considerable variation exists between these systems with respect to their component physiological parameters, triggers and the patient outcomes. There is no single system which has been validated to be universally applicable and thus there is no system that can be universally recommended. Most systems have the following parameters in common:

■ Heart rate
■ Respiratory rate
■ Systolic blood pressure
■ Level of consciousness
■ Temperature and oxygen saturation

As such it has been recommended that any system considered for implementation should include these parameters. Urinary output is also included in many scoring systems; however, its accurate determination requires catheterisation of the bladder which is not always appropriate and as such its inclusion may lead to the system not being able to be universally applied in all areas of a hospital. Finally, it is likely that using an appropriately low cut point to trigger the system is more important than the exact scoring system used.

Composition of response teams

When the patients are identified how best to respond? The search for better ways to correct tissue hypoxia continues, but the basic skills must also be addressed, airway protection, appropriate use of oxygen, fluid resuscitation and institution of inotropic support when necessary. These skills are more commonly used in certain areas of healthcare, particularly critical care, so it would seem appropriate that either these individuals take on the task of responders to the identified patients or they train other hospital staff to the level of competency in these skills through an education/exchange programme. The question exists as to whether this role should be a senior doctor with extensive critical care experience or whether the role could be adequately discharged by a nurse with similar experience appropriately supported by medical staff when required but also empowered by well-formulated protocols covering aspects of care both ward based and relating to ICU admission. There are, however, many others within the healthcare team whose skills may be brought to bear on these patients, a good example of this are physiotherapists whose specialist skills may be commonly required in respiratory dysfunction. Clearly many of the issues of who should form the response team are determined by who could form a response team in an individual hospital. The resources to provide twenty-four hour cover by an intensive care consultant, senior nurse, physiotherapist, senior physician and surgeon are clearly not available to many units outside a few large teaching hospitals. Thus, the composition of any response team should be decided locally based on the available staff as long as appropriate skills are universally available.

Summary and conclusions

Patients are being failed by modern healthcare systems. Too many patients displaying clear physiological precedents of impending critical events continue to deteriorate, resulting in cardiac arrest, death or unplanned ICU admission. One way of altering this process is by identifying these patients through track and trigger systems which assist ward staff to identify early deterioration and then empower them to act appropriately and oblige them to directly call a response team or senior help. This response team, whose members are appropriately trained and equipped with extensive experience of managing critically unwell patients, then institutes the best practices of modern critical care, thus affording the pa-

Quality and safety in critical care: Rapid response, medical emergency or outreach teams?

D

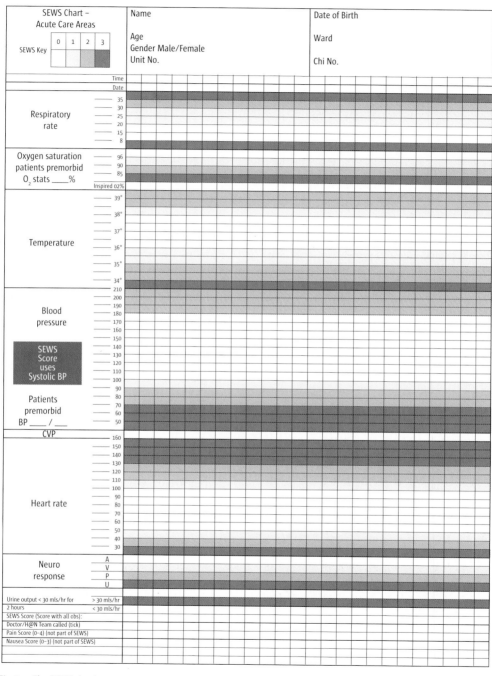

Fig. 3   The SEWS chart

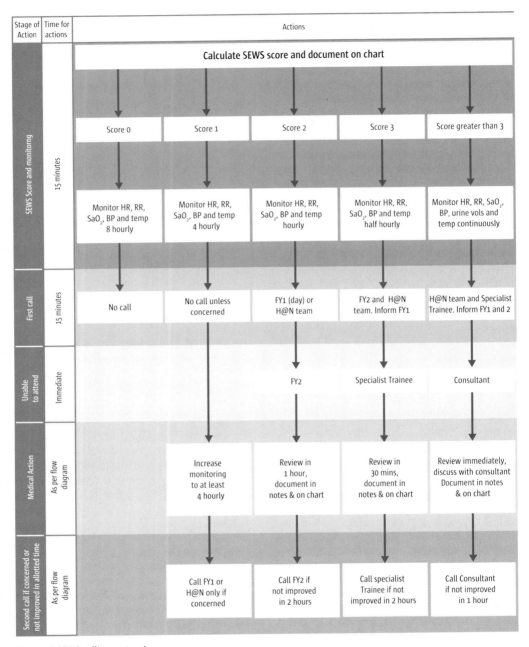

Fig. 4   A SEWS calling protocol

tient the best possible chance of attaining a positive outcome. This has been referred to as outreach, medical emergency teams or rapid response teams. As part of worldwide efforts to improve patient safety many have called for the universal implementation of response teams. Despite the apparent sense of this concept, a clear evidence base to support its use does not exist. However, this may be due to the methods of study uti-

Quality and safety in critical care: Rapid response, medical emergency or outreach teams?

D

lised or perhaps lack of efficacy of the system itself. We do, however, have evidence that the current system is failing and need to consider how to improve this situation urgently. The universal use of an appropriate track and trigger system may allow identification of many of the patients who deteriorate and allow the activation of a response especially if the trigger point is appropriately low. There is no clear evidence to identify a TTS that is best; however, different types of systems have been shown to have strengths and weaknesses and there are some key physiological parameters which should be included. Similarly there is no clear consensus as to who the component members of the response team should be, and any decision about this area would be dependent on the level of available resources. One thing, however, is certain, that given the current upswell of political pressure behind this concept, some form of rapid response, outreach or medical emergency team will soon become a much more familiar sight in hospitals throughout the world and those who work in the setting of critical care will be integral to its effective functioning.

The authors

Brian H. Cuthbertson, Prof.[1]
Paul Holder, MD[2]
[1]Health Services Research Unit and
Intensive Care Unit | University of
Aberdeen | Aberdeen, UK
[2]Consultant Department of Anaesthetics
and Intensive Care | Aberdeen Royal
Infirmary | Aberdeen, UK

Address for correspondence
Brian H. Cuthbertson
Professor of Critical Care
Health Services Research Unit and
Intensive Care Unit
University of Aberdeen
AB25 2ZD Foresterhill, Aberdeen, UK
E-mail: b.h.cuthbertson@abdn.ac.uk

References

1. Brennan TA, et al. Incidence of adverse events and negligence in hospitalized patients: Results of the Harvard medical practice study. N Eng J Med 1991; 324: 370–376.
2. McGlynn EA, et al. The quality of health care delivery to adults in the United States. N Eng J Med 2003; 348: 2635–2645.
3. Goldhill et al. Physiological values and procedures in the 24 hrs before ICU admission from the ward. Anaesthesia 1999; 54: 529–34.
4. Resuscitation Guidelines 2005: Resuscitation Council UK.
5. Department of Health. An organisation with a memory: Report of an expert group on learning from adverse events in the NHS chaired by the chief medical officer. Department of Health HMSO 2000.
6. Kohn LT, Corrigan JM, Donaldson MS Eds. To err is human: Building a safer health system 1999, Institute of medicine, National Academy Press.
7. Lee A, Bishop G, Hillman K, Daffurn K. The medical emergency team Anaesth Intensive Care 1995; 23: 183–6.
8. Priestly G, Watson W, Rashidian A, et al. Introducing critical care outreach: a ward-randomised trial of phased introduction in a general hospital. Intensive Care Med 2004; 30: 1398–1404.
9. Ball C, Kirby K, Williams S. Effect of the critical care outreach team on patient survival to discharge from hospital and readmission to critical care: non-randomised population based study. BMJ 2003; 327: 1014–7.
10. Garcea G, Thomasset S, McClelland L, Leslie A, et al. Impact of a critical care outreach team on critical care readmissions and mortality. Acta Anaes Scand 2004; 48: 1096–1100.
11. Bellomo R, Goldsmith D, Uchino S, Buckmaster J, et al. Prospective controlled trial of medical emergency team on postoperative morbidity and mortality rates. Crit Care Med 2004; 32: 916–921.
12. Buist MD, Moore GE, Bernard SA, et al. Effects of a medical emergency team on reduction of incidence of and mortality from unexpected cardiac arrests in hospital: preliminary study. BMJ 2002; 324: 1215.
13. Bristow PJ, Hilman KM, Chey T, et al. Rate of in-hospital arrest, deaths and intensive care admissions: the affect of a medical emergency team. Med J Austral 2000; 173: 236–40.
14. Leary T, Ridley S. Impact of an outreach team on readmissions to a critical care unit. Anaesthesia 2003; 58: 328–32.
15. MERIT study investigators. Introduction of the medical emergency team (MET) system: a cluster-randomised controlled trial. Lancet 2005; 365: 2091–97.
16. Rowan K. Evaluation of outreach services in critical care. http://www.sdo.nihr.ac.uk/sdo742004.html
17. McBride J, Knight D, Piper J et al. Long-term effect of introducing an early warning score on respiratory rate charting on general wards. Resuscitation 2005 65: 41–4.
18. Goldhill DR, Worthington L, Mulcahy A et al. The patient-at-risk team: identifying and managing seriously ill ward patients. Anaesthesia 1999 54: 853–60.

E. Protocolised medicine

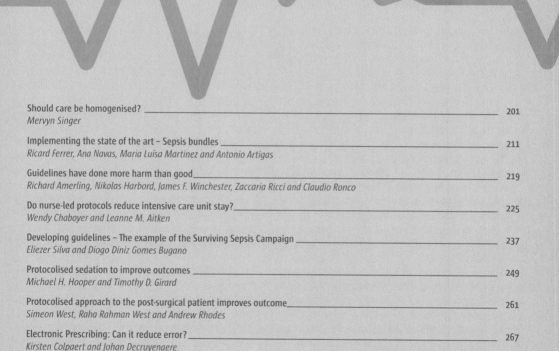

Mervyn Singer

Should care be homogenised?

Introduction

Much like the London street map, intensive care has evolved without formal planning. As a consequence there is a higgledy-piggledy mix of styles to fit a multitude of eclectic tastes and, often, very little consistency. Every so often, a thought process is bulldozed to build a new road but, not infrequently, this falls into disrepair, leads to nowhere in particular, or simply goes round in circles. Fashions come and go, and are routinely rediscovered or reinvented. Bandwagons roll at speed before rust sets in and the wheels fall off. Critical care still wrestles with the conflicting pulls of art versus science, of impulse versus dogma, of innovation versus constancy. Does a finding in a multi-centre trial population relate to a particular individual with a specific set of clinical circumstances? Can care ever be homogenised? This article will explore these dilemmas and will attempt to steer between the Scylla and Charybdis of rigid homogenised practice versus freewheeling care based on experience and hunch.

Evidence-based medicine (EBM)

According to David Sackett, the godfather of EBM,

"Evidence-based medicine is the conscientious, explicit and judicious use of current best evidence in making decisions about the care of individual patients." [1]

EBM seeks to apply scientific method to clinical practice by assessing and weighting available evidence to judge the risks and benefits of any particular treatment or strategy. It acknowledges that areas such as quality and value-of-life determinations are, by necessity, subjective, and that these can only be partially subject to scientific method. The hierarchy of evidence is evaluated to provide the best prediction of outcomes, with regular updating as new evidence becomes available.

The practitioner of EBM has to strike an awkward balance between treatment of an individual patient based on the best available medical knowledge on how to treat that specific patient, and systematic reviews that evaluate the best studies on specific topics, that clearly cater to populations in general, rather than a particular case. This dilemma is well covered by David Eddy [2]. He highlighted how the EBM movement sprang from the realisation that practitioners of the "art of medicine" – who believed in the correctness of their thoughts and actions based on a composite of prior knowledge of the patient, past experiences with similar patients, and their awareness of the literature – were frequently wrong. Whereas quality of performance was previously taken for granted, it became increasingly challenged, particularly with the recognition of the wide variations in practice patterns that could not all be compatible with optimal management. Indeed, many of the practices were deemed inappropriate by the standards of experts in the field. There was also an increasing appreciation of the complexity of decision-making, as well as the often flawed reasoning and considerable uncertainty that accompanied and frequently compromised the management options taken by an individual physician.

In 1985 a US governmental health technology committee estimated that a mere 15% of medical practices were based on solid clinical trials [3]. Increasingly, practices taken for granted were often discredited when subjected to scrutiny by formal trials, yet implementation of the results from these randomised clinical trials (RCT) was often patchy and slow. This led to the development of guidelines and protocols that have been increasingly led by specialist societies and by quasi-governmental bodies. This has been particularly apparent in the UK; recommendations made by the National Institute for Health and Clinical Excellence (NICE) <www.nice.org.uk> on drugs and interventional procedures strongly influence funding decisions by healthcare purchasers, yet are frequently challenged by specialist clinicians and patient groups. In the US, guidelines and protocols are increasingly being demanded by insurance companies and hospital administrators, perhaps with as much of an eye on financial penalty and potential litigation as on the obvious mantra of improving patient care. Independent organisations such as the Massachusetts-based Institute for Healthcare Improvement <www.ihi.org/> which "works to accelerate improvement by building the will for change, cultivating promising concepts for improving patient care, and helping healthcare systems put those ideas into action" [4] are also attempting to influence healthcare provision through governments and insurance companies (who also count among their major sponsors) by mandating "proven" bundles of care that have never actually been formally proven, particularly as a bundle of measures.

Evidence-based medicine can be been roughly divided into:

- *Evidence-based guidelines (EBG)*, i.e. practice at the organisational/institutional level with production of guidelines, policy and rules and
- *Evidence-based individual decision (EBID) making*, i.e. practice by the individual healthcare provider [2].

EBG are generated by multidisciplinary teams who use explicit, rigorous techniques to generate generic guidelines that address the needs of patient populations. These will indirectly affect the individual patient through influencing overall decision-making. On the other hand, EBID is undertaken by individual physicians who use implicit and personal methods to bring more research and evidence into their day-to-day practice. EBID thus directly influences individual decisions in discrete patients.

Eddy suggests these two approaches should be integrated [2]. He argues the concept of "medicine" is clearly broader than individual physician decision-making and also involves guidelines, quality improvement, performance measurement, disease management and public policy. Medicine would thus be best served if both individual physicians and those who design the guidelines and policies follow evidence-based methods. This would remove the traditional reliance upon consensus-based guidelines and policies, and would bring non-medical healthcare providers such as pharmacists, nurses, administrators, and public health workers to the fore. Importantly, what may make sense from the narrow viewpoint of an individual physician and patient may be at variance from the broader perspective of a programme or population. Concerns regarding costs, available resources, and efficiency are obvious examples. However, he stresses that EBG must be tailored to individual cases, a process that EBID should facilitate. He acknowledges that many problems fall through "the cracks of guidelines", and thus EBID is necessary to bring evidence-based medicine to the individual patient. The educational approach of EBID, which requires training to improve scrutiny of data and research, helps physicians to understand the rationale for EBG. Physicians thus become better and more accepting participants, especially when the evidence contradicts a time-honoured practice.

Critical care

Translating Eddy's sage words into the critical care environment requires both a historical perspective and an appreciation of current perceived "state-of-the-art" practice.

An historical perspective

We should not forget that critical care is a new specialty that has been forced to develop quickly. Although its origins stretch back to the Copenhagen polio epidemic of 1952–53 [5], it did not become generally established within most hospitals until the 1970s, essentially to meet an increasing requirement for sophisticated postoperative care of patients undergoing ever more complex surgical procedures. The introduction of novel invasive monitoring techniques (such as pulmonary artery catheterisation) and specialised support equipment (including advanced ventilators and renal replacement techniques) mandated sub-specialty training that, in some countries, has evolved to full specialty status. Alongside the training of intensive care clinicians, specialised training has also been developed for other critical care practitioners including nurses, physiotherapists and respiratory therapists.

Against this background of haphazard growth and development, different practice patterns have evolved, both locally and at the national level. A good example is the markedly contrasting use of colloids and crystalloids between Europe and North America and, within Europe, the variation in use of albumin, synthetic starches and gelatins [6]. These patterns often evolved from local anaesthesia practices, from familiarity with a particular product, and, not infrequently, from an almost complete lack of an evidence base in the critically ill. Likewise, many drugs were introduced into critical care practice without specific licensed indications, for instance, the use of opiates and sedatives. An early and notable example of a belated recognition of harm was by Watt and Ledingham who noted a marked jump in mortality rate in their Glasgow Shock-Trauma Unit in 1982–3 [7]. On further scrutiny they found this predominantly affected multiple trauma patients staying more than five days who received, in addition to opiates, an infusion of etomidate (77 %

mortality) as opposed to benzodiazepine (28 % mortality). On banning etomidate, overall mortality levels fell to previous levels. They subsequently demonstrated that etomidate depressed adrenal function and this led to withdrawal of its use for medium- to long-term sedation in intensive care. Yet, nothwithstanding this finding, and multiple studies showing that even a single dose may depress adrenal function for more than 24 hours in critically ill patients [e.g. 8], etomidate is still widely used for rapid sequence intubation.

Likewise, many devices were introduced without any analysis of safety or efficacy. The classic example is the pulmonary artery catheter which rapidly gained primacy until a retrospective analysis published by Connors et al. in 1996 [9], using a database collected for a multicentre evaluation of end-of-life decision-making, suggested a 39 % increase in mortality rate through its use in the first 24 hours of intensive care. This met with howls of outrage from the critical care community and a rapid rebuttal by an expert panel drawing together representatives of all the major societies such as SCCM, ESICM and ATS [10]. Yet, in an accompanying editorial [11], Mitch Fink was

> "... struck by a sense of cognitive dissonance. Over and over again, the answer to the question, 'Does management with the pulmonary artery catheter improve outcome in patients with (fill in the blank),' is an emphatic 'yes,' despite the absence of any solid data to support the conclusion. In the majority of the clinical situations analyzed, the authors concede that no credible evidence is available to support right-heart catheterization, and then go on to make a recommendation for the continued use of the PA catheter!"

The Connors paper and the ensuing response triggered a crucial turning point in critical care research. Health agencies now actively sought to fund large, academic multicentre studies in France, the US and the UK to formally evaluate the safety and clinical effectiveness of the catheter in critically ill patients in general [12, 13] and, specifically, in patients with heart failure [14] and acute lung injury [15]. While the harmful effect suggested by Connors was not reproduced in any of the studies, neither could benefit be demonstrated in any population taken as a whole. However, this overall neutrality does not preclude an advantage to some individuals but detriment to others.

Non-commercial, academic multicentre trials were still in their infancy at this stage. No benefit had been reported in 1987 from high-dose methylprednisolone in sepsis [16] nor, in 1995, from supranormal haemodynamic optimisation in critical illness [17]. The creation of clinical trials groups in Canada (CCCTG), the US (ARDS-NET) and Australasia (ANZICS CTG) enabled large numbers of patients to be enrolled into studies addressing important fundamental questions such as optimal haemoglobin level [18], tidal volume ventilation [19], and benefits of low dose dopamine [20]. Active multicentre trials groups are now functioning in England, Scotland, Spain, France, Italy and across Europe, to name but a few. Continued trialling of commercial products has also added to the burgeoning list of high-quality multicentre clinical trials. In addition, many other randomised, controlled studies, either from a single centre or a limited number of centres have produced considerable data and, in some cases, impacted considerably upon contemporary practice [e.g. 21, 22].

Despite this proliferation of knowledge in recent years, there are still many outstanding questions to be addressed and increasing doubt as to the worth of large multicentre trials of patients with syndromes such as sepsis. A recent publication by Ospina-Tascón et al. [23] described 72 multicentre adult critical care RCTs enrolling > 50 patients, with mortality as the primary outcome measure. Only ten reported a positive impact of the studied intervention on mortality, while seven reported a detrimental effect and 55 studies showed no statistical difference. They acknowledged a potential lack of efficacy of the tested intervention but also highlighted other issues that may have affected study outcomes including methodological limitations such as inadequate sample size, inadequate allocation concealment, poor quality of reporting, and the marked heterogeneity of the ICU patient population. As they noted, "classifying patients using broad definitions, like sepsis or ARDS, may hinder any objective demonstration of superiority of an intervention."

Current "state-of-the-art" practice and expert guidelines

We currently have an unresolved conundrum on how to best manage patients. On the one hand, there are numerous evidence-based guidelines while, on the other hand, EBG may not necessarily apply to an individual patient where particular circumstances may dictate an alternative approach. This is not to say that either side of the argument is necessarily wrong but the current knowledge base is often insufficient to make a definitive statement. Furthermore, on closer inspection, the expert guidelines are often interpretations of evidence that suit a particular current bias rather than an absolute reporting of incontrovertible fact.

Using the Surviving Sepsis Campaign (SSC) guidelines as a well-known exemplar, the first iteration in 2004 [24] made no mention of selective digestive decontamination (SDD), despite the evidence base at the time [25] exceeding most, if not all, of that supporting the other recommendations. The 2008 SSC guidelines [26] did cover the topic but the expert group chose to arrive at no recommendation for its use. Despite acknowledging multiple papers showing its utility in preventing infection and perhaps reducing mortality when used as a prophylactic measure, and its lack of harm, "the guidelines group was evenly split on the issue of SDD, with equal numbers weakly in favor and against recommending the use of SDD". They used the justification that there were "no studies of SDD specifically focused on patients with severe sepsis or septic shock." Yet the same document made numerous other practice recommendations despite a similar lack of sepsis-specific studies. This including stress ulcer prophylaxis and deep venous thrombosis prophylaxis where even ICU population-specific studies are few and far between.

Why should there be such a discrepancy in evaluating evidence? The 2008 SSC guidelines used GRADE criteria for assessing the quality of evidence and strength of recommendation. This new system ranges from Grade A (high) to Grade D (very low); randomised, controlled studies are initially graded "A" then downgraded on "limitations, inconsistency or imprecision of the results, indirectness of the evidence and possible reporting bias" [26]. The guidelines group then vote on the strength of recommendation based on

- "strong", where the benefits of adhering to a recommendation (better health outcomes, less burden on staff and patients, cost savings) were felt to clearly outweigh any undesirable effects (harm, more burden, greater costs); or
- "weak" where the benefits of adhering to a recommendation would probably outweigh the undesirable effects;

however, the voting panel lacked confidence due to continuing uncertainty regarding the overall risk/benefit ratio. This new evaluation system was recently criticised by Antonelli and Mercurio [27] who pointed out that "being a consensus of a majority of experts, this methodology does not always represent the state of the art or of science, and the strength of recommendation could change as a result of including new participants in the process." They instanced the strong recommendation of goal-directed fluid therapy on the basis of one single-centre (open) RCT conducted in an emergency room [22] that has never been replicated in a critically ill ICU population.

The validity of an expert opinion (individual or consensus) has not, to my knowledge, been properly dissected. How expert panels are constituted is rarely transparent, and the risk of selection bias is high. While industry links are criticised [26], less attention is paid to academic competing interests that can vary from grant funding to enable continuation of the expert's research to demolition of a lifetime's work and reputation. Again, referring to the SSC guidelines [26], they did attempt to be explicit on this point, however:

> "[...] the committee considered the issue of recusement of individual committee members during deliberation and decision making in areas where committee members had either financial or academic competing interests; however, consensus as to threshold for exclusion could not be reached."

Secondly, the impact of expert opinion (and of conflicting expert opinion) on the intensive care practitioner is of uncertain magnitude. While industry routinely targets opinion leaders ("OLs") at a regional/national level, and key opinion leaders ("KOLs") at an international level to both advise and market their products, as they clearly

feel this constitutes an important influence [29], the impact of expert guidelines on influencing practice has not been fully evaluated. An educational programme in Spain to improve uptake of the SSC guidelines [30] only succeeded in increasing compliance in the 6-hour resuscitation bundle from 6.3% to 12.9%, with a decline to 7.3% in long-term follow-up; notably, the early administration of broad-spectrum antibiotics – a non-controversial issue – significantly fell over this period (65.4% pre-education, 71% post-education, 56.7% long-term follow-up, p < 0.001).

Evolution versus revolution?

So what impels an intensive care clinician to practice in a certain way? Many factors may be invoked: experience, external influences (peers, guidelines, industry, hospital or governmental mandates), prejudice, culture, perceived safety concerns, marketing, ignorance, laziness, budgetary concerns, and so forth. But why have certain stratagems, such as tight glycaemic control [21], restricted blood use [18] and low tidal volume ventilation, caught the imagination, whereas others have shown only limited uptake? Is the introduction of simple, quick manoeuvres, or those that can be delegated (e.g. to nursing staff), viewed more favourably over more complex or expensive therapies or strategies? Are academic study findings viewed with less distrust that commercially-sponsored trials? We certainly have not evaluated the psychological make-up of the intensive care practitioner. Drawing an analogy with the business world, it is useful to invoke the work of Everett Rogers. He described diffusion of innovation as a means of explaining how, why, and at what rate new ideas and technology were taken up within members of a social system [31]. Innovators and early adopters are the first to select a new practice or technology, followed by the majority who do so more cautiously and, then finally, by a group of "laggards" who tail well behind in their rate of adoption (see Fig. 1). Rogers highlighted conditions that increase or decrease the likelihood of a new idea, product or practice being adopted, identifying attitude as a key element. This attitude is often reflective of the adopter's own personality traits (see Tab. 1). His Innovation Decision Process described five stages

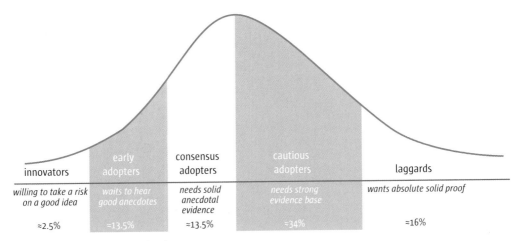

Fig. 1   Rogers' Adoption Innovation Curve

Tab. 1   Personality traits dictating speed of adoption of new ideas

	Innovators	Early adopters	Consensus adopters	Cautious adopters	Laggards
Risk taking	Rewards innovation	Rewards trial and speed	Rewards results	Rewards stability	Penalises failures
Planning & review	Seeks forgiveness rather than permission	Tries and sees	Structured & disciplined	Detailed & exacting	Defensive
Education	Teaching	Learning	Thinking	Watching	Waiting
Recruits	Innovators	Leaders	Performers	Experienced	Anyone

passing from *knowledge* of an innovation, to forming an *attitude* toward the innovation, taking a *decision* to adopt or reject, *implementing* the new idea and, finally, *confirming* this decision.

Another useful analogy can be drawn from the Bass equation (see Fig. 2) that predicts the diffusion pattern as a function of internal ("social contagion") and external ("innovation factor") influences [32]. This model was initially used to predict the uptake of a new consumer device based on the influence of advertising campaigns but has been successfully applied to healthcare and adoption of new technologies, e.g. electronic health records [33]. Eventually, a saturation point is reached until new evidence is produced, or a "new, improved" model is launched, to boost interest.

A final point to discuss is well covered by Reade et al. [34]. While acknowledging the utility

$$T = \frac{Ln^{q/p}}{p+q}$$

t = time to peak sales of a product
p is the coefficient of innovation, external influence or advertising effect,
q is the coefficient of imitation, internal influence or word-of-mouth effect.

Fig. 2   Bass equation that predicts the uptake of an innovation or novel technology or product

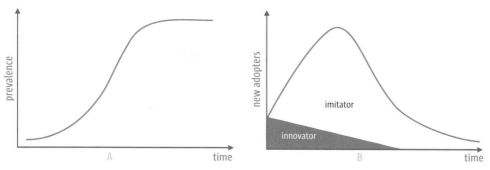

Fig. 3   Bass diffusion model showing 'S'-shaped uptake curve of new product (panel A) and replacement of innovators by imitators (panel B)

of practice guidelines, they query whether guideline committees should drive rather than reflect consensus. Should clinicians be impelled to follow recommendations perhaps against their own better judgment, or where local outcomes are already superior to trial data [35]? They also make valid points about the ability to extrapolate practices to poorer, less resourced countries, the ability to challenge guideline-driven dogma in prospective trials, and the threat of litigation if guidelines are not followed. I concur with their view that "guidelines should define broad goals rather than dictate exact replication of process." They propose replacing the recommended course with an entire map clearly marked with areas of certainty and uncertainty to enable the practitioner to steer a safe course for the patient.

Conclusion

Intensive care is still in its relative infancy. In the next few decades we will become far more sophisticated through the introduction of a range of biomarkers that can identify suitable patients to receive directed treatment at appropriate dose and time, and for the optimal duration. In the interim, we have to apply a common-sense approach, aided and abetted but not rigidly dictated by the literature and by expert guidelines. The clinician needs structure within which to operate effectively but this must not be a straitjacket, diminishing independent thought and flexibility of action. Guidelines should thus offer a template from which the clinician can and should be allowed to deviate after careful consideration of the pros and cons posed by a particular

problem. Homogenisation of care will, one day, be appropriate when we have sufficient knowledge and the right diagnostic tools. The time is not yet ripe.

Acknowledgements

This work was undertaken at UCLH/UCL who received a proportion of funding from the Department of Health's NIHR Biomedical Research Centres funding scheme.

The author

Mervyn Singer, Prof.
    Professor of Intensive Care Medicine
    Department of Medicine &
    Wolfson Institute of Biomedical Research
    University College London
    Cruciform Building, Gower St
    London WC1E 6BT, UK
    E-mail: m.singer@ucl.ac.uk

References

1. Sackett DL, Rosenberg WM, Gray JA, Haynes RB, Richardson WS. Evidence based medicine: what it is and what it isn't. BMJ 1996; 312: 71–2.
2. Eddy DM. Evidence-based medicine: a unified approach. Health Affairs. 2005; 24:9–17.
3. Committee for Evaluating Medical Technologies in Clinical Use, Assessing Medical Technologies. Washington: National Academies Press, 1985,pp 5.
4. http://www.ihi.org/ihi/about (Accessed 8th February 2009).

5. Andersen EW, Ibsen B. The anaesthetic management of patients with poliomyelitis and respiratory paralysis. Lancet 1954; i:786–88

6. Schortgen F, Deye N, Brochard L; CRYCO Study Group. Preferred plasma volume expanders for critically ill patients: results of an international survey. Intensive Care Med 2004; 30:2222–9.

7. Watt I, Ledingham IM. Mortality amongst multiple trauma patients admitted to an intensive therapy unit. Anaesthesia 1984; 39:973–81.

8. Absalom A, Pledger D, Kong A. Adrenocortical function in critically ill patients 24 h after a single dose of etomidate. Anaesthesia 1999; 54:861–7.

9. Connors AF Jr, Speroff T, Dawson NV, Thomas C, Harrell FE Jr, Wagner D et al for the SUPPORT Investigators. The effectiveness of right heart catheterization in the initial care of critically ill patients. JAMA 1996; 276:889–97.

10. Pulmonary Artery Catheter Consensus conference: consensus statement. Crit Care Med. 1997; 25:910–25.

11. Fink MP. The flow-directed, pulmonary artery catheter and outcome in critically ill patients: have we heard the last word? Crit Care Med 1997; 25:902–3.

12. Richard C, Warszawski J, Anguel N, Deye N, Combes A, Barnoud D et al; French Pulmonary Artery Catheter Study Group. Early use of the pulmonary artery catheter and outcomes in patients with shock and acute respiratory distress syndrome: a randomized controlled trial. JAMA 2003;290:2713–20.

13. Harvey S, Harrison DA, Singer M, Ashcroft J, Jones CM, Elbourne D et al. PACMan Study Collaboration. Assessment of the clinical effectiveness of pulmonary artery catheters in management of patients in intensive care (PAC-Man): a randomised controlled trial. Lancet. 2005; 366:472–477.

14. The ESCAPE Investigators and ESCAPE Study Coordinators. Evaluation study of congestive heart failure and pulmonary artery catheterization effectiveness: the ESCAPE trial. JAMA 2005;294:1625–33.

15. National Heart, Lung, and Blood Institute Acute Respiratory Distress Syndrome (ARDS) Clinical Trials Network, Wheeler AP, Bernard GR, Thompson BT, et al. Pulmonary-artery versus central venous catheter to guide treatment of acute lung injury. N Engl J Med. 2006; 354:2213–24.

16. The Veterans Administration Systemic Sepsis Cooperative Study Group. Effect of high-dose glucocorticoid therapy on mortality in patients with clinical signs of systemic sepsis. N Engl J Med. 1987; 317:659–65.

17. Gattinoni L, Brazzi L, Pelosi P, Latini R, Tognoni G, Pesenti A et al for the SvO2 Collaborative Group. A trial of goal-oriented hemodynamic therapy in critically ill patients. N Engl J Med 1995; 333:1025–32.

18. Hébert PC, Wells G, Blajchman MA, Marshall J, Martin C, Pagliarello G et al for the Transfusion Requirements in Critical Care Investigators, Canadian Critical Care Trials Group. A multicenter, randomized, controlled clinical trial of transfusion requirements in critical care. N Engl J Med 1999; 340: 409–17.

19. The Acute Respiratory Distress Syndrome Network. Ventilation with lower tidal volumes as compared with traditional tidal volumes for acute injury and the acute respiratory distress syndrome. N Engl J Med 2000; 342:1301–8.

20. Australian and New Zealand Intensive Care Society (ANZICS) Clinical Trials Group. Low-dose dopamine in patients with early renal dysfunction: a placebo-controlled randomised trial. Lancet 2000; 356: 2139–43.

21. van den Berghe G, Wouters P, Weekers F, Verwaest C, Bruyninckx F, Schetz M et al. Intensive insulin therapy in the critically ill patients. N Engl J Med 2001; 345:1359–67.

22. Rivers E, Nguyen B, Havstad S, Ressler J, Muzzin A, Knoblich B et al for the Early Goal-Directed Therapy Collaborative Group. Early goal-directed therapy in the treatment of severe sepsis and septic shock. N Engl J Med 2001; 345:1368–77.

23. Ospina-Tascón GA, Büchele GL, Vincent J-L. Multicenter, randomized, controlled trials evaluating mortality in intensive care: doomed to fail? Crit Care Med 2008; 36: 1311–22.

24. Dellinger RP, Carlet JM, Masur H, Gerlach H, Calandra T, Cohen J et al for the Surviving Sepsis Campaign Management Guidelines Committee. Surviving Sepsis Campaign guidelines for management of severe sepsis and septic shock. Crit Care Med. 2004; 32:858–73.

25. van Saene HK, Petros AJ, Ramsay G, Baxby D. All great truths are iconoclastic: selective decontamination of the digestive tract moves from heresy to level 1 truth. Intensive Care Med. 2003; 29:677–90.

26. Dellinger RP, Levy MM, Carlet JM, Bion J, Parker MM, Jaeschke R et al. Surviving Sepsis Campaign: international guidelines for management of severe sepsis and septic shock: 2008. Crit Care Med. 2008; 36:296–327.

27. Antonelli M, Mercurio G. The 2008 international guidelines for management of severe sepsis and septic shock: merits and weaknesses. Minerva Anestesiol. 2009; 75:27–9.

28. Eichacker PQ, Natanson C, Danner RL. Surviving sepsis–practice guidelines, marketing campaigns, and Eli Lilly. N Engl J Med 2006; 355:1640–2.

29. Moynihan R. Key opinion leaders: independent experts or drug representatives in disguise? BMJ. 2008; 336:1402–3.

30. Ferrer R, Artigas A, Levy M, Blanco J, González-Díaz G, Garnacho-Montero J et al. Improvement in Process of Care and outcome after a multicenter severe sepsis educational program in Spain. JAMA 2008; 299:2294–2303.

31. Rogers, EM. Diffusion of innovations, Glencoe: 1962 Free Press, Chapter 7.

32. Bass, F. A new product growth model for consumer durables. Management Science 1969; 15: 215–27.

33. Ford EW, Menachemi N, Phillips MT. Predicting the adoption of electronic health records by physicians: when will health care be paperless? J Am Med Inform Assoc. 2006; 13:106–12.

34. Reade M, Warrillow SJ, Myburgh JA, Bellomo R. Guidance in sepsis management: navigating uncharted waters? Crit Care 2008; 12:R428.

35. Ho BC, Bellomo R, McGain F, Jones D, Naka T, Wan L, et al. The incidence and outcome of septic shock patients in the absence of early-goal directed therapy. Crit Care 2006; 10:R80.

Ricard Ferrer, Ana Navas, Maria Luisa Martinez and Antonio Artigas

Implementing the state of the art – Sepsis bundles

Introduction

Sepsis is one of the most prevalent conditions among hospitalised patients and one of the main causes of hospital mortality [1]. Severe sepsis accounts for one in five admissions to intensive care units (ICUs) and is a leading cause of death in non-cardiac ICUs [2, 3]. In Spain, the incidence of severe sepsis is 104 cases per 100,000 adult residents per year with a hospital mortality of 20.7%, and the incidence of septic shock is 31 cases per 100,000 adult residents per year with a mortality of 45.7% [4]; these figures are similar to those reported in other European countries [5]. In the United States, both the incidence of severe sepsis (300 cases per 100,000 persons per year) and the mortality rate (28.6% = 215,000 deaths annually) are higher [1]. Sepsis places a significant burden on healthcare resources, accounting for 40% of total ICU expenditure; the total cost of treating sepsis in the year 2000 was estimated at $ 7.6 billion in Europe and $ 16.7 billion in the United States. Surprisingly, a recent survey done in the general population of Europe and United States showed that 88% of the interviewees had never heard the term "sepsis" and that 58% of those who recognised the term did not know that sepsis is a leading cause of death [6].

In recent years there have been unprecedented advances in the understanding of the epidemiology, patho-physiology, and treatment of sepsis syndrome [7; 8]. Several recently published studies have demonstrated that different interventions and treatments can decrease mortality among patients with sepsis. These data from rigorously performed randomised controlled trials, combined with previous data for beneficial interventions not specific to sepsis management, such as prophylaxis against deep vein thrombosis and stress ulcer, show it is possible to significantly reduce mortality in patients with severe sepsis and septic shock. Early appropriate antibiotic therapy [9, 10], early goal-directed therapy (EGDT) [11], corticosteroids [12], recombinant human activated protein C or drotrecogin alfa (activated) [13], tight glucose control [14], and lung-protective ventilation strategies [15] have all been associated with survival benefits.

These and other therapeutic advances led to the development of the Surviving Sepsis Campaign (SSC) guidelines [16] as part of a plan to reduce severe sepsis mortality by 25% by 2009. To improve the care for patients with sepsis, the SSC and the Institute for Healthcare Improvement recommend implementing two sepsis bundles. A bundle is a group of interventions that produce better outcomes when executed together than when implemented individually. The individual bundle elements are built on evidence-based practices, and the evidence for each element is strong enough for it to be considered a generally accepted practice. The recommended SSC bundles were elaborated in partnership with the Institute for Healthcare Improvement and are available at its website: http://www.ihi.org/IHI/Topics/CriticalCare/Sepsis/. The bundles are:

■ The resuscitation bundle, including lactate determination, early cultures and antibiotics, and EGDT, describes seven tasks that should begin immediately but must be accomplished within the first 6 hours of presentation for patients with severe sepsis or septic shock. Some items may not be completed if the clinical conditions described in the bundle do not prevail in a particular case, but clinicians must assess for these elements.

Sepsis resuscitation bundles (first 6 hours)

1. *Measure serum lactate.*
2. *Obtain blood cultures prior to antibiotic within 3 hours from time of presentation for ED admissions and 1 hour for non-ED ICU admission.*
3. *Administer broad-spectrum antibiotics within 3 hours from time of presentation for ED admissions and 1 hour for non-ED ICU admission.*
4. *In the event of hypotension and/or lactate > 36 mg/dl:*
   ■ *Deliver an initial minimum of 20 ml/kg of crystalloid (or colloid equivalent).*
   ■ *Apply vasopressors for hypotension not responding to initial fluid resuscitation to maintain mean arterial pressure (MAP) of 65 mmHg.*
5. *In the event of persistent hypotension despite fluid resuscitation (septic shock) and/or lactate > 36 mg/dl:*
   ■ *Achieve central venous pressure (CVP) of 8 mmHg.*
   ■ *Achieve central venous oxygen saturation (ScvO$_2$) of 70 %.*

■ The management bundle including optimisation of glycemic control, respiratory inspiratory plateau pressure, and determination of the need for corticosteroids or drotrecogin alfa (activated). Efforts to accomplish these goals should begin immediately, but these items may be completed within 24 hours of presentation for patients with severe sepsis or septic shock.

Sepsis management bundle (first 24 hours)

1. *Administer low-dose steroids for septic shock in accordance with a standardised ICU policy.*

2. *Administer drotrecogin alfa (activated) in accordance with a standardised ICU policy.*
3. *Maintain glucose control higher than the lower limit of normal, but < 150 mg/dl.*
4. *Maintain inspiratory plateau pressures < 30 cm-H$_2$O for mechanically ventilated patients.*

Several studies that are going to be described in this chapter have suggested that quality improvement efforts based on the SSC guidelines and bundles are associated with better outcome.

Surviving Sepsis Campaign implementation

Unfortunately, the gaps between evidence and practice have long been huge. Indeed, most available data suggest that the results of clinical trials and observational studies have not brought about substantial changes in clinical practice in sepsis care. Few emergency departments have implemented protocols for early resuscitation of patients with severe sepsis, delayed and inappropriate antibiotic administration remains common, and many patients with acute lung injury receive mechanical ventilation with potentially injurious tidal volumes. Moreover, physicians tend to overestimate their adherence to the recommendations in the sepsis bundles [17]. Based on the results of a national survey in the United States, Carlbom and Rubenfeld identified several reasons for failure to implement the sepsis bundles: lack of available nursing staff, inability to monitor central venous pressure in the emergency department, challenges in identifying septic patients, and difficulties in transferring care from the emergency department to the ICU [18]. Protocolised care has led to improved outcome for other conditions, like trauma, myocardial infarction, and cerebral infarction; thus, it is likely that protocolised care for sepsis including early diagnosis and delivery of recommended care would also lead to improvements in outcome.

A project to improve compliance with the current therapeutic recommendations is underway in hospitals throughout the world. The first step involves creating a change team comprising doctors, nurses, and others involved in treating patients with severe sepsis to organise care. The change team should include representatives from all departments with an interest in the change process. This team is responsible for all aspects of implementation, including daily planning, documentation, communication, education, monitoring, and evaluation. Within the team, a leader or leadership group prepared to champion the effort can help remove barriers, provide resources, monitor progress, and offer suggestions from an institutional perspective. Engendering evidence-based change through motivational strategies while monitoring and sharing the impact with healthcare practitioners is the key to improving outcome in severe sepsis [19].

Clinical studies

Change teams track and report how often the evidence-based measures recommended in the SSC are used, so there is a growing body of literature about the impact of these guidelines. Table 1 summarises the experience of some of the representative hospitals and networks in applying the SSC recommendations and sepsis bundles.

The first evidence of an effect of sepsis bundles on patient care came from Birmingham, England. Gao and colleagues [20] conducted a prospective observational study on 101 consecutive adult patients who presented severe sepsis or septic shock on medical or surgical wards or during emergency care at two acute National Health Service Trust teaching hospitals in England. The main outcome measures were the rate of compliance with the sepsis resuscitation and management bundles and the difference in hospital mortality between patients in whom care was compliant and those in whom it was not. Overall compliance with the sepsis bundles was 52%; compliance was associated with a lower hospital mortality compared with noncompliance (29% vs. 55%, p = 0.045).

Micek et al. [21] demonstrated that the implementation of a protocol for the management of septic shock in the emergency department was significantly associated with more rigorous fluid resuscitation, greater administration of appropriate initial antibiotic treatment (71.7% vs. 86.76, p = .043), less need for vasopressors at the time of transfer to the ICU (100% vs. 71.7%, p < .001), lower 28-day mortality (48.3% vs. 30%, p = .040), and shorter hospital stay (12.1 + 9.2

days vs. 8.9 + 7.2 days, P = .038). A secondary analysis of this emergency department protocol for sepsis indicates that this approach to patient management can result in substantial cost savings [22]. Median total costs were significantly lower after the protocol was implemented ($ 16,103 versus $21,985, p = .008). Mean hospital stay was also 5 days shorter among the post-intervention population (p = .023]. A Cox proportional hazard model indicated that the protocol was associated with lower per-patient costs, and restricting the analysis to only survivors did not alter the cost savings. These data suggest that protocols for the management of septic shock should be routinely employed.

Kortgen et al. [23] assessed in Germany the impact of a resuscitation algorithm (standard operating procedure) for organ dysfunction and septic shock. These investigators concluded that an approach combining EGDT, intensive insulin therapy, hydrocortisone administration, and rhAPC administration in selected cases improved outcome. Mortality was lower after implementation of the standard operating procedure in comparison with the historical control group (27% vs. 53%, p<0.05).

Shapiro and colleagues [24] enrolled 116 septic patients, 79 of whom had septic shock, in a study to evaluate a sepsis treatment protocol that incorporated empirical antibiotics, EGDT, rhAPC, steroids, intensive insulin therapy, and lung-protective ventilation (MUST: multiple urgent sepsis therapies). Compared with 51 historical controls, protocol patients received more fluids, earlier antibiotics, more appropriate empiric antibiotic coverage, more vasopressors in the first 6 hours, and tighter glucose control. Although mortality in the protocol group was only 18%, the study was not able to demonstrate a reduction in mortality because it was not adequately powered and the historical control group introduced a potential selection bias. This limitation underlines the need for multicentre trials to establish the collective effect of combining available evidenced-based sepsis therapies. Talmor et al. [25] evaluated the cost-effectiveness of the MUST protocol and concluded that is possible to save lives with a moderate increase in treatment costs. These increased costs in the study cohort were largely driven by higher ICU costs associated with longer ICU stay. The base case estimate

Tab. 1   Clinical studies evaluating the Surviving Sepsis Campaign recommendations

Author	Year	Number of hospitals/Country	Patient location at study inclusion	Study design	Number and type of patients	Intervention	Mortality
Gao	2005	2 / England	Critical care unit	Prospective observational	n = 101 Medical/surgical	Sepsis resuscitation and management bundles	Resuscitation: 49 % vs. 23 % (p < 0.01) Management: 50 % vs. 29 % (p = 0.16)
Micek	2006	1 / Missouri (USA)	Emergency department	Before/after	n = 120 Medical/surgical/trauma	EGDT + antibiotics	48.3 % vs. 30 % (p = 0.04)
Kortgen	2006	1 / Germany	Critical care unit	Retrospective cohort	n = 60 Medical/surgical	SOP*	53 % vs. 27 % (p < 0.05)
Shapiro	2006	1 / Massachusetts (USA)	Emergency department	Prospective intervention cohort with historical controls	n = 116 Medical/surgical	MUST protocol**	29.4 % vs. 20.0 % (p = 0.3)
Trzeciak	2006	1 / New Jersey (USA)	Emergency department	Retrospective cohort with historical controls	n = 38 Medical/surgical	EGDT	43.8 % vs. 18.2 % (p = 0.09)
Nguyen	2007	1 / California (USA)	Emergency department	Prospective observational cohort	n = 330 Medical/surgical	Sepsis bundle***	39.5 % vs. 20.8 % (p = 0.01)
Jones	2007	1 / North Carolina (USA)	Emergency department	Prospective interventional cohort	n = 156 Medical/surgical	EGDT	27 % vs. 18 %
Ferrer	2008	77 ICUs / Spain	Critical care unit	Before/after	n = 2566 Medical/surgical/trauma	Educational programme based on SSC guidelines	44.0 % vs. 39.7 % (p = 0.04)

EGDT: Early goal-directed therapy
SOP* (standard operating procedure): Early goal-directed therapy, glycemic control, low dose hydrocortisone, drotrecogin alfa.
MUST protocol** (multiple urgent sepsis therapies): Antibiotics, early goal-directed therapy, drotrecogin alfa, steroids, intensive insulin therapy and lung-protective ventilation.
Sepsis bundle***: Central venous pressure and central venous oxygen saturation monitoring within 2 hours, antibiotics within 4 hours, complete early goal-directed therapy at 6 hours, steroids and monitor for lactate clearance.

is that implementing the MUST protocol costs $ 16,309 per quality-adjusted life year expectancy gained and $ 11,264 per life year gained. These cost-effectiveness ratios are similar to, or better than, those for many healthcare strategies used in ICUs in the United States [26].

Nguyen and colleagues [27] enrolled 330 patients who met the criteria for severe sepsis or septic shock in a two-year prospective observational cohort study that examined the effect of implementing a severe sepsis bundle in the emergency department. The bundle comprised the following five elements:

1. Initiation of central venous pressure (CVP)/central venous oxygen saturation (ScvO$_2$) monitoring within 2 hours.
2. Delivery of broad-spectrum antibiotics within 4 hours.
3. Completion of an EGDT trial at 6 hours.
4. Delivery of corticosteroids to vasopressor-dependent patients and to those with suspected adrenal insufficiency.
5. Ongoing monitoring for lactate clearance.

The bundle was introduced as a quality indicator, and regular feedback was routinely provided to modify physicians' behaviour in the early management of severe sepsis and septic shock. Compliance with the bundle increased from zero at the start of the study to 51.2 % at the end of the study period. During the emergency department stay, patients in whom the bundle was completed received more CVP/ScvO$_2$ monitoring, more antibiotics, and more corticosteroids than patients in whom the bundle was not completed. In a multivariate regression analysis including the five elements of the bundle, completion of EGDT was significantly associated with decreased mortality (odds ratio 0.36; 95 % CI, 0.17 to 0.79; p = .01). In-hospital mortality was lower in patients in whom the bundle was completed than in patients in whom the bundle was not completed (20.8 % versus 39.5 %, p < .01). The authors concluded that implementation of a severe sepsis bundle as a quality indicator in the emergency department, with regular feedback to modify physicians' behavior, decreased in-hospital mortality.

Also in 2007, Jones et al. [28] published the results of a two-year prospective interventional trial that sought to determine the clinical effectiveness of implementing EGDT as a routine protocol in the emergency department. The authors prospectively recorded pre-intervention clinical and mortality data on consecutive eligible patients for 12 months. Next, they introduced an EGDT protocol and recorded clinical and mortality data for an additional 12 months. Before starting the study, the investigators defined the clinical effectiveness of the intervention as a 33 % relative reduction in

mortality (the relative mortality reduction found in the original EGDT trial by Rivers [11]). A total of 156 patients were enrolled in the study: 79 in the 12 months immediately before the intervention and 77 in the 12 months immediately after the intervention. Patients in the post-intervention period received significantly greater crystalloid volume and frequency of vasopressor infusion during initial resuscitation than patients in the pre-intervention period. In-hospital mortality was 27 % before the intervention compared with 18 % after the intervention but this difference did not reach statistical significance. This study provided external validation of the clinical effectiveness of EGDT for treating sepsis and septic shock in the emergency department.

The first multicentre study to address the implementation of the SSC guidelines directly was the Edusepsis study [29]. Edusepsis assessed compliance with the SSC guidelines before and after an educational programme in 77 medical-surgical ICUs homogeneously distributed around Spain. Compliance with the recommendations of the SSC guidelines was measured in a cohort of patients before the educational programme, in a cohort after the programme, and in a third cohort from a subset of the ICUs one year later. The educational programme consisted of training physicians and nursing staff from the emergency department, medical and surgical wards, and the ICU in the definitions of severe sepsis and sepsis shock, early recognition of severe sepsis and septic shock, and the treatment bundles included in the guidelines.

A screening tool that included definitions of sepsis and organ dysfunction was used to actively screen all ICU patients for the presence of severe sepsis or septic shock at admission from the emergency department or wards and daily thereafter. A total of 2,319 patients fulfilled the criteria for severe sepsis or septic shock during the pre-intervention and post-intervention periods. An additional 254 patients were included in the third cohort one year later to assess the long-term effects of the educational programme. At baseline, compliance was higher than 50 % for only three process-of-care variables: blood cultures before antibiotics, early administration of broad-spectrum antibiotics, and adequate inspiratory plateau pressure during mechanical ventilation. Compliance with process-of-care variables improved after the educational programme: resuscitation bundle (5.3 % vs. 10.0 %; p < .001) and management bundle (10.9 % vs. 15.7 %; p = .001). In-hospital mortality was also lower after the educational programme (44 % vs. 39.7 %, p = 0.036); however, as in other studies, the decrease in mortality observed in this study might derive from better identification of patients with severe sepsis or from improved compliance with the guidelines, or both.

The Edusepsis study identified several areas for improvement: The rate of compliance with the EGDT-related variables remained below 50 % after the educational programme. Improvements in process-of-care and mortality were especially evident in the hospitals with the worst performance before the educational programme, suggesting that educational programmes are more useful in hospitals where baseline compliance is low. At long-term follow-up, compliance with the resuscitation bundle returned to baseline but compliance with the management bundle and mortality remained stable with respect to the post-intervention period, suggesting that the effect of the educational programme is not sustained and that "plan-do-study-act" cycles or other strategies like incentives or ongoing performance measurement should be applied.

When the individual characteristics of these studies are compared, it becomes clear that although they have much in common, they also have important differences. Notably, not all used a bundle strategy, and some studied only EGDT. Most studies that included a bundle strategy did not use the exact bundle specified in the SSC specifications; likewise, the specifications for EGDT were different in most studies. Moreover, the designs of the studies were substantially different, including purely retrospective designs, before/after designs, prospective designs with historical controls, and entirely prospective studies. Nevertheless, while these differences make it difficult to reach firm conclusions about the benefits of implementing the SSC bundles in particular, they do allow us to conclude in a more general sense that protocolising care for severe sepsis results in benefits for these patients. Increased compliance with the chosen strategies had favourable effects on the process of care and/or on mortality. In all reported studies, thus, the interventions in the SSC bundles are likely to reduce mortality caused by severe sepsis and septic shock. These observa-tional trials provide confidence that the benefits in the care of patients with severe sepsis found in clinical trials can be brought to the bedside.

Finally, we await the publication of the aggregated data coming from the SSC international database. Providers have been recruiting and entering patients in this registry since January 2005 and more than 15,000 patients have been included. The exploration of this registry will determine whether guideline dissemination and applying the SSC bundles has sustained effects on patient care and outcome.

Summary

The initial management of patients with severe sepsis is critical for outcome. The implementation of the measures included in the SSC guidelines are associated with lower morbidity and mortality with little to no additional costs, so the guidelines should become the standard of care for the management of severe sepsis. No longer is it acceptable to simply publish practice guidelines and hope that quality improvement happens at a local level. Development of guidelines should be followed by rigorous testing, and, when results are positive, by implementation efforts.

Future analysis of which recommendations are associated with greater reductions in mortality will allow focusing quality improvement efforts on these therapies. Further analysis of data from all these observational studies could help answer this question.

The authors

Ricard Ferrer, MD
Ana Navas, MD
Maria Luisa Martinez, MD
Antonio Artigas, PhD, MD
    Critical Care Center | Hospital de Sabadell |
    CIBER Enfermedades Respiratorias |
    Instituto Universitario Parc Tauli |
    Universidad Autónoma de Barcelona, Spain

Address for correspondence
    Ricard Ferrer
    Critical Care Center, Hospital de Sabadell
    Parc Tauli s/n
    08208 Sabadell, Spain
    E-mail: rferrer@tauli.cat

References

1. Angus DC, Linde-Zwirble WT, Lidicker J, Clermont G, Carcillo J, Pinsky MR. Epidemiology of severe sepsis in the United States: analysis of incidence, outcome, and associated costs of care. Crit Care Med 2001 Jul;29(7):1303–10.

2. Brun-Buisson C, Doyon F, Carlet J, Dellamonica P, Gouin F, Lepoutre A, et al. Incidence, risk factors, and outcome of severe sepsis and septic shock in adults. A multicenter prospective study in intensive care units. French ICU Group for Severe Sepsis. JAMA 1995 Sep 27;274(12):968–74.

3. Guidet B, Aegerter P, Gauzit R, Meshaka P, Dreyfuss D. Incidence and impact of organ dysfunctions associated with sepsis. Chest 2005 Mar;127(3):942–51.

4. Esteban A, Frutos-Vivar F, Ferguson ND, Penuelas O, Lorente JA, Gordo F, et al. Sepsis incidence and outcome: contrasting the intensive care unit with the hospital ward. Crit Care Med 2007 May;35(5):1284–9.

5. Alberti C, Brun-Buisson C, Burchardi H, Martin C, Goodman S, Artigas A, et al. Epidemiology of sepsis and infection in ICU patients from an international multicentre cohort study. Intensive Care Med 2002 Feb;28(2):108–21.

6. Rubulotta FM, Ramsay G, Parker MM, Dellinger RP, Levy MM, Poeze M. An international survey: Public awareness and perception of sepsis. Crit Care Med 2009 Jan;37(1):167–70.

7. Abraham E, Singer M. Mechanisms of sepsis-induced organ dysfunction. Crit Care Med 2007 Oct;35(10):2408–16.

8. Wheeler AP. Recent developments in the diagnosis and management of severe sepsis. Chest 2007 Dec;132(6):1967–76.

9. Garnacho-Montero J, Garcia-Garmendia JL, Barrero-Almodovar A, Jimenez-Jimenez FJ, Perez-Paredes C, Ortiz-Leyba C. Impact of adequate empirical antibiotic therapy on the outcome of patients admitted to the intensive care unit with sepsis. Crit Care Med 2003 Dec;31(12):2742–51.

10. Kumar A, Roberts D, Wood KE, Light B, Parrillo JE, Sharma S, et al. Duration of hypotension before initiation of effective antimicrobial therapy is the critical determinant of survival in human septic shock. Crit Care Med 2006 Jun;34(6):1589–96.

11. Rivers E, Nguyen B, Havstad S, Ressler J, Muzzin A, Knoblich B, et al. Early goal-directed therapy in the treatment of severe sepsis and septic shock. N Engl J Med 2001 Nov 8;345(19):1368–77.

12. Annane D, Sebille V, Charpentier C, Bollaert PE, Francois B, Korach JM, et al. Effect of treatment with low doses of hydrocortisone and fludrocortisone on mortality in patients with septic shock. JAMA 2002 Aug 21;288(7):862–71.

13. Bernard GR, Vincent JL, Laterre PF, LaRosa SP, Dhainaut JF, Lopez-Rodriguez A, et al. Efficacy and safety of recombinant human activated protein C for severe sepsis. N Engl J Med 2001 Mar 8;344(10):699–709.

14. van den BG, Wouters P, Weekers F, Verwaest C, Bruyninckx F, Schetz M, et al. Intensive insulin therapy in the critically ill patients. N Engl J Med 2001 Nov 8;345(19):1359–67.

15. Ventilation with lower tidal volumes as compared with traditional tidal volumes for acute lung injury and the acute respiratory distress syndrome. The Acute Respiratory Distress Syndrome Network. N Engl J Med 2000 May 4;342(18):1301–8.

16. Dellinger RP, Carlet JM, Masur H, Gerlach H, Calandra T, Cohen J, et al. Surviving Sepsis Campaign guidelines for management of severe sepsis and septic shock. Intensive Care Med 2004 Apr;30(4):536–55.

17. Brunkhorst FM, Engel C, Ragaller M, Welte T, Rossaint R, Gerlach H, et al. Practice and perception–a nationwide survey of therapy habits in sepsis. Crit Care Med 2008 Oct;36(10):2719–25.

18. Carlbom DJ, Rubenfeld GD. Barriers to implementing protocol-based sepsis resuscitation in the emergency department–results of a national survey. Crit Care Med 2007 Nov;35(11):2525–32.

19. Levy MM, Pronovost PJ, Dellinger RP, Townsend S, Resar RK, Clemmer TP, et al. Sepsis change bundles: converting guidelines into meaningful change in behavior and clinical outcome. Crit Care Med 2004 Nov;32(11 Suppl):S595-S597.

20. Gao F, Melody T, Daniels DF, Giles S, Fox S. The impact of compliance with 6-hour and 24-hour sepsis bundles on hospital mortality in patients with severe sepsis: a prospective observational study. Crit Care 2005;9(6):R764-R770.

21. Micek ST, Roubinian N, Heuring T, Bode M, Williams J, Harrison C, et al. Before-after study of a standardized hospital order set for the management of septic shock. Crit Care Med 2006 Nov;34(11):2707–13.

22. Shorr AF, Micek ST, Jackson WL, Jr., Kollef MH. Economic implications of an evidence-based sepsis protocol: can we improve outcomes and lower costs? Crit Care Med 2007 May;35(5):1257–62.

23. Kortgen A, Niederprum P, Bauer M. Implementation of an evidence-based "standard operating procedure" and outcome in septic shock. Crit Care Med 2006 Apr;34(4):943–9.

24. Shapiro NI, Howell MD, Talmor D, Lahey D, Ngo L, Buras J, et al. Implementation and outcomes of the Multiple Urgent Sepsis Therapies (MUST.protocol. Crit Care Med 2006 Apr;34(4):1025–32.

25. Talmor D, Greenberg D, Howell MD, Lisbon A, Novack V, Shapiro N. The costs and cost-effectiveness of an integrated sepsis treatment protocol. Crit Care Med 2008 Apr;36(4):1168–74.

26. Talmor D, Shapiro N, Greenberg D, Stone PW, Neumann

PJ. When is critical care medicine cost-effective? A systematic review of the cost-effectiveness literature. Crit Care Med 2006 Nov;34(11):2738–47.

27. Nguyen HB, Corbett SW, Steele R, Banta J, Clark RT, Hayes SR, et al. Implementation of a bundle of quality indicators for the early management of severe sepsis and septic shock is associated with decreased mortality. Crit Care Med 2007 Apr;35(4):1105–12.

28. Jones AE, Focht A, Horton JM, Kline JA. Prospective exter-nal validation of the clinical effectiveness of an emergency department-based early goal-directed therapy protocol for severe sepsis and septic shock. Chest 2007 Aug;132(2):425–32.

29. Ferrer R, Artigas A, Levy MM, Blanco J, Gonzalez-Diaz G, Garnacho-Montero J, et al. Improvement in process of care and outcome after a multicenter severe sepsis educational program in Spain. JAMA 2008 May 21;299(19):2294–30

Richard Amerling, Nikolas Harbord, James F. Winchester,
Zaccaria Ricci and Claudio Ronco

Guidelines have done more harm than good

Introduction

In previous critiques of practice guidelines we have brought out methodological, philosophical, political and economic objections that are, in the aggregate, quite devastating [1]. Practice guidelines all suffer from major deficiencies, no matter how they are developed. They are heavily based on opinion, poor quality or no data, and are many years in the making. Many are obsolete by their publication date, or become so soon thereafter. Even guidelines based on prospective, randomised trial data are subject to opinion and bias. Guidelines cloak themselves with science, yet are inherently unscientific, and, unproven. We are asked to accept on faith that achieving certain numerical targets (soft endpoints) will lead to improved real outcomes (hard endpoints). To date, there is nothing to support such a belief. Poor guidelines can have an impact on thousands of patients.

Though guidelines never claim to replace the judgment of the individual practitioner working with an individual patient, in practice, that is exactly what is happening. Governments and other payers of medical bills use guidelines to control costs by so-called "payment for performance". Implementation involves payment based on achievement of benchmarks set out in various practice guidelines. Politicians and bureaucrats hope that guidelines coupled with powerful and all-pervasive

health information technology will enable them to exert increasing levels of control over medical practice. In this view, practice guidelines threaten medical professional autonomy.

Another aspect of guideline medicine that is receiving increasing scrutiny is the relationship with industry. It is clear that most guidelines are funded by the pharmaceutical and medical instrument industry. This funding is usually indirect, in the form of unrestricted grants to specialty societies and organisations. While we are unlikely to uncover any "smoking gun" memos showing industry's hand in creation of specific guidelines, such influence can be inferred from the all-too-common recommendations coming out of the working groups to use more industry products. There is also nearly universal industry funding of individual panel members. It is hard to see how such financial conflicts of interest could not influence the guideline development process. Again, we can infer from these facts that industry gets to have a say in who does and does not participate in a guideline-writing panel. (See for example the National Heart Lung and Blood Institute website http://www.nhlbi.nih.gov/guidelines/index.htm. Careful review of hypertension and cholesterol guidelines reveals progressive lowering of treatment targets, ensnaring millions of fundamentally healthy people into drug therapy. Please note the financial disclosures of the panel members.)

Practice guidelines advance the notion that institution of a process can obviate the need for individual clinical excellence. Nowhere is this concept more dangerous than in the field of intensive care medicine. In no other area is patient outcome more affected by the dedication, skill, knowledge, intelligence, attention to detail, and creativity of individual clinicians, nurses and technicians. It is with this perspective that we will now deconstruct the latest from the Surviving Sepsis Campaign (SSC): International guidelines for management of severe sepsis and septic shock: 2008 [2]. It is beyond the scope of this article to review every recommendation, most of which are non-controversial and widely accepted. For example, is it necessary to recommend that cultures be obtained before antibiotic treatment? It is difficult to imagine anyone working in intensive care medicine that would ever think to do otherwise. Rather, we will focus on methods, funding and some of the more controversial guidelines.

Methodology and funding

The current document builds on previous editions from 2001 and 2004 and includes "an updated search into 2007". There is no mention of a precise cutoff after which publications are not included. It is safe to say that data from most of 2007 and all of 2008 are not included, especially since the guidelines were published in late 2007. Labeling these guidelines "2008" is misleading.

The 2004 effort was funded by "unrestricted educational grants from industry through the Society of Critical Care Medicine (SCCM), the European Society of Intensive Care Medicine (ESICM) and the International Sepsis Forum (ISF)". They point out that both ESICM and SCCM receive "unrestricted industry funding to support SSC activities" but that "none of this funding was used to support the 2006–2007 committee meetings". First, if funding is to support SSC activities, by definition it is not "unrestricted". Second, money is fungible and, once given, can be used for any purpose. The distinction between non-specific and directed funding is strictly cosmetic.

They try to separate the "process of guidelines revision and the SSC," the latter being heavily funded by Eli Lilly and Company for use in the "performance improvement initiative". Again they state, "No industry funding was used in the guidelines revision process". As we note above, this artificial distinction is lost to actual dollars or euros being spent out of SSC accounts. And the "performance improvement initiative" is a road show designed to force implementation of the guidelines [3].

Regarding individual members and actual or potential conflicts of interest, only 8 of 24 did not disclose any. The committee "considered" having individual members recuse themselves in case of conflict, but "a consensus as to threshold for exclusion could not be reached". Rather, they "agreed to ensure full disclosure and transparency". This should have, in our view, included approximate amounts received from the listed sources. Knowing the paltry scale of academic medical salaries, we assume the amounts in most instances represent a significant percentage of total earnings, and could therefore easily be seen as a source of bias.

The Methods section deals with the formation of subgroups, development of searches for predefined questions, the schedule of meetings, and strategies for conflict resolution. The process is unbearably cumbersome and top-heavy. It also defines the GRADE system used to rank evidence. This assigns a letter from A to D for high- to poor-quality evidence, respectively, and a number – 1 for a strong, 2 for a weak recommendation. "Strong" means "the desirable effects of adherence (beneficial health outcomes, less burden on staff and patients, and cost savings) will outweigh the undesirable effects (harms, more burden and greater costs)". "Weak" means "desirable effects ... *probably* will outweigh the undesirable effects, but the panel is not confident about these tradeoffs" (emphasis added). With the possible exception of costs, isn't this precisely the risk-benefit calculation that clinicians make at the bedside dozens of times each day?

As clarification they add that "strong" recommendations are those that "most well-informed patients would accept," and that "most clinicians would use in most situations". What is a "well-informed patient," and why do we need guidelines for these practices?

In the document, "strong" is translated as "we recommend," whereas "weak" becomes "we suggest". Thus are interventions without clear consensus transformed into positive endorsements. In our experience, the major distinction between "recommend" and "suggest" is lost in translation, especially when guidelines are used in advertising campaigns.

Interestingly, the strength rating [1 or 2] can outweigh the evidence quality grade (A–D). This gives the lie to the notion that these guidelines are truly "evidence-based."

Glucose control

The Grade 1B recommendation to reduce blood glucose in ICU patients with severe sepsis and hyperglycemia was apparently based solely on the Leuven protocol, which showed improved mortality and shorter length of stay in post-cardiac surgery patients randomised to receive intensive insulin therapy targeting normoglycemia [4] There is no basis for extending this observation beyond this limited setting. Studies performed in other patients do not show improved mortality with intensive insulin and have much higher rates of hypoglycaemia [5, 6, 7, 8, 9]. Though some of these were not published at the time the SSC guidelines were released, the authors clearly knew the results and refer to them in the Rationale section. More recently, Weiner published a meta-analysis of studies in any language in which adult intensive care patients were randomly assigned to tight vs. usual glucose control [10]. Of 1,358 identified studies, 34 randomised trials (23 full publications, 9 abstracts, 2 unpublished studies) met inclusion criteria. Twenty-nine randomised controlled trials (RCTs) totalling 8,432 patients contributed data for this meta-analysis. Hospital mortality did not differ between tight glucose control and usual care overall. There was also no significant difference in mortality when stratified by glucose goal (very tight: < 110 mg/dl or moderately tight: < 150 mg/dl) or intensive care unit setting (surgical, medical, medical-surgical). Tight glucose control was not associated with a significantly lower risk of requiring dialysis, but was associated with a significantly increased risk of hypoglycaemia (glucose < 40 mg/dl).

In addition to this plethora of negative studies, it is hard to conceive of a physiologic basis by which transient glycemic control could yield significant clinical benefits. It is reasonable to imagine a benefit of insulin therapy in post-cardiac surgery patients who, on top of massive post-operative stress, are bombarded with pharmacologic doses of catecholamines. Here it is indeed possible that insulin might restore heavily skewed catabolic-anabolic balance and provide actual benefit.

This controversial guideline is likely to be obliterated by the results of a large RCT involving 6,000 patients comparing glucose levels of 80–110 mg/dl versus 140–180 mg/dl that is currently underway (Normoglycemia in Intensive Care Evaluation and Survival Using Glucose Algorithm Regulation, or NICE-SUGAR). Until these results are presented, it would seem prudent to maintain blood glucose levels within a more conventional range (110–190 mg/dl) rather than < 150 proposed by SSC [11].

It also seems odd that after endorsing intensive insulin therapy to fairly low targets, the SSC recommends care in the interpretation of low glucose levels obtained by point of care testing, suggesting these values "may *overestimate* arterial blood or plasma glucose levels" (emphasis added).

In the interim, this guideline may lead to overzealous use of insulin in ICU patients with attendant increases in hypoglycaemic episodes and likely mortality.

Recombinant human activated protein C (rhAPC)

It was easy for seasoned guideline critics to identify this section as the *raison d'être* for the creation of this set of guidelines (and indeed, for the entire SSC). Here we have an expensive new bio-engineered marvel, unjustly handicapped by less than stellar clinical results. Time to round up some experts, get a favorable guideline, and take it on the road!

The committee acknowledges the strength of evidence (high quality) to support their recommendation *against* the use of APC in patients "with severe sepsis and low risk of death, most of whom will have APACHE II scores of < 20". They cite a consistent lack of benefit and increase in serious bleeding within this subgroup, demonstrated in two randomised controlled trials [12, 13] described as "methodologically strong, (and) precise".

In consideration of "adult patients with sepsis-induced organ dysfunction associated with a clinical assessment of high risk of death, most of whom will have APACHE II > 25", the committee "suggests" the use of rhAPC if there are no contraindications. Remember how this terminology was created (see above). It is remarkable that the committee suggests the use of rhAPC and simultaneously acknowledges the moderate quality of evidence in its favor. The committee fails to forthrightly disclose the ongoing safety concerns with rhAPC while tacitly promoting its use in this subgroup. In fact, the FDA has approved APC for use only in this subgroup, and without prospective evidence of benefit, while asking the manufacturer (Eli Lilly) to conduct further research [3] As of February 2009, the FDA is still conducting a safety review of rhAPC and has not expanded the indication. There is obvious bias in the manner in which the committee relegates controversy over the single favorable RCT (PROWESS) to a misleading focus on subgroup analyses. *Possible* benefit to patients with high risk of death in a subgroup analysis of PROWESS led to the FDA indication *despite* concerns with the study. The guidelines also attempt to reconcile the unfavourable results of the ADDRESS trial with the favourable PROWESS trial. Furthermore, there appears to have been endorsement despite discordant views within the committee; with a vote required to resolve the issue and the details relegated to an appendix (D) to the guidelines, effectively eliminating the discord. The guideline endorsing use of rhAPC is an example of "profit-maximising under the guise of science" [14].

Assuming PROWESS and ADDRESS dosing of rhAPC (24 mcg/kg/hr for a 96-hour infusion), treating a 70 kg patient would cost from $ 10,600 to $ 14,800 at current retail pharmacy prices. This is not mentioned in spite of the inclusion of cost of treatment in the "strong vs. weak" component of the GRADE system. It is widely known that concerns over the safety and cost of rhAPC has left sales hundreds of millions of dollars short of initial projections. Monetary support for the generation of these guidelines and their promotion is principally the work of the manufacturers and marketers of rhAPC (*Xigris*®), Eli Lilly.

Widespread use of this agent based on guideline implementation may well lead to excessive bleeding and increased morbidity and mortality, and increase costs unnecessarily.

Conclusion

Practice guidelines are harmful to patients and to the medical profession because they promote a collectivist, as opposed to an individualised, approach to medical care. If we as a profession do not stop producing these anti-scientific treatises, we will all soon be forced to practice according to them by the centralised payers. We risk becoming "useful idiots" both of our bureaucratic paymasters, and of industrial concerns hoping to transform a sow's ear into a silk purse.

The authors

Richard Amerling, MD[1]
Nikolas Harbord, MD[1]
James F. Winchester, MD[1]
Zaccaria Ricci, MD[2]
Claudio Ronco, MD[2]

[1]Division of Nephrology and Hypertension | Beth Israel Medical Center | New York, NY USA
[2]Department of Nephrology and Intensive Care | St. Bortolo Hospital, Vicenza, Italy

Address for correspondence
Richard Amerling
Division of Nephrology and Hypertension
Beth Israel Medical Center
350 East 17th Street
New York, NY 10003, USA
E-mail: ramerlin@chpnet.org

References

1. Amerling R, Winchester JF, Ronco C. Guidelines have done more harm than good. Blood Purif 2008;26:73–76
2. Dellinger RP et al. Surviving Sepsis Campaign: International guidelines for management of severe sepsis and septic shock: 2008. Intensive Care Med DOI 10.1007/s00134-007-0934-2
3. Eichacker PQ, Natanson C, Danner RL. Surviving sepsis – practice guidelines, marketing campaigns, and Eli Lilly. N Engl J Med 2006;355:1640–1642
4. Van den Berghe G, Wouters P,Weekers F, Verwaest C, Bruyninckx F, Schetz M, Vlasselaers D, Ferdinande P, Lauwers P, Bouillon R (2001) Intensive Insulin Therapy in Critically Ill Patients. N Engl J Med 345:1359–1367
5. Van den Berghe G, Wilmer A, Hermans G, Meersseman W, Wouters PJ, Milants I, Van Wijngaerden E, Bobbaers

H, Bouillon R. Intensive insulin therapy in the medical ICU. N Engl J Med 2006; 2:449–61.

6. Brunkhorst FM, Engel C, Bloos F, Meier-Hellmann A, Ragaller M, Weiler N, Moerer O, Gruendling M, Oppert M, Grond S, Olthoff D, Jaschinski U, John S, Rossaint R, Welte T, Schaefer M, Kern P, Kuhnt E, Kiehntopf M, Hartog C, Natanson C, Loeffler M, Reinhart K; German Competence Network Sepsis (SepNet). Intensive insulin therapy and pentastarch resuscitation in severe sepsis. N Engl J Med 2008; 358:125–139.

7. Devos P, Preiser J, Melot C. Impact of tight glucose control by intensive insulin therapy on ICU mortality and the rate of hypoglycaemia: final results of the glucontrol study [European Society of Intensive Care Medicine 20th Annual Congress abstract 0735]. Intensive Care Med 2007; 33(suppl 2):S189.

8. Treggiari MM, Karir V, Yanez ND, Weiss N, Daniel S, Deem S. Intensive insulin therapy and mortality in critically ill patients. Crit Care 2008; 12(1):R29.

9. Vriesendorp TM, DeVries JH, van Santen S, Moeniralam HS, de Jonge E, Roos YB, Schultz MJ, Rosendaal FR, Hoekstra JB. Evaluation of short-term consequences of hypoglycemia in an intensive care unit. Crit Care Med 2006; 34:2714–2718.

10. Wiener RS, Wiener DC, Larson RJ. Benefits and Risks of Tight Glucose Control in Critically Ill Adults A Meta-analysis. JAMA 2008; 300:933–944.

11. Bellomo R. Does intensive insulin therapy protect renal function in critically ill patients? Nat Clin Pract Nephrol 2008; 4:412–3.

12. Bernard GR, Vincent JL, Laterre PF, LaRosa SP, Dhainaut JF, Lopez-Rodriguez A, Steingrub JS, Garber GE, Helterbrand JD, Ely EW, Fisher CJ Jr; Recombinant human protein C Worldwide Evaluation in Severe Sepsis (PROWESS) study group (2001) Efficacy and safety of recombinant human activated protein C for severe sepsis. N Engl J Med 344:699–709

13. Abraham E, Laterre PF, Garg R, Levy H, Talwar D, Trzaskoma BL, François B, Guy JS, Brückmann M, Rea-Neto A, Rossaint R, Perrotin D, Sablotzki A, Arkins N, Utterback BG, Macias WL, Administration of Drotrecogin Alfa (Activated) in Early Stage Severe Sepsis (ADDRESS) Study Group (2005). Drotrecogin alfa (activated) for adults with severe sepsis and a low risk of death. N Engl J Med 353:1332–1341

14. Brase T. "Evidence-Based Medicine": Rationing Care, Hurting Patients. American Legislative Council. December 2008

Wendy Chaboyer and Leanne M. Aitken

Do nurse-led protocols reduce intensive care unit stay?

Introduction

Over the past two decades, evidence-based practice (EBP) has emerged as the gold standard in providing patient care [1]; however, much has been written about the difficulties in implementing research evidence into clinical practice [2]. One strategy to address these difficulties is the development of protocols. Protocols standardise processes of care, providing clinicians with guidance on acceptable practice [3, 4]. This guidance may be especially valuable in environments such as the intensive care unit (ICU), where patient problems are complex and their associated clinical decisions often have multiple solutions. Protocols identify when care should be initiated and adjusted and who the authorised decision-makers are for that care [5]. They may be consensus- or evidence-based, and are most commonly developed by multidisciplinary teams. Protocols are distinguished from clinical practice guidelines (CPGs) in their specificity. That is, protocols are detailed, precise plans for health problems and/or for regimens of therapy [6, 7], whereas CPGs are statements or principles [7], thus are broader in nature. This chapter reviews the evidence on three nurse-led protocols, glycemic control, ventilation weaning and sedation control, with a focus on their effect on patient outcomes including ICU length of stay (LOS). Factors that influence protocol adherence are also examined.

What is the evidence on nurse-led protocols in ICU?

A number of ICU-specific protocols have been developed, some of which may be considered nurse-led, however, it important to note that most protocols involve more than one disciplinary group. For example, Takala et al.'s [8] protocols for cardiovascular management, sedation and weaning provide directions primarily to nurses, and could be termed nurse-led, but they also identify when medical staff are to become involved. This section critically examines recent studies related to three nurse-led protocols: glycemic control, ventilation weaning and sedation.

Nurse-led glycemic control protocols

Knowledge of the detrimental effects of hyper- and hypoglycaemia has led to the emergence of protocols to control blood glucose (BG). The results of a landmark study that showed that tight glycemic control was associated with better outcomes [9, 10] has fuelled the development and testing of a number of nurse-led glycemic control protocols. In fact, tight glycemic control is recommended by a number of leading bodies in the United States such as the Joint Commission on Accreditation of Healthcare Organizations, the Institute for Healthcare Improvement and the American Thoracic Society, despite the fact that evidence for such an approach is currently limited [11].

A number of practice surveys have been undertaken to understand current clinical practices surrounding glycemic control. Surveys have been undertaken in Canada [12], England [13], Australia and New Zealand [14], and the Netherlands [15]. Canadian doctors and nurses identified clinically meaningful thresholds for hypoglycaemia at 4 mmol/l (median) and hyperglycemia at 10 mmol/l (median), with nurses reporting significantly higher thresholds than doctors [12]. Almost half (46%) reported concerns with glucometer accuracy [12]. Other concerns included patient discomfort (42%), difficulty obtaining capillary blood (34%), glucometer availability (34%) and increased nurses workload (22%) [12]. In a survey of 71 English hospitals the median upper BG limit was 7.0 mmol/l in 66 units that had an upper limit and median lower limit of 4.1 mmol/l in the 56 units that had a lower limit [13]. A survey of 29 Australian and New Zealand ICUs identified that 10% (n = 3) used an intensive insulin regime for all patients and 31% (n = 9) used it in selected patients [14]. Schultz and colleagues [15] surveyed participants at the Dutch Society of Intensive Care annual meeting and found that 69% of over 100 respondents were practising intensive insulin therapy with 26% reporting BG limits of 80–110 mg/dl. Collectively, these practice surveys suggest tight glycemic control is not a universal standard, with a number of practice issues making such control difficult, even when desired.

The research evidence may shed light on reasons for a lack of uptake of glycemic control protocols. Table 1 contains a summary of eight studies [9, 16–22] that focused on clinical outcomes from nurse-led protocols. These studies were undertaken predominantly in the United States [16, 19, 20], Belgium [9, 18], with one study each in the United Kingdom [17], New Zealand [21] and Germany [22]. Sample sizes ranged from 213 [19] to 1,600 [16], with three studies including more than 1,000 patients [9, 16, 18].

The protocols tested were very detailed in nature, thus only a short overview is provided here. The actual protocol was published in half of the manuscripts. Interestingly, one study used a protocol that involved both insulin and nutrition algorithms [21] and three studies used aggressive, early feeding along with the insulin protocol [9, 17, 18]. A fourth study administered insulin and pentastarch [22]. Target BG was fairly consistently set at 80–110 mg/dl (4.4–6.1 mmol/l) in five studies [9, 18, 20, 22], with a higher upper limit in one study [17] and 91–130 mg/dl in one study [19]. One study had an upper limit of < 140 mg/dl [16]. Only three studies were randomised controlled trials (RCTs) [9, 18], two of which were from single sites. No studies were identified that used ICU LOS as a primary outcome, however, six studies measured it as a secondary outcome. Of these, three were retrospective before and after studies [16, 19, 20], two were single-centred RCTs [16, 18] and one was a multi-site study that was stopped early due to safety concerns [22]. Other outcomes measured included ICU, hospital and 28-day mortality, organ dysfunction and therapies such as mechanical ventilation time.

In two studies a decrease in ICU LOS was shown with tight glycemic control [16, 18] but not in four other studies [9, 19, 20, 22] although a decrease was demonstrated in subgroups whose ICU LOS was greater than 5 days [9] and greater than 2 weeks [19]. In terms of other clinical outcomes, ICU mortality showed improvement in one study [9] but no change in three others [18, 20, 21], however, it was decreased in subgroups whose ICU LOS was ≥ 3 days [18] and in patients who stayed longer in the ICU [21]. Hospital mortality was decreased in one study [16] but not the other [18]. Days of mechanical ventilation showed no improvement in one study [20] but was shorter in the subgroup of patients with ICU LOS > 5 days [9] and one study demonstrated quicker weaning in the subgroup staying in ICU ≥ 3 days [18]. In two studies kidney dysfunction [16, 18] and in one study renal replacement therapy [9] were all significantly less in the intervention group. Blood stream infection and critical illness polyneuropathy were both significantly less in the intervention group in one study [9] and in another there was a decrease in the proportion of patients requiring blood transfusions [16].

This review highlights that the studies to date remain inconclusive regarding the clinical benefits of nurse-led glycemic control protocols, with most of the evidence being generated from single-site RCTs or before and after studies. Studies do suggest that beneficial effects of tight glycemic control on ICU LOS may be found in those with prolonged ICU LOS. No studies described protocol adherence and none used ICU LOS as the primary outcome, yet other work has shown that protocol violations can occur about half of the time [23–25]. A lack of power and/or adherence may be two reasons why findings to date are equivocal. Importantly, actually obtaining moderate to tight glycemic control is difficult [26]. In fact, one group has identified 12 barriers to achieving glycemic control in the ICU such as communication among health care providers, fear of hypoglycaemia and health care utilisation [26]. Further, it is probably important to use a consistent BG source for titrating insulin, given BG differences between laboratory and bedside monitoring [27, 28]. The results of the recently completed but not yet published, multi-national Normoglycemia in Intensive Care Evaluation and Survival Using Glucose Algorithm Regulation (NICE-SUGAR) RCT may provide new and more definitive evidence on the benefits of such protocols.

The eight studies reviewed here tested a variety of nurse-led protocols. Meijering et al.'s [29] systematic review of clinical trials using insulin/glucose algorithms in critically ill patients provides recommendations for a feasible and reliable algorithm. They recommend a protocol with continuous insulin infusions combined with frequent BG determination (hourly to every four hours) and the use of the last two BG values to determine the insulin infusion rate. They note that while there is a concern about hypoglycaemia, it occurs rarely (< 4–5 % or less). In our review of the research, protocols in two studies led to more hypoglycaemia [18, 22] but not in three other trials [16, 20, 21]. Meijering et al. [29] recommend BG 4–8 mmol/l although they acknowledged that the best BG has yet to be determined. Importantly, they recognise that frequent BG determinants may increase nurses' workload, which may not facilitate acceptance of the protocol, a factor important for successful implementation.

Nurse-led ventilation weaning protocols

Strategies to improve ventilation weaning practices, primarily through the introduction of protocols, have been implemented and evaluated for some time [30–32]. These protocols have taken a number of different forms and been led by different members of the health care team including nurses, respiratory therapists and physicians. We review only those protocols that are led by nurses; some of these protocols may also have the option, but not mandatory requirement, of being led by a respiratory therapist.

Approaches to ventilation weaning differ between clinicians, patient populations and regional world practices [33], although all weaning processes have the aim of reducing the duration of ventilation and the consequent risk of adverse events associated with mechanical ventilation. Common elements of most weaning protocols include:

- adequate assessment of the patient's state of wakefulness;
- assessment of the patient's readiness to wean based on pre-determined criteria;
- a systematic process for weaning using a limited selection of ventilatory options;
- ongoing assessment of the patient's condition throughout the weaning process, with the ability to return the patient to greater ventilatory support if their condition deteriorates;
- assessment of the patient's readiness to be extubated based on pre-determined criteria; and
- appropriate education of staff responsible for implementing the weaning protocol.

Although not always required, some weaning protocols included the need to consult with and/or gain approval from senior members of the nursing or medical team prior to progressing beyond specified points, for example prior to extubating a patient. Studies have primarily reported the outcome measures of duration of mechanical ventilation, weaning and ICU length of stay. A small number of studies have also reported complications such as re-intubations and incidence of ventilator-acquired pneumonia (see Tab. 2).

A total of eight studies were reviewed [34–41]. The protocols were developed and tested in the UK [34, 36, 41], Europe [39] and the USA [35, 37, 38, 40]. Sample sizes included in the studies have generally been significant, ranging from 73 [34] to 928 [37] with four including more than 500 patients [37, 38, 40, 41].

Tab. 1 Studies that measured clinical outcomes from nurse-led glycemic control protocols

First Author (Year); Country	Setting and Sample	Protocol	Methods	Outcomes
Van den Berghe (2001); Belgium [9]	1,548 adult surgical ICU patients receiving MV, in a tertiary teaching hospital (n = 780 control, n = 765 intervention)	Target: BG 80–110 mg/dl; Protocol described but not included	Single-centre RCT	ICU deaths and RRT significantly less in the intervention group than the control group (4.6 % vs. 8.0 % and 4.8 % vs. 8.2 % respectively); BSI and CIP both significantly less in the intervention group than the control group (4.2 % vs. 7.8 % and 28.7 % vs. 51.9 % respectively); Of patients with ICU LOS > 5 days, ICU LOS and MV days was significantly less in the intervention group than the control group (12 vs. 15 days and 10 vs. 12 days respectively).
Krinsley (2004); USA [16]	1,600 adult medical, surgical ICU patients in a university-affiliated community teaching hospital (n = 800 before, n = 800 after)	Target: < 140 mg/dl; Protocol included	Before and after	Hospital mortality significantly decreased by 29.3 % after protocol (14.8 % vs. 20.9 %); Mean ICU LOS decreased significantly from 3.6 to 3.2 days; Number of patients with renal dysfunction decreased significantly after protocol (3 vs. 12); Significant reduction in proportion of patients requiring packed red blood cells after protocol (20.5 % vs. 25.2 %).
Thomas (2005); UK [17]	891 medical, surgical ICU patients (n = 288 before, n = 502 after, n = 101 after modification)	Target: 4.4–7.1 mmol/l; Web-based insulin calculator; Protocol included; Modified van de Berghe's [9] protocol	Retrospective service evaluation	No difference in mortality during the three time periods; OR for death for BG > 8.0 mmol/l was 2.1 compared to values < 6.1 mmol/l.
Van den Berghe (2006); Belgium [18]	1,200 adult medical ICU patients in a tertiary teaching hospital (n = 605 control, n = 595 intervention)	Target: BG 80–110 mg/dl; Same protocol as van den Berghe [9]; Protocol described but not included	Single centre RCT	No difference in ICU or hospital mortality; Significantly earlier weaning and earlier discharge from ICU and hospital in the intervention (hazard ratio 1.21, 1.15 and 1.16 respectively); Newly acquired kidney injury significantly less in the intervention group than the control group (5.9 % vs. 8.9 %); Subgroup ICU LOS ≥ 3 days the intervention group had significantly decreased hospital mortality group (43.0 % vs. 52.5 %), quicker weaning, and quicker discharge from ICU and hospital (hazard ratio 1.43, 1.34 and 1.58 respectively).

First Author (Year); Country	Setting and Sample	Protocol	Methods	Outcomes
Quinn (2006); USA [19]	213 adult medical and surgical patients in a community teaching hospital (n = 143 before, n = 70 after)	Target: BG 91–130 mg/dl; Protocol included	Retrospective before and after chart review	No significant difference in ICU LOS; Protocol decreased ICU LOS in patients whose ICU LOS was > 14 days (RR 4.6; 95 % CI 0.5–8.7).
Dortch (2008); USA [20]	552 adult acute and subacute ICU trauma patients in a tertiary university hospital (n = 309 paper-based before, n = 243 CPOE after)	Target: 80–110 mg/dl; Protocol included	Retrospective before and after evaluation of paper-based vs CPOE	No difference in ICU LOS, days of MV or mortality.
Chase (2008); NZ [21]	784 general ICU patients (n = 413 before with no protocol used, n = 371 after SPRINT)	Target: 4.4–6.1 mmol/l; Protocol not included but refers to previous publications that included it	Retrospective before and after change in clinical practice (i.e. not research)	No difference in ICU mortality.
Brunkhorst (2008); Germany [22]	488 adult severe sepsis patients in 18 ICUs in academic tertiary hospitals (n = 241 control, n = 247 intervention)	Target: BG 80–110 mg/dl; Same as Van den Berghe (2001); Protocol described but not included	2 x 2 factorial RCT	Trial stopped early for safety reasons (intensive insulin therapy group significantly higher severe hypoglycaemia (12.1 % vs. 2.1 %); No difference in 28-day mortality; No difference in ICU LOS but a trend towards longer ICU stays in the intensive insulin therapy group (p = 0.06).

BG: Blood glucose
LOS: Length of stay
RR: Relative risk
CPOE: Computerised care provider order entry
BSI: Blood stream infection
RRT: Renal replacement therapy
Pt: Patient

MV: Mechanical ventilation
RCT: Randomised controlled trial
CIP: Critical illness polyneuropathy
MPC: Model predictive control
SPRINT: Special relative insulin nutrition tables
HDU: High dependency unit

Tab. 2   Studies that measured clinical outcomes from nurse-led ventilation weaning protocols

First Author (Year); Country	Setting and Sample	Protocol	Methods	Outcomes
Anderson (1995); UK [34]	73 cardiac, thoracic, vascular surgery patients (32 pre, 41 post)	Criteria to be assessed by nurses prior to and during weaning process, decision to extubate made by senior nurse, process could be discontinued at any point	Pre-test – post-test	Descriptive reduction in length of MV – no statistical analysis reported.
Kollef (1997); USA [35]	357 ICU patients (179 intervention, 178 control)	Assessment of readiness to wean, with ongoing monitoring and extubation against pre-determined criteria	RCT	Reduced duration of MV before weaning commencement and total duration of MV in intervention group.
Crocker (2002); UK [36]	ICU patients, number not stated	Nurse-led weaning protocol – detail not provided	Retrospective audit	Descriptive data suggesting reduction in duration of ventilation, no statistical analysis.
Grap (2003); USA [37]	928 medical ICU patients (469 pre, 459 post)	Criteria to be assessed by RNs or respiratory therapists prior to and during weaning process, rapid shallow breathing index prior to weaning, spontaneous breathing trial to be conducted, decision to extubate made by physician	Pre-test – post-test	Reduced MV duration and number of ventilator shifts.
Dries (2004); USA [38]	650 surgical ICU patients (314 pre, 336 post)	Initial sedation assessment, followed by weaning criteria assessment by either RNs or respiratory therapists, followed by weaning trial, then extubation assessment, decision to extubate discussed with physicians	Pre-test – post-test	Reduced number of days of MV and use ratio (days of MV/days in ICU) in post-test period; Reduced incidence of VAP and reintubation in post-test period.
Tonnelier (2005); France [39]	104 general ICU patients requiring > 48 hrs MV; 104 matched historical controls	Criteria to be assessed by nurses prior to and during weaning process, physician approval required to extubate, process could be discontinued at any point	Case control	Reduced MV duration (cases: 16.6 ± 13 days; controls: 22.5 ± 21 days) and ICU LOS (cases: 21.6 ± 14.3 days; controls: 27.6 ± 21.7 days); No difference in unsuccessful MV discontinuation, mortality or ventilator-associated pneumonia rates.

First Author (Year); Country	Setting and Sample	Protocol	Methods	Outcomes
Hoffman (2005); USA [40]	526 subacute MICU patients (250 NP, 276 fellows)	All care, including weaning and extubation, managed by either an Acute Care Nurse Practitioner or Critical Care/Pulmonary fellows. Both care providers received oversight from an attending physician.	Non-randomised, repeated measures	No difference in ICU length of stay or duration of MV.
Blackwood (2006); Northern Ireland [41]	661 general ICU patients (197 pre, 214 post, 250 comparison unit)	Intervention consisted of 3 elements: ■ readiness to wean criteria ■ guidelines for reduction in ventilatory support ■ weaning plan	Pre-test – post-test, with additional comparison control group	After adjustment for confounders no difference in length of MV and intubation, re-intubations or mortality between phases in either group, increased ICU stay and tracheostomy rate in post phase in intervention group.

MV: Mechanical ventilation
VAP: Ventilator-associated pneumonia
LOS: Length of stay

Evidence of benefit from nurse-led weaning protocols is divided, with a number of studies suggesting a reduction in duration of mechanical ventilation [35, 37–39]. In contrast, there are other studies that report no difference in duration of mechanical ventilation [40, 41]. Importantly, no studies have identified an increased duration of mechanical ventilation and the small number of studies that investigated potential complications found either no change or a decrease in incidence [38, 39, 41].

It is likely that weaning protocols provide benefits in some institutions and models of critical care delivery, while not in others [7]. At this point the characteristics that determine when weaning protocols provide benefits have not been identified. Unfortunately, none of the studies examining ventilation weaning protocols reported data describing how consistently the protocols were adhered to. As a result, it is not possible to make comment on whether the potential benefits could be improved through increased protocol adherence.

Nurse-led sedation protocols

Sedation represents another area of critical care practice that is heavily influenced by nursing practice and is recognised as significantly influencing patient outcomes [42]. There is evidence to suggest that sedation requirements are not managed as effectively as possible, with one report of only 43 % of patients being assessed for sedation needs despite 72 % of patients receiving sedatives [43]. Other studies have demonstrated a link between aspects such as wakefulness and experience of pain during ICU admission and long-term psychological recovery (see Tab. 3). Specifically, development of delusional memories has been associated with administration of greater amounts of sedation as well as increased levels of agitation [44], while recall of delirious memory during admission to ICU has been associated with more severe symptoms of post-traumatic stress [45].

Recognition of the importance of appropriate sedation management has led to the development of clinical practice guidelines that, among other things, recommend the use of a sedation guideline, algorithm or protocol to guide assess-

Tab. 3   Studies that measured clinical outcomes from nurse-led sedation protocols

First Author (Year); Country	Setting and Sample	Protocol	Methods	Outcomes
Brook (1999); USA [47]	321 medical ICU patients requiring mechanical ventilation	Sedation protocol where nurses determined whether analgesics, sedatives or both were required, the dose and whether administration was continuous or intermittent and when to wean and withdraw medications	RCT	Significant reduction in duration of MV, ICU and hospital LOS and number of tracheostomies; No difference in mortality, development of organ failure or reintubation.
Brattebo (2002); Norway [48]	285 surgical ICU patients ventilated for > 24 hours; 147 in control period, 138 in intervention period	Nurse led sedation protocol incorporating sedation scoring system and protocol	Prospective pre-test – post test	No significant differences in duration of MV or ICU LOS.
De Jonghe (2005); France [49]	102 medical ICU patients requiring MV ≥ 24 hours; 54 in control group, 48 in intervention group	Sedation algorithm based on regular assessments of consciousness and tolerance to the ICU with sedative administration increased or decreased accordingly by nurses	Prospective pre-test – post-test	Significant reduction in duration of MV and time to arousal in intervention group.
Elliott (2006); Australia [50]	322 general ICU patients requiring MV; 159 in the control group, 163 in the intervention group	Nurse-led sedation algorithm incorporating regular sedation assessment and administration of diazepam, midazolam, morphine or fentanyl.	Prospective pre-test – post-test	No significant difference in duration of MV, Experience of Treatment in ICU questionnaire and incidence of tracheostomies and self-extubations; ICU LOS was significantly shorter in control group.
Quenot (2007); France [51]	423 medical ICU patients requiring MV ≥ 48 hours; 226 in control group, 197 in intervention group	Nurse-implemented sedation protocol with midazolam or propofol administered according to sedation scores	Prospective pre-test – post-test	Significant reduction in duration of MV, extubation failure, incidence of VAP, time from end of sedative infusion to extubation, ICU and hospital LOS in intervention period.
Bucknall (2008); Australia [52]	312 general ICU patients; 153 in protocol group where sedation was directed by formal protocol, 159 in usual care group	Nurse led sedation protocol incorporating unrestricted sedative drug regimen to achieve desired levels of sedation, drugs used included morphine, midazolam and propofol	RCT	No significant differences in duration of MV, ICU or hospital LOS, ICU or hospital mortality or in the incidence of tracheostomy or self-extubation between protocol and usual practice groups.

First Author (Year); Country	Setting and Sample	Protocol	Methods	Outcomes
Arias-Rivera (2008); Spain [53]	365 medical – surgical ICU patients ventilated for > 48 hours; 176 in control period, 189 in protocol period	Nursing-driven protocol of sedation incorporating midazolam, propofol and/or morphine in specified increments to achieve a target sedation score	Retrospective pre-test – post-test	No difference in duration of intubation, ICU LOS or mortality between the two periods; Reduction in days of weaning (3±3 vs. 4±4 days) and increase in ventilator free days (19±7 vs. 17±9 days) during intervention period.

MV: Mechanical ventilation
VAP: Ventilator-associated pneumonia
LOS: Length of stay

ment and therapy [46]. Despite this recommendation there is evidence to suggest that sedation guidelines remain poorly implemented, with less than 50% of critical care units in Canada, USA and Denmark indicating such use [42].

The outcomes reported in the studies examining the impact of nurse-led sedation protocols have been remarkably similar to those outcomes used in ventilation weaning studies, with duration of mechanical ventilation, ICU and hospital LOS and events such as tracheostomy, self-extubation and reintubation being the most common. In this chapter we only report those sedation protocols that are nurse-led and do not include any protocols where another health care professional, such as a pharmacist, had an integral role. We also do not review any protocols related to specific interventions such as daily wakening.

The seven studies [47–53] that are reviewed here represent practice from a broad international perspective, with four studies from various countries in Europe [48, 49, 51, 53], two studies from Australia [50, 52] and one study from the USA [47]. In a similar fashion to the earlier protocols reviewed, most studies have included a substantial sample size, with only one study with less participants than 250 [49], with the remainder ranging from 285 [48] to 423 [51].

Although sedation protocols have widespread support, there is mixed evidence regarding the benefits that can be achieved with the implementation of such protocols. A number of studies have demonstrated the benefits associated with nurse-led sedation protocols [47, 49, 51, 53], with other studies not demonstrating a benefit [48, 50, 52]. No pattern to explain these conflicting results is obvious from the published reports. Protocols that were implemented were remarkably similar, with all incorporating a sedation assessment instrument, then an algorithm-based process for manipulating the amount of medication a patient received. Most protocols incorporated both sedation and analgesia medications into the algorithm. Only one protocol included a specific pain assessment instrument [49], although some protocols incorporated a general prompt such as 'is pain likely?' [47, 50, 52].

When considering whether the setting may have influenced the results, the majority of studies were conducted in closed ICUs [47, 50, 52, 53], although the remainder of the reports did not disclose the nature of their unit [48, 49, 51]. Patient-to-nurse ratios did vary between the units, with two of the three studies reporting no benefits conducted in Australian ICUs with patient/nurse ratios of 1:1 [50, 52]. The remaining study that found no benefit did not report staffing levels [48] while all other units that reported nurse staffing levels had a ratio of 2:1 or 3:1. This feature may provide some partial explanation of the results, with the higher level of nurse staffing ensuring more frequent assessment and manipulation of medications without the added guidance of a sedation protocol.

Only one of the studies examining the implementation of a sedation protocol reported data related to protocol adherence [54]. Prior to introduction of the sedation protocol a sedation score was only documented 27 % of the time, with this improving to 57 % during the period post implementation of the protocol. Similarly, the percentage of patients where full adoption of the protocol was apparent increased following implementation of the protocol [54].

What influences protocol adherence?

Both researchers and clinicians traditionally believed that disseminating research findings would be sufficient to change practice; however, more recently, there has been recognition that active change management processes are required. This section briefly describes influences on protocol adherence. Davis [55] describes six factors that influence uptake of guidelines including:

- quality of the guideline;
- characteristics of the health care professionals;
- characteristics of the practice setting;
- incentives;
- regulation; and
- patient factors.

It is likely that uptake of protocols may also be influenced by these factors. Further, well planned and designed change interventions are likely required to ensure guideline adherence [4]. From their review of 18 strategies Grol and colleagues [4] conclude that seven (interactive small group sessions, educational outreach visits, reminders, computerised decision support, introduction of computers in practice, mass media campaigns and combined interventions) are generally effective in changing practice.

In the case of the three nurse-led protocols reviewed in this chapter, it appears essential to have an inter- or multi-professional approach to protocol adoption [48]. Further, to improve patient care and outcomes, the professional group primarily responsible for protocol execution may not be as important as consistency in implementation, which is influenced by compatibility of the protocol with current unit values, and work practices [4]. Given nurses are the most consistent member of the intensive care health care team present with the patient, it makes sense that they are responsible for implementing a protocol that requires consistent assessment to be effective.

Conclusion

Protocols are detailed, precise plans for patient therapies that guide clinicians' decision-making and standardise care. Nurse-led protocols are those that predominantly reflect the care nurses provide, however, they generally also include recommendations for when involvement of medical officers or other professional groups should be sought. To date, evidence for the benefits of three nurse-led protocols, glycemic control, ventilation weaning and sedation, is mixed. Importantly, most studies did not examine protocol adherence, yet it seems self-evident that the extent to which a protocol is implemented will influence its impact on patient outcomes. It is also likely that other organisational factors such as staffing levels may influence both the implementation and outcomes of nurse-led protocols, which complicates answering questions such as 'Do nurse-led protocols decrease ICU stay?'

The authors

Wendy Chaboyer, RN, PhD[1]
Leanne Aitken, RN, PhD[2]
[1]Director, Research Centre for Clinical and Community Practice Innovation |
Griffith University Gold Coast Campus |
Griffith University, Queensland Australia
[2]Professor of Critical Care Nursing |
Research Centre for Clinical and Community Practice Innovation | Griffith University and Princess Alexandra Hospital, Brisbane, Queensland, Australia

Address for correspondence
Wendy Chaboyer
Director, Research Centre for Clinical and Community Practice Innovation
Griffith University Gold Coast Campus
Griffith University
4222 Queensland, Australia
E-mail: W.Chaboyer@griffith.edu.au

References

1. Evidence-based medicine. A new approach to teaching the practice of medicine. JAMA 1992;268:2420–5.
2. Kleinpell RM. Promoting research in clinical practice: strategies for implementing research initiatives. AACN Adv Crit Care 2008;19:155–61.
3. Huttin C. The use of clinical guidelines to improve medical practice: main issues in the United States. Int J Qual Health Care 1997;9:207–14.
4. Grol R, Grimshaw J. From best evidence to best practice: effective implementation of change in patients' care. Lancet 2003;362:1225–30.
5. Ilott I, Rick J, Patterson M, Turgoose C, Lacey A. What is protocol-based care? A concept analysis. J Nurs Manag 2006;14:544–52.
6. Morris AH. Treatment algorithms and protocolized care. Curr Opin Crit Care 2003;9(3):236–40.
7. Chatburn RL, Deem S. Respiratory controversies in the critical care setting. Should weaning protocols be used with all patients who receive mechanical ventilation? Respir Care 2007;52:609–19.
8. Takala J, Dellinger RP, Koskinen K, St Andre A, Read M, Levy M, et al. Development and simultaneous application of multiple care protocols in critical care: a multicenter feasibility study. Intensive Care Med 2008;34:1401–10.
9. van den Berghe G, Wouters P, Weekers F, Verwaest C, Bruyninckx F, Schetz M, et al. Intensive insulin therapy in the critically ill patients. N Engl J Med 2001; 8;345:1359–67.
10. van den Berghe G, Wouters PJ, Bouillon R, Weekers F, Verwaest C, Schetz M, et al. Outcome benefit of intensive insulin therapy in the critically ill: Insulin dose versus glycemic control. Crit Care Med 2003;31:359–66.
11. Angus DC, Abraham E. Intensive insulin therapy in critical illness. Am J Respir Crit Care Med 2005 1;172:1358–9.
12. McMullin J, Brozek J, Jaeschke R, Hamielec C, Dhingra V, Rocker G, et al. Glycemic control in the ICU: a multicenter survey. Intensive Care Med 2004;30:798–803.
13. Mackenzie I, Ingle S, Zaidi S, Buczaski S. Tight glycaemic control: a survey of intensive care practice in large English hospitals. Intensive Care Med 2005;31(8):1136.
14. Mitchell I, Finfer S, Bellomo R, Higlett T. Management of blood glucose in the critically ill in Australia and New Zealand: a practice survey and inception cohort study. Intensive Care Med 2006;32:867–74.
15. Schultz MJ, Spronk PE, Moeniralam HS. Tight glycaemic control: a survey of intensive care practice in the Netherlands. Intensive Care Med 2006;32:618–9; author reply 20–1.
16. Krinsley JS. Effect of an intensive glucose management protocol on the mortality of critically ill adult patients. Mayo Clin Proc 2004;79:992–1000.
17. Thomas AN, Marchant AE, Ogden MC, Collin S. Implementation of a tight glycaemic control protocol using a web-based insulin dose calculator. Anaesthesia 2005;60:1093–100.
18. van den Berghe G, Wilmer A, Hermans G, Meersseman W, Wouters PJ, Milants I, et al. Intensive insulin therapy in the medical ICU. N Engl J Med 2006;354(5):449–61.
19. Quinn JA, Snyder SL, Berghoff JL, Colombo CS, Jacobi J. A practical approach to hyperglycemia management in the intensive care unit: evaluation of an intensive insulin infusion protocol. Pharmacotherapy. 2006;26:1410–20.
20. Dortch MJ, Mowery NT, Ozdas A, Dossett L, Cao H, Collier B, et al. A computerized insulin infusion titration protocol improves glucose control with less hypoglycemia compared to a manual titration protocol in a trauma intensive care unit. JPEN J Parenter Enteral Nutr 2008;32:18–27.
21. Chase JG, Shaw G, Le Compte A, Lonergan T, Willacy M, Wong XW, et al. Implementation and evaluation of the SPRINT protocol for tight glycaemic control in critically ill patients: a clinical practice change. Crit Care 2008;12:R49.
22. Brunkhorst FM, Engel C, Bloos F, Meier-Hellmann A, Ragaller M, Weiler N, et al. Intensive insulin therapy and pentastarch resuscitation in severe sepsis. N Engl J Med 2008;358:125–39.
23. Shulman R, Finney SJ, O Sullivan C, Glynne PA, Greene R. Tight glycaemic control: a prospective observational study of a computerised decision-supported intensive insulin therapy protocol. Crit Care 2007;11:R75.
24. Laver S, Preston S, Turner D, McKinstry C, Padkin A. Implementing intensive insulin therapy: development and audit of the Bath insulin protocol. Anaesth Intensive Care 2004;32:311–6.
25. Chant C, Wilson G, Friedrich JO. Validation of an insulin infusion nomogram for intensive glucose control in critically ill patients. Pharmacotherapy. 2005;25:352–9.
26. Anger KE, Szumita PM. Barriers to glucose control in the intensive care unit. Pharmacotherapy 2006;26:214–28.
27. Finkielman JD, Oyen LJ, Afessa B. Agreement between bedside blood and plasma glucose measurement in the ICU setting. Chest 2005;127:1749–51
28. Cook A, Laughlin D, Moore M, North D, Wilkins K, Wong G, et al. Differences in glucose values obtained from point-of-care glucose meters and laboratory analysis in critically ill patients. Am J Crit Care 2009;18:65–71.
29. Meijering S, Corstjens AM, Tulleken JE, Meertens JH, Zijlstra JG, Ligtenberg JJ. Towards a feasible algorithm for tight glycaemic control in critically ill patients: a systematic review of the literature. Crit Care 2006;10:R19.
30. Cohen IL, Bari N, Strosberg MA, Weinberg PF, Wacksman

RM, Millstein BH, et al. Reduction of duration and cost of mechanical ventilation in an intensive care unit by use of a ventilatory management team. Crit Care Med 1991;19:1278–84.

31. Wood G, MacLeod B, Moffatt S. Weaning from mechanical ventilation: physician-directed vs a respiratory-therapist-directed protocol. Respir Care 1995;40:219–24.

32. Esteban A, Frutos F, Tobin MJ, Alia I, Solsona JF, Valverdu I, et al. A comparison of four methods of weaning patients from mechanical ventilation. Spanish Lung Failure Collaborative Group. N Engl J Med 1995;332:345–50.

33. Dries DJ. Weaning from mechanical ventilation. J Trauma 1997;43:372–84.

34. Anderson J, O'Brien M. Challenges for the future: the nurse's role in weaning patients from mechanical ventilation. Intensive Crit Care Nurs 1995;11:2–5.

35. Kollef MH, Shapiro SD, Silver P, St John RE, Prentice D, Sauer S, et al. A randomized, controlled trial of protocol-directed versus physician-directed weaning from mechanical ventilation. Crit Care Med 1997;25:567–74.

36. Crocker C. Nurse led weaning from ventilatory and respiratory support. Intensive Crit Care Nurs 2002;18:272–9.

37. Grap MJ, Strickland D, Tormey L, Keane K, Lubin S, Emerson J, et al. Collaborative practice: development, implementation, and evaluation of a weaning protocol for patients receiving mechanical ventilation. Am J Crit Care 2003;12:454–60.

38. Dries DJ, McGonigal MD, Malian MS, Bor BJ, Sullivan C. Protocol-driven ventilator weaning reduces use of mechanical ventilation, rate of early reintubation, and ventilator-associated pneumonia. J Trauma-Injury Infection & Crit Care 2004;56:943–51.

39. Tonnelier JM, Prat G, Le Gal G, Gut-Gobert C, Renault A, Boles JM, et al. Impact of a nurses' protocol-directed weaning procedure on outcomes in patients undergoing mechanical ventilation for longer than 48 hours: a prospective cohort study with a matched historical control group. Crit Care 2005;9:R83–9.

40. Hoffman LA, Tasota FJ, Zullo TG, Scharfenberg C, Donahoe MP. Outcomes of care managed by an acute care nurse practitioner/attending physician team in a subacute medical intensive care unit. Am J Crit Care 2005;14:121–30; quiz 31–2.

41. Blackwood B, Wilson-Barnett J, Patterson CC, Trinder TJ, Lavery GG. An evaluation of protocolised weaning on the duration of mechanical ventilation. Anaesthesia 2006;61:1079–86.

42. Schweickert WD, Kress JP. Strategies to optimize analgesia and sedation. Crit Care 2008;12:S6.

43. Payen JF, Chanques G, Mantz J, Hercule C, Auriant I, Leguillou JL, et al. Current practices in sedation and analgesia for mechanically ventilated critically ill patients: a prospective multicenter patient-based study. Anesthesiology 2007;106:687–95.

44. Samuelson K, Lundberg D, Fridlund B. Memory in relation to depth of sedation in adult mechanically ventilated intensive care patients. Intensive Care Med 2006;32:660–7.

45. Weinert CR, Sprenkle M. Post-ICU consequences of patient wakefulness and sedative exposure during mechanical ventilation. Intensive Care Med. 2008;34:82–90.

46. Jacobi J, Fraser GL, Coursin DB, Riker RR, Fontaine D, Wittbrodt ET, et al. Clinical practice guidelines for the sustained use of sedatives and analgesics in the critically ill adult. Crit Care Med 2002;30:119–41.

47. Brook AD, Ahrens TS, Schaiff R, Prentice D, Sherman G, Shannon W, et al. Effect of a nursing-implemented sedation protocol on the duration of mechanical ventilation. Crit Care Med 1999;27:2609–15.

48. Brattebo G, Hofoss D, Flaatten H, Muri AK, Gjerde S, Plsek PE. Effect of a scoring system and protocol for sedation on duration of patients' need for ventilator support in a surgical intensive care unit. Bmj 2002;324:1386–9.

49. De Jonghe B, Bastuji-Garin S, Fangio P, Lacherade J-C, Jabot J, Appere-De-Vecchi C, et al. Sedation algorithm in critically ill patients without acute brain injury. Crit Care Med 2005;33:120–7.

50. Elliott R, McKinley S, Aitken LM, Hendrikz J. The effect of an algorithm-based sedation guideline on the duration of mechanical ventilation in an Australian intensive care unit. Intensive Care Med 2006;32:1506–14.

51. Quenot JP, Ladoire S, Devoucoux F, Doise JM, Cailliod R, Cunin N, et al. Effect of a nurse-implemented sedation protocol on the incidence of ventilator-associated pneumonia. Crit Care Med 2007;35:2031–6.

52. Bucknall TK, Manias E, Presneill JJ. A randomized trial of protocol-directed sedation management for mechanical ventilation in an Australian intensive care unit. Crit Care Med 2008;36:1444–50.

53. Arias-Rivera S, Sanchez-Sanchez Mdel M, Santos-Diaz R, Gallardo-Murillo J, Sanchez-Izquierdo R, Frutos-Vivar F, et al. Effect of a nursing-implemented sedation protocol on weaning outcome. Crit Care Med 2008;36:2054–60.

54. Elliott R, McKinley S, Aitken L. Adoption of a sedation scoring system and sedation guideline in an intensive care unit. J Adv Nurs 2006;54:208–16.

55. Davis DA, Taylor-Vaisey A. Translating guidelines into practice. A systematic review of theoretic concepts, practical experience and research evidence in the adoption of clinical practice guidelines. CMAJ 1997;157:408–16.

Eliezer Silva and Diogo Diniz Gomes Bugano

Developing guidelines –
The example of the Surviving Sepsis Campaign

Introduction

Evidence-based medicine (EBM) is defined as "integrating individual clinical expertise with the best available external clinical evidence from systematic research" [1]. Despite the development of more efficient tools for research and reporting, and the incorporation of this technique in health education, physicians face three great obstacles in using EBM in everyday practice: increasing amount of information, conflicting results, and lack of pragmatic trials able to answer questions about unselected patients.

Clinical guidelines developed by experts have arisen as a solution for this dilemma, since they summarise all evidence and apply it to clinically relevant questions, using expert opinion to provide recommendations when evidence is insufficient. In addition, they are useful for detecting areas of uncertainty on which research should focus; for standardising patient care, for aiding a comparison of health services and health policy planning and for improving patient care. These are some reasons why the number of clinical guidelines is growing every day, jumping from 444 in 1993 to 4,975 in 2006 [2].

The incorporation of clinical guidelines into practice has demanded improvement of their quality, which has led to the creation of entities specialised in developing better tools for the development of guidelines, such as

the National Institute for Health and Clinical Excellence (NICE, England), the Scottish Intercollegiate Guidelines Network (SIGN, Scotland), and the Agency for Healthcare Research and Quality (AHRQ, United States). Furthermore, the Institute for Healthcare Improvement (IHI), a non-profit organisation aiming to improve healthcare around the world, has also helped societies in implementing evidence-based best practice in the critical care field.

Some years ago, a very select group of researchers and clinical physicians decided to establish guidelines for the management of severe sepsis. The key drivers for this decision were the high prevalence and associated mortality rate. This academic group, called International Sepsis Forum, published the guidelines in 2001 [3] using the best evidence available and classifying it using the Sackett's methodology [4]. One year later, in October 2002, during the European Society of Intensive Care Medicine (ESICM) annual congress, the Surviving Sepsis Campaign was launched through the "Barcelona Declaration" – a document calling critical care providers, governments, health agencies and laypeople to join the fight against sepsis. The aim of the campaign was to reduce the sepsis mortality rate by 25 % within 5 years. In 2004, this group reported new guidelines for severe sepsis and septic shock, updating those published in 2001 [5]. These guidelines have changed considerably over time and are a good example of the evolution of the science behind the development of guidelines. Recently, a new update of these guidelines was published [6].

The aim of this chapter is to analyse different methods employed for guideline development, using the Surviving Sepsis Campaign as the background. We expect readers to understand the strengths and weaknesses of each method and to be able to implement them at the bedside.

Committees, nominal group technique, Sackett technique and ISF 2001 guidelines

Guideline development has the following main steps (see the following box): creation of a group responsible for defining the scope of the guidelines; selection of a set of clinically relevant questions which should be addressed by the guidelines; search for all relevant articles in the literature and evaluation of the quality of the evidence provided by them; discussion and application of this evidence to the proposed questions; elaboration of recommendations and implementation of these recommendations.

Main steps of guideline development

Selecting topic
Determining scope
Identifying and adopting existing clinical practice guidelines (CPG)
Formatting multidisciplinary guideline development group
Dealing with conflicts of interest
Involving guideline consumers
Establishing clinical questions
Grading outcomes (e.g.: death is a more important outcome than nausea)
Systematic search
Grading evidence
Including/excluding evidence
Comparison of desired/undesired effects
Appraising research
Developing recommendations
Developing implementation strategy
Writing summary
Planning for evaluating CPG impact, revising and updating

As mentioned above, in 2001, the International Sepsis Forum (ISF) proposed a systematic review and summary of the evidence regarding the care of patients with severe sepsis and septic shock. Basically, 9 experts in the areas of critical care medicine and infectious diseases were divided into 9 workgroups and each was responsible for summarising the evidence of one aspect of the studied patients: definition of sepsis, diagnosis of infection, antibiotics in sepsis, haemodynamic support, source control, airway and lung in sepsis, immunological therapy (currently available and experimental treatments), and other supportive therapies. Studies have different designs, which makes them susceptible to different biases and changes their ability to answer clinical questions. To asses study quality, the procedure proposed by Sackett was used.

The Sackett classification was proposed in 1989 in a guideline for antithrombotic therapy [4]. Basically, it considers that the best evidence for patient intervention comes from randomised controlled trials (RCT), followed by uncontrolled trials, observational studies, case series and expert opinion. Guideline recommendations based on RCTs are less susceptible to biases and therefore should be considered stronger than recommendations based on weaker evidence. The full grading for evidence (I–V) and recommendations (A–E) is summarised in Table 1.

Tab. 1 Sackett classification of evidence and recommendations [modified from Sackett DL. Rules of evidence and clinical recommendations on the use of antithrombotic agents. Chest 1989 Feb;95(2 Suppl):2S-4S]

Grading of evidence	
I	Large randomised trials with clear-cut results
II	Small randomised trials with uncertain results
III	Non-randomised; contemporaneous controls
IV	Non-randomised; historical controls
V	Uncontrolled studies, case series, expert opinion
Grading of recommendation	
A	More than one level I investigation
B	One level I investigation
C	Evidence level II
D	Evidence level III
E	Evidence levels IV or V

Members of each group were asked to present their evidence-based recommendations for the proposed questions to the whole guideline committee. However, evidence is still weak for most interventions and recommendations depend strongly on personal experience and values, which invariably leads to disagreements. Disagreements were solved using the nominal group technique. In the nominal group technique, all guideline participants express their points of view and then discuss the disagreements, trying to reach a consensus. Discussion ends when an agreement is reached or after a pre-defined time spam. After the discussion, each individual proposes new recommendations and the guideline organisers summarise all opinions. In 2001, after the discussion, another 9 experts were asked to create new recommendations, which were summarised by 3 guideline organisers.

The final guidelines were published in 2001 as a special supplement of the Intensive Care Medicine Journal and contained 83 recommendations [3].

Delphi approach, sepsis bundles and the SSC 2004 guidelines

Being based on research, guidelines should change over time following new evidence, and scheduling an update is a crucial step of guideline development. Besides that, after the publication of the 2001 guidelines it was evident that the care of patients with severe sepsis varied widely in different services and this contributed to different outcomes. To deal with this issue, in October 2002, during the European Society of Critical Care Medicine (ESICM) annual congress, the Surviving Sepsis Campaign was launched. The campaign was divided into 3 phases, the campaign divulgation being the first one. Phase II involved the creation of new guidelines and phase III the implementation of these guidelines and evaluation of results.

The nominal group technique allows discussion and agreement, which probably leads to more accurate conclusions. However, it has some drawbacks. Firstly, the difficulty of conducting a discussion with larger groups of individuals impairs the enrolment of representatives from different specialities, countries and values, making the generalisation of guidelines more difficult. Secondly, live discussions can be influenced by factors such as fatigue and pressure exerted by some participants on others, reducing the quality of the proposed recommendations. Finally, the nominal group technique makes guideline development a longer and more expensive process. For example, NICE takes 18 months and 15 meetings to generate each guideline, which ideally should be updated every two years [7].

An alternative is the Delphi approach [8]. First, a group of experts is selected and a series of questionnaires is sent to them. Participants give their answers to the proposed questions individually and provide explanations for their choices. Then, recommendations are summarised and mailed to every participant for re-evaluation. Finally, the participants, again anonymously, provide their new recommendations and the guideline organisers generate the final statement.

The SSC Steering Committee used a mixed approach for the development of the 2004 guidelines [9]. First, Delphi rounds were done; then, disagreements were solved using the nominal group technique. If the meetings were unable to reach a conclusion, new Delphi rounds were done for the remaining issues.

Finally, the main objective of the SSC was reducing mortality through the implementation of guidelines. To achieve that, the Advisory Board and the Steering Committee, working with the Institute for Healthcare Improvement, made the 2004 guidelines widely available through the Internet, lectures and printed material. Besides that, the IHI developed the concept of "bundles" to help healthcare providers deliver the best possible care for patients undergoing particular treatments with inherent risks. A bundle is a structured way of improving the processes of care and patient outcomes: a small, straightforward set of practices – generally three to five – that, when performed collectively and reliably, have been proven to improve patient outcomes (www.ihi.org). Physicians and institutions should be prepared to provide them to severe sepsis patients in the first hours after the diagnosis (or after the first sepsis-induced organ dysfunction).

The whole process involved 40 experts and other individuals, increasing costs even further. These were covered by the participation of more groups (11 organisations) and educational grants

Tab. 2 Comparison of the 2001, 2004 and 2008 guidelines

	2001	2004	2008		
Participants	18 experts	46 experts	56 experts		
Method	Nominal	Nominal/Delphi	Nominal/Delphi		
Recommendations	88	53	83		
Level of evidence	Sackett	Sackett	GRADE		
A	9 (10.2%)	5 (9.5%)		1	2
B	10 (11.4%)	12 (22.6%)	A	7	0
C	24 (27.3%)	5 (9.5%)	B	15	6
D	16 (18.2%)	4 (7.5%)	C	16	18
E	29 (32.9%)	27 (50.9%)	D	14	7
Groups	1	11	16		
Industry funding	no	yes	no		
AGREE					
Scope and purpose	67%	100%	100%		
Stakeholder involvement	25%	33%	50%		
Rigour of development	86%	86%	86%		
Clarity and presentation	100%	100%	100%		
Applicability	0%	0%	0%		
Editorial independence	100%	100%	100%		

from private groups. This highlights another important step in guideline development: dealing with conflicts of interest. Before the process of guideline development started, all participants were asked to state their personal conflicts of interest. Participants were not assigned to workgroups in which these conflicts of interest would be significant, and no one from these funding parties was allowed in guideline meetings.

This process yielded the 2004 guidelines [5] with 53 recommendations and 2 bundles: resuscitation (with 6 recommendations that should be implemented in 6 hours), and management (with 4 recommendations to be implemented in 24 hours).

SSC 2008 guidelines and GRADE system

With the growing number of guidelines being developed and updated, many mechanisms were developed to evaluate the quality of guidelines. The AGREE (Appraisal of Guidelines Research and Evaluation collaboration) appraisal tool is the most widely used one, because it is simple, highly reproducible, and validated [10, 11]. AGREE evaluates guidelines in 6 domains: scope and purpose, stakeholder involvement, rigour of development, clarity and presentation, applicability and editorial independence. When the 2004 and 2001 guidelines are compared (see Tab. 2), there is an improvement in definition of scope and purpose, probably motivated by the experience with the previous guideline and the clear objectives of the SSC, and there is better stakeholder involvement, a consequence of the Delphi approach, which allows for the participation of more individuals. Another interesting trend is the proportional increase in grade B recommendations, with a reduction in grades C and D, which may indicate research focused on answering clinically relevant questions after the 2001 guidelines.

Tab. 3   GRADE classification and its meaning for patients, clinicians and policy-makers

Factors that may decrease the strength of evidence	
Poor quality of planning or implementation	
Inconsistency of results (including subgroup analysis)	
Indirectness of results (differing population, intervention, control outcomes, comparison)	
Imprecision of results	
High likelihood of reporting bias	
Factors that may increase the strength of evidence	
Large magnitude of effect (RR > 2 with no plausible confounders)	
Very large magnitude of effect (RR > 5) with no threats to validity	
Dose-response gradient	
Underlying methodology	
A	RCT
B	Downgraded RCT or upgraded observational studies
C	Well-done observational studies
D	Case series or expert opinion
Implication of strong or weak recommendations	
Strong	
Patients	Most will want the recommended action
Clinicians	Most patients should receive the recommended action
Policy-makers	Recommendations can be adopted as policy in most situations
Weak	
Patients	Most will want the action, but many will not
Clinicians	Choices will vary based on clinician's and patient's values
Policymakers	Unlikely to be included as a policy

Criticism of the 2004 guidelines centred on the high costs, which demanded external funding, and the disadvantages of the Sackett method for grading evidence. The Sackett method overestimates the value of randomised controlled trials. It considers evidence from all RCTs equally strong and immune to subjectivity. However, methodological issues might weaken the evidence arising from a RCT, while massive, consistent effects in an observational study may strengthen the evidence derived from them. Besides that, the Sackett grading system is confounding, because many interventions with low levels of evidence are actually recommended and used in clinical practice.

Recently, the GRADE (Grading of Recommendations Assessment, Development and Evaluation) [12] system has been proposed as a substitute for Sackett and has been adopted by more than 20 associations for grading evidence (BMJ, Cochrane, World Health Organization, American College of Physicians, American Thoracic Society, and others) [13]. GRADE divides evidence into 4 groups: strong (A), intermediate (B), weak (C) and very weak (D), with clear meaning for patients, clinicians and healthcare policy makers (see Tab. 4). Randomised controlled trials are still considered a source of strong evidence and observational studies of weak evidence; however, their level of evidence may be raised or lowered according to standard criteria (see Tab. 3). Recommendations are classified as 1 (strong) or 2 (weak), meaning that guideline developers agreed completely or partially with that specific recommendation.

The 2008 guidelines were created following a mixed approach. First, experts from all participating organisations defined guideline scopes and relevant questions. Then, small specialist working groups (15–20 individuals) summarised evidence on each subject and proposed recommendations. These results were discussed in 2 nominal groups and whenever there was much disagreement, all guideline participants were asked to participate in the discussion using a Delphi approach via e-mail. To resolve all remaining issues, a final nominal group was held, and participants were asked to place their recommendation (strong or weak) and level of evidence in a GRADE grid, which was transferred to a computer. The software summarised all answers as votes: a recommendation was considered weak if at least 50 % of participants voted in favour of that specific intervention and less than 20 % voted against it; if more than 70 % were in favour, classification was "strong"; if no criteria were met, no recommendation was made [14].

Using the mixed approach and the GRADE grid system significantly lowered costs and, with the collaboration of 16 organisations from different countries, the 2008 guidelines were issued without any support from private sources.

Finally, all this effort culminated in the 2008 guidelines, with 83 recommendations [6]. In the original paper the authors depicted the main interventions which should be implemented in the first hours after the diagnosis of severe sepsis (see Tab. 4 and 5).

Implementation issues

Unfortunately, clinicians change very slowly. Historically, transfer of research from the workbench to the bedside is a long, tortuous process – one that is not driven by anything very clear and seemingly based more on fads and coincidence than on a keen, evidence-based evaluation of the literature. Phase III of the campaign hopes to change that. After publication of the guidelines [5, 6], the Steering Committee of the SSC and the Advisory Board, in collaboration with the IHI, specified several tools in order to facilitate, at the bedside, the implementation of every evidence-based recommendation for the management of severe sepsis. These tools include educational programmes designed to increase awareness and agreement with the recommendations, checklists or bundles to help ensure that patients receive the intervention, and performance measures designed to provide feedback regarding how often patients receive the evidence.

Briefly, the SSC steering committee proposed voluntary participation of every institution around the world through distribution of a secure database allowing for data collection and transfer, and offered simple means for providing practice audit and feedback to local clinicians. About 20,000 patients with severe sepsis were included in this worldwide database and the data was recently submitted to publication as an original article.

Besides the submission to publication of the global data, we have observed some reports from different regions including Spain and Brazil. The Severe Sepsis Educational Program in Spain was recently detailed in a very exciting paper published in JAMA [15]. The authors describe a connection of their programme implementation with a reduction in mortality rate. The main attributes of the educational programme included

- implementation in almost 60 medical-surgical intensive care units located throughout Spain,
- training physicians and nursing staff from the emergency department, wards, and ICU,
- an audit process to check adherence to the proposed severe sepsis bundles,
- a multidisciplinary team coordinated by a local chair (champion leader), and
- feedback from the coordinating centre with the baseline period data compared with global baseline period data (audit and feedback).

The authors were able to demonstrate a 10 % reduction in relative risk of death.

Similarly, in Brazil, the Latin American Sepsis Institute has organised the campaign implementation across the country [16]. The SSC was disclosed via panels, banners, and folders coordinated by the Institute, and manuals, lecture presentations, official documents and forms, databases, reference bibliography, multimedia storage (videocassette recorder, compact disc, and digital video disc), and data collection charts were

Tab. 4   2008 recommendations for initial resuscitation and infection issues [from Dellinger RP, Levy MM, Carlet JM, Bion J, Parker MM, Jaeschke R, et al. Surviving Sepsis Campaign: international guidelines for management of severe sepsis and septic shock: 2008. Intensive Care Med 2008 Jan;34(1):17–60]

Initial resuscitation (first 6 hours)

- Begin resuscitation immediately in patients with hypotension or elevated serum lactate >4mmol/l; do not delay pending ICU admission (1C)
- Resuscitation goals: (1C)
  - Central venous pressure (CVP) 8–12 mmHg*
  - Mean arterial pressure ≥65 mmHg
  - Urine output ≥0.5 ml/kg/h
  - Central venous (superior vena cava) oxygen saturation ≥ 70 %, or mixed venous ≥ 65 %
- If venous O_2 saturation target not achieved: (2C)
  - Consider further fluid
  - Transfuse packed red blood cells if required to haematocrit of ≥30 % and/or
  - Dobutamine infusion max 20 µg/kg/min

* A higher target CVP of 12–15 mmHg is recommended in the presence of mechanical ventilation or pre-existing decreased ventricular compliance

Diagnosis

- Obtain appropriate cultures before starting antibiotics provided this does not significantly delay antimicrobial administration. (1C)
  - Obtain two or more blood cultures (BCs)
  - One or more BCs should be percutaneous
  - One BC from each vascular access device in place > 48 h
  - Culture other sites as clinically indicated
- Perform imaging studies promptly in order to confirm and sample any source of infection, if safe to do so (1C)

Antibiotic therapy

- Begin intravenous antibiotics as early as possible, and always within the first hour of recognizing severe sepsis (1D) and septic shock (1B)
- Broad-spectrum: one or more agents active against likely bacterial/fungal pathogens and with good penetration into presumed source (1B)
- Reassess antimicrobial regimen daily to optimise efficacy, prevent resistance, avoid toxicity & minimise costs (1C)
- Consider combination therapy in Pseudomonas infections (2D)
- Consider combination empiric therapy in neutropenic patients (2D)
- Combination therapy no more than 3–5 days and deescalation following susceptibilities (2D)
- Duration of therapy typically limited to 7–10 days; longer if response slow, undrainable foci of infection, or immunologic deficiencies (1D)
- Stop antimicrobial therapy if cause is found to be non-infectious (1D)

Source identification and control

- A specific anatomic site of infection should be established as rapidly as possible (1C) and within first 6 hrs of presentation (1D)
- Formally evaluate patient for a focus of infection amenable to source control measures (e.g.: abscess drainage, tissue debridement) (1C)
- Implement source control measures as soon as possible following successful initial resuscitation (1C) Exception: infected pancreatic necrosis, where surgical intervention is best delayed (2B)
- Choose source control measure with maximum efficacy and minimal physiologic upset (1D)
- Remove intravascular access devices if potentially infected (1C)

- Indicates a strong recommendation
- Indicates a weak recommendation

Tab. 5 2008 recommendations for haemodynamic support and adjunctive therapy [from Dellinger RP, Levy MM, Carlet JM, Bion J, Parker MM, Jaeschke R, et al. Surviving Sepsis Campaign: international guidelines for management of severe sepsis and septic shock: 2008. Intensive Care Med 2008 Jan;34(1):17–60]

Fluid therapy

- Fluid-resuscitate using crystalloids or colloids (1B)
- Target a CVP of ≥ 8 mmHg (≥ 12 mmHg if mechanically ventilated) (1C)
- Use a fluid challenge technique while associated with a haemodynamic improvement (1D)
- Give fluid challenges of 1000 ml of crystalloids or 300–500 ml of colloids over 30 min. More rapid and larger volumes may be required in sepsis-induced tissue hypoperfusion (1D)
- Rate of fluid administration should be reduced if cardiac filling pressures increase without concurrent haemodynamic improvement (1D)

Vasopressors

- Maintain MAP ≥ 65 mmHg (1C)
- Norepinephrine or dopamine centrally administered are the initial vasopressors of choice (1C)
  - Epinephrine, phenylephrine or vasopressin should not be administered as the initial vasopressor in septic shock (2C)
  - Vasopressin 0.03 units/min may be subsequently added to norepinephrine with anticipation of an effect equivalent to norepinephrine alone
  - Use epinephrine as the first alternative agent in septic shock when blood pressure is poorly responsive to norepinephrine or dopamine (2B)
- Do not use low-dose dopamine for renal protection (1A)
- In patients requiring vasopressors, insert an arterial catheter as soon as practical (1D)

Inotropic therapy

- Use dobutamine in patients with myocardial dysfunction as supported by elevated cardiac filling pressures and low cardiac output (1C)
- Do not increase cardiac index to predetermined supranormal levels (1B)

Steroids

- Consider intravenous hydrocortisone for adult septic shock when hypotension remains poorly responsive to adequate fluid resuscitation and vasopressors (2C)
- ACTH stimulation test is not recommended to identify the subset of adults with septic shock who should receive hydrocortisone (2B)
- Hydrocortisone is preferred to dexamethasone (2B)
- Fludrocortisone (50 µg orally once a day) may be included if an alternative to hydrocortisone is being used which lacks significant mineralocorticoid activity. Fludrocortisone is optional if hydrocortisone is used (2C)
- Steroid therapy may be weaned once vasopressors are no longer required (2D)
- Hydrocortisone dose should be ≤ 300 mg/day (1A)
- Do not use corticosteroids to treat sepsis in the absence of shock unless the patient's endocrine or corticosteroid history warrants it (1D)

Recombinant human activated protein C (rhAPC)

- Consider rhAPC in adult patients with sepsis-induced organ dysfunction with clinical assessment of high risk of death (typically APACHE II ≥ 25 or multiple organ failure) if there are no contraindications (2B, 2C for post-operative patients)
- Adult patients with severe sepsis and low risk of death (e.g.: APACHE II< 20 or one organ failure) should not receive rhAPC (1A)

■ Indicates a strong recommendation
▨ Indicates a weak recommendation

Tab. 6   Main actions to improve compliance [from Teles JM, Silva E, Westphal G, Filho RC, Machado FR. Surviving sepsis campaign in Brazil. Shock 2008 Oct;30 Suppl 1:47–52]

Initiatives	Commentary
Triage	Improvement in the initial recognition of septic shock patients
Managed protocols	Execution of clinical protocol audited by a nurse
Sepsis and rapid-response team	Specialised group to rapidly identify and treat patients in shock with a multidisciplinary team using evidenced-based protocols
Reward system	Strategy to motivate the ones who adequately make the attendance
Sepsis checklist	Specific list to be used during the attendance
Banners	Strategy to disseminate the knowledge and share information regarding results
Sepsis packs	All materials and drugs promptly available in a box

made available. The Latin American Sepsis Institute, a non-profit foundation, was created in July 2004, aiming to share sepsis information with scientific and lay communities in Latin America, demonstrating the Latin American medical community's good level of maturity along with some experts' initiatives and efforts by several anonymous collaborators, thus offering an effective tool against sepsis. Table 6 shows the main actions promoted by the Institute to increase awareness of sepsis and adherence to the severe sepsis guidelines. Preliminary data has shown a 10% absolute reduction in mortality rates.

Impact of SSC implementation around the world

As mentioned before, the SSC implementation aims at reducing the relative risk of death by 25% within 5 years. Besides that, the implementation process could also reduce hospital length of stay, direct costs of sepsis management, and indirect costs, including absenteeism and early death. In parallel, there is an impact on quality process improvement in other areas of the institution.

There are several studies that show the positive impact of the SSC implementation. A couple of years ago, Gao and coworkers [17] were able to demonstrate an association between 6-hour bundle adherence and lower mortality rate (49% versus 23%, relative risk (RR) 2.12; 95% confidence interval 1.20 to 3.76). Regarding 24-hour bundle adherence, similar results were observed, although a statistically significant difference was not achieved.

Other studies have also shown similar results. Micek et al. [18] showed that a standardised set of instructions for the management of septic shock in the emergency department (ED) was associated with more rigorous fluid resuscitation, greater administration of appropriate initial antibiotic treatment and a lower 28-day mortality rate. More recently, in a before-after study, Jones et al. [19] published data on the implementation of a routine protocol based on early-goal directed therapy in the ED. They reported a lower mortality rate after protocol implementation with a 9% absolute and 33% relative reduction in mortality. The study demonstrates that the creation of a working team and the optimisation of processes and interventions may dramatically reduce the mortality of severe sepsis and septic shock.

Future trends

If the AGREE criteria are applied to the 2008 SSC guidelines, there would be two main issues: stakeholder involvement and applicability. In fact, many professionals who deal with the direct care of severe sepsis patients were consulted, but there were still some who were underrepresented and there were no representatives of patients. Regarding applicability, the 2008 Guidelines predicted the development and evaluation of different implementation techniques, but none was formally recommended by the committee. However, the worldwide implementation of the SSC Guidelines has been closely monitored and some implementation methods have been proved superior to the others. Preliminry data of this implementation have been reported and submitted to publication.

When the recommendations are evaluated, there are only 14 % of 1A recommendations and 57 % level 1 recommendations based on evidence rated C or D, showing that most strong recommendations are being given despite insufficient evidence. Research should focus on this area. There is a tendency for only doing research if it brings interesting results for the pharmaceutical industry [20], what might explain the low level of evidence of established interventions in severe sepsis. A process for overcoming this difficulty has recently been proposed in the "Workshop Integrating and Coordinating Efforts in Guideline Development: COPD as a Case in Point", organised by the American Thoracic Society (ATS) and European Respiratory Society (ERS) [21]. Ten steps have been proposed:

- Development of a standardised database of existing evidence and gaps in the evidence
- Formulation of questions that are important for patients and clinicians and include relevant stakeholders
- Organisation of collaborative evidence reviews relevant for answering the questions. Each organisation should focus on reviews in its own area of expertise (epidemiology, antibiotics etc.)
- Adopting GRADE as the common metric for quality of evidence and strength of recommendations
- Consideration of comorbidities: most research focuses on highly selected patients and does not answer everyday questions. Guideline development panels should focus on the need of pragmatic trials (large, unselected patient groups)
- Identify ways that help guideline consumers (clinicians, patients and others) understand and implement guidelines using the best available tools. Integrate quality-of-care indicators, adherence of institutions/clinicians to guidelines. Create material suitable for different scenarios
- Deal with conflicts of interest (COI) and guideline sponsoring transparently: central COI database, with common disclosure categories and definitions
- Support development of decision aids to assist implementation of value- and preference-sensitive guideline development: How to adapt global guidelines to specific values
- Maintain a collaboration of international organisations
- Examining collaborative models for funding guideline development and implementation

Conclusion

Several reports have demonstrated an association between Surviving Sepsis Campaign implementation and lower mortality rates. Even if guideline development has some drawbacks, this process should be encouraged in order to improve healthcare and reduce costs and deaths.

The authors

Eliezer Silva, MD, PhD[1]
Diogo Diniz Gomes Bugano[2]
[1]Intensive Care Unit | Hospital Israelita | Albert Einstein | São Paulo/SP, Brazil
[2]University of São Paulo | São Paulo/SP, Brazil

Address for correspondence
Eliezer Silva
Hospital Israelita
Intensive Care Unit
Avenida Albert Einstein 627 5th Floor
05651-901 Sao Paulo, Brazil
E-mail: eliezer@einstein.br

References

1. Sackett DL, Rosenberg WM, Gray JA, Haynes RB, Richardson WS. Evidence based medicine: what it is and what it isn't. BMJ 1996 Jan 13;312(7023):71–2.
2. Turner T, Misso M, Harris C, Green S. Development of evidence-based clinical practice guidelines (CPGs): comparing approaches. Implement Sci 2008;3;45.
3. Summary of Recommendations. Intensive Care Med 2001;(27 Suppl 1):S128-S134.
4. Sackett DL. Rules of evidence and clinical recommendations on the use of antithrombotic agents. Chest 1989 Feb;95(2 Suppl):2S-4S.

5. Dellinger RP, Carlet JM, Masur H, Gerlach H, Calandra T, Cohen J, et al. Surviving Sepsis Campaign guidelines for management of severe sepsis and septic shock. Crit Care Med 2004 Mar;32(3):858–73.

6. Dellinger RP, Levy MM, Carlet JM, Bion J, Parker MM, Jaeschke R, et al. Surviving Sepsis Campaign: international guidelines for management of severe sepsis and septic shock: 2008. Intensive Care Med 2008 Jan;34(1):17–60.

7. Raine R, Sanderson C, Black N. Developing clinical guidelines: a challenge to current methods. BMJ 2005 Sep 17;331(7517):631–3.

8. Clark LH, Cochran SW. Needs of older Americans assessed by Delphi procedures. J Gerontol 1972 Apr;27(2):275–8.

9. Hutchings A, Raine R, Sanderson C, Black N. A comparison of formal consensus methods used for developing clinical guidelines. J Health Serv Res Policy 2006 Oct;11(4):218–24.

10. Vlayen J, Aertgeerts B, Hannes K, Sermeus W, Ramaekers D. A systematic review of appraisal tools for clinical practice guidelines: multiple similarities and one common deficit. Int J Qual Health Care 2005 Jun;17(3):235–42.

11. Development and validation of an international appraisal instrument for assessing the quality of clinical practice guidelines: the AGREE project. Qual Saf Health Care 2003 Feb;12(1):18–23.

12. Atkins D, Best D, Briss PA, Eccles M, Falck-Ytter Y, Flottorp S, et al. Grading quality of evidence and strength of recommendations. BMJ 2004 Jun 19;328(7454):1490.

13. Guyatt GH, Oxman AD, Vist GE, Kunz R, Falck-Ytter Y, Alonso-Coello P, et al. GRADE: an emerging consensus on rating quality of evidence and strength of recommendations. BMJ 2008 Apr 26;336(7650):924–6.

14. Jaeschke R, Guyatt GH, Dellinger P, Schunemann H, Levy MM, Kunz R, et al. Use of GRADE grid to reach decisions on clinical practice guidelines when consensus is elusive. BMJ 2008;337:a744.

15. Ferrer R, Artigas A, Levy MM, Blanco J, Gonzalez-Diaz G, Garnacho-Montero J, et al. Improvement in process of care and outcome after a multicenter severe sepsis educational program in Spain. JAMA 2008 May 21;299(19):2294–303.

16. Teles JM, Silva E, Westphal G, Filho RC, Machado FR. Surviving sepsis campaign in Brazil. Shock 2008 Oct;30 Suppl 1:47–52.

17. Gao F, Melody T, Daniels DF, Giles S, Fox S. The impact of compliance with 6-hour and 24-hour sepsis bundles on hospital mortality in patients with severe sepsis: a prospective observational study. Crit Care 2005;9(6):R764-R770.

18. Micek ST, Roubinian N, Heuring T, Bode M, Williams J, Harrison C, et al. Before-after study of a standardized hospital order set for the management of septic shock. Crit Care Med 2006 Nov;34(11):2707–13.

19. Jones AE, Focht A, Horton JM, Kline JA. Prospective external validation of the clinical effectiveness of an emergency department-based early goal-directed therapy protocol for severe sepsis and septic shock. Chest 2007 Aug;132(2):425–32.

20. Tricoci P, Allen JM, Kramer JM, Califf RM, Smith SC, Jr. Scientific evidence underlying the ACC/AHA clinical practice guidelines. JAMA 2009 Feb 25;301(8):831–41.

21. Schunemann HJ, Woodhead M, Anzueto A, Buist S, Macnee W, Rabe KF, et al. A vision statement on guideline development for respiratory disease: the example of COPD. Lancet 2009 Feb 28;373(9665):774–9.

Michael H. Hooper and Timothy D. Girard

Protocolised sedation to improve outcomes

Introduction

Intensive care unit (ICU) patients, especially those being mechanically ventilated, are at especially high risk for experiencing psychological distress and pain during their critical illness [1]. Thus, clinicians frequently administer sedative and analgesic medications in the ICU to alleviate anxiety and pain as well as to treat potentially dangerous agitation, which is experienced by two out of every three mechanically ventilated ICU patients [2]. Indeed, the need to provide sedation or analgesia in the ICU using pharmacologic agents is widely accepted by medical professionals.

The delivery of sedative agents, however, can adversely impact clinical outcomes for critically ill patients; it cannot be assumed that sedative medications are always delivered in the safest manner possible. Kollef and colleagues [3], for example, showed that patients receiving continuous intravenous sedation spent more time on the ventilator than those receiving sedation via intermittent boluses. Patients treated with continuous sedation also had longer ICU and hospital stays and higher reintubation rates than those treated with intermittent boluses. Thus, deep sedation – still widely implemented in many ICUs [4, 5] – puts patients at increased risk for the complications and medical errors that are more likely to occur during prolonged ICU stays

[6]. In addition, sedatives have been associated with other adverse short-term outcomes, e. g., delirium [7], and poor long-term outcomes, such as posttraumatic stress disorder [8].

In the past ten years, concerns over these deleterious effects of sedation have prompted the investigation of a variety of approaches to safely deliver sedation to ICU patients; a number of important strategies have been developed and studied, including employment of sedation scales [9–13], daily interruption of sedatives [14, 15], and use of analgesics and/or novel sedative agents in lieu of benzodiazepines [16–19]. For patients to benefit from these research findings, however, the effective strategies identified in clinical trials must be applied in clinical practice, a process that is often delayed and may stall completely [20].

By standardising clinical decision-making, protocolised sedation has the potential to greatly improve the translation of research findings into clinical practice and thereby improve patient safety and outcomes. Often executed by ICU nurses, sedation protocols have been examined in over a dozen clinical investigations during the past decade [14, 15, 21–32], the results of which have prompted many ICUs to adopt sedation protocols for local use. A recent international survey of 1, 384 ICU practitioners, in fact, found that seven out of every ten respondents reported using a sedation protocol. In this chapter, we will first describe the strategies utilised in effective sedation protocols (see Tab. 1) and then review the clinical trials (see Tab. 2) supporting the use of sedation protocols to guide the delivery of sedation and analgesia in the ICU while minimising potential adverse side effects.

Pain management in sedation protocols

Pain is pervasive in the ICU; both surgical and non-surgical patients commonly experience moderate to severe pain during their ICU stay [33]. Not only is pain inherently unpleasant, it may incite or intensify adverse neurologic or physiological effects, including agitation, delirium, myocardial ischemia, respiratory failure, and hypercoagulability [34]. Adequate treatment of pain, therefore, is of central importance for the safety of the ICU patient.

In five studies of sedation protocols, pain management is specifically prioritised (see Tab. 1), as recommended in the Society of Critical Care Medicine's clinical practice guidelines: "Sedation of agitated critically ill patients should be started only after providing adequate analgesia and treating reversible physiological causes" [35]. Fentanyl, having a rapid onset and short duration of action, was the analgesic most commonly included in these protocols. In sufficient doses, fentanyl can cause sedation as well as adequate analgesia.

Recent clinical trials have suggested that analgesia-based sedation using remifentanil – which is rapidly metabolised in an organ-independent manner with an elimination half-life < 10 minutes – leads to earlier extubation than benzodiazepine-based sedation [16]. Future trials are needed to determine whether sedation protocols that incorporate novel analgesics such as remifentanil are superior to current approaches to sedation in the ICU.

Sedation scales point the way through sedation protocols

A sedation scale provides ICU practitioners with an objective tool by which to measure the effectiveness of sedation in individual patients. When used appropriately, a sedation scale can improve communication between members of the ICU team, promote consistency in sedative administration, and increase precision of medication titration as a patient's needs change during their ICU stay. The use of a validated sedation scale is therefore recommended in the Society of Critical Care Medicine's clinical practice guidelines, which recommend that a sedation scale be used when establishing a sedation goal or target and when regularly assessing and documenting response to therapy [35].

The practice of monitoring level of sedation in the ICU has changed significantly during the past 2 decades with the advent and validation of simple yet reliable sedation scales, which allow ICU staff to quickly and objectively determine a patient's level of sedation. Recent surveys [36, 37] suggest that, more than 30 years after it was introduced, the Ramsay scale [9] remains the most commonly used sedation scale in ICUs. Other frequently used scales include the Richmond Agitation-Sedation Scale (RASS) [12], the Sedation-Agitation Scale (SAS) [11], and the Motor Activity Assessment Scale (MAAS) [10].

In every study of sedation protocols except for the two that center on daily interruption of sedatives, sedation scales are used in the sedation protocol to measure response to therapy and guide titration of sedatives (see Tab. 1). Even the protocols that did not include validated sedation scales (examined in two studies) relied upon objective criteria to determine response to sedatives or, more accurately, response to interruption of sedatives. Three sedation protocol studies utilised the Sedation-Agitation Scale [29, 30, 32], three relied on the Ramsay scale [21, 22, 26], and two used the Richmond Agitation-Sedation Scale [25, 31]. Each of these, as well as some other sedation scales, were the centerpiece of a sedation protocol that improved outcomes compared with non-protocolised delivery of sedation, suggesting that the specific scale chosen for use in an ICU is not necessarily important; it is vital, though, that some sedation scale be chosen and implemented in a way that facilitates reliable and frequent use by ICU staff.

It is unclear whether the same level of sedation should be set as the goal for all patients (e.g., Brook et al. [21] targeted Ramsay 3 – response to commands only – for all patients managed with the sedation protocol) or if the sedation target

E

Tab. 1 Strategies utilised in sedation protocols

Strategy	Rationale	References
Prioritise analgesics	Target a common etiology of agitation/anxiety/delirium	[21, 22, 26, 30, 31]
Use a sedation scale to guide dose titration	Detect oversedation and undersedation, individualise therapy	[21–32]
Discourage continuous infusions	Reduce accumulation of drug, avoid oversedation	[21, 26, 31]
Daily interruption of sedatives	Reduce accumulation of drug in the setting of continuous delivery	[14, 15]
	Facilitate trials without sedation to determine patient needs	

Tab. 2 Studies evaluating sedation protocols*

Reference	n	Patient Population	Outcomes Improved by Protocol
Studies favoring sedation protocols			
Randomised controlled trials			
Brook et al., 1999 [21]	321	Medical	Ventilator time, ICU & hospital LOS, tracheostomy
Kress et al., 2000 [14]	128	Medical	Ventilator time, ICU LOS
Girard et al., 2008 [15]	335	Medical	Ventilator-free days, ICU & hospital LOS, one-year survival
Tobar et al., 2008 [32]	40	General	Oversedation
Cohort studies			
MacLaren et al., 2000 [22]	158	Medical-surgical-neurologic	Pain, discomfort
Brattebo et al., 2002 [23]	285	Surgical	Ventilator time
De Jonghe et al., 2005 [24]	102	Medical	Time to arousal, ventilator time
Chanques et al., 2006 [25]	230	Medical-surgical	Pain, agitation, ventilator time, nosocomial infection
Quenot et al., 2007 [27]	423	Medical	VAP, ventilator time, extubation failure, ICU & hospital LOS
Arias-Rivera et al., 2008 [28]	356	Medical-surgical	Successful extubation, oversedation
Marshall et al., 2008 [30]	156	Medical	Ventilator time, ICU & hospital LOS
Robinson et al., 2008 [31]	143	Trauma	Ventilator time, ventilator-free days, hospital LOS
Studies showing no difference			
Randomised controlled trials			
Bucknall et al., 2008 [29]	312	Medical-surgical-trauma	None
Studies favoring non-protocolised sedation			
Cohort studies			
Elliot et al., 2006 [26]	322	General	None improved, but ICU LOS worsened

*Pilot studies that were not powered to detect differences in outcomes are not shown.
Abbreviations: ICU, intensive care unit; LOS, length of stay; VAP, ventilator-associated pneumonia.

should be individualised according to each patient's perceived needs for sedation. Eight of the studies of sedation protocols applied one goal to all patients, whereas the other six studies encouraged individualised goals.

Intermittent rather than continuous delivery of sedatives

Sedative and analgesic medications are typically administered intravenously in the ICU, as either intermittent boluses or continuous infusions, with that latter being most common. In a multicenter, prospective cohort study that assessed the management of pain and sedation among 1,381 adult ICU patients throughout France, Payen and colleagues [4] found that > 90 % of sedatives and opioids were administered via continuous intravenous infusion. This may be due, in part, to the fact that most clinical trials evaluating specific sedative agents in the ICU have done so using continuous infusions [16, 18, 19, 38–40].

Compared with intermittent dosing of sedatives, the continuous method of administration has some important disadvantages. Sedative agents are more likely to accumulate and exert prolonged effects when administered continuously rather than intermittently, and acute increases in infusion rate for the treatment of agitation often may not be followed by an appropriate decrease in infusion rate once agitation is controlled. Thus, Kollef and coworkers [3] hypothesised that use of continuous intravenous sedation would be associated with prolongation of mechanical ventilation compared with intermittent bolus administration of sedation. Indeed, they confirmed their hypothesis in a prospective cohort study examining outcomes among 242 mechanically ventilated ICU patients; compared with those receiving intermittent bolus sedation or no sedation, patients receiving continuous intravenous sedation had worse outcomes, including prolongation of mechanical ventilation, delayed discharge from the ICU and hospital, more organ system failure, and a higher reintubation rate [3].

Though intermittent dosing is not a viable option for some sedative medications used in the ICU, e.g., propofol and dexmedetomidine, benzodiazepines and most opiates can be effectively administered via intermittent intravenous bolus. In three studies of sedation protocols, continuous intravenous dosing was explicitly recommended only after intermittent boluses had failed to achieve the desired level of patient comfort (see Tab. 1) [21, 26, 31]. In one of these studies, use of the protocol did not reduce the percentage of patients who received a continuous sedation infusion (approximately 41 % of patients in both treatment groups), but the duration of continuous infusions was significantly reduced from 5.6 ± 6.4 days in the non-protocol group to 3.5 ± 4.0 days in the protocol group [21]. In another study, there was no change in the frequency of fentanyl or propofol infusions with use of the protocol, but patients in the protocol group were much less likely to receive a lorazepam infusion compared with patients in the control group (14 % vs. 39 %) [31]. In both of these studies, as described in more detail later in this chapter, outcomes were improved when sedation was directed by a protocol. One other study [26] whose protocol discouraged use of continuous sedative infusions did not observe an improvement in outcomes; no data, unfortunately, were provided indicating whether the protocol effectively reduced the frequency or duration of continuous infusions.

Daily interruption of sedatives

Despite the disadvantages of continuous sedative delivery, many ICU patients will be treated for a variety of reasons with sedative agents that must be delivered via continuous intravenous infusions or will require that a sedative typically given intermittently be administered continuously instead. Compared with that provided by intermittent delivery of sedatives, continuous infusions can provide a more constant level of sedation; such infusions are needed to maintain comfort for some patients.

To offset the potential for oversedation associated with continuous sedation and to facilitate frequent assessments of a patient's need for sedation, the drugs can be discontinued at specific intervals (typically once daily) so that the patient awakens. This approach, referred to initially as "daily interruption of sedatives" and later as a "daily wake up," "sedation vacation," or "spontaneous awakening trial," reduces the overall exposure to sedatives (especially benzodiazepines) despite relying on continuous infusions as the method of delivery.

Two studies of sedation protocols used daily interruption of sedatives as the focal point of the protocol (see Tab. 1). In both, the cumulative doses of benzodiazepines were significantly lower, and outcomes were dramatically improved, among patients managed with the protocol compared with those managed according to usual care.

Reviewing the evidence

Although an earlier study had examined the effectiveness of general sedation guidelines [41], the first controlled investigation of a sedation protocol in the ICU was published only one decade ago. Subsequently, thirteen additional studies have been conducted such that five randomised controlled trials and nine prospective pre-post studies provide evidence regarding the efficacy of sedation protocols in the ICU (see Tab. 2). A multitude of protocols exist, but they commonly use both an objective method for assessing response to therapy (typically a validated sedation scale) and a sedative delivery algorithm that incorporates the patient's measured level of sedation in decision-making. Whereas the protocols studied have differed in agents administered, methods of measuring level of sedation, and algorithms for determining the frequencies and doses of sedative delivered, the results have nearly unanimously shown sedation protocols to be superior to non-protocolised administration of sedation.

Prompted by their observation that continuous sedation is associated with prolonged time on the ventilator, Brook and colleagues [21] conducted a seminal study during which 321 mechanically ventilated medical ICU patients were randomised to management with a sedation protocol implemented by nurses or to sedation according to usual care. The protocol incorporated three of the previously described strategies for effective sedation, prioritising analgesia, using a sedation scale to guide dose titration, and discouraging continuous sedative infusions (see Fig. 1). For patients in the control group, alternatively, every change in sedation had to be ordered by the treating physicians. Compared with physician-ordered sedation, management with the sedation protocol resulted in a significant reduction in duration of mechanical ventilation (124.0 ± 153.6 hours vs. 89.1 ± 133.6 hours, p = .003) as well as length of stay in the ICU (7.5 ± 6.5 days vs. 5.7 ± 5.9 days, p = .01) and hospital (19.9 ± 24.2 hours vs. 14.0 ± 17.3 days, p < .001). In addition, patients in the sedation protocol group were less likely than patients in the control group to undergo tracheostomy (6 % vs. 13 %, p = .04).

Since Brook et al. conducted their trial in a single medical ICU in the United States, it was unclear whether similar sedation protocols could improve outcomes in medical ICUs at other institutions. Three prospective pre-post studies subsequently compared sedation protocols to sedation according to usual care in medical ICUs in other parts of the world. De Jonghe and colleagues [24], for example, studied 102 mechanically ventilated medical ICU patients in France and found that the 48 patients managed with a sedation protocol spent less time on the ventilator than the 54 patients in the control group (4.4 [2.1–9.8] days vs. 10.3 [3.5–17.2] days, p = .01) as well as less time unarousable after initiation of mechanical ventilation (2 [2–5] days vs. 4 [2–9] days, p = .006). In a study conducted in another French medical ICU, Quenot and coworkers [27] found that a nurse-implemented sedation protocol not only reduced time on the ventilator, in the ICU, and in the hospital, but also reduced the incidence of ventilator-associated pneumonia. Compared with 15 % of patients in the control group who developed ventilator-associated pneumonia, only 6 % of patients managed with the sedation protocol experienced this complication of mechanical ventilation (p = .005). In the most recent study to examine a sedation protocol in a medical ICU, Marshall et al. [30] compared outcomes among 78 patients managed with a clinical pharmacist-enforced sedation protocol to those among 78 patients treated prior to implementation of the pharmacist-enforced protocol. Though sedation guidelines were available during the control period, patients enrolled at that time had longer stays on the ventilator (p = .0004), in the ICU (p = .002), and in the hospital (p = .001) than patients treated with the pharmacist-enforced protocol.

In these studies, medical ICU patients consistently benefited from management with seda-

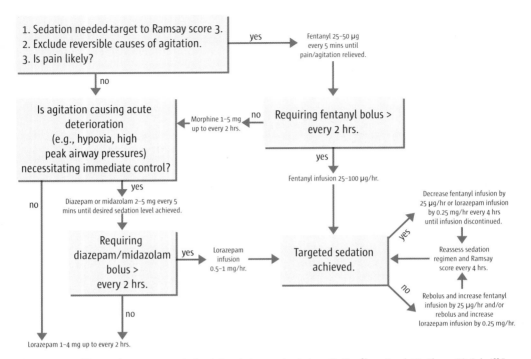

Fig. 1   Protocol for nursing management of sedation during mechanical ventilation [from Brook AD, Ahrens TS, Schaiff R, Prentice D, Sherman G, Shannon W, et al. Effect of a nursing-implemented sedation protocol on the duration of mechanical ventilation. Crit Care Med 1999;27:2609–15, with kind permission of Wolters Kluwer Health].

tion protocols, but additional data was needed to assess the impact of sedation protocols in ICUs that included surgical, trauma, or other ICU patients. MacLaren and colleagues [22] conducted the first such investigation, studying 158 patients mechanically ventilated in a combined medical-surgical-neurologic ICU in Canada. Though duration of mechanical ventilation and ICU length of stay were not significantly changed by the sedation protocol, patients treated with the protocol were less likely than patients in the control group to report pain (percentage of modified visual analog measurements representing pain, 6% vs. 10%; p < .05) or to demonstrate signs of discomfort (percentage of modified Ramsay sedation scores representing discomfort, 11% vs. 22%; p < .001). Chanques et al. [25] later confirmed that pain and agitation are reduced when a sedation protocol – even one that simply requires nurses to use validated pain and sedation scales and notify physicians of the results – is implemented in a medical-surgical ICU. In their

investigation, the 130 patients who were systemically evaluated with pain and sedation scales had a lower incidence of pain (p = .002) and agitation (p = .002) than the 100 patients managed according to usual care. Additionally, similar to the results observed in a medical ICU by Quenot et al., Chanques and coworkers found that nosocomial infections were less common in the intervention group than in the control group (8% vs. 17%, p < .05). Though not demonstrated in the early investigation by MacLaren et al., three studies including surgical and/or trauma patients showed that duration of mechanical ventilation is significantly reduced through use of a sedation protocol [23, 25, 31].

Some have expressed concern that nursing-implemented sedation protocols might dramatically increase the amount of time nurses spend delivering sedation and monitoring its effects [42]; little data exists to address this concern. In the only study to examine the effect of a sedation protocol on nursing workload, Arias-Rivera and

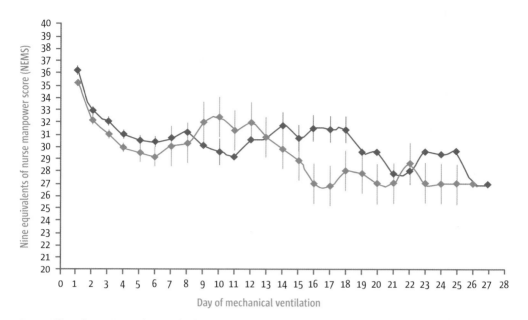

Fig. 2   Effect of a nursing-implemented sedation protocol on nursing workload. In the only study to examine this relationship, there was no significant difference in the daily mean (sem) of the Nine Equivalents of Nurse Manpower score
(NEMS) between patients managed with a sedation protocol (light gray box) and those whose sedation was delivered according to usual care (dark gray box). [from Arias-Rivera S, Sanchez-Sanchez MM, Santos-Diaz R, Gallardo-
Murillo J, Sanchez-Izquierdo R, Frutos-Vivar F, et al. Effect of a nursing-implemented sedation protocol on weaning
outcome. Crit Care Med 2008;36:2054–60, with kind permission of Wolters Kluwer Health].

colleagues [28] found that the Nine Equivalents of Nurse Manpower score (NEMS) was not significantly different pre- and post-implementation of a nursing-driven sedation protocol (see Fig. 2). Additional research is needed to determine the manpower costs of sedation protocols.

All of the sedation protocols studied in the investigations described to this point in the chapter promoted a strategy known as goal-directed or patient-targeted sedation; the protocols direct nurses to gradually titrate sedatives until a targeted level of sedation is achieved. The sedation goal or target is determined by members of the ICU team on an ongoing basis. One potential shortcoming of this approach is that the ICU team may overestimate a patient's need for sedation; in this circumstance, the protocol will direct nurses to give more sedation than the patient needs since the target is set at a deeper level of sedation than is required for the patient's comfort. Kress and colleagues [14] sought to avoid this potential problem by developing a protocol that allowed

the sedated patient to wake up each day during a period of sedative interruption. While the sedatives were held – a period of time now referred to as a spontaneous awakening trial – the patient was observed for signs of wakefulness or intolerance; if the patient awoke without agitation, anxiety, pain or other signs of intolerance, i.e., if they passed the spontaneous awakening trial, then the ICU team would know that sedatives were not needed at that time.

In a single-center trial, which enrolled 128 mechanically ventilated medical ICU patients receiving continuous IV sedation, Kress et al. [14] found that their sedation protocol involving daily interruption of sedatives significantly reduced duration of mechanical ventilation (p = .004) as well as ICU length of stay (p = .02) when compared with sedation according to usual care. This benefit was not accompanied by an increase in adverse events. Only 3% of patients in the sedation protocol group self-extubated compared with 7% of patients in the control group (p = .88). In fact, Schweickert and coworkers [43] conducted a thorough retrospective analysis of in-hospital complications experienced by patients enrolled in the Kress trial – including ventilator-associated pneumonia, upper gastrointestinal hemorrhage, bacteremia, barotrauma, venous thromboembolic disease, cholestasis, and sinusitis – and found that the overall complication rate was 2.8% in the sedation protocol group vs. 6.2% in the control group (p = .04). The authors concluded that complications related to a longer stay in the ICU and on mechanical ventilation were less likely to occur when patients were managed with the sedation protocol; the daily interruption of sedatives protocol was an important determinant of patient safety.

A major concern that might lead the ICU team to overestimate a patient's need for sedation is the potential for psychological harm during an ICU stay. To assess whether daily interruption of sedation promotes psychological harm by reducing sedative exposure, Kress and coworkers [44] interviewed patients enrolled in their original trial as well as other patients not enrolled in that trial but recruited contemporaneously. Patients were assessed for PTSD, depression, and anxiety by a psychologist blinded to details of the patient's ICU stay; none of the patients who were managed with the sedation protocol were diagnosed with PTSD compared with the 32% of patients managed with sedation according to usual care (p = .06). No differences were found between the groups in terms of anxiety or depression.

In the only multicenter randomised controlled trial to assess a sedation protocol, Girard and coworkers [15] examined the efficacy and safety of a "wake up and breathe" protocol that paired spontaneous awakening trials (i.e., daily interruption of sedatives) with spontaneous breathing trials. In this Awakening and Breathing Controlled (ABC) Trial, the investigators sought to extend the benefits of a sedation protocol by coordinating it with a ventilator weaning protocol that had already been proven beneficial [45, 46]. Among the 167 patients randomised to management with the wake up and breathe protocol, 895 spontaneous awakening trials were conducted; only 5% (42 of 895) of these trials resulted in signs of anxiety, agitation, or pain, a low rate that was achieved through the careful appli-

cation of a safety screen prior to each spontaneous awakening trial. Compared with the 168 patients in the control group, those managed with the sedation protocol spent on average 3 more days off the ventilator (p = .02), and they were discharged 4 days earlier from the ICU (p = .01) and hospital (p = .04). Additionally, this was the first clinical trial to demonstrate that a sedation protocol can significantly improve survival; management with the wake up and breathe protocol resulted in a 14% absolute reduction in the risk of death up to 1 year after enrollment (see Fig. 3; p = .01).

Of the fourteen investigations that compared either goal-directed sedation protocols or daily interruption of sedation protocols to non-protocolised delivery of sedation, only two failed to demonstrate the benefits of protocolised sedation. In the only randomised controlled trial that did not find a sedation protocol to be superior to non-protocolised sedation, Bucknall et al. [29] compared outcomes between 155 general ICU patients managed with a sedation protocol and 161 patients whose sedation was delivered without a protocol. No significant differences were observed in duration of mechanical ventilation, length of stay in the ICU and hospital, tracheostomy placement, or other outcomes. In addition, neither the total doses nor the average infusion rates of the sedatives commonly used in this trial, including propofol and midazolam, were significantly altered via use of the sedation protocol. This strongly suggests that the usual practice of sedative delivery in the participating ICU was actually similar to that dictated by the protocol, a fact that would not be true for most ICUs that implement an evidence-based sedation protocol. The authors noted that patients in their ICU are cared for in a 1:1 ratio by nurses who manage both the sedation and ventilation of the patient. Thus, this trial suggests that sedation protocols may not be of significant benefit in ICUs with high nurse:patient ratios and existing sedation practices that are similar to those promoted by protocols.

In the other investigation that did not find sedation protocols to be beneficial, Elliott and colleagues [26] examined the effect of a sedation protocol in a pre-post study of 322 general ICU patients and found that most outcomes were similar between groups. ICU length of stay, how-

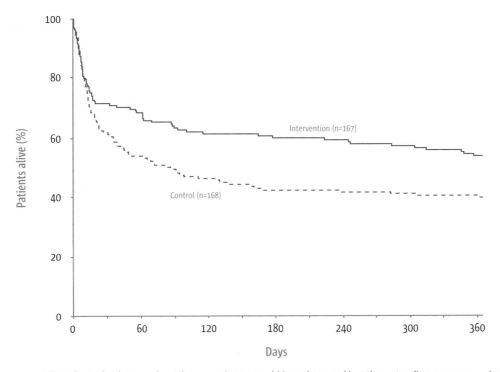

Fig. 3   Effect of paired sedation and ventilator weaning protocol (the wake up and breathe protocol) on one-year survival in medical ICU patients receiving mechanical ventilation. An unadjusted Cox proportional-hazard analysis showed that patients in the intervention group were 32 % less likely to die at any instant during the year following enroll-ment than patients in the control group (hazard ratio for death, 0.68; 95 % CI, 0.50 to 0.92; p = 0.01). [from Girard TD, Kress JP, Fuchs BD, Thomason JW, Schweickert WD, Pun BT, et al. Efficacy and safety of a paired sedation and ventilator weaning protocol for mechanically ventilated patients in intensive care (Awakening and Breathing Con-trolled trial): a randomised controlled trial. Lancet 2008;371:126–34, with permission from Elsevier].

ever, was increased for patients managed with the sedation protocol (p = .04). The study was conducted in Australia, as was that of Bucknall et al., where a 1 : 1 ratio of nurses to patients is common. The authors did not report the dos-es of sedatives used during the trial, so it is un-known whether the protocol actually increased or decreased (as is most common) the amount of sedation delivered. In addition, the pre-post design of this study makes it vulnerable to selec-tion bias, since patients enrolled during the se-dation protocol period may have been different from those enrolled earlier. Thus, the results of this study should not be taken to outweigh the results of the twelve studies that found sedation protocols to improve outcomes compared with non-protocolised delivery of sedation in the ICU.

Barriers to the use of sedation protocols

Despite the publication of numerous studies sup-porting sedation protocols during the past de-cade, the use of sedation protocols as part of rou-tine care has been limited. Recent surveys have found that goal-directed sedation protocols are employed in 30 %-70 % of ICUs and less than 40 % of ICUs use daily interruption of sedation protocols regularly [36, 37, 47, 48]. To understand the infrequent use of these sedation strategies, Tanios et al. [48] identified barriers to sedation protocols in a survey of 904 Society of Critical Care Medicine members. The most common rea-sons that goal-directed sedation protocols were not used were lack of a physician order (35 %), lack of nursing support (11 %), and fear of oversedation (7%). Alternatively, the reasons for not using a daily interruption of sedatives protocol included concern about inducing respiratory compromise (26%), lack of nursing acceptance (22%), concerns regarding patient-initiated device removal (19%), and worry about patient discomfort (13%). Most of these concerns were addressed with the publication of the Awakening and Breathing Controlled Trial [15], which showed that daily interruption of sedatives rarely causes respiratory compromise or patient discomfort; these results were not available at the time Tanios et al. conducted their survey. ICUs can address the barriers to goal-directed sedation protocols by implementing ICU-wide policies allowing use of such protocols without an explicit physician order and by educating ICU staff regarding the benefits of sedation protocols.

Conclusion

Treatment with sedative and analgesic medications is undoubtedly an essential component of quality care for patients in the ICU, since pain, discomfort, anxiety, and agitation are commonly experienced by critically ill patients, but overuse of these medications imparts harm to patients. Thus, physicians and other members of the ICU team are obligated to use agents and methods of sedation that minimise negative side-effects. Numerous observational studies and randomised trials have proven that sedation protocols can improve patient safety by reducing pain and agitation while simultaneously reducing oversedation, decreasing ventilator time, and hastening time to discharge from the ICU and hospital. When combined with protocolised ventilator weaning, e.g., in the wake up and breathe protocol, sedation protocols may even improve long-term survival for mechanically ventilated ICU patients.

The authors

Michael H. Hooper, MD[1]
Timothy D. Girard, MD, MSCI[2, 3]
[1]Fellow | Division of Allergy, Pulmonary and Critical Care Medicine | Vanderbilt University School of Medicine | Nashville, Tennessee
[2]Instructor in Medicine | Division of Allergy, Pulmonary and Critical Care Medicine
and Center for Health Services Research | Department of Medicine | Vanderbilt University School of Medicine | Nashville, Tennessee
[3]Tennessee Valley Geriatric Research, Education and Clinical Center (GRECC) Service | Department of Veterans Affairs Medical Center | Tennessee Valley Healthcare System | Nashville, Tennessee

Address for correspondence
Michael H. Hooper
6th Floor MCE
Nashville TN 37232–8300, USA
E-mail: Michael.Hooper@Vanderbilt.Edu

References

1. Turner JS, Briggs SJ, Springhorn HE, Potgieter PD. Patients' recollection of intensive care unit experience. Crit Care Med 1990;18:966–8.
2. Fraser GL, Prato BS, Riker RR, Berthiaume D, Wilkins ML. Frequency, severity, and treatment of agitation in young versus elderly patients in the ICU. Pharmacotherapy 2000;20:75–82.
3. Kollef MH, Levy NT, Ahrens TS, Schaiff R, Prentice D, Sherman G. The use of continuous i.v. sedation is associated with prolongation of mechanical ventilation. Chest 1998;114:541–8.
4. Payen JF, Chanques G, Mantz J, Hercule C, Auriant I, Leguillou JL, et al. Current practices in sedation and analgesia for mechanically ventilated critically ill patients: a prospective multicenter patient-based study. Anesthesiology 2007;106:687–95.
5. Weinert CR, Calvin AD. Epidemiology of sedation and sedation adequacy for mechanically ventilated patients in a medical and surgical intensive care unit. Crit Care Med 2007;35:393–401.
6. Valentin A, Capuzzo M, Guidet B, Moreno RP, Dolanski L, Bauer P, et al. Patient safety in intensive care: results from the multinational Sentinel Events Evaluation (SEE) study. Intensive Care Med 2006;32:1591–8.
7. Pandharipande P, Shintani A, Peterson J, Pun BT, Wilkinson GR, Dittus RS, et al. Lorazepam is an independent risk factor for transitioning to delirium in intensive care unit patients. Anesthesiology 2006;104:21–6.
8. Girard TD, Shintani AK, Jackson JC, Gordon SM, Pun BT, Henderson MS, et al. Risk factors for posttraumatic stress disorder symptoms following critical illness requiring mechanical ventilation: a prospective cohort study. Crit Care 2007;11:R28.
9. Ramsay MA, Savege TM, Simpson BR, Goodwin R.

Controlled sedation with alphaxalone-alphadolone. Br Med J 1974;2:656–9.

10. Devlin JW, Boleski G, Mlynarek M, Nerenz DR, Peterson E, Jankowski M, et al. Motor Activity Assessment Scale: a valid and reliable sedation scale for use with mechanically ventilated patients in an adult surgical intensive care unit. Crit Care Med 1999;27:1271–5.

11. Riker RR, Picard JT, Fraser GL. Prospective evaluation of the Sedation-Agitation Scale for adult critically ill patients. Crit Care Med 1999;27:1325–9.

12. Sessler CN, Gosnell MS, Grap MJ, Brophy GM, O'Neal PV, Keane KA, et al. The Richmond Agitation-Sedation Scale: validity and reliability in adult intensive care unit patients. Am J Respir Crit Care Med 2002;166:1338–44

13. Ely EW, Truman B, Shintani A, Thomason JW, Wheeler AP, Gordon S, et al. Monitoring sedation status over time in ICU patients: reliability and validity of the Richmond Agitation-Sedation Scale (RASS). JAMA 2003;289:2983–91.

14. Kress JP, Pohlman AS, O'Connor MF, Hall JB. Daily interruption of sedative infusions in critically ill patients undergoing mechanical ventilation. N Engl J Med 2000;342:1471–7.

15. Girard TD, Kress JP, Fuchs BD, Thomason JW, Schweickert WD, Pun BT, et al. Efficacy and safety of a paired sedation and ventilator weaning protocol for mechanically ventilated patients in intensive care (Awakening and Breathing Controlled trial): a randomised controlled trial. Lancet 2008;371:126–34.

16. Breen D, Karabinis A, Malbrain M, Morais R, Albrecht S, Jarnvig IL, et al. Decreased duration of mechanical ventilation when comparing analgesia-based sedation using remifentanil with standard hypnotic-based sedation for up to 10 days in intensive care unit patients: a randomised trial [ISRCTN47583497]. Crit Care 2005;9:R200–R210.

17. Carson SS, Kress JP, Rodgers JE, Vinayak A, Campbell-Bright S, Levitt J, et al. A randomized trial of intermittent lorazepam versus propofol with daily interruption in mechanically ventilated patients. Crit Care Med 2006;34:1326–32.

18. Pandharipande PP, Pun BT, Herr DL, Maze M, Girard TD, Miller RR, et al. Effect of sedation with dexmedetomidine vs lorazepam on acute brain dysfunction in mechanically ventilated patients: the MENDS randomized controlled trial. JAMA 2007;298:2644–53.

19. Riker RR, Shehabi Y, Bokesch PM, Ceraso D, Wisemandle W, Koura F, et al. Dexmedetomidine vs midazolam for sedation of critically ill patients: a randomized trial. JAMA 2009;301:489–99.

20. Lenfant C. Shattuck lecture–clinical research to clinical practice–lost in translation? N Engl J Med 2003;349:868–74.

21. Brook AD, Ahrens TS, Schaiff R, Prentice D, Sherman G, Shannon W, et al. Effect of a nursing-implemented seda-

tion protocol on the duration of mechanical ventilation. Crit Care Med 1999;27:2609–15.

22. MacLaren R, Plamondon JM, Ramsay KB, Rocker GM, Patrick WD, Hall RI. A prospective evaluation of empiric versus protocol-based sedation and analgesia. Pharmacotherapy 2000;20:662–72.

23. Brattebo G, Hofoss D, Flaatten H, Muri AK, Gjerde S, Plsek PE. Effect of a scoring system and protocol for sedation on duration of patients' need for ventilator support in a surgical intensive care unit. BMJ 2002;324:1386–9.

24. De Jonghe B, Bastuji-Garin S, Fangio P, Lacherade JC, Jabot J, Appere-De-Vecchi C, et al. Sedation algorithm in critically ill patients without acute brain injury. Crit Care Med 2005;33:120–7.

25. Chanques G, Jaber S, Barbotte E, Violet S, Sebbane M, Perrigault PF, et al. Impact of systematic evaluation of pain and agitation in an intensive care unit. Crit Care Med 2006;34:1691–9

26. Elliott R, McKinley S, Aitken LM, Hendrikz J. The effect of an algorithm-based sedation guideline on the duration of mechanical ventilation in an Australian intensive care unit. Intensive Care Med 2006;32:1506–14.

27. Quenot JP, Ladoire S, Devoucoux F, Doise JM, Cailliod R, Cunin N, et al. Effect of a nurse-implemented sedation protocol on the incidence of ventilator-associated pneumonia. Crit Care Med 2007;35:2031–6.

28. Arias-Rivera S, Sanchez-Sanchez MM, Santos-Diaz R, Gallardo-Murillo J, Sanchez-Izquierdo R, Frutos-Vivar F, et al. Effect of a nursing-implemented sedation protocol on weaning outcome. Crit Care Med 2008;36:2054–60.

29. Bucknall TK, Manias E, Presneill JJ. A randomized trial of protocol-directed sedation management for mechanical ventilation in an Australian intensive care unit. Crit Care Med 2008;36:1444–50.

30. Marshall J, Finn CA, Theodore AC. Impact of a clinical pharmacist-enforced intensive care unit sedation protocol on duration of mechanical ventilation and hospital stay. Crit Care Med 2008;36:427–33.

31. Robinson BR, Mueller EW, Henson K, Branson RD, Barsoum S, Tsuei BJ. An analgesia-delirium-sedation protocol for critically ill trauma patients reduces ventilator days and hospital length of stay. J Trauma 2008;65:517–26.

32. Tobar AE, Lanas MA, Pino PS, Aspee LP, Rivas VS, Prat RD, et al. Protocol based sedation versus conventional treatment in critically ill patients on mechanical ventilation. Rev Med Chil 2008;136:711–8.

33. Puntillo KA. Pain experiences of intensive care unit patients. Heart Lung 1990;19:526–33.

34. Epstein J, Breslow MJ. The stress response of critical illness. Crit Care Clin 1999;15:17–33.

35. Jacobi J, Fraser GL, Coursin DB, Riker RR, Fontaine D, Wittbrodt ET, et al. Clinical practice guidelines for the sustained use of sedatives and analgesics in the critically ill adult. Crit Care Med 2002;30:119–41.

36. Patel RP, Gambrell M, Speroff T, Scott TA, Pun BT, Okahashi J, et al. Delirium and sedation in the intensive care unit: survey of behaviors and attitudes of 1384 healthcare professionals. Crit Care Med 2009;37:825–32.

37. Mehta S, Burry L, Fischer S, Martinez-Motta JC, Hallett D, Bowman D, et al. Canadian survey of the use of sedatives, analgesics, and neuromuscular blocking agents in critically ill patients. Crit Care Med 2006;34:374–80.

38. Kress JP, O'Connor MF, Pohlman AS, Olson D, Lavoie A, Toledano A, et al. Sedation of critically ill patients during mechanical ventilation. A comparison of propofol and midazolam. Am J Respir Crit Care Med 1996;153:1012–8.

39. McCollam JS, O'Neil MG, Norcross ED, Byrne TK, Reeves ST. Continuous infusions of lorazepam, midazolam, and propofol for sedation of the critically ill surgery trauma patient: a prospective, randomized comparison. Crit Care Med 1999;27:2454–8.

40. Hall RI, Sandham D, Cardinal P, Tweeddale M, Moher D, Wang X, et al. Propofol vs midazolam for ICU sedation : a Canadian multicenter randomized trial. Chest 2001;119:1151–9.

41. Devlin JW, Holbrook AM, Fuller HD. The effect of ICU sedation guidelines and pharmacist interventions on clinical outcomes and drug cost. Ann Pharmacother 1997;31:689–95.

42. Brochard L. Sedation in the intensive-care unit: good and bad? Lancet 2008;371:95–7

43. Schweickert WD, Gehlbach BK, Pohlman AS, Hall JB, Kress JP. Daily interruption of sedative infusions and complications of critical illness in mechanically ventilated patients. Crit Care Med 2004;32:1272–6.

44. Kress JP, Gehlbach B, Lacy M, Pliskin N, Pohlman AS, Hall JB. The long-term psychological effects of daily sedative interruption on critically ill patients. Am J Respir Crit Care Med 2003;168:1457–61.

45. Ely EW, Baker AM, Dunagan DP, Burke HL, Smith AC, Kelly PT, et al. Effect on the duration of mechanical ventilation of identifying patients capable of breathing spontaneously. N Engl J Med 1996;335:1864–9.

46. Girard TD, Ely EW. Protocol-driven ventilator weaning: reviewing the evidence. Clin Chest Med 2008;29:241–52.

47. Martin J, Franck M, Fischer M, Spies C. Sedation and analgesia in German intensive care units: how is it done in reality? Results of a patient-based survey of analgesia and sedation. Intensive Care Med 2006;32:1137–42.

48. Tanios MA, de WM, Epstein SK, Devlin JW. Perceived barriers to the use of sedation protocols and daily sedation interruption: a multidisciplinary survey. J Crit Care 2009;24:66–73.

Simeon West, Raha Rahman West and Andrew Rhodes

Protocolised approach to the post-surgical patient improves outcome

Introduction

In the UK, NCEPOD (the National Confidential Enquiry into Patient Outcome and Deaths)[1] has revealed over 20,000 patients a year are dying following surgery, giving an in-hospital mortality of 0.8–1.0 %. It is recognised that the vast majority of these deaths are occurring in patients with multiple medical comorbidities, primarily cardiovascular or respiratory, and that the severity of these diseases is often being underestimated. These deaths represent the tip of the iceberg in terms of total patient harm following surgical procedures.

A scattergun use of intensive care resources can go some way to improve the outcome of a small minority of these patients. Limited bed numbers are only one of the reasons that a large proportion of the post-surgical deaths are occurring on general wards [2], and increasing the bed numbers would take a massive investment in infrastructure and staff. A study of 4.1 million non-cardiac surgical cases showed a high-risk group accounted for 12.5 % of surgical procedures, but over 80 % of the deaths [3]. In a follow-up study [4] in a large NHS hospital population, it has been shown that of 2,414 identified high-risk patients (9.3 % of total procedures), only 852 (35.3 %) were admitted to a critical care unit at any time. Of the 294 post-surgical deaths, only 144 (49 %) were admitted at any time to a critical care

unit. Even if we can identify all of these high-risk cases preoperatively, to treat them all on an intensive care unit for sufficient length of time to make a difference would require vast resources.

So are there ways in which the detrimental outcomes of surgery can be mitigated? The report by the Improving Surgical Outcomes Group in 2005 [3] gives us a number of recommendations ranging from improved high-risk recognition and assessment starting at MDT meetings, right through to the increased use of our limited intensive care resources. They highly stressed the importance of the use of haemodynamic optimisation using a cardiac output algorithm. The use of protocol-based goal-directed therapy using haemodynamic flow monitoring appears to offer a significant benefit in patient outcome. In this chapter we consider the choice of protocol, monitor and their place in improving patient safety.

Haemodynamic flow Monitoring

The findings of Shoemaker et al. over 20 years ago [6, 7, 8] first alerted the medical world to the fact that high-risk surgical patients, unable to increase their oxygen delivery in response to increased demand, had a significantly higher mortality. It has been further postulated that oxygen debt developing at the time of surgery is the cause of postoperative organ dysfunction and ultimately death, and if this debt is repaid within the first 8 hours post surgery, the incidence of postoperative complications decreases [9]. These landmark studies were performed using data from pulmonary artery catheters, and others have taken this work and shown a significant benefit in pre-optimisation for the high-risk surgical patient using protocols involving fluids and inotropes [10, 11].

Observational work had questioned the safety of the use of the pulmonary artery catheter [12, 13] and a number of trials have been designed to investigate this apparent danger [14, 15, 16]. None has shown the use of the pulmonary artery catheter to be an independent risk factor for increased mortality; however, no great benefit from its use was shown. Takala argues this is unsurprising as most trials had no specific protocols for haemodynamic optimisation using the data collected, and so clinicians were left to interpret and use the values as they saw fit. Furthermore it is only in the use of appropriately designed protocols and the selection of the at risk patient that we can see benefits in the use of this monitoring device [17].

As a result of this debate, rightly or wrongly, the pulmonary artery catheter has fallen out of favour in the general ICU setting. Interestingly, recent subgroup analysis of the results from the PAC-Man trial has shown that in a very small subset of patients (n = 64), post-surgical patients admitted to the intensive care unit after a deterioration and managed with PAC showed a significant improvement in hospital mortality (18).

It is clear that the insertion of a PAC alone does not improve patient outcome, and that levels of knowledge surrounding the use of its measured values are generally poor [19, 20, 21]. Coupled with the unproven doubts over its safety, and the lack of intensive care beds to safely perform preoperative optimisation, the role of goal-directed therapy in improving patient outcome could have become a dead end. Fortuitously, there have been a number of minimally invasive cardiac output monitors presented to market in recent years, these include the Cardio Q™ oesophageal Doppler monitor (Deltex Medical, Chichester, UK), the LiDCOplus system (LiDCO Ltd., Cambridge, UK), the PiCCO system (PULSION Medical Systems, Munich, Germany) along with a number of others.

The safety advantage of these systems over the PAC is logical as the avoidance of the requirement to cannulate the pulmonary artery reduces a potential risk to the patient. However, each carries its own new risks – for example, malposition of the oesophageal Doppler probe in the left main bronchus (22). Furthermore, the practical use of the monitors is somewhat limited by their design, with the oesophageal Doppler more portable, but largely unusable in the non-intubated patient, whereas the LiDCO requires an arterial line, and has a calibration process which perhaps makes its use more suited to the intensive care setting pre- or postoperatively.

In summary, the monitor used probably matters little; however, the way in which the data is used is of paramount importance. Safety concerns over the PAC are largely unfounded in terms of the evidence base, but now that well-validated studies are emerging using less invasive cardiac output monitors, it seems logical and more practical to use them in its place. Goal-directed therapy protocols, by virtue of removing the doubt in how to respond to the readings, go some way to bridge the gap in clinicians' knowledge in order to clearly benefit the patient's outcome.

Goal-directed therapy

Replacing the oxygen debt is the fundamental principle behind goal-directed therapy. Shoemaker's original work comparing survivors and non-survivors(8) monitored haemodynamic variables using pulmonary artery catheters, and found significant disparity between the groups. The median values in the survival group were cardiac index > 4.5 litre/min/m and a tissue oxygen delivery (DO2I) > 600 ml/min/m, and these variables have been subsequently postulated as targets to be achieved by manipulation using fluids and inotropes. A large number of protocol-driven studies have set out to demonstrate benefit in attaining these targets and how they may be replaced by surrogate markers of oxygen delivery (such as $S_{cv}O_2$ or serum lactate). As outlined earlier, the role of the PAC in monitoring these variables has largely been taken over by less invasive haemodynamic monitors, we consider the current evidence for the use of protocol-driven haemodynamic optimisation using the available monitoring, and the potential outcome benefit to patient safety.

Preoperative GDT

Due to the high pressures for intensive care beds, initial work on preoperative optimisation using protocols, such as by Wilson et al. [11], has been difficult to replicate outside of clinical trials. Subsequently, no work has been done using less invasive monitoring to investigate this avenue.

Perioperative GDT

The oesophageal Doppler has proved a useful tool in a simple perioperative goal directed approach, a number of studies [23–29] have shown improvement in hospital stay and morbidity. For example, Wakeling et al. [28] performed a single-blinded randomised control trial using a simple fluid therapy protocol consisting of colloid boluses of 250 ml, followed by assessment of stroke volume (SV) and central venous pressure (CVP); if the SV increased by 10% and the CVP increased < 3 mmHg, the bolus was repeated, if not, the measurements were repeated every 10 minutes until SV fell by 10%, then the process was restarted. They showed a reduction in morbidity as assessed by Post-Operative Morbidity Score (POMS) of 37.5% vs. 59.3% in the control group (p = 0.013), along with a reduction of hospital stay to 10 days in the treatment group vs. 11.5 days in the control (p = 0.031). Interestingly, neither treatment group nor control group reached the haemodynamic targets postulated by Shoemaker (median 535 vs. 435 m/min/m, p = < 0.05), this could reflect that a potential further benefit from postoperative fluid optimisation could be achieved, or that it is the trend towards increased oxygen delivery that is important with this monitor, rather than the actual numerical value.

A recent meta-analysis by Walsh et al. [30] included 4 trials [25, 27, 28, 29] of the use of oesophageal Doppler in major abdominal surgery. They were guarded in their findings, given the small total number of patients (n = 393); however, they showed a significant reduction in postoperative stay and complication rates. They also remarked that the differences in total fluid volumes given to the treatment group vs. control group was minimal; however, the type of fluid was largely colloid. They also reiterated Noblett's [29] postulation that the significant difference was that the treatment arm was given the majority of the fluid in the first 40 minutes. The driving force behind the early perioperative use of colloids was the protocol, regardless of the measurement taken (either stroke volume or corrected flow time). It is not enough just to give large volumes of colloid to every patient without monitoring, it is the individualisation due to the protocol that leads to the outcome benefits. This can be demonstrated by the wide range of total volumes given in the Wakeling et al study [28], which ranged from 500–5,000 ml of gelofusin.

Clearly, oesophageal Doppler is a useful tool for goal-directed therapy; however, the oral route of insertion currently precludes its use in awake patients limiting its usefulness in continuing goal-directed therapy in the postoperative period. Work on soft, nasal probes is ongoing, giving the potential for continued optimisation.

Postoperative GDT

The concept of oxygen debt being replaceable within the first 8 hours post-insult has led researchers to look at postoperative goal-directed therapy in high-risk surgical patients.

Initial studies were done by Polonen et al. [31] using SvO_2 and lactate as clinical endpoints for optimisation in post-cardiac surgical patients, and by McKendry et al. [32] using a nurse-led, oesophageal Doppler-based protocol, also in post-cardiac surgical patients. Both studies showed improvements in postoperative morbidity and length of hospital stay; of note, the McKendry study showed that by the application of a clear protocol, fluid optimisation can be carried out by trained nursing staff.

Pearse and colleagues [33] utilised the LiDCO-plus system to direct their protocolised postoperative optimisation after major surgery. A total of 122 patients were randomised to control or treatment group. The control group (n = 60) received colloid boluses to achieve sustained rises in their central venous pressure, whereas the treatment

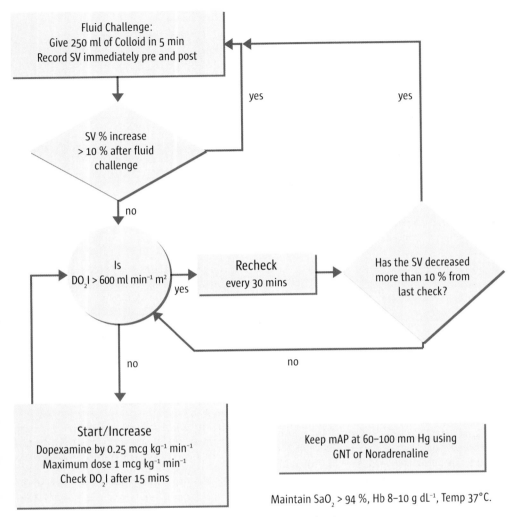

Fig. 1   Semantic flowchart for the post operative resuscitation of surgical patients

group (n = 62) were treated according to the protocol in Fig. 1. They achieved DO2I goals for 49 (79%) of the treatment group vs. spontaneous achievement in 27 (45%) of the control arm (p = 0.0002). A high proportion of those in the treatment arm not achieving DO_2I goals was associated with cessation of dopexamine because of tachycardia.

There were fewer patients with complications in the protocol arm 27 (44%) vs. 41 (68%) (relative risk 0.63; 95% confidence interval 0.46 to 0.87; p = 0.003) and this was associated with a reduction in hospital stay 17.5 days vs. 29.5 days (41% reduction, 95% confidence interval 0 to 81; p = 0.001). Post-hoc analysis of the results showed no significant difference in myocardial events, despite the use of dopexamine in the treatment arm [34]. The protocol has been adapted and is used routinely in all major postoperative surgical cases admitted to St George's intensive care unit. It is estimated that 500 patients could be treated, with up to 20 lives saved per year [35].

The future

Much work is ongoing into the role of new, less invasive technologies within the operating theatre environment that may help elucidate better targets for goal-directed resuscitation. These targets include variables assessing the microcirculation, the cellular levels of oxygen and the central venous saturation ($S_{cv}O_2$) as a surrogate marker for oxygen demand. A multicentre study of high-risk surgical patients by Bracht et al. [36] has shown low perioperative $S_{cv}O_2$ is associated with postoperative complications, although a target value is more difficult to define. A large, protocolised randomised controlled trial may yet reveal a benefit in patient outcome from the use of this marker, though at present it cannot be recommended.

Summary

Up to 20,000 patients a year are dying following surgery in the UK, with many more suffering significant complications leading to continued morbidity. One of the ways to reduce this unacceptable risk is by the use of protocol-driven haemodynamic optimisation, the method used probably matters little, although there are practical implications for each method that may preclude their use in certain situations, such as the inability to use an oesophageal Doppler probe in the awake patient (though ongoing work may yet solve this limitation).

The use of protocols per se is driving the timing and individualisation of fluid and inotrope therapy, and these go some way to bridge the gap in clinicians' knowledge that was self-evident in the past use of pulmonary artery catheters for the same purpose. The timing of fluid optimisation appears to be the key intervention in the high-risk groups, and it is the use of protocols that drives this early, judicious use of fluid. The perceived improved safety profile of the less invasive monitors is increasing their use in the wider anaesthetic community, and this is likely to result in a greater proportion of high risk patients treated early. Time will tell whether this translates into an improvement in surgical mortality.

The authors

Simeon West, MD
Raha Rahman West, MD
Andrew Rhodes, FRCP, FRCA
    Department of Intensive Care Medicine |
    St George's Healthcare NHS Trust | London, UK

Address for correspondence
    Andrew Rhodes
    Department of Intensive Care Medicine
    St George's Healthcare NHS Trust
    London SW17 0QT, London, UK
    E-mail: andyr@sgul.ac.uk

References

1. National Confidential Enquiry into Perioperative Deaths. The 2003 Report of the National Confidential Enquiry into Perioperative Deaths. 20 November 2003.
2. National Confidential Enquiry into Perioperative Deaths. The 2002 Report of the National Confidential Enquiry into Perioperative Deaths. 11 November 2002.
3. Pearse RM, Harrison DA, James P, et al. Identification and characterisation of the high-risk surgical population in the United Kingdom. Critical Care. 2006; 10: R81.
4. Jhanji S,Thomas B, Ely A,Watson D, Hinds CJ and Pearse RM. Mortality and utilisation of critical care resources amongst high-risk surgical patients in a large NHS trust. Anaesthesia, 2008; 63:695–700.
5. Modernising Care for Patients Undergoing Major Surgery. The 2005 report of the Improving Surgical Outcomes Group.June 2005.
6. Shoemaker WC. Cardiorespiratory patterns of surviving and nonsurviving postoperative patients. Surg Gynecol Obstet 1972; 134: 810–814.
7. Shoemaker WC, Czer LS. Evaluation of the biologic importance of various hemodynamic and oxygen transport variables: which variables should be monitored in postoperative shock? Crit Care Med 1979; 7: 424–431.
8. Shoemaker WC, Montgomerry ES, Kaplan E, Elwyn DH. Physiologic patterns in surviving and nonsurviving shock patients. Use of sequential cardiorespiratory variables in defining criteria for therapeutic goals and early warning of death. Arch Surg 1973; 106: 630–636.
9. Shoemaker WC, Appel PL, Kram HB. Haemodynamic and oxygen transport responses in survivors and nonsurvivors of high-risk surgery. Crit Care Med 1993; 21: 977–90.
10. Boyd O, Grounds RM, Bennet ED. A randomized clinical trial of the effect of deliberate peri-operative increase of oxygen delivery on mortality in high-risk surgical patients. JAMA 1993; 270:2669–707.

11. Wilson J, Woods I, Fawcett J, et al. Reducing the risk of major elective surgery: randomised controlled trial of preoperative optimisation of oxygen delivery. BMJ 1999;318:1099–1103.

12. Connor AF, Jr., McCaffree DR, Gray BA. Evaluation of right-heart catherization in the critically ill patient without acute myocardial infarction. N Engl J Med. 1983;308(5):263–267.

13. Robin ED. Death by pulmonary artery flow-directed catheter. Time for a moratorium? Chest. 1987; 92(4):727–731.

14. Rhodes A. Cusack RJ, Newman PJ, Grounds RM, Bennett ED. A randomised, controlled trial of the pulmonary artery catheter in critically ill patients. Intensive Care Medicine. 2002;28(3):256–264.

15. Harvey S, Harrison DA, Singer M, Ashcroft J, Jones CM, Elbourne D, Brampton W, Williams D, Young D, Rowan K: Assessment of the clinical effectiveness of pulmonary artery catheters in management of patients in intensive care (PAC-Man): a randomized controlled trial. Lancet 2005; 366:472–477

16. Sandham, JD; Hull, RD; Brant, RF; Knox, L; Pineo, GF; Doig, CJ; Laporta, DP; Viner, S; Passerini, L; Devitt, H; Kirby, A; Jacka, M.; Canadian Critical Care Clinical Trials Group. A randomized, controlled trial of the use of pulmonary-artery catheters in high-risk surgical patients. N Engl J Med. 2003;348:5–14.

17. Takala J. The pulmonary artery catheter: the tool versus treatments based on the tool. Critical Care 2006; 10:162

18. Harvey SE, Welch CA, Harrison DA, Rowan KM, Singer M. Post Hoc Insights From PAC-Man-The U.K. Pulmonary Artery Catheter Trial. Crit Care Med. 2008;36(6):1714–1721.

19. Iberti TJ, Fischer EP, Leibowitz AB, Panacek EA, Silverstein JH, Albertson TE. A multicenter study of physicians' knowledge of the pulmonary artery catheter. Pulmonary Artery Catheter Study Group. JAMA 1990;264:2928–2932.

20. Iberti TJ, Daily EK, Leibowitz AB, Schecter CB, Fischer EP, Silverstein JH. Assessment of critical care nurses' knowledge of the pulmonary artery catheter. The Pulmonary Artery Catheter Study Group. Crit Care Med 1994;22:1674–1678.

21. Gnaegi A, Feihl F, Perret C. Intensive care physicians' insufficient knowledge of right-heart catheterization at the bedside: time to act? Crit Care Med. 1997;25(2):213–20.

22. Hilkens MM, van Haren FHF, van Hoeven JG. Unexpected left main stem bronchus cardiac output measurement. Intensive Care Medicine 2003;29(7):1201.

23. Mythen MG, Webb AR. Peripoperative plasma volume expansion reduces the incidence of gut mucosal hypoperfusion during cardiac surgery. Arch Surg 1995;130:423–429.

24. Sinclair S, James S, Singer M. Intraoperative intravascular volume optimization and length of stay after repair of proximal femoral fracture; Randomized controlled trial. BMJ 1997;315:909–912.

25. Gan TJ, Soppitt A, Maroof M, et al. Goal-directed intraoperative fluid administration reduces length of hospital stay after major surgery. Anaesthesiology 2002;97:820–826.

26. Venn R, Steele A, Richardson P, Polniecki J, Grounds M, Newman P. Randomized controlled trial to investigate influence of the fluid challenge on duration of hospital stay and perioperative morbidity in patients with hip fractures. Br J Anaesth 2002;88:65–71.

27. Conway DH, Mayall R, Abdul-Latif MS, Gilligan S, Tackaberry C. Randomised controlled trial investigating the influence of intravenous fluid titration using oesophageal Doppler monitoring during bowel surgery. Anaesthesia 2002;57:845–849.

28. Wakeling HG, McFall MR, Jenkins CS et al. Intraoperative oesophageal Doppler guided fluid management shortens post-operative hospital stay after major bowel surgery Br J Anaesth 2005;95:634–42.

29. Noblett SE, Snowden CP, Shenton BK, Horgan AF. Randomized clinical trial assessing the effect of Doppler-optimized fluid management on outcome after elective colorectal resection. Br J Surg 2006; 93: 1069–76.

30. Walsh SR, Tang T, Bass S, Gaunt ME. Doppler-Guided Intra-Operative Fluid Management During Major Abdominal Surgery: Systematic Review and Meta-Analysis. Int J Clin Pract. 2008;62(3):466–470.

31. Polonen P, Ruokonen E, Hippelainen M, Poyhonen M, Takala J. A prospective, randomised study of goal-orientated haemodynamic therapy in cardiac surgical patients. Anaesth Analag 2000;90:1052–59.

32. McKendry M, McGloin H, Saberi D, Caudwell L, Brady AR, Singer M. Randomised controlled trial assessing the impact of a nurse delivered, flow monitored protocol for optimisation of circulatory status after cardiac surgery. Br Med J 2004; 329:258

33. Pearse R, Dawson D, Fawcett J, Rhodes A, Grounds RM, Bennett ED. Early goal directed therapy afetr major surgery reduces complications and duration of stay. A randomised, controlled trial. Crit Care 2005;9:R687–93.

34. Pearse R, Dawson D, Fawcett J, Rhodes A, Grounds RM, Bennett ED. The incidence of myocardial injury following post-operative Goal Directed Therapy. BMC Cardiovascular Disorders 2007;7:10.

35. Bennett ED. Advances in protocolizing management of high risk surgical patients. Crit Care 2006;10:124.

36. Collaborative Study Group on Perioperative ScvO2 Monitoring. Multicentre Study On Peri- and Postoperative Central Venous Oxygen Saturation In High-risk Surgical Patients. Crit Care. 2007;10(6)

Kirsten Colpaert and Johan Decruyenaere

Electronic Prescribing: Can it reduce error?

Introduction

Physicians traditionally use hand-written or sometimes only verbally communicated orders for patient care, which are then transcribed by various individuals before being carried out. Hand-written orders often use non-standard abbreviations and suffer from poor legibility which may lead to errors and cause injuries to patients. Using information/communication technology (ICT) for entry of medical orders theoretically offers many advantages: less delay in order completion, reduced errors related to handwriting, transcription or verbal communication, potential ordering of entry at the point of care and even off-site, possibility of error checking and decision support at the moment of electronic order entry.

According to the Institute of Medicine (IOM) report entitled "To Err is Human", written a decade ago, at least 770,000 injuries and 7,000 deaths occur annually in the United States due to medication errors (MEs) [1]. The report suggests the widespread implementation of hospital-based "computerised physician order entry" (CPOE) as a means of improving the safety and quality of healthcare delivery. This is in accordance with the Leapfrog Group, a consortium of private and public purchasers, who identified CPOE as one of three safety initiatives with the greatest potential in reducing deaths due to medical errors [2]. More recently, the British Department of Health also recommended the wider use of electronic prescribing tools to narrow down the incidence of medication errors [3].

CPOE refers to the electronic prescription of physician instructions, and in that way replaces verbal or written paper-based orders. Some, however, prefer to use the term "computerised provider order entry" or "computerised prescriber order entry" for referring to the same electronic prescription, as beside physicians, nurse practitioners and physician assistants can also use CPOE.

Intensive care units (ICUs) are typically extremely data-rich environments with around-the-clock changes of physiologic parameters and updated test result data [4]. Furthermore, there is an overwhelming amount of up-do-date therapeutic options, new medications and interactions, together with an increased vulnerability of the critical care patient to delayed or suboptimal care [5]. Donchin et al. already showed that, on average, 1.7 errors occur per patient per day [6], and every patient will experience at least one potential life-threatening error during his/her ICU stay. As a result critical care patients find themselves in the most perfect environment to benefit from the potential advantages of CPOE.

In this review, we will discuss the potential benefits and risks of electronic prescribing in critical care.

The importance of medication errors

Medication errors (MEs) often have tragic consequences for patients, as many serious MEs result in preventable adverse drug events (ADEs). These drug-related errors are categorised into six groups, according to the stage they occur in: prescription (ordering), transcription, preparation, dispensing, administration and monitoring errors. The earlier an error occurs in the medication process, the more likely it is to be intercepted before it reaches the patient [7]. Nurses and pharmacists manage to intercept up to 70 % of prescription errors on general wards [8]. More than half of those errors occur in the administration stage, followed by medication prescription errors [9]. Transcription errors are mainly due to illegible handwriting, use of abbreviations, unit misinterpretation and mistakes in reading [10], and can easily be waived by using electronic prescription. Although most of the MEs are harmless, or can be intercepted in time, 1 out of 100 do result in an adverse drug event (ADE), and approximately 1 out of 5 ADEs could be life-threatening [7, 11]. Even more alarming is the fact that almost half of all ADEs are judged preventable, and most of these errors occur in the ordering stage of the medication process [8].

The incidence of ADEs is almost twice as high in ICU settings as in general wards [12]. This can be attributed to the high number of drugs used, the preference for intravenous administration and the continuously evolving occurrence of organ failure in ICU patients [12, 13]. ICU patients not only have a higher incidence of ME inside the ICU, discharge to the general ward also poses an important problem, as up to three quarters of patients' habitual medications are stopped at ICU admission, but fail to be resumed after ICU or hospital discharge [14, 15].

Difficulties in medication error reporting

For several reasons, the evaluation of the numerous studies reporting on medication error is cumbersome. Firstly, the ambiguity in the classification of medication errors makes comparison between different studies problematic. The classification of MEs developed by the National Coordinating Council for Medication Error Reporting and Prevention [16] is rarely used, and most authors use a less extensive self-modified classification. Secondly, the different types of study design make evaluation of ME or ADE even more difficult. For example, if the patient's chart is being reviewed, the main focus is on detecting preventable MEs. However, if the clinical pharmacist is prospectively involved in the process of error recording, mainly the potential and actual prescription errors and/or administration errors will be registered. Lastly, there is the issue of error reporting. While most studies work with the least efficient method of voluntary error reporting [17, 18], chart reviewing is already more accurate in detecting MEs. Only a few studies use the most accurate method (direct observation), mainly because it is also the most labour-intensive method [19]. The incidence of reported errors clearly depends on the method used.

Benefits of electronic prescribing

The computerised physician order entry system

It is important to realize that not all CPOE systems have the same features (see Tab. 1). Standard CPOE only allows for standardised order entry, which means that only electronic orders are accepted in a standard and complete format, thereby ensuring especially the legibility of orders. Nowadays, almost all CPOE systems include some facilities for "clinical decision support" (CDS) of varying sophistication. Basic CDS may include suggestions or default values for drug doses, routes, and frequencies. More sophisticated CDS can perform drug-allergy checks, drug-laboratory value checks, drug-drug interaction checks, in addition to providing reminders about corollary orders (e.g. prompting the user to order glucose checks after ordering insulin, or prompting osmolality checks after ordering mannitol). The most advanced CDS includes the integration of guidelines to assist the physician at the time of drug prescription [20]. Those most sophisticated systems provide physicians with an environment that is more appropriate for the complexities of today's medicine than a paper-based setting [21].

Furthermore, as will be discussed in the following, many studies conducted earlier evaluated home-grown CPOE systems. However, the

Tab. 1 Advantages of CPOE systems in comparison with the paper-based setting [reprinted from Best Practice & Research Clinical Anaestesiology, 23, Colpaert K and Decruyenaere J, Computerized physician order entry in critical care, 27–38, 2009, with permission from Elsevier]

CPOE without CDS
Faster to the pharmacy, resulting in less delay in order completion
Free of handwriting identification problems
Possibility of ordering at the point of care or even off-site
Support for inventory management
Potential for automatic billing
Potential to identify the prescribing physician

CPOE with basic CDS
Default values for drug doses, routes and frequencies
Less subject to error associated with similar drug names
Able to avoid specification errors, such as trailing zeros

CPOE with advanced CDS
Drug allergy checks
Drug-laboratory value checks
Drug-drug interaction checks
Able to generate reminders for corollary orders
Able to integrate with drug guidelines
Able to avoid incorrect drug choices e.g. for antibiotic therapy
Able to suggest dose adaptations according to evolution of renal function
Potential for significant economic savings
■ Suggest enteral route over parenteral route
■ Reduce overprescribing
■ Suggest more cost-effective alternatives
■ Suggest appropriate duration of drug therapies

CPOE = Computerised physician order entry
CDS = Clinical decision support

development of a homegrown clinical intensive care information system has become virtually unachievable in recent years, mainly due to the complexity of interfacing with monitors, ventilators and syringe pumps. Indeed, most ICUs now decide to purchase a commercial ICU information system. This market is divided among a few big players and a handful of smaller companies, and all of those commercial ICU information systems come with built-in CPOE. It would be advisable for all those dedicated ICU information systems to be subjected to in-depth investigations regarding the effect of their incorporated CPOE on MEs and ADEs.

Effect of CPOE on medication errors in the general ward

Most studies evaluating the impact of electronic prescribing on medication errors are conducted in general wards and, unfortunately, most are non-randomised trials. The first article evaluating a CPOE system was published in 1994 by Evans et al. [22] Since then, a few dozen relevant articles have been published evaluating the impact of CPOE on medication errors in general adult or paediatric wards [12, 18, 22–37]. Most of those earlier studies were conducted with home-grown systems [12, 18, 23–32], and only focused on a small spectrum of drugs, i.e. nefrotoxic or anti-infective medications [22–24, 27, 29–31]. Looking at the impact of electronic prescribing compared to handwritten orders, there seems to be an overall positive effect of up to almost 90%, depending on the type of error reported [37–40], as is clearly shown in the review of Ammenwerth [39]. However, one study mentioned in this review failed to show a significant decrease in error reporting [41], and another even demonstrated an increase in errors [42] (see Fig. 1). Other studies evaluated an upgrade of their CPOE system, i.e. the introduction of decision-support tools on top of their existing CPOE system, and all found a significant decrease in medication errors [23–24, 29, 33, 34–36].

Few studies demonstrated reductions in adverse drug events (ADEs), varying between 20 and 80% [12, 18, 22]. Due to the low incidence of ADEs, most studies are not powerful enough for definitive conclusions to be drawn.

Effect of CPOE on medication errors in the adult intensive care unit

With respect to the critical care environment, the number of studies is rather limited. Over the last 10 years, only 9 relevant studies have been conducted in centres previously working with paper-based prescriptions (see Fig. 1). Two of those early studies were performed by Bates et al. [12, 18], who showed a significant reduction in serious MEs in both general and intensive care patients, although the most recent study could not demonstrate a benefit for ADEs. Another study by Evans [30], solely evaluating anti-infective medication, demonstrated both a reduction in MEs and ADEs. Since then, 3 additional studies have been performed in adult ICUs [43–45], all evaluating a commercial CPOE. Fraenkel et al. [45] evaluated the introduction of a clinical information system with incorporated CPOE and found

a significant reduction in the number of medication incidents and intravenous incidents. Shulman et al. [43] reported that the total proportion of MEs was significantly lower with CPOE than with hand-written prescription (4.8% vs. 6.7%; p < 0.04) [24]. The third study [44], performed in our centre, evaluated a newly installed intensive care information system with incorporated CPOE and a moderate level of CDS. The incidence of MEs was significantly lower in the CPOE unit compared with the paper-based prescribing unit (3.4% vs. 27.0%; p < 0.001). There was an almost complete elimination of prescribing errors in the CPOE unit compared with the paper-based prescribing unit. Intercepted MEs, non-intercepted potential ADEs, and ADEs were also significantly reduced in the CPOE unit, although less impressively than the prescribing errors.

CPOE theoretically also offers the potential to reduce administration errors, because most electronic orders contain information for nurses on how to prepare medication solutions, the administration route and the infusion rate. However, as far as we know, investigations studying the effect of CPOE on administration errors in the ICU are lacking.

Effect of CPOE on medication errors in paediatric wards

Most commercial systems are constructed primarily for adult patients, and therefore require adaptations including age-specific algorithms before being ready for implementation in a paediatric intensive care unit (PICU). Worth noting is the fact that the incidence of medication errors is the same as in the adult population, but the potential to cause harm is 3 times as high, thereby emphasising the importance of strategies to avoid such errors [46]. The data, however, are promising: All studies conducted in general wards [47–52] as well as in PICUs [31, 32, 53–54] show a significant decrease in medication errors after the introduction of CPOE (see Fig. 1). Regarding the reduction in potential ADEs or preventable ADEs, data remain scarce, but are always in favour of CPOE [31–32, 54]. Furthermore, the addition of CDS in CPOE seems to offer a greater potential for reducing MEs in paediatric in-patients [46], i.e. the most recent commercial systems will probably have an even greater effect.

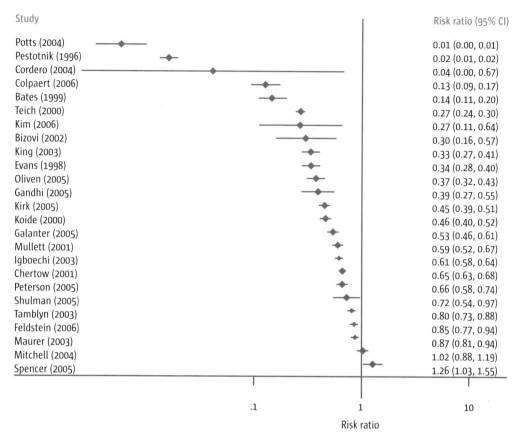

Study	Risk ratio (95% CI)
Potts (2004)	0.01 (0.00, 0.01)
Pestotnik (1996)	0.02 (0.01, 0.02)
Cordero (2004)	0.04 (0.00, 0.67)
Colpaert (2006)	0.13 (0.09, 0.17)
Bates (1999)	0.14 (0.11, 0.20)
Teich (2000)	0.27 (0.24, 0.30)
Kim (2006)	0.27 (0.11, 0.64)
Bizovi (2002)	0.30 (0.16, 0.57)
King (2003)	0.33 (0.27, 0.41)
Evans (1998)	0.34 (0.28, 0.40)
Oliven (2005)	0.37 (0.32, 0.43)
Gandhi (2005)	0.39 (0.27, 0.55)
Kirk (2005)	0.45 (0.39, 0.51)
Koide (2000)	0.46 (0.40, 0.52)
Galanter (2005)	0.53 (0.46, 0.61)
Mullett (2001)	0.59 (0.52, 0.67)
Igboechi (2003)	0.61 (0.58, 0.64)
Chertow (2001)	0.65 (0.63, 0.68)
Peterson (2005)	0.66 (0.58, 0.74)
Shulman (2005)	0.72 (0.54, 0.97)
Tamblyn (2003)	0.80 (0.73, 0.88)
Feldstein (2006)	0.85 (0.77, 0.94)
Maurer (2003)	0.87 (0.81, 0.94)
Mitchell (2004)	1.02 (0.88, 1.19)
Spencer (2005)	1.26 (1.03, 1.55)

Risk ratio

Fig. 1   Risk ratios of 25 studies analysing the effect of electronic prescribing on medication errors [reprinted from J Am Med Inform Assoc, 15(5), Ammenwerth E, Schnell-Inderst P, Machan C, Siebert U. The effect of electronic prescribing on medication errors and adverse events: a systematic review, Pages 585–600, 2008, with permission from Elsevier]

Other beneficial effects related to electronic prescribing

Drug monitoring

Monitoring drug therapy is a very time-consuming task, especially in drugs with a narrow therapeutic/toxic range. Moreover, problematic drugs are well documented and their pharmacology is well understood, making them perfect candidates for computer modelling. A 2008 reprint of a Cochrane review evaluated the evidence for computerised advice on drug dosage [55] and found that it increases the initial dose of the drug, resulting in a more rapid achievement of a therapeutic se-rum level. It also reduced the risk of toxic drug levels and the length of hospital stay.

Computerised alerts

Computerised alerts may greatly improve the quality of care. CPOE can be an essential component – combined with other sources of electronic clinical information – in generating relevant electronic clinical alerts.

A recent study has shown that integration of two data sources (CPOE data on blood product prescription and blood gas values from the laboratory) can screen for post-transfusion acute respiratory lung injury (TRALI) [56]. The computer alert system not only detected the patients faster, but also more efficiently than did the clinicians.

Computerised guidelines

Implementing guidelines and achieving good compliance is a real challenge. However, CPOE may be a powerful tool to increase compliance with evidence-based guidelines in critical care [4]. One example is the multicentre trial on transfusion requirements in critical care, which demonstrated that a liberal transfusion strategy is associated with a trend towards increased mortality and increased costs [57]. The "Transfusion in the ICU Interest Group" has shown that the implementation of an institutional protocol and decision support through CPOE could effectively decrease inappropriate red cell transfusion and their associated transfusion complications rate [58], although hospital mortality was not affected.

Another example of a successful guideline adherence with CPOE is the study by Boord et al. [59], who demonstrated that a computer-based insulin infusion protocol in a surgical ICU improved glycaemia control compared to the previous manual protocol, and reduced time to insulin therapy initiation.

Celi et al. also demonstrated that an artificial intelligence tool to predict fluid requirements in the intensive care unit could, at least theoretically, prevent hypotensive episodes requiring fluid boluses in the course of the day [60].

Hazards of electronic prescribing

Medication errors

CPOE introduces possible dangers by introducing new types of errors. Several reports describe potential harm by enhancing the probability of prescription errors, such as inconsistent or duplicate orders [43–44, 61–62]. Alarming is the fact that some of these errors are severe and even life-threatening. Causes were related to deficiencies in the CPOE system itself or to human shortcomings (such as physicians bypassing the normal way of prescribing). In the ICU study of Shulman et al. [43], two errors led to patient harm

resulting in an increased length of ICU stay. Furthermore, three electronic prescriptions could potentially have led to permanent harm or even death, had they not been intercepted. The authors concluded that moderate and major errors remain a significant concern with CPOE. In our study [44] there was an increase in double prescriptions, and in new problems with serum drug monitoring. A thorough evaluation, however, quickly identified those problems within our CPOE system resulting in correcting actions before any harm was done.

Indeed, the main reason for induction of severe MEs are configuration errors and the fact that physicians accept the proposed suggestions for drug doses or routes with minimal reflection [63]. Computerisation induces a false sense of security, a misconception that when technology suggests a course of action, errors are avoided.

Advanced CDS has other specific potential pitfalls, mainly prompted by too frequent alerts and warnings, which can interrupt work flow, causing those messages to be ignored or overridden.

Therefore, the importance of thoroughly evaluating a newly installed CPOE system must not be underestimated. For example, in our centre every new drug configuration or change to an existing one is first e-mailed to a core group of ICU physicians for evaluation, and double-checked by clinical pharmacists before implementation.

Communication

Another substantial problem of introducing CPOE in the ICU is the potential breakdown in communication between physicians and nurses. Indeed, a recent study has shown that CPOE may undermine the efficiency and safety of the medication process by impeding nurse-physician collaboration [64].

A different kind of communication inconsistencies is the poor linking between electronic medical records and related technologies, such as CPOE, or other software applications created by different companies.

Implementation problems

Han et al. found an unexpected increase in mortality coincident with the implementation of CPOE in a paediatric ICU [65]. The study by Delbeccaro et al. conducted one year later could not confirm this, and, on the contrary, even described a trend toward decreased mortality 5 months after implementation [66]. Notwithstanding the fact that both authors use the same commercial system, both studies are almost non-comparable due to differences in design and implementation processes. The latter included, for instance, a more standardised predefined order-set. There were also significant differences in implementation between the 2 centres. Implementing ICT in healthcare is not only a technical activity, but also has important social and psychological aspects. As a result, the implementation strategy in particular is of the utmost importance. Alignment with the formal and informal organisation and workflow in the clinical setting [67] is therefore essential.

Problems with upgrading

Even with an optimised implementation process and configuration, newly emerging problems may still appear after upgrades [45, 68]. Every end-user should be aware of this, and must be motivated to notify the responsible configuration member(s) of the staff in order to get the problem solved as quickly as possible. In the case of more labour-intensive adaptations where commercial support is needed, it may unfortunately take several weeks, possibly even months, before new software patches fix the problem and are ready to be installed.

Publication bias

Negative reactions in the popular press and scientific literature may potentially yield self-censorship [39]. As can be seen on the "Bad Health Informatics Can Kill" website, constructed by the Working Group on Assessment of Health Information Systems of the European Federation of Medical Informatics (EFMI), there are many examples of failed CPOE introduction, as well as other medical ICT problems (available at http://iig.umit.at/efmi/). Apparently, many of these negative examples never do make it into international scientific literature, resulting once more in a negative publication bias.

Conclusion

From a purely theoretical perspective, CPOE or electronic prescribing, offers several inherent error-preventing advantages – such as legibility – over classical handwritten orders. The real potential of CPOE can be realised if combined with decision support for correct drug dosing, drug-drug interactions and advice for optimal drug administration. Indeed, several studies have confirmed that CPOE can improve the safety of ICU medicine by reducing medication errors, especially minor errors. While several studies also show important reductions in the more important ADE incidence, a few reports do point to the introduction of new types of severe errors by CPOE. CPOE configuration must therefore form the subject of a constant and iterative quality improvement programme. Given the potential of CPOE to reduce errors, it is worrisome that the adoption rate of CPOE in the ICU remains low, mainly due to the high implementation cost. There is clearly a need for governmental financial incentives to lower the implementation threshold.

The authors

Kirsten Colpaert, MD[1]
Johan Decruyenaere, MD, PhD[2]
   [1]Intensivist | Department of Intensive Care Medicine | Ghent University Hospital | Ghent, Belgium
   [2]Professor of Medicine | Head of Department | Department of Intensive Care Medicine | Ghent University Hospital | Ghent, Belgium

Address for correspondence
   Kirsten Colpaert
   Department of Intensive Care Medicine
   Ghent University Hospital
   De Pintelaan 185
   9000 Ghent, Belgium
   E-mail: kirsten.colpaert@ugent.be

References

1. Kohn LT, Corrigan J, Donaldson MS. Institute of Medicine. To Err Is Human: Building a Safer Health System. Washington, DC: National Academia Press;1999.
2. The leapfrog Group for Patient Safety: Rewarding Higher Standards. Www. Leapfroggroup.org. Accessed 16-06-2008.
3. Smith J. Building a Safer National Health System for Patients: Improving Medication Safety. London: Department of Health, 2004. Available at: http://www.dh.gov.uk/en/Publicationsandstatistics/Publications/PublicationsPolicyAndGuidance/DH_4071443. Accessed on March 6nd, 2009.
4. Rothschild J. Computerized physician order entry in the critical care and general in-patient setting: a narrative review. J Crit Care 2004;19(4):271–8.
5. Nebeker JR, Hoffman JM, Weir CR. High rates of adverse drug events in a highly computerized hospital. Arch Intern Med 2005;165(10):1111–6.
6. Donchin Y, Gopher D, Olin M. A look into the nature and causes of human errors in the intensive care unit. Crit Care Med 1995;23(2):294–300.
7. Bates DW, Cullen DJ, Laird N, Petersen LA, Small SD, Servi D et al. Incidence of adverse drug events and potential adverse drug events. Implications for prevention. ADE prevention Study Group. JAMA 1995;274(1):29–34.
8. Leape LL, Bates DW, Cullen DJ, Cooper J, Demonaco H, Gallivan T et al. Systems analysis of adverse drug events. ADE Prevention Study Group. JAMA 1995;274(1):35–43.
9. Krähenbühl-Melcher A, Schlienger R, Lampert M, Haschke M, Drewe J, Krähenbühl S. Drug-related problems in hospitals: a review of the recent literature. Drug Saf 2007;30(5):379–407.
10. Moyen E, Camiré E, Stelfox HT. Clinical review: Medication errors in critical care. Crit Care 2008;12(2):208.
11. Allan EL, Barker KN. Fundamentals of medication error research. Am J Hosp Pharm 1990;47(3):555–71.
12. Bates DW, Teich JM, Lee J, Seger D, Kuperman G, Ma'Luf N et al. The impact of computerized physician order entry on medication error prevention. J Am Med Inform Assoc 1999;6(4):313–21.
13. Cullen DJ, Bates DW, Leape LL. Adverse Drug Event Prevention Study Group. Prevention of adverse drug events: a decade of progress in patient safety. J Clin Anesth 2000;12(8):600–14.
14. Herout PM, Erstad BL. Medication errors involving continuously infused medications in a surgical intensive care unit. Crit Care Med 2004;32(2):428–32.
15. Campbell AJ, Bloomfield R, Noble DW. An observational study of changes to long-term medication after admission to an intensive care unit. Anaesthesia 2006;61(11):1087–92.
16. Bell CM, Rahimi-Darabad P, Orner AI. Discontinuity of chronic medications in patients discharged from the intensive care unit. J Gen Intern Med 2006;21(9):937–41.
17. National Coordinating Council for Medication Error Reporting and Prevention NCC MERP). NCC MERP Taxonomy of Medication Errors Office of the Secretariat, US Pharmacopeia 1998.
18. Bates DW, Leape LL, Cullen DJ, Laird N, Peterson L, Teich J et al. Effect of computerized physician order entry and a team intervention on prevention of serious medication errors. JAMA 1998;280(15):1311–6.
19. Flynn EA, Barker KN, Pepper GA. Comparison of methods for detecting medication errors in 36 hospitals and skilled nursing facilities. Am J Health Syst Pharm 2002;59(5):436–446.
20. Overhage JM, Tierney WM, Zhou XH, McDonald CJ. A randomized trial of "corollary orders" to prevent errors of omission. J Am Med Inform Assoc 1997;4(5):364–75.
21. Kuperman GJ, Gibson RF. Computer physician order entry: benefits, costs, and issues. Ann Intern Med 2003;139(1):31–9.
22. Evans RS, Pestotnik SL, Classen DC. Preventing adverse drug events in hospitalized patients. Ann Pharmacother 1994;28(4):523–7.
23. Chertow GM, Lee J, Kuperman GJ, Burdick E, Horsky J, Seger DL et al. Guided medication dosing for in-patients with renal insufficiency. JAMA 2001;286(22):2839–44.
24. Peterson JF, Kuperman GJ, Shek C, Patel M, Avorn J, Bates DW. Guided prescription of psychotropic medications for geriatric in-patients. Arch Intern Med 2005;165(7):802–7.
25. Maurer C, Lecointre K, Cachin N, Latawiec K, Ouadfel F, Lahmek P, Fauvelle F, Piquet J. Impact of medical prescription computerisation on the incidence of adverse drug effects. Rev Mal Respir 2003; 20:355–63.
26. Oliven A, Michalake I, Zalman D, Dorman E, Yeshurun D, Odeh M. Prevention of prescription errors by computerized, on-line surveillance of drug order entry. Int J Med Inform 2005;74(5):377–86.
27. Pestotnik SL, Classen DC, Evans RS, Burke JP. Implementing antibiotic practice guidelines through computer-assisted decision support: clinical and financial outcomes. Ann Intern Med 1996;124(10):884–90.
28. Teich JM, Merchia PR, Schmiz JL, Kuperman GJ, Spurr CD, Bates DW. Effects of computerized physician order entry on prescribing practices. Arch Intern Med 2000;160(18):2741–7.
29. Kirk RC, Li-Meng Goh D, Packia J, Min Kam H, Ong BK. Computer calculated dose in paediatric prescribing. Drug Saf 2005;28(9):817–24.
30. Evans R, Pestotnik S, Classen D, et al. A Computer-Assisted Management Programme for Antibiotics and Other Antiinfective Agents. NEJM 1998;338(4):232–260.

31. Mullett CJ, Evans RS, Christenson JC, Dean JM. Development and impact of a computerized paediatric antiinfective decision support programme. Paediatrics 2001;108(4):E75.

32. Potts AL, Barr FE, Gregory DF, Wright L, Patel NR. Computerized physician order entry and medication errors in a paediatric critical care unit. Paediatrics 2004;113:59–63.

33. Koide D, Ohe K, Ross-Degnan D, Kaihara S. Computerized reminders to monitor liver function to improve the use of etretinate. Int J Med Inform 2000;57(1):11–9.

34. Galanter WL, Didomenico RJ, Polikaitis A. A trial of automated decision support alerts for contraindicated medications using computerized physician order entry. J Am Med Inform Assoc 2005;12(3):269–74.

35. Feldstein AC, Smith DH, Perrin N et al. Reducing warfarin medication interactions: an interrupted time series evaluation.Arch Intern Med 2006;166(9):1009–15.

36. Tamblyn R, Huang A, Perreault R, Jacques A, Roy D, Hanley J et al. The medical office of the 21st century (MOXXI): effectiveness of computerized decision-making support in reducing inappropriate prescribing in primary care. CMAJ 2003;169(6):549–56.

37. Shamliyan TA, Duval S, Kane RL. Just what the doctor ordered. Review of the evidence of the impact of computerized physician order entry system on medication errors. Health Serv Res 2008;43(1):32–53.

38. Eslami S, de Keizer N, Abu-Hanna A. The impact of comuterized physician medication order entry in hospitalized patients-A systematic review. Int. J Med Inform 2007; doi:10.1016/j.ijmedinf.2007.10.001

39. Ammenwerth E, Schnell-Inderst P, Machan C, Siebert U. The effect of electronic Prescribing on medication errors and adverse drug events: a systematic review. J Am Med Inform Assoc 2008;15(5):585–600.

40. Wolfstadt JI, Gurwitz JH, Field TS. The effect of computerized physician order entry with clinical decision support on the rates of adverse drug events: a systematic review. J Gen Intern Med 2008;23(4):451–8.

41. Mitchell D, Usher J, Gray S. Evaluation and audit of a pilot of electronic prescribing and drug administration. J Inform Tech Health care 2004;2(1):19–29.

42. Spencer DC, Leininger A, Daniels R, Granko RP, Coeytaux RR. Effect of a computerized prescriber-order-entry system on reported medication errors. Am J Health Syst Pharm 2005;62(4): 416–9.

43. Shulman R, Singer M, Goldstone J, Bellingan G. Medication errors: a prospective cohort study of hand-written and computerised physician order entry in the intensive care unit. Crit Care 2005;9(5):R516–21.

44. Colpaert K, Claus B, Somers A, Vandewoude K, Robays H, Decruyenaere J. Impact of computerized physician order entry on medication prescription errors in the intensive care unit: a controlled cross-sectional trial. Crit Care 2006;10(1):R21.

45. Fraenkel D, Cowie M, Daley P. Quality benefits of an intensive care clinical information system. Crit Care Med 2003;31(1): 120–5.

46. Fortescue EB, Kaushal R, Landrigan CP, et al. Prioritizing strategies for preventing medication errors and adverse drug events in paediatric in-patients. Paediatrics 2003;111(4):722–9.

47. Fontan JE, Maneglier V, Nguyen VX, Loirat C, Brion F. Medication errors in hospitals: computerized unit dose drug dispensing system versus ward stock distribution system. Pharm World Sci. 2003;25(3):112–7.

48. King WJ, Paice N, Rangrej J, Forestell GJ, Swartz R. The effect of computerized physician order entry on medication errors and adverse drug events in paediatric in-patients. Paediatrics 2003;112(3 Pt 1):506–9.

49. Upperman JS, Staley P, Friend K, Neches W, Kazimer D, Benes J et al. The impact of hospitalwide computerized physician order entry on medical errors in a paediatric hospital. J Pediatr Surg. 2005;40(1):57–9.

50. Kim GR, Chen AR, Arceci RJ, Mitchell SH, Kokoszka KM, Daniel D et al. Error reduction in paediatric chemotherapy: computerized order entry and failure modes and effects analysis. Arch Pediatr Adolesc Med. 2006;160(5):495–8.

51. Kirk RC, Li-Meng Goh D, Packia J, Min Kam H, Ong BK. Computer calculated dose in paediatric prescribing. Drug Saf. 2005;28(9):817–24.

52. Walsh KE, Landrigan CP, Adams WG, Vinci RJ, Chessare JB, Cooper MR et al. Effect of computer order entry on prevention of serious medication errors in hospitalized children. Paediatrics. 2008;121(3):e421–7.

53. Cordero L, Kuehn L, Kumar RR, Mekhjian HS. Impact of computerized physician order entry on clinical practice in a newborn intensive care unit. J Perinatol 2004;24(2):88–93.

54. Holdsworth MT, Fichtl RE, Raisch DW, Hewryk A, Behta M, Mendez-Rico E, Wong CL, Cohen J, Bostwick S, Greenwald BM. Impact of computerized prescriber order entry on the incidence of adverse drug events in paediatric in-patients. Paediatrics. 2007 Nov;120(5):1058–66.

55. Durieux P, Trinquart L, Colombet I, Niès J, Walton RT, Rajeswaran A et al. Computerized advice on drug dosage to improve prescribing practice. Cochrane Database of Systematic Reviews 2008, Issue 3.Art. No.: CD002894.

56. Finlay-Morreale HE, Louie C, Toy P. Computer-generated Automatic Alerts of Respiratory Distress after Blood Transfusion. J Am Med Inform Assoc 2008;15(3):383–385.

57. Hébert PC, Wells G, Blajchman MA. A multicentre, randomized, controlled clinical trial of transfusion requirements in critical care. Transfusion Requirements in Critical Care Investigators, Canadian Critical Care Trials Group. N Engl J Med 1999;340(6):409–17.

58. Rana R, Afessa B, Keegan MT, Whalen F, Nutall G, Evenson L et al. for the Transfusion in the ICU Interest Group. Evidence-based red cell transfusion in the critically ill: quality improvement using computerized physician order entry. Crit Care Med 2006;34(7):1892–7.

59. Boord JB, Sharifi M, Greevy RA, Griffin M, Lee V, Webb T, May M, Waitman L, May A, Miller R. Computer-based insulin infusion protocol improves glycemia control over manual protocol. J Am Med Inform Assoc 2007;14(3):278–87.

60. Celi L, Hinske LC, Alterovitz G, Szolovits P. An artificial intelligence tool to predict fluid requirement in the intensive care unit: a proof of concept study. Crit Care 2008;12:R151

61. Senholzi C, Gottlieb J. Pharmacist interventions after implementation of computerized prescriber order entry. Am J Health Syst Pharm 2003;60(18):1880–2

62. George D, Austin-Bishop N. Error rates for computerized order entry by physicians versus nonphysicians. Am J Health Syst Pharm 2003;60(21):2250–2.

63. Nadzam DM, Macklis RM. Promoting patient safety: is technology the solution? Jt Comm J Qual Improv 2001;27(8):430–6.

64. Pirnejad H, Niazkhani Z, Van der Sijs H. Impact of a computerized physician order entry system on nurse-physician collaboration in the medication process. Int J Med Inform 2008;77(11):735–44.

65. Han YY, Carcillo JA, Venkataraman ST, Clark RS, Watson SR, Nguyen T et al. Unexpected increased mortality after implementation of a commercially sold computerized physician order entry system. Paediatrics 2005;116(6):1506–12.

66. Del Beccaro MA, Jeffries HE, Eisenberg MA, Harry ED. Computerized provider order entry implementation: no association with increased mortality rates in an intensive care unit. Paediatrics 2006;118(1):290–5.

67. Ammenwerth E, Talmon J, Ash J, Bates D, Beuscart-Zéphir M.-C, Duhamel A et al. Impact of CPOE on Mortality Rates – Contradictory Findings, Important Messages. Methods of Information in Medicine 2006; 45(6):586–593.

68. Keuhn B. IT vulnerabilities highlighted by errors, malfunctions at Veterans' Medical Centre. J Am Med Assoc 2009; 301:919–20.

69. Colpaert K and Decruyenaere J. Computerized physician order entry in critical care. Best Practice & Research Clinical Anaestesiology, 2009; 23:27–38.

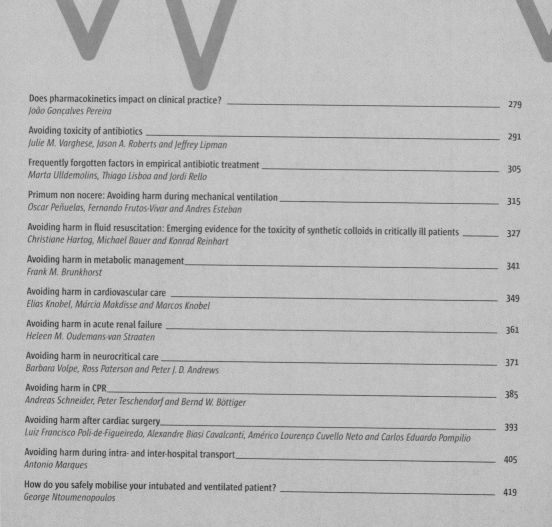

F. First do no harm

João Gonçalves Pereira

Does pharmacokinetics impact on clinical practice?

Introduction

Characteristically, critically ill patients show a wide range of organ dysfunctions related to the severe acute illness and often require several measures to control the underlying disease, like organ support, surgery and a variety of drugs such as sedatives, analgesics, vasopressors, inotropes, gastric acid suppressants and antimicrobials.

The efficacy of a drug is dependent on its ability to achieve an effective concentration in the target tissue. However, the risk of toxicity limits the dose which can be administered. The safe concentration range of a drug, that is to say, below the toxicity threshold but maintaining its efficacy, is called therapeutic range. In critically ill patients that range can be very narrow, thereby increasing the risks of toxicity.

In fact, critically ill patients are a unique challenge in drug dosing because of the increased cardiac output, capillary leak and modification of serum proteins, serum levels and binding properties. Additionally, increased renal and hepatic clearance or, on the contrary, organ failure, may change drug concentration in an unpredictable way [1].

Therapeutic procedures, notably large-volume infusions, contribute to altering the concentration-time relationship of many drugs. Besides, in patients with organ failure, especially renal and/or hepatic, drug accumulation and increased toxicity can occur (see Fig. 1).

The safety of a drug implies the prevention of its accumulation and of direct tissue injury. However, it also means prevention of underdosing, as failure to achieve an active concentration could result in an important risk for the patient, like hypotension (insufficient vasopres-

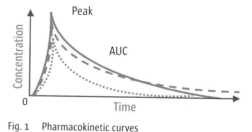

Fig. 1   Pharmacokinetic curves
Normal concentration-time profile of drugs administered by intravenous route (continuous line) is changed by critical illness, with lower peak concentration and area under the curve (dotted line). Half-life is dependent on clearance and may be increased. During organ failure (dashed line) peak concentration may also be lower (volume of distribution is increased), but smaller clearance prolongs half-life.
AUC – Area under the concentration-time curve

sors), agitation and delirium (inadequate sedation), fluid accumulation (insufficient diuretics) or sepsis and resistance selection (inappropriate antibiotics).

Pharmacokinetic (PK) monitoring is likely to be useful when there is a strong relationship between drug concentration and the pharmacological response [2]. Unfortunately, therapeutic drug monitoring is only available for a small number of drugs.

Nevertheless, many drugs, like sedatives or vasopressors, can be titrated according to the desired effect. Other drugs, like antibiotics, are not easily assessed, at least during the first hours of their use.

The knowledge of these PK changes may help to select appropriate dosage and intervals that contribute to therapeutic success and prevent toxicity.

Basic principles of pharmacokinetics

Pharmacokinetics refers to the study of drug concentration during a timeframe and its distribution in different tissues of the body, namely its absorption, bioavailability, distribution, protein binding, and also its metabolism and excretion. Clinical PK is the application of these principles to design individualised dosage regimens which optimise therapeutic response while minimising the chance of an adverse drug reaction.

When drugs are given extravascularly, absorption occurs through several physiological barriers. Bioavailability is the drug proportion which actually reaches systemic circulation. Distribution occurs when drug molecules leave the vascular system to different compartments, either tissues or organs. Their chemical conversion is called metabolism. Excretion is the irreversible elimination of a drug from the body [3].

In this context, it is critical to have knowledge of several primary PK parameters, like volume of distribution (Vd), clearance (Cl), half-life ($t_{1/2}$), peak and minimum serum drug concentration, area under the concentration-time curve (AUC).

The one-compartment PK model is the most useful in intensive care. In fact, although it simplifies complex underlying principles of drug distribution, it can roughly predict the concentration of drugs overtime.

Most drugs follow linear PK (its concentration changes proportionally with dose). However, some, such as phenytoin, present a saturable or Michaelis-Menten PK: After a certain threshold, concentration increases disproportionally with dose, because its Cl is enzyme-dependent and falls with increasing concentration. Other drugs have an autoinduction Cl (e.g. carbamazepine) or saturable plasma binding sites (e.g. valproate), and their Cl increases with high concentrations. These nonlinear PK drugs may be very difficult to titrate [3], especially in elderly patients.

Pharmacodynamics (PD) relates drug concentration and pharmacological response. However, drug effect is usually not proportional to drug concentration because pharmacological effects depend on the ability of a drug to form a complex with a receptor. Once these are saturated, a maximum response will be obtained. Often adverse effects of drugs follow the same type of concentration-response relationship. As a result, to obtain maximal pharmacological effect it is sometimes necessary to tolerate some toxicity [3, 4].

Absorption

Circulatory dysfunction in critical illness results in a decreased perfusion of muscles, skin and gut. Therefore, absorption from those sites is usually slow, erratic and sometimes incomplete. The first-pass effect, the hepatic elimination of enterically absorbed drugs before systemic circulation is reached, also influences systemic concentration.

Moreover, hypoperfusion is frequently exacerbated by mucosal oedema and dysfunction, venous congestion, hypomotility or diarrhoea. Also, the administration of crushed tablets via a nasogastric tube, mixed with enteric nutrition, may alter its chemical stability and bioavailability and may result in tube clogging. Therefore, the use of liquid dosage forms is preferable whenever possible [5].

Bioavailability of intravenously administered drugs approaches 100% and should be the preferred route for the critically ill patient, being necessary to ensure adequate plasma drug concentrations. However, some drugs, like fluoroquinolones, fluconazol, doxycicline and acetaminophen, have excellent oral absorption and can therefore be safely administered via the enteric route after patient stabilisation.

Acetaminophen may even be used to quantify absorption from the GI tract [6].

Distribution

Serum concentration of a drug depends of the amount delivered, its bioavailability and the Vd. The Vd is a mathematical construct and refers to the size of a compartment necessary to account for the total amount of the drug, assuming that its concentration is the same in the whole body, as the one measured in plasma [Vd = (dose * bioavailability)/concentration]. It is usually expressed in l/kg of body weight. Drugs that distribute mainly in the extracellular fluid have low Vd, whilst drugs that have rapid cellular uptake have high Vd (in excess of 0.6 l/kg).

In general, Vd is above normal in critically ill patients. Volume resuscitation, blood products, vasopressors, positive pressure ventilation, surgical procedures, capillary leak and reduction in albumin serum concentration, all contribute to an increase in Vd. Therefore, with the same dose, peak concentrations are usually lower.

However, if drug Cl remains unchanged, a rise in Vd proportionally increases the $t_{1/2}$ since $t_{1/2} = Vd/(Cl*0.693)$. This might be a useful effect for drugs that depend on time to act, but a major disadvantage for concentration-dependent agents.

The rate and extent of distribution of a drug in tissues is determined by cardiac output, regional blood flow, permeability of the capillary and tissue membranes to the drug and the drug's relative distribution between tissue and blood.

Drug doses may need to be altered depending on their tissue penetration. Many antimicrobials do not penetrate well in cerebrospinal fluid and higher doses may be necessary. By contrast, at excretory sites, such as the urine, drugs may concentrate and use of lower doses may be appropriate [7].

In critically ill patients misdistribution of blood flow in microcirculation (e.g. in septic shock), resulting in compromised tissue perfusion, may further decrease drug effect [8].

Serum albumin level is usually decreased, resulting in an increased Vd for drugs that bind to it (phenytoin, midazolam) and a higher free drug fraction. However, the latter leads to greater tissue distribution, thereby reducing plasma drug concentrations. Overall, changes in protein binding usually do not result in changes in unbound exposure. However, caution is advisable when monitoring levels of highly bound drugs (like phenytoin). Increasing serum concentration through changes in dose may cause increased free drug exposure and toxicity [9].

Excretion

In the hyperdynamic septic patients, there is usually an increased renal and hepatic blood flow and often an increased drug Cl [1, 10]. Conversely, patients with low cardiac output often have low drug Cl.

Oliguria also leads to drug accumulation and toxicity. However, critically ill patients with renal failure also present increased Vd and, therefore, need normal or even higher loading doses to achieve adequate serum levels, notably with antibiotics. Nevertheless, maintenance doses should be reduced (or intervals enlarged) to avoid accumulation and toxicity.

Prescription guidance is well-established in chronic renal failure. However, in acute renal failure there is often a narrow therapeutic range between ensuring effectiveness and preventing toxicity. Under renal replacement therapy, drug Cl is usually less than that provided by normal native kidneys. Consequently, $t_{1/2}$ is prolonged and dosage intervals need to be increased. However, there is a significant risk of underdosing, when doses previously defined for stable patients with chronic renal failure are used in critically ill patients [11, 12].

The effect of liver dysfunction on drug concentrations is less well defined, with numerous interactions, which allows prescription only on an individual basis.

Drug hepatic metabolism can be classified into

- high extraction ratio, dependent almost exclusively on blood flow, and
- low extraction ratio, which depends on free drug fraction and intrinsic Cl (4).

Cirrhosis, which alters blood flow, predominantly affects the first group, whilst hepatocellular injury causes accumulation of intrinsic Cl-dependent drugs. These are observed in drugs metabolised by the cytochrome P450 enzyme system, which is particularly sensitive to hypoxia and to ischemic insults.

Of note, patients with liver disease often have decreased renal Cl, although with a normal serum creatinine. Thus, dose reduction may be necessary even for renally cleared drugs [13)].

Drug pharmacokinetics

Sedatives and analgesics

Ideally, a sedative should have a rapid and predictable onset, be readily cleared without accumulation, easy to titrate, non-toxic and inexpensive. However, all sedatives show limitations and adverse effects. In addition, because sedatives are

Tab. 1   Pharmacokinetic changes in drugs commonly used in critically ill patients and procedures to improve patient safety
Whenever possible, routine PK monitoring should be used, especially in unstable patients and patients with renal failure. Titration to endpoints may also help prevent either accumulation and toxicity or underdosing.
Vd – Volume of distribution; $t_{1/2}$ – Half-life; MIC – Minimal inhibitory concentration

Drug	PK changes in critically ill patient	PK safety procedure
Sedatives	Accumulation	Titrate with sedation scales
		Daily interruptions of continuous infusions
	Organ failure accumulation	Use drugs not dependent on failing organ metabolism or excretion
Opioid analgesics	Accumulation	Use of multimodal analgesia
		Daily interruptions of continuous infusion
		Use of drugs with short $t_{1/2}$
	Organ failure accumulation	Use drugs not dependent on failing organ metabolism or excretion
Vasopressors	None	Titrate to haemodynamic endpoints
Inotropes	None	Titrate to haemodynamic endpoints
Diuretics	Accumulation in oliguria	Do not use in oliguric patients
Antibiotics		
β-Lactams	Increased Vd and underdosing	Maximum loading dose
		Extended-time infusions
		Continuous infusion (except carbapenems)
Aminoglycosides	Increased Vd and underdosing	Maximum loading doses (even in renal failure). Monitor peak serum levels
	Accumulation	Large intervals. Monitor trough levels.
		Use PK monitoring and informatic support to select dose and intervals
Vancomycin	Increased Vd and underdosing	Monitor serum levels
		Continuous infusion
Fluoroquinolones	None	High doses (according to MIC)

often administered by continuous infusion, their PK parameters, derived from short-term administration, may not be predictive of their behaviour, since these drugs and their active metabolites show multicompartmental behaviour.

Midazolam is a benzodiazepine, highly protein-bound (95%), with a short $t_{1/2}$ (90 min) and a large Vd (0.8–1.5 l/kg). It is the most predictable and easy benzodiazepine to titrate. However, it presents wide interpatient variability [14] especially in critically ill patients. Changes in Vd and hepatic metabolism may lead to its accumulation. Also in renal failure, extremely high levels of its glucuronide metabolite may be observed. Although this molecule is much less active than its parent compound, it contributes to prolonged sedation [15].

Propofol is commonly used for sedation because of its rapid onset and offset. Like benzodiazepines, propofol activates the GABA receptors to produce central nervous system depression. Propofol is cleared faster than midazolam and is rapidly eliminated from the central compartment. Recovery times and blood propofol concentrations were found to be similar after 24, 48, 72, and 96 hours of drug infusion [16]. Propofol is metabolised in the liver and cleared by the kidneys. However, extrahepatic Cl also occurs.

Clearance of propofol is usually slower in critical care and elderly patients than in the general population, probably reflecting a decreased hepatic blood flow. Propofol infusion syndrome, a rare but fatal complication, has been reported and seems to be related to infusion rates over 4 mg/kg/h [16].

Titration of sedatives can be made using sedation scales [17]. Also, daily interruptions of sedative infusions (until awakening) have proven to be safe, reduce the need for ventilation and prevent the risk of accumulation and toxicity [18, 19].

Opioid analgesics are extensively used in critically ill patients to provide analgesia, reduce anxiety and relieve the discomfort from the tracheal tube, potentially avoiding sedatives and neuromuscular blocking agents. They are often given by prolonged intravenous infusion. Therefore, changes in their PK may lead to accumulation and ventilation weaning delay.

Fentanyl and its derivatives are highly lipid-soluble and, with the exception of remifentanyl, are metabolised in the liver with a high extraction

ratio metabolism. In the critically ill patients these drugs show an increased Vd and prolonged $t_{1/2}$.

Alfentanyl is largely bound to α1-acid glycoprotein that is increased in the critically ill. In these patients hepatic Cl may be significantly impaired, leading to its accumulation, with respiratory and cough depression, especially in elderly patients [20] Therefore, daily interruptions [18] of these analgesics and use of multimodal analgesia (with other classes) may increase patient safety [16].

Remifentanyl-based analgosedation is safe and may reduce weaning time and ICU length of stay [21]. Its unique metabolism, by non-specific esterases found in plasma and tissues, results in rapid and predictable Cl independent of renal and hepatic function and of infusion time [20].

Vasopressors, inotropes and diuretics

Catecholamines, like norepinephrine or epinephrine, are among the most widely used drugs in intensive care and are easily titrated by their effects on the circulatory system, especially blood pressure and cardiac output.

These drugs are cleared mainly by monoaminoxidase (widely distributed) and also in the liver, and have a short $t_{1/2}$ (a few minutes), even in the presence of severe organ failure [2].

Dopamine is a vasopressor that combines α- and β-adrenergic activity with renal, dopaminergic receptors. The failure of the dopaminergic dose of dopamine to improve outcome led to its efficacy being challenged, but more recent data has rehabilitated its value [22].

Dopamine has a short $t_{1/2}$ but significant interpatient variability. This Cl variability is also present in dobutamine, and seems related to differences of hepatic intrinsic Cl [15]. Therefore, a fixed dose of dopamine can yield a wide range of plasma concentrations.

Critical illness or organ failure does not cause significant variation of these drugs' PK. Therefore, vasopressors and inotropes should be titrate according to hemodynamic endpoints, although the best strategy is not clear [23].

Loop diuretics are used extensively in intensive care to help eliminate fluid retention, which might have deleterious effects, at least after haemodynamic stabilisation, without any effect on GFR [24].

Furosemide is highly protein-bound and therefore hypoalbuminaemia increases its Vd. However, its activity is related to the amount of drug that is excreted in urine. Its Cl is proportional to renal function and it accumulates in oliguric patients, potentiating the nephro- and ototoxicity of other drugs, like aminoglycosides. Therefore, furosemide should be stopped if patients remain oliguric despite its use [25].

Antibiotics

Infection, whether community- or hospital-acquired, is an important cause of morbidity and mortality in critically ill patients [26]. Treatment of the septic patient is based on supportive management, while appropriate antibiotics and focus control provide specific therapy.

It has been shown that timely administration of empirical, appropriate antibiotic therapy in severe infection reduces hospital mortality [27–29]. However, for an antibiotic to be effective it has to reach bacteria in an appropriate concentration, during a certain period of time, according to its PD profile [30]. Therefore, an antibiotic with *in vitro* activity against the infecting bacteria, in a dose high enough to achieve suitable concentration in the infected tissue, according to its PD characteristics, should be started as soon as possible in order to obtain maximum killing rates and eradicate all infectious microorganisms. That also reduces the risk of selection of resistant strains.

However, antibiotic PK changes in critically ill patients, namely the Vd increase and the Cl increase or decrease, make its concentration difficult to predict. Moreover, antibiotic efficacy is not easily assessed, as its effects are usually unnoticeable before 48 hours of therapy. Lack of routine drug monitoring also makes it difficult to distinguish underdosing from lack of *in vivo* organism susceptibility.

Antibiotics pharmacodynamics

Antibiotics behave differently depending on the pathogen at which they are directed and on their pharmacological classes. One of the major characteristics of these drugs, which determine their timeframe activity, is whether their killing rate depends on drug concentration or on the duration of exposure [31]. The second major characteristic is the post-antibiotic effect (PAE) [7], the persistent effects that last after antimicrobial concentration fall under the minimal inhibitory concentration (MIC). Antibiotics that inhibit nucleic acid or protein synthesis tend to have a larger PAE [32].

Some drug classes, such as β-lactams (e.g. penicillins, cephalosporins, and carbapenems), have a slow continuous rate of killing that is almost entirely related to the time during which their concentration exceeds a certain threshold, usually a low multiple of the MIC of the infecting organism (T>MIC-dependent).

Concentration-dependent antibiotics, like aminoglycosides, show rapid concentration-dependent killing and PAE, which increases with the ratio between their peak concentration and MIC (Peak:MIC) [33]. Also, the area under the antibiotic concentration-time curve in comparison with the MIC (AUC:MIC) is important for explaining antimicrobial activity of antibiotics, such as fluoroquinolones [34].

When choosing a drug dose to attain the desired target, it is important to recognise the range of MICs that might be found clinically. The higher the MIC, the lower the probability of attaining its PK/PD target. Therefore, high antibiotic doses, according to their PD profile, should be used to ensure bacterial killing and patient safety.

However, these high antibiotics doses also increase the risk of toxicity to the host. Nevertheless, loading doses with at least the maximum recommended antibiotic dose should be given to all patients, to achieve therapeutic targets and bacterial death as soon as possible. Loading dose is only dependent on the Vd [1, 7, 32], which is increased in critically ill patients, and is not dependent on age or any organ failure.

β-Lactams

This class of drugs attaches and blocks penicillin-binding proteins, which are responsible for the stability of peptidoglycan from the bacterial cell wall. Bacteria death occurs when a considerable portion of these proteins are occupied. As the drug concentration increases, its effect quickly maximises and higher drug concentrations do not result in significantly greater bacterial killing. On the contrary, if antibiotic concentration falls, bacteria proliferate almost immediately, especially Gram-negative organisms. Therefore T > MIC is the major PK/PD parameter that correlates with efficacy [35].

In fact, these antibiotics are time-dependent with little PAE (with the exception of carbapenems) [36]. A T > MIC of 40–50 % of the dosing interval (30 % for carbapenems) has been shown to provide infection resolution [37].

The current unavailability of β-lactams monitoring of serum levels makes it difficult to prevent underdosing in critically ill patients. In fact, these antibiotics are predominantly extracellular and, therefore, have increased Vd [10, 38] and Cl (if renal function is preserved) [1]. Besides, thrombosis of the microcirculation may impair the antibiotic penetration in tissues, like muscle or fat [39, 40].

Since β-lactams are T>MIC-dependent, giving small doses with short time intervals or using continuous infusion (preceded by a loading dose), maximises time of bacteria exposure to active drug levels and may improve patient outcome. The use of this method is associated with a mean concentration of antibiotics higher than with conventional dosing (provided that the same amounts are administered) [41], although significant interpatient steady-state concentration variability may be observed [42].

Although clinical trials showing a better outcome with continuous infusion of β-lactams are still lacking, there are at least theoretical arguments, results from animal studies and case reports supporting the efficacy and safety of continuous or prolonged infusions [43].

Lodise et al. used prolonged infusions (4 h) of piperacillin tazobactam to treat *Pseudomonas aeruginosa* infection (N = 102) in a mixed hospital population during a period of two years. The control group was the population (N = 92) treated with the same antibiotic (30-min infusion) during the two previous years [44]. Overall there was no mortality benefit (8.8 % vs. 15.2 %; p = 0.17, respectively). In the more severe group (APACHE II > 16) the clinical benefit was statically significant, with reduction of mortality rate (12.2 % and 31.6 %; p = 0.04) and length of stay (18 vs. 27.5 days; p = 0.02). Also, Roberts et al. found continuous infusion of ceftriaxone (given

for at least 4 days) to reduce mortality (adjusted for age and SOFA score) in critically ill patients, when compared with ceftriaxone given in bolus (odds ratio for survival – 22.8; p = 0.008) [45]. In these studies there were no reports of increased adverse reactions.

In severe infection, where the risk of underdosing is even higher, continuous infusion of β-lactams has proven to be safe, with at least comparable therapeutic efficacy, and may even improve patient survival and help prevent the emergence of resistant strains.

Carbapenems, though with a significant PAE, may also benefit from extended-time infusion [46]. However, it should be noted that, since these antibiotics are not stable after reconstitution at room temperature, they are not suitable for continuous infusion but only for an extended infusion strategy. Moreover, imipenem should be avoided in renal failure patients, to prevent cilastatin accumulation.

Aminoglycosides

Aminoglycosides have a broad spectrum of action against Gram-negative bacteria, including the non-fermentative *Pseudomonas* and *Acinectobacter*. They block protein synthesis, leading to cell death.

These are extracellular drugs poorly bound to proteins and, therefore, also susceptible to PK changes occurring in the critically ill patients.

There is extensive *in vitro* evidence relating the peak aminoglycoside concentration with killing rate and outcome. Kashuba et al. [47] were able to show an *in vivo* relationship between aminoglycoside exposure (Peak:MIC higher than 10 in the first 48h) and infection resolution. Therefore, a peak reduction or an increase in MIC may cause therapeutic failure.

Using a Monte Carlo simulation, Nicolau et al. [48] calculated that a high gentamicin dose of at least 7 mg/kg (at extended 24 h intervals) was required to achieve that PK/PD target.

Even with these high doses, the increased Vd of critically ill patients may prevent the achievement of this Peak:MIC ratio. In a study from our group [49], despite a gentamicin median loading dose of 7,4 mg/kg, only 31,3 % of patients (N = 32) had a gentamicin peak higher than 20 µg/ml. The

Vd was elevated (0.41 l/kg) and without correlation with either SOFA score, Charlson score, age, or renal failure. Only female gender was predictive of an increased Vd (0.51 vs 0.39 l/kg; p = 0.002).

Other groups obtained similar results. Tang et al. found in 79 critically ill patients an increase in gentamicin Vd (0.43 vs 0.29 l/kg) and lower $t_{1/2}$, compared with a control of a non-septic group [50]. In another study of 40 critically ill patients, gentamicin Vd in the first 48 hours of therapy was also elevated, 0.43 l/kg [51]. By contrast, on the seventh day of therapy, Vd was already significantly lower (0.29 l/kg, p < 0.001) and close to "normal" (0.26 l/kg). Such a marked decrease (> 35%) in only 7 days reflects the PK variations in these patients and reinforces the need for close PK monitoring. Rea et al. note a very high Vd, 0.76 l/kg in a 102, mixed critically ill population. In their study only 20% of patients had a gentamicin peak higher than 20 µg/ml, despite receiving a dose of 7 mg/kg [52].

The fear of oto- and nephrotoxicity may prevent the use of high aminoglycoside doses even in severe sepsis. In a study of 373 patients treated with gentamicin, a decrease of 0.5% per day in creatinine clearance was noted. However, these changes did impact neither patient outcome nor the incidence of clinically significant renal failure [53].

Moreover, those high doses of aminoglycosides, given at extended intervals, do not increase nephrotoxicity [54]. In fact, binding of aminoglycosides to renal and vestibular tissue is a saturable process and, as a consequence, after a certain concentration, higher dosing should not cause more toxicity. Extended intervals may provide an increase of aminoglycoside tissue clearance time and even contribute to decreasing the drug's renal cortical accumulation [55].

A third reason to use these high aminoglycoside doses at extended intervals is the adaptative resistance of the Gram-negative bacteria when exposed to this class of antibiotics, which peaks at 12 h but reverses completely with long antibiotic-free time ([56)].

Vancomycin

Vancomycin is a glycopeptide that inhibits bacterial cell wall synthesis. It is not orally absorbed. It is eliminated in a considerable extent,

80%–90% unchanged via the renal route, within 24 h [57]. Vancomycin should be administered intravenously, with a standard infusion time of at least 1 h, to minimise infusion-related adverse effects (red man syndrome). In patients with normal creatinine clearance, vancomycin has a $t_{1/2}$ of 4–6 h and a Vd of 0.2–1.25 l/kg. However, in critically ill patients, its Vd is increased and therefore its concentration is lower (for the same dose). Conversely, in patients with renal failure, Cl is impaired and drug accumulation occurs [1].

Vancomycin acts against Gram-positive cocci, including methicillin-resistant *Staphylococcus aureus* (MRSA) and penicillin-resistant *Streptococcus pneumoniae*. However, its clinical activity may be limited by its poor tissue distribution, although inflamed tissues allow improved vancomycin concentration (e.g. 300% increase in cerebral spinal fluid [57]).

The penetration of vancomycin in the lung changes considerably and seems to range between 10 and 25% (more in the inflamed lung) [31]. Moreover, proteins in the infected tissue may bind to it and compromise its efficacy even further.

The outcome of vancomycin-treated patients has been related to the AUC:MIC or T > MIC. An AUC:MIC in plasma as high as 350 has been correlated with therapeutic success [58].

However, in a study of MRSA hospital-acquired pneumonia, Jeffres et al. were unable to find any correlation between the outcome and vancomycin either in trough levels or AUC (survivors' vancomycin AUC 351; non-survivors' vancomycin AUC 354; p = 0.941) [59]. Although these results can be disturbing, the authors did not measure MIC. Therefore, its is not possible to rule out a correlation between survival and AUC:MIC. In fact, an increase in bacteria MIC to only 2 µg/ml may prevent the achievement of these high AUC:MIC ratios.

Continuous infusion has been proposed as a method to achieve these high T>MIC or AUC:MIC. With a target concentration as high as 20 to 25 µg/ml, this infusion method may have some advantages over conventional dosing, provided that the same daily dose is used [60].

Vancomycin nephrotoxicity has been related in the past to impurities in the manufacturing process. Despite these drawbacks, today nephrotoxicity is reported to be less than 5%. However, a possible synergistic toxicity effect with aminogly-cosides has also been reported [57].

Consequently, careful monitoring of serum concentrations is recommended since it allows optimisation of efficacy and prevention of toxicity.

Fluoroquinolones

Because of excellent tissue penetration, fluoro-quinolone antibiotics can be used in the management of a large range of infections. These antibiotics block the topoisomerases, which are responsible for the stabilisation of DNA, thereby preventing bacteria replication.

Fluoroquinolones have a high Vd and present both renal and hepatic Cl. Therefore, their PK parameters are not significantly affected by critical illness. Also, renal failure is not associated with significative drug accumulation, unless the patient also has concomitant liver pathology [1].

Fluoroquinolones are concentration-dependent antibiotics. Research has shown that achieving a Peak:MIC ratio of 10 for ciprofloxacin is predictable of bacterial eradication [1]. However, concerns about neurotoxicity of such high concentrations may preclude its use. Therefore, the AUC:MIC is the parameter usually associated with outcome.

Forrest et al. studied ciprofloxacin in Gram-negative infections in critically ill patients. The authors concluded that the achievement of an AUC:MIC > 125 was associated with a successful clinical outcome. For Gram-positive organisms, an AUC:MIC of 30 was necessary for microbiological eradication [61]. Therefore, an increase in bacteria MIC may cause therapeutic failure.

Van Zanten et al. evidenced that ciprofloxacin in a dose of 400 mg *bid* only achieved an effective AUC:MIC for bacteria with a MIC less than 0.25 µg/ml [62]. Using the same antibiotic in critically ill patients, Lipman et al. showed that 400 mg *tid* was both safe and provided an AUC:MIC that was bactericidal against most organisms [63].

A major concern when using these antibiotics is their potential for selecting resistant mutants. A higher AUC:MIC may reduce that risk [61].

Prevention of resistance

Although necessary to treat infection, antibiotics are also responsible for selection of resistant microorganisms, especially when long courses of antibiotics are used. Critically ill patients are especially prone to resistant bacteria, due to the frequent use of broad-spectrum antibiotics and patient-to-patient transmission.

Selection of resistance to antibiotics appears to be strongly associated with suboptimal antimicrobial exposure, whilst its prevention is related to the ability to reach the PK/PD parameters needed for therapeutic success [64]. In fact, Thomas et al. identified, in patients treated with 5 different antibiotic regimens, that an AUC:MIC in excess of 100 was necessary to prevent the selection of antimicrobial resistance [65].

Usually bacteria inoculum presents sub-populations with spontaneous chromosomal point mutations, which makes them less susceptible to the antibiotic. The concentration required to kill the less susceptible bacteria is called the mutant prevention concentration (MPC).

The exposure of bacteria to an antibiotic concentration able to kill the wild-type subpopulation but not the less susceptible mutant subpopulation, promotes the selection of resistance [66]. The reduction of antibiotics time course, the use of doses to achieve maximum concentrations according to PK, the selection of drugs with the lower MIC and MPC and the use of optimum PK/PD relationship, facilitate maximal bacterial killing and are therefore strategies to prevent bacteria resistance, which contributes to patient safety.

Conclusion

Changes of PK in critically ill patients puts such patients at risk for either underdosing or prolonged drug exposure. Therefore, conventional dosing should be replaced by monitoring concentration and/or titration by effect.

Future strategies include combining patient characteristics (sex, biometry, liver and renal function, genetics) and PK profile, from serum and tissue (microdyalisis) measurements, to select doses and intervals. For antibiotic therapy, microbiological data is also important to determine the optimum therapeutic strategy. These strategies may help to improve clinical outcome, without compromising the patients' safety.

The author

João G. Pereira, MD
Unidade de Cuidados Intensivos Médicos
Hospital de São Francisco Xavier
Centro Hospitalar Lisboa Ocidental
Estrada do Forte do Alto do Duque
1449-005 Lisboa, Portugal
E-mail: joaogpster@gmail.com

Bibliography

1. Roberts JA, Lipman J. Antibacterial dosing in intensive care: pharmacokinetics, degree of disease and pharmacodynamics of sepsis. Clin Pharmacokinet2006;45:755-73.
2. Bodenham A, Shelly MP, Park GR. The altered pharmacokinetics and pharmacodynamics of drugs commonly used in critically ill patients. Clin Pharmacokinet1988;14:347-73.
3. Bauer L. Applied clinical pharmacokinetics. 2nd ed: The McGraw-Hill Companies; 2008.
4. De Paepe P, Belpaire FM, Buylaert WA. Pharmacokinetic and pharmacodynamic considerations when treating patients with sepsis and septic shock. Clin Pharmacokinet2002;41:1135-51.
5. Beckwith M, Feddema S, Barton R, Graves C. A Guide to Drug Therapy in Patients with Enteral Feeding Tubes: Dosage Form Selection and Administration Methods. Hospital Pharmacy2004;39:225-37.
6. Crome P, Rizeq M, George S, Braithwaite RA, Jones PW. Drug absorption may be delayed after stroke: results of the paracetamol absorption test. Age Ageing2001;30:391-3.
7. Estes L. Review of pharmacokinetics and pharmacodynamics of antimicrobial agents. Mayo Clin Proc1998;73:1114-22.
8. Levitt DG. The pharmacokinetics of the interstitial space in humans. BMC Clin Pharmacol2003;3:3.
9. Brundage R, Mann H. General Principles of Pharmacokinetics and Pharmacodynamics. In: Fink M, Abraham E, Vincent J, Kochanek P, editors. Textbook of Critical Care. Philadelphia: Elsevier; 2005. p. 1573-85.
10. Weinbren MJ. Pharmacokinetics of antibiotics in burn patients. J Antimicrob Chemother1999;44:319-27.
11. Fish DN, Teitelbaum I, Abraham E. Pharmacokinetics and pharmacodynamics of imipenem during continuous renal replacement therapy in critically ill patients. Antimicrob Agents Chemother2005;49:2421-8.
12. Thalhammer F, Horl WH. Pharmacokinetics of meropenem in patients with renal failure and patients receiving renal replacement therapy. Clin Pharmacokinet2000;39:271-9.
13. Morgan DJ, McLean AJ. Clinical pharmacokinetic and pharmacodynamic considerations in patients with liver disease. An update. Clin Pharmacokinet1995;29:370-91.
14. Shafer A, Doze VA, White PF. Pharmacokinetic variability of midazolam infusions in critically ill patients. Crit Care Med1990;18:1039-41.
15. Power BM, Forbes AM, van Heerden PV, Ilett KF. Pharmacokinetics of drugs used in critically ill adults. Clin Pharmacokinet1998;34:25-56.
16. Mistraletti G, Donatelli F, Carli F. Metabolic and endocrine effects of sedative agents. Curr Opin Crit Care2005;11:312-7.
17. Sessler CN, Jo Grap M, Ramsay MA. Evaluating and monitoring analgesia and sedation in the intensive care unit. Crit Care2008;12 Suppl 3:S2.
18. Kress JP, Pohlman AS, O'Connor MF, Hall JB. Daily interruption of sedative infusions in critically ill patients undergoing mechanical ventilation. N Engl J Med2000;18;342:1471-7.
19. Sessler CN, Wilhelm W. Analgesia and sedation in the intensive care unit: an overview of the issues. Crit Care2008;12 Suppl 3:S1.
20. Wilhelm W, Kreuer S. The place for short-acting opioids: special emphasis on remifentanil.Crit Care 2008;12 Suppl 3:S5.
21. Park G, Lane M, Rogers S, Bassett P. A comparison of hypnotic and analgesic based sedation in a general intensive care unit. Br J Anaesth2007;98:76-82.
22. Povoa PR, Carneiro AH, Ribeiro OS, Pereira AC. Influence of vasopressor agent in septic shock mortality. Results from the Portuguese Community-Acquired Sepsis Study (SACiUCI study).Crit Care Med2009;37:410-416.
23. Holmes CL. Vasoactive drugs in the intensive care unit. Curr Opin Crit Care2005;11:413-7.
24. Chappell D, Jacob M, Hofmann-Kiefer K, Conzen P, Rehm M. A rational approach to perioperative fluid management. Anesthesiology2008;109:723-40.
25. Mehta RL, Pascual MT, Soroko S, Chertow GM. Diuretics, mortality, and nonrecovery of renal function in acute renal failure. JAMA2002;288:2547-53.
26. Brun-Buisson C. The epidemiology of the systemic inflammatory response. Intensive Care Med2000;26 Suppl 1:S64-74.
27. Povoa P, Coelho L, Almeida E, Fernandes A, Mealha R, Moreira P, et al. C-reactive protein as a marker of ventilator-associated pneumonia resolution: a pilot study. Eur Respir J2005;25:804-12.
28. Kollef MH, Sherman G, Ward S, Fraser VJ. Inadequate antimicrobial treatment of infections: a risk factor for hospital mortality among critically ill patients. Chest1999;115:462-74.
29. Garnacho-Montero J, Ortiz-Leyba C, Herrera-Melero I, Aldabo-Pallas T, Cayuela-Dominguez A, Marquez-Vacaro

JA, et al. Mortality and morbidity attributable to inadequate empirical antimicrobial therapy in patients admitted to the ICU with sepsis: a matched cohort study. J Antimicrob Chemother2008;61:436–41.

30. Hyatt JM, McKinnon PS, Zimmer GS, Schentag JJ. The importance of pharmacokinetic/pharmacodynamic surrogate markers to outcome. Focus on antibacterial agents. Clin Pharmacokinet1995;28:143–60.

31. Craig WA. Basic pharmacodynamics of antibacterials with clinical applications to the use of beta-lactams, glycopeptides, and linezolid. Infect Dis Clin North Am2003;17:479–501.

32. Mehrotra R, De Gaudio R, Palazzo M. Antibiotic pharmacokinetic and pharmacodynamic considerations in critical illness. Intensive Care Med2004;30:2145–56.

33. Moore RD, Lietman PS, Smith CR. Clinical response to aminoglycoside therapy: importance of the ratio of peak concentration to minimal inhibitory concentration. J Infect Dis1987;155:93–9.

34. Ambrose PG, Bhavnani SM, Owens RC, Jr. Clinical pharmacodynamics of quinolones. Infect Dis Clin North Am2003;17:529–43.

35. Craig WA, Ebert SC. Continuous infusion of beta-lactam antibiotics. Antimicrob Agents Chemother1992;36:2577–83.

36. Dreetz M, Hamacher J, Eller J, Borner K, Koeppe P, Schaberg T, et al. Serum bactericidal activities and comparative pharmacokinetics of meropenem and imipenem-cilastatin. Antimicrob Agents Chemother1996;40:105–9.

37. Turnidge JD. The pharmacodynamics of beta-lactams. Clin Infect Dis1998;27:10–22.

38. Gomez CM, Cordingly JJ, Palazzo MG. Altered pharmacokinetics of ceftazidime in critically ill patients. Antimicrob Agents Chemother1999;43:1798–802.

39. Joukhadar C, Frossard M, Mayer BX, Brunner M, Klein N, Siostrzonek P, et al. Impaired target site penetration of beta-lactams may account for therapeutic failure in patients with septic shock. Crit Care Med2001;29:385–91.

40. Tomaselli F, Dittrich P, Maier A, Woltsche M, Matzi V, Pinter J, et al. Penetration of piperacillin and tazobactam into pneumonic human lung tissue measured by in vivo microdialysis. Br J Clin Pharmacol2003;55:620–4.

41. Lopez E, Soy D, Miana MT, Codina C, Ribas J. [Reflections on betalactam antibiotics administered by continuous infusion]. Enferm Infecc Microbiol Clin2006;24:445–52.

42. Benko AS, Cappelletty DM, Kruse JA, Rybak MJ. Continuous infusion versus intermittent administration of ceftazidime in critically ill patients with suspected gram-negative infections. Antimicrob Agents Chemother1996;40:691–5.

43. Mouton JW, Vinks AA. Is continuous infusion of beta-lactam antibiotics worthwhile? – efficacy and pharmacokinetic considerations. J Antimicrob Chemother1996;38:5–15.

44. Lodise TP, Jr., Lomaestro B, Drusano GL. Piperacillin-tazobactam for Pseudomonas aeruginosa infection: clinical implications of an extended-infusion dosing strategy. Clin Infect Dis2007;44:357–63.

45. Roberts JA, Boots R, Rickard CM, Thomas P, Quinn J, Roberts DM, et al. Is continuous infusion ceftriaxone better than once-a-day dosing in intensive care? A randomized controlled pilot study. J Antimicrob Chemother2007;59:285–91.

46. Krueger WA, Bulitta J, Kinzig-Schippers M, Landersdorfer C, Holzgrabe U, Naber KG, et al. Evaluation by monte carlo simulation of the pharmacokinetics of two doses of meropenem administered intermittently or as a continuous infusion in healthy volunteers. Antimicrob Agents Chemother2005;49:1881–9.

47. Kashuba AD, Nafziger AN, Drusano GL, Bertino JS, Jr. Optimizing aminoglycoside therapy for nosocomial pneumonia caused by gram-negative bacteria. Antimicrob Agents Chemother1999;43:623–9.

48. Nicolau DP, Freeman CD, Belliveau PP, Nightingale CH, Ross JW, Quintiliani R. Experience with a once-daily aminoglycoside program administered to 2,184 adult patients. Antimicrob Agents Chemother1995;39:650–5.

49. Pereira J, Martins A, Povoa P. Evaluation of gentamicin first dose pharmacokinetics in septic critically ill patients: pilot study (Abst); 29th International Symposium on Intensive Care and Emergency Medicine. Crit Care2009;13

50. Tang GJ, Tang JJ, Lin BS, Kong CW, Lee TY. Factors affecting gentamicin pharmacokinetics in septic patients. Acta Anaesthesiol Scand1999;43:726–30.

51. Triginer C, Izquierdo I, Fernandez R, Rello J, Torrent J, Benito S, et al. Gentamicin volume of distribution in critically ill septic patients. Intensive Care Med1990;16:303–6.

52. Rea RS, Capitano B, Bies R, Bigos KL, Smith R, Lee H. Suboptimal aminoglycoside dosing in critically ill patients. Ther Drug Monit2008;30:674–81.

53. Buchholtz K, Larsen CT, Hassager C, Bruun NE. Severity of gentamicin's nephrotoxic effect on patients with infective endocarditis: a prospective observational cohort study of 373 patients. Clin Infect Dis2009;48:65–71.

54. Watling SM, Dasta JF. Aminoglycoside dosing considerations in intensive care unit patients. Ann Pharmacother1993;27:351–7.

55. Verpooten GA, Giuliano RA, Verbist L, Eestermans G, De Broe ME. Once-daily dosing decreases renal accumulation of gentamicin and netilmicin. Clin Pharmacol Ther1989;45:22–7.

56. Barclay ML, Begg EJ, Chambers ST, Thornley PE, Pattemore PK, Grimwood K. Adaptive resistance to tobramycin in Pseudomonas aeruginosa lung infection

in cystic fibrosis. J Antimicrob Chemoth-
er1996;37:1155–64.

57. Rybak MJ. The pharmacokinetic and pharmacodynamic properties of vancomycin. Clin Infect Dis2006;42 Suppl 1:S35–9.

58. Moise PA, Forrest A, Bhavnani SM, Birmingham MC, Schentag JJ. Area under the inhibitory curve and a pneumonia scoring system for predicting outcomes of vancomycin therapy for respiratory infections by Staphylococcus aureus. Am J Health Syst Pharm2000;57 Suppl 2:S4–9.

59. Jeffres MN, Isakow W, Doherty JA, McKinnon PS, Ritchie DJ, Micek ST, et al. Predictors of mortality for methicil-lin-resistant Staphylococcus aureus health-care-asso-ciated pneumonia: specific evaluation of vancomycin pharmacokinetic indices. Chest2006;130:947–55.

60. Kasiakou SK, Sermaides GJ, Michalopoulos A, Soteriades ES, Falagas ME. Continuous versus intermittent intravenous administration of antibiotics: a meta-analy-sis of randomised controlled trials. Lancet Infect Dis2005;5:581–9.

61. Andes D, Anon J, Jacobs MR, Craig WA. Application of pharmacokinetics and pharmacodynamics to

antimicrobial therapy of respiratory tract infections. Clin Lab Med2004;24:477–502.

62. van Zanten AR, Polderman KH, van Geijlswijk IM, van der Meer GY, Schouten MA, Girbes AR. Ciprofloxacin pharmacokinetics in critically ill patients: a prospective cohort study. J Crit Care2008;23:422–30.

63. Lipman J, Scribante J, Gous AG, Hon H, Tshukutsoane S. Pharmacokinetic profiles of high-dose intravenous ciprofloxacin in severe sepsis. The Baragwanath Ciprofloxacin Study Group. Antimicrob Agents Chemother1998;42:2235–9.

64. Burgess DS. Pharmacodynamic principles of antimicro-bial therapy in the prevention of resistance. Chest1999;115(3 Suppl):19S-23S.

65. Thomas JK, Forrest A, Bhavnani SM, Hyatt JM, Cheng A, Ballow CH, et al. Pharmacodynamic evaluation of factors associated with the development of bacterial resistance in acutely ill patients during therapy. Antimicrob Agents Chemother1998;42:521–7.

66. Zhao X, Drlica K. Restricting the selection of antibiotic-resistant mutant bacteria: measurement and potential use of the mutant selection window. J Infect Dis2002;185:561–5.

Julie M. Varghese, Jason A. Roberts and Jeffrey Lipman

Avoiding toxicity of antibiotics

Antibiotics are commonly used in intensive care units. The toxicities associated with antibiotics are many and the incidence and severity of the different reactions vary depending on the different classes of antibiotics and particular drugs within each class.

Table 1 provides basic definitions and terminology that relate to this topic of antibiotic toxicities and adverse drug reactions [1–3].

Immunologically mediated adverse drug reactions can be further characterised according to the Gell & Coombs classification [4] (see Tab. 2).

In patients with existing adverse drug reactions, re-dosing with the causative agent is sometimes required in the absence of other alternative therapies. Drugs may be "re-challenged" or "desensitised" depending on the previous response to the drug. Re-challenge is the term used to describe the re-commencement or re-exposure of a drug in a patient who has had a previous reaction to the agent [5]. For less severe, non-IgE-mediated reactions (for example morbilliform or maculopapular rash) and in the absence of therapeutic alternatives, re-challenge of the agent may be considered in some circumstances. For IgE-mediated Type 1 hypersensitivity reactions only, desensitization may be considered an option

if the use of other alternative agents is not clinically possible [6, 7]. If a patient has previously developed a severe dermatological reaction such as Stevens-Johnson syndrome, future use of the drug is contraindicated and rechallenge or desensitisation should not be attempted [8].

Desensitisation protocols are available for some antibiotics including penicillins and sulfonamides and should be undertaken under careful medical supervision as there is the possibility of the ADR recurring [6]. The nature of the reaction that can occur during the desensitisation process will depend on the type of reaction that the patient experienced on previous exposure to the drug. After desensitisation, a patient should be maintained on the drug for the duration of the treatment required. The desensitisation is not permanent and the effect is usually lost within 48 hours of stopping the agent [7]. Thus, if a subsequent treatment is required after antibiotic therapy has been interrupted, then the desensitisation protocol will need to be repeated [7].

Time of onset of toxicity varies depending on the type of toxicity. Anaphylaxis, for example, usually occurs immediately [8]. Ototoxicity on the other hand may take days or weeks to develop. Some toxicities, for example, cholestatic

Tab. 1   Definitions & terminology [data from [1–3]]

Term	Definition	Characteristics	
Adverse drug reactions	Unintended drug-related events that can generally be classified into Type A & Type B reactions	**Type A reactions**	**Type B reactions**
		Predictable	Non-predictable (idiosyncratic)
		Dose-related	Unrelated to dose
		Usually reflects an excess of a drug's primary or secondary pharmacological action	Not related to the pharmacological properties of the drug
		Incidence and morbidity high	Incidence and morbidity low
		Mortality low	Mortality high
		Can be avoided with careful dosage adjustments	Cannot be avoided and may be immunologically mediated
		Examples include drug-induced toxicity, side effects and drug-drug interactions.	Examples include allergic or hypersensitivity reactions, idiosyncratic reactions & drug intolerances
Toxicity	The effects caused by high levels of the drug in the body	Usually caused by excessive dosing or impaired drug clearance	
Side effects	Adverse drug reactions that are not immunologically mediated nor related to toxic levels of the drug in the body	Usually occurs at therapeutic doses	
Allergic or hypersensitivity reactions	Reactions that are dependent on one or more immunologic mechanisms	Can be further classified according to the Gell & Coombs classification system (see Tab. 2)	
Idiosyncratic reactions	Uncharacteristic reactions not explainable in terms of known pharmacologic actions of the drug		
Drug interolerance	Undesired effect produced by the drug at therapeutic or sub-therapeutic dosages	E.g. nausea and diarrhoea caused by many antibiotics	

hepatitis associated with flucloxacillin may be related to the duration of therapy and there may be an increased risk of toxicity with prolonged therapy [9].

The severity of the different types of reactions may vary, with some reactions being considered more significant than others. For instructive purposes, haematologic adverse events (e.g. neutropenia) can be considered more serious than mild nausea. There may also be different degrees of severity; for example, dermatological reactions may range from a simple rash to the more severe skin reactions like Stevens-Johnson syndrome and toxic epidermal necrolysis (TEN) [5]. With the more severe type reactions, re-challenge of the causative agent would not be recommended [8]. The incidence of ADRs may also vary between different patient populations, with some patient groups more prone to ADRs than others. For example, there is an increased incidence of adverse reactions to trimethoprim-sulfamethoxazole in patients with HIV infection [10, 11].

In the intensive care setting, identification of drug-related adverse effects is particularly chal-

Tab. 2 Classification of immunologic hypersensitivity reactions based on the Gell and Coombs Classification System

Classification	Characteristics	Examples
Type 1	IgE-mediated Immediate hypersensitivity reactions	Urticaria Bronchospasm Anaphylaxis
Type 2	IgG- or IgM-mediated Cytotoxic hypersensitivity reactions	Haemolytic anaemia Thrombocytopenia
Type 3	Immune complex reactions involving antigen-antibody immune complexes	Serum sickness Drug fever
Type 4	Delayed-type hypersensitivity reactions Mediated by T-cells	Contact dermatitis

lenging. Disease pathophysiology, organ dysfunction and commencement of multiple drug therapies at similar times makes it difficult for the clinician to identify whether an observed symptom is in fact a drug-related adverse effect and if so, which drug is likely to be causative. Some drug-related adverse effects that occur may go unrecognised when the symptoms and signs of the reaction are incorrectly identified or diagnosed as a new or worsening medical condition and treated as such.

Critically ill patients with renal or hepatic impairment are at increased risk of developing antibiotic toxicities due to impaired drug clearance or metabolism. Dosage adjustments in critically ill patients with organ failure can minimise the likelihood of Type A adverse drug events which are mainly dose-related toxicities. Therapeutic drug monitoring (TDM) of antibiotics is recommended where possible not only to maximise efficacy but also to minimise toxicities associated with antibiotics. TDM is also useful to assist identification of whether an observed symptom is likely to be caused by a particular drug.

Another factor which complicates identification of drug-related adverse effects for clinicians is the low level of research conducted on drug-related adverse effects (both toxicities and hypersensitivities) in critically ill patients. Most data that exists on drug-related adverse effects is derived from pharmaceutical company-run drug registration trials in healthy volunteers and distinct patient populations or from post-marketing surveillance. The frequency and nature of drug-related

adverse effects in critically ill patients is extrapolated from such data and therefore may not be accurate. Indeed the likelihood of drugs commonly used in the ICU causing drug-related adverse effects thus far unrecognised, such as pulmonary, renal or other organ toxicity, may be quite high. Although it is not within the scope of this chapter to resolve these issues, this chapter does aim to focus on what are considered to be the most common and most significant toxicities for each class of antibiotic. Table 3 summarises the incidence and severity of adverse effects documented for antibacterial, antiviral and antifungal classes of drugs.

Antibacterials

Beta-lactams

The most commonly reported adverse drug reactions to penicillins and cephalosporins include rash and nausea. A rash is common with penicillins while true anaphylaxis reactions are rare, typically only occurring in 0.01% of people [12]. If possible, a thorough history of any previous allergic reactions should be obtained and documented, particularly including details such as the exact nature and type of reaction that has occurred in the past. There is a 5–10% risk of cross-sensitivity between penicillins and cephalosporins [13]. Aztreonam (the only monobactam antibiotic) does not significantly cross-react with penicillins or cephalosporins (except for ceftazidime) [14]. In some cases of patients with a pre-

Tab. 3   The incidence and severity of adverse effects for various antibacterial, antiviral and antifungal drugs

Antibacterials				
	Adverse effects	Incidence	Severity	Comments
Penicillins	Anaphylaxis	+	+++	
	Dermatological toxicity	+++	+	Rash and urticaria
	Haematological toxicity	++	++	Blood dyscrasias including haemolytic anaemia
	Nephrotoxicity	++	++	Acute interstitial nephritis
	Neurotoxicity	+	+++	Seizures with high doses of penicillins
	Hepatotoxicity	+++	++	Cholestatic hepatitis with flucloxacillin and dicloxacillin
	Electrolyte abnormalities	++	++	High sodium content in some parenteral penicillins
	Fever	+++	+	
	Diarrhoea	+++	++	
Cephalosporins	Anaphylaxis	+	+++	
	Dermatological toxicity	+++	+	Rash
	Haematological toxicity	++	++	Neutropenia, thrombocytopenia, haemolytic anaemia
	Nephrotoxicity	++	++	Acute interstitial nephritis
	Hepatotoxicity	++	++	Elevated liver function tests
	Fever	+++	+	
	Diarrhoea	+++	++	
Carbapenems	Anaphylaxis	+	+++	
	Dermatological toxicity	++	+	Rash
	Haematological toxicity	++	++	Blood dyscrasias
	Nephrotoxicity	++	++	
	Neurotoxicity	+	+++	Seizures with imipenem and ertapenem
	Hepatotoxicity	++	++	Elevated liver function tests
	Fever	++	+	
	Diarrhoea	+++	++	
Aminoglycosides	Anaphylaxis	+	+++	
	Nephrotoxicity	+++	+++	Acute tubular necrosis
	Ototoxicity	+++	+++	Vestibular & cochlear ototoxicity
	Neurotoxicity		+++	Neuromuscular junction blockade with rapid infusions

Antibacterials				
	Adverse effects	Incidence	Severity	Comments
Glycopeptides	Anaphylaxis	+	+++	
	Nephrotoxicity	++	+	
	Haematologic toxicity	+	++	Thrombocytopenia, leucopenia, neutropenia
	Ototoxicity	+	++	
	Red man syndrome		++	Infusion rate-related reaction that occurs with rapid infusions
Lincosamides	Anaphylaxis	+	+++	
	Diarrhoea	+++	++	*C.difficile*-associated diarrhoea
	Hepatotoxicity	++	+	Elevated liver enzymes
	Haematological toxicity	+	++	Blood dyscrasias
Macrolides	Anaphylaxis	+	+++	
	Neurotoxicity	+	+++	Seizures
	Cardiotoxicity	+++	+++	QT Prolongation with erythromycin & clarithromycin
	Hepatotoxicity	++	+	Cholestatic hepatitis
	Diarrhoea	++	+++	
Quinolones	Anaphylaxis	+	+++	
	Nephrotoxicity	++	++	Acute interstitial nephritis
	Neurotoxicity	+	+++	Seizures with ciprofloxacin
	Cardiotoxicity	++	+++	QT Prolongation with moxifloxacin
	Hepatotoxicity	++	+	Elevated liver enzymes
	Diarrhoea	++	+++	
	Tendon damage	++	++	Tendonitis and rarely tendon rupture
Co-Trimoxazole	Anaphylaxis	+	+++	
	Haematologic	++	++	Neutropenia, thrombocytopenia
	Nephrotoxicity	++	++	Acute interstitial nephritis
	Dermatological	+++	+++	Rare but serious Stevens-Johnson syndrome, toxic epidermal necrolysis
	Neurotoxicity	+	++	Headache, drowsiness, lowered mental acuity
	Hepatotoxicity	+	+	Hepatitis
	Electrolyte abnormalities	+++	++	Hyperkalaemia
	Fever	+++	+	
	Diarrhoea	+++	++	

Antibacterials				
	Adverse effects	**Incidence**	**Severity**	**Comments**
Linezolid	Haematological	++	++	Thrombocytopenia, leucopenia, neutropenia
	Anaphylaxis	+	+++	
	Neurotoxicity	++	++	Optical/peripheral neuropathy with long-term use (>4 weeks)
	Diarrhoea	++	++	
Colistin	Nephrotoxicity	+++	++	Acute tubular necrosis
	Neurotoxicty	+++	++	Paraesthesia, dizziness, ataxia, confusion, visual effects
Antivirals				
Aciclovir	Nephrotoxicity	++	+++	Obstructive nephropathy
	Anaphylaxis	+	+++	
	Neurotoxicity	+	++	Hallucinations, seizures
Ganciclovir	Haematological toxicity	+++	+++	Neutropenia, thrombocytopenia, anaemia
	Neurotoxicity	++	++	Hallucinations, seizures
	Hepatotoxicity	++	+	Raised liver enzymes
Antifungals				
Azoles	Anaphylaxis	+	+++	
	Cardiotoxicity	++	+++	QT Prolongation
	Hepatotoxicity	++	++	Elevated liver enzymes
	Dermatological toxicity	++	+	Rash is common
Amphotericin	Anaphylaxis	+	+++	
	Nephrotoxicity	+++	+++	Acute tubular necrosis
	Haematological	+++	++	Anaemia is common
	Fever	+++	++	Fever may be part of infusion-related reactions
	Electrolyte abnormalities	+++	++	Hypokalaemia & hypomagnesaemia
Echinocandins	Fever	+++	++	
	Anaphylaxis	+	+++	

The incidence of a particular adverse drug reaction is rated as follows:
+ (rare – incidence of less than 0.1 %)
++ (infrequent – incidence between 0.1 % and 1 %)
+++ (common – incidence of 1 % or more)
The severity of a particular adverse drug reaction is rated as follows:
+ (mild – not requiring treatment)
++ (moderate – requiring treatment or hospitalisation *or* resulting in non-permanent disability)
+++ (severe – potentially life-threatening reaction *or* resulting in permanent disability)
The classification of severity in Table 3 *refers to the worst-case scenario of a particular adverse drug reaction.*

vious Type I hypersensitivity reaction to penicillin where the use of an alternative agent is not possible, desensitisation may be considered [6, 7].

Haematologic adverse events such as neutropaenia, thrombocytopaenia and haemolytic anaemia are rare but possible adverse effects associated with the beta-lactam antibiotics. Ticarcillin, and to a lesser extent, piperacillin, when given in high doses may cause bleeding abnormalities that can include extended bleeding times and impaired platelet aggregation [15, 16].

Electrolyte disturbances are possible particularly with high parenteral doses. The penicillins are formulated as sodium salts for injection and some penicillins such as benzylpenicillin, piperacillin and ticarcillin have a high sodium content. For instance, each 3 g ticarcillin with 100 mg clavulanic acid contains 15.6 mmol or 360 mg of sodium and this should be considered especially in patients who are sodium-restricted [17].

Neurotoxicity is a possible adverse effect of this class and can manifest as confusion, twitching and myoclonus. Beta-lactam antibiotics can also induce seizures and this is dependent on the seizure threshold of the patient as well as the effect of the drug on the CNS receptors [18]. Rapid administration of large doses of intravenous penicillins should be avoided as it may result in seizures. Dose adjustment of penicillins is required in severe renal impairment as excessively high doses may also contribute to seizures [19].

Flucloxacillin more frequently than dicloxacillin may cause cholestatic hepatitis and there is an increased risk in the elderly (> 55 years) and with treatment courses of greater than 2 weeks [9]. Thrombophlebitis is common with the IV administration of dicloxacillin [20]. Acute interstitial nephritis, drug fevers and serum sickness-like syndromes are other rare adverse effects that have also been reported with the penicillins and cephalosporins.

Carbapenems

The carbapenems are broad-spectrum antimicrobial agents commonly used in the ICU setting. In patients with a history of penicillin allergy, the cross-sensitivity between penicillins and carbapenems has been reported to be between 9.2 and 11 % [14].

Neurotoxicity is one of the main adverse effects of the carbapenems. There is a 3 % reported risk of seizures with imipinem-cilastatin [21]. Imipenem is associated with seizures particularly when administered at high doses and in patients with pre-existing CNS disorders or renal impairment [21]. Dosage adjustment is required in patients with renal impairment. The concurrent use of imipenem with other drugs that can lower the seizure threshold should be avoided where possible. Meropenem has lesser neurotoxic effects and is considered appropriate for treatment of some forms of meningitis [22, 23]. Doripenem, a newly released carbapenem is reported to have the least neurotoxic effects [24].

Other less common adverse effects related to the use of carbapenems include blood dyscrasias and elevated liver function tests [22]. Monitoring of renal and hepatic function and complete blood counts are essential during treatment with carbapenems particularly with prolonged therapy.

Aminoglycosides

Nephrotoxicity and ototoxicity are the two main toxicities associated with the use of aminoglycosides. The incidence of aminoglycoside-related nephrotoxicity ranges from 5 to 25 % in most studies depending on the criteria used to define its occurence [25]. Aminoglycoside-associated nephrotoxicity is a Type A ADR and may develop within 5–10 days of initiation of the drug and typically presents as non-oliguric renal failure [26]. Renal failure is usually reversible after cessation of therapy although renal replacement therapy may be required until renal function improves [26]. Aminoglycoside-related nephrotoxicity is associated with the dose, duration of treatment and concurrent use of other nephrotoxic agents [27]. Other potential risk factors include decreased renal blood flow, volume depletion, pre-existing renal dysfunction and age [27].

Ototoxicity (both vestibular and cochlear) is difficult to diagnose in ICU patients and is generally irreversible [28]. Reported incidence in the literature varies between 2 % and 25 % and the true incidence is difficult to determine [28]. Some patients may have a genetic predisposition to ototoxicity and it has been shown that this is mediated by specific mutations in mitochondrial DNA [29].

Neuromuscular blockade that may result in respiratory depression can rarely occur, especially with rapid bolus injection of gentamicin or along with other factors such as concomitant use of neuromuscular blocking agents or in patients with pre-existing neuromuscular disease [30].

Glycopeptides

Vancomycin and teicoplanin are the two drugs in this class. Ototoxicity, nephrotoxicity and infusion rate-related reactions are the major adverse effects reported for the glycopeptides.

Glycopeptides as single-agent therapy may rarely cause hearing impairment but there is an increased risk with prolonged treatment, in patients with renal impairment and with concomitant ototoxic drugs (e.g. aminoglycosides) [31, 32]. Factors associated with increased risk of nephrotoxicity include concurrent treatment with aminoglycosides, prolonged treatment (> 21 days) and high vancomycin trough levels [33]. Monitoring of renal function and vancomycin trough concentrations is recommended to minimize toxicity.

"Red man syndrome" is an infusion rate-related reaction that occurs most frequently when vancomycin is administered too rapidly [34]. This is a non-immune hypersensitivity reaction for which no drug-specific antibodies are identified [35]. The "red man syndrome" is caused by a direct release of histamine after a rapid intravenous infusion of vancomycin, leading to symptoms that may include flushing of the face and neck and usually an upper torso rash. These symptoms may be treated with antihistamines [36]. Hypotension, although less common, is also a possible with the "red man syndrome" [34]. Patients who develop the "red man syndrome" can safely be administered vancomycin again but the infusion time should be extended to minimise this infusion-related reaction [37]. The incidence of "red man syndrome" is considered to have decreased over the past 30 years with the advent of newer formulations of vancomycin.

Lincosamides

Antimicrobial-associated diarrhoea is one of the most frequent adverse effects associated with the use of clindamycin. *Clostridium difficile* is the main causative organism identified in hospitalised patients and in severe cases is associated with pseudomembranous colitis [38, 39]. In the ICU setting there may be other causes of diarrhoea including other medications, other underlying medical conditions and the use of nutritional supplements. Early recognition of *C.difficile*-associated diarrhoea is essential to ensure prompt treatment with oral or IV metronidazole or oral vancomycin [39, 40]. Antidiarrhoeal agents should be avoided.

When administered intravenously, lincosamides should be infused slowly (over at least 1 hour) as rapid injection can lead to cardiac effects such as hypotension and cardiac arrest [41]. Other rare adverse effects of lincosamides include blood dyscrasias and hepatotoxicity.

Macrolides

Erythromycin and clarithromycin can prolong the QT interval leading to ventricular arrhythmias (e.g. torsades de pointes) [42]. Concomitant use of other drugs that also prolong the QT interval should be avoided if possible or used with careful monitoring. If the QT interval is > 500 millisec or if the interval increases by > 60 millisec over the baseline, the drug should be discontinued and replaced by an alternative [43]. Other factors that can also prolong the QT interval include electrolyte disturbances (e.g. hypokalaemia) and structural heart disease (e.g. coronary heart disease) [44]. Slow IV infusion is recommended as rapid IV administration of erythromycin can result in prolonged QT interval and the development of serious ventricular arrhythmias [45].

Macrolides also interact with many drugs and can cause clinically significant drug interactions by acting as inhibitors of CYP3A4. The potential for drug interactions are as follows (in decreasing order): erythromycin > clarithromycin > roxithromycin > azithromycin [46]. CYP3A4 inhibition will lead to increased plasma concentrations of CYP3A4 substrates causing Type A adverse drug reactions of these compounds.

The parenteral formulation of erythromycin can cause thrombophlebitis and should be diluted to a concentration of 1–5 mg/ml and infused over 60 minutes, or slowly via a central vein where possible [45]. Transient hearing loss can occur with the administration of large intravenous doses of erythromycin [32].

Quinolones

Possible toxicities associated with the quinolone class of antibiotics include neurotoxicity, nephrotoxicity and cardiotoxicity. The incidence of CNS adverse effects with quinolones is between 1 and 2 % and includes symptoms like dizziness, headache, somnolence and rarely seizures [47]. Among the quinolones, ciprofloxacin can induce seizures and should be used cautiously in patients with epilepsy or a history of CNS disorders.

Quinolones, especially ciprofloxacin, can be one of the causes of drug-induced acute interstitial nephritis. This is a rare, idiosyncratic hypersensitivity reaction that is non-dose-dependent. Discontinuation of the drug is required [26].

Gatifloxacin, levofloxacin and moxifloxacin have been reported to prolong the QT-interval and this may result in ventricular arrhythmias (including torsades de pointes) [44, 47]. Ciprofloxacin remains the safest quinolone in terms of QT prolongation [47].

Quinolones have also been reported to cause tendonitis and rarely tendon rupture, with the Achilles tendon the most common site of injury [47]. The risk of tendon growth retardation in paediatrics is well recognised, as is the increased risk of damage in the elderly and in athletes in training as well as persons using corticosteroids [47, 48]. In patients with renal impairment, dosage adjustment of ciprofloxacin and norfloxacin will be required to potentially reduce the risk of this adverse effect.

Trimethoprim + sulfamethoxazole (co-trimoxazole)

Drug-induced haematological adverse effects which include neutropenia and thrombocytopenia can occur with trimethoprim-sulfamethoxazole [49]. Monitoring of complete blood count is required particularly during prolonged or high-dose treatment. Dose adjustment is required in renal impairment to avoid drug accumulation. Hyperkalaemia can occur especially with higher doses and in patients with renal impairment as trimethoprim causes the retention of potassium.

Trimethoprim-sulfamethoxazole is contraindicated in patients who have a history of serious allergic reaction to trimethoprim or sulphonamides and related drugs (e.g. sulfonylureas, celecoxib and thiazide diuretics which all possess the sulphonamide moiety as part of their chemical structure). Patients allergic to trimethoprim-sulfamethoxazole in whom the use of this agent is considered clinically necessary may require desensitisation, and desensitisation protocols are available for this drug [7, 50]. HIV infection increases the incidence of allergic reactions to trimethoprim-sulfamethoxazole and desensitisation may allow for trimethoprim-sulfamethoxazole to be reintroduced in this group of patients [11, 50]. Severe skin reactions, for example, Stevens-Johnson syndrome and toxic epidermal necrolysis, are rare but potentially serious and life-threatening reactions, and the antibiotic should be stopped immediatedly and the patient should never be re-challenged with the same agent [51].

Linezolid

Linezolid is an oxazolidinone antibacterial that has a weak, reversible, non-selective monoamine oxidase (MAO) inhibitory activity. For this reason there is an increased likelihood of serotonin syndrome when linezolid is administered with other serotonergic drugs [52]. Where a patient is on a high dose of serotonergic agents (e.g. antidepressants), the dose should be tapered or reduced where possible before linezolid is initiated and the patient then carefully monitored for any signs of serotonin syndrome [52]. The use of other drugs such as tramadol and pethidine which can also contribute to serotonin toxicity should be avoided in patients on linezolid [53].

Haematologic adverse effects including thrombocytopenia, neutropenia and anaemia are the other major toxicity associated with linezolid use [54]. This myelosuppression caused by linezolid is usually reversible after discontinuation of the drug. Regular haematologic monitoring (at least once weekly) is recommended especially in patients receiving more than 14 days treatment with linezolid and those with pre-existing myelosuppression [54]. Other rare adverse effects of the drug include optic or peripheral neuropathy with linezolid therapy over 4 weeks [55].

Colistin

Colistin belongs to the polymyxin class of antibacterials and is used to treat infections caused by multi-drug-resistant Gram-negative organisms. Colistin may be administered intravenously or via the inhaled route [56, 57]. The most common systemic adverse effects reported in the early literature are nephrotoxicity and neurotoxicity with an incidence of about 20 % and 7 % respectively; however, more recent studies suggest that the incidence may be lower [58, 59]. Colistin can have a direct effect on the kidneys causing acute tubular necrosis [59]. Administration of colistin can also cause haematuria and proteinuria [58, 59]. Concomitant administration of other nephrotoxic drugs increases the risks of developing acute renal failure. Early discontinuation of the drug is necessary if acute renal failure develops in association with the use of colistin [58].

The neurotoxic effects of colistin include paraesthesia, dizziness, ataxia, confusion and visual disturbances, all of which may not be easily detected in critically ill patients [59]. Neuromuscular blockade which can lead to respiratory failure is also possible with the use of colistin [59]. Colistin administered via the inhaled route may cause bronchospasm or cough [56, 57, 60]. Bronchodilators can be used before each dose of nebulised colistin to prevent bronchospasm [61].

Antivirals

Aciclovir

Nephrotoxicity and neurological adverse effects have been reported with the use of aciclovir. High-dose IV aciclovir treatment may lead to crystal formation in the renal tubules resulting in obstructive nephropathy [62, 63]. The incidence of aciclovir-induced renal failure is reported to be between 12 % and 48 % [62]. Adequate hydration is important to maintain urinary flow and minimise crystal deposition in patients receiving IV aciclovir especially in high doses [62, 63]. Patients

who are at high risk of developing aciclovir-induced nephrotoxicity are those whose are fluid-depleted, those with pre-existing renal impairment and those receiving large doses of the drug [62]. Rapid intravenous bolus administration of aciclovir is also associated with nephrotoxicity, thus a slow IV infusion over 1–2 hours is recommended to avoid renal tubular damage [62, 64]. Acute renal failure that develops during treatment with aciclovir usually responds to rehydration, dosage reduction or cessation of the drug [62, 64].

Ganciclovir

Haematological toxicities including neutropenia, thrombocytopenia and anaemia are common adverse effects associated with ganciclovir [65, 66]. Complete blood count monitoring is required [67]. Neutropenia usually develops during the first 1–2 weeks of treatment and is generally dose-dependent and reversible [66]. Treatment should be stopped temporarily if severe neutropenia or thrombocytopenia occurs.

CNS adverse effects of ganciclovir range from headache and confusion to hallucinations and seizures [66]. Concurrent treatment with imipenem may increase the risk of seizures, thus the combination should be avoided [66–68]. Other possible adverse effects include raised liver enzymes and increased serum creatinine and blood urea concentrations [67]. Dosage adjustment is required in renal impairment [66].

Ganciclovir is considered to be carcinogenic and special handling using standard cytotoxic precautions will be required to protect staff [66].

Antifungals

Azoles

Azole antifungals interact with many drugs mainly through its action as a CYP450 enzyme inhibitor. Different azole antifungal agents have specificity for different CYP450 isoenzymes. Fluconazole inhibits CYP2C9 and CYP3A4 whilst most of the other azoles mainly inhibit CYP3A4 [69]. The potential for clinically significant drug interactions needs to be considered when azole antifungals are prescribed.

Elevated liver enzymes are common with the azole antifungals, and monitoring of liver function tests is warranted as hepatitis and hepatic failure can also occur less commonly [70, 71]. Ketoconazole, itraconazole, fluconazole and voriconazole may cause prolongation of the QT interval and concurrent use with other QT-prolonging drugs should be avoided due to increased risk of arrhythmia [44].

Fluconazole and voriconazole are available in intravenous injection form. The intravenous route of administration of voriconazole should be avoided if creatinine clearance is less than 50ml/min as the solvent in the injection formulation of voriconazole accumulates [71]. Voriconazole has also been reported to cause visual changes in up to 20% of patients; however, these are generally dose-related and reversible and usually resolve within an hour of dose administration [71]. Therapeutic drug monitoring for itraconazole, posaconazole and voriconazole is an option to ensure therapeutic drug levels and also to monitor for toxicity due to drug accumulation [72].

Amphotericin

The two main toxicities associated with amphotericin are nephrotoxicity and infusion-related reactions. Amphotericin is available in a number of different formulations including conventional amphotericin, amphotericin lipid complex and liposomal amphotericin [73–75]. Prescribers need to be careful when prescribing amphotericin to specify exactly which formulation is intended as the different forms have different dosing and infusion rates. Some of the adverse effects related to amphotericin occur at different rates depending on the different formulations used [76].

Nephrotoxicity is greatest with the conventional formulation of amphotericin compared to the lipid complex and liposomal formulations [77]. Treatment with other nephrotoxic agents (e.g. aminoglycosides, cyclosporin) may increase the likelihood of renal impairment with amphotericin [78]. Nephrotoxicity can be minimised by pre-hydration with 1L 0.9% sodium chloride daily before intravenous administration of amphotericin [79, 80]. In situations where nephrotoxicity is to be prevented, the conventional amphotericin formulation should be avoided and

the lipid complex or liposomal formulation of amphotericin or an alternative antifungal agent that is less nephrotoxic should be considered instead [26, 78, 81].

Infusion-related reactions such as fevers, chills and hypotension are common particularly with the conventional formulation of amphotericin but occurs less frequently with the newer formulations [73]. These reactions are most pronounced initially during treatment but lessen with repeated infusions of amphotericin. Paracetamol, antihistamines and hydrocortisone can be used to prevent or treat infusion reactions.

Hypokalaemia and hypomagnesaemia can occur as a result of the renal tubular damage cause by amphotericin [81]. Other adverse effects associated with amphotericin include blood dyscrasias and hepatotoxicity, hence monitoring of complete blood count and hepatic function is also recommended [73].

Echinocandins

Caspofungin, micafungin and anidulafungin are the three drugs in the echinocandin class of antifungal agents [82]. Caspofungin may cause infusion-related chills and fever as well as phlebitis at the injection site [83]. Rarely caspofungin can cause a possible histamine-mediated reaction that may include anaphylaxis, bronchospasm or facial swelling [83]. To avoid such effects, it is recommended that caspofungin be administered as an IV infusion over 60 minutes [83].

Dosing adjustments for caspofungin will be required in hepatic impairment; however, no dose modification is required in renal failure [84]. Among the antifungal agents, the echinocandins have a lower risk of toxicity compared to amphotericin [82]. There is also a lesser risk of drug interactions with the echinocandins compared to the azole antifungals [84].

Conclusions

Clinicians need to be aware of the incidence and severity of the various antibiotic-related toxicities. When making the decision to prescribe a drug, consideration should be given not only to the efficacy of the drug but also to its potential toxicities. Despite the significant toxicities of some drugs, their use may still be clinically appropriate when prudent monitoring is also undertaken. Risk factors that predispose patients to particular drug-related toxicities should be considered carefully and attention should be given to a patient's current clinical condition (including any renal or hepatic impairment), any pre-existing medical conditions, other concurrent medications and any potential drug interactions that may have a clinically significant impact on the potential for drug toxicity.

The authors

Julie M. Varghese, B Pharm (Hons)[1]
Jason A. Roberts, PhD, B Pharm (Hons)[1]
Jeffrey Lipman, MD, FJFICM[2]

[1]Royal Brisbane and Women's Hospital | Pharmacy Department | Intensive Care Unit | Herston Queensland, Australia | Burns Trauma and Critical Care Research Centre | The University of Queensland | Brisbane, Australia

[2]Royal Brisbane and Women's Hospital | Intensive Care Unit | Herston Queensland, Australia | Burns Trauma and Critical Care Research Centre | The University of Queensland | Brisbane, Australia

Address for correspondence
Jeffrey Lipman
Intensive Care Unit
Level 4 Ned Hanlon Building
Royal Brisbane and Women's Hospital
Butterfield St
4029 Herston Queensland, Australia
E-mail: j.lipman@uq.edu.au

References

1. Granowitz EV, Brown RB. Antibiotic adverse drug reactions and drug interactions. Critical Care Clinics 2008;24:421–442.
2. Beard K, Lee A. Introduction. In: Lee A, editor. Adverse Drug Reactions. 2 ed. London: Pharmaceutical Press; 2006.
3. Gruchalla RS. 10. Drug allergy. Journal of Allergy and Clinical Immunology 2003;111(2, Supplement 2):S48–S559.
4. Pichler WJ. Immune mechanism of drug hypersensitivity. Immunol Allergy Clin North Am 2004;24(3):373–397.
5. McKenna JK, Leiferman KM. Dermatologic drug reactions. Immunol Allergy Clin North Am 2004;24(3):399–423.
6. Castells M, Castells M. Desensitization for drug allergy. Curr Opin Allergy Clin Immunol 2006;6(6):476–481.
7. Solensky R, Solensky R. Drug desensitization. Immunol Allergy Clin North Am 2004;24(3):425–443.
8. Volcheck G. Clinical evaluation and management of drug hypersensitivity. Immunol Allergy Clin North Am 2004;24(3):357–371.
9. Devereaux BM, Crawford DH, Purcell P, et al. Flucloxacillin associated cholestatic hepatitis. An Australian and Swedish epidemic? Eur J Clin Pharmacol 1995;49(1–2):81–85.
10. van der Ven AJ, Koopmans PP, Vree TB, et al. Drug intolerance in HIV disease. J Antimicrob Chemother 1994;34(1):1–5.
11. Temesgen Z, Beri G. HIV and drug allergy. Immunol Allergy Clin North Am 2004;24(3):521–531.
12. Idsoe O, Guthe E, Willcox RR, et al. Nature and extent of penicillin side-reactions with particular reference to fatalities from anaphylactic shock. Bull World Health Organ 1968;38:159–188.
13. Kelkar PS, Li JTC. Cephalosporin Allergy. N Engl J Med 2001;345(11):804–809.
14. Frumin J, Gallagher JC. Allergic Cross-Sensitivity Between Penicillin, Carbapenem, and Monobactam Antibiotics: What Are the Chances? Ann Pharmacother 2009;43(2):304–315.
15. Brown C, Natelson E, Bradshaw M, et al. Study of the effects of ticarcillin on blood coagulation and platelet function. Antimicrob Agents Chemother 1975;7(5):652–657.
16. Gentry L, Jamsek J, Natelson E. Effect of sodium piperacillin on platelet function in normal volunteers. Antimicrob Agents Chemother 1981;19(4):532–533.
17. MIMS Australia, Timentin Product Information.
18. Chow KM, Hui AC, Szeto CC. Neurotoxicity induced by beta-lactam antibiotics: from bench to bedside. Eur J Clin Microbiol Infect Dis 2005;24(10):649–653.
19. Schliamser SE, Cars O, Norrby SR. Neurotoxicity of {beta}-lactam antibiotics: predisposing factors and pathogenesis. J Antimicrob Chemother 1991;27(4):405–425.
20. Diclocil injection (Dicloxacillin) [package insert]. Noble Park (VIC): Bristol-Myers Squibb Pharmaceuticals; 1998.
21. Calandra G, Lydick E, Carrigan J, et al. Factors predisposing to seizures in seriously III infected patients receiving antibiotics: Experience with imipenem/ cilastatin. The American Journal of Medicine 1988;84(5):911–918.
22. Linden P. Safety profile of meropenem: an updated review of over 6,000 patients treated with meropenem. Drug Saf 2007;30(8):657–668.
23. Norrby SR. Neurotoxicity of carbapenem antibiotics:

consequences for their use in bacterial meningitis. J Antimicrob Chemother 2000;45(1):5–7.

24. Horiuchi M, Kimura M, Tokumura M, et al. Absence of convulsive liability of doripenem, a new carbapenem antibiotic, in comparison with {beta}-lactam antibiotics. Toxicology 2006;222(1–2):114–124.

25. Hock R, Anderson RJ. Prevention of drug-induced nephrotoxicity in the intensive care unit. Journal of Critical Care 1995;10(1):33–43.

26. Pannu N, Nadim MK. An overview of drug-induced acute kidney injury. Critical Care Medicine 2008;36(4 Suppl):S216–223.

27. Appel GB. Aminoglycoside nephrotoxicity. The American Journal of Medicine 1990;88(3, Supplement 3):S16-S20.

28. Rizzi MD, Hirose K. Aminoglycoside ototoxicity. Curr Opin Otolaryngol Hed Neck Surg 2007;15(5):352–357.

29. Hu DN, Qui WQ, Wu BT, et al. Genetic aspects of antibiotic induced deafness: mitochondrial inheritance. J Med Genet 1991;28(2):79–83.

30. Gentamicin Injection BP [package insert].Bentley (WA): Pfizer (Perth) Pty Ltd;2005.

31. Wilson APR. Comparative safety of teicoplanin and vancomycin. Antimicrob Agents 1998;10(2):143–152.

32. Brummett RE, Fox KE. Vancomycin- and erythromycin-induced hearing loss in humans. Antimicrob Agents Chemother 1989;33(6):791–796.

33. Rybak MJ, Albrecht LM, Boike SC, et al. Nephrotoxicity of vancomycin, alone and with an aminoglycoside. J Antimicrob Chemother 1990;25(4):679–687.

34. Sivagnanam S, Deleu D. Red man syndrome. Critical Care 2003;7(2):119–120.

35. Demoly P, Hillaire-Buys D. Classification and epidemiology of hypersensitivity drug reactions. Immunol Allergy Clin North Am 2004;24(3):345–357.

36. Renz CL, Thurn JD, Finn HA, et al. Oral antihistamines reduce the side effects from rapid vancomycin infusion. Anesth Analg 1998;87(3):681–685.

37. Wlihelm MP, Estes LPD. Symposium on Antimicrobial Agents-PartXII.Vancomycin. Mayo Clin Proc 1999;74:928–935.

38. Bartlett JG. Narrative Review: The New Epidemic of Clostridium difficile-Associated Enteric Disease. Ann Intern Med 2006;145(10):758–764.

39. Kelly CP, Pothoulakis C, LaMont JT. Clostridium difficile Colitis. N Engl J Med 1994;330(4):257–262.

40. Johnson S, Gerding DN. Clostridium difficile Associated Diarrhea. Clinical Inf Dis 1998;26(5):1027–1034.

41. Aucoin P, Beckner RR, Gantz NM. Clindamycin-induced cardiac arrest. South Med J 1982;75(6):768.

42. Kao LW, Furbee RB. Drug-induced Q-T prolongation. Med Clin North Am 2005;89:1125–1144.

43. European Medicines Agency. The Clinical Evaluation of QT/QTc Interval Prolongation and Proarrhythmic Potential for Non-Antiarrhythmic Drugs [cited 2009 February 14]

Available from: http://www.emea.europa.eu/pdfs/human/ich/000204en.pdf

44. Owens RC, Jr. QT prolongation with antimicrobial agents: understanding the significance. Drugs 2004;64(10):1091–1124.

45. Erythrocin IV [package insert].Mosman(NSW):Link Medical Products Pty Ltd;2008.

46. von Rosenstiel N-A, Adam D. Macrolide Antibacterials: Drug Interactions of Clinical Significance. Drug Saf 1995;13(2):105–122.

47. Owens RC, Jr, Ambrose PG. Antimicrobial Safety: Focus on Fluoroquinolones. Clin Inf Dis 2005;41(s2):S144–S157.

48. Mehlhorn AJ, Brown DA. Safety Concerns with Fluoroquinolones. Ann Pharmacother 2007;41(11):1859–1866.

49. Aster RH, Bougie DW. Drug-Induced Immune Thrombocytopenia. N Engl J Med 2007;357(6):580–587.

50. Slatore CG, Tilles SA. Sulfonamide hypersensitivity. Immunol Allergy Clin North Am 2004;24(3):477–490.

51. Roujeau JC, Stern RS. Severe Adverse Cutaneous Reactions to Drugs. N Engl J Med 1994;331(19):1272–1285.

52. Bergeron L, Boule M, Perreault S. Serotonin Toxicity Associated with Concomitant Use of Linezolid. Ann Pharmacother 2005;39(5):956–961.

53. Bishop E, Melvani S, Howden BP, et al. Good Clinical Outcomes but High Rates of Adverse Reactions during Linezolid Therapy for Serious Infections: a Proposed Protocol for Monitoring Therapy in Complex Patients. Antimicrob Agents Chemother 2006;50(4):1599–1602.

54. Kuter DJ, Tillotson GS. Hematologic effects of antimicrobials:focus on the oxazolidinone linezolid. Pharmacotherapy 2001;21(8):1010–1013.

55. Corallo CE, Paull AE. Linezolid-induced neuropathy. Med J Aust 2002;177(6):332.

56. Falagas ME, Kasiakou SK. Colistin: The Revival of Polymyxins for the Management of Multidrug Resistant Gram Negative Bacterial Infections. Clin Inf Dis 2005;40(9):1333–1341.

57. Michalopoulos A, Kasiakou S, Mastora Z, et al. Aerosolized colistin for the treatment of nosocomial pneumonia due to multidrug-resistant Gram-negative bacteria in patients without cystic fibrosis. Crit Care 2005;9(1):R53 – R59.

58. Falagas ME, Kasiakou SK, Falagas ME, et al. Toxicity of polymyxins: a systematic review of the evidence from old and recent studies. Crit Care 2006;10(1):R27.

59. Koch-Weser J, Sidel VW, Federman EB, et al. Adverse Effects of Sodium Colistimethate. Annals of Internal Medicine 1970;72(6):857–868.

60. Madison J, Dodd M, Webb AK. Nebulized colistin causes chest tightness in adults with cystic fibrosis. Resp Med 1994;88(2):145–147.

61. Cunningham S, Prasad A, Collyer L, et al. Short report: Bronchoconstriction following nebulised colistin in cystic fibrosis. Arch Dis Child 2001;84(5):432–433.

62. Perazella MA. Crystal-induced acute renal failure. Am J Med 1999;106(4):459–465.

63. Izzedine H, Launay-Vacher V, Deray G. Antiviral drug-induced nephrotoxicity. Am J Kidney Dis 2005;45(5):804–817.

64. Aciclovir Intravenous Infusion (DBL) [package insert]. Melbourne (VIC):Hospira Australia Pty Ltd; 2004.

65. Crumpacker CS. Ganciclovir. N Engl J Med 1996;335(10):721–729.

66. Cymevene (ganciclovir) [package insert]. Dee Why (NSW): Roche Pty Ltd; 2006.

67. Noble S, Faulds D. Ganciclovir: An Update of its Use in the Prevention of Cytomegalovirus Infection and Disease in Transplant Recipients. Drugs 1998;56(1):115–146.

68. Primaxin [package insert]. Granville (NSW):Merck Sharp & Dohme (Aust.) Pty Ltd; 2007.

69. Gregg CR. Drug interactions and anti-infective therapies. The American Journal of Medicine 1999;106(2):227–237.

70. Diflucan (fluconazole) [package insert]. West Ryde (NSW):Pfizer Australia Pty Ltd;2006.

71. Vfend (Voriconazole) [package insert]. West Ryde (NSW): Pfizer Australia Pty Ltd; 2008.

72. Goodwin ML, Drew RH. Antifungal serum concentration monitoring: an update. J Antimicrob Chemother 2008;61(1):17–25.

73. Fungizone Intravenous (Amphotericin B) [package insert]. Noble Park (VIC): Bristol-Myers Squibb Pharmaceuticals; 2008.

74. Abelcet (Amphotericin B phospholipid complex) [package insert]. Berwick (VIC): Orphan Australia Pty Ltd; 2004.

75. AmBisome (Amphotericin B liposomal) [package insert]. East Melbourne (VIC): Gilead Sciences; 2007.

76. Chen SC, Sorrell TC. Antifungal agents. Med J Aust 2007;187(7):404–409.

77. Deray G. Amphotericin B nephrotoxicity. J Antimicrob Chemother 2002;49(suppl_1):37–41.

78. Luber AD, Maa L, Lam M, et al. Risk factors for amphotericin B- induced nephrotoxicity. J Antimicrob Chemother 1999;43(2):267–271.

79. Heidemann HT, Gerkens JF, Spickard WA, et al. Amphotericin B nephrotoxicity in humans decreased by salt repletion. Am J Med 1983;75(3):476–481.

80. Llanos A, Cieza J, Bernado J, et al. Effect of salt supplementation on amphotericin B nephrotoxicity. Kid Int 1991;40(2):302–308.

81. Taber SS, Mueller BA. Drug-associated renal dysfunction. Critical Care Clinics 2006;22(2):357–374.

82. Denning DW. Echinocandin antifungal drugs. The Lancet 2003;362(9390):1142–1151.

83. Cancidas (Caspofungin) [package insert]. Granville (NSW): Merck, Sharpe & Dohme (Aust.) Pty Ltd; 2005.

84. Wagner C, Graninger W, Presterl E, et al. The Echinocandins: Comparison of Their Pharmacokinetics, Pharmacodynamics and Clinical Applications. Pharmacology 2006;78(4):161–177.

Marta Ulldemolins, Thiago Lisboa and Jordi Rello

Frequently forgotten factors in empirical antibiotic treatment

I swear by Apollo Physician, by Asclepius, by Health, by Heal-all, and by all the gods and goddesses, making them witnesses, that I will carry out, according to my ability and judgment, this oath and this indenture (...); I will use treatment to help the sick according to my ability and judgment, but I will never use it to injure or wrong them. I will not give poison to anyone though asked to do so, nor will I suggest such a plan. But in purity and in holiness I will guard my life and my art. Into whatsoever houses I enter, I will do so to help the sick, keeping myself free from all intentional wrong-doing and harm. (...) Now if I keep this oath and break it not, may I enjoy honour, in my life and art, among all men for all time; but if I transgress and forswear myself, may the opposite befall me.

Hippocratic Oath   Hippocrates, 4th Century B.C.

Introduction

The myth of Icarus, who died trying to reach the sun with his artificial wings, reflects the inherent complexity of the human being that can lead to fatal consequences when pros and cons of our decisions are not sufficiently evaluated. Since ever, the physicians have been devoting their efforts to the complex task of fighting illness. However, they must not make the same mistake as Icarus, and measure carefully the optimal conditions of a therapy or procedure to, firstly, follow the Hippocratic instructions and do no harm.

Certainly, patient safety is a very important issue in critical care, and international organisms such as the Institute of Healthcare Improvement (IHI), the National Institute for Health and Clinical Excellence (NICE) or the Scottish Intensive Care Society Audit Group (SICSAG) have focused their efforts on harm prevention [1, 2, 3]. These organisations have elaborated guidelines and campaign materials that make recommendations related to safety aspects such as avoidance of adverse drug events and nosocomial infections, among others [1, 2, 3]. In fact, it is known that management of ICU infections is complex due to two main points: the critical sickness of patients (which produces severe variations in their pharmacokinetic parameters) and the complexity of nosocomial pathogens (whose prevalence and multidrug-resistant patterns are steadily on the rise [4]).

The EPIC study carried out in 17 European countries evidenced that 62 % of patients admitted to the ICU received antibiotic therapy, and more than half were treated with multiple agents [5]. Consequently, the choice of empirical antibiotic therapy represents one of the most challenging therapeutic decisions faced in daily practice, and prescription care bundles are increasingly needed for optimising antibiotic management [6, 7].

Care bundles are a group of evidenced-based recommendations that, implemented together, have a higher clinical impact in the clinical outcomes than each recommendation settled individually [6]. Recent, successful experiences in the ICU setting include using these recommendations for prevention of intravascular catheter-related bloodstream infections [8] or ventilator-associated pneumonia (VAP) [9].

The ideal antibiotic care bundle would be a package of measures to be followed by the intensivist and adapted to local needs and facilities. It should also be multidisciplinary, and include other healthcare professionals such as clinical microbiologists, biochemists or pharmacists, to optimise therapy and to prevent avoidable mistakes in antibiotic prescription.

The principal objectives of an acute care antibiotic care bundle would be to select the antibiotic most likely to adequately treat the patient and to also reduce the incidence of adverse events, the emergence of bacterial resistances and Clostridium difficile infections in a patient-specific approach [6]. As early as 2003, our group published evidence-based recommendations for VAP treatment, known as the "Tarragona Strategy", where the concept of a patient-specific approach was emphasised [10]. Currently, we are working on safety in critical care and pulmonary medicine [11, 12]. The FADO study, consisting of care bundles for the prevention of VAP, is still ongoing. Further efforts on the management of nosocomial infections, including care bundles, are planned for the foreseeable future.

The aim of this chapter is to propose the main points for an antibiotic care bundle focusing on the cornerstone of optimisation policy and highlighting the most frequently forgotten factors in the use of antibiotics in critically ill patients.

Top 10 false myths and mistakes in the use of antibiotics

1. *Administer narrow-spectrum antibiotic as empirical therapy.*
2. *Delay antibiotic prescription until culture results are known.*
3. *Choose the antibiotic guided exclusively by in vitro susceptibilities.*
4. *Overlook PK/PD when defining doses and administration schedules.*
5. *Do not consider albumin serum levels when*

prescribing highly-bound antibiotics and other drugs.
6. *Fail to identify patients with increased distribution volume that will need higher doses.*
7. *Underestimate creatinine clearances when prescribing the antibiotic doses.*
8. *Use standard dosing regimens that may lead to sub-therapeutic antibiotic concentrations.*
9. *Forget local patterns of bacterial resistance in the ICU.*
10. *Unnecessarily prolong antibiotic treatment leading to colonisation by resistant pathogens.*

The first critical hours

To avoid harming the patient, antibiotic therapy covering the offending pathogen has to be initiated without delay. Delays in the initiation of appropriate antibiotic therapy have been demonstrated to impact negatively on resolution. Nonetheless, it is crucial that the empirical antibiotic treatment chosen assure coverage of the most likely pathogens. However, therapeutic choice is unlikely to be supported by the microbiologic laboratory within the first hours of diagnosis, as microbiological identification and susceptibility test usually require 48 h. Empirical antibiotic therapy stewardship should have a balanced objective that includes the susceptibility of the infectious pathogen, but limits unnecessary selection pressure.

Adding complexity to the issue is the time factor. Since Ehrlich's concept of "hit hard and fast" (1913) we know that time is a crucial but frequently forgotten aspect of antibiotic treatment. Kumar et al. [13] reported that effective antimicrobial administration within the first hour of documented hypotension was associated with increased survival at hospital discharge (80 %) in adult patients with septic shock. Despite a progressive increase in mortality rate with increasing delays (a decrease in survival of 7.6 % after the first hour), only 50 % of septic shock patients received effective antimicrobial therapy within 6 h of documented hypotension.

For instance, many studies about VAP have reported consistent findings when assessing outcomes achieved with delayed appropriate therapy [14, 15, 16, 17]. Our group [15] described that a delay in the administration of effective therapy in critically ill patients with VAP significantly increased the mortality (greater than 20%) compared with episodes that were treated early. Luna et al. [16] reported that appropriate antibiotherapy administered prior to performing the bronchoalveolar lavage was associated with a lower mortality than delayed appropriate therapy. These results were confirmed by Kollef et al. [17], who reported a significant increase in the mortality when appropriate therapy was delayed.

Available evidence firmly encourages physicians to take early samples for the microbiology laboratory and administer without delay broad-spectrum empiric therapy as soon as infection is suspected. Early implementation of antibiotics may increase the likelihood of reducing the bacterial burden in the infection site, which consequently would lead to earlier resolution.

The importance of the right dosage

Drugs administered to critically ill patients exhibit significant variations in their pharmacokinetic behaviour. This is due to the changes in the physiology of the patients that may lead to either underdosing or overdosing and, consequently, to a suboptimal antibiotic management. Situations

such as variations in renal clearance, hypoalbuminaemia, massive fluid infusion, or inotropic agent administration (that may lead to high cardiac output states) are very common in severe sepsis. Direct implications consist in significant alterations of the distribution volume that should be taken into account when prescribing antibiotics and other drugs [20, 21, 22, 23, 24, 25]. An increase in the distribution volume leads to sublethal concentrations of the hydrophilic antibiotics in plasma and, therefore, in the target site. On the other hand, a decrease in the excretion of the drug may end in overdosing and toxicity. Consequently, it is important to adjust the doses depending on each individual patient situation.

The pharmacokinetic-pharmacodynamic (PK/PD) approach differentiates two subsets of antibiotics depending on how to achieve the best profile of activity. This classification and its considerations in dose prescription have been described in detail elsewhere [26, 27, 28]. Figure 1 illustrates the relevant parameters to evaluate in clinical antibiotic monitoring.

Briefly, administering the same dose of time-dependent antibiotics over a prolonged period of time or even continuously rather than in bolus results in higher killing activity against bacteria, as these antibiotics exhibit moderate post-antibiot-

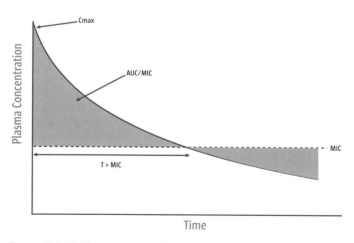

Fig. 1   Main PK/PD parameters. Single intravenous administration.
C_{max}: Maximum concentration
MIC: Minimum Inhibitory Concentration
T > MIC: Time over the Minimum Inhibitory Concentration
AUC/MIC: Area Under the Curve/Minimum Inhibitory Concentration

ic effects (PAE) [28]. Consequently, time-dependent antibiotics need to maintain their concentration in the target site over the minimum inhibitory concentration (MIC) of the causal bacteria
during a certain period of time between doses to
achieve the best outcomes. The most representative time-dependent antibiotics are β-lactams and
carbapenems. β-lactams, represented by penicillins and cephalosporins, exhibit moderate PAE
against Gram-positive bacteria and no PAE against
Gram-negatives [28]. Data from McKinnon et al.
suggest that for the treatment of severe infections
100 % t > MIC is associated with better clinical and
microbiological outcomes [27]. On the other hand,
carbapenems produce moderate PAE against
Gram-positive and Gram-negative bacteria, so
lower t > MIC, over 30–40 %, are required [25,
26, 28]. It has been reported that when the target
site concentration of beta-lactams decreases under MIC, the growth rate of remaining bacteria is
greatly increased [29, 30, 31, 32, 33, 34]. Roberts et
al. [33, 34] encourage physicians to instaurate long
or even continuous perfusions when prescribing
beta-lactam and carbapenem antibiotics, as maximal bacteria killing happens when the concentrations are maintained at 4–5 x MIC for a certain percentage of time among doses as described before
[28]. Extended and continuous infusion dosages
lead to a more consistent achievement of pharmacodynamic targets in both plasma and target tissues, as t > MIC reaches more than 90 %.

On the other hand, concentration-dependent
antibiotics exhibit prolonged PAEs, leading to a better profile of activity depending on the maximum
peak concentration achieved [25, 35, 36, 37, 38].
The most representative concentration-dependent
antibiotics are fluoroquinolones, aminoglycosides
and macrolides. The parameters that define PK/
PD breakpoints in concentration-dependent antibiotics are either AUC/MIC or C_{max}/MIC, or even
both. Once-daily aminoglycosides have been evaluated in several trials versus multidose regimens,
and single daily administration has shown to be
as efficacious or superior to traditional dosing for
the treatment of a wide variety of infections [37].
A C_{max}/MIC value of 10 is a generally accepted ratio to achieve [37]. Furthermore, available evidence
suggests that once-daily aminoglycosides are correlated with lower incidence of renal and ototoxic
adverse events compared with multiple administration [38, 39, 40, 41].

Regarding fluoroquinolones, their profile
of activity displays largely concentration-killing
characteristics, but also with some time-dependent effects. Both concentration-dependent pharmacodynamic targets, AUC/MIC and C_{max}/MIC,
should be considered for optimising fluoroqui-
nolone use in ICU patients [42]. Forrest et al.
defined that an AUC24/MIC > 125 with ciprofloxacin was associated with success in critically
ill patients [43].

Of note, it has been described that there is a
lower incidence of resistances in the ICU when
the PK/PD approach is considered in the antibiotic prescription. For concentration-dependent drugs, C_{max}/MIC over 10 have shown to decrease the emergence of bacterial resistance, and
so have extended t > MIC with time-dependent
antibiotics. On the other hand, maintaining sublethal concentrations increases the incidence of
resistant pathogens [33, 44].

The success of implementing the PK/PD approach in clinical practice should encourage physicians to deepen this approach and establish a
protocol of administration specific for each antibiotic behaviour.

Where is the infection site?

Nowadays, there is increasing interest in the
pharmacokinetic aspects of antibiotic therapy.
Factors such as peak concentrations, protein
binding or distribution are being evaluated in order to customise the therapy for each patient and
each infection.

It is crucial to consider penetration to the
specific tissue where the infection is located for
achieving the highest probability of eradicating
the pathogen. In vitro susceptibilities are not
enough when prescribing an antibiotic, because
depending on the percentage of drug that arrives
at the target site the reached concentrations will
differ significantly from the plasmatic ones, leading to probable underdosing.

Several studies have been conducted among
ICU patients to evaluate the penetration of different antibiotics to the target sites. For instance,
lung penetration is a key issue to be considered
when treating pulmonary infections. Vancomycin is a clear example of this relevance, as 1-hour
administration of 1 g vancomycin each 12 hours

was demonstrated to poorly penetrate into lung tissue (25 % of the plasma concentrations within the first hour post-infusion) and, therefore, was an inadequate dosage for the treatment of susceptible staphylococci [45]. However, a prospective multicentre multivariate analysis identified a better profile of activity when administering vancomycin in continuous infusion in MRSA pneumonia [46]. The election of other drugs such as linezolid for MRSA pneumonia treatment is based mainly on this concept, and is underemphasised in previous studies using a classic susceptibility-only approach [10].

Peritoneal penetration of the carbapenem doripenem was evaluated in patients having undergone abdominal surgery by Ikawa et al., [47] comparing concentrations in peritoneal exudate versus plasma. Their results show that doripenem penetrates significantly into peritoneal fluid, with achieved concentrations comparable to the plasmatics. Consequently bacterial exposure to the drug is correlated with the expected by plasma levels. Furthermore, Ikawa et al. designed carbapenem breakpoints for intraabdominal infections considering peritoneal penetration [48].

Many studies have been performed with antibiotics to define the relevance of the PK/PD component in the effect of antibiotics using microdialysis as the sampling technique [49, 50, 51 52, 53, 54]. Tomasselli et al. [50, 51] designed two studies to monitor the treatment of pneumonia with meropenem and piperacillin/tazobactam. They demonstrated the utility of this technique to evaluate both lung penetration and free-drug concentration in plasma over time. This elucidates the importance of continuous monitoring to achieve the breakpoints for each bacteria, adjusting doses and time of infusion. Similarly, Hutschala et al. [52] tested levofloxacin lung penetration in post-cardiac surgery pneumonia, and their results showed that penetration was lower than previously reported, as the pulmonary peak represented 38 % of plasma levels. Moreover, the study highlighted that a single dose of 500 mg was borderline sufficient for the treatment of *Klebsiella pneumoniae* pneumonia, but insufficient for *Pseudomonas aeruginosa*, as the desired breakpoint of 30–40 AUC/MIC for this antibiotic was not achieved [52].

Pharmacokinetic studies with microdialysis have also been performed to evaluate both pen-

etration and achieved levels of meropenem and imipenem in peritonitis [53, 54]. In the first case, the authors demonstrated that meropenem exhibits a penetration profile adequate for the treatment of pneumonia caused by susceptible organisms, but not always for intermediatly susceptible pathogens [53]. In the case of imipenem, slightly lower concentrations where documented in peritoneal fluid compared with serum, but the AUC relationship between plasmatic and peritoneal levels was close to the unit [54]. However, this study has several limitations for its practical application because it was performed in *in vivo* models, and findings may not be translated to the bedside.

Extrapolating this to clinical practice, there exists clear evidence to support re-evaluation of the antibiotic and dosage administered to the critically ill patient depending on both the host characteristics and the antibiotic patterns of distribution into the infected tissues.

Different settings = Different bugs

Another important aspect to be considered when prescribing antibiotics in the ICU is the resistance profile of each particular unit. In fact, different patterns of microbial resistances have been described among different hospitals and even different departments in the same hospital, which highlights the need for individualised algorithms to follow to control these outbreaks.

The ICU is a very propitious setting for bacterial resistance emergence. Antibiotic pressure, confined area and the presence of patients transferred from nursing homes are only some of the factors that produce an increase of prevalence of these less susceptible pathogens [55, 56, 57].

As mentioned above, different institutions exhibit very differential patterns of bacterial resistances. Data from the recent European study EU-VAP [58], which evaluated nosocomial pneumonia in 9 European countries, shows that *Acinetobacter baumannii* nosocomial pneumonia was very frequent in Turkish (52.7 %) and Greek (33.3 %) sites, while *Staphylococcus aureus* was the most prevalent in Spain (29.6 %), France (37.8 %), Belgium (12.2 %) and Ireland (22.2 %). *Pseudomonas aeruginosa* was the primary nosocomial pathogen causing pneumonia in Italy (27.6 %) and Portugal (16.2 %), whereas *Es-*

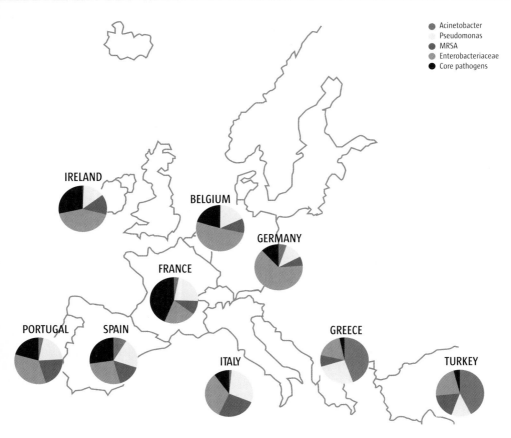

Fig. 2   Main nosocomial pathogens in pneumonia by countries (in percentage) [data from the EU-VAP study, Koulenti D, Lisboa T, Brun- Buisson C, et al. for EU-VAP/CAP study group. The Spectrum of Practice in the Diagnosis of Nosocomial Pneumonia in Patients Requiring Mechanical Ventilation in European ICUs. Crit Care MEd. 2009 (ahead of publication)]

cherichia coli was leading in Germany (21.7%) (see Fig. 2). This data shows important differences among countries regarding the most prevalent nosocomial bacteria [58], with important implications for empirical treatment choice.

This disparity when describing the most common bacteria in the ICU setting depending on each specific location evidences the need for studying the local susceptibilities in each department, incorporating this information to implement policies of resistance control.

When do antibiotics stop being useful?

Old paradigms postulated that prolonging treatment would result in better outcomes. More re-cent evidence suggests that antibiotic administration that is too long is associated with increases of the incidence of colonisation by antibiotic-resistant bacteria, *Clostridium difficile* infections and maximised risk of serious adverse events.

Traditionally, the recommended duration of therapy for ICU infections is arbitrary and ranges from 7–21 days depending on the infection site. The optimal duration of therapy remains unknown, but there is a clear trend in recent recommendations to favour shorter courses of treatment.

In pneumonia, some approaches to limit the duration of treatment have been evaluated, including short-course therapy (3 days) for low risk patients [59], arbitrarily defined 8 vs. 15 days [60], using de-escalation strategy [61], and, the most promising, an individualised discontinuation of treatment based on clinical response parameters [62].

Chastre et al. in 2003 compared two treatment arms of 8 versus 15 days of therapy in ventilator-associated pneumonia [60] and documented no significant difference on survival between both groups, which evidenced no benefit of prolonging the therapy to 15 days, except in patients with non-fermentative Gram-negative bacilli. However, it is important to note that patients indeed received a mean of 12.6 and 17.1 days of antibiotic (instead of the 8–15 days randomly assigned) due to the discretion of the physician in charge.

Another strategy to reduce total antimicrobial burden and minimise the selection pressure of broad-spectrum antibiotics is de-escalation. This approach includes an early start of broad-spectrum empirical treatment with adjustment of spectrum when microbiological data is available. The rationale of such a strategy is to hit "hard and fast" with an agent likely to cover the responsible pathogen, followed by narrow spectrum restriction guided by culture results, minimising the selection pressure. Our group studied the impact of this strategy in VAP patients and found de-escalation was feasible in about one-third of VAP patients [61]. Although rational, such a strategy should be evaluated in other nosocomial infections.

Mentzelopoulos et al. [63] reported in 2007 that a prolonged use of a combination of carbapenems and colistin predisposed to ventilator-associated pneumonia produced by pandrug-resistant *Pseudomonas aeruginosa* [49] in ICU patients without cystic fibrosis. This evidenced the importance of optimising the duration of antibiotic therapy for bacterial resistance control. Also in 2007, Aarts et al. [64] suggested that unnecessarily prolonging antibiotic administration might lead to worse outcomes, with a trend for higher mortality (OR for mortality = 3.8 95 %CI 0.9–15.5).

A customised approach based on clinical response to antibiotic treatment, using clinical variables and biomarkers (such as C-reactive protein or procalcitonin) may optimise management [65], allowing an individual, patient-specific approach for antibiotic treatment duration.

Although rational, such strategy is to be validated in randomised clinical trials.

Furthermore, *Clostridium difficile* infection, which significantly worsens the outcomes of critically ill patients in the acute care setting [64, 66], is clearly associated with previous use of antibiotics, especially clindamycin, cephalosporins, penicillins and fluorquinolones [67]. Minimising the duration of antibiotic treatment with these agents is a strategy to prevent the emergence of *Clostridium difficile* infection.

In summary, duration of therapy should be guided by clinical variables, biomarkers and microbiological response of the patient being re-evaluated after 72 hours to assess de-escalation.

Conclusion

The classical myths, such as Icarus', illustrate the potential damage of not measuring the strength and suitability of our actions. The extrapolation of the inner meaning of these stories should be implemented in daily medical practice, where the consequences of our decisions may significantly change outcomes.

Much has changed in our approach to safety over the past years. A checklist to avoid preventable mistakes in antibiotic prescription is provided below. It is a fact that difficult nosocomial infections in the intensive care units have seriously compromised patient safety and quality of care in these settings. Efforts for developing evidence-based care strategies should focus on the optimisation of antibiotic management and further research should be done into the design and validation of acute care antibiotic care bundles.

Proposed checklist for optimising antibiotic use in the ICU

1. *Were microbiological samples taken from the infection site and sent to the microbiology lab?*
2. *Was the optimal antibiotic administered within 2 hours from infection onset?*
3. *Were optimal dosage and penetration into the target site considered before prescribing?*
4. *Were local resistances taken into account when choosing the antibiotic and the dose?*
5. *Was the need for antibiotic reassessed after 72 h regarding clinical, microbiological and biochemical evolution?*

Acknowledgements

Supported in part by CIBER Enfermedades Respiratorias (CIBERES 06/06/0036) and AGAUR (2005/SGR/920).

The authors

Marta Ulldemolins, BPharm[1, 2]
Thiago Lisboa, MD[1, 2, 3]
Jordi Rello, MD, PhD[1, 2, 3]
  [1]Critical Care Department | University
  Hospital Joan XXIII- Tarragona, Spain
  [2]CIBER Enfermedades Respiratorias
  (CIBERES)
  [3]Rovira i Virgili University | IISPV-Tarragona,
  Spain

Address for correspondence
  Jordi Rello
  Critical Care Department
  Joan XXIII University Hospital
  Mallafre Guasch 4
  43007 Tarragona, Spain
  E-mail: jrello.hj23.ics@gencat.cat

References

1. Institute for Healthcare Improvement, 5 Million Lives Campaign. http://www.ihi.org/IHI/Programs/Campaign/Campaign/htm. (Accessed 14 February 2009).
2. National Institute for Health and Clinical Excellence. http://www.nice.org.uk/Guidance/CG2 (Accessed 14 February 2009).
3. Scottish Intensive Care Society Audit Group. http://www.sicsag.scot.nhs.uk/SubGroup/HAI.html (Accessed 14 February 2009).
4. Vidaur L, Sirgo G, Rodríguez AH, Rello J. Clinical approach to the patient with suspected ventilator- associated pneumonia. Respir Care. 2005; 57:965–74.
5. Vincent JL, Bihari DJ, Suter PM, et al. The prevalence of nosocomial infection in intensive care units in Europe. Results of the European prevalence of infection in intensive care (EPIC) Study. EPIC international advisory committee. JAMA 1995; 274:639–44.
6 Paterson DL. The role of antimicrobial management programs in optimising antibiotic prescribing within hospitals. Clin Infect Dis. 2006; 42:S90–5.
7. Cooke FJ, Holmes AH. The missing care bundle: antibiotic prescribing in hospitals. Int J Antimicrob Agents. 2007; 30:25–9.
8. Vandijck DM, Labeau SO, Secanell M, et al. The role of nurses working in emergency and critical care environments is the prevention of intravascular catether- related bloodstream infections. Int Emerg Nurs. 2009; 17:60–8.
9. Masterton R, Craven D, Rello J, Struelens M, et al. Hospital- acquired pneumonia guidelines in Europe: a review of their status and future development. J Antimicrob Chemother. 2007; 60:206–13.
10. Sandiumenge A, Diaz E, Bodí M, Rello J. Therapy of ventilator- associated pneumonia. A patient- based approach based on the ten rules of "The Tarragona Strategy". Intensive Care Med. 2003; 29:876–83.
11. Lisboa T, Craven DE, Rello J. Safety in critical care and pulmonary medicine. Should ventilator- associated pneumonia be a quality indicator for patient safety? Clin Pulm Med. 2009; 16; 28–32.
12. Lorente L, Blot S, Rello J. Evidence on measures for the prevention of ventilator- associated pneumonia. Eur Respir J. 2007; 30:1193–1207.
13. Kumar A, Roberts D, Wood KE, et al. Duration of hypotension before initiation of effective antimicrobial therapy is the critical determinant of survival in human septic shock. Crit Care Med. 2006; 34:1589–96.
14. Kuti EL, Patel AA, Coleman CI. Impact of inappropriate antibiotic therapy on mortality in patients with ventilator- associated pneumonia and bllodstream infection: a meta- analysis. J Crit Care. 2008; 23:91–100.
15. Rello J, Gallego M, Mariscal D, et al. The value of routine microbial investigation in ventilator- associated pneumonia. Am J Resp Crit Care Med. 1997; 156:196–200.
16. Luna CM, Vujacich P, Niederman MS, et al. Impact of BAL data on the therapy and outcome of ventilator-associated pneumonia. Chest. 1997; 111:676–85.
17. Kollef MH, Ward S. The influence of mini- BAL cultures on patient outcomes: implications for the antibiotic management of ventilator- associated pneumonia. Chest. 1998; 113:412–20.
18. Iregui M, Ward S, Sherman G et al. Clinical importance of delays in the initiation of appropriate antibiotic treatment for ventilator- associated pneumonia. Chest. 2002; 122:262–8.
19. Luna CM, Aruj P, Niederman MS, et al. for the Grupo Argentino de Estudio de la Neumonía Asociada al Respirador (GANAR) group. Appropriateness and delay to initiate therapy in ventilator- associated pneumonia. Eur Respir J. 2006; 27:158–164.
20. Roberts J, Lipman J. Antibacterial dosing in intensive care. Pharmacokinetics, degree of disease and pharmacodynamics of sepsis. Clin Pharmacokinet. 2006; 45:755–73.
21. Parrillo JE. Pathogenetic mechanisms of septic shock. New Eng J Med. 1993; 328:1471–8.
22. Kumar A, Schupp E, Bunnell E, Ali A, Milcarek B, Parrillo JE. Cardiovascular response to dobutamine stress predicts outcome in severe sepsis and septic shock. Crit Care 2008; 12:R35.

23. Domínguez de Villota E, Mosquera JM, Rubio JJ, et al. Assotiation of a low serum albumin with infection and increased mortality in critically ill patients. Intensive Care Med. 1980; 7:19–22.

24. Burkhardt O, Kumar V, Katterwe D et al. Ertapenem in critically ill patients with early- onset ventilator- associated pneumonia: pharmacokinetics with special consideration of free- drug concentration. J Antimicrob Chemother. 2007; 59:277–84.

25. Drusano GL. Pharmacokinetics and pharmacodynamics of antimicrobials. Clin Infect Dis. 2007. 45:S89–95.

26. Craig, WA. Pharmacokinetic/pharmacodynamic parameters: rationale for bacterial dosing of mice and man. Clin Infect Dis. 1998; 26:1–10.

27. McKinnon PS, Paladino JA, Schentag JJ. Evaluation of area under the inhibitory curve (AUIC) and time above the minimum inhibitory concentration (T > MIC) as predictors of outcome for cefepime and ceftazidime in serious bacterial infections. Int J Antimicrob Agents. 2008;31(4):345–351.

28. Craig WA. Interrelationship between pharmacokinetics and pharmacodynamics indetermining dosage regimens for broad- spectrum cephalosporins. Diagn. Microbiol. Infect. Dis. 1995; 22:89–96.

29. Craig WA. Pharmacokinetic and experimental data on beta- lactam antibiotics in the treatment of patients. Eur J Clin Microbiol Infect Dis. 1984; 3:575–8.

30. Vogelman B, Craig WA. Postantibiotic effects. J Antimicrob Chemother. 1985; 15:SA37–46.

31. Moulton JW, Vinks AA, and Punt NC. Pharmacokinetic-pharmacodynamic modeling of activity of ceftazimide during continuous and intermittent infusion. Antimicrob Agents Chemother. 1997; 41:733–738.

32. Nicolau DP. Pharmacodynamic optimisation of b-lactams in the patient care setting. Critical Care. 2008; 12:S2.

33. Roberts JA, Kruger P, Paterson DL, Lipman J. Antibiotic resistance- What's dosing got to do with it? Crit Care Med 2008; 36:2433–2440.

34. Roberts JA, Paratz JP, Lipman J. Continuous infusion of beta- lactams in the intensive care unit- Best way to hit the target? Crit Care Med. 2008; 36:1663–4.

35. Vogelman B, Craig WA. Postantibiotic effects. J Antimicrob Chemother. 1985; 15:S37- S46.

36. Vogelman B, Craig WA. Kinetics of antimicrobial activity. J Pediatr. 1986; 108:835–40

37. Lacy MK, Nicolau DP, Nightingale CH, et al. The pharmacodynamics of aminoglycosides. Clin Infect Dis. 1998; 27:23–7.

38. Rea RS, Capitano B. Optimizing use of aminoglycosides in the critically ill. Semin Respir Crit Care Med 2007; 28:596–603.

39. Zhanel GG, Ariano Re. Once daily aminoglycoside dosing: maintained efficacy with reduced nephrototoxicity? Ren Fail 1992; 14:1–9.

40. Ali MZ, Gotees MB. A meta- analysis of the relative efficacy and toxicity of single- day dosing versus multiple day dosing of aminoglycosides. Clin Infect Dis. 1997; 24:796–809.

41. Olsen KM, Rudis MI, Rebuck JA, et al. Effect of once-daily dosing vs. multiple daily dosing of tobramycin on enzyme markers of nephrotoxicity. Crit Care Med. 2004; 32:1678–82.

42. Benko R, Matuz M, Doro P, Peto Z, Molnar A, Hajdu E, Nagy E, Gardi J, Soos G. Pharmacokinetics and pharmacodynamics of levofloxacin in critically ill patients with ventilator- associated pneumonia. Int J Antimicrob Agents. 2007; 30:162–8.

43. Forrest A, Nix DE, Ballow CH, et al. Pharmacodynamics of intravenous ciprofloxacin in in seriously ill patients. Antimicrob Agents Chemother. 1993; 37:1073–81.

44. Burgess DS. Pharmacodynamic principles of antimicrobial therapy in the prevention of resistance. Chest 1999; 115:19S- 23S.

45. Cruciani M, Gatti G, Lazzarini L, et al. Penetration of vancomycin into human lung tissue. J Antimicrob Chemother. 1996; 38:865–9.

46. Rello J, Sole-Violan J, Sa- Borges M, et al. Pneumonia caused by oxacillin- resistant Staphylococcus aureus treated with glycopeptides. Crit Care Med. 2005; 33:1983–7.

47. Ikawa K, Morikawa N, Urakawa N, et al. Peritoneal penetration of doripenem after intravenous administration in abdominal- surgery patients. J Antimicrob Chemother. 2007; 60:1395–7.

48. Ikawa K, Morikawa N, Ikeda K, et al. Development of breakpoints of carbapenems for intraabdominal infections based on pharmacokinetics and pharmacodynamics in peritoneal fluid. J Infect Chemother. 2008; 14:330–2.

49. Roberts JA, Roberts MS, Robertson TA et al. A novel way to investigate the effects of plasma exchange on antibiotic levels: use of microdialysis. Int J Antimicrob Agents. 2008; 31:240–4.

50. Tomaselli F, Maier A, Matzi V, et al. Penetration of meropenem into pneumonic human tissue as measured by in vivo microdyalisis. Antimicrob Agents Chemother. 2004; 48:2228–32.

51. Tomaselli F, Dittrich P, Maier A et al. Penetration of piperacillin and tazobactam into pneumonic human lung tissue measured by in vivo microdyalisis. BR J Clin Pharmacol. 2002; 55:620–4.

52. Hutschala D, Skhirtladze K, Zuckermann A, et al. In vivo measurement of levofloxacin penetration into lung tissue after cardiac surgery. Antimicrob Agents Chemother. 2005; 49:5107–11.

53. Karjagin J, Lefeuvre S, Oselin K et al. Pharmacokinetics of meropenem determined by microdialysis in the peritoneal fluid of patients with severe peritonitis associated with septic shock. Clin Pharmacol Ther. 2008; 83:452–9.

54. Lefeuvre S, Marchand S, Lamarche I, et al. Microdialysis study of imipenem distribution in the intraperitoneal fluid of rats with or without experimental peritonitis. Antimicrob Agents Chemother. 2006; 50:34–7.

55. McGowan JE Jr. Antimicrobial resistance in hospital organisms and its relation to antibiotic use. Rev Infect Dis. 1983; 5:1033–48.

56. Kollef MH. Fraser V. Antibiotic resistance in the intensive care setting. Ann Intern Med. 2001; 134:298–314.

57. Richards MJ, Edwards JR, Culver DH, y col. Nosocomial infections in medical intensive care units in the United States. National Nosocomial Infections Surveillance System. Crit Care Med. 1999; 27:887–92.

58. Koulenti D, Lisboa T, Brun- Buisson C, et al. for EU-VAP/CAP study group. The Spectrum of Practice in the Diagnosis of Nosocomial Pneumonia in Patients Requiring Mechanical Ventilation in European ICUs. Crit Care MEd. 2009 (ahead of publication).

59. Singh N, Rogers P, Atwood CW, et al. Short- course empiric antibiotic therapy for patients with pulmonary infiltrates in the intensive care unit. Am J Respir Crit Care Med. 2000; 162:505–11.

60. Chastre J, Wolff M, Fagon JY, et al. Comparison of 8 vs 15 days of antibiotic therapy for ventilator- asosciated pneumonia in adults: a randomised trial. JAMA. 2003; 290:2588–98.

61. Rello J, Vidaur L, Sandiumenge A, Rodríguez AH, et al. De- escalation therapy in ventilator- associated pneumonia. Crit Care Med. 2004; 32:2183–90.

62. Park DR. Antimicrobial treatment of ventilator- associated pneumonia. Resp Care. 2005; 50:932–55.

63. Mentzelopoulos SD, Pratikaki M, Platsouka E, et al. Prolonged use of carbapenems and colistin predisposes to ventilator- associated pneumonia by pandrug- resistant Pseudomonas aeruginosa. Intensive Care Med. 2007; 33:1524–32.

64. Aarts MAW, Brun- Buisson C, Cook DJ et al. Antibiotic management of suspected nosocomial ICU- acquired infections: does prolonged empiric therapy improve outcome? Intensive Care Med. 2007; 33:1369–78.

65. Lisboa T, Seligman R, Díaz E, Rodríguez A, et al. C-reactive protein correlates with bacterial load and appropriate antibiotic therapy in suspected ventilator- associated pneumonia. Crit Care Med. 2008; 36:166–71.

66. Kelly CP, LaMont TJ. Clostridium difficile- More difficult than ever. N Eng J Med. 2008; 359:1932–40.

67. Gravel D, Miller M, Simor A, et al. And the Canadian Nosocomial Infection Surveillance program. Healthcare associated Clostridium difficile infection in adults admitted to acute care hospitals in canada: a canadian nosocomial infection surveillance program study. Clin Infect Dis. 2009; 48:568–76.

68. McFarland LW, Clarridge JE, Beneda HW, Raugi GJ. Fluorquinolone use and risk factors for Clostridium difficile-associated disease within a veterans administration health care system. Clin Infect Dis. 2007; 45:1141–51.

Oscar Peñuelas, Fernando Frutos-Vivar and Andres Esteban

Primum non nocere:
Avoiding harm during mechanical ventilation

Introduction

According to the available data it appears that approximately one-third of the patients admitted to the ICU will receive mechanical ventilatory support for more than 12 hours [1, 2]. Mechanical ventilation is part of basic life support, delays mortality in many patients with acute respiratory failure and is used to maintain adequate systemic oxygenation. However, over the last two decades, it has become evident that mechanical ventilation itself can augment or cause acute lung injury. Mechanical ventilation can increase alveolar-capillary permeability through the overdistension of the lung (volutrauma), worsening lung injury through the tidal recruitment/derecruitment of the collapsed alveoli (aletectrauma) and lead to even more subtle injury manifested by the activation of the inflammatory process (biotrauma). The mechanisms underlying the ventilation-induced lung injury (VILI) have been for the most part elucidated [3]. We propose: to highlight the main mechanisms related to VILI; review the different situations in which VILI can occur based on animal and clinical studies; to place these results into a clinical perspective of management to avoid VILI and to present ongoing new therapies for the treatment of VILI.

Mechanisms of VILI

According to the international conference consensus [4], VILI is defined as acute lung injury directly induced by mechanical ventilation in animal models. Since VILI is usually indistinguishable morphologically, physiologically, and radiologically from the diffuse alveolar damage of acute lung injury, it can only be discerned definitively in animal models. Definitive evidence that mechanical ventilation could cause damage to the lungs in humans is difficult to obtain, since it is clearly not possible to perform experiments in which humans are exposed to strategies of ventilation that are thought to be injurious, solely for the purpose of examining the lung injury that it could cause. Thus, a better term that might be used in many human studies is ventilator-associated lung injury (VALI). VALI is defined as lung injury that resembles acute respiratory distress syndrome (ARDS) and that occurs in patients receiving mechanical ventilation. VALI may be associated with pre-existing lung pathology. VALI refers to the additional injury imposed on a previously injured lung by mechanical ventilation in either the clinical setting or in experimental studies. The recognition that alveolar

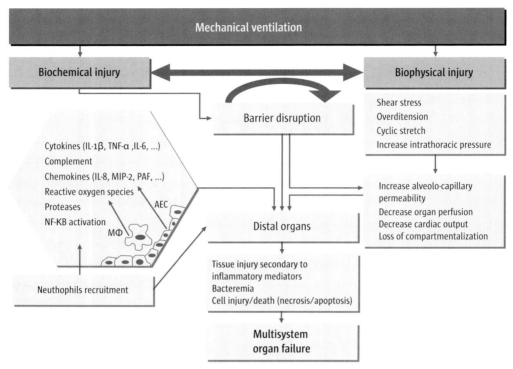

Fig. 1 Potential mechanisms of ventilator-induced lung injury. Summary effects of mechanical forces on lung injury [modified from Slutsky AR. Lung injury caused by mechanical ventilation. Chest 1999;116 (Suppl): 9S–15S] MΦ = alveolar macrophages.
AEC = alveolar epithelial type II cells.

overdistention rather than high proximal airway pressure is the primary determinant of the injury (i.e., volutrauma rather than barotrauma) has constituted a substantial shift in clinicians' thinking about the pathogenesis of VALI.

All the pathophysiological characteristics of ARDS (ventilation/perfusion mismatch and reduced compliance, lung oedema, atelectasis, pulmonary inflammation) may be worsened by inappropriate ventilator settings because of the non-homogeneous distribution of the normal lung regions mixed with consolidated, atelectatic regions and regions that can be recruited/derecruited depending on the particular ventilatory strategy used [5]. Full understanding of the mechanisms that mediate lung injury may permit potential strategies directed at preventing VALI and reducing the incidence of VILI-induced multiple organ failure.

Ventilation-induced lung injury and ventilation-associated lung injury can present following pathogenic characteristics (see Fig. 1).

Mechanical stretch of alveolar epithelial and endothelial cells

The conversion of physical signals such as contractile forces or external mechanical perturbations into chemical events is a fundamental cellular process that occurs at cell-extracellular matrix contact, which may compromise the balance of forces in alveolar epithelium. Thus, the increased mechanical stretch during injurious ventilation may contribute to lung injury [6–10].

Not only can the plasma membrane break, but so can the contact between cells. If such a disruption happens to the pulmonary endothelial and epithelial barrier, this will lead to haemorrhage and loss of compartmentalisation [11, 12].

These physical forces are mainly characterised as follows:

- Ventilation, especially with high ventilation pressures and zero positive end-expiratory pressure, can cause stress failure of the plasma membrane and of epithelial and endothelial barriers. Stress failure of the plasma membrane causes necrosis, which leads to liberation of both preformed inflammatory mediators and agents that stimulate other cells that are still intact to produce such mediators.
- Stress failure of the barriers causes loss of compartmentalisation with spread of mediators and bacteria throughout the body as a consequence.
- Less injurious ventilation strategies that do not cause tissue destruction can elicit release of mediators by more specific mechanisms, presumably through activation of stretch-activated signaling cascades (mechanotransduction, [13]).
- Ventilation with increasing positive pressures raises the pressure in the pulmonary circulation and thus vascular shear stress, both of which are known stimuli for endothelial cells.

In addition, pulmonary endothelium is a component of the alveolar-capillary unit that is vulnerable to injurious patterns, including mechanical stretch [14]. Recent data from microvascular endothelial cells and isolated perfused rat underline the role of endothelial responses to stretch-inducing VILI [15–17]. Kuebler et al. [15] showed that vascular stretch generated by ventilation increases nitric oxide by a signaling cascade involving phosphoinositide 3-OH kinase in lung endothelial cells, and that response is independent of the mechanical factors causing vascular distension. Shear stress is known to increase the activities of multiple transcription factors such as AP-1, NF-KB, Sp-1, and Egr-1. The actions of these transcription factors result in the induction of genes encoding for vasoactivators (prostacyclin, nitric oxide), adhesion molecules, monocyte chemoattractant protein-1, cytokines (IL-1, IL-6), and growth factors (platelet-derived growth factor, transforming growth factor-β) in endothelial cells.

Release of inflammatory mediators and polymorphonuclear (PMN) leukocyte recruitment and activation (biotrauma)

The role of the innate immune response and inflammation in the pathogenesis of VILI has been widely studied in recent years. PMN are an important component of the inflammatory response that characterises VILI. Polymorphonuclear leukocytes can be activated by mechanical ventilation, and the consequent release of elastase was correlated with the degree of systemic inflammatory response and multiple organ failure [18]. Although some have suggested that inflammation may not be integral to the initiation of VILI [19], clearly a preponderance of data in this field supports a major pathogenetic role for inflammation and lung neutrophil recruitment. Choudhury et al. [20] demonstrated that mechanical stress initiates pulmonary PMN sequestration early in the course of VILI, and this phenomenon is associated with stretch-induced inflammatory events leading to circulating leukocytes stiffening mediated by a L-selectin-dependent mechanism. PMN recruitment in VILI may be mediated by various chemoattractants and adhesion molecules derived from the several types of cells existing in the lung parenquima and air spaces [21].

The majority of biological markers identified in plasma, serum, pulmonary oedema fluid, and BAL fluid in experimental studies are cytokines and chemokines such as interleukin 6 (IL-6), interleukin 8 (IL-8), tumor necrosis factor alpha (TNF-a), vascular endothelium growth factor (VEGF), macrophage inflammatory protein 2 (MIP-2) [22–24]. Although none of these mediators distinguish ventilator-induced injury from other etiologies of lung injury, the temporal association between changes in levels of these proteins and changes in tidal volume or positive end-expiratory pressure (PEEP) along with inhibitor studies suggests a causative role. Importantly, the precise functional role of each mediator associated with ventilator-attributable lung injury is not completely understood.

Strong evidence has shown that mechanical damage of lung tissue may activate inflammatory mediators. In animal models, the strategy of mechanical ventilation influences local release of inflammatory mediators from the lung: The prevention of repeated collapse and reopening and overdistention reduces the release of these mediators. These mediators may also be released to the systemic circulation. It is possible, although not confirmed, that these alterations in the inflammatory response may modify lung injury itself or conceivably lead to a systemic inflammatory response and organ dysfunction [25, 26] that may occur in critically ill patients receiving mechanical ventilation due to the decompartmentalisation of inflammatory mediators during VILI [27].

Role of apoptosis/necrosis balance

Apoptosis is a process of controlled cell death, which is important in the development and remodelling of tissues that occur during the normal repair process. Whereas apoptosis occurs without corresponding inflammation of the surrounding tissue, necrosis is often associated with activation of the inflammatory response in the adjacent tissues. The same type of insult can induce either apoptosis or necrosis, but whether one mode of cell death is preferred over the other depends on the severity of the insult and the idiosyncrasy of the target cell.

Increasing evidence suggests a role of apoptosis in the maintenance of the alveolar epithelium under normal and pathologic conditions. Imai et al. [28] showed that low levels of mechanical stretch caused high levels of pulmonary apoptosis, whereas high levels of mechanical stretch were associated with decreased apoptosis and increased necrosis. The authors demonstrated that an injurious ventilatory strategy administered to the lung could lead to epithelial apoptosis in organ distal to the lung, such as the kidney or small intestine, mediated through soluble Fas ligand releasing. They concluded that this mechanism of ventilator-induced end-organ dysfunction might explain the high rate of multiorgan failure observed in patients with ARDS.

Mechanical stretch regulates pulmonary cell function and structure by mechanisms that include the expression of multiple genes. The stretch-induced activation of Akt-ERK 1/2 via a G-protein-dependent pathway has been shown to play a key role in linking external signals to nuclear response [29]. A novel hypothesis indicates

that mechanical deformation of pulmonary cells might trigger a G-protein-mediated pathway that activates Akt and ERK1/2 and inhibits apoptosis, thus leading to cell death by necrosis: Therefore inhibition of this pathway turns down the Akt-ERK1/2 inhibitory effect, enhancing apoptosis and preserving the alveolar epithelium exposed to stretch. Further studies are required to explore this novel hypothesis [30, 31].

Effects of injurious ventilation in healthy lungs

There are clinical data suggesting that patients without a diagnosis of ALI/ARDS may benefit from lower tidal volume. In a large international prospective observational study, Esteban et al. [1] observed that a plateau pressure greater than 35 cm H_2O was associated with an increased risk of death. Although not definitive, this study suggested that tidal volumes were too large (per lung size) in these patients, thereby causing an exaggeration of lung injury and eventually death.

In a multi-centre international study, Gajic et al. in a retrospective cohort study [32] showed that of 332 patients who did not have acute lung injury from the outset, 80 patients (24 %) developed acute lung injury within the first 5 days of mechanical ventilation. In a multivariate analysis, the main risk factors associated with the development of acute lung injury were the use of large tidal volume (odds ratio 1.3 for each ml above 6 ml/kg predicted body weight, p < .001). Furthermore, Gajic et al. found development of ARDS to be associated with the initial ventilator settings; large tidal volume (odds ratio 2.6 for tidal volume > 700 ml) and high peak airway pressure > 30 cmH_2O (odds ratio 1.6 for peak airway pressure > 30 cmH_2O) were independently associated with development of ARDS in patients who did not have ARDS at the onset of mechanical ventilation [33].

Several other investigators have prospectively tested the hypothesis that mechanical ventilation settings could be deleterious and induce or alter pulmonary inflammation in patients without lung injury at the onset of mechanical ventilation. The strongest evidence for benefit of protective lung ventilation in patients without ARDS comes from randomised clinical trials in postoperative patients [34–37]. In these studies, patients undergoing cardiac surgery were randomly ventilated with either tidal volume of 6 ml/kg of predicted body weight or 12 ml/kg of predicted body weight. After the mechanical ventilation period (lasting more than 5 hours) there were decreasing levels of inflammatory mediators such as interleukin-6 (IL-6), interleukin-8 (IL-8), or tumor necrosis factor alpha (TNF-α) in the bronchoalveolar lavage fluid sample after 6 hours, in patients ventilated with lower tidal volume.

Many mechanically ventilated patients are at risk of developing ALI/ARDS. Such patients may have lung injury but do not fulfill the ALI/ARDS consensus criteria at the start of mechanical ventilation. Patients without ALI but who have a predisposing condition, one or more "subsequent hits" can result in full-blown lung injury. Because nonprotective forms of mechanical ventilation may initiate or exacerbate pulmonary inflammation, use of large tidal volume may induce the "primary hit" or form a "second or third hit". Consequently, differences in results from several pathophysiologic studies on VILI in healthy lungs may be explained. Longer periods of mechanical ventilation with or without extrapulmonary "hits" may cause more injury than shorter periods of mechanical ventilation with no extrapulmonary challenges [38].

Effects of ventilation on previously injured lungs

ARDS is morphologically characterised by the distribution of the loss of lung aeration along the vertical axis, with a small number of normal alveoli located in the non-dependent lung and a large consolidated, non-aerated region located in the dependent lung [17–19]. The normally aerated compartment may receive the largest part of each breath and may therefore be hyperinflated and exposed to excessive alveolar wall tension and stress failure. Insufficient levels of PEEP may cause tidal recruitment/derecruitment of parts of the consolidated region and may therefore expose these regions to shear stress. These events may lead to a worsening of the pulmonary and systemic inflammatory response and distal organ dysfunction [39].

In a randomised clinical trial of mechanical ventilation in 44 patients with ALI/ARDS, Ranieri et al. [40] demonstrated that mechanical ventilation could induce a cytokine response that may be attenuated by a strategy to minimise overdistension and recruitment/derecruitment of the lung. Parsons et al. confirmed this finding in a large international randomised trial in 861 patients with ALI [41]. Plasma IL-6 and IL-8 were associated with morbidity and mortality and in ventilatory settings such a tidal volume was associated with an inflammatory response and showed that low tidal volume was associated with a more rapid attenuation of the inflammatory response.

Therefore, conventional mechanical ventilation of patients with ARDS is associated with local and systemic cytokine response and this response may be attenuated by a ventilatory strategy designed to minimise VILI-VALI.

Protection from ventilation-induced lung injury – First, do no harm

The most important factors that have been proposed as responsible for VALI are, firstly, high lung volume associated with elevated transpulmonary pressure and alveolar overdistension, and secondly, repeated alveolar collapse and reopening due to low end-expiratory volume.

The main objective of lung-protective mechanical ventilation strategies is to minimise regional end-inspiratory stretch, thereby decreasing alveolar damage as well as alveolar inflammation/decompartmentalisation [42, 43].

Ventilatory strategies to minimise the damage

Ventilatory strategies aimed at preventing or attenuating VALI have been tested in five randomised clinical trials in adults with ARDS [44–48]. Two trials showed significant increases in the odds ratio for survival of patients treated with low versus control tidal volume (henceforth referred to as the two beneficial trials) [44, 45]. In contrast, the other three trials showed a nonsignificant decrease in the odds ratio for this relationship [46–48]. In a recent meta-analysis comparing all these randomised clinical trials, Eichacker et al. [49] demonstrated that low tidal volumes have not produced consistent beneficial effects in clinical trials of patients with ALI and

ARDS. This analysis suggests that there were important post-randomisation differences in airway pressures in the control arms of the five trials to explain the discrepant results. On the basis of this meta-analysis, a parabolic relationship between mortality rates and changes in tidal volumes and resultant plateau airway pressures could provide an explanation for the contradictory findings in these five trials (see Fig. 2). Both high and low tidal volumes and airway pressures may be associated with increased mortality rate compared with common clinical practice. These trials established that as long as tidal volumes produce airway pressures between 28 cmH$_2$O and 32 cmH$_2$O there is no benefit from using low tidal volumes (i.e. 6 to 7 ml/kg of predicted body weight) and it may be harmful. Further clinical trials are necessary to determine whether lowered tidal volumes produce a survival benefit when compared with the intermediate tidal volumes (8–9 ml/kg) routinely used by participating physicians at the time of these trials.

Both experimental studies of VILI and clinical trials to minimise the potential impact of VALI have used the pressure-volume (P-V) curve of the respiratory system to assess mechanics and titrate ventilator settings. PEEP set above the lower inflection point (Pflex) and plateau pressure lower than the upper inflection point of the PV curve have been suggested as necessary to maintain recruitment and avoid overdistention, respectively [39]. The P-V curve inflection points can be difficult to identify and they are also affected by chest wall compliance (not just lung compliance), causing some uncertainty as to whether these points truly reflect lung recruitment and lung overdistention in clinical practice; this concern may be most important in patients with surgical conditions causing increased abdominal pressure and coincident acute lung injury, in whom PV curve inflection points have been shown to reflect chest wall rather than lung mechanics.

On the other hand, there is a controversy about the adequate level of PEEP applied to patients with mechanical ventilation and risk factors for the development of VILI. Numerous experimental studies showed that PEEP protected the lung in various models of VILI [22, 44]. Although the mechanisms of this protective effect are not fully elucidated, they may be mediated by PEEP-induced alveolar recruitment, which

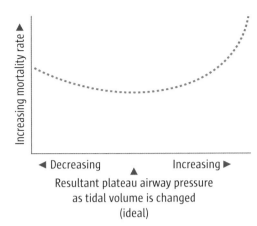

Fig. 2   Hypothetical model representing the relationship between tidal volumes and resultant plateau airway pressure and mortality rates. Mortality rates first decrease and then increase as tidal volume and plateau airway pressure decreases [Eichaker PQ, Gertenberger EP, Banks SM, Cui X, Natanson CA, 2002, A meta-analysis of ALI and ARDS trials testing low tidal volumes, Am Journal Respiratory and Critical Care Medicine; 166: 1510–428, Official Journal of the American Thoracic Society, © American Thoracic Society]

avoids cyclic airway collapse and reopening, protects lung surfactant and improves ventilation homogeneity. Recently, a randomised clinical trial [50] showing a strategy for setting the PEEP aimed at increased alveolar recruitment while limiting hyperinflation did not significantly reduce mortality but did improve lung function and reduce the duration of mechanical ventilation and the duration of organ failure. Meade and coworkers [51] compared in 1,083 patients two lung protective ventilation strategies, control group (n = 508) based on target tidal volumes of 6 ml/kg of predicted body weight, plateau pressure not exceeding 30 cm of water and conventional levels of PEEP with an experimental group (n = 475) based on target tidal volumes of 6 ml/kg of predicted body weight, plateau pressure not exceeding 40 cm of water, recruitment maneuvers and higher PEEP. The randomised clinical trial resulted in no significant decrease of mortality (all-cause hospital mortality) and resulted in similar rates of barotraumas and duration of mechanical ventilation.

Villar et al. [52] in a randomised and multicentre Spanish study with 95 patients with persistent ARDS showed that a mechanical ventilation strategy with a PEEP level set, on day 1, at 2 cmH_2O above the lower inflection point on the pressure-volume curve of the respiratory system (P_{flex}) and low tidal volume had a marked improvement in ICU mortality compared with a higher tidal volume and relative low PEEP (30.1 % vs. 54 %; p = 0.017), the mean difference in the number of additional organ failures post-randomisation was higher in the control group (p < 0.001) and no significant difference in barotrauma rates was observed. However, in a larger randomised clinical trial with 549 patients with ALI/ARDS who received mechanical ventilation with a tidal-volume goal of 6 ml/kg of predicted body weight and an end-inspiratory plateau pressure limit of 30 cmH_2O, clinical outcomes and organ failure-free days between the lower- and higher-PEEP study groups were similar whether lower or higher PEEP levels were used [53]. Furthermore, there were no significant differences between the study groups in the change in plasmatic interleukin-6, surfactant protein D, and intercellular adhesion molecule-1 (ICAM-1) from day 0 to day 3.

Although most of the studies justify the use of higher PEEP levels as part of a multifaceted protocolised lung-protective ventilation strategy designed to open the lung, there is an open controversy regarding the optimal level of PEEP for treating and/or preventing VILI in patients with ARDS. In a recent meta-analysis, Gordo et al. evaluated the effects of high PEEP versus conventional PEEP on mortality and on the risk of barotrauma in patients with the acute respiratory distress syndrome (ARDS). No effects of PEEP level on mortality (RR 0.73, 95 % CI: 0.49 to 1.10) or on the incidence of barotrauma (RR 0.50, 95 % CI: 0.14 to 1.73) were found. However, an analysis of the studies in which PEEP was individualised in function of Pflex showed a significant decrease in mortality (RR 0.59, 95 % CI: 0.43 to 0.82) (p = 0.001). The use of high or conventional PEEP in function of oxygenation does not affect mortality or the incidence of barotrauma in patients with ARDS. However, there might be a decrease in mortality associated with high PEEP individualised in function of the pulmonary mechanics of each patient [54].

Rescue therapies for preventing VILI in patients with ARDS

High-frequency oscillator ventilation (HFOV)

High-frequency oscillator ventilation (HFOV) is an unconventional form of mechanical ventilation that may improve oxygenation in patients with ARDS while limiting further lung injury associated with high ventilatory pressures and volumes delivered during conventional ventilation. Many investigators have hypothesised that the mechanical advantages of HFOV should lead to lower incidence of VILI. Indeed, HFOV has been found to reduce the morphologic findings of VILI, including hyaline membrane formation, alveolar leukocyte infiltration, and airway epithelial damage when compared with conventional ventilation. In addition, the expression of messenger RNA for tumor necrosis factor, several interleukins (IL-1beta, IL-6, IL-8, IL-10), transforming growth factor, and adhesion molecules were all reduced in animals receiving HFOV [55, 56], thus showing that HFOV might be a preferable option as a lung protection strategy for treating VILI in patients.

HFOV has seen widespread use for almost two decades in the neonatal population, but there is more limited experience with HFOV in adults. There are only two randomised clinical trials in adults with ARDS comparing HFOV to conventional ventilation which revealed encouraging results but failed to show a mortality benefit of HFOV over conventional ventilation [56, 57]. Further research is needed to clarify optimal patient selection, technique, the actual tidal volume delivered and the role of combining HFOV with other interventions such as recruitment maneuvers, prone positioning and nitric oxide. Ferguson and co-investigators [59] determined the safety, feasibility, and lung-recruitment efficacy of an explicit ventilation protocol combining high-frequency oscillatory ventilation and recruitment maneuvers in a prospective, multiple-centre, single-intervention pilot study. They showed that the combination of HFOV and recruitment maneuvers resulted in rapid and sustained improvement in oxygenation, likely through lung recruitment [55]. HFOV needs to be compared directly with CMV in a large randomised clinical trial with mortality as the primary outcome measure (ongoing multicentre trial led by Ferguson et al. [60]).

Mechanical ventilation in the prone position does not reduce mortality or duration of ventilation despite improved oxygenation and a decreased risk of pneumonia [61]. Therefore, it should not be used routinely for acute hypoxemic respiratory failure [62–65]. However, a sustained improvement in oxygenation may support the use of prone positioning in patients with severe hypoxemia.

In early/severe acute respiratory distress syndrome, pronation under positive end-expiratory pressure optimisation may reduce ventilator-induced lung injury risk [66, 67]. Future trials should examine the efficacy of maintaining the prone position for treating ventilator-induced lung injury.

New research fields in VILI:
Cellular therapy and regenerative medicine

Cell-based therapy is a very promising, novel treatment for ALI. Mesenchymal stem cells derived from bone marrow (MSCs) are multipotent cells that can be isolated from the bone marrow and expanded in culture relatively easily. Culture-expanded MSCs have been used in clinical settings to enhance haematopoietic stem cell engraftment in bone marrow transplant patients and in tissue regeneration therapy. In addition, on animal models of lung injury, in which administration of MSC attenuates inflammation, and injury. This effect reveals a central role for MSC in mitigating pro-inflammatory networks and amplifying anti-inflammatory signals involved in VILI.

Gupta et al. [68] showed the use of MSCs administered intratracheally as treatment of endotoxin-induced lung injury in mice. They demonstrated a marked decrease in mortality, primarily due to a decrease in ALI. Similar results were observed by Mei et al. [69]. MSCs were delivered intravenously 30 min after intratracheal instillation of lipopolysaccharide (LPS) to induce lung injury in mice. Administration of MSCs significantly reduced LPS-induced pulmonary inflammation, as reflected by reductions in total cell and neutrophil counts in bronchoalveolar lavage (BAL) fluid (53%, 95% confidence interval: 7%-101%; and 60%, 95% confidence interval: 4%-116%, respectively) as well as reducing levels of proinflammatory cytokines in both BAL fluid and lung parenchymal homogenates. Furthermore, administration of MSCs transfected with pANGPT1 (angiopoietin 1) resulted in nearly complete reversal of LPS-induced increases in lung permeability as assessed by reductions in IgM and albumin levels in BAL. Therefore, treatment with MSCs alone significantly reduced LPS-induced acute pulmonary inflammation in mice, while administration of pANGPT1-transfected MSCs resulted in a further improvement in both alveolar inflammation and permeability. The discoveries described herein have contributed to the novel concept of MSCs as a therapeutic modality in inflammatory diseases, including acute lung injury.

More preclinical work is needed to test the mechanisms of benefit and the potential therapeutic value of MSCs for VILI.

Conclusion

In summary, VILI is associated with excessive strain and airspace epithelial shear stress amplifying lung inflammation, exacerbating barrier disruption, and promoting ongoing pulmonary oedema formation and likely development of multisystem organ failure.

Nearly all patients with ARDS require mechanical ventilation and are therefore at risk for VILI/VALI. However, the proportion of patients receiving protective ventilatory strategies remains modest due to lack of congruent results in large randomised clinical trials and meta-analysis. Until future studies become available, clinicians should be aware in using ventilator settings that lead to plateau pressures higher than 30 cmH$_2$O in patients with/without ARDS (see Fig. 3). However, whether a truly safe ventilation strategy exists is uncertain. Although currently our ability to recognise ongoing VALI in patients is limited, experimental studies have indicated that measuring biological markers may be a valuable tool for identifying patients at risk, as well as for determining prognosis and understanding pathogenesis. Notably, the latest advances in the treatment of ALI, such as ventilation with lower tidal volume, constitute major improvements

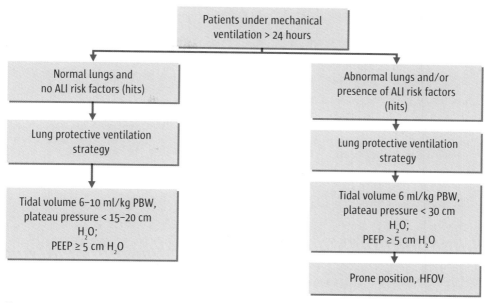

Fig. 3   Recommendations for the ventilator settings in patients under lung protective ventilation.
PBW = predicted body weight

in supportive care. However, clinical heterogeneity, such as different lengths of follow-up and higher plateau pressure in control arms in two trials, make the interpretation of the combined results difficult. The effects on long-term mortality are unknown, although the possibility of a clinically relevant benefit cannot be excluded [70]. For those reasons, these conclusions are neither directives nor recommendations for clinical application. Finally, the lung-protective strategy (ARDSnet strategy) might not be protective for all patients with ALI, and patients characterised by a larger amount of collapsed lung might be exposed to VILI despite tidal volume and pressure limitation. Therefore, the best ventilatory strategy should be ideally adapted to the size of the aerated lung [71].

Basic research on the mechanisms of VILI has led to the development of ventilatory strategies that have been shown to decrease mortality in randomised clinical trials. Future studies that identify patients at risk for VALI, test new ventilatory strategies and identify the underlying molecular mechanisms of the lung injury will alter our approach to mechanical ventilation. Only careful research and translational perspective in research will confirm or refute the current lung-protective ventilation strategy.

The authors

Oscar Peñuelas, MD
Fernando Frutos-Vivar, MD
Andres Esteban, MD, PhD
      Hospital Universitario de Getafe,
      Madrid, Spain | CIBER de Enfermedades
      Respiratorias, Madrid, Spain

Address for correspondence
      Andres Esteban
      Hospital Universitario de Getafe, Getafe
      Carretera de Toledo km 12,5
      CP 28905 Madrid, Spain
      E-mail: aesteban@ucigetafe.com

References

1.   Esteban A, Anzueto A, Frutos-Vivar F, Alía I, Brochard L, Stewart TE, et al, for the Mechanical Ventilation International Study Group. Characteristics and outcomes in adult patients receiving mechanical ventilation. JAMA 2002; 287: 345–355.
2.   Esteban A, Ferguson ND, Meade MO, Frutos-Vivar F, Apezteguia C, Brochard L, et al. VENTILA Group. Evolution of mechanical ventilation in response to

clinical research. Am J Respir Crit Care Med 2008; 177: 170-7.

3. Dreyfuss D, Saumon G. Ventilator-induced lung injury: lessons from experimental studies. Am J Respir Crit Care Med 1998; 157: 294-323.

4. International Consensus Conferences in intensive care medicine American Thoracic Society, European Society of Intensive Care Medicine, Societe de Reanimation Langue Francaise. Ventilator-associated lung injury in ARDS. Intensive Care Med 1999; 25: 1444-52.

5. Tobin MJ. Culmination of an era in research on the acute respiratory distress syndrome. N Engl J Med 2000; 342: 1360-1.

6. Fisher JL, Levitan I, Margulies SS. Plasma membrane surface increases with tonic stretch of alveolar epithelial cells. Am J Respir Cell Mol Biol 2004; 31: 200-8.

7. Tschumperlin DJ, Dai G, Maly IV, Kikuchi T, Laiho LH, McVittie AK, et al. Mechanotransduction through growth-factor shedding into the extracellular space. Nature 2004; 429: 83-6.

8. Fisher JL, Margulies SS. Modeling the effect of stretch and plasma membrane tension on Na+-K+-ATPase activity in alveolar epithelial cells. Am J Physiol Lung Cell Mol Physiol 2007; 292: L40-53.

9. Trepat X, Grabulosa M, Puig F, Maksym GN, Navajas D, Farré R. Viscoelasticity of human alveolar epithelial cells subjected to stretch. Am J Physiol Lung Cell Mol Physiol 2004; 287: L1025-34.

10. Uhlig U, Fehrenbach H, Lachmann RA, Goldmann T, Lachmann B, Vollmer E. Phosphoinositide 3-OH kinase inhibition prevents ventilation-induced lung cell activation. Am J Respir Crit Care Med 2004; 169: 201-8.

11. Vlahakis NE, Hubmayr RD. Cellular responses to capillary stress: plasma membrane stress failure in alveolar epithelial cells. J Appl Physiol 2000; 89: 2490-2496.

12. Haitsma, JJ, Uhlig S, Göggel R, Verbrugge SJ, Lachmann U, Lachmann B. Ventilator-induced lung injury leads to loss of alveolar and systemic compartmentalization of TNF-α. Intensive Care Med 2000; 26: 1515-1522.

13. Liu M, Tanswell AK, Post M. Mechanical force-induced signal transduction in lung cells. Am J Physiol Lung Cell Mol Physiol 1999; 277: L667-L683.

14. Orfanos SE, Mavrommati I, Korovesi I, Roussos C. Pulmonary endothelium in acute lung injury: from basic science to the critically ill. Intensive Care Med 2004; 30: 1702-14.

15. Kuebler WM, Uhlig U, Goldmann T, Schael G, Kerem A, Exner K, et al. Stretch activates nitric oxide production in pulmonary vascular endothelial cells in situ. Am J Respir Crit Care Med 2003; 168: 1391-8.

16. Haseneen NA, Vaday GG, Zucker S, Foda HD. Mechanical stretch induces MMP-2 release and activation in lung endothelium: role of EMMPRIN. Am J Physiol Lung Cell Mol Physiol 2003; 284: L541-7.

17. Dreyfuss D, Basset G, Soler P, Saumon G. Intermittent positive-pressure hyperventilation with high inflation pressures produces pulmonary microvascular injury in rats. Am Rev Respir Dis 1985; 132: 880-884.

18. Zhang H, Downey GP, Suter PM, Slutsky AS, Ranieri VM. Conventional mechanical ventilation is associated with bronchoalveolar lavage-induced activation of polymorphonuclear leukocytes: a possible mechanism to explain the systemic consequences of ventilator-induced lung injury in patients with ARDS. Anesthesiology 2002; 97:1426-33.

19. Ricard JD, Dreyfuss D, Saumon G. Production of inflammatory cytokines in ventilator-induced lung injury: a reappraisal. Am J Respir Crit Care Med 2001; 163: 1176-80.

20. Choudhury S, Wilson M.R, Goddard M.E, O'Dea KP, Takata M. Mechanisms of early pulmonary neutrophil sequestration in ventilator-induced lung injury in mice. Am J Physiol Lung Cell Mol Physiol 2004; 287: L902-10.

21. Belperio JA, Keane MP, Burdick M, Londhe V, Xue YY, Li K, et al. Critical role for CXCR2 and CXCR2 ligands during the pathogenesis of ventilator-induced lung injury. J Clin Invest 2002; 110: 1703-16.

22. Gurkan OU, O'Donnell C, Brower R, Ruckdeschel E, Becker PM. Differential effects of mechanical ventilatory strategy on lung injury and systemic organ inflammation in mice. Am J Physiol Lung Cell Mol Physiol 2003; 285: L710-8.

23. Chiumello D, Pristine G, Slutsky AS. Mechanical ventilation affects local and systemic cytokines in an animal model of acute respiratory distress syndrome. Am J Respir Crit Care Med 1999; 160: 109-16.

24. Wilson MR, Choudhury S, Goddard ME, O'Dea KP, Nicholson AG, Takata M. High tidal volume upregulates intrapulmonary cytokines in an in vivo mouse model of ventilator-induced lung injury. J Appl Physiol 2003; 95: 1385-93.

25. Tremblay, LN, Valenza R, Ribeiro SP, Li J, Slutsky AS. Injurious ventilatory strategies increase cytokines and c-fos m-RNA expression in an isolated rat lung model. J Clin Invest 1997; 99: 944-952.

26. Nin N, Peñuelas O, de Paula M, Lorente JA, Fernández-Segoviano P, Esteban A. Ventilation-induced lung injury in rats is associated with organ injury and systemic inflammation that is attenuated by dexamethasone. Crit Care Med 2006; 34: 1093-8.

27. Tutor JD, Mason CM, Dobard E, Beckerman RC, Summer WR, Nelson S. Loss of compartmentalization of alveolar tumor necrosis factor after lung injury. Am J Respir Crit Care Med 1994; 149: 1107-11.

28. Imai Y, Parodo J, Kajikawa O, de Perrot M, Fischer S, Edwards V, et al. Injurious mechanical ventilation and end-organ epithelial cell apoptosis and organ dysfunction in an experimental model of acute respiratory distress syndrome. JAMA 2003; 289: 2104-12

29. Vlahakis N.E, Hubmayr R.D. Response of alveolar cells to mechanical stress. Curr Opin Crit Care 2003; 9: 2–8.

30. Oudin S, Pugin J. Role of MAP kinase activation in interleukin-8 production by human BEAS-2B bronchial epithelial cells submitted ro cyclic stretch. Am J Respir Cell Mol Biol 2002; 27: 107–114.

31. Li LF, Ouyang B, Choukroun G, Matyal R, Mascarenhas M, Jafari B, et al. Stretch-induced IL-8 depends on c-Jun NH2 terminal and nuclear factor-kappaB inducing kinases. Am J Physiol Lung Cell Mol Physiol 2003; 285: L464-L475.

32. Gajic O, Dara SI, Mendez JL, Adesanya AO, Festic E, Caples SM, et al. Ventilator-associated lung injury in patients without acute lung injury at the onset of mechanical ventilation. Crit Care Med 2004; 32: 1817–24.

33. Gajic O, Frutos-Vivar F, Esteban A, Hubmayr RD, Anzueto A. Ventilator settings as a risk factor for acute respiratory distress syndrome in mechanically ventilated patients. Intensive Care Med 2005; 31: 922–926.

34. Wrigge H, Uhlig U, Baumgarten G, Menzenbach J, Zinserling J, Ernst M et al. Mechanical ventilation strategies and inflammatory responses to cardiac surgery: a prospective randomized clinical trial. Intensive Care Med 2005; 31: 1379–1387.

35. Zupancich E, Paparella D, Turani F, Munch C, Rossi A, Massaccesi S, et al. Mechanical ventilation affects inflammatory mediators in patients undergoing cardiopulmonary bypass for cardiac surgery: A randomized clinical trial. J Thorac Cardiovasc Surg 2005; 130: 378–383.

36. Reis Miranda D, Gommers D, Struijs A, Dekker R, Mekel J, Feelders R, et al. Ventilation according to the open lung concept attenuates pulmonary inflammatory response in cardiac surgery. Eur J Cardiothorac Surg 2005; 28: 889–895.

37. Choi G, Wolthuis EK, Bresser P, Levi M, van der Poll T, Dzoljic M, et al. Mechanical ventilation with lower tidal volumes and positive-end expiratory pressure prevents alveolar coagulation in patients without lung injury. Anesthesiology 2006; 105: 689–695.

38. Slutsky AS, Tremblay LN. Multiple system organ failure: is mechanical ventilation a contributing factor? Am J Respir Crit Care Med 1998; 157: 1721–1725.

39. Ranieri, VM, N. Brienza, S. Santostasi, Puntillo F, Mascia L, Vitale N, et al. Impairment of lung and chest wall mechanics in patients with acute respiratory distress syndrome. Am J Respir Crit Care Med 1997; 156: 1082–1091.

40. Ranieri VM, Suter PM, Tortorella C, De Tullio R, Dayer JM, Brienza A, et al. Effect of mechanical ventilation on inflammatory mediators in patients with acute respiratory distress syndrome: a randomized controlled trial. JAMA 1999; 282: 54–61.

41. Parsons PE, Eisner M.D, Thompson T, Matthay MA, Ancukiewicz M, Bernard GR, et al. Lower tidal volume ventilation and plasma cytokine markers of inflammation in patients with acute lung injury. Crit Care Med 2005; 33: 1–6.

42. Rouby JJ, Lu Q, Goldstein I. Selecting the right level of positive end-expiratory pressure in patients with acute respiratory distress syndrome. Am J Respir Crit Care Med 2002; 165: 1182–1186.

43. Muscedere JG, Mullen JBM, Gan K, Slutsky AR. Tidal ventilation at low airway pressures can augment lung injury. Am J Respir Crit Care Med 1994; 149: 1327–34

44. Amato MB, Barbas CS, Medeiros DM, Magaldi RB, Schettino GP, Lorenzi-Filho G, et al. Effect of a protective-ventilation strategy on mortality in the acute respiratory distress syndrome. N Engl J Med 1998; 338: 347–354.

45. Acute Respiratory Distress Syndrome Network. Ventilation with lower tidal volumes compared with traditional tidal volumes for acute lung injury and the acute respiratory distress syndrome. N Engl J Med 2000; 342: 1301–1308.

46. Stewart TE, Meade MO, Cook DJ, Granton JT, Hodder RV, Lapinsky SE, et al. Evaluation of a ventilation strategy to prevent barotrauma in patients at high risk for acute respiratory distress syndrome. N Engl J Med 1998; 338: 355–361.

47. Brochard L, Roudot-Thoraval F, Roupie E, Delclaux C, Chastre J, Fernandez-Mondejar E, et al. Tidal volume reduction for prevention of ventilator-induced lung injury in acute respiratory distress syndrome. Multicenter Trial Group on Tidal Volume Reduction in ARDS. Am J Respir Crit Care Med 1998; 158: 1831–1838.

48. Brower RG, Shanholtz CB, Fessler HE, Shade DM, White P Jr, Wiener CM, et al. Prospective, randomized, controlled clinical trial comparing traditional versus reduced tidal volume ventilation in acute respiratory distress syndrome patients. Crit Care Med 1999; 27: 1492–1498.

49. Eichaker PQ, Gertenberger EP, Banks SM, Cui X, Natanson CA. A meta-analysis of ALI and ARDS trials testing low tidal volumes. Am J Respir Crit Care Med 2002; 166: 1510–428.

50. Mercat A, Richard JC, Vielle B, Jaber S, Osman D, Diehl JL, et al. Expiratory Pressure (Express) Study Group. Positive end-expiratory pressure setting in adults with acute lung injury and acute respiratory distress syndrome: a randomized controlled trial. JAMA 2008; 299: 646–55

51. Meade MO, Cook DJ, Guyatt GH, Slutsky AS, Arabi YM, Cooper DJ, et al. Lung Open Ventilation Study Investigators. Ventilation strategy using low tidal volumes, recruitment maneuvers, and high positive end-expiratory pressure for acute lung injury and acute respiratory distress syndrome: a randomized controlled trial. JAMA 2008; 299: 637–45.

52. Villar J, Kacmarek RM, Pérez-Méndez L, Aguirre-Jaime A.

A high positive end-expiratory pressure, low tidal volume ventilatory strategy improves outcome in persistent acute respiratory distress syndrome: a randomized, controlled trial. Crit Care Med 2006; 34: 1311–8.

53. Brower RG, Lanken PN, MacIntyre N, Matthay MA, Morris A, Ancukiewicz M, et al. Higher versus lower positive end-expiratory pressures in patients with the acute respiratory distress syndrome. N Engl J Med 2004; 351:327–36.

54. Gordo-Vidal F, Gómez-Tello V, Palencia-Herrejón E, Latour-Pérez J, Sánchez-Artola B, Díaz-Alersi R. High PEEP vs. conventional PEEP in the acute respiratory distress syndrome: a systematic review and meta-analysis. Med Intensiva 2007; 31:491–501.

55. Imai Y, Nakagawa S, Ito Y, Kawano T, Slutsky AS, Miyasaka K. Comparison of lung protection strategies using conventional and high-frequency oscillatory ventilation. J Appl Physiol 2001; 91: 1836–1844.

56. Rotta A.T, Gunnarsson B, Fuhrman B.P, Hernan LJ, Steinhorn DM. Comparison of lung protective ventilation strategies in a rabbit model of acute lung injury. Crit Care Med 2001; 29: 2176–2184.

57. Derdak S, Metha S, Stewart T.E, Smith T, Rogers M, Buchman TG, et al. Multicenter Oscillatory Ventilation for the Acute Respiratory Distress Syndorme Trial (MOAT) Study Investigators. High frequency oscillatory ventilation for acute respiratory distress syndrome: a randomized, controlled trial. Am J Respir Crit Care Med 2002; 166: 801–808.

58. Bollen CW, van Well GT, Sherry T, Beale RJ, Shah S, Findlay G, et al. High frequency oscillatory ventilation compared with conventional mechanical ventilation in adult respiratory distress syndrome: a randomized controlled trial. Crit Care 2005; 9: 430–439.

59. Ferguson ND, Chiche JD, Kacmarek RM, Hallett DC, Mehta S, Findlay GP, et al. Combining high-frequency oscillatory ventilation and recruitment maneuvers in adults with early acute respiratory distress syndrome: Treatment with Oscillation and a Open Lung Strategy (TOOLS) Trial pilot study. Crit Care Med 2005; 33: 479–486.

60. The Oscillation for ARDS Treated Early (OSCILLATE) Trial Pilot Study. Clinicaltrial.gov

61. Sud S, Sud M, Friedrich JO, Adhikari NK. Effect of mechanical ventilation in the prone position on clinical outcomes in patients with acute hypoxemic respiratory failure: a systematic review and meta-analysis. CMAJ 2008; 178: 1153–61.

62. Pelosi P, Tubiolo D, Mascheroni D, Vicardi P, Crotti S, Valenza F, et al. Effects of the prone position on respiratory mechanics and gas exchange during acute lung injury. Am J Respir Crit Care Med 1998; 157: 387–393.

63. Mancebo J, Fernández R, Blanch L, Rialp G, Gordo F, Ferrer M, et al. A multicenter trial of prolonged prone ventilation in severe acute respiratory distress syndrome. Am J Respir Crit Care Med 2006; 173: 1233–9.

64. Guerin C, Gaillard S, Lemasson S, Ayzac L, Girard R, Beuret P, et al. Effects of systematic prone positioning in hypoxemic acute respiratory failure: a randomized controlled trial. JAMA 2004; 292: 2379–87.

65. Gattinoni L, Tognoni G, Pesenti A, Taccone P, Mascheroni D, Labarta V, et al. Prone-Supine Study Group. Effect of prone positioning on the survival of patients with acute respiratory failure. N Engl J Med 2001; 345: 568–73.

66. Papazian L, Gainnier M, Marin V, Donati S, Arnal JM, Demory D, et al. Comparison of prone positioning and high-frequency oscillatory ventilation in patients with acute respiratory distress syndrome. Crit Care Med 2005; 33: 2162–71.

67. Mentzelopoulos SD, Roussos C, Zakynthinos SG. Prone position reduces lung stress and strain in severe acute respiratory distress syndrome. Eur Respir J 2005; 25: 534–44.

68. Gupta N, Su X, Popov B, Lee JW, Serikov V, Matthay MA. Intrapulmonary delivery of bone marrow-derived mesenchymal stem cells improves survival and attenuates endotoxin-induced acute lung injury in mice. J Immunol 2007; 179: 1855–63.

69. Mei SH, McCarter SD, Deng Y, Parker CH, Liles WC, Stewart DJ. Prevention of LPS-induced acute lung injury in mice by mesenchymal stem cells overexpressing angiopoietin 1. PLoS Med 2007; 4: 1525–1537.

70. Petrucci N, Iacovelli W. Lung protective ventilation strategy for the acute respiratory distress syndrome. Cochrane Database Syst Rev 2007 Jul 18;(3): CD003844.

71. Terragni PP, Rosboch G, Tealdi A, Corno E, Menaldo E, Davini O, et al. Tidal hyperinflation during low tidal volume ventilation in Acute respiratory Distress Syndrome. Am J Respir Crit Care Med 2007; 175: 160–166.

Christiane Hartog, Michael Bauer and Konrad Reinhart

Avoiding harm in fluid resuscitation: Emerging evidence for the toxicity of synthetic colloids in critically ill patients

Meta-analyses and recent large-scale studies have shown that resuscitation in critically ill patients is equally effective with crystalloids or colloids. However, synthetic colloids are fraught with inherent risks. These include impairment of coagulation, renal failure and uptake into tissue with long-term adverse effects on morbidity and mortality in susceptible patients. Colloid adverse effects are dose-related, become manifest in the long term and have been shown for all HES solutions on the market including the modern HES 130/0.4. In comparison, crystalloid solutions are safe and considerably less costly. In overdosed larger volumes, crystalloid administration may be associated with tissue oedema, in particular abdominal compartment syndrome.

Textbook knowledge indicates that four to five times as much crystalloid as colloid volume is needed to achieve comparable volume effects. This theoretical assumption must be revised in view of latest study results which show that adequate resuscitation with equal outcomes is achieved by much less crystalloid fluid load, with ratios ranging between one to two.

The emerging evidence of toxicity of synthetic colloids in the critically ill patients is tipping the scales toward crystalloids for reasons of safety, side effects and containment of costs.

Introduction

Rapid and adequate administration of fluid is the mainstay of resuscitation in the critically ill patient. A study of resuscitation in septic patients has indeed emphasised the pivotal role of early and vigorous fluid therapy: In patients with severe sepsis and either blood pressure below 90 mm Hg or lactate above 4 mmol/L, rapid restoration of systemic oxygen delivery and improvement of tissue oxygenation within the first 6 hours after recognition of septic shock demonstrated significantly improved survival [1]. Early goal-directed resuscitation is one of the key consensus recommendations of an international panel of intensivists for best current care of patients with severe sepsis [2].

It is, however, less evident whether to choose crystalloid or colloid as first-line volume therapy. Systematic reviews have found that resuscitation is equally effective with crystalloid as with colloid solutions [3–5]. Given the limitations of such meta-analyses, it was even more convincing when large-scale prospective trials of fluid resuscitation confirmed that albumin, dextran and hydroxyethyl starch did not confer an outcome benefit over crystalloid solutions in adults and children

[6–9]. Recent consensus recommendations and practice parameters for fluid therapy in septic patients state that crystalloids and colloids may be given interchangeably [2, 10]. It is therefore not surprising that the utilisation of different fluids varies widely according to country and specialty [11–15]; marketing by pharmaceutical companies may also play a role [16]. A recent European observational study showed that 41% of patients received only crystalloids; HES and gelatin were used in 34% and 32% of patients, respectively, while albumin 20/25%, albumin 4/5% and dextran were used less commonly (8%, 5% and 5%, respectively) [17].

Colloids, which include albumin, hydroxyethyl starches (HES), gelatin and dextran, differ fundamentally from crystalloids because they generate colloid oncotic pressure. These solutions have theoretical advantages according to Starling's law by achieving faster plasma expansion with less administered volume. It is commonly believed that resuscitation with crystalloids will require two to four times more volume than colloids and that it takes longer to achieve desired haemodynamic endpoints [10]. This is deemed to be important because fluid may lead to oedema and increase in hydrostatic pressure, raising the complication rate and worsening outcome in acute lung injury, acute respiratory distress syndrome, acute pulmonary oedema and following surgery [18]. Moreover, synthetic colloids have potentially beneficial effects on microcirculation, rheology and serum levels of inflammatory mediators [19].

However, colloids are fraught with adverse effects. Synthetic colloids may lead to increased bleeding [20], acute renal failure [21, 22], and anaphylactoid reactions [23]. The non-synthetic colloid albumin which is derived from human blood carries the risk of infection [24].

Haemodynamic effects of crystalloids and colloids in critically ill patients

The current understanding and one of the arguments used in favor of colloids is that they expand the intravascular volume and increase myocardial preload faster than crystalloids [25]. However, larger studies and longer observation periods reveal that this effect is marginal and does not im-

prove clinical outcome in the ICU [6, 7, 9]. When septic patients with below-target values of CVP, central venous oxygen saturation (ScvO2) and mean arterial blood pressure (MAP) were resuscitated with HES or Ringer's, ScvO2 and MAP normalised equally fast with modified Ringer's lactate [9]. Children with Dengue shock syndrome who received colloids achieved initial cardiovascular stability more rapidly and showed a faster reduction in median haematocrit values during the first two hours (25%, 22% and 9% reduction for dextran, HES and Ringer's, respectively; p < 0.001). Subsequently, however, their haematocrit increased more than with Ringer's (5% increase for dextran or HES, 0% for Ringer's; p < 0.001). The authors explained this as a combination of fluid effects and vascular leak. Colloids exert a rapid effect followed by a rebound increase in vascular leak a few hours later. Overall time to final stabilisation was not different between groups [7].

It is commonly believed that the crystalloid volume needed to raise the circulating intravascular fluid volume to a similar degree is three to five times greater than colloid [26]. In experimental models, oncotic solutions achieved similar resuscitation goals with less than half the infusion volume of crystalloids [27, 28]. More recent clinical studies, however, reveal considerably smaller ratios of crystalloid to colloid volumes: 1.0–1.3 to normal saline [111], 1.4 to albumin in the SAFE study [6], 1.5 to HES in the VISEP study [9]. In septic children, initial resuscitation to the same clinical endpoints was achieved by a saline to gelatin ratio of 1.7 [8]. In a pig model of liver injury with uncontrolled bleeding, the volume expansion effects were approx. 75% for Ringer's lactate and 115% for HES 130/0.4, corresponding to a ratio of 1.53 [37].

It must therefore be concluded that the volume ratio needed for resuscitation may be closer to the range of 1.3–1.7. The advantage that was ascribed to colloids in theory therefore seems to dwindle in the face of practical evidence.

Albumin

Albumin has an excellent long-term safety record and serious adverse events reported from its use are rare; however, it is more costly than crystal-

Avoiding harm in fluid resuscitation:
Emerging evidence for the toxicity of synthetic colloids in critically ill patients

F

loids or synthetic colloids [30]. A highly contro-versial meta-analysis which focused on albumin alone found an increased mortality risk in criti-cally ill patients [31] and led to a steep decline in the use of albumin [32]. This finding was not con-firmed by subsequent meta-analyses and ran-domised controlled trials. The large intervention-al Saline versus Albumin Fluid Evaluation (SAFE) study randomised nearly 7,000 patients to receive either 4 % iso-osmotic albumin or nor-mal saline for resuscitation according to clinical status and response to treatment in a blinded fashion. There was no difference in outcome measures including 28-day mortality, length of stay in the ICU or in the hospital, number of or-gan failures or days on mechanical ventilation. The relative risk of death tended to be reduced in a subgroup of 603 patients with severe sepsis af-ter resuscitation with albumin (0.87, 95 % CI 0.74 to 1.02, p = 0.09) [6].

In a subgroup of patients with trauma, the relative risk of death during 28 days was higher in the albumin group (1.36 compared to 0.96 without trauma, p = 0.04); however, this was due to the greater number of patients with associ-ated brain injury who died after random assign-ment to albumin as opposed to saline (relative risk 1.62, 95 % CI, 1.12 to 2.34, p = 0.009). A post-hoc follow-up study of the enrolled patients with severe brain injury confirmed a significant-ly higher mortality at 24 months after treatment with albumin (relative risk 1.88, 95 % CI, 1.31 to 2.70; p < 0.001) [33].

In summary, 4 % iso-osmotic albumin is safe to use in the intensive care unit (ICU), except in patients with traumatic brain injury, and may have some potential benefit in patients with se-vere sepsis. Further trials are needed to deter-mine the relevance of this observation.

HES

Since introduction of the compound more than forty years ago, different types of HES solutions have been developed to lessen the rate of side ef-fects by changing molecular weight, degree and ratio of hydroxyethyl substitution. Whereas gela-tin is favoured in the UK, and more albumin is used in the US and Australia, HES 200/0.5 and 130/0.4 (with molecular weights of 200 and 130

kDa and substitution degrees of 0.5 and 0.4 re-spectively) are predominant in Europe [13–15], HES 70/0.5 is used in Japan. HES 450/0.7 and lately also HES 130/0.4 have been registered in the US, albeit on the basis of non-inferiority stud-ies with low cumulative doses and in low-risk patients or volunteers [34]. The clinical trials ros-ter supporting licensure of HES 130/0.4 in the US is made publicly available on the FDA web-site. Data was derived from 21 mainly non-infe-riority studies in patients without history of heart, kidney, liver, diabetes, or severe infectious dis-eases, history of coagulation disorders, known allergy to starch, BW > 100 kg, pregnancy, and lactation. In the single US volume replacement study, exclusion criteria also included previous cardiac surgery. Mean study period was 2 days, mean cumulative dose was 41.9 ml/kg, which is less than the recommended maximal daily dose of HES 130/0.4, and control fluids were mostly other HES or gelatin solutions. There are no studies on the safety of HES 130/0.4 in severe sepsis or intensive care patients with pre-existing renal impairment or risk of renal dysfunction. As will be shown below, HES 130/0.4 has in the meantime been associated with the whole range of adverse effects, including irreversible renal failure [35], increased bleeding [36, 37] and tissue uptake [38].

Renal impairment

Renal impairment may be due to a plurality of causes, including reabsorption of HES into renal tubular cells leading to osmotic nephrotic le-sions, or renal plugging due to hyperviscous urine. There is now considerable evidence on re-nal impairment by HES in ICU patients, ranging from acute renal failure in prospective multicen-tre studies in septic patients [9, 22] to chronic nephrotoxicity with secondary renal failure in liv-er transplant patients as long as 10 years after HES administration [39]. F. Schortgen et al. showed that septic patients who received 6 % HES 200/0.6 had significantly higher frequen-cies of acute renal failure (27/65 [42 %] vs. 15/64 [23 %], p = 0.028) than patients who received 3 % modified gelatin. Risk factors for acute renal fail-ure included use of hydroxyethyl starch $(2 \cdot 57[1 \cdot 13{-}5 \cdot 83], p = 0 \cdot 026)$ [22]. The VISEP study showed that recipients of 10% HES 200/0.5 had a higher risk of acute renal failure (34.9% vs. 22.8%, p = 0.002) and double the days on renal replacement therapy (650 of 3,554 vs. 321 of 3,471 total days, or 18.3% vs. 9.2%). Renal impairment correlated with the cumulative dose of HES, but not of Ringer's lactate. Importantly, patients who always received HES doses below the manufacturer's daily dose limit still had a higher risk for renal failure than patients receiving crystalloid (p = 0.04). HES recipients also had a lower median platelet count (p < 0.001) and received more units of packed red cells (p < 0.001) [9]. Renal changes can persist for many years. Renal biopsies performed at a mean of 5 years after liver transplantation in patients with chronic renal failure revealed, among other lesions, osmotic nephrotic lesions specifically related to the administration of hydroxyethyl starch [39].

It is important to note that studies called upon to rule out negative effects of HES solutions on renal function are flawed by inadequate comparators, e.g. other colloids like different HES solutions or gelatin, too short observation periods and inadequate endpoints for renal dysfunction [40–42]. With observation periods of 5 days or less and creatinine serum levels as marker of renal dysfunction, neither the Schortgen [22] nor the VISEP study [9] would have revealed the higher incidence of renal failure after HES administration. A recent, purely observational European multicentre study [17] suggested that HES was not associated with increased renal replacement therapy, yet HES recipients at baseline had less exposure to renal replacement therapy than patients not receiving HES (p < 0.001), and requirement for renal replacement therapy increased in the HES group (10.6 vs. 9.3%; p = 0.006), an effect which did not persist in a multivariate analysis of results from a subset of patients. Moreover, the mean cumulative dose of HES was less than 15 ml/kg. A recent comparison in cardiac surgical patients with 60-day follow-up concluded that HES 130/0.4 was as safe as 5% albumin; however, the cumulative dose during the 48-hour study period was only approximately 33 ml/kg, which is less than one recommended daily dose of 50 ml/kg [41].

Adverse effects on renal function have been noted in various clinical conditions and for diffe-

rent HES solutions, such as HES 70/0.4 in abdominal surgery [43], HES 130/0.4 in elderly cardiac surgical patients [44], HES 450/0.7 in renal transplantation [45], and HES 670/0.7 in cardiac surgery [46]. Renal failure with typical tubular lesions which was reversible has also been reported after transmaxillary buccopharyngectomy [47], after epidural anaesthesia for Caesarean section [48] and during haemodilution for cerebral ischemia and visual impairment [49]. Recently, chronic renal failure with osmotic nephrotic lesions and interstitial foam cells was reported by Hagne et al. in a patient who had been treated with a cumulative dose of 81 ml/kg HES 130/0.4 for septic shock [35].

Bleeding

In susceptible patients, administration of HES can lead to potentially fatal bleeding. A meta-analysis investigating in 653 cardiopulmonary bypass patients found that postoperative blood loss was significantly lower in patients exposed to albumin than in those exposed to HES 470 or 200 [50]. In 2004, the FDA issued a warning label on the package insert for hetastarch, stating that this solution "is not recommended for use as a cardiac bypass pump prime, while the patient is on cardiopulmonary bypass, or in the immediate period after the pump has been discontinued because of the risk of increasing coagulation abnormalities and bleeding in patients whose coagulation status is already impaired" [51]. In France, HES 200/0.62 was withdrawn from the market after a pharmacovigilance study documented 3 cases of fatal cerebral haemorrhage among 9 patients with subarachnoid haemorrhage and acquired von Willebrand's disease after HES exposure [52]. In patients with acute ischemic stroke and traumatic brain injury, HES products should be avoided because of their capacity to induce or aggravate bleeding [53, 54].

In septic patients, administration of 10% HES 200/0.5 led to a significant drop in platelet counts and coagulatory SOFA subscore compared to patients who received Ringer's lactate. Although the number of patients who received red cell transfusions did not differ, the number of red cell transfusion units was significantly increased in the patients exposed to HES [9].

Avoiding harm in fluid resuscitation:
Emerging evidence for the toxicity of synthetic colloids in critically ill patients

F

Tissue storage

Tissue storage is another potentially serious side effect [55] which is inherent to all artificial colloids. HES solutions are taken up in a variety of cells and tissues and can remain there for a long time. Duration of storage is unknown but depends on type of solution and amount infused [56]. In healthy volunteers 30–40% of the modern HES 200/0.5 solution which was cleared from the plasma was not eliminated renally but was stored elsewhere, probably in the cells of the reticuloendothelial system [57]. Tissue storage can manifest as *osmotic nephrotic lesions*, as *lysosomal storage disease with organ failure* and as intractable *pruritus*.

Osmotic nephrotic lesions are a non-specific histopathological finding characterised by vacuolisation and swelling of renal proximal tubular cells. They were described already in 1966 after HES administration in animals [58]. The lesions can be caused by different hyperosmotic compounds, such as hydroxyethyl starch, contrast media or immunoglobulins and show an accumulation of lysomomes in the cytoplasm with swelling, blebbing or rupture of the cell [59]. Per se, osmotic nephrotic-like lesions reflect a structural damage to the kidney that may be reversible but can also lead to renal impairment even in the absence of pre-existing kidney disease.

Osmotic nephrotic lesions have been associated with renal failure in various clinical conditions, such as in transplanted kidneys after HES administration to brain-dead organ donors [21, 60], after plasma exchange [61] and after surgery [47] and in patients who developed chronic renal insufficiency after HES administration during liver transplantation [39]. Recently, Hagne et al. found nephrotic lesions in the kidneys of a patient who developed chronic renal failures after treatment of septic shock with HES 130/0.4 (Voluven®) [35].

The kidney seems to be the most susceptible organ for HES uptake in critically ill patients. In a thorough post-mortem study of 12 ICU patients who died from multi-organ failure after acute respiratory distress syndrome (ARDS), HES uptake was detected by chemical analysis in kidney, liver, lung, spleen, pancreas, lymphnodes and intestinal mucosa, with kidneys showing the highest concentration of HES uptake (up to 26.4 mg/g) [57]. Patients had received a mean dose of 117 ml/kg HES 200/0.5 within a mean period of time of 41 ± 22 days. After repeated plasmapheresis with HES, a patient developed a foamy macrophage syndrome with hepatosplenomegaly, ascites and anaemia. Bone marrow was infiltrated with HES as long as 8 months afterwards [62]. Other patients developed lysosomal storage disease, with severe weight loss, organomegaly with ascites, myelofibrosis, polyneuropathy, and hydrocephalus with vasculitis of the choroid plexus and pituitary stalk oedema as a result of excessive tissue infiltration with foam cells [63] or thrombocytopenia and liver dysfunction [64]. These patients had received cumulative HES doses in the range of 250–400 ml/kg or more for plasmapheresis or in the ICU.

HES has also been found to be stored in the placenta (HES 200/0.5) [65]. In a study with 216 patients with severe hypertensive disorders of pregnancy, in which temporising management was combined with HES, HES did not improve maternal or fetal outcome [66]. However, there were more caesarean sections in the treatment groups and a trend towards less prolongation of pregnancy (median 7.4 vs. 11.5 days; p = 0.054) and more infants requiring oxygen treatment (66 vs. 46; p = 0.09).

Experimental evidence suggests that uptake may result in impairment of immune function [67, 68].

Intractatable *pruritus* is a result of HES uptake in the skin [69] most probably in cutaneous nerve fibres [70]. It is generally refractory to available therapies and can persist for up to 12–24 months [71]. The reported incidence ranges from 30% [72] to 54% [73] by retrospective analysis. In haemodilution therapy with 10% HES 200/0.5 compared to saline, pruritus was increased in the HES group and correlated with cumulative dose [74]. Patients answering a questionnaire after ICU treatment reported significantly more pruritus when they had received more than approx. 67 ml/kg cumulative dose [73]. Pruritus is associated with all HES solutions, notably also after HES 130/0.4 administration [34].

Long-term morbidity and mortality

In the recent Efficacy of Volume Substitution and Insulin Therapy in Severe Sepsis (VISEP) study, not only did 28-day mortality not differ between HES and crystalloid group (26.7% vs. 24.1%, p = 0.48) but 90-day mortality tended to be *higher* in the HES group (41.0% vs. 33.9%, p = 0.09). Further analyses revealed that this was due to a substantial subgroup of patients (n = 100) who had received high doses of HES on at least one day (defined as > 22 ml/kg body weight/day, 20 ml/kg/day being the dose limit recommended by the manufacturer). These patients also had received a cumulative dose of 136.0 ml/kg bodyweight and had an excessively high mortality rate of 57.9%, compared to the low-dose group with a median cumulative dose of 48.3 ml HES/kg and a mortality rate of 30.9%, p < 0.001 [9].

There is a lack of long-term outcome studies of HES, but some previous results suggest that HES in higher doses may lead to increased morbidity and mortality in patients at higher risk. A recent meta-analysis by Zarychanski et al., which included 22 trials with 1,866 patients, showed that patients receiving HES were more likely to receive renal replacement therapy [odds ratio [OR] 1.91 (95% confidence interval [CI] 1.22–2.99, I2 = 10.5%)]. This was also true for patients with severe sepsis or septic shock [OR 1.82 (95% CI 1.27–2.62, I2 = 0%)]. In high-quality trials [OR 1.27 (95% CI 0.94–1.73, I2 = 0%)], multicentre trials [OR 1.31 (95% CI 0.98–1.77,I2 = 0%)], and in reports indicating adequate allocation concealment [OR 1.29 (95% CI 0.96–1.73, I2 = 0%)], there was a trend toward increased risk of death associated with HES [75]. Analysis of discharge data from approx. 20,000 patients who had undergone CABG surgery showed that compared to non-protein colloid exposure including hetastarch or dextran, administration of albumin was associated with a lowered risk for hospital mortality (odds ratio, 0.80; 95% confidence interval, 0.67 to 0.96) [76]. Prospectively collected data from patients with subarachnoidal bleeding who received synthetic colloids (either 4% gelatin or 6% HES 200/0.5) showed that these had a more unfavourable neurological outcome at 6 months than patients receiving crystalloids (normal saline or Hartmann's solution). Odds for unfavourable outcome increased linearly with dose of colloid, while dose of crystalloids decreased unfavourable outcome [77]. In a retrospective analysis of patients who received orthotopic liver transplantation, starch infusion was

a risk factor development of sepsis and reduced patient survival [78].

Dextran

Dextrans are polydispersed mixtures of glucose polymers with molecular weights ranging from 10,000 Da to 150,000 Da. Dextran is used as prophylaxis and treatment of thromboembolism, distending medium during hysteroscopy, priming fluid in cardiopulmonary bypass, intracoronary perfusate during percutaneous transluminal coronary angioplasty, and plasma volume expander in shock. However, a recent Cochrane meta-analysis of trials with a total of 834 critically ill patients treated with either dextran or crystalloid found no evidence for efficacy (RR of 1.24 (95% CI 0.94 to 1.65) [4]. Wills et al. conducted a single-centre, randomised, double-blind comparison of Ringer's lactate, 6% dextran 70 and 6% HES 200/0.5 for emergency resuscitation of children stratified according to pulse pressure. The primary outcome measure was requirement for rescue colloid which was similar across treatment groups, the relative risk being 1.08 (95% CI 0.66 to 1.17; p = 0.38) for Ringer's compared with either colloid solution [7].

Dextrans strongly influence haemostasis, having considerable antithrombotic effects [79], decreasing von Willebrand factor [80] and also exerting potent anti-platelet and fibrinolytic activities [81]. In free-flap surgery, an increasing number of reports of significant morbidity related to low-molecular-weight dextran have questioned its use in microsurgery [82, 83]. A recent prospective trial evaluated the postoperative morbidity of low molecular weight dextran and aspirin prophylaxis in head and neck microsurgery in 100 consecutive patients with a 2-year followup. The method of prophylaxis had no effect on overall flap survival. However, the relative risk of pulmonary or cardiac complications was 3.9 or 7.2, depending on dextran dose, as compared to patients receiving aspirin [84]. Complications include postoperative pulmonary oedema and adult respiratory distress syndrome, possibly due to direct toxicity and/or volume overload, as well as "dextran syndrome", described as acute hypotension, hypoxia, coagulopathy and anaemia in a patient receiving dextran 70 as distending me-

Avoiding harm in fluid resuscitation:
Emerging evidence for the toxicity of synthetic colloids in critically ill patients

F

dium during hysteroscopy [85]. The pathophysiology of the dextran syndrome is postulated to include direct pulmonary toxicity, release of vasoactive mediators, activation of the coagulation cascade, intravascular intravasation of fluids, and haemodilution. When dextran 40 is used for resuscitation from shock, the total dose should not exceed 20 ml/kg during the initial 24 h or 10 ml/kg/d thereafter. Dextran syndrome also developed in a patient who accidentally received 52.3 ml/kg within three days [86].

Dextran administration is also associated with renal failure, as reported by Biesenbach et al. in 4.7% of 211 patients with acute ischaemic stroke who were treated with dextran 40 infusions. The incidence was higher in patients with pre-existing renal insufficiency. Of concern, half of the patients with renal failure died within 12 days of non-renal complications [87]. Dextran is also implicated in the formation of osmotic nephrotic lesions [59].

A high number of adverse events due to dextran 40 and 70 solutions are associated with anaphylactoid reactions caused by dextran-reactive immunoglobulin G antibodies. Between 1969 and 2004, the FDA received 366 clinical dextran adverse event reports, of which 90 (24.6%) were anaphylaxis/anaphylactoid events [88].

Gelatin

Gelatin solutions have been used as intravenous infusions since the First World War. They are produced by the breakdown of bovine collagen to yield solutions with a range of molecular weights. The latest Cochrane meta-analysis comparing colloid and crystalloid fluid therapy in a total number of 506 critically ill patients found no benefit for gelatin (pooled RR was 0.91 (95% CI 0.49 to 1.72)) [4]. In a well-conducted comparison between normal saline and gelatin for resuscitation therapy in 60 children with septic shock, both solutions performed equally in terms of haemodynamic stabilisation [8].

Anaphylactoid reactions and impairment of haemostasis are well-recognised complications of gelatin use and are four to six times more common after gelatin than after HES or dextran (pooled incidence rate ratio in comparison to albumin 12.4 (95% confidence interval 6.4–24.0))

[30]. Gelatins are also known to impair haemostasis. The US Federal Drug Administration (FDA) withdrew marketing approval for gelatin as plasma substitute in 1978 due to increased blood viscosity, reduced blood clotting and prolonged bleeding time [89]. There is now increasing evidence that gelatins influence platelet function, as well as blood coagulation by specific decrease of von Willebrand factor and factor VIII:c [90].

It is generally less well realised that the synthetic colloid gelatin, too, may impair renal function in susceptible patients. Gelatin elevated creatinine levels in 105 consecutive patients as compared with albumin as pump prime in cardiac surgery [91] and after cardiac surgery in comparison to HES 130/0.4 [40] and in patients undergoing aortic aneurysm surgery compared to HES 130/0.4 or HES 200/0.6 [92]. 4% gelatin solution and 6% HES 130/0.4 both raised four sensitive markers indicative of renal impairment (N-acetyl-beta-D-glucosaminidase, alpha-1-microglobulin, glutathione transferase-pi, and glutathione transferase-alpha) after cardiac surgery in patients over the age of seventy years [44]. Gelatin causes tubular cell injury in a dose-dependent manner, attenuating the tubular reabsorption of the low-molecular-weight protein beta2-microglobulin [93] and other low-molecular-weight proteins [94]. A retrospective analysis of approximately 3,000 patients in a surgical ICU receiving predominantly gelatin 4% or HES 130/0.4% revealed a similar incidence of acute renal failure and an increased independent risk at cumulative doses above 33 ml/kg of either HES (OR = 1.85, 95%CI: 1.01–3.41, p<0.001) or gelatin (OR = 1.99, 95%CI: 1.05–3.79, p = 0.035) [95]. The potentially harmful effect of gelatin on kidney function may have been masked in the past by studies which used nephrotoxic comparator compounds such as HES [22, 40, 43, 44, 96]. However, it is not clear which factors are responsible for renal failure. A recent multi-centre cohort study of over 1,000 ICU patients which classified gelatins together with 4% albumin as hypooncotic colloids found that these compounds were not associated with an increased risk of renal failure (OR 1.10 (0.59–2.45) [97].

As noted above, the use of synthetic colloids, either 4% gelatin or 6% HES 200/0.5 as fluid therapy increased need for blood transfusion, elevated inflammatory profiles, and decreased duration and strength of intact cerebral autoregulation, and dose-dependently increased the risk of unfavourable outcome at 6 months (OR 4.45, p = 0.035), while crystalloids decreased unfavourable outcome (OR 0.27, p = 0.005) [77].

Crystalloids

Crystalloids are generally safe to use, are less costly than colloids and do not induce coagulopathy beyond haemodilution. However, some unwanted effects may also be seen with crystalloid resuscitation. Saline-based fluids (including colloid plasma substitutes using saline solvent) can lead to the development of *hyperchloremic acidosis* which is usually self-corrective [98]. In surgical patients, volume therapy with normal saline required administration of bicarbonate, more total fluid and more blood products than with Ringer's, without, however, having a direct effect on ICU or hospital stay and number of adverse events [99].

In the critically ill, effects of surgery and its associated changes in the hormonal *milieu interne* are exaggerated by a systemic inflammatory response with development of capillary leak. A positive fluid balance is associated with morbidity and mortality in otherwise uncomplicated major elective surgery [100]. Crystalloid resuscitation should therefore be targeting a 'corridor of safety' avoiding both extremes of overt hypovolaemia or fluid overload. While avoidance of oedema formation is a prime objective and concern in visceral surgery, efforts to restrict fluids such as 'forced hypovolaemia' are associated with oliguria and occasionally renal shutdown and may impair nutritional microvascular blood flow in other vascular beds, such as the splanchnic circulation.

Sequelae of volume overload are particularly eminent, and the pathophysiological cascades of events have been worked out best for the patient with aggressive crystalloid resuscitation after major trauma: Manifestations of crystalloid overload might include ARDS and brain oedema in the patient with concomitant head injury [101–104]. Lately, development of secondary abdominal compartment syndrome (ACS) has claimed attention, i.e. ACS in the absence of abdominal injury which is associated frequently with haemorrhagic shock and early and excessive crystalloid resuscitation [105–109]. In a recent trial in patient cohorts with severe extremity injuries in the absence of abdominal trauma obtained from the Trauma Registry of the American College of Surgeons database, patients developing secondary ACS had significantly higher operating room crystalloid administration (9.9 l vs. 2.7 l), more frequent use of rapid infusing systems (12.5 % vs. 0.0 %) and multiple logistic regression identified early crystalloids as predictors of secondary ACS [110]. On the other hand, prospective trials comparing resuscitation with normal saline, 4 % gelatin, 6 % HES 200/0.5 and 5 % albumin in septic and non-septic ICU patients with acute lung injury showed that the type of fluid did not affect pulmonary permeability and oedema [29, 111]. Furthermore, in severe sepsis there was no difference in the pulmonary SOFA-subscore between the Ringer's lactate and the 10 % HES 200/0.5 group [9].

Isotonic versus hypertonic crystalloids

Hypertonic saline is still considered experimental in humans, except for the treatment of raised intracranial pressure and cerebral oedema following traumatic brain injury [112].

Use of hypertonic salt solutions might affect the fluid balance in general in a favourable way and might specifically reduce intracranial pressure (ICP) [113–116]. A single equimolar infusion of 7.45 % hypertonic saline solution is as effective as 20 % mannitol in decreasing ICP in patients with brain injury. In a recent study by Francony and coworkers, mannitol, however, exerted additional effects on brain circulation through a possible improvement in blood rheology [117]. Mannitol remains the first-line drug in intracranial hypertension of various origins, but hypertonic saline is an interesting rescue option to improve cerebral perfusion [112, 118, 119].

Similarly, recent guidelines for management of acute liver failure with higher grades of hepatic encephalopathy herald initial therapy with mannitol if intracranial pressure equals or exceeds 25 mmHg, supplemented if insufficient by hypertonic saline. Specifically, serum sodium should be maintained at least within high normal limits, and hypertonic saline administered to 145–155 mmol/l may be considered in patients

Avoiding harm in fluid resuscitation:
Emerging evidence for the toxicity of synthetic colloids in critically ill patients

F

with intracranial hypertension refractory to mannitol [120].

Data to support similar effects in body cavities other than the intracranial compartment is scarce but reflects an area of active research [113, 121, 122]. In patients being resuscitated from burn shock, hypertonic saline reduced the development of intra-abdominal hypertension compared to Ringer's lactate [123]. A recent meta-analysis could not arrive at a conclusion about the efficacy of hypertonic crystalloids for lack of adequate data in patients with trauma, burns, or those undergoing surgery [124].

Conclusion

Evidence to support the choice of either crystalloids or synthetic or natural colloids in the critically ill is tipping the scales toward crystalloids for reasons of safety, side effects and containment of costs. Crystalloids and colloids are equally effective but synthetic colloids have inherent adverse effects such as risk of bleeding and uptake into tissue. These effects are dose-dependent and may become manifest only after longer periods of time. In higher doses synthetic colloids may seriously increase long-term morbidity and mortality. Unfortunately, such adverse effects have also been demonstrated in the modern HES solution 130/0.4. Until adequate clinical trials investigating long-term outcome demonstrate their safety, all synthetic colloids should be avoided in the ICU since they do not confer any clinical benefit compared to crystalloids.

The authors

Christiane Hartog, MD[1]
Michael Bauer, MD[2]
Konrad Reinhart, MD[3]
  [1]Research Associate | Department of Anaesthesiology and Intensive Care Therapy | Jena University Hospital, Jena, Germany
  [2]Professor and Vice chair | Department of Anaesthesiology and Intensive Care Therapy | Jena University Hospital
  [3]Professor and Chair | Department of Anaesthesiology and Intensive Care Therapy | Jena University Hospital

Address for correspondence
  Konrad Reinhart
  Professor and Chair, Department of Anaesthesiology and Intensive Care Therapy
  Jena University Hospital
  Erlanger Allee 101
  07747 Jena, Germany
  E-mail: konrad.reinhart@med.uni-jena.de

References

1. Rivers EP, Nguyen HB, Huang DT, Donnino M. Early goal-directed therapy. Crit Care Med 2004;32:314–315; author reply 315.
2. Dellinger RP, Levy MM, Carlet JM, Bion J, Parker MM, Jaeschke R, et al. Surviving Sepsis Campaign: international guidelines for management of severe sepsis and septic shock: 2008. Crit Care Med 2008;36:296–327.
3. Alderson P, Schierhout G, Roberts I, Bunn F. Colloids versus crystalloids for fluid resuscitation in critically ill patients. Cochrane Database Syst Rev 2000:CD000567.
4. Perel P, Roberts I. Colloids versus crystalloids for fluid resuscitation in critically ill patients. Cochrane Database Syst Rev 2007:CD000567.
5. Roberts I, Alderson P, Bunn F, Chinnock P, Ker K, Schierhout G. Colloids versus crystalloids for fluid resuscitation in critically ill patients. Cochrane Database Syst Rev 2004:CD000567.
6. Finfer S, Bellomo R, Boyce N, French J, Myburgh J, Norton R. A comparison of albumin and saline for fluid resuscitation in the intensive care unit. N Engl J Med 2004;350:2247–2256.
7. Wills BA, Nguyen MD, Ha TL, Dong TH, Tran TN, Le TT, et al. Comparison of three fluid solutions for resuscitation in dengue shock syndrome. N Engl J Med 2005;353:877–889.
8. Upadhyay M, Singhi S, Murlidharan J, Kaur N, Majumdar S. Randomized evaluation of fluid resuscitation with crystalloid (saline) and colloid (polymer from degraded gelatin in saline) in pediatric septic shock. Indian Pediatr 2005;42:223–231.
9. Brunkhorst FM, Engel C, Bloos F, Meier-Hellmann A, Ragaller M, Weiler N, et al. Intensive insulin therapy and pentastarch resuscitation in severe sepsis. N Engl J Med 2008;358:125–139.
10. Hollenberg SM, Ahrens TS, Annane D, Astiz ME, Chalfin DB, Dasta JF, et al. Practice parameters for hemodynamic support of sepsis in adult patients: 2004 update. Crit Care Med 2004;32:1928–1948.
11. McIntyre LA, Hebert PC, Fergusson D, Cook DJ, Aziz A. A survey of Canadian intensivists' resuscitation practices in early septic shock. Crit Care 2007;11:R74.
12. Haljamae H. [Swedish practice routines for fluid therapy

are considerably changing]. Lakartidningen 2005;102:2659–2662, 2664–2655.

13. Schortgen F, Deye N, Brochard L. Preferred plasma volume expanders for critically ill patients: results of an international survey. Intensive Care Med 2004;30:2222–2229.

14. Boldt J, Lenz M, Kumle B, Papsdorf M. Volume replacement strategies on intensive care units: results from a postal survey. Intensive Care Med 1998;24:147–151.

15. Preferences for colloid use in Scandinavian intensive care units. Acta Anaesthesiol Scand 2008;52:750–758.

16. Miletin MS, Stewart TE, Norton PG. Influences on physicians' choices of intravenous colloids. Intensive Care Med 2002;28:917–924.

17. Sakr Y, Payen D, Reinhart K, Sipmann FS, Zavala E, Bewley J, et al. Effects of hydroxyethyl starch administration on renal function in critically ill patients. Br J Anaesth 2007;98:216–224.

18. Kellum JA, Cerda J, Kaplan LJ, Nadim MK, Palevsky PM. Fluids for prevention and management of acute kidney injury. Int J Artif Organs 2008;31:96–110.

19. Dieterich HJ. Recent developments in European colloid solutions. J Trauma 2003;54:S26–30.

20. Herwaldt LA, Swartzendruber SK, Edmond MB, Embrey RP, Wilkerson KR, Wenzel RP, et al. The epidemiology of hemorrhage related to cardiothoracic operations. Infect Control Hosp Epidemiol 1998;19:9–16.

21. Cittanova ML, Leblanc I, Legendre C, Mouquet C, Riou B, Coriat P. Effect of hydroxyethylstarch in brain-dead kidney donors on renal function in kidney-transplant recipients. Lancet 1996;348:1620–1622.

22. Schortgen F, Lacherade JC, Bruneel F, Cattaneo I, Hemery F, Lemaire F, et al. Effects of hydroxyethylstarch and gelatin on renal function in severe sepsis: a multicentre randomised study. Lancet 2001;357:911–916.

23. Lundsgaard-Hansen P, Tschirren B. Clinical experience with 120,000 units of modified fluid gelatin. Dev Biol Stand 1980;48:251–256.

24. von Hoegen I, Waller C. Safety of human albumin based on spontaneously reported serious adverse events. Crit Care Med 2001;29:994–996.

25. Rackow EC, Falk JL, Fein IA, Siegel JS, Packman MI, Haupt MT, et al. fluid resuscitation in circulatory shock: a comparison of the cardiorespiratory effects of albumin, hetastarch, and saline solutions in patients with hypovolemic and septic shock. Crit Care Med 1983;11:839–850.

26. Fink M, Abraham E, Vincent JL, Kochanek PM, eds. Critical Care Medicine. 2005, Elsevier Inc.: Philadelphia, USA.

27. Boura C, Caron A, Longrois D, Mertes PM, Labrude P, Menu P. Volume expansion with modified hemoglobin solution, colloids, or crystalloid after hemorrhagic

shock in rabbits: effects in skeletal muscle oxygen pressure and use versus arterial blood velocity and resistance. Shock 2003;19:176–182.

28. Zhang H, Voglis S, Kim CH, Slutsky AS. Effects of albumin and Ringer's lactate on production of lung cytokines and hydrogen peroxide after resuscitated hemorrhage and endotoxemia in rats. Crit Care Med 2003;31:1515–1522.

29. Boldt J, Scholhorn T, Mayer J, Piper S, Suttner S. The value of an albumin-based intravascular volume replacement strategy in elderly patients undergoing major abdominal surgery. Anesth Analg 2006;103:191–199.

30. Barron ME, Wilkes MM, Navickis RJ. A systematic review of the comparative safety of colloids. Arch Surg 2004;139:552–563.

31. Human albumin administration in critically ill patients: systematic review of randomised controlled trials. Cochrane Injuries Group Albumin Reviewers. BMJ 1998;317:235–240.

32. Roberts I, Bunn F. Egg on their faces. The story of human albumin solution. Eval Health Prof 2002;25:130–138.

33. Myburgh J, Cooper DJ, Finfer S, Bellomo R, Norton R, Bishop N, et al. Saline or albumin for fluid resuscitation in patients with traumatic brain injury. N Engl J Med. 2007;357:874–884.

34. FDA Center for Biologics Evaluation and Research. Product Product Approval Information – New Drug Applications. NDA REVIEW MEMO (MID-CYCLE). 6-MAR-2007. Last update 10-April-2008. Accessed on: 10-September-2008. Available from: http://www.fda.gov/CbER/nda/voluven.htm.

35. Hagne C, Schwarz A, Gaspert A, Giambarba C, Keusch G. HAES in septic shock – sword of Damocles? Schweizer Medical Forum 2009;in print.

36. Van der Linden PJ, De Hert SG, Deraedt D, Cromheecke S, De Decker K, De Paep R, et al. Hydroxyethyl starch 130/0.4 versus modified fluid gelatin for volume expansion in cardiac surgery patients: the effects on perioperative bleeding and transfusion needs. Anesth Analg 2005;101:629–634, table of contents.

37. Zaar M, Lauritzen B, Secher NH, Krantz T, Nielsen HB, Madsen PL, et al. Initial administration of hydroxyethyl starch vs lactated Ringer after liver trauma in the pig. Br J Anaesth 2009;102:221–226.

38. Leuschner J, Opitz J, Winkler A, Scharpf R, Bepperling F. Tissue storage of 14C-labelled hydroxyethyl starch (HES) 130/0.4 and HES 200/0.5 after repeated intravenous administration to rats. Drugs R D 2003;4:331–338.

39. Pillebout E, Nochy D, Hill G, Conti F, Antoine C, Calmus Y, et al. Renal histopathological lesions after orthotopic liver transplantation (OLT). Am J Transplant 2005;5:1120–1129.

40. Boldt J, Brosch C, Rohm K, Papsdorf M, Mengistu A. Comparison of the effects of gelatin and a modern

Avoiding harm in fluid resuscitation:
Emerging evidence for the toxicity of synthetic colloids in critically ill patients

F

hydroxyethyl starch solution on renal function and inflammatory response in elderly cardiac surgery patients. Br J Anaesth 2008;100:457–464.

41. Boldt J, Brosch C, Ducke M, Papsdorf M, Lehmann A. Influence of volume therapy with a modern hydroxyethylstarch preparation on kidney function in cardiac surgery patients with compromised renal function: a comparison with human albumin. Crit Care Med 2007;35:2740–2746.

42. Dehne MG, Muhling J, Sablotzki A, Dehne K, Sucke N, Hempelmann G. Hydroxyethyl starch (HES) does not directly affect renal function in patients with no prior renal impairment. J Clin Anesth 2001;13:103–111.

43. Kumle B, Boldt J, Piper S, Schmidt C, Suttner S, Salopek S. The influence of different intravascular volume replacement regimens on renal function in the elderly. Anesth Analg 1999;89:1124–1130.

44. Boldt J, Brenner T, Lehmann A, Lang J, Kumle B, Werling C. Influence of two different volume replacement regimens on renal function in elderly patients undergoing cardiac surgery: comparison of a new starch preparation with gelatin. Intensive Care Med 2003;29:763–769.

45. Deman A, Peeters P, Sennesael J. Hydroxyethyl starch does not impair immediate renal function in kidney transplant recipients: a retrospective, multicentre analysis. Nephrol Dial Transplant 1999;14:1517–1520.

46. Winkelmayer WC, Glynn RJ, Levin R, Avorn J. Hydroxyethyl starch and change in renal function in patients undergoing coronary artery bypass graft surgery. Kidney Int 2003;64:1046–1049.

47. De Labarthe A, Jacobs F, Blot F, Glotz D. Acute renal failure secondary to hydroxyethylstarch administration in a surgical patient. Am J Med 2001;111:417–418.

48. Dickenmann MJ, Filipovic M, Schneider MC, Brunner FP. Hydroxyethylstarch-associated transient acute renal failure after epidural anaesthesia for labour analgesia and Caesarean section. Nephrol Dial Transplant 1998;13:2706.

49. Waldhausen P, Kiesewetter H, Leipnitz G, Scielny J, Jung F, Bambauer R, et al. [Hydroxyethyl starch-induced transient renal failure in preexisting glomerular damage]. Acta Med Austriaca 1991;18 Suppl 1:52–55.

50. Wilkes MM, Navickis RJ, Sibbald WJ. Albumin versus hydroxyethyl starch in cardiopulmonary bypass surgery: a meta-analysis of postoperative bleeding. Ann Thorac Surg 2001;72:527–533; discussion 534.

51. Haynes GR, Havidich JE, Payne KJ. Why the Food and Drug Administration changed the warning label for hetastarch. Anesthesiology 2004;101:560–561.

52. Jonville-Bera AP, Autret-Leca E, Gruel Y. Acquired type I von Willebrand's disease associated with highly substituted hydroxyethyl starch. N Engl J Med 2001;345:622–623.

53. Wiedermann CJ. Complications of hydroxyethyl starch in

acute ischemic stroke and other brain injuries. Pathophysiol Haemost Thromb 2003;33:225–228; author reply 229–230.

54. Haynes GR. Is hydroxyethyl starch safe in brain injury? Anesth Analg 2004;99:620; author reply 620–622.

55. Thompson WL, Fukushima T, Rutherford RB, Walton RP. Intravascular persistence, tissue storage, and excretion of hydroxyethyl starch. Surg Gynecol Obstet 1970;131:965–972.

56. Sirtl C, Laubenthal H, Zumtobel V, Kraft D, Jurecka W. Tissue deposits of hydroxyethyl starch (HES): dose-dependent and time-related. Br J Anaesth 1999;82:510–515.

57. Lukasewitz P, Kroh U, Löwenstein O, Krämer M, Lennartz H. [Quantitative Untersuchungen zur Gewebsspeicherung von mittelmolekularer Hydroxyethylstärke 200/0,5 bei Patienten mit Multiorganversagen. Journal für Anästhesie und Intensivbehandlung 1998;3. Quartal:42–46.

58. Kief H, Engelbart K. [Reabsorptive vacuolization of the contorted main parts of the kidney (so-called osmotic nephrosis)]. Frankf Z Pathol 1966;75:53–65.

59. Dickenmann M, Oettl T, Mihatsch MJ. Osmotic nephrosis: acute kidney injury with accumulation of proximal tubular lysosomes due to administration of exogenous solutes. Am J Kidney Dis 2008;51:491–503.

60. Legendre C, Thervet E, Page B, Percheron A, Noel LH, Kreis H. Hydroxyethylstarch and osmotic-nephrosis-like lesions in kidney transplantation. Lancet 1993;342:248–249.

61. Peron S, Mouthon L, Guettier C, Brechignac S, Cohen P, Guillevin L. Hydroxyethyl starch-induced renal insufficiency after plasma exchange in a patient with polymyositis and liver cirrhosis. Clin Nephrol 2001;55:408–411.

62. Auwerda JJ, Wilson JH, Sonneveld P. Foamy macrophage syndrome due to hydroxyethyl starch replacement: a severe side effect in plasmapheresis. Ann Intern Med 2002;137:1013–1014.

63. Auwerda JJ, Leebeek FW, Wilson JH, van Diggelen OP, Lam KH, Sonneveld P. Acquired lysosomal storage caused by frequent plasmapheresis procedures with hydroxyethyl starch. Transfusion 2006;46:1705–1711.

64. Schmidt-Hieber M, Loddenkemper C, Schwartz S, Arntz G, Thiel E, Notter M. Hydrops lysosomalis generalisatus – an underestimated side effect of hydroxyethyl starch therapy? Eur J Haematol 2006;77:83–85.

65. Heilmann L, Lorch E, Hojnacki B, Muntefering H, Forster H. [Accumulation of two different hydroxyethyl starch preparations in the placenta after hemodilution in patients with fetal intrauterine growth retardation or pregnancy hypertension]. Infusionstherapie 1991;18:236–243.

66. Ganzevoort W, Rep A, Bonsel GJ, Fetter WP, van Sonderen L, De Vries JI, et al. A randomised controlled

trial comparing two temporising management strategies, one with and one without plasma volume expansion, for severe and early onset pre-eclampsia. BJOG 2005;112:1358–1368.

67. van Rijen EA, Ward JJ, Little RA. Effects of colloidal resuscitation fluids on reticuloendothelial function and resistance to infection after hemorrhage. Clin Diagn Lab Immunol 1998;5:543–549.

68. Alam HB, Stanton K, Koustova E, Burris D, Rich N, Rhee P. Effect of different resuscitation strategies on neutrophil activation in a swine model of hemorrhagic shock. Resuscitation 2004;60:91–99.

69. Stander S, Szepfalusi Z, Bohle B, Stander H, Kraft D, Luger TA, et al. Differential storage of hydroxyethyl starch (HES) in the skin: an immunoelectron-microscopical long-term study. Cell Tissue Res 2001;304:261–269.

70. Stander S, Evers S, Metze D, Schmelz M. Neurophysiological evidence for altered sensory function caused by storage of hydroxyethyl starch in cutaneous nerve fibres. Br J Dermatol 2005;152:1085–1086.

71. Bork K. Pruritus precipitated by hydroxyethyl starch: a review. Br J Dermatol 2005;152:3–12.

72. Gall H, Schultz KD, Boehncke WH, Kaufmann R. Clinical and pathophysiological aspects of hydroxyethyl starch-induced pruritus: evaluation of 96 cases. Dermatology 1996;192:222–226.

73. Kimme P, Jannsen B, Ledin T, Gupta A, Vegfors M. High incidence of pruritus after large doses of hydroxyethyl starch (HES) infusions. Acta Anaesthesiol Scand 2001;45:686–689.

74. Desloovere C, Knecht R. [Infusion therapy in sudden deafness. Reducing the risk of pruritus after hydroxyethyl starch and maintaining therapeutic success–a prospective randomized study]. Laryngorhinootologie 1995;74:468–472.

75. Zarychanski R, Turgeon AF, Fergusson DA, Cook DJ, Hebert P, Bagshaw S, et al. Renal outcomes following hydroxyethyl starch resuscitation: A meta-analysis of randomized trials. Intensive Care Med 2008;34:S91.

76. Sedrakyan A, Gondek K, Paltiel D, Elefteriades JA. Volume expansion with albumin decreases mortality after coronary artery bypass graft surgery. Chest 2003;123:1853–1857.

77. Tseng MY, Hutchinson PJ, Kirkpatrick PJ. Effects of fluid therapy following aneurysmal subarachnoid haemorrhage: a prospective clinical study. Br J Neurosurg 2008;22:257–268.

78. Nemes B, Sarvary E, Sotonyi P, Gerlei Z, Doros A, Galffy Z, et al. Factors in association with sepsis after liver transplantation: the Hungarian experience. Transplant Proc 2005;37:2227–2228.

79. Petroianu GA, Liu J, Maleck WH, Mattinger C, Bergler WF. The effect of In vitro hemodilution with gelatin, dextran, hydroxyethyl starch, or Ringer's solution on Thrombelastograph. Anesth Analg 2000;90:795–800.

80. Batlle J, del Rio F, Lopez Fernandez MF, Martin R, Lopez Borrasca A. Effect of dextran on factor VIII/von Willebrand factor structure and function. Thromb Haemost 1985;54:697–699.

81. Jones CI, Payne DA, Hayes PD, Naylor AR, Bell PR, Thompson MM, et al. The antithrombotic effect of dextran-40 in man is due to enhanced fibrinolysis in vivo. J Vasc Surg 2008;48:715–722.

82. Hein KD, Wechsler ME, Schwartzstein RM, Morris DJ. The adult respiratory distress syndrome after dextran infusion as an antithrombotic agent in free TRAM flap breast reconstruction. Plast Reconstr Surg 1999;103:1706–1708.

83. Hardin CK, Kirk WC, Pederson WC. Osmotic complications of low-molecular-weight dextran therapy in free flap surgery. Microsurgery 1992;13:36–38.

84. Disa JJ, Polvora VP, Pusic AL, Singh B, Cordeiro PG. Dextran-related complications in head and neck microsurgery: do the benefits outweigh the risks? A prospective randomized analysis. Plast Reconstr Surg 2003;112:1534–1539.

85. Ellingson TL, Aboulafia DM. Dextran syndrome. Acute hypotension, noncardiogenic pulmonary edema, anemia, and coagulopathy following hysteroscopic surgery using 32 % dextran 70. Chest 1997;111:513–518.

86. Wolfenden LL, Fessler HE. A 52-year-old man with pulmonary edema following large-volume transfusion. Chest 2004;125:1556–1560.

87. Biesenbach G, Kaiser W, Zazgornik J. Incidence of acute oligoanuric renal failure in dextran 40 treated patients with acute ischemic stroke stage III or IV. Ren Fail 1997;19:69–75.

88. Zinderman CE, Landow L, Wise RP. Anaphylactoid reactions to Dextran 40 and 70: reports to the United States Food and Drug Administration, 1969 to 2004. J Vasc Surg 2006;43:1004–1009.

89. DEPARTMENT OF HEALTH AND HUMAN SERVICES, Food and Drug Administration, 21 CFR Part 216 [Docket No. 98N-0655] List of Drug Products That Have Been Withdrawn or Removed From the Market for Reasons of Safety or Effectiveness Federal Register: October 8, 1998 (Volume 63, Number 195) pages 54082–54089 1998 [cited 3 February 2009]; Available from: http://www.fda.gov/ohrms/dockets/98fr/100898b.txt.

90. de Jonge E, Levi M. Effects of different plasma substitutes on blood coagulation: a comparative review. Crit Care Med 2001;29:1261–1267.

91. Himpe D, Van Cauwelaert P, Neels H, Stinkens D, Van den Fonteyne F, Theunissen W, et al. Priming solutions for cardiopulmonary bypass: comparison of three colloids. J Cardiothorac Vasc Anesth 1991;5:457–466.

92. Mahmood A, Gosling P, Vohra RK. Randomized clinical trial comparing the effects on renal function of hydroxyethyl starch or gelatine during aortic aneurysm surgery. Br J Surg 2007;94:427–433.

Avoiding harm in fluid resuscitation:
Emerging evidence for the toxicity of synthetic colloids in critically ill patients

F

93. Veldman BA, Schepkens HL, Vervoort G, Klasen I, Wetzels JF. Low concentrations of intravenous polygelines promote low-molecular weight proteinuria. Eur J Clin Invest 2003;33:962–968.

94. ten Dam MA, Branten AJ, Klasen IS, Wetzels JF. The gelatin-derived plasma substitute Gelofusine causes low-molecular-weight proteinuria by decreasing tubular protein reabsorption. J Crit Care 2001;16:115–120.

95. Schabinski F, Oishi J, Tuche F, Luy A, Sakr Y, Bredle D, Hartog C, Reinhart K, Effects of a predominantly hydroxyethyl starch (HES)-based and a predominantly non HES-based fluid therapy on renal function in surgical ICU patients. Intensive Care Med. 2009 Jun 17. [Epub ahead of print])

96. Wiesen P, Canivet JL, Ledoux D, Roediger L, Damas P. Effect of hydroxyethylstarch on renal function in cardiac surgery: a large scale retrospective study. Acta Anaesthesiol Belg 2005;56:257–263.

97. Schortgen F, Girou E, Deye N, Brochard L. The risk associated with hyperoncotic colloids in patients with shock. Intensive Care Med 2008;34:2157–2168.

98. Blanloeil Y, Roze B, Rigal JC, Baron JF. [Hyperchloremic acidosis druing plasma volume replacement]. Ann Fr Anesth Reanim 2002;21:211–220.

99. Waters JH, Gottlieb A, Schoenwald P, Popovich MJ, Sprung J, Nelson DR. Normal saline versus lactated Ringer's solution for intraoperative fluid management in patients undergoing abdominal aortic aneurysm repair: an outcome study. Anesth Analg 2001;93:817–822.

100. Lobo DN, Macafee DA, Allison SP. How perioperative fluid balance influences postoperative outcomes. Best Pract Res Clin Anaesthesiol 2006;20:439–455.

101. Hariri RJ, Firlick AD, Shepard SR, Cohen DS, Barie PS, Emery JM, 3rd, et al. Traumatic brain injury, hemorrhagic shock, and fluid resuscitation: effects on intracranial pressure and brain compliance. J Neurosurg 1993;79:421–427.

102. Feinstein AJ, Patel MB, Sanui M, Cohn SM, Majetschak M, Proctor KG. Resuscitation with pressors after traumatic brain injury. J Am Coll Surg 2005;201:536–545.

103. Wiedemann HP, Wheeler AP, Bernard GR, Thompson BT, Hayden D, deBoisblanc B, et al. Comparison of two fluid-management strategies in acute lung injury. N Engl J Med 2006;354:2564–2575.

104. Cotton BA, Guy JS, Morris JA, Jr., Abumrad NN. The cellular, metabolic, and systemic consequences of aggressive fluid resuscitation strategies. Shock 2006;26:115–121.

105. McNelis J, Marini CP, Jurkiewicz A, Fields S, Caplin D, Stein D, et al. Predictive factors associated with the development of abdominal compartment syndrome in the surgical intensive care unit. Arch Surg 2002;137:133–136.

106. Balogh Z, McKinley BA, Holcomb JB, Miller CC, Cocanour CS, Kozar RA, et al. Both primary and secondary abdominal compartment syndrome can be predicted early and are harbingers of multiple organ failure. J Trauma 2003;54:848–859; discussion 859–861.

107. Kirkpatrick AW, Balogh Z, Ball CG, Ahmed N, Chun R, McBeth P, et al. The secondary abdominal compartment syndrome: iatrogenic or unavoidable? J Am Coll Surg 2006;202:668–679.

108. Balogh Z, McKinley BA, Cocanour CS, Kozar RA, Valdivia A, Sailors RM, et al. Supranormal trauma resuscitation causes more cases of abdominal compartment syndrome. Arch Surg 2003;138:637–642; discussion 642–633.

109. O'Mara MS, Slater H, Goldfarb IW, Caushaj PF. A prospective, randomized evaluation of intra-abdominal pressures with crystalloid and colloid resuscitation in burn patients. J Trauma 2005;58:1011–1018.

110. Madigan MC, Kemp CD, Johnson JC, Cotton BA. Secondary abdominal compartment syndrome after severe extremity injury: are early, aggressive fluid resuscitation strategies to blame? J Trauma 2008;64:280–285.

111. van der Heijden M, Verheij J, van Nieuw Amerongen GP, Groeneveld AB., Crystalloid or colloid fluid loading and pulmonary permeability, edema, and injury in septic and nonseptic critically ill patients with hypovolemia. Crit Care Med. 2009;37:1275–1281.J Crit Care. 2009 May 7. [Epub ahead of print])

112. Wenham TN, Hormis AP, Andrzejowski JC. Hypertonic saline after traumatic brain injury in UK neuro-critical care practice. Anaesthesia 2008;63:558–559.

113. Toung TJ, Chen CH, Lin C, Bhardwaj A. Osmotherapy with hypertonic saline attenuates water content in brain and extracerebral organs. Crit Care Med 2007;35:526–531.

114. Jarvela K, Koskinen M, Kaukinen S, Koobi T. Effects of hypertonic saline (7.5 %) on extracellular fluid volumes compared with normal saline (0.9 %) and 6 % hydroxyethyl starch after aortocoronary bypass graft surgery. J Cardiothorac Vasc Anesth 2001;15:210–215.

115. Freshman SP, Battistella FD, Matteucci M, Wisner DH. Hypertonic saline (7.5 %) versus mannitol: a comparison for treatment of acute head injuries. J Trauma 1993;35:344–348.

116. Berger S, Schurer L, Hartl R, Messmer K, Baethmann A. Reduction of post-traumatic intracranial hypertension by hypertonic/hyperoncotic saline/dextran and hypertonic mannitol. Neurosurgery 1995;37:98–107; discussion 107–108.

117. Francony G, Fauvage B, Falcon D, Canet C, Dilou H, Lavagne P, et al. Equimolar doses of mannitol and hypertonic saline in the treatment of increased intracranial pressure. Crit Care Med 2008;36:795–800.

118. Horn P, Munch E, Vajkoczy P, Herrmann P, Quintel M,

Schilling L, et al. Hypertonic saline solution for control of elevated intracranial pressure in patients with exhausted response to mannitol and barbiturates. Neurol Res 1999;21:758–764.

119. Bratton SL, Chestnut RM, Ghajar J, McConnell Hammond FF, Harris OA, Hartl R, et al. Guidelines for the management of severe traumatic brain injury. II. Hyperosmolar therapy. J Neurotrauma 2007;24 Suppl 1:S14–20.

120. Stravitz RT, Kramer AH, Davern T, Shaikh AO, Caldwell SH, Mehta RL, et al. Intensive care of patients with acute liver failure: recommendations of the U.S. Acute Liver Failure Study Group. Crit Care Med 2007;35:2498–2508.

121. Gonzalez EA, Kozar RA, Suliburk JW, Weisbrodt NW, Mercer DW, Moore FA. Conventional dose hypertonic saline provides optimal gut protection and limits remote organ injury after gut ischemia reperfusion. J Trauma 2006;61:66–73; discussion 73–64.

122. Powers KA, Woo J, Khadaroo RG, Papia G, Kapus A, Rotstein OD. Hypertonic resuscitation of hemorrhagic shock upregulates the anti-inflammatory response by alveolar macrophages. Surgery 2003;134:312–318.

123. Oda J, Ueyama M, Yamashita K, Inoue T, Noborio M, Ode Y, et al. Hypertonic lactated saline resuscitation reduces the risk of abdominal compartment syndrome in severely burned patients. J Trauma 2006;60:64–71.

124. Bunn F, Roberts I, Tasker R, Akpa E. Hypertonic versus near isotonic crystalloid for fluid resuscitation in critically ill patients. Cochrane Database Syst Rev 2004:CD002045.

Frank M. Brunkhorst

Avoiding harm in metabolic management

"I do not want two diseases – one nature-made, one doctor-made."

(Napoleon Bonaparte, 1820)

"Until a favorable benefit-risk relationship is established in rigorous clinical trials (...) euglycemia is not an appropriate goal during critical illness in the routine clinical setting with current treatment methods."

(Philip E. Cryer, 2006) [1]

Changing the impact of hyperglycaemia in the ICU

A common finding in the intensive care unit (ICU) is hyperglycaemia, caused by insulin resistance in the liver and muscle, occurring also in patients without preexisting diabetes. Illness- or trauma-induced gluconeogenesis leads to increased hepatic glucose production even in the presence of hyperglycaemia and abundantly released insulin. The frequent need to use steroids for treatment of septic shock and high carbohydrate loads for enteral and parenteral nutrition only makes this problem worse [2]. In the past, hyperglycaemia has been considered an adaptive response, providing necessary glucose for the increased metabolic requirements of the brain, red cells, and wound healing. It was treated only when it exceeded levels above 200 mg/dl (> approximately 12 mmol/l). However, evidence is increasing that high glucose levels per se may paralyse the immune response. Among others, a retrospective study of 2,030 adults admitted to general hospital wards showed that hyperglycaemia (defined as fasting glucose levels of > 126 mg/dl; 7 mmol/l or random blood glucose > 200 mg/dl; 11.1 mmol/l) was present in 38 % of patients admitted, of whom one-third had no prior history of diabetes. ICU mortality was significantly raised in the group of patients with new hyperglycaemia as compared to known diabetics or normoglycemic patients (31 % versus 11 %) [3]. Based on these observations, it has been hypothesised that an intensive insulin therapy (IIT) to maintain euglycaemia as done in chronic type 1 diabetes may also be beneficial to prevent acute organ injury and death in the setting of critical illness.

Clinical trials of IIT in the ICU

In a frequently cited study, Van den Berghe and researchers from Leuven/Belgium demonstrated that controlling blood glucose levels by IIT decreased mortality and morbidity in a cohort consisting mainly of critically ill cardiosurgical patients (71%) requiring mechanical ventilation. Absolute ICU mortality reduction was 3.6% (4.6% IIT vs. 8.0% conventional treatment, n = 765; p < 0.04). Mortality reduction was greatest for subgroups of patients with ICU length of stay (LOS) > 5 days (10.6% IIT vs. 20.2% conventional treatment, p = 0.005) and for patients with APACHE II score 8–23 and patients with multiple organ failure with a proven septic focus regardless of a prior history of diabetes or hyperglycaemia [4]. Whether the beneficial effects on mortality and morbidity were due to normalisation of blood glucose levels or due to the drug insulin with its potential anti-inflammatory effects is still a matter of debate. From a multivariate logistic regression analysis of their data Van den Berghe concluded that the lowered blood glucose level rather than the insulin dose was related to reduced mortality (p < 0.0001) [5].

This had been further supported by Van den Berghe on the basis of a new single-centre study with approx. 1,200 patients performed in a medical ICU. The researchers found that IIT led to an absolute reduction of ICU mortality in a subgroup of patients with an ICU LOS > 3 days of 38.1% to 31.3% (absolute risk reduction: 6,8%; p < 0.02). In-hospital mortality was reduced from 52.5% to 44% (absolute risk reduction: 9,5%; p < 0.02) [6]. However, this trial has been criticised as completely negative because there was no benefit in the intention-to-treat population [7].

In the first multicentre RCT performed by the German publicly-funded network SepNet, efficacy and safety of IIT was compared to conventional insulin therapy in patients with severe sepsis and septic shock (VISEP study [8]). IIT vs. conventional insulin therapy did not significantly alter 28-day (24.7% vs. 26.0%; p = 0.74) or 90-day mortality rates (39.7% vs. 35.4%; p = 0.31). Subgroup analyses stratifying by prerandomisation APACHE II score, or categorising patients by different reasons for ICU admission, or determining if a history of diabetes was present or not,

did not show significant differences in survival comparing IIT vs. conventional insulin. In addition, an analysis excluding all patients discharged from the ICU before the third, seventh and tenth day did not reveal significant differences. In an exploratory Cox regression analysis, independent risk factors for time to death were APACHE II without age, age ≥ 60 years, and hypoglycaemia, but not the type of insulin treatment.

Finally, exploratory analyses stratifying by mean morning blood glucose levels (< 110 mg/dl, 110–150 mg/dl, > 150 mg/dl) did not show differences in survival rates. There were also no significant differences comparing IIT to conventional treatment for the secondary endpoints, including frequency of acute renal failure, need for renal replacement therapy, vasopressor use and ventilator-free days. IIT vs. conventional patients tended to have longer ICU lengths of stay (median 16.0 days; IQR, 8 to 30 vs. 13.5 days; IQR, 7 to 25; p = 0.06) and more patients received packed red cells (IIT: 191 of 247; 77.3% vs. conventional 197 of 290; 67.9%; p = 0.02).

The single-centre studies by Arabi (n = 523) and De La Rosa (n = 504) in mixed surgical and medical ICUs also failed to confirm the initial Leuven data [9]. Increased hypoglycaemia resulted in early termination of the European multicentre GLUCONTROL study (n = 1101) which also failed to confirm a beneficial effect of IIT [10]. The largest trial to date, the NICE-SUGAR study, will probably report results in March 2009. The NICE-SUGAR study used a web-based treatment algorithm to target normoglycaemia (blood glucose 4.5–6.0 mmol/l) and recruited 6,104 patients from 42 ICUs in Australia, New Zealand, Canada and the US [11]. Whatever the results of that trial, it is likely that significant questions will remain regarding the practice of IIT in critically ill adults.

In a recent meta-analysis [12] including 29 published randomised trials (RCT) totalling 8,432 patients hospital mortality did not differ between IIT and usual care overall (21.6% vs. 23.3%; RR, 0.93; 95% confidence interval [CI], 0.85–1.03). There was also no significant difference in mortality when stratified by glucose goal ≤ 110 mg/dl; 23% vs. 25.2%; RR, 0.90; 95% CI, 0.77–1.04; or ≤ 150 mg/dl; 17.3% vs. 18.0%; RR, 0.99; 95% CI, 0.83–1.18 or intensive care unit setting,

- surgical: 8.8% vs, 10.8%; RR, 0.88; 95% CI, 0.63–1.22;
- medical: 26.9% vs. 29.7%; RR, 0.92;95% CI, 0.82–1.04; or
- medical-surgical: 26.1% vs. 27.0%; RR, 0.95; 95% CI, 0.80–1.13.

Tight glycaemic control was not associated with significantly decreased risk for new need for dialysis (11.2% vs. 12.1%; RR, 0.96; 95% CI, 0.76–1.20), but was associated with significantly decreased risk of septicaemia (10.9% vs. 13.4%; RR, 0.76; 95% CI, 0.59–0.97). However, this could be shown only in a subgroup of surgical patients with an unusually low mortality (8%), compared to other RCTs in patients with severe sepsis (mortality 30–40%) [8].

More importantly, IIT significantly increased risk of severe hypoglycaemia (glucose < 40 mg/dl; 13.7% vs. 2.5%; RR, 5.13; 95% CI, 4.09–6.43).

Finally, in recent large landmark trial in more than 10,000 patients with type 2 diabetes, the use of intensive glucose control to target normal glycated haemoglobin levels for 3.5 years increased mortality and did not significantly reduce major cardiovascular events. Hypoglycaemia requiring assistance and weight gain of more than 10 kg were more frequent in the intensive-therapy group (p < 0.001). These findings identified a previously unrecognised harm of intensive glucose lowering in high-risk patients with type 2 diabetes [13].

Growing concerns about hypoglycaemia

Hypoglycaemia causes brain fuel deprivation that initially triggers a series of physiological and behavioural defenses but if unchecked results in functional brain failure that is typically corrected after the plasma glucose concentration is raised. Rarely, profound and, at least in primates, prolonged, hypoglycaemia causes brain death [14]. The sequence of responses to falling plasma glucose concentrations is illustrated in Figure 1. Notably, coma can occur at glucose levels in the range of 2.3–2.7 mmol/l (41–49 mg/dl) [15] as well as at lower glucose levels.

Dying brain cells, presumably neurons, have been reported following episodes of hypoglycaemia at plasma glucose levels of 1.7–1.9 mmol/l

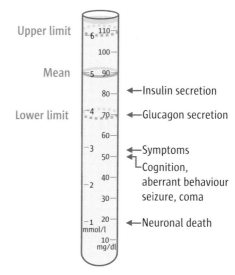

Fig. 1 Sequence of responses to falling arterial plasma glucose concentrations [reproduced with permission of American Society for Clinical Investigation, Hypoglycemia, functional brain failure and brain death, Cryer PE, J Clin Invest 2008; 117:868–870, permission conveyed through Copyright Clearence Center, Inc.]

(30–35 mg/dl) in rats [16]. As a result of the interplay of relative or absolute therapeutic insulin excess and compromised physiological and behavioural defences against falling plasma glucose concentrations, hypoglycaemia has been considered the limiting factor in the glycaemic management of diabetes [17]. It causes recurrent morbidity in most people with type 1 diabetes mellitus and in many with advanced type 2 diabetes mellitus and is sometimes fatal.

Hypoglycaemia occurs also spontaneously in hospitalised patients even without pre-existing diabetes or IIT. Kagansky et al. found that among 5,404 geriatric patients (> 70 years) 281 (5.2%) had documented hypoglycaemia (< 3.3 mmol/l or 60 mg/dl). Among predictors of developing hypoglycaemia, sepsis was associated with the highest risk (odds ratio 6.4, 95% CI 2.3–17.3). In-hospital mortality and 3-month mortality were about twice as high in the hypoglycaemic group (p < 0.001). However, hypoglycaemia in itself was not found to be a predictor of mortality but rather a marker for increased risk [18].

In this context, the high rates of hypoglycaemia found under IIT in critically ill patients are not without concern (see Tab. 1). In her first study on glycaemic control in surgical ICU patients, Van den Berghe reported an increased rate of hypoglycaemia (defined here as ≤ 40 mg/dl or 2.2 mmol/l) with 5.1 % in the intensive treatment group (39 patients) versus 1.02 % (6 patients) in the conventional treatment group (p < 0.009) [4]. In the second study of Van den Berghe in medical ICU patients [6] the rates of severe hypoglycaemia were considerably higher (18.7 vs. 3.1 %, p < 0.001 in the intention-to-treat population and 25.1 vs. 3.9 %, p < 0.001 in patients with an ICU stay > 3 days). In a recent study from the same group in pediatric ICU patients [19], hypoglycaemia (defined as blood glucose ≤ 40 mg/dl; 2.2 mmol/l) occurred in 87 (25 %) patients in the intensive group (p < 0·0001) versus 5 (1 %) patients in the conventional group. Hypoglycaemia defined as blood glucose less than 1.7 mmol/l (30 mg/dl) arose in 17 (5 %) patients versus 3 (1 %) (p = 0·001). A recent multicentre study in very-low-birth-weight (< 1500 g) infants was discontinued early because of concerns about futility with regard to the primary outcome and potential harm. There was an increased incidence of hypoglycaemia defined as < 2.6 mmol/l; 47 mg/dl (29 vs. 17 %, p = 0.005) and abnormalities detected on cranial ultrasound images in infants who were randomly assigned to receive early insulin infusions [20].

In a hitherto unpublished study from Cambridge, England, glycaemic control managed by the bedside nurse resulted in a mean morning laboratory glucose of 126 mg/dl (7.0 mmol/l) and was associated with a 42 % incidence of hypoglycaemia (defined as a blood glucose concentration of < 40 mg/dl; 2.2 mmol/l at any time) [31]. Unpublished data from the Netherlands also suggests that nurse-driven glycaemic control may lead to more severe hypoglycaemias. In the two ICUs studied retrospectively, there were more mild hypoglycaemias (patients with at least one blood glucose level < 79 mg/dl; 4.4 mmol/l) in (ICU-A: 10.0 % vs. 29.4 %; ICU-B 14.4 % vs. 19.9 %) and more severe hypoglycaemias (at least one blood glucose level < 40 mg/dl; 2.2 mmol/l) (0.9 % vs. 4.0 %; and 1.6 % vs. 3.3 %) than in the years before implementation of IIT. Age, higher APACHE-II scores and medical admission status were associated with an increased frequency of hypoglycaemias. The authors concluded that in a non-study "real life" setting, implementation of IIT without emphasis on specific training of ICU personnel and more frequent blood glucose measurements results in an increased frequency of hypoglycaemias [32]. In a recent observational study from Seattle a mixed cohort of ICU patients was studied over the period of implementation of an IIT protocol. Although there was a significant increase in the use of insulin during the study period, there was difficulty across the

Tab. 1 Rate of hypoglycaemia (glucose < 40 mg/dl; 2.2 mmol/l) in randomised clinical trials on IIT in the ICU
[adapted from Wiener RS, Wiener DC, Larson RJ et al. Benefits and risks of tight glucose control in critically ill adults: a meta-analysis. JAMA. 2008;300(8):933–944].
Of note, the definition of hypoglycaemia used in these trials is well below the glucose level that the American Diabetes Association considers to represent hypoglycaemia (glucose < 70 mg/dl; 3,9 mmol/l) [21]. Hypoglycaemias were calculated on a per-patient basis; for example, a patient with several episodes of hypoglycaemia only counts as 1 occurrence.

Setting	No. of studies	Intensive insulin therapy	Conventional insulin therapy	Relative risk (95 % confidence interval)
Surgical ICU [a]	4	48/967 (5.0)	8/987 (0.8)	5.37 (2.64–10.93)
Medical ICU [b]	2	112/599 (18.7)	20/609 (3.3)	3.65 (0.76–17.37)
Medical-surgical ICU [c]	9	290/1709 (17.0)	56/1742 (3.2)	4.95 (3.75–6.54)
Total	15	450/3275 (13.7)	84/3338 (2.5)	5.13 (4.09–6.43)

[a] see references: [4, 22, 23, 24]
[b] see references: [6, 25]
[c] see references: [8, 9, 10, 26, 27, 28, 29, 30] and Azevedo JRA et al., January 2008 (unpublished)

institution in meeting the strict glycaemic goals. A 4-fold increase in episodes of severe hypoglycaemia was observed. No reduction in mortality was observed in patients receiving IIT. Mortality seemed to be increased in IIT patients, particularly those with the shortest ICU stay (OR 1.47, 95 % CI 1.11, 1.93) [33]. Another cause for concern is a prospective randomised trial from Ghandi, who studied the role of an intensive insulin protocol intraoperatively in 199 cardiac surgery patients, no improvement in outcome was found. However, there was in fact a trend toward higher rates of stroke and death in patients treated with the intensive insulin protocol [34].

The German VISEP study was stopped early on account of an increased frequency of hypoglycaemia in the IIT group. 42 (17.0 %) intensive and 12 (4.1 %) conventional insulin patients experienced at least one episode of severe hypoglycaemia (p < 0.001). Significantly more of these hypoglycaemic episodes were reported as serious adverse events with intensive insulin than with the conventional insulin group (19 episodes; 7.7 percent vs. 7; 2.4 percent; p = 0.005). Although no serious adverse event was determined directly to result in death, the hypoglycaemic episodes with intensive insulin vs. conventional were more often classified as life-threatening (13 episodes; 5.3 percent vs. 6; 2.1 percent; p = 0.046) and requiring prolonged hospitalisation (6 episodes; 2.4 percent vs. 1; 0.3 percent; p = 0.052).

Krinsley et al. recently found from a series of 5,365 medical-surgical ICU patients, 102 of whom with at least one episode of hypoglycaemia, using case-control methodology and multivariable logistic regression analysis that even a single episode of severe hypoglycaemia (≤ 40 mg/dl; 2.2 mmol/l) was independently associated with increased risk of mortality [35].

However, the full extent of hypoglycaemic events in the published studies on IIT is unknown. This is because usual clinical warning signs and symptoms of hypoglycaemia may be masked by critical illness and sedation. Furthermore, glucose levels are measured only intermittently (every 1 to 4 h), so the full duration of hypoglycaemia and the number of unrecognised episodes is not determinable. Of concern, since the symptoms of hypoglycaemia are masked, insulin-induced hypoglycaemic coma may become

irreversible after only 30 min. [36] In clinical practice, where monitoring may be less vigilant, these serious adverse events, particularly those related to hypoglycaemia, could become more frequent and more likely to result in increased risk of death. So far, hypoglycaemic episodes have rarely been reported to result directly in death [37, 38]. On the other hand, it is conceivable that unrecognised adverse effects of hypoglycaemia on the brain or heart may have offset potential beneficial effects of IIT [17].

Concerns regarding glucose measurement

Concerns particularly of the nursing staff are faster laboratory turnaround and the accuracy of glucometer measurement in the ICU setting [39], highlighting the need to examine the limits of agreement between laboratory glucose measures and glucometers and the reliability of glucometer measures taken from the same sample [40]. Indeed one of the main strategies to increase acceptance of insulin protocols in the ICU may be a widespread use of highly reliable point-of-care testing (POCT) measures. Unfortunately, glucometers originally developed for out-of-hospital glucose control in the diabetic patient may not fulfil the needs for glucose control in the ICU, as the different methods used (glucoseoxidase, -hexokinase, -dehydrogenase) are influenced by common conditions in the critically ill, as low haematocrit, low oxygen saturation and drugs, particularly dopamine [41].

Due to a lack of precision (variation coefficient > 20 %) and low sensitivity in the normoglycaemic range of the presently available glucometers in whole blood, care should be taken to employ a device that can guarantee to detect hypoglycaemia safely and timely.

Moreover, systematic differences may occur as a result of differences in type of assay and the site and source of glucose sampling. This may be of concern when the targets of individual clinical trials are generalised among institutions that do not measure glucose in the same manner. Thus, determination of the appropriate methodology and targets for hospitalised patients must take these issues into account [42].

The second major issue is that glucose control is primarily nurse-driven and doctors do not

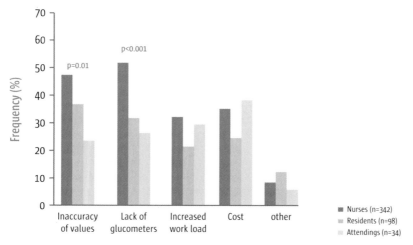

Fig. 2   Concerns about the use of glucometers in the ICU, results of a multicentre survey in Germany

seem to be involved on a daily basis [43]. Glycaemic control seems to be the first pharmacological intervention in the ICU that is driven primarily by nurses. Preliminary data from the German Competence Network SepNet indicates that while the importance of measuring blood glucose is generally realised by the whole ICU staff, nurses are significantly more concerned with increased frequency and accuracy of glucose measurements, i.e. with the practical aspects of implementation of glucose control (see Fig. 2). In order to achieve the desired blood glucose levels in a safe and consistent way to improve morbidity and mortality for the patient, the nurse/patient ratio in the ICU must be adequate to accommodate the increased workload and effort needed.

Glucose control by hypocaloric nutrition instead of insulin administration?

Some experts argue that administration of less glucose (e.g. in form of total parenteral nutrition) may be a more prudent way of approaching the problem. However, the reluctance of feeding the patient, especially in the pre- and postoperative period, is mostly based on tradition rather than on data. The methodological quality of interventional nutrition studies is poor compared to that of other studies in the critically ill, for example, sepsis studies [44]. There are also insufficient data to recommend either a high-fat/low-carbo-

hydrate or a low-fat/high-carbohydrate *enteral* formula in critically ill patients [45]. As new large-scale clinical studies are published, techniques will in all probability change in this area.

Conclusions

Subsequent trials have not borne out the results of IIT promised by the initial trial by van den Berghe et al. In critically ill adult patients, IIT is not associated with significantly reduced hospital mortality but is associated with an increased risk of severe hypoglycaemia. In our view, these findings warrant further research i) to prevent severe hypoglycaemia during IIT, namely by careful training of the nursing teams and use of continuous monitoring devices of blood glucose concentrations with reliable and accurate glucose sensors and continuously adapted insulin administration [46] to define the target range of blood glucose associated with the best risk-to-benefit ratio and taking into account daily variations of glucose levels [47] to characterise more accurately patients in whom IIT is associated with improved outcome. Currently, we have no other option than to abandon IIT until these pending issues are resolved [48].

Acknowledgements

Supported in part by the Competence Network Sepsis (SepNet) funded by the German Federal Ministry of Education and Research (BMBF), Grant No: 01 KI 0106

Postscript

After submission of this article the NICE-SUGAR trial has been published (New Engl. J. Med; 360:1283–97), showing – in accordance with the conclusions of this article – that a blood glucose target of less than 180 mg/dl resulted in a lower mortalilty than a target of 81–108 mg/dl. On the thesis of their results the authors do not recommend use of the lower target in critically ill adults.

The author

Frank Martin Brunkhorst, Prof., MD
    Department of Anaesthesiology and
    Intensive Care Medicine
    Friedrich-Schiller University of Jena
    Erlanger Allee 101
    07747 Jena, Germany
    E-mail: frank.brunkhorst@med.uni-jena.de

References

1. Cryer PE. Hypoglycaemia: the limiting factor in the glycaemic management of the critically ill? Diabetologia 2006; 49:1722.

2. Montori VM, Bistrian BR, McMahon MM. Hyperglycemia in acutely ill patients. JAMA 2002;288:2167–9.

3. Umpierrez GE, Isaacs SD, Bazargan N, You X, Thaler LM, Kitabchi AE. Hyperglycemia: an independent marker of in-hospital mortality in patients with undiagnosed diabetes. J Clin Endocrinol Metab 2002;87:978–82.

4. van den Berghe G, Wouters P, Weekers F, et al. IIT in the critically ill patients. N Engl J Med. 2001;345(19):1359–1367.

5. Van den Berghe G, Wouters PJ, Bouillon R, et al. Outcome benefit of IIT in the critically ill: Insulin dose versus glycemic control. Crit Care Med 2003;31:359–66.

6. van den Berghe G, Wilmer A, Hermans G, et al. IIT in the medical ICU. N Engl J Med. 2006;354(5):449–461.

7. Malhotra A. Intensive insulin in intensive care. New Engl J Med 2006; 354: 516–518.

8. Brunkhorst FM, Engel C, Bloos F, et al. IIT and pentastarch resuscitation in severe sepsis. N Engl J Med. 2008;358(2):125–139.

9. Arabi Y, Dabbagh O, Tamim H, et al. Intensive versus conventional insulin therapy: a randomized controlled trial in medical and surgical critically ill patients. Crit Care Med. 2008 Dec;36(12):3190–7, De la Rosa GD, Donado JH, Restrepo AH, et al. Strict glycemic control in patients hospitalised in a mixed medical and surgical intensive care unit: a randomized clinical trial. Crit Care 2008, 12:R120.

10. Devos P, Preiser J, Melot C. Impact of tight glucose control by IIT on ICU mortality and the rate of hypoglycemia: final results of the glucontrol study [European Society of Intensive Care Medicine 20th Annual Congress abstract 0735]. Intensive Care Med. 2007;33(suppl 2):S189.

11. Available from: http://www.clinicaltrials.gov/ct/gui/show/NCT00220987.

12. Wiener RS, Wiener DC, Larson RJ et al. Benefits and risks of tight glucose control in critically ill adults: a meta-analysis. JAMA. 2008;300(8):933–944.

13. The Action to Control Cardiovascular Risk in Diabetes Study Group. Effects of Intensive Glucose Lowering in Type 2 Diabetes. N Engl J Med 2008; 359:1519–1521.

14. Cryer PE. Hypoglycemia, functional brain failure and brain death. J Clin Invest 2008; 117:868–870.

15. Ben-Ami, H., Nagachandran, P., Mendelson, A., Edoute, Y. Drug-induced hypoglycemic coma in 102 diabetic patients. Arch. Intern. Med. 1999; 159:281–284.

16. Tkacs, N.C., Pan, Y., Raghupathi, R., Dunn-Meynell, A.A., Levin, B.E.. Cortical Fluoro-Jade staining and blunted adrenomedullary response to hypoglycemia after non-coma hypoglycemia in rats. J. Cereb. Blood Flow Metab. 2005; 25:1645–1655.

17. Cryer, P.E.. Diverse causes of hypoglycemia-associated autonomic failure in diabetes. N. Engl. J. Med. 2004; 350:2272–2279.

18. Kagansky N, Levy S, Rimon E et al. Hypoglycemia as a predictor of mortality in hospitalized elderly patients. Arch Intern Med 2003;163:1825–9.

19. Vlasselaers D, Milants I, Desmet L et al. IIT for patients in paediatric intensive care: a prospective, randomised controlled study. Lancet. Published online January 27, 2009 DOI:10.1016/S0140-6736(09)60044–1.

20. Beardsall K, Vanhaesebrouck S, Ogilvy-Stuart AL, et al. Early insulin therapy in very-low-birth-weight infants. N Engl J Med 2008;359:1873–84.

21. American Diabetes Association. Standards of medical care in diabetes–2008. Diabetes Care. 2008; 31(suppl 1):S12-S54.

22. Kia M, Botdorf J, Barber KR, et al. The effects of strict glycemic control in the critically ill general and vascular surgical patient. Paper presented at: 91st Annual Clinical Congress of the American College of Surgeons; October 16–20, 2005; San Francisco, California.

23. van Wezel HB, Zuurbier CJ, de Jonge E, et al. Differential effects of a perioperative hyperinsulinemic normoglycemic clamp on the neurohumoral stress response during coronary artery surgery. J Clin Endocrinol Metab. 2006;91(10):4144–4153.

24. Bilotta F, Caramia R, Cernak I, et al. IIT after severe traumatic brain injury: a randomized clinical trial [published online ahead ofprint March 29, 2008]. Neurocrit Care. doi:10.1007 /s12028–008–9084–9.

25. Bland DK, Fankhanel Y, Langford E, et al. Intensive ver-

sus modified conventional control of blood glucose level in medical intensive care patients: a pilot study. Am J Crit Care. 2005;14(5):370–376.

26. Mackenzie IM, Ingle S, Underwood C, Blunt M. Glycaemic control and outcome in general intensive care [abstract]. Proc Am Thorac Soc. 2005;2:A295.

27. Iapichino G, Albicini M, Umbrello M, et al. Tight glycemic control does not affect asymmetricdimethylarginine in septic patients [published online ahead of print May 27, 2008]. Intensive Care Med. doi:10.1007/s00134-008-1158-9.

28. Mitchell I, Knight E, Gissane J, et al. A phase II randomised controlled trial of IIT in general intensive care patients. Crit Care Resusc. 2006;8(4):289–293.

29. De la Rosa GD, Donado JH, Restrepo AH, et al. Strict glycemic control in patients hospitalised in a mixed medical and surgical intensive care unit: a randomized clinical trial. Crit Care 2008, 12:R120.

30. Henderson WR, Dhingra VK, Chittock DR, Ronco JJ. Survival using glucose algorithm regulation (sugar) trial–pilot data (in association with the Canadian Critical Care Trials Group) [abstract]. Proc Am Thorac Soc. 2005;2:A37.

31. Mackenzie I, Ingle S, Zaidi S, Buczaski S. Tight glycaemic control: a survey of intensive care practice in large English hospitals. Intensive care medicine 2005;31:1136.

32. Moeniralam H, Spronk P, Graat M et al. Tight glycemic control increases the incidence of hypoglycemia in intensive care unit patients. Critical Care 2005;9:P388.

33. Treggiari MM, Karir V, Yanez ND, et al. IIT and mortality in critically ill patients. Critical Care. 2008;12:R29.

34. Gandhi GY, Nuttall GA, Abel MD, et al. Intensive intraoperative insulin therapy versus conventional glucose management during cardiac surgery: a randomized trial. Ann Intern Med. 2007;146:233–243.

35. Krinsley JS, Grover, A. Severe hypoglycemia in critically ill patients: Risk factors and outcomes. Crit Care Med 2007, 35:2262–2267.

36. Sakel M. Schizophreniebehandlung mittels Insulin-Hypoglykämie sowie hypoglykämischer Schocks. Wiener Med Wschr 1934; 45: 1211–1214 32.

37. Bhatia A, Cadman B, Mackenzie I.Hypoglycemia and cardiac arrest in a critically ill patient on strict glycemic

control. Anesth Analg. 2006 Feb;102(2):549–51, Sinha S, Jayaram R, Hargreaves CG (2007) Fatal neuroglycopaenia after accidental use of a glucose 5 % solution in a peripheral arterial cannula flush system. Anaesthesia 62:615–20.

38. Korsatko S, Ellmerer M, Schaupp L et al. Hypoglycaemic coma due to falsely high point-of-care glucose measurements in an ICU-patient with peritoneal dialysis: a critical incidence report. Intensive Care Med. 2009 Mar;35(3):571–2.

39. McMullin J, Brozek J, Jaeschke R et al. Glycemic control in the ICU: a multicenter survey. Intensive Care Med 2004;30:798–803.

40. Brunkhorst FM, Wahl HG. Blood glucose measurements in the critically ill: more than just a blood draw. Crit Care10(6):178, Dungan K, Chapman J, Braithwaite SS, et al. (2007) Glucose measurement: confounding issues in setting targets for inpatient management. Diabetes Care 2006; 30(2):403–9.

41. Dungan K, Chapman J, Braithwaite SS, et al. Glucose measurement: confounding issues in setting targets for inpatient management. Diabetes Care 2007; 30(2):403–9. Review.

42. Dungan K. Glucose measurement in the hospital: Tips for clinicians. Review of Endocrinology, May 2007: 16–19.

43. Aragon D. Evaluation of nursing work effort and perceptions about blood glucose testing in tight glycemic control. American Journal of Critical Care 2006; 15:370–377.

44. Doig GS, Simpson F, Delaney A. A review of the true methodological quality of nutritional support trials conducted in the critically ill: time for improvement. Anesth Analg 2005;100:527–33.

45. Heyland DK, Dhaliwal R, Drover JW et al. Canadian clinical practice guidelines for nutrition support in mechanically ventilated, critically ill adult patients. JPEN J Parenter Enteral Nutr 2003;27:355–73.

46. Hovorka R. Continuous glucose monitoring and closed-loop systems. Diabet Med 2006;23:1–12, ii.

47. Egi M, Bellomo R, Stachowski E, et al. IIT in postoperative intensive care unit patients: a decision analysis. ARCCM 2006;173:407–13, and iii.

48. Marik P, Varon J. IIT in the ICU: Is it now time to jump off the bandwagon? Resuscitation 2007; 74:191–193.

Elias Knobel, Márcia Makdisse and Marcos Knobel

Avoiding harm in cardiovascular care

Introduction

It is estimated that medical errors are frequent in hospitalised patients, with adverse events occurring in approximately 3.7% to 16.6% of hospital admissions [1]. In its landmark report, "To Err Is Human," the Institute of Medicine (IOM) estimated that between 44,000 and 98,000 people die each year in hospitals in the United States from medical errors that could be avoided. These thousands of deaths are also associated with complex or urgent care and prolonged hospital stays [2]. In 2000 the IOM also published a report that examined the prevalence of medical errors and reviewed their potential causes [3].

Different types of human errors are associated with medical care. For instance, they might be errors of execution, called slips when they can be observed or lapses when they cannot, or they might be errors of planning, which are referred to as mistakes [4]. According to the "To Err Is Human" report, error of execution is defined as the failure of a planned action to be completed as intended, whereas error of planning is the use of a wrong plan to achieve an aim [3].

Any type of error has the potential to cause harm and when it happens, the error is referred to as a preventable adverse event. Negligent adverse events constitute a subset of preventable adverse events that are commonly seen in clinical practice, mostly related to medication error or non-compliance with evidence-based care.

According to the National Coordinating Council for Medication Error Reporting and Prevention (NCC MERP) a medication error is defined as "any preventable event that may cause or lead to inappropriate medication use or patient harm, while the medication is in the control of the health care professional, patient, or consumer." An analysis of case reports of fatal medication errors entered in the FDA's Adverse Event Reporting System showed that over 50% of the deaths related to medication errors occurred because of damages caused to the central nervous system, or because of the inappropriate use of antineoplastic or cardiovascular drugs [5].

In regard to non-compliance with evidence-based care, the failure to offer the patient the best treatment recommended on the basis of the best scientific knowledge has the potential to impact outcome and should be regarded as an error of planning [3].

The present article will focus on common preventable adverse events that have the potential to harm patients in acute cardiac care settings. The article will also examine promising strategies proposed to avoid these events.

Prevalence of errors in acute cardiac care

The exact prevalence of errors during treatment of acute cardiac diseases is difficult to determine because of the lack of data derived from well-designed clinical trials.

Available studies examining cardiac care settings suggest that a significant percentage of fatal and non-fatal adverse events may be preventable. One study showed that 14 % to 27 % of deaths due to cerebrovascular accidents, pneumonia, or myocardial infarction could have been avoided. Preventable deaths attributed to myocardial infarction reflected primarily errors in management, as compared with errors in diagnosis [6]. Another study found that 14 % of cardiac arrests occurred following an iatrogenic complication and that half of them could have been prevented [7]. These and other studies suggest that errors are very common in patients with cardiovascular disease and may account for adverse events, in both hospital and outpatient settings.

Errors in the initial approach to an acute cardiac patient

In the current era of high technology, clinical examination continues to play a key role in the evaluation of any acute cardiac patient. The lack of such evaluation or its inadequate application might lead to incorrect diagnosis and consequently to inappropriate therapy that might harm the patient.

In current medical practice, clinical diagnosis has been often relegated to a secondary role bypassed by the spreading utilisation of sophisticated, expensive, and not always efficient technologies. Such is the case with the approach used in patients presenting low cardiac output syndrome in the acute phase of myocardial infarction. In such cases, clinical evaluation of subjective signs of hypoperfusion such as altered sensorium, cold and clammy, skin, and oliguria, have been associated with an increase in 30-day mortality, independent of the haemodynamic variables [8].

Medication errors

Most common causes of medication errors

A Statement on Medication Errors in Acute Cardiac Care, published by the American Heart Association, didactically grouped medication errors in three main categories: drug name confusion errors, prescribing and dispensing errors, and errors of omission [9]. Based on that classification, some common causes of medication errors are discussed below.

Drug name confusion errors

In this common cause of medication error, the name of the dispensed drug looks or sounds like the one prescribed. Confusion may derive from brand or generic name similarities. But other common practices such as the use of abbreviations or acronyms, illegible handwriting, unfamiliarity with drug names, newly available products, similar packaging or labelling, and incorrect selection of a similar name from a computerised product list may also cause problems [10].

Failure during prescription, transcription, dispensing, and administering medication

Medication errors can occur at all levels of the medication-use system, from prescribing to dispensing. In the acute cardiac care setting, antithrombotics and fibrinolytics, both used in the treatment of acute coronary syndromes, constitute good examples of medication to be handled cautiously by experienced professionals, as any change in dose, duration, or intensity can result in an adverse effect on clinical outcome. Vasoactive drugs have frequently been linked to errors in administration, mainly due to wrong infusion rate in the intensive cardiac care unit setting [11, 12].

Among antithrombotic agents, heparin is one with the greatest potential to cause life-threatening adverse events. Inadvertent administration of high doses of heparin has been directly related to incidences of major haemorrhage. The rate of intracranial haemorrhage is significantly reduced in TIMI-9B in comparison to GUSTO II-a, as a consequence of a reduced dose regimen [13, 14]. This finding led to the current recommended regimen of an initial bolus of 60 U per kg (maximum 4,000 U) of unfractionated heparin (UFH) followed by an initial infusion of 12 U per kg per hour (maximum 1,000 U per hour). Monitoring involves aPTT measurements 6h after any dosage change. If significant changes in clinical status occur, it is recommended to adjust UFH infusion to a therapeutic level and to do a complete blood and platelet count to monitor for anaemia and heparin-induced thrombocytopenia, especially after prolonged infusions [15].

Another issue is the choice between unfractionated heparin (UFH) and low-molecular-weight heparin (LMWH). A meta-analysis of trials comparing these two treatments showed that the primary end points of death, namely myocardial infarction and major bleeding at 30 days, occurred significantly less often in patients receiving LMWH (enoxaparin) (11.1 % versus 12.9 %, odds ratio 0.84, 95 % CI 0.73–0.97). The main risk factors for bleeding in the enoxaparin group were older age and renal failure. In such cases, UFH should be preferred in order to avoid bleeding complications [16].

The efficacy of thrombolytic therapy in reducing morbidity and mortality related to ST-elevation Acute Myocardial Infarction (STEMI) has been widely reported. Since the publication of the ISIS 2 trial [17] that showed the effect of streptokinase, several other studies were conducted to test new thrombolytic agents. However, finding the right dosage and administration route so the adverse effects of these drugs are minimised while their benefits for coronary potency are provided, has been a challenge. It is well known that the more complex dosing and titration regimens are, the greater the risk of serious errors. Single-bolus and double-bolus fibrinolytic agents such as tenecteplase and reteplase have been associated with fewer medication errors than prolonged infusion agents such as t-PA or streptokinase [18, 19].

Digoxin has been commonly associated with medication errors in the hospital setting. Aging-related changes in renal function, body mass, and polypharmacy have all been linked with digoxin toxicity [20]

Errors of omission in the prescription of evidence-based medication

The benefits of certain cardiovascular drugs have been well established based on the findings of controlled randomised clinical trials. The failure to prescribe them may cause harm by potentially exposing the patient to avoidable adverse events.

Findings from the multinational GRACE (Global Registry of Acute Coronary Events) registry showed that one-third of the patients admitted in the acute phase of STEMI who were eligible for reperfusion therapy did not receive the treatment [21].

Female and elderly patients are especially prone to this kind of error. A recently published analysis showed that women are less likely to receive early aspirin treatment, early beta-blocker treatment, reperfusion therapy, or timely reperfusion [22]. In an analysis done of the GRACE registry, elderly patients admitted with acute coronary syndrome received less aspirin, beta-blockers, thrombolytic therapy, statins, and glycoprotein IIb/IIIa inhibitors while, on the other hand, receiving more calcium antagonists, which are drugs that are not recommended as first-line therapy for treating acute coronary syndromes [23].

Anticoagulant therapy with warfarin for stroke prevention in atrial fibrillation is also underutilised [24].

Some controversy exists when guideline recommendations are made on the basis of inconclusive evidence. This is the case with perioperative beta-blockers for the prevention of adverse clinical outcomes in patients submitted to noncardiac surgery. A recent meta-analysis of 33 trials found that perioperative beta-blockers were associated with a decrease in non-fatal myocardial infarction and myocardial ischaemia, but not with all-cause or cardiovascular mortality. Perioperative beta-blockers were also found to be associated with an increase in non-fatal strokes, perioperative bradycardia, and hypotension requiring treatment. The authors suggested that guideline recommendations on perioperative beta-blocker use should be softened until conclusive evidence is available [25]. The controversy is that perioperative withdrawal of chronically administered beta-blockers may result in increased cardiac morbidity and mortality. Among endovascular and vascular surgery patients, perioperative withdrawal of beta-blocker therapy has been associated with a 2.7-fold increase in 1-year mortality [26].

Adverse effects of medication

Many commonly used cardiovascular drugs have the potential to cause adverse reactions even if appropriately prescribed. Cardiac arrhythmias may be both treated and caused by the same antiarrhythmic agents, which may provoke adverse reactions due to their electrophysiologic actions [27, 28]. For instance, prolonged PR and QT intervals may lead to bradyarrhythmias or to malignant ventricular arrhythmias, such as *torsade de pointes*, which is a polymorphic ventricular tachycardia associated to drug-induced QT prolongation and the most important electrocardiographic presentation. The recognition of drug interactions that may increase the occurrence of such well-known adverse reactions is essential for avoiding harm. In regard to which anti-arrhythmic drug to use, the decision needs to consider the anti-arrhytmogenic potential of the drug. Probably the most important landmark in the pharmacological therapy for ventricular arrhythmias was the CAST study, which disclosed a significant increase of mortality related to class I anti-arrhythmic agents [29].

Drugs commonly used in clinical practice such as antibiotics may prolong QT interval and when used in combination with class III anti-arrhythmic agents may cause serious arrhythmias. Antibiotics (quinolones, antifungal drugs, and macrolides), triciclic antidepressants, beta-blockers, and digitalis are the main therapeutic agents involved in those interactions.

Cardiovascular diseases are often combined with renal insufficiency. Thus, it is important to check the patient's renal function and to perform any dose adjustment necessary to decrease the chance of errors related to inadequate dose regimen [30].

Many fashionable treatments for critically ill patients may cause harm. One example is the use of furosemide as first-line therapy for acute heart failure, hypovolemia, vasoconstriction, increased ventricular strain, increased sympathetic activation, and decreasing cardiac output; another is the use of catecholamines for severe heart failure and other forms of shock, increased fat β-oxidation, pro-arrhythmogenic and pro- and anti-inflammatory effects, altered immunity, and mitochondrial function [12].

Safety issues in the interventional cardiology setting

The extraordinary technological advances that have occurred over the past decades have allowed cardiac interventional procedures to be widely practised. Studies published by various institutions have shown that substantial variation in volume, patterns of proceedings, and practices and use of technology exists, which may impact the efficacy and safety of such interventions [31]. An adequate information system within the catheterisation laboratory is essential for implementing any quality monitoring and improvement programme [32]. Complications of percutaneous coronary interventions may be divided into the following categories for the purpose of assessing clinical competence: death, stroke, myocardial infarction, emergency coronary artery bypass graft surgery, vascular access site complications, excessive bleeding requiring treatment, contrast agent nephropathy, coronary perforation, and tamponade [33]. The first four are considered major complications; data derived from registries worldwide show these rates are below 1%, in spite of the increased complexity of the cases currently treated [34, 35, 36]. Even though such rates have remained low and stable, the availability of on-site support services such as cardiovascular surgery, coronary and intensive care units, vascular surgery, nephrology consultation and dialysis, neurology consultation and imaging services such as computed tomography, magnetic resonance imaging, and ultrasound are essential to enhance patient safety.

Catheterisation laboratories operating in facilities that lack those services should have very well-defined selection and exclusion criteria and establish a written agreement with a third-party centre for transfer and acceptance of patients within 60 minutes, in the event of emergency [32]. In any case, for catherisation laboratories, the existence of an adequate information system is essential for implementing any quality monitoring and improvement programme [32].

Vascular complications (defined as access site injury that requires procedural or surgical intervention, or bleeding that requires transfusion) are the most common complications of diagnostic and therapeutic percutaneous coronary procedures. The rate of vascular complications ranges from 2.6 % to 6.6 % and the strongest predictors of vascular complication are age ≥ 70, female sex, body surface area < 1.6 m², renal failure or creatinine > 2 mg/dl, emergent procedures, and the use of anti-GP IIb/IIIa agents during or after the procedure [37].

The risk of major bleeding after a percutaneous coronary intervention, defined as intracranial bleeding or clinically significant haemorrhage associated with a drop in haemoglobin concentration over 5.0 g/dl (or an absolute drop in the haematocrit of at least 15 % when haemoglobin dosage is not available), varies from 1.0 % to 5.4 %. It has been demonstrated that bleeding in the 30 days after a percutaneous coronary intervention is a strong and independent predictor of early and late mortality. Thus, the adoption of measures to reduce bleeding complications is important to improve patient outcome [38]. Using the femoral approach, the following factors have been identified as predictors of major bleeding post-PCI: older than 55, female, estimated glomerular filtration rate < 60 ml/min/1.73 m², pre-existing anaemia, administration of low-molecular-weight heparin within 48 hours pre-PCI, use of glycoprotein IIb/IIIa inhibitors, and intraaortic balloon pump use [39].

Contrast agent nephropathy, defined as an increase in serum creatinine occurring within the first 24 h after contrast exposure and peaking up to 5 days afterwards, is a major complication that affects patient outcome. The main risk factors for contrast agent nephropathy are occurrence of a compromised renal function (estimated glomerular filtration < 60 ml/min/1.73 m²), diabetes mellitus, volume depletion, use of nephrotoxic drugs, and haemodynamic instability. Higher contrast volumes (> 100 ml) are associated with higher rates of contrast-induced acute renal injury in patients at risk. Table 1 summarises key points and recommendations to prevent the occurrence of contrast-induced acute kidney injury [40].

Strategies to avoid or limit errors in cardiac care

To avoid or limit the occurrence of errors in cardiac care, hospitals and other healthcare facilities need to establish strategies and interventions at an organisational level, rather than relying on individual-level interventions.

It is important to recognise that errors do occur and then build a system that stimulates the reporting of those errors, specially of medication errors. Without error reporting, the design of strategies to promote changes for a safer system will be compromised.

Among the 14 barriers to medication error reporting identified in a survey involving representatives of four professions (physicians, pharmacists, advanced practitioners, and nurses) from four independently owned, non-profit nursing homes, 9 (60 %) were considered to be barriers at the organisational level. These include lack of a readily available medication error reporting system, lack of information on how to report errors, lack of feedback to the reporter, time-consuming reporting systems or forms, lack of a consistent definition of error, lack of an anonymous reporting system, lack of recognition that an error has occurred, and lack of a culture of reporting errors. At the individual level, these barriers were lack of knowledge of which errors should be reported, lack of knowledge of the usefulness of reporting errors, fear of disciplinary action, fear of being blamed, and fear of liability or lawsuits [41].

In order to identify opportunities for improvement, centres should adopt, select, and implement quality indicators to monitor their performance over time (to identify gaps and monitor the success of their improvement efforts) and to enable benchmarking with other centres. They should also formulate an integrated approach that takes care of patients from their arrival to their discharge. Also recommended are implementation of clinical protocols for recognition and management of procedural complications, providing regular feedback on outcomes to the administrative and clinical staff, and facilitating the active participation of staff in the formulation of improvement actions.

A set of demographic and clinical variables that may influence patient outcome must be systematically collected, analysed, and discussed with clinical and administrative staff.

In the acute coronary syndrome setting, performance measures targeted to patients who have STEMI and non-ST-elevation acute coronary syndromes (NSTACS) have been defined by ESC and ACC/AHA Task Force Writing Committees. The

Tab. 1   Key points and recommendations aimed to decrease the risk of contrast-induced acute kidney injury (AKI) [data from McCullough PA. Contrast-Induced Acute Kidney Injury. J. Am. Coll. Cardiol. 2008;5:1419–1428]

Key points	Recommendations
Assess baseline renal function	▪ Estimated glomerular filtration rate (eGFR) is a better index of renal function than serum creatinine.
Withhold nephrotoxic drugs	▪ Nonsteroidal anti-inflammatory drugs, calcineurin inhibitors, high-dose loop diuretics, aminoglycosides, and other nephrotoxic agents should be withheld when possible, for several days before contrast exposure.
Withhold metformin	▪ Metformin should be withheld before all contrast procedures because of the risk of lactic acidosis and should be restarted only after it is established that the patient has not developed AKI.
Volume expansion	▪ Isotonic crystalloid (saline or bicarbonate solution) appears to be more effective than half-normal saline. ▪ Intravenous fluids should be administered at a rate of 1.0 to 1.5 ml/kg/min, for 3 to 12 h before and 6 to 12 h after contrast exposure. ▪ There is not enough evidence that oral volume expansion is as effective as intravenous volume expansion.
Choice of contrast medium	▪ Iso-osmolar nonionic iodixanol has shown to have the lowest risk for contrast-induced AKI in patients with chronic kidney disease (CKD) and diabetes mellitus. Such isosmolal contrast media are recommended both by the American College of Cardiology/American Heart Association guidelines (Class I, Level of Evidence: A) and the National Kidney Foundation Kidney Disease Outcome Quality Initiative guidelines.
Volume of contrast	▪ Volume of contrast is an independent predictor of contrast-induced AKI, although in high-risk patients even small volumes of contrast can have adverse effects on renal function. In general, the volume of contrast should not exceed twice the baseline level of eGFR, in millilitres.
Dialysis and haemofiltration	▪ Lack of evidence that prophylactic dialysis reduces the risk of contrast-induced AKI. ▪ Haemofiltration performed 6 h before and 12 to 18 h after contrast has been shown to reduce mortality and need for haemodialysis in very high-risk patients (creatinine 3.0 to 4.0 mg/dl, eGFR 15 to 20 ml/min/1.73 m^2)
Pharmacologic strategies	▪ Currently there are no approved pharmacologic agents for the prevention of contrast-induced AKI. ▪ Ascorbic acid is the only agent tested in a multicentre, blinded, placebo-controlled trial that has been shown to reduce rates of contrast-induced AKI. The used dose was 3 g orally the night before and 2 g orally twice a day after the procedure. ▪ Heterogeneity of N-acetylcysteine studies precludes a conclusion on its effects. The REMEDIAL trial suggested that N-acetylcysteine combined with volume supplementation with sodium bicarbonate was more effective than N-acetylcysteine alone. The dose of N-acetylcysteine that reached better results was 1,200 mg given orally, twice a day, on the day before and after the procedure. ▪ Lack of benefit of fenoldopam, dopamine, calcium-channel blockers, atrial natriuretic peptide, and L-arginine. ▪ Furosemide, mannitol, and an endothelin receptor antagonist shown to be potentially detrimental.

Tab. 2 Performance measures in the acute coronary syndrome setting

Quality indicator	Description
Aspirin on admission and discharge	Rate of administration of aspirin within 24 hours before or after hospital arrival and at discharge
Beta-blocker on admission and discharge	Rate of prescription of beta-blockers within 24 hours before or after hospital arrival and at discharge
Angiotensin-converting enzyme inhibitor (ACE-I) or angiotensin receptor blocker (ARB) at discharge	Rate of prescription of ACE-I or ARB for patients with left ventricular systolic dysfunction at discharge
Statin at discharge	Rate of prescription of lipid-lowering medication (if LDL-C is ≥100 mg/dl) at hospital discharge
LDL cholesterol testing	Rate of LDL cholesterol testing during hospital stay
Smoking cessation counselling	Rate of patients receiving smoking cessation counselling during hospital stay

Tab. 3 Performance measures in the heart failure (HF) setting

Quality indicator	Description
Documentation of left ventricular (LV) systolic function	Rate of documentation of LV systolic function before arrival, during hospitalisation, or planned for after discharge
Angiotensin-converting enzyme inhibitor (ACE-I) or angiotensin receptor blocker (ARB) at discharge	Rate of prescription of ACE-I or ARB for patients with left ventricular systolic dysfunction at discharge
Beta-blocker at discharge	Rate of prescription of beta-blockers at discharge
Warfarin for HF patients with atrial fibrillation at discharge	Rate of prescription of warfarin in HF patients with chronic/recurrent atrial fibrillation
Smoking cessation counselling	Rate of patients receiving smoking cessation counselling during hospital stay
HF education at discharge	Rate of HF patients receiving instructions on physical activity, diet, discharge medication, follow-up appointment, weight monitoring, and symptom recognition at discharge

committees summarised the diagnostic, therapeutic, and patient education engagement strategies and dimensions of care that represent the strongest level of evidence and consensus [42]. The specific performance measures and the time and setting in which they should be applied are described in Table 2.

In the heart failure setting, Table 3 presents a set of performance measures that has been established for patients admitted with systolic dysfunction [43].

In the interventional cardiology setting it is recommended that operators and centres submit their data to large databases that allow for evaluation of risk-adjusted outcomes and benchmarking [33]. Such a recommendation demands the adoption of common data standards. This was the aim of the Cardiology Audit and Registration Data Standards (CARDS) project in which the European Society of Cardiology worked in partnership with the Department of Health and Children in Ireland and the Irish Cardiac Society to agree on data standards (variables, definitions, and coding) for a cardiology health information system. The system should support data collection on acute coronary syndromes, percutaneous coronary interventions, and clinical electrophysiology [44].

Another effort to mention is the initiative to help catheterisation laboratories with the development and implementation of continuous quality improvement (CQI) programmes. This was done with the creation of a web-based toolkit known as CathKIT sponsored by the American College of Cardiology Foundation and the Society for Cardiovascular Angiography and Interventions. The toolkit provides information and tools to assist the catheterisation laboratories in developing their own CQI initiatives while reinforcing best practices and adopting quality standards for clinical outcomes [45].

As for improving the rate of procedural complications, a non-randomised study to assess the impact of a CQI programme on adherence to quality indicators and outcomes related to percutaneous coronary interventions showed that at follow-up, the intervention group had higher use of preprocedural aspirin and glycoprotein IIb/IIIa blockers, lower use of postprocedural heparin, a lower amount of contrast media per case, lower rates of transfusions, vascular complications, contrast nephropathy, stroke, transient ischemic attack, and combined end points, when compared to the control group. The intervention consisted of feedback on outcomes, working group meetings, site visits, selection of quality indicators, and use of bedside tools for quality improvement and risk assessment [46].

Door-to-balloon time is defined as the time between arrival at the emergency department and the first balloon inflation during primary percutaneous coronary intervention (PCI). It is used to evaluate in-hospital delay for patients with ST-elevation myocardial infarction and has emerged as a key indicator to assess the promptness of intervention. Delays in door-to-balloon time have been associated with poorer outcomes [31]. When door-to-balloon time is improved, the rate of complications may be reduced and clinical outcomes improved as well.

Based upon clinical trials and registry analyses, a door-to-balloon time of less than 90 minutes has been established as the goal for primary PCI [47, 48]. However, published data indicate that only a minority of the acute care hospitals have been able to achieve this recommended goal. This has made some authors ask whether this 90-minute gold standard is feasible [49].

Door-to-balloon time is a complex process indicator that reflects the performance of the whole staff involved in initial diagnosis, decision-making, transport, and interventional procedure. To identify gaps in the process as a whole, several key subintervals such as door-to-electrocardiogram, electrocardiogram-to-lab, and lab-to-balloon time have been proposed. An analysis using data from 340 hospitals participating in the National Registry of Myocardial Infarction revealed that adjusted mean subinterval times in higher performing hospitals were 7.9 ± 1.7 minutes, 47.8 ± 7.1 minutes, and 29.0 ± 5.4 minutes for door-to-ECG, ECG-to-lab, and lab-to-balloon time, respectively [50].

Several strategies aiming to reduce door-to-balloon time have been proposed in recent years. A survey among 365 acute care hospitals identified six strategies strongly associated with a shorter door-to-balloon time. Three of the strategies focused on the activation of the catheterisation laboratory done

- by the emergency physician,
- by a single call to a central page operator, or
- while the patient is en route to the hospital.

These measures resulted in significant reduction in door-to-balloon times of 8.2, 13.8 and 15.4 minutes, respectively.

The other three strategies focused on setting the expectation that

- the catheterisation laboratory staff will be available within 20 minutes after being paged (–19.3 minutes),
- an attending cardiologist will always be on site (–14.6 minutes), and
- real-time data feedback on door-to-balloon time will be provided to both emergency department and catheterisation laboratory staff members (–8.6 minutes) [51].

The six core, evidence-based strategies to reduce door-to-balloon times advocated by the D2B Alliance for Quality, a new Guidelines Applied in Practice (GAP) programme launched by the American College of Cardiology, are

- the emergency department physician activating the catheterisation laboratory,
- one call activating the catheterisation laboratory,
- the catheterisation laboratory team being ready in 20 to 30 minutes,
- prompt data feedback being provided,
- achieving senior management commitment, and
- adopting a team-based approach. [Available at http://www.d2balliance.org.]

Operators' knowledge and skill, recognition and management of procedural complications, and in-hospital delay for patients with ST-elevation myocardial infarction are key points to be systematically monitored in interventional cardiology practice.

In regard to operators' and centres' experience, better outcome results have been observed when intermediate- and high-volume centres were compared to low-volume centres, especially for primary percutaneous intervention [52]. On the institutional side, it has been recommended that low-volume centres (less than 400 interventions per year) hold conferences with a more experienced centre. In the case of their data falling outside the risk-adjusted benchmarks in mortality or emergency CABG during 2 of 3 contiguous 6-month periods, an external audit should be made to identify opportunities for improvement. In very low-volume centres case-by-case analysis may be more appropriate than benchmarking for monitoring quality. On the operator side, the volume threshold has been set at 75 procedures per year. Also, it is recommended for operators to attend at least 30 hours of interventional cardiology continuing medical education every 2 years. They should have 5 (≥ 75 cases per year) to 10 (< 75 cases per year) randomly selected cases and all major complications reviewed each year by the catheterisation laboratory director or by a quality assessment committee able to provide feedback to the operator. As volume is not the only determinant of quality, even high-volume centres should consider adopting peer review procedures for evaluating their quality and outcomes on a continuous basis.

Conclusion

In summary, to provide a better treatment and offer the patient a safer system, health care facilities must create a culture of quality and safety that includes both administrative and clinical staff. This will demand a continuous effort to implement evidence-based guidelines, to build a readily available anonymous error reporting system, to analyse errors focused on the organisation level and not on the individual, to measure practices through quality indicators for monitoring, to compare their data with other institutions (benchmarking), to ensure that the staff receive feedback on performance procedures, and to design strategies that will promote a continuum of care, from admission to discharge, that are evidence-based and patient-focused.

The authors

Elias Knobel, MD, PhD, FAHA, MACP, FCCM[1,2]
Márcia Makdisse, MD, MSc, PhD[3]
Marcos Knobel, MD[4]
[1]Director emeritus and founder of the ICU | Hospital Israelita Albert Einstein | São Paulo, Brazil
[2]Associate Professor of Medicine | Federal University of São Paulo | São Paulo, Brazil
[3]Head of Cardiology | Hospital Israelita Albert Einstein | São Paulo, Brazil
[4]Medical Coordinator | Coronary Care Unit | Hospital Israelita Albert Einstein | São Paulo, Brazil

Address for correspondence
Elias Knobel
Hospital Israelita Albert Einstein
Av Albert Einstein 627/701
CEP 05651–901
Morumbi, São Paulo, Brazil
E-mail: knobel@einstein.br

References

1. Brennan TA, Leape LL, Laird NM, Hebert L, Localio AR, Lawthers AG, et al. Incidence of adverse events and negligence in hospitalized patients. Results of the Harvard Medical Practice Study I. N Engl J Med. 1991 Feb 7;324(6):370–6.
2. Weingart SN, Wilson RM, Gibberd RW, Harrison B.

Epidemiology of medical error. BMJ. 2000 Mar 18;320(7237):774–777.

3. Kohn LT, Corrigan M, Donaldson MS, eds, for the Committee on Quality Health Care in America, Institute of Medicine. To Err Is Human: Building a Safer Health System. Washington, DC: National Academy Press; 2000.

4. Reason, James T., Human Error, Cambridge: Cambridge University Press, 1990.

5. Phillips J, Beam S, Brinker A, Holquist C, Honig P, Lee LY, et al. Retrospective analysis of mortalities associated with medication errors. Am J Health Syst Pharm. 2001 Oct 1;58(19):1835–41.

6. Dubois RW, Brook RH. Preventable deaths: who, how often, and why? Ann Intern Med. 1988; 109: 582–589.

7. Bedell SE, Deitz DC, Leeman D, Delbanco TL. Incidence and characteristics of preventable iatrogenic cardiac arrests. JAMA. 1991 Jun 5;265(21):2815–20.

8. Hasdai D, Holmes DR, Jr., Califf RM, Thompson TD, Hochman JS, Pfisterer M, et al. Cardiogenic shock complicating acute myocardial infarction: predictors of death. GUSTO Investigators. Global Utilization of Streptokinase and Tissue-Plasminogen Activator for Occluded Coronary Arteries. Am Heart J. 1999 Jul;138(1 Pt 1):21–31.

9. Freedman JE, Becker RC, Adams JE, Borzak S, Jesse RL, Newby LK, et al. Medication errors in acute cardiac care: An American Heart Association scientific statement from the Council on Clinical Cardiology Subcommittee on Acute Cardiac Care, Council on Cardiopulmonary and Critical Care, Council on Cardiovascular Nursing, and Council on Stroke. Circulation. 2002 Nov 12;106(20):2623–9.

10. Rados C. Drug name confusion: preventing medication errors. FDA Consum. 2005 Jul-Aug;39(4):35–7.

11. Calabrese AD, Erstad BL, Brandl K, Barletta JF, Kane SL, Sherman DS. Medication administration errors in adult patients in the ICU. Intensive Care Med. 2001 Oct;27(10):1592–8.

12. Singer M, Glynne P. Treating critical illness: The importance of first doing no harm. PLoS Med. 2005 2(6): e167.

13. Randomized trial of intravenous heparin versus recombinant hirudin for acute coronary syndromes. The Global Use of Strategies to Open Occluded Coronary Arteries (GUSTO) IIa Investigators. Circulation. 1994; 90: 1631–1637

14. Antman EM. Hirudin in acute myocardial infarction. Thrombolysis and Thrombin Inhibition in Myocardial Infarction (TIMI) 9B trial. Circulation. 1996 Sep 1;94(5):911–21.

15. Anderson JL, Adams CD, Antman EM, Bridges CR, Califf RM, Casey DE, Jr., et al. ACC/AHA 2007 guidelines for the management of patients with unstable angina/ non-ST-Elevation myocardial infarction: a report of the American College of Cardiology/American Heart Association Task Force on Practice Guidelines (Writing Committee to Revise the 2002 Guidelines for the Management of Patients With Unstable Angina/ Non-ST-Elevation Myocardial Infarction) developed in collaboration with the American College of Emergency Physicians, the Society for Cardiovascular Angiography and Interventions, and the Society of Thoracic Surgeons endorsed by the American Association of Cardiovascular and Pulmonary Rehabilitation and the Society for Academic Emergency Medicine. J Am Coll Cardiol. 2007 Aug 14;50(7):e1-e157.

16. Murphy SA, Gibson CM, Morrow DA, Van de Werf F, Menown IB, Goodman SG, et al. Efficacy and safety of the low-molecular weight heparin enoxaparin compared with unfractionated heparin across the acute coronary syndrome spectrum: a meta-analysis. Eur Heart J. 2007 Sep;28(17):2077–86.

17. ISIS-2 (Second International Study of Infarct Survival) Collaborative Group. Randomised trial of intravenous streptokinase, oral aspirin, both, or neither among 17,187 cases of suspected acute myocardial infarction: ISIS-2. Lancet 1988; 2:349.

18. Cannon CP. Thrombolysis medication errors: benefits of bolus thrombolytic agents. Am J Cardiol. 2000 Apr 27;85(8A):17C-22C.

19. Van De Werf F, Adgey J, Ardissino D, Armstrong PW, Aylward P, Barbash G, et al. Single-bolus tenecteplase compared with front-loaded alteplase in acute myocardial infarction: the ASSENT-2 double-blind randomised trial. Lancet. 1999 Aug 28;354(9180):716–22.

20. Hanratty CG, McGlinchey P, Johnston GD, Passmore AP. Differential pharmacokinetics of digoxin in elderly patients. Drugs Aging. 2000 Nov;17(5):353–62.

21. Eagle KA, Goodman SG, Avezum A, Budaj A, Sullivan CM, Lopez-Sendon J. Practice variation and missed opportunities for reperfusion in ST-segment-elevation myocardial infarction: findings from the Global Registry of Acute Coronary Events (GRACE). Lancet. 2002 Feb 2;359(9304):373–7.

22. Jneid H, Fonarow GC, Cannon CP, Hernandez AF, Palacios IF, Maree AO, et al. Sex differences in medical care and early death after acute myocardial infarction. Circulation. 2008 Dec 16;118(25):2803–10.

23. Avezum A, Makdisse M, Spencer F, Gore JM, Fox KA, Montalescot G, et al. Impact of age on management and outcome of acute coronary syndrome: observations from the Global Registry of Acute Coronary Events (GRACE). Am Heart J. 2005 Jan;149(1):67–73.

24. Cohen N, Almoznino-Sarafian D, Alon I, Gorelik O, Koopfer M, Chachashvily S, et al. Warfarin for stroke prevention still underused in atrial fibrillation: patterns of omission. Stroke. 2000 Jun;31(6):1217–22.

25. Bangalore S, Wetterslev J, Pranesh S, Sawhney S, Gluud C, Messerli FH. Perioperative β blockers in patients having non-cardiac surgery: a meta-analysis. Lancet 2008; 372: 1962–76.

26. Hoeks SE, Scholte Op Reimer WJ, van Urk H, Jorning PJ, Boersma E, Simoons ML, et al. Increase of 1-year mortality after perioperative beta-blocker withdrawal in endovascular and vascular surgery patients. Eur J Vasc Endovasc Surg. 2007 Jan;33(1):13–9.

27. Podrid PJ. Aggravation of arrhythmia by antiarrhythmic drugs. In: Podrid PJ, Kowey PR,eds. Cardiac Arrhythmia: Mechanisms, Diagnosis, and Management. Baltimore: Williams & Wilkins, 1995;pp.507–22.

28. Kerin NZ, Somberg J. Proarrhythmia: definition,risk factors, causes, treatment, and controversies. Am Heart J 1994;128:575–85.

29. CAST Investigators. Preliminary report: effect of encainide and flecainide on mortality in a randomized trial of arrhythmia suppression after myocardial infarction. N Engl J Med 1989;321:406–12

30. Chertow GM, Lee J, Kuperman GJ, Burdick E, Horsky J, Seger DL, et al. Guided medication dosing for inpatients with renal insufficiency. JAMA. 2001 Dec 12;286(22):2839–44.

31. Moscucci M, Rogers EK, Montoye C, Smith DE, Share D, O'Donnell M, et al. Association of a continuous quality improvement initiative with practice and outcome variations of contemporary percutaneous coronary interventions. Circulation. 2006 Feb 14;113(6):814–22.

32. Bashore TM, Bates ER, Berger PB, Clark DA, Cusma JT, Dehmer GJ, et al. American College of Cardiology/ Society for Cardiac Angiography and Interventions Clinical Expert Consensus Document on cardiac catheterization laboratory standards. A report of the American College of Cardiology Task Force on Clinical Expert Consensus Documents. J Am Coll Cardiol. 2001 Jun 15;37(8):2170–214.

33. King SB, 3rd, Aversano T, Ballard WL, Beekman RH, 3rd, Cowley MJ, Ellis SG, et al. ACCF/AHA/SCAI 2007 update of the clinical competence statement on cardiac interventional procedures: a report of the American College of Cardiology Foundation/American Heart Association/American College of Physicians Task Force on Clinical Competence and Training (writing Committee to Update the 1998 Clinical Competence Statement on Recommendations for the Assessment and Maintenance of Proficiency in Coronary Interven-tional Procedures). J Am Coll Cardiol. 2007 Jul 3;50(1):82–108.

34. Togni M, Balmer F, Pfiffner D, Maier W, Zeiher AM, Meier B. Percutaneous coronary interventions in Europe 1992–2001. Eur Heart J. 2004 Jul;25(14):1208–13.

35. Anderson HV, Shaw RE, Brindis RG, Hewitt K, Krone RJ, Block PC, et al. A contemporary overview of percutane-ous coronary interventions. The American College of Cardiology-National Cardiovascular Data Registry (ACC-NCDR). J Am Coll Cardiol. 2002 Apr 3;39(7):1096–103.

36. Cardoso CO, Quadros AS, Mattos LA, et al. Use of drug-eluting stents in Brazil: The SENIC (National Registry of Cardiovascular Interventions) Registry. Arq Bras Cardiol 2007;89:322–326

37. Piper WD, Malenka DJ, Ryan TJ, Jr., Shubrooks SJ, Jr., O'Connor GT, Robb JF, et al. Predicting vascular complications in percutaneous coronary interventions. Am Heart J. 2003 Jun;145(6):1022–9.

38. Ndrepepa G, Berger PB, Mehilli J, Seyfarth M, Neumann FJ, Schomig A, et al. Periprocedural bleeding and 1-year outcome after percutaneous coronary interventions: appropriateness of including bleeding as a component of a quadruple end point. J Am Coll Cardiol. 2008 Feb 19;51(7):690–7.

39. Nikolsky E, Mehran R, Dangas G, Fahy M, Na Y, Pocock SJ, et al. Development and validation of a prognostic risk score for major bleeding in patients undergoing percutaneous coronary intervention via the femoral approach. Eur Heart J. 2007 Aug;28(16):1936–45.

40. McCullough PA. Contrast-Induced Acute Kidney Injury. J. Am. Coll. Cardiol. 2008;5:1419–1428.

41. Handler SM, Perera S, Olshansky EF, Studenski SA, Nace DA, Fridsma DB, et al. Identifying modifiable barriers to medication error reporting in the nursing home setting. J Am Med Dir Assoc. 2007 Nov;8(9):568–74.

42. Krumholz HM, Anderson JL, Brooks NH, Fesmire FM, Lambrew CT, Landrum MB, et al. ACC/AHA clinical performance measures for adults with ST-elevation and non-ST-elevation myocardial infarction: a report of the American College of Cardiology/American Heart Association Task Force on Performance Measures (Writing Committee to Develop Performance Measures on ST-Elevation and Non-ST-Elevation Myocardial Infarction). J Am Coll Cardiol. 2006 Jan 3;47(1):236–65.

43. Bonow RO, Bennett S, Casey DE, Jr., Ganiats TG, Hlatky MA, Konstam MA, et al. ACC/AHA clinical performance measures for adults with chronic heart failure: a report of the American College of Cardiology/American Heart Association Task Force on Performance Measures (Writing Committee to Develop Heart Failure Clinical Performance Measures) endorsed by the Heart Failure Society of America. J Am Coll Cardiol. 2005 Sep 20;46(6):1144–78.

44. Flynn MR, Barrett C, Cosio FG, Gitt AK, Wallentin L, Kearney P, et al. The Cardiology Audit and Registration Data Standards (CARDS), European data standards for clinical cardiology practice. Eur Heart J. 2005 Feb;26(3):308–13.

45. Dehmer GJ, Hirshfeld JW, Oetgen WJ, Mitchell K, Simon AW, Elma M, et al. CathKIT: improving quality in the cardiac catheterization laboratory. J Am Coll Cardiol. 2004 Mar 3;43(5):893–9.

46. Brindis RG, Dehmer GJ. Continuous quality improvement in the cardiac catheterization laboratory: are the benefits worth the cost and effort? Circulation. 2006 Feb 14;113(6):767–70.

47. McNamara RL, Wang Y, Herrin J, Curtis JP, Bradley EH, Magid DJ, et al. Effect of door-to-balloon time on mortality in patients with ST-segment elevation myocardial infarction. J Am Coll Cardiol. 2006 Jun 6;47(11):2180-6.

48. Silber S, Albertsson P, Aviles FF, Camici PG, Colombo A, Hamm C, et al. Guidelines for percutaneous coronary interventions. The Task Force for Percutaneous Coronary Interventions of the European Society of Cardiology. Eur Heart J. 2005 Apr;26(8):804-47.

49. Moscucci M, Eagle KA. Door-to-balloon time in primary percutaneous coronary intervention: is the 90-minute gold standard an unreachable chimera? Circulation. 2006 Feb 28;113(8):1048-50.

50. Bradley EH, Herrin J, Wang Y, McNamara RL, Radford MJ, Magid DJ, et al. Door-to-drug and door-to-balloon times: where can we improve? Time to reperfusion therapy in patients with ST-segment elevation myocardial infarction (STEMI). Am Heart J. 2006 Jun;151(6):1281-7.

51. Bradley EH, Herrin J, Wang Y, Barton BA, Webster TR, Mattera JA, et al. Strategies for reducing the door-to-balloon time in acute myocardial infarction. N Engl J Med. 2006 Nov 30;355(22):2308-20.

52. Magid DJ, Calonge BN, Rumsfeld JS, Canto JG, Frederick PD, Every NR, et al. Relation between hospital primary angioplasty volume and mortality for patients with acute MI treated with primary angioplasty vs thrombolytic therapy. JAMA. 2000 Dec 27;284(24):3131-8.

Heleen M. Oudemans-van Straaten

Avoiding harm in acute renal failure

To avoid harm in acute renal failure, the clinician should be aware of risk factors for acute kidney injury (AKI). Early recognition of AKI by the routine use of the RIFLE criteria is necessary to take preventive measures timely:

- Optimise circulation
- Apply prophylactic volume expansion
  - in patients at risk for contrast nephropathy
  - in rhabdomyolysis, tumour lysis syndrome
  - when using nephrotoxic drugs causing tubular obstruction
- Avoid high-molecular-weight hydroxy-ethyl starches in sepsis
- Monitor and treat intra-abdominal hypertension
- Avoid nephrotoxic drugs in patients with or at risk of AKI
- Apply therapeutic drug monitoring for drugs with a narrow therapeutic window
- Avoid the therapeutic use of low-molecular-weight heparins without anti-Xa monitoring when creatinine clearance is < 30 ml/min
- Provide sufficient protein
- Optimise antioxidant defence (ascorbic acid, selenium)
- Use citrate as an anticoagulant for renal replacement therapy

Acute renal failure (ARF) is a complex disease, because accumulation of uraemic toxins may cause deterioration of other organ functions as well. Furthermore, ARF in the setting of critical illness also gives retention of inflammatory mediators. In addition to the diminished excretion of solutes and water, the loss of tubular function confers loss of re-absorption, metabolic, endocrine and immunological functions as well. The aim of this contribution is to highlight the main conditions which may cause harm to the kidney or the patient with ARF and some interventions to prevent this harm.

Be aware of causes and risks of AKI

The main causes of AKI include hypovolaemia, ischaemia/reperfusion, sepsis or a systemic inflammatory response syndrome accompanying major surgery, trauma and pancreatitis, rhabdomyolysis, tumour lysis, radiocontrast or the exposure to nephrotoxic drugs and intra-abdominal hypertension. In addition, several underlying conditions increase the risk of AKI. Among these are pre-existing renal dysfunction, especially diabetic nephropathy, congestive heart failure, vascular disease and higher age [1, 2]. In most patients, more than one factor plays a role. Fortunately, several acute conditions are preventable by cautious clinical care.

Recognise acute kidney injury

Recently, the RIFLE (risk, injury, failure, loss of function, end-stage kidney disease) system has been developed to classify the severity of ARF by a poor man's marker of glomerular filtration rate: the change in serum creatinine and urinary output [3]. Nevertheless, a higher RIFLE stage predicts a higher mortality. Even RIFLE risk, a 50% increase in serum creatinine, confers increased mortality [4]. Routine use of RIFLE may improve patient outcome, because the diagnosis of AKI alerts the physician to take specific measures that protect patient and kidney from further injury.

Science and Art

Ideally, we should base treatment on evidence from randomised controlled trials (RCTs). However, the translation of evidence from RCTs into clinical measures at the bedside requires knowledge of the trial population, the specific conditions and limitations of the trials. For each individual, the clinician should weigh the risks and benefits of each intervention. 'Best clinical practice' may not always be optimal for each patient.

Optimise the circulation

While maintaining renal blood flow would be the best goal to prevent so-called 'prerenal' AKI, there is no reliable way to monitor renal blood flow in clinical practice. We can only try to optimise its main determinants: intravascular volume, perfusion pressure, cardiac output and abdominal pressure.

Maintain intravascular volume

Hypovolaemia is a known risk factor for the development of AKI, whereas intravascular fluid expansion is renal protective. Although there is broad consensus concerning this statement, there is no consensus about the degree of vascu-

lar filling, the best marker for fluid status and the ideal resuscitation fluid. Nevertheless, the use of high-molecular-weight hydroxy-ethyl starches (HES) should be avoided in patients with sepsis. A RCT comparing 6% HES 200/0.6-0.66 to gelatine in 129 septic patients showed lower serum creatinine levels in the group receiving gelatine [5]. A large RCT found a higher incidence of AKI, requirement of renal replacement therapy (RRT) and mortality with 10% HES 200/0.5 (n = 262) compared to Ringer's lactate (n = 275) [6]. The negative effects of HES were dose-related. Whether the more recently developed HES solutions are safe is not known yet. The infusion of albumin may reduce AKI and death in cirrhosis with spontaneous peritonitis [7].

Although hypovolaemia should be prevented, uncontrolled fluid infusion should be avoided as well. In a RCT comparing a conservative and a liberal fluid strategy in 1000 patients with acute lung injury the incidence of RRT tended to be higher in the liberal group [8]. In a post hoc group of 1120 patients with ARF of the Sepsis Occurrence in Acutely Ill Patients study, mean fluid balance was associated with higher 60-day mortality [9].

Maintain perfusion pressure

The use of vasopressors for renal protection is controversial. Vasopressors may cause splanchnic and renal ischaemia. However, in vasodilated hypotensive patients, restoration of blood pressure with noradrenalin is recommended after and along with tailored fluid resuscitation [10]. Though a small RCT in septic shock failed to demonstrate additional renal benefit of a target mean arterial pressure of > 80 mmHg over 65 mmHg [11], a higher pressure may be needed in patients with previous hypertension. Dopamine as the initial vasopressor in patients with shock was associated with more tachycardia, and a higher mortality in cardiogenic shock than noradrenalin (De Backer, preliminary results). Adrenalin has more metabolic side effects (hyperglycaemia, hyperlactataemia and hypokalaemia). Low-dose vasopressin (10 IU/h) may be helpful in noradrenalin refractory shock to increase blood pressure and diuresis, but has not ameliorated survival or AKI [12]. Terlipressin may be useful in impending hepatorenal syndrome. However, the drug is difficult to titrate, may have ischaemic side effects and superiority to noradrenalin is not proven.

Use vasodilators

Contrary to previous concepts, a 'renal-dose' dopamine has no benefit in preventing or ameliorating AKI in the critically ill [13]. However, the use of fenoldopam, a pure dopamine-A1 receptor agonist, may be renoprotective. A recent meta-analysis, including 1290 critically ill and surgical patients from 16 RCT, shows that fenoldopam reduces the incidence of AKI, need for RRT and hospital mortality [14].

Maintain cardiac output

Low cardiac output is associated with deterioration of renal function and is a risk factor for postoperative AKI in cardiac surgery [1]. In experimental sepsis, cardiac output appears as the main determinant of renal blood flow [15]. It therefore seems rational to optimise cardiac output. However, there are no RCTs showing that maintaining cardiac output protects against AKI.

Avoid intra-abdominal hypertension

Intra-abdominal hypertension (IAH) is a serious condition complicating trauma, prolonged abdominal surgery and massive fluid resuscitation. Complications are the result of impaired organ perfusion due to diminished preload, increased afterload and external compression. IAH is readily detectable by monitoring bladder pressure, which should be routinely done in patients at risk [16]. When intra-abdominal pressure is continually > 20 mmHg, organ failure can occur, a condition named intra-abdominal compartment syndrome. Early recognition and intervention are crucial to prevent further damage to the kidneys and others organs. Treatment consists of decompressive laparotomy with temporary closure enlarging the abdominal space. However, recovery of organ function is not uniform [17], possibly due to the timing of laparotomy and to the sever-

ity of underlying disease. If IAH occurs along with massive fluid resuscitation, RRT can be considered.

Avoid nephrotoxicity

Contrast nephropathy

Underlying renal dysfunction, especially diabetic nephropathy, seems to be the greatest risk factor for developing contrast nephropathy [2]. In patients at risk preventive measures are beneficial. Firstly, the avoidance of intravascular contrast should be considered. Secondly, non-steroidal anti-inflammatory drugs should be discontinued. Thirdly, low osmolal contrast media should be used and the intravascular contrast volume should be limited [18]. Fourthly, patients should be hydrated properly, aiming at an increase of extracellular volume and diuresis. Normal or half-normal saline can be used from 12 h before until 12 h after contrast infusion, or sodium bicarbonate (154 mmol/l) from 1 h before (3 ml/kg/h) and 6 h after contrast exposure (1 ml/kg/h). The latter regimen may be superior [19] and is especially recommended for emergency procedures. Whether specific medications provide additional protection remains to be proven. Differences in efficacy between studies may be related to the adequacy of hydration. Despite the proliferation of RCT and meta-analysis on the efficacy of N-acetylcysteine, we still do not know whether the drug is effective [20]. A single dose of 200 mg theophylline 30 min. before contrast infusion may be effective [21, 22]. Optimisation of anti-oxidant defence may be important because antioxidants play a role in contrast toxicity. Ascorbic acid, 3 g at least 2 h before followed by 2 g the night and morning after contrast administration was effective in one study [23], but not in others, possibly due to differences in baseline anti-oxidant defence.

Rhabdomyolysis, intravascular haemolysis and tumour lysis syndrome

Rhabdomyolysis, intravascular haemolysis and tumor lysis syndrome are examples of AKI caused by endogenous toxins. Mechanisms of renal toxicity in rhabdomyolysis include impaired renal perfusion due to hypovolemia and cardovascular depression. In addition, myoglobin exerts toxic effects by renal vasoconstriction mediated by nitric oxide scavenging, by forming intratubular casts, which are facilitated by hypovolaemia and acidosis, and by tubular toxicity in which free iron and oxidant stress play a role. Renal toxicity can be prevented by early and vigorous fluid infusion targeting vascular volume expansion and facilitating removal and tubular dilution of the toxin. The infusion of sodium bicarbonate in rhabdomyolysis and intravascular haemolysis counteracting tubular acidosis is physiologically rational, though evidence from clinical studies is sparse. Rasburicase, recombinant urate oxidase, reduces the risk of ARF in the tumour lysis syndrome.

Drug-induced nephropathy

Drugs may cause renal toxicity by altering renal haemodynamics (NSAIDs), tubular toxicity mediated by reactive oxygen species (aminoglycoside antibiotics, vancomycin, antivirals, and amphotericin B), by immunological mechanisms (penicillins), tubular obstruction (aciclovir, sulfonamides), by causing vasculopathy (calcineurin inhibitors, clopidogrel) or osmotic nephrosis (immunoglobulins, starches, dextrans) [24]. Drug-induced AKI is generally preventable. Potentially nephrotoxic drugs should be avoided in patients with or at risk of AKI. Therapeutic drug monitoring is mandatory for aminoglycosides, vancomycin, sulfonamides, antivirals and calcineuron inhibitors if and when these potentially nephrotoxic drugs are not avoidable, because nephrotoxicity is dose-related. Furthermore, prophylactic volume expansion to attain tubular dilution and facilitate removal of the drug reduces toxicity. Notably, continuous infusion of amphotericin-B is less nephrotoxic than 4-hour infusion [25].

Avoid toxic levels of drugs

In patients with ARF, drug dosing needs special attention. Underdosing leads to therapeutic failure while overdosing may have toxic effects. The clinician should know the pharmacokinetics and -dynamics of the drugs he/she prescribes [26]. For non-toxic drugs overdosing is preferred over underdosing. Special attention should be paid to drugs which are normally removed by the kidney, mostly hydrophylic drugs, and those with a narrow therapeutic range. Clearance by CRRT depends on treatment dose and sieving coefficient, which depends on the type of membrane, the filtration fraction and the replacement mode. Protein binding is important, because only the free fraction is available for filtration or dialysis. Critical illness affects protein binding. Also, tubular reabsorption plays a role for some drugs, explaining a higher removal rate with CRRT than expected on account of calculated filtrate flow. Furthermore, renal dysfunction may affect the volume of distribution and hepatic metabolism as well. General rules can be given [26], however, due to the many confounders prediction of actual drug levels may be unreliable. Therefore, therapeutic drug monitoring is mandatory for drugs with a narrow therapeutic window.

Therapeutic use of low-molecular-weight heparins

Low-molecular-weight heparins (LMWH) have a predictable anticoagulant response, which allows administration in a fixed dose without routine laboratory monitoring. However, several studies show that anti-Xa activity accumulates in elderly patients and those with renal dysfunction, while anti-IIa activity does not [27, 27, 28]. A meta-analysis found an increased risk of major bleeding in patients with a creatine clearance < 30 ml/min [29]. Recently, the multicentre Innohep in Renal Insufficiency Study in patients over 70 years of age with impaired renal function with thromboembolism was stopped after including 350 patients because mortality was higher with tinziparin than with unfractionated heparin (13 % vs. 5 %) (from: US Food and Drug Administration). The therapeutic use of LMWHs without anti-Xa monitoring should therefore be avoided in patients with renal dysfunction. The situation during CRRT may be different: enoxaparin passed AN69 and PS membranes [30], while no enoxaparin accumulation was observed during CVVH [31].

Avoid uraemic toxicity

Timing of renal replacement therapy

The accumulation of uraemic and inflammatory toxins may cause deterioration of other organ functions. For the removal of these toxins RRT is needed. However, removal by the natural kidney is far superior. This poses the dilemma of either starting an invasive treatment like RRT early or waiting for recovery of renal function. Only one RCT investigated whether timing of RRT affects outcome in critically ill patients with ARF. The results were inconclusive [32]. In contrast, non-randomised studies suggest that earlier timing is associated with better outcome [33]. Two large epidemiological surveys evaluate timing as well. In these studies, timing either reflects 'early or late' in relation to the course of ARF, or ARF occurring 'early or late' after ICU admission. Notably, patients with late recovery of renal function are not included. In one of these studies, mortality was lower when RRT was initiated early after ICU admission. In the other, later timing relative to ICU admission was associated with a worse outcome, longer duration of RRT and higher rate of dialysis dependency. In contrast, later timing in terms of serum urea was not related to mortality, while later timing defined by serum creatinine was associated with a lower mortality. The latter seemingly discordant results may partially reflect the problem of defining the severity of ARF by a biological marker.

It may be questioned whether a RCT is the proper instrument to determine the best timing of RRT, because it may be better to individualise timing. When we consider whether to initiate RRT or not we should realise that the consequences of uraemic toxicity, metabolic acidosis and fluid overload are likely more severe in the critically ill. Moreover, rapid recovery of renal function is unlikely when other organ failure persists. When deciding to initiate RRT, we may best regard ARF in the light of other organ failure. An early start may be beneficial in patients with AKI, persisting shock and persisting other organ failure, while waiting for renal recovery may be justified if the circulation has stabilised and other organ functions are improving.

Dosing of renal replacement therapy

Despite several RCTs, there is still no consensus on the best target dose. The issue seemed clear when two well-designed European RCTs showed that a higher dose of CVVH(D) [35–45 ml/kg/h] is associated with better survival than a lower dose (about 20 ml/kg/h) [34, 35]. However, two very recent RCTs and ours did not show this survival benefit. Our study evaluated similar dosages of CVVH, but showed no difference in mortality [36]. Tolwani randomised for an effluent dosage of 35 vs. 20 ml/kg/h of continuous venovenous haemodiafiltration (CVVHDF) with prefilter replacement. She found no difference in survival, possibly because the actual delivered dosage was 29 ml/kg/h, substantially lower than the targeted high dosage of 35 ml/kg/h [37]. The multicentre ARF Trial Network study evaluated intensity of RRT in 1,124 patients with AKI and failure of at least one nonrenal organ or sepsis. Patients receiving the intensive strategy underwent intermittent haemodialysis (IHD) or sustained low-efficiency dialysis (SLED) six times per week, or pre-dilution CVVHDF at 35 ml/kg/h; patients in the less-intensive group received the corresponding treatments thrice weekly and at 20 ml/kg/h. If the cardiovascular SOFA score was < 3, they received IHD, if the cardiovascular SOFA score was 3–4, CVVHDF or SLED were applied. Intensive renal support neither decreased mortality nor conveyed any other clinical benefit [38]. Before changing clinical practice on account of this study, several issues should be considered [39]. Firstly, the intensive group actually received a mean of 27 ml/kg/h instead of the intended 35 ml/kg/h. This implicates that especially the patients with instable haemodynamics who might have profited most from an intense strategy, received a lower than prescribed dose. Secondly, 65% of patients had received one session of IHD, SLED or CVVHDF for up to 24 h before randomisation. In the intensive group, 65% initially received a much lower dose, which may have influenced the results. Thirdly, a patient could subsequently receive IHD and CVVHD or SLED in any order, thus introducing many confounders within the randomised groups. Fourthly, the timing was not standardised. Length of stay in the ICU before randomisation was 6–7 days. These conditions differ from daily practice in many European centres.

A final conclusion concerning optimal dosage of RRT can therefore not yet be made. We look forward to the results of the ongoing dose/outcome RENAL trial in Australia and New Zealand. Awaiting these results, we may consider individualising the dose of RRT as we recommend with timing. A higher dose may be especially beneficial in hypermetabolic patients with AKI with persisting septic shock and other organ failure, while a lower dose may be sufficient if the circulation has stabilised, other organ functions are improving, or metabolism is not increased.

Optimising middle molecular clearance

Up to now, the concept of adequacy of RRT has focused on small molecular clearance. However, part of the uraemic toxicity is caused by the retention of middle- and higher-molecular-weight substances, β_2-microglobulin being a landmark middle molecule in chronic dialysis patients. Middle molecules retained in critical-illness-related AKI are granulocyte-inhibiting proteins and cytokines. High-flux membranes have the capacity to remove retention solutes of higher molecular weight. In a recent prospective clinical trial, 738 IHD patients were randomised to haemodialysis with either low- or high-flux membranes. Survival was not different in the overall population, however, patients with low serum albumin (a predefined stratum) on high-flux dialysis had significantly higher survival rates than low-albumin patients on low-flux dialysis [40]. Though these results can not be simply translated to the acute RRT setting, the specific benefit in the patients with low albumin, generally a reflection of chronic inflammation, suggest that high-flux membranes may be of benefit in the ARF setting as well. Preliminary studies with high-permeability haemofiltration in septic ARF show a substantial removal of interleukin-6 and a parallel decline of the plasma concentration. Increased middle molecular clearance also led to reduced vasopressor requirements and a restoration of monocyt function [41]. Further studies are needed to determine whether increased middle molecular clearance translates into clinical benefit.

Continuous vs. intermittent renal replacement therapy

Definite conclusions about the best mode of RRT cannot be given. Several RCTs are not conclusive [42]. Although intermittent haemodialysis techniques have much improved, there is broad clinical agreement regarding the preference of continuous techniques in haemodynamically instable patients allowing continuous and gentle control of fluid and electrolyte balance and a higher dose, which is especially important for patients with a high metabolic rate. In addition, renal recovery may be greater when continuous treatments are used [43, 44]. However, attention should be paid to reduce the possible risks of RRT, some of which are greater with continuous treatment.

Avoid complications of renal replacement therapy

Most risks are foreseeable and preventable by a strict protocol, routine monitoring and specific measures. It is crucial that RRT is performed by an experienced team, that physicians and nurses are trained and educated to understand the method and its potential risks.

Risks of renal replacement therapy
- *Haemodynamic instability*
- *Problems with vascular access*
- *Activation of coagulation causing circuit clotting*
- *Activation of inflammation by membrane and heparins*
- *Continuous anticoagulation causing bleeding*
- *Metabolic derangements (electrolytes, acid-base)*
- *Loss of beneficial substances:*
  - *Water-soluble vitamins*
  - *Trace elements such as selenium*
  - *Aminoacids, especially glutamine*
  - *Carnitine*
- *Loss of heat*
- *Inadequate dosing of drugs*
- *Malfunctioning of machines*
  - *User's mistakes*
  - *Technical errors*

Regional anticoagulation with citrate

During RRT, anticoagulation is needed because extracorporeal blood triggers coagulation. Heparins are the classical choice. However, extracorporeal use of heparins causes systemic anticoagulation as well, increasing the patient's risk of bleeding. For this reason, citrate is used. Citrate chelates calcium, decreasing ionized calcium in the circuit. Because calcium is a cofactor in the coagulation cascade, thrombin generation is inhibited. Citrate is partially removed by filtration or dialysis. The remains are rapidly metabolised if liver function and muscle perfusion are sufficient, liberating calcium. Systemic effects on coagulation are thus avoided. Many observational and non-randomised studies have shown that regional anticoagulation with citrate is feasible [45, 46]. In several, circuit life was longer with citrate and bleeding was less.

Citrate anticoagulation is complex, because citrate is a buffer as well, if at least metabolic conversion is adequate. To evaluate whether citrate anticoagulation is safe, we performed a RCT to compare regional anticoagulation with citrate to anticoagulation with the LMWH nadroparin in 200 critically ill patients with ARF. Circuit life was similar between groups and there was a trend toward less bleeding with citrate. Unexpectedly, citrate was far better tolerated than nadroparin, and most importantly, citrate appeared to confer a better patient and kidney survival [47].

Post hoc subgroup analysis revealed that citrate was especially beneficial in patients after surgery (not related to bleeding), with sepsis, higher than median SOFA score, and lower than median age, suggesting that in addition to less bleeding another mechanism might contribute to the survival benefit of citrate. The explanation is not known, citrate may be better or nadroparin may be worse. Anticoagulation with heparins is associated with the release of inflammatory mediators from activated polymorphnuclear leukocytes and platelets. This release is blunted with the use of citrate. This activation may not only be triggered by the membrane, but at least partially by heparin itself. Thus, regional anticoagulation with citrate seems to avoid several adverse effects of RRT, improving the safety of the intervention.

Optimise nutrition and anti-oxidant defence

Haemofiltration and haemodialysis do not replace most of the reabsorptive tubular functions. As a result, amino acids are lost relative to their plasma concentrations, which are highest for glutamine, a conditional essential amino acid. Water-soluble vitamins and trace elements are lost and low plasma concentrations are measured in patients on CRRT. Loss of these substances, especially of ascorbic acid and selenium, may further decrease the patient's immune defence. These losses are more pronounced with continuous treatment but are easy to replace. The role of ascorbic acid in the treatment of acute endothelial dysfunction has recently been stressed [48], while selenium supplementation may reduce mortality [49]. Thus, adequate supplementation of protein, water-soluble vitamins and selenium during CRRT avoids one of its possible harms.

Conclusion

To avoid harm in acute renal failure, the clinician should be aware of risk factors for acute kidney injury (AKI). Early recognition of AKI by the routine use of the RIFLE criteria is necessary to take preventive measures timely.

The author

Heleen M. Oudemans-van Straaten, MD, PhD
Department of Intensive Care
Onze Lieve Vrouwe Gasthuis
Oosterpark 9
1091AC Amsterdam, The Netherlands
E-mail: h.m.oudemans-vanstraaten@olvg.nl

References

1. Thakar CV, Arrigain S, Worley S, Yared JP, Paganini EP. A clinical score to predict acute renal failure after cardiac surgery. J Am Soc Nephrol 2005; 16(1):162–168.

2. McCullough PA. Acute kidney injury with iodinated contrast. Crit Care Med 2008; 36(4 Suppl):S204-S211.

3. Bellomo R, Ronco C, Kellum JA, Mehta RL, Palevsky P. Acute renal failure – definition, outcome measures, animal models, fluid therapy and information technology needs: the Second International Consensus

Conference of the Acute Dialysis Quality Initiative (ADQI) Group. Crit Care 2004; 8(4):R204-R212.

4. Hoste EA, Kellum JA. Incidence, classification, and outcomes of acute kidney injury. Contrib Nephrol 2007; 156:32–38.

5. Schortgen F, Lacherade JC, Bruneel F, Cattaneo I, Hemery F, Lemaire F et al. Effects of hydroxyethylstarch and gelatin on renal function in severe sepsis: a multicentre randomised study. Lancet 2001; 357(9260):911–916.

6. Brunkhorst FM, Engel C, Bloos F, Meier-Hellmann A, Ragaller M, Weiler N et al. Intensive insulin therapy and pentastarch resuscitation in severe sepsis. N Engl J Med 2008; 358(2):125–139.

7. Sort P, Navasa M, Arroyo V, Aldeguer X, Planas R, Ruiz-del-Arbol L et al. Effect of intravenous albumin on renal impairment and mortality in patients with cirrhosis and spontaneous bacterial peritonitis. N Engl J Med 1999; 341(6):403–409.

8. Wiedemann HP, Wheeler AP, Bernard GR, Thompson BT, Hayden D, deBoisblanc B et al. Comparison of two fluid-management strategies in acute lung injury. N Engl J Med 2006; 354(24):2564–2575.

9. Payen D, de Pont AC, Sakr Y, Spies C, Reinhart K, Vincent JL. A positive fluid balance is associated with a worse outcome in patients with acute renal failure. Crit Care 2008; 12(3):R74.

10. Bellomo R, Wan L, May C. Vasoactive drugs and acute kidney injury. Crit Care Med 2008; 36(4 Suppl):S179-S186.

11. Bourgoin A, Leone M, Delmas A, Garnier F, Albanese J, Martin C. Increasing mean arterial pressure in patients with septic shock: effects on oxygen variables and renal function. Crit Care Med 2005; 33(4):780–786.

12. Russell JA, Walley KR, Singer J, Gordon AC, Hebert PC, Cooper DJ et al. Vasopressin versus norepinephrine infusion in patients with septic shock. N Engl J Med 2008; 358(9):877–887.

13. Friedrich JO, Adhikari N, Herridge MS, Beyene J. Meta-analysis: low-dose dopamine increases urine output but does not prevent renal dysfunction or death. Ann Intern Med 2005; 142(7):510–524.

14. Landoni G, Biondi-Zoccai GG, Tumlin JA, Bove T, De LM, Calabro MG et al. Beneficial impact of fenoldopam in critically ill patients with or at risk for acute renal failure: a meta-analysis of randomized clinical trials. Am J Kidney Dis 2007; 49(1):56–68.

15. Langenberg C, Wan L, Egi M, May CN, Bellomo R. Renal blood flow and function during recovery from experimental septic acute kidney injury. Intensive Care Med 2007; 33(9):1614–1618.

16. De Waele JJ, De I, I, Malbrain ML. Rational intraabdominal pressure monitoring: how to do it? Acta Clin Belg Suppl 2007;(1):16–25.

17. De Waele JJ, Hoste EA, Malbrain ML. Decompressive laparotomy for abdominal compartment syndrome–a critical analysis. Crit Care 2006; 10(2):R51.

18. Cigarroa RG, Lange RA, Williams RH, Hillis LD. Dosing of contrast material to prevent contrast nephropathy in patients with renal disease. Am J Med 1989; 86(6 Pt 1):649–652.

19. Hogan SE, L'Allier P, Chetcuti S, Grossman PM, Nallamothu BK, Duvernoy C et al. Current role of sodium bicarbonate-based preprocedural hydration for the prevention of contrast-induced acute kidney injury: a meta-analysis. Am Heart J 2008; 156(3):414–421.

20. Bagshaw SM, McAlister FA, Manns BJ, Ghali WA. Acetylcysteine in the prevention of contrast-induced nephropathy: a case study of the pitfalls in the evolution of evidence. Arch Intern Med 2006; 166(2):161–166.

21. Bagshaw SM, Ghali WA. Theophylline for prevention of contrast-induced nephropathy: a systematic review and meta-analysis. Arch Intern Med 2005; 165(10):1087–1093.

22. Huber W, Eckel F, Hennig M, Rosenbrock H, Wacker A, Saur D et al. Prophylaxis of contrast material-induced nephropathy in patients in intensive care: acetylcysteine, theophylline, or both? A randomized study. Radiology 2006; 239(3):793–804.

23. Spargias K, Alexopoulos E, Kyrzopoulos S, Iokovis P, Greenwood DC, Manginas A et al. Ascorbic acid prevents contrast-mediated nephropathy in patients with renal dysfunction undergoing coronary angiography or intervention. Circulation 2004; 110(18):2837–2842.

24. Pannu N, Nadim MK. An overview of drug-induced acute kidney injury. Crit Care Med 2008; 36(4 Suppl):S216-S223.

25. Peleg AY, Woods ML. Continuous and 4 h infusion of amphotericin B: a comparative study involving high-risk haematology patients. J Antimicrob Chemother 2004; 54(4):803–808.

26. Bouman CS. Antimicrobial dosing strategies in critically ill patients with acute kidney injury and high-dose continuous veno-venous hemofiltration. Curr Opin Crit Care 2008; 14(6):654–659.

27. Mismetti P, Laporte-Simitsidis S, Navarro C, Sie P, d'Azemar P, Necciari J et al. Aging and venous thromboembolism influence the pharmacodynamics of the anti-factor Xa and anti-thrombin activities of a low molecular weight heparin (nadroparin). Thromb Haemost 1998; 79(6):1162–1165.

28. Samama MM, Gerotziafas GT. Comparative pharmacokinetics of LMWHs. Semin Thromb Hemost 2000; 26 Suppl 1:31–38.

29. Lim W, Dentali F, Eikelboom JW, Crowther MA. Meta-analysis: low-molecular-weight heparin and bleeding in patients with severe renal insufficiency. Ann Intern Med 2006; 144(9):673–684.

30. Isla A, Gascon AR, Maynar J, Arzuaga A, Corral E, Martin A et al. In vitro and in vivo evaluation of enoxaparin removal by continuous renal replacement therapies with acrylonitrile and polysulfone membranes. Clin Ther 2005; 27(9):1444–1451.

31. Joannidis M, Kountchev J, Rauchenzauner M, Schusterschitz N, Ulmer H, Mayr A et al. Enoxaparin vs. unfractionated heparin for anticoagulation during continuous veno-venous hemofiltration: a randomized controlled crossover study. Intensive Care Med 2007; 33(9):1571–1579.

32. Bouman CS, Oudemans-van Straaten HM, Tijssen JG, Zandstra DF, Kesecioglu J. Effects of early high-volume continuous venovenous hemofiltration on survival and recovery of renal function in intensive care patients with acute renal failure: a prospective, randomized trial. Crit Care Med 2002; 30(10):2205–2211.

33. Bouman CS, Oudemans-van Straaten HM. Timing of renal replacement therapy in critically ill patients with acute kidney injury. Curr Opin Crit Care 2007; 13(6):656–661.

34. Ronco C, Bellomo R, Homel P, Brendolan A, Dan M, Piccinni P et al. Effects of different doses in continuous veno-venous haemofiltration on outcomes of acute renal failure: a prospective randomised trial. Lancet 2000; 356(9223):26–30.

35. Saudan P, Niederberger M, De Seigneux S, Romand J, Pugin J, Perneger T et al. Adding a dialysis dose to continuous hemofiltration increases survival in patients with acute renal failure. Kidney Int 2006; 70(7):1312–1317.

36. Bouman CS, Oudemans-van Straaten HM, Tijssen JG, Zandstra DF, Kesecioglu J. Effects of early high-volume continuous venovenous hemofiltration on survival and recovery of renal function in intensive care patients with acute renal failure: a prospective, randomized trial. Crit Care Med 2002; 30(10):2205–2211.

37. Tolwani AJ, Campbell RC, Stofan BS, Lai KR, Oster RA, Wille KM. Standard versus high-dose CVVHDF for ICU-related acute renal failure. J Am Soc Nephrol 2008; 19(6):1233–1238.

38. Palevsky PM, Zhang JH, O'Connor TZ, Chertow GM, Crowley ST, Choudhury D et al. Intensity of renal support in critically ill patients with acute kidney injury. N Engl J Med 2008; 359(1):7–20.

39. Ronco C, Cruz D, van Straaten HO, Honore P, House A, Bin D et al. Dialysis dose in acute kidney injury: no time for therapeutic nihilism – a critical appraisal of the Acute Renal Failure Trial Network study. Crit Care 2008; 12(5):308.

40. Locatelli F, Martin-Malo A, Hannedouche T, Loureiro A, Papadimitriou M, Wizemann V et al. Effect of Membrane Permeability on Survival of Hemodialysis Patients. J Am Soc Nephrol 2008.

41. Haase M, Bellomo R, Morgera S, Baldwin I, Boyce N. High cut-off point membranes in septic acute renal failure: a systematic review. Int J Artif Organs 2007; 30(12):1031–1041.

42. Ricci Z, Ronco C. Dose and efficiency of renal replacement therapy: continuous renal replacement therapy versus intermittent hemodialysis versus slow extended daily dialysis. Crit Care Med 2008; 36(4 Suppl):S229-S237.

43. Uchino S, Bellomo R, Kellum JA, Morimatsu H, Morgera S, Schetz MR et al. Patient and kidney survival by dialysis modality in critically ill patients with acute kidney injury. Int J Artif Organs 2007; 30(4):281–292.

44. Bell M, Granath F, Schon S, Ekbom A, Martling CR. Continuous renal replacement therapy is associated with less chronic renal failure than intermittent haemodialysis after acute renal failure. Intensive Care Med 2007; 33(5):773–780.

45. Oudemans-van Straaten HM, Wester JP, de Pont AC, Schetz MR. Anticoagulation strategies in continuous renal replacement therapy: can the choice be evidence based? Intensive Care Med 2006; 32(2):188–202.

46. Joannidis M, Oudemans-van Straaten HM. Clinical review: Patency of the circuit in continuous renal replacement therapy. Crit Care 2007; 11(4):218.

47. Oudemans-van Straaten HM, Bosman RJ, Koopmans M, van der Voort PH, Wester JP, van der Spoel JI et al. Citrate anticoagulation for continuous venovenous hemofiltration. Crit Care Med 2009; 37(2):545–552.

48. Lehr HA, Germann G, McGregor GP, Migeod F, Roesen P, Tanaka H et al. Consensus meeting on "Relevance of parenteral vitamin C in acute endothelial dependent pathophysiological conditions (EDPC)". Eur J Med Res 2006; 11(12):516–526.

49. Heyland DK, Dhaliwal R, Suchner U, Berger MM. Antioxidant nutrients: a systematic review of trace elements and vitamins in the critically ill patient. Intensive Care Med 2005; 31(3):327–337.

Barbara Volpe, Ross Paterson and Peter J. D. Andrews

Avoiding harm in neurocritical care

Introduction

How do we know if we are doing harm or good?

For almost one hundred years, this question has generated interest and provided a challenge to improve the quality of health care. In 1854, Florence Nightingale took quick action to improve the deplorable conditions of the wounded, dramatically reducing mortality rates among soldiers from 40 % to 2 %, and recognised that only with knowledge could she help improve public health [1]. In 1914, Ernest Codman stated: "Every hospital should follow every patient it treats long enough to determine whether the treatment has been successful, and then to inquire 'if not, why not' with a view to preventing similar failures in the future." He instituted the first mortality and morbidity conferences and never ceased in his efforts to link care, errors, and end results and to measure, report, and improve [2]. He grouped errors by type, with errors due to surgical judgment, lack of care or equipment, lack of knowledge or skill. In addition to the errors there were four accidents and complications over which he had no known control. He thought these should be acknowledged by carers and the public and studied as how to prevent them in future. Consequently he established the Hospital Standardization Program,

which ultimately became the Joint Commission on Accreditation of Health Care Organizations (JCAHO) [3]. Despite these foundations, formal Quality Improvement (QI) principles have been adopted in health care only decades after they were developed. Shewhart and Deming were deeply intrigued by the issue of measurement of error in science and explained how a continuous evaluation of processes could improve quality and decrease defects [4]. In 1940, leaders of industries seeking to gain supremacy in the market formalised the principles of continuous QI, but only in 1980 did JCAHO mandate QI and performance measures for hospital accreditation [5]. Donabedian was a pioneer on outcome, process, and structure paradigm and promoter of their continual assessment to improve quality of care [7] (see Fig. 1). "To Err is Human" (1999) and "Crossing the Quality Chasm" (2001), the warning reports of the Institute of Medicine (IOM), estimated that 44,000–98,000 patients died in hospital each year because of medical errors and identified widespread quality problems including: the under-use, overuse, or misuse of medical care [8]. Harmful errors come from both health workers and system deficiencies that often increase patient vulnerability and decrease our effectiveness in protecting them [9]. Adverse events and severe errors occur more frequently in some "high-risk areas" within the health system. Critical cares, including neurocritical care, are such areas. The severity and instability of critically ill patients and their need for high-risk interventions and numerous medications lead to higher rates of iatrogenic injury and medical errors [9, 10]. Error is different from harm, but errors frequently do cause harm: In the ICU, iatrogenic complications are associated with a longer length of stay and a higher mortality rate, and adverse events can leave patients severely disabled [11]. Therefore, patient safety programs should be particularly directed to improve safety in these "high-risk areas".

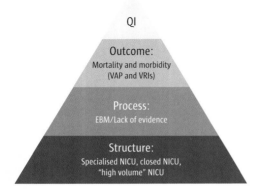

Fig. 1   Donabedian Model: Quality Improvement (QI)

Measure of safety: How to prevent harm

The IOM defined an error as a failure of a planned action or to use an incorrect plan to achieve an aim. An injury caused by medical management was the definition of an adverse event. A preventable adverse event was one attributable to error and a negligent adverse event was one in which the care provided failed to meet an acceptable standard [8]. In many circumstances an adverse event can be attributed to patient factors or to an unexpected or low-probability complication. By these definitions harm is not always due to errors or poor quality care. Not all adverse events cause harm, and those adverse events resulting from errors are not always due to negligence. If the patient dies or if there is a prolonged hospital stay, an injury or an impairment, harm has obviously occurred [12]. There is no literature dealing with the definition of harm, and defining harm will always involve some degree of ambiguity as well, as it is difficult to dif-

ferentiate between preventable and inevitable harm, with efforts to do so having low reliability and validity. Many organisations are working to try and improve safety: Health care organisations generally lack measures to evaluate their safety improvement, and we need empirical evidence to prove we are safer now than in the past.

Patient Safety Reporting System(s) (PSRS) are a common method for identifying patient safety topics, and recommended by the IOM. However, PSRS rates of reported adverse events contain significant bias because caregiver reporting is not reliable, the magnitude and direction of reporting biases are unknown, and the population at risk is unknown. In the trilogy of measures developed by Donebedian, *Outcome* (the health care results achieved) and *Process* (what is done by the caregivers) are measures with valid rates; however, *Structure* (how care is organised) is not a rate measure. An additional safety measure that is not a rate measure is *Culture* that describes the context in which care is delivered in a particular work unit and not in the hospital [13].

In the NICU setting, *Structure* is *the input* and refers to the type or size of the ICU, nature of staffing and availability of technology. *Process* is the collection of steps we pass through in the care of a patient that can include the use of available technology, trainee guidelines and supervision and communication among staff. Finally, there is *the output,* that is the *Outcome* including morbidity and mortality rates (the success of quality improvement projects depends on which projects all stakeholders find useful to build safety *Culture*) [13].

Outcome:
How often do we harm patients in NICU?

We currently have few valid measures of harm. *Mortality* is the classical outcome variable, but often requires sophisticated risk-adjustment models and therefore significant limitations remain [14]. Other safety outcome measures are being adopted despite limitations [15]. Specifically, length of stay in the NICU, unplanned readmission rates, duration of mechanical ventilation and incidence of complications are used. Quality of life after discharge could be an important outcome measure but is actually very difficult to assess. Perhaps the most robust measures of harm we have are *healthcare-associated infections*, which can be reduced by the use of quality improvement [16]. Approximately 10 % of ICU patients develop nosocomial infections. The major cause of nosocomial infections are the numerous devices essential for the intensive treatments. Urinary catheters cause 95 % of urinary tract infections that account for 31 % of all nosocomial infections in the ICU. Central lines are associated with 87 % of primary bloodstream infections that account for 19 % of nosocomial infections. Pneumonia is the most important nosocomial infection in NICUs and accounts for 27 % of nosocomial infections, of which 86 % are associated with mechanical ventilation (VAP) [17]. External ventricular drain (EVD)-related ventriculitis is a serious nosocomial complication in the NICU. The infection rate is high with reported incidence from 5 % to more than 20 % [18].

VAP, a "preventable harm"

VAP is the commonest severe nosocomial infection in NICU. The reported incidence of VAP is up to 56 % in ventilated head trauma patients [19]. This is partly explained by impaired consciousness and airway reflexes and the need for emergency tracheal intubation. Both can lead to oropharyngeal secretion aspiration [20]. It has also been shown that head injury (HI) induces immunosupression, very early compromise of local airway immune defenses, facilitating microorganism adhesion and persistence at mucosal surfaces [21]. In addition, the severity of traumatic injuries leads to a state of decreased response of both humoral and cell-mediated immunity [20, 22, 23, 23, 23, 23]. Most studies have found no link between the occurrence of VAP and mortality, but mortality varies depending on the responsible organisms. Especially gram-negative rods, responsible for late-onset VAP, including *P. Aeruginosa* and *A. Baumannii*, which are potentially resistant, and can increase the mortality rate [24]. VAP in TBI patients is an important cause of morbidity: longer duration of mechanical ventilation, longer intensive care unit and hospital lengths of stay, increasing the probability of suffering from complications associated with the management of the patient in the NICU

[25]. Drakulovic et al. showed a reduction in VAP by nursing patients on mechanical ventilation in a semi-recumbent position [26]. Kress et al. found that a formal daily interruption of sedation reduced the duration of mechanical ventilation [27]. When combined with peptic ulcer disease and deep venous thrombosis prophylaxis, these interventions can reduce infections and complication rates due to mechanical ventilation and decrease mortality. These processes have been defined as the ventilator bundle [28]. Leone et al. showed that selective digestive decontamination can decrease the rates of VAP caused by gram-negative bacteria [24]. The presence of a nasogastric tube is a risk factor for the development of VAP and early gastrostomy is associated with a lower frequency of VAP in patients mechanically ventilated for TBI [29]. Adequate, timely, and effective antibiotic therapy, use of the ventilator bundle and prevention of the colonisation of the patient after traumatic brain injury may reduce the occurrence of VAP and the harmful consequences.

Nosocomial EVD-related ventriculitis

External ventricular drainage (EVD) is an intracranial device for the treatment of elevated intracranial pressure secondary to acute hydrocephalus. However, these devices pose a risk of potentially life-threatening nosocomial catheter-associated infection that can result in ventriculitis or ventriculo-meningitis. Rates of ventriculostomy-related infections (VRIs) are between 0 and 22 %, but usually close to 10 % [30]. The pathogens predominantly responsible are gram-positive bacteria, especially multiresistant coagulase-negative staphylococci (CoNS) and methicillin-resistant staphylococcus aureus (MRSA). Gram-negative rods are less frequently isolated, but are associated with ventriculitis when present [31]. Risk factors associated with VRIs are the underlying neuro-critical illness: SAH or IVH, cranial fracture with CSF leak, craniotomy, ventriculostomy with irrigation and duration of catheter placement, and concomitant systemic infections. Most of these are not preventable in the NICU and consequently it is difficult to avoid the harm that may result. However, there are modifiable risk factors associated with CSF infections including: site of ventriculostomy, use of prophylactic antibiotics, catheter manipulation and CSF leak. *Duration of catheterisation* is extensively reported as a risk factor for VRIs, when no infections occurred before Day 3, whereas 85 % of infections occurred in patients who had been observed for 5 days or more without catheter replacement [30]. A retrospective study assessed the relationships between EVD duration, antibiotics and CSF infection: The EVD duration was significantly longer in infected and colonised EVDs. It was concluded that the incidence of infections is influenced more by duration and rate of EVD than the systemic administration of antibiotics [32]. Hoefnagel observed that in their NICU the duration of EVD drainage appeared to be a risk factor for infection and CSF sampling frequency was also a significant risk factor [33]. They proposed a new EVD protocol to decrease the number of EVD-related infections to a minimum. A higher incidence of EVD-related ventriculitis can be explained by low compliance with the protocol (EVD manipulation, absence of a tunneled EVD, absence of hair clipping, or shampooing, incorrect dressing change, inappropriate CSF bag or tap samplings). Patients with a protocol violation score of 0 or 1 showed no infection (EVD duration 2 to 42 days). The incidence of patient-related ventriculitis decreased from 12.2 % down to 5.7 % and the incidence of EVD-related ventriculitis from 9.9 % to 4.6 % [34]. The method of CSF surveillance may also affect the incidence of positive CSF cultures. Daily CSF sampling generates more positive CSF cultures than sporadic sampling. However, the majority of these additional positive cultures likely represent contaminants. Besides, more frequent access to a closed drainage system may increase the iatrogenic infection rate. A recent retrospective study suggested that daily CSF sampling does not decrease the time to detection of clinically relevant infections in children [35]. This relationship remains to be demonstrated in the adult population [30]. There is no consensus on the efficacy of prophylactic antibiotics in reducing EVD-related CSF infections. Randomised controlled trials of sufficient size, with appropriate blinding, are needed to address this issue. The use of prophylactic antibiotics selected more resistant organisms when VRIs occurred [36]. The placement of CSF diversion devices requires an appropriate technical expertise and surgical

training to minimise complications. The placement of intraventricular catheters by neurosurgeons remains a relatively safe and effective procedure that is associated with infrequent rates of symptomatic haemorrhage and infection [37] In reality, the placement of short-term EVDs in the NICU is safer than previously reported and can be maintained for the required duration of treatment with minimum infection rate [38]. Early diagnosis of VRIs is crucial for early treatment and course of the disease. The volume of intrathecal blood is an independent risk factor for VRI and may explain the equivocal diagnostic criteria in neurosurgical patients. The predictive value of following CSF cell counts is limited. The efficacy of CSF pleocytosis and altered CSF chemistry in predicting VRI deserve further investigation. The value of intrathecal interleukin-6 measurement has proved useful for predicting VRI and gives results one day earlier than the common diagnostic criteria. The predictive value of IL-6 for VRI was calculated as 89 %, with sensitivity and specificity respectively of 73.7 % and 91.4 % [39].

Process: How often do we do what we should?

Process measures provide timely data, rich in detail, which reflect the actual healthcare delivered at the bedside. Only through measuring processes can we evaluate if healthcare is provided using evidence-based recommendations. Evidence-based medicine should influence our daily practise in critical care; through interventions such as care bundles we should be able to improve clinical outcomes. Compared with other types of clinical research, the science of creating quality measures is currently underdeveloped. Healthcare needs many more process measures based on robust evidence. Especially in the NICU, further research must be conducted to validate care bundles [15].

Evidence-based medicine: Patients are safer through compliance with guidelines

We can improve clinical decision-making and patient care by bringing together best available evidence, patients' values and providers' preferences [40]. In critical care guidelines and protocols have been successful in improving performance of some care processes. Nevertheless, significant barriers exist to the use of evidence-based clinical practice guidelines including:

- lack of agreement between providers,
- lack of providers' ability to implement the guideline and
- even the providers' lack of awareness that guidelines even exist [41].

TBI is the major cause of death and disability among people below 40 years of age. Management guidelines for TBI have been developed, but the treatment of these patients has been variable. A systematic scenario-based survey was conducted among Canadian critical care clinicians and neurosurgeons treating patients with severe closed head injury. The awareness of the literature concerning therapeutic manoeuvres in those patients and the factors that affect their clinical utilisation were assessed. In the scenario of acute epidural hematoma with mass effect, clinicians reported mannitol and hypertonic saline as appropriate, however, the agreement was less strong when the use of the EVD, phenytoin, hyperventilation, nimodipine, and JVO were surveyed [42]. In another comparable scenario-based survey only 57% of critical care clinicians responded and reported EBM as being the most significant factor affecting use of a therapy. Except for the avoidance of corticosteroids which correlated well with the literature (51%), most neurocritical care clinicians did not correctly identify the highest published level of evidence for most therapies, showing the difficulty with translation of research into clinical practice [43]. A survey based on a questionnaire and directed to clinical managers in all Norwegian hospitals showed that the guidelines had significantly influenced the management of minor, mild and moderate head injury. However, physicians' decision-making in their daily practice seemed not be influenced by guidelines but by compliance with clinical leaders [44]. Studies suggest that compliance significantly improves the occurrence of good outcomes at discharge and reduces mortality and length of hospital stay. In 1995 a protocol following the Brain Trauma Foundation (BTF) guidelines was developed by members of a Level I trauma centre's interdisciplinary neurotrauma task force to evaluate whether the management of TBI according to BTF guidelines would reduce mortality and length of stay. The results of the study showed that in the 1995–96 cohort there was only 50% compliance with the protocol; by 1997–2000 compliance had risen to 88% and ICU length of stay was reduced by 5.4 days and the overall mortality rate showed a reduction of 4.0%. In 1997–2000, 61.5% of patients had a "good recovery" or only "moderate disability", an increase of more than 20%. Improving compliance with evidence-based clinical practice guidelines may have a significant impact on head injury care outcomes [45].

Are there characteristics of trauma centers associated with delivery of optimal care? In 2000 the Brain Trauma Foundation surveyed all designated trauma centres in the USA to address this issue. The survey identified predictors of guideline compliance including: Level I centres, use of treatments protocols, monthly patient volume, specialised neurological ICU, and presence of a neurosurgical residency programme. Full compliance was strongly and independently associated with three factors: centre designation, treatment protocols, neurosurgery residency programme. Full compliance with guidelines was rare, occurring only in 16% of surveyed centres. Noncompliance with guidelines such as failure to at least follow guidelines concerning indications for ICP monitoring occurred in 67% of surveyed trauma centres. Factors influencing guideline compliance were lack of neurosurgery residents or other neurosurgical assistants, no protocols to standardise nursing response to ICP measurements that in turn lead to ICP monitors being placed infrequently and use of outdated/harmful treatments (e.g. steroids). Potential barriers to caregivers' compliance with guidelines are:

- awareness,
- familiarity,
- agreement,
- self-efficacy,
- outcome expectancy,
- ability to overcome the inertia of previous practice and
- absence of external barriers to perform recommendations.

Patients with severe TBI should be directly transferred to centres with characteristics of EBM guideline compliance. This will avoid harm from non-compliance with guidelines [46].

Lack of evidence:
How do we know we are not doing harm?

Process measures must be valid and supported by evidence-based measures. Randomised controlled trials (RCTs) are the strongest level of evidence with lowest risk of bias. Furthermore, stronger levels of evidence are more likely to be accepted and put into practice [15].

How can we be sure we are not doing harm when we use interventions that are lacking evidence of effectiveness? **Hypothermia:** For over 50 years hypothermia has been a treatment option for patients with TBI. However, no clinical trials were performed until the last decade, reporting encouraging results of Phase II and Phase III RCTs. An increased risk of sepsis and pneumonia, possible ischaemia, coagulation abnormalities and atrial fibrillation are the main risks associated with induced systemic hypothermia. Twenty-two RCTs involving patients with TBI were included in The Cochrane Systematic review (2009) to estimate the effect of hypothermia on mortality and morbidity in this population of patients. Patients treated with hypothermia were less likely to die than those in the control group. A statistically non-significant reduction in death (compared with the control group) was reported by good allocation concealment trials and in the low-quality trials, patients treated with hypothermia were less likely to have favorable outcome. Three trials with good allocation concealment reported a statistically non-significant increase in pneumonia associated with hypothermia treatment. Due to uncertainties in its effects, hypothermia should only be given to patients taking part in an RCT with good allocation concealment [47]. The Eurotherm3235trial aims to answer: "Does therapeutic hypothermia (32–35°C) reduce morbidity and mortality rates at 6 months after traumatic brain injury assessed by the Extended Glasgow Outcome Scale?"

Hyperventilation, only one prospective randomised clinical trial has been reported concerning the effect of hyperventilation on clinical outcome; even so, raised ICP in TBI is commonly treated with hyperventilation despite evidence indicating possible negative effects of hyperventilation on oxygenation, metabolism and cerebral blood flow (CBF). Conflicting data may explain why some clinicians still use hyperventilation while others avoid it. Short-term hypocapnia when monitored with multimodality monitoring may be useful to control raised ICP [48]. Muizelaar et al. showed that patients with an initial Glasgow coma scale motor score of 4 or 5 and not hyperventilated, had a significantly better outcome at both 3 and 6 months after TBI compared with 5 days of hyperventilation [49]. Recommendations in the guidelines for the management of TBI state the following: "... in the absence of increased ICP, prolonged hyperventilation therapy ($PaCO_2$ < 25 mmHg) should be avoided." Moreover, "... the use of prophylactic hyperventilation ($PaCO_2$ < 35 mmHg) should be avoided during the first 24 h after severe TBI because it can compromise cerebral perfusion during a time when CBF is reduced." [50]

Vasopressors: Vasopressor-induced elevation of MAP causes a significant increase in cerebral perfusion and cerebral oxygenation after subarachnoid haemorrhage (SAH). In patients with SAH an improvement in regional CBF in ischaemic regions following dopamine- or phenylephrine-induced hypertension has been shown. Compared with hypertension alone, hypervolaemia and/or haemodiluition do not lead to an improvement in brain tissue oxygenation ($PtiO_2$) although they increase regional CBF. This might be due to a reduction in oxygen delivery in the setting of hypervolaemia and reduced hematocrit. Moreover, risks of hypervolaemic therapy have been widely reported, including cardiac failure, electrolyte abnormalities, cerebral edema, and bleeding abnormalities. Due to the potentially harmful effects of hypervolaemic therapy this should not be applied in SAH patients [51].

Osmotic therapy: Mannitol (20%) is the reference osmotheraphy to decrease cerebral water and ICP. However, there is some controversy about the onset of effect and duration and consequently no definitive quantitative information regarding the dosing of mannitol [52], there are no studies that report harms associated with these agents. Hypertonic saline (HS) is increasingly used for the management of raised intracranial pressure. Inappropriate and too rapid administration of hypertonic saline can lead to osmotic demyelination syndrome (ODS) or central pontine myelinolysis and extrapontinemyelinolysis related to the physiological balance of osmoles in the brain [53].

Medication process: High-risk steps for harm

In a prospective cohort study of incidents in ICUs in the USA, Pronovost et al. reported that 42 % of incidents caused harm [54]. In the ICU multiple risks occur at each stage of the medication process (from the supply of drugs and their storage in the clinical area to drug prescription, preparation, administration and monitoring the response to treatment) that have resulted in many reports of medication-related harm or potential harm to critically ill patients. Data collected in MICU and CCU found that 20.2 % of patients suffered adverse events and of those, 45 % were preventable and 11 % were life-threatening. Medication was involved in a large proportion of incidents: 47 % were due to adverse drug event (ADEs), non-preventable events were more than preventable ADEs. These were largely due to wrong dosage of medication; cardiovascular drugs 24 %, anticoagulants 20 % and anti-infective agents 13 % [55]. ICU patients often receive multiple medications by the intravenous route, either by bolus or continuous infusion; pharmaceuticals commonly delivered in such a way in NICU patients include analgesic, sedative and vasoactive agents. Erroneous infusion rates accounted for >40 % of overall errors in a multicentred evaluation of errors in several ICUs [56].

In a review of reports to the UK National Patient Safety Agency, the drugs most commonly involved with some patient harm were noradrenaline, insulin, and morphine. Different types of administration incidents made up 61 % of all incidents and caused the largest number involving harm. Errors in drug administration, technical failures of pumps, 12 labeling errors and incorrect infusion rates involved noradrenaline. Insulin was associated with very similar administration incidents but it was also associated with inappropriate or lack of glucose monitoring. Morphine most commonly resulted in pain. Prescription errors made up 26 % of all incidents. A high frequency of prescribing incidents involved failure to rewrite chart or drug, unit policy noncompliance, drugs indicated but not prescribed and ambiguous prescription dose. Admission to critical care is often associated with problems with communication between staff, particularly during transfer from theatre and recovery, and results in 5 % of all medication incidents.

To prevent many of the incidents described, particularly where bolus or high infusion rates of vasopressor are given, clear and appropriate color coded and labeled syringes must be used. Prescribing should also be kept as simple as possible and prescribers should be given education and feedback, access to drug information and advice from clinical pharmacists. Increasing complexity is known to increase error rates. Communication failure has previously been described as a cause of incidents: Good face-to-face handover with written information and correct labeling of infusions will reduce this problem. Electronic prescribing, the use of pre-prepared syringes and new pump technology may also reduce incidents; however, human error may still exist when manually entering information or when concentrations or doses are programmed into software and not reviewed for appropriateness [55, 57, 58].

Structural measures and safety culture: The input to avoid harm

Structural measures deal with the organisation of care and may include institutional variables (such a leadership structure for safety or processes for ensuring staff competency), task variables (such as presence of protocols) and team variables (adequacy of staffing and/or communication among team members). Structural measures of patient safety might include the presence of neuro-intensivists, nurse-to-patient ratios, pharmacist presence during ICU rounds, and the use of a comprehensive unit-based safety programme. Structure measures inform of defects; there are many sources from which to identify defects: outcome conferences, sentinel events and the most powerful – asking staff what happened and why, what can be done to reduce the probability that the defect will recur again, and how to know if the intervention was effective [13].

Staffing and centre effects: Specialised NICU, closed NICU, "high-volume" NICU

The organisation of an ICU is important because it can potentially reduce costs and improve outcomes. One such example is availability of intensivists. ICU staffing has been classified as low intensity (i.e. no intensivist available or elective intensivist consultation) or high intensity (i.e. mandatory intensivist consultation or closed ICU). High-intensity staffing is associated with lower hospital mortality and reduced hospital length of stay [59]. The main argument for mandating a neurointensivist is that the care of the critically ill neurologic patient requires training in clinical physiology of intracranial pressure, cerebral blood flow and metabolism, brain and neuromuscolar electrophysiology, postoperative care, and systemic complications of nervous system diseases. The effect of the availability of specialised neurocritical care teams (closed ICU) results in a decrease in hospital mortality rates and reduced hospital length of stay. In addition, high-intensity staffing reduces the number of significant medical complications [59, 60, 61]. The admission to a dedicated neuroscience critical care unit is associated with reduced mortality and hospital length of stay for patients with intracerebral haemorrhage [62, 63]. W. Mauritz et al. elucidated the reasons why patients with severe TBI admitted to Austrian ICUs between 1998 and 2004 did or did not receive ICP monitoring. A significant centre effect was found where patients were almost twice as likely to receive ICP monitoring if they were admitted to medium-sized centres. Largest and smaller centres had a lower rate of ICP monitoring. Since hospital mortality was significantly lower in the large centres, the lower rate of ICP monitoring is possibly due to more focused use (see Fig. 2). Finally, hospital mortality can be improved by admitting the patient with severe TBI to experienced centres with higher patient volumes [64]. Patel et al. analysed the largest trauma registry in Europe and compared outcome in patients with severe TBI managed in a hospital with a neurosurgical service and a similar cohort managed in hospitals without a neurosurgical service. 6921 patients suffered severe TBI between 1996 and 2003.The overall mortality was 44%. This crude mortality was significantly higher in the 33% of patients who were treated in a non-neurosurgical centre (see Fig. 3). The patients transferred to a non-neurosurgical centre had a 26% higher mortality than those treated in neurosurgical centres. Patients with an isolated non-surgical head injury had an 8% mean increase in mortality when treated in a non-neurosurgical

center versus those treated in a neurosurgical center. Patients with isolated non-surgical severe TBI treated in non-neurosurgical centres had an almost twofold increase in odds ratio of death, suggesting that this current neurosurgical triage practice is unsatisfactory. The reason for the aversion to transfer and admission of all head injuries to neurosurgical centres is unknown and may be due to the lack of good quality data for the effect of NICU/neurosurgical care or lack of resources at the specialist centres in the UK. Often early CT findings in patients with surgical lesion and the availability of neurosurgical or NICU facilities influence the fate of patients. However, patients with non-surgical lesions have a high mortality and make up to 55% of patients with severe head trauma. Moreover, non-surgical lesions often evolve into those requiring decompressive craniectomy. There is also evidence that outcome after trauma in comatose patients is better in high-volume centres than in those seeing fewer head injury patients. In accordance with current guidelines all patients with severe head trauma including patients with a non-surgical head injury should be transferred and treated in a setting with 24-hour neurosurgical/NICU facilities [65]. Despite the evidence supporting the intensivist model do we know what the optimal intensivist/patient ratio and composition of the clinical team are? In a study performed in the USA, an ICU quality improvement project was promoted. Critical changes in care systems were included to reduce the adverse events per ICU day by 50%, to reduce the rate of VAP by 25%, and to reduce device-related BSI by 44%. The results showed that adverse events and nosocomial infections declined following the introduction into the ICU of a care system with at least four components: multidisciplinary teams, use of bundles, use of flow meetings and change in culture. The most critical change to practice is multidisciplinary teams. The team approach led to improved communication among physicians, nurses, respiratory therapists, and pharmacists. The bundles promoted evidence-based medicine by acting as a reminder system. Flow meetings allowed timely decision-making and a prioritisation of activity [66]. Improving teamwork is crucial to improving patient safety.

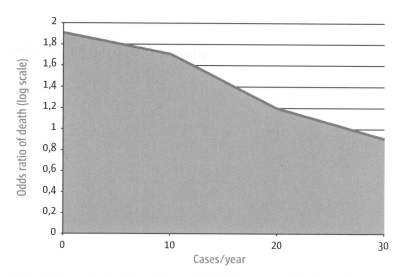

Fig. 2 Higher yearly admission rate is associated with a lower mortality. Center effect on Hospital mortality rate in patients with TBI [data from Mauritz W, Steltzer H, Bauer P, Dolanski-Aghamanoukjan L, Metnitz P. Monitoring of intracranial pressure in patients with severe traumatic brain injury: an Austrian prospective multicenter study. Intensive Care Med. 2008;34 (7):1208–1215]

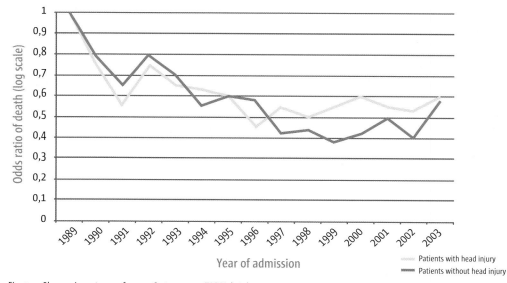

Fig. 3 Change in outcome from 1989 to 2003 – TARN database

Hospital transfer

Transportation of the critically ill patient imposes important risks – these are potentially more important to neuro-critical care patients. NICU patients must be transported to CT scanning/ imaging or to the operating room. In a cross-sectional case review of incident reports submitted to the Australian Incident Monitoring Study (AIMS-ICU) between 1993 and 1999, 61% of the reports identified patient/staff management problems, such as inadequate monitoring, incorrect set-up of equipment, artificial airway malpositioning, and incorrect positioning of patients and poor communication. Serious adverse outcomes occurred in 31%. Contributing factors were 46% system-based and 54% human-based. Important factors limiting harm are rechecking the patient and equipment, skilled assistance and prior experience. Guidelines/protocols for intrahospital transportation should be adopted [67].

Safety culture

Safety culture refers to values, attitudes, norms, benefits, practices, policies, and behaviors of personnel. The science of measuring safety culture is evolving: A number of tools are available to measure safety culture, but with limited validity and reliable data. The origin of a safety climate lies in the teamwork climate, perception of management, stress recognition, job satisfaction, and working conditions. A measurement of culture should include a presentation of results to staff as well as senior management, followed by focused intervention to improve culture. Critical changes in care systems can also lead to a change in culture. Changes that empower the team rather than caregivers individually, and overcoming cultural barriers, finding a common interest among caregivers by focusing efforts exclusively on patients is beneficial. Building a safety culture also means being aware of the limits of the care that has been provided; the lack of simple procedure to report errors is an important barrier. Error reporting should be as easy as possible and barriers to reporting such as time to report, ease of reporting, and comfort with reporting: culture, non-punitiveness, peer protection must be established [6].

Conclusions

There are no safe neurological intensive care units, only safe carers and systems for care delivery. Admission to high-volume, quality-assured centres delivering best EBM guidelines will promote safer care and reduce harm. More randomised controlled trials are needed to inform these guidelines, and tools to measure processes are as important as outcome measures.

The authors

Barbara Volpe, MD[1]
Ross Paterson, MD, MB, ChB[2]
Peter J. D. Andrews, MD, MB, ChB, FRCA[3]
  [1]Department of Anaesthesia and Intensive Care Policlinico "A.Gemelli" | Universita' Cattolica Del Sacro Cuore | Roma, Italy
  [2]Intensive Care Unit | Western General Hospital | Lothian University Hospitals
  [3]Intensive Care Unit | Western General Hospital | Lothian University Hospitals | University of Edinburgh

Address for correspondence
  Peter Andrews
  Intensive Care Unit
  Western General Hospital
  Lothian University Hospitals &
  University of Edinburgh
  EH4 2XU
  Edinburgh, UK
  E-mail: p.andrews@ed.ac.uk

References

1. Nightingale F. Notes on nursing what it is and what it is not. 1860.
2. Codman EA. The product of a hospital. Surg GynecolObstet. 1914;(18):491–496.
3. Codman EA. A study in hospital efficiency:as demonstrated by the Case Report of the First Five Years of the Privete Hospital. Private Printing. Reprinting by the Joint Commission of Accreditation of Healthcare Organizations:Illinois. 1916.
4. Hamby LS, Colacchio TA, Nelson EC. Application of quality improvement to surgical practice. Surgery. 2000;128 (5):836–844.
5. The Quality of Medical Care: Information for Consumers. Washington, DC: Congress of the U.S. Office of Technology Assessment. 1988.
6. Pronovost P, Sexton B. Assessing safety culture: guidelines and recommendations. Qual Saf Health Care. 2005;14 (4):231–233.
7. Donabedian A. The quality of care. How can it be assessed? JAMA. 1988;260 (12):1743–1748.
8. Kohn LT CJDM. To Err is Human: Building a Safer Health Care System. Washington, DC:National Academy Press. 2001.
9. Pronovost P, Wu AW, Dorman T, Morlock L. Building safety into ICU care. J Crit Care. 2002;17 (2):78–85.
10. Vande Voorde KM, France AC. Proactive error prevention

in the intensive care unit. Crit Care Nurs Clin North Am. 2002;14 (4):347–358.

11. Giraud T, Dhainaut JF, Vaxelaire JF, Joseph T, Journois D, Bleichner G et al. Iatrogenic complications in adult intensive care units: a prospective two-center study. Crit Care Med. 1993;21 (1):40–51.

12. Boyle D, O'Connell D, Platt FW, Albert RK. Disclosing errors and adverse events in the intensive care unit. Crit Care Med. 2006;34 (5):1532–1537.

13. Pronovost P, Holzmueller CG, Needham DM, Sexton JB, Miller M, Berenholtz S et al. How will we know patients are safer? An organization-wide approach to measuring and improving safety. Crit Care Med. 2006;34 (7):1988–1995.

14. Zimmerman JE DEWD. Comparing ICU populations: background and current methods. Springer. 2000;121–139.

15. Berenholtz SM, Pustavoitau A, Schwartz SJ, Pronovost PJ. How safe is my intensive care unit? Methods for monitoring and measurement. Curr Opin Crit Care. 2007;13 (6):703–708.

16. Pronovost P, Needham D, Berenholtz S, Sinopoli D, Chu H, Cosgrove S et al. An intervention to decrease catheter-related bloodstream infections in the ICU. N Engl J Med. 2006;355 (26):2725–2732.

17. Jain M, Miller L, Belt D, King D, Berwick DM. Decline in ICU adverse events, nosocomial infections and cost through a quality improvement initiative focusing on teamwork and culture change. Qual Saf Health Care. 2006;15 (4):235–239.

18. Beer R, Lackner P, Pfausler B, Schmutzhard E. Nosocomial ventriculitis and meningitis in neurocritical care patients. J Neurol. 2008;255 (11):1617–1624.

19. Kallel H, Chelly H, Bahloul M, Ksibi H, Dammak H, Chaari A et al. The effect of ventilator-associated pneumonia on the prognosis of head trauma patients. J Trauma. 2005;59 (3):705–710.

20. Berrouane Y, Daudenthun I, Riegel B, Emery MN, Martin G, Krivosic R et al. Early onset pneumonia in neurosurgical intensive care unit patients. J Hosp Infect. 1998;40 (4):275–280.21.

21. Ewig S, Torres A, El-Ebiary M, Fabregas N, Hernandez C, Gonzalez J et al. Bacterial colonization patterns in mechanically ventilated patients with traumatic and medical head injury. Incidence, risk factors, and association with ventilator-associated pneumonia. Am J Respir Crit Care Med. 1999;159 (1):188–198.

22. Schmand JF, Ayala A, Chaudry IH. Effects of trauma, duration of hypotension, and resuscitation regimen on cellular immunity after hemorrhagic shock. Crit Care Med. 1994;22 (7):1076–1083.

23. Cortinas SM, Lizan GM, Jimenez-Vizuete JM, Moreno CJ, Cuesta GJ, Peyro GR. [Incidences of early- and late-onset ventilator-associated pneumonia in a postanesthesia

and critical care unit]. Rev Esp Anestesiol Reanim. 2007;54 (3):147–154.

24. Leone M, Bourgoin A, Giuly E, Antonini F, Dubuc M, Viviand X et al. Influence on outcome of ventilator-associated pneumonia in multiple trauma patients with head trauma treated with selected digestive decontamination. Crit Care Med. 2002;30 (8):1741–1746.

25. Rincon-Ferrari MD, Flores-Cordero JM, Leal-Noval SR, Murillo-Cabezas F, Cayuelas A, Munoz-Sanchez MA et al. Impact of ventilator-associated pneumonia in patients with severe head injury. J Trauma. 2004;57 (6):1234–1240.

26. Drakulovic MB, Torres A, Bauer TT, Nicolas JM, Nogue S, Ferrer M. Supine body position as a risk factor for nosocomial pneumonia in mechanically ventilated patients: a randomised trial. Lancet. 1999;354 (9193):1851–1858.

27. Girard TD, Kress JP, Fuchs BD, Thomason JW, Schweickert WD, Pun BT et al. Efficacy and safety of a paired sedation and ventilator weaning protocol for mechanically ventilated patients in intensive care (Awakening and Breathing Controlled trial): a randomised controlled trial. Lancet. 2008;371 (9607):126–134.

28. Resar R, Pronovost P, Haraden C, Simmonds T, Rainey T, Nolan T. Using a bundle approach to improve ventilator care processes and reduce ventilator-associated pneumonia. Jt Comm J Qual Patient Saf. 2005;31 (5):243–248.

29. Kostadima E, Kaditis AG, Alexopoulos EI, Zakynthinos E, Sfyras D. Early gastrostomy reduces the rate of ventilator-associated pneumonia in stroke or head injury patients. Eur Respir J. 2005;26 (1):106–111.

30. Lozier AP, Sciacca RR, Romagnoli MF, Connolly ES, Jr. Ventriculostomy-related infections: a critical review of the literature. Neurosurgery. 2008;62 Suppl. 2:688–700.

31. Muttaiyah S, Ritchie S, Upton A, Roberts S. Clinical parameters do not predict infection in patients with external ventricular drains: a retrospective observational study of daily cerebrospinal fluid analysis. J Med Microbiol. 2008;57 (Pt 2):207–209.

32. Mahe V, Kermarrec N, Ecoffey C. [Infections related to external ventricular drainage]. Ann Fr Anesth Reanim. 1995;14 (1):8–12.

33. Hoefnagel D, Dammers R, Ter Laak-Poort MP, Avezaat CJ. Risk factors for infections related to external ventricular drainage. Acta Neurochir. (Wien) 2008;150 (3):209–214.

34. Korinek AM, Reina M, Boch AL, Rivera AO, De BD, Puybasset L. Prevention of external ventricular drain–related ventriculitis. Acta Neurochir. (Wien) 2005;147 (1):39–45.

35. Hader WJ, Steinbok P. The value of routine cultures of the cerebrospinal fluid in patients with external ventricular drains. Neurosurgery. 2000;46 (5):1149–1153.

36. Poon WS, Ng S, Wai S. CSF antibiotic prophylaxis for neurosurgical patients with ventriculostomy: a randomised study. Acta Neurochir. Suppl 1998;71:146–148.

37. Saladino A, White JB, Wijdicks EF, Lanzino G. Malplacement of Ventricular Catheters by Neurosurgeons: A Single Institution Experience. Neurocrit Care. 2008.

38. Clark WC, Muhlbauer MS, Lowrey R, Hartman M, Ray MW, Watridge CB. Complications of intracranial pressure monitoring in trauma patients. Neurosurgery. 1989;25 (1):20–24.

39. Schoch B, Regel JP, Nierhaus A, Wichert M, Mueller OM, Sandalcioglu IE et al. Predictive value of intrathecal interleukin-6 for ventriculostomy-related Infection. Zentralbl Neurochir. 2008;69 (2):80–86.

40. Sackett DL, Rosenberg WM, Gray JA, Haynes RB, Richardson WS. Evidence based medicine: what it is and what it isn't. BMJ 1996;312 (7023):71–72.

41. Cabana MD, Rand CS, Powe NR, Wu AW, Wilson MH, Abboud PA et al. Why don't physicians follow clinical practice guidelines? A framework for improvement. JAMA. 1999;282 (15):1458–1465.

42. Jacka MJ, Zygun D. Survey of management of severe head injury in Canada. Can J Neurol Sci. 2007;34 (3):307–312.

43. Jacka MJ, Des Ordons AR, Zygun D. Severe head injury: clinicians' awareness of the literature. Can J Neurol Sci. 2008;35 (4):458–471.

44. Heskestad B, Baardsen R, Helseth E, Ingebrigtsen T. Guideline compliance in management of minimal, mild, and moderate head injury: high frequency of noncompliance among individual physicians despite strong guideline support from clinical leaders. J Trauma. 2008;65 (6):1309–1313.

45. Fakhry SM, Trask AL, Waller MA, Watts DD. Management of brain-injured patients by an evidence-based medicine protocol improves outcomes and decreases hospital charges. J Trauma. 2004;56 (3):492–499.

46. Hesdorffer DC, Ghajar J, Iacono L. Predictors of compliance with the evidence-based guidelines for traumatic brain injury care: a survey of United States trauma centers. J Trauma. 2002;52 (6):1202–1209.

47. Sydenham E, Roberts I, Alderson P. Hypothermia for traumatic head injury. Cochrane Database Syst Rev. 2009;(1):CD001048.

48. Hutchinson PJ, Gupta AK, Fryer TF, Al-Rawi PG, Chatfield DA, Coles JP et al. Correlation between cerebral blood flow, substrate delivery, and metabolism in head injury: a combined microdialysis and triple oxygen positron emission tomography study. J Cereb Blood Flow Metab. 2002;22 (6):735–745.

49. Muizelaar JP, Marmarou A, Ward JD, Kontos HA, Choi SC, Becker DP et al. Adverse effects of prolonged hyperventilation in patients with severe head injury: a randomized clinical trial. J Neurosurg. 1991;75 (5):731–739.

50. Bratton SL, Chestnut RM, Ghajar J, Connell Hammond FF, Harris OA, Hartl R et al. Guidelines for the management of severe traumatic brain injury. XIV. Hyperventilation. J Neurotrauma. 2007;24 Suppl 1:S87-S90.

51. Muench E, Horn P, Bauhuf C, Roth H, Philipps M, Hermann P et al. Effects of hypervolemia and hypertension on regional cerebral blood flow, intracranial pressure, and brain tissue oxygenation after subarachnoid hemorrhage. Crit Care Med. 2007;35 (8):1844–1851.

52. Sorani MD, Morabito D, Rosenthal G, Giacomini KM, Manley GT. Characterizing the dose-response relationship between mannitol and intracranial pressure in traumatic brain injury patients using a high-frequency physiological data collection system. J Neurotrauma. 2008;25 (4):291–298.

53. Wang AH. Osmotic demyelination syndrome associated with 3 % hypertonic saline administration. Intern Med J. 2008;38 (3):219–220.

54. Pronovost PJ, Thompson DA, Holzmueller CG, Lubomski LH, Dorman T, Dickman F et al. Toward learning from patient safety reporting systems. J Crit Care. 2006;21 (4):305–315.

55. Rothschild JM, Landrigan CP, Cronin JW, Kaushal R, Lockley SW, Burdick E et al. The Critical Care Safety Study: The incidence and nature of adverse events and serious medical errors in intensive care. Crit Care Med. 2005;33 (8):1694–1700.

56. Calabrese AD, Erstad BL, Brandl K, Barletta JF, Kane SL, Sherman DS. Medication administration errors in adult patients in the ICU. Intensive Care Med 2001; 27 (10):1592–1598.

57. Alderson P, Roberts I. Corticosteroids for acute traumatic brain injury. Cochrane Database Syst Rev. 2005;(1):CD000196.

58. Thomas AN, Panchagnula U. Medication-related patient safety incidents in critical care: a review of reports to the UK National Patient Safety Agency. Anaesthesia. 2008;63 (7):726–733.

59. Pronovost PJ, Angus DC, Dorman T, Robinson KA, Dremsizov TT, Young TL. Physician staffing patterns and clinical outcomes in critically ill patients: a systematic review. JAMA. 2002;288 (17):2151–2162.

60. Suarez JI, Zaidat OO, Suri MF, Feen ES, Lynch G, Hickman J et al. Length of stay and mortality in neurocritically ill patients: impact of a specialized neurocritical care team. Crit Care Med. 2004;32 (11):2311–2317.

61. Varelas PN, Conti MM, Spanaki MV, Potts E, Bradford D, Sunstrom C et al. The impact of a neurointensivist-led team on a semiclosed neurosciences intensive care unit. Crit Care Med. 2004;32 (11):2191–2198.

62. Mirski MA, Chang CW, Cowan R. Impact of a neuro-science intensive care unit on neurosurgical patient outcomes and cost of care: evidence-based support for

an intensivist-directed specialty ICU model of care. J Neurosurg Anesthesiol. 2001;13 (2):83–92.

63. Diringer MN, Edwards DF. Admission to a neurologic/neurosurgical intensive care unit is associated with reduced mortality rate after intracerebral hemorrhage. Crit Care Med. 2001;29 (3):635–640.

64. Mauritz W, Steltzer H, Bauer P, Dolanski-Aghamanoukjan L, Metnitz P. Monitoring of intracranial pressure in patients with severe traumatic brain injury: an Austrian prospective multicenter study. Intensive Care Med. 2008;34 (7):1208–1215.

65. Patel HC, Bouamra O, Woodford M, King AT, Yates DW, Lecky FE. Trends in head injury outcome from 1989 to 2003 and the effect of neurosurgical care: an observational study. Lancet. 2005;366 (9496):1538–1544.

66. Jain M, Miller L, Belt D, King D, Berwick DM. Decline in ICU adverse events, nosocomial infections and cost through a quality improvement initiative focusing on teamwork and culture change. Qual Saf Health Care. 2006;15 (4):235–239.

67. Beckmann U, Gillies DM, Berenholtz SM, Wu AW, Pronovost P. Incidents relating to the intra-hospital transfer of critically ill patients. An analysis of the reports submitted to the Australian Incident Monitoring Study in Intensive Care. Intensive Care Med. 2004;30 (8):1579–1585.

Andreas Schneider, Peter Teschendorf and Bernd W. Böttiger

Avoiding harm in CPR

Introduction

Every year, an estimated 700,000 individuals undergo cardiopulmonary resuscitation (CPR) in the European Union, taking both out-of-hospital and in-hospital cardiac arrests into account [1–3]. The causes of cardiac arrest are as diverse as the patients. 50–60 % of cardiac arrests are caused by acute myocardial infarction [4–6]. The typical patient will, therefore, possess the classic cardiovascular risk profile. However, cardiac arrest can also occur in previously healthy patients, e.g. as a consequence of major trauma or intoxications.

Outcome after cardiac arrest remains poor. Spontaneous circulation can be restored in about 40–50 % of the patients, yet only about 5–15 % survive to hospital discharge [1–3]. Looking at these data, it becomes clear that there is hardly a second medical therapy next to CPR which is that closely linked to survival or death. In other words: CPR does not allow any mistakes.

Complications immanent to CPR

Like in any other invasive medical procedure, characteristic complications of CPR cannot always be avoided. Immediately during CPR, complications are often negligible compared to suc-cessful resuscitation of the patient's life. However, during the post-cardiac arrest period, it is crucial to be aware of the possible complications, to recognise and, if necessary, to treat them.

Skeletal injuries

External thoracic compressions during CPR frequently cause rib or sternal fractures. Hoke et al. systematically reviewed the literature to find a 13–97 % incidence of rib fractures and 1–43 % sternal fractures after CPR [7]. Rib fractures most commonly occur in the left hemithorax, and in many cases, multiple ribs are affected. Elderly patients are at particular risk, probably due to rather rigid thoraces and ossification of cartilages in conjunction with osteopenic bones.

It was suggested that at least some of the skeletal injuries might be caused by inaccurate hand placement during chest compression [8]. However, the truth is that chest fractures during CPR can never be fully excluded. Considering a compression depth of 4–5 cm, as it is requested by the CPR guidelines [9], breaking ribs might even be a prerequisite for effective chest compressions in some patients.

In most cases, rib or sternal fractures after CPR stay without clinical relevance. However, projecting bones can possibly cause pneumothorax, haematothorax or lung injuries, in rare cases even hepatic, splenic or gastric lesions. Serial rib fractures can lead to flail chest. It was hypothesised that flail chest might impair blood flow produced by external chest compression [7].

Oschatz et al. assessed 224 patients after cardiac arrest by chest radiograph to look for complications of CPR [10]. They found pneumothorax in 3 %, soft tissue emphysema in 1 % and serial rib fractures in 8 % of the patients. There was no difference as to whether CPR had been performed by bystanders or EMS personnel.

For several reasons, obtaining a chest radiograph should be a standard procedure after CPR. This is not only to look for fractures or the associated pleural or lung injuries, but also useful to assess for cardiopulmonary congestion or the position of the tracheal tube and central venous lines. Lederer et al. demonstrated that sensitivity of a chest radiograph to find rib or sternal fractures is below 25 % [11]. However, this is of solely academic interest, since it is the complications caused by fractures and not the fractures themselves which are important for the clinician.

Visceral injuries

Compared to the chest, injuries of abdominal structures during CPR are rare. Meron et al. retrospectively analysed 2558 patients who were admitted to a single hospital during 15 years after non-traumatic cardiac arrest [12]. They found only 15 patients (0.6 %) with major liver injuries and two patients (0.08 %) with splenic rupture. In an older autopsy study of non-selected patients after cardiac arrest, including those with trauma, liver injuries were noted in 20 of 705 patients (2.8 %), splenic rupture in 2 patients (0.3 %), gastric rupture in 1 patient (0.1 %) and omentum haemorrhage in 1 patient (0.1 %) [8].

Most typically, liver lesions affect the left lobe. It was, therefore, suggested that they are mainly caused by incorrectly placed hands during CPR, namely over the xiphoid process. Not surprisingly, patients with compromised coagulation, e.g. due to coumarin therapy, are at higher risk for symptomatic liver injury [12].

Liver rupture is followed by intraabdominal bleeding. Dropping levels of haematocrit are, therefore, the guiding symptom. Haemodynamics will hardly lead to the diagnosis of liver rupture, since most patients after cardiac arrest show instable haemodynamics. Whenever liver rupture is suspected, ultrasound examination of the abdomen should be performed. If necessary, a CT scan should be taken into account.

Airway complications

Regurgitation of gastric contents is common during cardiac arrest. In case of an open airway, this might lead to pulmonary aspiration. Mouth-to-mouth or bag-mask ventilation can further increase the risk by distending the stomach.

Oschatz et al., in their study analysing chest radiographs of patients after cardiac arrest admitted to hospital, found gastric distension in 41 of 155 mechanically resuscitated patients (26 %) and suspicion of aspiration in 29 of 155 (19 %) [10]. However, suspicion of aspiration was also found in patients resuscitated by electrical defibrillation only (2 of 18 = 11 %). These data are in line with Krischer et al. who, in their autopsy study, had a 29 % incidence of gastric distension and 11 % aspiration [8].

Stone et al. evaluated the incidence of gastric regurgitation at different time points as well as under different airway devices [13]. Prior to CPR, 84 of 797 (11 %) of patients had already regurgitated. During CPR, there was further regurgitation in 91 patients (10 %). After CPR, regurgitation occurred in an additional 15 patients (2 %). Regurgitation during CPR was markedly reduced by replacing bag-mask ventilation by primary insertion of a laryngeal mask airway (incidence 12.4 % in bag-mask ventilation only, 3.5 % in laryngeal mask only, 11.8 % in laryngeal mask following initial bag-mask ventilation).

On the one hand, ventilation is an integral part of CPR. On the other hand, when performing bag-mask ventilation (as well as mouth-to-mouth ventilation), this should always be done with the lowest pressure and tidal volume which is adequate to ensure proper ventilation. A tracheal tube or a supraglottic airway device such as the laryngeal mask airway might protect from aspiration. However, when inserted after initial aggressive bag-mask ventilation, they simply come too late.

Airway complications during CPR also include dental, oropharyngeal, laryngeal or tracheal injuries due to tracheal intubation. However, these events are rather sparse and hardly affect survival [8], but may cause legal consequences for the caregiver.

Therapeutic mistakes during CPR

As stated above, even the best emergency physician can never avoid all complications of CPR. However, problems arising from inaccurately chosen therapeutic strategies can hardly be called complications. Indeed, resuscitation success itself can be questioned by the wrong therapeutic focuses. In particular, all invasive measures are second to basic life support. Nothing is more important than continuous thoracic compressions.

Airway management

Tracheal intubation is considered the golden standard of airway management during CPR [9]. It provides protection from (further) aspiration and allows ventilation independent of chest compressions. However, one must not force intubation at any cost. There is a certain amount of skill and experience necessary to perform tracheal intubation. While this technique represents daily routine for the anaesthesiologist, physicians from other fields might sometimes lack continuous training.

Gries et al. calculated that emergency physicians in Germany perform an average of only nine out-of-hospital tracheal intubations per year [14]. These data are complemented by a recent study by Timmermann et al. who prospectively assessed 149 consecutive patients in Germany in whom out-of-hospital tracheal intubation was performed by emergency physicians recruited from different specialties [15]. Tracheal tube placement was verified on scene by an experienced anaesthesiologist using a combination of physical examination, direct laryngoscopy and capnometry. There was endobronchial intubation in 16 patients (10.7%) and oesophageal intubation in 10 patients (6.7%). In all cases, the tube position

could be corrected by the anaesthesiologist. In doing so, the vocal cords could be visualised in 8 of 10 patients with initially unrecognised oesophageal intubation (Cormack-Lehane laryngeal view grade I/II), only 2 patients presented with view of the epiglottis only (Cormack-Lehane grade III). 7 of 10 patients (70.0%) with initially unrecognised oesophageal intubation died within the first 24 hours of treatment as compared to 14 of 139 patients (10.1%) with correct tracheal tube position.

Wang et al. performed a similar study in the USA where out-of-hospital tracheal intubation was done by paramedics [16]. Covering 1953 patients from 40 different EMS centres, the tube was misplaced or dislodged in 3.1% of the cases, four or more intubation attempts were performed in 3.2%, successful intubation of the trachea failed in 18.4%.

In conclusion, the CPR guidelines state that "tracheal intubation ... should be attempted only if the healthcare provider is properly trained and has adequate ongoing experience with the technique" [9]. Intubation attempts must not lead to disregard of basic life support. Laryngoscopy should be performed without interruption of chest compressions and no attempt should last longer than 30 seconds [9]. If correct tracheal intubation is not achieved quickly, one should refrain from further attempts in favour of bag-mask ventilation. Supraglottic airway devices such as the laryngeal mask airway or the laryngeal tube may also represent an alternative method since they are much easier to insert.

Vascular access

Peripheral venous lines represent the method of choice to deliver drugs during CPR [9]. They are easy and fast to establish and are associated with few relevant complications. One might argue that a central venous catheter is a better way to deliver drugs like catecholamines. However, there is no indication to insert a central venous catheter during ongoing CPR. Not only would an interruption of chest compressions be needed, but also complications such as a pneumothorax or arterial puncture are not acceptable during CPR.

If peripheral intravenous access cannot be established, the guidelines name the intraosseous route as the second choice [9]. Intraosseous needles can be easily installed even without prior experience [17]. They provide a safe method to deliver drugs not only in children, but also in adults.

Adrenaline and some other drugs can also be given through the tracheal tube. However, this should be limited to those cases where neither the intravenous nor the intraosseous route is available [9]. Absorption through the lungs remains highly unpredictable during CPR. Niemann et al. retrospectively analysed 596 patients suffering from out-of-hospital cardiac arrest, finding that tracheal drug delivery as compared to intravenous administration was associated with impaired restoration of spontaneous circulation (15 % vs. 27 %), survival to hospital admission (9 % vs. 20 %) and survival to hospital discharge (0 % vs. 5 %) [18].

Recovery after successful CPR

Even medical laypersons know that the brain is extremely vulnerable to cardiac arrest. However, one must keep in mind that this sensitivity goes on during the post-cardiac arrest period. Modern therapies such as mild therapeutic hypothermia are known to improve (neuronal) outcome after cardiac arrest [19, 20]. However, considering these therapies must not lead to ignoring the fundamentals. The first goal of all therapeutic measures is to maintain physiological homoeostasis to establish an optimal environment for cerebral recovery.

Haemodynamics

Patients after cardiac arrest are usually haemodynamically unstable. One reason for this is so-called myocardial stunning. Following ischaemia, both systolic contractility and diastolic relaxation are impaired [21–23]. Moreover, systemic vasodilation and hypovolaemia contribute to haemodynamic instability. It seems that systemic inflammation largely contributes to these phenomena. The post-cardiac arrest period has even been called a "sepsis-like syndrome" [24].

In most patients after cardiac arrest, autoregulation of cerebral vessels is impaired or defective [25]. In healthy individuals, cerebral blood flow remains stable even if arterial blood pressure declines. In patients after cardiac arrest, however, cerebral circulation rapidly falls to critical amounts. Consistent with this, epidemiological studies show that hypotensive episodes are associated with increased mortality [26].

It seems clear that hypotension should be avoided after cardiac arrest. However, little is known besides that. Animal experimental data suggest that elevating blood pressure might improve outcome [27]. However, no data in this regard are available from clinical studies. The guidelines suggest to aim at the individual patient's normal blood pressure [9].

Due to the described haemodynamic instabilities, all patients after cardiac arrest should be provided with an arterial catheter for invasive blood pressure measurement. In some cases, supplementation by a pulmonary artery catheter or pulse contour analysis may be reasonable.

The first-line option to improve haemodynamics should be fluid substitution. Laurent et al. showed that stabilising the patient may require up to 8000 ml infusions within the first 72 hours [22]. Even if vasopressor or inotropic treatment is necessary, haemodynamics usually recover within 72 hours.

Blood glucose

Elevated blood glucose after cardiac arrest is associated with increased mortality and impaired neurologic recovery after cardiac arrest [26, 28].

In their classic randomised clinical trial, van den Berghe et al. showed that tight glucose control (80–110 mg/dl vs. 180–200 mg/dl) by intensive insulin therapy is able to improve outcome in a general intensive care setting [29]. However, in patients after cardiac arrest, the recommendation to do so has recently been questioned. Two small studies showed that only slightly elevated blood glucose (< 150 mg/dl) might not be associated with worsened outcome [30, 31]. It is possible that during tight glucose control with insulin, periods of hypoglycaemia that could impair outcome might not be recognised.

Ventilation

Adequate ventilation is extremely important in the post-cardiac arrest period in order to not further promote the effects of ischaemia. In cases of respiratory insufficiency, the patient should be intubated and mechanically ventilated. Both hypoventilation and hyperventilation must carefully be avoided. Any hyperventilation could lead to cerebral vasoconstriction and therefore reduction of cerebral blood flow [32]. If possible, ventilation should be adjusted to capnometry even in the preclinical setting. In the intensive care unit, blood gas analyses at regular intervals should go without saying.

During mild therapeutic hypothermia, there are, in principle, two theories on how to adjust ventilation parameters. Both aim at a "normal" pH of 7.4 and a "normal" CO_2 tension of 40 mmHg. However, with decreasing body temperature, autoprotolysis of water decreases (i.e. neutrality is at lower pH values) and gas solubility increases (i.e. gas tensions decrease). Blood gas analyses are always performed after heating the sample to 37°C. The question is whether to "correct" the measured values for the patient's body temperature. In an "alpha stat" approach, there is no such correction. It is supposed that normal values of pH 7.4 and CO_2 40 mmHg are only valid at 37°C, while other body temperatures require different values (which are not further investigated). In a "pH stat" approach, pH and gas tension at the patient's body temperature are calculated from the measured data. The idea is that pH 7.4 and CO_2 40 mmHg should always be considered normal independent of the current temperature.

It is not clear which approach is superior. There is a single animal experimental study in experimental ischaemic stroke in which pH stat ventilation reduced the infarct volume and brain oedema [33]. However, it is not known if this result can be transferred to human patients after cardiac arrest.

Body temperature

Elevated body temperature is common after cardiac arrest and is associated with impaired outcome [26]. However, the therapeutic goal is not normothermia, but hypothermia. Two randomised clinical trials have independently shown that cooling comatose adult patients after out-of-hospital cardiac arrest due to ventricular fibrillation to 32–34°C for 12–24 hours improves both

survival and neurological outcome [19, 20]. According to the CPR guidelines, therapeutic hypothermia should be considered in all unconscious patients after cardiac arrest unless there are specific contraindications such as severe cardiogenic shock or primary coagulopathy [9].

Despite the evidence, therapeutic hypothermia is still underused. Several surveys from both sides of the Atlantic have investigated the current implementation of therapeutic hypothermia [34–37]. Although the proportion of hospitals in which hypothermia is applied is steadily increasing, it might still be less than 50 % in total. Regarding the USA, it has been calculated that an additional 2298 patients per year could have a good neurological outcome if hypothermia was fully implemented [38].

Conclusions

Successful CPR requires effective, i.e. vigorous chest compressions. CPR is a matter of life or death. Therefore, the rescuer must not be influenced by the risk of complications such as skeletal injuries. Interruptions of chest compressions must be kept to a minimum. Thus, there is little space for elaborate invasive measures during ongoing CPR. In the post-cardiac arrest phase, avoiding harm means providing good critical care practice plus therapeutic hypothermia.

The authors

Andreas Schneider, MD
Peter Teschendorf, MD
Bernd W. Böttiger, MD
    Department of Anaesthesiology and
    Postoperative Intensive Care Medicine |
    University Hospital Cologne | Germany

Address for correspondence
    Andreas Schneider
    Department of Anaesthesiology and
    Postoperative Intensive Care Medicine
    University Hospital Cologne
    Kerpener Straße 62
    50937 Köln, Germany
    E-mail: andreas.schneider_@uk-koeln.de

References

1. Atwood C, Eisenberg MS, Herlitz J, Rea TD. Incidence of EMS-treated out-of-hospital cardiac arrest in Europe. Resuscitation. 2005;67:75–80.
2. Böttiger BW, Grabner C, Bauer H, Bode C, Weber T, Motsch J, Martin E. Long term outcome after out-of-hospital cardiac arrest with physician staffed emergency medical services: the Utstein style applied to a midsized urban/suburban area. Heart. 1999;82:674–679.
3. Peberdy MA, Kaye W, Ornato JP, Larkin GL, Nadkarni V, Mancini ME, Berg RA, Nichol G, Lane-Truitt T. Cardiopulmonary resuscitation of adults in the hospital: a report of 14 720 cardiac arrests from the National Registry of Cardiopulmonary Resuscitation. Resuscitation. 2003;58:297–308.
4. Müllner M, Hirschl MM, Herkner H, Sterz F, Leitha T, Exner M, Binder M, Laggner AN. Creatine kinase-MB fraction and cardiac troponin T to diagnose acute myocardial infarction after cardiopulmonary resuscitation. J Am Coll Cardiol. 1996;28:1220–1225.
5. Spaulding CM, Joly LM, Rosenberg A, Monchi M, Weber SN, Dhainaut JF, Carli P. Immediate coronary angiography in survivors of out-of-hospital cardiac arrest. N Engl J Med. 1997;336:1629–1633.
6. Vanbrabant P, Dhondt E, Billen P, Sabbe M. Aetiology of unsuccessful prehospital witnessed cardiac arrest of unclear origin. Eur J Emerg Med. 2006;13:144–147.
7. Hoke RS, Chamberlain D. Skeletal chest injuries secondary to cardiopulmonary resuscitation. Resuscitation. 2004;63:327–338.
8. Krischer JP, Fine EG, Davis JH, Nagel EL. Complications of cardiac resuscitation. Chest. 1987;92:287–291.
9. European Resuscitation Council. European Resuscitation Council guidelines for resuscitation 2005. Resuscitation. 2005;67:S1-S189.
10. Oschatz E, Wunderbaldinger P, Sterz F, Holzer M, Kofler J, Slatin H, Janata K, Eisenburger P, Bankier AA, Laggner AN. Cardiopulmonary resuscitation performed by bystanders does not increase adverse effects as assessed by chest radiography. Anesth Analg. 2001;93:128–133.
11. Lederer W, Mair D, Rabl W, Baubin M. Frequency of rib and sternum fractures associated with out-of-hospital cardiopulmonary resuscitation is underestimated by conventional chest X-ray. Resuscitation. 2004;60:157–162.
12. Meron G, Kurkciyan I, Sterz F, Susani M, Domanovits H, Tobler K, Bohdjalian A, Laggner AN. Cardiopulmonary resuscitation-associated major liver injury. Resuscitation. 2007;75:445–453.
13. Stone BJ, Chantler PJ, Baskett PJF. The incidence of regurgitation during cardiopulmonary resuscitation:
a comparison between the bag valve mask and laryngeal mask airway. Resuscitation. 1998;38:3–6.
14. Gries A, Zink W, Bernhard M, Messelken M, Schlechtriemen T. Realistic assessment of the physician-staffed emergency services in Germany. Anaesthesist. 2006;55:1080–1086.
15. Timmermann A, Russo SG, Eich C, Roessler M, Braun U, Rosenblatt WH, Quintel M. The out-of-hospital esophageal and endobronchial intubations performed by emergency physicians. Anesth Analg. 2007;104:619–623.
16. Wang HE, Lave JR, Sirio CA, Yealy DM. Paramedic intubation errors: isolated events or symptoms of larger problems? Health Aff. 2006;25:501–509.
17. Brenner T, Bernhard M, Helm M, Doll S, Völkl A, Ganion N, Friedmann C, Sikinger M, Knapp J, Martin E, Gries A. Comparison of two intraosseous infusion systems for adult emergency medical use. Resuscitation. 2008;78:314–319.
18. Niemann JT, Stratton SJ, Cruz B, Lewis RJ. Endotracheal drug administration during out-of-hospital resuscitation: where are the survivors? Resuscitation. 2002;53:153–157.
19. Bernard SA, Gray TW, Buist MD, Jones BM, Silvester W, Gutteridge G, Smith K. Treatment of comatose survivors of out-of-hospital cardiac arrest with induced hypothermia. N Engl J Med. 2002;346:557–563.
20. Hypothermia after Cardiac Arrest Study Group. Mild therapeutic hypothermia to improve the neurologic outcome after cardiac arrest. N Engl J Med. 2002;346:549–556.
21. Kern KB, Hilwig RW, Rhee KH, Berg RA. Myocardial dysfunction after resuscitation from cardiac arrest: an example of global myocardial stunning. J Am Coll Cardiol. 1996;28:232–240.
22. Laurent I, Monchi M, Chiche JD, Joly LM, Spaulding C, Bourgeois B, Cariou A, Rozenberg A, Carli P, Weber S, Dhainaut JF. Reversible myocardial dysfunction in survivors of out-of-hospital cardiac arrest. J Am Coll Cardiol. 2002;40:2110–2116.
23. Russ N, Böttiger B, Popp E, Schneider A, Teschendorf P. Early post resuscitation myocardial dysfunction in the rat is improved by Sevoflurane when administered during cardio pulmonary resuscitation. Eur J Anaesthesiol. 2008;25:ESAAP2–4.
24. Adrie C, Adib-Conquy M, Laurent I, Monchi M, Vinsonneau C, Fitting C, Fraisse F, Dinh-Xuan AT, Carli P, Spaulding C, Dhainaut JF, Cavaillon JM. Successful cardiopulmonary resuscitation after cardiac arrest as a "sepsis-like" syndrome. Circulation. 2002;106:562–568.
25. Sundgreen C, Larsen FS, Herzog TM, Knudsen GM, Boesgaard S, Aldershvile J. Autoregulation of cerebral blood flow in patients resuscitated from cardiac arrest. Stroke. 2001;32:128–132.

26. Langhelle A, Tyvold SS, Lexow K, Hapnes SA, Sunde K, Steen PA. In-hospital factors associated with improved outcome after out-of-hospital cardiac arrest. A comparison between four regions in Norway. Resuscitation. 2003;56:247–263.

27. Sterz F, Leonov Y, Safar P, Radovsky A, Tisherman SA, Oku K. Hypertension with or without hemodilution after cardiac arrest in dogs. Stroke. 1990;21:1178–1184.

28. Müllner M, Sterz F, Binder M, Schreiber W, Deimel A, Laggner AN. Blood glucose concentration after cardiopulmonary resuscitation influences functional neurological recovery in human cardiac arrest survivors. J Cereb Blood Flow Metab. 1997;17:430–436.

29. Van den Berghe G, Wouters P, Weekers F, Verwaest C, Bruyninckx F, Schetz M, Vlasselaers D, Ferdinande P, Lauwers P, Bouillon R. Intensive insulin therapy in the critically ill patients. N Engl J Med. 2001;345:1359–1367.

30. Losert H, Sterz F, Roine RO, Holzer M, Martens P, Cerchiari E, Tiainen M, Müllner M, Laggner AN, Herkner H, Bischof MG. Strict normoglycaemic blood glucose levels in the therapeutic management of patients within 12 h after cardiac arrest might not be necessary. Resuscitation. 2008;76:214–220.

31. Oksanen T, Skrifvars MB, Varpula T, Kuitunen A, Pettilä V, Nurmi J, Castrén M. Strict versus moderate glucose control after resuscitation from ventricular fibrillation. Intensive Care Med. 2007;33:2093–2100.

32. Buunk G, van der Hoeven JG, Meinders AE. Cerebrovascular reactivity in comatose patients resuscitated from a cardiac arrest. Stroke. 1997;28:1569–1573.

33. Kollmar R, Frietsch T, Georgiadis D, Schäbitz WR, Waschke KF, Kuschinsky W, Schwab S. Early effects of acid-base management during hypothermia on cerebral infarct volume, edema, and cerebral blood flow in acute focal cerebral ischemia in rats. Anesthesiology. 2002;97:868–874.

34. Kennedy J, Green RS, Stenstrom R. The use of induced hypothermia after cardiac arrest: a survey of Canadian emergency physicians. CJEM. 2008;10:125–130.

35. Merchant RM, Soar J, Skrifvars MB, Silfvast T, Edelson DP, Ahmad F, Huang KN, Khan M, Vanden Hoek TL, Becker LB, Abella BS. Therapeutic hypothermia utilization among physicians after resuscitation from cardiac arrest. Crit Care Med 2006;34:1935–1940.

36. Oksanen T, Pettilä V, Hynynen M, Varpula T. Therapeutic hypothermia after cardiac arrest: implementation and outcome in Finnish intensive care units. Acta Anaesthesiol Scand. 2007;51:866–871.

37. Wolfrum S, Radke PW, Pischon T, Willich SN, Schunkert H, Kurowski V. Mild therapeutic hypothermia after cardiac arrest. A nationwide survey on the implementation of the ILCOR guidelines in German intensive care units. Resuscitation. 2007;72:207–213.

38. Majersik JJ, Silbergleit R, Meurer WJ, Brown DL, Lisabeth LD, Morgenstern LB. Public health impact of full implementation of therapeutic hypothermia after cardiac arrest. Resuscitation. 2008;77:189–194.

Luiz Francisco Poli-de-Figueiredo, Alexandre Biasi Cavalcanti,
Américo Lourenço Cuvello Neto and Carlos Eduardo Pompilio

Avoiding harm after cardiac surgery

Introduction

Cardiac surgery is a complex procedure highly prone to harm. Postoperative complications may result from the frequent pre-existing comorbidities and/or because of the use of cardiopulmonary bypass (CPB). Besides the expected transient postoperative myocardial dysfunction and the marked change of normal physiology in several organs and systems, CPB, by causing blood contact with the synthetic surfaces of the extracorporeal circuits, can trigger a generalised inflammatory response, alter coagulation and promote widespread leukocyte-endothelial cell interaction, which all can compromise microcirculatory flow to several organs, leading to multiple organ dysfunction, important cause of morbidity and mortality.

In this chapter we discuss some strategies to reduce and/or avoid harm to patients undergoing CPB. We focus on general measures regarding quality and surgical safety programmes. We also discuss modifiable variables related to the postoperative management of pulmonary and renal dysfunctions, two of the most prevalent undesirable events associated with poor outcome after an apparently uneventful cardiac surgery.

Quality and safety programmes

Improvement in outcomes after coronary artery bypass grafting (CABG) has occurred in the last two decades, in spite of changes towards sicker patients undergoing surgery. Data including more than 5 million patients having isolated coronary artery bypass grafting in the United Stated from 1988 to 2005 (North American Registry), for instance, shows that patients are becoming more complex, with higher prevalence of comorbidities such as congestive heart failure, pulmonary disease, diabetes, and acute myocardial infarction [1]. The predicted risk increased from 2.6% to 3.7% (p < 0.0001), albeit risk-adjusted mortality took the opposite direction, decreasing from 6.2% to 2.1% (p < 0.0001). Inflation-adjusted charges also dropped by approximately 27%.

There are several possible explanations for this improvement in outcomes after CABG. However, feedback of outcome data coupled with an implicit or organised effort at quality improvement are considered the main reason for these advances [2, 3]. Quality improvement programmes using data audit and feedback for example were successful in reducing mortality rates [2, 4].

Public availability of surgeon- and institution-specific risk-adjusted outcomes

The high level of public interest in cardiac surgery outcomes has led to the publication of risk-adjusted mortality rates in the public domain in some states of the US since the mid-eighties [5]. Institutions from other countries such as the United Kingdom and Germany have also published their results on cardiac surgery [6, 7].

Some hypothesised that public reporting of mortality data would lead to increased public demand for CABG in those centres with better results. However, surveys to access how much the reporting of outcome data influenced physicians or patients' choice of institution for performing CABG have shown that its role was not important [8, 9]. Other aspects such as hospital reputation, geographic proximity and traditional referral patterns were more important determinants for selecting a cardiac surgery centre [10].

The reporting of risk-adjusted outcomes after CABG has been effective in reducing mortality rates by fostering a quality improvement culture [2, 3, 11]. However, studies have found that the public release of hospital- and physician-specific mortality rates has not led to improvements and failed to effectively guide consumers or change physicians' referral practices [8, 12].

Surgical safety checklist

The WHO Surgical Safety Checklist is a simple tool to ensure that very simple measures intended at preventing harm in surgery are implemented (see Tab. 1) [13]. The checklist is applied at three points: before starting anesthesia, immediately before incision and before moving the patient out of the operating room. At each of these points, members of the surgical team will orally confirm that basic items for safe anaesthesia, effective teamwork, prophylaxis against infection and other safety issues were addressed.

A "before/after" study evaluated the effects on deaths and major surgical complications of implementing the WHO Surgical Safety Checklist in eight hospitals in eight cities representing different economic circumstances and a variety of medical routine practices [14]. After implementation of the checklist, adherence to all of six safety indica-

tors improved from 34.2% to 56.7% (p < 0.001). Concurrently, death rate during hospitalisation and within the first 30 days decreased from 1.5% from 0.8% (p = 0.003), and complications decreased from 11.0% to 7.0% (p < 0.001). The effect was similar in higher- and lower-income sites.

Application of the WHO Surgical Safety Checklist is not costly or lengthy [14]. Measures recommended in the checklist are inexpensive, except for the pulse oximetry or prophylactic antibiotics, but these are already available in most institutions worldwide. Even though the implementation of the WHO checklist was evaluated in non-cardiac surgeries, all of its items are applicable to cardiac surgeries too. Therefore, it is likely that the checklist will also be beneficial in cardiac surgeries and its use should be encouraged.

Early extubation safety issues

The aims of the "fast track" after cardiac surgery is early extubation and shortening of ICU stay with subsequent cost reduction [15, 16, 17]. It is achieved by the use of faster anaesthetics at lower doses, normothermic temperature management and adoption of early extubation protocols. In addition, some institutions schedule patients eligible to fast-track protocol for operating in the morning, therefore allowing them to be discharged from the ICU on the same day, releasing the ICU bed for another patient.

Systematic reviews of randomised controlled trials comparing fast-track to conventional management protocols found reduced length of mechanical ventilation, ICU stay and in-hospital stay [18, 19]. Serious adverse events were rare and similar in both groups.

The selection of lower-risk patients for fast-tracking is of paramount importance. The use of a risk prediction model such as St Mary's fast-track failure propensity score may be very helpful to inform eligibility to a fast-track protocol (see Tab. 2) [19].

The following criteria should be met for proceeding to early extubation of heart surgery patients:

- Patient must be awake and cooperative with no evidence of neurologic deficits
- Haemodynamically stable without vasoactive drugs or intra-aortic balloon pump

Tab. 1   The WHO Surgical Safety Checklist [Copyright © Haynes, Weiser, Berry et al., A Surgical Safety Checklist to Reduce Morbidity and Mortality in a Global Popul. The New England journal of Medicine, 2009;360:491–499, Massachussetts medical Society. All rights reserved]

Sign-In

Before induction of anaesthesia, members of the team (at least the nurse and an anaesthesia professional) orally confirm that:

- The patient has verified his or her identity, the surgical site and procedure, and consent
- The surgical site is marked or site marking is not applicable
- The pulse oximeter is on the patient and functioning
- All members of the team are aware of whether the patient has a known allergy
- The patient's airway and risk of aspiration have been evaluated and appropriate equipment and assistance are available
- If there is a risk of blood loss of at least 500 ml (or 7 ml/kg of body weight, in children), appropriate access and fluids are available

Time-out

Before skin incision, the entire team (nurses, surgeons, anaesthesia professionals, and any others participating in the care of the patient) orally:

- Confirms that all team members have been introduced by name and role
- Confirms the patient's identity, surgical site, and procedure
- Reviews the anticipated critical events
  - Surgeon reviews critical and unexpected steps, operative duration, and anticipated blood loss
  - Anaesthesia staff review concerns specific to the patient
  - Nursing staff review confirmation of sterility, equipment availability, and other concerns
- Confirms that prophylactic antibiotics have been administered ≤ 60 min before incision is made or that antibiotics are not indicated
- Confirms that all essential imaging results for the correct patient are displayed in the operating room

Sign-out

Before the patient leaves the operating room:

- Nurse reviews items aloud with the team to confirm
  - Name of the procedure as recorded
  - That the needle, sponge, and instrument counts are complete (or not applicable)
  - That the specimen (if any) is correctly labeled, including patient's name
  - Whether there are any issues with equipment to be addressed

The surgeon, nurse, and anaesthesia professional review aloud the key concerns for the recovery and care of the patient

- Absence of new or uncontrolled arrhythmias
- Chest tube drainage of <100 ml/h for 2 hours
- Arterial pH > 7.35
- PaO_2 > 100 mmHg on FIO_2 < 50%
- Temperature of 35.5–36.5°C

The criteria for day 0 ICU transfer to a step-down unit (i.e. a high-dependency unit) are the following:

- At least 2 hours of observation after early extubation

Tab. 2   St Mary's fast-track failure propensity score to be used with nomogram
[reproduced from Vasilis C, fast track failure after cardiac surgery: Development of a prediction model, Critical Care
Medicine, 2009;34, 12, with kind permission of Wolters Kluwer Health]
ACS, acute coronary syndrome; LV, left ventricular; IABP, intra-aortic balloon pumping.
Complex procedure was defined as: any combined procedure (valve replacement and CABG), any dual valve or aortic
operation, and any other type of operation such as pericardial procedure, tricuspid valve operation, pulmonary
embolectomy, or chest wall reconstruction for sternal wound infection.

Risk Factor	Category	Score
No recent ACS (> 90 days)	Good LV function	0
	Moderate LV function	0.1
	Poor LV function	0.2
Recent ACS (≤ 90 days)	Good LV function	0.05
	Moderate LV function	0.7
	Poor LV function	1.2
Redo operations	None	0
	One	0.6
	More than one	2.8
Extracardiac arteriopathy	Absent	0
	Present	1.0
Preoperative IABP	No	0
	Yes	1.3
Serum creatinine, μmol/L	< 120	0
	120–150	0.5
	> 150	2.4
Complex surgery performed	No	0
	Yes	1.0
Operative urgency	Elective/scheduled	0
	Urgent/emergency	1.2

Total Score	0	1	2	3	4	5	6	7	8	>9
Probability of fast-track failure (%)	4.9	12.2	27.4	50.6	73.6	88.3	95.4	98.2	99.3	>99.8

- Stable haemodynamic status
- No significant bleeding
- No arrhythmias
- Normal EKG
- Normal neurological evolution

Avoiding harm to lungs and kidneys

Cardiopulmonary bypass (CPB) is commonly required to perform cardiac surgery; both can elicit a systemic inflammatory response syndrome
(SIRS) [20, 21], which is associated with many
postoperative complications and ultimately, multiple organ dysfunction. In addition to the contact
of the blood components with the artificial surfaces of the bypass circuits, ischaemia-reper-
fusion injury, endotoxaemia, hypothermia, and
operative trauma are all possible causes of SIRS
in this clinical setting [22].

The deleterious effects of CPB are mediated
by an acute-phase reaction where nuclear factor kappa B (NF-kB) plays a major role [23]. This
peptide is involved in the regulation of transcrip-

tion of many pro-inflammatory genes. It is activated by several stimuli such as interleukin-1 (IL-1), tumoral necrosis factor type alfa (TNF-α), Gram-negative lipopolissacarides (LPS), UV irradiation, growth factors, oxygen free radicals, oxidative stress and viral infections [24]. Once activated, NF-kB induces the adhesion molecule synthesis. Selectins (E, P and L), integrins and the members of the immunoglobulin superfamily expressed on the endothelial cell enable the activation, rolling, adherence, and finally, migration of leucocytes to intertitium, initiating inflammatory reaction. Recently, an elegant experiment performed by Evans et al. highlighted the role of leukocytes in inflammatory processes triggered by CPB [25].

This sequence of events is responsible for many of the postoperative complications such as the loss of vascular tone, capillary fluid leakage, and hypovolaemia leading to organ dysfunction. Additionally, it may explain the clinical settings observed during the postoperative period, varying from extreme vasodilation requiring vasoconstrictors, to low cardiac output syndrome and the development of significant respiratory and renal failures.

Postoperative pulmonary dysfunction

Acute lung injury (ALI) and acute respiratory distress syndrome (ARDS) as defined by the American-European Consensus [26] have a prevalence difficult to ascertain after cardiopulmonary bypass (CPB) and open-heart surgery. This occurs due to changes in definitions of ALI/ARDS since 1994, changes in surgical techniques and devices, and because lung injury presents in a continuum from a mild oxygenation defect to a full-blown ARDS. In previous studies, the incidence of ARDS after CPB has been found to be 1.0% to 1.7% [27, 28, 29]. More recent studies showed a slight decline of 1.32% [30] and 0.4% [31]. A large series addressing incidence and survival of ALI-associated postoperative respiratory failure was recently published [32]. The study included 4,420 consecutive patients undergoing high-risk elective surgeries for postoperative pulmonary complications. From this total, 1,381 were open-heart procedures. In this group, the incidence of ALI was 5.7%. The prevalence of the oxygenation

deficits was not measured, but we believe that it is very high. In spite of improvements in critical care and mechanical ventilation techniques, postoperative ARDS mortality rates remain around 50%. As a corollary, we need to focus on modifiable risk factors for ALI/ARDS and to evaluate some measures that could prevent these dramatic clinical scenarios.

Inflammation blocking

After these considerations, it seems logical that researchers work to find means that block inflammation after CPB. Two meta-analyses published recently addressed the effect of corticosteroids and statins on inflammatory reaction after CPB.

Meta-analysis by Whitlock et al. thoroughly reviews the perioperative use of steroids in CPB patients. The overall mortality rate was 3.2% and there was a trend towards a reduction with steroid therapy (RR 0.73, 95% CI 0.45 to 1.18, p = 0.20, I2 = 0%). There were no decreases in myocardial infarction, neurological events, duration of mechanical ventilation or infection rates. There was a significant decrease in new-onset atrial fibrillation in the steroid group (24.7%) in comparison to placebo (35.5%), with a significant risk reduction (RR 0.71, 95% CI 0.59 to 0.87, p = 0.001, I2 = 21%). Additionally, steroid use also resulted in a significant reduction in the length of stay (LOS) in the hospital in comparison to no steroids or placebo (WMD 20.59, p = 0.04).

In spite of the benefits of reduction in new-onset atrial fibrillation and hospital LOS, the dosage necessary to yield these effects is a subject of debate. Higher doses may induce a higher incidence of side effects such as gastrointestinal complications. The conclusion is that the current literature remains insufficient to make firm statements regarding safe steroid use in connection with CPB [34].

Another meta-analysis by Liakopoulos et al. [35] discusses the low (~40%) perioperative use of statins in cardiac surgery. The absolute risk reduction with statins on mortality yields a number-needed-to-treat (NNT) of 67 patients treated to save one life. To reduce atrial fibrillation, 23 patients need to be treated. Therefore, the conclusion is that statin use significantly reduces postoperative early mortality from all causes, the incidence of atrial fibrillation and stroke, and should be included in guidelines of cardiac surgery management [35].

Many attempts to maintain lung perfusion and diminish the inflammatory process during CPB have been performed. Lung-protective solutions [36], bilateral extracorporeal circulation [37] and heparin-coated circuits [38] are interesting strategies that require more definitive confirmation.

Mechanical ventilation

During CPB, the lungs remain hypoventilated in order to facilitate surgical access. Hypoventilation is associated with atelectasis, interstitial oedema, decreasing compliance, lung ischaemia, and higher incidence of infection, which all can result in postoperative ALI/ARDS [39]. Loeckinger et al. hypothesised that a CPAP of 10 cm-H2O during CPB could be beneficial to avoid these undesirable effects [40]. Using multiple inert gas elimination technique, they showed an improved ventilation/perfusion relationship and oxygenation in the postoperative period when CPAP was applied during CPB.

The open-lung approach constitutes two main strategies alleged to protect lungs: "Open up" the lung and "keep the lung opened" [41]. The first is accomplished with recruitment maneuvers [42], which are, however, considered dangerous and/or ineffective by other authors [43]. The second is also controversial, with low VT/high PEEP strategies [44]. Nevertheless, when applied after cardiac surgery, recruitment maneuvers improve oxygenation and increase end-expiratory volume, ameliorating anesthaesia-induced atelectasis. What is the best moment to institute these maneuvers is the subject of dispute [45]. Miranda et al. submitted cardiac surgery patients to two types of "open-lung approaches" [46]. In the first, recruitment maneuvers were initiated in parallel to the CPB ("early group"). In the second, recruitment maneuvers were initiated one hour after the completion of the procedure ("late group"). There was a control group with no recruitment maneuvers. Surprisingly, the late open-lung group showed no better results than controls. The early open-lung group, functional respiratory capacity was much better preserved, with 50 % higher values than in the control group on the first postoperative day suggesting that there is an early window in which this technique could be useful.

Zupancich et al. studied the influence of mechanical ventilation on pulmonary and systemic concentration of inflammatory mediators in patients undergoing CPB for cardiac surgery [47]. They hypothesised that mechanical ventilation with a non-protective strategy of high VT/low PEEP might further increase the concentration of inflammatory mediators caused by CPB. They could demonstrate that after CPB, the association of inflammatory process and non-protective ventilatory strategies in the postoperative period has addictive effects. This deleterious effect seems not to occur in non-cardiac surgeries, apparently due to the absence of CPB [48].

Postoperative acute renal dysfunction

The incidence of acute kidney injury after cardiac surgery varies between 5 and 30 %, depending on variable criteria available for definitions. Compromised renal function promotes a clear negative impact on outcome. In a large prospective cohort study in 4,118 patients who underwent cardiac and thoracic aortic surgery, even minimal increases or profound decreases of serum creatinine were associated with a substantial decrease in survival. In 2,441 patients in whom serum creatinine decreased, early mortality was 2.6 % in contrast to 8.9 % in patients with increased postoperative serum creatinine values. Mortality was lowest (2.1 %) in patients in whom serum creatinine decreased to a maximum of −0.3 mg/dl; mortality increased to 6 % in patients in whom serum creatinine remained unchanged or increased up to 0.5 mg/dl. Mortality was highest (32.5 %) in patients in whom creatinine increased 0.5 mg/dl or more [49].

More severe lesions, requiring renal replacement therapy, increased mortality up to 8 times [50]. A recent multicentre cohort of 3,500 adult cardiac surgery patients was performed to evaluate the relationships between three thresholds of acute renal dysfunction (> 25 %, > 50 %, and > 75 %) and mortality, according to the decrease in glomerular filtration rate within one week of surgery or the need for postoperative dialysis. All three thresholds were independently associated with a greater than 4-fold increase in the odds of death, with mortality rates of 10 %, 25 % and 39 %, respectively [51].

Therefore, it is crucial to identify potentially modifiable risk factors in order to promote interventions to minimise or prevent renal injury following cardiac surgery.

In a prospective study including more than 600 cardiac surgery patients, Palomba et al. [52] developed and validated a score to address the probability of postoperative kidney injury, AKICS – Acute Kidney Injury following Cardiac Surgery Score (see Tab. 3 and 4). This score not only includes preoperative clinical and laboratory variables, but also several intraoperative and postoperative events.

To reduce the impact of renal injury on cardiovascular surgery, several clinical interventions have been tested with limited or no success. Therefore, the initial approach should focus on the recognition of patients at risk for renal dysfunction. Protocols for optimised haemodynamic support in patients with renal dysfunction, serum creatinine levels greater than 1.2 mg/dl and myocardial dysfunction are needed.

Drug dosage revision, particularly regarding antibiotics, is required for patients with glomerular filtration rates less than 50 ml/min to avoid toxicity and further renal injury.

Glucose control

Mangano et al. identified diabetes as an independent factor for acute renal injury after cardiac surgery [53]. In parallel, Palomba et al. showed that preoperative hyperglycaemia (> 140 mg/dl) was associated with a seven-fold greater incidence of acute kidney injury after cardiac surgery [52]. Van Den Berghe et al. demonstrated that a glucose control protocol reduces the need for dialysis in critically ill patients [54]. However, the benefit of preoperative glucose control to prevent renal dysfunction has not been established.

Anaemia

Preoperative anaemia is a relevant risk factor for renal dysfunction. Karkouri and colleagues have demonstrated that a haemoglobin level lower

Tab. 3   AKICS score
[reproduced from Palomba H, de Castro I, Neto ALC, Lage S and Yu L. Acute kidney injury prediction following electic cardiac surgery: AKICS Score. Kidney International, 2007;72:624–631]
Minimum score = 0; maximum score = 20.
AKICS, acute kidney injury follwing cardiac surgery score; CHF, chronic heart failure; CPB, cardiopulmonary bypass, Cr, serum creatinine; CVP, central venous pressure; NYHA, New York Heart Association; Pre-op, preoperative.

Risk factor	Points
Combined surgery	3.7
CHF NYHA > 2	3.2
Pre-op Cr > 1.2 mg/dl	3.1
Low cardiac output	2.5
Age > 65 years	2.3
CPB time > 120 min	1.8
Pre-op capillary glucose > 140 mg/dl	1.7
CVP > 14 cm H_2O	1.7

Tab. 4   AKI risk according to risk categories
[reproduced from Palomba H, de Castro I, Neto ALC, Lage S and Yu L. Acute kidney injury prediction following electic cardiac surgery: AKICS Score. Kidney International, 2007;72:624–631]
AKI, acute kidney injury.

Risk categories	AKI categories (%)
0–4	1.5
4.1–8	4.3
8.1–12	9.1
12.1–16	21.8
16.1–20	62.5

than 10 g/dl increased by almost three-fold the incidence of moderate renal dysfunction [51]. Anaemia causes a reduction of oxygen delivery to the kidneys, particularly the medullary region, where partial oxygen tensions are normally lower. Moreover, anaemia promotes oxidative stress and reduces platelet function, thereby resulting in bleeding and increased operative time, with a negative impact on renal function. Anaemia correction with iron and erythropoietin are useful preoperative interventions.

N-acetylcysteine

The use of N-acetylcysteine (NAC) to reduce or prevent renal injury after cardiac surgery is controversial. Wijeysundera et at. were not able to show benefits in comparison to controls with the use of NAC before and up to four hours after the completion of CPB in patients with preoperative renal dysfunction [55]. On the other hand, Sisillo et al. showed benefits with NAC in patients undergoing cardiac surgery, probably due to the antioxidant properties of NAC reducing the CPB-induced oxidative stress [56].

Cardiopulmonary bypass or off-pump procedures

Several studies have shown that a CPB duration greater than 120 minutes plays a significant role in acute renal injury. However, the use of CPB remains controversial. Off-pump cardiac surgery is associated with less inflammatory response, lower citokine release and greater haemodynamic stability than regular CPB. However, Schwann et al. did not show renal protection benefits in patients undergoing off-pump cardiac repair [57]. More recently, Paganini et al. followed a cohort of more than 10,000 patients, including 1,300 patients in whom the off-pump technique was employed. The incidence of acute renal injury, defined as a 50 % reduction in previous renal function and the need for dialysis was two times greater after CPB [58].

Another important event in association with acute renal dysfunction is perioperative bleeding and the need for blood products. There is an almost linear relationship between the number of red blood cell units and the probability of acute renal injury [51]. Several studies also demonstrate the deleterious effects on renal function after combined cardiac surgeries. Increased surgical and CPB duration increases the likelihood of renal dysfunction.

Intra-aortic balloon pump

The need to use the intra-aortic balloon pump reflects severe myocardial dysfunction. The increase in serum creatinine levels is usually a consequence of a low flow state due to cardiogenic shock. However, the presence of widespread atherosclerotic vascular disease and hypoperfusion may contribute to acute renal dysfunction by causing muscular ischaemia and rhabdomiolysis. The released myoglobin impairs glomerular filtration and is toxic to the renal tubular cells. Volume expansion and urine alkalinisation may attenuate renal injury and reduce the potential for dialysis.

Contrast media

The use of contrast media is frequently require to define emergency surgical approaches as well as to clarify some postoperative complications. Contrast media may induce nefrotoxicity in cardiac surgery patients, particularly because they frequently present previous renal dysfunction and diabetes mellitus, the main risk factors for contrast-induced nephrotoxicity. The generation of oxygen free radicals has a pivotal role in the physiopathology of contrast-induced renal injury. Oxygen free radical scavengers such as N-acetylcysteine, 1.2 g every 12 hours, for 48 hours before and after the procedure, in addition to sodium bicarbonate with 154 mEq/l of sodium, 3 ml/kg/h as a boluses infusion, one hour before the contrast media injection and 1 ml/kg/h for 6 hours after the exam, reduced nephrotoxicity more efficiently than any measure alone [59]. Another kind of protection can be offered by the use of contrast media with low osmolarity, which can attenuate vasoconstriction and consequent renal injury.

Conclusion

A systematic search for improvement in processes to prevent error as well as spread a safety culture is of paramount importance to avoid harm after cardiac surgery. Additionally, it is crucial to identify potentially modifiable risk factors in order to promote interventions to minimise or prevent multiple organ dysfunction after cardiac surgery.

F

The authors

Luiz Francisco Poli-de-Figueiredo, MD, PhD[1]
Alexandre Biasi Cavalcanti, MD[2]
Américo Lourenço Cuvello Neto, MD[3]
Carlos Eduardo Pompilio, MD[4]

[1]Chairman, Department of Surgery |
University of São Paulo School of Medicine
and Intensive Care Unit | Hospital Alemão
Oswaldo Cruz | São Paulo, Brazil
[2]Intensive Care Unit | Hospital Albert
Einstein | São Paulo, Brazil
[3]Intensive Care Unit | Nephrology Division |
University of São Paulo School of Medicine
and Intensive Care Unit Hospital Alemão
Oswaldo Cruz | São Paulo, Brazil
[4]Intensive Care Unit | Department of
Gastroenterology | University of São Paulo
School of Medicine and Intensive Care
Unit | Hospital Alemao Oswaldo Cruz |
São Paulo, Brazil

Address for correspondence
Luiz Francisco Poli-de-Figueiredo
University of São Paulo School of Medicine
Av. Dr. Arnaldo, 455 suite 4215
São Paulo – SP – ZIP 01246–903, Brazil
E-mail: lpoli@usp.br

References

1. Song HK, Diggs BS, Slater MS, Guyton SW, Ungerlei-
   der RM, Welke KF. Improved quality and cost-effectiveness of coronary artery bypass grafting in the United
   States from 1988 to 2005. J Thorac Cardiovasc Surg
   2009;137:65–69.
2. O'Connor GT, Plume SK, Olmstead EM, Coffin LH, Mor-
   ton JR, Maloney CT, et al. A regional prospective study
   of in-hospital mortality associated with coronary artery bypass grafting. The Northern New England Cardiovascular Disease Study Group. JAMA 1991;266:803–
   809.
3. Hannan EL, Siu AL, Kumar D, Racz M, Pryor DB, Chassin
   MR. Assessment of coronary artery bypass graft surgery
   performance in New York. Is there a bias against taking
   high-risk patients? Med Care 1997;35:49–56.
4. Grover FL, Johnson RR, Marshall G, Hammermeister
   KE. Factors predictive of operative mortality among
   coronary artery bypass subsets. Ann Thorac Surg
   1993;56:1296–1306.
5. Halpin LS, Barnett SD, Henry LL, Choi E, Ad N. Public
   health reporting: the United States perspective. Semin
   Cardiothorac Vasc Anesth 2008;12:191–202.
6. Klein AA, Nashef SA. Perception and reporting of cardiac
   surgical performance. Semin Cardiothorac Vasc Anesth
   2008;12:184–190.
7. Gummert JF, Funkat A, Beckmann A, Schiller W, Hek-
   mat K, Ernst M, et al. Cardiac surgery in Germany during 2007: a report on behalf of the German Society for
   Thoracic and Cardiovascular Surgery. Thorac Cardiovasc
   Surg 2008;56:328–336.
8. Hannan EL, Stone CC, Biddle TL, DeBuono BA. Public
   release of cardiac surgery outcomes data in New York:
   what do New York state cardiologists think of it? Am
   Heart J 1997;134:1120–1128.
9. Schneider EC, Epstein AM. Influence of cardiac-surgery
   performance reports on referral practices and access
   to care. A survey of cardiovascular specialists. N Engl J
   Med 1996;335:251–256.
10. Shahian DM, Yip W, Westcott G, Jacobson J. Selection
    of a cardiac surgery provider in the managed care era.
    J Thorac Cardiovasc Surg 2000;120:978–987.
11. Peterson ED, Delong ER, Jollis JG, Muhlbaier LH, Mark
    DB. The effects of New York's bypass surgery provider
    profiling on access to care and patient outcomes in the
    elderly. J Am Coll Cardiol 1998;32:993–999.
12. Shahian DM, Normand SL, Torchiana DF, Lewis SM, Pas-
    tore JO, Kuntz RE, et al. Cardiac surgery report cards:
    comprehensive review and statistical critique. Ann Tho-
    rac Surg 2001 Dec;72(6):2155–68.
13. Surgical safety checklist. Internet site: http://www.who.
    int/entity/patientsafety/safesurgery/tools_resources/
    SSSL_Checklist_finalJun08.pdf 2009 (1st edition).
14. Haynes AB, Weiser TG, Berry WR, Lipsitz SR, Breizat AH,
    Dellinger EP, et al. A surgical safety checklist to reduce
    morbidity and mortality in a global population. N Engl J
    Med 2009;360:491–499.
15. Myles PS, Daly DJ, Djaiani G, Lee A, Cheng DC. A system-
    atic review of the safety and effectiveness of fast-track
    cardiac anesthesia. Anesthesiology 2003;99:982–987.
16. Hawkes CA, Dhileepan S, Foxcroft D. Early extubation for
    adult cardiac surgical patients. Cochrane Database Syst
    Rev 2003;(4):CD003587.
17. Poli de Figueiredo LF, Cavalcanti AB, Galas F, Hajjar LA.
    Fast track after cardiac surgery. In Controversies in In-
    tensive Care Medicine, Eds. Ruhen R, Moreno R, Ranieri
    M, Rhodes A. Mediizinisch Wissenschaftliche Verlags-
    gesellschaft, Berlin, 2008; p. 433–441.
18. Meade MO, Guyatt G, Butler R, Elms B, Hand L, In-
    gram A, et al. Trials comparing early vs late extuba-
    tion following cardiovascular surgery. Chest 2001;120(6
    Suppl):445S-453S.
19. Constantinides VA, Tekkis PP, Fazil A, Kaur K, Leonard R,
    Platt M, et al. Fast-track failure after cardiac surgery:
    development of a prediction model. Crit Care Med
    2006;34(12):2875–2882.

20. Wan S, LeClerc JL, Vincent JL. Inflammatory response to cardiopulmonary bypass: mechanism involved and possible therapeutic strategies. Chest 1997;112:676–692.

21. Kotani N, Hashimoto H, Sessler DI, Muraoka M, Wang JS, O'Connor MF, Matsuki A. Cardiopulmonary bypass produces greater pulmonary than systemic proinflammatory cytokines. Anesth Analg 2000;90:1039–1045.

22. Ascione R, Lloyd CT, Underwood MJ, Lotto AA, Pitsis AA, Angelini GD. Inflammatory response after coronary revascularization with or without cardiopulmonary bypass. Ann Thorac Surg 2000;69:1198–1204.

23. Paparella D, Yau TM, Young E. Cardiopulmonary bypass induced inflammation: pathophysiology and treatment. Eur J Cardiothorac Surg 2002;21:232–244.

24. Christman JW, Lancaster LH, Blackwell TS. Nuclear factor k B: a pivotal role in the systemic inflammatory response syndrome and new target for therapy. Intensive Care Med 1998;24:1131–1138.

25. Evans J, Haskard DO, Finch JR, Hambleton IR, Landis RC, Taylor KM. The inflammatory effect of cardiopulmonary bypass on leukocyte extravasation in vivo J Thorac Cardiovasc Surg 2008;135:999–1006.

26. Bernard GR, Artigas A, Brigham KL, et al. Report of the American-European consensus conference on ARDS: definitions, mechanisms, relevant outcomes and clinical trial coordination. The Consensus Committee. Intensive Care Med 1994; 20:225–232.

27. Messent M, Sullivan K, Keogn BF, et al. Adult respiratory distress syndrome following cardiopulmonary bypass: Incidence and prediction. Anesthesia 47:267–268, 1992.

28. Fowler AA, Hamman RF, Good JT, et al. Adult respiratory distress syndrome: Risk with common predispositions. Ann Intern Med 1983;98:593–597.

29. Christenson JT, Aeberhard JM, Badel P, et al: Adult respiratory distress syndrome after cardiac surgery. Cardiovasc Surg 1996;4:15–21.

30. Weiss YG, Merin G, Koganov E, et al. Postcardiopulmonary bypass hypoxemia: a prospective study on incidence, risk factors, and clinical significance. J Cardiothorac Vasc Anesth. 2000;14:506–513.

31. Milot J, Perron J, Lacasse Y, et al. Incidence and predictors of ARDS after cardiac surgery. Chest 2001;119:884–888.

32. Fernandez-Perez ER, Sprung J, Afessa B, Warner DO, Vachon CM, Schroeder DR ET al. Intraoperative ventilator settings and acute lung injury after elective surgery: a nested case control study. Thorax 2009;64:121–127.

33. Clark SC. Lung injury after cardiopulmonary bypass. Perfusion 2006; 21: 225_228.

34. Whitlock RP, Chan S, Devereaux PJ, Sun J, Rubens FD, Thorlund K, Teoh KHT. Clinical benefit of steroid use in patients undergoing cardiopulmonary bypass: a meta-analysis of randomized trials. European Heart Journal 2008;29:2592–2600.

35. Liakopoulos OJ, Choi YH, Haldenwang PL, Strauch J, Wit-twer T, Dörge H, et al. Impact of preoperative statin therapy on adverse postoperative outcomes in patients undergoing cardiac surgery: a meta-analysis of over 30 000 patients. European Heart Journal 2008;29:1548–1559.

36. Liu Y, Wang Q, Zhu X, et al. Pulmonary artery perfusion with protective solution reduces lung injury after cardiopulmonary bypass. Ann Thorac Surg 2000;69:1402–1407.

37. Richter JA, Meisner H, Tassani P, et al. Drew-Anderson technique attenuates systemic inflammatory response syndrome and improves respiratory function after coronary artery bypass grafting. Ann Thorac Surg 2000;69:77–83.

38. Ranucci M, Cirri S, Conti D, Ditta A, Boncilli A, Frigiola A, et al. Beneficial effects of Duraflo II heparin-coated circuits on postperfusion lung dysfunction. Ann Thorac Surg 1996;61:76–81.

39. Carvalho EMF, Gabriel EA, Salerno TA. Pulmonary protection during cardiac surgery: Systematic literature review. Asian Cardiovasc Thorac Ann 2008;16:503–507.

40. Loeckinger A, Kleinsasser A, Lindner KH, et al. Continuous positive airway pressure at 10 cm H2O during cardiopulmonary bypass improves postoperative gas exchange. Anesth Analg 2000;91:522–527.

41. Lachmann B. Open up the lung and keep the lung open. Intensive Care Med 1992;18(6):319–321.

42. Borges JB, Okamoto VN, Matos GFJ, et al. Reversibility of lung collapse and hypoxemia in early acute respiratory distress syndrome. Am J Respir Crit Care Med 2006;174:268–278.

43. Stapleton RD. Recruitment maneuvers in acute lung injury: what do the data tell us? Respir Care. 2008;53:1441–1449.

44. Brower RG, Lanken PN, MacIntyre N, et al. Higher versus lower positive end-expiratory pressures in patients with the acute respiratory distress syndrome. N Engl J Med. 2004;351:327–336.

45. Hedenstierna G. When shall the lung be opened up: during or after cardiac surgery? Crit Care Med. 2005 Oct;33(10):2425–6.

46. Miranda DR, Struijs A, Koetsier P, et al: Open lung ventilation improves functional residual capacity after extubation in cardiac surgery. Crit Care Med 2005; 33:2253–2258.

47. Zupancich E, Paparella D, Turani F, Munch C, Rossi A, Massaccesi S, Ranieri VM. Mechanical ventilation affects inflammatory mediators in patients undergoing cardiopulmonary bypass for cardiac surgery: A randomized clinical trial. J Thorac Cardiovasc Surg 2005;130:378–383.

48. Wrigge H, Uhlig U, Zinserling J, et al. The effects of different ventilatory settings on pulmonary and systemic inflammatory responses during major surgery. Anesth Analg. 2004;98:775–781.

49. Lassnigg A, Schmidlin D, Mouhieddine M, Bachmann LM, Druml W, Bauer P, Hiesmayr M. Minimal changes of

serum creatinine predict prognosis in patients aftercardiothoracic surgery: a prospective cohort study.J Am Soc Nephrol. 2004:15:1597–1605.

50. Chertow GM, Lazarus JM, Christiansen CL, Cook EF, Hammermeister KE, Grover F, Daley J. Preoperative renal risk stratification. Circulation. 1997;95:878–884.

51. Karkouti K, Wijeysundera DN, Yau TM, Callum JL, Cheng DC, Crowther M, Dupuis JY, Fremes SE, Kent B, Laflamme C, Lamy A, Legare JF, Mazer CD, McCluskey SA, Rubens FD, Sawchuk C, Beattie WS. Acute kidney injury after cardiac surgery: focus on modifiable risk factors. Circulation. 2009;119:495–502.

52. Palomba H, de Castro I, Neto AL, Lage S, Yu L. Acute kidney injury prediction following elective cardiac surgery: AKICS Score. Kidney Int. 2007;72:624–631.

53. Mangano CM, Diamondstone LS, Ramsay JG, Aggarwal A, Herskowitz A, Mangano DT. Renal dysfunction after myocardial revascularization: risk factors, adverse outcomes, and hospital resource utilization. The Multicenter Study of Perioperative Ischemia Research Group. Ann Intern Med 1998;128:194–203.

54. van den Berghe G, Wouters P, Weekers F, Verwaest C, Bruyninckx F, Schetz M,Vlasselaers D, Ferdinande P, Lauwers P, Bouillon R. Intensive insulin therapy in the critically ill patients.N Engl J Med. 2001;345:1359–1367.

55. Wijeysundera DN, Beattie WS, Rao V, Granton JT, Chan CT. N- acetylcysteine for preventing acute kidney injury in cardiac surgery patients with pre-existing moderate renal insufficiency.Can J Anaesth. 2007;54:872–881.

56. Sisillo E, Ceriani R, Bortone F, Juliano G, Salvi L, Veglia F, Fiorentini C, Marenzi G. N-acetylcysteine for prevention of acute renal failure in patients with chronic renal insufficiency undergoing cardiac surgery: a prospective, randomized, clinical trial. Crit Care Med 2008;36:81–86.

57. Schwann NM, Horrow JC, Strong MD 3rd, Chamchad D, Guerraty A, Wechsler AS. Does off-pump coronary artery bypass reduce the incidence of clinically evident renal dysfunction after multivessel myocardial revascularization? Anesth Analg. 2004;99:959–964.

58. Hix JK, Thakar CV, Katz EM, Yared JP, Sabik J, Paganini EP. Effect of off-pump coronary artery bypass graft surgery on postoperative acute kidney injury and mortality. Crit Care Med. 2006;34:2979–2983.

59. Briguori C, Airoldi F, D'Andrea D, Bonizzoni E, Morici N, Focaccio A, Michev I, Montorfano M, Carlino M, Cosgrave J, Ricciardelli B, Colombo A. Renal Insufficiency Following Contrast Media Administration Trial (REMEDIAL): a randomized comparison of 3 preventive strategies. Circulation. 2007;13;115:1211–1217.

Antonio Marques

Avoiding harm during intra- and inter-hospital transport

Introduction

Transport of the critically ill can be a challenging prospect, requiring skill and expertise beyond what most people (including health professionals) often recognise. Standard of care should, at a minimum, be of equal level as that provided at the point of origin. If inter-hospital transport is more easily valued (considering the time, terrain and easily identifiable risks), intra-hospital transport is often neglected in importance, and set aside as a chore for the younger and less trained professionals.

Realising that this can no longer be acceptable many intensive care specialists have come to recognise the importance of high-quality transport. This requires more than just adequately trained professionals and mandates great planning capability and logistical support.

Inevitably, various critical and emergency medicine organisations elaborated recommendations and standards to help define minimum requirements and help overcome and ease the logistical nightmare transport can sometimes be.

As more highly trained personnel became involved, various national scientific societies defined and adopted recommendations for good standard of care during transport.

Indeed, transport raises risks. Good planning and careful execution of the transport plan is a real risk management exercise.

What the present chapter aims to do is transmit basic thoughts, strategies and recommendations outlined in various more lengthy papers and reports, easing reader comprehension. Some references are made to landmark or especially interesting documents that have helped define the nature of good practice. Hence the main objective is to provide a planning tool, and not a lengthy review of the literature. Risk management implies simplicity and clarity. The objective is to contribute to a simple, hands-on practical approach for good clinical practice understanding and implementation.

Historical facts and current proposals

There are many recommendations available, both old and new. However, some are particularly important due to their timeliness and landmark statements. There are various visionary documents, striking in their forwardness and practicality.

The American College of Critical Medicine, the Society of Critical Care Medicine and the American Association of Critical Care Nurses were particularly proactive when, in 1992, they published the "Guidelines for the Transfer of the Critically Ill Patient" [2]. That same year, Critical Care Clinics dedicated a publication [3] to the comprehensive review of the "Transport of the Critically Ill". Others followed, most notably the British Intensive Care Society, in 1997 and 2002 with its "Guidelines for the Transport of the Critically Ill Adult" [4]. More recently, the American Critical Care Society updated its recommendations in 2004: "Guidelines for the inter- and intrahospital transport of critically ill patients" [5]. Others, trying to adapt to local realities (sometimes characterised by very severe and special conditions), also published specific policies, as for example the "Alaskan Trauma Triage, Transport & Transfer Guidelines" in 2002 [6]. Not all guidelines are general in nature as some have recommended specific policies for subsets of patients. For example, in 1999, on behalf of the Working Group on Neurosurgical Intensive Care of the European Society of Intensive Care: "Recommendations for intrahospital transport of the severely head injured patient" [7]. In 1997 [8], and more recently in 2008 [1], in conjunction with the Medical Order, the Portuguese Intensive Care Society took on the problem of systematising nationwide norms for good clinical practice in both intra and interhospital transport. These include air transport, clinical documentation, severity scores specific for transport (based on point-based evaluation tools: Etxebarria et al. [9]), decision trees and checklists for ease of decision and increased safety and prerequisite verification.

The present document draws much from these previous initiatives and tries to provide a summary of the basic risk management techniques employed by the different authors. Essential prerequisites for the implementation of the proposals mentioned herein are the recognition of the ethical responsibility caregivers have in this area of medicine, the importance of training as a tool for competency acquisition and the relevance of auditing and continuous project accompaniment. These will require strong organisational effort and determination, be it on the national, regional or local level.

Follow-up is essential for learning from experience, knowledge gathering and an honest appraisal of guideline implementation. Therefore, for successful application of the mentioned recommendations it is imperative that each institution define, clarify and implement an objective policy on critical care patient transport, including issues such as clinical and legal responsibility, medical team organisation (with specific training and regular experience), continuous education (in emergency care and specific areas such as flight physiology), incident reporting policies and regular auditing of the process and outcomes.

General principles

A critical care patient is defined as one whose survivability, either due to dysfunction or collapse of organ or system function, is dependent on advanced means of monitoring and treatment.

Transport of these patients involves considerable risk, but may be required between hospitals and/or different services within the same institution (such as for examinations or therapeutic manoeuvres not available or feasible in the present patient setting).

It is crucial to reflect upon the risk/benefit ratio that an additional exam or procedure can mean and how it will possibly influence outcome. If there is doubt as to the potential benefit, it is worth rethinking before setting out on a risky endeavour. Economical constraints should not put the patient in jeopardy or impede transport according to recognised safety standards.

Safe transport involves the following phases:
- Decision
- Planning
- Effective action

Decision

The decision whether or not to transport is a medical decision (medical act). As such, medical responsibility and liability involves not only the physician treating the patient, but also team leaders and service directors who have to devise and assume official policies (which should not be left to individual doctors or nurses to decide on an impromptu basis).

The various potential risks should be evaluated, such as hypoxia, hyper-/hypocarbia, haemodynamic instability, intracranial hypertension, and risk of secondary lesion to the spinal medulla, detecting situations where the apparent potential benefit does outweigh possible benefits and can cause clinical harm.

Planning

Planning implies a series of actions undertaken by the multi-professional team that will transport the patient dealing with: coordination, communication, stabilisation, team effort, equipment, the actual transport phase and the documentation of the whole process.

Planning should include: choice of referral destination, distance evaluation, travel time and possible aggravating factors (such as weather or relative patient risk). It should also imply careful transport team selection, in accordance with personnel availability and patient characteristics, not forgetting individual protection (insurance coverage in case of accident). Issues such as means of transport, level and complexity of monitoring, objectives for physiologic variables during transport (to maintain or avoid), ancillary equipment and treatment supplies (needed or potentially needed), as well as the provision of communication equipment, should also be dealt with.

Special attention should be paid to particularly high-risk moments: the first 5 minutes of transport, during handover of the patient and in prolonged transport situations (over 30 minutes). It is especially important to beware of accidental endotracheal extubation, loss of intravenous or arterial lines, inadequate oxygen reserve, mechanical ventilator malfunction, fallout or inadvertent clamping of thoracic drains and/or equipment battery failure – electrical power loss.

Effective action

The clinical level of care should not differ from that of the place of origin, with the possibility of actually elevating it in case of need. Transport responsibility only ceases on handover at destination (or on arrival at the base institution when the transport is undertaken only for doing an exam or procedure).

Ethical issues

The medical team, but first and foremost its leader, the head physician who accompanies the patient in whatever circumstances (primary/prehospital, secondary/inter-hospital or intra-hospital transport), is responsible for the level of care until handover. The respective institutions are responsible for the organisation of the necessary means for effective transport in accordance with recognised guidelines and official policies.

It is important that communication between the referring and accepting teams is previously established and maintenance of the desired level of care (at a minimum, identical to that at the referral facility) guaranteed.

Moreover, it is imperative that the indication for transport, just as the determination of the needed resources according to patient requirements, are regarded as medical decisions. As such, the relevant medical responsibility should be clearly assumed.

Education

Technical qualification, which is intimately related to training and clinical experience, constitutes one of the most important aspects in promoting and guaranteeing patient safety during transport.

For all, even for those professionals who regularly treat critical patients, it is important to invest in specific training. Beyond the expected basic competencies (i.e. advanced life support and trauma life support), it is important to consider issues such as the physiological effects of motion and vibration, air transport and, above all, safety.

Quality control

As in any serious clinical procedure, it is important to not only define recommendations as it is to develop and maintain a set of working orders that promote adequate data registration and regular audits.

Data registration

Clinical and legal responsibilities mandate thorough record-keeping. Audit programmes also rely on adequate data registration. All registration forms used during transport should include the following:
- Patient ID
- Referring physician/service/facility ID

- Receiving physician/service/facility ID
- Transfer medical team ID
- Time log
- Problems and diagnosis
- Summary of history of present illness and relevant past medical history
- Clinical status: airway, ventilation, circulation, neurological function, trauma/lesions, other
- Exam results
- Surgical interventions and results at referring facility
- Medical interventions and results at referring facility
- Procedures, medication, clinical stability and complications during transport

The development and implementation of algorithms and checklists can be very important to promote standardisation and good practice. Specifically, solutions based on status identification and predefined point scoring systems according to findings can objectively and rapidly help determine logistic need in relation to professional expertise, equipment and mode of transport.

Audit, comparing verified cases against reference norms, can and should be done at the service, institution and regional level (by major hospital area of influence). Clinical leadership is fundamental so as to guarantee credible good practice evaluation.

Intra-hospital transport

Critical care patients are frequently transported between emergency rooms, radiology services, operating theatres, postoperative recovery units and intensive care services.

Frequently, transport is done at the most vulnerable and dangerous moments. As these episodes may represent significant risk for secondary insults, it is imperative that staffing (in number and competency) and logistics be assured according to real clinical need.

Coordination

- Previous confirmation that the destination area is ready to receive the patient and, in case

of an exam, prepared to immediately initiate the relevant study.
- The chain of responsibility should be maintained during handoff between relevant physician and nursing teams.
- Information relevant to the patient's condition, instituted treatments and results should be duly recorded and communicated.
- Safety issues should always be respected, including cases of specific need relevant to infectious disease risk.

Professionals who accompany the patient

- The determination of the team composition should (ideally) be done according to previously defined good practice norms.
- Ideally, one of the accompanying professionals should be the nurse responsible for the patient.
- Both physician and nurse should accompany the patient who is (or is at risk of being) unstable or might need urgent intervention.
- When responsibility for the patient is not handed over to the destination service then the transport team should stay and accompany the patient throughout all procedures.

Equipment that accompanies the patient

- Portable vital signs monitor, with capabilities according to clinical necessity.
- Equipment for endotracheal intubation and ventilation.
- Oxygen source sufficient for the estimated trip time, plus an additional 30 minutes.
- Portable mechanical ventilator with monitoring capability of the minute volume and airway peak pressure, plus adjustable FiO_2 and positive end-expiratory pressure. Safety features should include peak airway pressure and disconnection alarms.
- Medication for sedation, haemodynamic compromise and resuscitation.
- Volume and drug infusion equipment, with adequate battery capacity.
- Hospitals should maintain transport equipment organised in predefined sacks/containers, ready for use at any time.

- Additionally, at any time during transport, airway suction and rapid access (under four minutes) to an emergency trolley is mandatory.

Monitoring during transport

- Level 1 – Mandatory
- Level 2 – Strongly recommended
- Level 3 – Ideal

Level 1 – Mandatory
- *Continuous vital sign monitoring with periodical registration*
- *Respiratory frequency*
- *FiO_2*
- *Pulse oximetry*
- *ECG*
- *Heart rate*
- *Arterial blood pressure (non-invasive)*
- *Airway pressure (in mechanically ventilated patients)*

- *Capnography (in mechanically ventilated patients). Service re-equipment plans should include acquisition of end-tidal CO_2 modules.*

Level 2 – Strongly recommended
- *Continuous measurement of invasive blood pressure (in potentially unstable patients)*
- *ECG with arrhythmia detection capability*

Level 3 – Ideal
(in selected patients according to clinical status)
- *Central venous pressure*
- *Pulmonary arterial pressure*
- *Intra-cranial pressure*

Evaluation for intra-hospital transport

A possible solution is the adoption of a point-based assessment tool such as that proposed by the Portuguese Intensive Care Society [1], a concept adapted from that described by Etxebarria et al. [9] (see Tab. 1).

Tab. 1   Evaluation for intra-hospital transport [adapted from Portuguese Intensive Care Society and Etxebarria et al. Prospective application of risk scores in the interhospital transport of patients. European Journal of Emergency Medicine 1998;5:1:13–18]

	0 Points	1 Point	2 Points
Artificial airway	No	Yes (with Guedel tube)	Yes (if intubated or recent tracheostomy)
Respiratory rate	10–14 (adult)	15–35 (adult)	Apneia or RR < 10 or RR > 35 or irregular
Respiratory support	No	Yes (with oxygen)	Yes (with mechanical ventilation)
Venous access	No	Peripheral access	Central venous access in unstable patient
Haemodynamic evaluation	Stable	Moderately stable (requiring volume < 15 ml/min)	Unstable (inotropic drug or blood products)
ECG monitoring	No	Yes (desirable)	Yes (in unstable patient)
Arrhythmia risk	No	Yes, low risk – no immediate risk/without necessity of immediate intervention (acute myocardial infarction over 48 hours)	Yes, high risk – immediate risk to life/with necessity of immediate intervention (acute myocardial infarction under 48 hours)
Pacemaker	No	Yes, definitive	Yes, temporary (external or endocavity)
Conscious level Glasgow Coma Scale	15	> 8 < or = 14	< or = 8
Technical/pharmacological support	None	Group I	Group II

	0 Points	1 Point	2 Points
Technical/ pharmacological support	None of the indicated drugs	Group I Naloxone, corticoides, mannitol, analgesic drugs	Group II Inotropic drugs, vasodilators, anti-arrhythmics, bicarbonate, thrombolitics, anti-convulsive drugs, general anaesthetics, thoracic drain with aspiration

Points	Level	Team	Monitoring	Equipment
0–2 (with only O_2 and IV line)	A	Auxiliary	None	None
3–6 (without any item worth 2 points)	B	Nurse	SpO_2, EKG, HR, non-invasive BP	Manual bag-mask ventilator + mask + Guedel tube
= or > 7 or < 7 if any item worth 2 points	C	Physician + nurse	SpO_2, EKG, HR, BP and capnography (if indicated)	Portable vital signs monitor, portable mechanical ventilator, advanced airway equipment plus rapid access to suction and emergency trolley

Inter-hospital (secondary) transport

The main indication for secondary transport of the critically ill patient is the inexistence of resources (human or other) in the referring institution to treat or give continuity to relevant treatment. Similarly, transport may be indicated because of specific exam or technique need not available in the hospital of origin.

Hence, the decision to transport implies an evaluation of the benefit/risk equation. Risk evaluation should include: factors that might affect cardio-respiratory stability, mechanical effects (vibration, acceleration/deceleration forces), temperature variations and transport mode availability and conditions (where weather will play a major role).

Proactive risk management mandates that all foreseeable techniques be applied before transport initiation (such as venous line access, endotracheal intubation, thoracic drainage, etc.). Pre-transfer stabilisation is very important [10, 11].

Also relevant is the need to inform the patient or his/her legal representative for consent, informing of the need for transport and destination.

The transport phase should be considered an extension of the care administered by the referring hospital, with legal and clinical responsibilities assumed by the same for the decision and planning issues. The team that effectively accompanies the patient is responsible for the operational phase.

The transfer process may represent one of the most vulnerable stages of patient management, where various factors, including hospital of origin and transfer duration, can have an impact on outcome [12].

Hospitals may not have the ideal resources for patient transport and may rely on third party teams for that purpose. Whatever the solution, the level of care (mainly determined by the level of expertise of the accompanying team) should not be downgraded in relation to the previous level guaranteed at the referring facility. The existence of specialised transfer teams may contribute to mortality reduction in critically ill trauma patients [13].

Transport coordination

- Initial (direct) contact between sending and receiving teams is mandatory, including registration of the name of the intervening parties.
- The receiving facility should confirm adequate capability to maintain/improve the level of care administered.
- Information should include a detailed report on clinical status, current treatment and response, as well as the estimated time of arrival.

- All relevant patient notes and exams should be furnished, including data on special considerations/risks.
- All relevant data registries should be maintained during transport and handed off to the receiving team.
- The choice of transport mode should consider the following: clinical situation (relative emergency), relevant medical interventions during transport, availability of resources, distance/duration of transport, with relevant consideration of weather conditions, transit flow, geographical difficulties and possible landing sites (if air transport is considered).
- Bidirectional means of communication should be constantly maintained.

Professionals who accompany the patient

- The team that accompanies the patient should include the routine members of the type of ambulance crew in question plus a physician and nurse (according to a previously assumed policy), both with experience in resuscitation and transport equipment use.

Equipment that accompanies the patient

- Portable vital signs monitor, with capabilities according to clinical necessity
- Defibrillator with external pacing capability
- Equipment for endotracheal intubation and ventilation
- Airway suction equipment
- Oxygen source sufficient for the estimated trip time, plus an added 50 % equivalent of the transport time
- Portable mechanical ventilator with monitoring capability of minute volume and airway peak pressure, with adjustable FiO_2 and positive end-expiratory pressure. Safety features should include peak airway pressure and disconnection alarms.
- Thoracic drain equipment
- Intravenous volume expanders, with relevant equipment for venous access and infusion
- Volume and drug infusion equipment, with adequate battery capacity

- Medication for sedation, analgesia, respiratory difficulty, haemodynamic compromise, convulsion treatment and resuscitation: adenosine, adrenaline, amiodarone, atropine, calcium, captopril, diazepam, dinitrate isosorbide, dobutamine, dopamine, etomidate, flumazenil, furosemide, heparin, hypertonic glucose, insulin, isoprenaline, labetalol, lidocaine, magnesium, manitol, methylprednisolone, midazolam, morphine, naloxone, nitroglicerine, noradrenaline, paracetamol, phenobarbital, propofol, salbutamol, sodium bicarbonate, suxametonium, thiopental, vecuronium, verapamil may be considered.

Monitoring during transport

- Level 1 – Mandatory
- Level 2 – Strongly recommended
- Level 3 – Ideal

Level 1 – Mandatory
- *Continuous vital sign monitoring with periodical registration*
- *Respiratory frequency*
- *FiO_2*
- *Pulse oximetry*
- *ECG*
- *Heart rate*
- *Arterial blood pressure (non-invasive)*
- *Airway pressure (in mechanically ventilated patients)*
- *Capnography (in mechanically ventilated patients). Service re-equipment plans should include acquisition of end-tidal CO_2 modules.*

Level 2 – Strongly recommended
- *Continuous measurement of invasive blood pressure (in potentially unstable patients)*
- *ECG with arrhythmia detection capability*

Level 3 – Ideal (in selected patients according to clinical status)
- *Central venous pressure*
- *Pulmonary arterial pressure*
- *Intra-cranial pressure*
- *Temperature*

Tab. 2 Evaluation for intra-hospital transport [adapted from Portuguese Intensive Care Society and Etxebarria et al. Prospective application of risk scores in the interhospital transport of patients. European Journal of Emergency Medicine 1998:5:1:13–18]

	0 Points	1 Point	2 Points
Artificial airway	No	Yes (with Guedel tube)	Yes (if intubated or recent tracheostomy)
Respiratory rate	10–14 (adult)	15–35 (adult)	Apneia or RR < 10 or RR > 35 or irregular
Respiratory support	No	Yes (with oxygen)	Yes (with mechanical ventilation)
Venous access	No	Peripheral access	Central access in unstable patient
Haemodynamic evaluation	Stable	Moderately stable (requiring volume < 15 ml/min)	Unstable (inotropic drugs or blood products)
ECG monitoring	No	Yes (desirable)	Yes (in unstable patient)
Arrhythmia risk	No	Yes, low risk – no immediate risk/ without necessity of immediate intervention (acute myocardial infarct over 48 hours)	Yes, high risk – immediate risk to life/with necessity of immediate intervention (acute myocardial infarction under 48 hours)
Pacemaker	No	Yes, definitive	Yes, temporary (external or endocavity)
Conscious level Glasgow Coma Scale	15	> 8 < or = 14	< or = 8
Support	None	Group I	Group II

	0 Points	1 Point	2 Points
Technical / pharmacological support	None of the indicated drugs	Group I Naloxone, corticoides, mannitol, analgesic drugs	Group II Inotropic drugs, vasodilators, anti-arrhythmics, bicarbonate, thrombolitics, anti-convulsive drugs, general anaesthetics, thoracic drain with aspiration

Points	Level	Vehicle	Team	Monitoring	Equipment
0–2 (with only O$_2$ and IV line)	A	Normal ambulance	Ambulance attendants	None beyond basic clinical	Standard EMS ambulance
3–6 (without any item worth 2 points)	B	Normal ambulance	Nurse	SpO$_2$, EKG, HR, non-invasive BP	Above stated plus vital signs monitor and IV drugs/volume expanders
= or > 7 or < 7 if any item worth 2 points	C	Land or Air Ambulance with medical team	Physician and Nurse	SpO$_2$, ECG, HR, BP and capnography (if indicated)	Above stated plus portable ventilator, advanced airway equipment, defibrillator/ pace, infusion pumps

Evaluation for inter-hospital transport

A possible solution is the adoption of a point-based assessment tool such as that proposed by the Portuguese Intensive Care Society [1], a concept adapted from that described by Etxebarria et al. [9] (see Tab. 2).

Air transport

Air transport can represent an efficient means to quickly transport a patient to the most adequate hospital site. Not only should the air ambulance itself be considered but also the health professional crew and their specific training for this type of transport (most often helitransport). The addition of a physician to the helicopter rescue team can reduce mortality in trauma patients [14].

Indications

- Estimated ground transport time over one hour
- Long transport distance, with helicopter use most efficient up to a 220 km radius [15]
- Provision of specialised medical team, even if within a short transport distance [16]
- Remote or inaccessible (by other means) locations

Contraindications

- Bad weather
- Unsafe landing conditions
- Violent/psychiatric patients
- Intraocular procedures with gas
- Intestinal occlusion
- Pneumothorax
- Diving accidents
- Pregnancy, in labour

Relative contraindications – Situations to ponder risks

- Trauma with possible air-filled cavities, most frequently head and/or chest (air spaces should be drained prior to transport as possible and flight should be kept at low altitudes).

Landing site safety precautions

- Clear zone with minimum diameter of 30–50 metres
- Ground inclination not greater than 10%
- Two-way road traffic blockade
- Stable ground (no sand or loose gravel)
- No posts, cables or wires in the vicinity
- No loose items on crew, medical team or patient
- Security perimeter to impair approach by unauthorised personnel
- Prohibition of any rear approach to the helicopter

Clinical considerations in patient preparation for flight

- Endotracheal tube cuff insufflation with saline (not air)
- If possible, patient stabilisation prior to transport (while awaiting arrival of aircraft)
- Secure airway and venous access
- Immobilise the patient

Specific problems during air transport
(for which medical teams should have training)

- Atmospheric pressure reduction with correspondent oxygen alveolar partial pressure and oxygen arterial saturation, with higher FiO_2 need to maintain oxygenation
- Gaseous space expansion (pneumoencephalus, pneumothorax, pneumoperitoneum, endotracheal tube cuff), with drainage need of closed gas spaces before transport (such as in the case of pneumothorax) or need to fly at low altitudes (such as in the case of pneumoencephalus)
- Need to leave all drains and catheters draining freely (no drain clamping)
- Haemorrhage increase, with bleeding control, possibly needing rapid infusion of volume expanders and amine perfusions
- Slowing down of intravenous infusions, with need of rapid infusion devices
- Oedema increase, with possible need to open fracture splints
- Hypothermia risk, with need to warm patient and IV fluids

- Nausea and vomit risk (with possible indication for pre-transport administration of prophylactic medication)
- Noise that hampers communication (equipment need for bi-directional communication between medical team members, and between medical team and the flight crew)
- Provision of visual alarms on monitors (not just sound alarms)
- Crew notification before cardiac defibrillation

How to avoid complications

All too frequently complications are due to insufficient resource allocation or lack of transport team experience. It is imperative that patient transport be viewed as an important stage in patient management and that health institutions implement the adequate norms and procedure policies.

It is not acceptable to have patient deterioration that is not due to the underlying clinical situation itself, but may be related to improper transport.

On the other hand, team and patient safety are paramount before any decisions are made.

The following issues should be valued to avoid complications:

- In each institution, a set policy for critical care patient transport should be defined, publicised and implemented. Identification of responsibilities is crucial
- Team structure (type and composition) should be defined according to clinical need, in accordance with a previously defined policy
- Team training in specific transport-related issues
- Organisation and maintenance of standardised transport equipment
- Checklist use for procedure, personnel and equipment review before call-out go-ahead
- Adequate patient stabilisation before transport [10, 11]
- Adequate patient preparation before air transport [17]
- Adequate care and fixation of all lines and tubes: endotracheal tube, venous and arterial lines, drains and catheters, especially during handoffs and patient movement between transport modalities or referral facility/transport vehicle/destination site transfers

- Immobilisation maintenance (of patient body and of patient relative to gurney/vehicle)
- Avoidance congested traffic routes
- Always plan for the unexpected (for example, keeping an extra supply of oxygen available)

Most frequent errors during the transport process

- Inadequate initial patient evaluation before transport (with incorrect summation of problems and inadequate patient preparation)
- Transport of haemodynamically unstable patients (surgical assessment and intervention may be necessary before transfer)
- Patient with airway at risk, not properly secured before transport (patients with airway/respiratory difficulty should be sedated and mechanically ventilated before transport)
- Failure to exclude pneumothorax after invasive interventions (central venous line placement)
- Failure to proceed with indicated drainage of gas/fluid-filled cavities before transport
- Inadequate venous line number, location, size and securing measures
- Inadequate vital sign monitoring
- Insufficient alarm provision/configuration of monitoring equipment
- Insufficient stock of IV fluids and of rapid infusion devices
- Incomplete list of medication

Secondary transport checklist

In order to facilitate routine case evaluation according to a standardised format, it may be helpful to use a pre-transport checklist – Portuguese Society of Intensive Care [1] (see Tab. 3). The use of such solutions can help to avoid frequent lapses and errors.

Conclusions

Preoccupation with good practice during transport of critically ill patients has long been evident, as documented in various guidelines and recommendations.

However, clinical practice often demonstrates disregard for best practices. Beyond simple norms and rec-

Tab. 3 Secondary transport checklist [adapted from Rua F, Sousa J, Freitas P, Marques A. Transporte de Doentes Criticos – Recomendações 2008. Portuguese Society of Intensive Care and Portuguese Medical Order 2008]

I	Transfer confirmation
	Patient identification registered
	Family/legal representative informed of transport and destination
	Direct hospital telephone number and ID of receiving physician
	Direct hospital telephone number and ID of referring physician
	Registration of transport medical team ID
II	**Patient evaluation**
	Cause and date of hospital admission
	Clinical history
	Previous medical history
	Reason for transfer
	Transfer notes
	Verification of relevant exams
	Evaluation of patient status according to previously defined reference, i.e. point scale to determine transfer logistics need
III	**Patient observation**
A	**Airway**
	Airway maintenance capacity during estimated time of travel
	Airway adjunct necessity
	Endotracheal intubation
	Exclude situations that suggest endotracheal intubation need
B	**Ventilation**
	Supplemental oxygen need
	Nasal prongs at _____ l/min
	Mask at FiO_2 _____ %
	Endotracheal intubation at _____ cm
	Artificial ventilation
	Ventilatory mode _____ Minute volume ___ RR ___ FiO_2 _____ PEEP ___
	Blood gas (___h ___ min) pH ___ paO_2 ___ $paCO_2$ ___ HCO_3 ___ FiO_2 ___
C	**Circulatory / haemodynamic stability**
	HR ___ BP ___ / ____ Non-invasive _____ Invasive _____
	Active haemorrhage within the last hour
	Transfusion support
	Vascular access: 2 peripheral IV lines ____G ____G, Central catheter _____, Arterial line _____

Urinary output _____ / last hour

Vasoactive amines: Dopamine _____ Dobutamine _____ Noradrenaline _____

D — Neurological evaluation

Convulsion within the last hour

Glasgow Coma Scale E ____ V ____ M ____

Signs of intra-cranial hypertension

Abnormal pupils _____

Sedation: Drug _____ RAMSAY _____

Psychomotor agitation

E — Trauma

Cervical spine immobilisation

Exclusion of pneumothorax or haemothorax

Exclusion of abdominal/pelvic haemorrhage

Long bone/pelvic immobilisation

F — Laboratorial evaluation (date _____ hour _____)

Hgb / HCT _____ / _____

Na+ _____

K+ _____

Glicemia _____

G — Monitoring at referral facility (last values before transport)

ECG

BP ____ / ____

SaO$_2$ _____

ET CO$_2$ _____ (if mechanically ventilated)

Temperature _____ site _____

Other: _____

H — Transport equipment verification (before patient transfer)

Oxygen reserve (necessary for trip + 50% reserve)

Vital signs monitor/defibrillator with external pace

Airway equipment

Medication (according to standard list)

IV — Before transfer

Confirmation of vacancy in receiving hospital, before leaving referring facility

Safe transfer to transport gurney/trolley

Change of mechanical ventilator

Change of IV perfusions

	Change of monitoring equipment
	Redundant fixation of tubes and lines
	Adequate patient and equipment fixation
	Cover patient (respect privacy and dignity)
	Knowledge of available (and location of) emergency equipment
	Data registration sheet on hand
V	**In the ambulance**
	Gurney/trolley fixation
	Equipment fixation and connection
	Patient observation at all times
	Final verification of equipment
	Registration of relevant data
VI	**During the trip**
	Registration of relevant vital sign/parameter data
	Registration of treatments/interventions and responses
	Registration of transport beginning and end time
VII	**Handoff at receiving hospital**
	History of present illness and previous medical history
	Reason for transfer
	Vital signs/parameters at arrival and treatments/interventions during transport
	Complications during transport
	Transmission of exam and administrative data
	Registration of handoff time and ID of physician responsible at receiving unit
VIII	**Return to referring hospital**
	Inform hospital of origin of transfer procedure completion
	Register time of arrival back at referring hospital
	Return equipment to normal storage site and report any abnormality
	Archive data log in proper place

ommendations, it is important to propose and implement tools that can help day-to-day practice in defining patient need, transfer team composition, vehicle and mode of transport and necessary equipment, in a standardised way.

There is clearly a need to honestly analyse and improve critical care patient transport (in a "no blame, no shame" environment). It is legitimate to promote an audit trail of the transfer process and, if the above mentioned tools (point scales and checklists) exist, it will be much easier to identify the reference points for comparison of actions done versus what should have been done.

We hope that the current recommendations, proposals and strategies can be of help in further structuring care during this most vulnerable phase of patient management.

The author

Antonio Marques, MD
   Director of Anaesthesiology, Intensive Care
   and Emergency Medicine
   Hospital de Santo Antonio –
   Centro Hospitalar do Porto
   Largo Prof Abel Salazar
   4099 – 001 Porto, Portugal
   E-mail: amarques.admn@hgsa.min-saude.pt

References

1. Rua F, Sousa J, Freitas, P, Marques A. Transporte de Doentes Criticos – Recomendações 2008. Portuguese Society of Intensive Care and Portuguese Medical Order 2008.
2. Guidelines practice/parameters committee of the American College of Critical Medicine. Guidelines for the Transfer of the Critically Ill Patient. American College of Critical Medicine, the Society of Critical Care Medicine and the American Association of Critical Care Nurses 1992. Critical Care Medicine 1993:21:6:931–937.
3. Carlson R, Geheb M (Consulting editors), Hageman J, Fetcho S (Guest editors) and Contributors. Transport of the Critically Ill. Critical Care Clinics July 1992:8:3:465–660.
4. Whiteley S, Gray A, McHugh P, O´Riordan B. Guidelines for the Transport of the Critically Ill Adult. Intensive Care Society 2002.
5. Warren J, Fromm R, Orr Richard, Rotello L, Horst H. American College of Critical Medicine. Guidelines for the inter and intrahospital transport of critically ill patients. Critical Care Medicine 2004:32:1:256–262.
6. Ingraham D (editor). Community Health and Emergency Medical Services – Alaska. Trauma Triage, Transport & Transfer Guidelines 2002.
7. Working Group on Neurosurgical Intensive Care of the European Society of Intensive Care. Recommendations for intrahospital transport of the severely head injured patient. Intensive Care Medicine 1999:25:1441–1443.
8. Sá J et al. Guia para o Transporte de Doente Críticos. Portuguese Society of Intensive Care 1997.
9. Etxebarria et al. Prospective application of risk scores in the interhospital transport of patients. European Journal of Emergency Medicine 1998:5:1:13–18.
10. Olson C, Jastremski M, Vilogi P et al. Stabilisation of patients prior to interhospital transport. American Journal of Emergency Medicine 1987:5:33–39.
11. Harrahil M, Bartkus E. Preparing the trauma patient for transfer. Journal of Emergency Nursing 1990:16:25–28.
12. Ridley S, Carter R. The effects of secondary transport on critically ill patients. Anaesthesia 1989:44:822–827.
13. McGinn G, MacKenzie R, Donnelly J, Smith E, Runcie C. Interhospital transfer of the critically ill trauma patient: the potential role of a specialist transport team in a trauma system. Journal of Accident and Emergency Medicine 1996:13:90–92.
14. Garner A, Rashford S, Lee A, Bartolacci R. Addition of physicians to paramedic helicopter services decrease blunt trauma mortality. Australia New Zealand Journal of Surgery 1999:69:697–701.
15. Schneider C, Gomez M, Lee R. Evaluation of Ground ambulance, rotor wing, and fixed wing aircraft services. Transport of the Critically Ill. Critical Care Clinics 1992:8:3:533–563.
16. Black J, Ward M, Lockey D. Appropriate use of helicopters to transport patients from incident scene to hospital in the United Kingdom: an algorithm. Emergency Medicine Journal 2004:21:355–361.
17. Anderson C. Preparing patients for aeromedical transport. Journal of Emergency Nursing 1987:13:229–231.

George Ntoumenopoulos

How do you safely mobilise your intubated and ventilated patient?

The prolongation of intubation and mechanical ventilation may be associated with complications such as ventilator-associated pneumonia, secretion retention, muscle weakness and reduced health-related quality of life. The mobilisation of the intubated and mechanically ventilated patient has been advocated as a means of reducing the complications of immobility and reducing time on mechanical ventilation and time in the critical care unit. Mobilisation may include a spectrum of activities from passive range of motion exercises for the limbs to sitting out of bed and ambulation. Mobilisation of the acutely ill, orally intubated and ventilated patient to sitting out of bed and ambulation is safe and feasible when appropriate criteria are fulfilled. Ambulation of the chronically critically ill tracheostomised patient is also safe, may improve functional outcomes and may be more realistically achieved. Randomised controlled trials are required to determine the safety and efficacy of mobilisation activities to achieve improvements in functional outcomes, time to wean from ventilation and time in the critical care unit and hospital. In addition, investigations of the effects of mobilisation activities on cardiopulmonary function, metabolic cost and inflammatory response will help clinicians to optimise appropriate strategies and the timing of commencement of intervention during the critical care stay.

Critical care, prolonged immobilisation and ventilation

Common complications resulting from critical care include deconditioning, muscle weakness, dyspnoea, depression and anxiety, and impaired health-related quality of life [1, 2]. Approximately 5–10 % of patients become chronically critically ill and require long-term mechanical ventilation [3]. Prolonged mechanical ventilation has been defined as the need for more than 21 days of mechanical ventilation [4]. Patients ventilated longer than 21 days are the most resource-critical recipients of critical care and they suffer from a significant burden of costly chronic critical illness and are at a greater risk of death in the first year after discharge from critical care [2]. Ambulation of the intubated and ventilated patient is not a new concept, it was promoted in the 1970s to reduce time to wean from ventilation and the negative sequelae of immobilisation [5] (see Fig. 1).

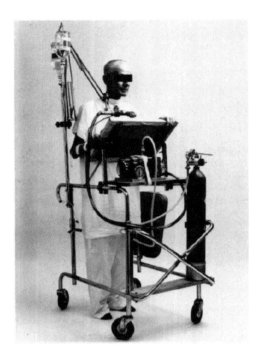

Fig. 1   Ambulation with ventilatory assistance in 1975
[reproduced with permission of American College
of Chest Physicians, from Early ambulation of
patients requiring ventilatory assistance, Burns JR,
Jones FL, Chest 1975;68:608; permission conveyed
through Copyright Clearance Center, Inc.]

Mobilisation during mechanical ventilation: Can we do better?

Deep sedation with infusions of sedatives and narcotics may be required during critical care [6]. Sedation can provide adequate patient comfort, cardiopulmonary stability, patient-ventilator synchrony and prevention of the accidental removal of invasive devices [7]. Adequate but not excessive sedation in the critically ill mechanically ventilated patient is a complex process [8]. Optimal sedation has been defined as "conscious sedation" [9] with the patient awake, cooperative and oriented. In a group of 42 intubated and ventilated patients "conscious sedation" could be maintained for 264 days of the total 582 days of ventilation [9]. In a randomised controlled trial of 104 intubated and mechanically ventilated patients, Schweickert et al. [10] demonstrated that the protocolised combination of a daily interruption of sedation with mobilisation activities significantly improved functional outcomes and reduced mechanical ventilation time.

The relatively common critical care complication of delirium, defined as an acute and fluctuating disturbance of consciousness and cognition, may impair the potential for rehabilitation even though other criteria have been fulfilled. Delirium is associated with increased mortality and impaired long-term cognition [11]. Risk factors for delirium include hypertension, alcoholism, increased severity of illness and use of sedatives and analgaesics [11]. The daily interruption of sedation combined with a ventilator weaning protocol can assist in reducing the time on mechanical ventilation, time in the ICU and hospital [12].

Bed rest unfortunately remains a common prescription in critical care [13, 14]. The transfer of acute respiratory failure patients to a critical care unit where patient activity or mobility is a key component of care can substantially improve the amount of ambulation achieved [14].

Mobilisation of the intubated and ventilated patient should minimise the loss of mobility and muscle strength, improve functional independence, optimise gas exchange, assist with secretion clearance and facilitate weaning from mechanical ventilation [15]. The mobility status of an acutely-ill patient may entail and progress from bedside activities such as physiotherapist-initiated and -delivered passive range of motion or passive repositioning into side-lying to patient-initiated bed mobility (e.g. rolling side to side, bridging) and sitting over the edge of the bed to sit-to-stand transfers and ambulation [16]. The factors that may affect the ability of the acutely ill patient to tolerate and/or participate in mobilisation include (but are not limited to) pre-morbid health, sedation level, cardiopulmonary and neuromuscular status, mechanical ventilatory requirements and the need for infusions of inotrope or vasoactive drug therapy. Back in 1992 Dean and Ross [17] proposed upright patient positioning and mobilisation out of bed as the most efficacious means to improve cardiopulmonary function. To challenge current physiotherapy practice, Dean and Ross purported that the adverse effects of chest physiotherapy including increased oxygen consumption and haemodynamic disturbances should be of concern for

How do you safely mobilise your intubated and ventilated patient?

F

the critically ill patient. However, we propose that the increases in oxygen consumption and haemodynamic stresses during chest physiotherapy [18] could be an unexplored therapy to elicit an "exercise response" in the deeply sedated and mechanically ventilated patient.

To date there have been eight trials to investigate various mobilisation activities (e.g. bed exercises, sitting over edge of bed, standing, ambulation) in the adult intubated and ventilated patient [14, 19–25].

Safety requirements for mobilisation

The critically ill patient has been viewed as being "too unwell" to tolerate mobilisation in the early phase of illness and hence the immobilisation may be prolonged [14, 15]. Stiller and Phillips [16] developed recommendations for the initiation of safe mobilisation of the critically ill patient. The key physiological recommendations include:

- Adequate pulmonary reserve and stability ($PaO_2/FiO_2 > 40$, $SaO_2 > 90\%$ and $< 4\%$ recent decrease)
- Adequate cardiac reserve (resting HR < 50% age-predicted maximal HR, BP < 20% variability recently and ECG normal with no evidence of MI or arrhythmia)
- Adequate haemoglobin and platelets
- Temperature $< 38°C$
- Blood glucose 3.5–20 mmol/l

Other important requirements for the safe mobilisation of the intubated and ventilated patient include patient consent, appropriate conscious and cognitive state of the patient, adequate muscle strength, adequate space for ambulation, adequate staffing, walking aids and portable cardiopulmonary monitoring and ventilator equipment (see Fig. 2).

During the mobilisation of a critically ill patient it is recommended [16] that there is an "appropriate incremental increase in HR AND initial rapid rise in systolic blood pressure, stable or slight decrease in diastolic blood pressure AND sinus rhythm and PaO_2/FiO_2 stable, $< 4\%$ decrease in SpO_2, respiratory pattern acceptable AND patient appears unstressed". Some of these non-specific recommendations may be difficult to interpret and apply in certain situations, for example in the patient with limited cardiopulmonary reserve.

Stiller et al. [26] investigated the applicability of the 2003 safety guidelines [16] in a group of 31 critically ill patients over 69 mobilisation episodes (39 episodes sitting on the edge of the bed, 19 episodes of sitting on the edge of the bed and progressing to standing, 10 episodes of sitting on the edge of the bed and stand transfer to a chair and finally sitting on the edge of the bed, standing and walking only on one episode). Of the 31 patients 18 were non-intubated and spontaneously breathing, 6 had a tracheostomy and were spontaneously breathing and 7 were on assisted ventilation via a tracheostomy. These 31 patients represented approximately 20% of the 129 patients admitted in the ICU. The main reasons for the exclusions included reduced conscious state, unstable cardiopulmonary function and other factors such as spinal and pelvic fracture. Heart rate, rhythm, blood pressure, transcutaneous arterial saturation in addition to patient appearance were monitored continuously before, during and up to one minute after ambulation with the patient returned to a resting position (position not described). Deterioration in the patient's condition and need for therapy intervention was documented. Heart rate and blood pressure increase although statistically significant was small in terms of clinical value, changing by approximately 10% or less. SaO_2 was stable throughout treatment for the group as a whole. On three of the 69 occasions of mobilisation (4.3%) a fall in SaO_2 occurred that required a temporary increase in FiO_2 which improved SaO_2 and did not necessitate any further intervention or termination of the mobilisation. Hence the authors concluded that mobilisation was well tolerated in this small group of patients (note only one episode included ambulation, most episodes involved sitting over the edge of the bed). However, it is unclear from the data reported if there were any group differences based on ventilation requirements. Of note, the two patients who experienced an arterial desatutration during ambulation were on mechanical ventilation. An increase in the inspired level of oxygen [20] and/or the level of respiratory support prior to, during and after mobilisation may assist to prevent or minimise the arterial desaturation and patient work of breathing and optimise the level of mobilisation achievable

Safe environment, adequate
staffing/skill level and
ambulation equipment
- Appropriate staffing
  (physiotherapists) and
  expertise with ambulation
  during mechanical ventilation
- Walking aids
- Portable ventilator and
  monitoring equipment

Patient consent, adequate patient
muscle strength, conscious and
cognitive level
- Patient consent and
  cooperation
- Adequate muscle strength
  (grade 3) major limb muscle groups
- Appropriate
  sedation/conscious level (RASS 0-1)
- Ability of patient to respond
  and move limbs to simple commands

**General safety issues for mobilisation
critically-ill patient**

No orthopaedic, neurological contra
indications or invasive medical
devices
- Raised intracranial pressure
- Unstable spinal/pelvic/lower
  limb fractures
- Femoral vascular continuous
  haemofiltration
- Intra-aortic balloon pump

Fig. 2   General safety issues for mobilisation of intubated and ventilated patients [data from 16 and 23].
RASS = Richmond agitation sedation score
The key physiological recommendations include:
- Adequate pulmonary reserve and stability ($PaO_2/FiO_2 > 40$, $SaO_2 > 90\%$ and $< 4\%$ recent decrease)
- Adequate cardiac reserve (Resting HR $< 50\%$ age predicted maximal HR, BP $< 20\%$ variability recently and ECG
  normal with no evidence MI or arrhythmia)
- Adequate haemoglobin and platelets
- Temperature $< 38°C$
- Blood glucose 3.5–20 mmol/l

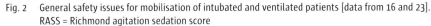

[27]. The cardiopulmonary limits to exercise proposed by Stiller and Phillips [16] may facilitate the safe mobilisation of the critically ill patient but may not provide an adequate exercise stimulus.

In a respiratory critical care unit, Bailey et al. [20] evaluated a larger number of ventilated patients (92/103 patients) during 1,449 mobilisation events in a respiratory critical care unit (all had been transferred from other acute critical care units). Mean age of the patients was 62.5 ± 15.5 years, respiratory ICU admission APACHE II score 17 ± 4.8 and total critical care unit length of stay (including previous ICU transferred from) of 22.7 ± 15.9 days. Of all the mobilisation events,

How do you safely mobilise your intubated and ventilated patient?

F

approximately half were undertaken with the patient intubated (600 events oral intubation and approximately 150 events with a tracheostomy). In contrast to the strict criteria of Stiller and Phillips [16], mobilisation was commenced with initial physiologic stabilisation based on three criteria including neurology (patient response to verbal stimulation), respiratory ($FiO_2 \leq 0.6$ and $PEEP \leq 10cm\ H_2O$), and circulatory (absence of orthostatic hypotension and catecholamine drips). Importantly, for patients who did not fully meet the respiratory or circulatory criteria they initiated a trial of activity with close monitoring for adverse events. Oxygen saturation was measured continuously before, during and after all activity events, whereas blood pressure was measured before and after an activity. Bailey et al. [20] classified adverse events as:

- fall to knees,
- tube removal,
- systolic blood pressure > 200 mmHg or less than 90mmHg,
- desaturation of < 80% and
- extubation.

Of note, there were only 14 adverse events of the total of 1,449 mobilisations (0.9%). The adverse events included five falls to knees, four systolic blood pressure < 90 mmHg, three oxygen desaturation < 80%, one naso-gastric tube removal, and one systolic blood pressure > 200 mmHg.

Morris et al. [23] also used relatively "liberal" criteria for commencement of a graduated programme of mobilisation (details of mobilisation programme in next section) in a group of 330 critically ill patients commenced within 48 hours of intubation. The following criteria were used to limit or to withhold mobility interventions including a decline in haemodynamic (mean arterial pressure < 65 mmHg, administration of a new pressor agent, new documented myocardial infarction, dysrhythmia requiring the addition of a new antiarrhythmic agent) or ventilatory status (frequent desaturations below 88%, an increase in the positive end expiratory pressure or a change to assist-control mode once in a weaning mode). If the mobility was withheld, the patients were re-evaluated the following day. Unlike Stiller and Phillips [16] there were no absolute limits in regards to FiO_2 and PEEP to withhold mobility. No deaths, near deaths or cardiopulmonary

resuscitation occurred during physiotherapy in either group. There were no adverse events such as accidental removal of a device. Similar to the findings of Bailey et al. [20], of all the combined passive and active sessions of mobilisation therapy, only 1.4% were not initiated because of high or low blood pressure and 0.9% of sessions were not initiated because of either too high or too low heart rate.

Changing the critical care culture to adopt a new paradigm of care involving rehabilitation in a medical critical care unit [7] is gathering momentum. Changes included a discontinuation of "bed rest" as the default activity level, early consultation with rehabilitation professionals and education of all staff in medical critical care regarding reducing heavy sedation and early rehabilitation [7]. The general considerations when deciding to initiate mobilisation out of bed were less restrictive than other authors [16], but may reflect the patient group (medical critical care). They included the responsiveness to sensory stimulation, respiratory stability (e.g. stable oxygen saturation, fraction of inspired oxygen < 0.60, and positive end-expiratory pressure < 10 cmH$_2$O, cardiovascular stability (e.g. no active cardiac ischaemia, hypotension, or increasing infusion of vasopressor medication), absence of an unstable fracture (e.g. spine).

For the severely deconditioned or medically unstable patient, the transcutaneous electrical stimulation of major limb muscle groups whilst resting in bed may provide an additional means of maintaining muscle strength and improving function. Zanotti et al. [25] report on a small randomised controlled trial of active limb exercises alone compared to active limb exercises plus twice-daily electrical stimulation for 28 days in a group of 24 bed-bound intubated and ventilated COPD patients. Muscle strength improved in both groups but significantly greater in the electrical stimulation group. Electrical stimulation in addition to active limb exercises also decreased the number of days needed to transfer from bed to chair.

The issue of the safe mobilisation of the critically ill patient is a complex issue. The detailed requirements reported by Stiller and Phillips [16] may enhance the safe mobilisation of the critically ill patient but the testing of their recommendations was in predominantly non-intubated patients [26]. These criteria may unfortunately restrict the mobilisation of the critically ill patient when compared to the requirements reported by other authors [7, 20, 23]. Further research is warranted to investigate the effect of mobilisation activities on cardiopulmonary function and measures of the "exercise" response to intervention. The measurement of the metabolic cost during the various mobilisation activities would provide detail of the exercise response to an intervention (to be discussed later). This will help clinicians to better understand the cardiopulomonary challenge posed by a mobilisation activity. Electrical stimulation of major lower limb muscle groups may prove to be a useful modality in the bedbound critically ill patient.

In a large prospective multi-centre observational study Zeppos et al. [28] recorded any adverse events associated with physiotherapy (mobilisation and respiratory) over a 3-month period in five intensive care units. A very detailed list of adverse events were described including an alteration in heart rate or blood pressure < or > 20% of resting values necessitating stopping the intervention or remedial action, a new arrhythmia (atrial fibrillation, increased number of ectopic beats, ST depression or elevation, increased magnitude of ST depression, bigeminy, trigeminy, ventricular tachycardia/fibrillation, asystole), arterial desaturation > 10% of baseline levels or a figure which necessitates stopping intervention or requires remedial action, pulmonary artery pressure (systolic) > 60 mmHg, pneumothorax detected immediately following intervention, agitation resulting in detachment of lines or equipment or requiring increased sedation, incorrect procedure, fall during mobilisation (e.g. transfer to chair, walking or tilt table), or a consultative event (e.g. asking the nurse to sit a patient out of bed) resulting in an episode as before within 30 minutes of the request. Of the 12, 281 physiotherapy interventions 27 interventions resulted in adverse physiological changes (0.2%). It is unclear how many of the total interventions involved mobilisation activities; however, only 2 of the total 27 adverse events involved either ambulation or passive limb movements, with resultant tachypnoea and a drop in blood pressure respectively. Overall, there was an extremely low incidence of adverse events, as demonstrated by others [20, 23].

Mobilisation: Description of activities

During critical illness it may be unrealistic and potentially unsafe to expect all patients to be sat out of bed, let alone to achieve ambulation during mechanical ventilation [19]. Bahadur et al. [19] reported on the number of occasions of sitting over the edge of the bed or sitting out of bed in a convenience sample of 30 patients intubated and ventilated via tracheostomy. Only 19 of the 30 patients were mobilised to sitting out of bed or over the edge of the bed. For the 11 patients not sat out of bed they demonstrated significantly higher mortality rate than the patients who were sat out of bed. There were no significant differences in age, gender, admission APACHE II score or length of ICU stay between the patients that did and did not sit out of bed. A graduated programme of mobilisation activities [23] may provide realistic goals for both the patient and staff (see Tab. 1).

The metabolic and cardiopulmonary stresses induced by mobilisation activities should determine the potential for therapeutic and/or detrimental effects. The passive repositioning of a patient into a portable chair to sit out of bed may not be "viewed" as rehabilitation [20, 26]. As activities such as "passive" chest physiotherapy can elicit an "exercise response" [18] there may be potential therapeutic benefits from many activities performed on patients yet to be elucidated.

Bailey et al. [20] defined mobilisation as attempts to sit on the edge of the bed and/or stand transfer to sit in a chair and/or ambulation. Before and after an activity period, assist-control ventilation was used as a means of rest if required. The FiO$_2$ was increased by 0.2 before the initiation of an activity and ventilator weaning was deferred in support of mobilisation as necessary. The goal of the activity protocol was to ambulate greater than 100 feet before discharge from the respiratory critical care unit.

Thomsen et al. [14] describe the activity protocol in a 104 patients with a mean age of 57.9 ± 18.1 years who were mechanically ventilated for at least 4 days prior to mobilisation. The mean duration of mechanical ventilation was 18 days and 30 days duration of hospitalisation. Thirteen, or 12%, of patients died during hospital stay. Similar to the investigation by Bailey et al. [20], these patients had been transferred to the

How do you safely mobilise your intubated and ventilated patient?

F

Tab. 1 Critical care mobilisation activities: Levels 1–4 based on conscious level, patient response to clinician commands and generalised muscle strength [adapted in part from 23, 25]

*ICU admission			ICU discharge
Level 1 Unconscious	**Level 2** Conscious**	**Level 3** Conscious	**Level 4** Conscious
■ Passive range of motion 3 x/day ■ Turns Q 2hrly ■ Consider use of electrical stimulation of major lower limb muscle groups**** ■ **When patient is able to respond to physiotherapist commands then progress to level 2**	■ Passive range of motion 3 x/day if indicated*** ■ Turns Q 2hrly ■ Active assisted/resistance exercises based on muscle strength ■ Consider use of electrical stimulation of major lower limb muscle groups ■ Sitting position minimum 20 minutes 3 x/day ■ **When patient can move arms against gravity then progress to level 3**	■ Passive range of motion 3 x/day if indicated*** ■ Turns Q 2hrly ■ Active assisted/resistance exercises based on muscle strength ■ Sitting position minimum 20 minutes 3 x/day ■ Sitting on the edge of the bed ■ **When patient can move legs against gravity then progress to level 4**	■ Passive range of motion 3 x/day if indicated*** ■ Turns Q 2hrly ■ Active assisted/resistance exercises based on muscle strength ■ Sitting position minimum 20 minutes 3 x/day ■ Sitting on the edge of the bed ■ **Stand transfer patient to sitting out in a chair at least 20 minutes/day**

* The patient should progress from level 1 through to level 4 during critical care; however, the patient's condition, conscious state and general muscle strength may change throughout the ICU stay and hence determine the level of therapy indicated.
** Patient considered alert enough when able to respond to 3 of 5 commands from the physiotherapist including "open/close your eyes", "look at me", "open your mouth and put your tongue out", "nod your head", and "raise your eyebrows when I have counted to 5".
*** If the patient is alert and has adequate muscle strength to perform active range of motion in major muscle groups (e.g. grade 3 muscle strength in all major groups), then passive range of motion may not be indicated.
**** Electrical stimulation may be indicated in the patient with severe muscle weakness [25].

respiratory critical care unit from another critical care unit. Thomsen et al. did not report on the use of mandatory modes of mechanical ventilation as rest periods before and or after ambulation. Early activity was commenced if patients fulfilled the same criteria as in the study by Bailey et al. Of the 40 % of patients who ambulated, they achieved an average ambulation distance of 238 feet by the time of RICU discharge. The authors did not describe any reporting of adverse events during the study.

Morris et al. [23] compared the outcomes of a structured rehabilitation programme from a "mobility team" in critical care to a usual care programme. Rehabilitation was commenced within 48 hours of intubation and 72 hours of admission to the medical critical care unit, being much earlier than other investigations. Only patients who survived to a hospital discharge were included in the outcome analyses as of the patients who died in the ICU few achieved sufficient wakefulness to be considered for physical therapy before their death, similar to the findings of Bahadur et al. [19]. Bahadur et al. reported that the critical care patients that could not be mobilised to sitting out of bed during ICU stay showed higher mortality rates than the patients who could be mobilised to sitting out of bed. Morris et al. [23] introduced a structured 4-level physiotherapy programme that was based on the patient's level of consciousness (see Tab. 1). Briefly all patients received passive limb range of motion and passive re-positioning, then, with increasing levels of consciousness with the patient able to interact with the physiotherapist, the next levels of intervention included active resisted range of motion exercises, sitting upright in bed, sitting over the edge of the bed, stand transfer to a chair to sitting out of bed. It is unclear whether ambulation was attempted. Of the total 3,032 patients admitted to the medical critical care unit, 1,605 were not intubated. Of the 1,427 intubated admissions (1,097 excluded due to predefined criteria), 330 met the study criteria and were assigned to the Usual care (n = 165) or the Protocol group (n = 165) with in-hospital mortality in 30/165 patients in Usual care group and 20/165 patients in the Protocol group. In the Usual care group 64/135 patients underwent at least one physiotherapy session at any time during their hospital stay compared with 116/145 patients of the Protocol group. Of the 64 Usual care patients who received physiotherapy, only eight patients had physiotherapy initiated during critical care compared with 106 of 116 Protocol patients. Of the patients who received at least one physiotherapy session Usual care patients received fewer sessions compared with protocol patients (4.1 sessions per patient vs. 5.5 sessions per patient). After adjustment for BMI, APACHE II and vasopressor usage, usual care patients were first out of bed in 11.3 days whereas protocol patients were first out of bed in 5.0 days. The change of focus in the critical care environment to one that encourages mobilisation out of bed can improve functional outcomes. A quick user guide on the equipment, staffing and processes required for the safe ambulation of an intubated and ventilated patient has been provided (see Tab. 2).

Tab. 2   Equipment/procedure safety checklist for ambulatory ventilation

Equipment
1. Portable ventilator (adequate battery backup)
2. Adequate number of full oxygen cylinders. Ensure both have flow meters and that one is connected to the ventilator
3. Emergency tracheostomy/reintubation kit available as per critical care guidelines
4. Manual resuscitation circuit
5. Portable haemodynamic/respiratory monitoring (heart rate, blood pressure, saturation)
6. Portable suction, suction catheters, gloves
7. Wheeled trolley for portable monitoring and other equipment
8. Wheeled seat/wheelchair with brakes
9. Walking aids as indicated (walking frame)

Action
1. Check the environment, have a clear path for ambulation
2. Consider increasing inspiratory support and/or oxygen for mobility as required
3. Ensure oxygen cylinders are functioning correctly
4. Ensure clear understanding of how to connect and disconnect oxygen cylinders
5. Ensure non-essential attachments and lines are disconnected (e.g. enteral feeding)
6. Connect patient to portable monitoring including transcutaneous saturation, ECG and blood pressure and check that are measures adequate before ambulation
7. Ensure checklist is complete and that the patient is safe and ready to mobilise before switching to portable ventilator

Staff required (3–4 people) and roles
1. Monitor/assist patient, ventilator circuit and connections. Assist mobility as required. This person should lead the session.
2. Monitor oxygen and move ventilator and be able to swap to 2nd oxygen cylinder as required
3. Monitor screen for vital observations and push trolley with monitor screen and other attachments

How do you safely mobilise your intubated and ventilated patient?

F

In a group of 39 chronic critically ill patients dependent on mechanical ventilation, Chiang et al. [21] tested the effect of a 6-week (5 day per week) physiotherapy programme that progressed in the following order:

1. Upper and lower extremity passive and active limb exercises with weights whilst the patient was in bed
2. Bedside functional mobility training focusing on turning in bed and transferring out of bed
3. Ambulation compared to a control group that only received assistance with activities of daily living such as bathing and toileting

All patients had been on mechanical ventilation for more than 14 days and had not received physiotherapy before. The patients in the physiotherapy group had significant improvements in limb muscle strength, mobility, cognitive function, activities of daily living and ventilator-free time compared to the control group.

Cardiopulmonary, metabolic and immunologic responses to mobilisation activities

Zafiropoulos et al. [29] reported on the respiratory and haemodynamic effects of early mobilisation in 17 ventilated abdominal surgery patients between days 1 to 6 after surgery (12 of the patients had COPD). All patients were orally intubated and mobilised whilst connected to a manual resuscitation bag. Measurement of lung volume, respiratory rate, minute ventilation, inspiratory and expiratory time via a pneumotachograph and respitrace, heart rate, blood pressure (systolic, diastolic and mean) and transcutaneously measured arterial saturation. Measurements were collected in the following standardised positions whilst breathing spontaneously on the manual resuscitation circuit: supine, sitting over the edge of the bed (by rolling onto their side and pushing up into sitting), standing, walking on the spot for one minute as able (the number of steps taken recorded), initially after sitting out of bed in a chair with the patient then returned back to ventilator and traditional ventilator settings. Subjects were provided with some assistance by physiotherapists as required to maintain safety. Termination of the study occurred if the following was observed: mean arterial blood pressure < 60 mmHg or

> 120 mmHg, ST segment depression on electrocardiogram (ECG) with anginal chest pain, respiratory rate > 35 bpm, SaO_2 < 90 %. Inclusion criteria were intubated and ventilated after abdominal surgery, able to follow and understand commands, less than 12.5 cm H_2O of CPAP, not requiring inotropes, no postoperative evidence of recent angina pectoris or recent MI (no ST or T wave changes on ECG), no evidence of motor block from an epidural that would affect the patient's ability to mobilise. The 17 subjects were on a range of pressure support (0–10 cm H_2O) and CPAP (range 5–12.5 cm H_2O) with an FiO_2 of 0.3–0.4. Mean number of days of intubation was 1.9 ± 1.6 days with a median size of endotracheal tube of 7.5. Fifteen subjects displayed bibasal atelectasis and consolidation and 2 subjects displayed unilateral basal consolidation as documented by a radiologist blinded to the study aims. Fifteen of the 17 subjects completed the study protocol for mobilisation. Two subjects were excluded based on the termination criteria due to haemodynamic instability prior to sitting over the edge of the bed. Mobilisation, as defined in this study, resulted in significant increases in tidal volume (27 % increase), respiratory rate (25 % increase) and minute ventilation when patients moved from supine to standing, but were not maintained after 20 minutes of sitting out of bed. No further changes in these parameters were observed with walking on the spot for one minute. Haemodynamic changes were observed as increases in blood pressure with patients initially sat over the edge of the bed with no changes in arterial blood gases. The major changes in ventilation were related to a positional change as walking on the spot for one minute did not elicit further increase beyond standing. This low level of exercise intensity may be safe but may not be of sufficient magnitude to further stimulate a cardiopulmonary response beyond standing.

Patient care activities such as patient re-positioning to side-lying and chest physiotherapy can affect metabolic and haemodynamic function [30] and provide an interesting insight to a potential therapeutic role for the critically ill patient. Horiuchi et al. [30] demonstrated that "passive" chest physiotherapy (chest wall percussion, vibrations) and positioning a patient into side-lying results in decreased mixed venous oxygen saturation, increased heart rate, blood pressure, minute ventilation and respiratory rate. There was an increased oxygen consumption (VO_2) with an associated increase in cardiac output, with the increased demand in oxygen that was met both by enhanced oxygen extraction and greater oxygen delivery. The authors thus proposed that the increase in physiologic activity during chest physiotherapy is secondary to both exercise-like and stress-like responses [30]. Sedation such as midazolam and fentanyl, often used to attenuate both the metabolic and haemodynamic stress responses to physiotherapy, may potentially "blunt" the therapeutic response. In the critically ill subset of patients who may not tolerate or be able to actively participate in more aggressive mobilisation activities (sitting out of bed or actively exercising), combinations of chest physiotherapy, passive limb range of motion or even electrical stimulation could be used to generate a cardiopulmonary exercise response and improve muscle strength.

Inflammation is a common problem for patients in the critical care unit and is frequently associated with serious and prolonged illness [31] and may be perceived to be one of the major contraindications or precautions to physiotherapy. There has been very limited research investigating the relationship between inflammation and physical activity in critically ill patients. The inflammatory response is often profoundly augmented in severe sepsis [32]. The balance between the pro- and anti-inflammatory cytokines is associated with critical illness outcome [32, 33]. IL-6 is generally proinflammatory, and high levels are associated with poor outcomes in heart failure, trauma and sepsis in the critical care unit [32, 34, 35]. IL-10 is an anti-inflammatory cytokine; both high and low levels have been associated with poor outcomes in critically ill patients and after cardiac arrest [32, 36]. There is limited information on the effects of exercise in hospitalised individuals. Long-term exercise in elderly people in the community lowers the levels of IL-6 compared with a control group only receiving education [37]. The promotion of physical activity early in acute illness has been advocated as a means to prevent the complications of bed rest, sedation, immobility [15]. The many cited potential precautions and contraindications to mobilisation [16] may prevent the development of a greater mobility culture in critical care. For example, one contraindication to early mobilisation may be the

perceived potential to cause an exacerbation of inflammation. The understanding of the link between activity levels and cytokines has the potential to assist in identifying the dose of activity that minimises dysfunctional inflammation and its adverse sequelae in ICU patients [31]. Therapeutic activity may also assist to preserve the patient's overall functional status by reducing inflammatory damage to skeletal and respiratory muscles [38]. However, there is limited information about the type, duration, and frequency of activity that may benefit acutely ill patients. In addition, the measurement of the activity levels in the critically ill patient is also challenging and there is no gold standard or even a universally used instrument.

Winkelman et al. [31] prospectively examined the relationships between the intensity and duration of physical activity and serum levels of IL-6, IL-10 and their ratio. In addition, they explored whether there are associations between activity, cytokines and patient outcomes such as length of ICU stay, weaning outcome and discharge destination. In this small observational study, two blood samples were drawn and cytokines were measured after activity periods that lasted for at least 10 minutes and after rest periods that lasted for at least 60 minutes. A total of 10 patients were included and they had been mechanically ventilated for more than 3 days, and had an ICU stay of 5–15 days and an absence of chemical and physical restraints. Average age of the patients was 62 years and on average they were observed during their 10th day of mechanical ventilation. Patients were calm and cooperative with a mean motor assessment and activity scale score of 2.7, with all patients able to spontaneously initiate head, hand, and/or leg movements. Mortality rate was 20%. Patients were only included if they had no recent surgery, cardiac or respiratory emergency in the last 24 hours preceeding data collection. All forms of patient activity were recorded (by direct observation and actigraphy); however, blood was only sampled for cytokines after at least 10 minutes of passive (initiated and supported by a healthcare worker) range of motion. There were small but significantly reduced IL6 values after activity compared with rest. The changes in IL10 and the IL6/IL10 ratio were not statistically significant but the study was underpowered. The average duration of activity in this sample of patients prior to collecting of blood for

How do you safely mobilise your intubated and ventilated patient?

F

analysis was 14.7 minutes, with actigraphy suggesting that these bouts of activity were infrequent throughout the 24-hour day. The level of activity used in this investigation may have been insufficient to elicit an appropriate immunomodulatory effect. The immunological effect of active and passive exercise in the septic patient requires elucidation. There is unclarity in the literature as to the most appropriate time to commence mobilisation activities during critical illness. In addition, it seems that the level and type of activity delivered in relation to disease status is the most likely variable that will affect the impact of the activity on the immune function.

Summary and recommendations

Mobilisation of the critically ill intubated and ventilated patient as described in the literature includes a range of activities from passive limb stretches to assistance with sitting over the edge of the bed and ambulation. The level of sedation, muscle strength, conscious state, medical status of the patient and "mobility culture" of the critical care unit may influence the form of activity that is feasible. The mobilisation of intubated and mechanically ventilated patients in critical care is safe and feasible in a large proportion of patients. Ambulation of the critically ill patient, however, requires appropriate physiological criteria and a coordinated approach with adequate staffing and equipment. The lightening of sedation should enhance the mobilisation of critical care patients and minimise the adverse sequelae of critical care.

The essential physiological requirements for the mobilisation of the intubated and ventilated patient out of bed are unclear; however, the progression of activities with close monitoring is recommended. Chest physiotherapy and passive limb stretches could be used in heavily sedated patients to elicit an exercise response and potentially maintain some level of cardiopulmonary fitness, but needs to be evaluated formally.

The adverse events associated with mobilisation are infrequent and often of only a temporary nature that can be easily remedied or minimised. Current/planned research should clarify the effects of exercise rehabilitation (including mobilisation/ambulation) in the acutely ill patient on major outcomes such as physical function, health-related quality of life and time on mechanical ventilation [39]. In addition, more detailed physiological investigations of cardiopulmonary, metabolic and immunologic effects of mobilisation activities will assist the development of optimal rehabilitation programmes from acute to chronic critical illness.

The author

George Ntoumenopoulos,
PhD, BAppSC, BSc, Grad Dip Clin Epid
Clinical Specialist Respiratory
Physiotherapist
Physiotherapy Department
Guy's and St Thomas' NHS Foundation Trust
Westminster Bridge Road
London SE1 7EH, UK
E-mail: georgentou@yahoo.com

References

1. Combes A, Cost M-A, Trouillet J-L, Baudot J, Mokhtari M, Gibert C et al. Morbidity, mortality, and quality-of-life outcomes of patients requiring ≥ 14 days of mechanical ventilation. Crit Care Med 2003;31:1373–1381.
2. Cox C, Carson S, Lindquist J, Olsen M, Govert J, Chelluri L et al. Differences in one year health outcomes and resource utilisation by definition of prolonged mechanical ventilation: a prospective cohort study. Crit Care 2007;11:R9.
3. Nierman D. A structure of care for the chronically critically ill. Crit Care Clin 2002;18:477–491.
4. MacIntyre N, Epstein S, Carson S, Scheinhorn D, Christopher K, Muldoon S. National Association for Medical Direction of Respiratory Care. Chest 2005;128:3937–3954.
5. Burns J, Jones F. Early ambulation of patients requiring ventilatory assistance. Chest 1975;68:608.
6. Weinert C, Calvin A. Epidemiology of sedation and sedation adequacy for mechanically ventilated patients in a medical and surgical critical care unit. Crit Care Med 2007;35:393–401.
7. Needham D. Mobilizing patient in the critical care unit. Improving neuromuscular weakness and physical function. JAMA 2008;300:1685–1690.
8. Schweickert W, Kress J. Strategies to optimise analgesia and sedation. Crit Care 2008;12(S3):S6.
9. Cigada M, Corbella D, Mistraletti G, Forster C, Tommasino C, Morabito A et al. Conscious sedation in the critically ill patient. J Crit Care 2008;23:349–353.
10. Schweickert W, Pohlman M, Pohlman A, Nigos C, Pawlik A, Esbrook C et al. Early physical and occupational therapy in mechanically ventilated critically ill patients: a randomised controlled trial. Lancet 2009;373:1814–1882.

11. Girard T, Prandharipande P, Ely W. Delirium in the critical care unit. Critical Care 2008;12:doi:1168/cc6149.

12. Girard T, Kress J, Fuchs B, Thomason J, Schweickert W, Pun B et al. Efficacy and safety of a paired sedation and ventilator weaning protocol for mechanically ventilated patients in critical care (Awakening and Breathing Controlled trial): a randomised controlled trial. Lancet 2008;371:126–134.

13. Winkelman C, Higgins P, Chen Y-J. Activity in the chronically critically ill. Dimens Crit Care Nurs 2005;24:281–290.

14. Thomsen G, Snow G, Rodriguez L, Hopkins R. Patients with respiratory failure increase ambulation after transfer to a critical care unit where early activity is a priority. Crit Care Med 2008;36:1119–1124.

15. Gosselink R, Bott J, Johnson M, Dean E, Nava S, Norrenberg M et al. Physiotherapy for adult patients with critical illness: recommendations of the European Respiratory Society and European Society of Critical Care Medicine Task Force on Physiotherapy for Critically Ill Patients. Intens Care Med 2008;34:118–1199.

16. Stiller K, Phillips A. Safety aspects of mobilising acutely ill inpatients. Physiotherapy Theory and Practice 2003;19:239–257.

17. Dean E, Ross J. Discordance between cardiopulmonary physiology and physical therapy. Toward a rational basis for practice. Chest 1992;101:1694–1698.

18. Weissman C and Kemper M. The oxygen uptake-oxygen delivery relationship during ICU interventions. Chest 1991;99:430–435.

19. Bahadur K, Jones G, Ntoumenopoulos G. An observational study of sitting out of bed in tracheostomised patients in the critical care unit. Physiotherapy 2008;94:300–305.

20. Bailey P, Thomsen G, Spuhler V, Blair R, Jewkes J, Bezdjian L et al. Early activity is feasible and safe in respiratory failure patients. Crit Care Med 2007;35:139–145.

21. Chiang L, Wang L, Wu C, H Wu, Y Wu. Effects of physical training on functional status in patients with prolonged mechanical ventilation. Phys Ther 2006;86:1271–1281.

22. Martin U, Hincapie L, Nimchuk M, Gaughan J, Criner G. Impact of whole-body rehabilitation in patients receiving chronic mechanical ventilation. Crit Care Med 2005;33:2259–2265.

23. Morris P, Goad A, Thompson C, Taylor K, Harry B, Passmore L et al. Early critical care unit mobility therapy in the treatment of acute respiratory failure. Crit Care Med 2008;36:2238–2243.

24. Nava S. Rehabilitation of patients admitted to a respiratory critical care unit. Arch Phys Med Rehabil 1998;79:849–854.

25. Zanotti E, Felicetti G, Maini M, Frachia C. Peripheral muscle strength training in bed-bound patients with COPD receiving mechanical ventilation. Chest 2003;124:292–296.

26. Stiller K, Phillips A, Lambert P. The safety of mobilisation and its effect on haemodynamic and respiratory status of critical care patients. Physiotherapy Theory and Practice 2004;20:175–185.

27. Dreher M, Storre J, Windisch W. Noninvasive ventilation during walking in patients with severe COPD: a randomised cross-over study. Eur Respir J 2007;29:930–936.

28. Zeppos L, Patman S, Berney S, Adsett J, Bridson J, Paratz J. Physiotherapy intervention in critical care is safe: an observational study. Australian Journal of Physiotherapy 2007;53:279–283.

29. Zafiropoulos B, Alison J, McCarren B. Physiological responses to the early mobilisation of the intubated, ventilated abdominal surgery patient. Australian Journal of Physiotherapy 2004;50: 95–100.

30. Horiuchi K, Jordan D, Cohen D, Kemper M, Weissman C. Insights into the increased oxygen demand during chest physiotherapy. Crit Care Med 1997;25:1347–1351.

31. Winkelman C, Higgins P, Chen Y, Levine A. Cytokines in chronically critically ill patients after activity and bed rest. Biol Res Nurs 2007;8: 261–271.

32. Gogos C, Drosou E, Bassaris H, Skoutelis A. Pro- versus anti-inflammatory cytokine profiles in patients with severe sepsis: A marker of prognosis and future therapeutic options. J Infect Dis 2000;181:176–180.

33. Bennermo M, Held C, Stemme S, Ercisson C, Silveira A, Green F et al. Genetic predisposition of the interleukin-6 response to inflammation: Implications for a variety of major diseases? Clinical Chemistry 2004;50:2136–2140.

34. Martin C, Boisson C, Haccoun M, Thomachot L, Mege J. Patterns of cytokine evolution (tumour necrosis factor and interleukin-6) after septic shock, haemorrhagic shock, and severe sepsis. Crit Care Med. 1997;25:1813–1819.

35. Oda S, Hirasawa H, Shiga H, Nakanishi K, Matsuda K, Nakamura M. Sequential measurement of IL-6 blood levels in patients with systemic inflammatory response syndrome (SIRS)/sepsis. Cytokine 2005;29:169–175.

36. Adrie C, Adib-Conquoy M, Laurent I, Monchi M, Vinsonneau C, Fitting C et al. Successful cardiopulmonary resuscitation after cardiac arrest as a "sepsis-like" syndrome. Circ 2002;106:562–568.

37. Niklas B, Hsu F, Brinkley T, Church T, Goodpaster B, Kritchevsky S et al. Exercise training and plasma C-reactive protein and interleukin-6 in elderly people. J Am Geriatr Soc 2008;56:2045–2052.

38. DeConnick N, Van Parijs V, Beckers-Bleukx G, Van den Bergh P. Critical illness myopathy unrelated to corticosteroids or neuromuscular blocking agents. Neuromusc Dis 1998;8:186–192.

39. Denehy L, Berney S, Skinner E, Edbrooke L, Warrillow S, Hawthorne G et al. Evaluation of exercise rehabilitation for survivors of intensive care: Protocol for a single blind randomised controlled trial. The Open Critical Care Medicine Journal 2008;1:39–47.

G. Safety during technical support

Gayathri Satkurunath, Andrew Rhodes and Maurizio Cecconi

Patient safety and physiological monitoring

The first post-operative care unit was opened in 1926 at the Johns Hopkins Hospital in Baltimore, USA, and it had 3 beds for neurosurgical patients. The first unit for ventilated patients was created in 1953 during the Copenhagen polio epidemic. Since then critical care units have increased the ability to monitor patients intensively and have allowed the collection of expertise to use increasingly complex equipment for this purpose.

Intensive care monitoring involves the frequent or continuous measurement of variables which are useful to ascertain the patient's physiological state. This is done in order to decide whether the patient is stable or whether his management needs to be changed.

Today there are many types of monitors available for many different variables. The properties of the ideal monitor are listed in Table 1. This chapter discusses the general principles involved in the safety aspects of monitoring and looks at a selection of the most commonly used monitors in the general intensive care unit.

In 2007, the UK National Patient Safety Agency (NPSA) investigated avoidable hospital deaths reported over a one-year period [1] and analysed these to determine the common factors found that led to patient deterioration. These included:

Tab. 1   Properties of an Ideal Monitor

Properties
Accurate and precise
Useful to the clinician
Improves patient outcome
Cheap
Simple to use and interpret
No risk to the patient
Easy to transport
Low maintenance
No artefactual results
Alarm for dangerous values needing emergency treatment

not taking observations, not recognising early signs of deterioration, not communicating observations that cause concern and insufficient training to understand the relevance of observations.

In the Australian Incident Monitoring Study [2] of events related to intra-hospital transfer of critically ill patients, 39 % were related to equipment problems and of these, battery or power

433

supply and monitor function were major problems. Inadequate monitoring was another significant problem detected.

In the Sentinel Events Evaluation (SEE) study [3], which was a multinational prospective observational study which covered 1,913 patients with 584 adverse events occurring, there was an unplanned dislodgement or disconnection of lines, catheters and drains in 158; equipment failure in 112 and inappropriate turn-off of alarms in 17.

These studies show that in addition to the technical aspects of the monitor which can lead to adverse events for the patient, the monitor needs to be part of an overall monitoring strategy in order to achieve the objectives of monitoring.

Mant [4] suggests a framework for a monitoring strategy:

1. **Minimum criteria for justification of monitoring**
   A clinically significant change of variable over time, a reliable test to detect that change and an effective intervention to improve the detected deterioration
2. **Choice of the best monitoring test**
   At different stages of monitoring, including a clear assignment of who should do the testing
3. **Specify and assess the monitoring strategy**
   Frequency of monitoring, action to take on the result, check whether the strategy works and is cost-effective
4. **Implementation**
   Training, equipment commissioning and quality assurance

Alarms

Most ICU monitors have alarms with the aim of improving early detection of severe physiological abnormalities which require immediate management. However, the total number of ICU alarm noises is high and this includes a high false-positive rate, with only a small amount of these being for truly life-threatening abnormalities [5]. Staff often do not respond to these alarms or turn them off without further management.

It has also been found that the amplitude of the alarm is often set too high, which leads to sleep deprivation and increased stress for patients and nurses. Misinterpretation of alarm sounds may lead to patient death or other significant adverse incidents [6]. A lower total number of alarms in the ICU with more appropriate alarm limits needs to be used to make them a more effective part of the monitoring strategy.

Pulse oximetry

This was introduced commercially in 1981, and it was shown that these monitors were better than anaesthetists at detecting hypoxic episodes [7]. A Cochrane review [8] of 4 trials showed that although the use of pulse oximeters reduced the number of hypoxic episodes there was no difference in perioperative morbidity or mortality. However, it was shown that staff in a large Danish randomised trial with over 20,000 patients did change their practice, using more oxygen and naloxone when oximeters were used [9]. In this trial there was a significant decrease in myocardial ischaemic events, 18% of anaesthetists said that they had helped them avoid a significant adverse event and 80% said they felt more secure with their use.

Although most of us are now fortunate enough to consider this a routine piece of anaesthetic and critical care equipment, there are still many countries where this is not the case [10]. Understanding its limitations is important for the safe use of a monitor. Causes of inaccurate readings include changes in haemoglobin, e.g. carbon monoxide poisoning or methaemoglobinaemia, factors that cause poor peripheral perfusion or affect light absorption and movement artifacts.

Assessing the plethysmographic waveform is useful to assess the strength of the pulse and the quality of the signal [11]. They are not accurate below 70%, as they have not been calibrated for that range. Users need to be particularly aware that a normal value does not exclude a respiratory deterioration, as it does not monitor adequacy of ventilation. Complications are rare: There have been reports of ischaemic pressure necrosis, blister injuries and limitation of movement in the area of monitoring leading to stiffness [12].

Pulse oximeters are currently available which are more accurate during movement or poor peripheral perfusion. In 2005 a pulse co-oximeter was invented which allows the non-invasive measurement of haemoglobin and the pleth variability index (PVI). Small trials have shown some success with PVI in the prediction of fluid responsiveness in ventilated patients [13].

Capnography

Capnography was first introduced into anaesthetic practice in 1978 and is useful for many functions in critical care. End-tidal CO_2 may be used to estimate $PaCO_2$, which is particularly useful in patient transfers where direct readings are not available. The waveform can be used to assess adequacy of ventilation, optimal PEEP setting, estimate alveolar deadspace, evaluate a weaning trial, detect patient/ventilator asynchrony and adequacy of cardio-pulmonary resuscitation. It can also be used as an immediate warning of circuit disconnection or leaks, extubation, bronchospasm, large pulmonary embolism or cardiac arrest.

There is still debate about whether this monitor should be a standard of care for all ICU patients. In anaesthesia it is part of the minimal monitoring standards but a side-stream analyser can be used which is cheaper, in the intensive care unit, however, this would regularly become blocked by humidity and secretions and therefore an in-line analyser is required. The Society of Critical Care Medicine also considers it a requirement for paediatric ICUs, but it is currently only "desirable" for adult mechanically ventilated patients.

Erroneous readings can be avoided by ensuring adequate calibration prior to use and checking regularly for water and secretions when using side-stream analysers as this may either interfere with the sampling flow or directly impair performance of the monitor. In patients with hypoventilation or with low tidal volume, the exhalation may not be complete and the alveolar gases may not have yet reached the main airways, and therefore, end-tidal CO_2 may be low and poorly represent $PaCO_2$ which is likely to be raised. In tachypnoeic patients the $ETCO_2$ may also underread if the analyser response time is longer than the respiratory cycle time of the patient [14].

Arterial catheters

These are used for continuous blood pressure monitoring or when frequent arterial blood gas sampling is required. Continuous invasive blood pressure monitoring is the optimal blood pressure monitor when non-invasive methods are inaccurate or not possible and for states where there are likely to be rapid changes in blood pressure.

A review of the literature from 1978–2001 showed that the incidence for serious complications (infection, permanent ischaemia and pseudoaneurysm formation) is <1% of arterial lines and this is similar for the radial, brachial and femoral arteries [15]. The most cannulated artery was the radial, and it had a temporary occlusion rate of 19.7%. The Allen test should be performed prior to insertion of a radial arterial line to detect patients without adequate collateral arterial supply.

The second most cannulated artery was the femoral artery, with a temporary occlusion rate of 1.18%, probably due to its larger size. Although some people advise against the use of the femoral artery due to its theoretically higher infection rate, the review and other studies [15, 16] have not found a difference in infection rates. In hypotensive patients, the femoral artery is usually easier to cannulate and the trace produced is more accurate and representative of aortic pressure than at more distal sites.

There currently is a prospective trial underway in North Carolina, USA, to compare the non-invasive oscillometric method with the accuracy of the invasive method in medical intensive care patients [17]. This may decrease the use of arterial blood pressure monitoring in certain critically ill patient groups.

Central venous pressure lines

These are often inserted with arterial lines as part of a "critical care package of treatment". They are useful as a monitoring tool and also as a central access for drug delivery. They have been associated with infectious (5–26%), mechanical (5–19%) and thrombotic complications (2–26%) [18] and the readings have often been misinterpreted. Their management has therefore been a focus by various groups trying to improve patient safety.

The National Institute for Clinical Excellence in the United Kingdom has recommended the use of 2-D ultrasound to guide insertion of internal jugular lines, and that it should be considered for both elective and emergency insertion [19]. Intensive therapy unit care bundles have been introduced to decrease the rate of catheter-related line sepsis. There has been guidance on a number of aspects of catheter management [20]: site of insertion, catheter material and coating, aseptic techniques for insertion and maintenance, dressings, sutures and strategy of replacement.

Central venous pressure is often used as a surrogate marker of the left ventricular end-diastolic pressure. This value or the variation with a fluid challenge can be used to ascertain adequate filling. However, this is not a reliable use and particularly in cardiac disease it may not indicate fluid responsiveness [21]. The value of CVP may also be influenced by the level of the PEEP set, depending on pulmonary compliance. Therefore, it is best measured at end-expiration.

In addition to the actual pressure, the waveform, which is often not considered, may also give useful information such as the presence of tricuspid regurgitation, cardiac tamponade and poor thoracic compliance [22].

The use of CVP lines which has become popular recently is to assess the central venous oxygen saturations as a surrogate marker of mixed venous oxygen saturation. Mixed venous oxygen saturation gives an indication of balance between global oxygen supply and demand. The Surviving Sepsis Campaign [23] recommends a target for central venous oxygen saturation of greater than or equal to 70% within the first 6 hours of resuscitation. Compared to mixed venous oxygen saturation via pulmonary artery catheterisation, the central venous oxygen saturation is a cheaper option with a lower complication rate. Several studies so far show good correlation, but in the subpopulations of shock and cardiac failure this has been controversial [24].

Pulmonary artery catheters

The pulmonary artery catheter (PAC), which was introduced into practice in 1970, has been considered the gold standard of haemodynamic monitoring. It seemed to make intuitive sense that having more information about the central dynamic haemodynamic state of the patient would lead to more appropriate management and a better outcome for critically ill patients.

Specific risks in addition to those found with central venous catheters include cardiac arrhythmias, pulmonary infarction, pulmonary artery rupture and endocardial damage [25]. There is an increased risk of infection and thrombosis after 48–96 hours and so it has been recommended that they be removed within 48 hours [26].

Initial widespread use of the PAC led to consideration of its risk-benefit ratio. In 1996, Conners et al. performed a retrospective case-controlled study which showed a higher mortality rate in patients whose treatment involved a PAC [27]. The controversy from this and other studies [28] led to a consensus conference [29] which found that there was insufficient evidence to assess whether PAC use changed patient outcome.

Recently, a Cochrane analysis [30] showed no difference in mortality with or without PAC use in general ICU patients and high-risk surgical patients. It also did not influence length of ICU or hospital stay. It has been suggested that lack of apparent benefit might also be related to incorrect measurement, inadequate training in interpretation of PAC derived variables or inappropriate subsequent management [26, 31]. Many of the studies that did not find any improvement in outcome with the use of the PAC were not coupled with a protocol in order to allow standardisation of interpretation and management. When a timed protocol was used, there have been studies which showed an improvement in outcome for these patients [32, 33].

The use of the PAC has been decreasing markedly [34, 35]. More research needs to determine whether it may be more beneficial in other subgroups, e.g. pericardiac surgery or in right heart failure, where it could provide specific information not provided by the less invasive techniques of cardiac output monitoring.

Doppler cardiac output monitors

Suprasternal Doppler assessment has not been widely practised due to the instability of probe position for repeated measurements over a prolonged period. The oesophageal Doppler has been refined by Singer et al. in 1989, [36] and since then has been increasingly used in clinical practice. Its use is restricted to patients who are sedated and ventilated and so can tolerate the probe. This probe unlike the PAC can be rapidly inserted, requires less technical skill and has fewer complications [37]. Contraindications include oesophageal pathology or surgery, severe coagulopathy, and an intra-aortic balloon pump (IABP) or severe aortic coarctation where there will be turbulent flow in the descending aorta [38].

In order to calculate the cardiac output, oesophageal Doppler technology uses two assumptions: that the descending aorta cross-sectional area can be assessed from a nomogram which depends on the age, height and weight of a patient, and that the proportion of cardiac output that goes to the descending aorta remains constant. However, the aortic cross-sectional area may vary with haemorrhage and the proportion of flow may vary with a lumbar epidural or aortic cross-clamping [38]. It has been validated against the thermodilution method and the Fick principle for cardiac output and preload [39, 40, 41]. There is much less information to validate the contractility and systemic vascular resistance variables produced.

A recent health technology assessment of its use showed a reduced hospital length of stay and fewer complications with intra-operative use and also in critically ill patients (although in this group only two studies, one of cardiac surgery and one of major trauma, were assessed) [42]. There was some evidence for a reduced number of deaths with its intraoperative use, but caution was advised with the interpretation of this due to low numbers in the meta-analysis and low overall mortality.

Pulse contour analysis

Cardiac output can be estimated indirectly by analysis of the pulse contour. This is also referred to as pulse pressure analysis. It is calibrated by a direct cardiac output estimation via transpulmonary thermodilution in PiCCO, lithium transpulmonary dilution in LiDCOplus/PulseCO and uses comparison against a historical control for the Vigileo/FloTrac. These minimally invasive techniques can be used on awake patients and require an arterial line and a venous line. They

require less technical skill for insertion, and since most intensive care patients already require these lines for other purposes, there is less excess risk involved compared to the PAC.

Concerns about the estimations used in pulse contour analysis [43] include: non-linearity of aortic compliance, which needs to be compensated for in the mathematical model; peripheral arterial pressure is used instead of aortic pressure, and although these may have a fixed relationship, resonance needs to be accounted for; damping from the catheter-transducer system may produce an inadequate signal; inadequate detection of every heartbeat, e.g. in arrhythmias, although this can be overcome by use of appropriately designed computer programmes; inter-individual variation of aortic properties means that although cardiac output changes can be tracked accurately with pulse contour analysis, the accuracy of the absolute value is best confirmed by a calibration technique such as thermodilution. The accuracy of these devices may also be affected by states with increased vascular turbulence such as aortic valve disease, IABP or severe peripheral vascular disease.

LiDCOplus is a technique which uses any arterial line and central or peripheral venous line. Lithium dilution has been validated against intrapulmonary thermodilution, [44] but recalibration is required every eight hours to maintain accuracy [45]. Calibration can be affected by chronic lithium therapy, severe hyponatraemia and temporarily by neuromuscular blocking drugs. It has shown patient benefit in post-operative goal-directed therapy with no change in mortality, but a significant reduction in hospital length of stay and complications [46].

PiCCO requires the presence of a central venous catheter and a specialised arterial line with a thermistor to detect the temperature change after a cold saline bolus. It has been validated against the PAC [47]. Although it is recommended that recalibration is performed eight-hourly, an observational study found that there was loss of accuracy after one hour which suggests that it should be recalibrated hourly.

The Vigileo monitor is the simplest pulse contour analysis to set up, it appears to track changes in cardiac output well, but has had conflicting validation results [48]. The algorithm has since been modified and awaits further assessment.

Accuracy and precision

Physiological monitoring involves measuring absolute values or detecting changes, so that therapy can be titrated toward achievement of an absolute value, a positive or negative change or towards maintenance of a stable value (null change).

When it is not possible to directly measure a variable, the monitor is not actually "measuring" but "estimating". A good example of this is the weighing scale which estimates mass. If jewellers used a weighing scale to buy and sell gold, a clever jeweller could buy one kg of gold at the equator and sell one kg at the North Pole and still have some spare gold. This is because the weighing scale measures weight, which is greater at the North Pole due to the different rotating force. Weighing scales are dynamometers as they measure the effect of the force of gravity applied to a mass. Jewellers actually have scales that measure mass and not weight.

In physiological monitoring, cardiac output monitors are not able to directly measure true cardiac output as this would be too invasive to be performed. There are many devices now which estimate cardiac output in different ways, but they need a good degree of accuracy and precision. Accuracy is a gauge of how close the measurement is to the real value. Precision is a gauge of how close repeated measurements are to each other.

If a highly precise cardiac output monitor is used, we can detect small real changes in that variable. But if a highly imprecise device is used, it may continuously provide us with changes that are simply the result of a poor level of precision. The precision is related to the minimum change that needs to be measured by a device in order to recognise a real change. For example, if we use a cardiac output monitor to detect changes in stroke volume after a fluid challenge, when choosing the cutoff value for the change for a positive response, we need to know the precision of the device. There is no point to use a cutoff value of 10 % if the level of precision of the device is ± 15 %.

If the target is an absolute value of cardiac output (i.e. to increase oxygen delivery to 600ml/min/m2) and the device is very precise, the therapy can be fine-tuned by looking at the changes, but the device needs to be highly accurate to know when the target is achieved.

Although jewellers are aware of the differences between measuring and estimating, clinicians are not always aware of this limitation of their monitoring device and may consider each number that the machine produces to be the true value.

Conclusion

The safe use of monitoring in patients requires a good knowledge of the monitor and individual consideration of the benefits the data may bring in comparison to the risks involved in its use.

In deciding the best test to choose, [49] it is important to assess clinical validity: whether it actually measures something that is useful therapeutically. For the haemodynamic tests discussed, they are often compared to what was previously considered the gold standard, thermodilution via the PAC, to assess their accuracy and precision [50]. But since this standard has not been shown to improve patient outcome, it may not prove to be the best comparator.

The best test should be free of systematic bias, which can be achieved by adequate calibration and understanding of the natural variation of the physiological variable, e.g. diurnal variation. In the intensive care unit, the tests must have fast response times and a large signal-to-noise ratio. The best test is also the most practical test, which is ideally cheap, simple to perform and non-invasive. However, sometimes the simplest test does not provide enough information to optimise the treatment of the most complex critically ill patient.

In reality we often make a compromise from what is ideal, in order to decide what tests should be available for the intensive care unit as a whole and of those, which is the most appropriate for the individual patient.

In order to produce the most benefits and least risk for the patient, the monitor should be part of a well-run monitoring strategy, as the monitor itself cannot improve patient outcome. It may be that where a lack of apparent benefit is seen with a particular monitor it is due to an inadequate strategy, e.g. lack of understanding of the derived data, or inappropriate subsequent treatment. Once the strategy is decided, it needs to be assessed and properly implemented to ensure effectiveness and safety.

The safe use of monitoring involves choosing the most appropriate monitor for the patient. But there is no point in using even the safest tool without a beneficial strategy and an understanding of the accuracy and precision of the numbers that we get.

The authors

Gayathri Satkurunath, MD, BSc, MRCP, FRCA
Andrew Rhodes, FRCP, FRCA
Maurizio Cecconi, MD
> Department of General Intensive Care |
> St George's Hospital | London, UK

Adress for correspondence
> Maurizio Cecconi
> Consultant
> Department of Intensive Care
> St George's Hospital
> SW17 0QT London, UK
> E-mail: mauriziocecconi@hotmail.com

References

1. National Patient Safety Agency (2007). Safer Care For the Acutely Ill Patient: Learning from serious incidents.
2. Beckmann U, Gillies DM, Berenholtz SM, et al. Incidents relating to the intra-hospital transfer of critically ill patients. An analysis of the reports submitted to the Australian Incident Monitoring Study in Intensive Care. Intensive Care Medicine 2004; 30(8):1579–1585.
3. Valentin A, Capuzzo M, Guidet B, et al. Patient safety in intensive care: results from the multinational Sentinel Events Evaluation (SEE) study. Intensive Care Med 2006; 32:1591–1598.
4. Mant D. A framework for developing and evaluating a monitoring strategy. In: Evidence-based medical monitoring: from principles to practice. Blackwell publishing 2008.
5. Chamrin MC, Ravaux P, Calvelo-Aros D, et al. Multicenter study of monitoring alarms in the adult intensive care unit (ICU): a descriptive analysis. Int Care Med 1999; 25:1360–1366
6. Edworthy J, Hellier E. Alarms and human behaviour: implications for medical alarms. Br J Anaesth 2006:97:12–17.
7. Moller JT, Jensen PF, Johannessen NW, et al. Hypoxaemia is reduced by pulse oximetry monitoring in the operating theatre and in the recovery room. Br J Anaesth 1992; 68:146–150.
8. Pedersen T, Dyrlund Pedersen B, et al. Pulse oximetry for perioperative monitoring. Cochrane Database Syst Rev 2003. issue 3

9. Moller JT, Johannessen NW, Espersen K, et al. Randomized evaluation of pulse oximetry in 20,802 patients: II. Perioperative events and postoperative complications. Anesthesiology 1993; 78(3):445–453.
10. Hodges SC, Mijumbi C, Okello M, et al. Anaesthesia services in developing countries: defining the problems. Anaesthesia 2007; 62:4–11
11. Place B. Pulse oximetry: benefits and limitations. Nursing Times 96 (26), 42
12. Jevon P and Ewens B. Monitoring Respiratory Function. In: Monitoring the Critically Ill Patient. Blackwell publishing 2004.
13. Cannesson M, Desebbe O, Rosamel P, et al. Pleth variability index to monitor the respiratory variations in the pulse oximeter plethysmographic waveform amplitude and predict fluid responsiveness in the operating theatre. Br J Anaesth 2008; 101(2):200–206
14. Bhavani-Shankar, Kumar AY. Capnometry and anaesthesia. Can J Anaesth 1992; 39(6):617–632
15. Scheer BV, Perel A and Pfeiffer U. Clinical review: Complications and risk factors of peripheral arterial catheters used for haemodynamic monitoring in anaesthesia and intensive care medicine. Crit Care 2002; 6(3):199–204.
16. Ricard, P, Martin, R and Marcoux, A. Protection of indwelling vascular catheters: incidence of bacterial contamination and catheter-related sepsis. Crit Care Med. 1985; 13:541–543.
17. Chatterjee AB and Chin R. Accuracy and Precision of oscillometric blood pressure monitoring in the calf and thighs of medical ICU patients when compared to invasive arterial blood pressure monitoring. Clinical Trials.Gov indentifier NCT00739700
18. McGee DC, Gould MK. Preventing complications of central venous catheterization. NEJM 2003; 348 (12):1123–1133
19. National Institute for Clinical Excellence. Guidance on the use of ultrasound locating devices for placing central venous catheters. Technology appraisal guidance no. 49. Sep 2002. www.nice.org.uk
20. O'Grady NP, Alexander M, Dellinger EP, et al. Guidelines for the prevention of intravascular catheter-related infections. Centers for Disease Control and Prevention. MMWR. Recommendations and reports: Morbidity and mortality weekly report. Recommendations and reports/ Centers for Disease Control 2002; 51(RR-10):1–29.
21. Marik PE, Baram M, Vahid B. Does central venous pressure predict fluid responsiveness? A systematic review of the literature and the tale of seven mares. Chest 2008; 134(1):172–178.
22. Magder S. Central venous pressure monitoring. Curr Opin Crit Care 2006; 12:219–227.
23. Dellinger RP, Levy MM, Carlet JM et al. Surviving Sepsis Campaign: International guidelines for management

of severe sepsis and septic shock: 2008. Crit Care Med 2008; 36:296–327.

24. Ladakis C, Myrianthefs P, Karabinis A et al. Central venous and mixed venous oxygen saturation in critically ill patients. Respiration 2001; 68:279–285.

25. American Society of Anesthesiologists Task Force on Pulmonary Artery Catheterization. Practice guidelines for pulmonary artery catheterization: an updated report by the American Society of Anesthesiologists Task Force on Pulmonary Artery Catheterization. Anesthesiology 2003; 99(4):988–1014.

26. Connors AF Jr, Potential misuse of the pulmonary artery catheter. Seminars in Resp Crit Care Med 1999; 20 (1):43–51.

27. Connors AF Jr, Speroff T, Dawson NV et al. The effectiveness of right heart catheterization in the initial care of critically ill patients. JAMA 1996; 276:889–897.

28. Cooper AB, Doig GS, Sibbald WJ. Pulmonary artery catheters in the critically ill. Critical Care Clinics 1996; 12:777–793.

29. Taylor RW Jr, Calvin JE, Matuschak GM. Pulmonary artery catheter consensus conference: the first step. Crit Care Med 1997, 25:2060–2063.

30. Harvey S, Young D, Brampton D, et al. Pulmonary artery catheters for adult patients in intensive care. Cochrane Database of Systematic Reviews 2006; Issue 3. Art No.: CD003408. DOI:10.1002/14651858.

31. Vincent JL, Pinsky MR, Sprung CL, et al. The pulmonary artery catheter: in medio virtus. Crit Care Med 2008; 36 (11):3093–3096.

32. Boyd O, Grounds RM, Bennett ED. A randomized clinical trial of the effect of deliberate perioperative increase of oxygen delivery on mortality in high-risk surgical patients. JAMA 1993; 270 (22):2699–2707.

33. Shoemaker WC, Appel PL, Dram HB, et al. Prospective trial of supranormal values of survivors as therapeutic goals in high-risk surgical patients. Chest 1988; 94 (6):1176–1186

34. Wiener RS, Welch HG. Trends in the use of the pulmonary artery catheter in the United States, 1993–2004. JAMA 2007; 298:423–429.

35. Carnendran L, Abboud R, Sleeper LA, et al. Trends in cardiogenic shock: Report from the SHOCK study. The should we emergently revascularize occluded coronaries for cardiogenic shock? Eur Heart J 2001; 22:472–478.

36. Singer M, Clarke J, Bennett ED. Continuous hemodynamic monitoring by esophageal doppler. Crit Care Med 1989; 17:447–452

37. Singer M. Esophageal Doppler monitoring of aortic blood flow: beat-by-beat cardiac output monitoring. Int Anesth Clin 1993; 31:99–125.

38. King SL, Lim MS. The use of the esophageal doppler monitor in the intensive care unit. Crit Care Resuss 2004;6:113–122.

39. Valtier B, Cholley BP, Belot JP, et al. Noninvasive monitoring of cardiac output in critically ill patients using transoesophageal doppler. Am J Resp Crit Care Med 1998; 158:77–83.

40. Cuschieri J, Rivers E, Caruso J, et al. A comparison of transesophageal doppler, thermodilution and fick cardiac output measurements in critically ill patients. Crit Care Med 1998; 26(Suppl) A62.

41. Madan AK, UyBarreta VV, Aliabadi-Wahle S, et al. Esophageal doppler ultrasound monitor versus pulmonary artery catheter in the hemodynamic management of critically ill surgical patients. J Trauma 1999; 46:607–612.

42. Mowatt G, Houston G, Hernandez R, et al. Systematic review of the clinical effectiveness and cost-effectiveness of oesophageal doppler monitoring in critically ill and high-risk surgical patients. Health Technol Assess 2009; 13(7):1–118

43. Van Lieshout JJ, Wesseling KH. Editorial II. Continuous cardiac output by pulse contour analysis? BJA 2001; 86(4):467–468.

44. Linton R, Band D, O'Brien T, et al. Lithium dilution cardiac output measurement: a comparison with thermodilution. Crit Care Med 1997; 25:1796–1800.

45. Cecconi M, Fawcett, Grounds RM, et al. A prospective study to evaluate the accuracy of pulse power analysis to monitor cardiac output in critically ill patients. BMC Anesthesiol 2008; 8:3

46. Pearse R, Dawson D, Fawcett J, et al. Early goal-directed therapy after major surgery reduces complications and duration of hospital stay. A randomized controlled trial. Crit Care 2005; 9:R687-R693.

47. Della Roca G, Costa MG, Pompei L, et al. Continuous and intermittent cardiac output measurement: pulmonary artery catheter versus aortic transpulmonary technique. Br J Anaesth 2002; 88:350–356.

48. Morgan P, Al-Subaie N, Rhodes A. Minimally invasive cardiac output monitoring. Curr Opin Crit Care 2008; 14:322–326.

49. Irwig L, Glasziou PP. Choosing the best monitoring tests. In: Evidence-based medical monitoring: from principles to practice. Blackwell publishing 2008.

50. Cecconi M, Rhodes A, Poloniecki J, et al. Bench-to-bedside review: The importance of the precision of the reference technique in method comparison studies – with specific reference to the measurement of cardiac output. Cit Care 2009; 13:201 (doi: 10.1186/cc7129).

Christian Putensen, Nils Theuerkauf, Thomas Muders, Hermann Wrigge
and Ulf Günther

Patient safety and respiratory support

Introduction

Mechanical ventilator support is one of the major supportive modalities used in intensive care. Traditionally, controlled or assisted mechanical ventilation is provided via an artificial airway or a mask to unload a patient's work of breathing and assure adequate gas exchange during the acute phase of respiratory insufficiency, until the underlying respiratory function has resolved [1]. The criteria used to determine when to terminate mechanical ventilation are essentially based on the clinical, and often, subjective assessment of the intensive care physician or on standardised weaning protocols [2, 3].

Despite technical and medical progress, outcome in mechanically ventilated patients with and without acute lung injury (ALI) or acute respiratory distress syndrome (ARDS) remains poor. Mortality in mechanically ventilated patients has been reported to vary between 35 % and 65 % with [4] and about 40 % in the absence of ALI/ARDS [5–7]. However, mechanically ventilated patients rarely die of hypoxia and/or hypercarbia but commonly develop a systemic inflammatory response that culminates in multiple organ system dysfunction syndrome and death [8].

Complications immanent to mechanical ventilation

As any other invasive medical procedure, characteristic complications of mechanical ventilation cannot always be avoided. Some complications associated with mechanical ventilation may be immediately life-threatening. Other complications and side effects may often be seen negligible compared to the benefit of improved gas exchange and the survival of the patient. However, these complications and side effects may later be of importance for the short- and long-term outcome of critically ill patients.

Airway-associated complications

Unplanned endotracheal extubation

Unplanned endotracheal extubation in intensive care patients occurs with an incidence ranging from 7.3 to 17 % [9–18] and can be further subdivided into unplanned self- and accidental extubations.

Self-extubation denotes every unplanned endotracheal extubation in which the tube is removed by the patient him-/herself, whereas accidental unplanned extubation emerges from the action of a third person. Dislocations of the endotracheal tube of up to 2 cm and subsequent accidental extubations may occur during positioning manoeuvres within the scope of nursing measures, during radiological and surgical procedures or by means of any change in the resting position of the head of intensive care patients, e.g. by flexion and extension of the cervical spine [19, 20].

The incidence of unplanned accidental endotracheal extubation in intensive care patients averages between 0.39 and 2.47% [11, 21–23]. A simple explanation for the occurrence of any tube dislocation consists in inadequate fixation of the endotracheal tube and in inappropriate surveillance on the part of the nursing staff.

On the other hand, pertinent critical care medicine textbooks specify that accidental extubation may also come about despite correct tube fixation and patient surveillance by bedside caregivers [22, 23]. These accidental extubations can be seen in intensive care patients independent of the mode of tube fixation and can only be reduced, but not entirely avoided, by means of particular prevention strategies [9, 19, 20, 24].

In a biennial trial dealing with the prevention of accidental endotracheal extubation by means of a strict protocol, Pesiri and coworkers [25] could merely show a reduction in the incidence of accidental extubation from 12 to 5%. Hence, by use of adequate prevention strategies, the occurrence of accidental endotracheal extubation cannot be prevented, but minimised in intensive care patients.

Tracheal and laryngeal injuries

Long-term complications of endotracheal intubation as well as tracheotomy such as inflammatory stenoses, tracheoesophageal and -innominate artery fistulas have been extensively documented in the literature [26–29].

Among all intubated patients, the reported incidence of post-intubation tracheal stenosis ranges from 10 to 22% [27, 30], but only 1–2% of the patients are symptomatic or have severe stenosis [31]. Today, severe post-intubation and post-tracheotomy tracheal stenosis have an estimated

incidence of 4.9 cases per million per year in the general population [32].

There are few reports dealing with acute airway lesions, of which tracheal rupture represents the most feared and potentially serious immediate complication, as severe respiratory insufficiency and subsequent death may occur. Most publications address single case reports and the true incidence of acute complications of airway access techniques can hardly be estimated, as the very large number of intubations performed daily on a worldwide basis is unknown.

The fact that most publications report on a single or few cases demonstrates the rarity of the condition. After intubation with a double-lumen tube, an incidence of approximately 0.1% has been reported [33, 34]. The frequency is presumably lower with the use of a single-lumen tube.

Nosocomial infections

Ventilator-associated pneumonia (VAP) is common and associated with high morbidity, mortality, and healthcare costs. VAP has a cumulative incidence of 10 to 25% and accounts for approximately 25% of all ICU infections and 50% of the antibiotics prescribed in the ICU [35–37]. Mortality rates for VAP vary between 20 and 70% and are highest in medical ICU patients. However, VAP is preventable, and many practices have been demonstrated to reduce the incidence of VAP and its associated complications [36].

Bacterial colonisation of the aerodigestive tract and entry of contaminated secretions into the lower respiratory tract are critical in the pathogenesis of VAP and major targets for prevention. The Canadian Critical Care Trials Group's initial comprehensive evidence-based clinical practice guidelines for VAP prevention recommend orotracheal intubation, new circuits for each patient, and changes if the circuits become soiled or damaged, but no scheduled ventilator circuit changes, changes of heat and moisture exchangers with each patient every 5 to 7 days and as clinically indicated, use of closed endotracheal suctioning system, use of subglottic secretion drainage in patients expected to be mechanically ventilated for > 72 h, semirecumbent positioning of 45°, and consideration of an oral antiseptic such as chlorhexidine or povidone-iodine [38].

Implementation of evidence-based clinical practice guidelines in daily routine care is rarely satisfactory.

The Institute for Healthcare Improvement recommends the use of bundles, generally three to five treatments that when performed collectively and reliably have been proven to improve patient outcome [39]. The components of the ventilator bundle are

- elevation of the head of the bed to 30–45°,
- daily "sedation vacation" and daily assessment of readiness to extubate,
- peptic ulcer disease prophylaxis, and [40]
- deep venous thrombosis (DVT) prophylaxis.

Because several institutions observed significant reductions in VAP rates this ventilator bundle was promoted as a tool for VAP prevention.

Although some studies have demonstrated a reduction of VAP in ICUs with implementation of the ventilator bundle or a modified VAP bundle, these results are difficult to interpret as bundle compliance rates were not reported, other specific VAP risk factors were not controlled, and clinical definition of VAP varied [41, 42]. Thus, other effective evidence-based strategies for VAP prevention should be considered in addition to the ventilator bundle or the development of a VAP bundle. Implementation of such prevention strategies in VAP bundles has been associated with VAP reduction [43, 44]. Prevention strategies used in VAP bundles included chlorhexidine antiseptic and subglottic secretion drainage. A meta-analysis that included five studies and 896 patients suggests that subglottic secretion drainage was effective in the prevention of early-onset VAP in patients expected to require mechanical ventilation > 72 h [45].

Use of the oral antiseptic chlorhexidine gluconate has been demonstrated effective in preventing VAP. A systematic review and meta-analysis of seven trials with 2,144 patients observed a reduction of VAP incidence with oral application of antiseptics, but this was not associated with reduced mortality, duration of mechanical ventilation or stay in the ICU [46]. Based on these observations oral application of chlorhexidine has been advocated in the most recent evidence-based VAP prevention clinical practice guidelines.

A randomised study in cardiac surgery patients mechanically ventilated > 48 h demonstrated that subglottic secretion drainage, when compared to conventional care, resulted in a reduction in VAP incidence, VAP episodes per 1000 days of mechanical ventilation, median length of ICU stay, and hospital antibiotic use [47].

Because the endotracheal tube lumen is a nidus for bacterial growth in biofilm, prevention of bacterial biofilm formation should decrease the risk of VAP. A recent multicentre, randomised clinical trial in patients mechanically ventilated > 24 h reports a reduction in VAP incidence with the use of silver-coated endotracheal tubes which prevent bacterial biofilm formation [48]. These results may explain that simply changing the airway from an oral endotracheal tube to a tracheostomy may not necessarily decrease the risk of VAP. Several trials focusing on early versus late tracheostomy show conflicting results regarding the effect of tracheostomy on VAP incidence. A systematic review and meta-analysis including 406 patients of five studies could not observe reduction in pneumonia, mortality, ventilator days, or length of ICU stay with early tracheotomy [49].

Non-invasive ventilation (NIV) provides ventilator support without the need for intubation or allows earlier removal of the endotracheal tube, thereby reducing complications related to prolonged intubation such as VAP. A meta-analysis observed decreased mortality, fewer days on mechanical ventilation, lower rates of VAP, and shorter ICU and hospital stays with NIV [50].

Cardiovascular effects

The application of a mechanical ventilator breath generates an increase in airway- and, therefore, in intrathoracic pressure, which in turn reduces the venous return to the heart. In normo- and hypovolaemic patients, this produces a reduction in right- and left-ventricular filling and results in decreased stroke volume, cardiac output and oxygen delivery (DO_2) [51]. To normalise systemic blood flow during mechanical ventilation, intravascular volume often needs to be increased and/or the cardiovascular system needs pharmacological support. Reducing mechanical ventilation to a level which provides adequate support for existing spontaneous breathing should help to reduce the cardiovascular side effects of ventilatory support [52].

Periodic reduction of intrathoracic pressure resulting from spontaneous efforts during mechanical ventilatory support promotes the venous return to the heart and right- and left-ventricular filling, thereby increasing cardiac output and DO_2 [53]. Experimental [54–57] and clinical [58, 59] studies show that assisted spontaneous breathing results in an increase in cardiac index. In addition, the outflow from the right ventricle which depends mainly on the lung volume, which is the major determinant of pulmonary vascular resistance, may benefit from a decrease in intrathoracic pressure during spontaneous breathing efforts[29] [58].

Conversely, mechanical support of each individual inspiration with PSV and identical airway pressures produces no increase or very little increase in cardiac index [58].

Increase in cardiac index observed during assisted spontaneous breathing when compared to controlled mechanical ventilation was a function of the pressure support level. This suggests that during assisted inspiration spontaneous respiratory activity may not always decrease intrathoracic pressures sufficiently to counteract the cardiovascular depression of positive pressure ventilation.

Patients with left-ventricular dysfunction may not benefit from augmentation of the venous return to the heart and increased left-ventricular afterload as a result of reduced intrathoracic pressure. Thus, switching abruptly from controlled to assisted mechanical ventilation with simultaneous reduction in airway pressure may lead to decompensation of existing cardiac insufficiency [60]. Räsänen et al. [61, 62] demonstrated the need of adequate ventilatory support and CPAP levels in patients with respiratory and cardiogenic failure.

Organ function and perfusion

By reducing cardiac output and the venous return to the heart, mechanical ventilation can have a negative effect on the circulation of the blood and, therefore, on the functioning of other organ systems.

In the kidney, the reduction in cardiac output and venous return causes, via a sympatho-adren-ergic reaction, vasoconstriction of the afferent renal arterioles with reduction and redistribution of the renal blood flow from the cortical to the juxtaglomerular nephrons [63]. This reduces the glomerular filtration rate and sodium excretion [64, 65]. The reduction in renal blood flow and increase in sodium content result at the macula densa, in conjunction with sympatho-adren-ergic stimulation, in activation of the renin angiotensin aldosterone system, which increases renal vasoconstriction and further slows the glomerular filtration rate and sodium excretion. As a result of stimulation of baroreceptors in the aorta, a drop in transmural blood pressure and the number of stretch receptors in the left atrium and lower intrathoracic blood volume, arginine vasopressin is released, causing vasoconstriction and the reabsorption of water at the distal tubules [66]. At the same time, less atrial natriuretic peptide, an arginine vasopressin antagonist, is released as there is less expansion of the atria [65, 67]. The increase in venous return and cardiac output, brought about by a rhythmic reduction in intrathoracic pressure during maintained spontaneous breathing, should significantly improve kidney perfusion and function during ventilation [68] (Hering).

In critically ill patients several investigations have observed a similar response of splanchnic blood flow to increase of PEEP. Berendes et al. [69] observed in 20 patients during abdominal surgery that an increase of PEEP in increments of 5 cm H_2O from 0 to 15 cm H_2O induced a parallel decrease in mixed venous and hepatic venous oxygen saturations. However, these changes only became significant at a PEEP level of 15 cm H_2O. In accordance, Winsö et al. [70] using flow probes found that PEEP decreased cardiac output and portal blood flow while splanchnic oxygen consumption was maintained by compensatory increase in splanchnic oxygen extraction during abdominal surgery. Compatibly, Aneman et al. [71] reported that mesenteric and hepatic oxygen consumption was not altered by the application of moderate PEEP at a level of 10 cm H_2O, despite a decrease in mesenteric and hepatic oxygen delivery. Aneman and coworkers [71] confirmed in these patients that hepatic arterial buffer response was preserved since the hepatic arterial blood flow increased to compensate the decrease in portal blood flow. Based on these results observed in anaesthetised patients during surgery it is difficult to conclude on critically ill patients. The effects of PEEP on splanchnic perfusion may be even more pronounced in patients with acute lung injury, especially if associated with hypovolaemia and sepsis per se causing deterioration in tissue perfusion [72].

In patients with ALI due to septic shock, Träger et al. [73] found that increase of the PEEP level up to 15 cm H_2O resulted in a decrease in cardiac output and hepatic vein oxygen saturation. Decrease of hepatic vein oxygen saturation was more pronounced at a PEEP level of 15 compared with 10 cm H_2O. Similarly, hepatic glucose production was maintained at PEEP levels up to 10 cm H_2O but decreased at PEEP levels of 15 H_2O. In contrast, Kiefer and coworkers [74] using continuous primed infusion of indocyanine green (ICG) observed no change in cardiac output and splanchnic blood flow when PEEP was increased in patients with acute lung injury. The different results found in these studies may be partially explained by differences in the external und total PEEP levels. Kiefer et al. [74] increased the total PEEP level determined with an end-expiratory occlusion manoeuvre in increments of 3 to 5 cm of H_2O. The maximal total PEEP level never exceeded 14 cm H_2O. Therefore, Kiefer et al. [74] also measured intrinsic PEEP which has been demonstrated to significantly increase intrathoracic pressures and deteriorate systemic blood flow. Thus, undetected intrinsic PEEP may result in higher total levels of PEEP and intrathoracic pressures which will result in deterioration in splanchnic blood flow and metabolism. However, a major limitation of the studies investigating the effect of PEEP on splanchnic perfusion is the small number of included patients. Therefore, the effect of PEEP splanchnic blood flow may have been confounded by some patients treated e.g. with adrenergic agents. Based on currently available data it can therefore be concluded that moderate levels of PEEP are usually well tolerated in critically ill patients, provided that fluid resuscitation is adequate and that cardiac output can be maintained.

Few data are available on the effects of PEEP gastrointestinal perfusion or metabolism. Experimental data show that gastric mucosal oxygenation may also be dissociated from the effects on cardiac output and splanchnic blood flow. Four-

nell et al. [75] observed in anaesthetised dogs that gastric mucosal oxygen saturation decreased at PEEP levels of 15 cm H_2O despite maintenance of cardiac output by a rapid fluid challenge. Currently, only one investigation studied the effects of PEEP on gut mucosal blood flow and oxygenation despite the wide clinical availability of various measurement techniques including gastric tonometry.

Ventilator-associated lung injury

Although mechanical ventilation provides essential life support, it can worsen lung injury [76]. Computed tomography (CT) images of patients with ARDS demonstrate a non-homogeneous distribution of pulmonary aeration. Normally aerated lung regions are relatively small but, receiving the largest part of tidal volume (V_T) [77, 78], may be exposed to excessive alveolar wall tension and stress due to overdistension [79, 80]. Atelectatic lung regions are prone to cyclic recruitment and derecruitment, leading to shear stress in adjacent aerated and non-aerated alveoli [81–83]. Whereas excessive stress or strain to lung tissues occurring during mechanical ventilation may result in structural damage of the lung parenchyma and barotraumas, ventilator-induced lung injury (VILI) is caused by moderate stress or strain to lung tissues occurring during mechanical ventilation, aggravating inflammation and diffuse alveolar damage [76, 84].

Lung-protective ventilation strategies (LPVS) include ventilation with small V_T and limited airway pressures to reduce VILI from overdistention while accepting hypercapnia and medium to high positive end-expiratory pressure (PEEP) levels to keep alveoli open throughout the ventilator cycle [85]. Hypercapnia and acidosis may increase intracranial pressure, pulmonary hypertension, depress myocardial contractility, decrease renal blood flow, and release endogenous catecholamines [86]. In addition, prevention of cyclic derecruitment with higher PEEP levels may contribute to overdistention of normally aerated alveoli, counterbalancing the benefits from low V_T and limited airway pressures ventilation cycle [85].

In the past years the effect of different LPVS on outcome in patients with ALI or ARDS has been investigated in randomised controlled trials (RCT). RCTs tested

- higher versus lower V_T ventilation at comparable PEEP [87–90],
- higher versus lower PEEP strategies during low V_T ventilation, [91–93] and
- lower V_T and PEEP titrated above the lower inflection point (IP) of the individual pressure volume curve versus higher V_T and low PEEP [94, 95].

The results of these RCTs were partially conflicting, which was explained by differences in study design and number of enrolled patients. These partially conflicting results from the RCTs may explain why the majority of critically ill patients is still ventilated with rather high V_T at low or even nil PEEP [4, 96]. Previous systematic reviews and meta-analysis did not focus strictly on the comparison between lower and higher V_T ventilation using comparable PEEP strategies but also included trials simultaneously reducing V_T while markedly increasing PEEP [97–99]. In addition, recent RCTs comparing higher versus lower PEEP strategies with lower V_T ventilation were not evaluated. Eichacker and colleagues [100] performed a systematic review without formal meta-analysis including 5 RCTs and a total of 1, 201 patients. These authors found a difference in the effect of lower V_T ventilation on mortality among RCTs. Because lower V_T ventilation did not improve outcome when higher V_T ventilation resulted in lower P_{ei} Eichacker and colleagues [100] concluded that the beneficial effect of lower V_T ventilation is restricted to settings in which higher V_T ventilation results in excessive P_{ei}. This conclusion is based on pooled mortality data observed at different times after randomisation. Moran and colleagues [97] analysed the same 5 RCTs and found no reduction in pooled 28-day or hospital mortality using a random effect model due to the high observed heterogeneity indicated by I^2 of 56.8%. The magnitude of heterogeneity was partially explained by including trials simultaneously testing lower and higher PEEP strategies. Petrucci and colleagues [98, 99], including 6 RCTs and a total of 1, 297 patients, found lower V_T ventilation to be associated with a reduction in the risk of hospital mortality and mortality at the end of the follow-up period for each trial. Recently, we performed

a meta-analysis according to the Cochrane Collaboration guidelines [101] including 9 RCTs with a total of 3, 596 patients (Putensen et al., Ann Int. Med., under review). In contrast to previous meta-analysis [97, 98], a distinction must be made between higher V_T ventilation using comparable PEEP strategies, lower versus higher PEEP at low V_T ventilation, and the combination of higher V_T and lower PEEP versus lower V_T and higher PEEP to better separate the effects of V_T and PEEP on mortality.

Evaluation of lower V_T ventilation using comparable PEEP strategies shows reduction in hospital mortality. However, the ARDS Network study [87] carries 86% of the weight in the pooled effect.

Previous [97–100] reports suggest that lower V_T ventilation did not improve outcome when higher V_T ventilation resulted in P_{ei} less or equal to 30 cm H_2O. However, all analyses could not demonstrate any advantage of high V_T ventilation. Thus, low V_T ventilation appears to be beneficial in acute lung injury or ARDS patients for routine clinical use if potential side effects as hypercapnia and respiratory acidosis are not contraindicated.

2 RCTs not demonstrating the advantages of lower V_T ventilation accepted pH thresholds of 7.00 and 7.05 before increasing V_T or buffering with sodium bicarbonate [88, 90]. Although ventilation with lower V_T may be associated with lower pH and a trend towards higher $PaCO_2$, mortality was not affected in these studies [88, 90].

Although all these trials [87–90] aimed at testing lower versus higher V_T ventilation using comparable PEEP strategies, PEEP levels were slightly higher with lower V_T ventilation on the first day of treatment. Poorer arterial oxygenation requiring higher FiO_2 to maintain the targeted oxygenation goal resulted in higher PEEP levels in all applied PEEP strategies [87]. Alveolar derecruitment and hence poorer oxygenation during lower V_T ventilation [102] may explain slightly higher FiO_2 and PEEP levels during lower V_T ventilation on day 1.

Ventilation with lower V_T and P_{ei} was not associated with reduction in the risk of barotrauma. Apparently, the higher V_T used in the trials [87–90] did not result in alveolar wall tension and stress sufficient to cause alveolar rupture and gross barotrauma. However, minor structural damage cannot be excluded. However, during higher V_T ventilation even moderate alveolar wall tension and stress may induce pulmonary and systemic inflammatory response [103]. The ARDSNet trial [87] reported lower blood concentrations of inflammatory mediators and lower incidence and less severity of organ dysfunction with lower V_T ventilation, which is generally believed to explain the beneficial effects of lower V_T ventilation on outcome. Based on these studies, routine use of low V_T in all ALI or ARDS patients has to be recommended.

Using different criteria for PEEP selection, three trials [91–93] demonstrated no difference in mortality comparing lower versus higher PEEP with lower V_T ventilation. Thus, random application of either higher or lower PEEP strategy in an unselected population with acute lung injury or ARDS does not significantly improve outcome. In two of these trials [92, 93] 7.8 to 34.6 % of patients needed rescue therapies to prevent decrease in P arterial oxygen saturation below 88 % at high FiO_2 levels. In the higher PEEP groups [92, 93] requirement of rescue therapies to prevent life-threatening hypoxaemia and mortality in patients who received rescue therapy were lower. Thus, higher PEEP strategies might be beneficial to prevent life-threatening hypoxemia in patients with severe ARDS.

Despite limitation of V_T, higher PEEP strategies increased P_{ei}, which may have contributed to overdistention of normally aerated alveoli, thereby counterbalancing small possible benefits of higher PEEP [80, 104–106]. However, higher PEEP strategies did not result in alveolar rupture and gross barotraumas when limiting V_T and P_{ei}.

To counteract possible cardiovascular depression caused by higher PEEP and P_{ei} fluid loading frequently associated with a positive fluid balance and/or vasopressors may be required, which has been shown to delay pulmonary recovery [107]. Because all these trials [92, 93, 107] did not consistently report fluid and cardio-vascular management the role of fluid and vasopressor management with respect to outcome is unclear.

Higher PEEP strategies during lower V_T ventilation did not improve hospital mortality and cannot be recommended in unselected ALI or ARDS patients. Higher PEEP strategies during lower V_T ventilation may be recommended to prevent life-threatening hypoxaemia.

Permissive hypercapnia

Hypercapnia is a consequence of lung-protective ventilatory strategies using small tidal volumes in patients with ALI and ARDS [94]. The cardio-circulatory changes related to permissive hypercapnia are substantial and occur not only because of the acute rise in arterial PCO_2, but also because of a decrease in intrathoracic pressure caused by reduction in tidal volume and hence end-inspiratory pressure [108]. Acute hypercapnia has important cardio-circulatory side effects due to an increase in myocardial contractility by stimulation of sympathetic nerve activity and a decrease in systemic vascular resistance which results in an increased cardiac index while maintaining arterial blood pressure [108]. The regional perfusion is variably modified by hypercapnia due to changes in local vascular tone. Hypercapnia associated with respiratory acidosis may cause vasoconstriction e.g. in the lungs and the kidneys while resulting in vasodilation in the brain.

Moreover, the cardio-circulatory instability frequently observed in patients with ALI and ARDS may be a confounding factor for the evaluation of the cardio-circulatory changes induced by hypercapnia. Thus even moderate hypercapnia may in the presence of cardio-circulatory instability result in a profound respiratory and metabolic acidosis.

Few studies in animals [109–113] and critically ill patients have assessed the effect of acute changes in arterial PCO_2 on hepatic and gut perfusion. Fujita and coworkers [111] observed no change in systemic circulation in dogs during hypocapnia with respiratory alkalosis by reducing instrumental deadspace volume, but a decrease in hepatic artery blood flow attributable to a direct vasoconstrictor effect.

Hypercapnia has been observed to increase hepatic and splanchnic blood flow [109–112] in a biphasic pattern. Initially, blood flow is reduced because of sympathetic stimulation, followed by an increase in blood flow caused by the direct vasodilator effect of carbon dioxide. Mas and coworkers [114] found in stable mechanically ventilated patients that moderate acute variations in arterial PCO_2 increased systemic perfusion while splanchnic perfusion, assessed by gastric mucosal-arterial PCO_2 difference (ΔPCO_2), did not change. Because most of these patients had normal basal ΔPCO_2, it is unclear if splanchnic perfusion may have changed in cases of previous intramucosal acidosis during hypercapnia. Apparently, under these conditions, the use of pHi to evaluate gastric perfusion appears unreliable.

Sitbon and coworkers [115] demonstrated that tidal volume reduction in patients with ARDS, despite resulting in increased cardiac output, did not improve gastric mucosal perfusion. However, the heterogeneity observed in the individual changes of gastric mucosal perfusion due to tidal volume reduction supports the concept that the direct local vasodilation of an elevated tissue PCO_2 may be opposed by the increased release of catecholamines in the systemic circulation. Compatible with these data, Kiefer [116] and coworkers observed in patients with ALI that splanchnic blood flow measured using primed continuous infusion of indocyanine green dye with hepatic venous sampling, gastric mucosal-arterial PCO_2 and splanchnic lactate/pyruvate exchange did not change significantly with an acute moderate increase in arterial PCO_2.

A major limitation of all investigations in critically ill patients is that only global splanchnic and intestinal perfusion can be determined. To investigate regional perfusion differences of the gut, e.g. to distinguish between perfusion of mucosal-submucosal and muscularis-serosal layers, one has to rely on experimental models using destructive methods like the microsphere techniques. Using coloured microspheres Hering and coworkers [117] demonstrated no marked increase in mucosal-submucosal blood flow to the stomach, the duodenum, the jejunum, and the colon during hypercapnia resulting in respiratory acidosis in induced lung injury.

Based on the clinical and experimental data it has to be concluded that despite an increased cardiac index it cannot be expected that splanchnic and gut perfusion is improved during permissive hypercapnia in critically ill patients.

Summary

Despite technical and medical progress, outcome in mechanically ventilated patients with and without acute lung injury (ALI) or acute respiratory distress syndrome (ARDS) remains poor. Thus, healthcare providers should devote particular attention to minimising complications associated with mechanical ventilation in critically ill patients.

Whereas results from large multicentre trials provide evidence for the implementation of low-tidal-volume ventilatory strategies, the choice of the "right" PEEP level in patients requiring mechanical ventilation due to acute lung injury or ARDS still remains an unsolved problem. As higher PEEP strategies during lower V_T ventilation did not improve hospital mortality, it cannot be recommended in unselected ALI or ARDS patients but may be so to prevent life-threatening hypoxaemia.

Implementation of prevention strategies in VAP bundles has been associated with VAP reduction; however, the particular measures still are matter of controversial discussion. Maintaining spontaneous breathing during ventilatory support is associated with improved pulmonary gas exchange and better systemic and intestinal blood flows.

Hypercapnia as a consequence of lung-protective ventilatory strategies leads to an increase in myocardial contractility and a decrease in systemic vascular resistance, resulting in a variable modification of regional tissue perfusion. Despite an increased cardiac index it cannot be expected that splanchnic and gut perfusion is improved during permissive hypercapnia in critically ill patients.

The authors

Christian Putensen, MD, PhD
Nils Theuerkauf, MD
Thomas Muders, MD
Hermann Wrigge, MD, PhD
Ulf Günther, MD
    Department of Anaesthesiology and
    Intensive Care Medicine | University
    Hospital Bonn | Bonn, Germany

Address for correspondence
    Christian Putensen
    Department of Anaesthesiology and
    Intensive Care Medicine
    University of Bonn
    Sigmund-Freud-Str. 25
    53105 Bonn, Germany
    E-mail: putensen@uni-bonn.de

References

1. Marini JJ. New options for the ventilatory management of acute lung injury. New Horiz 1993;1:489–503.
2. Ely EW, Baker AM, Dunagan DP, Burke HL, Smith AC, Kelly PT et al. Effect on the duration of mechanical ventilation of identifying patients capable of breathing spontaneously. N Engl J Med 1996;19;335:1864–1869.
3. Kollef MH, Shapiro SD, Silver P, St John RE, Prentice D, Sauer S et al. A randomized, controlled trial of protocol-directed versus physician-directed weaning from mechanical ventilation. Crit Care Med 1997;25:567–574.
4. Esteban A, Anzueto A, Frutos F, Alia I, Brochard L, Stewart TE et al. Characteristics and outcomes in adult patients receiving mechanical ventilation: a 28-day international study. JAMA 2002;287:345–355.
5. Lewandowski K, Metz J, Deutschmann C, Preiss H, Kuhlen R, Artigas A et al. Incidence, severity, and mortality of acute respiratory failure in Berlin, Germany. Am J Respir Crit Care Med 1995;151:1121–1125.
6. Luhr OR, Antonsen K, Karlsson M, Aardal S, Thorsteinsson A, Frostell CG et al. Incidence and mortality after acute respiratory failure and acute respiratory distress syndrome in Sweden, Denmark, and Iceland. The ARF Study Group. Am J Respir Crit Care Med 1999;159:1849–1861.
7. Vasilyev S, Schaap RN, Mortensen JD. Hospital survival rates of patients with acute respiratory failure in modern respiratory intensive care units. An international, multicenter, prospective survey. Chest 1995;107:1083–1088.
8. Vincent JL, Akca S, De MA, Haji-Michael P, Sprung C, Moreno R et al. The epidemiology of acute respiratory failure in critically ill patients(*). Chest 2002;121:1602–1609.
9. Barnason S, Graham J, Wild MC, Jensen LB, Rasmussen D, Schulz P et al. Comparison of two endotracheal tube securement techniques on unplanned extubation, oral mucosa, and facial skin integrity. Heart Lung 1998;27:409–417.
10. Betbese AJ, Perez M, Bak E, Rialp G, Mancebo J. A prospective study of unplanned endotracheal extubation in intensive care unit patients. Crit Care Med 1998;26:1180–1186.
11. Boulain T. Unplanned extubations in the adult intensive care unit: a prospective multicenter study. Association des Reanimateurs du Centre-Ouest. Am J Respir Crit Care Med 1998;157:1131–1137.
12. Chevron V, Menard JF, Richard JC, Girault C, Leroy J, Bonmarchand G. Unplanned extubation: risk factors of development and predictive criteria for reintubation. Crit Care Med 1998;26:1049–1053.
13. Christie JM, Dethlefsen M, Cane RD. Unplanned endotracheal extubation in the intensive care unit. J Clin Anesth 1996;8:289–293.
14. de LA, Alberti C, Azoulay E, Le ME, Cheval C, Vincent F et al. Impact of unplanned extubation and reintubation after weaning on nosocomial pneumonia risk in the intensive care unit: a prospective multicenter study. Anesthesiology 2002;97:148–156.
15. Epstein SK, Nevins ML, Chung J. Effect of unplanned extubation on outcome of mechanical ventilation. Am J Respir Crit Care Med 2000;161:1912–1916.
16. Popernack ML, Thomas NJ, Lucking SE. Decreasing unplanned extubations: utilization of the Penn State Children's Hospital Sedation Algorithm. Pediatr Crit Care Med 2004;5:58–62.
17. Razek T, Gracias V, Sullivan D, Braxton C, Gandhi R, Gupta R et al. Assessing the need for reintubation: a prospective evaluation of unplanned endotracheal extubation. J Trauma 2000;48:466–469.
18. Yeh SH, Lee LN, Ho TH, Chiang MC, Lin LW. Implications of nursing care in the occurrence and consequences of unplanned extubation in adult intensive care units. Int J Nurs Stud 2004;41:255–262.
19. Sugiyama K, Yokoyama K. Displacement of the endotracheal tube caused by change of head position in pediatric anesthesia: evaluation by fiberoptic bronchoscopy. Anesth Analg 1996;82:251–253.
20. Sugiyama K, Mietani W, Hirota Y, Matsuura H. Displacement of the endotracheal tube caused by postural change: evaluation by fiberoptic observation. Anesth Pain Control Dent 1992;1:29–33.
21. Carrion MI, Ayuso D, Marcos M, Paz RM, de la Cal MA, Alia I et al. Accidental removal of endotracheal and nasogastric tubes and intravascular catheters. Crit Care Med 2000;28:63–66.
22. Florette OG, Kirby RR. Airway Management. In: Civett JM TRKRe, 1997, eds. Philadelphia: Lippincott-Raven; 2009: 757–75.
23. Kapadia FN, Bajan KB, Raje KV. Airway accidents in intubated intensive care unit patients: an epidemiological study. Crit Care Med 2000;28:659–664.
24. Kaplow R, Bookbinder M. A comparison of four endotracheal tube holders. Heart Lung 1994;23:59–66.
25. Pesiri AJ. Two-year study of the prevention of unintentional extubation. Crit Care Nurs Q 1994;17:35–39.
26. Gelman JJ, Aro M, Weiss SM. Tracheo-innominate artery fistula. J Am Coll Surg 1994;179:626–634.
27. Grillo HC, Donahue DM, Mathisen DJ, Wain JC, Wright CD. Postintubation tracheal stenosis. Treatment and results. J Thorac Cardiovasc Surg 1995;109:486–492.
28. Mathisen DJ, Grillo HC, Wain JC, Hilgenberg AD. Management of acquired nonmalignant tracheoesophageal fistula. Ann Thorac Surg 1991;52:759–765.
29. Wood DE, Mathisen DJ. Late complications of tracheotomy. Clin Chest Med 1991;12:597–609.
30. Kastanos N, Estopa MR, Marin PA, Xaubet MA, gusti-Vidal A. Laryngotracheal injury due to endotracheal intubation: incidence, evolution, and predisposing factors. A prospective long-term study. Crit Care Med 1983;11:362–367.

31. HEAD JM. Tracheostomy in the management of respiratory problems. N Engl J Med 1961;264:587–91.:587–591.
32. Nouraei SA, Ma E, Patel A, Howard DJ, Sandhu GS. Estimating the population incidence of adult post-intubation laryngotracheal stenosis. Clin Otolaryngol 2007;32:411–412.
33. Borasio P, Ardissone F, Chiampo G. Post-intubation tracheal rupture. A report on ten cases. Eur J Cardiothorac Surg 1997;12:98–100.
34. Massard G, Rouge C, Dabbagh A, Kessler R, Hentz JG, Roeslin N et al. Tracheobronchial lacerations after intubation and tracheostomy. Ann Thorac Surg 1996;61:1483–1487.
35. Cocanour CS, Ostrosky-Zeichner L, Peninger M, Garbade D, Tidemann T, Domonoske BD et al. Cost of a ventilator-associated pneumonia in a shock trauma intensive care unit. Surg Infect (Larchmt) 2005;6:65–72.
36. Rello J, Ollendorf DA, Oster G, Vera-Llonch M, Bellm L, Redman R et al. Epidemiology and outcomes of ventilator-associated pneumonia in a large US database. Chest 2002;122:2115–2121.
37. Safdar N, Dezfulian C, Collard HR, Saint S. Clinical and economic consequences of ventilator-associated pneumonia: a systematic review. Crit Care Med 2005;33:2184–2193.
38. Muscedere J, Dodek P, Keenan S, Fowler R, Cook D, Heyland D. Comprehensive evidence-based clinical practice guidelines for ventilator-associated pneumonia: prevention. J Crit Care 2008;23:126–137.
39. Institute for Healthcare Improvement. http://www.ihi.org. 2009. Ref Type: Electronic Citation
40. Cook DJ, Fuller HD, Guyatt GH, Marshall JC, Leasa D, Hall R et al. Risk factors for gastrointestinal bleeding in critically ill patients. Canadian Critical Care Trials Group. N Engl J Med 1994;330:377–381.
41. Blamoun J, Alfakir M, Rella ME, Wojcik JM, Solis RA, Anees KM et al. Efficacy of an expanded ventilator bundle for the reduction of ventilator-associated pneumonia in the medical intensive care unit. Am J Infect Control 2009;37:172–175.
42. Westwell S. Implementing a ventilator care bundle in an adult intensive care unit. Nurs Crit Care 2008;13:203–207.
43. Lansford T, Moncure M, Carlton E, Endress R, Shik N, Udobi K et al. Efficacy of a pneumonia prevention protocol in the reduction of ventilator-associated pneumonia in trauma patients. Surg Infect (Larchmt) 2007;8:505–510.
44. Omrane R, Eid J, Perreault MM, Yazbeck H, Berbiche D, Gursahaney A et al. Impact of a protocol for prevention of ventilator-associated pneumonia. Ann Pharmacother 2007;41:1390–1396.
45. Dezfulian C, Shojania K, Collard HR, Kim HM, Matthay MA, Saint S. Subglottic secretion drainage for preventing ventilator-associated pneumonia: a meta-analysis. Am J Med 2005;118:11–18.
46. Chan EY, Ruest A, Meade MO, Cook DJ. Oral decontamination for prevention of pneumonia in mechanically ventilated adults: systematic review and meta-analysis. BMJ 2007;334:889-.
47. Bouza E, Perez MJ, Munoz P, Rincon C, Barrio JM, Hortal J. Continuous aspiration of subglottic secretions in the prevention of ventilator-associated pneumonia in the postoperative period of major heart surgery. Chest 2008;134:938–946.
48. Kollef MH, Afessa B, Anzueto A, Veremakis C, Kerr KM, Margolis BD et al. Silver-coated endotracheal tubes and incidence of ventilator-associated pneumonia: the NASCENT randomized trial. JAMA 2008;%20;300:805–813.
49. Griffiths J, Barber VS, Morgan L, Young JD. Systematic review and meta-analysis of studies of the timing of tracheostomy in adult patients undergoing artificial ventilation. BMJ 2005;330:1243-.
50. Burns KE, Adhikari NK, Meade MO. Noninvasive positive pressure ventilation as a weaning strategy for intubated adults with respiratory failure. Cochrane Database Syst Rev 2003;CD004127.
51. Pinsky MR. Determinants of pulmonary arterial flow variation during respiration. J Appl Physiol 1984;56:1237–1245.
52. Kirby RR, Perry JC, Calderwood HW, Ruiz BC, Lederman DS. Cardiorespiratory effects of high positive end-expiratory pressure. Anesthesiology 1975;43:533–539.
53. Downs JB, Douglas ME, Sanfelippo PM, Stanford W, Hodges MR. Ventilatory pattern, intrapleural pressure, and cardiac output. Anesth Analg 1977;56:88–96.
54. Falkenhain SK, Reilley TE, Gregory JS. Improvement in cardiac output during airway pressure release ventilation. Crit Care Med 1992;20:1358–1360.
55. Putensen C, Rasanen J, Lopez FA, Downs JB. Effect of interfacing between spontaneous breathing and mechanical cycles on the ventilation-perfusion distribution in canine lung injury. Anesthesiology 1994;81:921–930.
56. Putensen C, Rasanen J, Lopez FA. Ventilation-perfusion distributions during mechanical ventilation with superimposed spontaneous breathing in canine lung injury. Am J Respir Crit Care Med 1994;150:101–108.
57. Putensen C, Leon MA, Putensen-Himmer G. Timing of pressure release affects power of breathing and minute ventilation during airway pressure release ventilation. Crit Care Med 1994;22:872–878.
58. Putensen C, Mutz NJ, Putensen-Himmer G, Zinserling J. Spontaneous breathing during ventilatory support improves ventilation-perfusion distributions in patients with acute respiratory distress syndrome. Am J Respir Crit Care Med 1999;159:1241–1248.
59. Sydow M, Burchardi H, Ephraim E, Zielmann S, Crozier TA. Long-term effects of two different ventilatory modes on oxygenation in acute lung injury. Comparison of airway pressure release ventilation and volume-controlled inverse ratio ventilation. Am J Respir Crit Care Med 1994;149:1550–1556.

G

60. Lemaire F, Teboul JL, Cinotti L, Giotto G, Abrouk F, Steg G et al. Acute left ventricular dysfunction during unsuccessful weaning from mechanical ventilation. Anesthesiology 1988;69:171–179.

61. Rasanen J, Nikki P. Respiratory failure arising from acute myocardial infarction. Ann Chir Gynaecol Suppl 1982;196:43–7.:43–47.

62. Rasanen J, Heikkila J, Downs J, Nikki P, Vaisanen I, Viitanen A. Continuous positive airway pressure by face mask in acute cardiogenic pulmonary edema. Am J Cardiol 1985;55:296–300.

63. Manny J, Justice R, Hechtman HB. Abnormalities in organ blood flow and its distribution during positive end-expiratory pressure. Surgery 1979;85:425–432.

64. Annat G, Viale JP, Bui XB, Hadj AO, Benzoni D, Vincent M et al. Effect of PEEP ventilation on renal function, plasma renin, aldosterone, neurophysins and urinary ADH, and prostaglandins. Anesthesiology 1983;58:136–141.

65. Rossaint R, Jorres D, Nienhaus M, Oduah K, Falke K, Kaczmarczyk G. Positive end-expiratory pressure reduces renal excretion without hormonal activation after volume expansion in dogs. Anesthesiology 1992;77:700–708.

66. Marquez JM, Douglas ME, Downs JB, Wu WH, Mantini EL, Kuck EJ et al. Renal function and cardiovascular responses during positive airway pressure. Anesthesiology 1979;50:393–398.

67. Scholz J, Bednarz F, Roewer N, Schmidt R, Schulte am EJ. [The effects of incremental PEEP on atrial natriuretic peptide, right atrial pressure and the size of the right atrium in anesthetized patients]. Anasth Intensivther Notfallmed 1990;25 Suppl 1:20–4.:20–24.

68. Hering R, Peters D, Zinserling J, Wrigge H, von ST, Putensen C. Effects of spontaneous breathing during airway pressure release ventilation on renal perfusion and function in patients with acute lung injury. Intensive Care Med 2002;28:1426–1433.

69. Berendes E, Lippert G, Loick HM, Brussel T. Effects of positive end-expiratory pressure ventilation on splanchnic oxygenation in humans. J Cardiothorac Vasc Anesth 1996;10:598–602.

70. Winso O, Biber B, Gustavsson B, Holm C, Milsom I, Niemand O. Portal blood flow in man during graded positive end-expiratory pressure ventilation. Intensive Care Med 1986;12:80–85.

71. Aneman A, Eisenhofer G, Fandriks L, Olbe L, Dalenback J, Nitescu P et al. Splanchnic circulation and regional sympathetic outflow during preoperative PEEP ventilation in humans. Br J Anaesth 1999;82:838–842.

72. Bersten AD, Gnidec AA, Rutledge FS, Sibbald WJ. Hyperdynamic sepsis modifies a PEEP-mediated redistribution in organ blood flows. Am Rev Respir Dis 1990;141:1198–1208.

73. Trager K, Radermacher P, Georgieff M. PEEP and hepatic metabolic performance in septic shock. Intensive Care Med 1996;22:1274–1275.

74. Kiefer P, Nunes S, Kosonen P, Takala J. Effect of positive end-expiratory pressure on splanchnic perfusion in acute lung injury. Intensive Care Med 2000;26:376–383.

75. Fournell A, Scheeren TW, Schwarte LA. PEEP decreases oxygenation of the intestinal mucosa despite normalization of cardiac output. Adv Exp Med Biol 1998;454:435–40.:435–440.

76. Tremblay LN, Slutsky AS. Ventilator-induced lung injury: from the bench to the bedside. Intensive Care Med 2006;32:24–33.

77. Gattinoni L, Pelosi P, Crotti S, Valenza F. Effects of positive end-expiratory pressure on regional distribution of tidal volume and recruitment in adult respiratory distress syndrome. Am J Respir Crit Care Med 1995;151:1807–1814.

78. Terragni PP, Rosboch G, Tealdi A, Corno E, Menaldo E, Davini O et al. Tidal hyperinflation during low tidal volume ventilation in acute respiratory distress syndrome. Am J Respir Crit Care Med 2007;175:160–166.

79. Chiumello D, Carlesso E, Cadringher P, Caironi P, Valenza F, Polli F et al. Lung stress and strain during mechanical ventilation for acute respiratory distress syndrome. Am J Respir Crit Care Med 2008;178:346–355.

80. Rouby JJ, Puybasset L, Nieszkowska A, Lu Q. Acute respiratory distress syndrome: lessons from computed tomography of the whole lung. Crit Care Med 2003;31:S285-S295.

81. Halter JM, Steinberg JM, Schiller HJ, DaSilva M, Gatto LA, Landas S et al. Positive end-expiratory pressure after a recruitment maneuver prevents both alveolar collapse and recruitment/derecruitment. Am J Respir Crit Care Med 2003;167:1620–1626.

82. Marini JJ, Hotchkiss JR, Broccard AF. Bench-to-bedside review: microvascular and airspace linkage in ventilator-induced lung injury. Crit Care 2003;7:435–444.

83. Ranieri VM, Suter PM, Tortorella C, De TR, Dayer JM, Brienza A et al. Effect of mechanical ventilation on inflammatory mediators in patients with acute respiratory distress syndrome: a randomized controlled trial. JAMA 1999;282:54–61.

84. Tremblay LN, Slutsky AS. Pathogenesis of ventilator-induced lung injury: trials and tribulations. Am J Physiol Lung Cell Mol Physiol 2005;288:L596-L598.

85. Pinhu L, Whitehead T, Evans T, Griffiths M. Ventilator-associated lung injury. Lancet 2003;361:332–340.

86. Feihl F, Perret C. Permissive hypercapnia. How permissive should we be? Am J Respir Crit Care Med 1994;150:1722–1737.

87. Ventilation with lower tidal volumes as compared with traditional tidal volumes for acute lung injury and the acute respiratory distress syndrome. The Acute Respiratory Distress Syndrome Network. N Engl J Med 2000;342:1301–1308.

88. Brochard L, Roudot-Thoraval F, Roupie E, Delclaux C, Chastre J, Fernandez-Mondejar E et al. Tidal volume re-

duction for prevention of ventilator-induced lung injury in acute respiratory distress syndrome. The Multicenter Trail Group on Tidal Volume reduction in ARDS. Am J Respir Crit Care Med 1998;158:1831–1838.

89. Brower RG, Shanholtz CB, Fessler HE, Shade DM, White P, Jr., Wiener CM et al. Prospective, randomized, controlled clinical trial comparing traditional versus reduced tidal volume ventilation in acute respiratory distress syndrome patients. Crit Care Med 1999;27:1492–1498.

90. Stewart TE, Meade MO, Cook DJ, Granton JT, Hodder RV, Lapinsky SE et al. Evaluation of a ventilation strategy to prevent barotrauma in patients at high risk for acute respiratory distress syndrome. Pressure- and Volume-Limited Ventilation Strategy Group. N Engl J Med 1998;338:355–361.

91. Brower RG, Lanken PN, MacIntyre N, Matthay MA, Morris A, Ancukiewicz M et al. Higher versus lower positive end-expiratory pressures in patients with the acute respiratory distress syndrome. N Engl J Med 2004;351:327–336.

92. Meade MO, Cook DJ, Guyatt GH, Slutsky AS, Arabi YM, Cooper DJ et al. Ventilation strategy using low tidal volumes, recruitment maneuvers, and high positive end-expiratory pressure for acute lung injury and acute respiratory distress syndrome: a randomized controlled trial. JAMA 2008;299:637–645.

93. Mercat A, Richard JC, Vielle B, Jaber S, Osman D, Diehl JL et al. Positive end-expiratory pressure setting in adults with acute lung injury and acute respiratory distress syndrome: a randomized controlled trial. JAMA 2008;299:646–655.

94. Amato MB, Barbas CS, Medeiros DM, Magaldi RB, Schettino GP, Lorenzi-Filho G et al. Effect of a protective-ventilation strategy on mortality in the acute respiratory distress syndrome. N Engl J Med 1998;338:347–354.

95. Villar J, Kacmarek RM, Perez-Mendez L, guirre-Jaime A. A high positive end-expiratory pressure, low tidal volume ventilatory strategy improves outcome in persistent acute respiratory distress syndrome: a randomized, controlled trial. Crit Care Med 2006;34:1311–1318.

96. Esteban A, Ferguson ND, Meade MO, Frutos-Vivar F, Apezteguia C, Brochard L et al. Evolution of mechanical ventilation in response to clinical research. Am J Respir Crit Care Med 2008;177:170–177.

97. Moran JL, Bersten AD, Solomon PJ. Meta-analysis of controlled trials of ventilator therapy in acute lung injury and acute respiratory distress syndrome: an alternative perspective. Intensive Care Med 2005;31:227–235.

98. Petrucci N, Iacovelli W. Ventilation with smaller tidal volumes: a quantitative systematic review of randomized controlled trials. Anesth Analg 2004;99:193–200.

99. Petrucci N, Iacovelli W. Lung protective ventilation strategy for the acute respiratory distress syndrome. Cochrane Database Syst Rev 2007;CD003844-.

100. Eichacker PQ, Gerstenberger EP, Banks SM, Cui X, Natanson C. Meta-analysis of acute lung injury and acute respiratory distress syndrome trials testing low tidal volumes. Am J Respir Crit Care Med 2002;166:1510–1514.

101. Higgins JPT, Green S, editors. Cochrane Handbook for Systematic Reviews of Interventions 4.2.6 [updated September 2006] 49. The Cochrane Library. Chichester, UK: John Wiley & Sons, Ltd.; 2006.

102. Pelosi P, Goldner M, McKibben A, Adams A, Eccher G, Caironi P et al. Recruitment and derecruitment during acute respiratory failure: an experimental study 35. Am J Respir Crit Care Med 2001;164:122–130.

103. Ranieri VM, Suter PM, Tortorella C, De TR, Dayer JM, Brienza A et al. Effect of mechanical ventilation on inflammatory mediators in patients with acute respiratory distress syndrome: a randomized controlled trial. JAMA 1999;282:54–61.

104. Gattinoni L, Caironi P, Cressoni M, Chiumello D, Ranieri VM, Quintel M et al. Lung recruitment in patients with the acute respiratory distress syndrome 4. N Engl J Med 2006;354:1775–1786.

105. Gattinoni L, Caironi P. Refining ventilatory treatment for acute lung injury and acute respiratory distress syndrome 51. JAMA 2008;299:691–693.

106. Vieira SR, Puybasset L, Richecoeur J, Lu Q, Cluzel P, Gusman PB et al. A lung computed tomographic assessment of positive end-expiratory pressure-induced lung overdistension 38. Am J Respir Crit Care Med 1998;158:1571–1577.

107. Wiedemann HP, Wheeler AP, Bernard GR, Thompson BT, Hayden D, deBoisblanc B et al. Comparison of two fluid-management strategies in acute lung injury 39. N Engl J Med 2006;354:2564–2575.

108. Carvalho CR, Barbas CS, Medeiros DM, Magaldi RB, Lorenzi FG, Kairalla RA et al. Temporal hemodynamic effects of permissive hypercapnia associated with ideal PEEP in ARDS. Am J Respir Crit Care Med 1997;156:1458–1466.

109. Cardenas VJ, Jr., Zwischenberger JB, Tao W, Nguyen PD, Schroeder T, Traber LD et al. Correction of blood pH attenuates changes in hemodynamics and organ blood flow during permissive hypercapnia. Crit Care Med 1996;24:827–834.

110. Dutton R, Levitzky M, Berkman R. Carbon dioxide and liver blood flow. Bull Eur Physiopathol Respir 1976;12:265–273.

111. Fujita Y, Sakai T, Ohsumi A, Takaori M. Effects of hypocapnia and hypercapnia on splanchnic circulation and hepatic function in the beagle. Anesth Analg 1989;69:152–157.

112. Johnson EE. Splanchnic hemodynamic response to passive hyperventilation. J Appl Physiol 1975;38:156–162.

113. Laffey JG, Jankov RP, Engelberts D, Tanswell AK, Post M, Lindsay T et al. Effects of therapeutic hypercapnia on mesenteric ischemia-reperfusion injury. Am J Respir Crit Care Med 2003;168:1383–1390.

114. Mas A, Saura P, Joseph D, Blanch L, Baigorri F, Artigas A et al. Effect of acute moderate changes in PaCO2 on global hemodynamics and gastric perfusion. Crit Care Med 2000;28:360–365.

115. Sitbon P, Teboul JL, Duranteau J, Anguel N, Richard C, Samii K. Effects of tidal volume reduction in acute respiratory distress syndrome on gastric mucosal perfusion. Intensive Care Med 2001;27:911–915.

116. Kiefer P, Nunes S, Kosonen P, Takala J. Effect of an acute increase in PCO2 on splanchnic perfusion and metabolism. Intensive Care Med 2001;27:775–778.

117. Hering R, Viehofer A, Zinserling J, Wrigge H, Kreyer S, Berg A et al. Effects of spontaneous breathing during airway pressure release ventilation on intestinal blood flow in experimental lung injury. Anesthesiology 2003;99:1137–1144.

A.B. Johan Groeneveld, S. Azam Nurmohamed and Catherine S.C. Bouman

Patient safety during continuous renal replacement therapy

Introduction

During acute kidney injury (AKI) resulting in acute renal failure (ARF), some form of continuous renal replacement therapy (CRRT) is practised in most European intensive care units (ICUs) [1–3]. The technique varies among centres, however, including the route and composition of replacement fluid to compensate for the ultrafiltration, the type of fluid and mode of anticoagulation to keep the filter patent, on top of the continuing controversy on timing and dosing, particularly in sepsis [1–3]. In this chapter we will address safety issues and (potential) adverse effects of CRRT, mainly continuous veno-venous haemofiltration (CVVH), without or with dialysis (CVVHD) (see Tab. 1) [4]. We will not address safety issues regarding intermittent haemodialysis (IHD) in the ICU, which is less commonly practised in Europe for the treatment of AKI/ARF [2]. In this context it may be sufficient to state that continuous techniques supposedly are better tolerated haemodynamically than intermittent ones, even though randomised prospective studies showed no differences in haemodynamic tolerance or survival [5–8].

Tab. 1   Safety issues during CRRT

Vascular access problems
Fluid balancing
Electrolyte and acid-base disorders
Loss and dosing of drugs and (micro)nutrients
Contamination of circuit and replacement fluids
Coagulation and dosing of anticoagulants
Bleeding and blood loss
Biocompatibility
Alarms
Disconnections

Down time

Although the term continuous is used in CRRT, interruptions to treatment do occur, especially when the filter clots, technical problems occur, and when procedures are performed outside the ICU, such as surgery and radiological interventions. The longer the down time, i.e. the period when CRRT is not operative, the less effective the treatment. At present, there is little information on how many hours are spent off the filter each day during CRRT. In the study by Uchino et al. [9] in Australia, median filter down time was 3 hours, but is was as high as 8 hours in the study of Mehta et al. [6] in the USA. The lack of attention to the importance of minimising down time could be one of the reasons why CRRT has not shown a survival benefit over IHD.

Vascular access

CRRT requires well-functioning vascular access to a large vein, allowing high and uninterrupted blood flows in order to prevent clotting and facilitate ultrafiltration. Cannulation of the jugular, subclavian or femoral vein carries the risks of perforation, bleeding, thrombosis and, for femoral veins, formation of arteriovenous fistulas, among others [10]. Obviously, these risks are partly patient- and partly operator-dependent. Differences among access sites are relatively small. Nevertheless, the femoral route is preferred because of easy insertion and relatively low incidence of thrombosis, but the risk of infection may be elevated and immobilisation is required. Recirculation resulting in diminished clearance efficiency can be reduced by using a long catheter (with afferent and efferent ports far apart) and correct placement. The use of tunnelled catheters may prevent some of the long-term complications of untunnelled catheters, but they are harder to insert [11]. Subclavian access should probably be avoided because of the risk of thrombosis, or temporally limited and reserved for silicone catheters in order to prevent late-onset stenosis.

Ultrafiltration, replacement fluids, solute and thermal balance

Although a positive fluid balance during AKI/ ARF seems independently associated with mortality in the ICU [12] and thereby argues in favour of accurate monitoring, fluid balances calculated by weighing volumes of replacement and ultrafiltration fluids are prone to error, and more so

Tab. 2   Circulatory and metabolic complications of CRRT

Hypovolaemia and hypotension
Arrhythmias
Hypokalaemia
Hyper- and hyponatraemia
Metabolic acidosis and alkalosis
Hypophosphataemia
Hypomagnesaemia
Hypo- and hypercalcaemia
Hyper- and hypoglycaemia

when appropriate alarms are overridden [13–15]. A negative fluid balance if often aimed at, but exceedingly rapid withdrawal may contribute to hypotension and onset of atrial fibrillation (see Tab. 2) [3,15].

During CRRT the type and amount of replacement fluid used affects solute balance and concentration, and thus it is hard to draw general conclusions. Nevertheless, hypokalaemia, hypomagnesaemia and hypophosphataemia can be observed [15, 16]. Commercially available replacement fluids are often designed for low-dose CRRT and their use during high-dose CRRT volumes is more likely to disturb electrolyte and acid-base levels. There is some debate on the optimal buffer used in the replacement fluid, to combat metabolic acidosis and to prevent (overshoot) metabolic alkalosis. Lactate- or bicarbonate-buffered fluids seem comparable in this respect. Lactate-buffered fluids, however, carry the potential drawback of inducing some energetic loss and hyperglycaemia as excessive lactate is used for gluconeogenesis. The fluids may confound hyperlactataemia as a guide for cardiovascular compromise. Furthermore, it is suggested that excessive amounts of lactate can impair left ventricular function and thereby, oxygen delivery [17]. Acetate-buffered solutions are inferior with respect to acid-base balance. Citrate-buffered solutions may be equivalent to bicarbonate ones [18]. Only severe hepatic failure may be a major risk factor for harmful citrate accumulation and severe metabolic adverse effects.

The filter and extracorporeal circuit may also cause thermal loss, particularly in febrile patients, and cooling may even render some patients hypothermic, in spite of warmers in the extracorporeal circuit [19, 20]. However, it has been suggested that a fall in body temperature with the technique indeed partly accounts for potential beneficial effects of (high dose) CRRT in the treatment of severe sepsis and septic shock, even before full development of ARF. This may relate to reversal of peripheral vasodilation and diminished vasopressor requirements to maintain mean arterial pressure [19, 20]. On the other hand, harmful hypothermia should be avoided by warming techniques. Finally, there may be breaches in microbial integrity in commercial replacement fluid solutions, but the clinical significance hereof is not yet clear [21].

Loss of drugs and nutrients

The filtration of drugs and consequences for dosing, for instance of antibiotic and antifungal agents, remains a challenge [22]. There is considerable interpatient variation and studies may be contradictory, so that therapeutic drug monitoring (if available) is recommended. Indeed, observed drug clearances often do not follow predicted ones [22]. It may suffice to state that the more a drug is protein-bound the less filtration by the artificial kidney and the greater the dose adjustments presumably needed for drugs cleared by the kidneys [23]. Awareness is needed when some residual or recovering renal function may further complicate dosing.

An often overlooked phenomenon is that about 17% of infused aminoacids and 4% of glucose load infused with parenteral nutrition is lost in the ultrafiltrate [24, 25]. It is unknown what is lost during enteral nutrition and if and how this loss should be compensated. Nevertheless, protein intakes as high as 2.5 g/kg/day may be necessary to optimise protein balance [24]. Losses may further and unpredictably include those of folic acid and other water-soluble vitamins (ascorbic acid and thiamine), trace elements, etc., but the clinical significance thereof remains unclear [26–28]. Recent studies showed that calculated daily trace element loss attributed to CRRT is less than what is provided in a daily dose of trace elements supplementation product [26, 28].

Modes of anticoagulation and adverse effects

The extracorporeal circuit and the filter activate the clotting system [29, 30]. Hence, anticoagulation is needed to keep filters open and prevent down time, thereby enhancing the efficiency of CRRT [30, 31]. Bleeding is an adverse effect of systemic anticoagulation with unfractionated heparin, that can be overcome by using regional anticoagulation with the help of citrate, for instance [18, 30–34].

The use of fractionated low-molecular-weight heparins may be associated with increased risks for bleeding, due to, among other reasons, the difficulty of guiding such therapy [3]. Conversely, if dosed on the basis of anti-Xa levels, low-molecular-weight heparins may be associated with similarly low risks of bleeding than systemic administration of unfractionated heparin (low dose), while filter survival may be even prolonged with the former [35]. Obviously, heparin treatment also carries the risk of heparin-induced thrombocytopenia (and thrombosis, HITT), a difficult diagnosis in patients on CRRT [36]. CRRT may be associated with increased requirements of blood transfusions, determined by blood loss following filter clotting and impaired survival [37].

Biocompatability of filters

Filters used for CRRT can be made of cuprophane, cellulose acetate, and synthetic materials such as polysulphone, polymethyl metacrylate, polyamide or polyacrylonitrile, similar to filters used for IHD. It is largely unknown how these filters differentially affect innate immunity during contact of blood (cells) with the membrane during CRRT (as opposed to IHD), but the synthetic ones are considered "more biocompatible" due to a lesser degree of complement system activation than in the cuprophane and cellulose-based filters [38, 39]. This may even translate into better recovery of renal function and survival. The composition of the membrane could also affect the potential removal of circulating pro-inflammatory mediators either by adsorption or ultrafiltration [40–42]. Membranes with a special surface treatment (modification of the surface polarity) seem to have enhanced absorption properties especially when combined with high-volume haemofiltration [43].

However, the role of CRRT as adjunctive therapy for sepsis remains unclear [44].

Technical issues

Technical problems may arise from the blood pump. Blood pump failure leads to an abrupt discontinuation of blood flow through the extracorporeal circuit and clotting of the filter with subsequent loss of blood. A sudden decrease in negative afferent (arterial) pressure or rise in efferent (venous) pressure is usually caused by catheter problems, including kinking, thrombosis and obstruction against the vessel wall. A gradual increase in transmembrane pressure is indicative of clogging and saturation of the filter and/or gradual clotting. A sudden increase in the pressure is suggestive of kinking lines or clotting in the bubble trap. When the pressure in the circuit suddenly rises, the blood pump stops and this may, in turn, contribute to filter coagulation.

Conclusions

Modern techniques for CRRT seem relatively safe and efficient, even though studies on the rate of adverse effects and their impact on survival are lacking. Nevertheless, several sources of error and serious adverse effects can be identified that may be harmful and can be prevented. CRRT emergency teams and continuing education of the nursing staff involved in CRRT might help in this respect [45].

The authors

A.B. Johan Groeneveld, MD, PhD, FCCP, FCCM[1]
S. Azam Nurmohamed, MD[2]
Catherine S.C. Bouman, MD, PhD[3]
    [1]From the Departments of Intensive Care, Nephrology
    [2]Institute for Cardiovascular Research, VU Medical Centre, and the Department of Intensive Care
    [3]Academic Medical Centre, Amsterdam, The Netherlands

Address for correspondence
    A.B. Johan Groeneveld
    Department of Intensive Care
    VU Medical Centre
    De Boelelaan 1117
    1081 HV Amsterdam, The Netherlands
    E-mail: johan.groeneveld@vumc.nl

References

1. John S, Eckardt KU. Renal replacement strategies in the ICU. Chest 2007;132:1379–88.
2. Pannu N, Klarenbach S, Wiebe N, Manns B, Tonelli M. Renal replacement therapy in patients with acute renal failure: a systematic review. JAMA 2008;299:793–805.
3. Uchino S, Bellomo R, Morimatsu H, Morgera S, Schetz M, Tan I et al. Continuous renal replacement therapy: a worldwide practice survey. The beginning and ending supportive therapy for the kidney (B.E.S.T. kidney) investigators. Intensive Care Med 2007;33:1563–70.
4. Oudemans-van Straaten HM. Primum non nocere, safety of continuous renal replacement therapy. Curr Opin Crit Care 2007;13:635–7.
5. Lins RL, Elseviers MM, Van der Niepen P, Hoste E, Malbrain ML, Damas P et al. Intermittent versus continuous renal replacement therapy for acute kidney injury patients admitted to the intensive care unit: results of a randomized clinical trial. Nephrol Dial Transplant 2009;24:512–8.
6. Mehta RL, McDonald B, Gabbai FB, Pahl M, Pascual MT, Farkas A et al. A randomized clinical trial of continuous versus intermittent dialysis for acute renal failure. Kidney Intern 2001;60:1154–63.
7. Uehlinger DE, Jakob SM, Ferrari P, Eichelberger M, Huynh-Do U, Marti HP et al. Comparison of continuous and intermittent renal replacement therapy for acute renal failure. Nephrol Dial Transplant 2005;20:1630–7.
8. Vinsonneau C, Camus C, Combes A, Costa de Beauregard MA, Klouche K, Boulain T et al. Continuous venovenous haemodiafiltration versus intermittent haemodialysis for acute renal failure in patients with multiple-organ dysfunction syndrome: a multicentre randomised trial. Lancet 2006;368:379–85.
9. Uchino S, Fealy N, Baldwin I, Morimatsu H, Bellomo R. Continuous is not continuous: the incidence and impact of circuit "down-time" on uraemic control during continuous veno-venous haemofiltration. Intensive Care Med 2003;29:575–8.
10. Canaud B, Desmeules S, Klouche K, Leray-Moragues H, Beraud JJ. Vascular access for dialysis in the intensive care unit. Best Pract Res Clin Anaesthesiol 2004;18:159–74.

11. Schetz M. Vascular access for HD and CRRT. In: Acute kidney injury, Ronco C et al. (Eds), Karger, Basel; Contrib Nephrol 2007;156:275–86.

12. Payen D, de Pont AC, Sakr Y, Spies C, Reinhart K, Vincent JL. A positive fluid balance is associated with a worse outcome in patients with acute renal failure. Crit Care 2008;12:R74.

13. Ronco C, Ricci Z, Bellomo R, Baldwin I, Kellum J. Management of fluid balance in CRRT: a technical approach. Int J Artif Organs 2005;28:765–6.

14. Ronco C. Fluid balance in CRRT: a call to attention! Int J Artif Organs 2005;28:763–4.

15. Bagshaw SM, Baldwin I, Fealy N, Bellomo R. Fluid balance error in continuous renal replacement therapy: a technical note. Int J Artif Organs 2007;30:434–40.

16. Ratanarat R, Brendolan A, Volker G, Bonello M, Salvatori G, Andrikos E et al. Phosphate kinetics during different dialysis modalities. Blood Purif 2005;23:83–90.

17. Barenbrock M, Hausberg M, Matzkies F, de la Motte SS, Schaefer RM. Effects of bicarobonate- and lactate-buffered replacement fluids on cardiovascular outcome in CVVH patients. Kidney Intern 2000;58:1751–7.

18. Aman J, Nurmohamed SA, Vervloet MG, Groeneveld ABJ. Metabolic effects of citrate-based versus bicarbonate-based substitution fluid in continuous venovenous hemofiltration: a prospective sequential cohort study. In press.

19. Rokyta R, Jr., Matejovic M, Krouzecky A, Opatrny K, Jr., Ruzicka J, Novak I. Effects of continuous venovenous haemofiltration-induced cooling on global haemodynamics, splanchnic oxygen and energy balance in critically ill patients. Nephrol Dial Transplant 2004;19:623–30.

20. Pestaña D, Casanova E, Villagran MJ, Tormo C, Perez-Chrzanowska H, Redondo J et al. Continuous hemofiltration in hyperthermic septic shock patients. J Trauma 2007;63:751–6.

21. Moore I, Bhat R, Hoenich NA, Kilner AJ, Prabhu M, Orr KE et al. A microbiological survey of bicarbonate-based replacement circuits in continuous veno-venous hemofiltration. Crit Care Med 2009: in press.

22. Bouman CS. Antimicrobial dosing strategies in critically ill patients with acute kidney injury and high-dose continuous veno-venous hemofiltration. Curr Opin Crit Care 2008;14:654–9.

23. Meyer TW, Walther JL, Pagtalunan ME, Martinez AW, Torkamani A, Fong PD et al. The clearance of protein-bound solutes by hemofiltration and hemodiafiltration. Kidney Intern 2005;68:867–77.

24. Scheinkestel CD, Adams F, Mahony L, Bailey M, Davies AR, Nyulasi I et al. Impact of increasing parenteral protein loads on amino acid levels and balance in critically ill anuric patients on continuous renal replacement therapy. Nutrition 2003;19:733–40.

25. Berg A, Norberg A, Martling CR, Gamrin L, Rooyackers O, Wernerman J. Glutamine kinetics during intravenous glutamine supplementation in ICU patients on continuous renal replacement therapy. Intensive Care Med 2007;33:660–6.

26. Churchwell MD, Pasko DA, Btaiche IF, Jain JC, Mueller BA. Trace element removal during in vitro and in vivo continuous haemodialysis. Nephrol Dial Transplant 2007;22:2970–7.

27. Klein CJ, Nielsen FH, Moser-Veillobn PB. Trace element loss in urine and effluent following traumatic injury. J Parent Enter Nutr 2008;32:129–39.

28. Pasko DA, Churchwell MD, Btaiche IF, Jain JC, Mueller BA. Continuous venovenous hemodiafiltration trace element clearance in pediatric patients: a case series. Pediatr Nephrol 2009: in press

29. Bouman CS, de Pont AC, Meijers JC, Bakhtiari K, Roem D, Zeerleder S et al. The effects of continuous venovenous hemofiltration on coagulation activation. Crit Care 2006;10:R150.

30. Joannidis M, Oudemans-van Straaten HM. Clinical review: Patency of the circuit in continuous renal replacement therapy. Crit Care 2007;11:218.

31. van de Wetering J, Westendorp RG, van der Hoeven JG, Stolk B, Feuth JD, Chang PC. Heparin use in continuous renal replacement procedures: the struggle between filter coagulation and patient hemorrhage. J Am Soc Nephrol 1996;7:145–50.

32. Tolwani AJ, Prendergast MB, Speer RR, Stofan BS, Wille KM. A practical citrate anticoagulation continuous venovenous hemodiafiltration protocol for metabolic control and high solute clearance. Clin J Am Soc Nephrol 2006;1:79–87.

33. Nurmohamed SA, Vervloet MG, Girbes AR, Ter Wee PM, Groeneveld AB. Continuous venovenous hemofiltration with or without predilution regional citrate anticoagulation: a prospective study. Blood Purif 2007;25:316–23.

34. Oudemans-van Straaten HM, Bosman RJ, Koopmans M, van der Voort PHJ, Wester JPJ, van der Spoel JI, Dijksman LM, Zandstra DF. Citrate anticoagulation for continuous venovenous hemofiltration. Crit Care Med 2009;37:545–52.

35. Joannidis M, Kountchev J, Rauchenzauner M, Schusterschitz N, Ulmer H, Mayr A et al. Enoxaparin vs. unfractionated heparin for anticoagulation during continuous veno-venous hemofiltration: a randomized controlled crossover study. Intensive Care Med 2007;33:1571–9.

36. Holmes CE, Huang JC, Cartelli C, Howard A, Rimmer J, Cushman M. The clinical diagnosis of heparin-induced thrombocytopenia in patients receiving continuous renal replacement therapy. J Thromb Thrombolysis 2008; in press.

37. Cutts MWJ, homas AN, Kishen R. Transfusion requirements during continuous veno-venous haemofiltration – the importance of filter life. Intensive Care Med 2000;26:1694–7.

38. Himmelfarb J, Hakim RM. The use of biocompatible dialysis membranes in acute renal failure. Adv Ren Replacement Ther 1997;4:72–80.

39. Alonso A, Lau J, Jaber BL. Biocompatible hemodialysis membranes for acute renal failure. Cochrane Database Syst Rev 2008;(1):CD005283.

40. Grootendorst AF, van Bommel EF, van Leengoed LA, van Zanten AR, Huipen HJ, Groeneveld AB. Infusion of ultrafiltrate from endotoxemic pigs depresses myocardial performance in normal pigs. J Crit Care 1993;8:161–9.

41. Bouman CS, van Olden RW, Stoutenbeek CP. Cytokine filtration and adsorption during pre- and postdilution hemofiltration in four different membranes. Blood Purif 1998;16:261–8.

42. Rogiers P, Zhang H, Pauwels D, Vincent JL. Comparison of polyacrylonitrile (AN69) and polysulphone membrane during hemofiltration in canine endotoxic shock. Crit Care Med 2003;31:1219–25.

43. Rimmelé T, Assadi A, Cattenoz M, Desebbe O, Lambert C, Boselli E, et al. High-volume haemofiltration with a new ahaemofiltration membrane having enhanced adsorption properties in septic pigs. Nehprol Dial Transplant 2009;24:421–7.

44. Bouman CS, Oudemans-van Straaten HM, Schultz MJ, Vroom MB. Hemofiltration in sepsis and systemic inflammatory response syndrome: the role of dosing and timing. J Crit Care 2007;22:1–12.

45. Honore PM, Joannes-Boyau O, Gressens B. CRRT technology and logistics: is there a role for a medical emergency team in CRRT? In: Acute kidney injury, Ronco C et al. (Eds), Karger, Basel; Contrib Nephrol 2007;156:354–64.

Sophie Lorent and Daniel De Backer

Patient safety and infusion technology

Introduction

Infusion therapy is one of the interventions that are most frequently performed in critically ill patients. In addition to maintenance fluids, infusion of insulin, vasoactive agents, sedative agents and analgesics is often required. These agents have a short half-life and a narrow therapeutic window, undesired alterations in infusion rate may thus have major consequences. Intravenous drug adverse events are frequent in critically ill patients and these are associated with increased morbidity, ICU and hospital length of stay, and costs [1–4]. Errors in parenteral drug administration occur more often in the ICU than in the general ward, but this is directly correlated to a higher exposure to parenteral drugs, as the rate of events per exposure is similar in ICUs and general wards [5]. Nevertheless, many of these errors can probably be prevented.

Some of these events are intrinsically related to the drug (i.e. nephrotoxicity of aminoglycosides) but others are related to the infusion technology and may be prevented. A recent one-day observational study investigated errors in parenteral drug administration in critically ill patients in 113 ICUs worldwide [1]. In this study including 1,328 patients, 861 errors occurred in 441 patients and errors in infusion therapy accounted for one third of the errors. In this chapter we will discuss the

different aspects that need to be addressed to make infusion technology as safe as possible.

Drug-related factors

Stability of the product

Most of the infusion bags and syringes are stable for at least 24 hours, without significant risk of product degradation (physico-chemical stability: depends on the product) or bacterial growth (microbiological stability: 24 hours max., as most are not prepared in aseptic conditions). However, some products have limited stability once prepared. For example, esomeprazole is considered to be stable for 12 hours and drotrecogin alpha for 14 hours. Accordingly, when these substances are used as continuous infusion, syringes or infusion bags should be prepared just before use and replaced after a few hours (i.e. every 12 hours for esomeprazole). For some substances, the stability of the product depends of the type of diluent; for example, meropenem is considered to be stable for 8 hours if NaCl 0,9 % is used and only 3 hours in glucose 5 %. Therefore, a prolonged infusion should replace the continuous infusion for a meropenem infusion in glucose 5%. The reader should be aware that the solvent and additives may vary across different countries. As both solvent and additives may affect drug stability, the information available in textbooks may not always apply to the local product. In example, meropenem stability is reported to be 1 h after dilution in G5%ED in the US [6], 3 h in Belgium (product notice 2005) and 6 h in Canada [7].

It is important to note that we are regularly confronted with extraordinary conditions of drug administration (elevated dose or concentration, intrathecal infusion, ...) for which we do not have information regarding stability. Finally, some substances are inactivated by light (mostly by direct exposure to UV, and this depends both on the duration of exposure to the light and on the intensity of the light); specific tubing and syringes should be used during their administration/infusion (i.e. sodium nitroprusside, molsidomine).

may also result in physico-chemical interaction that may result in undesired effects. For instance, administration of ceftriaxone in a line perfused with calcium-containing solutions (Ringer's lactate, parenteral nutrition, ...) has been shown to produce calcium-ceftriaxone precipitation [8–10] that may accumulate in the lungs and kidneys of neonates and infants [9]. Similar accumulation has not been reported in adults but caution should be exercised not to use ceftriaxone together with calcium-containing solutions.

Specific tubing and bags made of PVC-free material sometimes need to be used. Some drugs in contact with PVC-containing material may lead either to phthalate liberation which is toxic for the patient (i.e. amiodarone, ciclosporine, ...) or to adsorption of the drug by the tubing or bag resulting in decreased efficacy (isosorbide dinitrate, tacrolimus, nimodipine). Specific syringes, infusion bags and tubing should be used to prevent these reactions.

Physico-chemical incompatibility with the drug

Ideally each product infused at a continuous rate should have its dedicated line. However, as several substances have to be infused simultaneously and as the number of lines is limited, it is not uncommon that we have to infuse multiple agents on the same infusion port. Physico-chemicals incompatibilities may lead to obstruction of a catheter, a loss of efficacy (therapeutic failure), the production of toxic derivatives, the risk of potentially fatal embolism and crystal deposits in organs. Physicians and nurses often pay attention to prevent co-infusion of drugs that may have physico-chemical interactions. For example, furosemide or insulin must be administrated on a dedicated line for this purpose, failing to observe this rule may result in precipitation or adhesion to tubing.

Co-administration of more than 2 products is very common in the ICU, but the only available information for Y-site injection compatibility of drugs concerns 2 substances. Indeed, stability is tested with the 2 substances in specific conditions, namely, the diluent, the final concentration, manufacturer and type of container [8]. Introduction of a third agent or modification of drug concentration may affect stability and compatibility. Intermittent administration of drugs

Inadvertent bolus

Great care should be taken to prevent inadvertent bolus. An inadvertent bolus may be precipitated by administrating a bolus of another drug in a non-dedicated line, resulting in a bolus of the infused drug. This may lead to catastrophic events: A bolus of remifentanil or nitroprusside may induce profound cardiovascular collapse, a bolus of vasopressor agents (dopamine, norepinephrine, vasopressin) may result in hypertension and tachycardia and sometimes even malignant arrhythmias. Often the bolus will be followed by a temporarily decreased administration rate due to wash-out of the line by the external agent. The duration of the temporarily decreased rate of administration depends on the infusion rate (it will be longer for a slow infusion rate as it will take more time to replenish the "dead space" of the line). Hence, a bolus of a vasoactive agent may result in haemodynamic instability, the duration of which depends on the half-life and infusion rate of the product. These products should be infused on a dedicated line.

Inadvertent drug infusion interruption

This may occur when the infusion bag or syringe has to be changed. This can be a catastrophic event with vasoactive agents. These agents have a short half-life (< 2 min) and abrupt interruption of infusion may rapidly lead to profound cardio-vascular instability. The only way to prevent these events is to use intelligent infusion pumps that have warnings and alarms when the infusion is close to an end and also to have reserve infusion bags or syringes prepared in advance. We do not recommend the use of a bolus of the agent when infusion is resumed as it may sometimes induce a huge and unnecessary overshoot. One may rather consider temporarily increasing the infusion rate in order to more rapidly restore the haemodynamic target level.

Should we use high or low concentrations for vasoactive agents?

When selecting a drug concentration, physicians should be aware of several factors. A highly concentrated drug has the advantage of limiting the amount of fluid administered, it also necessitates fewer syringe or infusion bag changes, limiting the number of human interventions. However, even though this limits the number of episodes of potential haemodynamic instability, their duration may be longer if a dedicated line is not used, as a result of dilution in the line.

Pump-related factors

Pumps are an important component of infusion therapy. Pumps need to continuously provide reliable infusion rates. Several factors play a role in the reliability of these pumps:

- Technical characteristics
- Alarms
- For some, a specific profile of administration and pharmacokinetic profile integration (i.e. drugs in operative anaesthesia)

The technical characteristics should take into account "dead space" of the line and precision for low fluid infusion because all parameters are specific to each type of syringe/infusion bag.

The alarm system should inform nurses when there is occlusion of tubing, or need for a change of syringe/infusion bag. Ideally, the alarm for near end of perfusion should integrate the perfusion speed in order to allow sufficient time for preparation of the new bag. Admittedly, most devices use either fixed volumes or user-defined volumes to trigger near end alarms, which may result in a variable time to end of infusion depending on infusion rate. This is quite paradoxical, as this would allow less time for preparation in case of high infusion speed which is more common when high doses are infused (and thus when patients are at higher risk of withdrawal). The staff should immediately react to these alarms in order to avoid problems related to drug infusion interruption (insufficient plasma levels of the drug, haemodynamic or metabolic instability due to interruption of therapy with short half-life drugs, ...).

The drug administration profile is an important setting of recent intelligent pumps. Defining a drug profile allows the user to use infusion settings specific to the drug infused. Using these settings helps to optimise increments in drug dosages and also to prevent use of doses that are higher than recommended. In addition, the bolus function can be deactivated for some drugs (i.e. remifentanyl, vasoactive drugs, ...). Bypassing the drug library should be strongly discouraged. In a large trial including 744 cardiac surgery admissions, 571 bypasses (representing close to 25 % of infusion therapies) were observed [11]. Some of the adverse drug events may have been prevented by avoiding bypasses of the drug library.

Finally, the drug administration profile also offers a clear identification of each syringe and infusion bag at the bedside, disclosing not only drug name but also its concentration. This limits the risk of inadvertent confusion between pumps.

Of note, although computer-driven infusion therapy is feasible, this technology is not yet recommended in the ICU. In the operating field, this technique is used for target-controlled infusion anaesthesia that can even be driven by various monitoring devices [12]. However, this technique is not yet used the ICU, mostly because of the multiple pathways involved and complexity of the patients that prevent closed-loop infusion. Nevertheless, closed-loop controlled infusion of norepinephrine has recently been shown to reduce norepinephrine weaning duration compared to manual adaptation of drug dosage [13].

Site of infusion-related factors

Another very important aspect is the vascular site at which the drug is infused. Due to their physical properties (or sometimes to properties of the excipient) many drugs are very irritating for the vessels and may promote phlebitis and vascular thrombosis. Accordingly, central venous access is often required for these agents (i.e. amiodarone, phenytoin, parenteral nutrition, ...). It is important to ensure proper placement of the catheter in a large central vein, not only at catheter placement but also throughout its use as it sometimes happens that the catheter is dislodged after nursing procedures or in patients with delirium (see Fig. 1 – Malpositioning of a central venous catheter). Malpositioning of a central catheter may have disastrous consequences as it may result in paravenous administration of the product, which is associated with decreased efficacy of the infusion (often requiring increase of infusion rate which further increases the extravasated volume) and subcutaneous skin necrosis.

Peripheral lines should be used with caution in infusion therapy; these can only be used for products that are not too irritating for the veins and that do not induce necrosis if infused subcutaneously (i.e. insulin, heparin).

Human/organisational factors

As expected, critically ill patients are particularly exposed to errors in infusion therapy, mostly because these patients often require repeated and/or prolonged use of infusion therapy [14]. The recent study of errors in parenteral administration of drugs [1] also helped to identify the factors associated with errors in infusion therapy. In addition to high patient severity and a large number of parenteral administrations and/or multiple vasoactive medications (all accompanied by a high exposure to intravenous therapy), a high level of ICU activity and low staffing were accompanied by an increased risk of error. Importantly, the use of an electronic prescribing system re-duced the risk of errors, as dilution, route and infusion rate are better specified. This observation confirmed some data suggesting that computerised physician order entry may decrease preventable errors by 50 % [15]. Another important factor was the labeling of syringes, which markedly reduced the risk of errors. Interestingly, advance preparation of syringes and solutions did not decrease the risk of errors.

Finally, pharmacist participation on medical rounds may also decrease by two-thirds the risk of infusion therapy errors [16].

Conclusions

Infusion of drugs is one of the most commonly performed interventions in ICU patients. Physicians and nurses should pay attention to factors that may interfere with the adequate delivery of the desired dose of the drug. Pharmacists may help to optimise drug infusion therapy (see Tab. 1).

The authors

Sophie Lorent, PharmD
Daniel De Backer, MD, PhD
    Department of Intensive Care | Erasme
    University Hospital | Université Libre de
    Bruxelles (ULB) | Brussels, Belgium

Address for correspondence
    Daniel De Backer
    Department of Intensive Care
    Erasme University Hospital
    Route de Lennik 808
    1070 Brussels, Belgium
    E-mail: ddebacke@ulb.ac.be

References

1. Valentin A, Capuzzo M, Guidet B, Moreno R, Metnitz B, Bauer P et al. Errors in administration of parenteral drugs in intensive care units: multinational prospective study. BMJ 2009;338:b814.
2. Valentin A, Capuzzo M, Guidet B, Moreno RP, Dolanski L, Bauer P et al. Patient safety in intensive care: results from the multinational Sentinel Events Evaluation (SEE) study. Intensive Care Med 2006;32:1591–1598.
3. Nuckols TK, Paddock SM, Bower AG, Rothschild JM,

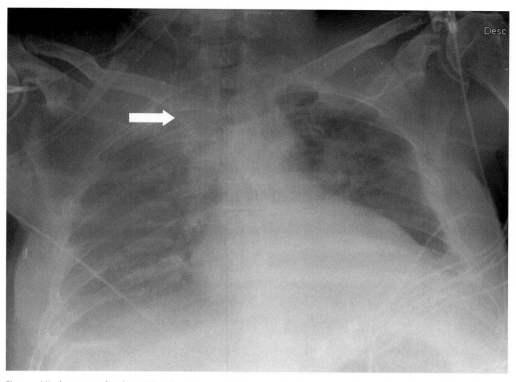

Fig. 1   Misplacement of catheter. This three-lumen catheter was pulled out progressively due to patient delirium. The tip of the catheter is indicated by the arrow.

Tab. 1   Factors associated with potential problems during drug infusion therapy

Problem	Action
Drug-related factors	
■ Stability	May depend on the solvent and additives
■ Interaction	Dedicated line, pharmacists
Pump-related factors	Use intelligent pump
Site of infusion-related factors	Dedicated line, check position of lines
Human-related factors	Electronic prescribing system, pharmacists on physician rounds

Fairbanks RJ, Carlson B et al. Costs of intravenous adverse drug events in academic and nonacademic intensive care units. Med Care 2008;46:17–24.

4. Rothschild JM, Landrigan CP, Cronin JW, Kaushal R, Lockley SW, Burdick E et al. The Critical Care Safety Study: The incidence and nature of adverse events and serious medical errors in intensive care. Crit Care Med 2005;33:1694–1700.

5. Cullen DJ, Sweitzer BJ, Bates DW, Burdick E, Edmondson A,

Leape LL. Preventable adverse drug events in hospitalized patients: a comparative study of intensive care and general care units. Crit Care Med 1997;25:1289–1297.

6. Trissel LA. Meropenem. In: Trissel LA, editor. Handbook on Injectable Drugs. Bethesda: American Society of Health-System Pharmacists, 2005.

7. Lacy CF, Armstrong LL, Goldman MP, Lance LL. Meropenem. In: Lacy CF, Armstrong LL, Goldman MP, Lance LL, editors. Drug Information Handbook International –

Canadian and International Drug Monographs. Hudson,Ohio: Lexi-Comp, 2005: 1006–1007.

8. Trissel LA. Ceftriaxone sodium. In: Trissel LA, editor. Handbook on Injectable Drugs. Bethesda: American Society of Health-System Pharmacists, 2005: 313–320.

9. Monte SV, Prescott WA, Johnson KK, Kuhman L, Paladino JA. Safety of ceftriaxone sodium at extremes of age. Expert Opin Drug Saf 2008;7:515–523.

10. Burkiewicz JS. Incompatibility of ceftriaxone sodium with lactated Ringers' injection. Am J Health Syst Pharm 1999;56:384.

11. Rothschild JM, Keohane CA, Cook EF, Orav EJ, Burdick E, Thompson S et al. A controlled trial of smart infusion pumps to improve medication safety in critically ill patients. Crit Care Med 2005;33:533–540.

12. Liu N, Chazot T, Genty A, Landais A, Restoux A, McGee K et al. Titration of propofol for anesthetic induction and maintenance guided by the bispectral index: closed-loop versus manual control: a prospective, randomized, multicenter study. Anesthesiology 2006;104:686–695.

13. Merouani M, Guignard B, Vincent F, Borron SW, Karoubi P, Fosse JP et al. Norepinephrine weaning in septic shock patients by closed loop control based on fuzzy logic. Crit Care 2008;12:R155.

14. Bates DW, Miller EB, Cullen DJ, Burdick L, Williams L, Laird N et al. Patient risk factors for adverse drug events in hospitalized patients. ADE Prevention Study Group. Arch Intern Med 1999;159:2553–2560.

15. Bates DW, Leape LL, Cullen DJ, Laird N, Petersen LA, Teich JM et al. Effect of computerized physician order entry and a team intervention on prevention of serious medication errors. JAMA 1998;280:1311–1316.

16. Leape LL, Cullen DJ, Clapp MD, Burdick E, Demonaco HJ, Erickson JI et al. Pharmacist participation on physician rounds and adverse drug events in the intensive care unit. JAMA 1999;282:267–270.

Carl S. Waldmann, Michael Imhoff and G. Daniel Martich

Patient safety and health informatics

Definitions

Health informatics is the development and assessment of methods and systems for the acquisition, processing and interpretation of patient data with the help of knowledge from scientific research [1].

Medical informatics is the discipline concerned with the systematic processing of data, information and knowledge in medicine and healthcare. The domain of medical informatics covers computational and informational aspects of processes and structures in medicine and healthcare [2].

Throughout this chapter health informatics will be used when referring to both health informatics and medical informatics as both terms are often used synonymously.

Overview

Information technology advances are spreading at an alarming rate except in healthcare. Physicians and other non-physician providers (NPP) rely on data quality, immediate access, and real-time updating as much as, if not more than, any other professional. Despite the recent fall in financial markets, we at least know the decrement in our retirement savings thanks to automation adopted long ago by Wall Street. The New York Stock Exchange developed its first automated quotation system in 1953, electronic ticker display boards in 1966 and by 1996 had a fully integrated technology network with wireless data system. Stock markets throughout the world have similarly relied on electronic transaction systems for years. Banks do not balance their books at the end of the day using paper and pen, but rather through electronic spreadsheets with linked databases. So, although you may "peek and shriek" the next time you look online at your 401K or other retirement plan, it is at least possible to do so and track it, unlike most personal health records.

Similarly, the airline industry, while not particularly solvent, is extraordinarily safe compared to other forms of travel. Airlines could not safely fly the thousands of flights with disparate equipment to all corners of the globe without electronic tracking and reservation systems. While many aspects of the airline industry may not be applicable to critical care medicine, the dramatic improvements in flight safety have also been achieved by the use of informatics and electronic decision support for different processes on the flight deck, in air-traffic control and on the ground [3]. Each of these industries can rightfully claim that efficiencies, greater productivity, and improved customer satisfaction have been a direct result of automation. In healthcare, the computer is to memory what the X-ray machine is to vision – a technology that vastly surpasses human limitations. The benefits of a computer-helper should quickly become evident in everyday practice.

In the ensuing manuscript, we will address key questions and discuss health informatics with a focus on patient safety.

Is there a need for CIS in critical care?

Perhaps the most gripping reason for development of clinical information systems (CIS) comes from the reports of the Institute of Medicine (IOM). The IOM, part of the National Academy of Sciences, is an adviser on scientific and technological matters to the US government. In June 1998, the IOM Quality of Health Care in America Committee was formed and ultimately concluded in its report "To Err Is Human" that up to 98,000 Americans die each year from preventable medical mistakes they experience during hospital admissions [4]. The report goes on to indicate that there are more deaths in hospitals each year from preventable medical mistakes than there are from motor vehicle accidents, breast cancer, or AIDS.

The single leading type of error is the medication error. Estimates range from 4% to 20% of all hospitalised patients encountering medication errors [5, 6]. These errors result in charges of $2,900 to $9,000 per error; preventing these errors can save litigation costs [7, 8, 9]. One of the oft-repeated recommendations from this IOM report is that information systems could reduce these mistakes considerably. The IOM strategy for improvement includes implementing computerised physician order entry, standardising processes for medication doses, dose timing, and dose scales in a given patient unit, and mandating external reporting of errors. This last recommendation on mandatory error reporting makes the invisible visible. Only once the errors are known and measured can they be managed. In the long run, the IOM understands that information technology and the electronic medical record are meant to support protocols such as standing orders, links to evidence-based care, alerts, and clinical decision support [10].

Information overload at the point of care

An intensive care unit is a data-rich environment. When so many data elements need to be turned into information and knowledge, errors occur because of sheer volume. A physician may be confronted with more than 200 variables during typical morning rounds [11]. However, even an experienced physician is often not able to develop a systematic response to any problem involving more than seven variables [12]. Moreover, humans are limited in their ability to estimate the degree of relatedness between only two variables [13]. This problem is most pronounced in the evaluation of the measurable effect of a therapeutic intervention. Personal bias, experience, and a certain expectation toward the respective intervention may distort an objective judgement [14].

While the first IOM report did not focus on care in intensive care units (ICUs), the report does suggest that critically ill patients are at a particularly high risk for adverse events. That ICU risk, as high as 17.7% for death or disability and nearly 46% for any type of adverse event, was highlighted in "To Err is Human." [15]. The abundance of information generated during the process of critical care can now be captured and stored using CISs which provide for complete medical documentation at the bedside. The clinical usefulness and efficiency of CISs has been shown repeatedly [16, 17, 18, 19].

The volume of scientific literature is growing exponentially. As of 1993, the number of systematic reviews in medicine increased 500-fold over a ten-year period [20]. It is impossible for the individual healthcare professional to keep track of all relevant medical knowledge even in very narrow subspecialties. This may also negatively affect patient safety, as physicians and caregivers may not be aware of the best possible and safest treatment when it is necessary. The penetration of new methods into daily practice may take as long as 10 to 15 years, far longer than in most other industries.

Compliance with guidelines and protocols

By 2009, the Physician Quality Reporting Initiative (PQRI) had nearly 200 measures developed by various organisations [21]. There are more than 50 new measures for 2009 and for the US, these will undoubtedly become the standard by which payment and reimbursement for physicians is determined. The PQRI measures list spans ambulatory, long-term, inpatient, surgical, and critical care with a good deal of potential overlap. Some of the critical care-related PQRI measures include the following:

- Perioperative care: Venous thromboembolism (VTE) prophylaxis (when indicated in all patients): Percentage of patients aged 18 years and older undergoing procedures for which VTE prophylaxis is indicated in all patients, who had an order for low-molecular-weight heparin (LMWH), low-dose unfractionated heparin (LDUH), adjusted-dose warfarin, fondaparinux or mechanical prophylaxis to be given within 24 hours prior to incision time or within 24 hours after surgery end time.
- Perioperative care: Discontinuation of prophylactic antibiotics (non-cardiac procedures): Percentage of non-cardiac surgical patients aged 18 years and older undergoing procedures with the indications for prophylactic antibiotics and who received a prophylactic antibiotic, who have an order for discontinuation of prophylactic antibiotics within 24 hours of surgical end time.

In Germany, in conjunction with disease-related groups (DRGs) as the sole method for inpatient reimbursement, healthcare authorities require hospitals to publish quality benchmarks and also accumulate accreditation data. This can realistically only be captured by means of an electronic patient record.

In the UK, a government initiative set up the Modernisation Agency for Critical Care to try and ensure standardisation of protocols for transfers and the introduction of care bundles for stress ulcer prophylaxis and VTE prophylaxis. The National Health Service (NHS) published a document "10 High Impact Changes" which included "*Change No. 6*: Increase the reliability of performing therapeutic interventions through a Care Bundle approach" [22]. The emergence of the sepsis care bundles to improve mortality from sepsis has not consistently had an effect as yet probably because of the lack of compliance with the bundles [23].

Now that over 80% of UK ICUs subscribe to Intensive Care National Audit and Research Centre (ICNARC), it has been possible for ICUs to measure themselves on case-mix-adjusted outcome against other units. Each of these initiatives, including data collection and standardisation, lend themselves perfectly to the use of CISs for the ICU.

Shortage of intensivists and intensive care beds

A recent report from the Organisation for Economic Co-operation and Development (OECD) highlighted the existing and dramatically increasing shortage of healthcare workers in nearly all developed countries [24]. This problem is very pronounced in intensive care medicine. It is well known, at least among intensivists, that in addition to a national and global shortages of nurses, there are too few intensivists to staff ICUs across the US and the world.

While intensivist-led care teams demonstrate improved mortality, it would be impossible to physically provide each ICU with enough intensivists on site to demonstrate the better outcomes. Therefore, one possible solution utilising information technology in the ICU is to create a system where intensivists and critical care nurses manage or consult patients in more than one ICU at a time. This can allow an intensivist to oversee between 50 and 100 critically ill patients instead of 8 to 16 when physically present in one ICU. One commerical model for such a virtual ICU care team is that established by VISICU [25]. The VISICU model is dependent on two essential factors:

a) Technology at the bedside capable of capturing vital signs, medication administration, documentation and laboratory information
b) Change of culture of hospital physicians to be receptive to suggestions by the offsite intensivist.

Another issue that adds to the shortage of critical care staff resources are the growing requirements for documentation including quality control measures and reimbursement data, as already mentioned above. This increasing documentation workload further directs scarce qualified staff resources away from actual patient care.

What should a CIS do for improving safety in critical care?

According to the IOM, quality care is that which is safe, effective (i.e. evidence-based), patient-centred, timely, efficient and equitable [26]. In the UK, the Department of Health is trying to introduce "Quality Metrics" in medicine and has asked each specialty to provide some quality indicators that can be measured. There is no doubt that the health informatics will be key in measuring compliance to the agreed quality metrics.

It is important to differentiate between minimum standards and quality indicators.

Minimum standards are those which should be maintained in intensive care units, regardless of size, location or resource; the Intensive Care Society ICS document "Standards for Intensive Care Units" enumerates some of these standards [27].

Quality indicators are standards which, if upheld, will likely improve the quality of patient care by means of improved safety, better patient outcomes, or greater efficiency. They must be relevant to deciding whether high-quality care is delivered. The staff collecting them must feel that they are important. They must be collectible, and as far as practicable must be evidence-based.

There are several approaches to defining quality measures used elsewhere. In the Netherlands, a review of quality measures by an expert panel using a consensus process has led to the adoption of 11 quality measures [28].

In the United States, the Joint Commission, which is responsible for accreditation of hospitals, stipulates four core measures [29]:

- measures to prevent ventilator-associated pneumonia,
- peptic ulcer disease prophylaxis,
- deep venous thrombosis prophylaxis and
- the incidence of central line-related blood stream infection.

The accrediting body in Australia, the Australian Council on Healthcare Standards, uses three indicators [30]:

- participation in the national patient database,
- the number of appropriate referrals not admitted to critical care and
- unplanned re-admissions within 72 hours.

However, the Australia and New Zealand Intensive Care Society collects the following data: mortality, length of stay, percentage of patients with length of stay greater than seven days, delayed admission, delayed discharge, theatre cancellation, emergency department bypass, catheter-related blood stream infection (CRBSI), infection with resistant organisms, VTE prophylaxis, pain assessment, blood transfusion threshold, ventilator-associated pneumonia prevention (including sedation break) and peptic ulcer disease prophylaxis.

In 2005, the Spanish Society of Critical Care and Coronary Care Units (SEMICYUC) produced a document enumerating 120 quality indicators for critical care, including levels of evidence for including the measures [31]. Of these, 20 were selected by a consensus process as core measures, including semirecumbent positioning of patients on ventilators, VTE prophylaxis, incidence of ventilator-associated pneumonia (VAP), stress ulcer prophylaxis and others common to other nations' quality indicators, but also included more difficult measures, such as surgical intervention for intracranial subdural or extradural haematoma, intra-cranial pressure measurement.

A point-of-care CIS allows the broadest control over the process of care. Outstanding examples for the management of process control are computerised protocols, clinical pathways, and guidelines. Order entry and decision support systems offer a unique opportunity to dramatically improve the quality of care while at the same time reducing overall costs [32, 33]. In the terminology of total quality management (TQM), an explicit method, e.g. a computerised protocol, is part of the stabilisation of the process necessary to improve quality [34, 35]. With the above background information, the major focus in healthcare informatics in the US has been computerised physician order entry (CPOE) with or without electronic decision support systems. While endorsed by the Leapfrog Group and recommended by the IOM, many hospitals and vendors are struggling to implement these extremely complex systems. Physician order entry can be considered the key to medical process control. It is probably the most complex functionality in any clinical information system.

Can clinical decision support improve safety?

Assuming that physicians and hospital organisations buy into the notion of process & change control as well as acceptance of evidence-based medicine in their daily practice, then the implementation of CIS, CPOE and, perhaps most importantly, clinical decision support (CDS) are possible. The goal of CDS is to supply the best recommendation under all circumstances [36]. In its 2001 report the IOM strongly recommends the use of sophisticated electronic CDS systems for radically improving safety and quality of care [20]. Clinical information systems that generate CDS-driven electronic reminders and CDS-assisted CPOE have proven to improve both quality and cost effectiveness of care [7, 37]. Electronic reminders can significantly improve physicians' compliance with guidelines, reduce the rate of human errors and make physicians more responsive to specific clinical events [36, 38].

The most detailed and explicit algorithms in clinical decision-making use rule-based computer systems [25, 39]. Using data from one of the most comprehensive clinical data repositories in the world (LDS Hospital, Salt Lake City, Utah, USA) the group of Morris developed a rule-based CDS for the mechanical ventilation of the critically ill [40]. Their CDS generates, on the basis of actual patient data, explicit, executable and reproducible instructions or recommendations for the next therapeutic step. Their study found that it was possible to control more than 95% of the ventilation times with these protocols, while intermediate and final clinical outcomes showed a beneficial effect [39].

Another tangible benefit of a CDS system is that the system can check all doctors' orders and where necessary cause them to be modified; in one large US institution, 400 out of 15,000 orders were altered. Most of these CDS-recommended changes were to avert potential adverse drug events [41].

Can CPOE and CDSS put patient safety at risk?

Until early into the third millennium CPOE and clinical decision support systems (CDSS) were hailed as the most effective means against medical error and for improving patient safety. Recent studies have cast doubt on this notion. It was repeatedly reported that CPOE and CDSS may introduce new types of medical errors, and that they mostly reduced the rate of less harmful errors while not eradicating the truly dangerous and potentially lethal medical errors [42, 43].

One broadly discussed study even reported increased mortality after introduction of a CPOE [44]. This study clearly showed, though, that the underlying issue was the lack of adaption of the CPOE processes to the clinical workflows.

A literature review on the aspect of overriding drug safety alerts from CPOEs found that alerts are ignored most of the time, overriding of alerts can result in patient harm, alerts are too sensitive and too unspecific most of the time, and that alerts often disrupt the clinical workflow [45]. Especially the two latter observations may lead to the problem of desensitisation that we also witness with medical device alarms, and that has been compared very well to the boy who cried wolf in the famous fable by Aesop.

Even against the background of these publications there is no reason to doubt that CIS, CPOE and CDSS can improve patient safety in critical care and beyond. But if we look more closely at those studies that support this notion, many of them have been done with "home-grown" systems that are fine-tuned to the clinical workflows of the respective institutions. Negative study results have been reported for systems that are evidently not well adapted to clinical workflows (although this may be possible with all available systems). It cannot be overemphasised how important the often tedious fine-tuning of these complex systems to the clinical needs and workflows is to achieve their full potential for the improvement of patient safety [46, 47].

Discussion

Why is there a reluctance to embrace information technology in healthcare?

In 1811, a social revolution began in Nottingham, England, called the Luddite movement. The Luddites, named for the fictitious leader known variably as "General Ludd," "King Ludd," or "Captain Ludd," set about destroying stocking frames, the new technology at the time. The rebellion was ultimately quelled, but not until much damage was done throughout England. Ultimately, 17 Luddites were executed because of their destructive behaviour.

Today, the term Luddite refers to any individual who opposes technological change and progress. Broadly characterising physicians with such a moniker would be a terrible generalisation and huge disservice to our profession. However, to understand that adoption of the newfangled computers at each ICU bedside by intensivists and critical care nurses is oftentimes less-than-enthusiastic because of a cultural divide would be accurate. Part of that cultural adoption barrier is the manner in which the new CIS is introduced into the hospital and ICU specifically. Appropriate training, education, support, and experience are needed for the user to become facile with CPOE and CIS. Remember, CPOE and CIS, in general, are tools. Much like any other new tool introduced into healthcare, there is a learning curve. Like CPOE, laparoscopic cholecystectomy is a tool. When laparoscopic cholecystectomies were introduced in the late 80s, complications were common and the procedure itself often took longer than a standard cholecystectomy. Now, laparoscopic cholecystectomies are the norm. They have less than a 2% complication rate, require shorter operative and recovery times, and patients have less visible incisions. The early experience in CPOE at a prominent children's hospital further emphasises the need to educate, train, adjust processes, and support the cultural changes associated with introduction of this new tool. That study found a coincident non-significant worsening in outcome in a sub-population of the critically ill children [44]. However, in a larger cohort of age-matched critically ill patients using the same CPOE system at another university children's hospital, the exact opposite finding was observed. The second study

identified a near-significant improvement in outcome in their population [48]. The improvement can be partly attributed to on-site observation by physicians, nurses, and IT professionals from the second site during the go-live at the first hospital. Adjustments to training, education, and process control were made prior to the second site go-live and voila! Successful adoption and deployment.

Medical errors are without any doubt one issue of major public interest and concern. The IOM report "To Err Is Human" describes a situation that is intolerable in the United States. There are studies that make it very likely that the problem of medical errors is as grave in Europe as in the US.

Information management given its broadest meaning to include communication among care-givers, process control and standardisation to achieve efficiencies is at the core of many efforts to reduce medical errors. Therefore, medical information management, with or without the help of computers, will play a decisive role in any solution posited for the growing concerns of quality in healthcare. The application of technology to the solution is a certainty given the complexity of the problem with the caveats of cost, timing and acceptance.

Specific recommendations from many groups focus on point-of-care CIS with CPOE and CDS systems. For the development of medical IT systems the implications are:

- The development of medical IT must be in point-of-care information systems integrated into the healthcare enterprise-wide information management approach.
- The integration of information and knowledge must be seamless along the continuum of care and across the entire healthcare enterprise.
- Clinical information systems, electronic order entry systems, clinical decision support systems, medical knowledge bases, and ultimately the electronic patient record provide the most powerful solutions to the problem of medical errors. These systems may even become in part legally compulsory or may be enforced by major payer groups.

It is also clear that IT must reach a critical mass to be effective. For instance, payback from a physician order entry system can only be expected if it covers most of the continuum of care. Despite the expensive nature of hardware and software for CIS, the total cost of ownership of these systems is often underestimated [49]. This means that massive up-front investments are needed. Moreover, most advanced online CDS systems require comprehensive patient information in electronic format, which can only be provided by clinical information systems.

On the other hand, there is increasing evidence that on a broad, hospital-wide scale clinical information technology can improve patient outcomes and reduce hospital cost [50].

Conclusion

There is no doubt that medical information management is one answer to the challenges of patient safety throughout the continuum and especially for the most critically ill patients. Standardisation of care, process control, physician order entry systems with online CDS, and the electronic patient record have the potential to make health care in general and intensive care in particular safer, improve quality of care, and reduce cost in the interest of all parties involved.

The authors

Carl S. Waldmann, MA, MB, BChir, FRCA, EDIC[1]
Michael Imhoff, MD, PhD[2]
G. Daniel Martich, MD[3]
   [1]Consultant Anaesthetist/Intensivist |
   Reading, UK
   [2]Associate Professor | Department for
   Medical Informatics | Biometrics and
   Epidemiology | Ruhr-University Bochum,
   Germany
   [3]Professor | Department of Critical Care
   Medicine | University of Pittsburgh School of
   Medicine | Chief Medical Information Officer |
   University of Pittsburgh Medical Center

Address for correspondence
   Carl Waldmann
   Intensive Care Unit
   Royal Berkshire Hospital
   London Road
   Reading RG1, UK
   E-mail: cswald@aol.com

References

1. Imhoff M, Webb A, Goldschmidt A. Health Informatics. Intensive Care Med 2001;27:179–86
2. Haux R. Aims and tasks of medical informatics. Int J Med Inf 1997;44:9–20
3. http://www.cnn.com/2009/TRAVEL/01/12/us.air. safety/ (accessed Jan 20, 2009)
4. Karlsson G, Johannesson M. Cost-effectiveness analysis and capital costs. Soc Sci Med 1998;46:1183–91
5. Leape LL. Error in medicine. JAMA 1994;272:1851–7
6. Leape LL, Bates DW, Cullen DJ, Cooper J, Demonaco HJ, Gallivan T, et al. Systems analysis of adverse druge events. JAMA 1995;274:35–43
7. Bates DW, Spell N, Cullen DJ, Burdick E, Laird N, Petersen LA, et al. The costs of adverse drug events in hospitalized patients. Adverse Drug Events Prevention Study Group. JAMA 1997;277:307–11
8. Classen DC, Pestotnik SL, Evans RS, Lloyd JF, Burke JP. Adverse drug events in hospitalized patients. Excess length of stay, extra costs, and attributable mortality. JAMA 1997;277:301–6
9. Raschke RA, Gollihare,B, WunderlichTA, Guidry JR, Leibowitz AI, Peirce JC, et al. A computer alert system to prevent injury from adverse drug events – Development and evaluation in a community teaching hospital. JAMA 1998;280:1317–20
10. http://www.iom.edu/Object.File/Master/7/824/james. pdf (accessed Jan 20, 2009)
11. Morris A. Algorithm-Based Decision-Making. In: Tobin JA, ed. Principles and Practice of Intensive Care Monitoring. New York: McGraw-Hill, 1998:1355–81
12. Miller G. The magical number seven, plus of minus two: Some limits to our capacity for processing information. Psychol Rev 1956;63:81–97
13. Jennings D, Amabile T, Ross L. Informal covariation assessments: Data-based versus theory-based judgements. In: Kahnemann D SPTA, ed. Judgement under uncertainty: Heuristics and biases. Cambridge: Cambridge University Press, 1982:211–30
14. Guyatt G, Drummond M, Feeny D, Tugwell P, Stoddart G, Haynes RB, et al. Guidelines for the clinical and economic evaluation of health care technologies. Soc Sci Med 1986;22:393–408
15. Andrews LB, Stocking C, Krizek T, Gottlieb L, Krizek C, Vargish T, et al. An alternative strategy for studying adverse events in medical care. Lancet 1997;349:309–19
16. Bosman RJ, Rood E, Oudemans-Van Straaten HM, Van der Spoel JI, Wester JP, Zandstra DF. Intensive care information system reduces documentation time of the nurses after cardiothoracic surgery. Intensive Care Med 2003;29:83–90
17. Imhoff M. A clinical information system on the intensive care unit: Dream or night mare? In: Rubi JAG, ed. Medicina Intensiva 1995, XXX. Murcia: Congreso SEMIUC. Murcia. Pictographia., 1995:17–22.

18. Imhoff M. Three years clinical use of the Siemens EMTEK System 2000: Efforts and Benefits. Clinical Intensive Care 1996;7 (Suppl.):43–7.

19. Imhoff M, Lehner JH, Löhlein D. Two year clinical experience with a clinical information system on a surgical ICU. In: Monduzi, ed. 7th European Congress on Intensive Care Medicine. Bologna: European Congress, 1994:163–6

20. Chalmers TC, Laus J. Meta-analytic stimulus for changes in clinical trial. Stat Methods Med Res 1993;2:161–72

21. http://www.cms.hhs.gov/PQRI/Downloads/2009PQRIMeasuresList.pdf (accessed Jan 20, 2009)

22. http://www.content.modern.nhs.uk/cmsWISE/HIC/HIC6/HIC6.htm

23. Gao F, Melody T, Daniels DF, Giles S, Fox S. The impact of compliance with 6-hour and 24-hour sepsis bundles on hospital mortality in patients with severe sepsis: a prospective observational study. Crit Care 2005;9:R764–70

24. OECD Health Policy Studies. The looming crisis in the health workforce. How can OECD countries respond? OECD 2008 (http://www.oecd.org/document/47/0,3343,en_2649_33929_36506543_1_1_1_1,00.html; accessed Feb 12, 2009)

25. Celi LA, Hassan,E, Marquardt,C, Breslow M, Rosenfeld B. The eICU: It's not just telemedicine. Crit Care Med 2001;29(suppl.):N183–9

26. Crossing the Quality Chasm, A New Health System for the 21st Century, Committee on Quality of Health Care in America, Institute of Medicine, National Academies Press, Washington, D.C., July 2001 23–38

27. http://www.ics.ac.uk/icmprof/downloads/ICSstandards4302.pdf (accessed Feb 12, 2009)

28. De Vos M, Graafmans W, Keesman E, Westert G, van der Voort PH. Quality measures at intensive care units: which indicators should we use? J Crit Care 2007;22:267–74

29. The Joint Commission. National Hospital Quality Measures – ICU. http://www.jointcommission.org/PerformanceMeasurement/MeasureReserveLibrary/Spec+Manual+-+ICU.htm (accessed June 21, 2008)

30. http://www.achs.org.au/pdf/Australasian_CIR_8th_Edition.pdf (last accessed Jan 20, 2009)

31. Delgrado MCM, Pericas LC, Moreno JR, Torra LB, Varela JB, Suero FC, et al. Quality indicators in critically ill patients. SEMICYUC 2005 (http://www.calidad.semicyuc.org/quality_indicators_SEMICYUC2006.pdf; accessed Feb 12, 2009)

32. Classen DC, Evans R, Pestotnik S, Horn SD, Menlove RL, Burke JP. The timing of prophylactic administration of antibiotics and the risk of surgica-wound infection. N Engl J Med 1992;326:281–6

33. Pestotnik SL, Classen DC, Evans RS, Burke JP. Implementing antibiotic practice guidelines through computer-assisted decision support: Clinical and financial outcomes. Ann Intern Med 1996;124:884–90

34. Teich JM, Glaser,JP, Beckley,RF, Aranow M, Bates DW, Kuperman GJ, et al. The Brigham integrated computing system (BICS): advanced clinical systems in an academic hospital environment. Int J Medl Inform 1999;54:197–208

35. Walton M. The Deming Management Method. New York: Putnam, 1986

36. McDonald CJ, Wilson,FJ, Jr. Physician response to computer reminders. JAMA 1980;244:1579–81

37. Balas EA, Weingarten S, Garb CT, Blumenthal D, Boren SA, Brown GD. Improving preventive care by prompting physicians. Arch Intern Med 2000;160:301–8

38. McDonald CJ. Protocol-based computer reminders, the quality of care and the non-perfectability of man. N Engl J Med 1976;295:1351–1355

39. Morris AH. Computerized protocols and beside decision support. Crit Care Clin 1999;15:523–45.

40. Thomsen GE, Pope D, East T, Morris AH, Kinder AT, Carlson DA, et al Clinical performance of a rule-based decision support system for mechanical ventilation of ARDS patients. Proc Annu Symp Comput Appl Med Care 1993;1993:339–43

41. Sharpe V Faden A. Medical Harm. Cambridge, UK: Cambridge University Press, 1998.

42. Koppel R, Metlay JP, Cohen A, Abaluck B, Localio AR, Kimmel SE, et al. Role of computerized physician order entry systems in facilitating medication errors. JAMA 2005;293:1197–203

43. Nebeker JR, Hoffman JM, Weir CR, Bennett CL, Hurdle JF. High rates of adverse drug events in a highly computerized hospital. Arch Intern Med 2005;165:1111–6

44. Han YY, Carcillo JA, Venkataraman ST, Clark RS, Watson RS, Nguyen TC, et al. Unexpected increased mortality after implementation of a commercially sold computerized physician order entry system. Pediatrics 2005;116:1506–12

45. van der Sijs H, Aarts J, Vulto A, Berg M. Overriding of drug safety alerts in computerized physician order entry. J Am Med Inform Assoc 2006;13(2):138–47

46. Wears RL, Berg M. Computer technology and clinical work: still waiting for Godot. JAMA 2005;293:1261–3

47. Bria WF. CPOE: the CURE for American healthcare or WMD? J Healthc Inf Manag 2005;19:9–10

48. Del Beccaro MA, Jeffries HE, Eisenberg MA, Harry ED. Computerized Provider Order Entry Implementation: No Association With Increased Mortality Rates in an Intensive Care Unit. Pediatrics 2006;118:290–5

49. Martich GD. Cervenak J. Eyes wide shut ... The "hidden" costs of deploying health information technology.. J Crit Care 2007;22:39–40

50. Amarasingham R, Plantinga L, Diener-West M, Gaskin DJ, Powe NR. Clinical information technologies and inpatient outcomes. Arch Intern Med 2009;169:108–14

Jean-Louis Teboul, Xavier Monnet and Christian Richard

Pulmonary artery catheter: Balance between safe and optimal use

Introduction

Over the years following its introduction in the 1970s [1], the pulmonary artery catheter (PAC) has found widespread application in intensive care units (ICU) and in the perioperative setting, despite a lack of high-quality evidence-based medicine supporting this practice [2]. The question of using a PAC has been a matter of debate for more than 25 years. The proponents of its use have argued that the ability of this tool to provide clinicians with relevant haemodynamic variables should improve the diagnosis and the management of a shock state. The opponents of its use have emphasised the complications associated with its insertion and maintenance, inaccuracies in measurements and difficulties in interpreting the data [3–5]. An increasing number of intensivists are reluctant to use this monitoring tool, possibly due to the combination of persistent doubts about its safety and lack of evidence of its efficacy to reduce mortality [6]. In this chapter, we first focus on the principles of optimal use of the PAC with emphasis on correct measurements and adequate interpretation of the main variables. We also review the safety procedures recommended for the routine use of the PAC. Finally, we summarise the issue of PAC impact on outcome.

Optimal use of the PAC-derived parameters

The PAC provides the physician with haemodynamic measures such as cardiac output, right atrial, pulmonary artery and pulmonary artery occlusion pressures (PAOP). It also provides tissue perfusion variables (mixed venous blood oxygen saturation (SvO_2), oxygen consumption, oxygen delivery, oxygen extraction and venous carbon dioxide pressure).

Cardiac output

Cardiac output is measured according to the thermodilution principle. Two methods of measurement are currently used. The intermittent thermodilution technique requires the injection of a saline bolus through the proximal (atrial) lumen of the catheter. The decrease of blood temperature is recorded downstream by the distal thermistor and cardiac output is calculated from the Stewart-Hamilton equation by an external processor. At least three measurements must be averaged for a reliable estimation of cardiac output. One advantage of this technique is that it provides the value of cardiac output at the time when it is measured.

The continuous thermodilution method is based on intermittent and automatic heating of blood by means of a proximal thermal filament and recording of the temperature changes by a distal thermistor. This continuous measurement of cardiac output has been demonstrated to agree with that provided by the intermittent technique [7], except for the high values of cardiac output that could be underestimated by the continuous method [8]. This technique presents the advantage of avoiding repeated manipulations of the lines and bolus injections. The major inconvenience is that it does not enable real-time monitoring of cardiac output since the average of successive cardiac output measurements is delayed as compared to the standard intermittent technique [9]. This limitation may be important if one attempts to monitor rapid changes induced by a haemodynamic treatment or to evaluate transient haemodynamic effects of a therapeutic challenge like the passive leg-raising test [10].

Pulmonary artery occlusion pressure

Technique of measurement

The inflation of the distal balloon of the catheter with 1.5 ml of air occludes a branch of the pulmonary artery approximately 13 mm in diameter. This occlusion stops the blood flow distal to the balloon to a pulmonary vein of similar diameter. The PAOP is the pressure obtained after inflating the distal balloon. Since a static column is created between the inflated balloon and the venous site where the blood flow resumes, PAOP is assumed to reflect the pressure in a large pulmonary vein and thus the left atrial pressure and eventually the left ventricular end-diastolic pressure [11].

Conditions for correct PAOP measurement and interpretation

Important pitfalls may preclude adequate acquisition of the measurement of PAOP. In this regard, American and European studies showed that almost 50% of physicians or nurses could not correctly assess PAOP from a non-equivocal pressure tracing [4, 5].

Before PAOP measurements can be correctly interpreted, numerous questions have to be addressed carefully.

Is the technique of pressure measurement suitable?

The correct measurement of PAOP requires a cautious calibration of the zero of the pressure gauge with respect to the atmospheric pressure. The catheter tip must be placed at the mid-axillary line. The fluid-filled catheter used for pressure measurement must be flushed to avoid clotting.

Is PAOP influenced by the variations in the intrathoracic pressure?

To minimise the influence of intrathoracic pressure on PAOP measurements, it is recommended to measure PAOP at the end of expiration, a time when intrathoracic pressure is close to atmospheric pressure (see Fig. 1). However, positive end-expiratory pressure (PEEP) or auto-PEEP may lead to overestimation of PAOP at end-expiration (see below).

Does PAOP always reflect the pressure in a large pulmonary vein?

For considering that the PAOP senses the pressure in the pulmonary vein where the blood flow resumes, one assumes that the blood column immobilised by the balloon inflation is uninterrupted. This may not be the case in the presence of high PEEP (or auto-PEEP) conditions that may result in squeezing of alveolar microvesssels downstream to the branch of the pulmonary artery where balloon inflation has occurred. This condition where PAOP may not reflect a pulmonary venous pressure but rather alveolar pressure can be easily identified by calculating the ratio of respiratory changes of PAOP over those of the pulmonary artery diastolic pressure, which are assumed to reflect the respiratory changes in intrathoracic pressure [12]. If this ratio is greater than 1.5, the PAOP is likely to reflect alveolar pressure and must not be interpreted as a pulmonary venous pressure [12].

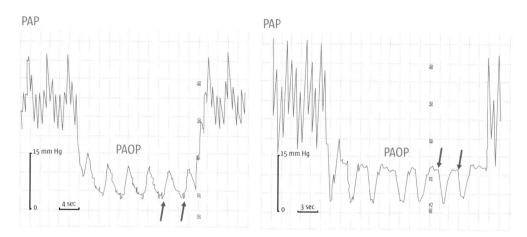

Fig. 1   Measurement of the pulmonary artery occlusion (PAOP) depending on the ventilatory mode.
To minimise the influence of intrathoracic pressure on PAOP measurements, it is recommended to measure PAOP at the end of expiration, a time when intrathoracic pressure is close to atmospheric pressure (arrows). During mechanical ventilation, the end-expiratory PAOP corresponds to the minimal pressure recorded during balloon inflation, while it corresponds to the maximal pressure recorded during balloon inflation in the case of spontaneous breathing [from Mebazza A, Gheorhiade M, Zannad FM and Parillo JE (Eds.), Acute heart Failure, with kind permission of Springer Science+Business Media]

Does the PAOP reflect the left ventricular end-diastolic pressure?

Even if reflected by PAOP, the left atrial pressure may differ from the left ventricular end-diastolic pressure in some clinical situations. The PAOP overestimates the left ventricular end-diastolic pressure in the case of significant mitral stenosis or mitral insufficiency. The PAOP underestimates the left ventricular end-diastolic pressure in the case of severe aortic insufficiency or in case of reduced left ventricular compliance.

Does the left ventricular end-diastolic pressure reflect the left ventricular preload?

The left ventricular preload is better related to the left ventricular transmural pressure (left ventricular end-diastolic pressure – intrathoracic pressure) than to the "intramural" left ventricular pressure. Accordingly, when high levels of PEEP are applied, the PAOP overestimates the left ventricular end-diastolic transmural pressure and hence the left ventricular preload, even at end-expiration. For correcting that overestimation, Teboul et al. proposed to evaluate the transmis-

sion of alveolar pressure to the intra-vascular system at end-expiration [13]. This transmission index (I_T) can be estimated by the ratio of DPAOP (difference between the PAOP values at end-expiration and end-inspiration) over DPalv (difference between plateau pressure and total PEEP) (see Fig. 2). Once I_T is calculated, the part of PAOP due to PEEP transmission can be estimated using the product of PEEP by I_T. This product must be subtracted from the end-expiratory PAOP and the corrected value of PAOP is obtained [13]. Unlike the nadir PAOP measurement proposed by Pinsky et al. [14], this technique is also suitable in the case of intrinsic PEEP [13]. Finally, the question whether the left ventricular preload is better assessed by left ventricular transmural end-diastolic pressure or volume is still a physiological debate. Because left ventricular compliance is different from one patient to another, PAOP must not correlate with left ventricular end-diastolic volume when a vast population of patients is considered [15]. Importantly, left ventricular end-diastolic dimensions better correlate with stroke volume than PAOP [16]. In patients studied after myocardial infarction, higher than normal values of PAOP have been

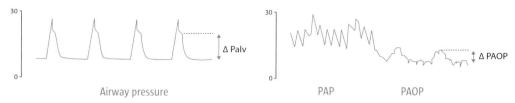

Fig. 2   Transmural pulmonary artery occlusion pressure.
The ∆PAOP/∆Palv (I_T) reflects the percentage of transmission of airway pressure to intrathoracic vessels. A "trans-mural" PAOP value can be calculated by subtracting the product of PEEP by I_T (Palv: alveolar pressure; PAP: pulmo-nary artery pressure; PAOP: pulmonary artery occlusion pressure) [from Mebazza A, Gheorhiade M, Zannad FM and Parillo JE (Eds.), Acute heart Failure, with kind permission of Springer Science+Business Media]

found associated with optimal left ventricular fill-ing conditions [17]. This suggests that in the case of reduced left ventricular compliance, a PAOP in the normal range may reflect an abnormally reduced left ventricular preload.

Does PAOP reflect the hydrostatic pulmonary filtration pressure?

The main determinant of pulmonary oedema for-mation is the hydrostatic pressure that exists in the capillary vessel (Pcp). Since the PAOP reflects the pressure in a large pulmonary vein, the dif-ference between PCp and PAOP is proportional to the blood flow through the pulmonary venous bed and the resistance of the pulmonary venous bed. Thus, PAOP underestimates Pcp, particu-larly in high blood flow states or in conditions where pulmonary venous resistance is elevated as during ARDS [18, 19]. The Pcp can be es-timated by observing the shape of the pulmonary artery pressure trace decay during the seconds following the inflation of the balloon. Schemati-cally, the decreasing pressure profile is con-sidered as bi-exponential: The initial fast decrease corresponds to the fast draining of blood through the low compliant arterial system; the ensuing slower decrease corresponds to the addition of the slower blood emptying through the capillary and venous beds [20]. The pressure recorded at the intersection between the two parts of the curve has been assimilated to Pcp [20]. However, this method is prone to numerous pitfalls in pathological conditions that make it difficult to apply routinely. Another approach is to estimate the resistance of the venous pulmonary bed. For this purpose, the PAC can be advanced with de-

flated balloon until wedging a small diameter ar-tery. The pressure measured at the distal tip of the PAC thus reflects the pressure into a small pulmonary vein of identical diameter at the op-posite side of the pulmonary bed [18]. The dif-ference between the PAOP (reflecting the pres-sure into a large pulmonary vein) and the distal wedge pressure is high in cases of high pulmo-nary venous resistance such as ARDS [18, 19] and alpha-agonist catecholamine therapy [21].

For which clinical purpose may the PAOP be used?

Diagnosing the mechanism of pulmonary oedema

As a rough estimate of Pcp, PAOP has been pro-posed to differentiate between hydrostatic and increased permeability pulmonary oedema. The value of 18 mmHg is often considered a cut-off value. However, hydrostatic pulmonary oedema can still be present although PAOP has already been normalised [22], and increased permeabil-ity pulmonary oedema can be associated with el-evated PAOP [23].

Whatever the nature of pulmonary oedema, PAOP cannot correlate with the amount of lung oedema. Therefore, a PAOP of 10 mmHg can be associated with low, normal or very high val-ues of extravascular lung water measured using transpulmonary thermodilution [24].

Using PAOP for guiding fluid resuscitation/fluid restriction

As a reflection of the left ventricular filling pres-sure, the PAOP has been proposed to reflect left ventricular preload. Nonetheless, as other static markers of cardiac preload, PAOP was demonstrated to be of little value for guiding fluid therapy in the critically ill [25] since it is a poor predictor of volume responsiveness [26]. Except for the lowest and the highest ranges of ventricular preload, a given value of any measure of ventricular preload can be associated with preload responsiveness in the case of normal ventricular contractility (steep part of the Frank-Starling curve) or with preload unresponsiveness in the case of decreased ventricular contractility (flat part of the Franck-Starling curve). As patients treated in ICUs often have already been resuscitated for several hours or days, ventricular preload (and thus PAOP) is rarely low in contrary to what may happen in patients admitted in the emergency room. Therefore, a given value of PAOP generally fails to predict the ability of the ventricle to positively respond to volume loading [25, 26]. On the other hand, it has been proposed to use PAOP as a safety parameter during volume loading [27]. In this regard, fluid administration could be discontinued when a predefined value of PAOP has been reached in order to prevent fluid-induced pulmonary oedema. The value of 18 mmHg is often cited as the PAOP value above which there is a high risk of pulmonary oedema occurring with fluid administration, although no study has validated it. Acute lung injury is a clinical situation where fluid management is a crucial issue. On the one hand, volume expansion may be required since this situation is frequently associated with sepsis and relative hypovolaemia; on the other hand, volume infusion may enhance pulmonary oedema formation since pulmonary vascular permeability is increased. Although there is some evidence of the superiority of conservative strategy over liberal strategy in terms of fluid management in acute lung injury [28], PAOP-guided therapy was not found to perform better than central venous pressure-guided therapy [29]. It must also be stressed that management based on the value of extravascular lung water was associated with better outcome than PAOP-guided management in a randomised study in critically ill patients [30].

Mixed venous oxygen saturation

The PAC provides measurement of SvO_2. Since the mixed venous blood results from the mix of all venous territories of the body, SvO_2 provides assessment of global tissue oxygenation, which is not provided by peripheral blood samplings.

Techniques of SvO_2 measurement

Two techniques are currently available. The first one requires blood sampling through the distal tip of the PAC (with deflated balloon). The second technique uses PAC models that enable a continuous in vivo monitoring of SvO_2 by means of fiberoptic spectrophotometry. This method avoids cumbersome repeated blood samplings and provides a continuous monitoring of SvO_2.

Significance and clinical use of SvO_2

SvO_2 is related to arterial oxygen saturation (SaO_2), oxygen consumption, to cardiac output and haemoglobin concentration (Hb) according to the formula derived from the Fick equation applied to oxygen:

$$SvO_2 = SaO_2 - [oxygen\ consumption/(cardiac\ output \times Hb \times 13.4)]$$

Thus, SvO_2 is a marker of the global balance between actual oxygen consumption and oxygen delivery, since cardiac output, Hb and SaO_2 are the key determinants of oxygen delivery. SvO_2 values range from 65% to 77% in healthy subjects.

A common mistake is to take SvO_2 as a surrogate of cardiac output. A better approach is to consider SvO_2 as a marker of adequacy of cardiac output with the actual metabolic conditions. In this regard, SvO_2 rather than cardiac output can be used to adjust the dose of inotropic drugs that have potential thermogenic effects [31, 32]. For example, phosphodiesterase inhibitors as well as β_1-agonist agents can increase myocardial and global oxygen consumption and may result in unchanged SvO_2 despite increase in cardiac output [33, 34]. Moreover, in patients with severe heart failure experiencing tricuspid regurgitation, thermodilution cardiac output may be erroneous and monitoring the cardiovascular treatment using SvO_2 could be a better approach [33].

The interpretation of SvO_2 and its changes is prone to some difficulties, which should be emphasised. Firstly, a low value of SvO_2 can be the consequence of a decrease in SaO_2. In this condition, SvO_2 can no longer be considered as a marker of the oxygen consumption/oxygen delivery balance. Secondly, a normal or high SvO_2 value can be observed in distributive shock states such as septic shock. In these conditions and contrary to what occurs in cardiogenic or hypovolaemic shock states, the decrease in oxygen consumption (relatively to oxygen demand) is not the consequence of a decrease in cardiac output but is related to impaired oxygen extraction capabilities. Therefore, in patients with septic shock where haemodynamic resuscitation has restored a normal or high cardiac output, values of $SvO_2 > 70\%$ can be achieved despite persistence of marked global tissue dysoxia. This emphasises the fact that SvO_2 is a marker of the global balance between oxygen delivery and oxygen consumption but not with oxygen demand. Thirdly, if oxygen consumption, Hb and SaO_2 are constant, the relation between SvO_2 and cardiac output is not linear, but hyperbolic. Under these conditions, while in low blood flow states changes in SvO_2 parallel changes in cardiac output, in hyperdynamic states marked changes in cardiac output will not significantly alter SvO_2. In this regard, when SvO_2 lies in its high or even normal range, any decrease in SvO_2 by at least 5% should be considered as clinically significant since it indicates a dramatic fall in oxygen delivery and/or an increase in oxygen demand. This should prompt the checking of Hb, SaO_2, cardiac output, and potential causes of increased oxygen demand and lead to appropriate treatment. Fourthly, in shock states characterised by oxygen supply/oxygen consumption dependency, changes in cardiac output will result in changes in oxygen consumption in the same direction such that SvO_2 will not change provided that oxygen delivery is less than its critical value. Fifthly, SvO_2 is the flow-weighted average of the venous saturation values from all organs of the body. Organs with high blood flow and low oxygen extraction, such as the kidneys, have a greater influence on SvO_2 than organs with low blood flow and high O_2 ex-

traction, such as the myocardium. During sepsis, the interpretation of SvO_2 is further complicated by disturbances of regional and local distribution of blood flow.

In summary, in the shock states SvO_2 and its changes must be cautiously interpreted. However, in any shock state (even of septic origin), monitoring SvO_2 is helpful since a low value of SvO_2 (for example < 65%) incites the clinician to increase oxygen delivery in order to improve global tissue oxygenation. Here, one must remember the utility of guiding therapy with central venous oxygen saturation (as a surrogate of SvO_2) in the early phase of severe sepsis, as reported by Rivers [34]. On the other hand, a high value of SvO_2 suggests that attempts to further increase oxygen delivery have little chance to improve tissue oxygenation and, ultimately, outcome [35].

Complications related to the PAC

Complications related to PAC insertion

The insertion of a PAC can lead to arterial puncture and bleeding, to pneumothorax, to the injury of the brachial plexus and to a gas embolism. More specifically, contact of the PAC with the atrio-ventricular node can induce transitory atrioventricular block. The introduction of the PAC through the tricuspid valve can induce ventricular extra-systoles and, more rarely, ventricular tachycardia [36]. These rhythmic complications, which are related to the duration of PAC insertion and to a pre-existing risk for arrhythmias, are spontaneously reversible in most cases [36].

Infectious and thrombotic complications

Bacterial colonisation of the PAC is relatively frequent but infectious endocarditis is rare. This risk is related to the duration of PAC use. Catheter infection is frequently associated with a venous thrombo-embolism. Heparin coating of the catheter could reduce such infectious and thrombo-embolic risks.

Complications related to the inflation of the PAC distal balloon

In the case of a too distal position of the PAC into the pulmonary artery, the inflation of the balloon can induce a rupture of a pulmonary artery branch [37]. This complication is rare but dramatic and can be treated by coil embolisation [37]. False aneurysm of the pulmonary artery related to the catheter is rare [38]. Long-time inflation of the distal balloon in a pulmonary branch may rarely result in infarction in the corresponding pulmonary region.

Complications related to PAC withdrawal

Just as its insertion, the withdrawal of PAC can induce transient ventricular arrhythmias [39]. Knotting of the catheter is possible at any level, especially if its insertion has been long and difficult. Such a knot makes the extraction of the catheter difficult. Although the percutaneous extraction of the catheter and the knot are usually possible, it sometimes requires surgical intervention [40].

In summary, various complications may occur during insertion and stay of the PAC, but are most often minor. Serious complications occur in less than 0.5 % of the patients [41]. The adverse side-effects related to the insertion or use of the PAC are clearly related either to poor experience of the user or to the duration of PAC insertion.

Safety procedures

The incidence of almost all PAC-related adverse effects can be reduced provided that some safety procedures are followed carefully. Some contra-indications to PAC insertion must be respected. Among these are the common contra-indications for central venous catheterisation (bleeding risk, etc.). PAC use may be discouraged in patients with cardiac pacemakers due to the risk of knotting with the electrodes in the veins or in the cardiac cavities. In patients with ventricular hyperexcitability, the benefit of PAC use can be counterbalanced by the risk of inducing cardiac arrhythmias during its insertion. Finally, the pressure waves must be displayed on the monitor during the insertion procedure.

The risk of infection is reduced if the duration of PAC use is shortened. Usually, the PAC should be removed after a maximum of three or four days. This amount of time is usually sufficient for elucidating the haemodynamic trouble that led to the PAC insertion.

The risk of adverse effects related to distal balloon inflation is limited. For avoiding balloon rupture, the inflation should be stopped as soon as a resistance appears. The balloon must be inflated with saline and not with air so that the risk of embolism in case of balloon rupture is minimised. In order to avoid pulmonary infarction the balloon must be carefully deflated as soon as PAOP has been measured.

PAC use and outcome of critically ill patients

Considering the advantages and disadvantages of the PAC, a debate has emerged over whether its use may cause harm or benefits in the critically ill. The debate was most seriously raised by the study by Connors et al. [3], showing an increase in mortality rate, in the cost and in the length of hospitalisation related to PAC utilisation. However, this study was observational and enrolled a very heterogeneous population of patients. Recent randomised studies compared outcome of severely ill patients who received PAC vs. patients who did not [42–44]. No differences in terms of outcome were observed in these randomised clinical trials. A meta-analysis of 13 randomised studies later confirmed that in critically ill patients, the use of the PAC neither increased mortality or hospital length of stay nor conferred benefit [45]. These neutral results can be explained by three reasons. The first is the lack of management protocols triggered by PAC data in most of the studies included in the meta-analysis. However, in recent randomised studies, PAC-guided therapy did not perform better than clinical evaluation-guided therapy in congestive heart failure [46] or than central venous catheter-guided therapy in acute lung injury [29]. The second reason is that the increased accuracy of diagnosis potentially provided by use of the PAC did not lead to improved survival since haemodynamic data triggered use of therapies which did not affect or even worsened outcome. In this regard, the use of inotropic therapy in patients with decompensated heart failure may affect outcome negatively [47]. The third reason explaining the neutral results of the meta-analysis [45] is that inaccuracies in measurement and interpretation of PAC data may have resulted in inappropriate decisions. This underscores the need for physicians and nurses to receive training in haemodynamic data interpretation to better use the PAC.

Conclusion

The PAC provides an outstanding view of the haemodynamic situation, from cardiac output to tissue oxygenation. It has been regarded as the unique monitoring tool for decades. Not only is it considered helpful in the management of circulatory disorders but has also enabled a comprehensive approach to the haemodynamic physiology, especially during shock states. Nevertheless, use of the PAC is now decreasing, most likely because it appears as an invasive and cumbersome procedure and because some negative studies have introduced doubt regarding its clinical benefit. In addition, the PAC is now in competition with less invasive haemodynamic monitoring devices (pulse contour analysis, transpulmonary thermodilution) or ultrasonographic methods that have emerged in recent years and which are becoming increasingly popular.

The authors

Jean-Louis Teboul, MD, PhD
Xavier Monnet, MD, PhD
Christian Richard, MD
    Service de réanimation médicale |
    Centre Hospitalier Universitaire de Bicêtre |
    Assistance Publique – Hôpitaux de Paris |
    Université Paris 11 | Le Kremlin-Bicêtre,
    France

Address for correspondence
    Jean-Louis Teboul
    Service de réanimation médicale
    Centre Hospitalier Universitaire de Bicêtre
    78, rue du Général Leclerc
    94 270 Le Kremlin-Bicêtre, France
    E-mail: jean-louis.teboul@bct.aphp.fr

References

1. Swan HJ, Ganz W, Forrester J, Marcus H, Diamond G, Chonette D. Catheterization of the heart in man with use of a flow-directed balloon-tipped catheter. N Engl J Med 1970, 283:447–451.
2. Hall JB. Searching for evidence to support pulmonary artery catheter use in critically ill patients. Jama 2005, 294:1693–1694.
3. Connors AF, Jr., Speroff T, Dawson NV, Thomas C, Harrell FE, Jr., Wagner D, et al. The effectiveness of right heart catheterization in the initial care of critically ill patients. SUPPORT Investigators. Jama 1996, 276:889–897.
4. Iberti TJ, Fischer EP, Leibowitz AB, Panacek EA, Silverstein JH, Albertson TE. A multicenter study of physicians' knowledge of the pulmonary artery catheter. Pulmonary Artery Catheter Study Group. Jama 1990, 264:2928–2932.
5. Gnaegi A, Feihl F, Perret C. Intensive care physicians' insufficient knowledge of right-heart catheterization at the bedside: time to act? Crit Care Med 1997;25:213–220.
6. Wiener RS, Welch HG. Trends in the use of the pulmonary artery catheter in the United States, 1993–2004. Jama 2007, 298:423–429.
7. Boldt J, Menges T, Wollbruck M, Hammermann H, Hempelmann G. Is continuous cardiac output measurement using thermodilution reliable in the critically ill patient? Crit Care Med 1994;22:1913–1918.
8. Dhingra VK, Fenwick JC, Walley KR, Chittock DR, Ronco JJ. Lack of agreement between thermodilution and fick cardiac output in critically ill patients. Chest 2002;122:990–997.
9. Poli de Figueiredo LF, Malbouisson LM, Varicoda EY, Carmona MJ, Auler JO Jr, Rocha e Silva M. Thermal filament continuous thermodilution cardiac output delayed response limits its value during acute hemodynamic instability. J Trauma 1999;47:288–293.
10. Monnet X, Teboul JL. Passive leg raising. Intensive Care Med 2008;34:659–63.
11. Teboul JL, Zapol WM, Brun-Buisson C, Abrouk F, Rauss A, Lemaire F. A comparison of pulmonary artery occlusion pressure and left ventricular end-diastolic pressure during mechanical ventilation with PEEP in patients with severe ARDS. Anesthesiology 1989;70:261–266.
12. Teboul JL, Andrivet P, Ansquer M, Axler O, Douguet D, Zelter M, et al. A bedside index assessing the reliability of pulmonary occlusion pressure during mechanical ventilation with positive end-expiratory pressure. J Crit Care 1992;7:22–29.
13. Teboul JL, Pinsky MR, Mercat A, Anguel N, Bernardin G, Achard JM, et al. Estimating cardiac filling pressure in mechanically ventilated patients with hyperinflation. Crit Care Med 2000;28:3631–3636.

14. Pinsky M, Vincent JL, De Smet JM. Estimating left ventricular filling pressure during positive end-expiratory pressure in humans. Am Rev Respir Dis 1991;143:25–31.

15. Raper R, Sibbald WJ. Misled by the wedge? The Swan-Ganz catheter and left ventricular preload. Chest 1986;89:427–434.

16. Kumar A, Anel R, Bunnell E, Habet K, Zanotti S, Marshall S, et al. Pulmonary artery occlusion pressure and central venous pressure fail to predict ventricular filling volume, cardiac performance, or the response to volume infusion in normal subjects. Crit Care Med 2004;32:691–699.

17. Crexells C, Chatterjee K, Forrester JS, Dikshit K, Swan HJ. Optimal level of filling pressure in the left side of the heart in acute myocardial infarction. N Engl J Med 1973;289:1263–1266.

18. Teboul JL, Andrivet P, Ansquer M, Besbes M, Rekik N, Lemaire F, et al. Bedside evaluation of the resistance of large and medium pulmonary veins in various lung diseases. J Appl Physiol 1992;72:998–1003.

19. Nunes S, Ruokonen E, Takala J. Pulmonary capillary pressures during the acute respiratory distress syndrome. Intensive Care Med 2003;29:2174–2179.

20. Cope DK, Allison RC, Parmentier JL, Miller JN, Taylor AE. Measurement of effective pulmonary capillary pressure using the pressure profile after pulmonary artery occlusion. Crit Care Med 1986;14:16–22.

21. Teboul JL, Douguet D, Mercat A, Depret J, Richard C, Zelter M. Effects of catecholamines on the pulmonary venous bed in sheep. Crit Care Med 1998;26:1569–1575.

22. Bindels AJ, van der Hoeven JG, Meinders AE. Pulmonary artery wedge pressure and extravascular lung water in patients with acute cardiogenic pulmonary edema requiring mechanical ventilation. Am J Cardiol 1999;84:1158–1163.

23. Ferguson ND, Meade MO, Hallett DC, et al. High values of the pulmonary artery wedge pressure in patients with acute lung injury and acute respiratory distress syndrome. Intensive Care Med 2002; 28:1073–1077.

24. Boussat S, Jacques T, Levy B, Laurent E, Gache A, Capellier G, et al. Intravascular volume monitoring and extravascular lung water in septic patients with pulmonary edema. Intensive Care Med 2002;28:712–718.

25. Osman D, Ridel C, Ray P, Monnet X, Anguel N, Richard C, et al. Cardiac filling pressures are not appropriate to predict hemodynamic response to volume challenge. Crit Care Med 2007;35:64–68.

26. Michard F, Teboul JL. Predicting fluid responsiveness in ICU patients: a critical analysis of the evidence. Chest 2002;121:2000–2008.

27. Vincent JL, Weil MH. Fluid challenge revisited. Crit Care Med 2006;34:1333–1337.

28. Wheeler AP, Bernard GR, Thompson BT, Schoenfeld, Wiedemann HP, deBoisblanc B, et al. Pulmonary-Artery versus Central Venous Catheter to Guide Treatment of Acute Lung Injury. N Engl J Med 2006;354:2213–2224.

29. Wiedemann HP, Wheeler AP, Bernard GR, Thompson BT, Hayden D, deBoisblanc B, et al. Comparison of Two Fluid-Management Strategies in Acute Lung Injury. N Engl J Med 2006;354:2564–2575.

30. Mitchell JP, Schuller D, Calandrino FS, Schuster DP. Improved outcome based on fluid management in critically ill patients requiring pulmonary artery catheterization. Am Rev Respir Dis 1992;145:990–998.

31. Teboul JL, Annane D, Thuillez C, Depret J, Bellissant E, Richard C. Effects of cardiovascular drugs on oxygen consumption/oxygen delivery relationship in patients with congestive heart failure. Chest 1992;101:1582–1587.

32. Teboul JL, Graini L, Boujdaria R, Berton C, Richard C. Cardiac index vs oxygen-derived parameters for rational use of dobutamine in patients with congestive heart failure. Chest 1993;103:81–85.

33. Nunez S, Maisel A. Comparison between mixed venous oxygen saturation and thermodilution cardiac output in monitoring patients with severe heart failure treated with milrinone and dobutamine. Am Heart J 1998;135:383–388.

34. Rivers E, Nguyen B, Havstad S, Ressler J, Muzzin A, Knoblich B, et al. Early goal-directed therapy in the treatment of severe sepsis and septic shock. N Engl J Med 2001; 345:1368–1377.

35. Gattinoni L, Brazzi L, Pelosi P, Tognoni G, Pesenti A, Fumagalli R. A trial of goal-oriented hemodynamic therapy in critically ill patients. SvO$_2$ Collaborative Group. N Engl J Med 1995;333:1025–1032.

36. Sprung CL, Pozen RG, Rozanski JJ, Pinero JR, Eisler BR, Castellanos A. Advanced ventricular arrhythmias during bedside pulmonary artery catheterization. Am J Med 1982;72:203–208.

37. Mullerworth MH, Angelopoulos P, Couyant MA, Horton AM, Robinson SM, Petring OU, et al. Recognition and management of catheter-induced pulmonary artery rupture. Ann Thorac Surg 1998;66:1242–1245.

38. Ferretti GR, Thony F, Link KM, Durand M, Wollschläger K, Blin D, et al. False aneurysm of the pulmonary artery induced by a Swan-Ganz catheter: clinical presentation and radiologic management. Am J Roentgenol 1996;167:941–945.

39. Damen J. Ventricular arrhythmias during insertion and removal of pulmonary artery catheters. Chest 1985;88:190–193.

40. Koh KF, Chen FG. The irremovable swan: a complication of the pulmonary artery catheter. J Cardiothorac Vasc Anesth 1998;12:561–562.

41. Ivanov R, Allen J, Calvin JE. The incidence of major morbidity in critically ill patients managed with pulmonary artery catheters: a meta-analysis. Crit Care Med 2000;28:615–619.

42. Rhodes A, Cusack RJ, Newman PJ, Grounds RM, Bennett ED. A randomised, controlled trial of the pulmonary artery catheter in critically ill patients. Intensive Care Med 2002;28:256–264.

43. Richard C, Warszawski J, Anguel N, Deye N, Combes A, Barnoud D. Early use of the pulmonary artery catheter and outcomes in patients with shock and acute respiratory distress syndrome: a randomized controlled trial. Jama 2003;290:2713–2720.

44. Harvey S, Harrison DA, Singer M, Ashcroft J, Jones CM, Elbourne D, et al. Assessment of the clinical effectiveness of pulmonary artery catheters in management of patients in intensive care (PAC-Man): a randomised controlled trial. Lancet 2005;366:472–477.

45. Shah MR, Hasselblad V, Stevenson LW, Binanay C, O'Connor CM, Sopko G, et al. Impact of the pulmonary artery catheter in critically ill patients: meta-analysis of randomized clinical trials. Jama 2005;294:1664–1670.

46. Binanay C, Califf RM, Hasselblad V, O'Connor CM, Shah MR, Sopko G, et al; ESCAPE Investigators and ESCAPE Study Coordinators. Evaluation study of congestive heart failure and pulmonary artery catheterization effectiveness: the ESCAPE trial. JAMA 2005;294:1625–1633.

47. Bayram M, De Luca L, Massie MB, Gheorghiade M. Reassessment of dobutamine, dopamine, and milrinone in the management of acute heart failure syndromes. Am J Cardiol 2005;96:47G-58G.

H. Training, teaching, and education

Julian F. Bion

Approaches to improving the reliability and safety of patient care

Introduction

We are well accustomed to the reality of imperfection in human affairs. Indeed, so well accustomed that we readily accept that healthcare has an inevitable failure rate which excuses error on the basis that medicine is not an exact science. Combine this with the historical concept of healthcare as a charitable gift to patients and beneficent intent as sufficient for professional regulation, and the scene is set for a level of tolerance of error and adverse events in healthcare which would be completely unacceptable in any other high-risk industry.

The Institute of Medicine's Report "To Err is Human" in 2000 [1] marked a turning point in attitudes of individuals and whole systems to safety. Using data from retrospective case note review studies [2–4] which demonstrated high levels of adverse events (4–16 % of patients) and avoidable harm, this and subsequent reports [5] called for concerted action to improve patient safety. Studies in other countries [6–10] and a systematic review [11] reinforced these data, and in 2005 the World Health Organisation formed the World Alliance for Patient Safety [12] to integrate national efforts with a series of biannual worldwide clinical challenges – first for hand hygiene, next for wrong site surgery.

Progress has been slow however [13, 14], which suggests that the concept of safety does not speak directly to clinicians and others responsible for healthcare delivery. An alternative way of expressing the problem may be to focus on reliability of care. Safety means the absence of error, a negative concept, whereas reliability means delivery of best practice, which is more in tune with the concept of professionalism, is more positive, and provides a clear benchmark for audit. Improve reliability, and safety must follow.

Unreliable care – the gap between desired and actual practice expressed as the proportion of errors to total opportunities for error – is very common. Civil aviation is often cited as having the greatest reliability, with an error rate of 10^{-6} (fewer than 10 errors per million opportunities); by comparison, blood transfusion services and anaesthesia achieve around 10^{-4}, but the rest of healthcare rarely does better than 10^{-2} (more than 10 errors per 100 opportunities) [15, 16]. Interventions based on education and prevention are the least reliably delivered [15], perhaps because they are the least rewarding to deliver. The most frequently cited are errors of drug administration or in operative procedures [11], though again this might be a feature of their ease of detection. Underlying (or root) causes are not well described; they include communication failures in around 80 % of errors [17].

Improving reliability of care means changing human behaviour. There is now a large literature on change management in healthcare, and yet sustained quality improvement seems to be one of the most difficult of all tasks for health systems trying to improve patient outcomes [18, 19]. The few examples of verifiably successful and sustained large-scale quality improvement collaborations [20] are counterbalanced by many of limited, or no, efficacy [21]. Grol, Berwick and Wensing [22] have called for much greater research investment and methodological rigour in quality improvement initiatives.

Environmental factors: Acuity and control

Reliability improvement is particularly challenging in emergency care [23] because of the need to intervene quickly in the context of life-threatening illness, unpredictable pathways, diagnostic uncertainty, and rapidly changing physical states; in the ICU this state may persist for comparatively long periods of time – many days or weeks – with care required at all hours of day and night, with multiple transitions between teams and geographical areas, and lapses and discontinuities in communication. Process control, absolutely essential for reliability improvement, is difficult to maintain in these circumstances [24–26]. The intensive care unit should therefore be one of the safest and most reliable environments in the hospital, since the ICU concentrates resources, knowledge and skills to ensure high-quality process control. However, even allowing for the markedly increased opportunities for error which exist in critical illness, current evidence suggests that there are substantial opportunities for improvement in the care of critically ill patients both inside and outside the ICU. Almost 15 years after the now classic study of Yoel Donchin [27], errors and adverse events remain common in ICU patients. In a direct observational study, Giraud and colleagues [28] found that 124 of 400 (31 %) consecutive patients admitted to an ICU had 316 iatrogenic complications, a rate of 2.5 complications per patient. In a review [29] of the medical records of 295 consecutive patients admitted to a medical ICU, 42 (14 %) had one or more complications of care during their treatment. Two studies using voluntary reporting systems found that one or more errors occurred during the care of 13–20 % of patients admitted to an ICU, a rate of 26–89 errors/1,000 patient days [30, 31]. Similar event rates are noted for paediatrics, with 220

adverse events during 730 paediatric ICU nursing shifts, a rate of 60 per 1,000 patient days [32]. Healthcare-related complications in ICU patients are associated with prolonged hospital stays and higher mortality [28, 29].

Theories and models of behaviour

The complex interplay between environment and people, between systems and human factors (in our case, between the healthcare system, the practitioner and the patient) has attracted a number of behavioural theories and frameworks which attempt to explain the gap between intention and behaviour. The practical utility of these theories is uncertain. Michie et al. [33] used iterative consensus methods to develop a 12-domain framework for classifying, studying and implementing behaviour change interventions [34] which may be useful for descriptive purposes. Ethnography allows in-depth exploration of the social world [35] and issues relating to patient safety [36–38]. One such ethnographic tool is the normalisation process model [39, 40] which provides a theoretical framework for examining the way in which complex interventions may become routinely embedded (normalised) in everyday practice. Ethnographic approaches are attractive because they use direct observation in the workplace.

Barriers and facilitators for changing behaviour

Most clinicians have at some point been encouraged to adopt new interventions which subsequently failed to demonstrate benefit or were found to cause harm [41], and a degree of scepticism may be appropriate. Frequent "top-down" government initiatives implemented locally by individuals without direct clinical responsibility are unlikely to be adopted with enthusiasm by front-line staff confronting the daily complexities of patient care, particularly when too many organisations are involved with overlapping responsibility for hospital accreditation, clinical practice standard development, training provision, professional education, and patient safety itself. The effort required for quality improvement is often not recognised and rewarded in the same way as other research interventions, and the research methodologies are perceived as less robust, which makes it more difficult to demonstrate success [42]. "Change" will therefore only result in improvement if it is approached in a systematic and integrated manner which takes into account the interrelationships between the intervention itself, the individuals who will implement it, the system in terms of social, cultural and organisational factors, and the tools and metrics available to assess performance and outcomes. The apparent efficacy of "simple" interventions such as financial incentives [43–46] does not mean that fiscal reward is the solution to unreliability; it means that quality improvement requires a systems approach to changing behaviour, as demonstrated in the VA studies [47]. Understanding the reasons for failure to deliver high-reliability care is essential prior knowledge for designing improvement projects.

Defining best practice

The use of best practice guidelines as benchmarks for assessing the reliability of care seems simple enough. However, some clinicians are deeply opposed to what they see as an attempt to limit clinical freedom and standardise the treatment of individual patients. Moreover, while evidence-based medicine provides an important framework for guideline development, it does not in itself obviate the need to make judgements. The GRADE system [48] makes it easier to consider separately the strength of evidence and the strength of the recommendation, an important distinction for quality improvement work where it may be impossible to conduct randomised controlled trials of established treatments (for example, timing of antibiotics for septic shock, rationing access to intensive care units, or hand hygiene). When evidence is weak, indirect, or conflicting, the process of arriving at a judgement to use, or not use, a particular intervention can be clarified by formal consensus techniques based on private polling of opinion within nominal groups [49]. Patterns of polling can show consensus, polarisation, or equipoise; and give a clear measure of strength of opinion. This makes it easier to issue authoritative recommendations to clinicians, as well as providing an estimate of uncertainty or identify those interventions which require further research.

Given the relative lack of impact of guidelines on clinical practice and the difficulty of operationalising large numbers of recommendations, quality improvement groups are starting to use care "bundles" in an attempt to improve implementation. The principles of creating care bundles are described in Table 1. First proposed by the Institute for Healthcare Improvement (IHI), bundles have been adopted by the Joint Commission in the USA [50] and the National Health Service in the UK [51], and have been used to facilitate implementation of the Surviving Sepsis Campaign guidelines [52]. Advantages of bundling include synergism, reducing complexity, and enforcing best practice. Potential disadvantages include disagreements about component elements, and concerns over legal implications of implementation "failure" or clinical freedom. Evidence that bundling (or standard order sets) are effective depends on the extent to which the components themselves are implemented; even modest improvements in process may result in improvements in survival from sepsis [53], but this study also demonstrates how difficult it is to change human behaviour in terms of reliability enhancement.

Tab. 1   Principles of bundling

Include high-evidence or strong recommendation interventions
Include interventions which gap analyses have shown are performed unreliably
Minimise the number of components
Interventions should share same time and location
Aim to complete all elements

Human factors

Human factors include fatigue [54, 55], burnout [56] and depression [57]. Attitudinal and behavioural barriers to implementing best practice vary widely between individuals, making generalisability difficult [58, 59]. Knowledge deficits are less common than implementation deficits [60, 61]. Competence-based training is important in defining educational outcomes, but it needs to be accompanied by a strong focus on attitudes and behaviours to ensure that excellence becomes a habit. Communication failures are one of the most common underlying causes of error [62–76], identified in around 80 % of multiple error sequences [17]. Changing the behaviour of people, and thus of whole systems, takes courage, persistence, willingness to learn from others, and leadership from in front. Patients also need to be empowered as partners in improving their own outcomes.

The system: Social and organisational factors

James Reason has described "blaming front-line individuals, denying the existence of systemic error-provoking weaknesses, and the blinkered pursuit of productive and financial indicators" as features of the vulnerable systems syndrome [77]. Systems are only as good as the individuals within them; structures and traditions can enhance or impede, but not replace, individual effort. The organisational structure should therefore be based on clear and widely shared strategic aims. Absence of strategic direction or visible front-line leadership permits fragmentation and loss of discipline. Vertical hierarchies and professional "silos" inhibit effective communication and transdisciplinary learning, a particular problem for acutely ill patients whose journey through the healthcare system crosses speciality and geographical boundaries. The differing authority and power of doctors, nurses, and patients makes it difficult in some cultures to challenge and correct errors, a major problem in acute care where system tolerances may be low. In a survey of three paediatric cardiac surgical centres, 60 % of respondents stated that it was difficult to discuss mistakes in their working environment, 71 % had no debriefing after adverse events, 39 % that guidelines were often ignored, and 27 % that clinical disagreements were not effectively resolved [78].

Team-working may mean some loss of professional autonomy, but this is not incompatible with taking personal responsibility, having pride in one's work, and leadership. Good role models and effective opinion leaders are essential in developing an organisation which is patient-focused, transparent, reflective, self-critical, supportive and forward-looking. Resources must be made available for all aspects of reliability improvement, including staff development.

Improvement tools

There is no single ideal method or tool for implementing and sustaining changes in clinical practice. Multifaceted interventions may be no more effective than properly applied single interventions [21]. Some interventions are of necessity multifaceted, for example rapid response (medical emergency or outreach) teams, in which case the content of the intervention should be made explicit. It is also important to distinguish between the intervention (e.g. earlier antimicrobials for sepsis) and the vehicle for delivery (e.g. outreach care, education).

Mortality and morbidity meetings are of limited use without measurable actions and objectives. Mortality rates may be better interpreted using control charts, as case mix adjustment methods have yet to demonstrate convincing links with quality of care [79]. Gap analyses can provide convincing evidence of the need for quality improvement: Clinicians consistently overestimate their adherence to best practice [80].

Plan-do-study-act (PDSA) cycles were developed as a method for enabling small-scale rapid change evaluations to grow into systems-wide performance improvement. Like care bundles, systematic evaluations of efficacy are lacking, but the technique has face validity as a useful tool for initiating change at a local level.

Clinical decision support is most effective if it is provided at the point of care and incorporated in routine workplace activities. Computerised reminders for therapies or laboratory investigations are most helpful if they reduce clinical work, for example by providing automated prescriptions for validation. Requesting documentation of the reasons for deviating from established guidelines also improves compliance.

Educational interventions such as passive distribution of materials, small group teaching, and educational outreach or academic detailing have evanescent effects unless accompanied by specific action plans or reinforcement. Reliability improvement needs to be built into life-long learning, for example by integrating best practice guidelines with national and international competency-based training programmes across disciplines [81]. Given the frequency with which human factors such as failures in communication, or attitudes and behaviours, drive unreliable care, educational programmes should focus on increasing self-awareness and insight amongst clinicians at as early a stage in their training as possible – certainly starting at undergraduate level. Multisource feedback (360 appraisal) when properly conducted has considerable potential in this respect [82].

Safety climate measurement is derived from work undertaken in high-risk industries such as aviation, and petrochemical and nuclear power generation. Safety "climate" is preferred to the earlier term of "culture" since the latter is an even more nebulous concept. Questionnaire surveys are used to determine the views of staff about their working environment and their attitudes towards safety. The Agency for Healthcare Research and Quality (AHRQ) has developed a 44-item questionnaire with additional data requested about the respondent [83]. This has undergone translation and psychometric testing in other countries [84]. However, while the psychometric properties of these instruments have been tested in healthcare, their utility and predictive power is very uncertain [85]; of 11 studies we have found which report the use of safety climate surveys to assess safety interventions, none reported any link with patient outcomes and other effects were modest or absent (data on file). Most studies report low response rates (usually less than 50%). Much of the literature from industry appears in non-peer-reviewed formats. This is clearly an area ripe for further transdisciplinary research, and the intensive care environment seems an ideal place for detailed examination since it combines acuity, high risk, process control, multi-tasking, teamworking, and ease of data acquisition, with safety issues as a high priority.

Planning and executing a quality improvement project

Quality improvement research is challenging not only because it involves changing behaviour but because equipoise is often absent for interventions which have become embedded in routine practice and which do not lend themselves to analysis by prospective randomised controlled trial. A systematic approach to planning is essential, presented in Figure 1. This synopsis is based on work by Pronovost, Cook, Curtis and our own experiences [86–88]. The first two steps are perhaps the most important, to understand the current "environment" and to gather broad support for the project. Involvement and support of frontline colleagues is essential; one way to do this is to encourage audit and gap analyses by trainees or undergraduates as a local project, across disciplines if appropriate. This may need to be accompanied by surveys of current behaviour, knowledge, and barriers to change. The "new" behaviour is the intervention, which requires consideration of all the components in the patient journey where the intervention could be applied. Improvement tools should be as simple as possible, and designed with the active involvement of those who will use them. Each step should contribute to understanding of long-term change, best achieved through training programmes – at national and international level when based on strong scientific evidence and systematic reviews, but also at local level in seminars and tutorials.

Conclusions

Reliable delivery of best practice care is the best way to promote patient safety. This means modifying behaviour – whether amongst clinicians, managers or patients themselves. Changing behaviour requires systems-wide commitment at all levels in the organisational hierarchy. Standardised care reduces opportunities for error, but challenges clinicians to make judgements about what constitutes best practice without inhibiting continued research and further refinement of clinical guidelines. Engagement in, and ownership of, quality improvement initiatives by front-line staff with the involvement of patients is central to success.

The author

Julian F. Bion, MBBS, MRCP, FRCP, FRCA, MD
  Professor of Intensive Care Medicine
  University of Birmingham
  University Dept Anaesthesia & ICM
  N5, Queen Elizabeth Hospital
  Edgbaston, Birmingham B15 2TH, UK
  E-mail: J.F.Bion@bham.ac.uk

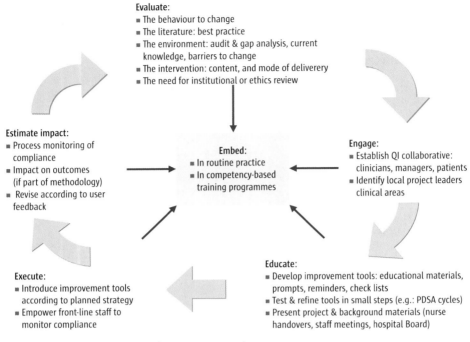

Evaluate:
- The behaviour to change
- The literature: best practice
- The environment: audit & gap analysis, current knowledge, barriers to change
- The intervention: content, and mode of deliverery
- The need for institutional or ethics review

Estimate impact:
- Process monitoring of compliance
- Impact on outcomes (if part of methodology)
- Revise according to user feedback

Embed:
- In routine practice
- In competency-based training programmes

Engage:
- Establish QI collaborative: clinicians, managers, patients
- Identify local project leaders clinical areas

Execute:
- Introduce improvement tools according to planned strategy
- Empower front-line staff to monitor compliance

Educate:
- Develop improvement tools: educational materials, prompts, reminders, check lists
- Test & refine tools in small steps (e.g.: PDSA cycles)
- Present project & background materials (nurse handovers, staff meetings, hospital Board)

Fig. 1   Planning and executing a quality improvement project

References

1. Kohn LT, Corrigan JM, Donaldson MS (Eds). To Err is Human: building a safer health system. Institute of Medicine. National Academy Press, Washington 2000.
2. Brennan TA, Leape LL, Laird NM, Hebert L, Localio AR, Lawthers AG, Newhouse JP, Weiler PC, Hiatt HH. Incidence of adverse events and negligence in hospitalized patients. Results of the Harvard Medical Practice Study I: The New England Journal of Medicine 1991;324:370–376.
3. Leape LL, Brennan TA, Laird N, Lawthers AG, Localio AR, Barnes BA, Hebert L, Newhouse JP, Weiler PC, Hiatt H. The nature of adverse events in hospitalized patients. Results of the Harvard Medical Practice Study II: The New England Journal of Medicine 1991;324:377–384.
4. Wilson RM, Runciman WB, Gibberd RW, Harrison BT, Newby L, Hamilton JD. The Quality in Australian Health Care Study: Med J Aust. 1995;163:458–471.
5. Institute of Medicine. Committee on Quality of Health Care in America. Crossing the quality chasm: a new health system for the 21st century. National Academy Press, Washington, D.C 2001.
6. Vincent C, Neale G, Woloshynowych M. Adverse events in British Hospitals: preliminary retrospective record review: BMJ 2001;322:517–519.
7. Davis P, Lay-Yee R, Briant R, Ali W, Scott A, Schug S. Adverse events in New Zealand public hospitals I: occurrence and impact: N Z.Med J 2002;115:U271.
8. Davis P, Lay-Yee R, Briant R, Ali W, Scott A, Schug S. Adverse events in New Zealand public hospitals II: preventability and clinical context: N Z.Med J 2003;116:U624.
9. Baker GR, Norton PG, Flintoft V, Blais R, Brown A, Cox J, Etchells E, Ghali WA, Hebert P, Majumdar SR, O'Beirne M, Palacios-Derflingher L, Reid RJ, Sheps S, Tamblyn R. The Canadian Adverse Events Study: the incidence of adverse events among hospital patients in Canada: Canadian Medical Association Journal 2004;170:1678–1686.
10. Adverse events in large NHS Hospital. Criterion-based retrospective case-note review. Qual Saf Health Care 2007;16:434–439. doi: 10.1136/qshc.2006.021154.
11. de Vries EN, Ramrattan MA, Smorenburg SM, Gouma DJ, Boermeester MA. The incidence and nature of in-hospital adverse events: a systematic review. Quality and Safety in Health Care 2008;17:216–223. doi:10.1136/qshc.2007.023622.
12. World Alliance for Patient Safety. World Health Organisation. www.who.int/patientsafety/en/
13. Altman DE, Clancy C, Blendon RJ. Improving Patient Safety – Five Years after the IOM Report. N Engl J Med 2004;351:2041–3.

14. Vincent C, Aylin P, Franklin BD, Holmes A, Iskander S, Jacklin A, Moorthy K. Is health care getting safer? BMJ 2008;337:a2426. doi:10.1136/bmj.a2426.

15. McGlynn EA, Asch SM, Adams J, Keesey J, Hicks J, DeCristofaro A, Kerr EA. The Quality of Health Care Delivered to Adults in the USA. NEJM 2003;348:2635–2645.

16. Stafford RS, Radley DC. The underutilization of cardiac medications of proven benefit, 1990 to 2002. J Am Coll Cardiol 2003;41:56–61.

17. Woolf SH, Kuzel AJ, Dovey SM, Phillips RL. A String of Mistakes: The Importance of Cascade Analysis in Describing, Counting, and Preventing Medical Errors. Ann Fam Med 2004;2:317–326. DOI: 10.1370/afm.126.

18. Cabana MD, Rand CS, Powe NR, Wu AW, Wilson MH, Abboud PA, Rubin HR. Why don't physicians follow clinical practice guidelines? A framework for improvement. JAMA 1999;282(15):1458–65.

19. Bero LA, Grilli R, Grimshaw JM, Harvey A, Oxman AD, Thomson MA. Closing the gap between research and practice: an overview of systematic reviews of interventions to promote the implementation of research findings. The Cochrane Effective Practice and Organization of Care Review Group. BMJ 1998;317(7156):465–8.

20. Pronovost P, Needham D, Berenholtz S, Sinopoli D, Chu H, Cosgrove S, Sexton B, Hyzy R, Welsh R, Roth G, Bander J, Kepros J, Goeschel C. An intervention to decrease catheter-related bloodstream infections in the ICU. N Engl J Med 2006;355(26):2725–32.

21. Grimshaw JM, Thomas RE, MacLennan G, Fraser C, Ramsay CR, Vale L, Whitty P, Eccles MP, Matowe L, Shirran L, Wensing M, Dijkstra R, Donaldson C. Effectiveness and efficiency of guideline dissemination and implementation strategies. Health Technol Assess 2004;8(6):1–72.

22. Grol R, Berwick DM, Wensing M. On the trail of quality and safety in health care. BMJ 2008;336:74–76 (12 January), doi:10.1136/bmj.39413.486944.AD.

23. Bion JF, Heffner J. Improving Hospital Safety For Acutely Ill Patients. A Lancet Quintet. I: Current Challenges In The Care Of The Acutely Ill Patient. Lancet 2004;363:970–7.

24. Angus DC, Black N. Improving care of the critically ill: institutional and health-care system approaches. Lancet 2004;363:1314–20.

25. Jarman B et al. Explaining differences in English hospital death rates using routinely collected data. BMJ 1999;318:1515–1520.

26. Braithwaite RS et al. Acutely ill hospitalised patients referred to intensive care: a high risk group for error. Qual. Saf. Health Care 2004;13:255–259.

27. Donchin Y, Gopher D, Olin M, Badihi Y, Biesky M, Sprung CL, Pizov R, Cotev S. A look into the nature and causes of human errors in the intensive care unit: Crit Care Med. 1995;23:294–300.

28. Giraud T, Dhainaut J-F, Vaxelaire J-F, et al. Iatrogenic complications in adult intensive care units: A prospective two-center study. Crit Care Med 1993;21:40–51.

29. Rubins HB, Moskowitz MA: Complications of care in a medical intensive care unit. J Gen Intern Med 1990;5:104–109.

30. Osmon S, Harris CB, Dunagan WC, et al. Reporting of medical errors: An intensive care unit experience. Crit Care Med 2004;32:727–733.

31. Flaatten H, Hevroy O. Errors in the intensive care unit (ICU). Experiences with an anonymous registration. Acta Anaesth Scand 1999;43:614–617.

32. Tibby SM, Correa-West J, Durward A, et al. Adverse events in a paediatric intensive care unit: Relationship to workload, skill mix and staff supervision. Intensive Care Med 2004;30:1160–1166.

33. Michie S, Johnston M, Abraham C et al. Making psychological theory useful for implementing evidence based practice: a consensus approach. Qual Saf Health Care 2005;14:26–33.

34. Bryman A. Integrating quantitative and qualitative research: how is it done? Qualitative Research 2006;6:97–113.

35. Bosk C. Forgive and Remember: managing medical failure. Chicago: Chicago University Press, 1979.

36. Waring J, Harrison S, McDonald R. A culture of safety or coping? Ritualistic behaviours in the operating theatre. Journal of Health Services Research and Policy. 2007;12,Suppl 1:S1-3-9.

37. Taxis K, Barber N. Causes of intravenous medication errors: an ethnographic study. QSHC 2003;12:343–7.

38. Smith AF, Pope C, Goodwin D, Mort M. Interprofessional handover and patient safety in anaesthesia: observational study of handovers in the recovery room. BJA 2008;101:332–7.

39. May C, Finch T, Mair F et al. Understanding the implementation of complex interventions in health care: the normalization process model. BMC HSR 2007;7:148.

40. May C. A rational model for assessing and evaluating complex interventions in health care. BMC HSR 2006;6:86.

41. Rubenfeld DG. Surrogate measures of patient-centered outcomes in critical care. In: Sibbald WS, Bion JF (Eds). Evaluating critical care: using health services research to improve quality. Springer, Berlin 2001.

42. Pronovost P, Wachter R. Proposed standards for quality improvement research and publication: one step forward and two steps back Qual. Saf. Health Care 2006;15:152–153. doi:10.1136/qshc.2006.018432

43. Roland M. Linking Physicians' Pay to the Quality of Care – A Major Experiment in the United Kingdom. NEJM 2004;351:14.

44. Lindenauer PK, Remus D, Roman S, Rothberg MB, Benjamin EM, Ma A, Bratzler DW. Public Reporting and Pay for Performance in Hospital Quality Improvement. NEJM 2007;356:486–496.

45. Clarkson JE, Turner S, Grimshaw JM, Ramsay CR, Johnston M, Scott A, Bonetti D, Tilley CJ, Maclennan G, Ibbetson R, MacPherson LMD, Pitts NB. Changing Clinicians' Behavior: a Randomized Controlled Trial of Fees and Education. J Dent Res 2008;87(7):640–644.

46. Epstein AM, Lee TH, Hamel MB. Paying Physicians for High-Quality Care. NEJM 2004;350:406–410.

47. Jha AK, Perlin JB, Kizer KW, Dudley RA. Effect of Transformation of the VA Health Care System on Quality of Care. NEJM 2003;348:2218–27.

48. GRADE Working Group. Grading quality of evidence and strength of recommendations. BMJ 2004;328:1490–8.

49. Jaeschke R, Guyatt GH, Dellinger P, Schünemann H, Levy MM, Kunz R, Norris S, Bion J. Use of GRADE grid to reach decisions on clinical practice guidelines when consensus is elusive. BMJ 2008;337:327–337.

50. Raising the Bar with Bundles. Joint Commission Perspectives on Patient Safety. April 2006; V6, Issue 4.

51. http://www.clean-safe-care.nhs.uk/ (accessed May 12th 2009)

52. Dellinger RP, Levy MM, Carlet JM, Bion J, Parker MM, Jaeschke R et al. Surviving Sepsis Campaign: International guidelines for management of severe sepsis and septic shock: 2008. Special Article. Critical Care Medicine 2008;36(1):296–327.

53. Ferrer R, Artigas A, Levy MM, Blanco J, González-Díaz G, Garnacho-Montero J, Ibáñez J, Palencia E, Quintana M, de la Torre-Prados MV, for the Edusepsis Study Group. Improvement in Process of Care and Outcome After a Multicenter Severe Sepsis Educational Program in Spain JAMA 2008;299 (19):2294–2303.

54. Barger LK, Cade BE, Ayas NT, Cronin JW, Rosner B, Speizer FE, Czeisler CA for the Harvard Work Hours, Health, and Safety Group. Extended Work Shifts and the Risk of Motor Vehicle Crashes among Interns. N Engl J Med 2005;352:125–34.

55. Landrigan CP, Rothschild JM, Cronin JW, et al. Effect of reducing interns' work hours on serious medical errors in intensive care units. N Engl J Med 2004;351:1838–1848.

56. West CP, Huschka MM, Novotny PJ, Sloan JA, Kolars JC, Habermann TM, Shanafelt TD. Association of Perceived Medical Errors With Resident Distress and Empathy A Prospective Longitudinal Study. JAMA 2006;296:1071–1078.

57. Fahrenkopf AM, Sectish TC, Barger LK, Sharek PJ, Lewin D, Chiang VW, Edwards S, Wiedermann BL, Landrigan CP. Rates of medication errors among depressed and burnt out residents: prospective cohort study. BMJ 2008;336:488–491 (1 March), doi:10.1136/bmj.39469.763218.BE.

58. Cabana MD, Rand CS, Powe NR, Wu AW, Wilson MH, Abboud PA, Rubin HR. Why don't physicians follow clinical practice guidelines? A framework for improvement. JAMA 1999;282(15):1458–65.

59. Tan JA, Naik VN, Lingard L. Exploring obstacles to proper timing of prophylactic antibiotics for surgical site infections. Quality and Safety in Health Care 2006;15:32–38; doi:10.1136/qshc.2004.012534.

60. Bahal A, Karamchandani D, Fraise AP, McLaws ML. Hand hygiene compliance: universally better post-contact than pre-contact in healthcare workers in the UK and Australia. British Journal of Infection Control 2007;8:24–28.

61. Shapey IM, Foster MA, Whitehouse T, Jumaa P, Bion JF. Central Venous Catheter Related Bloodstream Infections – Improving post-insertion catheter Care. Journal of Hospital Infection 2008 (in press).

62. Baggs JG, Schmitt MH, Mushlin AI, Mitchell PH, Eldrege DH, Oakes D. Association between nurse–physician collaboration and patient outcomes in three intensive care units. CCM 1999;27:1991–8.

63. Reader T, Flin R, Lauche K, Cuthbertson B. Non-technical skills in the intensive care unit. BJA 2006;96:551–9.

64. Edmondson A. Psychological safety and learning behaviour in work teams. Adm Sci Q 1999;44:350–83.

65. Thomas EJ, Sexton JB, Helmreich RL. Discrepant attitudes about teamwork among critical care nurses and physicians. CCM 2003;31:956–9.

66. Miller PA. Nurse–physician collaboration in an intensive care unit. Am J Crit Care 2001;10:341–50.

67. Sutcliffe KM, Lewton E, Rosenthal MM. Communication failures: an insidious contributor to medical mishaps. Acad Med 2004;79:186–94.

68. Pronovost PJ, Berenholtz SM, Dorman T, Lipsett PA, Simmonds T, Haraden C. Improving communications in the ICU using daily goals. J Crit Care 2003;18:71–5.

69. Dodek PM, Raboud J. Explicit approach to rounds in an ICU improves communication and satisfaction of providers. ICM 2003;29:1584–8.

70. Shortell SM, Zimmerman JE, Rousseau DM et al. The performance of intensive care units: does good management make a difference? Med Care 1994;32:508–25.

71. Render ML, Hirschhorn L. An irreplaceable safety culture. Crit Care Clin 2005;21:31–41.

72. Boyle D, Kochinda C. Enhancing collaborative communication of nurse and physician leadership in two intensive care units. J Nurs Adm 2004;34:60–70.

73. Baker GR, King H, Macdonald JL, Horbar JD. Using organizational assessment surveys for improvement in neonatal intensive care. Pediatrics 2003;111:419–25.

74. Zimmerman JE, Shortell SM, Rousseau DM, et al. Improving intensive care: observations based on organizational case studies in nine intensive care units: a prospective, multicenter study. CCM 1993;21:1443–51.

75. Sexton JB, Thomas EJ, Helmreich RL. Error, stress and teamwork in medicine and aviation: cross sectional surveys. BMJ 2000;320:745–9.

76. Reader TW, Flin R, Mearns K, Cuthbertson BH. Interdisciplinary communication in the intensive care unit. BJA 2007;98 (3):347–52.

77. Reason JT, Carthey J, de Leval MR. Diagnosing "vulnerable system syndrome": an essential prerequisite to effective risk management. Quality in Health Care 2001;10:ii21-ii25.

78. Bognár A, Barach P, Johnson JK, Duncan RC, Birnbach D, Woods D, Holl JL, Bacha EA. Errors and the Burden of Errors: Attitudes, Perceptions, and the Culture of Safety in Pediatric Cardiac Surgical Teams. Ann Thorac Surg 2008;85:1374–81.

79. Shojania KG, Forster AJ. Hospital mortality: when failure is not a good measure of success. CMAJ 2008;179 (2). doi:10.1503/cmaj.080010.

80. Brunkhorst FM, Engel C, Jaschinsky U, Ragaller M, Rossaint R, Seeger W, Bloos F, Löffler M, Reinhart K, and the German Competence Network Sepsis (SepNet). Treatment of Severe Sepsis and Septic Shock in Germany: the Gap between Perception and Practice – Results from the German Prevalence Study. Infection 2005;33 (Suppl 1):49.

81. The CoBaTrICE Collaboration. Consensus Development of an International Competency-Based Training Programme in Intensive Care Medicine. Intensive Care Medicine 2006;32:1371–83.

82. Wood L, Hassell A, Whitehouse A, Bullock A, Wall D. A literature review of multi-source feedback systems within and without health services, leading to 10 tips for their successful design. Medical Teacher, Vol. 28, No. 7, 2006, pp. e185–e191.

83. Agency for Healthcare Research and Quality. http://www.ahrq.gov/qual/errorsix.htm (accessed May 12th 2009)

84. Smits M, Christiaans-Dingelhoff I, Wagner C, Wal G, Groenewegen P. The psychometric properties of the ‚Hospital Survey on Patient Safety Culture‘ in Dutch hospitals. BMC Health Serv Res 2008;8:230–9.

85. Flin R, Burns C, Mearns K, Yule S, Robertson E M. Measuring safety climate in health care. Qual Saf Health Care 2006;15:109–115.

86. Pronovost PJ, Berenholtz SM, Goeschel CA, Needham DM, Bryan Sexton J, Thompson DA, Lubomski LH, Marsteller JA, Makary MA, Hunt E. Creating High Reliability in Health Care Organizations. Health Services Research 2006;41(4p2):1599–1617. doi:10.1111/j.1475-6773.2006.00567.x.

87. Cook DJ, Montori VM, McMullin JP, Finfer SR, Rocker GM. Improving patients' safety locally: changing clinician behaviour. Lancet 2004:363:1224–30.

88. Curtis RJ, Cook DJ, Wall RJ, Angus DC, Bion J, Kacmarek R, Kane-Gill SL, Kirchoff KT, Levy M, Mitchell PH, Moreno R, Pronovost P, Puntillo K. Intensive care unit quality improvement: a 'how-to' guide for the interdisciplinary team. Critical Care Medicine 2006;34:211–8.

Fred Rincon, Neeraj Badjatia and Stephan A. Mayer

Core curriculum and competencies for advanced training in neurocritical care – The American way

Training, teaching and education

Introduction

The subspecialty of neurocritical care involves comprehensive multisystem care of the critically ill neurological patient. In the ICU the neurointensivist functions as the primary coordinator of both neurological and medical aspects of care in a multidisciplinary environment. The maturation of neurocritical care as a subspecialty is reflected by recent efforts in the United States to establish a system for formally accrediting neurocritical care training programmes and certifying intensivists with special qualifications in neurocritical care. In 2008, neurointensivists were added to the Leapfrog Group's ICU physician definition of intensivists (www.leapfroggroup.org).

Rationale and scope of training in neurocritical care

The organisation of closed ICUs that provide around-the-clock availability of intensivists is important because this model has been shown to reduce costs, improve outcomes, and decrease hospital length of stay (LOS) [1]. There is new data showing similar benefits when critically ill neurological patients are cared for in specialty neuro-ICUs [2–5]. These benefits may be the result of

1. organisational improvements, including the development of urgent inter-hospital transfer systems,
2. the uniform institution of best medical practices,
3. improved access to specialised neuroimaging, monitoring, and therapeutic techniques, and
4. the creation of physician and nursing care teams with special expertise in caring for neurological patients.

In day-to-day practice neurointensivists focus on subtle changes in the neurological exam, interactions between the brain and other organ systems, and cerebral physiology, including intracranial pressure, cerebral blood flow and metabolism, neuropharmacology and electroencephalography. Common physiologic derangements such as hypotension and hypoxia, fever, hyperglycaemia, anaemia and hyponatraemia have specific consequences in the setting of acute brain injury and require different management strategies than are required in the setting of general medical illnesses. In this light, the neurointensivist delivers both life support and brain support using a combination of medical, neurological and critical care skills.

A fundamental guiding principle of neurocritical care is the concept of creating and maintaining a physiologically optimised environment for the comatose injured brain. Advanced neuromonitoring techniques, including direct measurement of cerebral blood flow, brain tissue oxygen tension, and brain metabolism using microdialysis will increasingly allow the neurointensivist to individualise and fine-tune physiological drivers such as blood pressure and brain temperature. Expertise in the prognostication of severe brain injury, the delivery of compassionate end-of-life care, brain death and organ donation, and related legal and ethical issues further add to the neurointensivst's unique skill set.

Training in neurocritical care

In 2007, the United Council of Neurological Subspecialties (UCNS, www.ucns.org) created the first nationwide system for accrediting US neurocritical care fellowship programmes and certifying neurointensivists. Of an estimated 30 fellowship training programmes, 14 have been accredited by the UCNS since 2007. At the same time, 91 physicians passed the first UCNS board examination in 2007, and an additional 124 passed the examination in 2008.

At the present time, eligibility for UCNS certification requires succesful completion of an accredited medical school curriculum in the US or Canada (www.aamc.org and www.aacom.org) or non-accredited medical education with succesful certification by the Educational Commission for Foreign Medical Graduates (www.ecfmg.org). In addition, applicants for UCNS neurocritical care certification must have completed a residency in a neurology, neurosurgery, anaesthesiology, internal medicine, emergency medicine, pediatrics, or surgery programme accredited by the American College of Graduate Medical Education (www.acgme.org) or the Royal College of Physicians of Canada. A "practice track" currently exists for physicians who meet the above requirements and can submit evidence that they have clinical experience equal to that of a two-year

UCNS neurocritical care fellowship (a minimum of 12 months of intensive care experience). As of 2013, however, eligibility for UCNS Neurocritical Care certification will require successful completion of a two-year UCNS fellowship.

There is currently no pathway for UCNS certification of neurointensivists from the European Union or other parts of the world who have not met the above requirements. However, the Neurocritical Care Society (NCS) is interested in working with non-US organisations to help create a global standard for certifying neurointensivists in the future.

UCNS guidelines for programme accreditation in neurocritical care

UCNS training programmes must exist in the context of a group of critical care physicians who provide comprehensive and around-the-clock ICU coverage to a specified population of critically ill neurological patients. This may occur in a dedicated neurological ICU, or in the setting of one or more medical-surgical ICUs. A participating institution must assume the ultimate responsibility for the programme and candidate training, but multiple institutions can be part of the curriculum as long as continuity of the educational experience is assured.

Currently, the period of training is two years, exclusive of any ACGME-accredited training programme, including vascular neurology. The core curriculum for neurocritical care fellowship training is evenly split between neurological and medical diseases and conditions that commonly complicate acute neurological illnesses. The standards for fellowship training are consistent with the Society of Critical Care Medicine's stipulation that a two-year fellowship must include a minimum of 12 months of ICU time in which the trainee functions as a *primary provider* of critical care; a consultative role is not sufficient.

The *Core Curriculum and Core Competencies in Neurocritical Care* establishes a set of cognitive and procedural skills (see Tab. 1) that must be acquired by the fellow during the two years of training (available at www.ucns.org). Knowledge of pathophysiology and therapies for neurological and medical diseases, as well as the acquisition of skills for the interpretation and use

Tab. 1   Diagnostic and treatment modalities specific to neurocritical care

- ICP monitoring
- Ventricular and spinal drainage
- Surface and depth electrode EEG monitoring
- Noninvasive cerebral oximetry
- Induced hypothermia for cardiac arrest and ICP control
- Fever control
- Brain tissue oxygen tension ($PbtO_2$) monitoring
- Invasive cerebral blood flow monitoring
- Transcranial Doppler ultrasonography
- Jugular venous oxygen saturation monitoring
- Cerebral perfusion imaging (SPECT, CT, and MR perfusion)
- Barbiturate coma
- Haemostatic therapy for intracranial bleeding
- Antifibrinolytic therapy for aneurysm rebleeding
- Intravenous thrombolytic therapy for acute ischaemic stroke
- Intra-arterial thrombolysis and clot retrieval for acute ischaemic stroke
- Intrathecal thrombolytic therapy for intraventricular haemorrhage
- Cerebral microdialysis
- Hyperosmolar therapy
- Multimodality data acquisition and analysis

ICP, Intracranial pressure
EEG, Electroencephalograph
SPECT, Single-photon emission computed tomography
CT, Computed tomography
MR, Magnetic resonance

of conventional monitoring and neuromonitoring techniques, are required. Airway management skills, including endotracheal intubation, are fundamental to the practice of critical care medicine and must be included in the curriculum of UCNS-accredited training programmes. A fellowship need not be based in a dedicated neuro-ICU, as long as the trainee participates in the care of a well-defined subpopulation of neurological patients. To allow flexibility, rotations through non-neurological ICUs are encouraged, but are not mandatory.

In addition to the specific cognitive and procedural competencies listed in the *Core Curriculum and Core Competencies in Nerocritical Care*, the programme must require its trainees to obtain competence in six core areas of medical practice, consisent with ACGME criteria:

- Patient care
- Medical knowledge
- Practice-based learning and improvement
- Interpersonal and communication skills
- Professionalism
- Systems-based practice

Programmes must define the specific knowledge, skills, behaviours, and attitudes required, and provide educational experiences as needed in order for their trainees to demonstrate accomplishment in these areas.

Fellowship directors must devote a minimum of 50 % of their clinical practice to neurocritical care and other primary faculty members (for instance, neurosurgeons or neuroanaesthesiologists who play an educational role in the programme) must devote a minimum of 25 %. Qualifications for both the programme director and faculty members should include certification in their primary specialty and UCNS neurocritical care certification or eligibility through fellowship training or practical clinical experience to sit for this examination ("practice track criteria"). Additionally, they should demonstrate a strong interest and competence in neurocritical care, and must support the goals and objectives of the educational programme of which they are members.

Not all aspects of fellowship training must be provided by the primary faculty. Fellows might learn airway skills from anaesthesiologists, or be trained in the placement of intracranial monitors by neurosurgeons affiliated with the training programme. There should be no more than one fellow per faculty member of a programme at any given time, and faculty members must practise in a setting in which they can provide continuous ICU coverage for their patients. Thus, a single neurointensivist can direct a UCNS fellowship if he or she trains one fellow every two years, and is part of a critical care practice group that provides daily coverage for the neuro-ICU patient population.

Certification in neurocritical care

On 26 October 2005, the medical subspecialty of neurolocritical care attained a major milestone in the US when it gained formal recognition and acceptance by the UCNS, a nonprofit organisation committed to the establishment of training standards for neurological subspecialty fellowships outside of the American Board of Medical Specialties (ABMS). With the establishment of this board, a formal pathway to accredit training programmes and certify physicians who devote their practice to the comprehensive multisystem management of neurological patients with life-threatening illness is now available. The UCNS Neurocritical Care Examination Committee included 10 experts in the field of neurocritical care who were nominated by sponsoring organisations such as the American Academy of Neurology, the Neurocritical Care Society, and the Society of Neurosurgical Anesthesia and Critical Care. As of 31 December 2008, 215 diplomates have been awarded the special certificate in neurocritical care; the third certification exam will be offered in December of 2010. For physicians without UCNS-accredited training in neurocritical care the practice track, or "grandfather" pathway, for certification will be discontinued in 2012.

The future of neurocritical care

Neurocritical care has experienced rapid growth since its inception in the mid-1980s, gaining reputation and respectability among the medical specialties by developing a distinct identity which has clearly changed the practice of neurology and neurosurgery. One indicator of the current state of the field is the rapid growth of the Neurocritical Care Society, a multidisciplinary nonprofit organisation that currently has nearly 1,000 members representing 24 countries around the world (www.neurocriticalcare.org). Ongoing efforts to realise the mission of the NCS – the promotion of quality patient care, training and education, research, interdisciplinary collaboration, and professional advocacy – will continue to expand the scope and influence of this new and rapidly-growing medical specialty.

The authors

Stephan A. Mayer, Prof., MD, FCCM[1]
Fred Rincon, MD, MSc, FACP[2]
Neeraj Badjatia, MD, MSc[3]
[1]Department of Neurology and
Neurological Surgery | Columbia University
College of Physicians & Surgeons | Director,
Neurological Intensive Care Unit | New York
Presbyterian Hospital | Columbia, USA
[2]Division of Critical Care Medicine and
Cardiovascular Disease | Cooper University
Hospital | Camden, New Jersey, USA
[3]Department of Neurology & Neurosurgery |
College of Physicians and Surgeons |
Columbia University | New York, USA

Address for correspondence
Stephan A. Mayer
New York Presbyterian Hospital/Columbia
Milstein Hospital Building
177 Fort Washington Avenue
MHB-8 Center
New York, NY 10032, USA
E-mail: sam14@columbia.edu

References

1. Pronovost PJ, Angus DC, Dorman T, Robinson KA, Dremsizov TT, Young TL. Physician staffing patterns and clinical outcomes in critically ill patients: A systematic review. JAMA 2002;288:2151–2162.
2. Mirski MA, Chang CW, Cowan R. Impact of a neuroscience intensive care unit on neurosurgical patient outcomes and cost of care: Evidence-based support for an intensivist-directed specialty ICU model of care. J Neurosurg Anesthesiol 2001;13:83–92.
3. Suarez JI. Outcome in neurocritical care: Advances in monitoring and treatment and effect of a specialized neurocritical care team. Crit Care Med 2006;34:S232–238.
4. Varelas PN, Eastwood D, Yun HJ, Spanaki MV, Hacein Bey L, Kessaris C, Gennarelli TA. Impact of a neurointensivist on outcomes in patients with head trauma treated in a neurosciences intensive care unit. J Neurosurg 2006;104:713–719.
5. Diringer MN, Edwards DF. Admission to a neurologic/neurosurgical intensive care unit is associated with reduced mortality rate after intracerebral hemorrhage. Crit Care Med 2001;29:635–640.
6. Guidelines for advanced training for physicians in critical care. American College of Critical Care Medicine of the Society of Critical Care Medicine. Crit Care Med 1997;25:1601–1607.
7. Mayer SA, Coplin WM, Chang C, Suarez J, Gress D, Diringer MN, Frank J, Hemphill JC, Sung G, Smith W, Manno EM, Kofke A, Lam A, Steiner T. Program requirements for fellowship training in neurological intensive care: United council for neurologic subspecialties guidelines. Neurocritical Care 2006;5:166–171.
8. Mayer SA, Coplin WM, Chang C, Suarez J, Gress D, Diringer MN, Frank J, Hemphill JC, Sung G, Smith W, Manno EM, Kofke A, Lam A, Steiner T. Core curriculum and competencies for advanced training in neurological intensive care: United council for neurologic subspecialties guidelines. Neurocritical Care 2006;5:159–165.
9. Rincon F, Mayer SA. Neurocritical care: A distinct discipline? Curr Opin Crit Care 2007;13:115–121.

I. Risk management

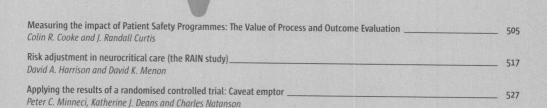

Colin R. Cooke and J. Randall Curtis

Measuring the impact of Patient Safety Programmes: The Value of Process and Outcome Evaluation

The publication of the Institute of Medicine's (IOM) report *"To Err Is Human: Building a Safer Health System"* [1] intensified the attention dedicated to patient safety in healthcare throughout the world. After its publication professional societies, hospital associations, accrediting bodies, healthcare payers, and investigators accelerated their effort to improve patient safety and now devote considerable resources toward ensuring that care delivered to patients is safe. The field of intensive care has been particularly receptive to this focus on patient safety. This effort within intensive care medicine is reflected by the rapid increase in the number of medical publications related to patient safety and intensive care since 1999 (see Fig. 1). While there are many individual success stories of improved patient safety at the local level, the national and international impact of these efforts remains unclear. A persistent barrier to understanding how regional, national, and international efforts improve patient safety is the lack of accurate and widely used measures to characterise progress.

Importance of measuring results of patient safety programmes

There is a large body of work concerning the measurement of outcomes of healthcare [2, 3]

and a considerable amount of this work is specific to critical care [4–12]. As we strive to improve patient safety in the intensive care unit, it is important that we quantify the success of our efforts in order to document and build on our accomplishments and to redirect time and resources from efforts that are unsuccessful. The objectives of this chapter are to summarise key concepts and outline a practical approach to the measurement of success (or failure) of patient safety programmes in the intensive care setting. We aim to provide a practical guide for leaders interested in beginning the process of improving patient safety in their own institutions.

Safety and quality continuum

The IOM Roundtable on Quality of Care identified the three main threats to quality care: underuse (failure to provide beneficial services), overuse (providing unnecessary potentially harmful services), and misuse (preventable complications of indicated services) [13, 14]. In the strictest sense, improving safety only addresses the misuse domain proposed by the IOM; however, one can easily argue that patient safety is compromised when

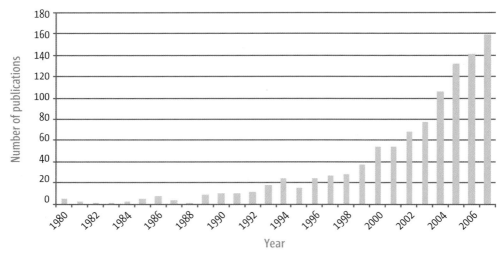

Fig. 1   Number of publications in intensive care medicine, by year. PubMed search using the medical subject headings "intensive care", "intensive care units", or "critical care" and "safety", "safety management", or "medical errors", limited to human studies.

patients do not receive beneficial therapies (errors of omission) or receive unnecessary, potentially harmful ones (errors of commission). Other authors have described the important similarities and differences between patient safety and quality in this book, but as the science behind safety interventions and quality improvement has evolved the distinction between the two has blurred [15]. We consider patient safety as an integral component of the quality of care framework that encompasses all three domains proposed by the IOM and focus on the lessons learned in measuring both patient safety and quality of healthcare [14].

Overview of measurement of quality and safety

Measurement of the quality of healthcare in a quantitative way requires a structured and quantitative approach. However, there is also much value in qualitative approaches to assessing the success of patient safety programmes. A complete patient safety programme evaluation should usually include a mixed methods approach integrating qualitative programme evaluation as well as quantitative evaluation.

The advantages of a mixed methods approach to evaluating patient safety initiatives as summarised by Brown and colleagues [16] include:

- triangulation – use of different methods to get at the same underlying truth through corroboration of findings;
- understanding – to elaborate and explain results of patient safety initiative;
- development – to generate theory;
- qualitative studies which may uncover early problems with safety programmes that can be addressed through modification of the initiative.

Integrating observations obtained through qualitative and quantitative methods in safety research requires judgment resulting in subjectivity, but this is no different than the subjectivity involved in any scientific endeavour, such as generalising the results of a randomised trial to individual patients. For this reason, ensuring transparency throughout the measurement development process is important to assure stakeholders of the validity of the results.

Qualitative approach

Qualitative research has its origins in the social sciences and is traditionally used to characterise complex entities not easily addressed through hypothesis testing such as human behaviour or social interaction. Quantitative methods test theory and seek the answer to questions such as *whether* a safety intervention improves outcomes or *how much* a safety programme increases use of evidence-based care. Qualitative methods construct theory and seek the answer to questions such as *why*, *how*, and *what* [17]. In contrast to quantitative approaches where numeric data is of primary interest, data collection in qualitative research includes focus groups, structured interviews, and participant observation which capture ideas, emotions, or social phenomena. The appropriate selection of methods for analysis of qualitative data is an important factor for consideration [18]. For an understanding of the barriers or successful aspects of patient safety programmes, content analysis [19] will often be an appropriate method. However, other analytic methods are available for more in-depth examination of safety and quality of care issues including grounded theory [20, 21] and ethnography [22].

In the context of patient safety, qualitative methods can be used prior to and throughout the safety measurement process. When identifying targets for patient safety initiatives, focus groups of ICU stakeholders may help identify the threats to patient safety of greatest importance locally. Similarly, interviews along with behavioural observation and social interaction among individuals in the ICU allow for the experiences of staff, patients, and their families to be captured in the assessment of a safety improvement initiative. Such information may explain reasons for success of an intervention or perhaps uncover theory as to why an intervention is failing, thereby providing hypotheses that can later be tested by quantitative methods. Finally, unanticipated hazards of a patient safety initiative, such as consumption of alcohol-based hand rubs by alcoholic patients for example, [23] may be uncovered through qualitative research.

As a further example of the use of qualitative research to inform patient safety programme evaluation, when approaching 'hand washing adherence' as a target for safety measurement, qualitative methods can characterise local barriers to provider hand washing prior to central catheter insertion. Results from this qualitative evaluation could then be used to develop a survey to assess the practice of all providers. Upon implementing a hospital-wide policy to improve hand washing

that addresses the previously determined barriers, qualitative methods could be used to understand the reasons for variability of hand washing adherence across different ICUs. A number of additional examples of the use of qualitative research to characterise patient safety in critical care are available [24–28].

Quantitative approach

A quantitative approach to patient safety programme evaluation requires that the complex concept of quality in healthcare be conceptualised in a systematic way that facilitates its measurement. Those attempting to measure the success of a patient safety programme will benefit by first understanding the conceptual model developed by Donabedian including three components that characterise healthcare: structure, process and outcome [29, 30]. Although these components are not necessarily mutually exclusive, the concepts provide a useful framework for understanding and measuring the quality of healthcare and therefore are useful for measuring the success of patient safety programmes.

Structure represents the first component of the quality of care model and can be defined as the way care delivery is organised. ICU structure varies across all levels of healthcare, within countries, regions of a single country, and even within individual hospitals. Sources of structural variation include how the ICU is integrated into the hospital or healthcare system, the number of beds in the ICU, the extent to which patients are managed by providers with critical care training, the type and amount of technology available, and the number, roles, workload, and responsibilities of ICU staff and the interactions between staff. Variation in these structural features can affect the care delivered to patients and ultimately patient safety. For example, studies suggest that patients managed in a closed ICU by physicians with critical care training have fewer adverse events and lower mortality than patients managed in open ICUs by generalists without critical care training [31]. However, a recent study showed that greater exposure to intensivists may be associated with worse outcomes for some patients and raises question about the most appropriate organisation of intensive care and the most appropriate allocation of intensive care resources [32]. Additional structural features such as daily rounds that integrate pharmacists and other ICU staff in a multidisciplinary team, and greater nurse staffing, may improve the care delivered to patients [33–35]. As these and other studies demonstrate, our knowledge of exactly how ICU structure affects the safety of patients is immature but evolving.

Process represents the second component of the quality of care model. Processes generally refer to what we do, or fail to do, for patients and their families. This encompasses everything from family conferences to protocolised care to individual medical and surgical therapies. Delivering error-free care in the ICU requires the synchronous efforts of large numbers of clinical and non-

clinical processes. This complexity creates greater opportunity for breaks in the chain linking the results of a study to what is actually delivered to the patient. For example, just because data exist that show lower rates of catheter-related blood stream infections when the skin is disinfected with chlorhexidine-based solutions, does not guarantee that this knowledge is translated effectively into clinical practice [36]. Another important process of care is timely transfer of patients into the ICU, between the ICU and other parts of the hospital or between different clinicians within the ICU [37]. Ensuring that critically ill patients and their families receive comprehensive processes of care and that these processes are implemented correctly, when appropriate, will make great strides toward optimum patient safety.

Tab. 1   Advantages and disadvantages of structure, process and outcome measures [modified from Curtis et al., Intensive care unit quality improvement: A "how-to" guide for the interdisciplinary team. Crit Care Medicine, 34, 2006, 211–8]

	Structure Measure	Process Measure	Outcome Measure
Do patients care about this?	Less understandable or relevant to patients	Less understandable or relevant to patients	Yes; very important to patients
Do providers care about this?	Yes; however, knowledge of how structure affects patient safety is immature	Yes; it relates directly to what providers are doing	Yes; however, providers are wary of confounding and may request risk-adjustment models
Obtain measure from routinely collected data?	Not usually	Usually	Sometimes; additional data that are not routinely collected may be needed
Interpretable for feedback and quality improvement?	Provides clear feedback to ICU management about organisation of delivered care	Provides clear feedback about what providers are actually doing	Difficult for providers to definitively know where to target efforts because outcomes are usually affected by several different processes
Directly measures prevention?	No	Yes	No
Need for risk adjustment?	No	No; however, need to clearly define eligible patients	Yes; need different models for each outcome
Time needed for measurement?	Less	Less	More (for risk-adjustment)
Patient sample size requirements?	Not applicable	Smaller	Larger
Responsiveness to improvement efforts?	May be difficult to change	More	Less

Outcomes represent the third component of the quality of care model and refer to the results we achieve. Critical care clinicians and researchers have traditionally dedicated the most effort to measuring and improving patient outcomes because outcomes are what patients and providers care about most. In fact, critical care has led the way in developing risk-adjustment mortality models and standardised mortality ratios as a means to measure the safety of care for groups of patients. Nonetheless, limitations such as the variability of definitions and data quality between models, the extent to which case-mix and socioeconomic variables are accounted for in such models, and the possibility for chance as an explanation for outcome differences indicate that risk-adjusted measures cannot fully assess patient safety in an individual institution or ICU [9, 38]. ICU quality and patient safety are also determined by other outcomes, including morbid events (e.g. nosocomial infections, venous thromboembolism, or serious adverse drug events [39]), cognitive or other organ dysfunction, health-related quality of life, and patient and family satisfaction with care. For these reasons, it is suitable to think of the many 'qualities' of care rather than a singular quality of care and to have a broad definition of the term 'safety' [10].

Critical care clinicians interested in measuring patient safety should understand the structure-process-outcome model and select aspects of greatest local importance, that are likely to have the greatest impact on patient safety in their setting, and that they can feasibly improve. There are a number of advantages and disadvantages of using structures, processes, or outcomes when trying to improve patient safety (see Tab. 1). Structure is arguably the most challenging domain to change; clinicians may wish to target processes or outcomes first. Outcome measures are intuitively important targets for clinicians, but they are often less responsive to improvement efforts and more prone to bias than process measures [10, 40, 41]. This is partly because adverse outcomes occur less frequently than deficiencies in their associated processes of care. In addition, processes are usually easier to measure and modify [42]. Although many processes within healthcare systems influence outcomes, not all of these processes are modifiable. Nonetheless, a comprehensive patient safety programme will

usually address measures within each of these three domains and may also consider the structures, processes, and outcomes outside the ICU which affect the safety and quality of care for critically ill patients and their families [6].

Measures of safety and quality in intensive care

A good safety measure is defined by a number of features [43–45]. The measure must be important, valid, reliable, responsive, interpretable, and feasible. Table 2 contains a description of each of these features. Although testing the validity, reliability and responsiveness of every safety measure chosen by a critical care team is unnecessary, the team should ascertain that these attributes of the measure have been determined and reported in the medical literature. The team must also assess the overall importance of the candidate measure to local stakeholders because importance may vary between different ICUs. The team should also consider the interpretability and feasibility of a measure before starting a project because these attributes may differ across ICUs based on factors such as the team's experience with patient safety measurement (for interpretability), or the availability of computerised clinical information systems (for feasibility).

Developing a patient safety measurement programme

Developing a patient safety measurement programme requires implementing a sequence of steps to ensure the measurement programme succeeds. We will review the important features of these steps.

Step 1: Form the measurement team

Measuring patient safety is generally not a one-person or one-discipline task; for best results it requires sharing commitment by unifying individuals from several clinical disciplines into an interdisciplinary ICU safety team. The team should include individuals with training and experience in patient safety or quality measurement.

Tab. 2   Features defining an ICU good quality measure [modified from Curtis et al., Intensive care unit quality improvement: A "how-to" guide for the interdisciplinary team. Crit Care Medicine, 34, 2006, 211–8]

A good ICU safety measure should be important, valid, reliable, responsive, interpretable, and feasible. Each of these characteristics is briefly described below with a focus on their relevance for the ICU quality improvement team.

An **important** measure for patient safety programmes should generally be high-prevalence outcomes or outcomes associated with considerable morbidity and mortality. For a structure or process measures to be important, it must be strongly linked to clinically important outcomes.

A **valid** measure refers to the extent to which a measure reflects what it is supposed to measure. Validation may include comparing the measure to other measures such as a gold standard (criterion validity) or to other measures or constructs that should give similar results (construct validity).

A **reliable** measure refers to the extent to which a measure yields the same result when assessed by a different rater (inter-rater reliability) or the extent to which repeated measurement provides the same result when the factor being measured hasn't changed (intra-rater reliability).

A **responsive** measure refers to the extent to which the measure is sensitive to change introduced by the patient safety improvement process. An important component of a responsive measure is that there is room for improvement in the measure and that the measure is capable of detecting that improvement. There should be a gap between current performance and desired performance that the measure can identify.

An **interpretable** measure is easily understood by the target audience including critical care clinicians, ICU management, and hospital leadership.

A **feasible** measure is useful because it is relatively easy to obtain and can be collected with available resources. Feasibility will vary depending on the resources that are available and should be assessed for every measure before implementing a patient safety project.

Most successful patient safety measurement programmes incorporate multiple individual projects under common interdisciplinary leadership. Lasting change is rarely achieved without strong interdisciplinary leadership, even when individual ICU clinicians champion specific patient safety measurement projects. Leadership is needed at each stage of the process, from the initial identification of a target to the evaluative phase. Successful leaders have to dedicate time and commitment for the programme to succeed.

Step 2: Identify the targets for measuring and improving patient safety

The next step for developing a patient safety measurement programme is to identify the opportunities and resources that might influence the choice of where to begin. The first project should be feasible and likely to succeed so that the team can utilise this experience to build on its successes. Ambitious projects that consume resources and have lower likelihood of success should be avoided. Such projects may discourage team members from pursuing successive projects and undermine the leadership of the team.

There are a multiple potential patient safety measures that can serve as the foundation of a patient safety measurement project. Table 3 shows potential patient safety measures categorised by structure, process and outcome. Process measures can be considered a type of surrogate outcome. As such, the process measures selected for a measurement project should be unambiguously linked to improved outcomes in randomised trials. In general, it is advisable to begin a safety measurement programme focusing on a single target to ensure feasibility; even though single measures may fail to capture the complexity of a patient safety problem.

Multiple processes may interact synergistically with no individual process producing great benefits or risks. Bundles better address this issue by measuring multiple processes of care linked to patient outcomes. For example, in the context of central venous catheter insertion, mea-

Tab. 3   Possible ICU patient safety measures [modified from Curtis et al., Intensive care unit quality improvement: A "how-to" guide for the interdisciplinary team. Crit Care Medicine, 34, 2006, 211–8]

STRUCTURE MEASURES
Intensivist-led rounding team
Higher nurse-to-patient ratios
Multidisciplinary team rounds
Computerised order entry

PROCESS MEASURES
DVT prophylaxis[1]*
Stress ulcer prophylaxis[1]*
Ventilator-associated pneumonia prevention strategies ▪ HOB elevation[1]* ▪ Heat & moisture exchangers & filters[1]
Central venous catheter blood stream infection prevention strategies ▪ Hand hygiene ▪ Maximal barriers ▪ Chlorhexidine[1] ▪ Avoidance of femoral site[1] ▪ Avoid routine replacement[1]
Protocol-driven ventilator weaning[1] ▪ Targeted sedation protocols ▪ Daily sedation vacation* ▪ Daily assessment of extubation readiness*
Severe sepsis[1] ▪ Early fluid resuscitation ▪ Early antibiotics ▪ Corticosteroids for shock ▪ Activated protein C for shock
Low tidal volume ventilation in ALI/ARDS[1]
Noninvasive ventilation for hypercarbic respiratory failure
Appropriate transfusion threshold[1]
Delayed transfer out of ICU or into ICU
Palliative care ▪ Symptom measurement & management at end of life ▪ Family conferences ▪ Directives regarding CPR, basic & advanced life support

OUTCOME MEASURES
Unplanned extubation rate
Ventilator-associated pneumonia rate
CVC blood stream infection rate
Multi-resistant organism infection rate
Serious adverse drug event rate
Family satisfaction
Unscheduled readmissions within 24–48h of ICU discharge
Mortality (absolute and severity-adjusted)

[1]Process measures strongly linked to outcomes in randomised trials.
*Part of the 'ventilator bundle' proposed by the Institute for Healthcare Improvement (www.ihi.org).

suring and improving 'hand washing adherence' may do little to improve overall patient safety if proper sterile precautions are being implemented in a minority of patients. Measuring global adherence to hand washing, maximal barrier precautions in addition to other catheter-related blood stream infection prevention strategies may provide a more comprehensive understanding of safety surrounding catheter insertion. Process measures that compose the 'ventilator bundle' proposed by the Institute for Healthcare Improvement (IHI), JCAHO, and the Volunteer Hospitals of America, Inc. may be particularly useful in ventilator-associated pneumonia prevention strategies. Other organisations have also developed their own lists of potential ICU safety or quality bundles including JCAHO [46], IHI [47], and individual investigators [48].

Patient safety in the ICU is an evolving field and novel safety measures will likely emerge as research progresses. This is particularly true for process and structural measures. For example, 24-hour intensivist staffing, medical emergency teams (MET) and specific nurse-to-patient ratios may eventually become validated structural safety measures if future studies support their effectiveness.

Step 3: Identify preliminary baseline performance on safety measures

A necessary step in the design and launch of a successful measurement project is to understand the current safety and quality of care and the barriers to implementing a patient safety project. Therefore, gathering preliminary baseline data about the safety of patients' care is an important early step [8]. This initial assessment may involve accessing available clinical or administrative databases. For example, microbiologic databases combined with clinical information may be a useful starting place for assessing rates of catheter-related blood stream infections [49]. More direct methods of establishing baseline data are observational studies such as chart reviews. Finally, qualitative studies that either directly observe patient care or capture provider perspectives can be useful to characterise behaviours that bear on safety improvement efforts and identify potential barriers to improvement.

Step 4: Develop the data collection system for measuring patient safety

Often a basic baseline assessment is necessary before one can build an effective data collection system. During the baseline assessment the team can collect information about the pertinent data sources, the data available from each source, and the validity and reliability of such data. Once the baseline assessment is complete, the patient safety measurement team can use this information to design an effective data collection system for ongoing assessment of patient safety. Without accurate baseline data, it is impossible for the team to document improvements. The target measure must be carefully operationalised using discrete, measurable components and a specific improvement goal should be explicitly stated prior to deployment of any safety improvement initiatives. Specific, detailed, rigorously developed definitions for the measure ensure the risk of bias in the measurement is minimal. Valid measures should have the ability to be expressed as rates in order to provide an estimate of how fast a target is changing in a specified population. In general, the team should consider the following features:

- **A unit of analysis**, or denominator, of the measure needs to be chosen. Common denominators are defined in relation to a patient sample (e.g. per 100 patients) or standardised for patient exposure (e.g. per 1000 patient days). For example, the latter might be chosen to express the number of catheter-related bloodstream infections per 1000 catheter days. Careful consideration of whether days for patients with two catheters should be double counted would be important for assigning each patient the appropriate denominator.
- **The event or outcome of interest** becomes the numerator of the measure and must also be defined. For example, 'catheter-related blood stream infection' needs to be defined. Because the presence of infection at another site may result in bacteraemia unrelated to the catheter, ascertainment of all potential sources of infection in each patient would be important. Organisations such as JCAHO and IHI are defining, operationalising, and evaluating safety measures that can be used by the safety improvement team [46, 47]. For example, current guidelines exist for defining catheter-

related blood stream infections [50]. Adhering to such examples for defining the event or outcome of interest can facilitate comparison of local safety standards to benchmarks.

- **Data collection methods**: Are the data already being collected? If not, how easily can they be obtained? Will physician order sheets, pharmacy databases, microbiology or laboratory databases, or clinician self-reports be used? Whenever possible, build measurement into daily workflow and capitalise on existing data sources to minimise additional effort [51, 52]. Regardless of the data source, perform a small-scale pilot before embarking on wide-scale measurement.

Choosing when and how often to collect data requires a balance between feasibility and precision. Frequent measurements may increase the precision of estimates and provide greater opportunity for real-time feedback, but require more time and effort. Although reducing the frequency of measurements makes measurement more feasible, it may hide important variation in safety and may reduce the likelihood that clinicians will adjust their practice. Pilot testing of the measurement system may also identify problems with feasibility or target measure definitions prior to full implementation.

Deciding who will perform the measurement will vary across ICUs and depends on what is being measured and how. Busy clinicians may find it difficult to engage in this potentially time-consuming aspect of safety improvement. Explicitly incorporating safety initiatives into the mission of an ICU and explicitly embedding responsibility for safety improvement into specific job descriptions will help. A potential predictor of success is the integration of project activities into clinicians' usual workload. However, this alone is insufficient. Provision of educational materials, data collection methods training, reliability testing of key measures, and ongoing audit of data accuracy are necessary tasks for whoever is performing the measurement.

Step 5: Develop a system for reporting patient safety data

A successful patient safety measurement project requires transparent and informative data reporting. Most critical care clinicians are too busy to analyse and interpret data by themselves and therefore rely on efficient data reporting to gain understanding of the state of patient safety in their unit. In the absence of timely and useful data reporting, interest can wane and projects may lose momentum. In contrast, easily interpretable and actionable data empower the ICU team, affirm that safety and quality efforts are making a difference, and increase the chances for sustainability of the programme.

When deciding how measurement data should be reported, consider the specific aims outlined during the planning phase, the background of the target audience, and local familiarity with existing data reports. Soliciting suggestions about the design and interpretability of patient safety results from target audiences may ultimately improve comprehension when actual patient safety data are officially released. Possible formats include text, tables and figures; each has advantages and disadvantages. Though a familiar vehicle for communication, text may take more space and be less attractive to the busy clinician. Tables succinctly display both descriptive and numerical variables, are easily assembled, and hold large amounts of information. However, tables are less useful for showing the variability of data over time and quickly become overwhelming when numerous targets are displayed. Graphs and figures (e.g. control charts, run charts, instrument panels, report cards) can visually display data over time and easily display multiple targets, but may require more expertise to create. Regardless of the chosen format(s), data should be clearly labelled and simply displayed. The most meaningful formats show not only past but present performance [53].

Determining when to report data depends partly on how often the target is actually measured. For process measures, monthly or even weekly reports may be more relevant, particularly if clinicians work in one-week blocks and feedback is being given about their week.

As with data collection, deciding who will analyse and report the data depends on what is being measured and the available resources. The data analyst should be familiar with computational databases, methods to minimise and assess for errors in data entry, and have the relevant statistical expertise and clinical understanding to create valid summaries presented in a format that faithfully represents the results. This may include formal significance testing to evaluate the likelihood that chance is an explanation for any changes seen in the target measure.

Evaluating and sustaining the patient safety measurement programme

A key step in evaluating patient safety measurement programmes is taking a scientific approach to evaluating whether the target safety measure is changing. In other words, the patient safety programme itself should be subjected to an evaluation process. Team members should seek answers to questions such as: Is the measurement programme working? How well is it working? What are the costs and benefits of the programme? What are the theories as to why it is or is not working? What are the factors causing variable success? Should the programme be modified? Without formal evaluation of the programme, it is impossible to judge whether it is successful and sustainable.

After generating initial results, challenges may arise when trying to sustain the improvements. A study examining the factors predicting continued clinician involvement in quality improvement projects found the following predictors: continuous use of the same quality improvement model, taking courses in the science of quality improvement, and remaining employed in the same unit [54]. This study provides important lessons on enhancing the sustainability of a patient safety measurement programme and encourages a focus on consistency of efforts, staff training, and staff retention. Other issues that may be important include simple methods for data collection, transparent presentation of results, sustaining the energy and morale of the patient safety team and bedside clinicians, and continued interdisciplinary leadership and collaboration.

Sustaining a patient safety measurement programme requires ongoing reassessment of the methods being used to collect data. When a project starts, the champions may have to manually collect data. Later, automated data collection methods may become available to obtain data from the electronic medical record or other electronic sources such as billing data. If such automation is possible, maintenance of the project will be greatly facilitated. If not, the team needs to ensure that sufficient resources are allocated to sustain the data collection. In the future, computerised clinical information, clinical decision support, and computer order entry systems will generate safety reports, thereby automating this aspect of data collection and reporting for selected process and outcome measures and making this step easier for ICU clinicians.

Although patient safety measurement programmes can accomplish much within the ICU, it is helpful if hospital administration supports the programme [55]. A key task for patient safety leaders is to portray their programme in terms that are meaningful to diverse stakeholders within and outside of the ICU [56]. For clinicians, the most meaningful motivation is improving patient care and tangible benefits will help ensure they stay engaged. For programme managers and leaders, the key aim may be improving programme outcomes. For hospital administrators, it may be improving reputation in the region, based on improving outcomes and increasing market penetration for ICU care.

Summary

As the complexity of modern healthcare increases, the opportunity for compromise in patient safety has never been greater. Throughout the world, organisations and individuals are actively implementing programmes to decrease the risk of such errors. A necessary first step toward improving patient safety requires measuring the safety of care delivered to patients. A rigorous, scientific, multidisciplinary, and mixed-methods approach to each step of the measurement process ensures the greatest chance for measurement success, and eventually, the validity of improvement in patient safety. We have outlined a step-by-step approach to the process of measuring patient safety. Successful implementation of a tangible measurement project can provide incentive for further investment potentially launching greater and more comprehensive safety improvement programmes in an ICU. The eventual goal for measuring safety is to provide data that helps us understand ways to improve the processes and structures within which we provide care [10]. However, the collection of data can only take us so far. Establishing a culture of safety involving multidisciplinary teamwork that values leadership, transparency, and reducing blame is an equally important piece of a safety measurement programme. The ultimate responsibility of improving the care of patients lies with people, not data. Nonetheless, an accurate and efficient measurement system is an essential component of meeting this responsibility.

The authors

Colin R. Cooke, MD, MSc
J. Randall Curtis, MD, MPH
    Division of Pulmonary and Critical
    Care | Department of Medicine |
    University of Washington, Seattle, WA

Address for correspondence
    J. Randall Curtis
    Harborview Medical Center
    University of Washington
    325 Ninth Avenue, Box 359762
    Seattle, Washington 98104, USA
    E-mail: jrc@u.washington.edu

References

1. Kohn KT, Corrigan JM, Donaldson MS, eds. To Err Is Human: Building a Safer Health System. Washington, DC: Committee on Quality of Health Care in America, Institute of Medicine, National Academy Press; 1999.
2. Donabedian A. The seven pillars of quality. Arch Pathol Lab Med 1990;114:1115–8.
3. Lomas J. Quality assurance and effectiveness in health care: an overview. Qual Assur Health Care 1990;2:5–12.
4. Frutiger A, Moreno R, Thijs L, Carlet J. A clinician's guide to the use of quality terminology. Working Group on Quality Improvement of the European Society of Intensive Care Medicine. Intensive Care Med 1998;24:860–3.
5. Rubenfeld GD, Angus DC, Pinsky MR, Curtis JR, Connors AF, Jr., Bernard GR. Outcomes research in critical care: results of the American Thoracic Society Critical Care Assembly Workshop on Outcomes Research. The Members of the Outcomes Research Workshop. Am J Respir Crit Care Med 1999;160:358–67.
6. Angus DC, Black N. Improving care of the critically ill: institutional and health-care system approaches. Lancet 2004;363:1314–20.
7. Bion JF, Heffner JE. Challenges in the care of the acutely ill. Lancet 2004;363:970–7.
8. Cook DJ, Montori VM, McMullin JP, Finfer SR, Rocker GM. Improving patients' safety locally: changing clinician behaviour. Lancet 2004;363:1224–30.
9. Lilford R, Mohammed MA, Spiegelhalter D, Thomson R. Use and misuse of process and outcome data in managing performance of acute medical care: avoiding institutional stigma. Lancet 2004;363:1147–54.
10. Pronovost PJ, Nolan T, Zeger S, Miller M, Rubin H. How can clinicians measure safety and quality in acute care? Lancet 2004;363:1061–7.
11. Garland A. Improving the ICU: part 2. Chest 2005;127:2165–79.
12. Garland A. Improving the ICU: part 1. Chest 2005;127:2151–64.
13. Chassin MR, Galvin RW. The urgent need to improve health care quality. Institute of Medicine National Roundtable on Health Care Quality. JAMA 1998;280:1000–5.
14. Leape LL, Berwick DM. Five years after To Err Is Human: what have we learned? Jama 2005;293:2384–90.
15. Brown C, Hofer T, Johal A, et al. An epistemology of patient safety research: a framework for study design and interpretation. Part 1. Conceptualising and developing interventions. Qual Saf Health Care 2008;17:158–62.
16. Brown C, Hofer T, Johal A, et al. An epistemology of patient safety research: a framework for study design and interpretation. Part 4. One size does not fit all. Qual Saf Health Care 2008;17:178–81.
17. Giacomini MK, Cook DJ. Users' guides to the medical literature: XXIII. Qualitative research in health care A. Are the results of the study valid? Evidence-Based Medicine Working Group. JAMA 2000;284:357–62.
18. Hsieh HF, Shannon SE. Three approaches to qualitative content analysis. Qual Health Res 2005;15:1277–88.
19. Clarke EB, Luce JM, Curtis JR, et al. A content analysis of forms, guidelines, and other materials documenting end-of-life care in intensive care units. J Crit Care 2004;19:108–17.
20. Curtis JR, Engelberg RA, Wenrich MD, et al. Studying communication about end-of-life care during the ICU family conference: development of a framework. J Crit Care 2002;17:147–60.
21. Curtis JR, Engelberg RA, Wenrich MD, Shannon SE, Treece PD, Rubenfeld GD. Missed Opportunities during Family Conferences about End-of-life Care in the Intensive Care Unit. Am J Respir Crit Care Med 2005.
22. Cassell J, Buchman TG, Streat S, Stewart RM. Surgeons, intensivists, and the covenant of care: administrative models and values affecting care at the end of life – Updated. Crit Care Med 2003;31:1551–7; discussion 7–9.
23. Meyer P, Baudel JL, Maury E, Offenstadt G. A surprising side effect of hand antisepsis. Intensive Care Med 2005;31:1600.
24. Cook DJ, Meade MO, Hand LE, McMullin JP. Toward

understanding evidence uptake: semirecumbency for pneumonia prevention. Crit Care Med 2002;30:1472–7.

25. Rocker GM, Cook DJ, Martin DK, Singer PA. Seasonal bed closures in an intensive care unit: a qualitative study. J Crit Care 2003;18:25–30.

26. Sinuff T, Cook DJ, Giacomini M. How qualitative research can contribute to research in the intensive care unit. J Crit Care 2007;22:104–11.

27. Sinuff T, Kahnamoui K, Cook DJ, Giacomini M. Practice guidelines as multipurpose tools: a qualitative study of noninvasive ventilation. Crit Care Med 2007;35:776–82.

28. Rusinova K, Pochard F, Kentish-Barnes N, Chaize M, Azoulay E. Qualitative research: adding drive and dimension to clinical research. Crit Care Med 2009;37:S140–6.

29. Donabedian A. Continuity and change in the quest for quality. Clin Perform Qual Health Care 1993;1:9–16.

30. Donabedian A. Aspects of medical care administration: specifying requirement for health care. Cambridge, MA: Harvard University Press; 1973.

31. Pronovost PJ, Angus DC, Dorman T, Robinson KA, Dremsizov TT, Young TL. Physician staffing patterns and clinical outcomes in critically ill patients: a systematic review. Jama 2002;288:2151–62.

32. Levy MM, Rapoport J, Lemeshow S, Chalfin DB, Phillips G, Danis M. Association between critical care physician management and patient mortality in the intensive care unit. Ann Intern Med 2008;148:801–9.

33. Young MP, Gooder VJ, Oltermann MH, Bohman CB, French TK, James BC. The impact of a multidisciplinary approach on caring for ventilator-dependent patients. Int J Qual Health Care 1998;10:15–26.

34. Leape LL, Cullen DJ, Clapp MD, et al. Pharmacist participation on physician rounds and adverse drug events in the intensive care unit. JAMA 1999;282:267–70.

35. Lankshear AJ, Sheldon TA, Maynard A. Nurse staffing and healthcare outcomes: a systematic review of the international research evidence. ANS Adv Nurs Sci 2005;28:163–74.

36. Kalassian KG, Dremsizov T, Angus DC. Translating research evidence into clinical practice: new challenges for critical care. Crit Care 2002;6:11–4.

37. Carlet J. Quality assessment of intensive care units. Curr pin Crit Care 1996;2:319–25.

38. Werner RM, Asch DA. The unintended consequences of publicly reporting quality information. Jama 2005;293:1239–44.

39. Federal Drug Administration. The FDA Safety Information and Adverse Drug Event Reporting Program www.fda.gov/medwatch/report/hcp.htm.

40. Rubin HR, Pronovost P, Diette GB. From a process of care to a measure: the development and testing of a quality indicator. Int J Qual Health Care 2001;13:489–96.

41. Rubin HR, Pronovost P, Diette GB. The advantages and disadvantages of process-based measures of health care quality. Int J Qual Health Care 2001;13:469–74.

42. Brook RH, McGlynn EA, Cleary PD. Quality of health care. Part 2: measuring quality of care. N Engl J Med 1996;335:966–70.

43. McGlynn EA. Selecting common measures of quality and system performance. Med Care 2003;41:I39–47.

44. McGlynn EA. Introduction and overview of the conceptual framework for a national quality measurement and reporting system. Med Care 2003;41:I1–7.

45. Flowers J, Hall P, Pencheon D. Public health indicators. Public Health 2005;119:239–45.

46. Joint Commission on Accreditation of Healthcare Organizations, National Hospital Quality Measures – ICU. (Accessed Jan 12, 2009, at www.jointcommission. org/PerformanceMeasurement/MeasureReserve Library/Spec+Manual+–ICU.htm.).

47. Institute for Healthcare Improvement, Critical Care. (Accessed Jan 12, 2009, at www.ihi.org/IHI/Topics/ CriticalCare/.).

48. Pronovost PJ, Berenholtz SM, Ngo K, et al. Developing and pilot testing quality indicators in the intensive care unit. J Crit Care 2003;18:145–55.

49. Bellini C, Petignat C, Francioli P, et al. Comparison of automated strategies for surveillance of nosocomial bacteremia. Infect Control Hosp Epidemiol 2007;28:1030–5.

50. CDC/NHSN surveillance definition of health care–associated infection and criteria for specific types of infections in the acute care setting (Accessed December 26th, 2008 at www.cdc.gov/ncidod/dhqp/pdf/NNIS/ NosInfDefinitions.pdf).

51. Nelson EC, Splaine ME, Batalden PB, Plume SK. Building measurement and data collection into medical practice. Ann Intern Med 1998;128:460–6.

52. Nelson EC, Splaine ME, Plume SK, Batalden P. Good measurement for good improvement work. Qual Manag Health Care 2004;13:1–16.

53. Dodek PM, Heyland DK, Rocker GM, Cook DJ. Translating family satisfaction data into quality improvement. Crit Care Med 2004;32:1922–7.

54. Wallin L, Bostrom AM, Harvey G, Wikblad K, Ewald U. Progress of unit based quality improvement: an evaluation of a support strategy. Qual Saf Health Care 2002;11:308–14.

55. Dlugacz YD, Stier L, Lustbader D, Jacobs MC, Hussain E, Greenwood A. Expanding a performance improvement initiative in critical care from hospital to system. Jt Comm J Qual Improv 2002;28:419–34.

56. Ferlie EB, Shortell SM. Improving the quality of health care in the United Kingdom and the United States: a framework for change. Milbank Q 2001;79:281–315.

57. Curtis JR, Cook DJ, Wall RJ, et al. Intensive care unit quality improvement: A "how-to" guide for the interdisciplinary team. Crit Care Med 2006;34:211–8.

David A. Harrison and David K. Menon

Risk adjustment in neurocritical care (the RAIN study)

Acute traumatic brain injury (TBI) is a major public health problem and a leading cause of death and disability worldwide; it is the leading cause in people aged under 40. Each year, about 1.5 million people die from TBI. In the UK National Health Service (NHS), adult patients with TBI are rarely managed by a single service; they are managed by a succession of services from first contact to definitive care; definitive care not always being provided in a dedicated neurocritical care unit. Despite guidelines recommending that all patients with severe TBI be treated within a specialist neuroscience centre, many (particularly those without surgical lesions) are currently neither treated in nor transferred to one. Research is required to determine which locations for neurocritical care are associated with improved outcomes for adult patients with TBI. While conventional randomised controlled trial methodology may be impractical in this setting, the presence of variation in the way services are organised and delivered can allow them to be compared using observational methods. This is only possible if a valid, reliable, appropriate and accurate risk prediction model exists. The Risk Adjustment In Neurocritical care (RAIN) study aims to validate risk prediction models for TBI in a neurocritical care setting and apply these models to answer vitally important questions regarding the organisation and delivery of neurocritical care services.

Risk prediction in adult, general critical care

Risk prediction models take information from early in an episode of care and use this information to calculate the predicted risk of an outcome of interest, most often mortality. They serve many purposes at both the aggregate and individual patient levels [1]. Aggregate data from risk prediction models form the basis for comparative audit, permitting comparison of risk-adjusted outcomes both between institutions and within institutions over time. In prospective research studies, risk predictions can be used to stratify patients on study entry, and adjustment for strong predictors of outcome can increase study power and reduce the required sample size [2]. In observational research, a good risk prediction model, taking account of all major known confounders, is essential to reduce the selection bias resulting from the non-random selection of which patients receive which treatments. At the individual patient level, the output of a risk prediction model provides an objective estimate of outcome that can be used to inform discussion with the patient and their family and provide realistic expectations based on the outcomes of many thousands of similar patients rather than the more limited experience of a single clinician. Within the healthcare team, risk prediction models provide a common shared language that can be used to quickly summarise and communicate the severity of illness. However, such models can only support, not replace, clinical judgement, and should not be in isolation as the basis for clinical decisions [3].

Risk prediction models have been in established use in adult, general critical care units for over 25 years, since the publication of the original Acute Physiology And Chronic Health Evaluation (APACHE) model in 1981 [4]. In the UK, the first large-scale validation of a risk prediction model was the Intensive Care Society's APACHE II Study in Britain and Ireland, 1987–1989 [5, 6]. This study produced recalibrated coefficients for the APACHE II model, and led, in 1994, to the formation of the Intensive Care National Audit & Research Centre (ICNARC) and the Case Mix Programme, the national comparative audit of patient outcome in adult, general critical care units in England, Wales and Northern Ireland. ICNARC has continued to pioneer developments in risk prediction in the Case Mix Programme, most recently through the validation and recalibration of a number of general risk prediction models [7] and subsequent development of a new model, the ICNARC model [8].

Risk prediction in neurocritical care – Why not use a general model?

Unlike adult, general critical care, no data are routinely collected in the UK National Health Service (NHS) for risk-adjusted comparison of outcomes from neurocritical care. However, there are significant limitations to using models developed and validated for general critical care for patients receiving neurocritical care. Using a spectrum of measures for calibration and discrimination, risk prediction models, successfully developed and validated for adult admissions to general critical care units showed significant departure from perfect calibration in patients with head injuries admitted to adult, general and dedicated neurocritical care units (see Fig. 1) [9]. The inclusion and handling of variables of specific prognostic importance in TBI is often poor [9]. For example, the APACHE II model assumes

that any patient that is sedated for the entire first 24 hours in the critical care unit is deemed neurologically normal, which has previously led to suggestions that pre-sedation values of the Glasgow Coma Scale (GCS) should be used for these patients [10]. The only general model to take any account of changes detected on computed tomography (CT) scan is the Mortality Prediction Model (MPM) II, and the inclusion of CT information in this model is limited to the presence of an intracranial mass effect. Furthermore, all risk prediction models for adult, general critical care use an outcome of mortality at discharge from acute hospital, which is not considered adequate for neurocritical care where longer-term (e.g. six-month) mortality and functional outcome, such as the Glasgow Outcome Scale (GOS), are more valid outcomes [11].

Risk prediction in traumatic brain injury

A number of specific models for TBI exist. However, a recent systematic review by the Cochrane Injuries Group found that most models are limited by being based on small samples of patients, having poor methodology, and rarely being validated on external populations [12]. Of 102 models for TBI identified in the review, only seven models had undergone any form of external validation, and only two models by Hukkelhoven et al [13] – one for mortality and one for unfavourable outcome at six months – met minimal criteria of being developed using appropriate methods on data from at least 500 patients in multiple centres, and validated in an external population from different centres. These models were based on 2,269 patients with moderate or severe TBI (GCS ≤ 12) enrolled in two randomised controlled trials (RCTs), one in the United States and Canada and the other in Europe, Israel and Australia. The model for unfavourable outcome at six months was validated in an observational database of 796 patients with moderate or severe TBI in 55 European countries from the core data survey of the European Brain Injury Consortium (EBIC). The model for six-month mortality was validated in the EBIC data and also in an observational database of 746 patients with non-penetrating severe TBI (GCS ≤ 8) in four US centres from the Trauma Coma Databank (TCDB).

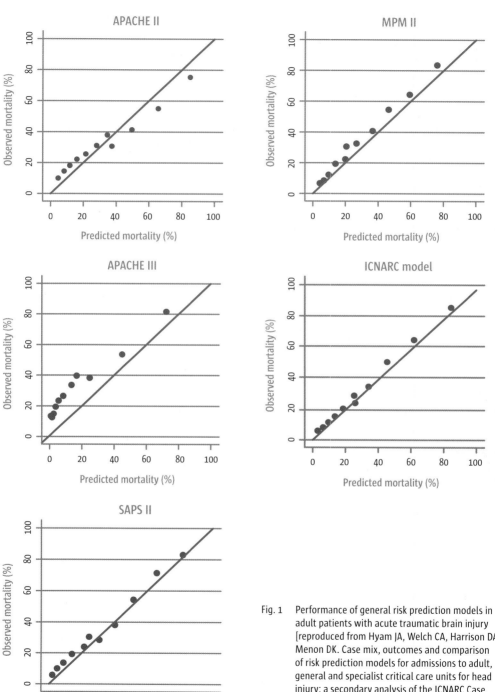

Fig. 1 Performance of general risk prediction models in adult patients with acute traumatic brain injury [reproduced from Hyam JA, Welch CA, Harrison DA, Menon DK. Case mix, outcomes and comparison of risk prediction models for admissions to adult, general and specialist critical care units for head injury: a secondary analysis of the ICNARC Case Mix Programme Database. Crit Care 2006;10 Suppl 2:S2 under the Creative Commons Attribution License]

One further model by Signorini et al. [14], identified from the systematic review, is also of relevance to identifying the best method for risk-adjustment in UK neurocritical care, being based on data from patients in a single UK centre, all of which were admitted to the critical care unit. This model was developed on 372 patients, and validated in a further 520 patients from the same centre, to predict survival at one year following TBI. The model incorporates age, GCS, Injury Severity Score (ISS), pupil reactivity and presence of haematoma on CT.

The authors of the systematic review went on to develop new models for 14-day mortality and unfavourable outcomes at six months aimed at addressing the shortcomings identified in their review [15]. Separate models were derived using only "basic" (demographic and clinical) variables and incorporating additional CT variables, and different models were reported for high-income countries and for low- and middle-income countries. These models were based on 10,008 patients with TBI (GCS ≤ 14) in the Corticosteroid Randomisation After Significant Head injury (CRASH) RCT [16, 17]. Of these, 2,482 patients were recruited from high-income countries, including 1,391 patients from 45 centres in the UK. The model for unfavourable outcomes at six months in high-income countries was validated in the International Mission for Prognosis And Clinical Trial (IMPACT) database [18, 19], a database combining data from 9,205 patients with moderate or severe TBI from eight RCTs and three observational studies (including the development and validation data from the Hukkelhoven models). The authors acknowledge that "further prospective validation in independent cohorts is needed to strengthen the generalisability of the models."

Further models for TBI have recently been developed using the IMPACT database and validated in CRASH data [20]. Three models of increasing complexity were presented for both mortality and unfavourable outcome at 6 months. The "core" model consists of weights for age, GCS motor score and pupil reactivity. The "extended" model additionally incorporates hypoxia, hypotension, CT classification, traumatic subarach-

Tab. 1   Prognostic factors included in the Hukkelhoven, Signorini, CRASH and IMPACT risk prediction models for outcome following acute traumatic brain injury

	Hukkelhoven	Signorini	CRASH		IMPACT		
			basic	CT	core	extended	lab
Demographic							
Age	X	X	X	X	X	X	X
Clinical							
GCS		X	X	X			
GCS motor score	X				X	X	X
Pupil reactivity	X	X	X	X	X	X	X
Injury Severity Score		X					
Major extracranial injury			X	X			
CT classification	X	X		X		X	X
Hypoxia	X					X	X
Hypotension	X					X	X
Laboratory							
Glucose							X
Haemoglobin							X

noid haemorrhage and epidural haematoma. Finally, the "lab" model also incorporates weights for glucose and haemoglobin. The prognostic factors incorporated in the Hukkelhoven, CRASH and IMPACT are summarised in Table 1.

Figures 2 and 3 show the external validation of the CRASH and IMPACT models for unfavourable outcome. On external validation using the EBIC dataset, the Hukkelhoven model for unfavourable outcome had an AUC of 0.83, out-

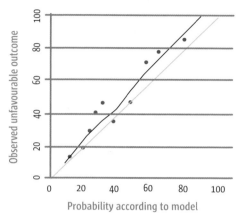

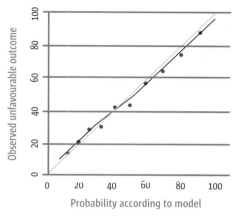

- Risk of outcome in 10ths of patients with similar predicted probabilities
— Relation between observed frequency and predicted probability of death or severe disability
— Ideal relation between observed and predicted frequency of outcome in model with perfect calibration

Fig. 2   Validation of CRASH high-income countries basic (L) and CT (R) models against IMPACT dataset. AUC for prediction of unfavorable outcome: 0.77 in both, but note the much poorer calibration of the basic model [reproduced from Predicting outcome after traumatic brain injury: practical prognostic models based on large cohort of international patients, MRC CRASH Trial Collaborators, 336, 425–429, 2008 with permission from BMJ Publishing Group Ltd.]

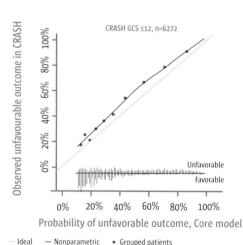

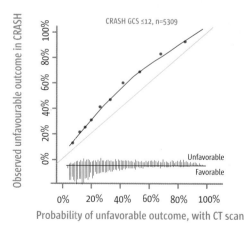

— Ideal   — Nonparametric   • Grouped patients

Fig. 3   Validation of IMPACT core (L) and extended (R) models for unfavourable outcome against CRASH high-income countries dataset. AUC for model: 0.78; for extended model 0.80. Both models tended to underestimate the rates of unfavourable outcome [reproduced from Predicting outcome after traumatic brain injury: development and international validation of prognostic scores based on admission characteristics, Steyerberg EW, Mushkudiani N, Perel P, Butcher I, Lu J, McHugh GS et al., PLoS Med, 5, e165, 2008 under the Creative Commons Attribution License]

performing that in the development data. The Signorini model predicted mortality only, and sufficient data were not available in the CRASH dataset to validate the IMPACT lab model.

While these recent developments in risk prediction models for TBI indicate potentially significant improvements over previously available models, these models still have limitations regarding their external validity (generalisability) for use in evaluating neurocritical care of patients with TBI in the NHS [21]. All these models were developed using some or all data from RCTs. Even when trials are pragmatic, as was the case for the CRASH trial, using data from an RCT to develop a prognostic model may impact on generalisability through self-selection of centres to participate in the trial, selection of patients enrolled in the trial, and the potential for all patients enrolled in a trial (in both active and control arms) to receive a better standard of care than usual [22]. Much of the data used in developing and validating these models is old. Only the CRASH database contains data from within the last 10 years, with the Hukkelhoven models based on data from the early 1990s, and the IMPACT data collected between 1984 and 1997. Models based on data from multiple sources are limited by differences in definitions of variables, timings of measurements, and inclusion criteria between the different data sources. The CRASH models for high-income countries are clearly of the most direct relevance to UK practice, as over half of all patients recruited to CRASH from high-income countries came from centres in the UK. However, in the CRASH trial as a whole, only 50 % of patients were admitted to critical care [16]. This figure may have been higher within the UK but, nonetheless, applying these models to a critical care setting is likely to introduce a selection bias and may invalidate the models' accuracy. It is clear that all these models require further prospective validation, and potentially recalibration, before they can be applied with confidence for research and audit in neurocritical care in the NHS.

Delivery of neurocritical care for traumatic brain injury in the NHS

In the NHS, adult patients with TBI are rarely managed by a single service; they are managed by a succession of services from first contact to definitive critical care, definitive critical care not always being provided in a dedicated neurocritical care unit. Despite recently updated guidelines from the National Institute of Health and Clinical Excellence (NICE) recommending that all patients with severe TBI be treated within a regional neuroscience centre where 24-hour neurosurgical services are available [23], many (particularly those without surgical lesions) are currently neither treated in nor transferred to one. A combination of geography, bed availability, local variation and clinical assessment of prognosis can often determine the location of definitive critical care for an adult patient with TBI. The Neurocritical Care Stakeholder Group, established to offer expert advice to the UK Department of Health and to commissioners, indicated in their 2006 audit report that, within the NHS, only 67 % of beds ring-fenced for neurocritical care were in dedicated neurocritical care units and that neurocritical care unit occupancy rates exceeded 90 % [24]. Most neurocritical care for adult patients with TBI was delivered either in dedicated neurocritical care units (42 %) or in general critical care units within a neuroscience centre (35 %). However, despite clear guidelines and the progressive regionalisation of neurosurgical care, 23 % of patients with TBI were treated in general critical care units outside a neuroscience centre. Local critical care consultant opinion indicated at least 83 % of these patients required transfer to a neuroscience centre. No data were available, or are routinely collected, within the NHS for risk-adjusted comparisons.

Where adult patients with TBI should be optimally treated is an important question for the NHS, both in terms of outcomes and costs. Belief and limited evidence has underpinned the establishment, and continuing expansion, of dedicated, neurocritical care facilities in the UK [25, 26] but no formal evaluation has been undertaken. A recent, large, multicentre observational research study using data from 60 % of all emergency departments in England and Wales, participating in the Trauma Audit and Research Network (TARN), has suggested benefit from managing severe head injuries in specialist neuroscience centres [27]. However, this research is acknowledged to be inconclusive due to lack of adjustment for all known confounders and the use of an unvalidated risk prediction model. It also does not address the issue of general versus specialist critical care units within neuroscience centres.

Further research is required to determine which locations for neurocritical care are associated with improved outcomes for adult patients with TBI, particularly for those who do not require surgical interventions such as placement of an external ventricular drain or craniotomy/craniectomy, a recommendation for future research in the recently revised NICE guideline [23]. A key issue for policy-makers is whether the additional initial costs of more specialised care are justified by subsequent reductions in morbidity costs and/or improvements in patient outcomes.

The transfer of critically ill patients is not without risk, and any benefit from transferring patients, or from instituting a bypass system such that patients with suspected traumatic brain injuries are taken directly to a neuroscience centre, must be weighed against the risks involved in the transfer itself. An analysis of the distance of ambulance journeys to hospital (in a mixed cohort of emergency, non-cardiac arrest patients) indicated that the absolute increase in mortality may be as much as 1 % for every additional 10 km travelled [28]. The question of the level of severity of TBI that warrants transfer has not been fully adressed. Patients may be either too severely ill for transfer to be appropriate, or not severe enough, such that the risks associated with the transfer outweigh any possible benefit.

While conventional RCT methodology is likely to be impractical in this setting, the presence of variation in the way services are organised and delivered can allow them to be compared using observational methods. This is only possible if a valid, reliable, appropriate and accurate risk prediction model exists. The Risk Adjustment In Neurocritical care (RAIN) study seeks to address both the validation of a risk adjustment methodology and the application of this methodology to answering these important questions on the service delivery and organisation of neurocritical care for TBI.

The Risk Adjustment In Neurocritical care (RAIN) study

The RAIN study was established with two primary aims:

- to validate risk prediction models for acute TBI in the setting of neurocritical care in the NHS; and
- to use these models to evaluate the optimum location and comparative costs of neurocritical care in the NHS.

The study will run in the majority of specialist neuroscience centres in the UK, including both dedicated neurocritical care units and mixed general/neurocritical care units, and also in adult, general critical care units from outside neurosurgical centres, recruited from the Case Mix Programme. This mix of units will enable us to identify all the variations in the pathways that patients take through the different services. During 18 months of data collection, detailed data will be collected on consecutive patients with acute TBI, sufficient to calculate risk predictions from the Hukkelhoven, Signorini, CRASH and IMPACT models. Abstraction of prospective administrative and clinical data will be undertaken by data collectors trained to collect a dedicated core dataset for RAIN according to precise rules and definitions. All data will undergo extensive validation, both locally and centrally, for completeness, illogicalities and inconsistencies. We will obtain copies of the admission CT in a randomly selected sample of 10 % of patients, weighted to include more patients from outside neuroscience centres, where patient throughput will be lower. These will be centrally viewed and assessed, and the reports generated will be compared to the corresponding submitted data to identify any systematic discrepancies.

All patients will be followed up centrally for mortality and functional outcome (extended Glasgow Outcome Scale and EQ-5D) at six months following their injury. Consensus recommendations have suggested that patients with TBI should be followed up using generic as well as disease-specific measures of health-related quality of life [29]. The use of EQ-5D will enable the calculation of quality-adjusted life years (QALYs) as the best global measure of cost-effectiveness. Strategies proven to improve response rates to postal questionnaires will be employed to ensure maximum possible response [30]. Non-respondents will be followed up with a further postal questionnaire and finally by telephone interview. In the minority of cases where the patient or their consultee does not respond, medical teams involved in the care of the patient will be contacted to attempt to determine the primary outcome measure for the study: whether the patient had a favourable or unfavourable outcome. As after a head injury patients can show dramatic personality changes and a variety of cognitive deficits, it is important that we have data covering these outcomes in order to determine why some patients make a better recovery than others.

The risk prediction models will be validated with measures of discrimination (the ability to separate survivors from non-survivors or those with favourable outcomes from those with unfavourable outcomes), calibration (the degree of agreement between the observed and predicted outcomes) and overall goodness-of-fit. If the calibration is poor, then the best model(s) will be recalibrated to provide revised coefficients specific to UK neurocritical care. The analysis will be based on methods used previously for the validation of risk prediction models for adult, general critical care [7, 8] and for evaluating general risk prediction models in patients with TBI [9]. A sample size requirement of 3,400 patients was calculated to give 80 % power to detect as statistically significant (p < 0.05) a 10 % relative difference in the area under the receiver operating characteristic (ROC) curve between two models, allowing for 9 % loss to follow-up. The strengths and weaknesses of each model will be assessed, including consideration of factors such as the purposes for which each model is suited, the choice of outcome variable, and the ease of data collection, in addition to statistical performance.

The cost analysis will take a health and personal social services perspective [30]. For each recruited patient, each day during the hospital stay will be assigned to an appropriate cost category using daily organ support data. Information will be collected on hospital readmissions and use of community health services post-discharge at six-month follow-up, allowing calculation of the total six-month hospital and community health service costs for each patient. The effect of location of neurocritical care on six-month mortality and unfavourable outcomes will be evaluated using multilevel logistic regression models [31]. Using a multilevel model enables adjustment for both patient-level factors, including the selected risk prediction model, and unit-level factors, such as the volume of cases, the size of the unit and, most importantly, the type (specialist or general) and location (neuroscience centre or not) of the unit. The cost-effectiveness analysis will use the six-month EQ-5D, health services questionnaire and survival data to report six-month risk-adjusted QALYs. These endpoints will be valued at different levels of willingness to pay for a QALY gain to report risk-adjusted incremental net benefits of each location of neurocritical care. Finally, a cost-effectiveness model will extrapolate from the risk-adjusted estimates of six-month cost and outcomes to project risk-adjusted cost-effectiveness over the lifetime. An extensive sensitivity analysis will investigate whether the conclusions about the relative cost-effectiveness of care delivery are robust to assumptions made about model specification.

Summary

The RAIN Study will first develop an appropriate methodology for risk adjustment in neurocritical care by validating existing risk prediction models for TBI, and then apply this methodology to answer vitally important questions regarding the appropriate model for organisation and delivery of neurocritical care services for this patient group.

Acknowledgements

The RAIN Study is funded by the National Institute for Health Research (NIHR) Health Technology Assessment (HTA) programme. The views expressed in this publication are those of the authors and not necessarily those of the NHS, the NIHR or the Department of Health. The NIHR HTA programme is funded by the Department of Health.

The authors

David A. Harrison, MA, PhD[1]
David K. Menon, MD, PhD, FRCP, FRCA, FmedSci[2]
[1]Intensive Care National Audit & Research Centre (ICNARC) | Tavistock House | Tavistock London, UK
[2]University Department of Anaesthesia | Addenbrooke's Hospital and University of Cambridge | Cambridge CB2 2QQ, UK

Address for correspondence

David A. Harrison

Intensive Care National Audit & Research

Centre (ICNARC)

Tavistock House, Tavistock Square

London WC1H 9HR, UK

E-mail: david.harrison@icnarc.org

References

1. Gunning K, Rowan K. ABC of intensive care: outcome data and scoring systems. BMJ 1999;319:241–4.
2. Hernández AV, Steyerberg EW, Butcher I, Mushkudiani N, Taylor GS, Murray GD et al. Adjustment for strong predictors of outcome in traumatic brain injury trials: 25 % reduction in sample size requirements in the IMPACT study. J Neurotrauma 2006;23:1295–303.
3. Skrobik Y, Kavanagh BP. Scoring systems for the critically ill: use, misuse and abuse. Can J Anaesth 2006;53:432–6.
4. Moreno RP, Jardim AL, Godinho de Matos R, Metnitz PGH. Principles of risk-adjustment in the critically ill patient. In: Kuhlen R, Moreno R, Ranieri M, Rhodes A (Eds). 25 Years of Progress and Innovation in Intensive Care Medicine. Berlin: Medizinisch Wissenschaftliche Verlagsgesellschaft, 2007.
5. Rowan KM, Kerr JH, Major E, McPherson K, Short A, Vessey MP. Intensive Care Society's APACHE II study in Britain and Ireland–I: Variations in case mix of adult admissions to general intensive care units and impact on outcome. BMJ 1993;307:972–7.
6. Rowan KM, Kerr JH, Major E, McPherson K, Short A, Vessey MP. Intensive Care Society's APACHE II study in Britain and Ireland–II: Outcome comparisons of intensive care units after adjustment for case mix by the American APACHE II method. BMJ 1993;307:977–81.
7. Harrison DA, Brady AR, Parry GJ, Carpenter JR, Rowan K. Recalibration of risk prediction models in a large multicenter cohort of admissions to adult, general critical care units in the United Kingdom. Crit Care Med 2006;34:1378–88.
8. Harrison DA, Parry GJ, Carpenter JR, Short A, Rowan K. A new risk prediction model for critical care: the Intensive Care National Audit & Research Centre (ICNARC) model. Crit Care Med 2007;35:1091–8.
9. Hyam JA, Welch CA, Harrison DA, Menon DK. Case mix, outcomes and comparison of risk prediction models for admissions to adult, general and specialist critical care units for head injury: a secondary analysis of the ICNARC Case Mix Programme Database. Crit Care 2006;10 Suppl 2:S2.
10. Livingston BM, Mackenzie SJ, MacKirdy FN, Howie JC. Should the pre-sedation Glasgow Coma Scale value be used when calculating Acute Physiology and Chronic Health Evaluation scores for sedated patients? Scottish Intensive Care Society Audit Group. Crit Care Med 2000;28:389–94.
11. Hayes JA, Black NA, Jenkinson C, Young JD, Rowan KM, Daly K et al. Outcome measures for adult critical care: a systematic review. Health Technol Assess 2000;4:1–111.
12. Perel P, Edwards P, Wentz R, Roberts I. Systematic review of prognostic models in traumatic brain injury. BMC Med Inform Decis Mak 2006;6:38.
13. Hukkelhoven CW, Steyerberg EW, Habbema JD, Farace E, Marmarou A, Murray GD et al. Predicting outcome after traumatic brain injury: development and validation of a prognostic score based on admission characteristics. J Neurotrauma 2005;22:1025–39.
14. Signorini DF, Andrews PJD, Jones PA, Wardlaw JM, Miller JD. Predicting survival using simple clinical variables: a case study in traumatic brain injury. J Neurol Neurosurg Psychiatry 1999;66:20–5.
15. MRC CRASH Trial Collaborators. Predicting outcome after traumatic brain injury: practical prognostic models based on a large cohort of international patients. BMJ 2008;336:425–9.
16. CRASH Trial Collaborators. Effect of intravenous corticosteroids on death within 14 days in 10008 adults with clinically significant head injury (MRC CRASH trial): randomised placebo-controlled trial. Lancet 2004;364:1321–8.
17. CRASH Trial Collaborators. Final results of MRC CRASH, a randomised placebo-controlled trial of intravenous corticosteroid in adults with head injury—outcomes at 6 months. Lancet 2005;365:1957–9.
18. Maas AI, Marmarou A, Murray GD, Teasdale GM, Steyerberg EW. Prognosis and clinical trial design in traumatic brain injury: the IMPACT study. J Neurotrauma 2007;24:232–8.
19. Marmarou A, Lu J, Butcher I, McHugh GS, Mushkudiani NA, Murray GD et al. IMPACT database of traumatic brain injury: design and description. J Neurotrauma 2007;24:239–50.
20. Steyerberg EW, Mushkudiani N, Perel P, Butcher I, Lu J, McHugh GS et al. Predicting outcome after traumatic brain injury: development and international validation of prognostic scores based on admission characteristics. PLoS Med 2008;5:e165.
21. Menon D, Harrison D. Prognostic modelling in traumatic brain injury. BMJ 2008;336:397–8.
22. Black N. Why we need observational studies to evaluate the effectiveness of health care. BMJ 1996;312:1215–8.
23. National Collaborating Centre for Acute Care. Head injury: Triage, assessment, investigation and early management of head injury in infants, children and adults. London: Royal College of Surgeons of England, 2007. [Available from http://www.nice.org.uk/cg56].
24. Neurocritical Care Stakeholder Group. Neurocritical care

capacity and demand. London: Neurocritical Care Stakeholder Group, 2006. [Available from http://www.nasgbi.org.uk/NCCcapacityReport.aspx].

25. Menon D. Neurocritical care: turf label, organizational construct, or clinical asset? Curr Opin Crit Care 2004;10:91–3.

26. Smith M. Neurocritical care: has it come of age? Br J Anaesth 2004;93:753–5.

27. Patel HC, Bouamra O, Woodford M, King AT, Yates DW, Lecky FE. Trends in head injury outcome from 1989 to 2003 and the effect of neurosurgical care: an observational study. Lancet 2005;366:1538–44.

28. Nicholl J, West J, Goodacre S, Turner J. The relationship between distance to hospital and patient mortality in emergencies: an observational study. Emerg Med J 2007;24:665–8.

29. Bullinger M, Azouvi P, Brooks N, Basso A, Christensen AL, Gobiet W et al. Quality of life in patients with traumatic brain injury—basic issues, assessment and recommendations. Restor Neurol Neurosci 2002; 20:111–24.

30. National Institute for Health and Clinical Excellence. Guide to the methods of Technology Appraisal: draft for consultation. London: National Institute for Health and Clinical Excellence, 2007.

31. Grieve R, Nixon R, Thompson SG, Cairns J. Multilevel models for estimating incremental net benefits in multinational studies. Health Econ 2007;16:815–26.

Peter C. Minneci, Katherine J. Deans and Charles Natanson

Applying the results of a randomised controlled trial: Caveat emptor

Introduction

The large prospective randomised controlled trial (RCT) has become an essential tool and the "gold standard" for evaluating therapies. To determine the value of a therapy in a broad patient base, RCTs often enroll heterogeneous patient populations at multiple centres. Subsequently, the bedside clinicians must interpret the results of these large RCTs and decide whether to change their practice.

Prior to applying the results of an RCT in clinical practice, a series of issues concerning the RCT should be considered. First, did the trial include a control group that accurately reflects prevailing medical practices outside of the trial? If not representative of current practice, then was the control group potentially disadvantaged in any way? Second, if the control group was appropriate, were the methods used rigorous, limiting potential bias, and are the results of the RCT internally consistent? For instance, are the results consistent across patient subgroups, during the entire period of enrollment, and at all investigating centres? Finally, are the results of the RCT externally consistent with the available data about the therapy in the literature including preclinical data, retrospective data, and across clinical trials?

An additional concern when interpreting the results of a large RCT investigating a specific treatment regimen in a heterogeneous patient population is that it likely included several clinically important patient subgroups. In this case, the RCT may demonstrate an overall beneficial effect, but this statistical benefit may be powered by marked clinical improvement in one subgroup with smaller harmful effects in others. Conversely, a therapy may be beneficial in a specific subpopulation, but the overall result of a trial may demonstrate no beneficial treatment effect. These issues are amplified in RCTs performed in critically ill patient populations. The critically ill population represents a heterogeneous group of patients with many different comorbid conditions who develop diseases that have varying degrees of severity. This heterogeneity in both the disease process and patient population may create subpopulations in which the investigated treatment may have differing effects.

The purpose of this chapter is to raise awareness about the inherent difficulties and risks in interpreting and applying the results of an RCT. We recognise that designing and performing such trials remains an ongoing challenge; the following discussion serves to raise awareness of issues surrounding clinical trial interpretation that have been demonstrated through retrospective analyses of completed trials. In this chapter, we will present examples from the literature to discuss the need for a trial to include a usual care control group to generate informative results and the importance of assessing the rigor of the methodology and the consistency of the results of an RCT prior to accepting and implementing a therapy.

Interpreting a critical care RCT: The importance of a usual care control group

When interpreting an RCT, several issues should be considered when determining if the results are valid and generalisable to clinical practice. These include determining if the control group in the trial is reflective of prevailing medical practices, evaluating the consistency of the results throughout the trial and across patient subgroups, and assessing whether the trial methodology minimised selection bias.

A usual care control group is necessary to determine if the results of an RCT are better or worse than current practice and whether the results are generalisable. The consequences of not including a usual care control group can be demonstrated in recent RCTs investigating therapies already used in clinical practice. These trials examined existing therapies that are usually adjusted in response to changes in disease severity in heterogeneous critically ill patient populations [1–12]. In these RCTs, patients were randomised to fixed levels of a titrated therapy independent of disease severity. Randomisation prevented clinicians from adjusting treatment levels based on severity disease and created "practice misalignments" [7]. Subgroups of patients within each study arm received therapy levels inconsistent with prevailing medical practices outside of the trial. Within the group of patients receiving the low level of fixed therapy, a segment of patients received insufficient therapy based on important clinical factors such as disease severity. In contrast, within the group of patients receiving the high level of fixed therapy, a segment of patients received excessive therapy for their level of disease severity. Compared to patients receiving usual care, these misaligned subgroups may have worse outcomes and may substantially contribute to the outcome differences detected between the trial arms. More importantly, these trials did not compare outcomes of either trial arm to a group of patients receiving usual titrated care; therefore, neither arm in the trial can be demonstrated to be superior to usual care. Consequently, the trial's ability to change clinical practice is limited. The following example demonstrates how the lack of a usual care control group in an RCT can lead to practice misalignments and make the results of an RCT uninformative to clinical practice. (Of note, more detailed descriptions and analyses of the practice misalignments in the following example have been previously reported [7]).

The Transfusion Requirements in Critical Care (TRICC) trial compared two blood transfusion strategies in critically ill patients [10]. Independent of co-morbidities, patients were randomised to either a liberal (10 g/dl of haemoglobin) or restrictive (7 g/dl) transfusion threshold. This trial did not have a control group reflective of usual care where transfusion thresholds were titrated based on the patient's severity of disease [11, 13]. The TRICC trial enrolled 838 patients and demonstrated that hospital mortality was higher with a liberal transfusion threshold compared to a restrictive transfusion threshold (28.1% vs. 22.2%, p = 0.05) [10]. The results of the TRICC trial have been interpreted by many clinicians to mean that most critically ill patients should only receive red cell transfusions when their haemoglobin concentration falls below 7.0 g/dl. However, patients with varying degrees of disease severity were assigned to treatments independent of need, creating subgroups of patients within each arm of the trial receiving treatments that were contrary to usual care outside of the trial (see Fig. 1) [7]. Patients with ischaemic heart disease who would usually be transfused at higher haemoglobin levels had transfusions restricted until their haemoglobin level dropped below 7 g/dl; these patients were placed at increased risk for coronary ischaemia and compromised oxygen delivery. Conversely, younger and healthier patients who would usually be transfused at lower haemoglobin levels received transfusions as soon as their haemoglobin level dropped below 10 g/dl; these patients were subjected to the risks of blood transfusion and potential volume overload. In addition, the TRICC trial did not compare outcomes of either trial arm to a group of patients receiving usual titrated care. The comparison of practice misalignments that are different in each arm make the reported results of this trial difficult to interpret and the lack of a usual care control group makes the results of this trial uninformative to clinical practice.

A

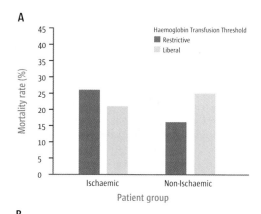

B

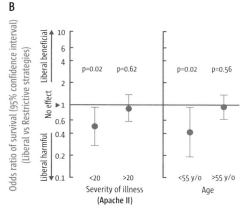

Fig. 1   Practice misalignments in the Transfusion Requirements in Critical Care (TRICC) trial

Panel A: In the TRICC trial, the presence of ischaemic heart disease significantly changes the treatment effect of the two transfusion strategies (p = 0.03) [7, 10]. In patients with ischaemic heart disease, a liberal transfusion strategy decreased mortality compared to a restrictive transfusion strategy. In patients without ischaemic heart disease, a liberal transfusion strategy increased mortality compared to a restrictive transfusion strategy.

Panel B: Younger (age < 55) and healthier patients (APACHE ≤ 20) had a significantly lower odds ratio of survival with a liberal transfusion strategy compared to a restrictive transfusion. These results suggest that increased harm in the groups of misaligned younger and healthier patients may have led to the overall beneficial effect of a restrictive transfusion strategy reported in the TRICC trial. [reproduced from Deans K et al., Randomization in clinical trials of titrated therapies: Unintented consequences of using fixed treatment protocols, Crit Care Med, 2007, 35(6):1509–1516]

Another example of the importance of incorporating usual care into RCTs can be demonstrated in the first RCT examining intensive insulin therapy (IIT) in critically ill patients [14]. In this trial, IIT significantly increased survival compared to conventional ICU blood glucose management in a single surgical ICU. Of note, the practice in this surgical ICU was to begin a continuous glucose infusion (200–300 grams/day) on the day of ICU admission and to institute total parental nutrition, total enteral nutrition or a combination of the two on the following day. The results of this study led many clinicians to use IIT in the management of critically ill patients, including medical patients and patients with sepsis. However, closer inspection of the trial methodology may have raised concerns about accepting and widely applying IIT. Firstly, few surgical ICUs have a nutrition policy as aggressive as the one utilised by the ICU in this trial; this raises questions about the generalisability of the results of this RCT to other surgical ICUs. In addition, the trial population did not include large numbers of medical ICU patients or patients with sepsis, suggesting that these results may not be generalisable to these patient populations. Two subsequent RCTs in septic patients and medical ICU patients comparing IIT to a usual care control group failed to demonstrate a survival benefit of IIT (see Fig. 2) [15, 16]. These results suggest that the beneficial effect of IIT in the initial trial may have been related to the inclusion of a control group not reflective of usual care at other institutions or is specific to critically ill surgical patients. Either way, a closer evaluation of the initial RCT may have demonstrated the limited generalisability of its results.

Interpreting a critical care RCT: Evaluating internal consistency

In addition to examining the appropriateness of a control group to inform clinical practice, the internal consistency of the results of an RCT should be evaluated by assessing the consistency of the treatment effect during the entire period of enrolment, across all participating centres, and across patient subgroups. Results from the PROWESS trial, the first large RCT of recombinant human activated protein C (rhAPC), dem-

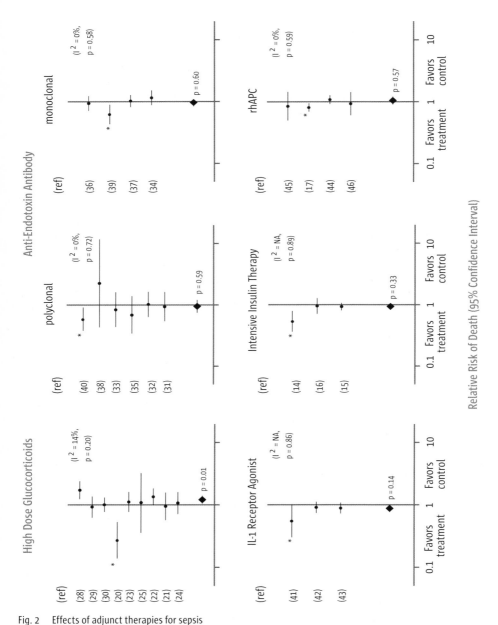

Fig. 2 Effects of adjunct therapies for sepsis

Each panel depicts the relative risk of death and 95 % CI (closed circle and horizontal line respectively) for each individual randomised controlled trial for one of six adjunct therapies for sepsis. An asterisk denotes any trial with p < 0.05. A summary statistic for all of the trials in each panel except the initial beneficial RCT is depicted by the diamond. The I-square and p-value for heterogeneity are reported for the summary statistic in each panel. For each of the six therapies, the RCTs performed after the initial beneficial trial demonstrated either no effect or harmful effects of the therapy. Il-1: Interleukin-1, rhAPC: Recombinant human activated protein C

[reproduced from Intensive Care Med 2008; 34: 1955–60, Once is not enough: clinical trials in sepsis, Sweeney DA, Danner RL, Eichacker PQ, Natanson C, Figure 1, with kind permission of Springer]

onstrate how issues with internal consistency can affect the interpretation and acceptance of the results of an RCT [17]. Near the midpoint of the PROWESS trial, a protocol amendment modified enrolment criteria to more effectively exclude patients who were likely to die from non-sepsis-related causes [18, 19]. In addition, a new drug preparation was introduced and trial sites were changed with 20 sites eliminated and 45 sites added [18, 19]. The timing of these changes divided the PROWESS trial into two parts, with rhAPC demonstrating markedly different treatment effects in the two parts of the trial [18, 19]. Compared to control, rhAPC did not decrease mortality during the first portion of the trial (30% vs. 28%, p = 0.57); however, rhAPC significantly decreased mortality during the second portion of the trial (31% vs. 22%, p = 0.0012). In addition, analysis of the entire trial demonstrated a negative effect of rhAPC at the 20 sites eliminated after the first part of the trial and a strong beneficial effect of rhAPC at the sites added in the second part of the trial. Furthermore, the treatment effect of rhAPC during the entire trial varied based on severity of illness, age, and the presence of chronic illness. Subgroup analysis demonstrated that the beneficial effects of rhAPC were most prominent in more severely ill patients with APACHE II scores > 25. In addition, rhAPC demonstrated marked benefit in patients 80–90 years old but no benefit in patients < 50 years old; these age-related effects may in part be explained by improved efficacy of rhAPC in patients with comorbid chronic health problems [19]. In patients who had chronic health points allocated in their APACHE II scores (n = 345), rhAPC markedly decreased mortality compared to controls (28% vs. 47%) [19]. In contrast, rhAPC did not improve mortality in patients who did not have chronic health points allocated in their APACHE II scores (n = 1345) [19]. The inconsistent results in the PROWESS trial across its first and second parts, across subgroups of patients, and at the different groups of enrolment sites raise concerns about the validity of the results and suggest that caution should be used when interpreting and applying the results of this trial.

Interpreting a critical care RCT: Assessing for potential bias

When interpreting the results of an RCT, the trial methodology should also be evaluated to determine if bias was minimised. An RCT investigating the effects of high-dose steroids in patients with septic shock underscores the importance of closely evaluating the methods of a trial when interpreting its results [20]. In 1976, an RCT examining the effects of high-dose steroids in patients with septic shock demonstrated a significant improvement in survival with steroid therapy compared to controls [20]. After publication of this trial, high-dose steroid therapy became widely accepted and administered to patients with septic shock. Over 7 years later, additional RCTs examining high-dose steroids in septic patients began reporting their results. Five subsequent RCTs failed to demonstrate an improvement in survival with high-dose steroids, and eventually this therapy was abandoned (see Fig. 2) [21–25]. A closer evaluation of this trial may have raised concerns about accepting its results. This trial enrolled "septic shock patients consecutively admitted" at a single institution over eight years [20, 26]. All patients were enrolled by a single investigator and the publication included the results of simultaneous prospective and retrospective trials at the institution [20, 26]. These issues raise concerns for unintentional selection bias and question the validity of the results.

Interpreting a critical care RCT: Evaluating internal consistency

Once a beneficial effect has been demonstrated in an RCT with a control group reflective of usual care and the internal consistency and validity of the results have been evaluated, then the external consistency of the trial should be assessed. The trial results should be interpreted within the context of the available literature to confirm that the treatment effects in important patient subgroups and across clinical trials are consistent with previously reported results. Not surprisingly, RCTs with internal validity issues may also have issues with external consistency; the results of these RCTs may not be reproducible in other clinical trials.

In the case of an RCT demonstrating the first beneficial effects of a therapy in critically ill patients, cautious acceptance and application may be warranted, particularly if the control does not represent usual care, the methods are not rigorous, or the results are not internally consistent. A recent analysis noted that multiple different adjunct therapies for sepsis have demonstrated benefit in an initial large RCT with subsequent trials failing to reproduce the beneficial effects (see Fig. 2) [27]. High-dose steroids were the earliest therapy to demonstrate this pattern. As discussed above, there were methodologic concerns with the initial RCT reporting an improvement in survival with high-dose steroid therapy in patients with septic shock [20]. In addition to those concerns, an evaluation of the external consistency showed others were not able to reproduce of the results of this trial (see Fig. 2) [26, 27]. Furthermore, this trial reported the lowest mortality with steroid treatment of any study to date [28–30]. Taken together with its internal issues, the results of this trial should have been interpreted cautiously.

Similar patterns of an improvement in survival in septic patients in an initial RCT followed by a lack of a beneficial effect in subsequent RCTs have occurred with anti-endotoxin antibody therapies [31–40], interleukin-1 receptor antagonists [41–43] and more recently with intensive insulin therapy (IIT) [14–16] and recombinant human activated protein C (rhAPC) [17, 44–46] (see Fig. 2). As discussed above, the first trial examining intensive insulin therapy (IIT) in critically ill patients was performed in a single surgical ICU with an aggressive nutrition policy and enrolled few medical ICU patients and patients with sepsis [14]. The two subsequent RCTs comparing ITT to a usual care control group in septic patients and medical ICU patients have failed to demonstrate a survival benefit of IIT [15, 16]. This example illustrates the importance of determining the applicability of the trial methodology and patient population with the clinical practices and patient population in your ICU prior to accepting and applying the results of an RCT.

In the initial large RCT testing the efficacy of rhAPC (PROWESS), rhAPC significantly decreased mortality in patients with severe sepsis compared to placebo (30.8 vs. 24.7 %; p = 0.005)

[17]. Despite issues with internal consistency, rhAPC was approved for clinical use by the U.S. FDA and the European Medicine Agency in subgroups of patients in which it demonstrated the largest improvements in survival (patients with an APACHE II score > 25 and patients with severe sepsis and multi-organ failure respectively) [19, 27]. Similar to other adjunct therapies for sepsis, the treatment effects of rhAPC have been inconsistent in subsequent trials. Two RCTs investigating the effects of rhAPC in children (RESOLVE) and in adults with sepsis and a low risk of death (ADDRESS) were both stopped early for futility [44, 46]. Of note, in the severely ill adult patients at a high risk of death in the ADDRESS trial, the treatment effects of rhAPC were inconsistent with the effects demonstrated in the PROWESS trial; in the ADDRESS trial, rhAPC did not decrease mortality in patients with an APACHE II > 25 (n = 324) or in patients with two or more organ failures (n = 872) [47]. In addition, compared to controls, rhAPC led to increased rates of serious bleeding events in both the RESOLVE and ADDRESS trials which exceeded the rates of bleeding reported in the PROWESS trial [48]. Because of these inconsistent results of rhAPC across trials, an additional large RCT (PROWESS-Shock) is being planned to examine the effects of rhAPC in severely ill septic patients at high risk of death [27, 49]. The pattern of inconsistent findings across RCTs for adjunct therapies for sepsis highlights the limitations of interpreting the beneficial effects of a therapy reported in a single RCT with internal inconsistencies.

Another example of the importance of assessing the external consistency of an RCT can be seen with clinical trials evaluating low tidal volume ventilation in patients with ARDS. The ARDS Network low tidal volume ventilation (ARMA) trial showed a significant improvement in mortality of patients with ARDS when tidal volumes were changed to 6 ml/kg compared to changing them to 12 ml/kg [1]. This trial also did not have a control group representative of usual care where tidal volumes were titrated based on measures reflective of severity of lung injury (e.g. compliance). When comparing the results of the ARMA trial to other available data at the time of their publication, meta-analyses have demonstrated that there were significantly varying effects in the published RCTs evaluating low tidal volume ventilation in patients with ARDS [9, 50]. These differing effects could be explained by differences in the control groups of the trials (see Fig. 3). Each trial randomised control patients to different tidal volume levels which subsequently led to different changes in airway pressures. In the trials in which the mean post-randomisation plateau airway pressure in the control groups remained less than 31 cm H_2O, there was no effect of low tidal volume ventilation on survival [51–53]. In contrast, the trials in which the mean post-randomisation plateau airway pressure in the control groups was greater than 31 cm H_2O demonstrated improved survival with low tidal volume ventilation [1, 54]. The inconsistent results across these RCTs and the potential explanation for the varying treatment effects raise concerns over the validity and generalisability of the results of the ARMA trial.

Conclusions

A critical evaluation and interpretation of an RCT is necessary because applying a therapy with inconsistent or unconfirmed results may place patients at increased risk and may increase mortality. In the example of high-dose steroids, a meta-analysis has demonstrated increased mortality with high-dose steroid therapy. In the cases of IIT and rhAPC, patients in the treatment groups had higher rates of hypoglycaemia and serious bleeding events respectively. In the TRICC and ARMA trials, a previous analysis demonstrated harmful effects of each treatment strategy in specific patient subgroups. These retrospective examples suggest that a beneficial treatment effect in a single RCT with methodological concerns or inconsistencies should be interpreted and applied with caution until confirmed in a subsequent trial.

Clinical trials are an essential tool to evaluate medical therapies but need to be interpreted carefully. Clinicians need to evaluate the control group to ensure it represents prevailing medical practices and is not disadvantaged in any way. The results of an RCT should then be assessed for internal consistency including a thorough examination of trial methodology and the treatment's effects throughout the trial and across patient subgroups. Subsequently, the results of completed trials should be interpreted within the larger body of available data to assess for the consistency of treatment effects in specific patient subgroups and across clinical trials.

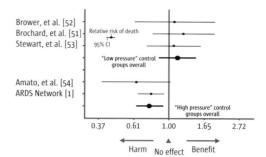

Relative risk of death with low tidal volume ventilation

Fig. 3   Effects of low tidal volume ventilation on mortality of patients with ARDS.
The relative risk of death and 95% confidence interval with low tidal volume ventilation is depicted for each of the individual randomised clinical trials and for the trials with "low-pressure" control groups (mean plateau pressure ≤ 31 cm H_2O, n = 3) and "high-pressure" control groups (mean plateau pressure > 31 cm H_2O, n = 2) trials [9, 50]. The effects of low tidal volume ventilation on mortality were dependent of the post-randomisation mean plateau pressure of the control groups (p = 0.004). In trials with "high pressure" control groups, low tidal volume ventilation significantly decreased mortality. In contrast, in trials with "low pressure" control groups, low tidal volume ventilation led to a nonsignificant increase in mortality. [reproduced from Minneci PC et al. A Critical Review of Randomized Controlled Trials of Tidal Volume Reduction During ARDS. In: Dreyfuss D, Hubmayr RD, Saumon G, eds. Ventilator Induced Lung Injury. New York: Marcel Dekker, Inc.; 2006:519–536]

In addition, prior to applying the results of an RCT in clinical practice, physicians should assess the consistency of the trial methodology and participants with their own practices and patient population. Finally, at least for RCTs in critically ill septic patients, cautious acceptance and application of a therapy based on a beneficial effect demonstrated in a single trial may be warranted until the results have been confirmed in a subsequent trial. This is especially important if the initial trial lacks methodological rigor, a control group reflective of usual care, or has issues with internal consistency.

The ideal critical care RCT would be a large multicentre trial with a control group reflective of usual care and unbiased blinded randomisation that generated consistent results at all participating centres, across important patient subgroups and throughout the duration of the trial; these results would be physiologically plausible and consistent with other available data including preclinical experiments, retrospective studies and smaller clinical trials. Unfortunately, the ideal trial may never be able to be performed, therefore, the clinician needs to carefully evaluate and interpret an RCT prior to accepting and applying the results.

Acknowledgements

The content of this manuscript represents the opinions of the individual authors and is not the official opinion of the National Institutes of Health, the United States Government, the University of Pennsylvania School of Medicine or the Children's Hospital of Philadelphia.

The authors

Peter C. Minneci, MD, MHSc[1, 2]
Katherine J. Deans, MD, MHSc[1,2]
Charles Natanson, MD[3]
    [1]Department of Surgery | The Children's
    Institute for Surgical Science | The Children's
    Hospital of Philadelphia | Philadelphia, PA
    [2]Department of Surgery | University
    of Pennsylvania School of Medicine |
    Philadelphia, PA
    [3]Critical Care Medicine Department |
    National Institutes of Health | Bethesda, MD

Address for correspondence
    Peter C. Minneci
    Department of Surgery
    University of Pennsylvania School of
    Medicine
    The Children's Institute for Surgical Science
    The Children's Hospital of Philadelphia
    34th St and Civic Center Boulevard
    Abramson Research Center, Rm 1116
    Philadelphia, PA 19104, USA
    E-mail: minneci@email.chop.edu

References

1. Ventilation with lower tidal volumes as compared with traditional tidal volumes for acute lung injury and the acute respiratory distress syndrome. The Acute Respiratory Distress Syndrome Network. N Engl J Med 2000; 342:1301–8.

2. Amato M, Brochard L, Stewart T, Brower R. Metaanalysis of tidal volume in ARDS. Am J Respir Crit Care Med 2003; 168:612; author reply 612–3.

3. Brower RG, Matthay M, Schoenfeld D. Meta-analysis of acute lung injury and acute respiratory distress syndrome trials. Am J Respir Crit Care Med 2002; 166:1515–7.

4. Brower RG, Rubenfeld G, Thompson BT. Meta-analysis of tidal volumes in ARDS. Am J Respir Crit Care Med 2003; 168:255–6.

5. Deans KJ, Minneci PC, Cui X, Banks SM, Natanson C, Eichacker PQ. Mechanical ventilation in ARDS: One size does not fit all. Crit Care Med 2005; 33:1141–3.

6. Deans KJ, Minneci PC, Eichacker PQ, Natanson C. Defining the standard of care in randomized controlled trials of titrated therapies. Curr Opin Crit Care 2004; 10:579–82.

7. Deans KJ, Minneci PC, Suffredini AF, Danner RL, Hoffman WD, Ciu X, et al. Randomization in clinical trials of titrated therapies: unintended consequences of using fixed treatment protocols. Crit Care Med 2007; 35:1509–16.

8. Eichacker PQ, Banks SM, Natanson C. Meta-analysis of tidal volumes in ARDS (Letter). Am J Respir Crit Care Med 2003; 167:798–800.

9. Eichacker PQ, Gerstenberger EP, Banks SM, Cui X, Natanson C. Meta-analysis of acute lung injury and acute respiratory distress syndrome trials testing low tidal volumes. Am J Respir Crit Care Med 2002; 166:1510–4.

10. Hebert PC, Wells G, Blajchman MA, Marshall J, Martin C, Pagliarello G, et al. A multicenter, randomized, controlled clinical trial of transfusion requirements in critical care. Transfusion Requirements in Critical Care Investigators, Canadian Critical Care Trials Group. N Engl J Med 1999; 340:409–17.

11. Hebert PC, Wells G, Martin C, Tweeddale M, Marshall J, Blajchman M, et al. A Canadian survey of transfusion practices in critically ill patients. Transfusion Requirements in Critical Care Investigators and the Canadian Critical Care Trials Group. Crit Care Med 1998; 26:482–7.

12. Parshuram C, Kavanagh B. Meta-analysis of tidal volumes in ARDS. Am J Respir Crit Care Med 2003; 167:798; author reply 798–800.

13. Consensus conference. Perioperative red blood cell transfusion. Jama 1988; 260:2700–3.

14. van den Berghe G, Wouters P, Weekers F, Verwaest C, Bruyninckx F, Schetz M, et al. Intensive insulin therapy in the critically ill patients. N Engl J Med 2001; 345:1359–67.

15. Brunkhorst FM, Engel C, Bloos F, Meier-Hellmann A,

Ragaller M, Weiler N, et al. Intensive insulin therapy and pentastarch resuscitation in severe sepsis. N Engl J Med 2008; 358:125–39.

16. Van den Berghe G, Wilmer A, Hermans G, Meersseman W, Wouters PJ, Milants I, et al. Intensive insulin therapy in the medical ICU. N Engl J Med 2006; 354:449–61.

17. Bernard GR, Vincent JL, Laterre PF, LaRosa SP, Dhainaut JF, Lopez-Rodriguez A, et al. Efficacy and safety of recombinant human activated protein C for severe sepsis. N Engl J Med 2001; 344:699–709.

18. Eichacker PQ, Natanson C. Recombinant human activated protein C in sepsis: inconsistent trial results, an unclear mechanism of action, and safety concerns resulted in labeling restrictions and the need for phase IV trials. Crit Care Med 2003; 31:S94–6.

19. Mackenzie AF. Activated protein C: do more survive? Intensive Care Med 2005; 31:1624–6.

20. Schumer W. Steroids in the treatment of clinical septic shock. Ann Surg 1976; 184:333–41.

21. Effect of high-dose glucocorticoid therapy on mortality in patients with clinical signs of systemic sepsis. The Veterans Administration Systemic Sepsis Cooperative Study Group. N Engl J Med 1987; 317:659–65.

22. Bone RC, Fisher CJ, Jr., Clemmer TP, Slotman GJ, Metz CA, Balk RA. A controlled clinical trial of high-dose methylprednisolone in the treatment of severe sepsis and septic shock. N Engl J Med 1987; 317:653–8.

23. Lucas CE, Ledgerwood AM. The cardiopulmonary response to massive doses of steroids in patients with septic shock. Arch Surg 1984; 119:537–41.

24. Luce JM, Montgomery AB, Marks JD, Turner J, Metz CA, Murray JF. Ineffectiveness of high-dose methylpred-nisolone in preventing parenchymal lung injury and improving mortality in patients with septic shock. Am Rev Respir Dis 1988; 138:62–8.

25. Sprung CL, Caralis PV, Marcial EH, Pierce M, Gelbard MA, Long WM, et al. The effects of high-dose corticosteroids in patients with septic shock. A prospective, controlled study. N Engl J Med 1984; 311:1137–43.

26. Minneci PC, Deans KJ, Banks SM, Eichacker PQ, Natanson C. Meta-analysis: the effect of steroids on survival and shock during sepsis depends on the dose. Ann Intern Med 2004; 141:47–56.

27. Sweeney DA, Danner RL, Eichacker PQ, Natanson C. Once is not enough: clinical trials in sepsis. Intensive Care Med 2008; 34:1955–60.

28. Bennett IL, Finland M, Hamburger M, Kass EH, Lepper M, Waisbren BA. The effectiveness of hydrocortisone in the management of severe infection. JAMA 1963; 183:462–465.

29. Klastersky J, Cappel R, Debusscher L. Effectiveness of betamethasone in management of severe infections. A double-blind study. N Engl J Med 1971; 284:1248–50.

30. Thompson WL, Gurley HT, Lutz BA, Jackson DL, Kyols LK, Morris IA. Inefficacy of glucocorticoids in shock (double-blind study). Abstr. Clin Res 1976; 24:258A.

31. Prophylactic intravenous administration of standard immune globulin as compared with core-lipopolysac-charide immune globulin in patients at high risk of postsurgical infection. The Intravenous Immunoglobulin Collaborative Study Group. N Engl J Med 1992; 327:234–40.

32. Treatment of severe infectious purpura in children with human plasma from donors immunized with Escherichia coli J5: a prospective double-blind study. J5 study Group. J Infect Dis 1992; 165:695–701.

33. Baumgartner JD, Glauser MP, McCutchan JA, Ziegler EJ, van Melle G, Klauber MR, et al. Prevention of gram-negative shock and death in surgical patients by antibody to endotoxin core glycolipid. Lancet 1985; 2:59–63.

34. Bone RC, Balk RA, Fein AM, Perl TM, Wenzel RP, Reines HD, et al. A second large controlled clinical study of E5, a monoclonal antibody to endotoxin: results of a prospective, multicenter, randomized, controlled trial. The E5 Sepsis Study Group. Crit Care Med 1995; 23:994–1006.

35. Calandra T, Glauser MP, Schellekens J, Verhoef J. Treatment of gram-negative septic shock with human IgG antibody to Escherichia coli J5: a prospective, double-blind, randomized trial. J Infect Dis 1988; 158:312–9.

36. Greenman RL, Schein RM, Martin MA, Wenzel RP, MacIntyre NR, Emmanuel G, et al. A controlled clinical trial of E5 murine monoclonal IgM antibody to endotoxin in the treatment of gram-negative sepsis. The XOMA Sepsis Study Group. Jama 1991; 266:1097–102.

37. McCloskey RV, Straube RC, Sanders C, Smith SM, Smith CR. Treatment of septic shock with human monoclonal antibody HA-1A. A randomized, double-blind, placebo-controlled trial. CHESS Trial Study Group. Ann Intern Med 1994; 121:1–5.

38. McCutchan JA, Wolf JL, Ziegler EJ, Braude AI. Ineffective-ness of single-dose human antiserum to core glycolipid (E. coli J5) for prophylaxis of bacteremic, gram-negative infections in patients with prolonged neutropenia. Schweiz Med Wochenschr 1983; 14:40–45.

39. Ziegler EJ, Fisher CJ, Jr., Sprung CL, Straube RC, Sadoff JC, Foulke GE, et al. Treatment of gram-negative bacteremia and septic shock with HA-1A human monoclonal antibody against endotoxin. A randomized, double-blind, placebo-controlled trial. The HA-1A Sepsis Study Group. N Engl J Med 1991; 324:429–36.

40. Ziegler EJ, McCutchan JA, Fierer J, Glauser MP, Sadoff JC, Douglas H, et al. Treatment of gram-negative bacteremia and shock with human antiserum to a mutant Escherichia coli. N Engl J Med 1982; 307:1225–30.

41. Fisher CJ, Jr., Dhainaut JF, Opal SM, Pribble JP, Balk RA, Slotman GJ, et al. Recombinant human interleukin 1

receptor antagonist in the treatment of patients with sepsis syndrome. Results from a randomized, double-blind, placebo-controlled trial. Phase III rhIL-1ra Sepsis Syndrome Study Group. Jama 1994; 271:1836–43.

42. Fisher CJ, Jr., Slotman GJ, Opal SM, Pribble JP, Bone RC, Emmanuel G, et al. Initial evaluation of human recombinant interleukin-1 receptor antagonist in the treatment of sepsis syndrome: a randomized, open- label, placebo-controlled multicenter trial. The IL-1RA Sepsis Syndrome Study Group. Crit Care Med 1994; 22:12–21.

43. Opal SM, Fisher CJ, Jr., Dhainaut JF, Vincent JL, Brase R, Lowry SF, et al. Confirmatory interleukin-1 receptor antagonist trial in severe sepsis: a phase III, randomized, double-blind, placebo-controlled, multicenter trial. The Interleukin-1 Receptor Antagonist Sepsis Investigator Group. Crit Care Med 1997; 25:1115–24.

44. Abraham E, Laterre PF, Garg R, Levy H, Talwar D, Trzaskoma BL, et al. Drotrecogin alfa (activated) for adults with severe sepsis and a low risk of death. N Engl J Med 2005; 353:1332–41.

45. Bernard GR, Ely EW, Wright TJ, Fraiz J, Stasek JE, Jr., Russell JA, et al. Safety and dose relationship of recombinant human activated protein C for coagulopathy in severe sepsis. Crit Care Med 2001; 29:2051–9.

46. Nadel S, Goldstein B, Williams MD, Dalton H, Peters M, Macias WL, et al. Drotrecogin alfa (activated) in children with severe sepsis: a multicentre phase III randomised controlled trial. Lancet 2007; 369:836–43.

47. Gardlund B. Activated protein C (Xigris) treatment in sepsis: a drug in trouble. Acta Anaesthesiol Scand 2006; 50:907–10.

48. Eichacker PQ, Natanson C. Increasing evidence that the risks of rhAPC may outweigh its benefits. Intensive Care Med 2007; 33:396–9.

49. Finfer S, Ranieri VM, Thompson BT, Barie PS, Dhainaut JF, Douglas IS, et al. Design, conduct, analysis and reporting of a multi-national placebo-controlled trial of activated protein C for persistent septic shock. Intensive Care Med 2008; 34:1935–47.

50. Petrucci N, Iacovelli W. Ventilation with smaller tidal volumes: a quantitative systematic review of randomized controlled trials. Anesth Analg 2004; 99:193–200.

51. Brochard L, Roudot-Thoraval F, Roupie E, Delclaux C, Chastre J, Fernandez-Mondejar E, et al. Tidal volume reduction for prevention of ventilator-induced lung injury in acute respiratory distress syndrome. The Multicenter Trail Group on Tidal Volume reduction in ARDS. Am J Respir Crit Care Med 1998; 158:1831–8.

52. Brower RG, Shanholtz CB, Fessler HE, Shade DM, White P, Jr., Wiener CM, et al. Prospective, randomized, controlled clinical trial comparing traditional versus reduced tidal volume ventilation in acute respiratory distress syndrome patients. Crit Care Med 1999; 27:1492–8.

53. Stewart TE, Meade MO, Cook DJ, Granton JT, Hodder RV, Lapinsky SE, et al. Evaluation of a ventilation strategy to prevent barotrauma in patients at high risk for acute respiratory distress syndrome. Pressure- and Volume-Limited Ventilation Strategy Group. N Engl J Med 1998; 338:355–61.

54. Amato MB, Barbas CS, Medeiros DM, Magaldi RB, Schettino GP, Lorenzi-Filho G, et al. Effect of a protective-ventilation strategy on mortality in the acute respiratory distress syndrome. N Engl J Med 1998; 338:347–54.

55. Minneci PC, Deans KJ, Banks SM, Natanson C, Eichacker PQ. A Critical Review of Randomized Controlled Trials of Tidal Volume Reduction During ARDS. In: Dreyfuss D, Hubmayr RD, Saumon G, eds. Ventilator Induced Lung Injury. New York: Marcel Dekker, Inc.; 2006:519–536.

J. Ethical issues

Christiane Druml

Protecting the patients, supporting the investigators, transparency for the public – The role of research ethics committees

Introduction

Without medical research there would be no advances in medicine. Many treatments we rely on today would not have been developed without clinical research. Competence of physicians can only be maintained by continually challenging medical practice. Even if physicians do not do research themselves they are depending on others who are engaged in research. Physicians are required to learn continually by obtaining information through medical journals, through medical congresses and other professional programmes. They are obliged to be able to interpret results of published clinical trials in order to apply them to their patients. They are also required to know about the structure and methodology of clinical research and should be familiar with institutions integrated in the research process.

Historical aspects

It is now more than 30 years that ethics committees have been institutionalised as an integral part of clinical research through the first amendment of the Declaration of Helsinki, adopted in Tokyo 1975 [1]. The vote of an ethics committee, which was originally just an opinion or advice

given by the peers of the investigator, without any legal consequences, now has – many years later – a defined legal status. Today, no clinical research project could be started, nor published in a good scientific journal, without the positive vote of an ethics committee.

The history of the protection of persons involved in clinical research started after World War II as a result of the doctors' trial with the formulation of the Nuremberg Code in the year 1947 [2]. It stated as a prerequisite for human experiments that nobody could be included in a clinical research project without his clearly expressed informed consent. The World Medical Association (WMA) was also established in 1947, the year the Nuremberg Code was written. Aware of the problems and pitfalls of medical research involving human subjects, the WMA established a set of principles regarding clinical research: the Declaration of Helsinki. The Declaration still of today is the most important document regulating clinical research. While it is not a law, but a document which is regarded as "soft law" without strict legal value, it constitutes an important statement for physicians engaged in clinical research.

The Declaration of Helsinki was revised in 1975, 1983, 1989, 1996, 2000 and 2008.

The amendment which is most important for the research community is the revision of 1975, when the involvement of ethics committees was introduced. Since then, every research proposal involving human subjects has to be submitted for review and approval to a committee that is independent of the investigator and sponsor.

Bioethics committees, research ethics committees and clinical ethics committees

There are three types of ethics committees, each of them with a clearly defined role:

Bioethics committees are bodies which are established to advise a government, a parliament or another legislative or political body from an ethical point of view on all social, scientific and legal issues arising from the scientific developments in the life sciences. This includes in particular the submission of recommendations for practical use and suggestions for enacting legal provisions as well as the preparation of expert opinions on specific issues. Such issues are: stem cell research, nanotechnology, end-of-life issues and others. Bioethics committees consist of experts in the medical field, the life sciences, genetics, philosophy, theology and law (see http://www.bka.gv.at/bioethics). The institution of such bioethics committees is relatively new. President Mitterand established the French National Bioethics Committee (CCNE) in the year 1983. It is one of the oldest in existence. Other countries established similar committees later, e.g. the Italian National Bioethics Committee in 1988, the Portuguese National Council of Ethics for the Life Sciences in 1990, the Belgian Advisory Committee on Bioethics in 1993 and the Austrian Bioethics Commission at the Federal Chancellery in 2001. Typically, bioethics committees would not discuss or approve individual research projects.

Research ethics committees are – as mentioned above – founded on the basis of the Tokyo amendment of the Declaration of Heldsinki dated 1975. The name "Ethics Committee" is the term most widely used, but those bodies are also known under the name "Institutional Review Board" (IRB) or "Human Subjects Committee" or, as in France, "Comité de Protection des Personnes" (CPP). In Europe, the establishment of these committees by European Union member states has been a mandatory step in the implementation of clinical drug trial governance.

Clinical ethics committees are the third type of ethics committee. They are the youngest of these three institutions. They are interdisciplinary teams in a hospital dealing with specific problems of individual patients which arise in medical practice and are too complex to deal with for a single treating physician. The main concern is to provide support on ethical issues like end-of-life issues, allocation of therapies or organs and others.

Laws and guidelines – European legislation

Although the European Clinical Trials Directive 2001/20/EC[1] was only aimed at research projects concerning medicinal products, some countries have – while transforming it into national law – established a regulatory framework in such a way that it also applies to other types of clinical studies, such as studies with medical devices, studies involving physical interventions, psychological questionnaires, the use of human biological material or research on sensitive data [3].

The European Clinical Trials Directive entered into force with the goal to "simplify and harmonise" European research including the ethical review of clinical research. Specific legal requirements have been in effect in the EU member states since 2004, among them the so-called "single-opinion procedure" for multi-centre clinical research projects. "Single opinion" means that for multi-centre clinical trials the positive vote of one ethics committee per European member state is sufficient – there is no need to submit the protocol for review and approval to each single ethics committee concerned.

The goal of this European directive was to enhance the competitiveness of European research, especially in comparison with clinical research in the United States. However, as ethical issues are at the EU member states' own discretion, the systems still differ widely throughout Europe. Member states like France or the United King-

---

1   Directive 2001/20/EC of the European Parliament and of the Council of 4 April 2001 on the approximation of laws, regulations and administrative provisions of the Member States relating to the implementation of good clinical practice in the conduct of clinical trials on medicinal products for human use

dom, where a specific system of provision of "one single opinion" already existed before the European directive became effective, have less problems to comply with the law than member states where ethical review had been predominantly local [4]. In these countries the ethics committees did not like the idea of giving up influence and power and argued that they needed to "protect their patients".

The European project ICREL – Impact on Clinical Research of European Legislation [5], which was funded to *measure and analyse* the direct and indirect *impact of the Clinical Trials Directive 2001/20/EC* and related legislations in the European Union on all categories of clinical research and on the different stakeholders, i.e. commercial and non-commercial sponsors, ethics committees and competent authorities, showed in its final conference on the results its survey that further guidance is needed. This survey was conducted in 2008 and provided metrics – objective arguments – to adapt the current legislation. It demonstrated that in order to improve Europe's attractiveness and competitiveness for clinical research a better balance of several issues is needed. The highest level of patient protection, and optimal information for sponsors, competent authorities, ethics committees and academic investigators regarding multi-centre national and international research projects can only be achieved when changes in the regulatory framework for clinical research are considered.

Function of ethics committees – Review of clinical research protocols

The function of ethics committees is a very important one: They have been established to prevent misconduct in clinical research and their prime obligation is to protect clinical trial participants in research projects. But another, very important objective is to support the investigator and his/her investigational plan, and thirdly, to give public assurance that clinical research is conducted in a transparent and ethical way. So investigators should not perceive the paperwork, time and effort required for submission as an annoying plight, but as support and a further step in the field of research integrity.

Ethics committees have to evaluate, among other things, the relevance of the trial, the design of the trial in terms of its aims, scientific validity and risk/benefit ratio, the suitability of the researcher, available facilities and supporting staff, recruitment of trial subjects and methods of obtaining informed consent.

Number of ethics committees in Europe, membership and procedures

Although ethics committees are regulated by European legislation, they still constitute a very heterogeneous issue in Europe, as highlighted by the following examples:

The number of ethics committees which are institutionalised in the different European member states varies greatly. While countries like Germany with a population of 82 million has 53 ethics committees, Italy with roughly 62 million inhabitants has more than 170 ethics committees, or even more than 900, according to another source. Belgium, a comparatively small country with 11 million inhabitants, counted until September 2006 the astonishing number of 215 ethics committees. Austria with a population of 8 million has 27 ethics committees, Sweden with 9 million inhabitants has 8 ethics committees [6] (see Tab. 1).

Another area of divergence is the number of members: While France requires 28 members, 14 lay members and 14 experts, the number required in Germany is 7–15 depending on state legislation or university policy. In Poland, where there are 52 ethics committees and one appeal committee at the Ministry of Health, the required number of members is 11–15. In Sweden there are 16 members including the chair. It is required that the chair is an acting or retired judge. 5 members have to represent public interests. In Denmark the number of members is 7–15, 4 of whom must be lay members. In Portugal there are institutional research ethics committees which have 7 members, and one national research ethics committee which is responsible for "human medicines" and has 21 members, a president appointed by the prime minister, a vice-president and five members representing the government and nine members representing other institutions.

Tab. 1 Number of ethics committees in European Union member states

Country	Inhabitants in 1,000[*]	Number of ethics committees[+]	Number of ethics committees (including local ethics committees)
Austria	8,356.7	27	
Belgium	10,741.0	35	215
Bulgaria	7,602.1	103	
Czech Republik	10,474.6	9	> 100
Cyprus	801.6	1	
Denmark	5,519.3	8	
Estonia	1,340.3	2	
Finland	5,325.1	25	
France	64,105.1	40	
Germany	82,062.2	53	
Greece	11,262.5	1	
Hungary	10,029.9	1	
Ireland	4,517.8	13	40
Italy	60,090.4	264	> 900
Latvia	2,261.1	5	
Lithuania	3,350.4	2	
Luxembourg	491.7	1	
Malta	412.6	1	
Netherlands	16,481.1	31	
Poland	38,130.3	55	
Portugal	10,631.8	1	
Romania	21,496.7	1	
Slovakia	5,411.1	9	89
Slovenia	2,053.4	1	
Spain	45,853.0	136	
Sweden	9,259.0	8	
United Kingdom	61,612.3	126	

[*Source: Eurostat. News release 179/2008–15 December 2008 – http://epp.eurostat.ec.europa.eu]
[+Source: EFGCP Ethics Working Party, Subgroup on Ethics Committees Reviewing Investigational Medicinal Products within the European Union: The Procedure for the Ethical Review of Protocols for Clinical Research Projects in the European Union, Int. J. Pharm. Med.2007, 21:1–113 update 2008 – http://www.efgcp.be/html.asp?what=efgcpreport.htm&L1=5&L2=1#report]

Spain has institutionalised, so-called "reference committees" which are authorised by the regional governments. A reference committee has to deal with the other "involved committees" if the application is submitted for a multi-centre trial. This means that all involved committees have to provide comments on the protocol. The reference committee is only entitled to give its "single opinion" after having considered all opinions from the other involved committees.

Germany also introduced a regulation where the "competent" committee has to review the application, but in the case of multi-centre clinical trials this has to be achieved in cooperation with all the other involved committees, called "local" committees, who have to assess the qualification of the investigator and suitability of the study sites. The local committees can also comment on the protocol, but their opinion is only relevant insofar as the local situation is concerned.

In France the situation is much less complicated: The sponsor submits the application to the ethics committee of the region where the coordinating investigator is based. This opinion is valid for all other sites without the cooperation of other local committees. In Hungary, too, the situation is uncomplicated as there is only one research ethics committee at the National Institute of Pharmacy (NIP).

Composition of ethics committees

Research ethics committees in Europe are typically composed of scientists and lay members: physicians, members from the nursing profession, members with legal expertise, a pharmacist, someone with ethical expertise or a philosophical or theological background, a statistician, somebody from a representative patient organisation, and others. Their main obligation is to review research protocols for clinical trials within a certain timeframe. In many European member states the review of a research protocol by the ethics committee is an integral part of the review of this protocol by the competent authority. Thus, ethics committees play an even greater role in the evaluation of clinical research.

Training of ethics committee members and clinical investigators

There is no formal requirement instituted for initial and ongoing training and education for ethics committee members throughout Europe. Training is necessary in issues like ethics and laws, methods of clinical research and the current standard operating procedures of the spe-

cific ethics committees in regard to the meetings and to the obligations ethics committee members have in order to observe their duties. Members are chosen for their specific expertise in a certain field like nursing or law, or being a physician. But the other qualifications regarding clinical research are neither required nor taught. There are practically only rudimentary requirements for training in the individual European member states. Only the United Kingdom has raised awareness and implemented regulations (see http://www.nres.npsa.nhs.uk). This definitely needs to be changed, as there are more and more training requirements clinical investigators need to meet to fulfil their role in an ethical way. There is no reason why ethics committee members should not bet put under the same scrutiny as clinical investigators [7].

Conflicts of interest

Investigators are required to announce any conflict of interest concerning an application. More and more start-up companies are founded from within university hospitals and other institutions and an increasing number of investigators are shareholders in such companies and thus have financial and academic conflicts of interests.

Any conflict of interest should not only be announced in regard to the application procedure to the ethics committee, but also to the participants of the clinical trial, be they patients or healthy volunteers. Any participant should have the possibility to decide freely if the expectations connected to participation are disproportionate to the possible results and benefits of the clinical trial. It is a crucial role of ethics committees to observe whether transparency is provided regarding any conflicts of interest.

Remuneration of ethics committee members

Except for certain ethics committees where the members are compensated with a small attendance fee, members generally work on an honorary basis. This means that they are not paid for their work, a situation which was acceptable 30 years ago, when the submission of clinical research projects was scarce and thus the time spent for the review was limited. But now, in 2009, the workload is heavy – ethics committees usually meet monthly and have to review, discuss and vote on a great number of protocols. It is not acceptable anymore to ask for "free" assessment of the submitted applications. If one counts the preparation time for a meeting, reading the protocols, the external reviews, the informed consent documents and all the other pertaining documents, many hours of uncompensated work are spent by highly qualified professionals.

Gender issues

Another issue of importance is the gender issue. This issue applies in two ways: the representation of women among the members of an ethics committee – committees are constituted of "men and women", but there is no reference to a percentage or quota; and the recommendation for the inclusion of women in clinical research projects [8].

Ethics committees should have guidelines describing the requirement for the inclusion of women in biomedical and behavioural research involving human subjects including clinical drug trials. Since a primary aim of clinical research is to provide scientific evidence leading to an improved standard of care and/or a change in health policy, it is important to determine whether the intervention or therapy being studied affects women or men differently [9].

If a research project is submitted for review, inclusion of both genders has to be provided. If only men are to be included and the studied therapy or intervention also affects women, the protocol has to give evidence of the reasons. Financial reasons should not be accepted (e.g. a greater number of included patients needed due to hormonal differences in the feminine cycle in a protocol in the field of endocrinology than if the inclusion criteria apply only to men).

Vulnerable populations

The consideration of the subject's autonomy is a cornerstone of medical research, autonomy being a value which is inextricably linked to the notion of research ethics and its principles. Subjects act autonomously when they are capable acting with self-determination, but not every human being is in a state or situation to execute this self-determination. Such human beings are called "vulnerable" and need to be under special protection, they have to be protected from any forms of exploitation or abuse.

Vulnerability is not absolute: While some groups of persons can always be considered vulnerable due to their status (e.g. children), others are vulnerable only due to the specific situation: persons can be vulnerable in a given situation, but not in another situation – for example, a student is a vulnerable person in regard to the hierarchical position in which he/she is in in relation to the teacher. This student might consent to participate in a proposed research project led by his/her teacher because the student might expect a reward for participating or harm if refusing to participate. In another setting, outside the school or university, this same student is not regarded as vulnerable.

Which groups are considered vulnerable? There are vulnerabilities in various contexts, like persons in hierarchical situations: students, employees, members of the armed forces, members of the police (see box below).

Other persons are vulnerable in another context

- *Children are always considered to be vulnerable, as they are not legally entitled to decide for themselves*
- *Women are still underprivileged in many societies, therefore they need to be placed under special protection*
- *Elderly and very old persons*
- *Temporarily incapacitated persons (emergency situations and intensive care)*
- *Mentally ill persons*
- *Immigrants*
- *Asylum seekers*
- *Nomads*
- *Ethnic and racial minorities*
- *Unemployed persons*
- *Homeless persons*
- *Prisoners*
- *Illiterate persons*

These persons are not generally excluded from participation in a research project, as this would also mean to exclude them from any potential benefit of research and violate the principle of justice. But there are certain requirements which have to be met in order to avoid exploitation and harm. It has to be assured that those persons consent in a free way without any outside pressure. Ethics committees must execute prudence while reviewing such protocols.

Temporarily incapacitated patients – Emergencies and intensive care research

As stated above, temporarily incapacitated patients are also considered vulnerable and are under special protection. What is the problem regarding these patients? As they are incapacitated due to an emergency situation – e.g. myocardial infarction, stroke, sepsis – they cannot give informed consent personally as they are unconscious or heavily sedated. Due to the nature of their condition, which was not foreseeable, they have no legal representative who can decide for them.

The situation differs widely throughout Europe as the Clinical Trials Directive has not regulated it in a pan-European way, but has referred to the national legislation of the European member states. The national legal situation has to be observed in regard to their inclusion in a clinical trial [10].

There are three possible solutions in regard to inclusion in a clinical trial:

1. The rapid nomination of a legal representative who gives his consent to the inclusion of the patient.
2. The possibility provided for by law for surrogate consent.
3. A "waiver of consent" as stated in the national law [11]. A waiver of consent means that if certain requirements are fulfilled, the patient can be included in the clinical trial without his/her own or legal representative's consent.

The requirements can be the following:
- The research is essential to validate data obtained in clinical trials on persons able to give consent or by other research methods.
- The research has to relate directly to the life-threatening or debilitating clinical condition from which the incapacitated adult suffers

- The risk threshold and the degree of distress shall be specially defined and constantly monitored.
- The protocol has been reviewed by an ethics committee with expertise in the field of emergency/intensive care research.
- The participation of the patient has to be in accordance with his/her presumed will
- The research project is necessary to "save the life, restore the health or ease the pain" of the patient.
- The prospect of a potential direct benefit for the patient has to be given. The interest of the patient always prevails over those of science and society.
- If the patients regain consciousness, it is mandatory to obtain informed consent if the clinical trial continues.

It is important to note that all such obtained data have to be included in the analysis according to the intention-to-treat principle as it counts all events in all randomised patients. It would lead to a tremendous bias and possibly give rise to incorrect results, even to the manipulation of "unwanted results" if data can be withdrawn after a treatment has been administered, especially in a patient group suffering from life-threatening diseases [12].

There is no possibility of doing research which includes temporarily incapacitated patients if the national law has not adopted specific legislation (e.g. in Finland). However, this is the worst-case scenario, because it excludes patients who are maximally dependent on novel therapies from any benefits of research.

There are still societies that perceive patients to have the "highest degree of protection" by not being included in research projects. But is it ethical to refuse to do intensive care research ("protecting the patients") and at the same time accept the results of clinical trials in this population which have been achieved in other countries?

Conclusion

Much has been achieved in the past years; ethics committees have not only been established in Europe or the United States, but also in other countries around the world where clinical research is being conducted. Apart from the World Medical Association's Declaration of Helsinki, other organisations operating internationally, such as the World Health Organisation (WHO), the United Nations Educational, Scientific and Cultural Organisation (UNESCO), the Council for International Organizations of Medical Sciences (CIOMS) and others, have issued guidelines to structure and regulate clinical research also in those countries where no specific laws are in place, so that the research projects can be conducted in a standardised way and investigators and ethics committee members can be trained. This is important as in developing countries the facilitation and promotion of clinical research projects is also necessary for the population to obtain the care for many diseases and conditions that they would not receive otherwise. Furthermore, regulation is important as many research projects are collaborations between industrialised countries and developing countries. Ethical review of those projects is required in each participating country and has to be dealt with in a standardised and accepted way to avoid exploitation of the poorer populations.

Ethics committees play an important role in guaranteeing transparency in clinical research. They are stakeholders in the conduct of clinical research according to the existing Good Clinical Practice Guidelines. In the future, they will have an even greater role to play in regard to scientific integrity and will re-evaluate the way in which clinical research projects are conducted, from submission to the publishing of the final report [13].

The author

Christiane Druml, LLD
    Ethics Committee of the Medical University
    of Vienna
    Borschkegasse 8 b
    1090 Vienna, Austria
    E-mail: christiane.druml@meduniwien.ac.at

References

1. World Medical Association (2002) World Medical Association Declaration of Helsinki: Recommendations Guiding Physicians in Biomedical Research Involving Human Subjects. Adopted by the 18th World Medical Assembly Helsinki, Finland, June 1964. Amended by the 29th World Medical assembly, Tokyo, Japan, October 1975; 35th World Medical Assembly, Venice, Italy, October 1983; 41st World Medical Assembly, Hongkong; 48th General Assembly, September 1989, Somerset West, Republic of South Africa, October 1996 and the 52nd General Assembly, Edinburgh, Scotland, October 2000 and the Note of Clarification on Paragraph 29 added by the World Medical Association General Assembly, Washington 2002
2. Lemaire F. The Nuremberg doctors' trial: the 60th anniversary. Intensive Care Med. 2006 Dec;32(12):2049–52
3. Sweden: The Act on Ethics Review of Research Involving Humans (2003:460)
4. Druml C, Singer EA, Wolzt M. Report of the 1st meeting of the "Vienna Initiative to Save European Academic Research (VISEAR)". Wien Klin Wochenschr. 2006 Apr;118(5–6):Suppl 1–12.
5. ICREL – Impact on Clinical Research of European Legislation, http://www.efgcp.be/icrel
6. EFGCP Ethics Working Party, Subgroup on Ethics Committees Reviewing Investigational Medicinal Products within the European Union: The Procedure for the Ethical Review of Protocols for Clinical Research Projects in the European Union, Int. J. Pharm. Med.2007, 21:1–113 update 2008 – (http://www.efgcp.be/html. asp?what=efgcpreport.htm&L1=5&L2=1#report)
7. Davies H, Wells F, Druml C. How can we provide effective training for research ethics committees members? A European assessment. J Med Ethics. 2008 Apr;34
8. Recommendations with Gender Reference for Ethics committees and Clinical Studies; Opinion of the Bioethics Commission at the Federal Chancellery, Austria (Nov 15, 2008) http://www.bundeskanzleramt.at/ DocView.axd?CobId=33153
9. Guidelines regarding the inclusion of women in clinical research, Ethics Committee of the Medical University of Vienna, http://www.meduniwien.ac.at/ethik
10. Lemaire F, Bion J, Blanco J, Damas P, Druml C, Falke K, Kesecioglu J, Larsson A, Mancebo J, Matamis D, Pesenti A, Pimentel J, Ranieri M. ESICM Task Force on Legislation Affecting Clinical Research in the Critically Ill Patient. The European Union Directive on Clinical Research: present status of implementation in EU member states' legislations with regard to the incompetent patient. Intensive Care Med. 2005 Mar;31(3):476–9. Epub 2005 Feb 15.
11. Druml C.Informed consent of incapable (ICU) patients in Europe: existing laws and the EU Directive.Curr Opin Crit Care. 2004
12. EMEA European Medicines Agency, ICH Topic E 9. Statistical Principles for Clinical Trials
13. Druml C. 30 Jahre Ethikkommission der Medizinischen Universität Wien: Garant für integre und transparente Forschung. Wien, Klin Wochenschr. 2008;120(21–22):645–6

Jose-Maria Dominguez-Roldan, Claudio Garcia-Alfaro and
Fernando Hernandez-Hazañas

Performing safe and timely identification of the organ donor

Introduction

One of the most important and difficult topics in the management of an intensive care unit (ICU) is the accurate and optimal definition of the admission and discharge criteria of patients. It is well known that ICU care is costly, and consequently ICU beds are a limited resource. An appropriate and rational utilisation of ICU resources is required.

The recovery of health and/or the limiting of risk for patients are the main goals of ICUs. So, from a general point of view, patients with severe and reversible medical or surgical events, with reasonable expectations of recovery of their health, are the "standard clients" of an intensive care unit. Patients without critical illnesses but with high risks derived from their events can also be considered potential beneficiaries of ICU care. In these patients, preventive ICU care endeavors to decrease these risks. The relatives of patients admitted to the ICU could be also considered second-level beneficiaries of the activities of ICUs.

With the development of organ donation and transplantation programmes, new possibilities of survival and improvement of quality of life are offered to patients with organ failure. Nowadays, renal, heart, liver and lung transplantation are successful programmes, fulfilling expectations of patients without other possibilities of survival and/or improvement in their quality of life. However, the achievement of these therapies requires the commitment of successful organ donation programmes. At present, the main source of organs for transplantation are from brain-dead patients.

Intensive care units not only play an important role in patient care after transplant surgery, but are also the cornerstone of the organ donation process. The diagnosis of brain death can be only performed in patients with mechanical ventilation and cardiocirculatory support. Organ retrieval for transplantation can also occur in the patient after cardiac death but the majority of organ retrievals still occur from brain-dead donors. Consequently, ICUs have a significant role and responsibility in organ procurement for transplantation. Conversely, recipients of transplants can also be considered beneficiaries of the ICU [1].

ICUs are at a crossroads, balancing the administration of expensive resources with the decisions of admitting patients to the ICU or not admitting them, as well as fulfilling their responsibility as intensivists in the organ procurement programme because of the potential benefit to recipients.

Criteria for admission of patients to the ICU. Has it influenced the rate of organ donation?

From a theoretical point of view, ICU admission criteria should select patients who are likely to benefit from ICU treatment and should exclude patients in which ICU care would provide no greater benefit than conventional care in the ward. This would support the theory that patients "too well to benefit from ICU care" and patients "too sick to benefit" should not be admitted to the ICU because of the inability to provide effective critical care services.

The identification of the patient population who are "too well" or "too sick" to benefit, is not an easy task. The definition of specific criteria of "substantial benefit of admission to the ICU" must take into consideration: the physiological state, co-morbidities and the reflection of what is a "reasonable result" of the medical process, including the grade of therapeutic intensity necessary for the recovery of the patient and the available resources.

The classification of patients into categories (according to the severity of the illness and the anticipated maximum therapeutic level in the ICU) can be a valuable strategy during the ICU admission process. A useful tool for this purpose is the prioritisation model proposed by the American Society of Critical Care Medicine, which classifies patients into five different categories of therapeutic intensity and different goals. The subgroup 4B of this model includes "patients with terminal and irreversible illness facing imminent death" (too sick to benefit from ICU care). For example: severe irreversible brain damage; irreversible multi-organ system failure; metastatic cancer unresponsive to chemotherapy and/or radiation therapy (unless the patient is on a specific treatment protocol); patients with decision-making capacity who decline intensive care and/or invasive monitoring and who receive comfort care only; braindead non-organ donors; patients in a persistent vegetative state and patients who are permanently unconscious, etc.

It is not clear in most protocols for ICU admission what is the right procedure for patients with an acute severe neurological state who are not brain-dead but have a small chance of survival. These patients, with ominous prognoses, may evolve to brain death, or may develop a chronic and severe disability. Once patients are identified as potential beneficiaries of the medical treatment of the ICU, the rejection of ICU admission or the admission for the possibility of becoming organ donors are the only options.

From an ethical point of view, the admission of patients to the ICU for the purpose of organ donation supports the ethical principle of beneficence, because it is looking for an additional beneficence for potential organ donors. However, the admission of those patients does not strictly fulfil the ethical principles of autonomy, beneficence (of the patient) and non-maleficence (that must rule the management of the ethical rights of patients) and distributive justice (an ICU with a non-brain-dead patient could limit the possibility of admission of other patients). The admission of an incompetent patient to an intensive care unit and the use of ventilator support, intensive therapy and monitoring with the only goal of benefiting other patients is a relevant change in the manner of performing medicine that has come after the development of ICUs and solid organ transplantation programs. However, there is an intense debate about the appropriateness of such action. While some intensivists are reluctant to consider this kind of admission based on ethical arguments, others consider it a responsibility of ICU doctors. In an Australian survey regarding the opinion of doctors on this topic more than 60 % of intensivists who responded to a questionnaire [2] (on attitudes towards organ donation) agreed that admitting severely brain-injured patients to the ICU for the sole purpose of organ donation was acceptable. In an observational study developed in a neurological ICU consisting of 621 consecutive patients [3], analysis of the repercussions of admitting patients "too ill to benefit from ICU" regarding mortality and organ donation showed that global mortality (15.45 %; 10.14 % due to brain death) decreased 2 % when "4B" category patients were excluded. The admission of this group of patients provided 25 % more organ donors compared to the hypothetical situation of not admitting 4B category patients to the ICU. This means that a relevant number of recipient patients benefited from the programme in which 4B patients were admitted.

The controversy between the two options (admission/no admission) is still an open debate. The elective ventilation and transfer of selected patients with serious and progressive neurological deterioration from general wards or emergency departments to intensive care units, before confirming brain death (namely, the admission of "4B" category patients with severe neurological damage and high risk of brain death), versus the potential possibility of retrieving transplantable organs, could collide with several ethical and medical values:

- Is the admission of this patient an appropriate action of intensivists considering there is a very low probability of health recovery? The dilemma is that there is a difference between the diagnosis of death and the timing of death.
- If a patient is still not intubated and mechanically ventilated and there are sensible reasons for not intubating according to their medical prognosis, is it ethical to intubate them based only on the potential of organ donation? Should this procedure be limited to individuals who have given prior informed consent not only for organ donation but also for mechanical ventilation?
- Should doctors seek the agreement of relatives for the initiation of artificial ventilation to preserve organ function before death has been diagnosed? What information should the family receive regarding the reasons for admission to the ICU?
- Who should assume the economic cost generated after the ICU admission of these "potential donor" patients?
- In case brain death does not occur in the intensive care unit, must the patient be transferred back to the ward?
- How can one consider, from an ethical point of view, the survival of a patient with a severe disability after admission and management in the ICU when the only reason for admission was potential for donation [4]?
- What would be the right decision if the admission of a patient is requested in a full ICU and the only bed is where an imminent brain death is expected but not fulfilled?

There are many ethical and medical questions with no simple answers that arise with the emergence of these new ethical issues in the ICUs. The balance between real beneficiaries (patients in ICU) and potential beneficiaries (potential organ recipients) must be framed not only by its ethical aspect, but also by its strategic, and economical repercussions.

Dilemmas in the ICU regarding organ donation

- *Admission to ICU of neurological non-brain-dead patients with low risk of benefit from ICU*
- *Withdrawal of treatment in neurological patients*
- *Definition of "potential organ donor"*
- *Initiation of mechanical ventilation in severe non-brain-dead patients that could be potential organ donors*

Withdrawal of treatment in neurocritical patients

When it is not possible to maintain life for long periods without any hope of recovery, the withdrawal of treatment is an issue that must be taken into account in intensive care units. Intensive care medicine usually offers support for organ systems, but it does not necessarily always offer restoration to health. Treatment is withdrawn when death is felt to be inevitable but also when, despite continued treatment, the clinical results (in terms of health recovery) are not proportional to the therapy level (futile therapy).

Treatment withdrawal in neurological patients has specific issues which must be considered. The severe disturbance of consciousness of critical neurological patients frequently makes it difficult to implement the ethical principle of autonomy (one of the basic concepts of ethical practice). In general, patients with acute neurological events often have not manifested their wishes regarding withdrawal of treatment in the ICU. On the contrary, this kind of decision is more common in patients with chronic and progressive neurological medical processes.

A new ethical critical point can occur in neurological patients admitted to the ICU for treatment when the decision to withdraw all life-sustaining therapy (except ventilation and circulatory support) is taken. It is possible that individuals may have made their decision explicit to become donors after death. However, it would be infrequent that this explicit willingness to donate would include neurological withdrawal of treatment with an undetermined time-frame of sustained non-therapeutic ventilation until brain death. This could be a problematic situation, from both an ethical and legal perspective, because it may constitute battery if informed consent is not obtained for this procedure. The withdrawal of treatment in neurological patients [5] will probably involve brain death of the patient and a new ethical element bears discussion: As a consequence of the withdrawal of treatment and subsequent brain death, there will be potential benefits for the organ recipients if donation and transplantation is performed.

The fundamental ethical principles demand that withdrawal of treatment in a neurological patient admitted to the ICU must be based on the willingness of the patient, having expressed such wishes previously, or based on inquiry and discussion with the closest relatives or surrogates. Nevertheless, a new element of controversy is possible: In cases where patients have not previously indicated their wishes regarding donation, and no possibilities, is it ethical to withdraw treatment and maintain circulatory and ventilator support with the aim of potential organ donation? In a global view of the present situation regarding this matter, it can be stated that there is no agreement on it. In those countries where the "opt-in" system of organ donation (where individuals are asked to register their willingness to be a donor after their death) this situation is probably ethically acceptable. It is true that the donation of organs always bears beneficence for other sick persons. Nevertheless, it should not be forgotten that modern ethics in most of the developing countries bestows a superior level on the ethical principle of autonomy than on the principle of beneficence (beneficence to third parties). Conversely, in those countries or medical schools where the "opt-out" system (which means that unless people opt out of the register or family members object, hospitals would be allowed to use their organs for transplantation) for organ donation is practised, the beneficence principle for the person that receives the organ through transplantation would receive a higher ethical value.

Apropos these previous reflections, treatment withdrawal in severe neurological patients must always be based on the current medical evaluation of the clinical situation, plus ethical considerations, and should never be conditioned by the fact that the patient may become a potential organ donor.

The commitment of ICU doctors to organ donation

Organ transplantation programmes today are recognised as a relevant and successful area of modern medicine. Linked to it, organ donation is an essential and relevant field indispensible for the development of transplantation. On the other hand, organ donation is considered an extension of end-of-life care [1–7]. Consequently, intensivists who regularly manage end-of-life care issues must be aware of the relevance of their role in the organ procurement programmes.

Several reasons place the role of the intensivist as one of the key elements in the programmes of organ donation and transplantation. The main reason is that donation of organs from brain-dead patients takes place exclusively in cases where patients with severe cerebral damage are mechanically ventilated and supported as a heart-beating donor. Consequently, organ donation is included as an area of knowledge and scientific activity of critical care medicine. Diagnosis of brain death and donor maintenance are areas of knowledge and expertise of ICU doctors. In addition, there are also other motivations for intensivists to support organ donation:

- The frequent admission of patients with severe liver dysfunction or refractory cardiac failure whose only therapeutic possibility is a liver or heart transplant;
- intensivists' frequent involvement in post-surgical care after transplantation of solid organs (kidney, liver, heart), which has justified the creation of another area of relevant knowledge, such as immunosuppression therapies in the ICU and the treatment of infections by certain opportunistic organisms which occur in these patients.

The commitment of ICU care providers to organ procurement has been directly related to successful organ procurement programmes. In Spain (currently with the highest rate of organ donation) several factors, including the specific role of ICU professionals, could have influenced the high donation rates. The role of the hospital transplant coordinator is also widely accepted as one of the main reasons. Most hospital transplant coordinators are doctors with part of their time dedicated to organ procurement. They are responsible for the process of organ procurement and donation within hospitals. A survey of Spanish transplant coordinators showed that 75.7% of transplant coordinators were doctors with intensive care medicine specialisation, 8.1% were anaesthesiologists and 6.7% nephrologists [8]. The coordination of organ procurement in Spanish hospitals is based on the abovementioned model where the doctor, usually supported by nurses, commonly has an intensive care background. In Spain, the ratio of doctors/nurses in these teams is 86.5/13.5%. The overall team is composed of 52% doctors, 27.7% nurses and others; with 70.3% working part-time and 27% full-time.

A potential conflict of interest has been perceived by some authors regarding the participation of intensivists in the organ procurement and organ donation process. This controversy can be easily refuted because most of the issues concerned (brain death diagnosis, management of brain death, information of the family about the death, etc.) are included in the area of knowledge of intensive care as well as in the training programme for this specialty. On the other hand, to put into question the professionalism and ethical basis of the intensivist makes no sense, mainly because the most relevant parts of end-of-life care (including brain death diagnosis) are extensively described and/or even regulated by guidelines, ethical committees, recommendations and even national legislations. In addition to this, all these ethical doubts can be minimised by the integration into the processes of organ procurement organisations or designated medical specialists not directly related to the patient where organ donation has been requested.

"Potential organ donor"
a controversial concept

The evidence shows that a greater rate of brain death patient diagnosis is directly correlated with a greater number of organ donors, and consequently a greater number of patients that obtain the benefits of the transplantation.

In addition, early identification of potential donors is a crucial element for the optimisation of transplant programme results. The early identification and monitoring of potential organs donors is the major objective for improving transplant results. A proactive attitude in organ donor detection and a decrease in the time between diagnosis of death and organ retrieval would result in the facilitation of the support treatment after brain death and a greater quality of the organs retrieved, as well as a diminished risk of cardiac arrest after the diagnosis of the brain death.

Several strategies have been described to increase the detection of brain-dead patients or patients with a high risk of brain death [9–10] by considering a more efficient method of identifying ward and emergency department patients with severe neurological processes that may be consistent with a high risk of brain death and ICU admission of such patients as potential organ donors.

However, the following of non-brain-dead patients as potential donors or reporting individuals as potential organ donors who are not yet in brain death could create an ethical conflict for some health professionals in the ICU. An impending conflict could appear in this situation: Are the care providers advocates for the patients under their care or the advocacy of the potential organ recipient [11]?

When different strategies of organ procurement organisations are observed, it is evident that there are not only relevant differences in the logistical implementation of tracking potential organ donors, but also significant differences in defining a "potential organ donor".

The Instituto Nacional Central Unico Coordinador de Ablacion e Implante of Argentina (INCUCAI), created a proactive donor detection plan performed by physicians from intensive care units across that country. This programme monitored 9,343 patients admitted to ICUs in a coma (level of consciousness lower than 8 points of the Glasgow Coma Scale). This surveillance showed that 40% of patients died due to cardiac arrest, 30% died after brain death, and 30% were discharged from the ICU. 7% (654 patients) of the whole group of patients were organ donors [12]. In the aforementioned series, the most frequent mechanism of brain damage was gunshot injury, and spontaneous intracerebral haemorrhage.

One of the conclusions of this study was that a surveillance programme of comatose patients is a valuable tool for identifying potential organ donors. However, not all authors agreed on the concept of a "potential organ donor". Some groups used the term "potential organ donor" which applied only to brain-dead persons as, for example in the document "Conditions for Coverage for Organ Procurement Organizations (OPOs); Proposed Rule (Organ Donor Potential means the number of patients whose age is 70 or less meeting death by neurological criteria, based on generally accepted practice parameters for determining brain death, who do not have any of the following clinical indications: ...)" [13] or in the papers of Madsen et al. [14] For other groups [15] the expression "potential donor" referred to patients with confirmed brain death, or likelihood of progression to brain death, with no medical contraindications for organ donation. These authors expanded the concept of "potential donor" to patients who either had features consistent with brain death (but in whom brain death was not formally diagnosed) or in whom brain death would most likely have developed in the first three days of admission to the ICU if airway support and oxygenation was continued.

Other arguable scenarios include the fact that in some countries and states, the legislation recommends or even stipulates that all ICUs/hospitals must notify the transplant agencies/organ procurement organisations or transplant coordinator teams regarding all deaths and "impending" deaths for all patients younger than the age limit in the management protocols of potential donors. The positive side of these regulations is that the purpose of this notification is screening for possible organ donation and consequently increasing the number of transplants. However, besides the previously mentioned ethical problem of advocacy for patients admitted to the ICU versus advocacy for potential organ recipients there also exists a relevant consideration: the definition of "imminent death". This notification involves the provision of information about these patients to an external agency, including their name, age, diagnoses and risk factors for blood-borne infections.

Identification of neurological patients "too sick to benefit from ICU therapy"

The identification of those patients who can benefit from ICU admission is parallel to the identification of patients "too ill" to benefit from ICU therapy. It is for this reason that it is advisable to use an objective system of evaluation to identify and evaluate the patients who must be managed in the ICU.

Evaluation of the severity of acute neurological patients before accepting them for treatment in the ICU must take into account not only their probability of survival of the event after discharge from the ICU but also the probability of severe permanent neurological damage with lasting severe disability. Frequently, patients with severe neurological diseases are not conscious, which means that the decision for ICU admission is based on expectations of survival and the outcomes must be consistent with previously expressed wishes of the patient (if known) and discussion/information exchange with the relatives.

To establish the prognosis for patients with severe neurological injury is not a simple task. The challenge lies in the difficulties associated with predicting survival as well as future recovery of neurological functions and quality of life. However, some clinical and instrumental tools can be useful for obtaining an estimation of the risk of death in neurological patients admitted to the ICU. Some clinical neurological scales are frequently used for estimating the risk of the appearance of some clinical pathological phenomena (vasospasm, surgical risk, etc.) associated with neurological diseases. In the same way, the use of some clinical data is able to identify groups of patients with a high risk of poor outcomes or death. It must be taken into account that risk evaluation is valuable for groups of patients with the same pathological condition not having the same potential evaluation of risk for individual patients.

It must be also considered that the pathology of the central nervous system includes a broad spectrum of syndromes and diseases [16]. Consequently there are several different clinical tools and scales which can be applied to most of them, mainly related to the level of consciousness, but some of them are specific for each clinical picture. One of the more frequently applied scales for evaluating the severity of head-injured patients is the Glasgow Coma Scale. This scale tries to approach the level of processing of neurological signals in the central nervous system. The Glasgow Coma Scale, which ranges from 3 to 15 points, is related to the highest level that the external stimulus (pain, voice, etc.) reaches in the brain and brainstem. This scale is strongly associated with the prognosis, particularly in the lower scores (lower than 8 points), where a higher mortality rate exists in the patients with a very low score (lower than 5 points).

In cases of subarachnoid haemorrhage, there are several scales associated with the evaluation of risk in these patients, such as the Hunt and Hess Scale, Fisher Scale, World Federation of Neurosurgeons Scale (WFNS), etc. In spite of their extensive use, these scales were not initially described to try to predict the mortality of the patients with subarachnoid haemorrhage, but to foresee some specific phenomena frequently associated with aneurysmal haemorrhage. The Hunt and Hess scale was initially used to define the estimated risk of clipping the aneurysm in patients with previous subarachnoid haemorrhage; the Fisher Scale had the intention of defining subgroups of patients with similar risk of vasospasm, etc.

Just as the clinical scales, instrumental evaluation can also be useful for the appraisal of the risk of brain death. Computerised tomography (CT) is probably the image test most commonly used to weigh up the severity of intracranial lesions. Consequently, Computerised tomography findings can also be used as a feasible tool for brain death risk evaluation purposes.

Some researchers have investigated which intracranial lesions and decreasing clinical neurological states have a more significant association with brain death. A group study [17] was conducted which observed patients with spontaneous subarachnoid haemorrhage admitted to the ICU with good (survival) and bad outcome (brain death). The CT scan and the clinical findings of both groups were compared, showing that the patients with a 1–2 Hunt and Hess grade had a significantly lower risk of brain death than patients with a higher grade; WFNS showed a greater chance of detection of the risk of brain death than the scale of Hunt and Hess, mainly in those patients who had levels of 4–5 on the World Federation of Neurosurgeons Scale. Patients with

a CT scan showing a frontal haematoma (associated with subarachnoid haemorrhage) had a greater risk of brain death than patients with cerebral haematoma in the parasilvian region. However, haematoma volume was not able to predict a poor outcome. The Fisher scale was not associated with a higher risk of brain death; on the contrary, intraventricular bleeding (evaluated by the Graeb Scale) was a predicting factor of prognosis.

The analysis of CT scans of patients with acute ischaemic stroke [18] showed evidence that the unilateral absence of ambiens cistern was statistically more frequent in the patients who developed brain death. In this last group the midline shift had significantly higher values compared to the group of patients with ischaemic stroke who survived. Other CT scan data, such as the presence of insular ribbon sign or the existence of hyperdensity in the middle cerebral artery, were not a discriminating factor between patients of good/bad outcome. For this study the CT scan analysed was the one just before admission to the ICU, not the worst CT scans in the evolution of patient.

In cases of spontaneous intracerebral haemorrhage, a series of useful radiological markers can identify patients with a greater risk of brain death [19]. A report from our research group was able to reveal that there are signs in the tomography of the brain associated with a high probability of death: the compression of the fourth ventricle, the existence of compression of the ambiens cistern, a haematoma volume greater than 50 cc, a midline shift higher than 10 mm, and intraventricular bleeding with a Graeb score greater than 9 points. In this same series, the location of haematomas at the pons, mesencephalus or putamen was associated with greater mortality compared with the thalamic or lobar location. In severely head-injured patients, the connection of some intracranial lesions and brain death was also observed [20]. Thus, the existence of hemispheric swelling (see Fig. 1) and subdural haematoma associated with intracerebral bleeding had a significantly higher incidence in the patients with a bad outcome.

Besides the studies previously mentioned, other instrumental tests, such as transcranial Doppler sonography, have been proposed as a strong tool for the indirect evaluation of blood flow in the arteries of the base of the skull, and consequently for the assessment of the risk of

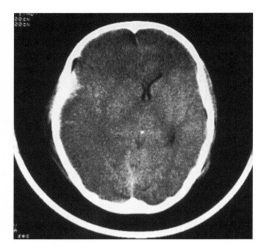

Fig. 1 CT scan of a head-injured patient with small subdural haematoma, hemispheric swelling and significant midline shift, signs significantly associated with brain death.

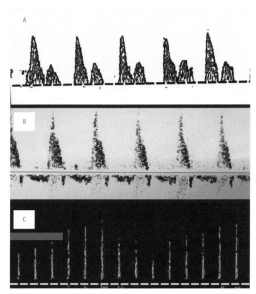

Fig. 2 Transcranial Doppler sonography readings compatible with cerebral circulatory arrest.
A: Systolic- diastolic separation pattern,
B: Reverberating flow pattern,
C: Systolic spike pattern.

cerebral circulatory arrest phenomenon linked to brain death. The lack of cerebral blood flow is closely related to brain death. Its demonstration at the level of the circle of Willis is a sign that supports the diagnosis of death. In addition to this, the progressive decrease of intracranial arterial flow is a warning sign for a critical neurological condition. Therefore, transcranial Doppler sonography is able to confirm the lack of flow in the middle cerebral arteries, anterior cerebral arteries, posterior cerebral arteries and basilar arteries. The presence of a specific sonographic pattern [21] (reverberating flow, systolic spikes, or diastole-systole separation pattern) (see Fig. 2) supports the diagnosis. The development of refractory progressive signs of decreasing flow in the arteries of the base of the skull is also a sign of risk of potential brain death.

It is obvious that the use of one of these elements alone (clinical exam, CT scan, or transcranial Doppler sonography) is not sufficient to establish a definite prognosis of the severe neurological patient. On the other hand, admission scoring systems were designed as probabilistic methods for determining survival in the ICU population and were not designed to predict outcome for individual patients. However, a joint use of all these tests is a strong strategy to establish an accurate prognosis, so if the patient is not still admitted to the ICU, it can help to know if there is a reasonable basis for the admission to the ICU for a therapeutic purpose with the probability of good results. Conversely, the combined use of the previously mentioned data can support the decision of not admitting to ICU because of the low probability of benefits. In this case, the option of ICU admission can be weighed up against some of the medical, ethical, organisational, and legislative aspects described above.

Summary

- At present, neurological critical care patients that evolve to brain death are the most important source of donor organs for transplantation.
- All organ donors in brain death are submitted to interventional ventilator therapy, so they must be admitted to intensive care units.
- Most cases of brain death occur in the ICU as a consequence of unsuccessful neurological therapy. A small percentage of patients are admitted to the ICU in brain death.

- Some patients with cerebral damage fulfill the pre-requisites for being admitted to ICU even though they are too ill to gain benefit from the admission. Some intensivists agree (but there is no general agreement) that these patients should be admitted to the ICU as potential organ donors.
- Patients' categorisation at admission to the intensive care unit can help to identify the level of therapeutic treatment that should be established for each patient. The categorisation of patients in the group "too ill to gain benefit from ICU" can help identify patients with a high risk of brain death and the possibility of organ donation after admission.
- Some researchers have paid attention to the identification of clinical and instrumental findings that correlate with a high probability of brain death.
- The admission of non-brain-dead patients to the ICU with a very low probability of good outcome can create ethical dilemmas open to controversy.
- There is no unanimity between different medical schools about a homogenous use of the term "potential organ donor".
- The withdrawal of treatment in neurological patients in the ICU can also raise discussion and ethical debate.
- The withdrawal of treatment for a neurological patient in the ICU is always independent of the possibility of organ donation and it is always governed by medical and ethical criteria.
- The evidence shows that besides the organisational aspects of organ procurement systems, the commitment of intensive care doctors is an essential part of organ donation programmes. The role of intensivists is relevant in organ donation and thus in the benefits of transplantation, and its consequence is the survival and improvement of quality of life for organ recipients.

The authors

Jose-Maria Dominguez-Roldan MD, PhD[1]
Claudio Garcia-Alfaro MD, PhD[2]
Fernando Hernandez-Hazañas MD, PhD[2]
    [1]Clinical Chief | Critical Care Department | Hospital Universitario Virgen del Rocío | Sevilla, Spain
    [2]Intensive Care Specialist | Critical Care Department | Hospital Universitario Virgen del Rocío | Sevilla, Spain

Address for correspondence
    Jose-Maria Dominguez-Roldan
    Hospital Universitario Virgen del Rocio
    UCI-HRT
    Avda Manuel Siurot s/n
    41013 Sevilla, Spain
    E-mail: jmdominguez@telefonica.net

References

1. Procaccio F, Barbacini S, Meroni M, Sarpellon M, Verlato R, Giron GP. Deaths with acute cerebral lesion and heart-beating potential organ donors in the Veneto region. Minerva Anestesiol 2001: 67:71–78.
2. ANZICS Survey on Brain Death and Organ Donation 2006 (from the final report-2008 of the National Clinical Taskforce on Organ and Tissue Donation. http://www.anzca.edu.au/events/asm/asm2008/abstracts/organ-donation-organ-harvesting-or-end-of-life-care.html
3. Domínguez-Roldán JM, Garcia Alfaro. Model of categorization of patients at admission in ICU. A useful tool for making compatible. Quality Indicators of ICU and Quality Indicators of Organ Procurement Programs. C. Abstracts book of 5th European Transplant Coordinators Organization Annual Meeting 2008
4. Wallace, P. G M. Elective ventilation of potential organ donors. BMJ 1995; 311: 121c
5. Varelas PN, Abdelhak T, Hacein-Bey L. Withdrawal of life-sustaining therapies and brain death in the intensive care unit. Semin Neurol 2008 28:721–735
6. Truog RD, Campbell ML, Curtis JR, Haas CE, Luce JM, Rubenfeld GD, Rushton CH, Kaufman DC; American Academy of Critical Care Medicine. Recommendations for end-of-life care in the intensive care unit: a consensus statement by the American College of Critical Care Medicine. Crit Care Med 2008;36:951–963
7. Rocker GM, Cook DJ, Shemie SD. Brief review: Practice variation in end of life care in the ICU: implications for patients with severe brain injury. Can J Anaesth 2006;53:811–819
8. Manyalich M, Cabrer C, Vilardell J, Miranda B.Functions, responsibilities, dedication, payment, organization, and profile of the hospital transplant coordination in Spain in 2002. Transplant Proc. 2003;35:1631–1635
9. Matesanz R. Factors that influence the development of an organ donation program. Transplant Proc. 2004;36:731–741.
10. Bozzi G, Matesanz R, Saviozzi A, RossiFerrini PL. Summary: the quality improvement program in organ donation of the Tuscany region. Transplant Proc. 2004;36:421–425
11. Dodek P. Mandatory reporting of "imminent" death to

identify organ donors: history, controversy, and potential solutions Can J Anesth 2003; 50: 955–960

12. Bustos JL, Surt K, Soratti C. Glasgow coma scale 7 or less surveillance program for brain death identification in Argentina: Epidemiology and outcome. Transplant Proc. 2006;38):3691–3699.

13. Comments to CMS Medicare and Medicaid Programs; Conditions for Coverage for Organ Procurement Organizations (OPOs) Proposed Rule. www.unos.org/SharedContentDocuments/OPO_CMS_CoC_FINAL_1-3-05.doc

14. Madsen M, Bøgh L. Estimating the organ donor potential in Denmark: a prospective analysis of deaths in intensive care units in northern Denmark. Transplant Proc. 2005;37:3251–3259.

15. Opdam HI, Silvester W. Identifying the potential organ donor: an audit of hospital deaths. Intensive Care Med. 2004;30:1391–1397

16. Kompanje EJ, Bakker J, Slieker FJ, Ijzermans JN, Maas AI. Organ donations and unused potential donations in traumatic brain injury, subarachnoid haemorrhage and intracerebral haemorrhage. Intensive Care Med. 2006 2006;32:211–222

17. Dominguez-Roldan JM, Garcia-Alfaro C, Diaz-Parejo P, Barrera-Chacon JM, Caldera-Gonzalez A, Murillo-Cabezas F. Identification of subarachnoid hemorrhages with high risk of evolution to brain death. Transplant Proc. 2002;34:1–10

18. Dominguez-Roldan JM, Jimenez-Gonzalez PI, Garcia-Alfaro C, Hernandez-Hazañas F, Murillo-Cabezas F, Perez-Bernal J. Identification by CT scan of ischemic stroke patients with high risk of brain death. Transplant Proc. 2004;36:2561–2563.

19. Dominguez-Roldan JM, Barrera-Chacon JM, Martin-Bermudez R, Santamaria-Milsut JL, Flores-Cordero JM, Jimenez Gonzalez P. High-risk spontaneous cerebral hematomas leading to brain death: early detection of potential organ donors. Transplant Proc 1999;31:2591–2596..

20. Dominguez-Roldán JM, Murillo-Cabezas F, Muñoz-Sanchez A, Gonzalez-Menendez E. High-risk cerebral injuries leading to cerebral death: early detection of potential organ donors. Transplant Proc 1992;24:21–30.

21. Dominguez-Roldan JM, Garcia-Alfaro C, Jimenez-Gonzalez PI, Rivera-Fernandez V, Hernandez-Hazanas F, Perez-Bernal J. Brain death due to supratentorial masses: diagnosis using transcranial Doppler sonography. Transplant Proc 2004;36:2891–2900.

K. Future approaches

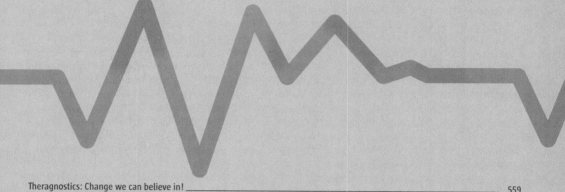

Guillaume Dubreuil, David Grimaldi, Nicholas Heming and Jean-Paul Mira

Theragnostics: Change we can believe in!

Theragnostics is a treatment strategy that combines therapeutics with diagnostics. It associates both a diagnostic test that identifies patients most likely to be helped or harmed by a new medication, and targeted drug therapy based on the test results. Genomics, proteomics, and functional genomics are biology tools essential for the progress of molecular theragnostics. These tools generate the genetic and protein information required for the development of diagnostic assays. Theragnostics includes a wide range of subjects, including personalised medicine, pharmacogenomics and molecular imaging to develop efficient new targeted therapies with adequate benefit/risk ratios for patients and a better molecular understanding of how to optimise drug selection. Futhermore, theragnostics aims to monitor treatment response, to increase drug efficiency and safety. In addition, theragnostics could help avoid the unnecessary treatment of patients for whom therapy is not appropriate, which would result in significant drug cost savings for the healthcare system. However, the introduction of theragnostic tests into routine healthcare requires both a demonstration of cost-effectiveness and the availability of appropriate, accessible testing systems. This chapter reports validation studies in oncology, infectious and cardiovascular diseases that have demonstrated the benefits of such an approach in well-defined subpopulations of patients, moving the subject from the field of drug development process towards clinical practice and routine application. Theragnostics may change the usual business model of pharmaceutical companies from the classical blockbuster model towards targeted therapies.

Introduction

In 2004, the Food and Drug Administration (FDA) released an important report entitled "Innovation/Stagnation: Challenge and Opportunity on the Critical Path to New Medical Products" (http://www.fda.gov/oc/initiatives/criticalpath/whitepaper.pdf). This "Critical Path Initiative" is an FDA effort to modernise the sciences through which FDA-regulated products are developed, evaluated, and manufactured. In particular, the report underlined the scientific reasons for the recent decrease of the number of approved innovative medical products (23 new drug approvals by the FDA in 2006) and called for a concerted effort to modernise available scientific tools (e.g. *in vitro* tests, computer models, qualified biomarkers, and innovative study designs). This productivity decline in the pharmaceutical industry has increased during the last decade with a pharmaceutical research and development investment that has doubled, associated with a worldwide decrease of the rate of submission of new chemical entities.

Paradoxically, at the same time, the diagnostic industry has been the target of a number of cost-cutting exercises by governments and financial partners aimed at restricting the use of diagnostic tests. More recently, the pharmaceutical industry received similar demands for proof of efficiency, safety, and cost-effectiveness. However, pharmaceutical and diagnostic companies have certainly found a common answer to these regulatory and financial constraints in the emerging field of *theragnostics* in which the developing technologies and capabilities of the diagnostic division are applied to improve the efficiency and economics of new drugs. In this way, theragnostics is clearly a concept that responds to FDA expectations.

The term theragnostics or theranostics was probably first used by the CEO of PharmaNetics, John Funkhouser, in describing his company's business model in developing diagnostic tests directly linked to the application of specific therapies. Considering diagnostics as the ability to define a disease state, John Funkhouser defined theragnostics as "the ability to affect therapy or treatment of a disease state". Hence, theragnostics is a treatment strategy for individual patients that associates both a diagnostic test that identifies patients most likely to be helped or harmed by a new medication and targeted drug therapy based on the test results. Clinicians and patients will embrace theragnostics when it will provide information that fills an essential knowledge gap deemed clinically important to the diagnosis, prognosis, treatment and monitoring of patients with serious disease [1].

Theragnostics covers a wide range of topics that includes

- predictive medicine,
- personalised medicine,
- integrated medicine and
- pharmacodiagnostics.

Theragnostics tests differ from traditional ones (troponin, lactate, procalcitonin, blood glucose, ...) because they are based on sophisticated recent technologies. Hence theragnostics may be considered as the possible end result of new advances made in pharmacogenomics and drug discovery using genetics, molecular biology and microarray chips technology. As illustrated in the FDA's "Table of Valid Genomic Biomarkers in the Context of Approved Drug Labels", which portrays a view on valid genomic biomarkers in the context of FDA-approved drug labels (http://www.fda.gov/cder/genomics/genomic_biomarkers_table.htm), theragnostics has three principal key applications [2]:

1. Identification of subgroups of patients presenting a profile likely to give a positive response to a given treatment: Targeted therapies (Efficiency)
2. Identification of subgroups of patients at risk of aggravated side effects during treatment: Pharmacogenomics (Safety)
3. Monitoring the response to a treatment (Efficacy and Safety)

This review describes the principles of theragnostics and its current and future applications.

Improved efficiency with targeted therapies by theragnostics

It is usually well admitted that it is very important to find indicators that may help physicians predict which of their patients will respond to therapy. However, this evidence is not always easy to complete, and may become an economic and societal concern with the development and commercialisation of very expensive drugs that should be prescribed to a limited number of well-defined patients. The first key application of theragnostics (and probably the most important for the drug industry) consists in identifying the population of patients in which a therapy will be effective through detection by theragnostics tests. Hence, for patients, theragnostics means *more effective care* and the possibility of *avoiding useless treatments* that might have harmful side effects.

In an ideal world, the new drug and the diagnostic test will be co-developed and approved by the FDA at the same time. Such was the case in September 1998, a key date for theragnostics, which may be considered the birth date of this new concept. On that date, the FDA granted simultaneous approval for both trastuzumab (Herceptin®) for the treatment of stage IV breast cancer and the HER2 protein test (HercepTest®) for diagnosis of HER2 overexpression. Since then, many significant advances in cancer and infectious disease management have focused on the development and introduction of molecularly targeted therapy based on theragnostic tests.

Tumour protein detection test: The birth of theragnostics

Despite advances in the diagnosis and treatment of breast cancer, which is staged between I and IV, more than 44,000 women in the United States die each year of metastatic disease [3]. Approximately 25 to 30 percent of stage IV breast cancers show significant overexpression of a growth factor receptor, human epidermal growth factor receptor 2 (HER2). Women with breast cancers that overexpress HER2 have an aggressive form of the disease with a significantly poorer overall prognosis. Amplification of HER2 has been shown to have a direct role in the pathogenesis of these cancers, thereby providing an opportunity to target a therapeutic agent directly against this alteration [4]. Trastuzumab is a humanised monoclonal antibody to HER2 which is effective by binding to the HER2 expressed on the cell surface of the tumour cells and provides a new and highly effective tool in targeting stage IV breast cancer overexpressing HER2 [4]. Two diagnostic tests, HercepTest and Path-Vysion, are used to detect susceptible tumours, which allows treatment to be limited to patients most likely to benefit from the drug. Uptake of trastuzumab into clinical practice for treatment of HER2 overexpressing stage IV breast cancer was rapid because knowledge of a tumour's HER2 expression status has immediate consequences on the selection of the most appropriate treatment [3–5].

Other examples of drugs that have been co-approved along with an eligibility diagnostic test for the selection of patients are cetuximab along with the eligibility test (DakoCytomation EGFR pharmDx™ test kit) for immunohistochemical evidence of positive EGFR expression in the colorectal carcinoma and imatinib and all members of the tyrosine kinase inhibitor family along with the eligibility test for the expression of the t(9;22) translocation fusion gene Bcr-Abl (chronic myelogenous leukemia (CML) and Philadelphia chromosome-positive acute lymphoblastic

leukemia (Phi+ALL)) or the tyrosine-kinase receptor c-Kit (gastro-intestinal stromal tumours, GISTs). Hence, in patients with Philadelphia chromosome-positive CML unresponsive to interferon, imatinib provides a significant survival advantage [6].

In contrast, erlotinib and gefitinib, which are epidermal growth factor receptor (EGFR) inhibitors indicated for patients diagnosed with non-small-cell lung cancer, cannot be strictly considered as molecularly targeted therapies [7]. Their approval by the FDA did not yet include a validated eligibility diagnostic test for EGFR status designed to select patients whose tumours were more likely to respond to their action. Immunohistochemistry, fluorescence in situ hybridisation, and mutational analyses of the EGFR gene have all been proposed as candidates to help predict response or survival benefit from EGFR-targeted therapy in patients with non-small cell lung cancer [8]. However, further prospective validation from ongoing randomised studies will be needed to fully determine which assays are best to help predict patient outcome. In addition, it will be critical for these assays to undergo standardisation before widespread clinical use.

Nucleic acid-based tests for targeted therapies

For the above-mentioned molecular therapies, the target is represented by one or more tumour-specific molecular features. Among them, Philadelphia chromosome highlights the importance of theragnostics DNA-based biomarkers. The idea that genetics play a role in therapeutical response has become more prevalent in recent years in a number of diseases. Identifying the presence of genetic variants or a certain set of gene expression profiles in a patient may predict whether he or she will respond to therapy.

Human genetic variations for targeted treatment

It is only little more than 50 years ago that Watson and Crick discovered the structure of DNA and six years since the human genome sequence and its first single-nucleotide polymorphism (SNP) map were published in the same issue of Nature [9]. The Human Genome Project shows a high degree of similarity between the DNA sequences of two individuals, defining us as a species; on the other hand, it revealed differences in DNA sequences that make each human being unique. These differences are either qualitative, in the form of SNPs and haplotypes, or quantitative such as deletion/insertion, duplications and large-scale rearrangements like the Philadelphia chromosome [10]. Genomics-based knowledge promises the ability to approach each patient as a unique biological individual, thereby completely changing our paradigms and improving efficacy. In oncology, some emerging tests support this promise.

As mentioned above, the Philadelphia chromosome or Philadelphia translocation is a specific chromosomal abnormality that is associated with CML and can be easily detected [11]. It is due to a reciprocal translocation designated as t(9;22) (q34;q11), which means an exchange of genetic material between region q34 of chromosome 9 and region q11 of chromosome 22. The presence of this translocation is a highly sensitive test for CML, which was the first malignancy to be linked to a clear genetic abnormality [11]. As a result of the translocation, part of the BCR gene from chromosome 22 is fused with the ABL gene on chromosome 9. This abnormal BCR-ABL fusion gene generates a continuously active tyrosine kinase, which controls the cell cycle, speeding up cell division and inhibiting DNA repair, causing genomic instability and making the cell more susceptible to developing further genetic abnormalities. The action of the bcr-abl protein is the pathophysiologic cause of CML, leading to the development of targeted therapies (such as imatinib) which specifically inhibit the activity of the BCR-ABL protein [12]. These tyrosine kinase inhibitors can induce complete remissions in CML, confirming definitively the central importance of BCR-ABL as the cause of CML. Hence, advances in understanding molecular and genetic mechanisms underlying cancer ontogenesis may lead to an individualised management of disease. Similarly, women carrying a BRCA1 or BRCA2 germline mutation are at very high risk of breast and/ or ovarian cancer. The detection of these mutations is easy and reliable using the BRACAnalysis test, which has been one of the first patented DNA-based theragnostics tests. This diagnosis helps to decide whether to perform prophylactic surgery, essentially prophylactic bilateral salpingo-oophorectomy which is superior to bilateral prophylactic mastectomy and/or chemoprevention and/or intensified surveillance, including breast magnetic resonance imaging screening [13, 14].

Gene expression profiles for targeted treatment

Beyond panels of individual genetic alleles, the entire gene expression profile derived from DNA microarray studies (transcriptome) has the potential to add much information to the analysis of biological phenotypes. With this technology, physicians can determine which genes have been "turned on" and which have been "turned off" and can identify sensitive changes in the gene expression over time. Transcriptome can distinguish normal and diseased tissues, classify the various stages of the disease (severity, progression, resolution), and select patterns of gene expression with prognostic and predictive value. Similar global approaches are being developed using patterns of disease-specific SNPs, microRNA and epigenetic changes associated with DNA methylation [15, 16].

Perhaps the most successful application of this progress has been the characterisation of human cancers, including the ability to predict clinical outcomes. As a consequence, gene expression signatures are used for the development of new targeted therapeutics based on better detection and classification of tumours. For instance, differences in gene expression profile can be used to detect tumours that already demonstrate gene expression changes associated with increased risk of metastasis, in order to propose more aggressive treatment. A number of studies have identified prognostic and predictive gene "signatures" whose prediction of disease outcome and response to treatment is superior to conventional prognostic indicators. Moreover, a relatively small number of genes seem able to predict response to breast cancer or B lymphoma therapy. Although the results are promising, further optimisation and standardisation of the technique and properly designed clinical trials are required before microarrays can reliably be used as tools for clinical decision-making [17].

MicroRNAs and MicroRNAs expression profiles for targeted treatment

MicroRNAs (miRNAs) are small (~22 nucleotides) non-coding RNAs that were discovered over 12 years ago in the nematode *Caenorhabditis elegans* [15]. Comparing human, worm, fruit fly, and plant genome sequences allowed miRNA research to accelerate in the past few years. Soon after miRNAs were found in humans, researchers were calculating the number of miRNA genes and focusing on their targets; they went on in 2005 to using them as a signature of cancer in cells and as a potential tool for reducing gene expression.

MiRNAs are believed to serve fundamental roles in many biological processes through regulation of gene expression by targeting messenger RNAs (mRNAs) through translational repression or RNA degradation. Approximately 500 miRNA genes have been identified in the human genome. Many fundamental biological processes are modulated by miRNAs, and an important role for microRNAs in carcinogenesis is emerging. Hence, miRNAs have been shown to regulate oncogenes, tumour suppressors and a number of cancer-related genes controlling cell cycle, apoptosis, cell migration and angiogenesis [18]. Some miRNAs and their target sites were found to be mutated in cancer and miRNAs expression profile studies demonstrate that many miRNAs are deregulated in human cancers and are designated as oncogenic miRNAs (OncomiRs). Furthermore, expression patterns of miRNAs are systematically altered in cancers (lymphoma, leukemia, carcinomas, ...). In colon adenocarcinomas, for example, high miR-21 expression is clearly associated with poor survival and poor therapeutic outcome [19]. Hence miRNAs match not only the criteria for ideal therapeutic targets because they are causally associated with disease, but also for ideal diagnostic biomarkers because they are easy to measure and have strong associations with clinical outcomes [15]. It is predictable that they will have major importance in the development of theragnostics in the coming years.

Microbially-based theragnostics tests

As reported above, remarkable examples already illustrate the power of theragnostics to target therapy in oncology. Theragnostics will also provide new information about the response of certain patients to specific drugs, and then lead to the development of theragnostics tests in others key areas such as infectious diseases.

Infectious diseases, mainly bacterial infections, are responsible for more than 17 million deaths worldwide and represent the leading cause of death in ICUs. Adequate antimicrobial therapy is the essential starting point of their therapy. However, use of antimicrobials to treat patients without bacterial infection, as well as the common use of broad-spectrum antimicrobials, is associated with an increasing rate of resistance which complicates treatment and multiplies healthcare costs. Bacterial identification and antibacterial susceptibility testing methods currently used in clinical microbiology laboratories require at least two days because they rely on the growth and isolation of microorganisms. However, prompt initiation of adequate treatment is a major determinant of success of infectious diseases, underlying the urgent need for rapid and accurate diagnostic tests. Molecular theragnostic testing for infectious diseases is an emerging concept in which molecular biology tools are used to provide rapid (less than one hour), accurate and more informative diagnostic microbiology assays, thus enabling better therapeutic interventions and the development of new and more specific antimicrobial agents or futuristic drugs. Two examples illustrate how theragnostics influences infectious disease diagnosis and treatment.

Theragnostics and preventive medicine in infectiology

Methicillin-resistant *Staphylococcus aureus* (MRSA) is a major cause of nosocomial infection throughout the world. Rates of infection and colonisation vary substantially between different hospitals both within and between different countries (4% at admission in ICUs in the United States). MRSA is a significant contributor to prolonged hospital stay, poor clinical outcome and increased healthcare costs especially amongst surgical patients. The major method for instituting control is the microbiological identification of patients either colonised or infected with MRSA, followed by isolation of these patients to prevent cross-infection [20]. Screening swabs for detection and follow-up of treated carriers of MRSA in high-risk units has been recommended in different guidelines and has been shown to be an effective and cost-avoidant strategy for achieving a sustained decrease of MRSA infections throughout the hospital. MRSA detection has largely relied on conventional culture methods on agar plates, which can take 48–72 h to obtain a result leading to isolation of the patient for three to four days (sometimes more). In recent years a number of different molecular methods for the rapid detection of MRSA have been described. Among them, the IDI-MRSA test is highly specific for detecting MRSA in nasal swabs with a 91.7 % sensitivity and a processing time of about 2 hours [21]. Although it is more expensive, IDI-MRSA offers greater detection of MRSA colonisation, independent of the swab site, than do conventional selective agars [22]. PCR screening for MRSA with this test on admission to critical care units has been demonstrated to be feasible in routine clinical practice, and to provide quicker results than culture-based screening, leading to a better management of both colonised and infected patients and permitting a significant reduction in subsequent MRSA transmission [23]. Hence, assays based on the detection of nucleic acids of microbial agents offer enormous potential for the rapid and accurate diagnosis of infections including detection and identification of the causal microorganism(s), as well as the detection and characterisation of genes or mutations associated with antimicrobial resistance and virulence. It may be anticipated that the optimal selection of appropriate antimicrobials by clinicians will be gradually improved as an increasing number of rapid molecular diagnostic tools become commercially available. The maraviroc story is a good example of this "future".

Theragnostics and new targeted anti-microbial agents

HIV infects target cells by binding of its envelope gp120 protein to CD4 and a co-receptor on the cell surface. *In vivo*, the different HIV-strains use either CCR5 or CXCR4 as co-receptor. CCR5-using strains are named R5 viruses, while CXCR4-using strains are named X4. As X4 viruses usually occur in the later stages of the disease, co-

receptor usage is used as a marker for disease progression. Interest in co-receptors increases as a consequence of the development of a new class of antiretroviral drugs, namely the co-receptor antagonists [24]. So far, CXCR4 blockers are not allowed to be used in clinical practice due to their severe side effects. In 2007 maraviroc, a member of the CCR5 co-receptor antagonists family was approved by the FDA for the treatment of HIV-infected adult patients who are infected with an HIV-1 virus that is solely CCR5-tropic, who have evidence of viral replication and who are resistant to multiple antiretroviral agents [25]. Interestingly, both tropism and treatment history should guide the use of maraviroc, which has demonstrated *in vitro* activity against a wide range of CCR5-tropic clinical isolates, including those resistant to the four currently existing drug classes of antiretroviral agents. In contrast, CXCR4-tropic and dual-tropic HIV-1 entry are not inhibited by maraviroc. Hence, the knowledge of patients' viral population tropism before the initiation of and during therapy with compounds such as maraviroc may be critical in order to optimise treatment strategies. Besides traditional phenotypic assays, there are at least four phenotypic recombinant virus assays (RVA) available to predict co-receptor usage. The detection of minority variants is a limitation of all population-based assays and varies between 1 and 10 %, depending on the assay used. However, recombinant virus assays combine efficiency and accuracy, thus making them suitable for the clinical management of HIV-infected individuals treated with co-receptor antagonists [24, 26]. The two pivotal phase III trials for maraviroc, MOTIVATE-1 and -2, were conducted using the Trofile CCR5 co-receptor assay developed by Monogram Biosciences that was approved for commercial use by the FDA on August 6, 2006. In these studies maraviroc, in combination with optimised background therapy (OBT), demonstrated superior virologic and immunologic treatment outcomes than OBT alone in treatment-experienced patients infected with CCR5-tropic HIV-1. Therefore the FDA recommends that maraviroc only be used after a test has been done to determine that the patient only has virus using the CCR5 co-receptor. The drug should be part of a combination therapy regimen. However, cost is an issue. Whereas the price for maraviroc is similar to second-generation protease inhibitors that have been developed to treat experienced patients ($ 29 a day), the price for the assay is a steep $ 2,000!

In addition to targeting drugs to increase efficacy, theragnostics also helps in identifying patients who might be susceptible to dangerous side effects of medications.

Theragnostics to increase drug safety

In the United States, serious adverse drug reactions (ADR) cause or lead to 6 % of all hospitalisations (over 2 million hospitalised patients), even when drugs are appropriately prescribed and administered, and contribute to 100,000 deaths annually (fourth to sixth leading cause of death) [27]. Regarding the importance of this healthcare problem, the FDA has been operating the Adverse Event Reporting System since 1998. It collects all reports of ADR submitted directly to the agency or through drug manufacturers. Analysis of this database reveals that, from 1998 through 2005, the number of reported serious and fatal ADRs have increased by a factor of 2.7 (15,107 deaths in 2005) [28]. Thus, the second key application of theragnostics, which consists in identifying the population at risk of aggravated side effects during therapy, is becoming an increasingly important instrument as physicians, patients, regulatory authorities and payers seek innovative ways to improve the risk/benefit ratio of drugs. Classical causes of the extraordinary variation in patient response to medications are well known: age, organ function, drug interaction, etc. The Human Genome Project opened new opportunities for using genetic information to individualise drug therapy, called pharmacogenetics or pharmacogenomics. Although the terms are sometimes used interchangeably, pharmacogenetics is the study of how inherited DNA variations, typically in just a few genes, affect drug metabolism or toxicity. Hence, depending of the medication, individual genetic variation can account for as much as 95 % of variability in drug disposition and effects [27]. Pharmacogenomics is a broader term that covers all the technologies that can be used in high-throughput screening [29].

Considerable research has focused on understanding the molecular mechanisms behind ADRs during drug development and clinical practice. Therefore, current analyses estimate the cost of bringing a new drug to the market at around $ 880–1,000 million over 15 years. The goal of integrating pharmacogenomics into the research and development process is to make this process more efficient, to come up with better drugs not only to help in decision-making, but also to avoid withdrawal of the drug postmarketing due to an emerging side effect which will have been predicted. The National Institutes of Health, through the Pharmacogenetics Research Network (PGRN), are promoting the discovery of new genes that affect drug metabolism, as well as stronger correlations between known polymorphisms and drug effects or adverse events. The search for pharmacogenomic biomarkers focuses mainly on genes encoding drug-metabolizing enzymes, whose mutations can lead either to elevated levels of the drug itself and/or of its reactive metabolites or to ineffective underdosing. In contrast, for immune-mediated toxic effects, convincing data are actually restricted mainly to the genes of the major histocompatibility complex class I.

Variations of drug-metabolising enzyme genes

The right dosage regimen for an individual patient is one that provides an acceptable balance between benefits and the risk of adverse effects. However, traditional approaches in drug development and clinical practice to getting this right dose vary greatly with the therapeutic area of the drug and with the drug's benefit/risk ratio. Most of the dosing paradigms are simple and easy for physicians and patients to understand and respect the principle of population-acceptable safety and efficacy. This is often referred to as the "one-dose-fits-all" concept of dosing. In current practice, for a few medications doses are adjusted *a priori* for patient characteristics known to, or suspected to, change the exposure profile of the drug (e.g. age, renal function, body mass), and may be also adjusted *a posteriori* based on response. Too often, however, for drugs with a narrow therapeutic index, the "one-dose-fits-all" dosing paradigm is not precise enough and new approaches are needed to define the right dose to avoid or minimise ADRs.

Warfarin is a perfect example of this need for *a priori* strategies to individualise dose. It has been more than half a century since the FDA approved warfarin as an oral anticoagulant. Since then, warfarin became the most prescribed anticoagulant worldwide with more than 23 million prescriptions in 2003 in the United States alone. Despite this marketing success and decades of experience, the safety of warfarin is still an area of intense scrutiny and controversy because the rate of minor and major adverse events from this well-known drug is still among the highest of all commonly prescribed outpatient drugs in the world [30].

The major challenges for prescribers wanting to administer warfarin are linked to biological heterogeneity associated with patient comorbidities and to the very narrow therapeutic index of the drug. As a consequence, there is greater than 10-fold inter-individual variability in the dose required to attain a therapeutic response [30]. For this reason, initial dosing of warfarin begins as a "trial and error" exercise with frequent *a posteriori* adjustments of dose based on the individual observed anticoagulant response as measured by the International Normalised Ratio (INR). With the expansion of knowledge on genetic biomarkers related to the pharmacokinetics and pharmacodynamics of warfarin, clinical pharmacologists can now estimate the therapeutic warfarin dose by genotyping patients for single nucleotide polymorphisms (SNPs) that affect warfarin metabolism or sensitivity. Hence, pharmacogenetic analysis of two genes, the warfarin metabolic enzyme, cytochrome CYP2C9 and warfarin target enzyme, vitamin K epoxide reductase complex 1 (VKORC1), confirmed that the variants of these two genes account for 30 to 50 % of the variability of warfarin dosage. Studies have shown that patients carrying the allelic variants CYP2C9*2 and/or CYP2C9*3 variants or the common *VKORC1* haplotype A/A (or haplotype*2) are warfarin-sensitive and typically require lower warfarin doses to reach a therapeutic INR with a minimal risk of bleeding [31]. A recent large study confirmed that the presence of each variant is a significant predictor of time to the first INR over 4. Only the *VKORC1* haplotype A/A was associated with a decreased time period to the first INR within the therapeutic range [32]. This result supports the August 2007 decision of the FDA to update the label of warfarin to include information on pharmacogenetic testing and to encourage, but not require, the use of this information in warfarin dosage when initiating warfarin therapy. Pharmacogenetic-guided dosing of warfarin is a promising application of "personalised medicine". Two recent trials of genotype-guided versus standard warfarin therapy have recently confirmed the feasibility and the benefits of this approach [33, 34]. Moreover, in the last 5 years, at least 4 studies observed a significant difference in "warfarin sensitisers" allele frequency due to ethnic considerations, definitely burying the one dose fits all concept [35–38]. Hence algorithms incorporating genetic (CYP2C9 and VKORC1), demographic, and clinical factors to estimate the warfarin dosage, could potentially minimise the risk of overdose during warfarin induction.

Similar examples of genetic variants responsible for serious ADRs have been described in oncology. The chemotherapy drug irinotecan is one of the most important drugs used in advanced colorectal cancers despite some unpredictable adverse effects (diarrhea and neutropenia). To understand why some patients experience severe adverse effects while others do not, pharmacogenetic analysis of metabolic pathways has been realised and has suggested that the drug is particularly toxic in a subset of patients homozygous for UGT1A1*28, a variant sequence in a promoter region of the UGT1A1 gene, that codes for the bilirubin detoxifying enzyme, UDP-glucuronosyltransferase. About 10 % of patients are homozygous for the genetic variant, which boosts their chances of developing a dangerously low level of white blood cells, a known side effect of the drug [39]. As a consequence, the FDA has revised the package insert of irinotecan in order to warn of the association between toxicity and UGT1A1*28.

In addition to UGT1A1, thiopurine methyltransferase (TPMT), which metabolises the anti-cancer drug 6-mercaptopurine, is also a well-known candidate for current theragnostics application, because TPMT-deficient patients are at risk of severe bone marrow toxicity at otherwise normal drug dosages. Physicians now routinely prescreen children with leukemia with the thiopurine methyltransferase test that aims to predict the risk of severe neutropenia for the purine drugs azathioprine and 6-mercaptopurine at relatively low cost [40]. As with irinotecan, the FDA decided that evidence indicates sufficient benefit to warrant informing prescribers, pharmacists and patients of the availability of pharmacogenetic tests and their possible role in the selection and dosing of 6-mercaptopurine and has approved label changes of this drug to include pharmacogenetic testing as a potential means to reduce the rate of severe toxic events.

In December 2004, the FDA approved Roche Molecular Systems' AmpliChip Cytochrome P450 (CYP450) test, an array that detects 29 variations in two genes, *CYP2D6* and *CYP2C19*. These enzymes play key roles in drug metabolism, and genetic variations in the genes can affect the rate of drug metabolism. The product, which is now available, could have major implications for dosing and choice of therapy for a variety of pharmaceuticals, including cardiovascular drugs and antidepressants. While cytochrome p450s genes are important, they are not the only ones to affect drug response. As many as 180 genes could affect drug metabolism, including metabolic enzymes, transporters, and other proteins. These genes have at least 2,000 different variants, and a truly comprehensive metabolic genotyping panel would have to test for all of them. The Affymetrix® Drug-Metabolizing Enzymes and Transporters (DMET) Early Access solution provides a solution to this challenge, by combining molecular inversion probe technology with universal microarrays. The DMET solution profiles 1,069 drug metabolism biomarkers and automatically interprets data into a commonly used format that can be integrated into clinical trial workflows [41].

Expected adverse events, focus, anticipate!

"Primum non nocere" – Hippocrates
(460–370 BC)

In 2000, a post-hoc analysis of the Scandinavian Simvastatin Survival Study identified a population carrying the Epsilon4 (ε4) allele coding for the apolipoprotein E gene associated with a two-fold increased risk of dying of coronary heart disease after surviving a myocardial infarction. This increased mortality risk disappeared under simvastatin treatment [42]. Hence, ε4 carriers seem

to be a subpopulation with a major benefit from simvastatin therapy.

However, if statins are the most effective medication to reduce cardiovascular events in at-risk patients and particularly in ε4 carriers, they are also associated with muscle-related complications, ranging from myalgia to rhabdomyolysis. For the period from January 1, 1990 to March 31, 2002, the FDA database reports 3,339 cases of statin-associated rhabdomyolysis. Thompson and colleagues identified 612 cases of rhabdomyolysis in the United States from November 1997 through March 2000 requiring hospitalisation or being life-threatening in 64 % of cases, with death occurring in 7.8 % of patients [43]. This incidence of fatal rhabdomyolysis is estimated to be 0.15/million prescriptions [44] which is colossal considering that Lipitor® and Zocor® were the two top-selling drugs in the US in 2006 for almost 14 billion dollars (Bloomberg News, February 2006).

This potential serious adverse event has an economical impact on healthcare costs and on pharmaceutical industry investment, as illustrated in 1997 when MERCK stopped the development of a simvastatin sustained-release formulation due to a significant increase in side effects [45]. In August 2008, the SEARCH Collaborative Group identified common variants of SLCO1B1 (coding for OATP1B1, a polypeptide that mediates hepatic uptake of statins) associated with an increased risk of statin-induced myopathy [46]. This work highlighted a subpopulation of patients carrying these variants who could benefit from a decrease in statin doses in order to avoid this potentially lethal adverse effect. The challenge remains to develop a routine genotyping-test in order to optimise statin therapy regarding each patient's profile.

Hypersensitivity reactions and variations of MHC class I genes

Among the validated pharmacogenetics biomarkers, some HLA allelic variants have been consistently associated with immune-mediated toxic effects of medications from different classes, such as carbamazepine, ximelagatran or abacavir. Abacavir is a nucleoside reverse transcriptase inhibitor that has been prescribed to almost

1 million HIV patients during the past decade and which is used in combination with other medications to treat human immunodeficiency virus (HIV) infection [47]. In caucasians, hypersensitivity reactions (HSR) occur within the first 6 weeks of therapy, in 5 to 8% of patients receiving this drug. Signs and symptoms of abacavir HSR are non-specific (fever, rash, vomiting, diarrhea) making the diagnosis challenging, particularly in medically complex patients. Clinical management is aimed at supportive therapy and discontinuation of abacavir. Rechallenge with abacavir is contraindicated due to the risk of precipitating a life-threatening reaction. Since 2002, several small studies demonstrated that identification of patients at risk of developing abacavir hypersensitivity through routine genetic screening for human leukocyte antigen (HLA) HLA-B*5701 led to a drastic reduction of HSR associated with abacavir, representing a significant advance in the field of pharmacogenomics, with an apparent 100% negative predictive value. Recently, these results have been confirmed in a very large double-blind prospective study which showed that HLA-B*5701 screening reduces the risk of hypersensitivity reaction to abacavir, confirming that a pharmacogenetic test can be used to prevent a specific toxic effect of a drug [48]. Even if 94% of caucasians do not carry the HLA-B*5701 allele, all data suggest that pharmacogenetic screening for HLA-B*5701 before abacavir prescription is cost-effective [48, 49].

Theragnostics to monitor treatment response

The third key application of theragnostics is to monitor drug efficacy in order to adjust the most effective and non-toxic drug dosage. Recent advances in the understanding of the molecular pathways of disease have been a method to design medical diagnostics that can be used to monitor therapy. Like previously, most theragnostics applications for drug monitoring are focused on the field of antiviral drugs, as illustrated by viral load measurement which indicates the effectiveness of HIV anti-retroviral treatment, and oncology, as shown by theragnostics imaging and monitoring of novel anti-cancer drugs.

Theragnostics imaging in oncology

As reported previously in this review, anti-cancer drug development is a major area of research that has received a lot of attention from theragnostics to improve both drug targeting and safety. Imaging monitoring of response to new anti-cancer drugs has undergone an evolution (and a revolution) from structural imaging modalities to targeting functional metabolic activity at cellular level, to better define responsive and non-responsive cancerous tissues. Positron emission tomography (PET) is already a major contributor to this progress and it may be predicted that the development of novel PET tracers and improvements in technology will continue to augment the potential of PET and enhance its attractiveness as an instrument to facilitate drug development [50].

PET is a non-invasive functional imaging technology that provides rapid, reproducible in vivo assessment and quantification of several key biological processes important in cancer development and progression that are targeted by anti-cancer therapies. Previously, estimation of responses to new biological drugs used inaccurate measures of efficacy, such as changes in tumour size or serial invasive testing by tumour biopsies. PET provides information complementary to conventional anatomic imaging, demonstrating utility in a range of cancer settings from diagnosis, tumour stratification and staging [51].

The traditional example is PET imaging with the biomarker F-18 fluorodeoxyglucose (18F-FDG), reflecting tumour glucose metabolism, which offers relevant unique information regarding treatment response. Several mechanisms may influence the enhanced glucose uptake in cancer cells, including upregulation of glucose transporters, increase in the activities of hexokinase and AKT, which appears to play a key role in the control of glucose metabolism together with proteins which are involved in the signalling pathway, such as mTOR, the target of rapamycin. Moreover, it has been shown that changes in tumour glucose metabolism precede changes in tumour size underlying the sensibility of the method and directly reflect drug effects at a cellular level (high specificity). Thus, it has been demonstrated in patients with gastrointestinal stromal tumours and other sarcomas who received treatment with imatinib that PET with 18F-FDG is appropriate for treatment monitoring [52]. 18F-FDG PET not only enables the prediction of therapeutic response early in the course of the disease but also determines the viability of residual masses after completion of treatment.

PET has also been used to examine other drug-induced metabolism modification, cellular proliferation and tissue perfusion [51]. Changes induced by immuno-modulating drugs such as apoptosis, telomere activity, or growth factor levels can be studied using specific radiolabelled PET tracers, whereas conventional imaging modalities may not prove useful in such scenarios [53].

Theragnostics imaging is also very useful in monoclonal antibody (mAbs) therapy. MAbs have been approved for use as diagnostics and therapeutics in a broad range of medical indications, but especially in oncology. Immuno-PET uses PET technology to track and quantify mAbs *in vivo* and to monitor mAb-based therapy. The availability of proper positron emitters, sophisticated radiochemistry, and advanced PET-computed tomography scanners has been crucial in these developments. For example, PET pharmacokinetic studies will allow a rapid assessment of novel mAbs biodistribution before the decision whether or not to proceed with the development of a new drug is made. Immuno-PET will play an important future role in the improvement and tailoring of therapy with existing mAbs, and in the efficient development of novel mAbs.

Monitoring of new cancer drugs

A growing number of patients with advanced non-small-cell lung cancer (NSCLC) require second-line treatment after progression or relapse following frontline therapy. Gefitinib is a selective inhibitor of the epidermal growth factor (EGFR) tyrosine kinase, which is overexpressed in many cancers, including relapsing NSCLC. If different genetic biomarkers (germline polymorphisms in EGFR gene and high EGFR copy number) are associated with gefitinib efficacy, their role in predicting drug response is still under examination because of conflicting results in different studies. Moreover, in clinical practice, the use of specific cancer biomarkers necessary

for genetic biomarker testing is hampered by the lack of sufficient tumour tissue especially for lung cancer patients. However, it has been reported that drug action can be monitored in available surrogate tissue, such as buccal mucosa epithelial cells or normal skin [54]. Thus, epithelial cells obtained from buccal mucosa of patients with an objective response to gefitinib presented a reduction in expression of p-EGFR, p-MAPK, and p-AKT after gefitinib treatment, highlighting the *in vivo* efficacy of this tyrosine kinase inhibitor, whereas the mucosa epithelial cells from patients with progressive (drug-resistant) disease had increased or unchanged phosphoproteome. Unfortunately, some NSCLC non-responders still had evidence of EGFR downstream signaling inhibition with gefitinib, suggesting that redundant signaling pathways might regulate the growth and/or survival of NSCLC.

Perspectives and conclusions

Blockbuster versus targeted business model for new drug research and development

For the past 30 years, large pharmaceutical companies have maintained an unchanging core focus on the blockbuster model of drug development (typically defined as products with annual revenues in excess of $1 billion). The success of blockbuster drugs compensated for the numerous molecules that unpredictably did not make it out of phase 1 or 2 clinical testing. In the past few years, this model has come under intense pressure on several fronts. First, the absolute need to prove clinical efficacy and cost-effectiveness of new medicines has increased the costs and decreased the productivity of research and development [2]. Meanwhile, reimbursement is getting tougher as insurers become increasingly reluctant to pay the high price of innovative drugs and threaten to limit reimbursement levels. Finally, the switch to generic drugs is becoming routine once a blockbuster drug loses its patent protection. Theragnostics that fuses therapeutic and diagnostic medicine has the potential to positively impact these challenges and may change the classic business model. Through pharmacogenetics and pharmacogenomics, this strategy has the capability to lead to improved productivity by using molecular biomarkers to enrich clinical trials with known responders, to exclude those at risk for serious adverse events, and to individualise dosing of drugs to patients' genetic profiles. Theragnostics also has the potential to reduce risks and costs, potentially speeding market admission and, ultimately, enhancing the commercial success of the medicine by two mechanisms. Firstly, theragnostics' liability to identify appropriate patients and measure efficacy with objective diagnostic criteria has a huge potential to increase sales. Secondly, the life cycle of the new drug is expanded, because the medication is tightly linked to a diagnostic test which has patent protection beyond the expiry of the medicine patent.

Even if narrowing the market by targeting a subpopulation appears to be highly undesirable from a business perspective, the current commercial imperative is to lower costs by improving the clinical development success rate. Thus non-targeted therapies that are marginally effective may turn out to have a substantial benefit when paired with an appropriate theragnostics test. Similarly, it may be possible with theragnostics to explore, in the same series of trials, the efficacy of targeted and non-targeted approaches. Such development programmes could salvage some new drugs and improve overall success. This new model is strongly supported by the FDA, which released voluntary genomic data guidance meant to assist both regulatory agencies and pharmaceutical companies in evaluating the potential benefit of implementing theragnostics tests during the preclinical and clinical phases of drug development (http://www.fda.gov/cder/genomics/FDAEMEA.pdf).

Theragnostics and personalised medicine: A political issue

On August 4, 2006, Senator Barack Obama introduced a bill entitled the "Genomics and Personalized Medicine Act of 2006" (S. 3822), that mandates technology convergence between pharmaceuticals and diagnostics with the stated intention to "improve access to and appropriate utilization of valid, reliable, and accurate molecular genetic tests by all populations, thus helping to secure the promise of personalized medicine for all Americans." In particular senator Obama's bill recognises the enormous potential of pharmacogenomics to "better target the delivery of healthcare, facilitate the discovery and clinical testing of new products, and help determine a patient's predisposition to a particular disease or condition." Ultimately, this would "increase the efficacy and safety of drugs and reduce healthcare costs." (http://www.theorator.com/bills109/s3822.html)

To achieve these aims, very innovative measures are proposed:

- Creation of a "Genomics and Personalized Medicine Interagency Working Group" within the Department of Health & Human Services
- Incentive actions to encourage genomics and biobanking research
- Enhancement of genomics workforce training
- An income tax credit for patients paying for genetic tests or the research related to that test

This legislation has the potential to provide significant incentives to the industry to expand and accelerate pharmacogenomic research efforts, with the intent of speeding up the approval process for new drugs and providing additional companion diagnostic tests. Finally, this legislation may force current industrial players into new and unexpected alliances, thereby reshaping the process through which pharmacogenomic products are brought to the market.

In summary, it is becoming increasingly clear that the development of new technologies, both genetic and non-genetic, offers new opportunities for a better understanding of the underlying mechanisms of disease. These advances will facilitate the development of new classes of targeted medicine as well as sensitive and specific diagnostic tests. It is very likely that the maximum value for these advances will be gained where the diagnostic and therapeutic applications of this knowledge are brought together in the developing field of theragnostics.

The authors

Guillaume Dubreuil, MD[1]
David Grimaldi, MD[1]
Nicholas Heming, MD[1]
Jean-Paul Mira, MD, PhD[1, 2]
  [1]Centre Hospitalier Universitaire Cochin-Port-Royal | Service de réanimation médicale | Assistance Publique- Hôpitaux de Paris | Paris, France
  [2]Institut Cochin | INSERM U567 | Université Paris Descartes | Faculté de médecine | Paris, France

Address for correspondence
  Jean-Paul Mira
  Cochin University Hospital
  Medical Intensive Care Unit
  27 rue du faubourg St Jacques
  75014 Paris, France
  E-mail: jean-paul.mira@cch.aphp.fr

References

1. Wilson C, Schulz S, Waldman SA. Biomarker development, commercialization, and regulation: individualization of medicine lost in translation. Clin Pharmacol Ther 2007;81(2):153–5.
2. Ozdemir V, Williams-Jones B, Glatt SJ, Tsuang MT, Lohr JB, Reist C. Shifting emphasis from pharmacogenomics to theragnostics. Nat Biotechnol 2006;24(8):942–6.
3. Dawood S, Ueno NT, Cristofanilli M. The medical treatment of inflammatory breast cancer. Semin Oncol 2008;35(1):64–71.
4. Revillion F, Lhotellier V, Hornez L, Bonneterre J, Peyrat JP. ErbB/HER ligands in human breast cancer, and relationships with their receptors, the bio-pathological features and prognosis. Ann Oncol 2008;19(1):73–80.
5. Olver IN. Trastuzumab as the lead monoclonal antibody in advanced breast cancer: choosing which patient and when. Future Oncol 2008;4(1):125–31.
6. Jabbour E, Cortes JE, Ghanem H, O'Brien S, Kantarjian HM. Targeted therapy in chronic myeloid leukemia. Expert Rev Anticancer Ther 2008;8(1):99–110.
7. Wheatley-Price P, Shepherd FA. Epidermal growth factor receptor inhibitors in the treatment of lung cancer: reality and hopes. Curr Opin Oncol 2008;20(2):162–75.
8. Eberhard DA, Giaccone G, Johnson BE. Biomarkers of response to epidermal growth factor receptor inhibitors in Non-Small-Cell Lung Cancer Working Group: standardization for use in the clinical trial setting. J Clin Oncol 2008;26(6):983–94.
9. Lander ES, Linton LM, Birren B, et al. Initial sequencing and analysis of the human genome. Nature 2001;409(6822):860–921.
10. Birney E, Stamatoyannopoulos JA, Dutta A, et al. Identification and analysis of functional elements in 1% of the human genome by the ENCODE pilot project. Nature 2007;447(7146):799–816.
11. Craddock C. Molecularly targeted therapy in myeloid leukaemias. Clin Med 2007;7(6):632–5.
12. de Kogel CE, Schellens JH. Imatinib. Oncologist 2007;12(12):1390–4.
13. Fatouros M, Baltoyiannis G, Roukos DH. The predominant role of surgery in the prevention and new trends in the surgical treatment of women with BRCA1/2 mutations. Ann Surg Oncol 2008;15(1):21–33.
14. Roukos DH, Briasoulis E. Individualized preventive and therapeutic management of hereditary breast ovarian cancer syndrome. Nat Clin Pract Oncol 2007;4(10):578–90.
15. Calin GA, Croce CM. MicroRNA signatures in human cancers. Nat Rev Cancer 2006;6(11):857–66.
16. Sears C, Armstrong SA. Microarrays to identify new therapeutic strategies for cancer. Adv Cancer Res 2007;96:51–74.
17. Reis-Filho JS, Westbury C, Pierga JY. The impact of expression profiling on prognostic and predictive testing in breast cancer. J Clin Pathol 2006;59(3):225–31.
18. Blenkiron C, Miska EA. miRNAs in cancer: approaches, aetiology, diagnostics and therapy. Hum Mol Genet 2007;16 Spec No 1:R106–13.
19. Schetter AJ, Leung SY, Sohn JJ, et al. MicroRNA expression profiles associated with prognosis and therapeutic outcome in colon adenocarcinoma. Jama 2008;299(4):425–36.
20. Cooper BS, Stone SP, Kibbler CC, et al. Isolation measures in the hospital management of methicillin resistant Staphylococcus aureus (MRSA): systematic review of the literature. Bmj 2004;329(7465):533.
21. Huletsky A, Lebel P, Picard FJ, et al. Identification of methicillin-resistant Staphylococcus aureus carriage in less than 1 hour during a hospital surveillance program. Clin Infect Dis 2005;40(7):976–81.
22. van Hal SJ, Stark D, Lockwood B, Marriott D, Harkness J. Methicillin-resistant Staphylococcus aureus (MRSA) detection: comparison of two molecular methods (IDI-MRSA PCR assay and GenoType MRSA Direct PCR assay) with three selective MRSA agars (MRSA ID, MRSASelect, and CHROMagar MRSA) for use with infection-control swabs. J Clin Microbiol 2007;45(8):2486–90.
23. Cunningham R, Jenks P, Northwood J, Wallis M, Ferguson S, Hunt S. Effect on MRSA transmission of rapid PCR testing of patients admitted to critical care. J Hosp Infect 2007;65(1):24–8.
24. Jones J, Taylor B, Wilkin TJ, Hammer SM. Advances in antiretroviral therapy. Top HIV Med 2007;15(2):48–82.
25. Carter NJ, Keating GM. Maraviroc. Drugs 2007;67(15):2277–88; discussion 89–90.
26. Mueller MC, Bogner JR. Treatment with CCR5 antagonists: which patient may have a benefit? Eur J Med Res 2007;12(9):441–52.
27. Phillips KA, Veenstra DL, Oren E, Lee JK, Sadee W. Potential role of pharmacogenomics in reducing adverse drug reactions: a systematic review. Jama 2001;286(18):2270–9.
28. Moore TJ, Cohen MR, Furberg CD. Serious adverse drug events reported to the Food and Drug Administration, 1998–2005. Arch Intern Med 2007;167(16):1752–9.
29. Evans WE, Relling MV. Moving towards individualized medicine with pharmacogenomics. Nature 2004;429(6990):464–8.
30. Yin T, Miyata T. Warfarin dose and the pharmacogenomics of CYP2C9 and VKORC1 – rationale and perspectives. Thromb Res 2007;120(1):1–10.
31. Flockhart DA, O'Kane D, Williams MS, et al. Pharmacogenetic testing of CYP2C9 and VKORC1 alleles for warfarin. Genet Med 2008;10(2):139–50.
32. Schwarz UI, Ritchie MD, Bradford Y, et al. Genetic determinants of response to warfarin during initial anticoagulation. N Engl J Med 2008;358(10):999–1008.

33. Anderson JL, Horne BD, Stevens SM, et al. Randomized trial of genotype-guided versus standard warfarin dosing in patients initiating oral anticoagulation. Circulation 2007;116(22):2563–70.

34. Caraco Y, Blotnick S, Muszkat M. CYP2C9 genotype-guided warfarin prescribing enhances the efficacy and safety of anticoagulation: a prospective randomized controlled study. Clin Pharmacol Ther 2008;83(3):460–70.

35. Johnson JA. Ethnic differences in cardiovascular drug response: potential contribution of pharmacogenetics. Circulation 2008;118(13):1383–93.

36. Limdi NA, McGwin G, Goldstein JA, et al. Influence of CYP2C9 and VKORC1 1173C/T genotype on the risk of hemorrhagic complications in African-American and European-American patients on warfarin. Clin Pharmacol Ther 2008;83(2):312–21.

37. Sanderson S, Emery J, Higgins J. CYP2C9 gene variants, drug dose, and bleeding risk in warfarin-treated patients: a HuGEnet systematic review and meta-analysis. Genet Med 2005;7(2):97–104.

38. Tham LS, Goh BC, Nafziger A, et al. A warfarin-dosing model in Asians that uses single-nucleotide polymorphisms in vitamin K epoxide reductase complex and cytochrome P450 2C9. Clin Pharmacol Ther 2006;80(4):346–55.

39. Ando Y, Fujita K, Sasaki Y, Hasegawa Y. UGT1AI*6 and UGT1A1*27 for individualized irinotecan chemotherapy. Curr Opin Mol Ther 2007;9(3):258–62.

40. Maitland ML, Vasisht K, Ratain MJ. TPMT, UGT1A1 and DPYD: genotyping to ensure safer cancer therapy? Trends Pharmacol Sci 2006;27(8):432–7.

41. Dumaual C, Miao X, Daly TM, et al. Comprehensive assessment of metabolic enzyme and transporter genes using the Affymetrix Targeted Genotyping System. Pharmacogenomics 2007;8(3):293–305.

42. Gerdes LU, Gerdes C, Kervinen K, et al. The apolipoprotein epsilon4 allele determines prognosis and the effect on prognosis of simvastatin in survivors of myocardial infarction: a substudy of the Scandinavian simvastatin survival study. Circulation 2000;101(12):1366–71.

43. Thompson PD, Clarkson P, Karas RH. Statin-associated myopathy. Jama 2003;289(13):1681–90.

44. Staffa JA, Chang J, Green L. Cerivastatin and reports of fatal rhabdomyolysis. N Engl J Med 2002;346(7):539–40.

45. Davidson MH, Stein EA, Dujovne CA, et al. The efficacy and six-week tolerability of simvastatin 80 and 160 mg/day. Am J Cardiol 1997;79(1):38–42.

46. Link E, Parish S, Armitage J, et al. SLCO1B1 variants and statin-induced myopathy–a genomewide study. N Engl J Med 2008;359(8):789–99.

47. Hughes CA, Foisy MM, Dewhurst N, et al. Abacavir Hypersensitivity Reaction: an Update (March) (CE). Ann Pharmacother 2008.

48. Mallal S, Phillips E, Carosi G, et al. HLA-B*5701 screening for hypersensitivity to abacavir. N Engl J Med 2008;358(6):568–79.

49. Phillips E, Mallal S. Drug hypersensitivity in HIV. Curr Opin Allergy Clin Immunol 2007;7(4):324–30.

50. Yu EY, Mankoff DA. Positron emission tomography imaging as a cancer biomarker. Expert Rev Mol Diagn 2007;7(5):659–72.

51. Facey K, Bradbury I, Laking G, Payne E. Overview of the clinical effectiveness of positron emission tomography imaging in selected cancers. Health Technol Assess 2007;11(44):iii-iv, xi-267.

52. Goldstein D, Tan BS, Rossleigh M, Haindl W, Walker B, Dixon J. Gastrointestinal stromal tumours: correlation of F-FDG gamma camera-based coincidence positron emission tomography with CT for the assessment of treatment response – an AGITG study. Oncology 2005;69(4):326–32.

53. Avril N, Propper D. Functional PET imaging in cancer drug development. Future Oncol 2007;3(2):215–28.

54. Loprevite M, Tiseo M, Chiaramondia M, et al. Buccal mucosa cells as in vivo model to evaluate gefitinib activity in patients with advanced non small cell lung cancer. Clin Cancer Res 2007;13(21):6518–26.